The Complete Peerage of England, Scotland, Ireland, Great Britain, and the United Kingdom

THE COMPLETE
PEERAGE

THE COMPLETE
PEERAGE

OF ENGLAND SCOTLAND IRELAND
GREAT BRITAIN AND THE
UNITED KINGDOM

EXTANT EXTINCT OR DORMANT

BY G.E.C.

NEW EDITION, REVISED AND MUCH ENLARGED

EDITED BY

THE HON. VICARY GIBBS

VOLUME I
AB-ADAM TO BASING

LONDON
THE ST. CATHERINE PRESS LTD.
8 YORK BUILDINGS ADELPHI

1910

TO

GEORGE EDWARD COKAYNE

CLARENCEUX KING OF ARMS

THIS SECOND EDITION OF

THE COMPLETE PEERAGE

TO WHICH THE HIGHEST PRAISE THAT CAN

BE GIVEN IS THAT IT FOLLOWS FAITHFULLY

ON THE LINES LAID DOWN IN THE FIRST

IS DEDICATED BY

HIS HUMBLE PUPIL AND GRATEFUL NEPHEW

VICARY GIBBS

" People don't know how entertaining a study it
[genealogy] is Who begot whom is a most
amusing kind of hunting; one recovers a grand-
father instead of breaking one's own neck—and
then one grows so pious to the memory of a
thousand persons one never heard of before."

Horace Walpole to the Rev
Mr. Cole, 5 June 1775.

PREFACE

I T is hoped that a second edition of *The Complete Peerage* may find favour for the following reasons:—

The period which has elapsed since the original work was published has been marked by the appearance of a multitude of volumes in which public Records, private Letters, Memoirs etc., have been printed, providing a great fund of material for rendering these pages more complete and for increasing their precision and interest. The present Editor has spared no pains to utilise to the utmost these sources of information, on which he has been engaged for more than fifteen years. It would be tedious to set out all the authorities that have been gone through, but as an illustration it may be mentioned that the *Close Rolls*, *Patent Rolls*, and *Papal Letters*, so far as they have been printed, all the publications of the *Historical Manuscripts Commission*, and the obituaries of the *Gentleman's Magazine* have been systematically searched for matter bearing on the Peerage; every number, also, of the *London Gazette*, since its first issue in 1665 has been examined by the Rev. A. B. Beaven, and his notes of the official dates of public appointments, as gazetted, have been utilised throughout. It will be found, accordingly, that a large addition has been made not only to the facts and dates, but also to those thumb-nail sketches of character, and particulars of life and manners, which enlivened the work in its earlier form and contributed so much to its popularity. In the House of Lords also, since the first edition appeared, some important cases have been decided, and the results of these will be incorporated, together with comments on their features and their bearing on peerage law. Lastly, the changes in the peerage itself, since the first volume of the original edition was published—more than 20 years ago—have already made a new one needful, extinctions, creations, promotions and successions, involving no small alteration.

As regards the plan or scope of the work very little change has been made, and none at all except after confer-

ence with the former Editor. Baronies by tenure not being Peerage dignities, and having only been dealt with in the first edition under the letter "A", have, except in one or two cases such as Abergavenny and Berkeley, disappeared altogether. As G. E. C. wrote, when deciding to discontinue them, "The reproduction of such accounts without accurate supervision (which the Editor has neither the will nor the capacity to bestow) does more harm than good."

The heirs apparent of living Peers, who come within its scope, are set out in the body of the work in all cases, and not merely, as in the previous edition, when they enjoyed a courtesy title.

The longer notes have been removed to appendices, because in some cases they so much reduced the text on a page as to interfere with its continuous and convenient examination. Where notes have been added which did not appear in the first edition, the present Editor has affixed his initials; where notes which did so appear have been altered or modified, the Editor has sometimes attached his initials and sometimes not, being conscious that whichever course he elected to pursue he must lay himself open to one of two charges, that of saddling G. E. C. with opinions for which he is not responsible, or that of claiming credit for remarks which are in truth due to another.

In those parts of the book which deal with the mediæval period an attempt has been made to describe people by the Christian names and Surnames which they may be supposed to have borne and by which they were known to their contemporaries, and not by the charter Latin equivalents or (even less suitably) by anglicized variants of the Latin, as has been the custom in all Peerages since the time of Dugdale. As this matter will be found fully discussed in vol. iii, Appendix C, it is not necessary to dilate further on it here. The brackets which appear round the Surnames of Peers are not meant to support the foolish modern phantasy that peers have no Surnames, but are merely inserted for convenience, with a view to indicating where the Christian names end and the Surnames begin.

The text is confined to giving, concisely and precisely so far

as they have been obtainable, particulars of the parentage, birth,
honours, orders, offices, public services, politics, marriage, death
and burial, of every holder of a Peerage.   In the above list the
only novel item is that of the politics, which have been systematically recorded from the period of the Exclusion Bill agitation of
1679-81 (when the terms Whig and Tory first came into general
use as party definitions) to the present day.   The Editor hopes
that this additional information (which has not hitherto been
obtainable in a collected form, and is not easy to procure individu-
ally in the case of the less prominent politicians of the period
before the Reform Bill of 1832) will not be without interest to
the general reader, while it cannot fail to be of service to the
future historian and biographer.(ª)   The party designations allotted
in the text, as well as the notes appended in particular cases, to
explain the political divagations of peers whom it is difficult to
classify under one definite epithet, have all been furnished by the
Rev. A. B. Beaven, whose familiarity with the minute details of
the political and party history of England since the Restoration is
probably unrivalled. (ᵇ)

Many more authorities have been cited in this than in the
former edition, but it has been found impossible
AUTHORITIES   to quote them habitually on account of the
intolerable size to which such a course would
have swollen these volumes—e.g., such a typical (though imaginary)
sentence as the following . — " He m., 14 April 1627, at Boston,
co. Lincoln, at her age of 17, and without the knowledge of her
parents, Jane, only child of Sir John Smith, Mayor of Boston
(1620), by Jane, da. of James Jones, of York, Leatherseller, "
might well have been built up from a dozen different sources,
and might entail references to (1) a Parish Register, (2) a Newsletter, (3) a Peerage, (4) a Diary like Luttrell's, (5) an entry in a
Bible, (6) a note in a genealogical magazine, (7) a private letter
to the Editor from a friend with genealogical tastes, (8) Correspondence printed by the Hist. MSS. Com., (9) Pedigrees both
of Smith and Jones, (10) an unedited MS. at the British Museum,
Record Office, or College of Arms, etc.   Accordingly, as a general

---

(ª) The *Dictionary of National Biography* is conspicuously lacking in such details
with regard to members of both Houses of Parliament who were not, and even some
who were, ' front bench ' men.

(ᵇ) See Appendix I in this volume.

**

rule, authorities have only been given where the statements seem likely to be doubted or where they conflict with accounts previously given by writers of standing In many cases a reference to the original English or Scottish Records (now available) has been substituted for notes referring to Dugdale, Douglas, Courthope, or other Peerage writers.

As this work is concerned rather with the history of the peerage than with the events of the moment, it has been thought well to exclude from this edition any account of persons who have become peers, whether by succession or creation, since the death of Queen Victoria, an event which practically synchronizes with the close of the 19th century. Thus a definite point of termination has been secured which will be the same through all the volumes.

In the notes, the editor has allowed himself a free hand

NOTES " Quidquid agunt homines nostri est farrago libelli. " Many of them will be found to contain passages from Swift, Hervey, Walpole, Macky, and other such writers, whose crisp epigrammatic style lends itself readily to quotation; but it should be borne in mind that (whether flattering or the reverse), these nearly contemporary comments are largely coloured by political or personal prejudice, truth being often sacrificed to smartness. If, however, not merely the unfairness but the triviality of some of these sketches should be urged against them, the defence of Francis Osborn (in his *Queen Elizabeth*) seems applicable, who remarks—" Neither can I apprehend it a greater folly in me to register the yellownesse of Queen Anne's hair with other levities, which may seem pertinent to posterity though trivial now, yet of as high concernment as Cæsar's nose. "

Anyone who reads this part of the work will go " from grave to gay, from lively to severe, " and, as the fancy takes him, may turn from the canonized Earl of the 14th to the bigamous Baron of the 19th century He may learn who were the Scottish nobles slain at Flodden, or discover how two noble ladies were locked up in " the Cage " for being drunk and disorderly.

The present Editor would certainly not have tried unassisted to draw the " bow of Ulysses, " but he has been

ACKNOW-LEDGMENTS fortunate in securing not only, as he would confidently have expected, the constant advice and assistance, dating back now for many years, of G.E C., the " onlie begetter " of this work, but also of those whose names follow in alphabetical order, on whom he had no sort of claim for the cordial and valuable co-operation which they have given

Oswald Barron has kindly undertaken to furnish the armorial bearings of all peers of England or Great Britain, a difficult task, for which his fitness will be generally recognised, and which was not attempted in the first edition.

The Rev. Alfred B Beaven has not only supplied information as to the politics of peers as already mentioned, but has also revised, and (where necessary) corrected, and added to, all statements with reference to the offices, honours, orders, or seats in the House of Commons, held by peers—no light labour—and last but not least has carefully read and commented on all proofs.

*George Dames Burtchaell, Athlone Pursuivant and Registrar of the Office of Arms (Dublin), has carefully and systematically revised the Irish portions of the work, and has devoted much labour to investigation with regard to some of the early and obscure Irish titles which will be found acknowledged *in loco*. He has also read all proofs relating to Irish peers and been ready to help in any case of difficulty.

Sir Henry Maxwell Lyte, K.C.B., Deputy Keeper of the Public Records, has given the benefit of his special knowledge with regard to some of the early baronies by writ, and both officially and unofficially has done everything in his power to aid the Editor.

Sir James Balfour Paul, Lyon King of Arms, as all who know him will anticipate, has been most obliging not only in fulfilling the same important function concerning Scotland which G D. Burtchaell has undertaken with regard to the sister island, but has observed without a murmur the " conveyance " of matter from his *Scots Peerage* into the following pages.

*John Horace Round needs no trumpet from the present writer to be the herald of his fame , he also has been good enough, in spite of many conflicting claims upon his time, to examine the proofs, and though it would be grossly unfair to saddle him with any sort of responsibility for statements in this work, yet if no errors should hereafter be detected bearing upon

---

(*) Those marked with an asterisk also assisted G E.C in the compilation of the first edition.

peerage law, their absence may safely be attributed in large measure to his immense knowledge and watchful eye.

*George Wentworth Watson. Those who read the *Genealogist* will know something of the capacity of this writer, but of the extent to which the present Editor is indebted to him they can have no knowledge, and he finds it quite impossible to overstate his sense of obligation. The special articles which he has re-written are duly acknowledged in their place, but these do not represent a tithe of the assistance which he has rendered, for he has scrutinised every word, nay every comma, of the proofs with a minuteness which could not have been surpassed.

Besides the above many others have aided in a greater or less degree by sending communications, and the Editor desires to express his hearty thanks to H. W. Forsyth Harwood, Editor of *The Genealogist*, H. J. Ellis, of the British Museum, W. H. B. Bird, D. G. Warrand, Sir James Ramsay, Major Francis Skeet, H. Stuart Moore, Josiah Wedgwood, M.P., W. F. Carter, A. Crawley-Boevey, and to all who have helped in and looked kindly on this enterprise.

The list of those to whom the Editor is under obligation must not be concluded without mentioning his publisher, H. A. Doubleday, whom zeal has led, and knowledge has enabled, to make many valuable suggestions for the improvement not only of the form but of the matter of these pages.

It will be seen therefore that, if the Editor should be found to have attempted something greater than he was capable of accomplishing, he will not be able to plead in excuse the lack of competent and generous helpers. Whatever may be thought of the work on other grounds, he is satisfied that it will not deserve the praise that has been accorded to other peerages, namely :—
" The best thing in fiction that the English have ever done. "

Nor is it only to men but to books also that the Editor must proclaim himself a debtor. J. H. Round's recently published *Peerage and Pedigree* has proved most useful, *The Scots Peerage* has already been mentioned, but to this should be added Ruvigny's *Jacobite Peerage*, Crisp's quaintly named but useful *Visitations*, Burke's and other annual *Peerages*, and similar works as to which want of space has prevented acknowledgment in the cases where they have been laid under contribution.

(*) See note on previous page.

EARLY WRITS

In an historic peerage the compiler is constantly confronted with the difficulty that it is impossible to reconcile the facts of history with the Law of Peerage. More especially is this the case when the question arises of how to describe men who were summoned to Parliament by writ before the time of Henry V. Take for example the incidental mention of, say, Ferrers of Groby ; when we find that in the most formal documents Henry IV never describes this man otherwise than William de Ferrers of Groby knight, it seems both inaccurate and anachronistic to describe him as Lord Ferrers of Groby. On the other hand, he cannot conveniently be described otherwise in the article " Ferrers, " and it seems unreasonable to give no indication that the Sir William de Ferrers of one part of the work is the same as the Lord Ferrers of another.

On the whole the best compromise in the case of a man summoned at an early date to Parliament, appears to be to refer to him when mentioned incidentally as Sir (—) (—) [Lord —], and, when he is dealt with directly in the article which gives an account of him, to set out the dates of his writs of summons and to add " whereby he is held to have become Lord—."

To write a peerage from a purely historic standpoint would be to exclude a number of men summoned at an early date to Parliament whose descendants in some cases are now sitting in the House of Lords in virtue of those summonses. To write a peerage from a purely legal standpoint would be to produce a work demonstrably and grotesquely untrue in fact.

Even in the case of a peerage written from a strictly legal standpoint, the arbitrary, conflicting, and unhistoric, decisions of the House of Lords would render it impossible for the compiler to feel any confidence that he had correctly decided as to who should, and who should not, figure in his work as peers, or that even if his list were correct at the moment of going to press it would be so six months later. *E.g.*, the decision on the Mowbray and Segrave Case in 1877 had the effect, not only of treating the writs of 1264 as bad, although all the men then summoned might have been (on account of the precedency of 1264 having been allowed to the baronies of Despenser and de Ros) included in former peerages, but it held the hitherto universally discredited writs of

1283 to be good, and by so doing accomplished the *ex post facto* creation of, or gave a new precedence to, 99 peers, or rather, to be strictly accurate, it did so as far as the supposed intentions of King Edward I are concerned. But in fact, owing to the unreasonable though desirable doctrine that proof of sitting is necessary before a man can establish his right to a peerage under a writ of summons, this startling pronouncement has very small *practical* effect on any one living at the present day. It is not, however, only as regards the past that the decision in 1877 as to the writs of 1283 is important, but in view of the number of such summonses to councils and other gatherings, it has opened up a wide field for the conversion in the future of knights and gentlemen of the Edwardian period into hereditary noblemen. It may be quite true that with regard to the living the Crown is the 'sole fountain of honour,' but with regard to the dead and gone that position has been usurped by the Committee for Privileges.

Until 1877 the first valid writs of summons, setting aside the anomalous cases of Ros and Despenser, were supposed to have issued in 1295, but in consequence of the decision in the Mowbray and Segrave Case the Editor has felt bound to set out all the men summoned in 1283; for obviously all those that were summoned at the same date as Roger Mowbray were as much, or as little, peers as Roger himself.

Nevertheless, there is no ground for supposing that, because the House of Lords held Roger's peerage to have originated in the writ of 1283, they would treat another claimant whose claim rested on the same basis in the same fashion. For although we must all recognise the truth of what the learned Sir Francis Bacon advances in the Ros Case (27 April 1616), that "matters of honour before so honourable judges cannot but receive an honourable determination," yet it is much to be hoped that before such another occasion arises, sufficient light on the history of the subject will have penetrated into that august Chamber to prevent their Lordships repeating this decision. Remembering, however, the unanimous finding of the Committee for Privileges in the case of the Earldom of Norfolk in 1906, when the plainest historic facts were ignored because they did not square with *later* legal decisions, such a hope seems somewhat over-sanguine. Finality can never be reached as to who were and who were not peers until the Lords' decisions are based upon some recognised principle; hitherto they have been settled by the opinions of the small body sitting at the time, who did not as a rule possess expert knowledge, or else by the importance of the claimant

The Mowbray and Segrave Case, in 1877, constituted, or implied, a reversal of the two previous awards in the Cases of Despenser and de Ros (1603 and 1616). The decision in the Case of the Earldom of Wilts in 1869 constituted a reversal of the extraordinary one in the Case of the Earldom of Devon in 1831, and no one can safely predict what the Lords will do from what the Lords have done.

The fact that an account is given of all the men summoned in 1283, and of all those who can be proved to have sat in the Parliament of 1290, forms a new and important feature which alone would differentiate this from any similar work.

It is not proposed to deal in this Preface with the large and difficult question of how far any summonses by writ can be held *in their origin* to have created a peerage dignity ; that matter will be discussed in an Appendix to the last volume if the writer should happily live to complete this work. He may however here say that he is abundantly convinced that there was no such thing as a peer of Parliament (*i e.* a man who obtained a higher status *because* he had received a summons), at any rate in Edwardian times. To dogmatise as to what was, or was not, legally a good summons to Parliament is impossible, having regard to the fact that the Committee for Privileges has never (as J. H. Round has pointed out) laid down what constitutes a Parliament, although it has been regarded as necessary for this purpose that the Lords temporal, the Lords Spiritual, and the Knights of the Shire and Burgesses should be summoned.

It is, however, thought that this is as good a place as any other to discuss the DOUBTFUL WRITS, as to the validity of which different opinions have been held from time to time ; this, accordingly, the Editor will proceed to attempt.

WRITS OF 1264

The first writs on record of any summons to Parliament are those of 24 December (1264) 49 Henry III, and thereon Courthope [p. xxv *sub* " Baronies by Writ "] remarks, " Very little can be gathered from it as it does not contain the names of one third part of the [Feudal] Baronial body, and though issued in the King's name, the King was himself a prisoner to the Earl of Leicester, the leader of the rebellious Barons, who [*i.e.* which Earl], it may fairly be inferred, summoned only those Barons who took part with him against the Royal cause. " The true date of these writs is, so far as laymen are concerned, 24 December, though owing to the fact that some of the clergy were summoned ten days earlier, *viz.*, 14 December, to meet at the same time and place, that date is often wrongly substituted ; *e.g.*, Courthope divides the laymen summoned on 24 December impartially between the two dates. The number of the laity summoned at this date was 23, of whom 5 were Earls.

The full list is as follows ·—

Comiti Leyc'	Radulfo Basset de Drayton'
Comiti Glouc'	Henrico de Hasting'
Comiti Norf' et Marescallo Angl'	Galfrido de Lucy
Comiti Oxon'	Roberto de Ros
Comiti Derb'	Johanni de Eyvill'
Radulfo de Cameys	Ade de Novo Mercato
Rogero de Sancto Johanne	Waltero de Colevill'
Hugoni le Despenser Justic' Angl'	Willelmo Marmyun
Johanni filio Johannis	Rogero Bertram
Willelmo de Munchenes'	Radulfo Basset de Sapecot'
Nicholao de Segrave	Gilberto de Gaunt
Johanni de Vescy	

The first occasion on which a writ of this date was treated as being capable of founding an hereditary peerage was in 1604, when the Barony of Despenser was allowed to Dame Mary Fane, and confirmed to her with such pre-eminence as Hugh le Despenser, Justiciar of England (1264), enjoyed. The second occasion was shortly afterwards, in 1616, when the Barony of Ros was recognised as originating in the said writ of 1264. The same view was again held on 5 Feb. 1666/7, and again on 7 May 1806, when the question of the inheritance of that Barony was at issue. On none of these occasions does the point that these writs were bad, as having issued in rebellion, appear to have been taken ; and it was not until the Mowbray and Segrave Case in 1877 that this very reasonable view was definitely adopted, although it should be remembered that previously (in 1841) the writs of 1264 were ignored in the Hastings Case.

WRITS OF 1283

These writs are recorded—merely—on the Welsh Rolls (*m. 2 dorso*), and are consequently ignored by Dugdale in his *Summons to the Great Councils and Parliaments*. The summonses were to 11 Earls; including Wilham DE VALENCE, who, though summoned as 5th among the Earls is not designated Earl of Pembroke ; also including Gilbert DE UMFREVILLE, EARL OF ANGUS, and Robert DE BRUS, EARL OF CARRICK, who, though so designated, can hardly be supposed, even if the writs be accounted good, to have been summoned as English Earls, but should rather be held to have been summoned, according to modern doctrine, as Barons, (ª) the mention of the Scottish Earldoms being merely an act of courtesy. (ᵇ)

In addition to the Earls, summonses were issued to 99 other persons, who must, if the writs be good, be accounted as Barons. The full list is as follows :—

Gilberto de Clare Comiti Glouc' et Hertford	Johanni de la Mare
Edmundo fratri Regis Comiti Lanc'	Henrico Husee
Rogero le Bygod Comiti Norff' et Mar' Angl'	Rogero de Lanc'
	Nicholao de Meynill'
Johanni de Warenn' Comiti Surr'	Roberto de Tateshal'
Henrico de Lacy Comiti Lincoln'	Ricardo de Grey
Willelmo de Valenc'	Roberto de Brus domino Vallis Anand
Hunfrido de Bohun Comiti H'ef' et Essex'	Galfrido de Nevill'
	Johanni de Stayngreve
Willelmo de Bello Campo Comiti Warr'	Radulfo de Thony
	Waltero de Wygeton'
Roberto de Veer Comiti Oxon'	Roberto filio Walteri de Davintre
Gilberto de Umfraunvill' Comiti de Anegos	Rogero la Zusche
	Roberto filio Rogeri
Roberto de Brus Comiti de Carrik	Johanni de Wauton'
Ade le Despenser	Normanno de Arcy
Petro de Gousl'	Johanni de Sancto Johanne
Reginaldo de Grey	Willelmo de Vescy
Gilberto de Gaunt	Thome de Berkel'
Nicholao de Segrave	Rogero de Colevill' de Byham
Matheo de Lovayn	Almarico de Sancto Amando

(ª) Again, as Bacon truly observes in the Ros case "the name of barons is subject to equivocation."

(ᵇ) Compare the similar case of Atholl under that title

***

Galfrido de Lucy
Johanni filio Galfridi * de Sancto
  Johanne
Nicholao de Cryoll'
Gilberto Pecche
Johanni de Bohun de Sussex'
Johanni de Wahull'
Philippo de Kyme
Johanni de Balliolo
Rogero de Moubray
Hugoni le Despenser
Radulfo Pypard
Roberto de Everingham
Johanni de Sullye
Ade de Bavent
Alexandro de Balliolo de Chileham
Willelmo filio Warini de Monte
  Canis'
Willelmo de Monte Canis' de Ed-
  wardeston'
Ricardo filio Johannis
Johanni Giffard de Brimmesfeld
Radulfo de Crumwell'
Johanni de Breus'
Ricardo de Breus'
Petro de Malo Lacu
Roberto de Ros
Johanni de Eyvill'
Willelmo Bardolf
Thome de Furnivall'
Willelmo de Huntingfeld
Radulfo Basset de Welledon'
Johanni de Bosco
Radulfo Basset de Drayton'
Theobaldo de Verdun
Marmeduco de Tweng'
Willelmo de Ros
Willelmo de Say

Rogero de Somery
Waltero de Facunberg'
Johanni de Bella Aqua
Thome filio Willelmi de Creistok
Johanni de Vallibus
Thome de Moleton' de Hoyland
Thome de Moleton' de Gillesland
Roberto de Grey
Reginaldo de Argenteym
Willelmo de Ferrar'
Gerardo de Insula
Rogero de Leyburn'
Johanni de Bello Campo
Alano de Plukenet
Hugoni Poinz
Johanni de Cogan
Radulfo de Albin'
Henrico de Urtiaco
Simoni de Monte Acuto
Olivero Dynant
Hugoni de Curtenay
Willelmo Martyn
Willelmo de Breus'
Maugero de Sancto Albino
Nicholao de Monte Forti
Philippo de Albin'
Rogero Exraneo
Edmundo de Mortuo Mari
Nicholao Baroni de Stafford
Andree de Estleye
Simoni Basset
Griffino filio Wenunwen
Petro Corbet
Johanni Extraneo
Roberto de Mortuo Mari
Willelmo le Botiller de Wemme
Fulconi filio Warini

There were also summonses to Knights of the Shire, and to
Burgesses from 21 cities or towns, but none to the Clergy.

In 1830-34 Palgrave threw a certain official halo over these

(*) *Sic* on the Roll, but it should be " Rogeri ". It may be added that in this
list, both as printed in the *Lords' Reports*, and in Palgrave's *Parliamentary Writs*, the
words " Davintre " and " Hoyland " have been misread, and there are also a few
minor mistakes common to both (G. W. Watson)

writs by recognising them in his *Parliamentary Writs* as good with this exception, until 1877, it had never, as far as the Editor knows, been suggested that writs summoning men to Shrewsbury to attend the trial of David ap Griffith, at least "super hoc et aliis locuturi" important as the event was in marking the development of parliamentary institutions, could confer on them hereditary titles. Nevertheless at that date the Lords, as it would seem, quite lightly and unadvisedly, and without realising the important bearing of their action, but apparently desiring to offer some *solatium* for disallowing a writ of 1264, held that one of 1283 was valid for that purpose. The question of the validity of these writs is fully discussed by J. H. Round in his *Peerage and Pedigree* (1910), where he deals with the treatment of them in the successive cases of Mowbray, Wahull, and Fauconberg. In this last case the validity of a writ of this date was keenly argued and was based on its acceptance in the Mowbray case. Unfortunately the Resolutions adopted by the Committee, while studiously ignoring these writs, leave it, perhaps, open to doubt whether they have been definitely rejected. J H. Round has now advanced against them the further argument that "no fewer than half the 'barons' summoned were never summoned to a Parliament of clear validity" (*Peerage and Pedigree*, vol. i, pp. 261-2), which is certainly significant. The argument which appeared to have most weight with Lord Halsbury, who sat on the Committee, was that because a statute was passed by the assembly in 1283, that constituted it a Parliament. Yet, as has been pointed out, Magna Charta is numbered among the Statutes, but no one will suggest that it was a regular Parliament which met at Runnymede. Even if the fact that the Clergy were not summoned were not a fatal flaw, when it is remembered that as late as the first Parliament of James I the peers of England of all ranks only numbered 82, the notion that Edward I, into whose head it never entered to make peers at all, ever contemplated such a wholesale creation as that of 99 Barons in one day is so preposterous, that the mere number alone should have made the Lords hesitate to render the law of Baronies by writ ridiculous by adopting it. (ª) If however it be answered that Edward I never had any such intention, but that many of these men had been peers of Parliament long before, the retort can only be "produce your evidence."

(ª) See Preface to 1st edition, note " a, " as reprinted on p. xxx of this volume.

J. H. Round points out that Bishop "Stubbs writing in
1875 declared there to be no valid writs between 1264 and 1295,
so the production (in 1877) of 1283 [as valid] was a revolution,"
and that Sir Thomas Hardy, who became head of the Record Office,
stated in evidence (1841) that there were no writs of summons to
Parliament between 1264 and 1295 (*Peerage and Pedigree*, vol. i,
p. 254). He further observes that Sir H. Nicolas had previously
(1825) stated the writs of 1294 to be "the earliest on record
excepting that of 1264" proving that he also ignored the writs
of 1283.

PARLIAMENTS OF 1290

In this year two Parliaments were held, one after the Feast
of St. Hilary, and another after Easter [2 Apr]. As to the first
of these, there are no writs of summons thereto on record. It
appears, however, from an entry in the proceedings, that Edmund,
Earl of Cornwall, had come to that Parliament "ad mandatum
domini Regis : " presumably, therefore, a writ had been issued to
him for that purpose, and so to others.

As to the second Parliament, no writs to Earls or Barons are
in evidence ([a]) but, there is a memorandum stating that, "in crastino
S. Trinitatis anno xviij [*i. e.* 29 May 1290]," a grant was made
to the King, in full Parliament, of an Aid to marry his daughter,
by certain persons named, who, besides five Bishops and the Elect
of Ely, were as follows :—

Edmundus frater domini Regis	Humfridus de Bohun Comes
Willelmus de Valenc' Comes Penebrock	Hereford et Essex'
	Robertus de Tipetot
Gilbertus de Clare Comes Glouc' et Hertford	Reginaldus de Grey
	Johannes de Hastinges
Johannes de Warenn' Comes Surr'	Johannes de Sancto Johanne
Henricus de Lacy Comes Linc'	Ricardus filius Johannis

([a]) There are, however, writs enrolled (*Close Roll*, 18 Edw. I, *m.* 9d), dated
14 June, to the Sheriffs of counties, directing them each to elect *duos vel tres* knights
of the shire to be at Westminster "a die Sancti Johannis Baptiste proximo futuro
in tres septimanas ad ultimum" [*i. e* before 15 July, some time after Parliament
met] "ad consulendum et consentiendum pro se et communitate illa [comitatus] hiis
que comites barones et proceres predicti tunc duxerint concordandum." No writs
are known to have been issued to the authorities of any town.

Willelmus le Latymer   Walterus de Huntercomb'
Rogerus de Monte Alto   Nicholaus de Segrave et ceteri
Willelmus de Brewose   magnates et proceres tunc in
Theobaldus de Verdun   Parliamento existentes. (ª)

The scant knowledge that we have about the constitution of this Parliament, and the fact that, in spite thereof, the Lords in 1841 decided that the then Lord Hastings' Barony originated at this date, because his ancestor could then be proved to have sat, makes it desirable to consider this Parliament when doubtful writs are being discussed.

The imperfection of the present state of our acquaintance with the development stage of our parliamentary history is emphasised by the discovery of C. Hilary Jenkinson that burgesses were summoned to the first Parliament of Edward I, at Easter 1275. Until April of the present year (1910) it was not known that representatives of the towns had ever been summoned before the Assembly or Parliament of 1283, except in the case of Simon de Montfort's rebel Parliament in 1264.

That the assembly of May 1290, however constituted, proceeded to pass Statutes, including among them the well-known *Quia Emptores*, is certain, and if Lord Halsbury's opinion *ut supra* is to be accepted, that fact alone constitutes it a genuine Parliament. Fortunately, whether the Parliament was good or bad, for the purpose of converting its members into hereditary noblemen, the effect on the Peerage can be but small.

In the first place only eleven men of Baronial rank are known to have sat; in the second, nearly all of those were summoned to an undoubted Parliament 5 years later,—in fact only two, Robert de Poynings and John de St. John, were never summoned again—and finally, as has been intimated already, the fact that the Committee for Privileges recognised the sitting in 1290 as originating the Barony in the Hastings case, is no criterion as to the line which a differently constituted Committee may take in the future. It is of course quite absurd to look for the same regularity and precision in the summoning of Parliaments during the period of transition and development *temp.* Edward I, as when these matters have been settled and ordered for centuries, *temp.* Edward VII.

The exact amount of irregularity in the constitution of an

(ª) *Parl Rolls*, vol. 1, p. 25 : Palgrave, *Parl Writs*, vol. 1, p. 20

early parliamentary gathering which the Lords' tribunal may be prepared to overlook for the purpose of creating a man a peer or of furnishing his peerage with a high precedence, is governed by the sweet pleasure of the judicial body for the moment, is not regulated by known laws, and consequently cannot be determined beforehand. So we come back to the crucial question, What constitutes a Parliament for Peerage purposes? And this query nobody answers, for nobody knows.

WRITS OF 1294

The observations of Sir N. Harris Nicolas (p. 141) on these writs are as follows :—

" REGINALD DE CLYVEDON was, with about sixty other persons, sum. 8 June (1294), 22 Edw. I, to attend the King, wherever he might be, to advise on the affairs of the Realm ; but there is very considerable doubt if that writ can be considered as a regular writ of summons to Parl , as none of the higher temporal Nobility nor any of the spiritual Peers were included in it ; nor was there any day fixed for the meeting. It is also to be observed that the writ in question is the earliest on record, excepting that of (1264) 49 Hen. III, that the majority of the persons summoned in (1294) 22 Edw. I were never again summoned excepting in 25 Edw. I, that several of those persons were not considered as Barons by Tenure, and that of those who were Barons by Tenure and summoned on those occasions, many were never included in any subsequent summons to Parliament. The writ of (1294) 22 Edw. I has, however, on one occasion (in the case of the Barony of Ros) been admitted as a writ of summons to Parliament at the bar of the House of Lords, but the last 'General Report of the Lords' Committee appointed to search for matters touching the Dignity of a Peer of the Realm,' appears to confirm the objections here expressed. "

The criticisms of G.W. Watson on the above disquisition are as follows :

" It appears from the foregoing remarks that Nicolas must have been under some misapprehension when he took these writs into consideration. For the only writ concerned in the Ros Case (1616, ' before the Commissioners for the office of Earl Marshal') was one of 1264 and not one of 1294. It would seem indeed that

no writs of this latter date have ever been brought forward in any
Case, nor are they even mentioned in the *Lords' Reports*, vol. i,
p. 208.   It may be further observed that the person whom Nicolas
here calls *Reginald* de Clyvedon is described, and rightly described,
in the enrolment (*Gascon Roll*, 22 Edw. I, *m.* 8d) as *Reymond* de
Clivedon : also that under " Ros, " Nicolas has confused the writ
of 1294 to William de Ros (of Hemsley) with that to William de
Ros of Ingmanthorpe, though both these persons were summoned,
and distinguished from each other in the writs   It remains to
be added that Courthope has copied Nicolas in all these particulars "

WRITS OF 1297

The validity of the writs of 1297 as regular writs of summons to Parliament (such as would now be held to originate a
Peerage) is discussed at great length in *Nicolas* (p. 242), under
" FITZ JOHN, " in a long and elaborate note which is reprinted in
Courthope, with a few slight alterations.   The doubt of such validity
was suggested by the following note (written, apparently, by John
Vincent, son of the well known Augustine Vincent) in a copy of
the summonses in the College of Arms   " This can be no summons [to Parl.], because it is only directed to the Temporality. "

As to the reason for the clergy not being summoned, Hamilton
Hall, in *N. & Q.*, 8th Ser., vol. xi, p. 1, points out that they
were all then outlawed, Pope Boniface VIII and the Primate
Winchelsey having advanced the proposition (very unlikely to be
admitted by a needy and resolute King) that Church property
should pay no taxes.

J. H. Round points out that, according to Stubbs *(Constitutional History)*, " Six earls and eighty-nine barons and knights had
been invited, and most of them attended, " but the clergy and
commons were not summoned.   It was in this historic assembly,
which met at Salisbury, 24 February 1296/7, having been summoned 26 January preceding, that the earls of Hereford and Norfolk
defied the king, who exclaimed to Norfolk ' By God, Earl, you
shall either go or hang, ' and was met by the rejoinder, ' By God,
King, I will neither go nor hang '   It was probably owing to this
assembly being styled a *parliamentum* in the marginal heading on
the Close Roll that it seems to have been accepted without question

as a 'Parliament' in 1677, when the solitary writ of summons produced in the Frescheville claim (see FRESCHEVILLE) was to this assembly. But in the Wahull claim (1892), when this was one of the two 'Parliaments' to which writs of summons were produced, Lord Selborne said, in his Judgment, "it seems to me clear that the Assembly appointed to meet at Salisbury in 1297, to which Thomas de Wahull was summoned, was not a proper Parliament." Nevertheless, a writ of summons to it had been accepted as valid (in 1877) in the Mowbray and Segrave Case (see Round's *Peerage and Pedigree*, vol. i, pp. 255, 260). It should be added that the strange error of Dugdale (followed by Nicolas), who carelessly read *Mathie* as *Mathei*, which led him to suppose that the 'Parliament' was summoned for 21 September (instead of 24 February), was first pointed out in 1823. See the *Lords' Reports*, 2nd edition, vol. i, p. 470, note 55. In *N & Q.*, 5th Ser., vol. v, p. 103, James Greenstreet gives 94 coats of arms of the magnates there assembled, which he calls "The First Nobility Roll," being the earliest *dated* roll of arms known to exist.

WRITS OF 1342

The only other doubtful writs about which it is needful to say anything are those of 25 February (1341/2) 16 Edward III, and they do not require detailed examination. For some unknown reason they been have treated as good by peerage writers, but there seems no justification for looking on the assembly summoned by them as other than a council. The matter is of some importance, for though, so far as the Editor is aware, no attempt has ever been made to establish the validity of a writ of this date before the Committee of Privileges, yet of the multitude of men then summoned some were never summoned on any other occasion. Stubbs in his *Constitutional History* remarks that "Edward did not venture to summon a Parliament" in this year. The objections to these Writs, shortly stated by J. H. Round in a letter to the Editor, are as follows : — "The summonses are headed " de consilio summonito " [not " de Parliamento summonito " as is the case in 1341 and 1343] and are addressed only to the Archbishop of Canterbury, seven bishops, nine Earls and the Earl of Angus, and to a great number of Barons, but to no Knights [of the

Shire] or citizens. Clearly this is no Parliament The summons was put in evidence in the Meinill case, but Counsel stated that this was only a summons to a council. " To the above need only be added, that whereas to the undoubted Parliaments of 1341 and 1343 there were, excluding Earls, 45 and 40 persons summoned respectively, to this intermediate council of 1342 the attendance of 96 persons was ordered.

So little regard do the voluminous *Lords' Reports* attach to this gathering, that in the chapter " On the constituent Parts of the Legislative Assemblies [N B. not merely the Parliaments] of England during the reign of Edward the Third " it is entirely ignored in its chronological place (vol. i, p. 316), the writers passing straight from the consideration of the Parliament of 15 to that of 17 Edward III.

✳✳✳✳

PREFACE

TO THE FIRST EDITION (*)

This work is intended as an alphabetical "*Synopsis*" of the ENTIRE HEREDITARY PEERAGE, extant, extinct, or dormant, of England, Great Britain and the United Kingdom, as also of Scotland and Ireland (including such Peerages as have been created for life only by charter or patent), containing a short account of each Peer, and stating also (where it can be ascertained) the date and place of birth, baptism, marriage, death and burial, not only of all the Peers themselves, but of their respective wives, together with other particulars, including the name and description of the father and mother of each Peer and Peeress.

The succession to the title is shown, and the plan generally adopted is almost the same as in the "SYNOPSIS OF THE PEERAGE OF ENGLAND" (a work of infinite labour and merit), edited by that well-known antiquarian genealogist, Sir Nicholas Harris Nicolas, G.C.M.G., in 1825   Of this work (after his death), a new edition, under the name of the "HISTORIC PEERAGE OF ENGLAND," was issued in 1857, with many very valuable additions, by one who was thoroughly competent for such a work, *viz*, William Courthope, late (1854-66) Somerset Herald.   Both these works, however (besides that upwards of a quarter of a century has now [1887] elapsed since the publication of the latter), take *no notice* of the Peerage *of Scotland or Ireland,* and (though most useful, and indeed indispensable, to all genealogists) contain, *even as to the English Peers,* a somewhat meagre (though generally accurate) account ; while *no notice* whatever is taken *of their alliances.*

This work includes such eldest sons or grandsons of Dukes, Marquesses, or Earls, who, having been styled by a *courtesy* title as heirs apparent to such Peerages, have died in the lifetime of their respective fathers or grandfathers.   Of these the account is placed immediately after the notice of such their ancestors.

With respect to BARONIES BY TENURE (of which a fuller and more

---

(*) The Preface to volume 1 of the first edition is here reprinted with the additions made by G.E.C in later volumes.

accurate account than any hitherto published is greatly to be wished), they are not included, save in two or three cases, such, more especially, as Abergavenny, Berkeley, &c., where it has been contended that the tenure *per Baroniam* constituted the actual peerage. Baronies by Tenure are a class of dignities which are best dealt with by themselves, and the account of them given in *Nicolas* and reproduced in *Courthope* is, when tested by the light of the researches made during the last threescore years, very inaccurate, besides also that a vast number of such Baronies are altogether omitted in those publications.

The object of the present work being not only to amplify and continue any previous account of the hereditary Peerage of England, &c., but to insert therewith that of Scotland and Ireland, some difficulty arises in determining, with respect to these last two kingdoms, as to what in them constituted a Peerage, in the same sense as that term *(mutatis mutandis)* is applied to England.

As to Scotland, an accurate distinction between such Barons as may be considered Peers (*i.e.*, the Greater Barons, who were 'Lords of Parliament') and such (*i e*, the Lesser Barons) as held only a territorial Barony, is, at an early period, hardly attainable. In this work an account will be given of such Scotch Baronies only as were Lords of Parl , or which (though, in some cases, almost imperceptibly) developed afterwards into such. One of the best authorities on such a subject, the well-known John Riddell ('*Scotch Peerage Law*,' edit. 1833, p. 89, note 2) remarks that in Scotland 'we had no hereditary Lordships of Parl. till about [1437-1463] the reign of James II.' [S]. R. R Stodart, Lyon Clerk Depute, in a letter (1885) to the Editor, writes that 'It does not seem that there were Barons by tenure here [S] as in England, or rather, one might say that the *Minor Barons* were *all Barons by tenure*; they certainly were not Lords of Parl.' G. Burnett, Lyon, adds, in a similarly directed letter (1889), that 'the Scotch Parl., as it existed in the 14th and 15th centuries and the greater part of the 16th, was an assemblage in one Chamber of three separate orders of the Community, the Prelates, *Barons* and Burgesses. *The Earls belonged to the order of Barons. All* Barons in the old sense, *i.e.*, landholders *holding their land as a Barony*, had the right, or, more properly speaking, were under the obligation, to attend the meeting of the Estates, sometimes expressed as part of the *reddendum* of a charter. By the less considerable landowners the obligation to be present was often held a grievous burden, and a statute of James I [S], in March 1427/8, enacted that the Small Barons should be excused from attending Parl , provided they sent two or more wise men from each Sheriffdom to represent them. Though this act, as well as a later one, was a failure as to its main object (Parliamentary representation) it was probably held to afford a quasi-sanction to the habitual absence of the *Small Barons*, with the bestowal of a new title, that of *Lord of Parliament*, on the more considerable of the order, who might regard parliamentary attendance as a privilege rather than a burden, contributed further to the same result. No such creations, however, existed prior to the time (1406-37) of James I [S], who created

but few, though his successor (1437-60) James II [S], created a good
many, but many Barons even at that period, who attended the meetings
of the estates, were not Lords of Parliament.' The distinction between
the Greater Barons [S] (who were Lords of Parl.), and the Lesser Barons
(who were not such Lords) is emphasised in the creation (14 Apr. 1616) of
Sir David Carnegy *in Baronem Majorem et Dominum Parliamenti* [S].

As to IRELAND, where no comprehensive account of the entire Peerage
exists, and where one cannot (as in England) be guided by the writ of
summons (which in Ireland was merely incidental to, and not creative
of the Peerage), (ᵃ) the Editor has not attempted to deal with any title of
honour in that kingdom, which may have existed as an hereditary Peerage
of parliament and have become *extinct* prior to the reign of Henry VII,
other than with such among them as had been created, before that period,
by patent or charter, (of which there appear altogether to have been but
twelve), and with the Earldom of Cork, which in all probability was so
created. (ᵇ) In addition to these, and to such Peerages as were *existing* in the
reign of Henry VII, and (of course) such as *thereafter* were created, some
account will be given of the few feudal Baronies which had developed
before that reign, into the hereditary Peerages then existing, such as those
of Slane, Howth, &c. Of the twelve Peerages created by *patent* before
the reign of Henry VII as above-mentioned, the holders of five were
among the fifteen Irish Peers (ᶜ) who were summoned by that King in 1489

(ᵃ) The case of the Barony of La Poer (or Power of Curraghmore) is but an
apparent contradiction to this statement, for the decision concerning it (in 1767) was
grounded on the *erroneous* report of the Attorney and the Solicitor General for Ireland,
that this ancient feudal Barony (of which the Peerage dignity was created *by patent*,
33 Hen VIII, to Richard Power, the then feudal Lord, "*et hæredibus masculis de
corpore exeuntibus*") was a *Barony created by writ*, and, consequently, one *in fee*.
With this anomaly, the *entire* Irish Baronage is composed exclusively of the male heirs
of the Peers recognised in 1489 by Henry VII, and of those since ennobled by *letters
patent*. So clearly was the fact recognised (even at so late a time as the end of the
17th century) that no writ of summons created a Peerage of Ireland, that when
James II, shortly after the revolution, wished to confer a *hereditary* Irish Peerage, he
(being then unwilling, in those troublous times, to rely solely on letters patent) introduced *express words* to that effect in the writ of summons, which otherwise would
have been (like the Irish writs of his predecessors) merely personal.

(ᵇ) These were seven Earldoms (which, with the Earldom of Cork, were apparently, all that ever existed before that date), four Baronies, and one Viscountcy, *viz.*
the *Earldoms* of Ulster (1205), Carrick (1315), Kildare (1316), Louth (1319),
Ormonde (1328), Desmond (1329) and Waterford (1446) The *Baronies* of
Trimleston (1461/2), Portlester (1461/2), Ratowth (1468) and Rathwire* (1476);
also the *Viscountcy* of Gormanston (1478).

* As to the existence of Rathwire as a peerage title see Appendix A., p. 458, note
" a " in this volume. V.G.

(ᶜ) *Viz*, three EARLS, *i e*, Kildare, Ormonde and Desmond (all three Earldoms
having been created by patent), three VISCOUNTS, *i.e.*, Buttevant, Fermoy and
Gormanston (of which the last alone had been, in 1478, created by patent), and nine
BARONS, *i.e*, Athenry, Kingsale, Kerry and Lixnaw, Slane, Delvin, Killeen, Howth,

to Greenwich, but the remaining ten of those so summoned (two Viscounts and eight Barons) possessed Peerages, the mode of whose creation is, and probably will ever remain unknown ; (ª) it certainly was not by writ,(ᵇ) and probably, in the earlier cases at all events, not by patent. These ten may be called *Prescriptive Peerages*, of which the holders were, in 1489, acknowledged as Hereditary Peers of Parliament by Henry VII.

As to Scotland and Ireland, the Editor, though he has not in all cases implicitly adopted the views therein contained, is under the greatest obligation to two most valuable works · one entitled " Inquiry into the Law and Practise in Scottish Peerages, &c., " by John Riddell · the other, " Feudal Baronies in Ireland during the Reign of Henry II, " by William Lynch, F.S.A. (ᶜ) The early dates (1181, &c) assigned to some of the Irish Baronies have always been a great difficulty, one, it is feared, that has not been very adequately dealt with in this work, but (since its issue) the

---

Trimleston and Dunsany, of which Trimleston alone had been (in 1461/2) created by patent. The Earl of Waterford (Earl of Shrewsbury in England) was not summoned, neither was Lord Portlester, who did not die till 1496. The Baronies of Ratowth and of Rathwire * were probably under forfeiture

* See note * on previous page.

(ª) Even with respect to the Baronies of Killeen and Dunsany, two of the most modern prescriptive peerages, nothing can be ascertained as to the mode of their creation   Camden merely states that " Christopher Plunket was advanced [*evectus est*] to the dignity of Baron of Killeen, having inherited Killeen (*i.e* , the *manor*) from the family of Cusack. " The Barony so created (though the name and estate were inherited through a *female*) was, according to the established rule of the Irish Baronage, one descendible to the *issue male* of the grantee, and has, as such, twice passed over the heir general in favour of the heir male. The writ under which Lord Killeen's male ancestor, Richard Plunkett of Rathregan, sat in the Parliament of 48 Edw. III did not entitle him (as in England) to any hereditary Peerage.

(ᵇ) Until the 10th year of Henry VIII the power of summoning these Parliaments was in the chief Governor of Ireland though he issued his writ in the Royal name and style   No act of any *subject*, however exalted, can, in any case, create a Peer, and indeed (excepting in the case of the Barony of La Poer) none of the families so summoned ever attempted to advance any such claim. See " Remarks upon the Ancient Baronage of Ireland " [Dublin 1829, 8vo., pp. 158], page 16, 31, &c , which little work is a very clear account of these dignities, probably written by William Lynch, the Author of " Feudal Baronies in Ireland. "

(ᶜ) " Lynch is the ablest writer, no doubt, upon the subject, but, we must remember, a partisan   Lynch wrote with the object of establishing, as a rule of law, a presumption in favour of heirs male in the descent of Irish dignities. Betham, in spite of his official position [Ulster King of Arms, 1820-53] was so poor an advocate (in his *Dignities Feudal and Parliamentary*, 1830) of the opposite view, that we cannot wonder at G.E.C. following Lynch throughout. . . .   The native tribal principle, invincibly in favour of Agnates, strove here, as elsewhere, against the principles of English law. We imagine that at first the latter prevailed especially within the Pale, but with the ebb of the English rule the native principle revived, and even the Anglo-Normans (Hibernis Hiberniores) adopted, in the wilder parts, the old tribal system, or at least elaborately entailed their estates upon heirs male   Thus there arose, in practise, a system of male succession, altho', in our opinion, it had not

solution thereof has been thus ably indicated. 'The origin of the difficulty is, we would suggest, that whereas in England the *creation* of a Barony [if not by letters patent] is reckoned to date from the first proved *writ* of summons; in Ireland the writ of summons has been comparatively ignored, and dignities traced to the earliest period at which their possessors were Barons by *tenure*. This principle, tho' pressed upon them, has always been rejected by our own House of Lords, so that the apparent superior anti-quity of Irish over English Baronies has no foundation in fact. ' The anomalous precedency accorded to the Barony of Abergavenny seems, however, a case (probably the only case) in which the English Peers have in modern times recognised some such right.

As TO ENGLAND, Courthope's work (above mentioned) is an almost infallible guide as far as it extends ; some matters, however, have been changed since (1857) the date of its issue. The validity of the writ of (1264) 49 Hen. III (to Montfort's parl.) which had been accepted in the cases of Le Despencer (1604) and of De Ros (1806) has been disallowed in 1877 (in the decision on Mowbray) whereby it 'has raised a question of precedence as yet insoluble ' It had previously, in 1841, been ignored in the Hastings Case. The theory that the next valid writ to 1264 was that of 24 June (1295) 23 Edw. I, (though the late Dep. Keeper of the Records, the well-known Sir Thomas Duffus Hardy, expressly stated in 1841, in the Hastings case, that he had made search for any intermediate writs of summons and found none) has also been upset by their Lordships' decision in 1877 (in the Mowbray and Segrave case) who allowed the validity of the writ of summons to Shrewsbury, 28 June (1283) 11 Edw. I, 'apparently without the slightest conception that they were establishing a precedent of the most momentous consequence. When it is added that the contested writs of 1294 and 1297 were also allowed to be put into evidence without question ([a]) and that the writ of 1283 affects a hundred ['] Baronies, it will be seen that the Mowbray decision (1877) unconsciously worked a revolution, and that the histories of baronies by writ must now be undertaken *de novo*. ' ([b]) The decision in 1841 in the Hastings case (ignoring the writ of 1264) recognised the *sitting* in 1290 (no record being found of writs of summons) as the *date* of that dignity.

---

prevailed at first. It is largely due to this development that the houses of the *Conquistadores* present so long and illustrious a descent in the male line, instead of merging in heiresses, as in England would have been their fate. " (*Quarterly Review*, for Oct. 1893, vol. 177, p 410, in an able article headed " The Peerage ").

([a]) These writs, however, were very possibly not questioned, as nothing turned upon them The number of writs (already held to be valid) under which (by the decision of 1673), a peerage descendible to heirs general is now held to have been created, is great, and the persons summoned in such writs are "legion " It is curious, too, that these (now deemed) hereditary peerages should have been created in batches of 100 or so, and that, too, by the early Plantagenet kings, generally supposed to have been more chary of such creations than their successors.

([b]) Article headed " The Peerage " in the *Quarterly Review* for Oct. 1893.

The account of existing Peers, or even of existing Peerages, forms but a small part of this work   An acknowledgement is however due to the various Editors of the Annual Peerages for such information as may have been taken therefrom, *e.g.*, from " Dod " it may have been culled that a certain Peer was born in Wilton Crescent, educated at Harrow &c. , from " Lodge " that some nobly born lady of an uncertain age was actually born on some precise (though possibly ancient) date ; from " Foster, " that a marriage or birth occurred at some hitherto unascertained and unsuspected period ; as also a full account of all the places for which the embryo Peer was M P., with the dates thereof, and many other precise and well verified dates ; while from " Burke "—but who can say what can, or rather what can not, be found in the closely printed and well-arranged pages of that most energetic and chivalrous King of Arms ? His are the Extant and Extinct Peerage, the Extant and Extinct Baronetage, the Landed Gentry, the Vicissitudes of Families, the Anecdotes of the Aristocracy, &c , &c , &c. The amount of indebtedness which all who write on a kindred subject must feel to this all comprehensive and indefatigable genealogical writer cannot be too deeply acknowledged

The account of the *Family estates* is taken from Bateman's " Great Landowners of Great Britain and Ireland," 1883. An earlier edition was pub. in 1878. A still earlier one, which related to England *alone* (being called " The Acre-ocracy of England ") was pub. in 1876. It should also be mentioned that, early in 1886 (about two years after this publication had commenced) a *most important* work, as far as the higher grades (Dukes to Viscounts) of the *English* Peerage is concerned, has appeared. It is entitled (somewhat strangely, inasmuch as it is *not* by an " *official,* " nor under " *official* " sanction, and [alas l] does *not* (excepting in some few *special* instances) contain the " *Barons* ") " *The official Baronage* of England, by James E. Doyle. " [3 vols. 4to.].   The great value of this work consists in the long list of the various appointments held by the Peers therein mentioned, the dates whereof (of which a free use has been made in this work), having been sought out, with wonderful and most commendable industry, from the original authorities by the indefatigable Editor.

Among the persons who energetically assisted the Editor during the progress of the work (1884-97) are, taking first those who have passed away before its completion in the order of their death, [1] Edmund Montagu BOYLE, *d.* 11 Aug. 1885 aged 40 ; [2] Robert Riddle STODART, Lyon Clerk Depute (1863-86) *d.* 19 Apr. 1886, aged 58 ; [3] Walford Dakin SELBY, of the Public Record Office, Editor (1884-88) of *The Genealogist,*" N.S., vols 1 to 5 (in which work, from Jan 1884 to Dec. 1889, the first two vols. of this Peerage were first issued), who *d.* 3 Aug 1889 aged 45, and as to whom see *The Genealogist,* N.S., vol. vi, pp 65-68 ; [4] George BURNETT, LL D , Lyon King of Arms (1866-90) who *d.* 24 Jan. 1890, as to whom see *The Genealogist,* N.S , vol. vi, pp 213-215 ; [5] Sir Bernard BURKE, Ulster King of Arms (1853-92), above mentioned, who *d* 12 Dec. 1892, aged 80, as to whom see *The Genealogist,* N S., vol. ix, p. 186 ; [6] Michael J. M. SHAW-STEWART, sometime in the Bombay Civil Service, *d* 3 Apr 1894, aged 65. Among those that are still, (ª) happily, among us, are [7] J. Horace ROUND, LL.D., author of *Geoffrey de Mandeville, &c.*; [8] G. Wentworth WATSON, M.A ; [9] Joseph BAIN, F.S.A. (Scot) (ᵇ) ; [10] R E. CHESTER-WATERS, M A (ᶜ) ; [11] The Rev John WOODWARD, F.S A. (ᵈ) author of a valuable work on Heraldry , [12] B Wyatt GREEN-FIELD, F S A (ᵉ) ; [13] Sir Albert W. WOODS, K C B , (ᶠ) Garter, as well as several other members of the College of Arms, London ; [14] George Dames BURTCHAELL, M A., (ᵍ) whose assistance has been invaluable ; [15] W. Duncombe PINK, of Leigh, co. Lancaster ; and last, but by no means least, [16] The Hon. Vicary GIBBS, M P., not only for contributing numerous dates, and names of persons and places, but for supplying many notices of peers and peeresses, generally from contemporary sources (more especially those in vols. vi to viii), and for various valuable suggestions The Editor takes this opportunity of mentioning that during the course of this work, a large number of Letters, Memoirs, Journals, Obituaries and other kindred writings have (with the assistance of friends) been carefully examined, with the result not only of correcting and amplifying many vague and doubtful statements appearing in works bearing on the Peerage, but of checking and confirming a still larger number Such a field is practically inexhaustible, and, if this enquiry be pursued, it will, as printing makes more and more of such works accessible, be possible in the future to approach much nearer, not only to correctness, but also to completeness, than in this so styled *Complete Peerage* has hitherto been attained.

In conclusion, the Editor, though fully (most fully) aware how many errors and imperfections there must (almost of necessity) be in a work of this nature, and how little competent (more especially as regards the intricacies of the Scotch Peerage) he is to deal with it, trusts that the manifest advantage of an arrangement by which *any* correction for *any* Peerage can *at once* be effected, and be thereafter capable of *at once* being referred to, will in a great measure compensate for the numerous sins of omission and commission which are herein.

G. E. C. 1887.

(ª) *i.e.* early in 1897.
(ᵇ) Living early in 1909
(ᶜ) Died 25 Nov. 1898, aged 60.
(ᵈ) Died 4 June 1898, aged 60.
(ᵉ) Died 16 Sep. 1897.
(ᶠ) Afterwards (1903) G C.V.O. ; died 7 Jan 1904, aged 87.
(ᵍ) Afterwards (1908) Athlone Pursuivant and Registrar of the College of Arms, Dublin, being probably the ablest Genealogist (among the many able ones) that has ever existed in that office.

EXPLANATION

OF THE PLAN OF THE WORK, AND OF THE
ABBREVIATIONS USED

1. The Roman numerals indicate the number of persons who have borne a dignity, while the Arabic ones show how many of the same family have inherited it.

2. A slanting line between the figures of a date indicates that it refers to the first part of the year preceding 26 March, before the style was changed in England, and a horizontal line that it refers to the *regnal* year. Thus "He *d*. Jan. 1601/2" means a death which after 2 Sep 1752 would have been regarded as occurring in January 1602 ; whilst the words "He *d*. 1299-1300" would indicate a death in 28 Edw. I, *i.e.* between 20 Nov. 1299 and 20 Nov. 1300

3. The *date* after the Roman numeral is that of the creation of, or succession to, the dignity. When such date is not accurately known, the name of the king in whose reign it is supposed to have occurred is substituted.

4. The *limitation* of all patents of creation is to be understood as being to the heirs male of the body of the grantee, unless otherwise stated.

5. All Peerages and other dignities are to be considered as either of England, Great Britain, or of the United Kingdom, unless followed by the letters [S.] or [I.], which respectively denote them to be of Scotland or of Ireland.

7. In Scottish Peerages the title is given as in the Appendix to *Douglas*, in Irish Peerages as in *Lib. Hib.*, unless at variance with any higher authority.

8. In the account of each Peer or Peeress, as also of any Peer connected with him or her *by alliance*, the *surname* is given within brackets ; but when a Peer is but *incidentally* mentioned, his surname is often omitted, more especially if it is the *same* as the title of the Peerage

9. The words "*Knight*" and "*Esquire*" are omitted. The former is applicable, in this work, to all who have the designation of "Sir" before their names, unless expressly stated to be Baronets.

10. All wills and administrations are to be considered, unless stated otherwise, as having been registered in the Prerogative Court of the Archbishop of Canterbury, or, after its abolition, in the Principal Registry, London.

*****

ABBREVIATIONS

Besides those for the different orders of Knighthood, for the University degrees, &c , and such as are in general vogue, the following are made use of in this work.

admon , administration.
afsd., aforesaid.
ap., apparent
Arch., *Archæologia*, 4to., 1809.
b., *born*.
bap., *baptized*.
Barr., Barrister at Law.
bur., *buried.*
cod., codicil.
coh., coheir.
Coll. Top. et Gen., *Collectanea Topographica et Genealogica*, 8 vols., large 8vo., Nichols & Son, London, 1834-43.
Coll. Gen., *Collectanea Genealogica*, edited by J. Foster, large 8vo., vol. i, 1881, &c.
Collins, Collins' *Peerage of England*, edited by Sir E. Brydges, 9 vols., 8vo., 1812. (The 1st edition is in 1 vol., 8vo., 1709.)
Compendium [E.], *Compendium*, *English Peerage*, small 4to., 1st to 13th edit. 1718-69.

„	[S.]	„	Scottish	„	„	1st to 7th edit. 1720-64.
„	[I.]	„	Irish	„	„	1st to 5th edit. 1722-56.

   This is the first printed Peerage of Ireland ; followed, three years afterwards, by *Crossley*, as below.
cont., contract.
Courthope, Courthope's *Historic Peerage of England*, 8vo., 1857.
Crawfurd, Crawfurd's *Peerage of Scotland*, folio, 1716. This is the first printed Peerage of Scotland (2nd and 3rd edition in 1719).
Crossley, Crossley's *Peerage of Ireland*, folio, 1725.
cr., *created.*
Cruise, Cruise on *Dignities*, 2nd edit , 8vo., 1823.
d., *died.*
diem cl. ext., (writ of) *diem clausit extremum.*
da., daughter.
dat., dated.
disp., dispensation.
Douglas, Douglas' *Peerage of Scotland*, 2nd edition, edited by J. P. Wood, 2 vols., folio, 1813. The 1st edition is in 1 vol., folio, 1764.
Dugdale, Dugdale's *Baronage of England*, 2 vols., folio, 1675-76, the first and greatest work on the English Peerage.

ABBREVIATIONS

ed., educated.

[E.], Kingdom of England.

Ex Hist., *Excerpta Historica*, large 8vo., 1831

Fac. off., Faculty office, London.

Fun. Cert., Funeral Certificate.

Gen., *Genealogist*, edited by G W. Marshall, 8vo., 7 vols., 1877-83

[G.B.], Kingdom of Great Britain

Han Sq., Hanover Square, Middlesex.

h , heir.

Her and Gen., *Herald and Genealogist*, edited by J. G. Nichols, 8 vols , 8vo , 1863-74.

Hewlett, Hewlett's *Dignities in the Peerage of Scotland, which are dormant or forfeited*, 8vo., 1882.

Hewlett's Jur., Hewlett's *Jurisdiction in regard to Scottish Titles of Honour*, small 8vo., 1883.

Hist. MSS. Com , Historical Manuscripts Commission.

[I.], Kingdom of Ireland.

Inq , Inquisition.

Inq. p. m., Inquisition *post mortem*.

J.P , Justice of the Peace.

lic , licence.

Lib. Hib., *Liber Munerum Publicorum Hiberniæ*, 19 Stephen to 7 Geo. IV, two enormous folio vols., 1852.

Lodge, Lodge's *Peerage of Ireland*, 2nd edit., edited by M. Archdall, 7 vols , 8vo , 1789. The 1st edition is in 4 vols., 8vo , 1754

Lond. off., Bishop of London's office.

L C.C., London County Council.

Lords' Reports, first, second, third and fourth *Reports on the dignity of a Peer of the Realm from the Lords' Committees*, 4 vols , folio, 1826.

Lynch, Lynch's *Feudal Baronies in Ireland*, 8vo., 1830.

Maidment, Maidment's *Genealogical Collections*, 4to., pp. 172, 1882. Privately printed.

m., married.

mar. lic., marriage licence.

mar. settl , marriage settlement

matric, matriculated.

M.I., monumental inscription.

Misc. Gen. et Her., *1st s.*, ditto, *2nd s.*, ditto, *3rd s.*, *Miscellanea Genealogica et Heraldica*, edited by J. J Howard, large 8vo , *1st series*, 2 vols., 1868-76 ; *2nd series*, 4 vols., 1874-83 ; *3rd series*, vol. 1, 1884, &c.

N and Q., *Notes and Queries;* first issued on 3 Nov. 1849.

Nicolas, Nicolas' *Synopsis of the Peerage of England*, 2 vols., small 8vo , 1825.

Nichols' *Wills*, *Royal and Noble Wills*, 1087 to 1508, edited by J. Nichols, 4to., 1780. (*)

(*) In Nichols' *Wills* each document is given in its own language and at full length, whereas in *Test Vet* those that are not in English are translated, and many are abridged.

off., office.

pr., proved.

P.C., Privy Councillor.

Rep , Representative.

Riddell, Riddell's *Law and Practice in Scottish Peerages,* 2 vols , 8vo., 1842.

Robertson, Robertson's *Proceedings relating to the Peerage of Scotland,* 1707 to 1788, 4to. Edinburgh, 1790.

[S.], Kingdom of Scotland.

Segar, "Baronagium Genealogicum," by Sir W Segar, Garter (1603-33), continued to 1740 by his great-grandson, Simon Segar, a most valuable MS., 3 vols., folio, in the College of Arms, London. (ᵃ)

Selden, Selden's *Titles of Honour,* 3rd edit., folio, 1672. The 1st edition is 4to., 1614.

s , son.

s.p., sine prole.

s.p.legit., sine prole legitimâ

s.p m , sine prole masculâ.

s.p.m s , sine prole masculâ superstite.

s p.s., sine prole superstite

spec., special.

Sq , square.

St., Saint

Str , street

suc , succeeded.

sum., summoned

Summons, Summons of the Nobility to the Parliaments, 1264 to 1685, by Sir W Dugdale, Garter, 1677-86, folio, 1685.

surv., surviving.

Test. Vet., Testamenta Vetusta, 1190 to 1560, edited by Sir N. H. Nicolas, large 8vo., 1826

Top and Gen., Topographer and Genealogist, edited by J G. Nichols, 3 vols., 8vo , 1846-58

[U.K.], the United Kingdom.

unm., unmarried.

v f., vitâ fratris.

v.m., vitâ matris.

v p., vitâ patris

V.C.H., Victoria History of the Counties of England, ed. by H. A. Doubleday and William Page.

Vic. Gen., Vicar General's office, London.

Visit., The Heralds' Visitation of the county.

Westm , Westminster.

yr., younger.

yst., youngest.

(ᵃ) This MS was used by Edmondson for his *Peerage,* 5 vols., folio, 1764 , vol. vi, folio, 1784.

CONTENTS

Vol. 1

EDITOR'S NOTE

While this volume was in the press it was found advisable to make a change in the Appendices. Appendix A in this volume was originally to have contained a list of the Irish Peerage before the 16th Century. This list is postponed to vol. xi. The references to it in the following notes consequently require to be cancelled, and the words " appendix A in vol. xi " substituted

Note " a " p. 24
Note " b " p. 290
Note " b " p. 291
Note " b " p. 292
Note " c " p. 292

Appendix E in volume II has also been changed, wherefore, on p. 281, note " c "

for vol. II, Appendix E
read vol. iii, Appendix H

ERRATUM

p. 74, note " a "

for Appendix F
read Appendix E

THE COMPLETE
PEERAGE

A

AB-ADAM see AP-ADAM

ABBEY LEIX

See "DE VESCI OF ABBEY LEIX, Queen's County, " Viscountcy [I.] *(Vesey)*, *cr.* 1776 (the 2nd BARON KNAPTON [I.], being the grantee.).

i.e., "DE VESCI OF ABBEY LEIX, Queen's County, " Barony [U.K.] *(Vesey)*, *cr.* 1884 ; *extinct* 1903 ; see as above, under the 4th Viscount [I.].

ABBOTS LANGLEY

See "RAYMOND OF ABBOTS LANGLEY, co. Hertford, " Barony *(Raymond)*, *cr.* 1731 ; *extinct* 1753.

ABERBROTHWICK

i.e., "HAMILTON, AVANE, ABERBROTHWICK AND BOTHWELLHAUGH, " Barony [S.] *(Stewart)*, sometimes (but apparently erroneously as to the two last-named titles) said to have been *cr.* 1581, with the EARLDOM OF ARRAN [S.], which see ; *forfeited* 1585.

BARONY [S.]   1. JAMES (HAMILTON), 2nd MARQUESS OF HAMILTON
I. 1608.   [S.], received from · James VI [S.] the lands, patronages
                  and titles belonging to the Abbey of Aberbrothwick, the
same being, by charter dat. 5 May 1608, erected into a temporal Lordship in his favour *with the title of a Lord of Parliament*, *i.e.* "LORD ABERBROTHWICK " [S.].   See "HAMILTON, " Marquessate of [S.], *cr.* 1599, under the 2nd Marquess.

ABERCARN

See "LLANOVER OF LLANOVER and ABERCARN, co. Monmouth, " Barony, *cr.* 1859, *extinct* 1867.

2

ABERCORN

BARONY [S.]

I. 1603.

EARLDOM [S.]

I. 1606.

1. James Hamilton, Master of Paisley, (ª) s. and h. ap. of Claud (Hamilton), 1st Lord Paisley [S.], by Margaret, da. of George (Seton), 6th Lord Seton [S], was M.P. [S] for Linlithgow 1597, and, being P.C. and Gent of the Bedchamber to James VI [S.], obtained in 1600 the office of Sheriff of co. Linlithgow to him and his heirs male, and in 1601, a grant of the *lands of Abercorn, &c.*, in that co , subsequently erected into a free Barony. On 5 Apr. 1603, he was *cr.* LORD (ᵇ) ABERCORN, co. Linlithgow [S.], to him and his heirs male and assigns whatever. In 1604 he was on the Commission which treated of a proposed Union of Scotland with England. On 10 July 1606, he was *cr.* EARL OF ABERCORN, LORD PAISLEY, HAMILTON, MOUNTCASTELL, and KILPATRICK [S.], to him and his heirs male whatever. On 20 May 1615 he was appointed one of the Council of the province of Munster, having previously by Privy Seal, Westm., 31 Mar. 1613, obtained a Royal Warrant " to hold [*in Ireland*] the place and precedency of an Earl in Parliament as he did at the Council table and in all other places. " (ᶜ) He received large grants of land in the Barony of Strabane, co. Tyrone, and built a castle thereon He *m.* Marion, 1st da. of Thomas (Boyd), 5th Lord Boyd [S], by Margaret, da. of Sir Matthew

(ª) The eldest sons of Scottish Peers were said *to be Peers*, and (presumably as such) were declared, in Dec 1708, incapable of sitting in the House of Commons as members for any shire or burgh in Scotland. The title of ' Master ' was as early as ' the beginning (at least) of the 15th century borne by the heirs apparent of the noblemen of the 1st class ', such was the case of ' Robert, Master of Atholl, ' grandson and h. ap [1437] of Walter (Stewart), Earl of Atholl [S]. It was, in some cases, as in that of Forrester, 1651, expressly conferred, while on certain occasions (as in that of the Earldom of Lennox, 17 Sep. 1490) both the father and the son (the h. ap.) are given the same peerage title, the fee of such title having been resigned by the former, though the life-rent was reserved (See *Riddell*, p 114)

(ᵇ) See p. 9 note " e ".

(ᶜ) On 11 March 1613/4 (1) the Earl of Abercorn [S.] , (2) Lord Henry O'Brien, s. and h. ap. of the Earl of Thomond, [I.] ; (3) Lord Audley [E.], afterwards Earl of Castlehaven [I] , (4) Lord Ochiltree [S.], afterwards, 1619, Baron Castle Stewart [I], and (5) Lord Burleigh (*Qy* Lord Balfour of Burleigh [S]), were sum. by writ to the Irish House of Lords, it being enacted that the said Earl of Abercorn should ' hold the place and precedency of an Earl in parl., ' &c. This singular warrant, granted to a person in no way connected with the Irish Peerage, appears to have been generally classed with the summons issued to the eldest s. and h. ap. of an Irish Peer. This classification is strengthened by the fact that on the same day, also by Privy Seal, occurs the 1st of such summons to the Irish House of Lords, viz., the s of the Earl of Thomond, as Baron of Ibrackan. Of these summons of the h. ap. there were in all but nine, viz. (1) the said Lord Ibrackan, in 1613 , (2) the s. of the Duke of Ormonde, as Earl of Ossory, in 1662, (3) the s of the Earl of Clancarty, as Viscount Muskerry, also in 1662; (4) the s. of the Earl of Cork, as Viscount Dungarvan, in 1662/3 , (5) the s. of the Earl of Meath, as Baron of Ardee, in 1665 , (6) the

CAMPBELL, of Loudoun.   He *d. v.p.*, at Monkton, 23 Mar., and was *bur.* 29 Ap. 1618, in the Abbey Church, Paisley, aged 43.   Will dat. 7 June 1616, pr. 26 June 1624.   His widow, a prominent Rom. Cath. who was excommunicated in the Kirk of Paisley 20 Jan. 1628, *d.* in the Canongate, Edinburgh, 26 Aug., and was *bur.* 13 Sep. 1632, with her husband.

II. 1618.   2. JAMES (HAMILTON), EARL OF ABERCORN, &c. [S.], s. and h.   In the lifetime of his father and grandfather, he, though only about thirteen years of age, was, on 8 May 1617 (the Privy Seal being dat. 18 Oct. 1616), *cr.* LORD HAMILTON, BARON OF STRABANE, co. Tyrone [I.], with rem. to the heirs male of the body of his father.   Soon after this he *suc.* to his father's Peerages in Scotland, and in 1621 he *suc.* his grandfather as LORD PAISLEY, co. Renfrew [S.], a Peerage *cr.* 29 July 1587.   On 11 Nov. 1633 he resigned his Irish Peerage in favour of his yr. br., Claud Hamilton, on whom the Irish estates were settled.   Being a Rom. Cath., he was excommunicated by the general assembly of the Church of Scotland in 1649, and ordered out of that kingdom.   On 11 Sep. 1651, by the death, *s.p.m.*, of his cousin, William, 2nd DUKE OF HAMILTON [S.], he became the *male representative of the illustrious house of Hamilton*, though he inherited none of the estates or titles of the senior line.([a])   He *m.*, about 1632, Catharine, Dowager DUCHESS OF LENNOX [S.], da. and h. of Gervase (CLIFTON), LORD CLIFTON OF LEIGHTON BROMSWOLD, by Catharine, da. and h. of Sir Henry DARCY, of Leighton afsd. She (who by Royal Lic., 28 Nov. 1632, was entitled, notwithstanding her marriage, to retain her title, rank, and precedency as Duchess of Lennox [S.]), *d.* in Scotland, and was *bur.* " without ceremonie " 17 Sep. 1637, aged about 45.   Will dat. 12 Aug. 1637, pr. 15 Jan. 1638/9.   He was then living, but " more than 400,000 merks in debt. "   He *d.* about 1670.

---

s. of the Earl of Clanricarde, as Baron Dunkellin, in 1711 ; (7) the s. of the Earl of Meath (again), as Baron of Ardee in 1714 ; (8) the s. of the Earl of Granard, as Baron Forbes in 1725; and (9) the s. of Viscount Strabane (Earl of Abercorn [S.]), as Baron Mountcastle, in 1735/6.   As to the precedency of Peers in the *English* Parl. granted by Royal Warrants since the Statute of Precedency of 31 Hen. VIII, see Appendix C. at the end of this volume.

([a]) As h. male of the body of James (Hamilton) Earl of Arran [S.] (so *cr.* 11 Aug. 1503, in consequence of his marriage with the Princess Margaret of Scotland), it is not improbable that he was entitled to that Earldom.   (See Pedigree on p. 4). The original limitation thereof to heirs male of the body, was extended by the second, and possibly by the 1st, of two charters thereafter granted, *viz.* (1) on 16 Jan. 1512/3 the limitation of the lands and BARONIES OF HAMILTON, &c. was extended to several bastard sons of the grantee and to others therein named (of the name of Hamilton) " and the heirs male of their bodies respectively, which failing, to the nearest heir male whatever " of the grantee.   (2) On 15 Sep. 1650, by another charter, the BARONIES OF HAMILTON &c., together with the EARLDOM OF ARRAN, were granted to James, the 2nd Earl, and the heirs male of his body, which failing, to five other persons (therein named) of the name of Hamilton, in like manner, which failing, " to his nearest heirs [*query*, heirs male] bearing the arms and name of Hamilton. "   See Wood's *Douglas*, vol. i, pp. 697-699.

TABULAR PEDIGREE OF THE EARLS OF ABERCORN [S.]

shewing their descent from, and since 1651, their representation in the male line of the family of Hamilton Earls of Arran [S.], of the Lady Mary Stewart, 1st da. of James II of Scotland, as also of the Dukes of Châtellerault in France. To the first (*Hamilton*) EARL OF ARRAN [S.], and the heirs *male* of his body, the Roman numerals I to XV are successively prefixed. The descent of the Earl of Derby, the heir *of line*, & the descent of the Duke of Hamilton [S.] (who is *neither* h. male, nor h. of line) from the same three sources is also shewn.

Thomas Boyd, *styled* Master = Mary, 1st da. of JAMES II, = James Hamilton, *cr*. Lord of Boyd, *cr*. Earl of Arran | King of Scotland, *d*. 1488 ? | Hamilton [S.] 1445, *d*. 1479. [S.] 1467 ; *d*. about 1472.

issue extinct.

I. James, Lord Hamilton [S.] *b*. 1475 ? *cr*. Earl of Arran [S.] 1503, *d*. 1529 ?

II. James, Earl of Arran, REGENT of Scotland, &c, who was *cr*. in 1548/9, Duke of CHATELLERAULT in France ; *d*. 1575.

III. James, Earl of Arran, insane, *d*. *s.p.* 1609.

John Hamilton, *cr*. Marquess of Hamilton [S.] 1599, *d*. 1604.

Claud Hamilton, *cr*. Lord of Paisley [S.] 1587, *d*. 1621.

IV. James, 2nd Marquess of Hamilton, afterwards 4th Earl of Arran, *d*. 1625.

James Hamilton, *cr*. 1606, Earl of Abercorn [S.] *d*. *v.p.* 1618.

V. James, 3rd Marquess, &c., *cr*. Duke of Hamilton [S.] with a spec. rem. 1643, *d*. 1649, *s.p.m.s.*

VI. William, 2nd Duke of Hamilton, &c. *d*. 1651, *s.p.m.s.*

VII. James, 2nd Earl of Abercorn, *d*. about 1670.

Claud, Lord Strabane [I.] *d*. 1638.

Sir George Hamilton.

(House of Douglas)
William Douglas = Anne, *suo jure cr*. Earl of Selkirk | Duchess of Ha-[S.] 1646 & Duke | milton, the *heir* of Hamilton [S.] | *of line d*. 1716. 1660, *d*. 1694.

Susanna, *m*. 1668 John (*Kennedy*), Earl of Cassillis [S.].

VIII. George, 3rd Earl of Abercorn, *d*. unm. about 1680.

James, Lord Strabane [I.], *d*. *s.p.* 1655.

George, Lord Strabane, [I.] *d*. 1668.

Colonel James Hamilton, *d*. *v.p.* June 1673.

James, 4th Duke of Hamilton, *d*. 1712.

IX. Claud, Lord Strabane [I.], afterwards 4th Earl of Abercorn, *d*. *s.p.* 1690.

X. Charles, 5th Earl of Abercorn, *d*. *s.p.s.* 1701.

XI. James, 6th Earl of Abercorn, *d*. 1734.

James, 5th Duke of Hamilton, *d*. 1742.

XII. James, 7th Earl of Abercorn, *d*. 1744.

James, 6th Duke of Hamilton, *d*. 1758.

Archibald, 9th Duke of Hamilton, *d*. 1819.

XIII. James, 8th Earl of Abercorn, *d*. unm. 1789.

John Hamilton, Capt. R.N., *d*. 1755.

James George, 7th Duke of Hamilton, *d*. *s.p.* 1769.

Douglas, 8th Duke of Hamilton, *d*. *s.p.* 1799. *(House of Stanley)*

Elizabeth, *m*. Edward (*Stanley*) Earl of Derby, she *d*. 1797. He *d*. 1834.

Alexander, 10th Duke of Hamilton, *d*. 1852.

XIV. John James, 9th Earl of Abercorn, *cr*. Marquess of Abercorn 1790, *d*. 1818.

Edward, 13th Earl of Derby *d*. 1851.

William, 11th Duke of Hamilton *d*. 1863.

James Hamilton, *styled* Viscount Hamilton, s. and h. ap., *d.v.p.* 1814.

Edward Geoffrey, 14th Earl of Derby *d*. 1869.

William, 12th Duke of Hamilton, *b*. 1845, *a descendant* of, but neither heir male nor heir of line to the 1st Earl of Arran. *d*. *s.p.m.* 1895.

XV. James, Marquess of Abercorn, *b*. 1811, *cr*. Duke of Abercorn [I.] 1868. *Heir male of the Body* to the 1st Earl of Arran *d*. 1885.

Edward Henry, Earl of Derby, *b*. 1826. *Heir of line* to the 1st Earl of Arran.

Dukes of Abercorn.

[JAMES HAMILTON, *styled* LORD PAISLEY, s. and h. ap. He *m.*, 28 Apr. 1653, at St. Bartholomew's-the-Less, London, Catharine,(ª) da. of Sir John LENTHALL, Marshal of the King's Bench, by Hester, da. of Sir Thomas TEMPLE, 1st Bart., of Stowe, which John (ᵇ) was a br. of William LENTHALL, of Burford, Oxon, Speaker of the House of Commons. He *d. v.p.* and *s.p.m.* before 1670. His widow's admon. as " of Burford, Oxon, widow," 20 July 1696.]

III. 1670 ?   3. GEORGE (HAMILTON), EARL OF ABERCORN, &c. [S.], 3rd, but 1st surv. s. and h., *b.* about 1636. He was living in 1670, but *d.* unm. at Padua, in Italy, before 1683.

IV. 1680 ?   4. CLAUD (HAMILTON), EARL OF ABERCORN, &c. [S.], also LORD HAMILTON, BARON OF STRABANE [I.], cousin and h. male. He was s. and h. of George, 4th LORD STRABANE [I.] (by Elizabeth, da. and h. of Christopher FAGAN, of Feltrim, co. Dublin), who was br. and h. of James, 3rd Lord Strabane [I.], being s. of Claud, 2nd Lord Strabane [I.], which Claud was yr. br. of James, 2nd Earl of Abercorn, who had (as before mentioned) resigned in his favour the Irish Peerage of Strabane. He was *bap.* 13 Sep. 1659, at St. Audoens, Dublin. On 14 Apr. 1668, he *suc.* his father in the Irish Peerage and estates. He was P.C. [I.], and Lord of the Bedchamber to James II, with whom he went to France at the Revolution, and for whom he commanded a regiment of Horse, in 1689, in Ireland, where he was killed when re-embarking for France, after the battle of the Boyne, 1 July 1690. He *d.* unm. After his death he was outlawed [I.], 11 May 1691, when his *Irish Peerage* and estates were *forfeited.*

V. 1690.   5. CHARLES (HAMILTON), EARL OF ABERCORN, &c. [S.], and afterwards, also, LORD HAMILTON, BARON OF STRA-BANE [I], br. and h. By Royal Letters, 24 May 1692, he obtained a *reversal* of his brother's *attainder*, and *suc.* to the *Irish Peerage* and estates accordingly. On 31 Aug. 1695 he took his seat in the Irish House of Lords, and in 1697 signed the declaration for the succession to the Crown, &c. On 16 July 1697, he was tried at Oxford for the murder of Mr. Prior of Burford, and acquitted. (ᶜ) He *m.* Catharine, widow of William LENTHALL (*bur.* 5 Sep. 1686), of Burford, Oxon, only da. and h. of James HAMILTON, *styled* LORD PAISLEY, abovenamed, by Catharine, da. of Sir John LENTHALL, afsd., Marshal of the King's Bench. He *d., s.p.s.,* at Strabane, June 1701. Will dat. 7 Aug. 1697, pr. 16 May 1704. His widow *d.* 24 May 1723, aged about 70, in Pall Mall, and was *bur.* in the Richmond vault in Henry VII's Chapel, Westm. Abbey. Will dat. 17 Aug. 1722, pr. 24 May 1723.

(ª) She had previously borne "some children " to Sir William Fleming. Baillie's *Letters*, vol. iii, p. 366. V.G.

(ᵇ) See *Gent. Mag.* N.S. vol. v, p. 570, for pedigree, with proofs enlarging that in Le Neve's *Knights.* V.G.

(ᶜ) *Hist. MSS. Com.* 12th Rep., App., Pt. 7, and Luttrell's *Diary.* V.G.

VI. 1701.   6 James (Hamilton), Earl of Abercorn, &c. [S.],
            also Lord Hamilton, Baron of Strabane [I.], under
the spec. rem in the creation (1617) of that dignity, cousin and h. male,
being s. and h of Col. James H , by Elizabeth, da. of John (Colepeper),
1st Lord Colepeper, which Col. James was s and h. ap. of Sir George H.,
of Donalong, co. Tyrone (ᵃ), 1st Bart. [I], who was 4th s. of the 1st Earl.
On 6 June 1673 he *suc.* his father (who *d v p*, being mortally wounded
3 June in a sea-fight with the Dutch), whose post as Groom of the Bedchamber
to Charles II he obtained.   M.P. for Tyrone 1692, and again 1695.   He
was Col. of a regiment to James II, but, deserting that King at the Revolution, assisted William III during the siege of Londonderry, by bringing relief
to that city.   Accordingly, on 2 Sep 1701, he was *cr.* BARON MOUNT-
CASTLE, co. Tyrone, and VISCOUNT STRABANE [I.], and took his
seat (as such) 21 Sep. 1703 in the Irish House of Lords.   On 3 Oct. 1706
he took his seat in the Scottish House   He was P.C [I] to Queen Anne,
Geo. I., and Geo. II.   He *m.* (Lic. at Fac. off. 24 Jan. 1683/4), Elizabeth
(then aged about 15), only child of Sir Robert Reading, of Dublin, Bart.
[I.] (so *cr.* 1675), by Jane, Dowager Countess of Mountrath [I.], da. of
Sir Robert Hannay, Bart. [S.].   He *d* aged 73, 28 Nov, and was *bur.*
3 Dec. 1734, in the Ormonde vault in Henry VII's Chapel, Westm.
Abbey.   Will dat. 5 May 1731, pr 2 Dec. 1734.   His widow *d* aged 86,
in Sackville Str., Midx., 19, and was *bur* 22 Mar. 1754, with her husband.
Will dat. 5 Apr. 1739, pr. 20 Mar. 1754.

VII. 1734.   7. James (Hamilton), Earl of Abercorn, &c. [S],
            also Viscount Strabane, &c. [I.], 2nd, but 1st surv. s.
and h., *b.* 22 Mar. 1685/6, *styled* Lord Paisley from 1701 till he *suc.* to the
peerage.   F.R.S., 10 Nov 1715   Author of *Calculations and Tables on the
attractive Power of Loadstones* (1729).   P.C. of England 20 July 1738, of
Ireland 26 Sep. 1739   He *m.*, in 1711, before 18 Apr., (Lic. at Fac off.
26 Mar. 1711, to *m.* at Widford, Herts), Anne, 1st surv da of Col. John
Plumer, of Blakesware, in Ware, Herts, by Mary, 1st da of William Hale,
of King's Walden in that co.   He *d.* in Cavendish Sq., aged 57, 11, and
was *bur.* 16 Jan 1743/4, with his father in Westm Abbey.   Admon.
25 Feb. 1743/4   His widow (who was *b.* 29 June and *bap* 3 July 1690
at Ware), *d* in London, 7, and was *bur.* 13 Aug. 1776, with her husband,
aged 86.   Will dat. 24 June 1771, pr. 10 Aug. 1776.

VIII. 1744.   8. James (Hamilton), Earl of Abercorn, &c. [S.],
            also Viscount Strabane, &c. [I.], s. and h., *b.* 22 Oct.
1712, in Queen Sq., St. Geo. the Martyr, Holborn   He was sum. *v.p.*,

(ᵃ) This Sir George *m.* Mary, (*d* Aug. 1680) sister of the famous James
(Butler), Duke of Ormonde, and had 6 sons and 4 daughters.   Of these (besides
the abovenamed Col. James H) the most celebrated were Elizabeth, Comtesse de
Gramont, Sir George Hamilton (husband of Frances Jennings, afterwards Duchess
of Tyrconnel [I]), and Count Anthony Hamilton, author of the well known
Mémoires de Gramont   See note *sub* James, Viscount Strabane [1701].

on 23 Mar. 1735/6, as BARON MOUNTCASTLE (I.) to the Irish House of Lords, and took his seat the same day. (ª) In 1761, 1768, 1774, 1780, and 1784 he was chosen a Rep. Peer (Tory) [S.]. On 11 Mar. 1766 he voted against the Repeal of the American Stamp Act, and on 17 Dec. 1783 against Fox's India Bill. On 24 Aug. 1786, he was *cr.* a Peer of Great Britain (ᵇ) as VISCOUNT HAMILTON (ᶜ), with a spec. rem., failing his issue male, to his nephew, John James HAMILTON. In 1745 he purchased the Barony of Duddingston, co. Edinburgh (where he built a mansion), and in 1764 the Lordship of Paisley, co. Renfrew (being the inheritance, anciently, of his paternal ancestors), where, in 1779, he laid out a new town. He also built a magnificent house at Baronscourt, near Londonderry. He *d.* unm. at Boroughbridge (on a journey), 9 Oct. 1789, in his 77th year, and was *bur.* in the Abbey of Paisley. (ᵈ) Will dat. 24 May 1785, pr. 14 Oct. 1789.

IX. 1789.	9 and 1. JOHN JAMES (HAMILTON), EARL OF ABER-
MARQUESSATE	CORN, &c. [S.], also VISCOUNT STRABANE, &c. [I.], also
	VISCOUNT HAMILTON, (under the spec. rem. above-
I. 1790.	mentioned), nephew and h., being posthumous s. and

h. of John H., Capt. R.N. (by Harriet, widow of Richard ELIOT of Port Eliot, Cornwall, and illegit. da. of the Rt. Hon. James CRAGGS), which John H. was next br. to the 8th Earl, but. *d.* Dec. 1755, *v.f.*, aged 41. He was *b.* July 1756, and *bap.* at St. Geo., Han. Sq. M.P. (Tory) for East Looe 1783-4, and for St. Germans 1784-9. On 15 Oct. 1790, he was *cr.* MARQUESS OF ABERCORN. P.C. [I.] 1 Feb. 1794, K.G. 17 Jan. 1805. He *m.*, 1stly, 20 June 1779, at St. Marylebone, Midx., Catharine, 1st da. of Sir Joseph COPLEY, 1st Bart., by Mary, da. of John BULLER, of Morval, Cornwall. She *d.* at Bentley Priory, Midx., 13, and was *bur.* 19 Sep. 1791, at Stanmore. He *m.*, 2ndly, 4 Mar. 1792, in Grosvenor Sq., Midx., his 1st cousin, Lady Cecil HAMILTON (raised to the precedency of an Earl's da. by Royal Warrant, 27 Oct. 1789) (ᵉ), 5th and yst. da. and coh. of his

---

(ª) See p. 2 note " c, " where all such summons, *v.p.*, of eldest sons of Irish peers are enumerated.

(ᵇ) In consequence of this creation, by a resolution of the Committee for Privileges on 13 Feb. 1787 (52 to 38 votes), duly confirmed by the House of Lords, he ceased to be a Rep. Peer [S.]. This resolution was the first on this subject, and was some-what militated against by the fact of the Duke of Atholl [S.] having sat in the House from 14 Mar. 1737 till the gen. election in 1741 as a Peer of Great Britain (Lord Strange), as well as a Rep. Peer [S.]. See *Robertson*, pp. 181 and 430. See also note *sub* William, DUKE OF QUEENSBERRY [1778.]

(ᶜ) Described in the signet office docquet as Vt. Hamilton of Hamilton, co. Lei-cester, but on the patent roll referred to as (merely) " *Viscount Hamilton.* "

(ᵈ) For illustrations of his stiff manners, " Castilian pomp, " pride, eccentricity, and unpopularity, see several rather amusing stories in *Gent. Mag.* for Oct. 1789. V.G.

(ᵉ) This was certainly a most unusual proceeding, as neither her father (who *d. s.p.m.* 26 Nov. 1787) nor any of his issue ever could have *suc.* to the title, he having been a yr. br. of Capt. John H., ancestor of the *then* Peer. This favour was not extended to any of her four elder sisters ; indeed the precedency was only that of the

uncle, the Hon and Rev George HAMILTON, Canon of Windsor, by Elizabeth, da. of Lieut. Gen. Richard ONSLOW. She was *b* 15 Mar. 1770, was separated from her husband 1798, and *divorced* by Act. of Parl., Apr. 1799. (ª) He *m*, 3rdly, 3 Apr. 1800, in Dover Str., St. Geo, Han. Sq., Lady Anne Jane HATTON, (widow of Henry HATTON, of Great Clonard, co. Wexford), da of Arthur Saunders (GORE), 2nd EARL OF ARRAN [I.], by his 1st wife, Catharine, da. of William (ANNESLEY), 1st VISCOUNT GLERAWLEY [I.]. He *d.* at Bentley Priory, Stanmore, (ᵇ) 27 Jan., and was *bur.* 5 Feb. 1818, at Stanmore. Will dat 18 Mar. 1809, pr. 9 May 1818. His widow, who was *b* Apr. 1763, *d.* 8 May 1827, at Naples. Will pr. June 1827.

[JAMES HAMILTON, *styled* VISCOUNT HAMILTON, s. and h. ap. by 1st wife, *b.* at Petersham Lodge, Surrey, 7 Oct, and *bap* 4 Nov. 1786, at Petersham. Matric. Oxford (Ch. Ch.), 24 Oct. 1805. M.P for Dungannon 1805-7, and for Liskeard 1807-12. He *m.*, 25 Nov. 1809, in London, Harriet, da. of the Hon. John DOUGLAS (2nd s. of James, xv (14th) EARL OF MORTON [S.]), by Frances, 1st da. of Edward (LASCELLES), 1st Earl of HAREWOOD. He *d., v.p.*, 27 May 1814, in Upper Brook Str. His widow *m.*, 8 July 1815, George (GORDON), 4th EARL OF ABERDEEN [S.], and *d.* 26 Aug. 1833.]

MARQUESSATE	2. 10. and 1. JAMES (HAMILTON), MARQUESS OF
II.	ABERCORN &c., (ᶜ) grandson and h., being s. and h. of
	James HAMILTON, *styled* VISCOUNT HAMILTON, and
EARLDOM	Harriet his wife, abovenamed. He was *b.* 21 Jan. 1811,
and	in Seamore Place, Mayfair. Ed. at Harrow, and at Ch.
BARONY [S.].	Ch., Oxford. Lord Lieut of co. Donegal, 1844; K.G.,

---

da. of *an* Earl, *viz*, one of a creation of 1789, not of 1606, as if her father had *suc.* to the Earldom. The explanation of this special favour is, according to Wraxall, (*Posth. Mem.* vol 1, pp. 63-4) highly discreditable to all the parties concerned, and implies that she had been the Marquess's mistress during his first wife's lifetime. Wraxall adds that the Marquess had used his influence with Pitt to obtain the honour for her, though not " without strong marks of repugnance being evinced by their Majesties. " George Selwyn writes to Lady Carlisle, 9 Nov. 1786, " Mr. Hamilton now Lord Hamilton but *toujours magnifico* will have one of his cousins a Lady as if she had been an Earl's daughter, and no other of her sisters. He will himself be Duc de Châtellerault, to which I know that he has no more pretensions than I should have to an estate that an ancestor of mine had sold a century ago. " V.G.

(ª) She *m.*, 2ndly, 23 May 1799, Capt. Joseph COPLEY, afterwards 3rd Bart. (on account of adultery with whom she had been divorced), the br. of the 1st wife of her former husband, and *d* 19 June 1819. He *d* 21 May 1838.

(ᵇ) " He is stated to have always gone out shooting in his Blue Ribbon, and to have required his housemaids to wear white kid gloves when they made his bed. It is also alleged that having learnt of his second wife's contemplated elopement, he sent her a message begging her to take the family coach, as it ought never to be said that Lady Abercorn left her husband's roof in a hack chaise. " (G.E. Russell, *Collections and Recollections*, 1898). V G.

(ᶜ) As to the Dukedom of Châtellerault, to which he was served h. male of the

X. 1818.	12 Dec. 1844; P.C. 25 Feb. 1846; Groom of the Stole
DUKEDOM [S.]	to the Prince Consort, 1846-59; LL.D. Cambridge, 5 July 1847; D.C.L. Oxford, 4 June 1856; LL.D. Dublin,
1. 1868.	together with the PRINCE OF WALES and H.R.H. the

Duke of Cambridge, 21 Apr. 1868; a Governor of Harrow School; sometime Col. in the Donegal Militia; Major-Gen. of the Royal Archers, the King's Body Guard of Scotland; LORD LIEUT. OF IRELAND (for the first time) July 1866 to Dec. 1868. On 10 Aug. 1868 he was *cr.* MARQUESS OF HAMILTON ([a]) of Strabane, co. Tyrone, and DUKE OF ABERCORN [I.]. Grand Master of Freemasons [I.] 1874 till his death. From Feb. 1878 to Dec. 1876 he was (for the second time) LORD LIEUT. OF IRELAND. He was subsequently ENVOY EXTRAORDINARY ([b]) to Italy for the investiture (at Rome, 2 Mar. 1878) of King Humbert with the Order of the Garter. Chancellor of the University of Ireland, 1881. A Conservative in politics. He *m.,* 25 Oct. 1832, from Gordon Castle, at Fochabers, co. Banff, Louisa Jane, 2nd da. of John (RUSSELL), 6th DUKE OF BEDFORD, by his 2nd wife, Georgiana, 5th da. of Alexander (GORDON), 4th DUKE OF GORDON [S.]. He *d.* 31 Oct. 1885, in his 75th year, at Barons-court, and was *bur.* there. ([c]) Will dat. 13 Mar. 1869 to 2 Feb. 1877, pr. 27 Feb. 1886, over £144,000. His widow, who was *b.* 8 July 1812, member (3rd class) of the V.A., ([d]) *d.* at Coats Castle, Pulborough, Sussex, 31 Mar., and was *bur.* 5 Apr. 1905, at Chenies, Beds. Will pr. above £24,000.

DUKEDOM [I.]		2, 3, and 11. JAMES (HAMILTON),
II.		DUKE OF ABERCORN [1868], MAR-
		QUESS OF HAMILTON OF STRABANE
MARQUESSATE [G.B.]		[1868], VISCOUNT STRABANE [1701],
III.	1885.	LORD HAMILTON, BARON OF STRABANE [1617], and BARON OF MOUNTCASTLE
EARLDOM and		[1701], in the peerage of Ireland, also
BARONY [S.]		MARQUESS OF ABERCORN [1790] and VISCOUNT HAMILTON [1786] in that
XI.		of Great Britain, also Earl OF ABER-CORN [1606], LORD PAISLEY [1587],

body in Scotland, 13 Jan. 1862, and to which he unsuccessfully asserted his rights before the Conseil d'Etat in Paris in 1866, see Appendix B in this volume.   V.G.

([a]) This creation was *by promotion* (!!) of his Irish Viscountcy of Strabane, a mode of procedure supposed to be authorised by the Act of the Irish Union, but (excepting in this instance) not acted upon since 1831, when its absurdity and possible illegality were noticed. If the Viscountcy of Strabane has been " promoted, " what has become of it ? It cannot both exist in its former state, and yet have been "promoted," to a higher.

([b]) See list of these Garter missions in vol ii, Appendix B.

([c]) Of his seven daughters, all were married to Peers, *viz.,* (1) to the Earl of Lich-field; (2) to the Earl of Durham; (3) to the Duke of Buccleuch [S.]; (4) to the Earl of Mount Edgcumbe; (5) to the Earl Winterton [I.]; (6) to the Duke of Marl-borough; and (7) to the Marquess of Lansdowne.

([d]) A photograph of her and her 101 descendants was taken in July 1894.

3

Lord Abercorn ([a]) [1603], Lord Paisley, Hamilton, Mount Castell
and Kilpatrick (1606), in that of Scotland, ([b]) 1st s. and h. He was
b. 24 Aug. 1838, at Brighton; was *styled* Viscount Hamilton till 1868, and
Marquess of Hamilton 1868 to 1885; ed. at Harrow, and at Ch. Ch.,
Oxford; B.A. 1860; M.A. 1865; was M.P. (Conservative) for co. Donegal 1860-80; Sheriff of co. Tyrone 1863; a Lord of the Bedchamber to the
Prince of Wales 1866-85, and Groom of the Stole 1886-1891; attached to
the Garter mission to Denmark, Apr. 1865; C.B. (civil) 1865; Knight of
the Dannebrog of Denmark, of the St. Anne of Russia, and of the Iron-
Crown of Austria; sometime Hon. Col. 5th Batt. Royal Inniskilling
Fusiliers; Lord Lieut. of co. Donegal, 1885; Grand Master of Freemasons
[I.] 1886; Chairman of the British South African Company   K.G. 10 Aug.
1892   Special Envoy to the Courts of Denmark, Sweden, Norway, Prussia,
and Saxony, to announce the accession of H.M. King Edward VII, 1901.
Lord High Constable [I] at the Coronation of Edward VII, 9 Aug. 1902.
He *m.*, 7 Jan. 1869, at St Geo, Han Sq., Mary Anna, 2nd da of Richard
William Penn (Curzon-Howe), 1st Earl Howe, by his 2nd wife, Anne,
2nd da. of Admiral Sir John Gore, K.C.B. She was b. 23 July 1848.

[James Albert Edward Hamilton, *styled*, since 1885, Marquess of
Hamilton, 1st s. and h. ap. , b. 30 Nov. 1869, in Hamilton Place, Piccadilly, the Prince of Wales being one of his sponsors. Ed. at Eton.
Sometime Capt. 1st Life Guards. M.P. Londonderry City 1900   Treasurer
of the Household, 1903-5. He *m*, 1 Nov 1894, at St. Paul's, Knightsbridge, Rosaline Cecilia Caroline, only da. of Charles George (Bingham),
4th Earl of Lucan [I.], by Cecilia Catherine, da. of Charles (Gordon-
Lennox), 5th Duke of Richmond. She was b. 26 Feb. 1869.]

[James Edward Hamilton, *styled* Lord Paisley, b. 29 Feb. 1904, for
whom the King stood sponsor].

Family Estates.—These, in 1883, consisted of 76,500 acres in Ireland
(*viz.* 60,000 in co. Tyrone and 16,500 in co. Donegal), worth £ 41,000 a
year, and of 2,162 in Scotland (*viz.* 1,500 in co. Edinburgh and 662 in co.
Renfrew), worth £ 11,900 a year. ([c]) *Total*, 78,662 acres, worth about

---

Her s. Lord Claud H. writes that in Dec. 1904 she had 162 living descendants ! V.G.

([a]) Sir James B Paul points out that the anomalous style for a Scots peerage
" Baron of Abercorn " given in Wood's *Douglas* is merely that writer's translation of
the common form " *Dominus de Abercorn* " which occurs in the Register of the Great
Seal in the charter to Abercorn, and freely elsewhere.   V.G.

([b]) The Duke of Abercorn, the Marquess of Lansdowne since 1895, and the Earl
of Verulam, are the only Peers (in 1909) who, besides their Peerage of Parliament,
possess Peerages both in Scotland and Ireland   From 1688 to 1715 the famous Duke
of Ormonde, from 1836 to 1889 the Dukes of Buckingham and Chandos, and from
1840 to 1868 the Marquesses of Hastings enjoyed the same distinction

([c]) Bentley Priory in Harrow (near Stanmore), Midx , which, since 1788, had
been the property and chief residence of the family, was sold by the 1st Duke, some
90 years subsequently, to Sir John Kelk, Bart.   It is now (1909) an hotel, the land
having been laid out for villas.

£53,000 a year. *Principal Seats.*—Baronscourt, near Newtown Stewart, co. Tyrone, and Duddingston House, co. Edinburgh

ABERCROMBIE

BARONY [S.]   1 Sir James Sandilands, (ᵃ) of Abercrombie, other-
I. 1647.   wise St. Monance, co. Fife, s. and h. of Sir James S , the
younger (who *d. v.p.*), by Agnes (ᵇ), 2nd da. of David
(Carnegie), 1st Earl of Southesk [S.], *suc.* his grandfather, Sir James
Sandilands, the elder, in Oct. 1644, and, being then of full age, was served
heir to him, 5 and 16 July 1645. On 10 July 1646 he obtained a charter
of the Barony of Abercrombie, &c., and by patent, dat. at Carisbroke Castle,
12 Dec. 1647, he was *cr.* LORD OF ABERCROMBIE [S.]. (ᶜ) In five
years' time, " being a riotous youth " (ᵈ), he had wasted all his property, and, having in 1649 sold his Castle of Newark and other estates, co.
Fife, for 67,000 marks, to Lieut. Gen. David Leslie, he embarked at
Kirkcaldy, in 1650, for the Continent, whence he returned in 1658. He
m , 1stly, (contract 4 Aug. 1643) Jean Crichton, (ᵉ) da. of Patrick Lichtoun,
of Dunninald, co. Forfar. He *m.*, 2ndly, in 1663, Christian Fletcher,
widow of James Grainger, Minister of Kinneff (who *d.* between 14 Jan.
and 20 May 1663). He was living 27 Feb. 1666/7. His widow was
living 21 Aug. 1686. (ᶠ)

II. 1670 ?   2. James (Sandilands), Lord Abercrombie [S.], only
to   s. and h. by 1st wife, *b.* 1645, but owing to his father's
1681   misconduct, not *bap.* till 30 Apr 1650, at Abercrombie.
He *d.* unm. in poverty and obscurity at Kinneff, co.
Fife, (ᵍ) in 1681, when the *peerage* became *extinct.* (ʰ)

(ᵃ) This account of the family, which differs very much from that given in
Wood's *Douglas*, is taken from the *History of the Carnegies, Earls of Southesk*, by
[Sir] W. Fraser. Edinburgh, 2 vols, 4to, 1867.

(ᵇ) Her marriage contract, with £10,000 " tocher, " is dat. Aug. 1610.

(ᶜ) To him and the heirs male of his body, and that they " indignitabuntur et
nominabuntur *Domini de Abercrombie* omni tempore futuro. " In the return of the
Lords of Session [S.], 12 June 1739, it is stated that " it does not appear that either
the patentee, or any successor of his in that right, ever sat or voted in Parl. "—See
Robertson, pp 214 and 218.

(ᵈ) See *Lamont.*

(ᵉ) A letter from her husband was read 25 Sep. 1649 at the Provincial Synod of
Fife, withdrawing a charge against her of incontinence. He confessed to drunkenness,
keeping bad company, etc. (with which he had been charged), and was publicly
censured by the Presbytery for having scandalised his wife. V.G.

(ᶠ) It was she who " carried away the crown of Scotland in her lap, when
Dunnottar Castle was about to be surrendered to the English. " *(Scots Peerage)* For
this service she had a grant from the Estates, in 1661, of 1000 marks, *i.e.* £100. V.G.

(ᵍ) See Wood's *East Neuk of Fife.*

(ʰ) " Lord Abercrombie " indeed appears on the Union Roll [S.], 1 May 1707,

ABERCROMBY OF ABOUKIR AND TULLIBODY

BARONY   1. MARY ANNE ABERCROMBY (2nd da. and coh. of
I. 1801.   John MENZIES, of Ferntower, in Crieff, co. Perth, by Ann,
              da. of Patrick CAMPBELL of Monzie), widow of Lieut.
Gen. Sir Ralph Abercromby, K.B., late Commander-in-chief against the
French in Egypt, was, on 28 May 1801, in reward for her late husband's
gallant conduct, *cr.* BARONESS ABERCROMBY OF ABOUKIR AND
TULLIBODY, co. Clackmannan, with rem. of the Barony to the heirs
male of her body by her said late husband. He was s. and h. of George
A., of Tullibody, afsd., by Mary, da of Ralph DUNDAS, of Manour, co.
Perth, and was *b.* 25 Oct. 1734 (ª) ; ent. Rugby school 12 June 1748 ;
suc. his father 8 June 1800. Cornet 2nd Dragoon Guards, 1756 ; Capt.
3rd Dragoons 1762 ; Col. 103rd Foot 1781-83 ; Major Gen. 1787 ; Col.
7th Dragoon Guards 1795-96 ; Col. 2nd Dragoons 1796-1801 ; M.P. for
co. Clackmannan, 1774-80 and 1796-98 ; K.B. 22 July 1795 ; P.C. [I.]
1798 ; Gov. of Inverness 1798-1801. He *m.*, 17 Nov. 1767, at Ferntower
afsd. (marr. reg. at Alloa). Having served in several campaigns, he was
made Lieut. Gen in the army 1797. He landed his troops at Aboukir
early in 1801, but being mortally wounded in the battle of Alexandria
21 Mar., he *d.* 28 Mar. 1801, on board H.M S. *Foudroyant,* in Aboukir
Bay, and was *bur.* in the Commandery of the Grand Master, at Malta. (ᵇ)
Monument at St. Paul's, London, by grant of the House of Commons.
Will pr. June 1801. His widow, the *suo jure* BARONESS, *d.* 11 Feb 1821,
at Charlotte Sq., Edinburgh. Will pr. Aug. 1821.

II. 1821.   2. GEORGE (ABERCROMBY), BARON ABERCROMBY OF
                 ABOUKIR AND TULLIBODY, s. and h , *b.* 14 Oct. 1770, at
Tullibody. Advocate, 5 July 1794 ; M.P. (Whig) for Edinburgh, 1805-6 ;
for co. Clackmannan, 1806-7, and 1812-15. Lord Lieut. of co. Stirling
1837-43. He *m.,* 20 Jan. 1799, at Edinburgh, Montague, 3rd da. of
Henry (DUNDAS), 1st VISCOUNT MELVILLE, by his 1st wife, Elizabeth, da.
of David RENNIE, of Melville Castle. She, who was *b.* 29 Apr. 1772,
d. 10 Mar. 1837. He *d.* 15 Feb. 1843, at Airthrey Castle, aged 72. Will
dat. 16 Dec. 1841, pr. 19 Apr. 1843. Both *bur.* at Tullibody.

III. 1843.   3. GEORGE RALPH (ABERCROMBY), BARON ABERCROMBY
                  OF ABOUKIR AND TULLIBODY, s and h , *b.* 30 May 1800,
at Edinburgh. Major 3rd Dragoons 1826, and Col. ; M.P. (Whig) for
co. Clackmannan, 1824-26, and 1830-31 ; for co. Stirling, 1838-41 ; for cos.

---

but so also do five other peerages then extinct or dormant. See note *sub* ii LORD
RUTHVEN OF FREELAND.

(ª) See *Scottish Nation* as to his baptism being 26 Oct. 1734.

(ᵇ) Not a very great commander, but a high-minded, hard-working, sensible, and
humane soldier. "As he looked out from under his thick shaggy eyebrows, he gave
one the idea of a very good-natured lion." V.G.

Clackmannan and Kinross, 1841-42. Lord Lieut. of co. Clackmannan 1840-52. He *m.*, 3 Apr. 1832, at 17 Ainslie Place, Edinburgh, Louisa Penuel, da of John Hay FORBES, a Judge of Session as Lord Medwyn, by Louisa, da. of Sir Alexander CUMMING-GORDON, 1st Bart., of Altyre He, who was blind, *d.* 25 June 1852, aged 52, at Airthrey Castle. Will dat. 23 July 1844, pr. 23 Sep. 1852. His widow *d.* 20 Apr 1882, in Chapel Str., Mayfair. Will dat. 24 Nov. 1875, pr. 17 July 1882. Both *bur.* at Tullibody.

IV. 1852.　　　4. GEORGE RALPH CAMPBELL (ABERCROMBY), BARON ABERCROMBY OF ABOUKIR AND TULLIBODY, s and h., *b.* at Leamington, co Warwick, 23 Sep., and *bap.* there 2 Nov. 1838 ; D.L. for co. Stirling, 1860. A Liberal in politics. He *m.*, 6 Oct. 1858, at Camperdown House, co. Forfar, Julia Janet Georgiana, only da. of Adam (DUNCAN), 2nd EARL OF CAMPERDOWN, by Juliana Cavendish, 1st da. and coh. of Sir George Richard PHILIPS, of Weston, 2nd Bart. She, who was *b.* 24 Jan. 1840, at Naples, was one of the Ladies of the Bedchamber to Queen Victoria, Apr. 1874 to Mar. 1885, and a member (3rd class) of the V. A.

Family Estates —These, in 1883, consisted of 10,407 acres in co. Perth ; 3,707 in co. Clackmannan and 1,150 in co Stirling. *Total*, 15,264 acres, worth £14,959 a year. *Principal Residence.*—Tullibody Castle, co. Clackmannan. *Note.* The Stirling estate including Airthrey Castle, formerly the chief seat of the family, was sold between 1883 and 1905.

ABERDARE OF DUFFRYN

BARONY.　　　1. HENRY AUSTIN BRUCE, 2nd s. of John Bruce BRUCE-
I. 1873.　　　PRYCE of Duffryn, co. Glamorgan (whose surname was for-
　　　　　merly KNIGHT, afterwards [1805] BRUCE, and subsequently [1837] BRUCE-PRYCE) by his 1st wife, Sarah, 2nd da. of Rev. Hugh Williams AUSTIN, Rector of St. Peter's, Barbados, *b.* 16 Apr. 1815, at Duffryn. Barrister (Linc. Inn), 1837 ; J.P and D L for co. Glamorgan, 1847 ; M.P. (Liberal) for Merthyr Tydvil, 1852-68, and for Renfrewshire, 1869-73 , Under Secretary of State for Home Department, 1862-64 ; Vice-President of the Council on Education, and P C. 26 Apr. 1864 ; Secretary of State for Home Department, 1868-73 On 23 Aug. 1873 he was *cr.* BARON ABERDARE OF DUFFRYN, co. Glamorgan ; He was made President of the Council, Aug. 1873 to Feb. 1874 ; F.R.S. 20 Jan. 1876. Hon. D.C.L (Oxford), 1880. Pres. Roy. Geog. Soc. 1880-84 and 1885-86. G C.B. (Civil) 7 Jan. 1885. He *m.*, 1stly, 6 Jan 1846, Annabella, only da. of Richard BEADON, of Clifton, co. Gloucester, by Annabella, sister of William, 1st Baron HEYTESBURY, and da. of Sir William Pierce Ashe A'COURT, 1st Bart. She *d.* 28 July 1852. He *m.*, 2ndly, 17 Aug. 1854, Norah Creina Blanche, 7th da. of Lieut. Gen. Sir William Francis Patrick NAPIER, K.C.B., by Caroline Amelia, 2nd da of Gen the Hon. Henry Fox. He *d.* 25 Feb. 1895, of influenza, at 39 Prince's Gardens, aged 79, and

was *bur.* at Mountain Ash, co. Glamorgan. (ᵃ) His widow *d.* at Pen Pole House, Shirehampton, co. Gloucester, 27, and was *bur.* 30 Apr. 1897, at Mountain Ash afsd., aged 70.   Will pr. at £3,209

II. 1895.   2. HENRY CAMPBELL (BRUCE), BARON ABERDARE OF
              DUFFRYN, 1st s. and h., by 1st wife, *b.* 19 June 1851, at
Duffryn ; ed. at Rugby, and at Berlin ; Major 3rd Vol. Batt. Welsh Reg. A Liberal in politics. He *m*, 10 Feb. 1880, at St Geo, Han. Sq, Constance Mary, only da. of Hamilton BECKETT, by Sophia Clarence, da. and coh. of John Singleton (COPLEY), BARON LYNDHURST.

[HENRY LYNDHURST BRUCE, 1st. s. and h. ap., *b.* 25 May 1881 ; Capt. 3rd Batt. Royal Scots, *m.*, 11 Oct. 1906, in London, "Camilla Antoinette, da. of the late Reynold CLIFFORD, of independent means," according to the register of marriage. (ᵇ)]

Family Estates.—These, in 1883, consisted of 3,950 acres in co. Glamorgan, worth £12,113 a year. *Principal Residence.*—Duffryn, near Aberdare, co. Glamorgan.

ABERDEEN (County of)

EARLDOM[S.]   1. SIR GEORGE GORDON, of Haddo, co. Aberdeen,
I. 1682.   Bart. [S.], 2nd s. of Sir John G., 1st Bart. [S], by Mary,
              da. of William FORBES, of Tolquhoun, *b.* 3 Oct. 1637 ; *suc.* his eldest br. in the Baronetcy and estate of Haddo in 1665. He became an Advocate 7 Feb. 1668, M.P. for co. Aberdeen 1669-74, 1678, and 1681-2. P.C. 1678, one of the Lords of Session 1 June 1680, President 1 Nov. 1681, and having been made HIGH CHANCELLOR [S.] 1 May 1682, was, on 30 Nov. 1682, *cr.* LORD HADDO, METHLICK, TARVES, and KELLIE, VISCOUNT OF FORMARTINE, and EARL OF ABER-DEEN (ᶜ) [S]. In June 1684 he resigned office, and though at the Revolution he was imprisoned in Edinburgh Castle for refusing to take the oath of allegiance to William III, he took it subsequently to Queen Anne. He *m.* (cont. 1671) Anne, 1st da. of George LOCKHART, of Torbrecks, by

---

(ᵃ) An amiable man of fine presence and popular in society, he was an industrious, but not a gifted nor a successful, politician. He was one of the few Peers who supported Gladstone when that Minister gave way to the Irish demand for *Home Rule.* V.G.

(ᵇ) No evidence is forthcoming as to the occupation habitat or nationality of Mr. Clifford, only an assurance as to his " means. "   The lady was a " Gibson girl " on the Gaiety stage, *i.e.* a young woman chosen because her features recalled the type of female beauty which the American artist Gibson affects ; a correspondent, though on what authority I know not, writes that, previously, she was a Scandinavian steerage emigrant to Nova Scotia, and, he believes, then known as "Ottersen " V G.

(ᶜ) The patent is printed at length in the appendix to Crawfurd's *Lives of Officers of State.* It sets forth the death of the grantee's father in the Royal cause, his own " splendid abilities " &c

Anne, da. of Sir James LOCKHART, of Lee. In 1672 she became h. to her br., William L. She was *bur* 19 July 1707, at Methlic. He *d.* 20 Apr. 1720, at Kellie, in his 83rd year. Will. dat. 5 May 1706.

[GEORGE GORDON, 2nd s. (ª) and h. ap , *bap* at Methlic, 6 Aug. 1674, *styled* LORD HADDO after 1682, *d.* unm. *v.p.*, between 1 July 1694 (ᵇ) and 1708]

II 1720.   3. WILLIAM (GORDON) EARL OF ABERDEEN, &c. [S.], 4th (ᶜ) but 1st surv. s. and h., *bap.* 22 Dec. 1679, at Methlic. He, being then *styled* LORD HADDO, was chosen M.P. (Tory) for co. Aberdeen 1 June 1708, but declared by the House of Commons, 18 Jan. 1708/9, incapable of sitting for any shire or borough in Scotland, as being the eldest s. of a Scottish Peer. (ᵈ) On 1 June 1721 he was elected a Rep. Peer, and again in 1722, but not in 1727. He took a decided part against Ministers and all the Court measures. He *m.*, 1stly, in 1708, before 12 Oct., Mary, 1st da. of David (LESLIE), EARL OF LEVEN AND MELVILLE [S.], by Anne, 1st da. of James (WEMYSS), Lord BURNTISLAND [S.]. Her father was at that time Governor of Edinburgh Castle, in which the bridegroom's father was prisoner. She, who was *b.* July 1692, *d. s p m*, and was *bur.* 29 Jan. 1709/10, at Methlic. He *m.*, 2ndly, 25 Apr. 1716, at Huntingtower, Susan, (ᵉ) 4th da. of John (MURRAY) 1st DUKE OF ATHOLL [S.], by his 1st wife, Catharine, da. of William (DOUGLAS), DUKE OF HAMILTON [S.]. She, who was *b.* 15 Apr. 1699, *d.* in childbed, 22 June 1725, and was *bur.* at Methlic. He *m.*, 3rdly, 9 Dec. 1729, at Bellie Parish Church, Fochabers, Anne, 3rd da. of Alexander (GORDON), 2nd DUKE OF GORDON [S.], by Henrietta, da of Charles (MORDAUNT), EARL OF PETERBOROUGH and MONMOUTH. He *d.* 30 Mar. 1745, at Edinburgh, in his 66th year. Will dat. 3 Jan. 1736. His widow *d.* there 26 June 1791, in her 78th year.

III. 1745.   3. GEORGE (GORDON), EARL OF ABERDEEN, &c. [S.], s and h. by 2nd wife, was *b.* 19, and *bap.* 20 June 1722, at Methlic ; was *styled* LORD HADDO till 1745. Chosen a Rep. Peer [S.] 1747-61, and 1774-90.(ᶠ) He *m.*, before 22 Aug.1759, Catharine Elizabeth, da. of Oswald HANSON, of Wakefield, co. York. He *d.* 13 Aug. 1801, at Ellon House, in his 80th year. His widow *d.* 15 Mar 1817, in her 83rd year, at Rudding Park, and was *bur.* at Methlic. Admon. Aug. 1820.

[GEORGE GORDON, *styled* LORD HADDO, s. and h. ap., *b.* 28 Jan. 1764; *m.*, 18 June 1782, at Gilmerton, Charlotte, sister of Gen. Sir David BAIRD,

---

(ª) The 1st s., John, *bap* 7 Sep. 1673, at Methlic, was *bur.* there 17 June 1675. V.G.

(ᵇ) At this date he is described as "a very solid young gentleman, and who will one day make an able man, if he gets good breeding." (*Letters of James, Earl of Perth*, Camden Soc., p. 34.) V G.

(ᶜ) The 3rd s., James, *bap.* 11 Aug. 1676, at Methlic, *d. v.p.* and *s.p*   V.G.

(ᵈ) See p. 2, note "a."

(ᵉ) She is called Anne in the Funeral entries in the Lyon Office.

(ᶠ) He voted against Pitt's Regency Bill. V G.

Bart , and da. of William Baird, of Newbyth, co. Haddington. Grand
Master of Freemasons 1784-86. He *d. v p.*, 2 Oct. 1791, of a fall from
his horse, at Formartine House, and was *bur.* at Methlic. His widow *d.*
8 Oct 1795, at Clifton, co. Gloucester. Admon. Nov. 1796.]

IV. 1801.   4. George (Gordon, afterwards Hamilton-Gordon),
          Earl of Aberdeen, &c. [S], grandson and h., being s. and
h. of George Gordon (*styled* Lord Haddo) and Charlotte his wife abovenamed. He was *b* 28 Jan 1784, at Edinburgh ; was *styled* Lord Haddo,
1791 till 1801 ; ed. at Harrow, and at St. John's Coll., Cambridge ; M A.
1804 ; attached in 1801 to the embassy to negotiate with Napoleon at
Amiens, where the treaty for peace was signed Mar. 1802 ; Rep. Peer [S.]
1806-18 ; K.T. 16 Mar. 1808 ; F.R.S. 28 Apr. 1808 ; Grand Cross of
St. Stephen of Austria, 4 Sep. 1813 ; ambassador to Austria, 1813, where he
prevailed with the Emperor to join (by the treaty of Toplitz, Sep 1813) the
allied Sovereigns against (his s.-in-law) Napoleon. (ª)   On 1 June 1814 he
signed the treaty of Paris on behalf of his Sovereign, and on the same day
was *cr.* a Peer of the United Kingdom as VISCOUNT GORDON OF
ABERDEEN, co. Aberdeen. P.C. 22 July 1814. By Royal lic., 13 Nov.
1818, he took the name of Hamilton before that of Gordon. (ᵇ) After
fourteen years' retirement he again took office, Jan. to June 1828 (under the
Wellington administration), as Chancellor of the Duchy of Lancaster.
From June 1828 to Mar. 1830, and again from Sep. 1841 to 1846, he was
Secretary of State for Foreign Affairs. Finally, Dec. 1852 to Feb. 1855,
he was First Lord of the Treasury, and as such, Prime Minister, the
chief event in his tenure of office being the bloody Crimean Campaign.
His cabinet fell from the idea that through his feebleness we had " drifted
into the war." (ᶜ) K.G. 7 Feb. 1855. (ᵈ) Trustee Brit. Museum from 1812,
and Lord Lieut. of co. Aberdeen from 1846, till his death ; Ranger of

(ª) " He has high birth and dignity, a sound and cultivated understanding, im-
penetrable discretion, and polite but somewhat grave and reserved manners. " (J.W.
Ward, Letter dat. 1813) V.G.

(ᵇ) The ground on which he petitioned for this licence was his *connection* with the
family of Hamilton, and his being guardian to (his wife's child) the young Marquess of
Abercorn , as neither he nor his surv. children had any of the blood or estates of the
Hamiltons, the reason alleged for taking such name appears very inadequate. Accordingly it was, with good judgment, formally abandoned by the 7th Earl, 9 Oct. 1900

(ᶜ) See *Annual Register*, 1860, pp. 376-383. He was a Tory and Conservative
till 1846 ; afterwards leader of the Pittites in the H of L. V.G.

(ᵈ) He was granted the very rare distinction of being permitted *to retain the order
of the Thistle together with that of the Garter.* Exclusive of the blood royal, twelve
Knights of the Thistle (since its re-establishment in 1687) have been elected to the
Garter, *viz.* ·—(1) The Duke of Argyll [S.], K.G 1709/10; (2) *The Duke of
Hamilton* [S.], *Duke of Brandon* [G.B.] K.G. 1712 ; (3) the Earl of Essex, K.G.
1737/8 ; (4) The Earl of Bute [S], K G. 1762 ; (5) The Earl of Carlisle, K.G.
1793 ; (6) The Duke of Buccleuch [S], K G 1794 ; (7) The *Duke of Roxburghe*
[S.], K.G. 1801 , (8) The Duke of Montrose [S.], K.G. 1812 ; (9) The Duke of
Buccleuch [S.], K G. 1835 , (10) The *Earl of Aberdeen* [S.], K.G. 1855 ; (11) The

Greenwich Park 1845-60; Chancellor of King's Coll, Aberdeen, 1847-60; Elder Br. of the Trin House 1853-60. He *m.*, 1stly, 28 July 1805, at Bentley Priory, in Stanmore, Midx. (spec. lic), Catherine Elizabeth, 1st surv. da. of John James (HAMILTON), 1st MARQUESS OF ABERCORN, by his 1st wife, Catherine, da. of Sir Joseph COPLEY, Bart. She was *b.* 10 Jan. 1784, and *d. s.p.m.s.*, 29 Feb. 1812, at Argyll House, St. James's He *m.* 2ndly, 8 July 1815, Harriet, *styled* Dowager VISCOUNTESS HAMILTON (being widow of James, s. and h. ap. of the afsd. 1st MARQUESS OF ABERCORN), 2nd da of Hon John DOUGLAS (s. of James, XV (14th) EARL OF MORTON [S], by Frances, da. of Edward (LASCELLES), 1st EARL OF HAREWOOD She was *b.* 8 June 1792, and *d.* 26 Aug. 1833, at Argyll House He *d.* there, 14 Dec. 1860, in his 77th year, and was *bur.* at Stanmore, as were both his wives. (ª)

[...... GORDON, *styled* LORD HADDO, s. and h. ap , by 1st wife, *b.* and *d.* 23 Nov 1810]

V 1860. 5. GEORGE JOHN JAMES (HAMILTON GORDON), EARL OF ABERDEEN, &c [S], also VISCOUNT GORDON OF ABERDEEN, 1st surv. s and h. by 2nd wife, *b.* 28 Sep 1816, at Bentley Priory , *styled* LORD HADDO till 1860. Ed. at Harrow, and at Trin. Coll., Cambridge ; M.A. 1837, M.P. (Liberal) for co Aberdeen 1854-60. He *m.*, 5 Nov. 1840, at Taymouth Castle, co Perth, Mary, sister of George, 10th EARL OF HADDINGTON [S.], and 2nd da of George BAILLIE, of Jerviswood, by Mary, da. of Sir James PRINGLE, 4th Bart. [S.]. He *d.* 22 Mar 1864, at Haddo House, aged 47. His widow *d.* 3 Apr. 1900, at Kennet, Alloa, aged 85. Will pr. Dec 1900, at £15,845. Both were *bur.* at Methlic

VI. 1864. 6. GEORGE (HAMILTON GORDON), EARL OF ABERDEEN, &c. [S.], also VISCOUNT GORDON OF ABERDEEN, s. and h., *b.* 10 Dec. 1841, at Holyrood ; *styled* LORD HADDO from 1860 to 1864 He *d.* unm. (being drowned while serving in the ship *Hera* on a voyage from Boston to Melbourne), 27 Jan. 1870, aged 28.

VII. 1870. 7. JOHN CAMPBELL (HAMILTON GORDON), EARL OF ABERDEEN, VISCOUNT OF FORMARTINE, LORD HADDO, METHLICK, TARVES and KELLIE [S.] ; also VISCOUNT GORDON OF ABERDEEN,

---

Earl of Zetland, K.G. 1872 ; and (12) The Duke of Argyll [S], K G. 1883. Of these twelve, only four, (*viz.* those whose names are in *italics*) one of whom was an English Duke, and another Prime Minister and senior K.T , have retained both orders. As to (2) the Duke of Hamilton [S.], he *d* within three weeks of his election, and it is not improbable that he might have resigned the order of the Thistle, according to precedent, before his installation, though he apparently wished to retain both orders. See Beltz, *Order of the Garter*, p. cxxiv, note. In the plate affixed to his stall in 1836 (124 years later) he is described as K T.

(ª) When a lad he avoided the control of his harsh and negligent grandfather by appointing as curators Dundas and Pitt, who forced the old man to agree to his being sent to Cambridge, Pitt drily writing that he "did not concur with his Lordship in considering that rank superseded the necessity for education" ! He was a sound

and a Baronet [S], 3rd and yst. (ᵃ) and only surv br and h., *b.* 3 Aug.
1847, at Edinburgh   Ed. at Univ. Coll. Oxford, B.A. 1871, M.A 1875.
His right to the Peerage was confirmed by the House of Lords 6 May
1872.   Lord Lieut. of co. Aberdeen, 1880 ; High Commissioner to the
General Assembly of the church of Scotland, 1881-85.   P.C 6 Feb 1886
Viceroy of Ireland, Feb. to Aug. 1886.   Gov. Gen. of Canada 1893-98.
G.C M.G., 1895.   LL.D. of the Univs. of Aberdeen, Toronto, Ottawa, &c.
Pres of the Highland and Agric. Soc. [S.] 1901-1902.   He *m.*, 7 Nov.
1877, at St. Geo., Han Sq., Isabel Maria, da. of Dudley Coutts (MARJORI-
BANKS), 1st LORD TWEEDMOUTH, by Isabella, da. of the Rt. Hon. Sir James
WEIR-HOGG, 1st Bart.   She was *b.* 14 Mar. 1857.

[GEORGE GORDON, *styled* LORD HADDO, s. and h. ap., *b.* 20 Jan. 1879,
in Grosvenor Sq., Midx.   Ed. at Harrow.   He *m.*, 6 Aug 1906, at the
Scottish Presbyterian Ch of St. Columba, Pont St , Chelsea, Mary Florence,
widow of E.S. COCKAYNE, of Sheffield, draper (ᵇ), da. of Joseph CLIXBY, of
Owmby Cliff, co. Lincoln.]

Family Estates.—These in 1883 consisted of 62,422 acres in co. Aberdeen, worth £44,112 a year.   *Principal Residence.*—Haddo House, co.
Aberdeen.

ABERDEEN (co. Aberdeen)

i.e. "GORDON OF ABERDEEN," Viscountcy *cr.* 1814   See "ABERDEEN"
Earldom of [S.], under the 4th Earl.

ABERDELGY

See "OLIPHANT OF ABERDELGY," Barony [S.] (*Oliphant*), *cr.* 1458, *dormant* since 1748 or 1751.

---

classical scholar, and had travelled far in the bypaths of literature   In Byron's verse
he is " the travelled thane, Athenian Aberdeen."
    " The cast of his features in later life was one of dignified sternness rather than
beauty "   He did much by planting to improve his estate at Haddo, and was something of a botanist   His s., Lord Stanmore, writes, " nothing could be more curious
than the way in which colleagues and friends, whenever at a loss, came to him for
information on the most varied topics, and rarely came in vain. "   (*The Holland House
Circle*, by Lloyd Sanders, pp 295-9)   " He belonged to that class of statesmen who are
great without being brilliant, who succeed without ambition, who without eloquence
become famous, who retain their power even when deprived of place.   He denied that
his vocation was politics, but his friends knew him better , they appreciated his clear head,
his tolerant nature, his vast experience, and his perfect integrity "   (J.T. Delane,
Ed. of *The Times*)   V.G.
    (ᵃ) The 2nd s., James Henry, *b.* 11 Oct. 1845, was killed at Cambridge, by the
accidental discharge of his gun, 12 Feb 1868, when an undergrad. at Trin. Coll. there.
    (ᵇ) " Miss Clixby *m.* one of the partners in a very flourishing Sheffield drapery
business   Her first marriage took place in 1881 " [*i.e.* when her 2nd husband was
but 2 years old].   See *M.A.P.*, 27 June 1906.   V.G.

ABERDOUR

In 1351 Sir James Douglas had the grant of the Barony of Aberdour [S.], co. Fife, from his uncle William, sometime Earl of Atholl [S], to whose barony of Dalkeith he *suc.* before 1369. His great grandson James, often regarded as Lord Dalkeith [S.], on 14 Mar 1457/8 was *cr.* Earl of Morton [S.]. William, the 6th Earl had, 16 Mar. 1638, a very comprehensive Charter of the lands, Earldom, and Barony of Morton, with all his other lands, and "Aberdour was at the same time erected into a burgh of Barony and the title was altered to EARL OF MORTON AND LORD ABERDOUR."(ª) Since that time the title of *Lord Aberdour* [S.] has been used as *the courtesy title* belonging to the eldest son of the Earl of Morton [S.]. See Morton, Earldom of [S.], *cr.* 1457/8.

i.e. "Aubigny, Dalkeith, Torboltoun, and Aberdour" Barony [S.] (*Stuart*), *cr.* 1581, with the Dukedom of Lennox [S.], which see ; *extinct* 1672.

ABERGAVENNY
or *(as it was at one time styled)* BERGAVENNY

On account of the notoriety of this dignity, and to assist in forming a judgment as to how far the possession of the castle and demesne of Abergavenny could be supposed to constitute a *Barony by tenure*, a brief account is here given of its possessors previous to 1392, the date when the (then) possessor was first summoned as "de Bergavenny." Before the period when a writ of summons converted a Barony into a *personal* instead of a *territorial* dignity, the owner of this castle, &c doubtless by its tenure possessed a Feudal Barony, which was, however, but *one* among very many others (ᵇ)

OWNERS of the LORDSHIP I. *temp.* Will. II.	Hamelin de Ballon (ᶜ) received the lordship of Over Gwent, including the castle of Abergavenny, (ᵈ) from William Rufus. (ᵉ) He *m.* Agnes, and had two sons,

(ª) *Reg Mag Sig*, as quoted in the *Scots Peerage*, vol vi. p. 375.

(ᵇ) The editor desires to express his obligation to G.W.Watson for having entirely rewritten the account of these early owners of the Castle, as also for many valuable corrections and additions to the accounts of the early Lords Bergavenny.

(ᶜ) For the earliest lords of Abergavenny see the paper on "The Family of Ballon," in J H Round's *Studies in Peerage and Family History*, pp. 189 *et seq.*, where Dugdale's errors are corrected. It is there shown that Hamelin, who took his name from his birthplace, Ballon in Maine, received his lands in England from William Rufus. He founded a Priory at Abergavenny. V.G

(ᵈ) The Castle "taketh his name from the river of *Gevenny*, whereon it is situate, and the British word *Abber* which signifieth a mouth," being built where the "*Gevenny* doth open itself to the end of the Uske." (Bird, *A Treatise of the Nobilitie*, enlarged by Serjeant Doderidge, 1642, p. 144.) V.G

(ᵉ) It appears from some charters of St Vincent at Le Mans, printed by Dom Martène (*Amplissima Collectio*, vol. i, 1724, c. 577-9), and analysed by J.H.Round (*Documents etc.*, nos. 1045-8), that "vir quidam nobilis et prudentissimus Hamelinus de

William and Matthew. He was living in 1103, and *d.* 5 Mar. 11— (*)

II *temp.* Henry I.   BRIEN FITZ COUNT, or OF WALLINGFORD, illegit. s. of
         Alan Fergent, Duke, or Count, of Britanny, was a Welsh
magnate before 16 Oct. 1119, being then possessed of the honour of
Abergavenny (*i e* Over Gwent), which he held either by grant to him and
his wife, Maud, Lady of Wallingford, (ᵇ) or else solely in her right
They transferred the honour to Miles, Earl of Hereford, (ᶜ) in 1141-2, to
be held of them and their heirs by the service of 3 knights.

III. 1141-2.   MILES OF GLOUCESTER, hereditary sheriff thereof, and
         the King's Constable, s. and h. of Walter FITZ ROGER de
PÎTRES, who held the former office. He was *cr.* EARL OF HEREFORD,
25 July 1141. He *m.*, 1121, Sibyl, da. and h. of Bernard DE NEUFMARCHÉ,
Lord of Brecon, (ᵈ) and *d.* 24 Dec. 1143. See fuller account under
" HEREFORD. "

IV. 1143.   ROGER, EARL OF HEREFORD and the King's Con-
         stable, s. and h. He was confirmed in all his father's
possessions by Henry II in 1155; this must be held to have included the
honour of Abergavenny. He *m.* in 1137-8, Cicely, 1st. da and coh. of
Payn FITZ JOHN, by Sibyl. (ᵉ) He *d* a monk of Gloucester, in 1155, *s p*
See fuller account under " HEREFORD "

---

castro Baladone natus atque propter industriam a rege Anglorum Wilhelmo filio
opinatissimi regis Wilhelmi amplissimis muneribus atque honoribus sublimatus" gave
to the Abbey " capellam sui castelli quod sibi supradictus gloriosus rex jam dederat
quod lingua Britannica Bergeuenis nominant. " He also gave all the tithes of all
Over Gwent *(Weneiscoit)*. These gifts were confirmed by King Henry I. (*ex inform.*
G.W.Watson) V.G.

(ᵃ) The *fundatoris genealogia* of Abergavenny (*Monasticon*, vol. iv, p 615) says that
he was s of Dru de Baladun, and that he *d s.p*, and gave Abergavenny and Over
Gwent to Brien *(filio comitis de Insula)*, s of his sister Lucy. But J H Round has
proved (*Peerage Studies*, pp. 198-206) that he left a da., Emmeline, who *m.* Reynold,
s of Roger, Earl of Hereford, and was mother of William, who, in 1166, entered a
claim to Abergavenny. The *genealogia*, which, however, as Round elsewhere remarks,
breaks down completely on being tested, states that Earl Miles was s. of Emma,
another sister of Hamelin   (*ex inform* G.W.Watson)   V.G

(ᵇ) According to an inquisition in the *Testa de Nevill* (p. 115), she was widow
of Miles Crespin (a Domesday tenant, who *d.* 1107), and da and h. of Robert d'Oilly
of Wallingford (another Domesday tenant) by the da. and h (Ealdgyth) of Wigod,
Lord of Wallingford *temp.* King Harold   But this inquisition is of too late a date to
be implicitly relied on   (*ex inform.* G W Watson.)   V G.

(ᶜ) J H Round has edited in his *Ancient Charters* (Pipe Roll Soc) pp 43-5, the
charter by which the Empress Maud granted to Miles, Earl of Hereford, and his heirs
the Castle and Honour to be held of Brien fitz Count and Maud of Wallingford his
wife and their heirs. Round infers from this important charter that Brien held the
castle in right of his wife   It will be observed that the charter merely creates an
under-tenancy   V.G.

(ᵈ) Round, *Ancient Charters*, no 6.

(ᵉ) *Idem*, nos. 21, 22.

V 1155. WALTER OF HEREFORD, (*) the King's Constable, next
br. and h. ; Sheriff of Gloucester and Hereford 1155-57,
and of Hereford 1157-1159. He *d. s.p.*

VI. 1160 ? HENRY OF HEREFORD, (*) the King's Constable, next br.
and h. He *d. s.p*, being slain by Seisyll ap Dyvnwal, on
an Easter Eve between 1159 and 1163, at Castle Arnold, near Abergavenny.
He was *bur.* at Llanthony in Wales (or at Llanthony without Gloucester)
His widow, Isabel, held 5 knights' fees in dower from her sister-in-law,
Margaret de Bohon, in 1166.

VII. 1163 ? MAHEL OF HEREFORD, the King's Constable, next br.
and h. He was present at the Council of Clarendon,
Jan 1163/4. He *d. s.p.*, and was *bur.* at Llanthony without Gloucester.

VIII. 1164 ? WILLIAM OF HEREFORD, the King's Constable, next
br. and h He held the honour for about a year, and
d. s.p. before 1166, being mortally hurt by a stone dropped from Bronllys
Tower, co Brecon

[In 1165, the King's household officers were in garrison at Abergavenny, apparently under the command of Walter de Beauchamp. (ᵇ)
According to Fane's Case, " the lands of Over-went were by Henry II
betaken to the custody of Seisill ap Yago, whom Seisill ap Dunwall slew. "]

IX. H[UGH] DE BEAUCHAMP, br. of Walter abovenamed, (ᶜ)
confirmed to the monks of Abergavenny all that " ante-
cessores mei Hamelinus de Balon et Brientius filius comitis et alii domini
de Bergeveni eis impenderunt. His testibus Gauterio et Richerio fratribus
domini " (ᵈ)

X 1173 ? WILLIAM DE BRIOUZE, (ᵉ) Lord of Briouze in Normandy,
and of Bramber, Sussex, s. and h of Philip de B, of the
same, by Aenor, da. and h. of Juhel son of Alvred, Lord of Barnstaple
and Totnes. He *m.*, in or before 1150, Bertha, 2nd sister and coh. of

(*) William de Briouze [no. XI] confirmed to the monks of Abergavenny all the
donations made by " Hamelinus de Balon et Brientius comitis filius et Walterus de
Herefort et Henricus de Herefort" (*Monasticon*, vol. IV, p 616) The *genealogia*, besides
erroneously making Walter junior to Henry, states that the latter received Over Gwent
from his grandfather Walter—who never held it. (*ex inform.* G.W Watson) V.G.
(ᵇ) *Pipe Roll*, 11 Hen II. The King's troops occupied the Castle till Easter 1166.
(ᶜ) They were probably brothers of William de Beauchamp, Sheriff of Hereford
1160-69, and sons of Walter de Beauchamp of Elmley. V.G.
(ᵈ) *Monasticon*, vol. IV, p. 616.
(ᵉ) Briouze-Saint-Gervais (formerly Braiose), arrond of Argentan, dept. of Orne.
His descendants spelt the name Brewes. In some 25 early references to this name,
not in charter latin, it appears as Breouse, Breuse, or Brewys (the last of which still
exists as a surname), but never as Braose, the form adopted in peerages, for which it
seems doubtful if there be any good authority For some discussion on mediæval
English names see vol. III, Appendix C V G.

William of Hereford abovenamed. Sheriff of Hereford, Easter 1173-1175, at which earlier date probably he already possessed the Lordship of Over Gwent. He was living in 1179.

XI.   WILLIAM DE BRIOUZE, Lord of Briouze, Bramber,
                   Brecon, Over Gwent, &c., s. and h. (ª). He *m*. Maud
DE ST. VALERY, "Lady of La Haie." In consequence of his well-known quarrel with King John, his lands were forfeited in 1208, and his wife and 1st s. starved to death in the dungeons of Corfe (or of Windsor) in 1210. He *d*. at Corbeil near Paris, 9, and was *bur*. 10 Aug. 1211, in the Abbey of St. Victor at Paris.

XII. 1215.   GILES DE BRIOUZE, 2nd s., Bishop of Hereford,
                   1200-1215. He seized his father's Welsh possessions in 1215, which seizin was, however, confirmed by the King, 21 Oct. 1215, on payment of a fine. He *d*. 13 Nov. 1215 [not 1216], at Gloucester, and was *bur*. in Hereford Cathedral.

XIII. 1216.   REYNOLD DE BRIOUZE, next br. He had seizin of his
                   father's lands 26 May 1216, but gave up Bramber in or after 1220 to his nephew John, s. and h. of his 1st br. William. He *m*., 1stly, Grecia, da. and in her issue coh. of William BRIEGUERRE OR BRIWERE, by Beatrice DE VAUX. He *m*., 2ndly, 1215, Gwladus Du, da. of Llewelyn ap Iorwerth, Prince of North Wales, by his 2nd wife, Joan, illegit. da. of King John. He *d*. between 5 May 1227 and 9 June 1228. His widow *m*., 2ndly, Ralph DE MORTIMER, of Wigmore, who *d*. 6 Aug. 1246, and was *bur*. at Wigmore Abbey. She *d*. at Windsor in 1251.

XIV. 1228.   WILLIAM DE BRIOUZE, s. and h. by 1st wife. He *m*.
                   Eve, da. and in her issue coh. of William (MARSHAL),
EARL OF STRIGUL AND PEMBROKE. He *d*. 2 May 1230, being hanged by Llewelyn abovenamed. His widow *d*. before 1246.

XV.   EVE DE BRIOUZE, da. and coh., heiress of Abergavenny.
                   She *m*., after 25 July 1238 (when his father, William de C., obtained her wardship and marriage together with the custody of Abergavenny and the other lands falling to her share), and before 15 Feb. 1247/8, William DE CANTELOU, (ᵇ) of Calne, Wilts, and Aston Cantlow, co.

(ª) He slaughtered Seisyll ap Dyvnwal (abovenamed) and a host of unarmed Welshmen, in the castle of Abergavenny in 1175, in revenge for the death of his uncle Henry of Hereford (*Brut y Tywysogion*, R. de Diceto, etc.). Seisyll was owner of Castle Arnold, and is said in an inaccurate version of the *Brut* to have captured Abergavenny in 1172, the slaughter being dated 1177 (*The Gwentian Chronicle*, Cambrian Arch. Assoc., p. 137). But the better version of the *Brut* (Rolls Ser., p. 218 ; *Y Brutieu*, in Welsh Texts, ed. Rhys and Evans, 1890, p. 330) on the contrary, states that Seisyll was captured in 1172 by the garrison of Abergavenny. (*ex inform.* G. W. Watson.) V.G.

(ᵇ) In the case for Lady Fane and her husband claiming the title (Collins,

Warwick. He *d.* at Calstone, Wilts, 25, and was *bur.* 30 Sep. 1254, at Studley Priory, co. Warwick. Writ of extent 15 Oct. 1254. She *d.* in 1255, about 20 and before 28 July.

XVI. 1255   GEORGE DE CANTELOU, only s. and h.; *b.* 29 Mar 1252, at Abergavenny He *m.* (cont. ratified by the King, 1 Sep. 1254) Margaret, da of Edmund (DE LACY), EARL OF LINCOLN, by Alasia, da. of Manfredo, MARQUIS OF SALUZZO. He was knighted 13 Oct. 1272, and had seizin of his lands 25 Apr. and 1 May 1273. He *d. s.p.*, 18 Oct. 1273.(ᵃ) His widow was *bur.* in the Church of the Black Friars at Pontefract.

XVII. 1273.   JOHN (HASTINGS), LORD HASTINGS, nephew and coh., being s. and h. of Sir Henry HASTINGS of Ashill, Norfolk, by Joan, sister and coh. of the last owner of Abergavenny. He was *b* 6 May 1262, *suc* his father in 1268/9, (ᵇ) and was sum. to Parl., 1295 to 1313, by writs directed "*Johanni de Hastinges.*" (ᶜ) Writ of *diem cl. ext.*, 28 Feb. 1312/3.

XVIII. 1313.   JOHN (HASTINGS), LORD HASTINGS, s. and h., *b* 30 Sep. 1286. He was sum. to Parl, 1313 to 1325, by writs directed "*Johanni de Hastinges,*" (ᶜ) and *d.* 1325.

See fuller account under "HASTINGS."

Baronies by Writ, &c., 1734, pp. 61-96) it is stated that "It pleased King Henry III to create Sir William de Cantelupe Lord of Bergavenny, *by his writ of summons to Parl.* by the name of William Cantelupe of *Bergavenny,* chevalier, as by the name of his chiefest mannor and seigniory." There is, however, not the slightest proof of the existence of this writ, which (as the said William *d.* in 1254) would be many years earlier than the earliest writ on record

  (ᵃ) His heirs were his sister Milicent, then of full age and wife of Eudes la Zouche, and his nephew John, the next owner of Abergavenny. Oswald Barron writes, "I question the accuracy of the form de Cantilupe, all my notes give Cantelowe or Cantlow as the accepted english version of this surname." Indeed Cantilupe has the air of being an anglicization of a lantinization rather than a real name. For some discussion on mediaeval English names see vol iii, Appendix C. V.G.

  (ᵇ) In 1301 he signed the letter to the Pope as "Johannes de Hastinges, *dñs de Bergeveny.*" Considerable stress is laid on this fact in a small work by Bird, (see note "d" p. 19) at the end whereof is a statement, "*That the Barony of Aburgavenny is a Barony by tenure.*" Any person, however, who looks at the list of these Barons (given in *Nicolas,* p. 762) will see how many of them were but *feudal* Lords of the place, whereof they wrote themselves "*Domini.*" The very next Baron to Lord Hastings is Henry Percy, "*dñs* de Topclive," yet no one, probably, would contend that the Barony of the Percy family was styled "Topcliffe;" that of Lovel, "de Dakking" (*i.e.* Docking, in Norfolk); that of de Vere, "de Swanschaumpis," &c, &c. John de Hastings was undoubtedly styled "Dominus de Bergeveny," "Seigneur de Berge-veny," &c, in many contemporary documents, but doubtless only from that Castle being his *chief* residence.

  (ᶜ) As Nicolas points out (see *post,* p. 25, note "c") the word '*Bergavenny*' never appears on any of the numerous writs issued to these two Barons The Barony they held was that of "HASTINGS," which Barony in 1841 was allowed, with the precedence of the sitting in 1290, to Sir Jacob Astley, Bart., the junior coheir of the junior coheiress thereof.

XIX 1325.

LAURENCE (HASTINGS), LORD HASTINGS, s. and h., *cr* EARL OF PEMBROKE, 1339. He *d.*

30 Aug. 1348.

XX. 1348.

JOHN (HASTINGS), EARL OF PEMBROKE, s. and h. ([a]) He *d.* 16 Apr. 1375. ([b])

XXI 1375.

JOHN (HASTINGS), s and h., never invested as Earl of Pembroke. He *d.* a minor, unm.,

30 Dec. 1389

See fuller account under PEMBROKE.

XXII. 1389.

BARONY.

I. 1392

1. WILLIAM BEAUCHAMP, cousin (*i.e.* s. of a sister of the grandmother) ([c]) of the *last* owner, (but in no way connected with any of the former owners previous to the marriage of his maternal aunt with the then Lord), *suc.* to the Castle and Honour of Abergavenny by virtue of the entail, made by John, Earl of Pembroke, abovenamed. ([b]) He was 4th s. of Thomas, EARL OF WARWICK, by Katharine, da. of Roger (MORTIMER), EARL OF MARCH. He served under the gallant Chandos, and subsequently, in the wars with France, with great distinction, and in 1375 (or 1376) was, by Edward III, nominated K.G. In 1383 he was Captain of Calais. Having *suc.*, as above mentioned, to the lands of

([a]) As to his styling himself Seigneur de Weiseford, see under "Wexford," in Ireland, in Appendix A in this volume.

([b]) In pursuance of a royal licence, dated 20 Feb. (1368/9) 43 Edw. III, the Earl enfeoffed certain persons of all his estates, except the manor of Ashill, Norfolk, and the feoffees redemised to him for 5 years from 20 Mar., 43 Edw. III. On 15 Apr (1372) 46 Edw III, styling himself *Johan de Hastynges conte de Pembrok seignur de Wesseford et Bergeveny*, he confirmed and granted the same estates to these feoffees and their heirs for ever. Finally, by letters patent written in his hostel in London, 5 May 1372, he directed the feoffees that, if he *d.* abroad, his debts should be paid, and that if he *d. s.p.* [he had then no child], the King should be enfeoffed of the castle and county of Pembroke, the castles and lordships of Tenby and Kilgerran, and the commote of Oysterlowe : and that they should give and grant the other castles, manors etc., which they had of his feoffment *ove la reversione du chastel la ville et seignurie de Bergev'* etc., to his cousin Monsieur William de Beauchamp and his heirs for ever, on condition that he bore the Earl's arms undifferenced (*enteres*), and that he took proceedings before the King *qil port non de cont de Pembrok a lui et a ses heirs*, and that if William declined these terms, they should enfeoff the Earl's cousin, William de Clynton, on the same conditions Wherefore, in the quinzaine of St. Michael (1375) 49 Edw. III, the Earl being dead in parts beyond seas, the feoffees appeared before the King's Council at Westm., and afterwards, in the same presence, William de Beauchamp accepted the above terms. But since the Earl had an heir of his body then living under age, it was decreed that the King should have the custody of the castles, manors, etc., till the age of the said heir. (Exemplification on the *Patent Roll,* 5 Mar. 1377, 51 Edw. III, *m* 29). (*ex inform.* G.W. Watson.) V G.

([c]) His precise relationship to the Earls of Pembroke is that his mother's sister, Agnes Mortimer (wife of Laurence, Lord Hastings, *cr.* Earl of Pembroke), was mother of John, Earl of Pembroke (who, in 1372, executed in his favour the deed of entail), and grandmother of John Hastings, who *d.* unm in 1389.

Abergavenny, he was sum to Parl., 23 July (1392), 16 Ric. II to 18 Dec. (1409) 11 Henry IV, ([a]) as a Baron, [LORD BERGAVENNY, or BEAUCHAMP DE BERGAVENNY ([b]), all the writs being directed "*Willelmo Beauchamp de Bergeveny,*" ([c]) In 1399 he was appointed Justiciary

---

([a]) There is proof in the Rolls of Parl. of his sitting.

([b]) In Pat. Roll 21 Mar. 1401/2 he is called "Lord Pembroke and Bergaveny."

([c]) The following note by Sir N. Harris Nicolas states that much doubt exists in his mind "whether, until the Writ of Summons of the 29th Hen. VI. to Edward Nevill, as 'Domino de Bergavenny,' the proper designation of the previous barons was not that of their family name. The first possessor of that territory after Writs of Summons were regularly issued was John de Hastings, who *d.* 6 Edw. II. and was *suc.* by his s. John de Hastings, who *d.* 18 Edw. II.; to these personages nearly thirty Writs of Summons were directed, and in no instance, in this number, does the word 'Bergavenny' occur, in addition to which the said John de Hastings was entitled to Summons to Parl. as s. and h. of his father Henry, Lord Hastings, a Baron of great note, and the barony in which they sat passed away upon the death of the last Earl of Pembroke, and was separated from the tenure of Bergavenny. From the creation of the 1st Earl of Pembroke till the death of the last, no inference on the subject is to be drawn, until the Writ of Summons to William Beauchamp, 16 Ric. II, who was sum. as 'Willielmo Beauchamp de Bergavenny.' This William Beauchamp not being related to the preceding Barons, and being summoned as 'de Bergavenny,' certainly affords at the first view strong grounds for the generally received opinion that he was sum. as Lord Bergavenny, by tenure of that Castle. On looking attentively into the point, however, a conclusion equally strong may be drawn, that it was merely an addition used to distinguish him from 'John de Beauchamp de Kydderminster.' In the previous reign, a John de Beauchamp was sum. as 'de Somerset,' and another John de Beauchamp, a younger son of Guy Earl of Warwick, as 'de Warwyck;' and before, contemporary with, and after this William de Beauchamp de 'Bergavenny,' numerous Barons were named in Writs of Summons with the addition of their place of residence, without such ever being supposed to be the title of their Baronies: as, therefore, in the only instances which occur of Writs of Summons being issued to the possessor of the Castle of Bergavenny, previous to that to William de Beauchamp, in the 16th Ric. II. they were never designated as 'de Bergavenny,'—and as examples of such additions were exceedingly frequent, without any similar inference being deduced from them,—there does not appear any greater cause for supposing that the designation in question was intended to express the title of the Barony, than there is for concluding such to have been the case either in the instances of John de Beauchamp 'de Somerset,' 'de Warwyk,' or in either [*sic*] of the numerous examples alluded to. In order, however, to obtain as much information as possible on the subject, it was necessary to inquire in what manner the Barons in question were described in the Rolls of Parliament previous to the reign of Henry VI., and the result of the examination is certainly in favour of William Beauchamp's being considered as Baron Bergavenny, though it does not positively establish the fact, whilst it confirms the opinion that his predecessors in the Lordship of Bergavenny never bore that name as the title of their dignity. The earliest instance when BERGAVENNY occurs as a title in the Rolls of Parl. is in the 21st Ric. II. 1397, five years after William Beauchamp was sum. to Parl. as 'Willielmo Beauchamp (de Bergavenny),' when he was described as 'Wm Beauchamp, Sr de Bergavenny.' In the 1st Hen IV. the names of 'Dns. de Roos, de Willoghby, de *Bergeveney*,' occur; and in the following year we find among the Barons then present, 'le Sr de Berga-

of South Wales and Governor of Pembroke. By deed, 20 Feb. (1395/6) 19 Ric. II, he entailed the Castle, &c., of Abergavenny on himself and his wife, and their issue male, with rem. to (his br.) Thomas, Earl of Warwick, and his heirs male for ever. He *m.* Joan, sister and eventually (1415) coh. of Thomas (FITZALAN), EARL OF ARUNDEL, da. of Richard, EARL OF ARUNDEL, by Elizabeth, da. of William (BOHUN), EARL OF NORTHAMPTON. He *d.* 8 May 1411. Will dat. 25 Apr. 1408, in which he directs to be *bur.* at the Black Friars, Hereford, pr. at Lambeth. (ª) *Inq. p. m.* 5 June 1411, at Hereford. His widow, who was *b.* 1375, held the Castle and Honour of Abergavenny in dower till her death. She *d.* 14 Nov. 1435. Will dat. 10 Jan. 1434/5, pr. 19 Nov. 1435. (ᵇ) In it she directs to be *bur.* by her husband. *Inq. p.m.* at the Guildhall, London, 15 Dec. 1435.

II. 1411.   2. RICHARD BEAUCHAMP, who, unless the Peerage be considered as one incident to the *tenure* of the Castle (which he never possessed), must be considered as LORD BERGAVENNY, or BEAUCHAMP DE BERGAVENNY, s. and h., *b.* in or before 1397, being 14 years old and upwards in June 1411. K.B. 8 Apr. 1413. Joint Warden of the Welsh Marches 1415. Capt. of Lances and Archers in Normandy 1418. He does not appear among the fourteen Barons in the Parl. of 16 Nov. 1417, nor among the thirteen Barons in that of 16 Oct. 1419, (ᶜ) but (in

---

venny.' In the 2nd Hen. IV. he is mentioned as 'William Sire de Bergavenny,' and in a similar manner on subsequent occasions. It must, however, be observed, on the other hand, that on the last and most solemn occasion when his name occurs in the Rolls of Parl., *viz.* among the Peers present at the settlement of the Crown in the 8th Hen. IV., he is in both places styled 'Will'mi Beauchamp de *Bergevenny*; and at the same time Henry Lord Scrop of Masham is mentioned as 'Henrici le Scrop *de Masham*', whilst other Barons are styled 'Reginaldi *Domini* de Grey de Ruthyn, William *Domini* de Ferrers, Thomæ *Domini* de Furnyvel,' &c. Richard Beauchamp, his s. and h., was never sum. to Parl. as a Baron, as he was *cr.* Earl of Worcester four years after he became of age; and though he is sometimes styled 'Lord of Bergavenny,' and his mother, both in the Rolls of Parl. and in her will, is called 'Lady of Bergavenny,' no conclusion is to be drawn therefrom, for this expression was more frequently applied to designate important manors and lordships than Parliamentary Baronies. On Edward Nevill's being sum. in the 29th Hen. VI. as 'Domino de Bergavenny,' such certainly became the title of his Barony : but it is to be considered that this occurred in the reign of Henry VI., a period, as is remarked elsewhere, fruitful in anomalies on subjects connected with the Peerage, and when even, as is stated in a subsequent page, some instances occur of the addition of 'Domino de,' &c., being used, without such designation being the title of the dignity possessed by the Baron to whose name it was appended. *Vide* the observations on this subject under Charleton, Dudley, and Grey of Powis. "—*Nicolas*, p. 9, note.

(ª) See *Test. Vet.*, p. 171.

(ᵇ) *Idem*, p. 224.

(ᶜ) This is one of the arguments urged as to the right of the Writ of Summons being incident to the tenure of the feudal Barony which was then in possession of (his mother) the widow of the late Baron. The able and learned author of the *Authorities, &c.* (1862), in the Berkeley claim (in his zeal for establishing the existence of territorial Peerages), actually asserts (p. 188, and elsewhere) *as a fact* that

his 23rd or 24th year), *viz* in Feb. 1420/1, (ª) was *cr.* EARL OF WORCESTER. He *m.*, 27 July 1411, at Tewkesbury, Isabel, sister and eventually (1414) sole *h* of Richard Le Despenser, apparently *de jure* Lord Burghersh, being da. of Thomas, [the attainted] Earl of Gloucester (Lord Le Despenser), by Constance, da. of Edmund, Duke of York. He *d. s.p.m.* (being mortally wounded at the siege of Meaux in France, 18 Mar. 1421/2), and was *bur.* 25 Apr. 1422 in Tewkesbury Abbey. At his death, his vast estates and the representation of his Barony devolved on his only da. and h. (as below), but the Earldom of Worcester apparently *reverted to the Crown.* His widow, (who was *b.* (posthumous) 26 July 1400, at Cardiff, and who was apparently *suo jure* Baroness Burghersh, and, but for the attainder, would have been *suo jure* Baroness Le Despenser) *m.* (by papal disp.) 26 Nov. 1423, at Hanley Castle, co. Worcester, as 2nd wife, her husband's cousin, Richard (Beauchamp) 5th Earl of Warwick, who *d.* 30 Apr., and was *bur.* 4 Oct. 1439, at Warwick. M.I. Will dat. 8 Aug. 1435. She *d* 27 Dec. 1439, at the Friars Minoresses, London, and was *bur.* 13 Jan. 1439/40, in Tewkesbury Abbey. M.I. Will. dat. 1 Dec. 1439, pr. 4 Feb 1439/40. *Inq. p.m* at Abingdon, June 1441.

III 1422.   3. Elizabeth Beauchamp, who, unless the Peerage be considered as one incident to the *tenure* of the Castle, must be considered as Baroness Bergavenny, or Beauchamp de Bergavenny, only da and. h ; *b.* at Hanley Castle, co. Worcester, 16 Sep. 1415. She *m.*, when very young, before 18 Oct. 1424 (ᵇ) [in 1426 her husband (as " *Dominus de Bourgevenny* ") (ᶜ) had summons to take, with the King himself, the order of Knighthood], Edward Nevill, 11th and yst. s. of Ralph, 1st Earl of Westmorland, being 9th s. by his 2nd wife, Joan (Beaufort), Dowager Lady Ferrers de Wemme, the legitimated da of John " of Gaunt," Duke of Lancaster In (1435) 14 Hen VI, she was found h. to her grandmother (who had held the lands of Abergavenny and others in dower), when she and her husband had livery of the lands of her inheritance, but *not* of the castle and lands of Abergavenny, to which her

this Richard " *was a commoner* until created an Earl, " arguing, from the mere circumstance of his being styled " Richard Beauchamp of Bergavenny, *Knight*" in the same instrument in which his mother is spoken of as " *Lady* Bergavenny, " that the Peerage (which, it should be remarked, was undoubtedly possessed by her late husband) was *vested (suo jure)* in her (and *not* in the s. and h) by her *tenure* of the Castle. At that time, however, and long afterwards, Peers were frequently (if, indeed not generally) described as above ; and in the writ to the escheator for the *Inq. post mortem* of this *very* Lady she is styled merely " Johanna, quæ fuit uxor Will'i de Bello Campo, *militis*," though, in the inquisition itself, her husband is alluded to as " nuper Dominus de Bergevenny." (*Berkeley Case*, Appendix 2, p. 59.)

(ª) The charter or patent for this creation does not seem to have been enrolled
(ᵇ) Will of her husband's father.
(ᶜ) *Foedera*, vol. x, p. 356. His name, however, does not occur in the chroniclers' lists of those knighted, consequent on this summons, by Henry VI, at Leicester, on Whitsunday, 19 May 1426 (See *Chron. of London*, ed. Kingsford, 1905, pp. 95 and 130)

PEDIGREE

Shewing the Owners of the Castle and Honour ot Abergavenny
(marked XVII to XXXV respectively), from 1273 to 1535.

First wife.═XVII. John, Lord Hastings (1290), 6th in descent from═Second wife.
William de Briouze, who acquired the Lordship of Aber-
gavenny before 1175. He *suc.* thereto in 1273, and *d.* 1313.

| XVIII. John, Lord Hastings, 1313 to 1325. ═ | Elizabeth, *m.* Roger, Lord Grey of Ruthyn. | Sir Hugh Hastings, in whose issue the Barony of Hastings vested in 1391 ; the abeyance being terminated accordingly in 1841. | Roger (Mortimer), Earl of March, *d.* 1330. ═ |

XIX. Laurence, Lord Hastings═Agnes   Thomas (Beauchamp),═Katharine
cr. Earl of Pembroke, 1339, | Mortimer.   Earl of Warwick, *d.* | Mortimer.
d. 1348.   1369.

| | (2) | | (1) |
| XX. John,═XXI. Anne Earl of Pembroke, *d.* 1375. | Manny, *held the Castle, &c.* in dower 1376. | XXIII. William Beauchamp,═XXIV. Joan Fitzalan, *suc.* to the Castle, etc. 1389, sum. as Lord Bergavenny 1392, *d.* 1411. | *held the Castle, etc.* in dower, *d.* 1435. | Thomas (Beau-champ) Earl of Warwick, s.&h. *d.* 1401. |

XXII. John Hastings, *d.* | Richard (Beauchamp)═Isabel Despenser═XXV. Richard, Earl of Warwick, h.
s.p. 1389. | *cr.* Earl of Worcester, | sole heir of the (at- | *male* of his uncle in 1422. In Nov.
   1420, *d.* before his | tainted) BARONY | 1435 he *suc. to the Castle, &c.* (under
   mother, *s.p.m.* 1422. | OF LE DESPENSER, | the entail of 1396), and had seizin
    | *d.* 1439. | thereof 18 Feb. 1435/6, *d.* 1439.

XXVI. Sir Edward═Elizabeth   XXVII. Henry,   Richard (Nevill)═XXIX. Anne, who in 1449
Nevill, sum. as Lord | only da. and | *cr.* Duke of War- | Earl of Warwick | became *coheir* of her
Bergavenny 1450, | h. of her | wick. *d. s.p.m.* | and Salisbury, *d.* | mother. She was some-
d. 1476. | father, | 1446. | 1471. | time *seized of the Castle*
    d. 1448. | ═ | | *&c., d.* about 1490.

| George, Lord Bergavenny, 1482 to 1492. In 1439 he had become *coheir* of his grandmother Isabel Despenser. He *d.* 1492. | XXVIII. Anne, da. & h., d. young 3 Jan. 1448/9. | XXX. ═Isabel, George, | da. & Duke of | coheir, Clar- | *m.* 1469, ence, | *d.* 1476. *held the Castle, &c., jure uxoris, d.* 1477/8. | Anne,═XXXI. Ed- da. & | Richard ward coheir, | III, *held* IV. *d.s.p.s.* | *the Castle* ═ 1485. | *&c. jure uxoris, d.* 1485. | Edmund (Tudor), Earl of Rich-mond. ═ | XXXIII. Jas-per (Tudor), Duke of Bedford, *to whom the Castle &c. was granted* by Henry VII in 1485/6, *d. s.p.* 1495. |

XXXV. George, Lord Bergavenny,   Elizabeth═XXXII. Henry VII, *to*
1497 to 1535, *to whom the Crown*   of York, | *whom the Castle &c. es-*
restored the Castle, &c., d. 1535.   h. to the | *cheated* on the death of
                               Crown. | Richard III. He *d.* 1509.

XXXIV. Henry VIII, *who restored the Castle*
&c. to George (Nevill), Lord Bergavenny.

right did not accrue till 11 June 1446, even on the *most* favourable interpretation to the Nevill family of the entail of 1395/6, ([a]) unless, indeed, that entail is, from some unknown cause, to be considered as invalid, against her right as *heir at law* to her grandfather, the maker of the entail. She *d.* 18 June 1448, ([b]) aged 32, and was *bur.* at the Carmelites, Coventry. ([c])

([a]) On 11 June 1446 the *male* line of the Beauchamp family, who [under the entail 20 Feb. 1395/6, of William (Beauchamp), 1st Lord Bergavenny] were entitled to the castle and lands of Abergavenny, became *extinct* by the death, *s.p.m.*, of Henry (Beauchamp), Duke and Earl of Warwick. A grave question however remains as to *what* title the Earls of Warwick had therein. The words of the entail are, "Thomas, Earl of Warwick, and his *heirs male for ever.*" Under the construction that such estate constituted one *in fee*, the castle, &c, is stated to have been *held in fee*, in the *Inq. post mortem* of Richard, Earl of Warwick (who *d.* 1439), and of Henry, Duke of Warwick, his s. and h. It is to be noted that Coke says "where lands are given to a man and *his heirs male* he hath a *fee simple*, because it is not limited, by the gift, *of what body* the issue male shall be." Anyhow, the castle, &c, was for a long time afterwards withheld from this branch of the Nevill family by Anne, da. and h. of this Duke Henry, and Anne, sister of the said Duke, who *m.* Richard (Nevill), Earl of Warwick and Salisbury [on whose seal, of date 1 Feb. 4 Edw. IV (1464/5) is *Sigillum : ricardi: neuill comitis : warrewici : domini . de : bergeuenny :* See *Visit. of co. Huntingdon*, 1613, Camden Soc., p. 74.] Besides these, it was asserted in Fane's case that George, Duke of Clarence, and Richard, Duke of Gloucester, his [*i e* the Earl of Warwick and Salisbury's] sons-in-law, were successively seized of the castle and lordship as in right of their wives; that Henry VII granted the castle &c., to Jasper, Duke of Bedford ; and that after the death of Jasper *s.p.*, the property was restored by Henry VIII to George Nevill, Lord of Bergavenny, upon a petition of right. (Collins, *Baronies by Writ*, p. 79) " The fact seems to have been as thus stated, and therefore the Nevill family, during the seisin of the several persons before named, could not have been sum. to Parl. in consequence of their seisin of the Castle and Lordship of Bergavenny, not having such seisin " (*Lords' Reports*, vol. i, p. 443.) Sir Edward Nevill, however, asserted his wife's right as heir *at law* (notwithstanding the entail) and " Undeuly entred upon us in the place and Castel of Bergevenny, whereof the heir is our warde " See commands for his expulsion therefrom issued to the Duke of York by Henry VI on 15 Oct. [*qy.* 1447 ?] printed in Bentley's *Excerpta Historica* (1831), p. 6.

([b]) On the petition of Edward Nevill, lord of Bergevenny .—showing that he and Elizabeth late his wife as in her right were seized in their demesne as of fee of the castle, lordship, and manor of Bergevenny, until by Richard, late Earl of Warwick, contrary to law and equity they were disseized, on which they forthwith claimed the premises, and, on Richard's death, Henry, late Duke of Warwick, entered therein, on which they entered and were seized thereof, and had issue George . and afterwards Henry disseized them, and had issue Anne. And after Henry's death they entered and were seized thereof until they were expelled under colour of an inquisition, by which it was found that Henry *d.* seized of the premises, that the sd. Anne was his da. and h. and under age, and that the premises were held of the King and Crown. And Anne *d.* when the premises were in the King's hands :—the King gave him licence, 14 July 1449, to enter and possess the sd. castle, lordship, and manor (*Patent Roll*, 27 Hen. VI, *pars* ii, *m.* 7). If Edward Nevill ever actually obtained seizin under this grant, he must have been again disseized, by Anne, Countess of Warwick, sister of Henry abovenamed. (*ex inform.* G. W Watson). V.G.

([c]) P. Enderbie (*Cambria Triumphans*, 1661, bk. iii, between pp. 278 and 285)

III (*bis*). 1450.   SIR EDWARD NEVILL, ([a]) a year after the death of
his wife (as above), obtained, on 14 July 1449, licence
from Henry VI to enter on the lands, &c., of Abergavenny, and, from
5 Sep. (1450) 29 Hen. VI to 19 Aug. (1472) 12 Edw. IV, was sum. to
Parl. ([b]) as a Baron [LORD BERGAVENNY], ([c]) by writs directed
"*Edwardo Nevill domino de Bergevenny militi,*" and on and after 30 July
38 Hen. VI., "*Edwardo Neville de Bergevenny chivaler,*" though he does
not appear to have been seized, except for a short time, of the Castle and
lands of that name.   He *m.*, 2ndly, (by spec. disp., 15 Oct. 1448)
Katharine, da. of Sir Robert HOWARD, by Margaret, da. of Thomas
(MOWBRAY), DUKE OF NORFOLK ; she, with whom he had cohabited in the
lifetime of his 1st wife, was related to him in the third degree.   He *d.*
18 Oct. 1476. ([d])   His widow was living 29 June 1478.

IV. 1476.   4. GEORGE (NEVILL) LORD BERGAVENNY, 2nd but 1st
surv. s. and h. by 1st wife, *b.* at Raby Castle, and *bap.* at
Staindrop, co. Durham.   He was knighted at Tewkesbury, by Edward IV,
4 May 1471; was aged 36 and more ([e]) in 1476.   On 12 Jan. 1476/7, he had
livery of the lands of his parents, but he never had seizin of Abergavenny.
He was one of the Barons at the coronation of Richard III. ([f])   He was sum. to

---

recites a deed whereby "Edwardus Nevill miles et Elizabetha de Beauchamp domina
de Burgavenny " gave to Philip Thomas the advowson of the Church of [St. Bride]
"beate Frigitte in nostro dominio de Burgavenny... Sigilla nostra apposuimus in
castro nostro de Burgavenny vicessimo secundo die Julii anno regni Regis Henrici
sexti post conquestum vicessimo septimo [1449]." This charter, if genuine, must
be incorrectly transcribed, the date being some thirteen months after Elizabeth
Beauchamp's death. (*ex inform.* G. W. Watson.) V.G.

([a]) The origin of the Nevills is shewn by J.H. Round in his *Feudal England* to be
from Dolphin Fitz Uchtred (who received ' Staindropshire ' from the Prior of Durham
in 1131), whose grandson, Robert fitz Meldred, of Raby, *m.* Isabel de Nevill, and by
her was father of Geoffrey de Nevill (who took his mother's name) from whom the
Lords Abergavenny deduce a direct male descent. Some dates and facts (not to be
found elsewhere) are in an *Account of the noble family of Nevill, particularly of the
House of Abergavenny*, by Daniel Rowland, Esq., London, 1830, folio. The account
in Drummond's *Noble British Families* of this branch of the Nevill family is very
jejune.

([b]) There is proof in the rolls of Parl. of his sitting.

([c]) The Nevills, Lords Bergavenny, differenced the arms of Nevill of Raby
with a red rose on the saltire. (*ex inform.* Oswald Barron.) V.G.

([d]) The monument in the Priory Church at Abergavenny, formerly supposed to
be his, is now recognised as being of an earlier date. V.G.

([e]) In the 17 inquisitions taken after his father's death, it is uniformly stated
that "dictus Edwardus obiit die Jovis decimo octavo die mensis Octobris predicto
anno [r. R. Edwardi] sexto decimo et quod Georgius Nevill miles est suus filius et
heres propinquior et est etatis triginti et sex annorum et amplius " (Ch. *Inq. p. m.*,
Edw. IV, file 58, no. 66). 18 Oct. 1476 was, however, a Friday. (*ex inform.*
G. W. Watson). V.G.

([f]) For a list of the 35 peers there present see note *sub* ii (1) LORD DACRE DE
GILLESLAND.

Parl. (ª) 15 Nov. 1482 to 12 Aug. 1492, by writs directed *Georgio Nevyle de Bergevenny chr.* He *m.*, 1stly, Margaret, da. and h. of Sir Hugh FENNE, of Sculton Burdeleys, Norfolk, (ᵇ) and of Braintree, Essex, Treasurer of the Household to Henry VI. She *d* 28 Sep. 1485 He *m.*, 2ndly, as her 4th husband, Elizabeth, widow of John STOKKER, of St. George's, Eastcheap, (whose will was pr. 1485) and before that, widow of Richard NAYLOR (ᶜ), citizen of London (who was *bur.* at St. Martin's Outwich, London, and whose will was pr. 1483), and before that widow of Sir Robert BASSETT, Lord Mayor of London [1475-6.]. He *d.* 20 Sep. 1492, and was *bur.* at Lewes Priory, Sussex. Will dat. 1 July 1491, pr. 1492. (ᵈ) She *d.* 1500, and was *bur.* at St. Martin's Outwich afsd. (ᵉ) Will, in which she describes herself as of Berghdenne, in the parish of Chartham, Kent, widow, dat. 14 Apr. 1500, pr. 19 June following. (ᶠ)

V. 1492.   5. GEORGE (NEVILL), LORD BERGAVENNY, s. and h. by 1st wife, aged 16 and more at his mother's death. He was dubbed K.B., 4 July 1483, *v.p.* He was sum. to Parl. (ᵍ) 16 Jan. 1496/7 to 5 Jan. 1533/4 He served in the wars against France, and was in the battle of Blackheath, 17 June 1497, against the Cornish rebels. Was Constable of Dover Castle and Warden of the Cinque Ports. Chief Larderer at the coronation of Henry VIII, 24 June 1509, and again at that of Anne Boleyn, Queen Consort, 1 June 1533. (ᵍ) K.G. 23 Apr., and

---

(ª) There is proof in the Rolls of Parl. of his sitting.

(ᵇ) This manor is held by Grand Serjeanty " as Chief Larderer. " Service was performed accordingly by the Lords Abergavenny, or their deputies, at the coronations of James II, Queen Anne, and George I, George II, George III, and George IV. Hugh Fenne *d.* in 1476.

(ᶜ) " Alicia Naylor vidua Baronis de Abergavenny " is shown in the Visit. of Kent (1619) as wife of Walter Roberts. Query if this refers to this lady. V.G.

(ᵈ) See *Test. Vet.* p. 406.

(ᵉ) There has been much confusion as to the order of this lady's husbands. V.G.

(ᶠ) See *Test. Vet.* p. 441.

(ᵍ) Sir Roger Wilbraham, *temp.* Eliz., relates a smart retort, made apparently by this Lord, to Henry VIII. " The L. of Burgaveny had morgaged that house ; the King having an ynkling thereof at his meeting with him said 'God morow my L. of Burgaveny without Burgaveny ; ' the Lord more boldly than discreetly said to the King 'God morow my liege Lord, King of France without France. ' This tale is not only amusing, but has a practical bearing ; for if Abergavenny were a Barony by tenure, and if the fond " conceipt that the Castle and Lordship of A should draw the stile and dignity " were true, then a mortgage, which transfers the legal ownership, would have also transferred the peerage ; but the Lords having no notice of the transfer would have continued to summon Mr. Nevill, and by so doing would, (according to modern peerage law) have conferred a new peerage on him of the same date as the summons, while as soon as the mortgagee had foreclosed on Abergavenny and taken possession, they could not refuse him his writ of sum. to the ancient Barony. It is clear that such a process might recur, and that by now we might have a collection of Lords Abergavenny of various dates, which, as Euclid says, is absurd.

If it were possible for a Barony by tenure to exist in modern days, we should have from time to time the scandal of sales, and see advertisements such as this.—"At

installed 7 May 1513. To him, 18 Dec. 1512, (ᵃ) Henry VIII granted
the castle and lands of Abergavenny, &c., (ᵇ) which, in 1389, had
been inherited by William BEAUCHAMP, LORD BERGAVENNY (1392), whose
representative he was through his grandmother. His vast estates, derived
chiefly from the Beauchamp family, he entailed on himself and the heirs
male of his body, with rem. to his brothers Thomas and Edward respectively
in like manner, and this entail, made by his will, being confirmed by Act

the Mart, Tokenhouse Yard, on Tuesday the 21st, will be sold the castle of Abergavenny in Monmouthshire carrying with it the right to a seat in the H. of Lords with
high precedence. " Later on there would be the Newspaper account of the auction.
" We have to chronicle quite a " slump " in feudal Baronies since the " record " price
obtained for this unique lot in 18—. We understand that " Abergavenny " did not
reach the reserve, and that, like so many of our treasures, it will probably be disposed
of privately in America. The fall in values is explained by the fact that the present
Government freely supply a very similar though of course modern article, and have
practically cleared the Market of buyers " V G.

(ᵃ) On the death of Richard III, 22 Aug. 1485, the lordship of Abergavenny
appears to have been vested in the s. and h. of Isabel, Duchess of Clarence. For,
1 Feb. 1485/6, one of the servants of that lordship was appointed *during the minority
of Edward, Earl of Warwick* (*Privy Seals*, 1 Hen. VII, no. 667 : *Patent Roll, pars* 11,
m 13). However, shortly afterwards, 27 Feb. 1485/6, a grant in tail male was made
to Jasper, Duke of Bedford, of all the castles, lordships, and manors, of Glamorgan,
Morgannwg, Abergavenny, etc., to hold the same as from 21 Aug. last (*Privy Seals*,
1 Hen. VII, no 725 : *Patent Roll, pars* 11, *m* 5). This grant was repeated 15 and
21 Mar. 1487/8 (*Privy Seals*, 3 Hen. VII, no. 124 *Patent Roll, pars* 11, *m*. 20),
subsequent to a grant and confirmation, 13 Dec. 1487, to the King and his heirs
male, by Anne, Countess of Warwick, of *all* her castles, lordships, manors, etc.
(including the three abovenamed) except the manor of Erdington, co Warwick
(*Close Roll*, 3 Hen. VII, *m*. 11 d). Jasper *d.s.p.* in 1495, when Abergavenny escheated
to the Crown. Finally, 18 Dec. 1512, there is an order for George Nevile, Lord
Bergevenny, to have livery of lands as s. and h. of George, s. and h. of Edward,
Lord Bergevenny, and Elizabeth, his wife, which Edward and Elizabeth were seized
in right of the sd. Elizabeth of the castle and manor of Bergevenny, and disseized
by Richard, Earl of Warwick, against whom they claimed the premises, and on
his death entered on the same, and were again disseized by Henry, Duke of Warwick,
s. and h. of the sd. Earl, who *d.* seized of the premises in fee, leaving issue Anne, his
da and next h. (*Patent Roll*, 4 Hen. VIII, *pars* 11, *m*. 9). In the R.O. there is a roll
endorsed " A bill of lands and possessions assigned by the King's Highness to divers
uses," wherein, under " Lands and possessions restored," occurs " to Lord Burgavenny
£253-7-11½ " (*Cal. of Letters and Papers, temp.* Hen. VIII, vol. 11, no. 1363). (*ex
inform.* G. W. Watson). V.G.

(ᵇ) It had been granted by Henry VII to his 2nd s., Henry, Duke of York, who
is spoken of, 19 Apr. 1496, as Lord of Abergavenny (*Ancient Deeds*). The statement
that this George Nevill was *not* seized of the castle, made in *Nicolas*, p. xxxvii, is, of
course, not true as to *him*, though, as is correctly stated by Nicolas, it is true as to his
immediate predecessor ; the passage therein referred to, as being in Collins' *Baronies
by Writ* (p. 96), only says, " It shall be proved, " &c., but does not give *any* proof.
The account of the Barony of Bergavenny given in *Nicolas* (pp. xxx to xxxvii), is
much fuller than that given in the subsequent edition, edited by Courthope, as regards
the nature of its tenure and the proceedings concerning it in 1604.

of Parl. (31 Jan. (1555/6) 2 and 3 Philip and Mary), ([a]) preserved them intact to the succeeding Lords. P.C. 1516. He *m.*, 1stly, Joan, da. of Thomas (FITZALAN), EARL OF ARUNDEL, by Margaret, da. of Richard (WIDVILLE), EARL OF RIVERS. She *d. s.p.m.*, 14 Nov. ([b]) He *m.*, 2ndly, Margaret, da. of William ([c]) BRENT, of Charing, Kent, 'gentleman.' She was living 1515, but *d. s.p.s.* He *m.*, 3rdly, about June 1519, Mary, da. of Edward (STAFFORD), DUKE OF BUCKINGHAM, by Eleanor, da. of Henry (PERCY), EARL OF NORTHUMBERLAND. He *m.*, 4thly, Mary BROOKE, otherwise COBHAM, who had formerly been his mistress, and who survived him. He *d.* 1535, and was *bur.* at Birling (his heart being *bur.* at Mereworth), Kent. Will dat. 4 June 1535, pr. 24 Jan. 1535/6.

VI. 1535.   6 HENRY (NEVILL) LORD BERGAVENNY, s. and h by third wife, *b.* after 1527. He was sum. to Parl. 23 Jan. 1551/2 to 15 Oct. 1586. He was one of the 26 peers who signed the letters patent, 16 June 1553, settling the Crown on Lady Jane Grey ; K.B. 29 Sep. 1553 ; Chief Larderer at the coronation of Queen Mary 1 Oct. 1553. On 6 Oct. 1586 he was one of the Peers who tried Mary, Queen of Scots, at Fotheringhay. ([d]) He *m*, 1stly, before 31 Jan 1555/6, Frances, da. of Thomas (MANNERS), EARL OF RUTLAND, by his 2nd wife, Eleanor, da. of Sir William PASTON. She is mentioned as being among the "noble authors." She was *bur.* Sep. 1576, at Birling. He *m*, 2ndly, Elizabeth, da. and coh. of Stephen DARRELL, of Spelmonden, in Horsmonden, Kent, Chief Clerk of the Royal Kitchen, by Philippe, da. of

---

([a]) The "Act concerninge the restitucion of the heirs males of Sir Edward Nevyll knight" recites the petition of his eldest son *Edwarde Nevill esquier*, that the sd. Sir Edward, 4 Dec., 30 Hen. VIII, *was atteynted of highe treason and for the same was putt to execucion of deathe*, and in the Parl. 28 Apr.-28 June 31 Hen. VIII attainted and all his estates forfeited · that in the Parl. 22 Jan. 33 Hen VIII-12 May 35 Hen. VIII, the pet[r]. was restored in name and blood and made h. to the sd. Sir Edward and to all others to whom the sd. Sir Edward was h or might have been h if he had not been attainted : and also enabled to inherit all such honours, lordships, etc., which at any time should descend to him as h. of the body of the sd. Sir Edward or of any of his ancestors, but not to any honours etc. *which were the late sd. Sir Edward the father or which the King then had or was intitled to have by reason of the atteyndour*. The pet[r]. now seeks that, for lack of heirs male of the body of Henry N , now Lord a Burgavenny, he may have etc. all the honours, baronies, etc., which by the will of George N. kt., Lord a B. decd., were for lack of heirs male of his body, or of the body of Sir Thomas N. kt., decd., entailed etc. on Sir Edward N. kt. and the heirs male of his body. And that for lack of heirs male of the body of the pet[r]., the rem. should be to his br. Henry and the heirs male of his body, rem. to his br. George and the heirs male of his body, rem. to the heirs of the body of the sd. George, Lord a B., rem. to the heirs of the body of Sir Thomas N. kt., rem. to the Queen—Soit baille aux communz—A ceste bill lez communz sount assentuz—31 Jan. [1555/6] 2 and 3 Ph. and Mary. (*ex inform.* G. W. Watson.) V.G.

([b]) *Coll. Top et Gen.*, vol. i, p. 281.

([c]) In the Visit. of Kent (1619) his name is given as William John Brent, but the date seems too early for a man to have borne two Christian names. V G

([d]) For a list of these see note *sub* Henry, EARL OF DERBY, [1572].

Edward WELDON, Clerk of the Green Cloth. He *d. s.p.m.*, 10 Feb., at Comfort, in Birling, Kent, and was *bur.* 21 Mar. 1586/7, at Birling. (ᵃ) Admon. 9 May 1587, wherein he is styled " *Sir Henry Nevill, Baron of Abergavenny*," to " *Lady Elizabeth Nevill,*" the widow : Lady Mary Fane, the da., renouncing. His widow *m.* Sir William SEDLEY, 1st Bart., of Southfleet, Kent, (who *d.* 27 Feb. 1618) and was living Feb 1601/2.

VII. 1587.   7 EDWARD NEVILL, of Newton St. Loo, Somerset, cousin and h. male, who (ᵇ) in the grant of livery (1588)

(ᵃ) Mary, his da. and sole h (by his 1st wife), who, at the time of his death, was aged 32, and the wife of Sir Thomas FANE, was unquestionably entitled to any Barony *in fee* possessed by her late father. She, however, by patent 25 May 1604, was granted the Barony of LE DESPENSER (a Barony originating by writ of 1264), of which she was a coh. [see pedigree, p. 41]. As this was a much more ancient Barony than the Barony of Bergavenny, *under the writ of* 1392, which was all she could claim (being neither the representative nor even a descendant of any of the former holders), this *practically* put an end to her claim to the latter Barony. Whether or no her claim, and that of her representatives thereto, is *legally* barred by this, or by the subsequent proceedings of the Crown and the House of Lords, as to such Barony, is open to grave doubt. The Barony "came with a lass" (the h. gen. of the Beauchamps of Abergavenny) to the Nevills, and ought apparently to have left them " with a lass " (the h. gen. of the Nevills), and gone to the Fanes, more especially as the subsequent proceedings of the House in giving it a precedency *inferior* to that of Le Despenser (*cr.* by writ of 1264) shew that their Lordships held it to be a *personal* dignity of the Beauchamp family, and not one attaching to *the tenure of the Castle*, whose owners were Barons at a much earlier period

This Lady inherited, though only by agreement with the heir of entail (confirmed by Act of Parl. 35 Eliz.), the estate of Mereworth, Kent (which had come to the Nevills through the Beauchamps and Fitzalans), and also the manor and park of Althorne, Essex Her s. and h., Francis Fane, was, in 1624, *cr.* Earl of Westmorland, in which title till 1762 (when the h. male was no longer the h. gen) the Barony of Le Despenser continued merged.

(ᵇ) In Coke's *Reports* (vol. xii, p. 70) it is stated that this Edward had summons to Parl 2 and 3 Philip and Mary, but *d.* before Parl. met ; the writ is given at length, and Coke takes occasion to state that it was decided 8 Jac. I (1610-11) that the direction and delivery of the writ did not make him a Baron or Noble until he came to Parl. and there sat according to the commandment of the writ, and hence that no hereditary dignity was *cr.* by the writ directed to him in consequence of his never having sat under it. (See *Lord's Reports*, vol. i, pp. 482-486). As to Coke's statements, it should be noted that (i) *no* writ was addressed to " *Edward* Nevill de Abergavenny" for that Parl., though there is one, of the alleged date, 21 Jan , to " *Henry* Nevill de Bergavenny." (ii) In this same Parl., 31 Jan., is the petition above related [note "a " p. 33] of this same Edward as " Edward Nevill esquier " (iii) This Edward did not die, as Coke falsely asserts, in 1555/6, but lived till 1588/9, as in the text. Charity itself cannot suppose that such a wholesale misrepresentation of facts, which must indeed have been common knowledge, was anything but wilful. This, which is famous as " Lord Abergavenny's case," is the foundation of the doctrine that a writ does not create a barony unless a sitting under it is proved It is discussed at some length in J H.Round's *Peerage and Pedigree*, where the facts alleged by Coke are shown to be fictitious and a different version of the case is suggested. V.G.

of the lands of Henry, late Lord Bergavenny decd , is styled "Edwardus Nevill, *armiger, alias* dictus Edwardus Nevill, *dominus Bergavenny*," and who (according to the decision of 1604, and the place assigned to his son in the House of Lords) may perhaps be considered entitled to be reckoned as LORD BERGAVENNY. He was s. and h. of Sir Edward Nevill, of Addington Park, Kent, by Eleanor, Dowager LADY SCROPE of Upsall, da. of Andrews (WINDSOR), LORD WINDSOR, which Edward was 3rd son of George 4th, and br. of George 5th, Lord Bergavenny. He inherited the Castle, &c., of Abergavenny and the entire estates of the family, under the entail thereof to heirs male made by his uncle, the 5th Lord (as abovenamed), notwithstanding the attainder of his father, being enabled so to do under Act of Parl. beforementioned, ([a]) 2 and 3 Philip and Mary. He is spoken of as having been deaf. He *m.*, 1stly, Katharine, da. of Sir John BROME, of Halton, Oxon, by Margaret, da. of John ROWSE, of Ragley, co. Warwick. She was Maid of Honour to Queen Mary. He *m.*, 2ndly, Grisold, da. of Thomas HUGHES, of Uxbridge, Midx. He *d.* at Uxbridge, 10 Feb. 1588/9. *Inq. p. m.* at Maidstone, 7 July 1589, in which he is styled "Edward Nevill, decd., s. and h. of Sir Edward Nevill, Knt., also decd." Admon., in which he is styled "*Edward, Lord Abergavenny, alias Edward Nevill, Esq* ," granted 15 May 1590 to his s. Henry Nevill. His widow *m.*, about 1589, Francis (CLIFFORD), 4th EARL OF CUMBERLAND, who *d.* 21 Jan. 1640/1. She *d.* 15 June 1613, at Londesborough, and was *bur.* there M.I.

VIII. 1589.   8 or 1   EDWARD NEVILL, who on the same grounds
  „   1604.   as his father, may, on his death, be considered as entitled
                 to be reckoned as LORD BERGAVENNY, s. and h. by first wife.([b]) He was 38 years old in 1588/9. M.P. for Windsor 1588-89 and 1593. "Being seised of an estate in tail male by virtue of the Act of Restoration, 2 and 3 Philip and Mary (1555/6) in the Castle and Lordship of Bergavenny, he claimed in 1598 the dignity of Baron of Bergavenny, not, as has been generally supposed, on the sole ground that the dignity was attached to the Castle of Bergavenny, but that he, as being seised of that Castle, and as h. male of the last Lord, was the more eligible person. On this occasion the Lord Chief Justice of England (Sir John Popham) determined that there was ' no right at all in the h. male, and therefore he must wholly rely on the favour of the Prince—the common custom of England doth wholly favour the h. gen.—that Her Majesty may call by new creation the h. male, and omit the h. gen. during her life, but yet a right to remain to her [*i.e.* the h. general's] son, having sufficient supportacion. No entail can carry away dignity but by express words or patent ;' the Lord Chief Justice of the Common Pleas was of the same

---

([a]) See p 33, note "a".
([b]) A survey of his numerous estates in the counties of Sussex and Monmouth, together with some in Kent, Surrey, Norfolk, Suffolk, Essex, Warwick, Worcester, Hereford, Salop, Wilts, and Somerset, including " Burgavenny House" in the parish of St.Martin, Ludgate, London, is given in Rowland's *Nevill Family*, p.151, see *Ibid.* p.104

opinion. Upon these opinions Lady Fane, who, as da. and h. of Henry, Lord Bergavenny, claimed as h. gen., prayed to be allowed the Barony, but nothing further took place until 1604, when the claims being renewed, the House of Lords avoided a formal decision, being 'not so perfectly and exactly resolved as might give a clear and undoubted satisfaction to all the consciences and judgements of all the Lords for the precise point of Right;' it was agreed therefore that suit should be made to the King for ennobling *both* parties by way of restitution, the one to the Barony of Le Despencer, the other to the Barony of Bergavenny ; and by a further resolution it was determined that BERGAVENNY should go to Nevill, and LE DESPENCER to Fane ; this arrangement was approved of by the King, and a Writ of Summons was directed *Edwardo Neville de Bergavenny Chr.*, 25 May, 2 Jas. 1604, and letters patent dated the same day confirmed the dignity of Le Despencer to Lady Fane."—*Courthope*, p. 17. (ª)

This EDWARD (NEVILL), LORD BERGAVENNY, so sum. 1604 as above, though *neither h. nor even coh. of any Barony cr. by writ of* 1392, was allowed the same precedency (ᵇ) as had been enjoyed by the former lords. (ᶜ) This precedency was certainly *not* on account of his having been held to be a BARON BY TENURE, for the decision of the House was, " that the place,

---

(ª) The famous and prolonged struggle for the barony of Abergavenny between the heir-general and the heir male after the death of Henry, Lord Abergavenny is described and discussed by Sir Harris Nicolas in his *Barony of l'Isle* (1829), pp. 384-391.   It has also been investigated anew by J. H. Round in his *Peerage and Pedigree*, where it is shown that all previous accounts of it are inaccurate, and that there were three stages, at successive periods · (ı) Sir Thomas Fane, in right of his wife *versus* the elder Edward Nevill, (ıı) Lady Fane, as a widow, *versus* the younger Edward Nevill, under Queen Elizabeth ; (ııı) the same parties, under James I.   V G.

(ᵇ) That is to say a precedency based neither upon writ, nor tenure, but upon usage.   V.G.

(ᶜ) This appears to have been without a Royal Warrant.   See Appendix C in this vol. as to precedency of Peers *in Parl.* granted by Royal Warrant since the Statute of Precedency of 31 Hen. VIII.   The award made by Edward IV, 14 April 1473, in the case of the BARONY OF DACRE, is very similar to that made by James I as to the BARONY OF BERGAVENNY.   Edward IV, after awarding the old Barony to the h. *gen.*, declares that the h. *male* should be "called the LORD DACRE OF GILLESLAND, and he and the *heirs male* of the said Thomas, late Lord Dacre to have place in our Parl. *next adjoining* beneath the place the said Richard *Fenys*, Knt , LORD DACRE [the h. gen.] now hath."   Here then is a spec. *precedency*, extending even to Parl. (where, in *this* case, it has always been allowed), granted *by the Crown* to a newly created Barony Neither in the case of Dacre nor of Bergavenny was the King's award carried out by patent, but in both *by writ*.   The effect of this as to the Barony of Dacre of Gillesland was, that this Barony (when claimed in 1569 by Leonard Dacre the h. male of the body of the grantee, as against his nieces, the heirs gen.), was declared by the Commissioners of the Earl Marshal "to have commenced by writ 13 Edw. IV," and so "ought *not* to descend to the said Leonard as h. male."   The *royal award* which (in the case of Dacre, though not in that of Bergavenny) declared expressly it should be to heirs *male*, not having been carried out by letters patent, *went for nothing*.   It is difficult to see why the writ of 1604 in the case of Bergavenny (which has *not*, as in the

seat, precedency and pre-eminence of the Barons Le Despencer, *anciently was*, and *is* and ought to be before and *above* that of the Barons of Bergavenny," *i.e.* that a Barony *cr by writ* of 1264, was entitled to the precedence of one, which, IF *by tenure*, must have been long before that date, " for the territory of Bergavenny undoubtedly existed in the hands of tenants in chief of the Crown, *before* (1264) 49 Hen. III and, of persons who were certainly esteemed Barons of the Realm." (*Report of the Lords Committees on the Dignity of a Peer*, vol. 1, p. 440.). Unless we accept the theory that this writ was incidental either (i) to a *Patent* (hitherto undiscovered) of this date, or (ii) to the *tenure of the Castle*, it must (according to all modern Peerage law) have *cr.* a Barony in fee, and one *de novo* of the date of 1604. He *m.* Rachel, 3rd da. of John LENNARD, of Knole, near Chevening, Kent, by Elizabeth, da. of William HARMAN, of Ellam, in Crayford, in that co. She was *bur.* 15 Oct. 1616, at Birling, Kent. He *d.* at his house in Great St. Bartholomew's, London, 1, and was *bur.* 3 Dec. 1622, at Birling afsd. Will dat. 19 Jan. 1618/9 to 24 Nov. 1622, pr. 2 Dec. 1622.

IX. 1622.   9 *or* 2. HENRY (NEVILL), LORD BERGAVENNY, s. and h., *b.* before 1580. M.A. Oxford (incorp. from Cambridge) 9 July 1594. He was first sum. to the Parl. which met 12 Feb. 1623/4, and last to the " Long " Parl., which met 3 Nov. 1640. An intermediate writ, however, to the Parl. that met, 20 Jan. 1628/9, is directed (doubtless in error), " *Johanni* Nevill de Abergavenny." He *m.*, 1stly, before 1601, Mary, da. of Thomas (SACKVILLE), 1st EARL OF DORSET, Lord Treasurer of England, by Cecily, da. of Sir John BAKER, of Sisinghurst, Kent. He *m.*, 2ndly, before 1616, Catharine, yst. da. of George VAUX, by Elizabeth, da. of John (ROPER), 1st LORD TEYNHAM, which George was s. and h. ap. of William, 3rd LORD VAUX OF HARROWDEN. He was *bur.* 24 Dec. 1641, at Birling. His widow, who was under 12 in 1604, was *bur.* there 10 July 1649.

X. 1641.   10, 3, *or* 1. JOHN (NEVILL), LORD BERGAVENNY, 1st surv. s and h. male, (ª) being 1st s. by 2nd wife. He was 8 years old in 1622. He appears to have sat in Parl., (ᵇ) his name being among those sum. 8 May (1661) 13 Car. II. He *m.* Elizabeth, da.

case of Dacre, the support *even* of *a Royal edict* declaring the limitation to be to heirs *male*), is not to be similarly interpreted. For a list of persons sum in the name of, and anomalously granted the precedency of, an ancient Barony to which they were not entitled by descent, see Appendix D in this volume.

(ª) His elder br. (of the half blood), Sir Thomas Nevill, K.B, *d. v.p.*, and was *bur.* at Birling, 7 May 1628, leaving two sons (both of whom *d.* unm., one in 1637 and the other in 1639) and one da., viz., Margaret, *m.* Thomas Brooke of Madeley, Salop, who was aged 49 in 1663, when their grandson and h. ap., Basil Brooke, was aged 4 years. See Visit. of co. Stafford, 1663. Among their numerous descendants would vest any Barony in fee possessed by Edward Nevill, sum. by writ in 1604 as LORD BERGAVENNY.—See pedigree, p. 41.

(ᵇ) In Dugdale's *Summons* it is written in this case " *A*bergavenny, " but in the next (1685) as *B*ergavenny.

and coh. of John CHAMBERLAINE, of Sherborne Castle, Oxon, by Katharine, da. of Francis PLOWDEN, of Plowden, Salop. He *d. s.p.*, 23 Oct. 1662. Will dat. 2 Aug. 1661 (remaining, apparently, among the family deeds), devising his lands to his wife to sell for payment of his debts, &c. His widow *d.* between Nov. 1669 and 1694. Admon. 5 Jan. 1693/4 (wherein she is styled "*Elizabeth, Baroness Dowager of Abergavenny,*" of Sherborne, Oxon, widow), to a creditor ; Lady Mary Goring, sister and next of kin, renouncing.

XI. 1662.   11, 4, *or* 1. GEORGE (NEVILL), LORD BERGAVENNY, br. and h. He appears never to have been sum. to Parl. He *m.* Mary, sister of Sir Henry GIFFORD, of Burstall, co. Leicester, Bart., da. of Thomas GIFFORD, M.D., of Dunton Waylett, Essex, by Anne, da. and h. of Gregory BROOKSBY, of Burstall afsd. He *d.* 2, and was *bur.* 14 June 1666, at Birling. Will dat. 18 May 1666, pr. 16 July following. His widow *m.* (as his 2nd wife) Sir Charles SHELLEY, of Michelgrove, Sussex, 2nd Bart., who *d.* 1681. She was *bur.* 14 Nov. 1699, from St. Giles'-in-the-Fields, at St. Pancras, Midx. Will, in which she describes herself as seized of the manor of Portslade, Sussex, dat. 10 and pr. 22 Nov. 1699.

XII. 1666.   12, 5, *or* 2. GEORGE (NEVILL) LORD BERGAVENNY, only s. and h., *b.* 21 Apr. 1665, *suc.* to the title at a year old. His name appears in the roll of the Parl. of 1685 as "under age." The anomalous precedency of this barony in Parl. (as the premier one) was challenged, 8 Mar. 1669/70, by Lord Fitzwalter, who sat under a writ of 1295.(*) He was chief Larderer at the coronation of James II, 23 Apr.1685. He *m.* Honora, da. of John (BELASYSE), 1st LORD BELASYSE of Worlaby, by his 3rd wife, Anne, da. of John (PAULET), 5th MARQUESS OF WINCHESTER. He *d. s.p.*, 26 Mar., and was *bur.* 1 Apr. 1695, at St. Giles'-in-the-Fields, Midx. Will, in which he mentions no relations but speaks of his "now wife," dat. 30 July 1694, and pr. 29 Mar. 1695. (b) His widow *d.* 1, and was *bur.* 9 Jan. 1706/7, at St. Giles' afsd. M.I. Will dat. 5 June 1706, pr. 9 Jan. 1706/7 by Dame Barbara Webb, the sister.

XIII. 1695.   13, 6, *or* 1. GEORGE (NEVILL), LORD BERGAVENNY, cousin and h. male, 7 years old in Dec. 1666, being s. and h. of George Nevill, of Sheffield, Sussex (by Mary, da. of Sir Bulstrode

(*) Lord Fitzwalter on making good his claim to that title claimed, in virtue of the 1295 writ, "precedence of all Barons *now* sitting as Barons " (some Baronies, such as Mowbray, being then merged). (*ex inform.* J. H. Round.) V.G.

(b) On his death any Barony in fee possessed by his father would have passed to his niece, Frances, da. of Sir John Shelly, of Michelgrove, 3rd Bart., and only child of her mother, Bridget, only da. of George, xith Baron. She *m.* Richard, 5th Viscount Fitzwilliam [I.], and *d.* 1777, aged about 90. In 1837 the Earl of Pembroke and Edward Bourchier Hartopp were her representatives. See case of the claim to the Barony of Vaux of Harrowden ; see also pedigree, p. 41.

WHITELOCK), who was only s. and h. of Richard or Edward Nevill, the s. and h. ap. of Sir Christopher Nevill, of Newton St .Loo, Somerset, K.B., who was yst. s. of Edward, 8th, and br. of Henry, 9th Lord. He *suc.* his father in 1665, thirty years before he *suc.* to the Peerage. He took his seat in the House of Lords, 1 May 1695. Except on the theory that his writ was incidental either (1) to a *Patent* (hitherto undiscovered) of 1604 to his ancestor, or of 1695 to himself, or (11) to the *tenure of the Castle*, such writ must (according to all modern Peerage law) have *cr.* a Barony in fee and one *de novo* of the date of 1695. Gent. of the Bedchamber to George, Prince of Denmark. He *m.*, 22 Oct. 1698, (^a) at St. Anne's, Soho, Anne, da. of Nehemiah WALKER, of Midx., "a sea captain," from whom he apparently was separated after 8 Jan. 1711/12. (^b) He *d.* 11, and was *bur.* 19 Mar 1720/1, in his 63rd year, at Sheffield, Sussex. Will, in which he revokes all benefits hitherto made to his wife, Anne, dat. 16 Dec 1708 (with a cod. 24 Nov. 1720), pr. 17 Aug. 1723 (^c) His widow *m.*, (as his 2nd wife) 15 June 1744, John (WEST), 1st EARL DE LA WARR, who *d.* 16 Mar. 1766. She *d.* at Balderwood Lodge, Hants, 26 June 1748.

XIV. 1721.   14, 7, *or* 2. GEORGE (NEVILL), LORD BERGAVENNY, or ABERGAVENNY, 2nd, but 1st surv. s. and h., *b.* 16 May and *bap.* 26 Aug. 1702, at St. Martin's-in-the-Fields. Matric. at Univ. Coll. Oxford, 13 Sep. 1722. He *m.*, 21 Feb. 1722/3, at St. Mary Magd., Old Fish Str., Elizabeth, 1st sister and coh. of Gideon THORNICROFT, of Dodington and Linstead, Kent, and da of Col. Edward THORNICROFT, of Westm., by Mary, only da. and eventually sole h. of Sir William DELAUNE, of Sharsted, Kent. He *d. s.p.*, 15 Nov. 1723, of the small pox, in Soho Sq., and was *bur.* at Sheffield, Sussex. (^d) His widow (by whom he had two posthumous daughters, both of whom, *b.* 20 Nov., *d.* 1 Dec. 1723) *m* Alured PINCKE, of Lincoln's Inn, and Tottenham High Cross, Midx., who was *bur.* 6 Dec. 1755, at Tottenham afsd. She *d.* 4, and was *bur.* 12 Mar.

(^a) The following entry is in the St. Pancras Reg. "George Newton, Gent., and Mrs. Anne Walker married by License. (I understand this was my Lord Abergavenny but he did not own his quality) 10 Apr. 1697." No doubt he *m.* again at St. Anne's, Soho, 22 Oct. 1698, the validity of the first ceremony being doubted. V.G.

(^b) Lady Wentworth at that date writes :—" Here is a strange unnatural report of Lady Abargane, that she has in passion killed her own child, about 7 years old ; she having been a great while whipping it, my Lord being grieved to hear it cry so terribly, went into the room to beg for it, and she threw it with such a force to the ground, she broke the skull." V.G.

(^c) His will is signed "*Bergavenny,*" and this appears to be the last signature, so spelt, of any of these Lords According to Macky *(Characters),* he (about 1704) "was a little brown man, very lively, 30 [45] years old ; with, learning, wit and one of the best libraries in England." He was the "first Protestant Lord that bears that title." (Luttrell, *Diary,* 30 Mar. 1695.) V.G.

(^d) " A most ingenious sensible young gentleman, but very much deformed. " (T. Hearne, 1723.) VG

1778, aged 85, at Tottenham afsd. Will dat. 26 Oct. 1770, pr. 14 Mar. 1778, by her s., Alured Pincke of Sharsted Court afsd. ([a])

XV. 1723.   15, 8, *or* 3. EDWARD (NEVILL), LORD BERGAVENNY, or ABERGAVENNY, br. and h. Ed. at Wadham Coll., Oxford. He *m.*, 6 May 1724, ([b]) at the Fleet Chapel, London, Katharine, 1st da. of Lieut. Gen. William TATTON, of St. Margaret's, Westm., (who *d.* June 1736) by his 1st wife, who was dead before 1717. He *d.*, also of the small pox, *s p.*, 9 Oct. 1724, ([c]) in his 19th year, at his father-in-law's house, at Cowley near Uxbridge. Admon. 27 Oct. 1724, to " Gideon Harvey, Esq, curator of Katharine, Baroness Dowager of *Abergavenny*,"([d]) till her age of 21. His widow *m.*, 20 May 1725, his successor, William, LORD ABERGAVENNY, as under.

XVI. 1724.   16, 9, *or* 4. WILLIAM (NEVILL), LORD ABERGAVENNY, ([e]) cousin and h. male, being only s. and h. of Edward Nevill, Capt. R.N. (by Hannah, da. of Jervois THORPE), who was br. to George, 13th Lord. He *suc.* his father 12 Sep. 1701, twenty three years before he *suc.* to the Peerage. He took his seat in the House of Lords on 12 Nov. 1724. In 1730 he built a residence at Kidbrook in East Grinstead, Sussex (an estate purchased by sale of outlying lands), and ceased to inhabit the old mansion of the family at Birling. Capt. of the Yeomen of the Guard 1737. Master of the Jewel Office 10 Feb. 1738/9. He *m.*, 1stly, 20 May 1725, Katharine, Dowager LADY ABERGAVENNY, (widow of the last Lord) abovenamed. She *d.* 4, ([f]) and was *bur.* 12 Dec. 1729, at Kensington. ([g]) Shortly after her death he recovered £10,000 damages in an action against " Richard Lyddel, Esq., her Lord's intimate friend," for *crim. con.* He *m.*, 2ndly, 20 May 1732, Rebecca, da. of Thomas (HERBERT), 8th EARL OF PEMBROKE, by his 1st wife, Margaret, da. of Sir Robert SAWYER. He *d.* at Bath, 21, and was *bur.* 30 Sep. 1744, at East Grinstead, Sussex. Admon. 20 Nov. 1744 to his widow. She *d.* 20 Oct. 1758, at Gaddesden, Herts, and was *bur.* with her husband. Will dat. 1 Apr., pr. 7 Nov. 1758.

([a]) See *Misc. Gen. et Her.*, 3rd Series, vol. ii. p. 191, for pedigree of Pincke.

([b]) Register, in J. S. Burn, *Fleet Registers*, 1834, p. 94.

([c]) On his death any Barony in fee possessed by his father (who sat in the House in 1695) would have vested in his sisters, *viz.*, (1) Jane, *b.* 8 Mar. 1703, *m.* John Abel Walter, of Busbridge, Surrey, and *d.* 19 Mar 1786, leaving numerous descendants ; and (2) Ann, *b.* about 1715, who, like her mother (but unlike her brothers and sister, all of whom were her seniors), received no benefit under her father's will or codicil, and who *d.* unm. Mar. 1736/7, in her 22nd year.—See pedigree, p. 41.

([d]) Her father had *m* (26 Feb. 1716/7, at St. Mary Aldermary, London) Ann, da. of Gideon Harvey, M.D , Physician to the Tower of London.

([e]) In Garter's Roll, 13 Jan. 1729/30, the title first appears as " *Abergavenny*," and continues ever afterwards as such. The death of George, Lord *Bergavenny*, on 15 Nov. 1723, is noted on a previous roll.

([f]) The *Grub Street Journal* has a poem on her death, attributed to the Duke of Dorset, beginning " Young, thoughtless, gay, unfortunately fair." V.G.

([g]) Her yst. child, Edward, *b.* shortly before her death 19 Nov., was bap. 3 Dec. 1729, at St. Anne's, Soho.

PEDIGREE

Shewing the Descent of the Lords Bergavenny of Abergavenny
(marked respectively I to XVI), from 1392 to 1744.

I. William Beauchamp, *sum. by writ* 1392 = Joan Fitzalan, *held the as Lord Bergavenny, d.* 1411. | *Castle, &c., d.* 1435.

II. Richard (Beauchamp) *cr.* = Isabel Despenser, *sole heir* of the = Richard (Beauchamp), Earl Earl of Worcester 1420/1, *d.* | (attainted) BARONY of LE DES- | of Warwick, 2nd husband, *s.p.m.* 1421/2. | PENSER, *d.* 1439. | *d.* 1439.

See pedigree at p. 28

III. Sir Edward Nevill, *sum. by writ* = Elizabeth, only da. & h. 1450 as Lord Bergavenny, *d.* 1476. | of her *father, d.* 1448.

IV. George, Lord Bergavenny, 1482-92. In 1439 he had become *a coheir* (through his mother) to the attainted BARONY of LE DESPENSER, *d.* 1492

V. George, Lord Bergavenny, 1497-1534,   Sir Edward Nevill, beheaded 1538. *d.* 1535.

VI. Henry, Lord Bergavenny,   VII. ? Edward Nevill, [*Query*] 1552-86, *d. s.p.m.* 1586/7.   Lord Bergavenny, *d.* 1588/9.

Mary, da. & h., to whom the BARONY   VIII. Edward Nevill, *sum. by writ* 1604 OF LE DESPENSER was assigned in 1604.   as Lord Bergavenny, *d.* 1622. She was *heir gen. to William Beauchamp, sum. by writ* 1392 *as Lord Bergavenny;* as also to *Edward Nevill, sum. by writ* 1450   IX. Henry, Lord   Sir Christopher in the same title.   Bergavenny, *d.* 1641.   Nevill, *d.* 1649.

Sir Thomas Nevill   X. John, Lord   XI. George, Lord   Richard or Edward Nevill, K.B., *d.v.p.* 1628.   Bergavenny, *d.*   Bergavenny, *d*   *d. v.p.* 1643.   *s.p.* 1662.   1666.

Margaret, *m.* Thomas Brooke of Madeley,   XII. George, Lord   Bridget, *m.* Sir   George Salop, who was aged 49 in 1663. She was   Bergavenny, *d. s.p.*   John Shelley,   Nevill, *heir gen. to Edward Nevill sum. by writ* 1604   1695.   Bart. and *d.* 1687.   *d.* 1665. *as Lord Bergavenny.*

Frances (only child of her mother) *heir gen. to her grandfather*   XIII. George, Lord   Edward Nevill *the xjth Lord.*[a] She *m.* Richard, Viscount Fitz William [I.].   Bergavenny, *d.* 1720/1.   *d.* 1701.

XIV. George,   XV. Edward,   Jane, who (on the death of   XVI. William, Lord Aber- Lord Berga-   Lord Berga-   her sister Anne in 1736/7)   gavenny, sum. by writ 1724, venny, *d. s.p.*   venny, *d. s.p.*   became *heir gen. of her father*   the father of George, *cr.* Earl 1723.   1724.   *George Nevill, sum by writ*   of Abergavenny (1784), and   1695 *as Lord Bergavenny.*   ancestor of the succeeding   She *m.* John Abel Walter   Peers. He *d.* 1744.   and *d.* 1786.

[a] The xith Lord, however, appears never to have been sum. to Parl.

XVII. 1744.   1. George (Nevill), Lord Abergavenny, only surv.
EARLDOM.   s. and h., by 1st wife, *b.* 24 June, and *bap.* 14 July 1727,
                at St. Margaret's, Westm., the King, George II, being
I. 1784.   his godfather. Matric. at Oxford (Ch. Ch.) 14 Feb.
                1744/5. In July 1757 he was appointed Lord Lieut. of
Sussex, but resigned July 1761. On 17 May 1784 he was *cr.* VISCOUNT
NEVILL of Birling, Kent, and EARL OF ABERGAVENNY, co.
Monmouth. (ª) He *m.*, 5 Feb. 1753, at Stanmer, Sussex, Henrietta, widow
of the Hon. Richard Temple, of Romsey, Hants, sister of Thomas, 1st Earl
of Chichester, being da. of Thomas Pelham, of Stanmer afsd., by Annetta,
da. of Thomas Bridges. (ᵇ) She, who was *b.* 1, and *bap.* 22 Aug. 1730, at
St. Anne's, Westm., *d.* at Bristol, 31 Aug., and was *bur.* 8 Sep. 1768,
at East Grinstead. Admon. 24 July 1779 to her husband. He *d.* 9 Sep.
1785, and was *bur.* at East Grinstead. Will pr. Sep. 1785. (£1,200 *p.a.*
and £20,000.)

EARLDOM. ⎫   2. Henry (Nevill), Earl of Abergavenny,
II.   ⎪   &c., only s. and h., *b.* 22 Feb. and *bap.* 19 Mar.
          ⎬1785. 1755, at St. Geo., Han. Sq.; ed. at Ch. Ch.,
BARONY.   ⎪   Oxford; M.A. 8 Mar. 1776; M.P. for Seaford
XVIII.   ⎭   1784, and for co. Monmouth 1784-85. Recorder
                   of Harwich. K.T. 23 May 1814. About 1790
                   he repaired the old family place of Eridge (where

---

(ª) In this patent he is styled " George Lord Abergavenny. " The creation of
an Earldom of the *same* place as that of a Barony, but with a *different* limitation is very
objectionable as, in the event of their separating, the anomaly arises of *two* persons
being designated of one and the *same* place—*e.g.* in 1717 the Earldom of Ferrers (so
cr. 1711) became separated from the Barony of that name, and so continues; and in
1882 the Earldom of Berkeley (so *cr.* in 1679) became (apparently) separated from
the ancient Barony thereof. The Barony of Abergavenny however may be held to
have vested in the first Earl, either (1) by a Patent (hitherto undiscovered), granted
in 1604 (or even in 1450!) to his ancestor, or in 1724 to his father; or (2) by the
Tenure of the Castle. As to the former supposition it is *not usual* (though *not*
without a precedent) for the House of Lords to *imagine a patent* to exist, and to regulate
the descent of a Peerage accordingly. As to the Peerage being one *by tenure*, the
decision of the House, in 1604, that it was a Peerage *less* ancient than the Barony of
Le Despenser, is certainly greatly against such having been the *then* theory; and it is
one also that has not found greater favour in more modern times. The only other
alternative then that remains is (3) that the writ of 1724, (according to the modern
law in Peerage) *cr.* a Barony *de novo* of that date (1724), to which the House yielded
(as it has done in other cases, see Appendix D. at the end of this volume) the
precedence due to the ancient Barony of the same name existing (in this case) some
330 years previously.—See pedigree, p. 41.

(ᵇ) Hor. Walpole, writing to Lord Hertford 12 Feb. 1765, talks of a separation
being in contemplation on account of the Earl's infidelity, and remarks that " his
Lordship's heart is more inflammable than tender. " In 1774 he figures (" Lord A.
and Mrs. P. ") in the notorious *tête à tête* portraits in *The Town and Country Mag.*,
vol. vi, p. 452, of which a good account is given by Horace Bleackley in *N. & Q.*,
10th Series, vol. iv, pp. 241-2. V.G.

Queen Elizabeth had in 1573 been entertained by his ancestor), and adopted it as his chief residence. In 1805, he sold the newly acquired estate of Kidbrook He *m.* (spec. lic.), 3 Oct. 1781, ([a]) at Isleworth, Midx., Mary, only child of John ROBINSON, D.C.L., of Sion Hill and Wyke House in that parish, ([b]) many years Secretary to the Treasury, by Mary, da. of (—) CROWE, of Barbados. She *d.*, aged 36, at the Hot Wells, Clifton, co Gloucester, 26 Oct, and was *bur.* 5 Nov. 1796, at Isleworth. He *d.* aged 88, at Eridge Castle, 27 Mar, and was *bur.* 4 Apr. 1843, at East Grinstead. ([c]) Will pr. Apr. 1843.

[HENRY GEORGE NEVILL, *styled* VISCOUNT NEVILL, s. and h ap., *b.* 22 May, and *bap.* 20 June 1785, at Isleworth. He *d.* unm. *v.p.*, 8 Apr. 1806, at Moorgate, near Rotherham, co. York, and was *bur.* at East Grinstead.]

[RALPH NEVILL, *styled* VISCOUNT NEVILL, 2nd, but eventually 1st surv. s. and h. ap., *b.* 21 Dec. 1786, and *bap.* 22 Jan. 1787, at Isleworth. Capt. R.N. 1811, having served on the *Victory* at Trafalgar He *m.*, 2 Feb. 1813, at St. Paul's, Covent Garden, Mary Anne, da. of Bruce ELCOCK, of Sloane Str., Chelsea. He *d. s.p.* and *v.p.*, 20 May 1826, at Boulogne-sur-mer. Will pr. Sep. 1826. His widow *d.* 6 June 1828, aged 32, at Kensington. Will pr. Sep. 1828. Both were *bur.* at East Grinstead.]

EARLDOM.		3. JOHN (NEVILL), EARL OF ABERGAVENNY, &c.,
III.		3rd, but 1st surv s. and h , *b.* 25 Dec. 1789, and
	1843	*bap.* 27 Feb. 1790, at Isleworth afsd. Ed at
BARONY.		Christ's Coll., Cambridge; M.A. 1818. In holy
		orders; Rector of Burgh Apton with Holveston,
XIX.		Norfolk, 1818-1831, and Rector of Otley, Suffolk,
		1818-31. Chaplain to the Prince Regent 1818.

Being in delicate health he sat but once in the House of Lords. He *d.* unm., 12 Apr. 1845, aged 55, at Eridge Castle, Sussex. Will pr May 1845.

EARLDOM.		4. WILLIAM (NEVILL), EARL OF ABERGAVENNY,
IV.		&c., youngest br. and h., *b.* 28 June and *bap.*
	1845.	5 Aug. 1792, at Isleworth afsd. Ed. at Magd.
BARONY.		Coll., Cambridge. M.A 1816 In holy orders;
		sometime Rector of Birling, Kent, and Vicar of
XX.		Frant, Sussex Chaplain to William IV. He *m.*,
		7 Sep. 1824, Caroline, 2nd da of Ralph LEEKE, of

([a]) " Lord Abergavenny's son is certainly to marry Robinson's daughter. He gives her £25,000 down, which does not pay all the young man's debts. Lord A. gives them £1000 a year. He is a weak good-tempered young man. " (George Selwyn to Lord Carlisle, 13 June 1781) V.G.

([b]) A copious pedigree of this family of Robinson is entered at the College of Arms in " Norfolk xi " The political correspondence of this John Robinson, important for the secret history of George III's reign, is preserved at Eridge Castle. See *Hist. MSS. Com.*, 10th Report, and App. vi, pp 3-72. V G.

([c]) " Un richard misanthrope octogénaire que la malheur a poursuivi. " (Duchesse de Dino, *Chronique*, 16 Sep. 1831) V.G

Longford Hall, Salop, by Honoria Frances, only da. of Walter Harvey
THURSBY. He *d.* 17 Aug. 1868, at Birling Manor, Kent, in his 77th year,
and was *bur.* there. Will pr. 14 Oct. 1868, under £300,000. His widow *d.*
19 May 1873, at Birling Manor afsd. Will pr. 17 July 1875, under
£35,000.

EARLDOM.
V.
BARONY.
XXI.

5. WILLIAM (NEVILL), EARL OF ABERGAVENNY,
VISCOUNT NEVILL, and LORD ABERGAVENNY, 2nd,
but 1st surv. s. and h., *b.* 16, and *bap.* 19 Sep.
1826, at Longford. Ed. at Eton. An officer in
the 2nd Life Guards, 1849. On 14 Jan. 1876
he was *cr.* EARL OF LEWES, (ᵃ) Sussex, and
MARQUESS OF ABERGAVENNY, co. Mon-
mouth. (ᵇ) K.G., inv. at Windsor 22 Feb. 1886. He *m.*, 2 May 1848,
at St. Geo., Han. Sq., Caroline, sister of Harcourt, LORD DERWENT,
and 1st da. of Sir John VAN-DEN-BEMPDE-JOHNSTONE, 2nd Bart., by
Louisa Augusta, da. of the Hon. Edward VENABLES-VERNON-HARCOURT,
ARCHBISHOP OF YORK. She, who was *b.* Apr. 1826, *d.* 13 Sep. 1892,
at Eridge Castle, and was *bur.* at Eridge. Will pr. at over £9,200
gross, and over £2,100 net.

[REGINALD WILLIAM BRANSBY NEVILL, *styled* EARL OF LEWES, 1st
s. and h. ap., *b.* 4 Mar. 1853. Ed. at Eton. Lieut. West Kent Yeomanry,
1873-76. J.P. for Kent 1880.]

Family Estates.—These, in 1883, consisted of 15,364 acres in Sussex;
5,854 in Kent; 2,683 in co. Warwick; 2,639 in co. Monmouth; 1,664 in
co. Worcester; 319 in co. Hereford, and 11 in Norfolk. *Total,* 28,534
acres, worth £30,325 a year. *Principal Residence.*—Eridge Castle, near
Frant, Sussex.

(ᵃ) A moiety of the town of Lewes came to the Nevills through the Beauchamps
and Fitzalans (who possessed the entirety) from the old Earls of Warren and Surrey.
The other moiety went through the other coh. of the Fitzalans to the Mowbrays,
Dukes of Norfolk. See note *sub* Robert, Baron GERARD OF BRYN. [1876].

(ᵇ) His Lordship is not improbably h. *male* of the body of Ralph Nevill, Earl of
Westmorland, so *cr.* 29 Sep. 1397, and, as such, entitled to an Earldom, which (but
for the exceptional Earldom of Arundel now vested in the Dukes of Norfolk) would
be more ancient than any now existing, supposing the *attainder* of 1570 was reversed.
The attainted Earl *d. s.p.m.s.*, in 1601. Soon after his death, Edmund Nevill, styling
himself Lord Latimer (a Barony by writ of which, though he was h. *male*, he was *not*
h. general), claimed in 1605 the Earldom (being h. male of the body of the 1st Earl,
but by the *second* wife) on the ground that being cousin of the *half blood* (only) to the
attainted Earl, such attainder (being that of a person of whom he could not by the
[then] law of half-blood be heir) did not affect him. It was however decided against
his claim, and the honour declared to be *forfeited*. This Edmund *d.* about 1640
(before 2 Jan. 1645/6) *s.p.m.s.*, when Lord Bergavenny possibly became h. male of the
1st Earl. According, however, to Drummond's *Noble British Families*, p. 15, the
issue male of Thomas Nevill, of Pigotts in Ardleigh, Essex (who was of a senior line
to the House of Abergavenny, being yr. s. of the 2nd Lord Latimer), existed long
afterwards.

ABERNETHY

See " SALTOUN OF ABERNETHY," Barony [S.] (*Abernethy*, afterwards *Frazer*), *cr.* 1445.

---

i.e., " ABERNETHY AND STRATHEARN " [*rectius* ' STRATHDEARN ' in Moray], Barony [S.] (*Stewart*), *cr.* 1562, with the Earldom of MORAY [S.], which see.

---

i.e., " ABERNETHY AND JEDBURGH FOREST," Barony [S.] *(Douglas)*, *cr.* 1633, with the Marquessate of DOUGLAS [S.], which see.

---

i.e., " ANGUS AND ABERNETHY," Marquessate [S.], *(Douglas)*, *cr.* 1703, with the Dukedom of DOUGLAS [S.], which see; *extinct* 1761.

ABERRUTHVEN

i.e., " ABERRUTHVEN, MUGDOCK AND FINTRIE," Barony [S.] *(Graham)*, *cr.* 1707, with the Dukedom of MONTROSE [S.], which see.

ABINGDON

EARLDOM.   1. JAMES (BERTIE) ([a]) LORD NORREYS OF RYCOTE,
I. 1682.   younger s. of Montagu, 2nd EARL OF LINDSEY, being
     1st s. by his 2nd wife, Bridget, *suo jure* BARONESS
NORREYS, only da. and h. of Edward WRAY, Groom of the Bedchamber to
James I. He was *bap.* 16 June 1653, at St. Margaret's, Westm., and *suc.* to
the Barony, vested in his mother, 24 Mar. 1656/7. He first sat in Parl.
" *as a Peer by descent*," under the style of " James Norris de Rycot,"
13 Apr. 1675, ([b]) and was again sum. 17 Oct. 1679 and 1 Mar.
1679/80. On 30 Nov. 1682 he was *cr.* EARL OF ABINGDON,
Berks. He was Lord Lieut. of Oxon 1674-87, ([c]) High Steward of
Oxford City, 16 Sep. 1687, and was one of the most active of the Peers
who in 1688 ([d]) invited the Prince of Orange to mediate between James II

([a]) The Berties, Earls of Abingdon, bear the arms of Bertie as they are borne
by the Berties, Earls of Lindsey. The 2nd Earl of Abingdon put the arms of Venables in the 1st quarter of his shield. (*ex inform.* Oswald Barron.) V.G.

([b]) *Journals*, vol. xii, p. 653.

([c]) He was one of the 15 Lord Lieutenants who were dismissed by James II,
in 1687, for a list of whom see vol. ii, Appendix G.

([d]) For a list of these see vol. ii, Appendix H.

and his subjects, contributing £30,000 towards the Prince's expedition. When, however, he found that the Prince aimed at the Crown he steadfastly opposed him, (ª) and exerted all his influence against declaring the throne vacant. He was again, May 1689 to May 1697, Lord Lieut. of Oxon, was Chief Justice in Eyre south of Trent Nov. 1693 to May 1697, and was High Steward of Oxford. He *m.*, 1stly, 1 Feb. 1671/2, at Adderbury, Oxon, Eleanora, 1st da. and eventually sole h. of Sir Henry Lee, of Quarendon, 3rd Bart., by Anne, sister and coh. of Henry Danvers, and da. of Sir John Danvers, of Cornbury, Oxon. She, who was *bap.* 3 June 1658, at Ditchley, Oxon, *d.* suddenly 31 May, (ᵇ) and was *bur.* 6 June 1691, at West Lavington, Wilts. M.I. (ᶜ) He *m.*, 2ndly, (Lic. Bp. of Lond. 15 Apr. 1698, he aged 44, she 30, to *m.* at Stanwell, Midx.) Catherine, Dowager Viscountess Wenman [I], 1st da. and coh. of Sir Thomas Chamberlayne, 2nd Bart., by Margaret, da. of Edmund Prideaux. He *d.* of fever, in his 46th year, at his house in Deans Yard, Westm., 22, and was *bur.* 29 May 1699, at Rycote Chapel in the parish of Haseley, Oxon. M.I. Will dat. 27 July 1683, pr., with three cods., 3 Feb. 1699/1700. His widow *m.*, 3rdly, Francis Wroughton, of Estcourt, Wilts, who *d.* there 29 Apr. 1733, and was *bur.* at Long Newnton, Wilts. She *d.* 9·Feb. 1741/2, in her 83rd year, and was *bur.* there. M.I. Will (signed " Catherine Abingdon ") dat. 9 July 1741, pr. 5 Mar. 1741/2, by William Wroughton.

II. 1699.   2. Montagu (Bertie, afterwards Venables-Bertie), Earl of Abingdon, &c., s. and h. by 1st wife. He was M.P. for Berks 1689-90, for Oxon, 1690-99, P.C. to Queen Anne 21 Apr. 1702, and George I 1714; Constable and Lord Lieut. of the Tower of London 27 May 1702-5; Lord Lieut. of Oxon 10 June 1702-5, and

---

(ª) " He was the first peer of the realm who [in Nov. 1688] made his appearance at the quarters of the Prince of Orange." Hitherto the Earl had " been regarded as a supporter of arbitrary government. He had been true to James in the days of the Exclusion Bill. He had, as Lord Lieutenant of Oxfordshire, acted with vigour and severity against the adherents of Monmouth, and had lighted bonfires to celebrate the defeat of Argyle. But dread of Popery had driven him into opposition and rebellion." (Macaulay, *History of England.*) He had also shortly before (as some recompense for having been deprived of the Lieutenancy of Oxon owing to his zeal for the Protestant faith), been mentioned for the Chancellorship of the University of Oxford, which however was given to the young Duke of Ormonde, grandson to the late Chancellor.

" The Earl of Abingdon, with a party of 50 Horse is gone thro' Dorchester to join the Prince of Orange." (*Diary of Narcissus Luttrell*, under 17 Nov. 1688.) The following character of him when " past 40 years old " is given by Bishop Burnet with Swift's comment thereon in italics. " A gentleman of fine parts; makes a good figure in the counties of Oxon and Berks: is very high for Monarchy and Church; of a black complexion. "—" *Very covetous.* "

(ᵇ) A letter from Peregrine Bertie giving an account of her death is dated 2 *May* [*sic*] 1691, but this is probably a slip of the writer's pen for 2 June.—See *Hist. MSS. Com.*, 13th Rep., App., pt. vi, p. 248.

(ᶜ) See an elegy on her by the poet Dryden.

again 17 May 1712-15 ; Chief Justice in Eyre south of Trent 1702-6, and
again 1711-15 ; Recorder and High Steward of Oxford, &c. He was
also one of the Lords Justices, Regents of the Realm, 1 Aug. to 18 Sep.
1714, (ᵃ) nominated to govern the Kingdom after the death of Queen
Anne till the arrival of George I. He *m.*, 1stly, 22 Sep. 1687, (ᵇ) Anne
(styled " BARONESS KINDERTON " (ᶜ) on her monument), da. and h. of
Peter VENABLES, of Kinderton, co. Chester (generally known as " Baron of
Kinderton "), by Catharine, da. of Sir Robert SHIRLEY. In consequence
of this match he, by Royal lic. dat. 10 Nov. 1687, took the additional name
of VENABLES for himself and his issue by his said wife. She was *b.* 7 May
1674, and consequently was only thirteen at the time of her marriage. She
was Lady of the Bedchamber to Queen Anne during the whole of her
reign. She *d. s.p.*, 28 Apr. 1715, and was *bur.* at Rycote Chapel. M.I.
Admon. 25 June 1715. He *m.*, 2ndly, 13 Feb. 1716/7, at Beaconsfield,
Bucks (registered at Rycote), Mary, widow of Gen. Charles CHURCHILL, da.
and h. of James GOULD, of Minterne, Dorset, by Mary, 1st da. of William
BONDE, of Bestral, in that co. He *d. s.p.s.*, 16, and was *bur.* 27 June 1743,
at Rycote Chapel. Will dat. 3 Apr. 1736, pr. 1 July 1743. His widow,
who was accidentally burnt to death, *d.* 10 Jan. 1757. Will, in which she
directs to be *bur.* by her father at St. Peter's, Dorchester, dat. 3 Mar. 1742,
pr. 20 June 1757. (ᵈ).

[JAMES BERTIE, *styled* LORD NORREYS, only child, by 2nd wife, s. and
h. ap., *b.* 14, and *bap.* 26 Nov. 1717, at St. Margaret's, Westm. He
d. v.p., 25 Feb. 1717/8, of the small pox.]

III. 1743. 3. WILLOUGHBY (BERTIE), EARL OF ABINGDON, &c.
nephew and h., being s. and h. of the Hon. James BERTIE,
of Stanwell, Midx., (*d.* 18 Oct. 1735), by Elizabeth, (mar. lic.Vic. Gen. 4 Jan.
1691/2) da. of George (WILLOUGHBY), 7th LORD WILLOUGHBY OF PARHAM,
and sister and h. of John, the 8th Lord, which James was 2nd s. of the
1st Earl. He was *b.* 28 Nov. 1692, at Lindsey House, Westm., registered
at Stanwell, Midx. M.P. for Westbury 1715, but unseated on petition.

(ᵃ) For a list of these see note *sub* William, DUKE OF DEVONSHIRE [1684].
(ᵇ) Lady Roos congratulates him in a letter, dat. 22 Sep. 1687, on his marriage
to "so vast a fortune and pretty a lady as Mrs. Venables." V.G.
(ᶜ) " The possessors of some lands called, but improperly called, BARONIES
within the counties Palatine of Chester and Durham, and in some of the Palatinates
in Ireland, were called BARONS, but, *as they did not hold of the Sovereign*, they were NOT
PEERS of his Parliament " ; again " To the *Caput Baroniæ*, as in the cases of BURFORD,
DUDLEY, and others, the term BARONY was applied, although the possessions formed
only *a part* of the Ancient Territorial Barony. The possessors of the Manor of
Burford and of some other heads of Baronies were also styled BARONS ; but, *as they
had not the entire Baronies* which had given title to their predecessors, they were NOT
PEERS." See Fleming's note, p. 18, to *Authorities, &c.*, as to the Barony of Berkeley
being "a Peerage by tenure," 1862. KINDERTON in Cheshire was one of the most
considerable of these so-called Baronies.
(ᵈ) " A woman of great virtues." (T. Hearne.) V.G.

High Steward of Abingdon and Wallingford Nov. 1743. He *m.*, Aug. 1727, at Florence, Anna Maria, da. of Sir John Collins (ᵃ) [*query*, of Chute Lodge, Hants ?]. He *d.* 10 June 1760, and was *bur.* at Rycote Chapel. Will dat. 3 Dec. 1756, pr. 9 July 1760. His widow *d.* suddenly, 21 Dec. 1763, while visiting the Venetian Ambassador at Powis House. Will pr. Mar. 1764.

[James Bertie, *styled* Lord Norreys, s. and h. ap., *bap.* 25 Sep. 1735, at Gainsborough. He *d.* unm., *v.p.*, 12 Oct. 1745, being burnt in his bed, at Rycote, and was *bur.* there.]

IV. 1760.   4. Willoughby (Bertie), Earl of Abingdon, &c., 2nd, but 1st surv. s. and h., *b.* 16 Jan. and *bap.* 18 Feb. 1739/40, at Gainsborough. Ed. at Westm., and at Geneva. On 3 July 1759, being then a student at Oxford (Magd. Coll.), he was one of the three undergraduates chosen to address the Chancellor on his installation. M.A. 1761. Took his seat in the House of Lords 6 Feb. 1761. High Steward of Abingdon and Wallingford 1761. (ᵇ) He *m.*, 7 July 1768, at St. Geo., Han. Sq., Charlotte, yst. of the 3 surv. daughters and coheirs of Admiral Sir Peter Warren, of Warrenstown, in Ireland, K.B., by Susanna, da. of Stephen De Lancy, and Ann, formerly Ann van Cortlandt, spinster. She *d.*, of "a complaint in the stomach," at Rycote, 28 Jan., and was *bur.* 8 Feb. 1794, at Rycote Chapel. He *d.* 26 Sep. 1799, aged 60, and was *bur.* there. Will pr. May 1800.

[Willoughby Bertie, *styled* Lord Norreys, s. and h. ap., *b.* 8 Feb. and *d.* 20 Feb. 1779, aged twelve days.]

[Willoughby Bertie, *styled* Lord Norreys, 2nd s. and h. ap., *b.* 9 Apr. 1781, *d. v.p.*, an infant.]

V. 1799.   5. Montagu (Bertie), Earl of Abingdon, &c., 3rd, but 1st surv. s. and h., *b.* 30 Apr. 1784, and *bap.* at St. Geo., Han. Sq.; *cr.* D.C.L. of Oxford, 3 July 1810. He was Cup-bearer at the coronation of George IV, 19 July 1821; High Steward of

---

(ᵃ) "A gentleman of Scottish extraction." *Collins.*

(ᵇ) He was sentenced in the King's Bench to some months' imprisonment for libelling an attorney named Sermon. "A singular young man, not quite devoid of parts, but rough and wrong-headed, extremely underbred but warmly honest." (Hor. Walpole, *Journal*, Sep. 1777.) Lord Charlemont, in his *Memoirs*, describes him as "a man of genius, but eccentric and irregular almost to madness :" which account tallies with the view generally taken of his character. His talent for "Flute playing" is mentioned in the characters of *Men of Fashion* in 1782, (see Appendix H at the end of this volume) and again as under in a ballad describing the carousal "following the Cape Hunt" (pub. in *The Wiccamical Chaplet*, by G. Huddesford, 1804) where his brother Capt. Peregrine Bertie "*full* brother to a peer" had distinguished himself.
  "When tidings to Lord Abingdon were wrote with pen and ink,
  That Peregrine of Gattendon was overcome with drink,
  His Lordship strummed his fiddlestring as he sung with merry glee,
  Huzza ! of *Fiddlers* I'm the King; the King of *Fuddlers* he."

Abingdon 1826, and Lord Lieut. of Berks. He *m.*, 1stly, 27 Aug. 1807, at St. Geo., Han. Sq., Emily, sister of Henry, 3rd Viscount Gage [I], and 5th and yst da. of Gen. the Hon. Thomas Gage, by Margaret, da. of Peter Kemble, President of the Council of New Jersey. She, who was *b.* 25 Apr. 1776, in Park Place, St. James's, Westm., *d.* 28 Aug. 1838, in Eaton Sq., and was *bur.* in Rycote Chapel. He *m.*, 2ndly, 11 Mar. 1841, also at St. Geo., Han. Sq., Frederica Augusta, 5th da. of Vice-Adm. Lord Mark Robert Kerr, by Charlotte, *suo jure* Countess of Antrim [I.]. He *d.*, at Wytham Abbey, Berks, aged 70, 16, and was *bur.* 24 Oct. 1854, at Rycote Will pr. May 1855. His widow *d.* 26 Nov. 1864, at Eccleston Sq., Midx., aged 48, *s.p.*

VI. 1854. 6. Montagu (Bertie), Earl of Abingdon, &c., s. and h., by 1st wife, *b.* 19 June 1808, in Dover Str., Midx. Ed. at Eton, and at Trin. Coll., Cambridge. M.A. 1829. *Cr* D.C.L of Oxford 11 June 1834. M P. for Oxon 1830-31, and 1832-52, and for Abingdon 1852-54. Lord Lieut. of Berks 1855-81. High Steward of Oxford and Abingdon. He *m.*, 7 Jan. 1835, at Nuneham, Elizabeth Lavinia, only da. and h. of George Granville Vernon-Harcourt, of Nuneham Courtenay, Oxon, by his 1st wife, Elizabeth, 1st da. of Richard (Bingham), 2nd Earl of Lucan [I.] She *d.* 16 Oct. 1858, at Wytham Abbey afsd. He *d.* 8 Feb. 1884, in 18 Grosvenor Str., Midx. Will pr. 31 Mar. 1884, over £36,000.

VII. 1884. 7. Montagu Arthur (Bertie), Earl of Abingdon, and Lord Norreys, 1st s. and h., *b.* 13 May 1836, in Han. Sq. Ed. at Eton. Lieut. Col. Royal Berks Militia 1863-80. Hon Col. 1880. He *m.*, 1stly, 10 July 1858, at the Bavarian R.C. Chapel, Warwick Str., Golden Sq., London, Caroline Theresa, 1st da., and, in her issue, coh. of Charles Towneley, of Towneley, co. Lancaster, by Caroline, da. of William Philip (Molyneux), 2nd Earl of Sefton [I.]. She *d.* 4 Sep. 1873, at Wytham Abbey, Berks. He *m.*, 2ndly, 16 Oct. 1883, at the R C. Cathedral, Portsmouth, Mary, da. of Major Gen. the Hon. James Charlemagne Dormer, C.B., by Ella Frances Catherine, only da. of Sir Archibald Alison, Bart. She was *b.* 13 Oct. 1867.

[Montagu Charles Francis Bertie, *styled* Lord Norreys, 1st s and h. ap., by 1st wife, *b.* 3 Oct 1860 Assumed the name of Towneley Bertie in 1896. Sometime Capt 3rd Batt. Berks Regiment. Served in the S African War 1899-1900. He *m.*, 25 July 1885, at the R C. Chapel, Kingston on Thames, Rose Riversdale, sister of the 3rd and 4th Barons Wolverton, 1st da. of Vice-Adm. the Hon. Carr Glynn, C B., by Rose, da. of the Rev. Dennis Mahony, of Dromore Castle, co. Kerry. She was *b.* 10 Mar. 1860, and was granted, by Royal Warrant 1889, the rank of the da. of a Baron]

Family Estates.—These in 1884 consisted of about 21,000 acres, valued at about £28,000 a year ; *viz.*, above 8,000 in Oxon, rather less than 8,000 in Berks, and 66 acres in Bucks (which 16,000 acres or so were of the annual value of about £23,000) ; also above 4,500 acres in co. Lancaster, and 500 in co. York (part of the Towneley property), of the annual value (exclusive of mine rents) of about £5,000 in addition. Total 21,276 acres valued at £28,248 a year. *Principal Residence.*—Wytham Abbey, Berks.

ABINGER

BARONY.

I. 1835

1. JAMES SCARLETT, 2nd s. of Robert S., of Duckett's Spring, in St. James's Parish, Jamaica, by Elizabeth WRIGHT, widow, da. of Philip ANGLIN, of Paradise estate in that island, was *b.* there 1769 ; entered as a Fellow Commoner at Trin. Coll., Cambridge, at the age of fifteen ; B.A. 1790 ; M.A. 1794 ; LL.D. 1835 ; Barrister (Inner Temple) 1791 : King's Counsel 1816 ; M.P. for Peterborough 1819-30 (having been defeated, in 1822, for the University of Cambridge) ; M.P. for Malton 1830-31 : for Cockermouth 1831-32; and for Norwich 1832-34; Knighted 30 Apr. 1827; Attorney-Gen. for a short time in 1827, and again in 1829. On 24 Dec. 1834 (Sir Robert Peel being then Prime Minister), he was made LORD CHIEF BARON OF THE EXCHEQUER, and a few weeks afterwards, 12 Jan. 1835, was *cr.* BARON ABINGER, (ª) of Abinger, (ᵇ) in Surrey, and of the city of Norwich ; being the first Chief Baron who ever received a Peerage while in office. P.C. (ᶜ) He *m.*, 1stly, 22 Aug. 1792, Louise

---

(ª) The Scarletts, Lords Abinger, bear arms of Checky gold and gules with a lion rampant ermine and a quarter azure charged with a castle of three turrets silver. A grant of these arms was made to the first peer in 1835. The castle differences them from those borne in the 17th Century by Scarlett of Nayland and Copford, to whom this family, although descended out of Sussex, would seem to be of kin. (*ex inform.* Oswald Barron.) V.G.

(ᵇ) This estate, which had been purchased by him, was sold by his grandson, and the proceeds invested in an estate in Scotland.

(ᶜ) An amiable, popular man, of respectable character and genial disposition. His voice was low and mellifluous, his manner persuasive and easy, his face was round, jolly, rubicund, and intelligent in expression. In later life he became very portly. "Cautious, wary, astute, clear in his discernment, almost infallible in his judgment," he was an unrivalled *nisi prius* counsel, and his success with juries was almost miraculous, though not given to oratorical or any other form of display. He is the "Mr. Subtle" of Warren's Novel *Ten Thousand a year.* Like so many distinguished lawyers, he was not very successful in the House of Commons. He made a fairly good judge, though too much of the advocate still remained in him after his elevation. He is stated to have expressed his ability to convince any 12 jurymen of the truth of the Christian religion. When this was repeated to another judge now (1909) living, he retorted that if the case came before him he should stop it as there was no evidence to go to a jury ! He began life as a Whig, but changed sides during the Reform agitation in 1830. A Memoir of him by the Hon. Peter Scarlett was pub. in 1877. V.G.

Henrietta, 3rd da. of Peter CAMPBELL, of Kilmorey, co. Argyll. She *d.* 8 Mar. 1829. He *m.*, 2ndly (a few months before his death), 28 Sep 1843, at Ockley, Surrey, Elizabeth, widow of the Rev. Henry John RIDLEY, Rector of Abinger, and da. of Lee Steere STEERE, formerly L. S WITTS, of Jayes, in Wotton, Surrey, by Sarah, da. of Robert HARRISON, of London. He was struck with paralysis, after having sat through the whole day in Court, at Bury St. Edmund's, and *d.* there (five days afterwards), 7, and was *bur.* 14 Apr. 1844, at Abinger. Will pr 1844, under £18,800. His widow *d.* 13 Oct. 1886 at West Cliff House, Brighton, aged 84. Will pr. at Lewes, 9 Nov. 1886, under £40,000.

II.   1844.   2. ROBERT CAMPBELL (SCARLETT), BARON ABINGER, s. and h., by first wife, *b.* 5 Sep. 1794, in London Ed. at Trin Coll, Cambridge, B A. 1815, M.A. 1818. Barrister (Inner Temple) 1818 M.P for Norwich 1835-38; for Horsham 1841-44 Sometime British Minister at Florence. He *m.*, 19 July 1824, Sarah, 2nd da of George SMITH, Chief Justice of the Mauritius. He *d* 24 June 1861, at Abinger Hall, Surrey, aged 66, having survived his br -in-law, Lord Chanc. Campbell, but one day His widow *d.* 3 June 1878, in her 76th year, at Queen's Gate Terrace, South Kensington.

III.   1861.   3 WILLIAM FREDERICK (SCARLETT), BARON ABINGER, s. and h., *b.* 30 Aug. 1826 at Abinger Hall, Surrey. Ed at Eton, and at Trin Coll., Cambridge. Entered the army 1846, Capt. and Lieut. Col. Scots Fusilier Guards 1855, Major 1868, Lieut. Col. 1874, Major Gen. 1877, Lieut. Gen. 1882 Served in the Crimean War, 1854-56, and was at Alma, Inkermann, Balaklava, &c Retired on half-pay, Sep 1877. C B 2 June 1877; 5th class Medjidie. He settled in Scotland at Inverlochie Castle, co. Inverness. He *m*, 23 Dec 1863, at Christ Church Cathedral, Montreal, Helen (Ella, or Eileen), 2nd da. of George Allan MAGRUDER, Commodore in the U. S. Navy. He *d.* 16 Jan 1892, aged 65, at Inverlochie Castle, and was *bur.* at Inverlochie. Will pr. at £108,167 gross, and £93,933 net. His widow living 1909.

IV.   1892.   4. JAMES YORKE MACGREGOR (SCARLETT), BARON ABINGER [1835], only s. and h., *b.* 13 Mar. 1871, sometime Lieut. 2nd Batt. Cameron Highlanders He *d.* unm , suddenly, at supper at Montmartre, Paris, 11, and was *bur.* 19 Dec. 1903, at Inverlochie Castle Will pr. over £24,000 personalty. (ᵃ) He was *suc.* by his cousin, who does not come within the scope of this work.

Family Estates.—These, in 1883, consisted of 39,414 acres in co. Inverness, worth £4,346 a year, and 1,005 in Surrey valued at £689

(ᵃ) He left his estates to his successor, excluding, however, his next heir, and all who are Rom. Catholics.

a year. *Total* 40,519 acres, worth £5,035 a year. *Principal Residence* —Inverlochie Castle, near Kingussie, co. Inverness. The estate of Abinger, Surrey, was subsequently sold to Sir T. H. Farrer, who, in 1893, was *cr.* Baron Farrer of Abinger.

See " FARRER OF ABINGER, " co. SURREY, Barony *(Farrer)*, *cr.* 1893.

ABOUKIR

See " ABERCROMBY OF ABOUKIR, &c., " Barony *(Abercromby)*, *cr.* 1801.

ABOYNE

i.e., " ABOYNE " Barony [S.] *(Gordon)*, *cr.* 1627, with the Viscountcy of MELGUM [S.], which see ; *extinct* 1630.

VISCOUNTCY [S.]   1. GEORGE GORDON, *styled* LORD GORDON, and sometimes EARL OF ENZIE, s. and h.
I.   1632.   ap. of George, 6th EARL and 1st MARQUESS of HUNTLY [S.], and elder br. of John GORDON who had been *cr.* LORD ABOYNE and VISCOUNT MELGUM [S.] in 1627, was, soon after the death of his said younger br. (who *d.*, *s.p.m.*, Oct. 1630), by patent dat. 20 Apr. 1632, at Whitehall (reciting " the lamentable death of the late Viscount of Melgum "), *cr.* VISCOUNT ABOYNE [S.], with a *spec. rem.* after his father's or his own death (whichever should first happen), to his 2nd s. James GORDON and the heirs male of his body. This rem. took effect on the death of the Marquess (his father), 13 June 1636, when he, the said George Gordon, became 2nd MARQUESS OF HUNTLY [S.], and his yr. s. *suc.* (as below) to the Viscountcy.

For fuller particulars see " HUNTLY " [S.], under the second Marquess.

II. 1636 to 1649.   2. JAMES (GORDON), VISCOUNT ABOYNE [S.], 2nd s., but h. to the title under the *spec. rem.* He was a consistent and active but inefficient supporter of the Royal Cause, on which behalf he took and held Dumfries. He was defeated by Montrose (then fighting for the Covenanters) at the Bridge of Dee, 19 June 1639. He was excommunicated by the Gen. Assembly at Edinburgh, 24 Apr. 1644. He joined Montrose in Menteith in Apr. 1645, and his defection from him at Philiphaugh, 13 Sep. 1645, ruined the King's cause in Scotland. On 2 July following he became (by the death of his elder br.) 1st surv. s. and h. ap. of his father. He was excepted from pardon in 1648, and made his escape to France. He *d* unm. at Paris, Feb. 1648/9, a few days *after* (and, it is said, from grief occasioned *by*) the execution of his Royal Master (30 Jan.), and a few days *previous* to the execution of his father (22 Mar. 1648/9), for loyalty to the said King. His honours are presumed to have become *extinct* (ᵃ)

EARLDOM. [S.]   1. CHARLES GORDON, *styled* LORD CHARLES GORDON,
                            4th s. of George, 2nd MARQUESS OF HUNTLY [S], by
I. 1660.   Anne, 1st da. of Archibald (CAMPBELL), 7th EARL OF
                ARGYLL [S.], and br. of James, VISCOUNT ABOYNE [S.]
abovenamed, adhered firmly to the Royal cause during the Civil Wars, and suffered many hardships thereby, and was, in consideration thereof *cr.*, 10 Sep. 1660, LORD GORDON OF STRATHAVON and GLENLIVET, and EARL OF ABOYNE [S.]   He had a charter under the great seal in 1661 of the whole of the lands and lordship of Aboyne. He *m.*, 1stly, Margaret, da. of Alexander IRVINE, of Drum   She *d., s.p.m*, Dec. 1662. He *m*, 2ndly, (cont. 28 Aug. 1665) Elizabeth, only da. of

---

(ᵃ) Considerable insight as to the interpretation to be put upon the words "*Heirs male bearing the name and arms*" is afforded by this patent. "The use of the phrase *bearing the name and arms* was rare till 1615, and the fashion was not very prevalent till the time of Charles I, towards the end of whose reign it again fell out of common practice. From the table given of Peerages *cr* in connexion with his visit to Scotland in 1633, it is shewn that the stipulation is then, as it would appear, indiscriminately added or omitted. It was occasionally annexed to heirs male of the body, as well as to heirs male whatsoever, in either of which cases it could have no effect. " (Alex. Sinclair, *Dissertation upon Heirs male in grants of Scotch Peerages*, 1837, p 148   See also *Riddell*, pp 624-626, and pp. 1020-1021.)

In the patent by which this Viscountcy is *cr*., the former letters patent are recited whereby the King had conferred the title of Lord Aboyne and Viscount Melgum [S.], on the deceased Viscount Melgum " *et hæredes suos masculos nomen et insignia de Gordon gerentes*," and it is added that the said Viscount Melgum had died " *absque hæredibus masculis* DE CORPORE *suo legitime procreatis*, IN QUOS *dictus titulus Vice comitis conferendus fuit*, thus clearly proving that the dignity, though granted as above, was considered as confined to heirs male *of the body*. " *Ac volentes* (continues the patent) *ut prior titulus* [*i.e.*, that of Aboyne] REVIVAT [which expression shews its EXTINCTION], *et permaneat in personâ domini Gordon, &c* "   The patent proceeds to confer the dignity of Viscount Aboyne [S.] on the said Lord Gordon in the manner stated in the text, with a *spec. rem.* to his 2nd son, James, " *hæredesque suos masculos cognomen et insignia de Gordon gerentes* "

As this James *d* unm , 1648/9, this title, which was conferred with precisely the same limitation as that of Melgum, must similarly be held to be *extinct*. Sinclair suggests that it may be considered as having devolved on his next younger br., Lewis, who a few days later (on his father's death) became 3rd Marquess of Huntly [S.], and hence have passed on to the subsequent Marquesses. This suggestion can hardly be entertained, for, if so, one of the *younger* brothers of the Viscount Melgum [S.] (of whom we know that one, *viz*. Lord Adam Gordon, was alive in 1636 and at his father's funeral) ought to have *suc*. to *that* title in 1630, (the remainders being *exactly* the same), whereas we have the authority of the patent of Apr. 1632 that the Viscountcy of Melgum was then *extinct*.

John (Lyon), 2nd Earl of Kinghorn [S.], by his 2nd wife, Elizabeth, da. of Patrick (Maule), 1st Earl of Panmure [S.].   He *d.* Mar. 1681. (ª)

II. 1681.   2. Charles (Gordon), Earl of Aboyne, &c. [S.], s. and h. (ᵇ) Having been bred a "Papist" he qualified himself for taking his seat in the House, 27 July 1698, by taking the oath as a Protestant.   He *m.* his 1st cousin, Elizabeth, 2nd da. of (his maternal uncle) Patrick (Lyon), 3rd Earl of Strathmore and Kinghorn [S.], by Helen, 2nd da. of John (Middleton), 1st Earl of Middleton [S.].   He *d.* Apr. 1702.   His widow *m.* Patrick (Kinnaird), 3rd Lord Kinnaird [S.], who *d.* 31 Mar. 1715.   She *m.*, 3rdly, Capt. Alexander Grant, of Grantsfield, and *d.* Jan. 1739.

III. 1702.   3. John (Gordon), Earl of Aboyne, &c. [S.], s. and h.   Served h. to his father in Nov. 1702.   He *m.*, 20 June 1724, Grace, da. of George Lockhart of Carnwath, by Euphemia, 2nd da. of Alexander (Montgomerie), 6th Earl of Eglinton [S.].   He *d.* 7 Apr. 1732, at his seat of Charlton-Aboyne, Scotland.   His widow *m.*, Dec. 1734, James (Stuart), 8th Earl of Moray [S.], who *d.* 5 July 1767.   She *d.* 17 Nov. 1738, at Darnaway, co. Moray.

IV. 1732.   4. Charles (Gordon), Earl of Aboyne, &c. [S.], s. and h., *b.* about 1726.   After a long minority he entirely cleared his estate from debt, and actively improved it in other ways. He *m.*, 1stly, 22 Apr. 1759, at Edinburgh, Margaret, da. of Alexander (Stewart), 6th Earl of Galloway [S.], by his 2nd wife, Catherine, da. of John (Cochrane), 4th Earl of Dundonald [S.].   She *d.* 12 Aug. 1762, at Aboyne Castle.   He *m.*, 2ndly, 14 May 1774, at St. Geo., Han. Sq., Mary, da. of James (Douglas), 14th Earl of Morton [S.], by his 1st wife, Agatha, da. of James Halyburton, of Pitcur.   He *d.* 28 Dec. 1794, in St. Andrew's Sq., Edinburgh, in his 68th year.   His widow *d.* 25 Dec. 1816, aged 79, at Edinburgh.

V. 1794.   5. George (Gordon), Earl of Aboyne, &c. [S.], s. and h., by 1st wife, *b.* at Edinburgh, 28 June 1761. On 28 May 1836 he *suc.* as MARQUESS OF HUNTLY [S.], on the death of his cousin, George, 5th Duke of Gordon and 8th Marquess of Huntly [S.].   See "Huntly," Marquessate [S.], *cr.* 1599, under the 9th Marquess.

ACHESON

BARONY.   1. Archibald Acheson, *styled* Viscount Acheson, s. and h. ap. of Archibald, 2nd Earl of Gosford [I.], and I. 1847.   1st Lord Worlingham, was, on 18 Sep. 1847, *cr.* BARON

(ª) He was an author, and some of his poems are preserved.   They are said to be not without merit, but licentious in tone.   V.G.

(ᵇ) In a letter of James, Earl of Perth, dat. 30 Mar. 1694, he is called "a most sweet youth and humble like the dust of the street."   V.G.

ACHESON of Clancairney, co. Armagh. On 27 Mar. 1849 he *suc.* to his father's honours, when this Barony became *merged* in the Barony of WORLINGHAM (*cr.* 1835). See "GOSFORD," Earldom of [I.], *cr.* 1806, under the 3rd Earl

ACTON OF ALDENHAM

BARONY.   1. SIR JOHN EMERICH EDWARD DALBERG-ACTON, Bart.,
I. 1869.   of Aldenham Hall, Salop, s. and h. of Sir Ferdinand
                     Richard Edward DALBERG-ACTON, Bart., of the same, by
Marie Louise Pelina, only da. and h. of Emmerich Josef Wolfgang
Heribert, DUKE OF DALBERG, (ª) was *b.* 10 Jan. 1834, at Naples, and *suc.*
his father, as 8th Bart., 31 Jan 1837.   Ed at the R C. College at Oscott,
and under Dr. Döllinger at Munich   M P for Carlow, 1859-65 ; for
Bridgnorth, 1865, but was unseated on petition the following year.   D C.L.
Oxford, 1887, LL D. Cambridge, 1888   Hon. Fellow of All Souls,
Oxford, 1890 (an honour shared only with Mr. Gladstone).   A Lord in
Waiting, 1892-95   Regius Professor of Mod. Hist Cambridge, 1895.
On 11 Dec. 1869 he was *cr.* BARON ACTON OF ALDENHAM,
Salop. (ᵇ)   He *m*, 1 Aug. 1865, at St. Martin, in Upper Austria, Maria
Anna Ludomilla Euphrosina, 2nd da. of Johann Maximilian, COUNT OF
ARCO-VALLEY, by Anna Margareta Maria Juliana Pelina, COUNTESS MARES-
CALCHI ; (ᶜ) she was *b.* 11 Feb. 1841.   He *d.* 19 June 1902, at Tegernsee,
Bavaria. (ᵈ)   He was *suc.* by his s., who is outside the scope of this work.

(ª) He was only s of Wolfgang Heribert, Kämmerer von Worms, Reichsfreiherr von Dalberg zu Hernsheim, and was *cr* a Duke of the Empire by Napoleon, by letters patent, dated 14 Apr. 1810, and confirmed by Louis XVIII, 1 Feb. 1817, he was *cr* a Peer of France 17 Aug. 1815, and *d* at Hernsheim near Worms, 27 Oct 1833   (K Hopf, *Hist. Geneal. Atlas*, 1858-66, vol 1, no. 201 ; A. Révérend, *Armorial du Premier Empire*, 1895, vol 11, p. 3).   The arms quartered by the Lords Acton for this marriage differ somewhat from those of the Freiherren von Dalberg, which were, Quarterly, 1 and 4, Az , 6 fleurs-de-lis Arg , a chief *diminué* indented Or, for Kämmerer von Worms ; 2 and 3, Or, a cross moline Sa., for Dalberg.   To which the Duke added a chief Gu., semé with estoiles Arg (Siebmacher, under *Baden ;* Rietstap, etc) (*ex inform.* G W. Watson.)   V.G.

(ᵇ) Lord Acton of Aldenham bears arms of Gules with crosslets fitchy silver and two lions passant of the same   This is a Lestrange coat, borne by reason of the marriage of his ancestor Edward Acton with one of the daughters and coheirs of Fulk Lestrange of Longnor, a 14th century cadet of Lestrange of Blackmere   He quarters the arms of Dalberg as stated above. (*ex inform.* Oswald Barron.)   V.G.

(ᶜ) Johann Maximilian, Graf von und zu Arco-Valley, genannt Bogen, Herr zu Arco, St Martin, Valley etc , königl. bayerischer Kämmerer, etc. (*b.* 8 Apr. 1806, *d.* at Venice 23 Dec. 1875), *m.* 11 June 1832, Anna Margareta Maria Juliana Pelina, Contessa Marescalchi (*b.* 28 Aug. 1813, *d.* at Tegernsee 22 July 1885). Arco is in Tyrol, and Valley in Bavaria   (*Chronik der Grafen des H. R. R. von und zu Arco genannt Bogen*, 1886). (*ex inform* G. W. Watson)   V.G.

(ᵈ) He "is a theologian, a professor, a man of letters, a member of Society. When at intervals all too long he quits his retirement at Cannes or Cambridge, his

Family Estates.—These, in 1883 (besides 14 acres in Midx., valued at only £23 a year), consisted of 6321 acres in Salop, of the annual value of more than £7,500   *Principal Residence.*—Aldenham Hall, near Bridgnorth Salop.

ADARE

BARONY [I.]	1. Sir Richard ([a]) Quin, Bart., of Adare Manor, co. Limerick, on 31 July 1800 was *cr.* BARON ADARE, of Adare, co. Limerick , on 3 Feb. 1816
1 1800.	
VISCOUNTCY [I.]	he was *cr.* VISCOUNT MOUNT-EARL [I.]; and lastly, on 5 Feb. 1822, was *cr.* VISCOUNT ADARE
1 1822.	and EARL OF DUNRAVEN AND MOUNT-

EARL [I.].   See "Dunraven," Earldom [I.], 1822.

ADBASTON

See "Whitworth of Adbaston, co Stafford," Viscountcy *(Whitworth)*, *cr.* 1813, *extinct*, with the Earldom of Whitworth, 1825.

---

i e , "Adbaston, co. Stafford," Barony *(Whitworth)*, *cr.* 1815, with the Earldom of Whitworth, which see ; *extinct* 1825.

ADDERBURY

i.e., "Wilmot of Adderbury, co. Oxford," Barony *(Wilmot)*, *cr.* 1643; see "Rochester" Earldom, *cr.* 1652 ; *extinct* 1681.

ADDINGTON

BARONY.	1. John Gellibrand Hubbard, ([b]) of Addington Manor, Bucks, was 1st s. and h. of John Hubbard (*d.*

---

appearance is hailed with rejoicing by everyone who appreciates manifold learning, a courtly manner, and a delicately sarcastic vein of humour." (*Collections and Recollections*, 1898.)   A man of great personal charm and amiability, his liberal views and love of historic truth brought him into conflict with the narrower ultramontanes of his own communion   He collected an enormous library at Aldenham, but considering that he was perhaps the most learned and widely read man of his day, he left singularly little work behind him.   According to the '*Times*' obituary notice, " a decided indolence of disposition, a certain mental timidity, a distinct want of national fibre, were his main imperfections "   He was ennobled on the recommendation of Mr Gladstone, whom he adulated, and followed and encouraged in his political divagations.   He made no mark in either House of Parliament   V G.

([a]) In the patent for his Earldom he is called ' Valentine Richard.'

([b]) Lord Addington bears arms of Vert, a cheveron engrailed with plain cotices silver between three eagles' heads razed silver with collars gules flowered on both edges   The origin of these arms would appear to be in a grant made (*temp.*

16 Aug. 1847), of Stratford Grove, Essex, by Marianne, da of John MORGAN, of Bramfield place, Herts, was *b.* 21 Mar. 1805, at Stratford afsd. Head of the firm of " J. Hubbard *& Co,* " Russia Merchants, St Helen's place, London ; a director and sometime Governor of the Bank of England, Chairman of the Public Works and Exchequer Loan Committees, 1853-75; M.P. (Conservative) for Buckingham 1858-68, and for London 1874-87; P.C. 1874 On 22 July 1887, he was *cr.* BARON ADDINGTON, of Addington, Bucks. (ª) He *m.,* 19 May 1837, at Kew, Maria Margaret, 1st da. of William John (NAPIER), 9th LORD NAPIER OF MERCHISTOUN [S.], by Eliza, da of the Hon. James COCHRANE-JOHNSTONE. He *d.* 28 Aug. 1889, at Addington Manor afsd., in his 85th year. (ᵇ) Will pr. Mar 1890, at £111,985. His widow, who was *b.* 18 Mar. 1817, at Edinburgh, *d.* 18 Apr. 1896, at Addington Manor, aged 79.

II. 1889.　　　　　2 EGERTON (HUBBARD), BARON ADDINGTON, 1st s. and h., *b.* 29 Dec. 1842, at 26 Sussex Sq , Paddington ; ed. at Radley, and at Ch. Ch , Oxford ; B.A (1st class Hist.) 1865 ; M.A. 1866 ; partner in his father's firm in London, and in that of " Egerton Hubbard *&* Co. " of St. Petersburg ; M.P. for Buckingham 1874-80, and for North Bucks 1886-89. He *m.,* 3 June 1880, at Oakley, Hants, Mary Adelaide, 3rd da of Sir Wyndham Spencer PORTAL, 1st Bart., of Malshanger House, Hants, by Mary Jane, 1st da. of William Hicks BEACH, of Oakley Hall, in that county. She was *b* 20 Mar 1856, at Malshanger afsd.

[JOHN GELLIBRAND HUBBARD, s. and h. ap., *b.* at 23 Cadogan Place, Chelsea, 7 June, and *bap.* 18 July 1883, at Addington. Ed. at Eton ; matric. at Oxford (Ch. Ch.) Oct. 1902 ; B.A. 7 Nov. 1906 (2nd class Mod. Hist)]

Family Estates.—These, in 1883, consisted of 2,576 acres in Bucks, Beds, and Kent, worth £4,887 a year. *Principal Seat.*—Addington Manor, near Winslow, Bucks

AGHADOE

i.e., "ALLANSON AND WINN OF AGHADOE, co. Kerry," Barony [I.] (*Winn*), *cr.* 1797 with the Barony of HEADLEY [I], which see.

Henry VIII) to Hubbert of Calais of a shield of Azure with a cheveron silver between three swans' heads razed of the same, with golden crowns for collars. (*ex inform.* Oswald Barron) V.G.

(ª) Eight other Baronies had been already *cr.* that month (1 to 9 July), on the occasion of Queen Victoria's (first) " jubilee. " See note *sub* CHEYLESMORE

(ᵇ) He was author of several financial pamphlets, *e g , The Currency of the Country, Reform or Repeal the Income Tax,* etc.

AGHANVILLE

See " Downes of Aghanville, in King's County " Barony [I.]
(*Downes* afterwards *Burgh* and *De Burgh*), *cr.* 1822 ; *extinct* 1863.

AGHRIM

i.e., " Aghrim, co Galway, " Barony [I.] (*Butler*), *cr.* 1676 with the
Earldom of Gowran [I.], which see ; *extinct* 1677.

---

i.e., " Aghrim, co. Galway, " Barony [I.] (*de Ginkell*), *cr.* 1692 with
the Earldom of Athlone [I.], which see ; *extinct* 1844.

AILESBURY

EARLDOM   1. Robert (Bruce), Earl of Elgin, Lord Kinloss,
            and Lord Bruce of Kinloss [S.], also Baron Bruce of
1. 1664.   Whorlton, co York [E.], was only s and h. of Thomas,
1st Earl of Elgin, &c. [S.], and 1st Baron Bruce of Whorlton, by his
1st wife, Anne, da. of Sir Robert Chichester, of Raleigh, Devon, K.B.
He was *b.* before 1638, in the parish of St. Bartholomew the Less,
London (ᵃ)   He was one of the 12 commoners deputed, 7 May 1660, to
invite the return of Charles 11.   On 26 July 1660 he was, with the Earl
of Cleveland, appointed joint Lord Lieut. of Beds, and was M P. for that
co. 1661-63.   He *suc.* his father 21 Dec 1663, and, having been instrumental in procuring the Restoration, was, on 18 Mar 1663/4, *cr.* BARON
BRUCE OF SKELTON, co. York, VISCOUNT BRUCE OF AMPT-
HILL, Beds, and EARL OF AILESBURY, Bucks.   On 29 Mar. 1667
he was sole Lord Lieut. of Beds ; High Steward of the Honour of
Ampthill (ᵇ) 1670 ; joint Commissioner for the office of Earl Marshal,
20 June 1673 ; P.C Oct 1678 ; Gent of the Bedchamber ; Lord Lieut. of
Hunts 1681 ; Lord Lieut. of cos. Cambridge and Hunts 1685 , F.R.S.;
a few months before his death, at the coronation of James II, 23 Apr.
1685, he bore St. Edward's Staff, and on 30 July following was appointed
Lord Chamberlain of the Household. (ᶜ)   He *m.*, 16 Feb 1645/6,

---

(ᵃ) This fact (as well as the place of his marriage) is mentioned in the Earl's will.
(ᵇ) The Honour of Ampthill had been leased by the Crown in 1613 to Lord
Bruce [S], and was sold by the Earl of Ailesbury, in 1730, to the Duke of Bedford,
as was Houghton Park, the seat of the Bruce family (demolished in 1794), which was
partly in this parish and partly in Houghton Conquest.   Maulden, which was the
burial place of the Bruces, was also included in the sale
(ᶜ) " He was a learned person well versed in English history and antiquities. "
A. à Wood, *Fasti Oxonienses*, vol. i, p. 887.

at St. Alphage's, London Wall, Diana, 2nd da. of Henry (Grey), 1st Earl of Stamford, by Anne (heiress of Stamford), yst. da. and coh. of William (Cecil), 2nd Earl of Exeter. By her he had 8 sons and 9 daughters. He *d* at Houghton Park, Beds, 20, and was *bur.* 26 Oct 1685, aged 59, at Maulden in that co. (ᵃ) Will dat. 1, and pr. 15 Dec. 1685. His widow, who was *b.* in the same parish as her husband, (ᵇ) *d.* 8, and was *bur.* 12 Apr. 1689, at Maulden. Will dat. 14 Jan. 1685/6, pr. 26 Feb. 1689/90.

II. 1685.   2. Thomas (Bruce), Earl of Ailesbury, &c. [E], also Earl of Elgin, &c. [S.], 5th (ᶜ) but 1st surv. s. and h, *b.* 1656. M P. for Marlborough, 1679-81 ; for Wilts, 1685 Page of Honour, at the Coronation of James II, 23 Apr. 1685 Groom of the Bedchamber, 1685-88. Lord Lieut. of cos. Bedford and Huntingdon 1685-88. He was one of the few noblemen who offered their services to James II after the Prince of Orange had embarked for England, and was one of the four Peers (ᵈ) deputed to invite that King to return from Sheerness to Whitehall ; and when the King, two days later (18 Dec. 1688), was ejected from Whitehall, he was one of the four Peers (ᵉ) who accompanied him to Rochester The Earl returned to London, and took the oath to the Revolution Government. (ᶠ) He was accused of having conspired, in May 1695, to plan the restoration of King James, and was imprisoned in the Tower of London, Feb. 1695/6, but admitted to bail 12 Feb. 1696/7, and subsequently allowed to quit the Kingdom. He *m*, 1stly, 31 Aug. (or 30 Oct.) 1676, Elizabeth (who was raised, by royal warrant, 28 June 1672, to the precedency of a da. of the Duke of Somerset), 3rd da, but

(ᵃ) Ailesbury House or " St John's," Clerkenwell, Midx (where some of the 1st Earl's children were born, 1646-62) was the London residence of this family till they sold it in 1706. It was part of the old Hospital of St. John of Jerusalem, and came to the Bruce family through that of Cecil, to whom it had been granted by James I

(ᵇ) See p. 58, note "a."

(ᶜ) His elder brothers, Edward, *bur*. 21 Mar. 1662 at Maulden, Robert, *bur.* there 17 Feb. 1652, Charles, *bur.* there 19 Nov 1661, and Henry, all *d.* young, unm., and *v p.*, as did his yr br, Bernard, *bap.* 3 Sep 1666, at Ampthill, and *bur.* 31 May 1669, at Maulden   V G.

(ᵈ) These were the Earls of Ailesbury, Yarmouth, and Feversham [E.], and the Earl of Middleton [S.].

(ᵉ) These were the Earl of Ailesbury and the Earl of Lichfield [E.], the Earl of Dunbarton and the Earl of Arran, afterwards Duke of Hamilton, [S.].

(ᶠ) He took the oath, regarding it, to use his own expression, as "a Garrison one," and thinking, moreover, that those " who desired protection (from the *de facto* King) ought to take some oath. " He sent, however, a message to William that he would accept nothing so long as James or his son lived " Ailesbury and Dartmouth had as little scruple about taking the oath of allegiance [to William and Mary] as they afterwards had about breaking it ; " and in 1690, " Clarendon, who had refused the oaths, and Ailesbury, who had dishonestly taken them, were among the chief traitors "—See Macaulay, *History of England.* It is surely Whiggery run mad to brand as " Chief traitor " a man who only formally acknowledged the Revolution, and who preferred a long life in poverty, obscurity, and exile, to breaking the oath of allegiance which he had taken to King James. V.G.

only child that had issue, of Henry SEYMOUR, *styled* LORD BEAUCHAMP, by Mary, da. of Arthur (CAPELL) 1st LORD CAPELL, which Henry was s. and h. ap. of William, 1st MARQUESS OF HERTFORD, afterwards (1660) DUKE OF SOMERSET. (ᵃ) On 12 Dec 1671, by the death of her br., William, the 3rd Duke, the estates of Tottenham and Savernake forest, Wilts, devolved on her, as also the representation as senior coh. [heir of line] of Mary Tudor, sister of Henry VIII, through the families of Grey and Brandon. She *d.* in childbed, in the Tower (ᵇ) (of alarm at her husband's danger) 12, and was *bur* 27 Jan. 1696/7, aged 41, at Maulden. Bur. reg 1 May 1697, at St. Anne's, Soho. He *m.*, 2ndly, 27 Apr 1700, at Brussels, Charlotte Jacqueline, *suo jure* COUNTESS OF ESNEUX and BARONESS OF MELSBROECK, posthumous da. and h. of Louis Conrad D'ARGENTEAU, COUNT OF ESNEUX, by Marie Gilberte, only da. and h. of Jean DE LOCQUENGHIEN, BARON OF MELSBROECK. (ᶜ) She *d. s.p.m.*, (ᵈ) 13/23 July 1710, of fever, in her 31st year, at Brussels, and was *bur.* there in the Church of the Brigittines. (ᵉ)

(ᵃ) The Duke was grandson and h. of Edward Seymour, Earl of Hertford, by Katharine (next sister to the unfortunate Lady Jane Grey), da. and, in her issue, sole h. to Frances (wife of Henry Grey, Marquess of Dorset, afterwards Duke of Suffolk), the 1st da. and coh. of Mary Tudor, Queen Dowager of France, by Charles Brandon, Duke of Suffolk. According to the will of Henry VIII, he and his said ancestors would, since 1603, have been entitled to THE CROWN of England, to the exclusion of the House of Stuart

(ᵇ) " On 12 Jan. my dearest wife, who had just sat down to dinner, and asking what was the meaning of the cannon firing, they were so indiscreet as to tell her that the King was going to pass the Bill against Sir John Fenwick She fell backwards in her great chair and never spoke more. About 12 at night she was delivered of a daughter in the 8th month, and then expired . . . . No man ever had such a wife, and endowed with all the most rare qualities that ever woman enjoyed (*Memoirs of Thomas, Earl of Ailesbury*) V.G.

(ᶜ) Argenteau (in Flemish, Erckenteel) on the Meuse, and Esneux on the Ourthe, both in the province of Liége. The pedigree of Argenteau is in Butkens, *Trophées de Brabant*, 1724-6, vol. ii, pp. 222-227 : that of Locquenghien in *Annales de l'Acad. d'Archéol de Belgique*, 1st Series, vols. xi-xiv, 1854-7. The parents of Jean de Locquenghien were Charles (*b* 6 June 1591, *d* 14 Oct. 1670), *cr* Baron of Melsbroeck in Brabant by Philip, King of Castile, 17 Mar 1659 , and Mary (*m.* 23 Oct 1617, *d.* 18 Sep 1664), da. of William Middleton, a Scottish captain in the service of His Catholic Majesty. Both were *bur.* in the Church of the Brigittines at Brussels. (*ex inform.* G W. Watson.) V.G.

(ᵈ) " There was scarce her equal in goodness and sweetness, and generous to the last degree, the reverse of her mother." (*Memoirs of Thomas, Earl of Ailesbury*) V G.

(ᵉ) Her only child, Marie Thérèse Charlotte (*b.* 19/30 Sep. 1704, *d.* 19/30 Nov 1736), *m.* as 1st wife, 6/17 June 1722, Maximilian Emmanuel, Prince of Hornes (*b.* 31 Aug. 1695, *d* 12 Jan 1763) Their 2nd da and coh., Elisabeth Philippine Claude (*b.* 10 May 1733, *d.* 25 Jan. 1826), *m.* 22 Oct. 1751, Gustav Adolf, Prince of Stolberg-Gedern (*b.* 6 July 1722, *d.* 5 Dec. 1757). The latter's 1st da. and coh., Louise Maximilienne Caroline Emanuèle, *m.* Charles Edward Stuart, " the Young Pretender " See below under " ALBANY," titular Earl of (*ex inform* G W Watson.) V.G.

He *d.* there 16 Dec. ([a]) 1741, in his 86th year, and was *bur.* there with his 2nd wife. ([b]) Will pr. Jan. 1742.

III. 1741   3. CHARLES (BRUCE), EARL OF AILESBURY, &c. [E.], also
to   EARL OF ELGIN, &c. [S], 2nd ([c]) but only surv s and h
1747.   by 1st wife, *b* 29 May 1682. Charles II was one of his
         Godparents. He was M.P for Great Bedwyn 1705-08 ;
and was elected also in 1710, but sat for Marlborough 1710-11. On 29 Dec. 1711, he was sum. to the House of Lords, *v.p.*, in his father's Barony, as LORD BRUCE OF WHORLTON.([d]) On 17 Apr. 1746 he was *cr* BARON BRUCE OF TOTTENHAM, Wilts, with a *spec. rem.*, ([e])

([a]) T. A. Mann, *Histoire de Buxelles*, 1785, vol 1, p 241. According to Macky "he was very tall, fair complexioned " His remarkably interesting Memoirs, written about 1729, were pub by the Roxbrughe Club in 1890, and leave on the reader's mind the impression that the writer was a moderate, sensible, honest, truthful, and chivalrous partisan of the exiled Family. V G.

([b]) Urns containing their hearts are in the Mausoleum at Maulden, Beds. V.G.

([c]) His elder br. Robert, *b.* 6 Aug 1679, *d.* young, *v p*, and was *bur.* 22 July 1685, before his father was ennobled. V.G.

([d]) He was one of the twelve Peers who, not without some straining of the prerogative, were *cr.* within 5 days to secure a majority in the House of Lords for the Tory Administration. They are said to have been sarcastically asked by the Earl of Wharton, whether they tendered their votes separately, " *or by their foreman.*" Three of these were eldest sons of Peers of England, and consequently made no permanent addition to the Peerage, *viz.* ·

Bruce (s. and h. ap. of the Earl of Ailesbury), sum in his father's Barony.

Compton (s. and h. ap. of the Earl of Northampton), sum. in his father's Barony.

Paget (s. and h ap. of Lord Paget), *cr.* Lord Burton.

The other nine, arranged alphabetically as to their surnames and titles of Peerage, were—

Bathurst, *cr* Lord Bathurst
Dupplin, Lord, see Hay
Foley, *cr.* Lord Foley.
Granville, *cr* Lord Lansdown.
Hay, *styled* Lord Dupplin, being s. and h. ap. of the Earl of Kinnoul [S], *cr.* Lord Hay.
Lansdown, Lord, see Granville
Mansel, *cr* Lord Mansel.
Masham, *cr.* Lord Masham.
Middleton, Lord, see Willoughby.
Mountjoy, Lord, see Windsor
Trevor, *cr* Lord Trevor.
Willoughby, *cr.* Lord Middleton.
Windsor, Viscount Windsor [I.], *c)*. Lord Mountjoy
(See also note *sub* BATHURST.)

([e]) This *spec. rem.* is the more remarkable as he had female issue of his own, who *represented* him and his family, while the issue of his sister not only did *not represent* the family of Bruce, but were not even entitled to quarter their armorial ensigns. Of his three married daughters, the eldest, Mary (wife of Henry Brydges,

failing the heirs male of his body, to Thomas Bruce Brudenell, 4th and yst. s. of Elizabeth (his only surv sister), by George, 3rd Earl of Cardigan. He *m.*, 1stly, 7 Feb. 1705/6, at St. Giles-in-the-Fields, (fortune £60,000) Anne, 1st da. and coh. of William (Saville), 2nd Marquess of Halifax, by his 1st wife, Elizabeth, da. and h. of Sir Samuel Grimston, Bart, of Gorhambury, Herts. (ª) She *d.* 18, and was *bur* 25 July 1717, at Maulden afsd. He *m.*, 2ndly, 2 Feb. 1719/20, at Burlington House, Chiswick, Juliana, 2nd da. of Charles (Boyle), 3rd Earl of Burlington [E.], and 3rd Earl of Cork [I.], by Juliana, da. and h. of the Hon Henry Noel, of Luffenham, Rutland. She *d. s.p.*, 26 Mar., and was *bur.* 2 Apr. 1739, at Maulden. He *m.*, 3rdly, 18 June 1739, at Somerset House Chapel, Midx., (she 18 and he 57), (ᵇ) Caroline, only da. of Gen. John Campbell, of Mamore, afterwards (1761) 4th Duke of Argyll [S], by Mary, da. of John (Bellenden) 2nd Lord Bellenden [S.]. He *d s.p.m s.*, 10, and was *bur.* 16 Feb 1746/7, at Maulden. (ᶜ) Will pr. Apr. 1747. On his death the Earldom of Elgin, and the Barony of Bruce of Kinloss [S], devolved (under the *spec. rem.* in the patent of 1633) on his cousin and h. male, Charles (Bruce), 9th Earl of Kincardine [S]; the Barony of Kinloss [S], (*cr.* 1601) devolved, *de jure*, on (his grandson) the heir of line, but was not assumed by him, (ᵈ) while, as to the English Honours, the Earldom of Ailesbury, the Viscountcy of Bruce of Ampthill, and the Barony of Bruce of Skelton (all of which were *cr.* 1664), also the Barony of Bruce of Whorlton (*cr.* 1641), became *extinct*; but the Barony of Bruce of Tottenham (*cr.* 1746) devolved under the *spec. rem.* on his nephew, afterwards (1776) *cr.* Earl of Ailesbury, as below. His widow, who was *b.* 12 Jan. 1721, *m.*, 19 Dec. 1747, at Somerset House Chapel, Field Marshal the

---

afterwards Duke of Chandos), was (in 1889) represented by her descendant, the (last) Duke of Buckingham and Chandos (*d.* 1889), who thus became the senior coh (h. of line) to Mary Tudor, Queen of France, sister of Henry VIII (See p 60, note "a"). A lock of this lady's hair was among the articles in the sale of the effects of the (then) Duke of Buckingham, at Stowe, Bucks, in August 1848, and sold for the small sum of £7 10s It had been, however, acquired by purchase (not descent) in 1786, by the Duke of Chandos, but its authenticity was indisputable.

(ª) Although she was heiress in blood of the Grimstons of Gorhambury, her father left the family estates to his great nephew, William Luckyn, who took the name of Grimston, and was ancestor of the Earls of Verulam. V.G.

(ᵇ) Mrs Delaney writes, "Her father can give her no fortune; she is very pretty, modest, well behaved, and just 18, has £2000 a year jointure, and £400 pin money; they say he is cross, covetous and three score years old." V G

(ᶜ) Of his 2 sons, both by his 1st wife, (1) George, *d.* young; (2) Robert, M.P. for Great Bedwyn, *m.* 8 Feb. 1728/9, Frances, da of Sir William Blackett, Bart., of Wallington, co. Northumberland, and *d. s.p.* and *v.p.* 30 Aug 1738

(ᵈ) This was James Brydges, afterwards (1771) 3rd Duke of Chandos, s and h. of Mary, his 1st da. and coh. (by 1st wife), who had *d v.p.* This James *d s p m*, 1789, leaving an only da and h., Anna Eliza (*de jure* Baroness Kinloss [S]), mother of Richard Plantagenet, 2nd Duke of Buckingham and Chandos (who *d.* 1861), and grandmother of the 3rd Duke (*d.* 1889), who, on 21 July 1868, established his right, in virtue of this descent, to the Barony of Kinloss [S.] afsd

Hon. Henry Seymour-Conway, who *d.* 9 July 1795, aged 75, at Park Place, in Remenham, Berks. (ᵃ)   She *d.* 17 Jan 1803, aged 82, (ᵇ) in Upper Brook Str., St. Geo , Han. Sq. , will pr. Jan. 1803.

IV. 1776.   1 Thomas Bruce (Bruce-Brudenell), *afterwards,* Brudenell-Bruce), Baron Bruce of Tottenham, nephew, by the sister, being 4th and yst s. of George (Brudenell), 3rd Earl of Cardigan, by Elizabeth, sister of the whole blood to (the last Lord) Charles, 3rd Earl of Ailesbury, &c, and 1st Lord Bruce of Tottenham. He was *b.* 30 Apr., and *bap.* 13 May 1729, at St. James's, Westm. Ed 1737-46 at Winchester. On the death of his maternal uncle, 10 Feb. 1747, (whose vast estates in cos. Wilts and York, he inherited to the exclusion of his said uncle's daughters), he *suc.* to the BARONY OF BRUCE OF TOTTENHAM, under the *spec. rem.* above-mentioned. By royal licence, 29 Dec. 1767, he took the name of Bruce. He was Lord of the Bedchamber to George III. In May 1776 (ᶜ) he was made Governor to the Prince of Wales and Prince Frederick, but soon retired, being succeeded by his elder br., the Duke of Montagu. On 10 June 1776 he was *cr.* EARL OF AILESBURY, Bucks. Lord Lieut. of Wilts, 1780. K.T. 29 Nov. 1786. He *m.,* 1stly, 17 Feb. 1761, at the chapel in Tottenham Park, Wilts (registered at Great Bedwyn), Susanna, widow of Charles (Boyle), *styled* Viscount Dungarvan, da. and coh. of Henry Hoare, of Stourhead, Wilts, and of London, banker, by his 2nd wife, Susan, da. and h. of Stephen Colt   She, who was *b.* 15 Apr. 1732, *d.* 4 Feb. 1783, and was *bur.* at Maulden, Beds. He *m* , 2ndly, 14 Feb. 1788, by spec. lic., in St. James's, Westm , Anne, 3rd da. of John (Rawdon), 1st Earl of Moira [I.], by his 3rd wife, Elizabeth, *suo jure* Baroness Hastings   She, who was *b.* 16 May 1753, *d. s p.* in Seamore Place, Mayfair, 8, and was *bur* 16 Jan. 1813, at Maulden. He *d.* 19 Apr. 1814, in Seamore Place, afsd , aged 85, and was *bur.* at Maulden. Will pr. May 1814.

[George Bruce-Brudenell, *styled,* after 1776, Lord Bruce, 1st s. and h. ap , *b.* 23 Mar. 1762, *d.* unm. and *v.p.* 28 Mar. 1783.]

(ᵃ) This "well-known seat " (for a short time the residence of Frederick, Prince of Wales), was sold by his widow, the said Lady Ailesbury, to Lord Malmesbury.

(ᵇ) "She had been extremely handsome. She was mild, gentle . . . had read much, was fond of music, and had a wonderful genius for needlework. . . . She lived in the happiest union with her husband [i e. Gen. Conway]."—Horace Walpole, Sep. 1774. She had been married young, against her will, to the Earl   V G

(ᶜ) "A formal, dull, man, totally ignorant of and unversed in the world, and a Tory; very unexceptionable in character." [Horace Walpole, *Journal,* 28 May 1776.] The same writer speaks of his 1st wife, as at that date "living at Bath, mad. "   V.G.

V. 1814.

MARQUESSATE.

I. 1821.

2 and 1. CHARLES (BRUDENELL-BRUCE), EARL OF AILESBURY, &c., 3rd and yst., but only surv. s. and h. ([a]) by 1st wife, b. in Seamore place, Mayfair, 14 Feb., and bap. 24 Apr. 1773, at St. Geo., Han. Sq.; styled LORD BRUCE, 1783-1814; M P for Marlborough in 5 Parls., 1796-1814; Col Wilts Yeomanry, 1797, and of the Wilts Militia, 1811-27; K.T. 20 May 1819. He was cr., 17 July 1821, ([b]) VISCOUNT SAVERNAKE of Savernake Forest, Wilts, EARL BRUCE OF WHORLTON, co. York, and MARQUESS OF AILESBURY, ([c]) Bucks. He m, istly, 20 May ([d]) 1793, at Florence, Henrietta Maria, 1st da. of Noel (HILL), 1st BARON BERWICK OF ATTINGHAM, by Anna, da. of Henry VERNON. She d. in Grosvenor Sq., 2, and was bur. 11 Jan. 1831, at Maulden afsd. Admon. Jan. 1840. He m., 2ndly, 20 Aug. 1833, at Ham House in Petersham, Surrey, Maria Elizabeth, 2nd da of the Hon. Charles TOLLEMACHE, (3rd s. of Louisa, suo jure COUNTESS OF DYSART [S.]) by his 2nd wife, Gertrude Florinda, 1st da. of Gen. William GARDINER. He d. at Tottenham Park, 4, and was bur. 12 Jan. 1856, at Great Bedwyn, Wilts, aged 82. Will pr. July 1856 His widow, who was b. 27 Oct. 1809, d. 7 May 1893, aged 83 ([e]), and was bur. at Petersham. Will dat. 24 July 1891, pr. at £74,920 personalty.

MARQUESSATE.

II.

EARLDOM.

VI.

} 1856.

2 and 3 GEORGE WILLIAM FREDERICK (BRUDENELL-BRUCE), MARQUESS OF AILES-BURY, &c., 1st s. and h. by 1st wife; b. 20 Nov. 1804, in Lower Grosvenor Str., and bap. at St. Geo., Han. Sq., George III and his Queen being sponsors; styled LORD BRUCE, 1814-21, and EARL BRUCE, 1821-56; matric. at Oxford (Ch. Ch.), 2 Oct. 1822; M.P. for Marlborough, 1826-30; Lieut. Col. Com. Wilts Yeomanry, 1835, of which, in 1876, he became Hon Col.; was sum. to Parl v.p, 10 July 1838, in his father's Barony, as LORD BRUCE OF TOTTENHAM; suc. to the Marquessate of Ailesbury,

---

([a]) His next elder br. (the 2nd s. of his parents) Charles, was b. 7 Mar. 1767, and d 22 Jan. 1768. V.G.

([b]) This was one of the coronation peerages of George IV , for a list of which see vol. ii, Appendix F.

([c]) The (Brudenell-Bruce) Marquesses of Ailesbury, bear the arms of Brudenell:— Silver a cheveron gules between three hats of estate azure. Since 1767 this house has borne the arms of Bruce, Earl of Elgin, in the first quarter   Old examples commonly give the hats in the Brudenell shield as lined and turned up with gules (ex inform. Oswald Barron.) V.G.

([d]) Hist. MSS. Com, App., 15th Report, Part vii, p. 254. V.G.

([e]) For nearly 60 ['] years the " evergreen Maria Marchioness, " sprightly, gay and universally popular, was a constant frequenter of London parties and country race courses, and was to be seen in Hyde Park with flaxen hair (or wig), driving two ponies, generally preceded by two outriders. She was one of the four Marchionesses of Ailesbury who flourished from 1886 to 1891.

&c, some 16 years later, 4 Jan. 1856; Yeomanry Aide-de-Camp to the
Queen, and Colonel, 1857; P C. 1859; Master of the Horse, 1859-66,
and again 1868-74; Lord Lieut. of Wilts, 1863; K.G 25 May 1864.
By the death of his cousin, the 7th Earl of Cardigan, 28 Mar. 1868, he
suc. as EARL OF CARDIGAN [1661], BARON BRUDENELL OF
STONTON [1628], and a Baronet [1611]   He *m.*, 11 May 1837, at St.
Geo., Han. Sq., Mary Caroline, 3rd da. of George Augustus (HERBERT),
11th EARL OF PEMBROKE, by his 2nd wife, Catherine, only da. of Simon,
COUNT WORONZOW, of Russia   He *d. s p.*, 6 Jan. 1878, at Savernake,
aged 73, and was *bur.* there.   His widow, who was *b.* 22 Mar. 1813, *d.*
20 Jan. 1892, at 78 Pall Mall, and was *bur.* from Savernake, aged 78 ([ª])
Will pr. at £66,716.

MARQUESSATE. III. EARLDOM. VII.	1878.	3 and 4. ERNEST AUGUSTUS CHARLES (BRUDENELL-BRUCE), MARQUESS OF AILES-BURY, EARL OF CARDIGAN, &c, br. and h ; *b.* 8 Jan. 1811, at Warren's Hotel, St. James's Sq.; *styled* LORD ERNEST BRUCE, 1821-78; ed. at Eton, and at Trin. Coll, Cambridge; M.A. 1831 ; M P. for Marl-

borough in 11 Parls., 1832-78; a Lord of the Bedchamber, 1834-35:
P.C. 1841; Vice Chamberlain of the Household, 1841-46, and 1852-58.
He *m.*, 25 Nov 1834, at St. Geo, Han. Sq, Louisa Elizabeth, 2nd da of
John (HORSLEY-BERESFORD), 2nd BARON DECIES [I], by Charlotte Philadelphia, da. and h. of Robert HORSLEY.   He *d.* 18 Oct. 1886, at Savernake,
and was *bur.* at Great Bedwyn, aged 75.   Will pr. 14 Jan. 1887, above
£55,000 personalty.   His widow, who was *b.* Apr. 1814, *d.* 14 Oct. 1891,
at Villa Marbella, Biarritz, and was *bur.* at Great Bedwyn, aged 77 ([ª])
Will pr. 22 Jan. 1892, above £26,000 personalty.

MARQUESSATE. IV. EARLDOM VIII.	1886.	4. and 5. GEORGE WILLIAM THOMAS (BRUDENELL-BRUCE), MARQUESS OF AILES-BURY, EARL OF CARDIGAN, &c., grandson and h., being only s. and h. of George John BRUDENELL-BRUCE, Lieut. 14th Hussars, by Evelyn Mary, 2nd da. of William (CRAVEN), 2nd EARL OF CRAVEN, which George John

was 1st s. and h. ap, of the late Marquess, but *d. v.p.*, 28 May 1868,
aged 29, at Ajaccio in Corsica, ten years before his said father's accession
to the peerage.   He was *b.* 8 June 1863; ed. at Eton ; *styled* VISCOUNT
SAVERNAKE, 1878-86.   He *m*, 6 May 1884, at the Registry Office, St. Geo.,
Han. Sq, ([ᵇ]) " Julia HASELEY, ([ª]) aged 23, Spinster, " da. of " Thomas

---

([ª]) She was one of the four Marchionesses of Ailesbury who flourished from
1886 to 1891.

([ᵇ]) He was described as "G.W.T. Brudenell-Bruce, aged 21, Bachelor, Cab
Proprietor, Kendall's Mews, George Str., Marylebone," and his wife as "Julia Haseley, aged 23, Spinster, 72 Vincent Sq., Westm., " da. of "Thomas Haseley, deceased,

10

HASELEY." He *d. s.p.*, 10 Apr 1894, aged 30, at the house of his estate agent (Mr. Feltham), 121 Leander Road, Brixton, and was *bur.* from Savernake. (ᵃ) His widow *m.*, 28 Mar. 1901, David Waddle WEBSTER, of Arbroath, J.P. co. Forfar.

MARQUESSATE. V. EARLDOM. IX.	1894	5 and 6. HENRY AUGUSTUS, (BRUDE-NELL-BRUCE), MARQUESS OF AILESBURY [1821], EARL OF CARDIGAN [1661], EARL OF AILESBURY [1776], EARL BRUCE OF WHORLTON [1821], VISCOUNT SAVERNAKE [1821], BARON BRUDENELL OF STONTON [1628], and BARON BRUCE OF TOTTENHAM

[1746], also a Baronet [1611], uncle and h., being 3rd s. (ᵇ) of the 3rd Marquess. He was *b.* 11 Apr. 1842, in Curzon Str., Mayfair; was sometime Capt 9th Reg of Foot; *styled* LORD HENRY BRUCE, 1878-94; was M.P. for Wilts (Chippenham div.), 1886-92; Chairman of the well-known firm of "Meux & Co.," Brewers. He *m.*, 10 Nov. 1870, Georgiana Sophia Maria, 2nd da. of George Henry PINCKNEY, of Tawstock Court, Devon. She *d.*, suddenly, 23 June 1902, at 35 Albemarle Str.

[GEORGE WILLIAM JAMES CHANDOS BRUDENELL-BRUCE, *styled* since 1894, EARL OF CARDIGAN, only s and h ap.; *b.* 21 May 1873; sometime an officer in the 3rd batt. of the Argyll and Sutherland Highlanders. Major in the Wilts Imperial Yeomanry. Served in the S. African War 1899-1900. (ᶜ) He *m.*, 21 Mar. 1903, in Midlent, at St. Mark's, North Audley Str., Caroline Sydney Anne, only da of John MADDEN of Hilton Park, co.

---

no occupation." Witnesses "Arthur Thompson," and "Mary Jane Haseley." Each of the three Marquesses having left a widow, all of whom were alive in 1886, this lady was the junior of no less than 4 living Marchionesses of Ailesbury, and (having been generally known as *Doll Tester*) was spoken of in *The World* (Oct. 1886) as "The Marchioness Dorothy, née Tester, late of the refreshment department of the Theatre Royal, Brighton, and more recently, of the chorus at *The Empire* and elsewhere." As (besides these ladies) the mother of the 4th Marquess was also alive in 1886, "The Marchioness Dorothy " in the ordinary course of nature would have been the *fifth* (living) Marchioness. See note *sub* Charles, EARL OF PETERBOROUGH [1697], as to the marriages of Peers with actresses, singers, and dancers.

(ᵃ) A young man of low tastes, bad character and brutal manners, of whom a recent Prime Minister remarked that 'his mind was a dunghill, of which his tongue was the cock.' On 30 Sep. 1887 he was expelled for life from the Jockey Club, for fraud in connection with the running of his horse 'Everitt.' On 4 Mar. 1892 his total liabilities were stated in the Bankruptcy Court to be £345,462, of which £244,211 was unsecured. It has been said that his death was only mourned by the Radical Party, who thus lost, for their speeches, a most eligible example of hereditary legislators. It is said that he was kind to animals, and doubtless he had other good qualities, though obscured by ill training and worse associates. V.G.

(ᵇ) His next elder br., James Ernest Brudenell-Bruce, Barrister, *b.* 29 June 1840, *d.* unm. and *v.p.*, 21 June 1876, two years before his father *suc.* to the peerage.

(ᶜ) For a list of peers and heirs ap. of peers, serving in this war, see vol iii, Appendix B.

Monaghan, by Caroline, sister of Robert Bermingham (CLEMENTS), 4th EARL OF LEITRIM, 2nd. da. of the Hon. and Rev Francis Nathaniel CLEMENTS.]

[CHANDOS SYDNEY CEDRIC BRUDENELL-BRUCE, *styled* VISCOUNT SAVERNAKE, *b.* 26 Jan. 1904.]

Family Estates—These, in 1883, consisted of 37,993 acres in Wilts; 15,502 in co. York (then valued at £17,897 a year), and 1,556 in Berks. *Total*, 55,051 acres, worth £59,716 a year. Of these, however, 10,002 acres of the Yorkshire property (of the gross annual value of about £11,675) including the celebrated ruins of Jervaux Abbey, were sold in Feb. 1887, for £310,000, while as to the Wiltshire estate, it was, in 1891-92, agreed to be sold for £750,000, but the contract (though confirmed by the House of Lords in Aug. 1892) fell through, and that (deeply encumbered) estate remains (1909) in the family.

AILESFORD, see AYLESFORD
AILMER, see AYLMER
AILSA

BARONY.

1. 1806.

MARQUESSATE.

1. 1831.

I ARCHIBALD (KENNEDY), EARL OF CASSILLIS, &c, [S.], s. and h. of Archibald, the 11th Earl, by his 2nd wife, Anne, da. of John WATTS, of New York, was *b.* Feb. 1770. He raised an independent Company of Foot, 1790, and *suc.* his father in the Scottish Peerage 30 Dec. 1794. He was elected a REP. PEER [S] 1796-1806, and on 12 Nov. 1806 was *cr.* BARON AILSA, of Ailsa, co. Ayr. K.T. 17 July 1821. He was subsequently, 10 Sep. 1831, at the coronation of William IV (one of whose illegit. daughters his 2nd s had *m*), *cr.* MARQUESS OF AILSA, of the Isle of Ailsa, co Ayr. F.R S, &c. He was a consistent Liberal in politics, and voted for the " Reform Bill, " 14 Apr 1832. He *m*, 1 June 1793, at Dun, co. Forfar, Margaret, 2nd da. of John ERSKINE, of Dun afsd., by Mary, da. of William BAIRD, of Newbyth. He *d.* 8 Sep. 1846, at his residence, St. Margaret's, Isleworth, Midx, and was *bur.* at Dun, aged 76. Will. dat. 11 Sep. 1843, pr. Nov. 1846, at £160,000. His widow *d.* 5 Jan. 1848, of influenza, at St Margaret's afsd, aged 76. Will pr. Jan. 1848.

[ARCHIBALD KENNEDY, *styled* EARL OF CASSILLIS, s. and h. ap., *b.* 4 June 1794. M.P. for Evesham, 1830. He *m*, 1 May 1814, at Dun House, Eleanor, only da. and h. of Alexander ALLARDYCE, of Dunottar, co. Kincardine. (ᵃ) He *d. v.p.*, 12 Aug. 1832, at Cassillis House, co. Ayr. His widow, who was aged 17 in 1813, *d.* there 16 Nov. 1832.]

" (ᵃ) Lord Kennedy called upon me today full of the same blushes and bashfulness he exhibited while a boy, which dont become the papa of two lusty children. What a pity it was he did not first marry *Alma Mater*, and then go abroad, in place of espousing Miss Allardyce and growing mouldy at Dunotter! However, neither his

MARQUESSATE   2. ARCHIBALD (KENNEDY), MARQUESS OF AILSA,
BARONY.   &c., [U.K.], also EARL OF CASSILLIS, &c. [S.],
               grandson and h., being s. and h. of Archibald Ken-
II.   1846   nedy, *styled* Earl Cassillis, and Eleanor, his wife,
               abovenamed. He was *b.* 25 Aug 1816. Ed. at
Westminster Lieut. Rifle Brigade 1833. Capt. 17th Lancers 1838. Lord
Lieut. of Ayrshire, 1861. K.T. 7 Mar. 1859. He *m.*, 10 Nov 1846, in
London, Julia, 2nd da of Sir Richard Mounteney JEPHSON, 1st Bart., by
his 2nd wife, Charlotte Rochfort, da. of Lieut. Gen. Sir John SMITH,
K.C.B. He *d* 20 Mar. 1870, at Culzean Castle, from injuries received
in the hunting field. His widow *d.* at 19 Pont Str., S.W., 11, and was *bur.*
17 Jan. 1899, at Culzean Castle   Will pr. 22 Feb 1899, above £34,000.

III.   1870.   3. ARCHIBALD (KENNEDY) MARQUESS OF AILSA and
              BARON AILSA [U K.], also EARL OF CASSILLIS and LORD
KENNEDY [S.], s. and h., *b.* 1 Sep. 1847. Ed. at Eton. An officer in the
Coldstream Guards 1866-70. He *m.*, 1stly, 7 Mar. 1871, at St. Geo.,
Han Sq., Evelyn, 3rd da. of Charles (STUART), LORD BLANTYRE [S], by
Evelyn, 2nd da. of George Granville (SUTHERLAND-LEVESON-GOWER),
2nd DUKE OF SUTHERLAND. She was *b.* 24 June 1848, and *d.* 26 July
1888, at Culzean. Will resealed 31 Dec. 1888, above £17,000 personalty
[E. and S.]. He *m.*, 2ndly, 3 Nov. 1891, at St. Andrew's, Edinburgh,
Isabella, only da. of Hugh MacMASTER, a market gardener, of Kausani,
in the North-West Provinces of India

[ARCHIBALD KENNEDY, *styled* EARL OF CASSILLIS, s. and h. ap. by 1st.
wife, *b.* 22 May 1872, in Berkeley Sq., Midx   Capt. Royal Scots Fusiliers,
served in S Africa 1900-02 (2 medals and 5 clasps). (*)   Advocate Edinburgh, 1897. He *m.*, 20 Apr. 1903, at Ardwell, co Wigtown, Frances
Emily, 3rd da of Sir Mark John MacTAGGART-STEWART, 1st Bart., [1892],
by Marianne Susanna, only child of John Orde OMMANEY.]

Family Estates.—These, in 1883, consisted of 76,015 acres in co.
Ayr, of the annual value of £35,825. *Principal Residences.*—Culzean
Castle, and Newark Castle, co. Ayr.

AIR

VISCOUNTCY.   1. WILLIAM (CRICHTON), LORD CRICHTON OF SAN-
I.   1622.   QUHAR [S.], was, by patent dat at Newmarket, 2 Feb.
              1622, *cr.* LORD OF SANQUHAR and VISCOUNT

---

awkwardness, nor that of a country tailor, can spoil the look of blood and a very pleasing
manner. " (Ch. Kirkpatrick Sharpe, Aug. 1817.) He was a sportsman and a
great gambler, who dissipated his own and his wife's fortune   It appears from Chanc.
Proceedings, 15 July 1818, as to her mar. settlement, that she had landed estate in
Scotland valued at between £3000 and £4000 *p.a.*, and £30,000 in Bank Stock
(*Annual Reg.*, 1818)   V G

(*) For a list of peers, and heirs ap. of peers, serving in this war, see vol. III,
Appendix B.

I. 1633.   OF AIR [S.]. By a subsequent patent, dat. at Dunglass, 12 June 1633, he was *cr.* LORD CRICHTON OF SANQUHAR and CUMNOCK, VISCOUNT OF AIR and EARL OF DUMFRIES [S], with a *spec. rem.* (as to this creation) to heirs male for ever bearing the name and arms of Crichton. See DUMFRIES, Earldom of [S], *cr* 1633

AIRDES, see ARDES

AIREY

BARONY.

I.   1876

to

1881.

1. RICHARD AIREY, 1st s. and h. of Lieut. Gen Sir George AIREY, K.C.H. (*d.* 1833), by Catharine, yst. da. of Richard TALBOT, of Malahide Castle, co. Dublin, by Margaret, *suo jure* BARONESS TALBOT OF MALAHIDE [I.], was *b.* Apr. 1803, at Newcastle-on-Tyne Ed at Woolwich Academy. Ensign 34th Foot, 1821; Capt. 1825; Aide-de-Camp to the Commissioner of the Ionian Islands, 1827-30; to the Governor of British North America, 1830-32; Military Secretary there, 1832-35; Lieut. Col. 34th Reg., 1838; Assistant Adjutant Gen at the Horse Guards, 1838-47, Assistant Quarter-Master-Gen. there, 1851-53; Acting Quarter-Master-Gen. in the Crimea, 1854-55; was in command of a brigade at Alma, Balaklava, and Inkermann, and was at the capture of Sebastopol; Quarter-Master-Gen of the forces, 1855, when he received the local rank of Lieut. Gen. in Turkey He was *nom.* KCB, 5 July 1855, for his services against the Russians, was Col. of the 17th Foot, 1860; Governor and Commander-in-Chief at Gibraltar, 1865-70; G.C.B, 13 Mar. 1867; Col. of the 7th Foot, 1868; Adjutant Gen. of the Forces, 1870-76; Gen. in the Army, 1871-72. On 29 Nov. 1876, he was *cr.* BARON AIREY ([a]) of Killingworth, Northumberland. In Oct. 1877 he retired from the army. He *m.*, Jan. 1838, Harriet Mary Everard, 3rd da. of his maternal uncle, James (TALBOT), LORD TALBOT OF MALAHIDE [l.], by Anne Sarah, da and coh. of Samuel RODBARD, of Evercreech, Somerset. She *d.* 28 July 1881, in Lowndes Sq., Midx. He survived her but a few weeks, and *d. s p m.s*, 13 Sep 1881, at the Grange, Leatherhead, Surrey, when the title became *extinct.* ([b]) Both were *bur.* in the cemetery at Kensal Green, Midx.

([a]) Lord Airey of Killingworth bore arms of Azure a cheveron silver between three molets silver in the chief and a mural crown gold in the foot with three cinqfoils of the field on the cheveron. This modern shield seems to have been based upon the ancient arms of the Derbyshire Eyres, which were adopted without reason by more than one of the surname of Airey. (*ex inform.* Oswald Barron.) V.G

([b]) He appears to have been a hardworking, strong, efficient man, trained in the school of Wellington Owing to the attempt to throw on him the responsibility for the failure of the commissariat department in the Crimean War, he demanded an official enquiry, the result of which was to clear him of the charge. V.G

AIRLIE

BARONY [S]   1   SIR JAMES OGILVY, of Airlie and Lintrathen, co.
I.   1491.   Forfar, s. and h. of Sir John O.([a]), of the same, possibly by
                    Marion, 2nd da. of Sir William SETON, of Seton, b. about
1430, suc. his father about 1484 (in which year he was one of the guarantors
of the treaty of peace concluded with the English), was, on 28 Apr. 1491, cr.
LORD OGILVY OF AIRLIE [S.].   On 18 May following he went as
AMBASSADOR to Denmark.   He is said to have m., 1stly, about 1450,
Elizabeth KENNEDY, of the family of Cassillis. ([b])   He certainly m. Helen
GRAHAM, who was his wife 20 Nov. 1486.   He m. lastly Jean LYLE.   He
d. about 1504, before 25 Sep. 1504.   His widow d. about 1525.

II.   1504 ?   2.   JOHN (OGILVY), LORD OGILVY OF AIRLIE [S.], s.
                    and h. by 1st wife.   Knighted between 1494 and 1497.
He m., 1stly, before 14 Oct. 1472, Mariot or Marion   He m., 2ndly, Jean,
1st da of William (GRAHAM), LORD GRAHAM, of Kincardine [S], by Elene
DOUGLAS, apparently da. of George (DOUGLAS), 4th EARL OF ANGUS [S.].
He d before 9 Jan 1505/6 ([c])

III. 1505.   3.   JAMES (OGILVY), LORD OGILVY OF AIRLIE [S.], s.
                    and h. by 2nd wife.   He m. Isobel, da of Alexander
(LINDSAY), 8th EARL OF CRAWFORD [S], by Margaret, da. of (—) CAMPBELL,
of Ardkinglass.   He d. between 1513 and 29 Nov. 1524.

IV.   1520?   4.   JAMES (OGILVY), LORD OGILVY OF AIRLIE [S.], s
                    and h.   Served h to his father 29 Nov. 1524   On 5 Mar.
1542, he was appointed one of the Extraordinary Lords of Session.   He m.
Helen, da. of Henry (SINCLAIR), 1st LORD SINCLAIR [S], by Margaret, da.
of Patrick (HEPBURN), 1st EARL OF BOTHWELL [S.].   He d between 27
Nov. 1547 and 13 July 1548. ([d])   His widow d. between 1552 and 1562.

([a]) This Sir John O certainly m. Margaret, Countess of Moray, and Sir James
Balfour Paul, Lyon, writes, 31 May 1909, "There is not the slightest proof that he
m. a Marion Seton. "

([b]) Douglas is the only authority for this match.   The same writer gives him,
as a 2nd wife, Mary, da of Archibald (Douglas), 5th Earl of Angus [S], only child
by his last wife, Catherine, da of Sir William Stirling, of Keir   The dates, however,
show that in this latter case Douglas is in error, for Mary's parents m. about 1 June
1500, and she cannot, therefore, have been much over 3 years old at the date of her
supposed husband's death, which took place not later than Sep. 1504.   V.G.

([c]) Acta Dom. Conc , vol. xvii, p. 161.

([d]) The death of " James, Lord Airlie, May 1554, " is among the funeral entries
at the Lyon office , and this agrees with the retour to him of his great-great-grandson,
10 May 1630, where he is stated to have d. " about 1554 "   This date is, however,
totally inconsistent with the charter of 1549, granted by his grandson, as in the text.
See Crawford Peerage Case, p. 161, note.

V. 1548.   5. JAMES (OGILVY), LORD OGILVY OF AIRLIE [S.], grandson and h., *b.* about 1541, being s. and h. of James OGILVY, *styled* Master of Ogilvy, by Katherine, da. of Sir John CAMPBELL, of Cawdor, which James was s. and h. ap. of the 4th Lord, but *d v.p.*, 10 Sep. 1547, being killed at the battle of Pinkie. On 17 Dec. 1549 he granted an annuity, with consent of his mother and guardian, out of the lands of Airlie, to "Thomas, s. of the *deceased* James, Lord Ogilvy of Airly, grandfather of James, now Lord Ogilvy of Airly." He was one of the Commissioners who ratified the treaty of Berwick, 10 May 1560. When Queen Mary escaped from Lochleven, he repaired to her standard, and signed the association in her defence, 8 May 1568. He was imprisoned, accordingly, till James VI took the government on himself. By him he was sent as ENVOY to Denmark, to assist at the coronation of Christian IV, in 1596. He *m.* Jean, 1st da. of William (FORBES), 7th LORD FORBES [S.], by Elizabeth, da. and coh. of Sir William KEITH. He *d.* Oct. 1606, at Farnell. Will dat. 21 July 1606, pr. 20 Mar. 1607, ordering his burial "in the Isle of the Kirk of Kynnell"

VI. 1606.   6. JAMES (OGILVY), LORD OGILVY OF AIRLIE [S.], s. and h. He *m.*, 1stly, 11 Nov. 1581, "with great solemnity and triumph," in Holyrood House, Jean, 4th da. of William (RUTHVEN), 1st EARL OF GOWRIE [S.], by Dorothea, da. of Henry (STEWART), 1st LORD METHVEN [S.]. She *d.* 6 Jan. 1611/2. Will pr. 12 Jan. 1616/7. He *m.*, 2ndly, (cont. dat. 1613) Elizabeth, 6th and yst. da of Archibald NAPIER, of Merchistoun, by his 2nd wife, Elizabeth, da. of Robert MOUBRAY. He *d.* between Aug 1616 and Apr. 1618. His widow, who was living 1 May 1623, and apparently not then remarried, *m.* Alexander AUCHMOUTIE, Gent. of the Privy Chamber.

VII. 1617?   7. and 1. JAMES (OGILVY), LORD OGILVY OF AIRLIE EARLDOM [S.]   [S.], s. and h. by 1st wife, *b.* 1586. In reward of his own and his ancestors' loyalty, he, by pat. dat. at York I. 1639.   2 Apr. 1639, was *cr.* LORD OGILVY OF ALITH and LINTRATHEN, co. Forfar, and EARL OF AIRLIE [S.].(ᵃ) In 1644 he joined Montrose, and greatly distinguished himself in the victory over the Covenanters at Kilsyth, 15 Aug. 1645. He, with his 1st s., was excepted from pardon by the Articles of Westminster, 11 July 1646, and was excommunicated by the Gen. Assembly, 27 July 1646. His "forefaultour," however, was rescinded 17 Mar. 1647. He *m.*, (cont. dat. 22 Nov. 1610) Isabel, 2nd da. of Thomas (HAMILTON), 1st EARL OF HADDINGTON [S.], by his 1st wife, Margaret (*d.* Dec. 1596), da. of James BORTHWICK, of Newbyres. She was *b.* at Edinburgh, 18 Feb. 1595/6. He *d.* 1664/5. His wife surv. him.

(ᵃ) In July 1640 the Marquess of Argyll raided and devastated his lands and burnt his castle, leaving him "in all his lands not a cock to crow day,"—an event commemorated in the ballad "The bonnie House of Airlie." V.G.

EARLDOM [S.] ⎫
II ⎪
⎬ 1665.
BARONY [S] ⎪
VIII. ⎭

2 and 8. JAMES (OGILVY), EARL OF AIRLIE, &c. [S.], s. and h., *b.* about 1615. He was a devoted adherent of Charles I, and was twice taken prisoner by the Covenanters. On the last occasion, after his defeat under Montrose at Philiphaugh, 13 Sep 1645, he was sentenced to death, 26 Nov. 1645, but escaped out of the Castle of St. Andrew, the eve before his execution, in his sister's clothes. On 7 June, and 9 July 1649, two Acts of Parliament were passed in his favour. He was "an excommunicate Papist" in 1650. He was a prisoner in the Tower for several years under the Commonwealth, until Jan. 1656/7. After the Restoration, he had command of a troop of horse, and was made a P.C. In 1693 he was excused from attending Parl., owing to his great age. He *m.*, 1stly, (cont. 20 Mar. 1628/9) Helen, 1st da. of George (OGILVY), 1st LORD BANFF [S.], by his 1st wife, Margaret, da. of Sir Alexander IRVINE, of Drum. She was living Feb 1663/4. He *m.*, 2ndly, (cont. 31 Oct. 1668) Mary, Dowager MARCHIONESS OF HUNTLY [S.], da. of Sir John GRANT, of Freuchie, by Mary, da. of Walter (OGILVY), 1st LORD OGILVY OF DESKFORD [S]. He *d.* in 1703. (a) His widow was living 25 Dec. 1707.

EARLDOM [S.] ⎫
III. ⎪
⎬ 1703 to 1717
BARONY [S] ⎪
IX. ⎭

3 and 9. DAVID (OGILVY), EARL OF AIRLIE, &c. [S.], 2nd, but 1st surv. s. (b) and h. by 1st wife. He was served h. to his father in 1704. He *m.* (cont. 17 Apr. and 8 May 1696) Grizel, 1st da. of Patrick (LYON), EARL OF STRATHMORE and KINGHORN [S.], by Helen, 2nd da. of John (MIDDLETON), 1st EARL OF MIDDLETON [S.] He *d.* 1717, when, in consequence of the forfeiture of his s. and h., the title became under *attainder* (c) and so continued for 109 years. Will dat. 22 Mar. 1716, pr. 17 Aug. 1727.

The following is an account of the successive heirs to the Grantee of these Peerages, after the forfeiture :

(a) "A little, light man. . . . always very loyal, and a great follower of his cousin the great Marquess of Montrose." V.G.

(b) His elder br., James, *bap.* 6 Aug. 1633, at Banff, *d.* young. V.G.

(c) In the Airlie case it was held, that " if the attainted person *survived* the person in possession of the dignity, the title was *forfeited* "—See *Hewlett*, p 12 This was the unanimous opinion of the 12 English Judges, to whom the question had been referred, and " *it seems clear that*, IF *a Judgment had been asked* at the time [1814], and the opinion of Sir Vicary Gibbs and his brethren laid before the Committee, *it would have been confirmed*."—See *Maidment*, pp. 85-86. See also *Cruise*, p. 131, &c., and *Riddell*, pp. 724-730 There is great difficulty in reconciling this *opinion* (for it is *but* an opinion) with the *ratio decidendi* in the earlier case of Atholl. In that case (1764) it was held that the claimant, being son of the attainted person (Lord George Murray), though at *common law* he would have been *included* in the attainder, *came within the statute* "de donis" (12 Edw. I, c 1, modified by 26 Hen. VIII, c 13) and that thus

1717.   JAMES OGILVY, (*who, but for his attainder, would have been*) EARL OF AIRLIE, &c. [S], s. and h. He having, *v p*, when *styled* LORD OGILVY, taken part in the Rising of 1715, was *attainted* (ª) by Act, 1 Geo. I, cap. 43, 13 Nov. 1715, but obtained a pardon in 1725, and returned home. He *m.*, 6 Dec. 1730 (five weeks before his death), Anne, da. of David ERSKINE, of Dun, co. Forfar. He *d. s.p.* 12 Jan. 1730/1, at Edinburgh, of the small pox, and was *bur.* at Holyrood. His widow *m.*, 3 Apr. 1733, Sir Alexander MACDONALD, of Slate, Bart. [S], and *d.* 27 Nov. 1735, at Edinburgh, in her 27th year. He, who was titular 4th LORD SLATE [S.], *d.* 23 Nov. 1746, at Bernera.

1731.   JOHN OGILVY, *generally* (at that time) *considered* (as not having been affected by his brother's attainder), to be EARL OF AIRLIE, &c. [S.], br. and h., *b.* 1799. He took no part in the Rising of 1745. Under the Act of 1747 abolishing heritable jurisdictions, he was allowed £2,800 for the bailieries of the Regalities of Aberbrothock, Coupar, and Brechin. He *m.* (cont. 5 Dec. 1722) Margaret, only da. and h. of David OGILVY of Cluny. He *d.* 24 July 1761, at Cortachy, co. Forfar. His widow *d.* 1767.

1761.   DAVID OGILVY, *styling himself* EARL OF AIRLIE, &c. [S.], but more usually (before 1783) *styled* (by the courtesy title of) LORD OGILVY, s. and h., *b.* 16 Feb. 1725, at Cortachy. Ed. at Perth. On 3 Oct 1745 he joined (Prince) Charles Edward, "the young Chevalier," at Edinburgh with a Regiment of 300 men, mostly of his own clan. For this he was *attainted* by Act 19 Geo II, cap. 26. He escaped after the battle of Culloden to Norway, whence he went to France, where he commanded a Regiment of Foot, called "Ogilvy's Regiment," and rose to the rank of Lieut. Gen. in the French service He procured a *free pardon* under the Great Seal, 30 Mar. 1778, and, returning home, obtained a confirmation thereof by Parl. in 1783, Act 23 Geo. III, cap. 94. He *m.*, 1stly, (having eloped with her) Margaret, da of Sir James JOHNSTONE, of Westerhall, 3rd Bart. [S. 1700], by Barbara, da. of Alexander (MURRAY), 4th LORD ELIBANK [S.]. She was *b.* 30 Oct. 1724, and was so active in the Rising of 1745, that in June 1746 she was imprisoned in Edinburgh Castle, whence (in Nov) she escaped to France, where she *d.* 1757, aged 33. He *m.*, 2ndly, in 1770, Anne, 3rd da.

(passing over his attainted father, who was never tenant in tail in possession) he could take the dignity, as by gift, directly from his grandfather. In the case of Airlie, on the other hand, the opinion given was that the statute " de donis " *had no application to Honours*, and that the *common law* principle *must prevail, i e.* that every heir, belonging to the same estate-tail as the attainted person, suffers from the attainder, whether descended from him or not , it being only on the extinction of that estate-tail that the honours revive in favour of the representative of the next estate-tail.

(ª) He was attainted as " James Ogilvie Esq. commonly called Lord Ogilvie. " For a list of the Scots peerages forfeited at this time, and after 1745, see Appendix E in this volume. V.G.

of James STEWART of Blairhall, co Perth. She *d. s p.*, 27 Dec 1798, at Airlie Lodge, co. Forfar. He *d.* 3 Mar. 1803, at Cortachy afsd., in his 79th year.

1803. DAVID OGILVY, only s. and h., *b.* 4 Dec. 1751, at Auchterhouse, co. Forfar. He was insane, and never assumed the title. He *d.* unm., 6 Apr. 1812, at Kinnalty House, co. Forfar.

1812. WALTER OGILVY, *generally considered* (as not having been affected by the attainders of his collateral relatives in 1715 and 1745), to be EARL OF AIRLIE &c. [S], uncle and h. male, *b.* 1733. Admitted an Advocate at Edinburgh, 19 Feb 1757 Was of Clova. He laid claim to the title, but *d.* before any decision was given. He *m.*, 1stly, Margaret, da. of William FULLARTON, of Spynie, claiming to be LORD SPYNIE [S.]. She *d. s.p.*, 3 June 1780, at Balnaboth. He *m* , 2ndly, 12 Nov. 1780, at Forfar, Jean, da. of John OGILVY, M.D., of Balfour and Murkle, co. Forfar, by Margaret, da. of John OGILVY, of Innshewan. She *d.* 11 June 1818, at Cortachy afsd. He *d.* there, 10 Apr. 1819, aged 85.

1819. 4 and 10 DAVID OGILVY, *generally considered* (as not having been affected by
EARLDOM [S.] IV. the attainders of his collateral relatives in 1715 and 1745), *as* EARL OF AIRLIE,
1826. &c. [S.], 2nd, but 1st surv. s and h.,
BARONY [S.] X. *b.* 16 Dec. 1785. He was sometime Capt. 42nd Highlanders. Being great-grandson and h. male of David 3rd Earl, and having proved his right of succession to the title, *but for the attainder*, he obtained the *reversal* thereof, by Act of Parl., 26 May 1826, (ᵃ) and thus became *de facto* EARL OF AIRLIE, &c [S] He was Lord Lieut of co. Forfar. REP. PEER [S] 1833-49. He *m.*, 1stly, 7 Oct. 1812, Clementina, only da. and h. of Gavin DRUMMOND, of Keltie, co. Perth, by Clementina, sister and coh of Alexander GRAHAM, of Duntroon. She *d.* 1 Sep. 1835, in Park Crescent, Marylebone Admon. Mar. 1837. He *m* , 2ndly, 15 Nov. 1838, at 6 Heriot Row, Edinburgh, Margaret, only da. and h. of William BRUCE, of Cowden. She *d.* 17 June 1845, in childbed, at Brighton He *d.* 20 Aug. 1849, in Regent Str., Midx., aged 63. Will pr. May 1851.

(ᵃ) At this date the Royal assent was given to " An Act to restore David Ogilvy Esq. from the effects of the attainder of James, eldest son of David Earl of Airlie and of David Ogilvy taking upon himself the title of Lord Ogilvy " On the same day, by a similar Act, the attainder affecting the Earldom of Wemyss [S] was reversed, and the Earldom of Carnwath [S.] and the Barony of Duffus [S.] were restored to the respective heirs thereof. See Appendix F in this volume for a list of such restorations, as returned to the House of Lords 15 June 1885. V.G.

EARLDOM [S.]
V

BARONY [S.]
XI

1849.

5 and 11. David Graham Drummond (Ogilvy), Earl of Airlie &c. [S.], 2nd, but 1st surv. s. and h. by 1st wife, (ª) b. 4 May 1826, in London. Rep. Peer [S.] 1850-81. K.T. 12 Mar. 1862. High Commissioner to the Gen. Assembly of the Church of Scotland, 1872-73. LLD. Glasgow, 1879. He m., 23 Sep. 1851, at Alderley, co. Chester, Henrietta Blanche, 2nd da. of Edward John (Stanley), 2nd Lord Stanley of Alderley, by Henrietta Maria, 1st. da. of Henry Augustus (Dillon), 13th Viscount Dillon [I.]. He d. 25 Sep. 1881, at Denver, Colorado. His widow, who was b 3 July 1830, was living 1909.

EARLDOM [S.]
VI.

BARONY [S.]
XII.

1881.

6 and 12. David Stanley William (Ogilvy), Earl of Airlif &c [S], s and h., b. 20 Jan. 1856, at Florence. Ed at Eton, and at Balliol Coll., Oxford Lieut. 1st Regt. 1874; Scots Guards 1875; 10th Hussars 1876. Rep. Peer. [S.] 10 Dec. 1885 He served in the Afghan War, 1878-9; in the Soudan Expedition 1884; and in the Nile Expedition 1884-5, being slightly wounded at Abu Klea, 7 Jan. 1885, and again at El Gubat. He was twice mentioned in Despatches. Lieut. Col. 12th Lancers, Dec 1897, He went to S. Africa with his regt. at the outbreak of the Boer War; he was specially mentioned in Despatches for gallantry at Modder River, and was again wounded near Brandfort. He m., 19 Jan. 1886, at St. Geo., Han. Sq., Mabell Frances Elizabeth, 1st da. of Arthur Saunders William Charles Fox (Gore), 5th Earl of Arran [I], by his 1st wife, Edith Elizabeth Henrietta, da of Robert (Jocelyn), styled Viscount Jocelyn. She was b 10 Mar. 1866. He was killed, 11 June 1900, at Diamond Hill, in the Transvaal, aged 44. (ᵇ) Personalty above £44,000. His widow was living 1909.

EARLDOM [S.]
VII.

BARONY [S.]
XIII

1900.

7 and 13. David Lyulph Gore Wolseley (Ogilvy), Earl of Airlie, Lord Ogilvy of Airlie, and Lord Ogilvy of Lintrathen [S.], 1st s. and h. ap, b. 18 July 1893, at Cahir, co. Tipperary.

Family Estates.—These, in 1878, consisted of about 65,000 acres in co. Forfar, and about 5,000 in co. Perth. Total about 70,000 acres, of the annual value of above £28,000. Some of the lands (those at Craighead and

---

(ª) An elder br., Walter, was b in Paris 21 Sep 1823, and d. there 27 Mar. 1824. V.G.

(ᵇ) For a list of peers and heirs ap. of peers, serving in this war, see vol. iii, Appendix B. V.G.

Craignethie) have, however, since been sold.   *Chief Seat.*—Cortachy Castle, eight miles from Forfar.   This was partially destroyed by fire, 14 Sep 1883.

AIRTH

EARLDOM [S.]   1.   WILLIAM (GRAHAM), EARL OF MENTEITH
I. 1633.   [S.], having been, on 25 May 1630, served *h.*
                    of line to David (STEWART), EARL OF STRATHERN
[S.] (who was s. of Robert II, KING OF SCOTLAND), was, on 31 July
1631, confirmed in that dignity by Royal Charter " to him and his
heirs male and of entail, directing that he and they should thereafter be styled EARLS OF STRATHERN AND MENTEITH " [S.]   The
King's Charter, however, as well as the retour (finding the Earl to
be the h. of Prince David), were subsequently " *reduced* " by the
Court of Session, 1633.   The Earl having thus (for no fault of his
own) been deprived of the Earldom of Strathern, the King, to make
such deprivation less conspicuous, and, perhaps, for the purpose of
sinking the title of Menteith (as being connected with *Royal* descent),
erected the lands and Barony of AIRTH into an Earldom, and united
it by patent, 28 Mar. 1633, with the EARLDOM OF MENTEITH,
declaring its precedency to be that which was due to that Earldom,
therein defined as 6 Sep. 1428, (ᵃ) and " ordained the said Earl and
his heirs to be called in all time coming EARLS OF AIRTH and
to bruik and enjoy the honours, dignity, and precedence due to
them by virtue of the said Charter granted to the said Malise, Earl
of Menteith before all others " (ᵇ).   He *d.* in 1661, after 13 Apr.

II. 1661   2.   WILLIAM (GRAHAM), EARL OF AIRTH and
    to   MENTEITH [S.], grandson and h.   Having no issue,
    1694.   he resigned his territorial Earldoms (desiring also
                to resign, at the same time, the actual dignities of
the EARLDOMS OF MENTEITH AND OF AIRTH) in favour of James
(GRAHAM), MARQUESS OF MONTROSE [S.], and his heirs male, but
the King, while he accepted the resignation of the *territorial Earldoms*
and directed a charter of regrant to pass thereupon, refused to accept
a resignation of the *dignities*, or to interfere with the right of succession to them.   The Earl *d. s.p.* 12 Sep. 1694, when the *issue male*
of the 1st EARL OF AIRTH [S.] became *extinct.* (ᶜ)

[right margin:] Earldom of [S.], cr. 1427, under " MENTEITH," Earldom of [S.], the 7th and 8th Earls.   For fuller particulars see " MENTEITH,"

(ᵃ) This date is, oddly enough, in error by a year; it should be 6 Sep. 1427. In right of this clause of precedency the Earl of Menteith (who in the " decreet of Ranking " had been ranked as a creation of 1466) was (subsequently) placed next *below* " Mar " and next above " Rothes, " as appears in the records of Parl., 1639.   This militates against the theory that the date of 1457 (not 1404) was the one assigned at the " Ranking " to the Earldom of Mar.

(ᵇ) See *Earldoms of Strathern, Menteith, and Airth, with a report on the Claim* (1834) *of R B Allardice to the Earldom of Airth*, by Sir N.H Nicolas, 1842, p 98. See also Craik's *Romance of the Peerage*, 1848-9, vol. iii, pp. 362-4, for an interesting account of these Earldoms.

(ᶜ) Of his two sisters, whose seniority is doubtful, (1) Mary *m.*, 8 Oct. 1662, Sir

AIRTHRIE

i.e. "Airthrie," Viscountcy [S.] *(Hope)*, *cr.* 1703, with the Earldom of Hopetoun [S.], which see.

ALBANY

i.e., those parts of Scotland that are north of the Firths of Clyde and Forth.

DUKEDOM [S]   1. Robert Stewart, 3rd, but 2nd surv., s. of Robert,
I. 1398.   High Steward of Scotland, afterwards (1370-90)
Robert II, by his 1st wife, Elizabeth, da. of Sir Adam Mure, of Rowallan, was *b.* about 1340, and, while a young man (1361), became, in right of his wife, Earl of Menteith [S]. By agreement, 30 Mar. 1371, with Isabel, *suo jure* Countess of Fife [S.], he became, on her resignation, Earl of Fife [S.], by which latter title he was generally known   Great Chamberlain [S.] 1383-1407. He made two successful raids into England, one in 1385, and another in 1388. On 1 Dec. 1388, the King (his father), being aged, and his eldest br. (afterwards

John Allardice of Allardice, and *d.* Dec. 1720, leaving issue ; (2) Elizabeth *m*, Dec. 1663, Sir William Graham of Gartmore, Bart. [S.], and *d v.f*, leaving issue, which, according to some accounts, became *extinct* on the death of her great-great-grand-daughter Marie Bogle in 1821   The claim of the Allardice family to the title was opposed in 1839 by Nicholas Donnithorne Bishop, and Mary Eleanor his wife, da. and h. of James Andrew Bogle, alleged to have been a descendant of this Elizabeth Graham —See Burke's *Extinct Peerage*, *sub* "Graham, Earl of Strathern," *&c.* In 1834 Robert Barclay-Allardice (whose mother, Sarah Ann, was da. and h. of James Allardice, great-grandson and h. of Sir John A. and Mary Graham abovenamed) claimed the dignity of Earl of Airth [S.] as h. of line of the grantee, contending that the word "heirs" in the patent of 1633 must be read as "heirs of the body." To which the Lord Advocate objected that the patent only annexed the new dignity of Airth to the old one of Monteith, and that no person could be Earl of Airth [S] who was not *also* Earl of Monteith [S].   The case was frequently heard in 1839, and was adjourned 15 Aug. 1839.   In 1840, the same claimant presented a petition for the dignity of Earl of Strathern and Monteith [S], but no further steps were taken, and he *d.* in 1854   In 1870, Mrs. Barclay-Allardice, his only surv child, claimed the dignity of Countess of Airth [S], and was opposed by W. C Bontine (formerly Graham), who claimed to be h male of the body of the 1st Earl of Menteith, or Monteith [S.], and asserted this Earldom to be united with the Earldom of Airth.   The case was last heard 21 July 1871. See *Hewlett*, pp 74-76. G E C.
  Mrs. Barclay-Allardyce *d* 7 Aug. 1903, and in Nov 1904, her s, Robert B.-A. was contemplating the assertion of his claim as h. of line.   From press notices of that time it would appear that Robert Bontine Cunninghame Graham, 1st s of W.C. Bontine mentioned above, was prepared to contest the claim on the same ground as his father had done.   Another claimant was also announced in the *Daily Mail* of 19 Nov. 1904, as intending to assert his claim as h male, namely George Marshall Graham, *b* 18 Nov. 1852, at Edinburgh, and then of Kansas City, U.S A, s. and h. of James G. of Leichtown, Menteith, co. Perth. *(ex inform.* J. H. Round) V.G

Robert III) infirm, he was made, by Parl., GUARDIAN *(Custos)* OF
THE REALM [S.], and, as such, agreed to a treaty with the English in
1389 ; but on 27 Jan. 1398/9, he was superseded, by the appointment
of David, the h ap of the throne, as " King's Lieutenant, " with
as ample powers as his (David's) uncle (the said Duke) had as " Guardian." On the death, *s.p. legit.*, of his br. Alexander (STEWART), EARL
OF BUCHAN [S.], he appears to have been considered to have suc.
to that Earldom, (recognized to the said Alexander, 25 July 1382) which
he resigned 20 Sep. 1406. ([a]) In Mar. 1398 he, with his said nephew
David, had an interview at Haudenstank with John, Duke of Lancaster, and other English Commissioners, and shortly afterwards he and
his said nephew were each advanced to a Dukedom (the first Dukes ([b])
ever made in Scotland), he being, on 28 Apr. 1398, *cr.* DUKE OF ALBANY
[S.], in a solemn Council held at Scone. For his complicity in the arrest of
his said nephew, David, then Duke of Rothesay [S.], (who *d.* a prisoner in
Albany's Castle of Falkland, 27 Mar. 1402) he received a remission from
Parl ([c]) After his nephew's death, the Duke assumed the then vacant office
of " KING'S LIEUTENANT " [S] ; and by Charter, 2 Sep. 1403, was *cr.* EARL
OF ATHOLL [S.] during the life of the reigning King, with rem. (should he
die before the said King) to his 2nd s. John. By the death of the said King,
4 Apr. 1406, this Earldom consequently became *extinct.* At the council
held June 1406, after the death of his br. Robert III, he was made
REGENT [S.] *(Gubernator Scotiæ)*, the King (his nephew James I), being
then a prisoner in England, which Kingdom accordingly he again invaded
in 1417, but on this occasion without success. He *m*, 1stly, (disp.
9 Sep. 1361), Margaret, *suo jure* COUNTESS OF MENTEITH [S.], (who had
previously been the wife of Sir John MORAY of Bothwell *(d s p.* 1352),
of Thomas (ERSKINE), EARL OF MAR [S.], and of Sir John DRUMMOND of
Concraig) ([d]), da. of John GRAHAM, *jure uxoris* EARL OF MENTEITH [S], by
Mary, *suo jure* COUNTESS OF MENTEITH [S.]. She *d.* about 1380, between
21 July 1372 and 4 May 1380. He *m.* 2ndly, (Papal disp. 4 May

([a]) See under that title.

([b]) " It is probable that the superior title of John of Gaunt [as *Duke* of Lancaster]
led to some claim of precedence or respect not relished by the Scottish Princes. The h.
ap. to the throne was *cr.* Duke of Rothsay, a miserable *hamlet* in the Isle of Bute, while
the *whole island* would not have afforded a territorial title to a Baron , and the Earl of
Fife had the real style of the heir ap in the title of Duke of Albany or of *all* Scotland
North of the Firths of Clyde and Forth " (Pinkerton's *Scotland*, vol. i, p. 52)

([c]) The Parl declared that the Prince had *d.* from natural causes ; but whether
his death was from dysentery or from actual starvation seems doubtful. Sir Walter
Scott, though, as a historian, inclining to the (popular) belief in Albany's guilt,
expresses his entire disbelief in the sensational particulars taken from Boëce, which he
used with such thrilling effect in his *Fair Maid of Perth.*—See Lardner's *Cabinet
Cyclopædia*, vol i, p. 136. See also some remarks in vol iii of the *Exchequer Rolls*
[S.], Preface, p. xc. &c. ; and vol. iv, Preface, p. xlvii, &c., as to Albany's character
and acts as Regent.

([d]) See a note by " Sigma," suggesting that it was not she, but her mother, who
m Sir John Drummond, in *N. & Q.*, 7th Series, vol. x, pp. 163-4.

1380) ([a]) Muriel, 1st da. of Sir William KEITH, Marischal of Scotland, by Margaret, da. and h. of Sir Alexander FRASER, High Chamberlain [S.]. He *d.* 3 Sep. 1420, at Stirling Castle, aged above 80, and was *bur.* in Dunfermline Abbey. His widow *d* shortly before Whitsunday (1 June) 1449

II. 1420   2. MURDOCH (STEWART), DUKE OF ALBANY, EARL OF FIFE and EARL OF MENTEITH [S], s. and h. by 1st wife, *b.* probably 1362. Justiciar North of the Forth, 2 Apr. 1389. He was taken prisoner at the Scottish defeat on Homildon Hill, 14 Sep. 1402, and was detained in England till 1415, when he was exchanged for the Earl of Northumberland. He *suc* his father as REGENT [S] in 1420; and having accomplished the release of his cousin James I in 1424, attended him at his coronation at Scone The King, however, " was not slow in commencing the work of vengeance on the race by whom he had been long supplanted," ([b]) and, having obtained their conviction, at a Parl. held at Perth 25 Mar 1425, caused the Duke himself, his two elder surv. sons (Walter and Alexander), and his father-in-law the EARL OF LENNOX [S.], to be beheaded on the Castle Hill of Stirling. ([c]) He *m.* (settlement 17 Feb. 1391/2) Isabel, 1st da. and coh. of Duncan, EARL OF LENNOX [S.], by Helen, da of Gillespic CAMPBELL She was h. presumptive to the Earldom of Lennox [S.], her father having resigned it (to Robert II), and obtained a new grant thereof to himself and the heirs male of his body with rem. to her, her husband and the heirs of their bodies The Duke *d.* (as afsd.) 24 May 1425, and was *bur.* in the Blackfriars Church, Stirling, when, having been attainted, *all his honours* were *forfeited* His widow, *suo jure* COUNTESS OF LENNOX [S.], *d. s.p.s.*, at Inchmurrin Castle, Loch Lomond, either in 1458 or 1459 ([d])   •

[ROBERT STEWART, *styled* " OF FIFE " or MASTER OF FIFE, 1st s. and h. ap. He was a witness to charters 1407, 1409 and 1410. He *d. v.p.* and unm., between 1416 and July 1421.]

[SIR WALTER STEWART, *styled* " OF LENNOX, " and, after 1421, " OF FIFE, " 2nd, but 1st surv. s and h. ap.; Keeper of Dunbarton Castle. On

---

([a]) Robert Duke of Albany, and Isabella [*sic*] his wife, are mentioned in a petition to the Anti-Pope, dated Jan. 1417/8 The name "Isabella" is certainly an error V.G.

([b]) See Burke's *Vicissitudes of Families*, 1859, 1st Series, p. 95, *&c.*, where it is mentioned that Sir Robert Graham " the companion of these most unhappy Princes was released and lived to consummate his long-planned vengeance on the King in 1437 He it was, who, when James cried for mercy in his extremity, replied— 'Thou cruel tyrant, thou never hadst any mercy on Lords born of thy blood, therefore no mercy shalt thou have here '."

([c]) Whence he could see " his rich and romantic territory of Menteith and the hills of Lennox to which his Duchess was heir, and even descry the stately Castle of Doune, which had been his own Vice-Regal Palace " See Burke, *ut supra*

([d]) James Stewart, the only s. who had escaped from the vengeance of the King, *d. s.p. legit.* some time before 18 May 1451, leaving (by an Irish lady, named Macdonald) a son James, ancestor of the Stewarts of Ardvorlich.

24 Apr. 1421 he had dispensation to marry Janet, da. of Sir Robert
ERSKINE, but it is doubtful if the marriage was ever consummated. He
d.v p., probably *s.p legit.*, (ª) and *under attainder*, being executed at the
same time as his father, 24 May 1425.]

III. 1456?   1   ALEXANDER STEWART, 2nd s. of King JAMES II, *b.*
                about 1454, and before 8 July 1455. He was EARL OF
MARCH [S] before 8 July 1455, was *styled* "LORD OF ANNANDALE and
EARL OF MARCH" [S.] in an Act of Parl., 4 Aug. 1455, and soon afterwards
(certainly before 3 July 1458) was *cr.* DUKE OF ALBANY [S]. In 1479
his br. James III, on suspicion of conspiracy, arrested him and his br.
John, Earl of Mar [S.]. The latter died in prison, but the Duke
escaped to France, where he was honourably received by Louis XI.
In 1482 he (styling himself KING OF SCOTLAND) made an agreement
with Edward IV to pay homage to him, but, soon afterwards, he
appears to have been reconciled to his br., James III, who apparently,
about this time (Jan. 1482/3) must have *cr.* him EARL OF MAR AND
GARIOCH [S.], which dignity had belonged to his abovenamed br. In
1483, however, he renewed his treaty with the English, and placed his
Castle of Dunbar in their hands, and was "*forfeited*" in that year. Having
invaded Scotland he was routed near Lochmaben, 22 July 1484, and
escaped again into France. He *m.*, 1stly, Catherine, (ᵇ) 1st da of William
(SINCLAIR), EARL OF ORKNEY AND CAITHNESS [S.], by his 1st wife, Elizabeth,
Dowager COUNTESS OF BUCHAN [S.], da. of Archibald DOUGLAS, 4th EARL OF
DOUGLAS [S.]. She was divorced, 2 Mar. 1477/8, on account of propinquity
of blood, by sentence pronounced by the official of the district of Lothian
and ratified by Act of Parl, 15 Nov. 1516. He *m.*, 2ndly (cont. 16 Jan.
1478/9, (ᶜ) in France, Anne, da. of Bertrand DE LA TOUR, COUNT OF BOU-
LOGNE AND AUVERGNE, SEIGNEUR DE LA TOUR in Auvergne, by Louise, da.
of Georges DE LA TRÉMOILLE, SEIGNEUR DE LA TRÉMOILLE in Poitou. He is

---

(ª) He had many sons, all probably illegit , of whom the eldest, Andrew, was *cr.*
Lord Avondale [S.] in 1439. This Andrew, with his brothers Arthur and Walter,
was *legitimated* 17 Apr. 1479. Notwithstanding that Walter is included in this
Act, there may be *some* grounds for supposing it possible that he (*though he alone*) may
have been a s. by Janet Erskine, and consequently *legitimate*. The matter is discussed
in an able article on the Stewart Genealogy, by George Burnett, sometime Lyon
King of Arms, in the Preface to vol. IV of the *Exchequer Rolls* [S.].

(ᵇ) They had one s., Alexander Stewart, pronounced illegit by Act of Parl., 13
Nov. 1516. He was Bishop of Moray, 1527, *d.* 1534, and was *bur.* at Scone.—See
Douglas, vol. I, p. 59.

(ᶜ) The contract, between "excellens illustris et potens Princeps Alexander
Dux Albanie Comes Marchie Dominus Vallis Enandi et Mannie magnus Admirallus
Scotie et Gardianus marchiarum orientalium et occidentalium versus Angliam
fraterque germanus illustrissimi et excellentissimi Principis Scotorum Regis" and
"egregius et potens Dominus Bertrandus de Bolonia Comes Alvernie et Lauraguesii
Dominusque de Turre et nobilis et inclyta Domicella Anna de Bolonia ejus filia

said to have *d.* in 1485, in Paris, being accidentally killed at a tournament, and was *bur* in the Church of the Celestins there "By Act. of Parl., 1 Oct. 1487, the lands forfeited by Alexander, DUKE OF ALBANY, EARL OF ALBANY, EARL OF MARCH, MAR AND GARIOCH, LORD OF ANNANDALE AND MAN (ª) [S.], were annexed to the Crown. These lands were the Lordship and Earldom of March, the Baronies of Dunbar and Colbrandspath, with the Castle of Dunbar and tower and fortalice of Colbrandspath, and the Lordship of Annandale, with the Castle of Lochmaben." (ᵇ) His widow *m.* (cont. 15 Feb. 1486/7), (ᶜ) LOUIS DE LA CHAMBRE, COUNT OF LA CHAMBRE in Savoy, who *d.* at his castle of La Rochette in Savoy, 17 May 1517, aged 72, and was *bur.* in the Carmelite Monastery there. She *d.* 13 Oct. 1512, at La Rochette afsd., and was *bur.* with him. M I to both, there.

IV. 1505 ?   2. JOHN (STEWART), DUKE OF ALBANY [S.], (ᵈ) only
to   child by 2nd wife, and h , his elder br. (of the half blood)
1536.   having been pronounced illegit. He was appointed
                REGENT OF SCOTLAND during the minority of James V,
and arrived 18 May 1515 from France at Dunbarton, where he was inaugurated with great state, and even crowned After a profuse, weak, and inefficient regency of eight years, he finally quitted Scotland in Dec. 1523. He was Governor of Bourbonnais, Auvergne, Forez, and Beaujolais. He *m.* (cont. dat 13 July 1505), (ᵉ) his cousin, Anne, COUNTESS

emancipata a dicto Domino Comite, " dated "die decima sexta mensis Januarii anno Domini millesimo quatercentesimo septuagesimo nono," is in E. Baluze, *Hist. geneal. de la Maison d'Auvergne*, 1708, vol. ii, *preuves*, pp. 670-72. The marriage took place before 4 Dec. 1479 (*Idem*, p. 672). The erroneous date, 16 Feb. 1480, in *Anselme* (vol iv, p. 530), has been extensively copied. (*ex inform.* G.W Watson.) V.G.

(ª) The Isle of Man was granted by Robert I [S.] to Thomas (Randolph), Earl of Moray, on 20 Dec. 1313, according to *Scot Hist. Review*, vol iii, p 405, and certainly before 6 Dec. 1316 (Reg. Ho. Charters, no. 83), the extant copies of the charter of the Isle being dated 20 Dec. 1324. (*Scots Peerage*, vol. vi, p. 292, note 6.) See also *Riddell*, p. 102 &c., and Riddell's *Remarks, &c.*, 1833, p. 55, &c. The afsd. Earl of Moray is styled Lord of Annandale and Mann between 1316 and 1320, and his s. John is so styled, 1322-46, shewing that these Lordships were thus early united. In the reign of Robert II [S.] (1370-90], George (Dunbar), Earl of March &c [S.], the h. of the disponee, is called "*Dominus Vallis Annandiae et Manniae*." V.G.

(ᵇ) See *Douglas*, p. 59.

(ᶜ) Her marriage contract, dated "MCCCCLXXXVII xv Febr. indict. v" [*i.e.* 1486/7], and the epitaphs at La Rochette on her and her 2nd husband, are in *Baluze, ut supra, preuves*, p. 673. The date 7 May, in *Anselme*, is a misprint for 17 May. (*ex inform.* G.W. Watson.) V.G.

(ᵈ) There is no Act of Parl. nor any recorded charter extant, *restoring* to him the Dukedom *forfeited* by his father's attainder. He must have come of age about 1505, in which year also he married, and very possibly may have been then restored.

(ᵉ) The contract, "entre hault et puissant Prince Monseigneur Jehan Stuard Duc dAlbanie dune part et haulte et puissante Damoiselle Madamoiselle Anne de Boulogne fille aisnee de feu hault et puissant Seigneur Monseigneur Jehan en son vivant Comte de Boulogne et dAuvergne dautre part," dated "le xiii jour de Juillet lan MDV," is in *Baluze, ut supra, preuves*, p. 686 (*ex inform.* G W. Watson) V.G.

12

OF BOULOGNE AND AUVERGNE, 1st da. and coh. of his maternal uncle, Jean DE LA TOUR, COUNT OF BOULOGNE AND AUVERGNE, by Jeanne, da. of Jean DE BOURBON, COUNT OF VENDÔME. She was then under 10 years of age. She *d. s.p.* in June 1524, at the Castle of St. Saturin. (ª) Will dat. 16 June 1524. He *d. s.p. legit.*, 2 June 1536, at his Castle of Mirefleur in Auvergne, and was *bur.* in the Chapel of the Palace of Vic-le-Comte, when *all his honours* became *extinct.* (ᵇ)

V. 1541.   1. ARTHUR (STEWART), 2nd s. of JAMES V, by his 2nd wife, Marie, da. of Claude DE LORRAINE, DUKE OF GUISE, was *b.* at Falkland, Apr. 1541, and was *styled at his birth* DUKE OF ALBANY [S.]. He *d.* eight days after his baptism, 1541, and was *bur.* at Holyrood Chapel—when *the title* (if indeed it ever existed) became *extinct.*

VI. 1565.   1. HENRY (STEWART], EARL OF ROSS, &c. [S.], more generally known by his courtesy title of LORD DARNLEY, 1st s. and h. ap. of Matthew, 4th EARL OF LENNOX [S.], by Margaret, da. of Archibald (DOUGLAS), EARL OF ANGUS [S.], was, by charter 15 May 1565, (ᶜ) *cr.* LORD ARDMANNOCH and EARL OF ROSS [S.], under which designation he obtained, on 25 May, charter of the lands of Albany, and was soon afterwards, 20 July 1565, (ᶜ) *cr.* DUKE OF ALBANY [S.]. On 29 July 1565 he *m.* Queen Mary [S.] at Holyrood Chapel, having been proclamed KING OF SCOTLAND the day previous. His murder at Kirk o'Field, 10 Feb. 1566/7, as also the life and remarriage of the Queen, his widow, (ᵈ) and her execution, 8 Feb. 1586/7, are matters of national history. He was *bur.* privately in Holyrood Chapel.

VII. 1567.   2. JAMES (STEWART OR STUART), who, at his birth, was DUKE OF ROTHESAY, &c. [S.], and PRINCE OF SCOTLAND; became *also*, a few months afterwards, (in right of his deceased father) DUKE OF ALBANY, EARL OF ROSS, and LORD ARDMANNOCH [S.], only child and h. He was *b.* in Edinburgh Castle, 19 June 1566. By the abdication of his

---

(ª) Her sister, Madeleine, *m.* (cont. Saturday 16 Jan. 1518, *i.e.* 1517/8), Lorenzo de' Medici, Duke of Urbino, and *d.* 23 Apr. 1519, leaving an only child, Catherine, Countess of Auvergne and Lauraguais, *b.* 13 Apr. 1519, who *m.*, 28 Oct. 1533, Henry, Duke of Orléans, afterwards (1547) Henry II of France.

(ᵇ) These particulars as to his death &c., are given in the Obituary of the Chapel of Vic-le-Comte (Baluze, *ut supra, preuves,* p. 202), where he is styled " Duc d'Albanie Comte de Boulogne et d'Auvergne. " The arms depicted with the effigies of himself and his wife, reproduced by Baluze, vol. i, p. 358, are,—Quarterly ; 1, *Scotland ;* 2, the *Earldom of March ;* 3, the *Lordship of Man ;* 4, the *Lordship of Annandale.* (*i.e.* the same as in Laing's *Catalogue,* no. 790). And for his wife, *La Tour* quartering the *Comté of Auvergne,* over all the *Comté of Boulogne. (ex inform.* G.W. Watson.) V.G.

(ᶜ) See *sub* METHVEN.

(ᵈ) See *sub* BOTHWELL.

mother, 24 July 1567, he *suc.* to the throne of Scotland as JAMES VI, when *all his honours merged in the Crown.* On 24 Mar. 1603 he *suc.* to the throne of England as JAMES I.

VIII. 1600   1. CHARLES (STEWART OR STUART), 2nd s. of the above,
    to   was *b.* 19 Nov. 1600, at Dunfermline, and was when *bap.,*
    1625.   23 Dec. 1600, *cr.* LORD ARDMANNOCH, EARL
                 OF ROSS, MARQUESS OF ORMOND, and DUKE
OF ALBANY [S.]. (ª) On 6 Jan. 1605, his father being then King of England, he was *cr.* DUKE OF YORK. By the death of his elder br., 6 Nov. 1612, he became DUKE OF CORNWALL [E.] and DUKE OF ROTHESAY, &c. [S.], and, on 4 Nov. 1616, was *cr.* EARL OF CHESTER and PRINCE OF WALES. On 27 Mar. 1625 he *suc.* to the throne as CHARLES I, when *all his honours merged in the Crown.*

IX. 1660   1. JAMES (STEWART OR STUART), DUKE OF YORK, &c.
    to   (PRINCE JAMES OF ENGLAND AND SCOTLAND), 2nd s. of
    1685.   Charles I, *b.* 14 Oct. 1633, was by his father *cr.*, 27 Jan.
                 1644, DUKE OF YORK. By his br., Charles II, soon
after the Restoration, he was *cr.*, 31 Dec. 1660, DUKE OF ALBANY [S.]. On 6 Feb. 1684/5 he *suc.* to the throne as JAMES II [E.] and JAMES VII [S.], when *all his honours merged in the Crown.*

TITULAR   CHARLES EDWARD LOUIS PHILIP CASIMIR STUART (ᵇ)
EARLDOM   (generally spoken of as " Prince Charles Edward, "
I. 1766   " the Young Chevalier, " " the Chevalier de St.
    to   George, " or " the Young Pretender "), s. and h. of
    1788.   James Francis Edward, sometime DUKE OF CORNWALL
            (*titular* PRINCE OF WALES 1688-1701 and titular KING
OF ENGLAND &c. 1701-66), by Marie Clementine, 4th da. and coh. of Jacques Louis Henry SOBIESKI, PRINCE OF POLAND, was *b.* 31 Dec. 1720, at Rome, and *bap.* there the same day. On 25 Dec. 1723, he was invested at Rome with the order of the Thistle by his father. On 25 July 1745, he landed in Scotland and proclaimed his father as King, but was finally defeated, 16 Apr. 1746, at Culloden. On 1 Jan. 1766 he *suc.* his father, after which time (though on formal occasions he assumed the *titular style* of King, as " CHARLES III "), he appears to have generally *styled* himself [Comte d'Albanie] EARL OF ALBANY. He *m.*, privately and by proxy, at Paris, 28 Mar., and afterwards in person, in the Chapel of the

---

(ª) There is no record of this creation in the Great Seal Register, but in the Privy Seal, 6 Nov., and afterwards, the Prince is called Duke of Albany, Marquess of Ormond, Earl of Ross, and Lord Ardmannach. (*ex inform.* G. Burnett, sometime Lyon.)

(ᵇ) Material help in the rewriting of this article has been kindly rendered by that capable genealogist G.W. Watson. V.G.

Palazzo Compagnoni-Marefoschi, at Macerata in the March of Ancona, on Good Friday, 17 Apr. 1772, Louise Maximilienne Caroline Emmanuèle,([a]) 1st da. and coh. of Gustav Adolf, PRINCE OF STOLBERG-GEDERN, by Elisabeth Philippine Claud, 2nd da. and coh. of Maximilian Emmanuel, PRINCE OF HORNES AND OF THE EMPIRE. He *d.* of paralysis, ([b]) *s.p. legit.*([c])

([a]) For her descent from Thomas (Bruce), 2nd Earl of Ailesbury, see p. 60, note " e, " and for her descent from George, Duke of Clarence, see Ruvigny's *Blood Royal of Britain*.

([b]) " He goes regularly to the theatre, and always falls asleep at the end of the first act, being generally intoxicated. His face is red and his eyes fiery, otherwise he is not an ill looking man. The Countess is not handsome, being black and sallow, with a pug nose. Alfieri the Piedmontese is a constant attendant in her box. " (Swinburne, *Courts of Europe*.) V.G.

([c]) Two brothers (well known in London Society) claimed to be his legit. grandsons, viz. (i) John Sobieski Stuart, " *Count d'Albanie*, " who (with his br.) served in the advanced Guard of the French army at Waterloo, and *d. s.p.*, (ii) Charles Edward Stuart, " *Count d'Albanie*, " who left an only s., Charles Edward Louis Casimir Stuart, " *Count d'Albanie*, " sometime Col. in the Austrian army, who *d.s.p.* (see pedigree below). The father of the two brothers abovenamed appears to have been Capt. Thomas Allen, R.N. (yr. s. of Admiral John Carter Allen, an adherent of the House of Hanover, who was a claimant to the Earldom of Erroll [S.]), but according to their own account he was James Stuart, " *Count d'Albanie*, " legit. s. of the *titular* Charles III, though passed off by Adm. Allen as his own son. This tale, however, is conclusively refuted in an excellent article in the *Quarterly Review* for June 1847. See also *Northern Notes and Queries*, vol. iv, pp. 140 and 189, and vol. v, p. 45, as also an exhaustive article in the *Genealogical Mag.*, (1897) vol. i, p. 21.

The following pedigree of these gentlemanly impostors may be of interest.

John Carter Allen, afterwards Admiral of the White, (*d.* 2 Oct. 1800, leaving £100 to his 2nd s. Thomas, but £2,200 to an elder s.) said to have taken charge of (as his own s.) a s. of Charles Edward, *b.* 1773, (the year after the marriage with Louise of Stolberg) *viz.*

Capt. Thomas Allen, R.N., yr. s. (*b.* 1773) so named in the Admiral's=Katherine, da. of the Rev. will, but in 1822 called " Thomas Hay Allan, of Hay " and afterwards | Owen Manning, Vicar of " James, Count d'Albanie. " He *d.* 14 Feb. 1852, at 22 Henry Str., | Godalming, *m.* there 2 Oct. Clerkenwell, and was *bur.* at Old St. Pancras. He was sometimes | 1792. known by the name of Salmon.

John Hay Allen, afterwards called John Sobieski Stolberg Stuart, Count d'Albanie, 1st s., *m.* Georgiana, 2nd da. of Edward Kendall J. P., of Anstey, co. Warwick. He *d.s.p.* 13 Feb. 1872, and was *bur.* at Eskdale, co. Inverness, aged 74. His widow *d.* at Bath, 13 Feb. 1888.

Charles Stuart Hay Allen, afterwards called Charles Edward Stuart, Count d'Albanie, *b.* 4 June 1799, at Versailles, 2nd and yst. s., *m.* 9 Oct. 1822, in London, Anna Gardiner, widow, da. of the Rt. Hon. John de la Poer Beresford. He *d.* 25 Dec. 1880, and was *bur.* at Eskdale, aged 81.

Catherine Ma-=Count Ferditilda, only da. | nand de Lancastro. Count Charles Ferdinand Montesino de Lancastro et d'Albanie, only s., *d.* 28 Sep. 1873, in London.

Alice Mary Emily,=Charles 3rd da. of William George (Hay), 18th Earl of Erroll, *m.* 16 May 1874, and *d.* 7 June 1881.

Charles Louis Casimir Stuart, Count d'Albanie, only s., *d.s.p.* 8 May 1882, aged 57.

Edward Mary, *d.* unm. 22 Aug. 1873, at Beaumanoir on the Loire.

Louisa Sobieska, *m.* Edward, Count von Platt, of the Austrian Imp. Body Guard. She was living 1890.

Clementina, a nun, living 1890.

Alfred Edward, only s.

31 Jan. 1788, (*) aged 67, and was *bur.* in St. Peter's, Rome. M.I. Will
dat. 23-25 Mar. 1783, in which he refers to his da. as Duchess of Albany.(ᵇ)
A later will, dat. 22 Oct. 1784, making his da., the Duchess of Albany,
his universal h., is preserved in the archives of contract at Florence. (ᶜ)
His widow, (ᵈ) who was *b.* at Mons in Hainault 20 Sep. 1752, and *bap.*
there the same day, received a pension of £2000 *p.a.* from George III. (ᵉ)
She *d.* at Florence, 29 Jan. 1824, in her 72nd year, and was *bur.* at Santa
Croce, by the side of the poet Alfieri. (ᶠ) M.I. Will dat. 29 Mar. 1817.

TITULAR	1. CHARLOTTE (ᵍ) STUART, illegit. da. of Prince Charles
DUKEDOM	Edward abovenamed, by Clementina Maria Sophia, (ʰ)
I. 1783	Countess of "Alberstroff" (ⁱ) (so *cr.* by the Em-
to	peror), yr. da. of John WALKINSHAW, of Camlachie and
1789.	Barrowfield, co. Lanark, being 1st da. by his 3rd wife,
	Katherine, da. of Sir Hugh PATERSON, Bart. [S.], of

Bannockburn, was *b.* at Liège, and *bap.* there 29 Oct. 1753 as da. of

---

(*) A Requiem Mass was sung, 31 Jan. 1888, at the Church of the Carmelites,
Kensington, for the repose of his soul.

(ᵇ) *Hist. MSS. Com.,* 10th Report, vi. pp. 234-9. V.G.

(ᶜ) Printed in full by A. von Reumont, *Die Gräfin von Albany,* 1860, vol. ii,
pp. 316-321. V.G.

(ᵈ) She is thus described :—" of the middle height, blonde, with deep blue eyes, and
nose slightly turned up ; the complexion dazzlingly fair like that of an Englishwoman.
Her expression was maliciously gay. She seemed made to turn everybody's head."
(Bonstettin). "A well informed, shrewd, sensible, worldly person, and, as they tell me,
well looking in her day." (J. W. Ward. 1814.)

(ᵉ) " Her acquaintance with Alfieri, the poet (whom Card. York in 1785 asserted
to have been the origin and completer of the disunion between herself and the Prince),
began in 1777. After his death [at Florence,] 8 Oct. 1803, he was replaced as her
cavaliere servente by M. Fabvre, a French painter, whom she was said to have privately
married." (James Dennistoun, *Mem. of Sir Robert Strange,* 1855, vol. ii, p. 317.) V.G.

(ᶠ) On her monument she is styled " Aloysia e Principibus Stolbergiis Albaniae
Comitissa." In her will she calls herself " Luisa Carolina Massimiliana Albertina di
Stolberg... Vedova del fu Carlo Eduardo Stuart sotto la denominazione di Conte d'Albany ; " but her baptismal and marriage registers bear only the Christian names given
in the text. (*ex inform.* G. W. Watson.) V.G.

(ᵍ) " She is allowed to be a good figure, tall and well made, but the features of
her face resemble too much those of her father to be handsome." (Sir Horace
Mann). According to Dennistoun (*ut supra,* ii, 215), when Father Cowley, prior of the
English Benedictines at Paris, proposed to introduce her and her mother, Clementina
Walkinshaw, to Lady Strange, wife of Sir Robert, that Lady exclaimed, " Oh, the
vile jads ! if ye bring them here I'll put the door in their face." V.G.

(ʰ) Gen. Charles Edward Stuart, Baron Rohenstadt (1781-1854), *bur.* in Dunkeld
Cath., is said to have been son of Clementina by the Prince. Clementina *d.* Nov. 1802,
at Freiburg, in Switzerland. Her sister, Catherine, *d.* unm. in London, 11 Nov.
1794. Another sister, Maria Matilda, *d.* at Rome, 3 Oct. 1797, aged 70. V.G.

(ⁱ) This looks like a corruption of Albertsdorf. There is an Albertsdorf in
Lorraine, but perhaps this was a fancy title ; when it was obtained is unknown. V.G.

Mr. William Johnson and Lady Charlotte Pitt. She was legitimated by her father as Duchess of Albany, ([a]) by deed dat. 30 Mar. 1783, and recorded in the Parl. of Paris 6 Sep. 1784. She *d.* unm., in the Palace of Prince Giovanni Lambertini at Bologna, 17 Nov. 1789, of an abscess in the side, and was *bur.* there in the Church of St. Biagio. ([b])

See "YORK AND ALBANY," Duke of ; *cr.* 1717, *extinct* 1728.
"   "   "   *cr.* 1760, *extinct* 1767.
"   "   "   *cr.* 1784, *extinct* 1827.

DUKEDOM [U.K.]   1. *H.R.H.* LEOPOLD GEORGE DUNCAN ALBERT,
I. 1881.   PRINCE OF GREAT BRITAIN AND IRELAND, also DUKE
OF SAXONY, 4th and yst. s. of QUEEN VICTORIA, *b.*
7 Apr. 1853, at Buckingham Palace, Midx., and bap. there 28 June
following ; Matric. at Oxford (Ch. Ch.) 1872 ; P.C. 1874 ; D.C.L. Oxford
30 May 1876 ; F.S.A. 1876 ; K.G. 24 May 1869 ; K.T. 24 May 1871 ;
G.C.S.I. 25 Jan. 1877 ; G.C.M.G. 24 May 1880 ; and knight of several
foreign orders ; on 24 May 1881 he was *cr.* BARON ARKLOW, ([c]) EARL
OF CLARENCE, and DUKE OF ALBANY. Appointed Col. in the
Army and Hon. Col. 3rd Seaforth Highlanders, 1882. He *m.*, 27 Apr.
1882, at St. George's Chapel, Windsor, Helene Friederike Auguste, 5th da.
of Georg Victor, reigning PRINCE OF WALDECK AND PYRMONT, by Helene
Wilhelmine Henriette Pauline Mariane, 6th da. of Georg Wilhelm August
Heinrich Belgicus, DUKE OF NASSAU. He *d.* suddenly, at the Villa Nevada,
Cannes, in the South of France, in his 31st year, 28 Mar., and was *bur.*
5 Apr. 1884, in St. George's Chapel, Windsor. ([d])   His widow was *b.*
17 Feb. 1861, at Arolsen, in the Principality of Waldeck. Living 1909.

([a]) Her father in his will, 22 Oct. 1784, made her his universal heir :—"S.A.R. la Sig. Carlotta Stuart Duchessa d'Albany mia figlia naturale nata da me e dalla Sig. Clementina Walingshu in detto tempo ambedue in stato libero legittimata e restituita pienamente ai legittimi natali con una legittimazione plenaria per atto inserito nel Parlamento di Parigi con approvazione del Rè di Francia... gli 6 Settembre 1784." (A. von Reumont, *ut supra*, vol. ii, p. 317). (*ex inform.* G. W. Watson.) V.G.

([b]) The notice in the necrology of that church is as follows :—"1789, 17 Novembr. Carlotta ex regio sanguine Stuardo, Filia Caroli III quondam Iacobi idem III Angliae Regis, nata Leodii anno 1753, Bullonii enutrita, postea Luthetiae Parisiorum educata,... xv Kal. decembris ad primam noctis horam... regia virgo obdormivit in Domino." (A. von Reumont, *ibid.*, vol. ii, p. 321). (*ex inform.* G. W. Watson.) V.G.

([c]) A title being taken from each of the 3 Kingdoms, according to the general practice in the Royal Family since the reign of George III.

([d]) In the leading article of "*The Times*" newspaper, 29 Mar. 1884, is an appreciative notice of this amiable and cultivated young man.

II. 1884. 2 *H R.H.* Leopold Charles Edward George Albert, Prince of Great Britain and Ireland, Duke of Albany, Earl of Clarence and Baron Arklow, also Duke of Saxony, posthumous s and h., *b.* at Claremont, in Esher, Surrey, 19 July, and privately *bap.* there, 4 Aug. 1884 ; *suc.* to the peerage, as above, at his birth ; *suc.* his uncle, Prince Alfred, as Duke of Saxe Coburg and Gotha, 30 July 1900, G.C.V.O. 27 Jan. 1901 ; K.G. 15 July 1902. Knight of the Black Eagle, of the Elephant, &c. He *m.*, 11 Oct. 1905, at Glücksburg, Victoria Adelheid Helena Louise Marie Frederike, 1st da. of Frederik Ferdinand Georg Christian Carl Wilhelm, Duke of Schleswig-Holstein-Sonderburg-Glücksburg, by Victoria Frederike Augusta Marie Caroline Mathilde, 2nd da. of Frederik Christian August, Duke of Schleswig-Holstein-Sonderburg-Augustenburg. She was *b.* 31 Dec. 1885, at Grünholz in Denmark.

[*H.H.* Johann Leopold Wilhelm Albert Ferdinand Victor, Hereditary Prince of Saxe Coburg and Gotha, Duke of Saxony, s. and h. ap., *b.* 2 Aug. 1906, at the Castle of Callenberg, near Coburg.]

ALBEMARLE (ª)

DUKEDOM. 1. George Monck, (ᵇ) 2nd s. of Sir Thomas Monck, of Potheridge, Devon, by Elizabeth, da. of Sir George Smythe, of Madford in Heavitree, in that co, was *b.* at Potheridge, 6, and *bap* 11 Dec. 1608, at Lancross. His military achievements and general career are a matter of history. M.P. for Devon (Barebones Parl.) 1653, and again 1660 (having also been elected at the same time for Cambridge Univ.) until made a peer. He was one of the (62) members of Cromwell's House of Lords, being styled therein "George Monke, General in Scotland." For the active part he took in effecting the restoration of Charles II, at which time he was Commander in Chief of all the Forces for the Parl., and Joint Gen. of the Fleet, he was *nom.* by that King K.G., being el. and invested at Canterbury, 26 May 1660, and inst. 15 Apr. 1661. On 7 July 1660 he was *cr.* BARON

I.

1660.

(ª) Monck was the first person to bear precisely this title, and its history appears to be as follows. His predecessors were Earls or Dukes of Aumale, Aumarle, or Aubemarle, according to the various ways in which the word was spelt (Oswald Barron informs me that the last is the form which he has usually found in old documents.) Of these words the supposed latin equivalent employed in charters was *de Alba Marla*, and this expression was, somewhere in the 16th century, docked and anglicised into Albemarle For some remarks on mediæval English names, see vol. III, Appendix C.

(ᵇ) He bore for arms, Gules with a cheveron silver between three lions' heads razed of the same. These are the arms of the ancient Devonshire house of Monck of Potheridge, of which he became heir male on the death of his elder brother. (*ex inform.* Oswald Barron) V.G.

MONCK OF POTHERIDGE, BEAUCHAMP AND TEYES; (ª)
EARL OF TORRINGTON, Devon, and DUKE OF ALBEMAR-
LE. (ᵇ) A pension of £7000 a year, and the estate of New Hall, in Essex,
were granted to him and his heirs for ever. (ᶜ) P.C., Gent. of the Bed-

---

(ª) As to the unwarranted assumption of the title Teyes, as also that of three other
baronies, by John (Dudley), 1st Duke of Northumberland, see note under that title.

(ᵇ) "The General's title is Duke d'Albemarle (a place in Normandy belonging
to the Plantagenets from whom he derives himself), Earl of Toddington or Torrington: Viscount Coldstream, and Baron of Potheridge, his house. Coldstream is the
river in the north that lay between him and Lambert last year." (See letter from
Andrew Newport, dat. 26 June 1660. *Hist. MSS. Com.*, 5th Rep., App., p. 154.)
The explanation of these titles is by reason of the undermentioned descent; a descent,
however, which carries with it *no* representation of the titles thus taken. Alice, da.
and h. of Henry, Lord Teyes (or Tyas), *m.* Warin de Lisle. Their grandson, Warin,
Lord Lisle, left a da. and h., Margaret, who *m.* Thomas, Lord Berkeley, and had a
da. and h., Elizabeth, who *m.* Richard (Beauchamp), Earl of Warwick, and (*cr.* 1419)
Earl of Aumale. Margaret, one of the three daughters of this Earl and his said
wife, *m.* (as 2nd wife), John (Talbot), 1st Earl of Shrewsbury, and had a son, John,
cr. Viscount Lisle, 1452. His da., Elizabeth, coh. of the Barony of Teyes, *m.*
Edward Grey, *cr.* Baron and Viscount Lisle. Their da. and eventually, representative, *m.*, for her 2nd husband (the issue by her 1st husband, Edmund Dudley,
carrying away *her* representation), Arthur Plantagenet (illegit. s. of Edward IV), who
was *cr.* Viscount Lisle, 1533. Frances, one of his three daughters and coheirs (having
left issue by her 1st husband, John Basset, in whom *her* representation would vest) *m.*,
for her 2nd husband, Thomas Monck of Potheridge, the great-grandfather of George
Monck, *cr.*, as in the text, Baron Monck of Potheridge, Beauchamp and Teyes, and
Duke of Albemarle. This Frances was sister, *ex parte maternâ*, of John (Dudley),
Duke of Northumberland, who was styled, though improperly, Baron Tyas. The
Baronies indicated a descent not only from the last possessor (a life tenant) of that
title, but also (though but a bastard one) from the Royal Family, by whom alone
(with the exception of the abovenamed grant in 1419) this semi-royal Peerage had
hitherto been borne, after the extinction, in the 13th century, of the old (Norman) line
of Earls. The surname is spelt both as Monck and as Monk in the patent, though,
generally as the former, which is the spelling of the Barony *cr.* by the said patent.

(ᶜ) The following is drawn from Lord Clarendon's account of him :—"He was of
an ancient family in Devonshire, always very loyally affected, and being a yr. br., he
entered early into the life and condition of a soldier. When the troubles began in
Scotland, he betook himself to the service of the King, and was soon after sent into
Ireland, where he served with singular reputation of courage and conduct. He was
taken prisoner at Nantwich, and remained in the Tower to the end of the war, when
Cromwell prevailed upon him to engage himself again in the war of Ireland; and
from that time he continued very firm to Cromwell, who was liberal and bountiful to
him, and took him into his entire confidence. After the death of Cromwell, Monk
was looked upon as a man more inclined to the King than any other in great authority,
if he might discover it without too much loss or hazard. He had no fumes of
religion to turn his head, nor any credit with, or dependence upon, any who were
swayed by these trances." He is thus described by Lord Macaulay—"With very
slender pretensions to saintship, [he] had raised himself to high commands by his
courage and professional skill. His nature was cautious and somewhat sluggish."
Lord Clarendon also remarks that "He was cursed, after long familiarity, to marry a

chamber, Capt. Gen. and Master of the Horse, 1660.   Lord Lieut. of Ireland
1660-62.   P.C. [I.] 1661.   Lord Lieut. of Devon 1660, and of Midx. 1662;
Bearer of the Sceptre and Dove at the Coronation, 23 Apr. 1661; acting Lord
High Admiral, Mar. to June 1666.   First Lord of the Treasury, 1667-70.
He *m.*, 23 Jan. 1652/3, at St. George's, Southwark, Surrey, Anne, late, or
possibly actual, wife of Thomas RADFORD, or REDFORD, (ª) da. of John
CLARGES, a farrier in the Savoy, Strand, by his wife, Anne LEAVER.   He
d., at the Cockpit in Whitehall, 3 Jan. 1669/70, and was *bur.*, 29 Apr. 1670,
with a state funeral the next day, in Westm. Abbey.   Will dat. 8 June
1665, pr. 3 Jan. 1669/70, the day of his death.   His widow survived him
but three weeks.   She *d.* 29 Jan., and was *bur.* (nearly two months before
him) 28 Feb. 1669/70, in Westm. Abbey, aged 54.   Admon. 15 Dec.
1688 to her br., Sir Thomas Clarges.

II. 1670   2. CHRISTOPHER (MONCK), DUKE OF ALBEMARLE, EARL
   to   OF TORRINGTON and BARON MONCK, (ᵇ) only surv. s.
1688.   and h., said to have been *b.* in 1653.   M.P. for
              Devon 1667-70.   Gent. of the Bedchamber, 1670.   El.
K.G., 4 Feb. 1669/70 and inst. 28 May 1671.   Col. of a Reg. of Horse
1679, and of the 1st Horse Guards 1679-85.   P.C. 1675.   Lord
Lieut. of Devon 1675-85.   Chancellor of the Univ. of Cambridge
1682.   Recorder of Sandwich 1684, of Harwich 1685, and of Saffron-
Walden 1688.   Bearer of the Sceptre and Dove at the Coronation,
23 Apr. 1685.   High Steward of Totness; and of Colchester 1688, and

woman of the lowest extraction, the least wit, and less beauty. " According to
Pepys, 8 Mar. 1661, she was "ever a plain homely dowdy. "   He also says, 28 Dec.
1663, "I find him a very heavy dull man. "   "The Duke of A., in his drink, taking
notice, as of a wonder, that Nan Hide should be Duchess of York, 'Nay' says
Troutbeck, 'n'er wonder at that, I will tell you as great if not greater a miracle. '
And what was that but that our dirty Bess (meaning his Duchesse) should come to be
Duchesse of Albemarle. "   (*Pepys*, 4 Nov. 1666.)   Thomas, Lord Ailesbury, in his
Memoirs, written about 1729, says of him :—"He was naturally of heavy parts and
illiterate, but he supplied that by a good judgment, and secret to the last degree, and
most cautious in all his undertakings. "   V.G.

(ª) She *m.* her 1st husband 28 Feb. 1632/3, at St. Laurence Poultney, London.
He is said to have been (as was her father) a farrier, and was not improbably a s. of
that "Thomas Redford, farrier, servant to Prince Charles, " who was *bur.* 20 Nov.
1624, at St. Martin's-in-the-Fields.   She proved her father's will 1 Jan. 1648/9,
being then separated from her husband, but there is no evidence of his death before
her 2nd marriage.   See note under her burial in Col. Chester's *Registers of Westminster
Abbey.*   See also a curious account in Burke's *Extinct Peerage*, 1883, in a note under
"Monk, " as to the suit (15 Nov. 1700) of William Sherwin, the h.-at-law, *v.* Clarges.

(ᵇ) It is stated in "Pride *v.* the Earls of Bath and Montague, " in Salkeld's
Reports, vol. i, p. 120 (edit. 1795), Hilary term, 6 Will. III (King's Bench), that
"Duke Christopher was a *bastard* begotten of a woman who at the time of her marriage
with George, Duke of Albemarle, was married to another man who was then and is
yet living. "   It was objected that since Duke George and the said woman were dead,
the issue, who was dead also, could not be bastardized, who, when living, was reputed
legitimate, but the court held that this objection did not apply to bastardy of this sort.

of Barnstaple 1688. He was employed against Monmouth in June 1685, when he is said to have shewn neither capacity nor courage. He was appointed Gov. of Jamaica, 25 Nov. 1686. (ᵃ) He *m.*, 30 Dec. 1669, in the Cockpit, Whitehall, (Lic. Vic. Gen.) Elizabeth, 1st da. and coh. of Henry (Cavendish), 2nd Duke of Newcastle, by Frances, da. of the Hon. William Pierrepont. He *d.* in Jamaica, *s.p.s.*, 6 Oct. 1688, and was *bur.*, 4 July 1689, in Westm. Abbey, when *his honours* became *extinct.* Will dat. 4 July 1687. His widow (who was *b.* 22 Feb. 1654) *m.*, 8 Sep. 1692, as his 2nd wife, Ralph (Montagu), 1st Duke of Montagu, who *d.* 9 Mar. 1708/9. She was well known as " the mad Duchess. " She *d. s.p.s.*, at Newcastle House, Clerkenwell, Midx., 28 Aug., and was *bur.* 11 Sep. 1734, in Westm. Abbey, aged 80, or, according to the journals of the day, 96. Admon. 4 Nov. 1734.

Note.—So popular was this title of Albemarle, that, in 1661 (only a year after it had been conferred on George Monck), on the petition of John (Granville), Earl of Bath (so *cr.* 20 Apr. 1661), " the King passed a warrant, under the privy seal, whereby he obliged himself and recommended it to his successors, that, in case of failure of male issue to Gen. Monck, the title of Duke of Albemarle should descend to the said Earl of Bath and be continued in his family. " (See Heylin's *Help to English History*, 1783, p. 183.) In 1688 this event happened. The validity of the King's warrant had expired with his Majesty in 1685, so that a royal recommendation to his successor was all that remained; however, as will be seen below, this recommendation was acted upon, as far as it was in his power to do so, by the titular King James III, in 1721.

TITULAR DUKEDOM. I. 1696.	1. Henry Fitz-James, 2nd s. and yst. of the five illegit. children of James II, by Arabella Churchill, spinster, sister to John, Duke of Marlborough, and only da. of Sir Winston Churchill, was *b.* Aug. 1673.

At the age of 16 he was made Col. of a reg. of infantry, which he headed at the battle of the Boyne. In 1695, he and his br., the gallant Duke of Berwick, were *outlawed.* He was commonly known as " the

---

(ᵃ) " *An Expostulation* " addressed to him contains these lines :—
" Let a disbanded peer, kicked out of Court,
And made some upstart statesman's common sport,
Sneak like a dog, and beg he may be sent
With a great character to banishment. "
A note to *Absalom and Achitophel*, part ii, is more complimentary. " Son to the brave General Monk, and President of Wales. He was liberal, loyal, and a leading man among the friends of the King and the Duke. " Of his wife her father writes, 16 Mar. 1682/3 :—" I saw, when my daughter Albemarle was here, she was not mad, but there was a great consternation upon her, I suppose caused by her own folly and pride, and the malice of others. " V.G.

Grand Prior." On 13 Jan. 1696, he was *cr.* by his father James II (when in exile), DUKE OF ALBEMARLE, EARL OF ROCHFORD, AND BARON OF ROMNEY, (ª) and was placed in command of the Toulon fleet designed to invade England. He was, in 1702, made a Lt. Gen. and Admiral in France. He *m.*, 20 July 1700, Marie Gabrielle, only child of Jean D'AUDIBERT, COUNT OF LUSSAN, in Languedoc, by Marie Françoise, da. of Henri RAIMOND, SEIGNEUR DE BRIGNON, also in Languedoc. (ᵇ) He *d. s.p.m.s.,* (ᶜ) 16/27 Dec. 1702, at Bagnols in Languedoc. His widow *m.,* (ᵈ) at St. Eustache, Paris, 25 May 1707 (without the knowledge and much to the displeasure of her parents), John (DRUMMOND), 2nd EARL (*titular* DUKE) OF MELFORT [S.], who *d.* 29 Jan. 1754. She, who was *b.* about 1675, *d.* 15 May 1741, at St. Germain en Laye.

II. 1721.   1. GEORGE (GRANVILLE), BARON LANSDOWN, (1712) was *cr.*, by the titular King James III, 6 Oct. 1721, as "George Granville Esq," LORD OF LANSDOWN, Devon, VISCOUNT OF [—] co.[—], and EARL OF BATH, Somerset [E.,] with *rem.* to his heirs male, and on 3 Nov. following, as " George Granvill, commonly called LORD LANSDOWN, EARL OF CORBEIL AND LORD THORIGNI AND GRANVILLE in France and Normandy," he was *cr.* BARON LANSDOWN OF BIDEFORD, Devon, VISCOUNT BEVEL, EARL OF BATHE, MARQUIS MONK AND FITZHEMON, and DUKE OF ALBEMARLE [E.], with a *spec. rem.* failing heirs male of his body, to his br. Bernard and the heirs male of his body. (ᵉ)   He *d. s.p.m.*, 8 Jan. 1734/5. (ᶠ)

III. 1735   2. BERNARD (GRANVILLE), titular DUKE OF ALBEto   MARLE &c., nephew and h. under the *spec. rem.*, being 1776.   1st s. of Bernard G. of Buckland, co. Gloucester, by Mary, da. of Sir Martin WESTCOMBE, 1st Bart. (1700), which last named Bernard was yr. br. of the late Duke. He was *b.* 1700 ; served in the Army ; *suc.* his father 8 Dec. 1723, and his uncle 11 years later. He *d.* unm., at Calwich, co. Stafford, 2 July 1776, when the Dukedom, and other honours *cr.* 3 Nov. 1721, became extinct, but those conferred on 6 Oct. of that year devolved on his h. male.

EARLDOM, &c.   1. ARNOLD JOOST VAN KEPPEL, HEER VAN DER Voorst in Guelderland, BARON VAN KEPPEL, s. and h. I. 1697.   of Osewolt VAN KEPPEL, of the same (who *d.* 1685),

---

(ª) For a list of Jacobite Peerages see Appendix F at the end of this vol.

(ᵇ) See *Anselme*, vol. ix, p. 243.

(ᶜ) He had one da., Marie, a nun, who was living 20 June 1707. V.G.

(ᵈ) According to *Anselme, ut supra,* (1733), she " se remaria à — Mahoni, Colonel Irlandois. Ce mariage fut tenu caché, afin qu'elle pût conserver le titre duchesse d'Albemarle. " No confirmation has been found of this story. If she did marry Mahony, it must have been as her 2nd husband. V.G.

(ᵉ) There is a long preamble setting forth the promise made by Charles II to the Granville family, mentioned on p. 90.

(ᶠ) For fuller particulars see *sub* LANSDOWN OF BIDEFORD.

by Reinira Anna Gertruyde, da. of Johan VAN LINTELLO TOT DE MARS.
He was *b.* 1670, and attended the Prince of Orange, in 1688, to England
as a page of honour, who, soon after his accession to the throne of England
(as William III), made him (1691) Groom of the Bedchamber 1691-95, and
Master of the Robes 1695-97. He also granted him an enormous amount
of forfeited Irish lands, though Keppel was then but a handsome lad,
under age, who had rendered no service whatever to his adopted country. (ᵃ)
He attended the King in his several campaigns, and (having been in 1692
admitted into the Knighthood of Zutphen, and, subsequently, into that of
Holland and West Friesland), was, on 10 Feb. 1696/7, *cr.* BARON
ASHFORD, of Ashford, Kent ; VISCOUNT BURY, co. Lancaster ; and
EARL OF ALBEMARLE. (ᵇ) Major Gen. 1697. Col. of 1st troop of

(ᵃ) " Keppel had a sweet and obliging temper, winning manners and a quick,
though not a profound, understanding. Courage, loyalty, and secrecy, were common
between him and Portland." See Macaulay's *History of England*, where also it is
mentioned that of nearly three-quarters of the 1,700,000 acres that had been forfeited
in Ireland, " though a small part had been bestowed on men whose services to the
state well deserved a much larger recompence " (*e.g.*, the Earl of Athlone and the
Earl of Galway), the rest had been given to " the King's personal friends. Romney
had obtained a considerable share of the royal bounty. But of all the grants the
largest was to Woodstock, the eldest s. of Portland ; the next was to Albemarle. An
admirer of William cannot relate without pain that he divided between these two
foreigners an extent of country larger than Hertfordshire. " The facts are as follows.
To his discarded concubine, to six foreigners, and three others, the upright monarch
allotted over 600,000 acres in Ireland, besides an immense acreage in England of which
no precise estimate is available. It is not surprising that Parl. should have refused to
sanction all these grants, which were without parallel since the reign of Ric. II.
The list of the principal grants is as under :—

	acres
Viscount Woodstock, (s. and h. ap. of the Earl of Portland)	133,820
Arnold van Keppel, afterwards *cr.* Earl of Albemarle	108,634
Elizabeth Villiers, afterwards Countess of Orkney	95,649*
Richard Coote, *cr.* Earl of Bellomont	77,291
Henry Sydney, afterwards *cr.* Earl of Romney	49,518
William Nassau de Zulestein, afterwards *cr.* Earl of Rochford	39,871
Henri de Ruvigny, afterwards *cr* Earl of Galway	36,148
Godert de Ginkell, afterwards *cr.* Earl of Athlone	26,481
Marquis de Puissar	25,753
Lady Gravemore	21,006
* Valued at £337,943 ! Total	614,171

Of the above grants even more outrageous than that to his mistress, is the colossal
donation to the young Dutchman, Keppel, with which the Royal Corydon rewarded
the public (?) services of a handsome lad then barely of age, who was shortly after to
be adorned with an English Earldom. No wonder that Portland was jealous, that
mutinous Tories talked of Piers Gaveston, and that even Macaulay is driven to express
the above pained disapprobation of his hero's conduct. V.G.

(ᵇ) The late Lord Braybrooke (1825-58) states [erroneously] that he was *cr.*

Horse Guards, 1698/9-1710. El. K.G., 14 May, inst. 5 June 1700.
Having just returned from a special embassy to the Hague, he was present
at the death of the King, 8 Mar. 1701/2, (who bequeathed to him 200,000
guilders), after which event he retired to Holland, and took his seat among
the Nobles of the States General. He was appointed Gen. of their forces,
and was in command at Ramillies in 1706, at Oudenarde, 1708, &c. On
16 Apr. 1705, he was cr. LL.D. by the University of Cambridge. He was
defeated when fighting for the Imperialists at Denain, 13/24 July 1712,
and taken prisoner by the French. He m., 15/26 June 1701, at the
English church at the Hague, in Holland, Gertrude de Quirina, da. and
h. of Adam VAN DER DUYN, Lord of St. Gravenmoer in Holland, and
Master of the Buckhounds to William III. He d. (ª) 19/30 May 1718,
aged 48, at the Hague, and was bur. there. (ᵇ) Will. dat. 29 May 1718,
pr. 13 July 1721. His widow d. Dec. 1741, also at the Hague. Admon.
5 June 1742 to her son, the 2nd Earl.

II. 1718. 2. WILLIAM ANNE (VAN KEPPEL), EARL OF ALBEMARLE,
&c., only s. and h., b. at Whitehall, 5, and bap. 16 June
1702, at St. Martin's-in-the-Fields, the Queen (Anne) being his Godmother. He was educated in Holland, and was a Gen. in the service of
the United Provinces. Capt., with rank of Lieut. Col., in 1st Reg. of Foot
Guards, 25 Aug. 1717. Lord of the Bedchamber to the Prince of Wales,
Oct. 1722, which office he still held after the Prince's accession, till 1751.
K.B., 18 May 1725, on the revival of that order, but resigned in 1749 for
the Garter. Aide-de-camp to the King, 1724-34. Col. of 3rd troop of
Horse Guards, 4 June 1733. Gov. of Virginia, 26 Sep. 1737-54. Brig.
Gen. 2 July 1739; Maj. Gen. 20 Feb. 1741/2; Lieut. Gen., 26 Feb. 1744/5;
Col. Coldstream Guards 1744-54. He was at the battles of Dettingen (1743),
Fontenoy (1745), and Culloden (1746) ; after which he was, on 23 Aug.
1746, made Commander-in-Chief of the forces in Scotland. AMBASSADOR TO
FRANCE, 1749-54. El. K.G., 22 June 1749; inst. by proxy, 12 July 1750.
Groom of the Stole 1751-54. P.C. 12 July 1751. On 30 Mar. 1752,
he was one of the Lords Justices during the King's absence in Germany.

" Earl of Albemarle in Normandy, " adding, " the title having been doubtless selected
as one so frequently enjoyed by persons of the highest consideration, and not in any way
resting upon an hereditary claim." See N. & Q., 1st Ser., vol. ii, p. 466. Doubtless
this was the idea, though why Keppel was entitled to the highest consideration, does not
appear so clearly. The case was different (as regards merit) with Gen. Monck, and (as
regards pre-eminence) with all the previous holders. The grantee is in the patent styled
" Arnoldus Justus de Keppel, " and in the docquet " Arnold Joost van Keppel. "

(ª) " He is grown the gentleman of most application in the service, the most
affable and obliging in his behaviour, the best husband and most regular man in his
living that is in the States dominions ; only continues pretty expensive in his equipage
and housekeeping. " (J. Drummond to Robert Harley, 9 Dec. 1710.) He was,
according to Macky (when about 30 years old) " Beautiful in his person, " and a
few years earlier Bishop Burnet calls him " a cheerful young man. " V.G.

(ᵇ) The Keppels, Earls of Albemarle, bear arms of Gules with three scallops
silver. (ex inform. Oswald Barron.) V.G.

He *m.*, 21 Feb. 1722/3, at Caversham, Oxon, Anne, 2nd da. of Charles (LENNOX), 1st DUKE OF RICHMOND, by Anne, Dowager BARONESS BELASYSE, da. of Francis BRUDENELL, *styled* LORD BRUDENELL. He *d.*, suddenly, in his coach, after supper, at Paris, 22 Dec. 1754, and was *bur.* 21 Feb. 1755, in the Chapel in South Audley Str., Grosvenor Sq., Midx. Admon. 15 Feb. 1758, to a creditor. (ᵃ) His widow, who was *b.* 24 June 1703, and was one of the Ladies of the Bedchamber to Queen Caroline, *d.* 20 Oct. 1789, in New Str., Spring Gardens, Midx. Will pr. Nov. 1789.

III. 1754.   3. GEORGE (KEPPEL), EARL OF ALBEMARLE, &c., s. and h., *b.* 5 Apr., and *bap.* 4 May 1724, at St. Martin's-in-the-Fields. M.P. for Chichester, 1746-54. Served in the army under the Duke of Cumberland, to whom he was Lord of the Bedchamber. In command of the 20th Foot, 1 Nov. 1749. Major Gen., 1 Feb. 1756 ; Lieut. Gen., 1 Apr. 1759 ; Gen., May 1772. Col. of the King's own Reg. of Dragoons, 1755-72. P.C. and Keeper and Gov. of Jersey, 28 Jan. 1761. Commander-in-Chief at the reduction of the Havannas in 1762. El. K.G., 26 Dec. 1765 ; inst. 25 July 1771. He *m.*, 20 Apr. 1770, at Bagshot Park, in the parish of Windlesham, Surrey, Ann, yst. da. of Sir John MILLER, of Chichester, 4th Bart., by Susan, da. of Matthew COMBE, of Winchester, M.D. He *d.*, of inflammation of the bowels, 13, and was *bur.* 22 Oct. 1772, at Quidenham, Norfolk, aged 48. (ᵇ) Will pr. Oct. 1772. His widow *d.* 3 July 1824. Will pr. Feb. 1825.

IV. 1772.   4. WILLIAM CHARLES (KEPPEL), EARL OF ALBEMARLE, &c., only s. and h., *b.* 14 May, and *bap.* 8 June 1772, at St. Geo., Han. Sq. Master of the Buckhounds 1806-7. P.C. 1830. Master of the Horse 1830-34, and again 1835-41. G.C.H. (Civil), 1833. (ᶜ) He *m.*, 1stly, 9 Apr. 1792, at St. Geo., Han. Sq., (he 20, and she 16) Elizabeth, 2nd da. of Edward (SOUTHWELL), LORD DE CLIFFORD, by Sophia,

---

(ᵃ) "What made our friend, Lord Albemarle, Col. of a Regt. of Guards, Governor of Virginia, Groom of the Stole, and Embassador at Paris ?... It was his airs, his address, his manners, his graces." (Chesterfield's *Letters*, vol. ii, p. 253.) " His figure was genteel, his manner noble and agreeable." (Hor. Walpole, *Memoirs of Geo. II*, vol. i, p. 82.) " He was *par excellence* what is called a *galant homme*, noble, sensible, generous, full of loyalty, frankness, politeness, and goodness ; he united what is best and most estimable in the characters of English and French." (Marmontel's *Memoirs*, vol. i, p. 342.) V.G.

(ᵇ) He bought this estate for £63,000. He was one of 15 children, his next br. being the well-known Admiral, Viscount Keppel. He appears in 1769, (" Americanus and Eliza") [Mrs Anne *(sic)* G...N...R] among the notorious *tête à tête* portraits in *Town and Country Mag.* A good account of these by Horace Bleakley is in *N. & Q.*, 10th Ser., vol. iv, pp. 241-2.

(ᶜ) The Duke of Sussex writes to Coke of Norfolk in 1833, " you will laugh when I tell you that the King took Albemarle by surprise, and has made him a *Knight of the Thistle.* I do not think the members of the House enjoyed it, but it could not be helped." Albemarle had no connexion by blood or estate with Scotland, so apparently the King's blunder *was* helped by making him G.C.H. instead. V.G.

3rd da. of Samuel CAMPBELL. She was *b.* 11 Jan. 1776, and *d.* 14 Nov 1817, in labour of her 15th child, at Mr. Coke's, Holkham, Norfolk, and was *bur* at Quidenham. Admon. Nov. 1832. He *m.*, 2ndly, 11 Feb. 1822, in Upper Grosvenor Str , Charlotte Susannah, da. of Sir Henry HUNLOKE, 4th Bart., by Margaret, da. of Wenman COKE, of Longford, co. Derby. He *d.* 30 Oct. 1849, at Quidenham afsd., aged 67. Will pr Feb. 1850. His widow *d.* 1 *s p.*, 13 Oct. 1862, at Twickenham, aged about 85.

[WILLIAM KEPPEL, *styled* VISCOUNT BURY, s. and h. ap. by 1st wife, *b.* 1 Mar. and *bap.* 3 Apr. 1793, at St. James's, Westm.; *d. v p.*, 9 Apr. 1804, in Berkeley Sq., aged 11, and was *bur.* at Quidenham]

V. 1849.   5. AUGUSTUS FREDERICK (KEPPEL), EARL OF ALBEMARLE, *&c*, 2nd, but 1st surv. s and h. by 1st wife, *b* 2 June 1794 ; sometime an Officer in the 1st Reg Foot Guards, receiving the Waterloo medal   M.P. for Arundel, 1820-26. He *m.*, 4 May 1816, (spec. lic.) Frances, da. of Charles STEER, of Chichester, by Mary WOOD, of Jamaica   He *d s.p.*, 15 Mar. 1851, having been insane since some time before Dec. 1849. Admon. Mar. 1860. His widow *m.* (as his 2nd wife), 20 Aug. 1860, at Ashridge, Herts, Lieut. Col. the Hon. Peregrine Francis CUST, who *d.* 15 Sep. 1873. She *d. s.p.*, 16 May 1869, at the Hôtel de l'Europe, Lyons, France. Will pr. 30 June 1869, under £30,000.

VI. 1851.   6. GEORGE THOMAS (KEPPEL), EARL OF ALBEMARLE, br. and h., *b.* 13 June 1799, in Marylebone. Ed at Westm. School. Entered the 14th Foot, Apr. 1815, and served at Waterloo. Major Gen., 1858 ; Lieut Gen., 1866 ; Gen., 1874   Sheriff of co. Leitrim 1838. M.P. for East Norfolk, 1834-35 ; for Lymington, 1847-50. Private Sec. to Lord John Russell (when Premier), 1846-47; sometime Equerry to H.R.H. the Duke of Sussex. Groom in Waiting 1838-41.(ª) Author of *Memoirs of the Marquess of Rockingham, Fifty Years of my Life,*(ᵇ) *&c.* F.A.S., F.G.S., *&c.* He *m.*, 4 June 1831, at Willesden, Midx., Susan, 3rd da. of Sir Coutts TROTTER, 1st Bart., by Margaret, da. of the Hon. Alexander GORDON, 3rd s. of William, 2nd EARL OF ABERDEEN [S.]. She *d.* 3 Aug. 1885, at Lyndhurst, Hants, aged 79. He *d.* 21 Feb. 1891, at 8 Portman Sq., Marylebone, in his 92nd year, and was *bur.* at Quidenham.

VII. 1891.   7. WILLIAM COUTTS (KEPPEL), EARL OF ALBEMARLE, *&c.*, s. and h. ap., *b.* 15 Apr. 1832, in London. Ed. at Eton. Ensign and Lieut. 43rd Foot, 1843. Lieut. Scots Guards, 1848-53. Aide-de-Camp to Lord Frederick Fitz-Clarence in India ; retired, 1853. *Styled* VISCOUNT BURY 1851-91. M P. for Norwich, 1857-59 ; for Wick Burghs, 1860-65 ; for Berwick, 1868-74. Superintendent of Indian affairs

---

(ª) " His voice is loud, his manner confident and somewhat overbearing. " (*Gent. Mag.* Feb. 1857.)

(ᵇ) A review thereof, as to Westminster School, *&c*, is in *N & Q.*, 3rd Ser., vol. vii, p. 461.

for Canada, 1854-56. P.C., 1859. Treasurer of the Queen's Household, 1859-66. Lieut. Col. of the Civil Service Rifle Volunteers, 1860.
K.C.M.G., 24 Aug. 1870. On 6 Sep. 1876 he was *sum.*, *v.p.*, to the House
of Lords in his father's BARONY OF ASHFORD. Under Sec. for War, 1878-
80, and 1885-86. Was received into the Church of Rome, Easter Sunday,
13 Apr. 1879. Volunteer Aide-de-Camp to the Queen, 1881. He *m.*,
15 Nov. 1855, at Dundrum, Canada West, Sophia Mary, da. and coh. of
Sir Allen Napier McNab, of Dundrum, Bart. (sometime Prime Minister of
Canada), by his 2nd wife, Mary, da. of John STUART, Sheriff of Johnstown
district, Upper Canada. He *d.* of paralysis, 28 Aug. 1894, aged 62, and
was *bur.* at Quidenham. His widow living 1909.

VIII. 1894.   8. ARNOLD ALLAN CECIL (KEPPEL), EARL OF ALBE-
                   MARLE, VISCOUNT BURY and BARON ASHFORD [1697], 1st
s. and h., *b.* 1 June 1858, in Sloane Str., Chelsea ; ed. at Eton ; sometime
Lieut. Scots Guards ; Lieut. Col. Com. Civil Service Rifles (Vol.) ; *styled*
VISCOUNT BURY, 1891-94; M.P. for Birkenhead, 1892-94. He *m.*, 4 Jan.
1881, Gertrude Lucia, only child of Wilbraham (EGERTON), 1st EARL
EGERTON, by Mary Sarah, 1st da. of William Pitt (AMHERST), 2nd EARL
AMHERST OF ARRACAN. She was *b.* 9 Jan. 1861.

[WALTER EGERTON GEORGE LUCIAN KEPPEL, *styled* since 1894, VIS-
COUNT BURY, 1st s. and h. ap., *b.* 28 Feb. 1882. Lieut. Scots Guards ;
A.D.C. to Gov. Gen. of Canada, 1904. He *m.*, 9 June 1909, at St.
Margaret's, Westm., Judith Sydney Myee, 4th da. of Charles Robert
(WYNN-CARRINGTON), 1st EARL CARRINGTON, by Cecilia Margaret, 1st da.
of Charles (HARBORD), 5th BARON SUFFIELD. She was *b.* 27 Sep. 1889.]

Family Estates.—These, in 1883, consisted of about 7,500 acres in
Norfolk, and about 2,500 in co. Leitrim ; the former being worth about
£7,300 and the latter about £1,000, making a total of about £8,300
a year. *Principal Residence.*—Quidenham Hall, near Attleborough, Norfolk.

ALBINI or D'ALBINI, see DAUBENY

ALBION

TITULAR EARLDOM [I.]	1. "SIR EDMUND PLOWDEN, EARL OF AL-BION," so styled in the margin of his will, dat. 29
I. 1640 ? to 1659.	July 1655, pr. 27 July 1659. In the body of the said will he describes himself as "Sir Edmund PLOWDEN of Wansted, co. Southampton, Knt., Lord, EARL PALATINE, Governor and Capt.-Gen. OF
THE PROVINCE OF NEW ALBION in America, and a PEER OF	

THE KINGDOM OF IRELAND." (ª)   In this will (which is signed
"ALBION") he states that "I am seized of the Province and County
Palatine of New Albion as of free Principality and held of the Crown of
Ireland *of which I am a Peer*, (ª) which Honour, and Title and Province,
as ARUNDELL and many other Earldoms and Baronies, is assignable and
saleable with the Province and County Palatine as a local Earldom." (ᵇ)
He was 2nd s. of Francis PLOWDEN, of Plowden in Lidbury, Salop, by
Mary, da. of Thomas, and sister of Sir Richard FERMOR, of Somerton,
Oxon.   He was knighted in Ireland by the Lords Justices, 25 Dec.
1630.   He *m.* Mary, da. and h. of Peter MARRINER, of Wansted afsd.,
by Dorothy, his wife.   He *d.* July 1659.   His wife survived him.   Their
2nd s., THOMAS PLOWDEN, *suc.* under his father's will to "*the Province
and Earldom of Albion*," and he, by will, dat. 16 May, and pr. 10 Sep.
1698, left it to his 3rd s., FRANCIS PLOWDEN, who went out there to
prosecute his right, and *d.* in Maryland.   His descendants registered their
pedigree in 1774 at the College of Arms, London, but the *style* or *title* of
EARL OF ALBION seems *never* to have been assumed after 1659.

ALBUERA AND DUNGARVAN

See "BERESFORD OF ALBUERA AND DUNGARVAN," co. Waterford, Barony
(*Beresford*), *cr.* 1814 ; *extinct* with the VISCOUNTCY OF BERESFORD 1854.

ALCESTER

BARONY.   1. FREDERICK BEAUCHAMP PAGET SEYMOUR, G.C.B., 2nd,
I. 1882   but 1st surv. s. and h. of Col. Sir Horace Beauchamp SEY-
   to   MOUR, K.C.H. (who was s. of Admiral Lord Hugh SEYMOUR,
1895.   5th s. of Francis, 1st MARQUESS OF HERTFORD), by his 1st
               wife, Elizabeth Malet, da. of Sir Lawrence PALK, 2nd Bart.,
was *b.* 12 Apr. 1821, in Bruton Str., Midx. ; ed. at Eton ; entered the
Royal Navy, Jan. 1834 ; served in the Burmese War, 1852-53 ; in the
White Sea, 1854 ; in the Black Sea, 1855-56 ; in New Zealand, where he
was severely wounded, 1860-61 ; Rear Admiral 1870 ; commanded a de-
tached squadron, 1870-72 ; Junior Lord of the Admiralty, 1872-74, and
1883-85 ; commanded the Channel Squadron, 1874-77 ; Vice Admiral 1876 ;
Admiral 1880, and Commander-in-Chief of the Mediterranean Squadron,

(ª) There appears to be no authority for the existence of any Irish Peerage
either of the name of " ALBION " or of " PLOWDEN " but he may have considered
that he was a peer of Ireland, as holding a palatine earldom " of the crown of
Ireland. "   V.G.

(ᵇ) On 30 Oct. 1654, as "Sir Edmund Plowden, Earl of Albion, " he presented
Ezekiel Lawrence to the benefice of Luffam, (? Lasham) Hants.   (Loose sheets at
Lambeth Library.)

1880-83; in command at the destruction of the forts of Alexandria, 1882; C.B.,
16 July 1861 ; K.C.B., 2 June 1877 ; G.C.B., 24 May 1881 ; had Royal
lic., on 16 Nov. 1882, to accept the First class of the Order of Osmanieh ;
and, finally, on 24 Nov. 1882, was, as a reward for his distinguished services,
cr. BARON ALCESTER([a]) of Alcester, co. Warwick.   He was introduced
into the House on 12 Apr. 1883 by Lord Harlech and by (his companion
in the Egyptian campaign) Lord Wolseley.   Shortly afterwards he received
the freedom of the City of London, and the sum of £25,000 by vote of Parl.
in lieu of the usual annual grant.   D.C.L. Oxford 1885.   He *d.*, unm.,
at 22 Ryder Str., St. James's, aged 73, ([b]) 30 Mar. and was *bur.* 3 Apr.
1895, at Woking Cemetery, when the title became *extinct.*

ALDBOROUGH (co. Suffolk.)

"ALDBOROUGH co. Suffolk " Barony (*von der Schulenberg*), *cr.*
1722 with the EARLDOM OF WALSINGHAM, which see ; *extinct* 1778.

ALDBOROUGH (Ireland.)

VISCOUNTCY [I.]   1. JOHN (STRATFORD), BARON BALTINGLASS [I.],
                      was *b.* 1698, at Ormond, co. Tipperary ; ent. Trin.
I. 1776.   Coll. Dublin, 8 May 1715, aged 17.   He was
                      3rd s. of Edward STRATFORD, of Baltinglass, co. Wick-
EARLDOM [I.]   low, and of Belan, co. Kildare (who is said to have
I. 1777.   refused a Peerage from Will. III) by his 1st wife,
                      Elizabeth, da. of Euseby BAISLEY of Ricketstown, co.
Carlow; was Sheriff of Kildare 1727, of Wicklow 1736, and of Wexford 1739;
M.P. for Baltinglass, 1721-63 ; and on 21 May 1763, was *cr.* BARON
OF BALTINGLASS, co. Wicklow [I.], and on 22 July 1776 ([c]) was *cr.*
VISCOUNT ALDBOROUGH of Belan, co. Kildare [I].   On 9 Feb. 1777,
he was *cr.* "VISCOUNT AMIENS and EARL OF ALDBOROUGH
of the Palatinate of Upper Ormond " [I.]. ([d])   He *m.* Martha, da. and

---

([a]) For his arms see *sub* HERTFORD Marquessate.

([b]) He was a capable naval officer, and being a smart, dressy, genial man, was
known among his friends as " the swell of the ocean. "   V.G.

([c]) For a list of the profuse creations and promotions in the Irish Peerage in
1776, see vol. iii, Appendix H.

([d]) This creation has been compared with the enrolment in Chancery [I.].
The choice of the name of Amiens for a Peerage title is accounted for by referring
to a fulsome account of the ancestry of the family of Stratford (which, in *Lodge*
begins only in 1660) given in Owen, Davis, and Debrett's *Peerage*, 1790, vol. iii,
p. 156.   Here it is stated that the ancestor of the Stratford race, one "Gualtera [*sic*] de
Lupella, vulgarly called Lovel or Tonci, " came " from Amiens the capital of Picardy
in France, to England with William the Conqueror, &c. "   It may interest the
reader to know (on the same unquestionable authority) that " the arms of the noble
peer [Earl of Aldborough] are the same as those of Alexander the Great, &c., &c. "

coh. of the Ven Benjamin O'NEALE, Archdeacon of Leighlin, by Hannah, da. and coh. of Col Joshua PAUL. He *d.* 29 June, and was *bur.* 4 July 1777, aged 86. Will pr. in Prerog. Court [I] 1778. His widow *d* 11 Mar 1796, at her house in Kildare Str., Dublin, after a lingering illness, in her 90th year. Will pr. [I.] as "Countess Dowager," 1802.

EARLDOM [I.]   2. EDWARD, or EDWARD AUGUSTUS, (STRATFORD), EARL OF ALDBOROUGH, &c., s. and h. M.P. (Whig interest) for Taunton, Somerset, 1774, but was un-seated on petition, for bribery ; and for Baltinglass [I.] 1759-68, and 1775-77. A Governor of co. Wicklow 1778 ; F.R.S. May 1777 ; Hon. D.C.L. Oxford 3 July 1777. He voted in favour of the Irish Union in 1800. He *m*, 1stly, 29 July 1765, (spec. lic) at St. Geo., Han Sq, Barbara, 2nd da. and h. of the Hon. Nicholas HERBERT, of Great Glemham, Suffolk (7th s. of Thomas, 8th EARL OF PEMBROKE), by Anne, da. and coh of Dudley NORTH, of Great Glemham afsd. She, who was *b.* July 1742, *d. s.p.*, 11 Apr. 1785, of apoplexy, aged 42, and was *bur* at Glemham. M.I. Admon. 1788. He *m*, 2ndly, 24 May 1787 (spec. lic.) in the house of the Dowager Duchess of Chandos, in Grosvenor Sq., Anne Elizabeth, (a fortune of £50,000) only da. of John (HENNIKER), 1st LORD HENNIKER [I], by Anne, 1st da. and coh of Sir John MAJOR, 1st Bart. He *d. s.p.*, 2 Jan. 1801, aged about 60, at Belan, co. Wicklow, and was *bur* in St. Thomas's, Dublin.(ª) Will dat. 14 Sep. to 5 Oct. 1800, pr. Jan. 1803. His widow *m.*, Dec 1801, George POWELL, Barrister at Law, and *d. s.p.* at Aldborough House, Dublin, 14 July 1802. Admon. Jan. 1803.

VISCOUNTCY [I.]

II 1777.

III. 1801.   3. JOHN (STRATFORD), EARL OF ALDBOROUGH, &c. [I.], br. and h., M.P. for co. Wicklow 1776-90 ; for Baltin-glass, 1763-76 and 1790-1800 (ᵇ) A Governor of co. Wicklow 1795. He *m.*, Apr. 1777, Elizabeth, da. and h. of the Rev. Frederick HAMILTON (a grandson of William, DUKE OF HAMILTON [S.]), Archdeacon of Raphoe and Vicar of Wellingborough, Northants, by Rachel, da. of (———) DANIEL, of Ireland. He *d. s.p.m*, 7 Mar. 1823, at Belan, co. Kildare. His widow *d.* 29 Jan. 1846, at her hotel in Paris. (ᶜ)

IV. 1823.   4. BENJAMIN O'NEALE (STRATFORD), EARL OF ALD-BOROUGH, &c. [I.], br. and h. male, being 4th s. of the 1st Earl. A Governor of co. Wicklow 1777. M.P. for Baltinglass 1777-83 and 1790-1800. He *m.*, (lic. from Consistory Court, Dublin) 10 Jan. 1774, Martha, only da. and h. of John BURTON, of St. Anne's,

---

(ª) He was noted for his ability and eccentricity. V.G

(ᵇ) When Sir John Blaquiere writing of him says, "The support and gratitude of this very honourable family never to be depended upon." V.G.

(ᶜ) *Gent. Mag.* gives a circumstantial account of her death, at Bath, about May 1811, from an abscess, and adds that she had been a Dublin toast, and the best horse-woman in Ireland. V.G.

Dublin, by Sarah, sister and coh. of Mason Gerard, da. of Jonathan GERARD, of Dublin, brewer. She *d* 24 Aug. 1816. He *d.* at Stratford Lodge, 11, and was *bur* 12 July 1833, at Baltinglass, aged 87.

V. 1833.   5. MASON GERARD (STRATFORD), EARL OF ALDBOROUGH, &c. [I], s. and h., *b* 8 July 1784 He *m*, 2 Aug. 1804, at Kircudbright, Cornelia Jane, (ª) 1st da. of Charles Henry TANDY, of Waterford, by Cornelia, da. of Samuel KING, of Dublin, shoemaker. They were divorced *a mensâ et thoro* by decree of the Arches Court of Canterbury, 6 Dec. 1826. Some months earlier he established another lady in her stead, and *m.* (or rather went through the form of marriage with), 23 Sep 1826, at the British Embassy (ᵇ) Paris, Mary, (ᶜ) da of Samuel ARUNDELL (decd.), of Dursley, co. Gloucester, by Adriana, his wife. The Earl *d.* at Leghorn, 4, and was *bur.* there 8 Oct. 1849, aged 65. Will dat. Leghorn, 13 July 1849. His widow (Cornelia Jane) *d.* at a great age, 5 Aug. 1877, at Mulgrave Terrace, Kingstown, co. Dublin. Will dat 2 Sep. 1875, pr. in Dublin 3 Sep. 1877, under £12,000.

VI. 1849   6. BENJAMIN O'NEALE (STRATFORD), EARL OF ALD-
to   BOROUGH, VISCOUNT ALDBOROUGH, VISCOUNT AMIENS and
1875.   BARON OF BALTINGLASS [I], s. and h., *b.* 10 June 1808 at
Dublin ; sometime Capt. 15th Light Dragoons, retired 1842. His claim as an Irish Peer was allowed June 1854. He *d.* unm., 19 Dec. 1875, at Alicante, in Spain, when all his honours became *extinct*. Admon. 1 Mar. 1876 to his mother Cornelia Jane, Dowager Countess of Aldborough, widow.

Chief estates.—These were at Belan, co. Kildare, at Baltinglass, co. Wicklow, and at Mount Neale, co. Carlow. Stratford Lodge, in Balting-

(ª) "The readiest, quickest person in conversation, I have ever seen, was she quieter she would be more agreeable ; the truth is however, she knows too well the imprudences of her past life, and she is fighting for her place in Society by the perpetual exercise of her talents (*Creevey Papers*, Sep 1817) V G.

(ᵇ) The marriage entry runs, "The Hon. Gerard Mason Stratford, commonly called Viscount Amiens, *bach.*, with Mary Arundell of Chelsea, Midx., Spinster, a minor with consent of mother "

(ᶜ) In June 1854, she, as "Mary, widow of Mason Gerard, Earl of Aldborough," opposed, unsuccessfully, the claim of the 6th Earl to the Peerage, on behalf of her son, Henry Stratford. Having failed to establish the validity of her marriage, she was known henceforward as "Mrs. Gerard," and lived with her numerous family at Florence. She *d* about 1876 *The case of Mary Countess of Aldborough* was published. In this the will of the 5th Earl (as above) is quoted, wherein he alleges that he "never was married to a Miss Tandy, " and that his issue by her are "natural children, " and that he has "no legitimate child but those of Mary Arundell, Countess of Aldborough, " to whom and to whose children he leaves everything. A document sealed up with the will in an envelope (opened 19 Feb. 1850), states that, "before I ever saw Miss Tandy I was married to Miss Maria Teresa Devenport, who was then alive. " By his own showing the Earl must have been an exceptional scoundrel and bigamous betrayer of women under cover of pretended marriage.

lass, was built by the 3rd Earl ; while the 2nd Earl, about 1780, "founded in the center of one of the principal streets of Westm. [Oxford Street] *Stratford Place*, one of the principal ornaments of the metropolis ; and erected a superb edifice for his residence at the upper end of the street and square, which form a cul-de-sac." See Owen's *Peerage*, 1790. He appears also to have founded a town in co. Wicklow, called Stratford-upon-Slaney.

ALDEBURGH or ALDBROUGH (ª)

BARONY. 1. Sir William Aldeburgh, of Aldeburgh, now Ald-
I. 1371. brough, in Richmondshire, (ᵇ) s. and h. of Sir Ives A., of the
same, by Mary, his wife. (ᶜ) He was sometime *valettus*
to Edward Balliol, King of Scotland. (ᵈ) In 1364, Sir Robert de l'Isle of Rougemont enfeoffed him and Elizabeth, his wife, of the manor of Harewood, co. York. (ᵉ) He was sum. to Parl. 8 Jan. (1370/1) 44 Edw. III

(ª) The advance over previous accounts, in accuracy and completeness, of this article, and the notes thereon, are due to G.W. Watson, who has unreservedly placed his store of knowledge at the disposal of the Editor V.G.

(ᵇ) Aldbrough-juxta-Tees, near Stanwick, wapentake of Gilling West. (see p. 102 note "a" as to their arms) A distinct family of Aldeburgh, who bore entirely different arms, viz , Az a fesse Arg. between 3 cross crosslets Or (Ped. in Foster's *Yorkshire Visitations*, p. 279), took their name from Aldborough, near Boroughbridge, Claro wapentake, in the church of which place there is a well known brass to the memory of one of them The two families are nearly always confused with each other. V.G

(ᶜ) (i) Mary, widow of Sir Ives de A , gave to William, her s., lands in A. — 22 Edw. III. (ii) William, s. of Sir Ives de A , gave to John, s of William de Moubray, and to Margaret, John's wife, his manor of A. in Richmondshire ·—26 Edw. III. Seal.—A lion rampant charged with a fleur de lis. (*Glover's Collections*, Harl. MSS., no. 245, f. 147). (iii) Edw III confirmed to William, s. and h of Ives de A , lands in *Brokesmouth*, co. Roxbury, which Edward Balliol, King of Scotland, had given to Ives :—13 Nov 1347 (*Scottish Rolls*, 21 Edw III, m. 1). V.G.

(ᵈ) He is termed " vallettus magnifici principis Edwardi de Balliolo regis Scotie consanguinei nostri carissimi, " 22 Jan. 1350/1 to 6 Sep. 1352, and *miles* of the sd. King, 6 Aug 1353. (*Scottish Rolls*, 24-27 Edw. III, *passim*). The arms of Balliol were set up at Harewood Castle, where they still exist. V G

(ᵉ) Inq whether it would be to the detriment of the King or of others that Robert de l'Isle of Rougemont kt should enfeoff William de Aldeburgh kt. and Elizabeth his wife of two parts of the manor of Harewood, which he held in chief · and should concede that the third part of the sd. manor, which Maud, late the wife of John de l'Isle of Rougemont, father of Robert, held in dowry, should remain after Maud's death to William and Elizabeth (Writ 18 May 38 Edw. III, Inq 1 June following—Ch *Inq. ad quod damnum*, file 351, no. 16) Robert de l'Isle paid £70 *pro licencia feoffandi* the two parts of the manor, 16 June 1364. (*Fine Roll*, 38 Edw III, m 3). Most genealogists assume that Elizabeth was sister of Robert, though Ralph Brooke (*Discoverie of certaine Errours in the Britannia*, 1596, p 66) denies this, and says that she was sister of John, Robert's father But there is no known authority for either relationship The arms of L'Isle, and those of Aldeburgh (as above), occur among those seen by Glover at Harewood. (Foster, *ut supra*, pp. 466-8). V.G

to 8 Aug. (1386) 10 Ric. II, by writs directed *Willelmo de Aldeburgh'*, whereby he is held to have become LORD ALDEBURGH. (ᵃ)   His wife *d.* in or before 1378.   He *d.* 1 Apr. 1388. (ᵇ)

II. 1388.   2. Sɪʀ Wɪʟʟɪᴀᴍ Aʟᴅᴇʙᴜʀɢʜ, of Harewood, only s. and h., aged 30 and more at his father's death.   He was never sum. to Parl.   He *m.* Margery, widow of Peter ᴅᴇ Mᴀᴜʟᴀʏ *le septiesme*, and 2nd da. and coh. of Sir Thomas Sᴜᴛᴛᴏɴ, of Branceholme Castle and Sutton in Holderness, by Agnes, his wife. (ᶜ)   He *d. s.p.*, 20 Aug. 1391.   Will dat. 14 Nov. 1390, pr. 6 Sep. 1391.   His widow *d.* 10 Oct. following.   Will dat. 22 Sep. 1391, pr. 19 Oct. 1391. (ᵈ)   Both were *bur.* in the Church of the Friars Preachers at York. (ᵉ)   At his death any hereditary Barony, that may be held to have existed, fell into abeyance.

His coheirs in 1392 were his 2 sisters. (1) Elizabeth, aged 28 and more, widow of Sir Brian Stapleton (who was s. and h. ap. of Sir Brian Stapleton of Carlton, co. York, but *d. v.p.*).   She *m.*, 2ndly, between 7 Sep. 1393 and 16 July 1399, Sir Richard Redman, of Levens, co. Westmorland.   She *d.* 21 Dec. 1417, leaving Brian Stapleton her grandson and h.   Her husband *d.* 22 May 1426, leaving Richard Redman his grandson and h. (2) Sibyl, aged 25 and more, wife of Sir William Ryther, of Ryther, co. York, who *d.* about 1426.   She *d.* 3 Sep. 1439, leaving Sir William Ryther her s. and h. (ᶠ)   The Redmans and Rythers held Harewood in undivided moities for about 150 years.

(ᵃ) He sealed in 1363 with his arms of a lion rampant, and the same device is seen over the old gateway of his Castle of Harewood.   His descendants, the Redmans, quartered for Aldeburgh the arms of Gules a lion silver, with a fleur de lys azure on the shoulder.   (*ex inform.* Oswald Barron).   As to the distinct family of Aldeburgh and their arms see p. 101 note "b."   V.G.

(ᵇ) Inq., cos. York and Linc., 5 May and Monday after the Ascension (11 May) 1388 (writs *diem cl. ext.* 22 Apr. 11 Ric. II).   The jurors say "quod Willelmus de Aldeburgh senior chivaler obiit primo die Aprilis anno regni Regis Ricardi undecimo. Et quod Willelmus de Aldeburgh junior chivaler filius ipsius Willelmi de Aldeburgh senioris est heres ejusdem Willelmi propinquior et etatis triginta annorum et amplius." (Ch. *Inq. p.m.*, Ric. II, file 49, no. 3).   V.G.

(ᶜ) *Patent Rolls*, 28 Aug. 1395, 19 Ric. II, pars i, m. 1d.   V.G.

(ᵈ) His will, dated "Lunedy le xiiijme jour de Novembre" 14 Ric. II, and his wife's, dated "in die veneris proxime ante festum Michaelis ᴍᴄᴄᴄxᴄɪ," directing her burial with him at the Friars Preachers at York, are printed in *Test. Ebor.* (Surtees Soc.), vol. i, nos. 108, 122.   V.G.

(ᵉ) Their names occur in the list of those *bur.* in that Church (*Coll. Top. et Gen.*, vol. iv, pp. 76, 77, from *MSS. Coll. Arms*, L8).   Besides these, mention is made of "Elizabeth de Aldeburogh jadiz dame de Harwode" and of "Richart Redman chlr.   The former entry refers to the wife of the first William and not to his da., who, after her 2nd marriage, was called Elizabeth Redman.   There is a tomb at Harewood ascribed to Sir Richard Redman and his wife.   V.G.

(ᶠ) Inq., cos. Linc. and York, Thursday after St. Hilary (18 Jan.) and 16 May 1392 (writs *diem cl. ext.* 18 Oct. 15 Ric. II).   The jurors say "quod Willelmus de Aldeburgh chivaler obiit xx die Augusti ultimo preterito et quod Elizabetha que

ALDENHAM

BARONY.   1. Henry Hucks Gibbs, of Aldenham House, Herts,
I. 1896.   and Clifton Hampden, Oxon, 1st s. and h. of George
                  Henry Gibbs, of the same, senior partner in the firm of
"Antony Gibbs & Sons," Merchants of London (d. 21 Aug. 1842, aged
56), by Caroline da of the Rev. Charles Crawley, Rector of Stowe-nine-
Churches, Northants (br. of Sir Thomas Crawley-Boevey, Bart.), was
b. 31 Aug. 1819, in Powis Place, St Geo. the Martyr, Midx., and bap
4 Oct. at Stowe afsd. , ed. at Rugby and at Ex Coll., Oxford ; B.A. and
3rd class classics, 1841 ; M.A., 1844 ; partner (senior partner in 1875) of
the said house of "Antony Gibbs & Sons", a director and sometime
(1875-77) Governor of the Bank of England , F G.S. ; F S.A ; High
Sheriff of Herts, 1884 ; M P. (Conserv. interest) for London, 1891-92, and
was cr, 31 Jan 1896, BARON ALDENHAM (ª) of Aldenham, Herts,

---

fuit uxor Briani de Stapilton junioris chivaler et Sibilla quam Willelmus de Ryther
chivaler duxit in uxorem fuerunt sorores ipsius Willelmi de Aldeburgh et quod
sunt heredes ipsius Willelmi propinquiores.   Et dicunt quod dictus Willelmus de
Ryther et Sibilla uxor ejus habent prolem inter se legitime procreatam.   Et dicunt
quod dicta Elizabetha est etatis xxviij annorum et amplius et dicta Sibilla etatis xxv
annorum et amplius " (ii) By Inq , co York, 16 May 1392 (writ diem el ext
18 Oct 15 Ric. II), the jurors say " quod Margeria [que fuit uxor Willelmi de
Aldeburgh chivaler] obiit decimo die mensis Octobris ultimo preterito sine herede
de corpore suo per prefatum Willelmum de Aldeburgh. "   (Ch. Inq. p. m., Ric. II,
file 69, no 2)   (iii) By Inq , co York, 1 Mar 1433/4, (writ 5 Feb 12 Hen VI),
the jurors say " quod Elizabetha [que fuit uxor Ricardi Redeman militis] obiit
vicesimo primo die Decembris anno regni domini H nuper Regis Anglie patris domini
Regis nunc quinto   Et quod Brianus de Stapilton est filius et heres Briani de
Stapilton militis ac consanguinrus et heres propinquior predicte Elizabethe videlicet
filius et heres prefati Briani filii ejusdem Elizabethe   Et dicunt quod idem Brianus
filius prefati Briani fuit viginti et unius annorum et amplius die veneris proximo post
festum sancti Leonardi ultimo preterito [13 Nov.].   Et ulterius dicunt quod Ricardus
Redeman miles nuper vir prefate Elizabethe [vixit] usque vicesimum secundum diem
Maii anno regni domini Regis nunc quarto quo die prefatus Ricardus obiit. "
(Ch Inq p m, Hen. VI, file 63, no. 18). (iv) By Inq , co. York, 10 Sep 1426
(writ diem cl. ext. 8 Sep 5 Hen VI), the jurors say " quod [Ricardus Redman miles]
obiit die mercurie in septimana Pentecostes ultimo preterito [22 May].   Item
dicunt quod Ricardus Redman filius Mathei Redman militis est consanguineus dicti
Ricardi Redman militis et heres ejus propinquior videlicet filius predicti Mathei filii
predicti Ricardi Redman militis   Et fuit etatis novem annorum in festo sancti
Martini in yeme ultimo preterito et amplius [11 Nov]. " (Ch. Inq p. m, Hen VI,
file 28, no. 28). (v) By Inq , co York, Saturday after St. Michael (3 Oct) 1439
(writ diem cl. ext. 9 Sep. 18 Hen VI), the jurors say " quod Sibilla [Rither nuper
uxor Willelmi Rither militis] obiit die jovis proximo ante festum Nativitatis beate
Marie Virginis ultimo preterito et dicunt quod Willelmus Rither miles est filius et
heres predicte Sibille propinquior et etatis lx annorum et amplius. " (Ch. Inq p m ,
Hen. VI, file 101, no. 68). V.G.

(ª) Lord Aldenham bears arms of Silver three battle-axes sable with a border

being introduced 11 Feb. 1896. (*)   Trustee of the Nat. Portrait Gallery 1891-1907.   He *m.*, 6 May 1845, at Thorpe, Surrey, Louisa Anne, (ᵇ) 3rd da. of William Adams, LL.D., Fellow of the College of Advocates, Doctors Commons, London, by Mary Anne, (ᶜ) 3rd da. of the Hon. William Cockayne, (ᵈ) of Rushton Hall, co. Northampton, niece and coh. of Borlase, 6th Viscount Cullen [I.].   She, who was *b.* at 36 Southampton Row, 10 Sep. and *bap.* 9 Nov. 1818, at St. Geo., Bloomsbury, *d.* at St. Dunstan's, Regent's Park, 17, and was *bur.* 21 April 1897, at Aldenham, aged 78.   He *d.* at Aldenham, 13, and was *bur.* there 18 Sep. 1907, aged 88.   Will dat. 19 Mar. to 28 Aug. 1906, pr. Dec. 1907, over £703,700 gross. (ᵉ)   He was *suc.* by his s. and h., who is outside the scope of this work.

Family Estates.—These, in 1909, consisted of 3035 acres in Herts ; 1,309 in Oxon, 107 in Midx, and 21 in Berks.   *Total.*—4,472 acres, worth £9,438 a year.   *Principal Seat.*—Aldenham House, near Elstree, Herts.

See "Acton of Aldenham, Salop," Barony (*Acton*), cr. 1869.

ALDERHURST

See "Thring of Alderhurst, Surrey," Barony (*Thring*), cr. 1886.

---

nebuly sable.   The like arms without the border were borne by Gibbes of Venton in Devonshire, with whom the Aldenham family were connected, but from whom their descent is not established.   (*ex inform.* Oswald Barron.)   V.G.

(ᵃ) This was one of no less than 8 introductions on the same date, *viz.*, 1 Earl (Carrington), 1 Viscount (Peel of Sandy), and 6 Barons (Burghclere of Walden, James of Hereford, Glenesk, Rathmore of Shanganagh, Pirbright, and Aldenham).

(ᵇ) Her yst. br., George Edward Cokayne (formerly Adams), *b.* 29 Apr. 1825, was the original compiler of this work, and her 3rd s., Vicary Gibbs, *b.* 12 May 1853, is responsible for the 2nd edition.   V.G.

(ᶜ) She was granted, by Royal Warrant, dated 4 Sep. 1838, the precedency of the da. of a Viscount.

(ᵈ) In the time of his father (the 5th Viscount, who enjoyed that title above 86 years,) 1716, the spelling was altered from Cokayne to Cockayne.

(ᵉ) The Bp. of St. Albans, in an address at Hitchin, 30 Oct. 1907, says of him:— " Rarely are so many gifts and graces combined in a single person...   Rare culture, princely liberality, and admirable judgment were the embellishments, known and read of all men, of a character that was above all things essentially Christian.   It is for the deep humility, the earnest devotion, the fervent faith, the large charity, the loving churchmanship of the man that we specially thank God. "   In person he was tall, dark, handsome, and of fine presence ; in manners, bright, gracious, and unassuming ; in intellect, quick and versatile, having a brain stored with varied information which he would impart in the most pleasant and modest fashion ; in character, loyal, gentle, and affectionate.   He had a remarkable memory and gift for languages, and made a special study of philology, and of currency questions.   A staunch, outspoken Churchman and Tory, he yet contrived to maintain the friendliest relations with those who differed from him in opinion.   V.G.

ALDERLEY

See " STANLEY OF ALDERLEY, co. Chester, " Barony (*Stanley*), *cr.* 1839.

ALDERNEY

i.e., " ALDERNEY " Barony (*Prince of Great Britain, &c.*), *cr.* 1726, with the DUKEDOM OF CUMBERLAND, which see ; *extinct* 1765.

ALDITHLEY, see AUDLEY

ALDWORTH

See " TENNYSON OF ALDWORTH, Sussex, " Barony (*Tennyson*), *cr.* 1884.

ALEMOOR

i.e., " ALEMOOR AND CAMPCASTELL, " Barony [S.] (*Scott*), *cr.* 1660 with the EARLDOM OF TARRAS [S.], which see ; *extinct* 1693.

ALESBOROUGH *rectius* AYLESBOROUGH

ALEXANDER

The style of " Viscount Alexander " is used by the heir apparent of the Earls of Caledon [I.], whose surname is Alexander. These Earls, however, are not entitled to a Viscountcy of *Alexander*, but to a Viscountcy of *Caledon* [I.], *i.e.*, one of the same name as the Earldom ; See " CALEDON " Earldom [I.], *cr.* 1801.

ALEXANDER OF TULLIBODY

i.e., " ALEXANDER OF TULLIBODY, " Barony [S.] (*Alexander*), *cr.* 1630 with the VISCOUNTCY OF STIRLING [S.], and again 1633 with the EARLDOM OF STIRLING [S.], which see ; *dormant* since 1739.

ALEXANDRIA

i.e., " HUTCHINSON OF ALEXANDRIA AND KNOCKLOFTY, co. Tipperary, " Barony (*Hely-Hutchinson*), *cr.* 1801 ; see " DONOUGHMORE " Earldom, [I.], *cr.* 1800, under the 2nd Earl ; *extinct* (the Earldom, etc., remaining) 1832.

ALFORD

i.e., "ALFORD, co. Lincoln," Barony (*D'Auverquerque*), *cr.* 1698 with the EARLDOM OF GRANTHAM, which see ; *extinct* 1745.

---

i.e., "ALFORD, co. Lincoln," Viscountcy (*Cust*), *cr.* 1815 with the EARLDOM OF BROWNLOW, which see.

ALFORD(a)

TITULAR   1. John GRÆME, 1st s. and h. of James GRÆME (Sol.
EARLDOM.   Gen. for Scotland 1688), by Elizabeth, da. of Robert
I. 1760.   MORAY of Abercairney, was *cr.* a Bart. 6 Sep. 1726 by
James III, in reward for his services at the Court of
Vienna.   Chief Sec. of State, Apr. 1727.   On 20 Jan. 1760 he was *cr.*
Lord and Peer of Parl. as LORD NEWTON, VISCOUNT OF
FALKIRK, and EARL OF ALFORD [I.].   He *d. s.p.,* 3 Jan. 1773,
in the Scots College, Paris, when, apparently, his titles became *extinct.* (b)

ALINGTON OF KILLARD AND ALINGTON OF WYMONDLEY(c)

BARONY [I.]   1. WILLIAM ALINGTON, of Horseheath, co. Cambridge,
I. 1642.   and of Great Wymondley, Herts, (d) 4th s. and 9th child,
but only surv. s. and h. of Sir Giles A. of the same, by

(a) For a list of Jacobite Peerages, see Appendix F. at the end of this vol.
(b) His br. David G. in Scotland was his heir. V.G.
(c) Much help in rewriting this article has been given by G.W. Watson. V.G.
(d) The Lord of the manor of Great Wymondley is entitled to the office of
CHIEF CUPBEARER at the Coronation, it having been granted (at least so it is said)
on this tenure, by Will. I to Guy, *filius Teconis,* whose da. and h. brought it in marriage, *temp.* Stephen, to John de Argentine.   However this may be, it is certain that
Richard d'Argentine held Great Wymondley, *temp.* John, by the serjeantry of serving
with a silver cup at the King's Coronation (*Red Book of the Exchequer,* p. 507).
Richard d'Argentine, and Giles, his s. and h., subsequently held the same by a like
service (Ch. *Inq. p. m.,* 31 Hen. III, file 5, no. 12, and 11 Edw. I, file 33, no. 16).
Wymondley passed by an heiress, *temp.* Hen. VI, to the family of Alington.   The
service was performed by William, the 3rd Lord [I.] at the coronation of Charles II,
and by Hildebrand A. (afterwards the 5th Lord), on behalf of his nephew Giles,
the 4th Lord [I.], at the coronation of James II.   The manor (and office) continued
(save for a space of some 20 years or so after 1691) in the family of Alington
till the death of the last Lord in 1722/3, when it passed to his 3 nieces and coheirs,
the sisters of his nephew, the preceding Lord.   Sir Richard Grosvenor, Bart.,
husband of Diana, da. and h. of Sir George Warburton, Bart., by Diana, one of

his 1st wife, (ª) Dorothy, da. of Thomas (CECIL), 1st EARL OF EXETER, was *bap.* 14 Mar. 1610/1, at Horseheath, and *suc.* his father, who was *bur.* there 23 Dec. 1638 On 28 July 1642, he was *cr* BARON ALINGTON OF KILLARD, co. Cork [I.] (ᵇ) He *m.* (post nuptial settlt. 1 Oct. 1631) Elizabeth, da. of Sir Lionel TOLLEMACHE, 2nd Bart , by Elizabeth, da. of John (STANHOPE), 1st LORD STANHOPE OF HARRINGTON. He was *bur.* 25 Oct. 1648, at Horseheath. His widow *m* , about 1651, the Hon Sir William COMPTON, who *d.* 18 Oct. 1663. She was *bur.* at Horseheath, 14 Apr 1671 Will dat. 5 Apr 1669, pr. 17 Apr. 1671.

II. 1648   2. GILES (ALINGTON), BARON ALINGTON OF KILLARD
                      [I.], 2nd, but 1st surv. s. and h. He *d.* a minor and
unm., and was *bur.* at Horseheath, 20 Mar. 1659/60.

---

these 3 coheirs, (in right of ¼ of the manor inherited by his wife and of the other ¾ acquired by purchase), performed the office at the coronation of Geo. II, and it was again performed by his nephew Richard, 1st Lord Grosvenor, at the coronation of Geo III. In 1767, however, his Lordship sold the estate, when this honourable office, which had been some 350 years in his family, passed into the hands of strangers See Clutterbuck's *History of Hertfordshire*, vol. ii, pp 537-544

(ª) His 2nd wife, (another) Dorothy, da. of Michael Dalton (whom he *m.* 2 Dec. 1630, at West Wratting, co. Cambridge, he aged 58, she 24), was his niece, *i.e.* the da. of his half-sister, Mary (2nd wife of the said Michael), which Mary was da. of his (Sir Giles') mother, Margaret, by her 2nd husband, Edward Elrington. Several pedigrees mistake this *Sir* Giles A. for his 2nd son, Giles A , who *d.* in Feb 1613/4 at the age of twelve. "Sir Giles Alington was censured and fined in the Star Chamber £32,000, [*rectius*, Eccl. Ct. High Com. £12,000.] only for marrying the da. of his sister by the half blood He paid the fine to Sir Thomas Hutton, a young courtier." (Ch. Caesar's Commonplace Book, cited in *Clutterbuck*, vol. ii, p 540). He did penance in 1631. On 7 Jan. 1633/4 the offenders had "pardon for incest, provided they shall not hereafter cohabit." (Privy Seal, 48th *Rep.* Dep. Keeper, p. 491) [*ex inform* J. H. Round] The lady *d.* of the small pox before 24 Sep. 1638, the date of her husband's will. V.G.

(ᵇ) Though Irish peers, none of these Lords was ever in Ireland. As regards the creations, by the Stuart Sovereigns, of Peers who had no connexion with Ireland, the following extract from the *Lords' Journals* [I], 1 Aug 1634, is worthy of observation.—

"The Lords of the committee of Privileges being this day met, upon reading a Draught of a Petition to be presented unto His Majesty for making such noblemen as are resident in England liable to all publick charges and payments taxed by Parliament in this Kingdom, from whence the Titles of their Honours are derived, it is thought fit and so ordered, that His Majesty's Attorney General, with the advice of some of the Judges, shall reduce the contents of the said Petition, ready to be presented to the House tomorrow morning, to an Act, with limitation that every Earl deriving his Honour from this Kingdom, shall within two years next after this present Parliament, purchase in this Kingdom three Hundred Pounds pr. annum at least, and every Viscount Two hundred and fifty Pounds pr annum at least, and every Baron Two hundred Pounds pr. annum at least, with a clause therein contained that upon their Defaults of purchasing as aforesaid their Honours derived from this Kingdom to be void and annihilated to all intents and purposes whatsoever." Of course nothing further was heard of this attempt to curtail the Royal Prerogative. [*ex inform.* G. D. Burtchaell]. V.G.

III. 1660. 3 and 1. WILLIAM (ALINGTON), BARON ALINGTON OF
BARONY [E.] KILLARD [I.], br. and h., M.P. for Cambridge 28 Mar.
1. 1682. 1664 to 28 Mar. 1681. He served the Emperor against
the Turks in Hungary, &c. Was made Col. of a
regiment of foot, 13 June 1667. (ª) Major-Gen. of
the Land Forces, 1 May 1678. Constable of the Tower of London,
23 Apr. 1679-85. Lord Lieut. of co. Cambridge, 9 Mar. 1680/1-85. On
5 Dec. 1682 he was raised to the English Peerage, being cr. BARON
ALINGTON OF WYMONDLEY, (ᵇ) Herts. He m., 1stly, Catha-
rine, da. and h. of Henry STANHOPE, styled LORD STANHOPE (s. and h. ap. of
Philip, 1st EARL OF CHESTERFIELD), by Catharine, suo jure COUNTESS OF
CHESTERFIELD. She d. s.p., in childbed, 19 Nov., and was bur. 4 Dec. 1662,
at Horseheath. He m., 2ndly (Lic. Fac. Off. 30 July 1664, he about 30,
she about 16), Juliana, da. of Baptist (NOEL), 3rd VISCOUNT CAMPDEN, by
his 3rd wife, Hester, 2nd da. and coh. of Thomas (WOTTON), 2nd LORD
WOTTON, and sister of Catharine, COUNTESS OF CHESTERFIELD, abovenamed.
She was bap. 4 Feb. 1645/6, at Kensington, Midx.; d. s.p.m., 14 Sep. 1667,
and was bur. at Horseheath. Admon. 2 Dec. 1667 to her husband. He
m., 3rdly (Lic. Fac. Off. 5 July), 15 July 1675, (ᶜ) at Hackney, Midx.,
Diana, widow of Sir Greville VERNEY, da. of William (RUSSELL), 1st DUKE
OF BEDFORD, by Anne, da. and h. of Robert (CARR), EARL OF SOMERSET.
He d., suddenly, of apoplexy, at the Tower of London, 1, and was bur.
17 Feb. 1684/5, at Horseheath. Will dat. 16 May 1684, pr. 6 May 1685.
His widow d. at her house in Kensington, 13, and was bur. 24 Dec. 1701,
at Horseheath. Will. dat. 14 Feb. 1700/1, pr. 19 May 1702.

BARONY [I.] 4 and 2. GILES (ALINGTON), BARON ALING-
IV. TON OF KILLARD [I.], and BARON ALINGTON OF
WYMONDLEY [E.], 2nd, but 1st surv. s. and h.,
BARONY [E.] } 1685. by 3rd wife, b. 4 and bap. 20 Oct. 1680, at
II. Horseheath; (ᵈ) Ed. at Eton, where he d.,
young and unm., 18, and was bur. 22 Sep. 1691,
at Horseheath, when the English Peerage, i.e.
the BARONY OF ALINGTON OF WYMONDLEY, cr. 1682, became extinct.
Admon. 17 Oct. 1691 to his mother.

BARONY [I.] 5. HILDEBRAND (ALINGTON), BARON ALINGTON OF
V. 1691 KILLARD [I.], uncle and h. male, bap. 3 Aug. 1641, at
to Horseheath. Capt. in Lord Alington's Foot, 13 June
1723. 1667, and in Lord Huntingdon's, 20 June 1685. He d.
unm. 11, and was bur. 25 Feb. 1722/3, at Wethersfield,

(ª) "A young, silly Lord," writes Pepys, 17 Mar. 1667. V.G.
(ᵇ) The Lords Alington of Wymondley bore arms of Sable with a bend engrailed
between six billets silver. (ex inform. Oswald Barron.) V.G.
(ᶜ) "Lady Diana Verney will not have Lord A., some think she will marry
Lord Buckhurst." (Letter of E. Cholmeley to Lady Harley, 12 Apr. 1673.) V.G.
(ᵈ) His name appears as 'absent' in a list of peers present in, and absent from,
the Parl. [I.] of James II in May 1689, for which see vol. iii, Appendix D. V.G.

Essex, when the Irish Peerage, *i.e.* the BARONY OF ALINGTON OF KILLARD [I.], *cr.* 1642, became (also) *extinct.* Will. dat. 1 July 1685, pr. 3 Apr. 1723.

ALINGTON OF CRICHEL

BARONY   1. HENRY GERARD STURT, of Crichel, Dorset, s. and h.
I. 1876.   of Henry Charles S., of the same (sometime M.P. for
              that co.), by Charlotte Penelope, 2nd da. of Robert
(BRUDENELL), 6th EARL OF CARDIGAN, and sister and coh. of John Thomas, the 7th Earl. He was *b.* 16 May 1825, at Crichel. Ed. at Eton and at Ch. Ch., Oxford. *Suc.* his father 14 Apr. 1866. Was M.P. for Dorchester, 1847-56; and for Dorset, 1856-76. On 15 Jan. 1876 (ᵃ) he was *cr.* BARON ALINGTON OF CRICHEL, (ᵇ) Dorset. (ᶜ) He *m.*, 1stly, 10 Sep. 1853, his 1st cousin, Augusta, 1st da. of George Charles (BINGHAM), 3rd EARL OF LUCAN [I.], by Anne, 6th and yst. da. of Robert (BRUDENELL), 6th EARL OF CARDIGAN abovenamed. She, who was *b.* 7 Feb. 1832, *d.* 3 July 1888, at Alington House. He *m.*, 2ndly, 10 Feb. 1892, at St. Paul's, Knightsbridge, Evelyn Henrietta, da. of Henry Blundell LEIGH, 2nd s. of John Shaw LEIGH, of Luton Hoo, Beds. He *d.* at Crichel 17, and was *bur.* there 22 Feb. 1904. Will pr. above £43,000, leaving a set of waistcoat buttons to the King, and £100 to the Queen. He was well known in the sporting world. He was *suc* by his son, who is outside the scope of this work.

Family estates.—These, besides some small property (under 100 acres in each county) in Hants, Herts, Oxon, and co. Cambridge, consisted, in 1883, of about 15,000 acres in Dorset, and about 2,500 in Devon. Total about 17,500 acres, of the yearly value of about £24,000. The extremely valuable estate at Hoxton, Midx., derived by descent from the family of Pitfield, is not included. *Principal Residence.*—Crichel, near Wimborne, Dorset.

ALITH

i.e. "OGILVY OF ALITH and Lintrathen, co. Forfar" Barony [S.] (*Ogilvy*), *cr.* 1639 with the EARLDOM OF AIRLIE [S.], which see.

(ᵃ) As to the 8 creations in 1876, see note *sub* GERARD OF BRYN.

(ᵇ) Lord Alington of Crichel bears arms of Vert a fesse gold between three running colts silver, with three roses gules on the fesse, arms which were granted in 1691 to his ancestor, Anthony Sturt of London, whom Peter le Neve describes as "a meal man first, after a commissioner of excise." (*ex inform* Oswald Barron.) V.G.

(ᶜ) He was a descendant and co-representative of the former Lords Alington, through Catherine, 3rd da. (and eventually coh) of William, 3rd Lord [I] and 1st Lord [E.]. She *m.*, 28 Aug. 1694, Sir Nathaniel Napier, of More Crichel, Dorset, 3rd Bart., and their da. Diana (who became, in her issue, their sole h.), *m.* Humphrey STURT, of Horton, Dorset, great-great-grandfather of the said H.G. Sturt, *cr.* Lord Alington, in 1876, as above.

ALLANSON

i.e. "ALLANSON AND WINN of Aghadoe, co. Kerry," Barony [I.]
(Winn), *cr.* 1797, with the EARLDOM OF HEADLEY [I.], which see.

ALLEN AND ALLEN OF STILLORGAN

VISCOUNTCY [I.]   1. JOHN ALLEN of Stillorgan, co. Dublin, s. and
BARONY [I.]   h. of Sir Joshua A. of Mullynahack, near Dublin,
      Merchant and sometime (1673) Lord Mayor of that
I. 1717.   city, by Mary, (*d. c.* 1708) sister of Richard WYBROW,
      of co. Chester, Capt. of Horse in Ireland, and da. of
John WYBROW, of cos. Kerry and Limerick, was *b.* 13 Feb. 1660/1, in
Dublin. Ent. Trin. Coll., Dublin, 24 Nov. 1677, aged 16. Sheriff of co.
Dublin 1691, and *suc.* his father 8 July 1691. He was Capt. in the army
on the side of William III ; M.P. for co. Dublin 1692-93, for co. Carlow
1695-99, for co. Dublin again 1703-13, for co. Wicklow 1713-14, and for
co. Dublin again 1715-17. On 9 Oct. 1714, he was made P.C., and on
28 Aug. 1717 was *cr.* BARON ALLEN OF STILLORGAN, co. Dublin,
and VISCOUNT ALLEN in co. Kildare [I.]. (ª) He *m.*, (Lic. Prerog. I,
23 July) in 1684, Mary, sister of Robert, 19th EARL OF KILDARE [I.], and
1st da. of the Hon. Robert FITZGERALD, by Mary, da. and h. of James
CLOTWORTHY. She was *b.* 22 Aug. 1666, and was living 19 Aug.
1697. (ᵇ) He *d.* in London, 8, and was *bur.* 19 Nov. 1726, at St. James's,
Dublin. Will pr. Nov. 1726.

II. 1726.   2. JOSHUA (ALLEN), VISCOUNT ALLEN, *&c.* [I.], s. and
      h., *b.* 17 Sep. 1685, in Dublin. Ent. Trin. Coll., Dublin,
as Fellow Commoner, 1 July 1701. LLD. 1718. M.P. for co. Kildare
1709-26. Took his seat 28 Nov. 1727. He *m.*, 18 Nov. 1707, at Westminster, Margaret, da. of Samuel DU PASS, of Epsom, Surrey, first clerk in
the Secretary of State's office, by Dorothy, da. of Edward ELLIS, who contributed £24,000 to Charles II in his exile. He *d.* at Stillorgan, 5, and
was *bur.* 8 Dec. 1742, at St. James's, Dublin. Will pr. Apr. 1743. His
widow, who was *b.* in St. James's Rectory, Piccadilly, Midx., *d.* at Duke
Str., 4, and was *bur.* 9 Mar. 1758, in that parish. Will dat. 20 July
1754, 6 July and 9 Dec. 1755, pr. 24 Nov. 1758.

III. 1742.   3. JOHN (ALLEN), VISCOUNT ALLEN, *&c.* [I.], only
      surv. s. and h. M.P. for Carysfort 1733-42. On 29 Oct.
1743, he took his seat. He *d.* unm., 25 May 1745, "of a wound
received in a rencounter with one of the Guards at Dublin whom he shot."
Will pr. 1745, in Dublin.

(ª) The preamble to this creation is printed in *Lodge*, vol. v, p. 184.
(ᵇ) See will of that date of Elizabeth Mossom, widow, pr. in Dublin, 1698, as
quoted in *N. & Q.*, 3rd Series, vol. vi, p. 187.

IV. 1745.   4. JOHN (ALLEN), VISCOUNT ALLEN, &c. [I.], cousin
and h male, (ª) being s. and h. of the Hon. Richard A
(3rd and yst. s. of the 1st Viscount), by Dorothy, da and coh of Major
Samuel GREEN, of Killaghy, co. Tipperary.   He was Capt. of a troop of
horse ; M.P. for co. Wicklow 1742-45.   He took his seat in the House
of Lords [I.] 9 Oct. 1745.   After taking an active part against the Government, he retired from public life, and lived secluded at Punchestown,
co. Kildare.   He d. unm., 10 Nov. 1753, " at his seat near Naas, in
Ireland. "   Will pr. 1754.

V. 1753.   5. JOSHUA (ALLEN), VISCOUNT ALLEN &c., [I.], br. and
h., b. 26 Apr. 1728, took his seat 26 Nov. 1753.   Capt.
37th Regt., under Prince Ferdinand of Brunswick, during the campaigns
of 1758-60 ; was wounded at Minden in 1759.   Capt. 1st Regt. of Foot
Guards, 1763-75.   M.P. for Eye, Suffolk, 1762-70.   Obtained a pension
of £600 a year in 1770.   He m., 5 Aug. 1781, in Dublin, Frances, 1st da.
of Gaynor BARRY, of Dormstown, co. Meath, by Anne, da. of the Rev.
Richard RICHARDS, Rector of Killany, co. Monaghan.   He d. 1 Feb. 1816,
in Merrion Sq., Dublin.   His widow d. in Lower Grosvenor Str., 11, and
was bur. 20 Aug. 1833, at St. James's, Westm., aged 74.   Will pr.
Aug. 1833.

VI. 1816   6. JOSHUA WILLIAM (ALLEN), VISCOUNT ALLEN AND
to   BARON ALLEN OF STILLORGAN [I.], only s. and h.
1845.   Matric. Oxford (Ch. Ch.) 22 Oct. 1801, aged 18 ; M.A.
13 June 1804.   He served under Wellington in the
Peninsula, as an officer of the Guards.   He d. unm., 21 Sep. 1845,aged 64,
at Gibraltar, and was bur. there, when his honours became extinct. (ᵇ)

ALLESBOROUGH see AYLESBOROUGH

ALLINGTON

See " WELBY OF ALLINGTON, CO. LINCOLN," Barony (Welby), cr. 1894.

ALLOA

ALLOA, FERRITON AND FOREST, Barony [S.], cr. 22 Oct. 1715 with the
DUKEDOM OF MAR [S.], by the titular King James III.   See MAR, Earldom of [S.].

(ª) Much of the family property was inherited by the 2 sisters and coheirs of the
3rd Viscount.   See CARYSFORT and NEWHAVEN.
(ᵇ) He distinguished himself by his dashing conduct as a subaltern at Talavera,
and was known among his own generation as ' King Allen. '   Some curious anecdotes of
the eccentricities, &c., of this Nobleman are given in Burke's Romance of the Aristocracy,
1855, vol. 1, p. 305, &c.   " A penniless Lord and Irish pensioner, well behaved,
and not encumbered with too much principle. "   (T. Creevey, Oct. 1834)   V G

ALMARAZ

See " HILL OF ALMARAZ and of Hawkestone, Salop, " Barony *(Hill)*, *cr.* 1814, *extinct* 1842.

See " HILL OF ALMARAZ and of Hardwicke, Salop, " Barony *(Hill)*, *cr.* 1816.

ALMOND

i.e. " LIVINGSTON OF ALMOND, " Barony [S.] *(Livingston)*, *cr.* 1633.

Also " LIVINGSTON AND ALMOND, " Barony [S.], *cr.* 1641 with the EARLDOM OF CLARENDON [S.], *forfeited* 1715, which see.

ALMOND ([a])

TITULAR EARLDOM I. 1689.   1. Donna VICTORIA DAVIA-MONTECUCULI ([b]) was *cr.* by James II, when in exile, (warrant 3/13 Jan. 1688/9) COUNTESS OF ALMOND for life. ([c])

TITULAR EARLDOM [S.] I. 1698.   1. " Signor VIRGILIO DAVIA, Senator of Bologna, " was *cr.* by James II (when in exile at St. Germain) EARL OF ALMOND, VISCOUNT OF MONEYDIE and BARON DAVIA " in our ancient Kingdom of Scotland. " Drafts of the warrant and letters patent (in Latin and English), dat. 9 and 12 Apr. 1698, are still in existence. The preamble states that the honour was conferred on account of his own services to the Queen, but chiefly on account of the " extraordinary merits " of his wife " Donna Victoria DAVIA-MONTECUCULI, and her having attended on the person of our said dearest Consort even from her infancy with great zeal and fidelity, and particularly her having waited on our said dearest Consort in her hazardous passage out of England into France at the beginning of the late Revolution, and shared in all the many and great dangers and difficulties of her evasion, and that, as the misfortunes of our Royal Family increased, she has redoubled her endeavours to be still more and more usefull in performing all the duties of a faithfull servant, " &c. ([d]) The maiden name of this Lady appears to have been " Anna Victoria MONTECUCULI ; " she was " the companion

---

([a]) For a list of " Jacobite Peerages, " 1689-1760, see Appendix F at the end of this volume.

([b]) " A tall, well made woman, with a great deal of wit, much appreciated at our Court. " (St. Simon.) V.G.

([c]) See Stuart Papers, *Hist. MSS. Com.*, vol. i, p. 130, where also, pp. 127-8, is the preamble given in the text above.

([d]) The Rev. W.D. Macray, M.A., F.S.A., &c., has kindly furnished an epitome of the above, which is in full at ff. 469-474 of vol. 180 of the Nairne Papers, in Carte's collection in the Bodleian Library.

> of the childhood and the friend of the maturer years" of Mary Bea-
> trice (ᵃ) of Modena (the Queen of James II), being one of her Ladies
> of the Bedchamber, and remaining with her till (to the great grief of her
> Royal Mistress) she *d.* at St. Germain, Apr. 1703.

ALNWICK

See " PERCY OF ALNWICK, co. Northumberland, " Barony (*Percy*), *cr.*
1643, *extinct* 1652.

i.e. " ALNWICK, CO. NORTHUMBERLAND " Barony (*Percy*), *cr.* 1794 with
the BARONY OF LOVAINE, which see.

ALSOP-EN-LE-DALE

See "HINDLIP OF HINDLIP, co. Worcester, and OF ALSOP-EN-LE-DALE,
co. Derby, " Barony (*Allsopp*), *cr.* 1886.

ALTAMONT (ᵇ)

EARLDOM [I.]   1. JOHN BROWNE, of Westport, co. Mayo, s. and h.
I. 1771.   of Peter B. of the same, by Mary, da. of Denis DALY,
one of the Judges of the Court of Common Pleas [I.].
Matric. Oxford (Ch. Ch.) 17 July 1725, aged 16; Sheriff of co. Mayo
1731; M.P. for Castlebar, 1744-60, and Governor of Mayo; and, on
10 Sep. 1760, was *cr.* BARON MONTEAGLE of Westport, co. Mayo
[I.], taking his seat 22 Oct. 1761. On 24 Aug. 1768 he was *cr.*
VISCOUNT WESTPORT of Westport, co. Mayo [I.], taking his seat as
such 17 Oct. 1769. On 4 Dec. 1771, he was *cr.* EARL OF ALTA-
MONT, co. Mayo [I.], taking his seat on the Earls' Bench on the day

---

(ᵃ) She accompanied the unfortunate Queen on her escape to France, with her
infant son, from Whitehall, soon after midnight, Sunday, 9 Dec. 1688, conducted by
the chivalrous Count de Lauzun and his friend, M. St. Victor, of Avignon. Of
this party, also, were Lord and Lady Powis, Lady Strickland of Sizergh (sub-governess
of the Prince of Wales), Lord and Lady O'Brien of Clare [I.], the Marquis Montecuculi
[*Query*, her father or brother?], the Queen's Confessor, Père Givelui, the Queen's
Physician, Sir William Waldegrave, one of her bedchamber women, Signora Pelegrina
Turinie (whose husband was on guard when the Queen passed), and two Pages.—See
Agnes Strickland, *Lives of the Queens of England.*

(ᵇ) Four years before an Earl of Bellamont had been *cr.* Such names must be
regarded as examples of phonetic degeneration, being Italianised forms on the analogy
of 'Chiaramonte.' They must not be looked on as indicating a then low ebb of
classical knowledge in Ireland, nor as attributing a feminine gender to 'mons,' for
which, indeed, the quotation "Parturiunt montes" offers but a feeble excuse. Mount
Eagle, otherwise Croagh-Patrick, is the *high mountain* (2510 ft) near Westport, from
which the Earls of Altamont take their title. (*ex inform.* G.D. Burtchaell.) V.G.

16

following. He *m.*, Dec. 1729, Anne, sister of Arthur, 1st EARL OF ARRAN [I.], 1st da. of Sir Arthur GORE, of Newton Gore, 2nd Bart. [I.], by Elizabeth, 1st da. of Maurice ANNESLEY. She *d.* 7 Mar. 1771. He *d.* 4, and was *bur.* 7 July 1776, at Westport. Will pr. 1776, Prerog. Ct. Dublin.

II. 1776.   2. PETER (BROWNE), EARL OF ALTAMONT, &c. [I.], sometime Peter BROWNE-KELLY, having assumed the name of Kelly on his marriage, s. and h. Matric. Oxford (Ch. Ch.) 26 Oct. 1748, aged 17. He was formerly of Mount Browne, co. Mayo, and M.P. for that co. 1761-68. On 27 Jan. 1778, he took his seat in the House of Lords [I.]. He *m.*, 16 Apr. 1752, Elizabeth, da. and h. of Denis KELLY, of Lisduffe, co. Galway, and of Spring Garden, co. Mayo, formerly Chief Justice of Jamaica. She *d.* 1 Aug. 1765. He *d.* 28 Dec. 1780, at Westport. Will dat. 19 Aug. 1780, pr. 1781.

III. 1780.   3. JOHN DENIS (BROWNE), EARL OF ALTAMONT, &c. [I.], s. and h., *b.* 11 June 1756. Ed. at Eton. Sheriff of co. Mayo, 1779, and M.P. for Jamestown [I.] 1776-80. Took his seat in the House of Lords [I.] 22 Nov. 1781. P.C. [I.], 1785. On 31 Dec. 1800, he was *cr.* MARQUESS OF SLIGO [I.]. See " SLIGO," MARQUESSATE OF [I.], *cr.* 1800.

ALTHAM

BARONY [I.]   1. The HON. ALTHAM ANNESLEY, 2nd s. of Arthur (iii),
I. 1681.   2nd VISCOUNT VALENTIA [I.] and 1st EARL OF ANGLESEY, by Elizabeth, da. and coh. of Sir James ALTHAM of Acton, Midx., was *cr.* M.A. by the University of Oxford, 1 Feb. 1670/1. In consideration of his father's services and those of his mother's family, he, on 14 Feb. 1680/1, was *cr.* BARON ALTHAM (a) of Altham, co. Cork [I.], (b) with a *spec. rem.*, failing the heirs male of his body, to his yr. brothers respectively in like manner. (c) Having been *attainted* in his absence by the Irish Parl., May 1689, (d) of James II, as a resident in England, and his estate of £1400 a year sequestered, he was not introduced into the House of Lords [I.] till 22 Aug. 1695. He *m.*, 1stly, 3 Sep. 1678, at Leighton Buzzard, Beds, Alicia, da. and coh. of the Hon. Charles LEIGH (2nd surv. s. of Thomas, 1st LORD LEIGH), by his 1st wife, Anne, Dowager Lady HOLT, da. of Sir Edward LITTLETON, of Pillaton, co. Stafford. She *d. s.p.*, 4 June 1684, aged 23, at Stoneleigh, and was *bur.* there. M.I. at Leighton Buzzard. (e) He *m.*, 2ndly, July 1697,

---

(a) For his arms see *sub* ANGLESEY.

(b) He was sentenced, 26 Dec. 1686, to pay 100 marks, for speaking words against the King when he was drunk. (Luttrell, *Diary.*) V.G.

(c) The preamble of this patent is printed in *Lodge*, vol. iv, p. 129.

(d) For a list of peers present in, and absent from, this Parl., see vol. iii, Appendix D. V.G.

(e) The following must refer to her. " Anglesey House is in tears for the

Ursula, da. and in her issue sole h. of Sir Robert MARKHAM, 2nd Bart,
by Mary, da. and coh. of Sir Thomas WIDDRINGTON. He *d*. 26 Apr.
1699, of apoplexy, in London, or at Bath, Somerset. Admon. 31 July
1699, and 11 Jan. 1699/1700 [I.], granted to his widow. She, who was
b. in London, 1 Jan. 1678, *m*., 1701, Samuel OGLE, M.P., Commissioner
of the Revenue in Ireland. He *d*. 10 Mar. 1718. Will. pr. by his
widow, 14 May 1719. She *m*., 3rdly, 29 Dec. 1720, William VESEY,
M.P., and was *bur*. 16 May 1725, at St. Peter's, Dublin

II. 1699.   2. JAMES GEORGE (ANNESLEY), BARON ALTHAM [I.],
                   only s. and h. by 2nd wife. He *d*. an infant in 1697
or 1700. Admon [I] 15 Oct. 1702 to his mother.

III. 1700. ?   3. RICHARD (ANNESLEY), BARON ALTHAM [I.], uncle
                   and h., according to the *spec rem*. in the patent.   Matric.
at Oxford (Magd. Coll.), 15 Sep. 1669, being then aged 14 ; M.A. 1 Feb
1670/1 ; B.D. 1677 ; D.D. 1689 ; Preb. of Westm. 20 Sep. 1679 ;
Preb. of Exeter 23 Mar. 1680/1 ; Dean of Exeter 7 Apr 1681.   He never
took his seat in the House of Lords.   He *m*., before 1689, Dorothy, da.
of John DAVEY, of Ruxford, Devon   He *d*. in London, 19, and was *bur*.
25 Nov. 1701, in Westm. Abbey.   Will dat. 6 Oct. 1694, pr. 6 July 1713
(sic).   His widow's will (in which she directs to be *bur*. either in Westm
Abbey or Exeter Cathedral) dat 30 June 1715, pr. 18 Feb. 1717/8.

IV. 1701.   4. ARTHUR (ANNESLEY), BARON ALTHAM [I.], 1st s. and
                   h, 12 years old in 1701.   He took his seat 9 July 1711.
He *m*., 1stly, when a minor, 8 Apr. 1703, at St. Margaret's, Westm.,
Phillips, da. (*) of John (THOMPSON), 1st BARON HAVERSHAM, by his 1st
wife, Frances, da. of Arthur (ANNESLEY), 1st EARL OF ANGLESEY. She *d. s p.*,
May 1704. Admon. 22 June 1704, to Dorothy, Dowager Baroness Altham,
mother and guardian of her husband, and again 18 Jan. 1708/9, to her said
husband, he having attained the age of 21.   He *m*., 2ndly, 22 July 1707,
also at St. Margaret's, Westm., Mary SHEFFIELD, Spinster, illegit. da. of John
(SHEFFIELD), DUKE OF BUCKINGHAM.   She was separated from her husband
1717, when he established another person, Joan LANDY (whom he called
"Lady Altham") in her place. He *d*. (as was supposed (ᵇ)) *s.p.s.*) at Inchicore,

---

death and great loss of Lord Altamonts' [*sic*] Lady, who *d*. this sennight of small
pox." (Letter of Roger Herbert to the Earl of Rutland, 10 June 1684.)   V.G.

   (ᵃ) See Luttrell, *Diary*.

   (ᵇ) By the trial in the Irish Exchequer, mentioned below, the truth of the following statements, which appear more fully in a publication entitled *The adventures of
an unfortunate young Nobleman*, seems to be established.   It is stated, however, *(per
contra)* in the petition of George, 2nd Earl of Mountnorris, 7th Baron Altham, &c.
[I], for the Earldom of Anglesey (30 June 1819), that by a *subsequent* chancery suit
this "unfortunate young nobleman," James Annesley, was found to be a bastard s of
a maidservant named Landy (*i.e.* the Joan L. of the text).   According to his own
account, however, his descent was as follows :

V. 1727.   5. JAMES ANNESLEY (*de jure* BARON ALTHAM [I.], and in 1737
          de jure EARL OF ANGLESEY, &c. [E.]), only s. and h. of the 4th

near Dublin, 16, and was *bur* 18 Nov. 1727, at Ch. Ch., Dublin. (ᵃ) His widow *d.* 26 Oct. 1729, of paralysis, (ᵇ) and was *bur* at St Andrew's, Holborn, London.   Admon 18 May 1743, to her s, " James Annesley, Esq."

V   1727.   5. RICHARD (ANNESLEY), BARON ALTHAM [I.],
                           br and h., supposing the last Peer to have *d.*
s.p. legit He was *b.* 1694. His right of succession to the
Peerage was acknowledged by the House [I.], inasmuch as he
took his seat (as Baron Altham) 28 Nov 1727. On 1 Apr.
1737, he (by virtue of the same descent) *suc* his cousin Arthur
as VISCOUNT VALENTIA, &c. [I] (under which title he
took his seat [I.] 4 Oct. 1737), and as EARL OF ANGLE-
SEY, &c [E.].   He *d.* 14 Feb. 1761, *s.p. legit.* according to the
decision of the *English* House of Parl , (22 Apr 1771) whereby
the EARLDOM OF ANGLESEY and his other *English* honours
became (under the English decision) *extinct*, but the Irish dignities
devolved on his s., who, according to the decision of the *Irish*
House of Parl , 1765 (confirmed 1772), was *b.* in wedlock.

(right margin, rotated): For fuller particulars see "ANG-LESEY" Earldom of, *cr.* 1661, under the 6th Earl.

Lord Altham [I.], by Mary, his wife (formerly Mary Sheffield, spinster), abovenamed, *b.* at Dunmain, co Wexford, 1715, being an obstruction to the grant of some leases, which his father's extravagance rendered necessary, was removed to an obscure school, whence his death was announced   On his father's death, his uncle Richard (who had assumed the title of Lord Altham [I.] as stated in the text), sold him, as a slave, to an American planter. (Smollett devotes a chapter of Peregrine Pickle to the story, and Sir Walter Scott has evidently made use of his adventures in the construction of *Guy Mannering*) He escaped, however, to Jamaica, and thence, in Sep. 1740, to England, Admiral Vernon taking him under his care.   He began an action of ejectment against his uncle, then (as stated in the text) Earl of Anglesey, which came on for trial 11 Nov. 1743   The defence attempted was that, though s of the 4th Lord, he was not by his wife, but by one Joan Landy, spinster   This, however, was confuted, and the jury on the 15th day of the trial returned a verdict for the Plaintiff, who recovered the estates accordingly. (See Howell's *State Trials*, vol. xvii ; *Gent. Mag.,* xiv, pt i, p 503, pt. ii, pp. 405 and 605. See also an account of the trial in O'Flan-agan's *Chancellors of Ireland*, under 'Bowes ') Singularly enough, he appears never to have assumed the family honours either in England, or even in Ireland, where his legitimacy had thus been established. He *m* , 1stly, —, da. of — CHESTER, of Staines Bridge, Midx., who *d.* 22 Dec. 1749. He *m.,* 2ndly, 14 Sep 1751, at Bidborough, Kent, Margaret, da of Thomas I'ANSON, of Bounds, near Tunbridge. He *d.* at Blackheath, 5, and was *bur.* 14 Jan 1760, at Lee, Kent, as "James Annesley Esq."

VI. 1760.   6. JAMES ANNESLEY *(de jure* BARON ALTHAM, &c. [I.], and
                         EARL OF ANGLESEY, &c. [E.]}, s. and h., only s. by 1st wife.
He *d. s p.* 6 Nov 1763.

VII. 1763.   7. [——] ANNESLEY *(de jure* BARON ALTHAM, &c. [I], and
                         EARL OF ANGLESEY, &c. [E]}, br. and h., only s. of his father by
the 2nd wife. He *d.* unm, aged about 7 years, in 1764, when the *legitimate issue male of the 4th Lord* (assuming that it ever existed) became *extinct*. (See Burke's *Romance of the Aristocracy* (1855) vol ii, p 327, &c ; also Burke's *Vicissitudes of Families*, 3rd Series, (1863) vol. iii, p. 70, &c.)

(ᵃ) "So miserably poor, that he was actually *bur.* at the public expense." V.G.
(ᵇ) "Being reduced by disease and poverty to a state of extreme imbecility both of body and mind " V G

VI. 1761.   6. ARTHUR (ANNESLEY), VISCOUNT VALENTIA, ⎫
BARON MOUNTNORRIS and BARON ALTHAM [I.], s.
and h., *b.* 7 Aug 1744   He *suc* to the *Irish* dignities, but not to
the *English,* according to the decisions of the Houses of Parl. of
those respective Kingdoms.   Took his seat, as Viscount Valentia
[I.], 5 Dec. 1765, and again 7 Nov 1771   On 3 Dec. 1793, he was
cr. EARL OF MOUNTNORRIS [I.].   He *d.* 4 July 1816

VII. 1816   7. GEORGE (ANNESLEY), EARL OF MOUNTNORRIS,
to   VISCOUNT VALENTIA, BARON MOUNTNORRIS and
1844   BARON ALTHAM [I.], only surv. s. and h., *b.* 2 Nov
1769. He *d. s.p m.s.,* 23 July 1844, when (together
with the EARLDOM OF MOUNTNORRIS [I.]) the BARONY OF ALTHAM
[I.] became *extinct,* the issue male of the 1st Peer and of all
his brothers (who were included in the *spec. rem.*) having failed.
The BARONY OF MOUNTNORRIS and VISCOUNTCY OF VALENTIA [I.]
devolved on the h. male of the body of the 1st Viscount —See
" VALENTIA " [I.], under the (xith), 10th Viscount.   ⎭

(right margin, rotated) For fuller particulars see MOUNTNORRIS, Earldom of [I.].

ALTHORP

i e. " SPENCER OF ALTHORP, co. Northampton, " Viscountcy *(Spencer),*
cr. 1761, see SPENCER, EARLDOM, *cr.* 1765.

---

i e. " ALTHORP, co NORTHAMPTON, " Viscountcy *(Spencer), cr.* 1765
with the EARLDOM OF SPENCER, which see

ALTON

i.e. " ALTON co. STAFFORD," Marquessate *(Talbot), cr* 1694 with the
DUKEDOM OF SHREWSBURY, which see ; *extinct* 1718.

ALTRIE

BARONY [S.]   1. The Hon. ROBERT KEITH, 2nd s. of William, 4th EARL
1. 1587.   MARISCHAL [S.], by Margaret, da. and coh. of Sir William
KEITH, of Innerugie, co Banff, being Commendator of the
Cistercian Abbey of Deer, co. Aberdeen, had a grant of the lands thereof (ᵃ)
as a *Barony,* by charter 29 July 1587, with the title of LORD ALTRIE
(and a seat as a BARON (ᵇ) OF PARL.) to himself for life, with a *spec rem.*
to his nephew George, EARL MARISCHAL [S.], his heirs male and assignees

---

(ᵃ) See note *sub* HOLYROODHOUSE for some remarks on lands of religious houses,
granted with a Peerage [S.] to laics.
(ᵇ) See note *sub* CRAMOND as to this use of the word " Baron. "

in fee. In 1589 he was named as Envoy to Denmark, but excused himself on account of his age. He *m.* Elizabeth, da. and h. of Robert LUNDIE, of Benholm, co. Kincardine. He *d. s.p.m.*, between 1 July and 26 Sep. 1592, aged 63. (ª)

II. 1592.   2. GEORGE (KEITH), EARL MARISCHAL, LORD KEITH, and LORD ALTRIE [S.], nephew and h. male ; h. to this title according to the terms of the charter. He was s. and h. of William KEITH, *styled* LORD KEITH (1st br. of Lord Altrie [S.] abovenamed), who was s. and h. ap. of William, 4th EARL MARISCHAL [S.] also abovenamed. In the Earldom of MARISCHAL the Barony of Altrie [S.] continued *merged*, and with it was *attainted* in 1716. See " MARISCHAL, " Earldom of [S.].

ALVANLEY

BARONY.   1. RICHARD PEPPER ARDEN, (ᵇ) was 2nd s. of John
I. 1801.   ARDEN (or ARDERN), of Harden (or Hawarden) in Bred-
bury township, in the parish of Stockport, co. Chester, by Mary, sister and h. of Preston PEPPER, of Pepper Hall in South Cawton, co. York, and da. of Cuthbert P., of the same. He was *b.* at Bredbury, 20 May, and *bap.* at Stockport, 20 June 1744 ; ed. at the Grammar School at Manchester, 1752-63, and, in Oct. 1763, admitted a Fellow Commoner of Trin. Coll., Cambridge ; B.A. and 7th Wrangler, 1766; M.A. and Fellow, 1769 ; Barrister (Middle Temple), 1769 ; King's Counsel, 1780; Solicitor Gen., 1782-83, and again 1783-84; Attorney Gen. and Chief Justice of Chester, 1784-88. He was M.P. for Newtown, Isle of Wight, 1783-84 ; for Aldborough, co. York, 1784-90 ; for Hastings, 1790-94, and for Bath, 1794-1801. On 4 June 1788, he was made Master of the Rolls, and Knighted on the 18th. In May 1801, he was made Lord Chief Justice of the Common Pleas, and was, on 22 May 1801, *cr.* BARON ALVANLEY, (ᶜ) of Alvanley, (ᵈ) co. Chester.

(ª) The Editor has unfortunately not preserved his authority for this statement, which probably is to be found in *Hist. MSS. Com. The Scots Peerage* states that he was living 13 July 1594, and gives no authority, but this (*ex inform.* Sir J.B. Paul) must be that in a charter in the Reg. of the Great Seal, 15 July 1594, (by which the King grants to Robert Keith, Lord A.'s nephew, lands which that Lord had resigned) he is not designated as *quondam.* V.G.

(ᵇ) This is one of the 12 families (Arden, Ashburnham, Bruce, Cecil, Compton Drummond, Dunbar, Dundas, Harley, Hume, Nevill, and Perceval) treated of in that magnificently illustrated, but carelessly compiled work, Drummond's *Histories of Noble British Families*, 2 vols. large folio, 1846.

(ᶜ) Lord Alvanley bore arms of Gules with three crosslets fitchy and a chief gold. These arms are a differenced version of a coat of Arden or Arderne in whose earliest form the crosslets were six in number. (*ex inform.* Oswald Barron.) V.G.

(ᵈ) Alvanley was a manor, in the parish of Frodsham, Cheshire, which had been in the possession of the family since the time of Hen. III. See Foss's *Judges of England.*

P.C 1788. He *m.*, 9 Sep. 1784, at Hornsey, Midx., Anne Dorothea, sister of Edward, 1st LORD SKELMERSDALE, da of Richard WILBRAHAM (afterwards WILBRAHAM-BOOTLE), by Mary, da. and h. of Robert BOOTLE, of Lathom House, co. Lancaster. He *d.* at Frognal, Hampstead, or according to the *Annual Reg.* in Great George Str., Westm, 19, and was *bur.* 26 Mar. 1804, aged 59, in the Rolls Chapel, London. ([a]) Will pr. Apr. 1804. His widow *d.* 17 Jan. 1825, at the British Hotel, Edinburgh.

II. 1804. 2. WILLIAM (ARDEN), BARON ALVANLEY, 2nd, but 1st surv. s. and h., *b.* 8 Jan. and *bap.* 20 Feb. 1789, at the Rolls House, Chancery Lane, in St. Dunstan's-in-the-West, London. Sometime an officer in the Coldstream Guards, and afterwards Capt. 50th Reg. of Foot. He was well known as a wit and a spendthrift. ([b]) In May 1835 he fought a duel with Morgan John O'Connell, whose father (the well known "agitator") he asserted to have been "purchased" by Lord Melbourne on his accession to office, and who had called him "a bloated buffoon." He *d.* unm., 16 Nov. 1849. Admon. Dec. 1849

III. 1849 3. RICHARD PEPPER (ARDEN), BARON ALVANLEY, br. to and h., *b.* 8 Dec. 1792, and *bap.* 1 Feb. 1793, at the Rolls 1857. House afsd. Lieut. Col. in the army. He *m.*, 25 Apr. 1831, at St. James's, Westm., Arabella, 5th and yst. da. of William Harry (VANE), 1st DUKE OF CLEVELAND, by his 1st wife, Catherine, da. and coh. of Harry (PAULETT), 6th and last DUKE OF BOLTON. He *d s.p.*, 24 June 1857, in Bruton Str., when the title became *extinct.* Will pr. Aug. 1857. His widow, who was *b.* 2 June 1801, *d.* 26 Nov. 1864, at Thorpe Perrow, co. York.

ALVERSTONE

BARONY. 1. RICHARD EVERARD WEBSTER, of Winterfold, Surrey, I. 1900. 2nd s. of Thomas W., Q.C., of Beachfield, Sandown, Isle of Wight (*d.* 3 June 1875), by his 1st wife, Elizabeth

---

([a]) He is stated, in *The Rolliad*, to have once blundered into a joke, which was "that some resolutions passed between 6 and 7 a.m. were entitled no respect as the House was then at sixes and sevens. " " He was not a man of great oratorical powers, but possessed the qualities of intelligence, readiness and wit.... It would be vain to claim any great distinction for Lord Alvanley He was a learned lawyer and a successful politician .. the few productions that remain from his pen evince refinement, taste, and facility of expression. " (*Dict. of Nat. Biog.*) V.G.

([b]) Charles Greville in his *Memoirs*, 23 Jan. 1850, writes of him ·—" His constant spirits and good humour, together with his marvellous wit and drollery, made him the delight and ornament of Society. He was naturally of a kind and affectionate disposition, good natured, obliging, and inclined to be generous ; but he was to the last degree reckless and profligate about money ; he cared not what debts he incurred . . . . For the last four years of his life he was afflicted with painful diseases, and his sufferings were incessant, and intense. He bore them all with fortitude, and a cheerfulness which excited universal sympathy and admiration " Dighton's clever caricature of him is still (1909) in White's Club, St. James's Str. V.G.

Anne (*d.* 3 Dec. 1847), da. of Richard CALTHROP, of Swineshead Abbey, co. Lincoln ; was *b.* at 4 Chester Pl., 22 Dec. 1842, and was *bap.* 3 May 1843, at St. Peter's, Eaton Sq. ; ed. at King's Coll. School, at the Charterhouse, and at Trin. Coll. Cambridge.   M.A. 1869, Hon. LL.D. 1892, Hon. LL.D. Edinburgh and Aberdeen ; D.C.L. Oxford ; F.R.S.   Called to the Bar 1868; Q.C. 1878; Attorney Gen. 1885-86, 1886-92, and 1895-1900 ; Master of the Rolls May 1900 ; Lord Chief Justice of England Oct. 1900.   M.P. (Conserv. interest) for Launceston 1885, and for the Isle of Wight 1885-1900.   Knighted 9 July 1885 ; G.C.M.G., 7 Dec. 1893 ; *cr.* a Baronet 29 Jan. 1900, and P.C. in the same year.   On 18 June 1900, being then Master of the Rolls, he was *cr.* BARON ALVERSTONE (ª) of Alverstone, co. Southampton.   He *m.*, 20 Aug. 1872, at Withern, co. Lincoln, Louisa Mary, only da. of William Charles CALTHROP, M.D., of Withern afsd., by Louisa Jane, da. of the Rev. Christopher CARR, rector of Fletton, near Peterborough.   She, who was *b.* at Withern, *d.* 22 Mar. 1877, at Hornton Lodge, Kensington, and *bur.* at Norwood. (ᵇ)

AMBERLEY

i.e. "AMBERLEY OF AMBERLEY, co. Gloucester, and of ARDSALLA, co. Meath," Viscountcy *(Russell), cr.* 1861 with the EARLDOM OF RUSSELL, which see.

AMESBURY

See "DOUGLAS OF AMESBURY, Wilts, " Barony *(Douglas), cr.* 1786, *extinct* 1810.

BARONY.   1. CHARLES DUNDAS (ᶜ) of Barton Court, Berks, 2nd s.
I. 1832.   of Thomas D., of Fingask, co. Stirling, by his 2nd wife,
                 Janet, da. of Charles (MAITLAND), 6th EARL OF LAUDERDALE [S.], *b.* 5 Aug. 1751.   Ed. at Trin. Coll., Cambridge ; B.A. 1773, M.A. 1776.   He was M.P. (in the Whig interest) for Richmond 1775-80; for Orkney 1780-84 ; for Richmond (again) 1784-86 ; and for Berks

---

(ª) The arms granted to Lord Alverstone are described as " Azure two pallets or and five swans in cross proper between four annulets of the second. "   This is evidently a differenced version of the arms allowed by the heralds in the early seventeenth century to the Websters of Flamborough in Yorkshire. (*ex inform.* Oswald Barron.)   V.G.

(ᵇ) Their only s., Arthur Harold Webster, *b.* 16 June 1874, ed. at Charterhouse, and at Trin. Coll. Cambridge, *m.,* 10 May 1898, Gwladys Marie de Grasse, 2nd da. of Sir Francis Henry Evans, 1st Baronet [1902], but *d. v.p.* and *s.p.,* after an operation for appendicitis, at Shanklin, Isle of Wight, 8 Aug. 1902, and was *bur.* at Cranleigh, Surrey.

(ᶜ) The family of Dundas is one of the 12 given in Drummond's *Noble British Families* ; see p. 118 note (b).

1794-1832. On 16 May 1832, he was *cr.* BARON AMESBURY of Kintbury-Amesbury, and Barton Court, Berks, (ª) and Aston Hall, co Flint.   He *m.*, 1stly, Anne, da. and h. of Ralph WHITLEY, of Aston Hall afsd   She *d. s.p m.*, 29 Nov. 1812, aged 59, and was *bur.* at Kintbury, Berks, (ᵇ) being descended from the family of Raymond, of that place. M.I. He *m.*, 2ndly, 25 Jan. 1822, his cousin, Margaret, widow of Major Archibald ERSKINE, of Venlaw, and formerly of Charles OGILVY, being 3rd da. of the Hon. Charles BARCLAY, formerly MAITLAND, by his 1st wife, Isabel, da. and h of Sir Alexander BARCLAY, of Towie.   He *d. s p.m.*, (of cholera, about 6 weeks after his creation) 30 June 1832, aged 80, in Pimlico, Midx., when the title became *extinct.* M.I. at Kintbury (ᶜ) Will pr. Nov. 1832.   His widow *d.* 21 Apr. 1841, at Portobello, near Edinburgh. Will pr June 1841.

AMHERST

OF HOLMESDALE, AMHERST OF MONTREAL AND AMHERST OF ARRACAN

BARONY.

I. 1776 to 1797.

1. JEFFREY AMHERST, (ᵈ) 2nd s of Jeffrey A., of Riverhead, near Sevenoaks, Kent, (who *d.* there 21 Oct. 1750) Bencher of Gray's Inn, by Elizabeth, da. of Thomas KERRILL, of Hadlow, Kent, was *b.* 29 Jan. 1717, and as a boy was page to the Duke of Dorset ; Ensign in the 1st Reg. Foot Guards 1731 ; Lieut. Col. 1745, served under Ligonier at Roucoux, Dettingen and Fontenoy &c. 1745-47, and under the Duke of Cumberland at Lauffeld and Hastenbeck &c. 1747-57   He acquired great military fame by the following achievements in North America, where he was Com.-in-chief, 1758-64, *viz.*, the taking of Louisburg, 26 July 1758 ; of Fort du Quesne, 24 Nov. 1758 ; of Niagara, 25 July 1759, of Ticonderoga, 26 July 1759 ; of Crown Point, 4 Aug. 1759 ; of Quebec, 18 Sept. 1759 ; of Fort Levi, 25 Aug. 1760 ; of Isle au Noix, 28 Aug. 1760 ; of Montreal and (with it) all Canada, 8 Sep. 1760 ; and of St. John's, Newfoundland (retaken), 18 Sep. 1762.   Governor of Virginia 1759-68. On 23 Mar. 1761, he was *nom.* K.B.   He *suc.* to the estate of Riverhead 12 Dec. 1763, on the death, *s p.*, of his 1st br., Sackville A.   Governor of Guernsey, 1770-97. Lieut. Gen. of H. M's Ordnance, 1772-82. P C, 1772.

(ª) *suc.* Yet Amesbury is in Wilts. Kintbury-Amesbury is a part of Kintbury belonging formerly to the Priory of Amesbury.

(ᵇ) The only child Janet inherited Barton Court. She *m*, in 1808, as his 1st wife, James Deans, who took the name of Whitley-Deans-Dundas, and who, after her death, became in 1855 G C B., and in 1861 Admiral of the White. She *d* 30 Apr. 1846 (not 7 Dec. 1837), at Nice in her 63rd year, leaving male issue.   M.I. at Kintbury. Her husband *d.* 3 Oct. 1862, aged 76.

(ᶜ) Giving his death as on 30 June. V G

(ᵈ) " Provident, methodic, conciliating and cool."   (Horace Walpole, *George II.*) V.G.

He was *cr.*, 20 May 1776, BARON AMHERST OF HOLMESDALE, Kent.([a]) Major Gen. 1759; Lieut. Gen. 1765; Gen. 1778; Commander in chief 1778-82, and 1793-95. Col. 2nd Life Guards, and Gold Stick, 1788. Having no children to inherit his Peerage, he was, on 6 Sep. 1788, *cr.* BARON AMHERST OF MONTREAL,([b]) Kent, with a *spec. rem.* failing the heirs male of his body, to his nephew, William Pitt Amherst. In 1795 he refused an Earldom. FIELD MARSHAL, 30 July 1796. He *m.*, 1stly, 20 May 1753, at Gray's Inn Chapel, Midx., Jane, only surv. da. of Thomas DALISON, of Manton, co. Lincoln, and of Hamptons, Kent, by Jane, da. of Capt. Richard ETHERINGTON. She was *b.* 14 Feb. 1722, and *d. s.p.*, 7 Jan. 1765, at Tonbridge, aged 41, and was *bur.* at Plaxtole, Kent. He *m.*, 2ndly, 26 Mar. 1767, at her father's house in Clifford Str., St. James's, Westm., Elizabeth, 1st da. and coh. of Lieut. Gen. the Hon. George CARY (br. of Lucius Charles, 6th VISCOUNT FALKLAND [S.]), by Isabella, da. of Arthur INGRAM, of Barraby, co. York. He *d. s.p.*,([c]) at his seat of Montreal, in the parish of Riverhead afsd., 3, and was *bur.* 10 Aug. 1797,([d]) at Sevenoaks, when the BARONY OF AMHERST OF HOLMESDALE (*cr.* 1776) became *extinct*. Will pr. Aug. 1797. His widow *d.* 22 May 1830, in Hill Str., aged 90, and was also *bur.* at Sevenoaks. Will pr. July 1830.

BARONY.	2 and 1. WILLIAM PITT (AMHERST), BARON AMHERST
II. 1797.	OF MONTREAL, nephew and h., *suc.* to the peerage under the *spec. rem.*, being s. and h. of William A., Lieut.
EARLDOM.	Governor of Newfoundland (br. of the 1st Lord), by Elizabeth, da. of Thomas PATERSON. He was *b.* 14 Jan.
I. 1826.	1773, at Bath, Somerset. Ed. at Ch. Ch., Oxford; B.A., 1793; M.A., 1797. Envoy to the Court of Naples,

1809-11; P.C. 30 Dec. 1815; Lord of the Bedchamber 1804-13, 1815-23, and 1829-35; AMBASSADOR to China, 20 Jan. 1816, where, however, he was refused admission; subsequently GOVERNOR GEN. OF BENGAL, 1822-28. In 1835 he was *nom.* by Peel, when leaving office, GOVERNOR OF CANADA, but this was cancelled by the incoming Ministry. On 24 Feb. 1824, he was compelled by the pretensions of the King of Burmah to declare war ; the result being the annexation (among other places) of Arracan, whence he afterwards took the title of his Earldom. G.C.H. (Civil) 1834.

([a]) Earl Amherst bears the arms of his ancestors of the old Kentish house of Amherst, which are Gules with three jousting spears gold, the heads silver. (*ex inform.* Oswald Barron.) V.G.

([b]) For remarks on this and similar titles chosen to commemorate foreign achievements, see vol. iii, Appendix E. V.G.

([c]) He was an honourable and popular, if not a great man, who "proved himself worthy of high command by his quiet self control and skilful combinations." By the conquest of Canada he conferred a lasting service on his country, but his later official career calls for no encomium. V.G.

([d]) According to the "Black Book," a pension of £3000 a year was granted in 1803 (*sic*) to *Jeffrey* (*sic*), Lord Amherst and his heirs for ever.

On 19 Dec. 1826 he was *cr.* VISCOUNT HOLMESDALE, in Kent, and EARL AMHERST OF ARRACAN in the East Indies. (ª) He *m.*, 1stly, at St. Geo., Han Sq., 24 July 1800, Sarah, Dowager COUNTESS OF PLYMOUTH (widow of the 5th Earl), 1st da. and coh. of Andrew (ARCHER) 2nd BARON ARCHER OF UMBERSLADE, by Sarah, da. of James WEST. She, who was *b.* 19 and *bap.* 27 July 1762, at St George's afsd , *d.* at 66 Grosvenor Str., 27 May, and was *bur.* 5 June 1838, at Riverhead in Sevenoaks, Kent He *m.*, 2ndly, 25 May 1839, at Knole, Kent, Mary (also) Dowager COUNTESS OF PLYMOUTH (being widow of the 6th Earl), 1st da of John Frederick (SACKVILLE), 3rd DUKE OF DORSET, by Arabella Diana, da. of Sir Charles COPE, Bart. He *d.* at Knole House, 13, and was *bur.* 21 Mar. 1857, in the church of Sevenoaks. Will dat 17 Jan. 1845, to 19 Feb. 1852, pr 11 May 1857. His widow, who was *b.* 30 July 1792, and *bap.* at St. Geo , Han Sq , and who had become, in Feb. 1815, coh. of her br. the 4th Duke of Dorset, (inheriting the family estate of Knole, Kent), *d. s.p.*, 20 July 1864, at Bournemouth, in her 73rd year. Will dat. 21 Apr. 1860, to 3 May 1864, pr. 12 Apr. 1865.

EARLDOM.
II.
BARONY.
III.

2 and 3. WILLIAM PITT (AMHERST), EARL AMHERST OF ARRACAN, &c., 2nd, (ᵇ) but 1st surv. s. and h., *b.* 3 Sep. 1805, in Lower Grosvenor Str., Midx., and *bap.* at Montreal, in Sevenoaks. *Styled* VISCOUNT HOLMESDALE 1826-57 Ed. at Westm. school, and at Ch. Ch , Oxford ; 2nd class classics 1827 , B.A., 1828. He was M.P. for East Grinstead, 1829-32. He *m.*, 12 July 1834, at Sion House, in Isleworth, Midx., Gertrude, 6th da. of the Hon and Right Rev. Hugh PERCY, Bishop of Carlisle, (br. of George, 5th DUKE OF NORTHUMBERLAND), by his 1st wife, Mary, da. of Charles MANNERS-SUTTON, Archbishop of Canterbury. He *d.* 26 Mar. 1886, at Montreal afsd , aged 80, and was *bur.* at Riverhead. Will dat. 28 Aug. 1862, to 29 Oct 1877, pr 23 July 1886, over £109,000 personalty. His widow, who was *b.* 30 Aug 1814, *d* 27 Apr. 1890, at 32 Rutland Gate, aged 75, and was *bur.* at Riverhead. Will dat. 13 Jan. 1890, pr. 27 Oct. 1890.

EARLDOM.
III. 1886.
BARONY.
IV 1880.

3 and 4. WILLIAM ARCHER (AMHERST), EARL AMHERST OF ARRACAN [1826], VISCOUNT HOLMESDALE [1826] and BARON AMHERST OF MONTREAL [1788], 1st s. and h ; *b.* in Lower Brook Str., 26 Mar., and *bap* 3 May 1836, at St. Geo., Han Sq. ; ed. at Eton ; Capt in the Coldstream Guards, 1855-62, and served in the Crimean war, being present at Balaklava, Inkerman (where he was severely wounded), and the siege of Sebastopol; *styled* VISCOUNT HOLMESDALE, 1857-86; M.P. for West Kent, 1859-68 ; for Mid Kent, 1868-80. Was *sum.* to

(ª) See note (ᵇ) on previous page
(ᵇ) His elder br., Jeffrey, *b.* at Montreal, Sevenoaks, 29 Aug and *bap.* there 16 Oct. 1802, *d.* 2 Aug 1826, aged 23, at Barrackpore, unm and *v.p.* V.G

Parl , *v p* , 17 Apr. 1880, in his father's Barony, as BARON AMHERST OF MONTREAL. He *m.*, 1stly, 27 Aug. 1862, at Linton, Kent, Julia (who, by royal licence, 22 Oct. 1844, had been authorised, when a few months old, to bear the surname of CORNWALLIS only, in lieu of that of MANN), 2nd and yst da. and coh. of James (MANN, formerly CORNWALLIS), 5th and last EARL CORNWALLIS, and only child of his 3rd wife, Julia, 4th da. of Thomas BACON, of Redlands, Berks. She was *b.* 2, and *bap.* 23 July 1844, at Linton, and *suc.* to the estate of Linton Place, Kent, on the death of her father, 21 May, 1852. She (as VISCOUNTESS HOLMESDALE), *d. s.p.* 1, and was *bur.* 7 Sep. 1883, at Linton afsd. Will dat 17 Feb 1866, pr. 23 Feb. 1884, over £31,000. He *m.*, 2ndly, 25 Apr. 1889, at Christ Church, Down Str., Alice Dalton, Dowager COUNTESS OF LISBURN [I.], 1st da of Edmund PROBYN, of Huntley Manor, co. Gloucester, by Sophia, da. of Richard DALTON, of Knaith, co. Lincoln

Family Estates.—These, in 1883, consisted of 4,269 acres in Kent, 1,789 in co. Warwick, 834 in Sussex, and 741 in Essex   Total, 7,633 acres, valued at £8,781 a year. (ᵃ)   *Principal Residence.*—Montreal Park, near Sevenoaks, Kent.

AMHERST OF HACKNEY

BARONY.   1   WILLIAM AMHURST TYSSEN-AMHERST (formerly
I 1892.   TYSSEN-AMHURSI, and before that, DANIEL-TYSSEN'), of
                  Amherst, Kent, Didlington Hall, Norfolk, and Hackney,
co. London, 1st s and h. of William George TYSSEN-AMHURST (ᵇ), formerly DANIEL-TYSSEN, and before that, DANIEL, of the same (*d.* 30 Dec. 1885, aged 54), by Mary, 1st da. of Andrew FOUNTAINE, of Narford Hall, Norfolk, was *b.* there 25, and *bap.* 26 Apr 1835, at Narford; ed. at Eton, and matric. Oxford (Ch Ch.) May 1853 ; took (together with his father) the name of *Tyssen-Amhurst*, in lieu of that of *Daniel-Tyssen*, by royal lic. 6 Aug. 1852 ; High Sheriff of Norfolk, 1866 , took, by royal lic, 16 Aug. 1877, the name of *Tyssen-Amherst* in lieu of that of *Tyssen-Amhurst ;* was M P. for West Norfolk, 1880-85, and for South West Norfolk, 1885-92, and was *cr.*, 26 Aug. 1892, (ᶜ) BARON AMHERST OF HACK-

---

(ᵃ) The return made by Lord Holmesdale of his then wife's estates (those of the family of Mann, of Linton Place, Kent) early in 1883, was 18,053 acres (of which 16,209 were in Kent, 970 in Sussex and 874 in Stafford) valued at £30,744 a year These, after her death in Sep 1883, went to the family of Wykeham-Martin, descended from her 1st sister, Lady Jemima Isabella Wykeham-Martin, 1st da. of the 5th and last Earl Cornwallis.

(ᵇ) He was s and h. of William George Daniel, afterwards (1814) Daniel-Tyssen, of East Farleigh, Kent (*d.* 13 Jan. 1838), by Amelia, da. of John Amhurst, Capt. R.N (*d.* 1788, aged 64), h to her mother, Mary (her father's 2nd wife), da. and h of Francis John Tyssen, of Hackney abovenamed

(ᶜ) His claim to a peerage, like many others, appears to have been based on the fact that he was very wealthy, and had voted for some years with his party in the H. of Commons, though making no mark there.   What claim he can have had to the

NEY,(ᵃ) co London, (ᵇ) with a *spec. rem.* of that dignity, failing heirs male of his body, to his 1st da., Mary Rothes Margaret, wife of Lord William CECIL, and the heirs male of her body.   He *m.*, 4 June 1856, at Hunmanby, co. York, Margaret Susan, da. and h. of Admiral Robert MITFORD, of Mitford Castle and of Hunmanby afsd., by Margaret, da. of James DUNSMORE, of Edinburgh.   She was *b.* 8 Jan. 1835, at Lucker, Northumberland, and *bap* there.   He *d.*, suddenly, aged 73, at 23 Queen's Gate Gardens, 16, and was *bur.* 20 Jan. 1909, at Didlington afsd.   Will pr. Feb 1909, £67,457 gross, £341 ¹ net. (ᶜ)   He was *suc.* by his 1st. da. and h., under the *spec. rem.*, who is outside the scope of this work.

Family Estates.—These, in 1883, consisted of 9,488 acres in Norfolk, 240 in the East Riding of York, and 47 in Kent.   *Total,* 9,775 acres, worth £6,976 a year   *Principal Residence* —Didlington Hall, near Brandon, Norfolk.

AMIENS

i.e., " AMIENS, " VISCOUNTCY [I.] (*Stratford*), *cr.* 1777 with the EARLDOM OF ALDBOROUGH [I.], which see ; *extinct* 1875.

---

exceptional favour of a spec. rem. to his 1st da it is impossible to suggest.   (For a list of, and remarks on, spec rems granted to commoners, see vol iii, Appendix F)   It is also much to be regretted that he was allowed to take the title of Amherst, then enjoyed by a noble family to whom it had been granted for really eminent services to the State.   This action is the more unreasonable when it is remembered that the grantee was not an Amherst at all by male descent, and that if he did not fancy either of his other surnames, he could perfectly well have taken the simple title of " Hackney " where much of his property was situated   V G.   This was one of 8 Baronies conferred at the recommendation of Lord Salisbury, when leaving office, for a list of which see note *sub.* 1st LORD LLANGATTOCK.   No fewer than two of these, of which this was one, were granted with a special remainder.

(ᵃ) Lord Amherst of Hackney bore the undifferenced arms of the old Kentish family of Amherst (see Amherst, Earldom), quartering Daniel (his paternal coat) and Tyssen   (*ex inform.* Oswald Barron)   V.G

(ᵇ) See note *sub* WANDSWORTH, as to the "county of London."   In a letter, however, 22 Apr. 1897 (marked ₄₅₉₇ from the "London County Council, Estates and Valuation department," signed "Andrew Young, Valuer, pr. W.G." in reply to enquiries (made by G E.C), it is stated that "By the Local Government Act, 1888, and the Metropolis Management Act, 1885, Putney, which includes Roehampton, was incorporated and became part of *London,* ceasing from that time to form part of *Surrey !* "   It is presumed therefore that this remark (*mutatis mutandis*) applies generally to all other places now situated in the county (or "administrative county " as, at first, it was certainly designated) of London

(ᶜ) For the greater part of his life he had been a collector of rare books, MSS, Egyptian antiquities, and works of art, but owing to the rascality of his solicitor, who stole an immense quantity of his money, he was forced shortly before his death to sell his choicest treasures.   V.G.

AMORIE, see D'AMORIE

AMPTHILL

i.e., " BRUCE OF AMPTHILL, co. Bedford," Viscountcy (*Bruce*), *cr.* 1664 with the EARLDOM OF AILESBURY, which see ; *extinct* 1747. (ᵃ)

BARONY.

I. 1881.

1. ODO WILLIAM LEOPOLD RUSSELL, 3rd and yst. s. of Major-Gen. Lord George William RUSSELL, G.C.B. (br. to Francis Charles Hastings, 9th DUKE OF BEDFORD), by Elizabeth Anne, only da. and h. of the Hon. John Theophilus RAWDON, br. of Francis, 1st MARQUESS OF HASTINGS, was *b.* at Casa Bianca, Florence, 20 Feb., and *bap.* there 25 Mar. 1829. Baptism reg. at Woburn, Beds. Ed. at Westm. School. Attaché at Vienna, 1849 ; Foreign Office, 1851 ; Attaché at Paris, 1852 ; Constantinople, 1854 ; Washington, 1857 ; Florence, 1858 ; Naples, 1860 ; Special Service, Rome, 1860-70 ; Assistant Under Secretary of State for Foreign Affairs, 1870-71 ; AMBASSADOR to Berlin, 1871-84. Had royal warrant of precedence as the son of a Duke, 25 June 1872. P.C. 1872. G.C.B., 21 Feb. 1874. G.C.M.G., 24 May 1879. On 11 Mar. 1881, he was *cr.* BARON AMPTHILL of Ampthill, (ᵇ) co. Bedford. He *m.*, 5 May 1868, at Watford, Herts, Emily Theresa, 3rd da. of George (VILLIERS), 4th EARL OF CLARENDON, by Katherine, widow of John FOSTER-BARHAM, da. of Walter James (GRIMSTON), 1st EARL OF VERULAM. He *d.*, at his villa at Potsdam, near Berlin, 25 Aug., and was *bur.* 3 Sep. 1884, at Chenies, Bucks. Will pr. 17 Dec. 1884, above £45,000, reciting that over £75,000 Consols was in settlement. His widow, who was *b.* 9 Sep. 1843, at Grosvenor Crescent, Midx., was a Lady of the Bedchamber, 1885-1901 ; V. and A. 3rd class. Living 1909.

II. 1884.

2. ARTHUR OLIVER VILLIERS (RUSSELL), BARON AMPTHILL, s. and h., *b.* 19 Feb. 1869, at the Palazzo Chigi, Rome. Baptism reg. at the British Embassy there. Ed. at Eton ; matric. Oxford (New Coll.) 12 Oct. 1888 ; 3rd class history, 1891 ; B.A., 1892 ; Priv. Sec. to the Colonial Sec., 1895. Governor of Madras 1900-05. He *m.*, 6 Oct. 1894, at Madresfield, co. Worcester, Margaret, 3rd da. of Frederick (LYGON), 6th EARL BEAUCHAMP, by his 1st wife, Mary Catherine, only da. of Philip Henry, 5th EARL STANHOPE. She was *b.* 8 Oct. 1874.

[JOHN HUGO RUSSELL, s. and h. ap., *b.* 4 Oct. 1896.]

(ᵃ) See as to the honour of Ampthill, p. 58, note " b. "

(ᵇ) Following modern custom, Lord Ampthill bears the undifferenced arms of Russell, which belong to the ducal house of Bedford. (*ex inform.* Oswald Barron.) V.G.

ANCASTER

DUKEDOM.   1. ROBERT BERTIE, s and h. ap. of Robert (BERTIE),
3rd EARL OF LINDSEY, by his 2nd wife, Elizabeth, da. of
l. 1715.   Philip (WHARTON), 4th LORD WHARTON, was *b.* 20 Oct.
1660. M.P. for Boston 1685-87 and 1689-90, also el. for Preston 1689;
Chanc. of the Duchy of Lanc. 1689-97. On 27 Apr. 1690, he took his seat
in the House of Lords, having been *sum., v.p.,* on 19 Apr., in his father's
Barony, as LORD WILLOUGHBY DE ERESBY. On 8 May 1701,
he *suc.* his father as HEREDITARY LORD GREAT CHAMBERLAIN, (ᵃ) and also
as EARL OF LINDSEY, and took his seat, as such Earl, on 28 May.
Lord Lieut. of co. Lincoln 4 Apr. 1701-23. P.C. 19 June 1701, 18 Mar.
1702, and again 25 Nov 1708 and 1 Oct 1714   On 21 Dec. 1706, he was
cr. MARQUESS OF LINDSEY, with a *spec. rem.* as in the subsequent
creation of the Dukedom of Ancaster. Having been one of the Lords
Justices during the absence of George I in Hanover in 1715, he was, on
26 July 1715 (ᵇ) *cr.* DUKE OF ANCASTER AND KESTEVEN, (ᶜ) with
a *spec. rem.*, failing the heirs male of his body, to the heirs male of the
bodies of his father and mother abovenamed. He *m.,* 1stly, 30 July 1678,
at Westm. Abbey, Mary, da. and sole h. of Sir Richard WYNN, 4th Bart.
of Gwydyr, by Sarah, da. of Sir Thomas MIDDLETON, 1st Bart. of Chirk.
She *d.* 20 Sep 1689. He *m.,* 2ndly, 6 July 1705, Albinia, 1st da. of Major
Gen. William FARRINGTON, of Chislehurst, Kent, by Theodosia, sister and
coh. of Sir Edward BETENSON, Bart., and da. of Richard B., of Scadbury
in Chislehurst afsd. He *d.* at his seat, Grimsthorpe, co. Lincoln, 26 July,
and was *bur.* 16 Aug. 1723, aged 62, at Edenham, in that co. M.I. (ᵈ)
Will dat. 23 May 1719, pr, with 3 cods., 1 Apr. 1724. His widow,
who, in her issue, became (1758) h to her father, *m.* James DOUGLAS.
She *d.,* aged 46, 29 July, and was *bur.* 1 Aug. 1745, in Chislehurst
Church, Kent.

(ᵃ) See as to this great office vol. ii, Appendix D.

(ᵇ) By statute 1 Geo I. it was enacted that, notwithstanding the statute of 31
Hen. VIII. (whereby the Great Chamberlain takes precedence of all Peers of his
degree) this Dukedom should rank [only] according to the date of its patent. This
unjust infringement of the existing law came, however, to an end (on the extinction
of the peerage) in 1809 'when the precedence of the office of Great Chamberlain fell
again under the operation of the statute of 31 Hen. VIII.' (Sir C.G. Young's *Order
of Precedence,* p. 21).

(ᶜ) For his arms see LINDSEY, Earldom of.

(ᵈ) According to Macky, in his *Characters, c* 1704, he was "handsome in his
person; of a fair complexion, doth not trouble himself with affairs of state, but his
brother [Peregrine Bertie] is Vice Chamberlain and a Privy Counseller, a fine gentleman, has both wit and learning." The brother's merit seems hardly sufficient to have
gained the Earl two steps in the Peerage. Bishop Burnet's character of the Earl
with Swift's remarks thereon in italics, is as follows.—"A fine gentleman, hath both
wit and learning. *I never observed a grain of either.*"

[ROBERT BERTIE, *styled* LORD WILLOUGHBY, s. and h. ap. to his father when EARL OF LINDSEY, by his 1st wife ; *b.* 6 Feb. 1683/4 ; *d. v.p.*, unm., and under age, about 4 May 1704, at Wolfenbüttel, in the Duchy of Brunswick. Admon. 3 July 1704.]

II. 1723.   2. PEREGRINE (BERTIE), DUKE OF ANCASTER, &c., 2nd, but 1st surv. s. and h., by 1st wife, *b.* 29 Apr. 1686. Vice Chamberlain to Queen Anne, 14 Apr. 1702. *Cr.* D.C.L. at Oxford, 27 Aug. 1702. M.P. for co. Lincoln, 1708-15. P.C. 25 Nov. 1708, and 3 Jan. 1723/4-42. Was *sum., v.p.*, 16 Mar. 1714/5, to the House of Lords, in his father's Barony, as LORD WILLOUGHBY DE ERESBY. A Lord of the Bedchamber 1719-27 ; Lord Lieut. of co. Lincoln, 3 Feb. 1723/4. He officiated as LORD GREAT CHAMBERLAIN at the Coronation of George II. Lord Warden and Justice in Eyre North of Trent, 21 June 1734-42. He *m.*, June 1711, Jane, 3rd da. and coh. of Sir John BROWNLOW, of Great Humby, co. Lincoln, 3rd Bart., by Alice, da. of Richard SHERARD, of Lobthorpe, in that co. She *d.* at Grimsthorpe, afsd., 26 Aug., and was *bur.* 18 Sep. 1736, at Edenham. He *d.* 1, and was *bur.* 13 Jan. 1741/2, at Edenham. M.I. Will pr. May and Nov. 1742.

III. 1742.   3. PEREGRINE (BERTIE), DUKE OF ANCASTER, &c., s. and h., *b.* 1714. P.C. and Lord Lieut. of co. Lincoln, 20 Feb. 1741/2-78. Being attached to the House of Hanover, he raised a regiment for the *de facto* King in 1745. Lord of the Bedchamber 1755-65. Major Gen., 19 Mar. 1755. Lieut. Gen., 3 Feb. 1759. General, 25 May 1772. At the coronation, 22 Sep. 1761, he officiated as LORD GREAT CHAMBERLAIN, and from 13 Dec. 1766 to 1778 was MASTER OF THE HORSE.[a] He *m.*, 1stly, 22 May 1735, Elizabeth, (with £70,000) widow of Sir Charles Gunter NICOLL, K.B., da. and sole h. of William BLUNDELL, of Basingstoke, Hants. She *d., s.p.*, 17 Dec. 1743. Admon. 4 Apr. 1745 to her husband. He *m.*, 2ndly, 27 Nov. 1750, at Newmarket, co. Cambridge, Mary,[b] da. of Thomas PANTON, of Newmarket afsd., Master of the King's running horses, by Priscilla, his wife. He *d.* at Grimsthorpe, "of a bilious disorder," in his 65th year, 12, and was *bur.* 27 Aug. 1778, at Edenham. M.I. Will pr. Aug. 1778. His widow, who was Mistress of the Robes to Queen Charlotte, 1761-93, *d.* at Naples, 19 Oct. 1793. Will pr. Jan. 1794.

[PEREGRINE THOMAS BERTIE, *styled* MARQUESS OF LINDSEY, s. and h.

---

[a] "The Duke of Ancaster indeed was mentioned [for the L. Lieutenancy of Ireland in succession to Earl Harcourt], but 'Good God,' said Lord North, 'it is impossible to send into such a responsible station, such a very egregious blockhead, who is besides both mulish and intractable." (Sir John de Blaquiere, 18 Nov. 1776. *Harcourt Papers*, vol. x, p. 206.) V.G.

[b] She brought him a fortune of £60,000. Horace Walpole, in a letter to Mann, 9 July 1779, describes her as "natural daughter of Panton, a disreputable horse jockey." Walpole's statement that she was *natural* da. is untrue, and his error doubtless arose from the fact that, when he wrote, Panton, whose wife had *d.* in July 1778, was living with a mistress, one Sarah Tuting. V.G.

ap., by 2nd wife, *b.* 21 May 1755, in Berkeley Sq., Midx., *d.* 12 Dec. 1758, and was *bur.* at Edenham]

IV. 1778.   4. ROBERT (BERTIE), DUKE OF ANCASTER, &c., 2nd, but only surv. s. and h., by 2nd wife, *b.* 17 Oct. 1756, at Grimsthorpe. In his 21st year he served as a volunteer in North America. P.C. and Lord Lieut. of co. Lincoln, 12 Feb. 1779. He *d.* unm., in his 23rd year, of scarlet fever, at Grimsthorpe, 8, and was *bur.* 22 July 1779, at Edenham. (*) M.I. Will pr. July 1779.(*b*) On his death the hereditary office of LORD GREAT CHAMBERLAIN, as well as the BARONY OF WILLOUGHBY DE ERESBY (being a Barony in fee), *fell into abeyance* between his two sisters, till, on 18 Mar. 1780, the abeyance of the Barony was terminated in favour of Priscilla Barbara Elizabeth, the eldest coh. (*c*) See "WILL-OUGHBY DE ERESBY." His other Peerage honours devolved as under.

V. 1779   5. BROWNLOW (BERTIE), DUKE OF ANCASTER AND
   to   KESTEVEN, MARQUESS OF LINDSEY and EARL OF LINDSEY,
   1809.   uncle and h. male, *b.* 1 May 1729, at Lindsey House, Lincoln's Inn Fields, and *bap.* at St. Giles's-in-the-Fields, Midx. M.P. for co. Lincoln, 1761-79. P.C., and Lord Lieut. of co. Lincoln, 12 Feb. 1779. He *m*, istly, 11 Nov. 1762, at the house of Gen. Durand in Cork Str., St. James's, Westm., Harriot, only da. and h. of George Morton PITT, of Twickenham, Midx, Governor of Fort St. George, India, by Sophia, sometime wife of George DRAKE, da. of (—) BUGDEN. She, who was *bap.* 22 June 1745, at Twickenham, *d. s p.*, Apr., and was *bur.* 6 May 1763, at Edenham. Admon. 21 May 1765. He *m.*, 2ndly, 2 Jan. 1769, at St. James's, Westm., Mary Anne, yst. da. of Peter LAYARD, of Sutton Friars in Canterbury, Major in the army, by Mary Anne, da. and, eventually, coh. of James CROZE, a Captain in the Dutch navy. She, who was *b.* 5 Mar. 1743, at Sutton Friars afsd., *d.* 13 Jan 1804, in Saville Row, Midx. He *d. s.p.m.*, in his 80th year, at Grimsthorpe, 8, and was *bur.* 17 Feb. 1809, at Swinestead. Will pr. Mar. 1809. On his death (the issue male of the first Duke and of his brothers, who were included in the *spec. rem.*, having failed) the DUKEDOM OF ANCASTER AND KESTEVEN and the MARQUESSATE OF LINDSEY became *extinct*, while the EARLDOM OF LINDSEY devolved on his distant cousin and h. male, a descendant of the 2nd Earl. See "LINDSEY," Earldom of, *cr.* 1626, under the 9th Earl.

* * * * * *

(*) He was addicted to rioting and drunkenness In 1779, he and some woman of the town appear as "The Favourite of the Fair and the captivating Lais" [Miss St...y] in the *tête à tête* portraits in *Town & Country Mag.*, vol. xi, p. 233. See *N. & Q.*, 10th Series, vol. iv, p 462.

(*b*) "I hear he has left a legacy to a very small man that was always his companion, and whom, when he was drunk, he used to fling at the heads of the company, as others fling a bottle." (H. Walpole, *Letters*, 4 July 1779). V.G.

(*c*) This Lady inherited Grimsthorpe Castle and most of the Lincolnshire estates.

EARLDOM.   1. Gilbert Henry (Heathcote-Drummond-Wil-
I. 1872.   loughby), Lord Willoughby de Eresby [1313], Baron
Aveland[1856], and a Baronet[1732/3], only s. of Gilbert
John (Heathcote), 1st Baron Aveland, by Clementina Elizabeth, *suo jure*
Baroness Willoughby de Eresby, was *b.* 1 Oct. 1830, in Portman Sq.,
Marylebone ; ed. at Harrow, and at Trinity Coll. Cambridge ; M.P. for
Boston 1852-56, and for Rutland 1856-67, when he *suc.* his father as
Baron Aveland and a Baronet.   He was appointed, 24 Jan. 1871, Deputy
to his mother and her sister (the Dowager Baroness Carrington) in the
office of Lord Great Chamberlain, (a) which position he held till 22 Jan.
1901 (the end of the reign of the sovereign who conferred it), having
himself meanwhile become a coh. of that High Office, by the death,
13 Nov. 1888, of his mother.   On 4 May 1872, he took by royal lic. (as
did also his mother) the name of Heathcote-Drummond-Willoughby in
lieu of his patronymic Heathcote.   P.C. 1880.   Being through his said
mother (who was da. of Peter Robert (Burrell), Lord Willoughby de
Eresby and Baron Gwydyr, and grand-daughter of Peter (Burrell),
Baron Gwydyr (so *cr.* 16 June 1796), by Priscilla Barbara Elizabeth, *suo
jure* Baroness Willoughby de Eresby, elder of the two daughters of
Peregrine (Bertie), 3rd Duke of Ancaster) a descendant and a representative of the Dukes of Ancaster [a title *extinct* 8 Feb. 1809, as above], was
himself *cr.* EARL OF ANCASTER, 22 Aug. 1892.   He *m.*, 14 July 1863,
at St. Paul's, Knightsbridge, Evelyn Elizabeth, 2nd da. of Charles (Gordon),
10th Marquess of Huntley [S.], by his 2nd wife, Mary Antoinetta, da.
of the Rev. William Pegus.   She was *b.* 22 Mar. 1846.

[Gilbert Heathcote-Drummond-Willoughby, *styled* Lord Wil-
loughby de Eresby, 1st s. and h. ap.; *b.* at 23 Wilton Crescent, Midx., 20 July,
and *bap.* 10 Oct. 1867, at Normanton; was ed. at Eton, and at Trin. Coll.
Cambridge; B.A. 1889; M.A. 1893; M.P. for the Horncastle div. of co.
Lincoln 1894-1906.   He *m.*, 6 Dec. 1905, at St. Margaret's, Westm., Eloise,
1st da. of W.L. Breese, of New York State, by (—) da. of H.V. Higgins.]

Family Estates.—The Heathcote estates, belonging to Lord Aveland in
1883, consisted of 17,637 acres in co. Lincoln ; 13,633 in Rutland, and 5 in
cos. Derby and Huntingdon.   *Total,* 31,275 acres, worth £46,894 a year.
Those at that date belonging to the Baroness Willoughby de Eresby,
which, since 1888, have become united with the above, were 24,696 acres
in co. Lincoln (derived from the family of Willoughby) ; 30,391 in co.
Carnarvon, and 296 in co. Denbigh (both derived from the family of
Wynn (b) and estimated at £8,521 a year), besides 76,837 in co. Perth
(derived from the family of Drummond, and estimated at £28,965 a year).
Total, 132,230 acres, worth £74,006 year.   The two totals together making
163,505 acres, worth £120,900 a year.   *Principal Seats.*—Grimsthorpe
Castle, near Bourn, co. Lincoln ; Normanton Park, Rutland ; Gwydyr, (b)
near Llanwryst, co. Carnarvon, and Drummond Castle, near Crieff, co. Perth.

(a) As to this high office, see Appendix D at the end of vol. ii.
(b) By the marriage of the 1st Duke of Ancaster with the heiress of the family of

The Earl of Ancaster is one of the few noblemen who possess above 100,000 acres in the United Kingdom. See note *sub* BUCCLEUCH for a list of those who existed in 1883, at which date the lands then belonging to his mother, Baroness Willoughby de Eresby, but inherited by him in 1888, were considerably over that amount, viz., above 132,000, to which should be added above 31,000 inherited by him in 1867, from his father.

ANCRAM or ANCRUM

EARLDOM [S.]

I. 1633.

1. SIR ROBERT KERR (or CARR) of Ancrum, co. Roxburgh, s. and h. of William K., of the same, by Margaret, widow of Sir David HOME, of Fishwick, da. of Archibald DUNDAS, of Fingask. He was *b.* 1578, *suc.* his father 20 Dec. 1590; was served h. of his grandfather Robert Kerr (who had *d.* in 1588) in 1607; had charters of lands at Whitchester, 1611; of the Lordship of Newbottle, 1631; of the Barony of Langnewton, 1632, &c. He was a Capt. of the King's Body Guard to James VI [S.], which office he resigned in 1613. He was possibly K B. at the Coronation, 25 July 1603,(*) and was certainly, as a knight, M.P. for Aylesbury Jan. to Aug. 1625, and for Preston 1628-29.(*) Being much esteemed by Charles, Prince of Wales, he was made by him, when he became King (in 1625), a Gent. of the Bedchamber, and by patent(*) dat. 24 June 1633, was *cr.* EARL OF ANCRAME, LORD KERR OF NISBET, LANGNEWTOUN, AND DOLPHINSTOUN [S], with a *spec. rem* to his heirs male by his 2nd wife, Anne, which failing to his heirs male general. After the murder of the King he retired to Holland. He was a fervent loyalist, of high education, and an author of some note. He *m.*, 1stly, in 1605, Elizabeth, da. of Sir John MURRAY, of Blackbarony. She *d.* before 1620. He *m.*, 2ndly, in 1621 (after 6 Nov.), (*) Anne, widow of Sir Henry PORTMAN, 2nd Bart. (who *d. s.p.*, 12 Feb. 1621), da. of William (STANLEY), 6th EARL OF DERBY, by Elizabeth, da. of Edward (VERE), 17th

Wynn, of Gwydyr, co Carnarvon, he acquired that considerable estate, which afterwards gave its name to the Barony of Gwydyr, conferred in 1796 on the husband of his great-grand-daughter Priscilla, *suo jure* Baroness Willoughby de Eresby These Wynn estates, however, were sold, in or about 1895, to Earl Carrington, whose mother was sister and, in 1870, coh. to Alberic, Lord Willoughby de Eresby, after which acquisition he, by Royal lic., 24 Apr. 1896, took the name of Wynn before that of Carrington.

(*) It is more probable that this K.B was Robert Carr, then s. and h. ap. of (and in 1609 himself) the Earl of Lothian [S.] See Howe's continuation of Stow's *Chronicle*, p. 827, in which 'Newboth' is an obvious misprint for 'Newbottle,' and Nichols' *Progresses of James I*, vol. i, p 222, note 5 It is certain that the identification, Douglas' *Peerage*, vol. ii, p 134 (in Shaw's *Knights of England*, and Metcalfe's *Book of Knights*) of the K.B. with the future Earl of Somerset, is erroneous. V.G.

(*) About 1 Feb. 1620, he killed Charles Maxwell of Terregles, in a duel, which the latter had forced on him. For this he was tried at the Cambridge Assizes, found guilty of manslaughter, and banished for six months.

(*) Patent given in *Robertson*, p. 224. See also p. 206 of that work

(*) At this date Charles, Prince of Wales, wrote recommending him to the lady's mother as a suitor.

EARL OF OXFORD.   He *d.* at Amsterdam, shortly after 9 Dec. 1654, in great poverty, aged 76.   Admon. 2 July 1657, to his s. " Stanley Carr, Esq," and (on his death) again 14 May 1672, to his s. Earl Charles.   His widow, who was *b.* about 1600, *d.* at St. Paul's, Covent Garden, and was *bur.* 15 Feb. 1656/7, in Westm. Abbey.   Admon. 9 June 1657 to her s. Earl Charles.

II.   1654.   2. CHARLES (KERR), EARL OF ANCRAM, &c. [S.], 2nd s., being only s. by 2nd wife.   He (being then *styled* ' Lord CARR') was M.P. for St. Michael's, Mar. 1647 till secluded in Dec. 1648 ; and *suc.* to the peerage [S.] in Dec. 1654, according to the *spec. rem.* in the creation of that dignity.   He was subsequently (July to Dec. 1660) M.P. for Thirsk, and for Wigan (in 5 parls.), 1661-81, and 1685-87.   He *m.* shortly before 1 May 1662.   His wife, and a son, were living 5 Feb. 1675/6, but the latter *d. s.p.* and *v.p.*   He *d. s.p.s.*, in needy circumstances, between 1 and 11 Sep. 1690.

III.   1690.   3. ROBERT (KERR), EARL OF LOTHIAN, EARL OF ANCRAM, &c. [S.], nephew and h., being s. and h. of William, EARL OF LOTHIAN [S.], elder br. (of the half-blood) to the deceased, which William was 1st s. and h. of the 1st EARL OF ANCRAM [S.], and his only s. by the 1st wife.   He was *b.* 8 Mar. 1636 ; *suc.* his father, Oct. 1675, as EARL OF LOTHIAN, &c. [S.].   He was *cr.*, 23 June 1701, MARQUESS OF LOTHIAN [S.] ; see that dignity.

i.e. "ANCRAM," Earldom [S.] (*Kerr*), *cr.* 1701 with the MARQUESSATE OF LOTHIAN [S.], which see.

ANDOVER

i.e. "ANDOVER co. Southampton," Viscountcy (*Howard*), *cr.* 1622 ; see BERKSHIRE, Earldom, *cr.* 1626.

ANGLESEY

EARLDOM.   1. The Hon. CHRISTOPHER VILLIERS, of Ashley Park, in the parish of Walton on Thames, Surrey, 3rd s. of
I. 1623.   Mary, *suo jure* COUNTESS OF BUCKINGHAM, by Sir George VILLIERS, of Brokesby, co. Leicester, and yr. br. of George, 1st DUKE OF BUCKINGHAM, was Gent. of the Horse 1616, Gent. of the Bedchamber, and Master of the Robes 1617 ; and on 18 Apr. 1623, was *cr.* BARON VILLIERS OF DAVENTRY, co. Northampton, and EARL OF AN-GLESEY in Wales. (ᵃ)   Chief Steward of the Honour of Hampton Court, 1628.   He *m.* Elizabeth, da. of Thomas SHELDON, of Howby, co. Leicester.   He *d.* 3 Apr. 1630, at Windsor, and was *bur.* in St. George's Chapel there. (ᵇ)   Admon. 6 May 1630 to his widow.   She *m.*, 5 Aug.

(ᵃ) "There was talk here that the Earl of Anglesey (Kit Villiers) was banished the Court . . . .   The King saying, he would have no drunkards of his chamber." (Rev. J. Mead to Sir M. Stuteville, 23 Apr. 1625.)   V.G.

(ᵇ) See Nicolas, *Memoir of A. Vincent, Windsor Herald*, pp. 93-94, and see also (as to the 2nd Earl) the burial at St. Martin's, of *Carolus Villers, Comes.*

1641, at Sunbury, Midx., the Hon. Benjamin Weston, who, in her right, was of Ashley Park abovenamed, and who was *bap.* 4 Aug. 1614, at Roxwell, Essex. He *d. s p.*, in St. Andrew's, Holborn, in or before 1673. Admon. 26 June 1673. She *d.* 12, and was *bur.*, at night, 18 Apr. 1662, at Walton afsd. (ª) M.I. (ᵇ)

II. 1630   2. Charles (Villiers), Earl of Anglesey, and Baron
    to   Villiers of Daventry, only s. and h., *b.* about 1627 ; ent.
    1661.   Eton 1642. He *m.*, 25 Apr. 1648, at St Bartholomew-
the-Less, London, (Lic. Bp. of Lond., he 21 and she 23) Mary, Dowager Viscountess Grandison [I.], 3rd da. of Paul (Bayning), 1st Viscount Bayning, by Anne, da. of Sir Henry Glemham. He *d. s.p.*, of small pox, and was *bur.* at St. Martin's-in-the-Fields, Midx., 4 Feb. 1660/1, (ᶜ) when his honours became *extinct.* His widow (who was aged 6 at her father's death, 10 July 1629), *m.*, 3rdly, Arthur Gorges, of Chelsea, Midx., who *d. s.p*, 18 Apr. 1668, and was *bur.* there. Her admon., as of Blankney, co. Lincoln, 26 Jan 1671/2, granted to her da. Barbara, Duchess of Cleveland. Will dat. 30 Mar. 1671, pr. 16 Feb. 1676/7, by John Fanning, of Blankney afsd.

———————

III. 1661.   1. Arthur (Annesley), Viscount Valentia and
              Baron Mountnorris [I.], was, on 20 Apr. 1661, *cr.*
BARON ANNESLEY of Newport Pagnel, Bucks, and EARL OF ANGLESEY in Wales. (ᵈ) He was s. and h. of Francis, Viscount Valentia, Lord Mountnorris and a Baronet [I], by his 1st wife, Dorothy, da. of Sir John Philipps, of Picton, 1st Bart. He was *b.* in Fishamble Str., Dublin, 10, and *bap.* 20 July 1614, at St. John's, in that city. He is said to have been ed. at Magd. Coll., Oxford, 1630; B.A. 1634, and entered Lincoln's Inn the same year M P. for co Radnor 1647-53, for Dublin (Eng. Parl.) 1659-60, and for Carmarthen 1660. In 1645, and again in 1647, he

———————

(ª) Two knots of ribbon (with which her wrists had been tied up) remained in good preservation in 1710 (when the vault was first opened after her death), and were sent to her descendant, Sir John Shelley, Bart, grandson of Sir Charles Shelley, Bart., by her da. Elizabeth Weston. See Manning and Bray's *Surrey*, vol ii, p. 767—as also "*The Topographer* (1791), vol iii, p 304

(ᵇ) Lodge, in error, gives the death date and M.I. of Elizabeth (who *d.* 1662), widow of the 1st (Villiers) Earl of Anglesey, to Elizabeth (who *d* 1697/8) widow of iii (Annesley) Earl of Anglesey, and Betham follows him in the Annesley Pedigree registered in Ulster's Office. V.G.

(ᶜ) See note " b " on previous page.

(ᵈ) For an account of the ceremonies attending this creation, see note *sub* i Earl of Clarendon. Annesley, Earl of Anglesey, bore arms of Paly silver and azure with a bend gules, being the undifferenced arms of his ancestors the Annesleys of Annesley. His immediate ancestors, the Annesleys of Newport Pagnel, were, however, a family of lesser gentry, sprung from a younger son of the Annesleys of Ruddington, themselves a cadet branch from the main stock. The quartering by this family of the arms of Chandos has nothing the justify it. (*ex inform* Oswald Barron) V.G.

was one of the Commissioners to manage the Irish affairs under the Parl., but, after the murder of the King, took part with the Royalists. In 1658 he was empowered to treat at Brussels with the King's rebellious subjects. Early in 1660 he was President of the Council of State. Was sworn P.C. 1661, and was Vice Treasurer of Ireland, 1660-67. Treasurer of the Navy 1667-68. On 22 Nov. 1660, he *suc.* to his father's Irish Peerage (taking his seat by proxy 25 June 1661), and on 20 Apr. 1661, was *cr.* a Peer [E.] as above, and took his seat accordingly 11 May 1661. On 8 Mar. 1665 he received a pension of £600 a year, and on 22 Apr. 1673 was made LORD PRIVY SEAL, but was dismissed 9 Aug. 1682, from which time he lived chiefly at Blechington, Oxon.(*) He *m.*, 24 Apr. 1638, at Acton, Midx., Elizabeth, da. of Sir James ALTHAM, of Oxhey, Herts, by Elizabeth, da. and h. of Sir Richard SUTTON, of Acton afsd. He *d.* 6 Apr. 1686, at his house in Drury Lane, Midx., of quinsy, and was *bur.* at Farnborough, Hants.(*) Will dat. 23 Feb. 1685/6, pr. 18 June 1686, and again 3 July 1699. His widow was *b.* 9 Jan. 1620, and by *Inq.*, 2 Nov. 1630, was found the elder of the two sisters and coheirs(*) of Sutton Altham of Acton. She was *bur.* 26 Jan. 1697/8,(*) at St. Anne's, Soho, Midx. Will dat. 18 May 1686, pr. 22 Mar. 1697/8.

IV. 1686.   2. JAMES (ANNESLEY), EARL OF ANGLESEY, &c., [E.], also VISCOUNT VALENTIA, &c. [I.], s. and h. Matric. Oxford (Ch. Ch.) 4 Dec. 1661, aged 16. M.P. (Whig) for co. Waterford 1666, and for Winchester, 1679-81. On 10 May 1686 he took his seat in the English House of Lords, and on 17 Nov. 1688, joined the Bishops in their celebrated petition to James II. He *m.* (settl. dat. 17 Sep. 1669) Elizabeth, 4th da. of John (MANNERS), 8th EARL OF RUTLAND, by Frances, da. of Edward (MONTAGU), LORD MONTAGU OF BOUGHTON. He *d.* 1 Apr. 1690. Admon. 6 June 1690 to his widow. She *d.*, of cancer in the

(*) He had a most indifferent reputation. "Sir H. Cholmeley is confident my Lord A. is one of the greatest knaves in the world." (Pepys' *Diary*, 26 June 1667.) On 21 May 1669 he was soundly cudgelled by a Major Scott with whom he had declined a duel. "Arlington had a cruel dispute with Anglesey yesterday, and told him that he is a knave, which is too true." (W. Harbord to Earl of Essex, 28 Mar. 1674.) The great Duke of Ormonde also had a mean opinion of him, and writes, in 1680/1 of him as "a man I have seen detected in public of misinformation and mean artifices, for sordid sums, and yet never blush at the matter." Bp. Burnet describes him as "a man of grave deportment." V.G.
   The more interesting portions of his Diary, in which, among other things, he notes his wife's "Bedlam railing humour," are printed in the *Hist. MSS. Com.*, 13th Rep., pt. vi, p. 261 *et seq.* V.G.
   (*) See a curious anecdote about him in the *Memoirs* of Edward (Harley), Earl of Oxford, wherein it is stated that he was "buttler" to Sir Arthur Chichester, the Lord Lieut. of Ireland. (*N. & Q.*, 2nd Series, vol. i, p. 325.) His splendid library, of which the sale catalogue (4to.) contained pp. 286, was sold by auction, in London, 25 Oct. 1686. See *N. & Q.*, 1st Series, vol. x, pp. 286, 375, and 2nd Series, vol. xi, p. 443.
   (*) The other coh. was the Countess of Carbery [I.].
   (*) See note "b" on previous page.

breast, 7, and was *bur.* 10 Dec. 1700, at St. James's, Westm. Will dat. 10 Feb. 1699/1700, pr. 20 Jan. 1700/1.

V. 1690. 3. JAMES (ANNESLEY), EARL OF ANGLESEY, &c. [E.], also VISCOUNT VALENTIA, &c. [I.], s. and h., *bap.* 13 July 1674. (*) Matric. Oxford (Ch Ch.) 15 July 1690. He took his seat in the Irish House, 27 Aug., and in the English House 23 Nov. 1695. He *m.*, 28 Oct. 1699, at Westm. Abbey, "the Rt. Hon. Lady Catherine DARNLEY," (ᵇ) illegit. da. of JAMES II by Catherine (SEDLEY), *suo jure* COUNTESS OF DORCHESTER. They were separated by Act of Parl., 12 June 1701, on account of his cruelty. He *d. s.p.m.*, (ᶜ) 21 Jan. following (1701/2), and was *bur* at Farnborough, Hants. Will dat. 14 May to 9 Dec 1701, (ᵈ) pr. Prerog Ct. [I.]. His widow *m.*, 16 Mar. 1705/6 (Lic. at Fac. Office), at St. Martin's-in-the-Fields (as his 3rd wife), John (SHEFFIELD), 1st DUKE OF BUCKINGHAM, who *d.* 24 Feb 1720/1. She *d.* 14 Mar., and was *bur.* 8 Apr. 1743, at Westm. Abbey, aged 61.

VI. 1702. 4. JOHN (ANNESLEY), EARL OF ANGLESEY, &c. [E.], also VISCOUNT VALENTIA, &c. [I.], br. and h. male, *bap.* 18 Jan. 1676 at Farnborough. Took his seat in the English House, 3 Feb. 1701/2 ; P.C., Vice Treasurer, Receiver Gen. and Paymaster of the Forces [I.], 1710 He *m.*, 21 May 1706, (Lic. Fac. Office) Henrietta, *suo jure* BARONESS STRANGE, 1st da. and coh. (in 1714 sole h.) of William Richard George (STANLEY), 9th EARL OF DERBY, by Elizabeth, da of Thomas BUTLER, *styled* EARL OF OSSORY, s. and h. ap. of James, 1st DUKE OF ORMONDE. He *d. s.p.s.*, 18 Sep. 1710, and was *bur.* at Farnborough, (ᵉ) Hants. Will dat. 14 June 1708, pr. Sep. 1710, and [I.] 30 Nov. 1711. His widow *m.*, (as his 2nd wife) at the Chapel Royal, Whitehall, 24 July 1714, John (ASHBURNHAM), 1st EARL OF ASHBURNHAM, who *d.* 10 Mar. 1736/7. She *d. s.p.m.*, 26 June 1718, in her 31st year, and was *bur.* at Ashburnham.

VII. 1710. 5. ARTHUR (ANNESLEY), EARL OF ANGLESEY, &c. [E.], also VISCOUNT VALENTIA, &c. [I.], br. and h. male, sometime Fellow of Magd. Coll., Cambridge ; M.A., 1699 ; Gent. of the Privy Chamber 1691 ; M P. (Tory) for Cambridge Univ., 1702-10, and for New Roll [I.], 1703-10. High Steward of Cambridge Univ. 9 Feb. 1721/2 till his death. Took his seat in the English House, 23 Nov. 1710, and in the Irish House, 9 July 1711. P.C. [E.] 1710, and [I.]. Joint Vice Treasurer and Treasurer at War [I.] 1710-16. On the death of Queen Anne

---

(*) See his grandfather's Diary.

(ᵇ) She is so styled in her m. lic. from the Dean and Chapter of Westm.

(ᶜ) Catharine, his only da and h , *b.* Jan. 1700/1, *m.*, Sep 1718, William Phipps, by whom she had a son Constantine, [1], 1765.

(ᵈ) See the *Certiorari* Bundle at the P.R.O.

(ᵉ) Swift calls him "the great support of the Tories," and remarks on his death, "I could hardly have had a loss that would grieve me more." V.G.

he was made one of the Lords Justices, 1 Aug. to 18 Sep. 1714, (ª) until the arrival of George I from Hanover. A Governor of co. Wexford, Nov. 1727. He *m.*, on Sat. before 27 July 1701/2, (ᵇ) (Lic. Fac. Office 6 Jan., both above 21) his cousin, Mary, 3rd da. of John (Thompson), 1st Lord Haversham, by Frances, widow of Francis Wyndham, da. of Arthur (Annesley), 1st Earl of Anglesey. She *d.* at Woodstock, Oxon, 22 Jan. 1718/9, and was *bur.* at Farnborough afsd. He *d. s p.*, 1 Apr. 1737, at Farnborough, and was buried there. (ᶜ) Will dat. 18 Feb. 1735, pr. May 1737.

VIII. 1737 to 1761.	6. Richard (Annesley), Earl of Anglesey and Baron Annesley [E.], also Viscount Valentia, Baron Mountnorris, and (5th) Baron Altham [I.], cousin and h. male, (ᵈ) being yr. s. of Richard, 3rd Baron Altham [I.],

(by Dorothy, da. of John Davey), who was a yr. s of Arthur (in), 1st Earl of Anglesey, &c. [E], and (iii) 2nd Viscount Valentia, &c. [I.]. He was *b.* shortly after 1690, (ᵉ) became an Ensign in the army, but was struck off the half pay in 1715, about which time, being in needy circumstances, he appears to have sought his fortune by marriage (or marriages) as stated below. On 14 Nov. 1727 he *suc.* his elder br. as BARON ALTHAM [I], and his right thereto was acknowledged by his taking his seat as such. In 1737 he *suc.* his cousin (as above) in the Earldom of Anglesey and other titles [E. & I.], and took his seat in England, as an Earl, 10 May 1737, and in Ireland, as a Viscount, 4 Oct. 1737. (ᶠ) He was also a Governor of co. Wexford before 1745, in which county he fixed his residence at Camolin Park. He *m*, 25 Jan. 1715, (ᵍ) when he is stated to have been 21, (ʰ) at Northam, in North Devon, Ann, da. of Capt. John Prust, of Monkleigh, near Bideford, in that co., by Mary, da. of Thomas Ley. She, who was *b.* 21 Sep. and *bap.* 11 Oct. 1694, at Monkleigh, is said to have brought him a considerable fortune, and to have lived with him at Westminster, and at Waterford and Ross, but to have separated from him in 1719, returning to North Devon, where she *d. s.p.*, and was *bur.* (as Ann, Countess of Anglesey) 13 Aug. 1741, (ᵍ) at Monkleigh, Devon.

(ª) For a list of these see note sub II Duke of Devonshire "A person of true merit, and must be lamented of all good men." (Duke of Ormonde to E. Hamilton, 13 May 1737.) V.G

(ᵇ) Letter of Selina, Countess Ferrers, dat. 27 July. V.G

(ᶜ) See *Call Top. et Gen.*, vol. vii, p. 233.

(ᵈ) If, however, the statement of James Annesley, "*the unfortunate young nobleman*" (who claimed to be s. and h. of Arthur, 4th Lord Altham [I.], the elder br. of this Richard) be true, the said James (and not the abovenamed Richard) would have been the h. male. See full account of this under Altham.

(ᵉ) The Richard Annesley *bap* 31 Oct. 1689, and *bur.* 18 Nov. 1690, at Westm. Abbey, was his elder br.

(ᶠ) For an account of his conviction, 3 Aug. 1744, on the charge of assaulting "The Hon. James Annesley Esq.," the claimant to his estates and honours, see *State Trials,* vol. xviii, p. 197.

(ᵍ) Parish Reg, produced at the claim (in 1819) of George, Earl of Mountnorris [I.], to the Earldom of Anglesey.

(ʰ) See "Anglesey Case," 1771.

According to another account, (ᵃ) however, in the same year 1715, he *m.*, 1stly privately, and afterwards publicly (with a Lic. from the Consistorial Court of Dublin) (ᵇ), Anne, only da. of John SIMPSON, a wealthy clothier of Meath Str., Dublin, she being then about 15 years old.   This Anne is mentioned in her father's will (who *d.* 1730) under the name of " Lady Altham, " and was presented (after 1737) at the Vice Regal Court [I.], as " Countess of Anglesey. " (ᶜ)   This Lady, by whom he had three daughters, survived the Earl four years, so that, if her marriage be reckoned valid, (ᵈ) it would upset *both* the other ones.   On 15 Sep. 1741 (about a month after the burial of Anne, Countess of Anglesey first named), he *m* , (ᵉ) privately at his own house, Camolin Park, afsd., Juliana, da. of Richard DONOVAN, sometime a merchant of Wexford, by (—), da. of Richard NIXON, of the same co   This marriage, both the witnesses being dead, was *acknowledged* to have taken place as above, and was *again celebrated* in the same place, 8 Oct. 1752   The Earl *d.* 14 Feb. 1761, at Camolin Park.   Will dat. 7 Apr. 1759, pr. 1761, Prerog Ct. [I.]. (ᶠ)   His widow *m.* (as his 1st wife) Mathew TALBOT, of Castle Talbot, co Wexford, whose will was pr. 1795, and *d.* at Bath, Somerset, 20 Nov. 1776.   Will pr. 1771.

(ᵃ) See Burke's *Vicissitudes of Families*, 3rd series, 1863, p. 83, &c.

(ᵇ) No such Lic. exists.   (*ex inform*. G. D. Burtchaell, 1909)   V.G.

(ᶜ) It must be remembered, however, that the rival wife (Miss Prust) was also named Anne.

(ᵈ) There is a remarkable document signed by this Lady, on 22 Dec. 1726, wherein she binds herself never to prosecute her husband for bigamy, which certainly looks as if both these parties considered the marriage with Ann Prust to have been legal.   See claim to Earldom of Anglesey, in 1819.

(ᵉ) The certificate of this marriage was produced to the ENGLISH House of Lords on the trial for the English Peerage, but was discredited on the ground of forgery. The witness on whose testimony that decision was principally grounded was proved (*afterwards*) to have been perjured, and the decision itself (22 Apr. 1771), was but by a majority of *one*, thirteen Peers being present   In the following year, the validity of the marriage was again confirmed by the IRISH House (1 June 1772), and their decision appears (from the evidence produced) to have been in all probability the right one. *Both* the Earl *and Countess* testified to the marriage of 1741 on their death beds.   As to the Earl (though we are told that he was " a man very regular in *devotion*, and using frequent prayers in his family, at which he constantly assisted with great appearance of fervour "), his *devotion* to the fair sex certainly equalled, if it did not surpass his *spiritual* devotion, for we hear of *another* illegit s of his (by yet another woman, named Salkeld), one Richard Annesley, who *claimed the title* in 1770.   The *London Evening Post*, 4 Apr 1722, states this Richard to be the legit. s. of Earl Richard " by Anne, 2nd da. of William Salkeld, of the city of London, Merchant. "   (The date of 1742 is attributed to this marriage in a ped of Jackson—the name of Anne Salkeld's mother—in Morehouse's *History of Kirkburton, co York*, p. 172.   See *N. & Q.*, 7th Series, vol. ii, p. 16.)   The *possibility* of such a marriage is doubtful, as the Earl's 1st marriage (or marriages) was (or were) in 1715, soon after he was of age, and the subsequent marriage (the 1st of the two marriages with Juliana, who survived him) was within a month of the death of one of these wives, probably *the* 1st and lawful wife.   See *N. & Q.*, 2nd Series, vol. x, pp. 27 and 156, as also several notices in 2nd Series, vol. xi

(ᶠ) The statement in Vicars' *Irish Wills*, that his will was pr. 1759, is wrong.   V.G.

Note.—On the death of the Earl (14 Feb. 1761), ARTHUR ANNESLEY, his s. by the said Juliana (*b.* 7 Aug. 1744), though opposed by the next h., was held in Ireland to have *suc.* to the IRISH HONOURS, and took his seat in the House [I.] as VISCOUNT VALENTIA, 5 Dec. 1765 and 7 Nov. 1771.(ª) On his petitioning, however, for a writ of sum. to the Parl. of Great Britain as EARL OF ANGLESEY &c., the House of Lords for that kingdom (to whom it had been referred) decided, 22 Apr. 1771, that "the claimant had no right to the titles, honours and dignities claimed by his petition." (ᵇ) According, therefore, to these decisions, the ENGLISH titles of EARL OF ANGLESEY and BARON ANNESLEY had become *extinct* on 14 Feb. 1761, the Irish titles continuing.

The said Arthur, Viscount Valentia [I], was, on 3 Dec. 1793, *cr.* EARL OF MOUNTNORRIS [I.]. He *d.* 5 July 1816, and was *suc.* by his s. George, 2nd Earl of Mountnorris, &c. [I.]. The latter's claim as a Peer of Ireland was, on 6 Mar. 1817, admitted (by the House of Lords of the *United Kingdom*) not only as an Earl, but as a Viscount, and the holder of two Baronies [I], which last three peerages he could only possess *in right of inheritance* from his grandfather, Richard (viii) 6th Earl of Anglesey abovenamed. (ª) On the ground of this admission of his father's lawful birth, he petitioned, 30 Jan 1819, for his writ as "EARL OF ANGLESEY," &c, which petition was referred to the committee for privileges, but no further steps appear to have been taken in the matter. He *d. s p m.s*, 23 July 1844, when *the issue male of the* 1st EARL OF ANGLESEY and BARON ANNESLEY (to whom alone those honours were limited) became *extinct*, granting (as was held by the *Irish* House of Lords) that the s. of the 6th Earl (who *suc.* him in his Irish, but not in his English, honours) was *b.* in wedlock. The title of ANGLESEY, however, was (in accordance with the *English* decision of 1771, whereby it was held to have been *extinct* in 1761) made use of again, as a Peerage title, some thirty years *before* such extinction of issue had occurred.

MARQUESSATE.   1. HENRY WILLIAM (ᶜ) PAGET, s. and h. of Henry (PAGET), 1st (III) EARL OF UXBRIDGE, by Jane, 1st da.
I. 1815.   of Arthur CHAMPAGNE, Dean of Clonmacnoise [I.], was *b.* 17 May, and *bap.* 12 June 1768, at St Geo., Han. Sq.   Ed. at Westm. School, and at Ch. Ch., Oxford.   M.A. 28 June 1786.   M.P.

(ª) See under ALTHAM.
(ᵇ) On 10 May 1767, he *m*, at St James's, Westm., as "Earl of Anglesey," and signed the entry (curiously enough) as "ALTHAM-ANGLESEY," though "*Altham*" was but a *Barony* [I.], while "*Valentia*" (to which he was unquestionably equally entitled) was a *Viscountcy* [I.], and one of much older creation.
(ᶜ) He is called "Henry William *Bayly Peter Walter*, commonly called Lord Paget" in the reg of his marriage, 1795. See, as to the origin of the Bayly family, which was not Scotch, *Scottish N. & Q.*, vol. ii, p. 16.   As to the name Peter Walter, see note *sub* x LORD PAGET DE BEAUDESERT.

(Tory) for the Carnarvon boroughs, 1790-96, and for Milborne Port, 1796-1804 and 1806-10. In 1790 he raised a regiment (the 80th Foot or Staffordshire Volunteers) from his father's tenantry, of which he was subsequently Lieut. Col. In 1795 he was Lieut. Col. of the 16th Light Dragoons, and in 1797 of the 7th Light Dragoons; Col. thereof 1801-42 ; Col. of the Royal Horse Guards 1842-54; Major Gen. 1802; Lieut. Gen 1808; General 1819. He distinguished himself (being then *styled* LORD PAGET) in the campaign of the Duke of York, and subsequently, when commanding the Calvary, at Corunna, under Sir John Moore. On 13 Mar. 1812 he *suc.* his father as EARL OF UXBRIDGE AND LORD PAGET DE BEAUDESERT. At Waterloo, 18 June 1815, he commanded the cavalry of the Anglo-Belgian army, and contributed greatly to the success of that memorable battle, in which he received a wound, which entailed the loss of his leg. (ª) Three weeks after that action, on 4 July 1815, he was rewarded by being *cr.* MARQUESS OF ANGLESEY. G.C.B. 2 Jan. 1815. Knight of Maria Theresa of Austria, 21 Aug. 1815, and on the same date, Knight of St George of Russia. G.C.H., 1816. El. K.G. 19 Feb., inst. 2 Mar. 1818. P.C., 1827. Gold Stick 1842. FIELD MARSHAL, 1846. He was also twice, 1827-28 and 1846-52, Master Gen. of the Ordnance ; and twice, 1828 to 1829, when the Tory Govt. not approving of his conduct recalled him, and 1830 to 1833, having then gone over to the Whigs, LORD LIEUT. OF IRELAND. At the coronation of Geo. IV, 1821, he acted as LORD HIGH STEWARD. Lord Lieut. of Anglesey 1812-54, Lord Lieut. of co. Stafford 1849-54. He *m*, 1stly, 25 July 1795, at the Earl of Jersey's house in Grosvenor Sq., Caroline Elizabeth, 3rd da. of George Bussey (VILLIERS), 4th EARL OF JERSEY, by Frances, da. and h. of Philip TWYSDEN, Bishop of Raphoe [I.] She was *b.* 16 Dec. 1774. This marriage, after the birth of eight children, was dissolved at her own suit by the Scotch Courts in 1810. (ᵇ) He *m.,* 2ndly, in 1810, Charlotte, (ᶜ) the divorced wife of the Rt. Hon. Sir Henry Wellesley, G.C.B. (afterwards *cr.* LORD COWLEY), da. of Charles Sloane (CADOGAN), 1st EARL CADOGAN, by his 2nd wife, Mary, da. of Charles CHURCHILL. She was *b.* 11 July 1781, and *d.* 8 July 1853, at Uxbridge House, Old Burlington Str., Midx , aged 72. Admon Dec. 1853. The Marquess, who (with the exception of the Royal family) was the only Field Marshal at that time in the army, *d.* at Uxbridge House,

---

(ª) See an interesting account thereof and amusing epitaphs thereon in *N. & Q.*, 3rd Series, vol. ii, pp 249, 320 and 339.

(ᵇ) She *m.,* 29 Nov. 1810, George William (CAMPBELL), 6th DUKE OF ARGYLL [S] (who *d. s.p.,* 22 Oct. 1839), and *d.* 16 June 1835. " Lord Paget will not admire meeting his quondam wife with the higher rank of Duchess, and an obsequious husband, for he has always treated her with the most shameful contempt " (Lady Jerningham, Nov. 1810) V.G.

(ᶜ) He seduced this woman, then the mother of four children, and a verdict against him for £24,000, the full amount claimed in an action for *crim. con.,* a duel between him and her br., Capt. Cadogan, and two divorces, were the results of this misconduct.

afsd , in his 86th year, 29 Apr., and was *bur*. 6 May 1854, in Lichfield Cathedral. (ª) Will pr. July 1854.

II. 1854.   2. HENRY (PAGET), MARQUESS OF ANGLESEY, &c., s. and h. by 1st wife, *b*. 6 July 1797. Col. of the 42nd Foot. M.P. (Whig) for Anglesey, 1820-32   He was *sum. v.p.* to the House of Lords by writ, 15 Jan. 1833, in his father's Barony, as LORD PAGET DE BEAUDESERT. A Lord in Waiting 1837-39. State Steward to the Lord Lieut. [I.] 1828-29. P.C. 1839. Lord Chamberlain of the Household 1839-41. Lord Lieut. of Anglesey 1854-69. He *m*., 1stly, 5 Aug. 1819, at Altyre in Scotland, and again, 8 Feb. 1820, at St. Geo., Han. Sq , Eleanora, 2nd da. of John CAMPBELL, of Shawfield, by Charlotte Susan Maria, 2nd da. of John (CAMPBELL), 5th DUKE OF ARGYLL [S.]. She *d*. 3 July 1828, aged 29, at Twickenham. He *m*., 2ndly, 27 Aug. 1833, in Pimlico, Henrietta Maria, 3rd. da of the Rt. Hon. Sir Charles BAGOT, G C.B., by Mary Charlotte Anne, 1st. da. of William (WELLESLEY), 3rd EARL OF MORNINGTON [I.]. She, who was *b*. Sep 1815, *d* 22 Mar. 1844, in York Str , St. James's, and was *bur* at Lichfield, aged 28. He *m*., 3rdly, 8 Mar. 1860, Ellen Jane, the divorced wife of W. J. BELL, and da. of George BURNAND. By her he had no issue. He *d*. 6 Feb. 1869, suddenly, at Beaudesert. (ᵇ)   His widow *d*. 2 June 1874, at Worthing, Sussex, in her 44th year, and was *bur*. in the cemetery there.   M.I

III. 1869.   3. HENRY WILLIAM GEORGE (PAGET), MARQUESS OF ANGLESEY, &c., s. and h., being the only s. by 1st wife, *b*. 9 Dec. 1821.   Sometime an officer in the Grenadier Foot Guards. M.P (Liberal) for South Staffordshire, 1854-57. He *m*., 7 June 1845, at Horsham, Sussex, Sophia, da. of James EVERSFIELD, of Denne Park, Sussex, by Mary, 1st da of Robert H. CREW. He *d. s p*., 30 Jan. 1880, at Albert Mansions, Victoria Str., Westm.   His widow *d*. 7 Dec. 1901, at the Pantiles, Tunbridge Wells   Will dat. 28 Dec 1894 to 1 Dec. 1901, pr. Feb. 1902, at £8,632 gross, and £8,440 net.

IV 1880.   4. HENRY (PAGET), MARQUESS OF ANGLESEY, &c., half br. and h., being s. of the 2nd Marquess by his 2nd wife, *b*. 25 Dec. 1835.   He *m*., 1stly, 24 Aug 1858, at a Registry Office, Elizabeth, da. of Joseph NORMAN, said to have been a farmer in Kent. She *d. s.p.*, 5 Nov. 1873, aged 32.   He *m*., 2ndly, 2 Feb 1874, at the British Embassy, Paris, Blanche Mary, da. of John Christian Curwen BOYD, of Merton Hall, co. Wigtown, and of Prince's Gardens, Hyde Park, Midx.   She *d*. 14 Aug. 1877, at Boulogne-sur-Mer.   He *m*., 3rdly, 26 June 1880, also at the British Embassy, Paris, Mary Livingstone, widow

---

(ª) He was a brilliant, gallant cavalry officer, but neither a wise nor a virtuous man.   He was very popular in Ireland during his first, and very unpopular in his second, vice-royalty   V G.

(ᵇ) A keen sportsman, devoting his time to shooting, coursing, racing, and cricket , in morals he resembled his father.   V.G.

of the Hon. Henry Wodehouse, da. of the Hon. John P. King, of Sand-hills, Georgia, U.S A   He *d.* 13 Oct. 1898, at Plâs Newydd, after a long illness, and was *bur.* at Llanedwen, Anglesey.   Will pr. gross £535,395, net £22,978.   His widow was living at Versailles 1909.

V. 1898.   5. Henry Cyril (Paget), Marquess of Anglesey,
                 Earl of Uxbridge and Baron Paget de Beaudesert,
s. and h. by 2nd wife, *b.* 16 June, 1875.   Ed. at Eton.   Lieut. 2nd Vol. Batt. Royal Welsh Fusiliers   He *m.*, 20 Jan. 1898, at St. Mary's Rom Cath. Ch , Sloane Str., Chelsea, his cousin, Lilian, 1st da. of Sir George Chetwynd, Bart., by Florence Cecilia, yst. da. of Henry (Paget), 2nd Marquess of Anglesey.   She, who was *b.* 10 Mar. 1876, obtained a decree *nisi* of nullity of marriage, 7 Nov. 1900.   He became bankrupt for £544,000 in 1904. (ª)   He *d. s p.*, at Monte Carlo, 14, and was *bur.* 23 Mar. 1905, at Llanedwen afsd.   He was *suc.* by his cousin, who is outside the scope of this work.

Family Estates.—These, in 1883, consisted of about 1,000 acres in Dorset, worth about £800 a year ; about 10,000 acres in Anglesey, worth about £10,000 a year, and about 1,500 acres in co. Derby, and 17,500 in co. Stafford, worth, together, about £100,000 a year.   Total about 30,000 acres, worth about £110,000 a year.   *Principal Residences :*—Beaudesert Park, near Lichfield ; Plâs Newydd, Anglesey.

ANGLIA or EAST ANGLIA see "NORFOLK"

ANGUS

    This was one of the seven original Earldoms [Mormaerships] of Scot-land which, more or less, represented the seven provinces (*each* province consisting of *two* districts), of the Pictish Kingdom, afterwards called Alban, into which, prior to the 9th century, " transmarine Scotland " (*i.e.* the country north of the Firth of Forth and the Firth of Clyde) was by seven brothers divided. (ᵇ)   These divisions were : (1) Angus (being the name of the eldest brother), now co. Forfar, *with* Mearns, now co. Kincar-dine ; (2) Athole *with* Gowry, now the north and east part of co. Perth ; (3) Stratherne *with* Menteith, now the southern part of co. Perth; (4) Fife

---

(ª) He incurred debts, within 6 years, to the extent of £544,000, though his estates were worth £110,000 *p. a.*   His wardrobe and personal jewels, sold when he became insolvent, disclosed a preposterous accumulation, the latter realising £88,000. He seems only to have existed for the purpose of giving a melancholy and unneeded illustration of the truth that a man with the finest prospects, may, by the wildest folly and extravagance, as Sir Thomas Browne says, " foully miscarry in the advantage of humanity, play away an uniterable life, and have lived in vain. "   V G

(ᵇ) *Celtic Scotland*, by W.F Skene, 1880, vol. iii, cap. ii, *&c.*   In this is a map shewing the seven ancient divisions.   From this valuable work most of the above remarks are taken.

with Fothreve now together forming co. Fife ; (5) Mar *with* Buchan, now together forming cos. Aberdeen and Banff ; (6) Moray (Muref or Moreb) *with* Ross, now cos. Inverness and Ross ; and (7) Caithness *with* Sutherland. The district on the west being the Kingdom of Dalriada (now part of Argyll), is here omitted ; but in the 10th century the province of Arregaithel (Argyll) was *added*, which included not only the Dalriada, but the entire western seaboard of Scotland as far north as the old province of Caithness, which latter province was then omitted, having previously passed into the hands of the Norwegians. The ruler of each of these districts originally bore the title of " Ri " (*i.e.* King), being inferior only to the " Ardri " (*i.e.* Supreme King) ; but in the 10th century (with the exception of Argyll, and occasionally of Moray) each such ruler was styled " Mormaer, " *i.e.* Great Maer or Steward.

During the reign of Alexander I, in the foundation charter of the monastery of Scone bearing date either 1114 or 1115, the Mormaers of most of these provinces occur for the first time under the name of Earls. This charter was granted " with the consent of nine persons, two of whom have the simple designation of *Episcopus* [being] followed by seven others, six of whom have the word *Comes*, or Earl, after their names, and the only one who is not so designated is Gospatrick, whom we know to have been at the time (or shortly afterwards) Earl of Dunbar, and who probably represented that part of Lothian attached to Alexander's Kingdom. The other six must of course have represented the districts of transmarine Scotland which properly formed Alexander's dominions. . . . . The six persons who bear the title of *Comes*, are Beth, Mallus, Madach, Rothri, Gartnach, and Dufugan, and of these we can identify four, " ([a]) *viz.* (Mallus) Stratherne ; (Madach) Athole ; (Rothri) Mar ; and (Gartnach) Buchan. Doubtless another was (Dufugan) Angus. " *Beth, Comes* " is difficult of strict identification, not improbably he was Earl of Fife, but possibly Earl of Moray. ([b]) In this early part of the 12th century, out of the seven *original* provinces founded by the seven brothers, Caithness, was certainly, and Moray probably (though Fife possibly) wanting ; the two vacant places being supplied by Dunbar (from the Lowlands), and by Buchan, which had previously become separated from Mar.

" Thus the great Celtic Chiefs of the Country, to whom the Norwegians applied the Norwegian title of Jarl, which was a *personal* dignity though given in connection with a territory, now appear bearing the Saxon title of *Comes* or *Earl*, and the Celtic title of Mormaer, probably official in its origin, was now merged in a personal dignity. " ([c])

" From the time when the Celtic King Malcolm (1057-98) had *m.* the Saxon Princess Margaret, there had been an increasing Saxon influence in the government of the Celtic provinces, " and of his three sons (by that Princess) who, from 1098 to 1153, were successively Kings [S.], " the reigns of Edgar and Alexander I must be viewed as essentially those of Saxon

([a]) Skene's *Celtic Scotland.*
([b]) See (as to this point) Skene, *ut supra*, vol. iii, p. 62, note 36.
([c]) *Ibid*

monarchs, modelling their Kingdom in accordance with Saxon institutions, while the object of David was to introduce the *feudal system* of *Norman England* into Scotland, and adapt her institutions to *feudal forms.*" (ᵃ)

"David's object on his accession to the throne (1124) was to feudalise the whole Kingdom, by importing feudal forms and holdings into it, and to place the leading dignitaries of the Kingdom in the position of *crown vassals*, as well as to introduce a Norman Baronage. The relation of these old Celtic Earls, or Mormaers, towards the *districts* with which their names were connected was *not a purely territorial* one. It was more a relation towards the *tribes* who peopled it, than towards the *land*. David's desire, certainly, would be to place them, whenever opportunity offered, in the position of holding the land they were officially connected with, *as an Earldom of the Crown in Chief*, in the same manner as the Barons held their Baronies." (ᵇ)

"The process of *feudalizing* the Earldoms began under David I, and was carried on by his successors, Malcolm the Maiden, and William [1153-1214]. In the course of the twelfth century, (ᶜ) the seven Earls were gradually passing from the position of COMITES of the Sovereign to that of Feudal Lords, holding the lands, with which their position *had* been judicial, as an *Earldom of the Crown ;* the creation of six additional Earls, namely MENTEITH, GARIOCH, LENNOX, ROSS, CARRICK and CAITHNESS, formed part of the feudalizing scheme ; and though the Earls continued down to 1214 to be spoken of as seven in number, the Earldoms enumerated were not always the same. . . . . *Till* feudalized, the Earldoms of Scotland were distinctly *non*-territorial, and the Earls oftener designated by their names than their titles. The ancient Earldoms, when converted into

---

(ᵃ) See note " b " on previous page.

(ᵇ) Skene's *Celtic Scotland.*

(ᶜ) " After 1214, " said Lord Mansfield in his speech in the Sutherland case, " I think it clear that territorial peerages [S.] must have gone, because lands then became saleable. " This, however, is merely an *obiter dictum* (and not a very happy one) of his Lordship, and, in a legal point of view, these *dicta*, whether of Lord Mansfield, or of other Law Lords, " are acknowledged to have *none of the force of a decision* of the House of Lords sitting as a Court of Appeal, and [in this case] being founded on very imperfect knowledge of the facts about which they would generalize, they are of *still less value historically.* . History tells us that Scottish Earldoms only *began* to be territorial half a century before the time when Lord Mansfield supposed that they *ceased* to be so. Documentary evidence further tells that of the multitudes of extant and recorded charters of Earldom, original and by progress, from the earliest date to 1578, only five can be named (Carrick, 1318 ; Wigton, 1341 ; Glencairn, 1488 ; Moray, 1501 , and Mar, 1562), in which the dignity of EARL is directly mentioned, and in four out of these five there is an obvious reason for its specification. In 1578 the practice began to vary, and from that date to 1600, half the charters of Earldom (they were ten in all) did, and half did not, specify the dignity, yet in each and every case the grantee was recognised as Earl, and the line of heirs specified in their charters, original or by progress, *enjoyed the dignity*, as well as the lands. " See p 226, &c., of a very exhaustive treatise on the " Jurisdiction in Scottish Peerages, " in the *Journal of Jurisprudence, &c.*, vol. xxvii, pp. 225-244 , May 1883.

feudal holdings, were territorial *exactly as far* as the newer were, and no further. *All* the Scottish Earldoms had become feudalized before the end of the thirteenth century. . . . In the case of some of them . . . even at an early period, the lands became so sub-divided, that little remained of them but the chief messuage." (*)

In the early part of the reign (1153-1165) of Malcolm IV, the seven Earls of Scotland consisted of ANGUS, ATHOLE, FIFE, MAR, STRATHERNE and BUCHAN, together with DUNBAR from the Lothians. Of the two last named, Buchan, before 1114, had become separated from Mar, and had apparently taken the place of Caithness ; while Dunbar appears to have taken the place of Moray, which was the first of the Celtic Earldoms to break up (by the defeat and death of Angus, bearing the title of EARL OF MORAY), in the beginning of the previous reign [1124-53] of David I.

Malcolm IV (1153-65) added two new Earldoms, *viz.*, Ross and MENTEITH ; and continued the policy, inaugurated by David I, " for transforming the old Celtic Kingdom of the Scots into a feudal monarchy." (b) His successor, William the Lion (1165-1214), added four new Earldoms, *viz.*, GARIOCH, LENNOX, CARRICK, and CAITHNESS.

During the reign of Alexander II (1214-49) " We find the seven Earls of Scotland frequently making their appearance, apparently as a constitutional body, whose privileges were recognised. They first appear at the King's Coronation, and then consisted of the Earls of FIFE, STRATHERNE, ATHOLE, ANGUS, MENTEITH, BUCHAN and LOTHIAN [*i.e.* Dunbar]. With the exception of Menteith, which was a more recent Earldom, these are the same Earldoms whose Earls gave their consent to the foundation charter of Scone, but Menteith now comes *in the place of Mar*, perhaps owing to the controversy as to the rightful possessor of the latter Earldom, and Buchan was now held by a Norman Baron." (b) The seven Earls again appear in 1237, in the agreement of that date with England. They were, at that time, DUNBAR, STRATHERNE, ANGUS, ATHOLE, (with) LENNOX, MAR and Ross, these last three being in place of FIFE, MENTEITH and BUCHAN. Again the seven Earls appear, when the agreement was renewed in 1244, and, this time, Fife, Menteith and Buchan *re-appear* among them, while Angus (which had in 1243 passed to a Norman race), Lennox and Ross were omitted. Thus we see that, " though the number of seven was always retained, the constituent members were not always the same." (b) It would almost seem from the addition and subtraction of Lennox and Ross, in 1237 and 1244 respectively, that junior Earldoms were added to make up the number to seven, when, from any cause, the senior Earldoms were not available.

In 1251, the 2nd year of Alexander III, a solemn ceremony took

---

(a) See p. 590 of an able article, reviewing Hewlett's *Dignities in the Peerage of Scotland*, in *The Journal of Jurisprudence, or Scottish Law Magazine*, (vol. xxvi, pp. 575-591, Nov. 1882) wherein Hewlett's holding that the most ancient Earldoms [S.] were " in an especial sense *territorial*," is confuted : the Reviewer very conclusively demonstrating that " *exactly the reverse* is the case. "

(b) Skene's *Celtic Scotland*.

place in the presence of the seven Earls, but 30 years later they " were gradually losing their separate corporate existence, and were no longer able to maintain in this reign the functions they exercised in previous reigns, for when the succession to the throne was settled upon the da. of Alexander in 1284, we find them merged in the general *Communitas*, in which the entire body of the Earls, now amounting to thirteen, appear. " (ª)   In 1297, however, the seven Earls, being, at that time, BUCHAN, MENTEITH, STRATHERNE, LENNOX, ROSS, ATHOLE, and MAR, (in company with John Comyn of Badenoch), made a disastrous invasion of England ; but " after this, we hear no more of the SEVEN EARLS of Scotland. " (ª)

EARLDOM [S.]   1. " Dufugan, Comes, " who appears among the
I. 1115 ?   seven Earls in the charter of 1114 or 1115, (see remarks
             above) in all probability was Mormaer of Angus, though
in this charter (possibly for the first time) styled " *Comes,* " *i e.* EARL OF ANGUS [S.].   He was probably a descendant of Dubucan, Mormaer of Angus in the 10th century. (ᵇ)

II. 1135 ?   2. GILLBRIDE, (ᶜ) EARL OF ANGUS [S.], was at the battle
             of the Standard, 22 Aug. 1138, when the Scots were
totally defeated at Northallerton, co. York, and was (long afterwards) one of the hostages for King William the Lion [S.] in 1174.   He seems to have *m.*, 1stly, a da. of Gospatrick, EARL OF DUNBAR [S.].   He *m*, subsequently, the h of the EARLS OF CAITHNESS [S.], who was mother, by him, of Magnus, EARL OF CAITHNESS [S] in 1232. (ᵈ)   He *d.* about 1187.

III. 1187 ?   3. ADAM (ᵉ) EARL OF ANGUS, s. and h., witnessed a
             charter, *v.p.*, in 1164, as " son of EARL GILLBRIDE. "   He
is named in a charter, about 1187, as EARL OF ANGUS.   He *d.* before 1198.

(ª) Skene's *Celtic Scotland*.

(ᵇ) It is stated on the contemporary evidence of the " Pictish Chronicle " (a work of the 10th century) that Dubucan, s. of Indrechtaig, was Mormaer of Angus, and *d.* about 935, being *suc.* by his s. Maelbrigdi.   After him (according to the later chronicles), one Conchar was Mormaer of Angus.   He was father of Fynebole, Lady of Fettercairn, by whom King Kenneth McMalcom was treacherously slain, in 995, in revenge for the slaughter of her only son at Dunsinane.   See *Chronicles of the Picts and Scots*, edited by W.F. Skene, pp. 9, 175, 289.   The resemblance of the name of Dufugan to that of Dubucan " leads to the supposition that he may have filled that [*i.e.* the same] position, &c. "   See Skene's *Celtic Scotland*, vol. iii, p 60.

(ᶜ) " During the whole reign of David I (1124-53) these Earls [*i.e.* the seven Earls of the seven Provinces of transmarine Scotland], appear simply with the designation of *Comes*, without any territorial addition, with two exceptions which occur towards the end of his reign.   In the last year of David's reign, the Earl who *suc.* Gillemichel appears as Dunchad, *Comes de Fif*, and, along with him, for the first time appears Gillebride, *Comes de Angus.* " (Skene's *Celtic Scotland*, vol. iii, p 63.)   Thus the two Earldoms of Fife and of Angus appear to have been already territorialised.

(ᵈ) See Skene's *Celtic Scotland*, vol. iii, p. 450

(ᵉ) The credit for first calling attention to the existence of this obscure Earl belongs to Sir William Fraser.   See *Douglas Book*, vol. ii, pp 2, 3.   V G.

IV. 1197 ?   4   GILCHRIST, (ª) EARL OF ANGUS [S.], br. and h   He was witness in 1198 to a document in the Chartulary of Arbroath Abbey (no. 148), to which Abbey he was a great benefactor   He *d.* between 1207 and 1211.

V. 1210 ?   5   DUNCAN, EARL OF ANGUS [S.], s. and h.   He *d.* between 1207 and 1214.

VI. 1214 ?   6. MALCOLM, EARL OF ANGUS [S.], s and h , witnessed a charter as Earl of Angus (simply) 22 Apr. 1231, and is called Earl of Angus and Caithness in 1232, (ᵇ) most probably from having the last named Earldom in ward   He *m.* Mary, da. and h of Sir Humphrey BERKELEY.   He was living 1237, when he took part in the Convention of York, (ᶜ) but *d.* before 1242.

VII. 1240 ?   7   MAUD, *suo jure* COUNTESS OF ANGUS [S.], da. and h., ✗*m.* John COMYN✗who, in her right, became EARL OF ANGUS [S.], and *d. s.p ,* in France, 1242. She *m.,* 2ndly, in 1243, Gilbert DE UMFREVILLE, (ᵈ) Lord of Prudhoe and Redesdale in Northumberland, who may, in her right, have become EARL OF ANGUS [S.] (ᵉ) He was s and h of Richard de Umfreville, of the same, and did homage for his father's lands 8 Jan. 1226/7 (ᶠ)   He *d.* shortly before 13 Mar. 1244/5, (ᵍ) and was *bur.* in Hexham Priory. His widow *m.,* before 2 Dec. 1247, Richard OF CHILHAM, or OF DOVER, s. and h. of Richard FITZ ROY, an illeg. s of King John. (ʰ)

_____

(ª) It has been said, but this is doubtful, that his wife was Maud, or Marjory, sister of King William the Lion.

(ᵇ) *Chartulary of Moray,* no. 110.

(ᶜ) " The family of Ogilvie, who retained possession of a considerable portion of the Earldom [of Angus], appear to have been the *male* descendants of these old Celtic Earls, and they likewise gave a line to CAITHNESS, who possessed with the title of Earl one half of the lands of the Earldom [of Caithness].   Of the land of the Earldom of Angus, the district of Glenisla was alone included within the Highland line, and preserved its Gaelic population. "   Skene's *Celtic Scotland,* vol. iii, p 290.

(ᵈ) This family perhaps took its name from Amfréville-sur-Iton (Elect. de Pontde-l'Arche) , or, as M. Bémont states (*Rôles Gascons,* vol. iii, p. 119), from Offranville, near Dieppe.   Lower *(Dict of Family Names)* supposes that the name is *Humfredi villa,* the vill of Humphrey. Hodgson (*Northumberland,* pt. ii, vol. i, p. 8), from finding it sometimes written *Unfrancvilla,* thinks it means *bond-town.* Its usual latin equivalent was, however, *Umframvilla.*   V.G.

(ᵉ) The rewriting of the article on the Umfrevilles, Earls of Angus, has been most kindly undertaken by G W.Watson.   V.G.

(ᶠ) *Fine Roll,* 11 Hen. III, duplicate.   On the other roll *m.* 11, this date, by a slip, is written 8 Nov. (1226)   V.G

(ᵍ) On which date the Sheriff of Northumberland was ordered to take his lands into the King's hand (*Fine Roll,* 29 Hen. III, m. 12). M. Paris, who says, erroneously, that he *d.* in " septimana Passionis Dominicae " [2-8 Apr.] 1245, calls him " praeclarus baro, partium Angliae borealium custos et flos singularis, Gilebertus de Humfranvilla " *(Chron. Majora,* ed. Luard, vol. iv, p. 415.)   V.G.

(ʰ) See an article by G.J.Turner on *Richard Fitzroy,* in *Genealogist,* N.S., vol. xxii, p. 109.   V.G.

VIII. 1267 ?   8. GILBERT (DE UMFREVILLE), EARL OF ANGUS

Qy. EARLDOM [E.]   [S.], s. and h., *b.* about 1244. (ᵃ)   In 1265 he joined the rising of the Barons against the

I. 1299. [1283 ?]   King. He is styled EARL OF ANGUS in June 1267. (ᵇ) In 1281 he was one of the Nobles who swore to ratify the marriage of Margaret of Scotland with Eric, King of Norway. In 1291, being then Governor, not only of Dundee and Forfar Castles, but of the whole territory of Angus, he refused to surrender it to England unless under an indemnity from the King, and from all the Competitors to the Scottish Crown. On 24 June, 1 Oct., and 2 Nov. (1295) 23 Edw. I, and on 26 Aug. (1296) 24 Edw I, he was sum. to Parl. by writs directed *Gilberto de Umframvill'*, whereby he may be held to have become LORD UMFREVILLE, (ᶜ) and on 28 June (1283) 11 Edw. I,(ᵈ) and again from 6 Feb. (1298/9) 27 Edw. I to 26 Aug. (1307) 1 Edw. II, he was sum. to Parl. under the designation of EARL OF ANGUS, the writs being directed *Gilberto de Umframvill'* (or *Unfranvill'*) *comiti de Anegos.* (ᵉ) He *m.* Elizabeth, 3rd da. of Alexander (COMYN),

---

(ᵃ) Simon de Montfort obtained the custody of the lands and of the heir of Gilbert *de Umfraunvilia*, 15 June 1245, for a fine of 10,000 marks. *(Fine Roll,* 29 Hen. III, *m.* 8).

(ᵇ) In 1267 the King granted to Gilbert *de Humframvilla,* Earl of Angus, and his heirs, free warren in his demesne lands in Northumberland (16 June), and a market and fair at his manors of Overton, Rutland, and Kirkwhelpington, Northumberland (22 June) *(Charter Roll,* 51 Hen. III, *m.* 5 and 4.)

(ᶜ) As to how far these early writs of summons did in fact create any Peerage title, see Appendix A in the last volume. V.G.

(ᵈ) As to this supposed Parl., see Preface

(ᵉ) " Dugdale states that he was sum. in virtue of his Barony of Prudhoe, co. Northumberland; but by the late Francis Townsend, Esq, Windsor Herald, the writ of 25 Edw. I (1297) [*i.e.* the writ, dated 26 Jan. 1296/7, to attend an assembly at Salisbury, which at the time when Townsend wrote, was considered to have been a summons to Parl], was considered to have cr. an *English Earldom,* and certainly he and his descendants are always sum. with other Earls, but the editor [*i.e* Courthope, not Nicolas], is of opinion that no such English Earldom was intended to have been cr., but that the King, having in 1296 seized upon the sovereignty of Scotland, did, in directing summons to his Baron, Gilbert de Umfreville, in the following year, allow to him, in the way of courtesy, that title which had by marriage or otherwise been acquired in Scotland; he was therefore sum as a Baron, though by the appellation of an Earl · and it may be added, in confirmation of the opinion that no English Earldom was intended to be cr., that Henry de Beaumont, having *m.* Alice, da and h. of Alexander Comyn, Earl of Buchan, was sum. to Parl. from 1334 till his decease, 1340, as ' Henrico de Bello Monte Comiti de Boghan, ' but that his s and h, John Beaumont, having lost the Buchan property in Scotland, was no longer sum by the title of Buchan, but by that of Beaumont only. " *(Courthope,* p 24). The remarks of Townsend will be found in *Coll. Top et Gen,* vol vii, p. 383. He sensibly observes (referring to the manner in which this peerage altogether ceased after the death of Earl Gilbert in 1381), that this case seems to countenance the idea " that the descent of ancient dignities in general depended chiefly upon the will of the Crown."

The following remarks (made by J. H. Round on the above note) are subjoined—

EARL OF BUCHAN [S.], (ᵃ) by Elizabeth, 3rd da. and coh. of Roger (DE QUINCY), EARL OF WINCHESTER. He *d.* shortly before 13 Oct. 1307, (ᵇ) and was *bur.* in Hexham Priory. (ᶜ) His widow *d* shortly before 17 Feb. 1328/9. (ᵈ)

[GILBERT DE UMFREVILLE, s. and h. ap   He was brought before the

---

" Courthope's view is evidently based on the *Lords' Reports on the dignity of a Peer*, from which his argument is practically derived, and which were issued (1820-22) subsequent to Townsend's day. (See 1st Report, p. 432; 3rd Report, pp. 116, 117). The Reports incline rightly to the view ' that those Earls, though summoned by the names of Earls, were really summoned as Barons of the Realm. ' It may be added that the summonses were not addressed to them, as stated by Courthope, as ' Umfrevill (*sic*), Comiti de Anggos, ' but as ' Umframvill', Comiti de Anegos ; ' and a more serious error is committed by Courthope [as also by *Nicolas*, both of them following Dugdale's *Summons*] in the dates of the writs ; Gilbert, the father, not having been sum after 26 Aug. (1307) 1 Edw. II, while Robert, his son, was first sum. on 19 Jan. (1307/8) 1 Edw. II. The father and son are also confused by a most careless error in the *Lords' Reports* (3rd Report, p. 171), where the writ of 25 Edw I is twice said to have been addressed to Robert (*sic*) de Umframville "

With respect to the summons to Gilbert de Umfreville as Earl of Angus, there is in Camden's *Britannia*, (ed. Gough, vol. iii, p. 403) the following statement.— " The English lawyers indeed refused to allow this title in their proceedings, because Angus was no part of the Kingdom of England, till he produced in the court the writ by which the King had summoned him to parliament by the title of Earl of Angus "

(ᵃ) Her Christian name is sometimes given as Agnes, but of the marriage itself there is no doubt. Wyntoun, in his account of the Earls of Buchan, (*Cronykil*, ed. Macpherson, vol. ii, p. 35) states that of the " systris fywe " of Earl John—
" The thryd [had] Schyr Gylbert Wmfrayiyle,
Erle of Angws in that qwhile,
(Of Angws and of Ryddysdale
Erle he wes, and Lord all hale)
On that Lady eftyrwart
Of Wmframville he gat Robert :
On that Lady he gat alswa
Othir Brethyr to Robert ma. "

(ᵇ) Writ of *diem cl. ext.* 13 Oct. 1 Edw II. He *d.* seized of the castle or Prudhoe, the liberty of Redesdale (which included the castle of Harbottle and the manor of Otterburn), and the manors of Harlow and Birtley, etc , in Northumberland. (Ch. *Inq. p. m.*, Edw. II, file 2, no 21). V.G.

(ᶜ) According to the ancient Rolls of Arms, the Umfrevilles, Earls of Angus, bore, Gules semy of cross crosslets and a cinquefoil Or. On the effigy of this earl at Hexham the crosslets are however crosses *patoncées*, and in the arms cut on the battlements of Elsden castle, Northumberland, they are cross crosslets *patées*, which is much the same thing   The crest depicted with these latter arms is a cinquefoil, supporters two wolves, no doubt in allusion to the ancient tenure of Redesdale, the Umfrevilles holding " castrum de Herbotell et manerium de Otterburn de domino rege in capite per servicium custodiendi vallem et libertatem de Riddesdale ubi dicta castrum et manerium situantur a lupis et latronibus. " The earlier Umfrevilles sealed with a single cinquefoil.

(ᵈ) Writ of *diem cl. ext.* 17 Feb. 3 Edw. III. (Ch. *Inq. p. m.*, Edw. III, file 15, no. 26).

King's Council to answer for his contempt in striking one of the King's ministers at the Parl held at Berwick on the octave of the Assumption, 22 Aug. 1296.([a]) He *m.* Margaret, 1st da of Sir Thomas DE CLARE, Lord of Thomond in Connaught, by Julian, 2nd da. and eventually sole h. of Maurice FITZ MAURICE, Lord Justice of Ireland. He *d. v.p., s.p.,* before 23 May 1303. ([b]) His widow *m.,* before 30 June 1308, Sir Bartholomew BADLESMERE [LORD BADLESMERE], who *d* 14 Apr. 1322. She *d.* late in 1333.]

| EARLDOM [S.] IX. Qy. EARLDOM, [E] II. | 1307. | 9 and 2. ROBERT (DE UMFREVILLE), EARL OF ANGUS [S.], and LORD UMFREVILLE [E.], 2nd, but 1st surv. s. and h., aged 30 and more at his father's death. He did homage and had livery of his father's lands, 6 Nov. |

1307. He was sum., 18 Jan. 1307/8, to attend the coronation of Edward II, and by that King was appointed Joint King's Lieut. and Keeper in Scotland, 21 June 1308, Joint Guardian between Berwick and the Forth, 16 Aug. 1308, and a Commissioner to treat with the Scots, 14 Nov. 1308, 16 Feb. 1309/10, 22 Feb. 1315/6, and 18 Mar. 1317/8. ([c]) He was sum. to Parl. from 19 Jan. (1307/8) 1 Edw. II to 26 Dec. (1323) 17 Edw. II, by writs directed *Roberto de Umframvill' comiti de Anegos.* He *m.,* 1stly, before 20 Sep. 1303, Lucy, da. and in her issue h. of Sir Philip DE KYME [1st LORD KYME], by . . . . , da of Sir Hugh LE BIGOD, Chief Justiciar of England. He *m.,* 2ndly, Alienor. He *d.* Mar. 1325, and was *bur.* in the Abbey of Newminster. ([d]) Dower was assigned to his widow 10 and 19 July 1325. She *m.,* before 16 Aug. 1327 (at which date he was fined £10 and had pardon for

---

([a]) *Close Roll,* 24 Edw. I, *m.* 4, Aug. or Sep. 1296.

([b]) In a Ch. *Inq ad quod damnum,* Edw. I, file 43, no. 13 (writ 23 May 31 Edw. I), it is stated that Robert was s. and h. of Gilbert *de Umframvilla,* Earl of Angus, and then under age : and that Margaret, widow of Gilbert, s. of the sd. Gilbert, held Hambleton and Overton, Rutland, in dower.

([c]) His possessions in Scotland were confiscated by Robert Bruce, and he is styled in a charter *dudum comes de Anegus.* The English Kings of course did not recognise these proceedings by a usurper, and it seems futile to attempt to estimate the legal effect of this informal confiscation. It is, however, clear that, although the Umfrevilles were sum. under the title of Earl of Angus, among, and with precedence over several of, the English Earls, the Edwards had no idea that they had thereby created another (English) Earldom of Angus. Whether they did not do so, according to modern notions, which are far removed from ancient practice, is another question.

([d]) Writ of *diem cl. ext.* 12 Apr. 18 Edw. II (Ch. *Inq. p. m,* Edw. II, file 90, no. 78 : Exch. *Inq. p. m.,* Enrolments no. 14). According to the Obituary of Newminster (*Monast,* vol. v, p. 401), he *d. secundo idus Apr. ,* but this is a mistake, for the escheator seized his lands into the King's hand on 30 Mar. (Escheators' *Enrolled Accounts,* no. I, 18 Edw II, rot. 30 d, *New Escheats,* Northumberland).

marrying her without licence) Sir Roger MAUDUIT, of Eshot, Northumberland, sometime Chamberlain of Scotland, who *d.* before 24 Feb. 1350/1. She *d.* 31 Mar. 1368. (*)

EARLDOM [S.]
X.

Qy. EARLDOM [E.]
III.

} 1325 to 1381.

10 and 3. GILBERT (DE UMFREVILLE), EARL OF ANGUS [S.], and LORD UMFREVILLE [E.], 1st s. by 1st wife, aged 15 at his father's death. On doing homage, 6 July 1331, he had livery of his father's lands, and also of those of his grandmother, Elizabeth, Countess of Angus. He was one of the disinherited barons who invaded Scotland in 1332, and assisted in the victory of Edward Balliol at Dupplin Muir, 11 Aug. 1332. One of the commanders at the battle of Nevill's Cross, 17 Oct. 1346, where the King of Scots was taken prisoner, for whose redemption he was appointed a Commissioner, 18 June 1354. He was appointed a warden of the Marches 28 May and 15 July 1352, 9 July 1359, 11 Feb. 1366/7, 16 Oct. 1369, 5 July 1370, 25 June and 12 Oct. 1371, 25 Feb. 1371/2, and 3 May 1372. He was sum. to Parl. 27 Jan. (1331/2) 6 Edw. III to 26 Aug. (1380) 4 Ric. II, by writs directed *Gilberto de Umframvill'* (or *Umfravill'*) *comiti Danegos* (or *de Anegos*). He *m.*, 1stly, Joan, da. of Sir Robert WILLOUGHBY [1st LORD WILLOUGHBY], by Margaret, da. of Sir Edmund DEINCOURT [1st LORD DEINCOURT]. She *d.* 16 July 1350. He *m.*, 2ndly, before Oct. 1369, Maud, only da. of Sir Thomas LUCY [2nd LORD LUCY], by Margaret, 3rd da. and eventually coh. of Sir Thomas MULTON [1st LORD MULTON]. He *d. s.p.s.*, 6 Jan. 1380/1. (b) His widow, who had become sole h. of her family, 30 Sep. 1369, possessed, as a life tenant, the greater part of his property after his death. She *m.*, before 3 Oct. 1383, as 2nd wife, Henry (PERCY), 1st EARL OF NORTHUMBERLAND, and *d. s.p.*, 18 Dec. 1398. (c) The Earl, her 2nd husband, on whom and whose family she had entailed her paternal inheritance to the exclusion of her heir at law, and who also possessed Prudhoe, &c., after her death by virtue of an entail made by her 1st husband, 16 Aug. 1375, was slain, 20 Feb. 1407/8, at Bramham Moor.

[SIR ROBERT DE UMFREVILLE, 1st s. and h. ap., by 1st wife. He *m.* (Roy. Lic. for settlt. of lands, 20 Jan. 1339/40), Margaret, da. of Sir Henry PERCY [2nd LORD PERCY], by Idoine, da. of Sir Robert CLIFFORD [1st LORD CLIFFORD]. He *d. v.p., s.p.* His widow *m.*, as 2nd wife, before 25 May 1368, Sir William FERRERS [3rd LORD FERRERS OF GROBY], who *d.* 6, 7, or 8 Jan. 1370/1. She *d. s.p.*, 1, 3, 5 or 10 Sep. 1375, (d) at Gyng (now Buttsbury), Essex. Will dat. 26 Apr. 1374].

(*) Writ of *diem cl. ext:* 8 May 42 Edw. III. (Ch. *Inq. p. m.*, Edw. III, file 203, no. 58).

(b) Writs of *diem cl. ext.* 14 Jan. 4 Ric. II. (Ch. *Inq. p. m.*, Ric. II, file 17, no. 57: Exch. *Inq. p. m., Enrolments,* file 1091, nos 1, 2, and file 1335, nos 1, 2).

(c) Writs of *diem cl. ext.* 23 Dec. 22 Ric. II. (Ch. *Inq. p. m.*, Ric. II, file 106, no. 38).

(d) Writs of *diem cl. ext.* 26 Sep. 49 Edw. III. (Ch. *Inq. p. m.*, Edw. III, file 254, no. 52, and file 261, no. 12).

After the death of Gilbert, Earl of Angus, 6 Jan. 1380/1, ([a]) none of the descendants of his grandfather, Earl Gilbert, who was the first to be sum. to Parl., were sum. under the title of Earl of Angus or that of Lord Umfreville. The right of succession to the Barony of Umfreville, and (if any) to the Earldom of Angus, devolved as follows.—

I. 1381. 1. THOMAS DE UMFREVILLE, of Hessle, co. York, and Holmside, co. Durham, br. of the last Earl (of the half blood), being 3rd s.([b]) of Earl Robert, by his 2nd wife, Alienor. He inherited the castle of Harbottle and the manor of Otterburn, which fell to him under a fine of Easter 1378. He m.([c]) Joan, da. of Adam DE RODDAM. He d. 21 May 1387. ([d])

II. 1387. 2. SIR THOMAS DE UMFREVILLE, of Harbottle, &c., elder s., aged 26 at his father's death. Sheriff of Northumberland 1388-89, and M.P. for that co. in the Parliaments which met 3 Feb. 1387/8 and 17 Jan. 1389/90. He m. Agnes. He d. 12 Feb. or 8 Mar. 1390/1. ([e]) His widow d. 25 Oct. 1420. ([f])

III. 1391 3. SIR GILBERT DE UMFREVILLE, of Harbottle,
to Hessle, Kyme, &c., only s. and h., b. 18 Oct 1390, at
1421. Harbottle Castle, and bap. in the church there. ([g])
He inherited the Kyme property, co. Lincoln, on the death, 18 Dec. 1398, of Maud, Countess of Angus and Northumberland. He is said to have accompanied his uncle, Sir Robert de Umfreville, in an incursion into Scotland (1409-10) 11 Hen. IV. Some chroniclers (English and French) style him Earl of Kyme, ([h]) but no such title is ever given him in any formal document. ([i]) He was at the

---

([a]) His heir at law was his niece Alienor, then aged 40 and more, and widow of Sir Henry Tailboys, she being da. and h. of Elizabeth (the Earl's only sister of the whole blood who left issue), by Sir Gilbert Borrowdon. Her grandson, Walter Tailboys, inherited Harbottle, Otterburn, Kyme, &c., on the death of Sir Robert de Umfreville, K.G., 27 Jan. 1436/7.

([b]) The 2nd s., Robert, d.s.p. shortly before 10 Oct. 1379.

([c]) Or, rather, she was the mother of his two sons, Thomas and Robert, as to whose legitimacy there is considerable doubt. See Genealogist, N.S., vol. xxvi, pp. 129, sqq.

([d]) Writs of diem cl. ext. 25 May 10 Ric. II. (Ch. Inq. p. m., Ric. II, file 48, no. 43: Exch. Inq. p. m., I, file 54, no. 2, and Enrolments, file 1338, no. 4). Durham Inq., 10 June 1387. (Cursitor's Records, no. ii, f. 157).

([e]) Writs of diem cl. ext. 1 Apr. 14 Ric. II. (Ch. Inq. p.m., Ric. II, file 64, no. 50: Exch. Inq. p. m., I, file 57, no. 7).

([f]) Durham Inq. 3 Mar. 1420/1. (Cursitor's Records, no. ii, f. 197 d).

([g]) Writ de etate prob. 28 Jan. 13 Hen. IV. (Ch. Inq. p. m., Hen. IV, file 88, no. 54).

([h]) See further particulars under KYME.

([i]) According to John Hardyng, who was a follower of the Umfrevilles, this Gilbert and his uncle, Sir Robert, went with the Earl of Arundel in 1411 to support the Duke of Burgundy against the Armagnacs, and having distinguished himself [9 Nov. 1411] in an engagement at St. Cloud, near Paris, in which the English

battle of Agincourt in 1415, was appointed Captain of Caen, 30 Sep. 1417, and during the siege of Rouen, 1418-19, was commissioned, 3 Jan. 1418/9, with the Earls of Warwick and Salisbury, &c., to treat for the surrender of that city. He was appointed Captain of Pontoise 2 Feb., of Eu 12 Feb., and of Neufchâtel 21 Feb. 1418/9. (ᵃ) He *m.*, before 3 Feb. 1412/3, (ᵇ) Anne, 5th da. of Ralph (NEVILL), 1st EARL OF WESTMORLAND, by his 1st wife, Margaret, da. of Hugh (STAFFORD), 2nd EARL OF STAFFORD. He *d. s.p.*, being slain at the battle of Baugé in Anjou, 22 Mar. 1420/1. (ᶜ) Admon., as Gilbert Umfrevile kt. lord of Redesdale, 19 Feb. 1421/2, at Lambeth. (ᵈ)

His coheirs in 1421 were his 5 sisters. (1) Elizabeth, then aged 30, and wife of Sir William Elmeden, of Elmeden (now Embleton), co. Durham. She *d.* 23 Nov. 1424, leaving 4 daughters her coheirs. (2) Maud, then aged 28, and wife of Sir William Ryther, of Ryther, co. York. She *d.* 4 Jan. 1434/5, leaving William Ryther her s. and h. (3) Joan, then aged 26 (48 in 1437), and wife of Sir Thomas Lambert. She was living in 1446. (4) Margaret, then aged 24 (47 in 1437), and widow of William Lodington, of Gunby, co. Lincoln, Justice of the

---

were victorious, was on that day "proclaymed erle of Kyme" (*Chronicle*, ed. Ellis, p. 367). Possibly (as suggested by Sir J.H. Ramsay, *Lancaster & York*, vol. i, p. 131), the title of Count was then conferred on him by the French. He was certainly thereafter popularly known as an Earl—

> "To whiche Gilbert Umfrevile erle of Kyme
> Aunswered for all his felowes and there men
> They shuld all die together at a tyme."

And again, in the account of the battle of Baugé, where the Duke or Clarence was slain—

> "With him were slayne then therle Umfrevyle
> And syr John Graye the erle of Tankervyle."
>
> (Hardyng's *Chronicle*, pp. 368, 385).

To these Lords who were slain on the part of the English, can be added John, Lord Roos. The Earls of Somerset and Huntingdon, and Walter, Lord Fitz Walter, were taken prisoners in the same defeat.

(ᵃ) Henry V gave him, 1 Feb. 1418/9, Amfréville-sur-Iton in the bailiwick of Rouen, late of Pierre and Jean d'Amfréville. (*Norman Roll*, 6 Hen. V, *pars* ii, *m.* 28).

(ᵇ) Papal licence, 3 non. Feb. 3 John XXIII, to Gilbert Umfravyll, lord of Kyme, and Anne his wife. (*Cal. Papal Registers*, vol. vi, p. 385).

(ᶜ) Writ of *diem cl. ext.* 18 Apr. 9 Hen. V (Ch. *Inq. p. m.*, Hen. V, file 60, no. 56: Exch. *Inq. p. m.*, I, file 125, no. 3, and *Enrolments*, file 728, no. 5 (1)). Durham Inq., 26 Apr. 1423. (*Cursitor's Records*, no. ii, f. 211 d).

(ᵈ) His uncle Sir Robert de Umfreville, K.G., succeeded to the greater portion of his estates, and was thenceforward styled Lord of Kyme and Redesdale. He *d. s. p.*, 27 Jan. 1436/7 (Ch. *Inq. p. m.*, Hen. VI, file 83, no. 57 : Exch. *Inq. p. m.*, *Enrolments*, file 739, no. 3, and file 1363, no. 5), and not *sexto kal. jan.* 1436, as stated in the Obituary of Newminster, which has misled Dugdale, Beltz, and others.

Common Pleas, who *d.* 9 Jan. 1419/20. She *m.*, 2ndly, before 26 Apr. 1423, John Constable, of Halsham in Holderness (afterwards kt.). She *d.* 23 June 1444, leaving John Constable her s. and h. (5) Agnes, then aged 22 (46 in 1437), and wife of Thomas Haggerston, of Haggerston, co. Durham. She was living in 1446.(ᵃ) Among their lineal representatives the Barony of Umfreville, *cr.* by writ of summons (1295) 23 Edw. I, and the Earldom of Angus, (if considered as an English Earldom in fee, *cr.* by the summons under that title) are in abeyance, while the Scotch Earldom (disregarding the confiscation thereof) is in the representative of Agnes, wife of Thomas Claxton, and 1st da. and coh. of Elizabeth Elmeden, above mentioned. (ᵇ)

EARLDOM [S.]   1. JOHN STEWART, of Bonkyl, co. Berwick, s. and h.
XIV. 1329.   of Sir Alexander S., of the same, *suc.* his father 1319, and is *styled*, in a charter dat. 15 June 1329, EARL OF ANGUS [S.]. He was knighted 24 Nov. 1331, at the coronation of David II. He *m.*, by Papal disp. dat. 24 Oct. 1328 (being within the fourth degree of consanguinity), Margaret, 1st da. of Sir Alexander ABERNETHY. He *d.* 9 Dec. 1331. His widow was living 1370.

XV. 1331.   2. THOMAS (STEWART), EARL OF ANGUS [S.], only s. and h. He commanded at the taking of Berwick in Nov. 1355, and was one of the eight Lords, of whom three were to place themselves in the hands of the English as security for the release of David II. He was Great Chamberlain [S.] 1357 and 1358. On 18 Aug. 1359 he had a safe conduct for four ships of Flanders, with which he was to join Edward III at Calais, but he broke his engagement, and in Mar. 1359/60 was charged to return to England to fulfil his obligation as a hostage. He *m.*, by Papal disp. dat. 3 June 1353 (being within the fourth degree of consanguinity), Margaret, generally considered to have been da. of Sir William ST. CLAIR, of Roslin, by Isabel, da. and coh. of Malise, EARL OF STRATHERN, CAITHNESS, AND ORKNEY [S.], which Margaret was, however, more probably sister of the said Sir William. Being imprisoned in Dunbarton Castle, he *d.* there, of the plague, 1361. His widow *m.* Sir John SINCLAIR, of Herdmanstoun.

XVI. 1361.   3. THOMAS (STEWART), EARL OF ANGUS [S.], only s. and h. An infant at his father's death. He *d. s.p.*, 1377.

(ᵃ) Inq. on Gilbert and Robert de Umfreville, as above ; Durham Inq., 5 Apr. 1446. *(Cursitor's Records*, no. clxiv, nos. 72, 73, 74). It will be observed that each of the coheirs is described in 1421 as 10 years or so younger than she must actually have been.

(ᵇ) This is on the unlikely supposition that Thomas de Umfreville (*d.* 1391) was legitimate. Otherwise the representation would be in the heirs of Walter Tailboys (see p. 151, note "a "), if not extinguished by the attainder in 1461 of his s., William.

XVII. 1377. 4. MARGARET (STEWART), *suo jure* COUNTESS OF ANGUS [S.], eldest sister and h. of line. She *m.*, between 1361 and 1374, as his 2nd wife, Thomas, 13th EARL OF MAR [S.], the last Earl of Mar in the direct *male* line, who *d. s.p.*, 1377. Probably in her husband's lifetime, (a) but certainly very shortly afterwards, she became mother of a s., known as George *Douglas*, begotten by her late husband's br.-in-law, William (DOUGLAS), 1st EARL OF DOUGLAS [S.], whose wife Margaret, *suo jure* COUNTESS OF MAR [S.] (being sister and h. of Thomas, 13th Earl of Mar abovenamed), was then alive, and outlived her said husband. On 9 Apr. 1389 the Countess of Angus resigned the Earldom (reserving for herself the frank tenement thereof for life) in favour of the said GEORGE DOUGLAS, not however then styling him her s. or alleging any relationship to him; though in his marriage contract with the King's da., some eight years afterwards, she styles him "LORD OF ANGUS," and acknowledges him as her s. She, however, survived her said s., and was living 1417, being styled "Countess of Angus and Mar," (*viz.*, ANGUS, in her own right, and MAR, in right of her long deceased and only husband), but (of course) never styled "Countess of Douglas," as the wife of that Earl of Douglas (who was the father of her children) survived him. She *d.* before 23 Mar. 1417/8.

XVIII. 1389. 1. GEORGE (DOUGLAS), EARL OF ANGUS [S.], illegit. s. of William (DOUGLAS), 1st EARL OF DOUGLAS (b) [S.], by Margaret, *suo jure* COUNTESS OF ANGUS [S.], as above mentioned, was *b.* not later than 1378. On 9 Apr. 1389, by the resignation of his mother, the said Countess, he received a grant of THE EARLDOM OF ANGUS [S.] to himself and the heirs of his body, with rem. to Elizabeth, wife of Sir Alexander HAMILTON, of Innerwick (yst. and only sister of the said Countess), and the heirs of their bodies. (c) He *m.*, contract dat. 24 May 1397, the Lady Mary STEWART, 2nd da. of ROBERT III, by Annabel,

(a) The date of the birth of her s., George DOUGLAS (the future Earl of Angus [S.]), who *m.* in May 1397, and had three children within five years afterwards, would (if we suppose him to be 19, and no older, at his marriage) *just* allow of his being *b.* a year after the death of his mother's husband, the Earl of Mar [S.].

(b) The Earldom of Douglas [S.] was entailed, 26 May 1342, on the *heirs male of the body* of Earl William, whom failing, to a certain William Douglas and Archibald Douglas respectively in like manner. On the death, *s.p.*, in Aug. 1388, of James, 2nd Earl of Douglas [S.], who was the only legit. s. of the said Earl William, this George Douglas (the Earl of Angus mentioned in the text), would, *if legitimate*, have, of course, as h. male of the body, *suc.* to his father's Earldom of Douglas [S.]. Under the actual circumstances, however, that Earldom devolved (according to the entail of 1342) on the Archibald Douglas abovenamed. "This singular Douglas entail now above 500 years old, is given by Mr. Riddell in [his] *Stewartiana*, pp. 83 and 84, apparently from the Torphichen charter chest" [the family of Sandilands being the representatives of the House of Douglas]. See Sinclair's remarks on the *status* of George Douglas, 1st Earl of Angus [S.].

(c) This limitation was altered in 1547. See under (xxiii) 6th Earl.

da. of Sir John DRUMMOND, of Stobhall. He was taken prisoner at the battle of Homildon Hill, and *d.* of the pestilence in England, in the same year, 1402. His widow *m.*, 2ndly, 1404, Sir James KENNEDY the yr, of Dunure. He was killed, *v.p.*, before 8 Nov. 1408. In July 1409 his widow had Papal disp. to *m.* (as his 2nd wife) Sir William CUNNINGHAM, but there is no clear evidence that the marriage ever took place. He *d.* between 7 Aug 1413 and Dec. 1415. She *m*, 3rdly, (as his 2nd wife) 13 Nov. 1413, (*) William (GRAHAM), 1st LORD GRAHAM [S.], who was living 10 Aug 1423. She *m.*, 4thly, 1425, Sir William EDMONSTONE, of Duntreath. She was living 1458, having had issue by all four husbands, and was *bur.*, with her last husband, in the Church of Strathblane.

XIX. 1402.   2 WILLIAM (DOUGLAS), EARL OF ANGUS [S.], s. and h. He was one of the negotiators for the release of James I [S.] in 1423. Was AMBASSADOR to England, 1430, and Warden of the Middle Marches, 1433. He defeated the English at Piperden, 10 Sep. 1435. (ᵇ) He *m.* (betrothal dat. 12 Dec. 1410) by disp. dat 1425, Margaret, only da. of Sir William HAY, of Yester, by his 1st wife, Jean, da. and coh. of Hew GIFFORD, of Yester. He *d.* Oct. 1437. His widow was living as late as 22 Apr. 1484.

XX. 1437.   3. JAMES (DOUGLAS), EARL OF ANGUS [S.], s. and h., served h. to his father 27 Feb. 1437/8. He was *forfeited* 1 July 1445, but the attainder was probably soon *reversed.* He *d. s.p.*, and apparently unm., (ᶜ) in 1446, before 9 Sep.

XXI. 1446. (ᵈ)   4. GEORGE (DOUGLAS), EARL OF ANGUS [S.], br., though often supposed to be uncle, (ᵉ) and h. He was one of the Commissioners to conclude a treaty with England, 1449 and 1459, and was AMBASSADOR there, 1451 He adhered to James II during the Douglas rebellion in 1454, and was rewarded with large grants of

---

(*) The Editor has unfortunately not preserved the authority for this date, but there is no reason to doubt its correctness, as the marriage unquestionably took place before 15 May 1416   V G.

(ᵇ) Sometimes considered as the battle commemorated in " Chevy Chase, " this Earl being the Earl Douglas therein mentioned. See note *sub* NORTHUMBERLAND.

(ᶜ) As to his alleged marriage with the Lady Jean STEWART, 3rd da. of JAMES I (to whom he was contracted 18 Oct 1440, but who *m.*, 1458/9, James (Douglas), 1st Earl of Morton [S.]), see such statement confuted in the *Exchequer Rolls* [S.], vol vi, Preface, pp lv and lvi

(ᵈ) There is a puzzling entry in the *Exchequer Rolls* [S.], vol. v, pp. 371-372, implying that an Earl George had succeeded an Earl *William* in 1448 or 1449 The supposition that William may be a clerical error for James is hardly sufficient explanation, inasmuch as the same record states (p 246) that Earl James, though alive in 1445, was dead and was succeeded by Earl George in 1446.

(ᵉ) That statement is refuted by Godscroft's MS., and by a document, dated 26 June 1450, at Durham, in which appears the ' Relaxatio Willielmi Douglas, comitis de Angus, patris comitis moderni' and by other proofs in Fraser's *Book of Douglas*, vol ii, pp. 45-6.

lands of that family. He was accounted the head of the party known
as the "Old Lords" during the minority (1460) of James III. When
Henry VI was a fugitive in Scotland in 1461, he engaged to give the Earl
lands of the yearly value of 2000 marks, and to erect them into a Dukedom.
Early in 1462 he obtained a victory over the English at Alnwick. He *m.*,
probably before 1446, Isabel, only da. of Sir John SIBBALD, of Balgony,
co. Fife. He *d.* 14 Nov. 1462, or, according to his son's retour, 12 Mar.
1462/3, and was *bur.* at Abernethy. His widow *m.*, 2ndly, in or before
1477, John CARMICHAEL, of Balmedie. She *m.*, 3rdly, after 1479, as his
2nd wife, Sir Robert DOUGLAS, of Lochleven, who was slain at Flodden,
9 Sep. 1513. She *d.* between 1500 and Feb. 1502/3.

XXII. 1462.   5. ARCHIBALD (DOUGLAS), EARL OF ANGUS [S.], popu-
               larly called "Bell the Cat," (*) and "The Great Earl,"
s. and h. He was but 9 years old at his father's death. He was Warden of
the East Marches, 11 Apr. 1481, and was continued in that office by James
IV, with whom he was in great favour. He was P.C., and was HIGH
CHANCELLOR [S.] 1493-98. His advice to the King against the fatal
engagement at Flodden being insultingly received, he quitted the field
shortly before the fight, bidding his two sons remain, both of whom were
there slain, with their King. He *m.*, 1stly, (b) 4 Mar. 1467/8, Elizabeth,
only da. of Robert (BOYD), 1st LORD BOYD [S.], by Mariot, da. of Sir
Robert MAXWELL, of Calderwood. She *d.* before 21 Feb. 1497. He *m.*,
2ndly, about 1498, Janet, 2nd wife, or possibly mistress, of Sir Alexander
GORDON (who was slain at Flodden, 9 Sep. 1513), da. of John (KENNEDY),
2nd Lord KENNEDY [S.], by his 2nd wife, Elizabeth, Dowager COUNTESS OF
ERROLL [S.]. There are charters by him, dat. 20 July and 25 Sep. 1498,
of lands granted to her for life, "with rem. to the heirs male procreated or
to be procreated betwixt them." She, however, must soon have deserted
him, for on 1 June 1501, she obtained a charter (under the name of "Janet
Kennedy, Lady Bothwell") from James IV (by which King she was
mother of James Stuart, *cr.* (as an infant) EARL OF MORAY [S.] in 1501),
on condition of her remaining "*absque marito seu alio viro, cum Rege, &c.*"
In 1531, Janet Kennedy founded a prebend in the collegiate church of

(*) This name was thus acquired. The nobles having, in 1483, resolved to
check the favouritism of James III, there was quoted in their conclave the "*Fable
of the Mice,*" wherein it is suggested that, to warn them of the approach of the *Cat,*
some one should place a bell round her neck; but the proposition fell to the ground,
as none had the courage to do so. On this Angus exclaimed "I will bell the Cat,"
and forthwith organised measures which resulted, not only in the execution of the
favourites, but in the murder of the King himself, in 1488. G.E.C.
    The too partial family historian, Hume of Godscroft, writes of him thus :—
"Upright and square in his actions, sober and moderate in his desires. . . . one fault
he had, that he was too much given to women, otherwise there was little or nothing
that was amiss." Sir Herbert Maxwell (1902) more truly pronounces his career to
have been "in most of its features deplorable, and in none of them glorious." V.G.
    (b) On 30 Sep. 1461, when a child, he was contracted to *m.* Catherine, 4th and
yst da. of Alexander, 1st Earl of Huntley, but the marriage never took place.

St. Mary-in-the-Fields, near Edinburgh, for the soul of the deceased
Archibald, EARL OF ANGUS, formerly her husband. He *m.*, lastly, in 1500,
Katherine, da of Sir William STIRLING, of Keir, by Margaret, da. of James
CRICHTON, of Ruthvendeny. She signed a discharge as "Katryne Ctess of
Angus" 10 Aug. 1510, but on 14 May 1513, she is designated simply as
Katherine Stirling, and she was then probably separated from the Earl,
and living with Alexander, Lord HOME, by whom she had an illegit. s.
about this time. The Earl *d.* at the Priory of St. Ninian or Whithorn,
in Galloway, between 29 Nov. 1513 and 31 Jan 1513/4.

[GEORGE DOUGLAS, MASTER OF ANGUS, possibly *styled* LORD DOUGLAS,
s. and h. ap. by 1st wife, *b.* about 1469. He *m.*, before Mar. 1487/8,
Elizabeth, widow of Sir David FLEMING, of Monycabo, and 2nd da. of John
(DRUMMOND), 1st LORD DRUMMOND [S.]. He *d. v p.*, 9 Sep 1513, being
slain at the battle of Flodden. His widow was living 21 Aug. 1514.] (ª)

XXIII. 1514.   6. ARCHIBALD (DOUGLAS), EARL OF ANGUS [S.], grandson
                  and h, being s. and h. of George DOUGLAS, *styled* MASTER
OF ANGUS or LORD DOUGLAS, and Elizabeth his wife abovenamed. He
was *b.* about 1490, and was one of the most distinguished men of his time.
From 1517 to 1521 he was one of the Council of Regency, and again, 1523-26.
In 1526, when the King, James V, attained his majority of 14 years,
the Earl exercised supreme power for two years, and in Aug. 1527 was
made HIGH CHANCELLOR [S] In 1528, however, sentence of *forfeiture*
(which was reversed Mar. 1542/3) was pronounced against him, and he
retired to England, where he was made P.C. On the death of the King
in 1542, he returned to Scotland, and distinguished himself at the battle of
Ancrum muir, in 1545; and of Pinkie, in 1547. On 31 Aug. 1547, he
resigned his Earldom and had a regrant of the same "*sibi et suis hæredibus
masculis et suis assignatis quibuscunque.*" (ᵇ) He *m.*, 1stly (cont. 26 June
1509), Margaret or Mary, 2nd da. of Patrick (HEPBURN), 1st EARL OF
BOTHWELL [S.], by Janet, only da. of James (DOUGLAS), 1st EARL OF MORTON
[S.]. She *d. s p.s.*, in childbed, 1513. He *m.*, 2ndly, 6 Aug. 1514,
Margaret, QUEEN DOWAGER OF SCOTLAND, formerly the Lady Margaret
TUDOR, (ᶜ) 1st da. of HENRY VII. They were *divorced* 11 Mar. 1526/7.

(ª) When George Douglas, her "*filius carnalis et ballivus*" gave an instrument of
seizin. [Query illegit. elder br. of the whole blood to the xxiii Earl] *Hist. MSS.
Com.*, Report 1902, MSS. of David Milne Home.

(ᵇ) This regrant was confirmed 11 Nov. 1564, and ratified by Parl. 19 Apr.
1567, the then h. of line, Lady Margaret Douglas, having previously (1565), with
consent of her husband and of her 1st s. and h. ap. (see note "b" next p.), renounced
all right to the Earldom. Action of reduction was brought, some years afterwards,
by James VI as h. of line, but determined against him, 7 Mar. 1588/9. He
thereupon agreed to relinquish all further claim to the Earldom on receipt of 35,000
merks from his opponent; payment of this sum was enforced by the Session 14 Aug
1589; final acquittance dated 9 Jan 1590; and contract, whereby the King renounced
that Earldom to William, Earl of Angus [S], his heirs male and of tailzie, ratified by
Act of Parl, 1592.

(ᶜ) Her portrait was painted by Holbein. V.G.

She, who was *b.* 28 Nov. 1489, (ᵃ) at Westm., *d.* 18 Oct. 1541, at Methven, and was *bur.* in the Carthusian monastery of St. John, at Perth. (ᵇ) He *m.*, 3rdly, after her death (having never recognised the said divorce), 9 Apr. 1543, Margaret, only da. of Robert (MAXWELL), 4th LORD MAXWELL [S.], by his 1st wife, Janet, da. of Sir William DOUGLAS, of Drumlanrig. He *d.* at Tantallon Castle, Jan. 1556/7, of erysipelas, and was *bur.* at Abernethy. His widow *m.*, before Sep. 1560, Sir William BAILLIE, of Lamington. She *d.* 1593. Will pr. 15 May 1594 at Edinburgh.

[JAMES DOUGLAS, *styled* MASTER OF ANGUS, or LORD DOUGLAS, only s. and h. ap., by 3rd wife, *d.* an infant, and *v.p.*, Feb. 1547/8.]

XXIV. 1557.   7. DAVID (DOUGLAS), EARL OF ANGUS [S.], nephew
Jan.   and h. male, being s. and h. of Sir George D., of Pitten-
           driech, by Elizabeth, da. and h. of David DOUGLAS, of Pittendriech afsd., which George was next br. of the last Earl. He, who was *b.* about 1515, *suc.* his father 10 Sep. 1547, but is said to have been inactive and sickly. He *m.* (cont. dat. 8 May 1552, at Linlithgow) Margaret or Elizabeth, widow of James JOHNSTONE, Laird of Johnstone, da. of Sir John HAMILTON, of Clydesdale (illegit. s. of James, 1st EARL OF ARRAN [S.]), by Janet, 1st. da. and coh. of Alexander, 3rd LORD HOME [S.]. He *d.* June 1557, at Cockburnspath. His widow *m.* Sir Patrick WHITELAW of that ilk, who *d.* before 1571.

XXV. 1557.   8. ARCHIBALD (DOUGLAS), EARL OF ANGUS, and after-
June.   wards (1585) EARL OF MORTON [S.], only s. and h. He
           was but two years old when he *suc.* his father. On 15 Dec. 1567 he carried the Crown at the meeting of the first Parl. of James VI. He was known as "*the good Earl.*" In 1584 he joined the nobles against the King, and was *attainted* 22 Aug. in that year, but *pardoned* in 1585. By act of indemnity and letters of rehabilitation, 29 Jan. 1585/6, he *suc.* to the EARLDOM OF MORTON [S.], which had been under *attainder* since the death of the last Earl in 1581. He *m.*, 1stly, 13 June 1573, at Stirling, Mary (not Margaret), (ᶜ) da. of John (ERSKINE), EARL OF MAR [S.] and Regent of Scotland, by Annabella, da. of Sir William MURRAY, of Tullibardine. She *d. s.p.*, 3 May 1575, and was *bur.* at Holyrood. He *m.*, 2ndly, 25 Dec. 1575, Margaret, (ᵈ) yst. da. of George (LESLIE), 4th EARL OF ROTHES [S.],

---

(ᵃ) iv kl. Dec. "This sat'day was borne at Westm' at nyght aft' the ixᵗ hour' a qᵃrt' my ladi M'garet the ijᵈ child to the King Harri the vijᵗ aᵒ doᶦ 1489." (King's MSS, 2A. xviiia, *Coll. Top. et Gen.*, vol. i, p. 280). V.G.

(ᵇ) Margaret, their only child, *b.* 18 Oct. 1515, *m.* Matthew (STUART), 4th EARL OF LENNOX [S.], and was mother of Henry, *styled* LORD DARNLEY, the father of James VI. In consequence of this descent the King claimed the Earldom, as mentioned in a previous note. The Queen Dowager *m.*, 3rdly, immediately after her divorce, Henry STEWART, who, in 1525, was *cr.* LORD METHVEN [S.], but by him had no surv. issue.

(ᶜ) See his letter, 1 May 1573, acknowledging tocher. (*Hist. MSS. Com.*, Mar MSS., p. 30.) Her tocher was 8000 merks. V.G.

(ᵈ) On 29 Nov. 1581 a Parliamentary confirmation of certain Baronies was

by his 1st wife, Margaret, illegit. da. of William (CRICHTON), 3rd LORD
CRICHTON [S.]. From her he was divorced 1587. He *m*, 3rdly, directly
afterwards, being asked in church on the Sunday following (cont. dat.
29 July 1587), Jean, widow of Robert DOUGLAS the yr., sometimes called
MASTER OF MORTON (who *d*. 1584), and 1st da. of John (LYON), 8th LORD
GLAMIS [S.], by Elizabeth, da. of Alexander (ABERNETHY), LORD SALTOUN
[S.]. He *d*. 4 Aug. 1588, *s p m*., and probably *s p.s.*, (ᵃ) at Smeaton, near
Dalkeith, probably of consumption, his death being attributed to sorcery. (ᵇ)
Will pr. 3 Mar 1588/9 at Edinburgh. (ᶜ) His widow *m*., 3rdly, before
July 1592, Alexander (LINDSAY), 1st LORD SPYNIE [S.], who *d*. July 1607.
She was living 7 Aug 1607, but *d*. before 23 Feb. 1611.

XXVI. 1588.   9. WILLIAM (DOUGLAS), EARL OF ANGUS(ᵈ) [S], cousin
                   and h. male, being s. and h of Sir Archibald DOUGLAS, of
Glenbervie, co. Kincardine, by his 1st wife, Agnes, 4th da. of William
KEITH, 3rd EARL MARISCHAL [S.], which Archibald (who *d*. 1570) was s.
and h. of Sir William D., the 2nd s. of Archibald, the 5th Earl, the said
Sir William (with his elder br., the Master of Angus), having been slain at
Flodden, 9 Sep 1513.   He was *b*. about 1532   At the coronation,
7 May 1590, of Anne, the Queen Consort, he bore (*not* the Crown, but)
the Sword. Shortly before his death he obtained a charter, in 1591, confirming all the ancient privileges of the family of Douglas to himself and his
heirs male. (ᵉ) He *m*. (cont dat. 14 Feb. 1551/2), Gille (Egidia), da. of
Sir Robert GRAHAM, of Morphie, co. Kincardine. He *d*. 1 July 1591,
of fever, at Glenbervie, and was *bur*. there, in his 59th year. M.I   Will
pr. 26 May 1593, at Edinburgh. His widow was living 1606.

XXVII. 1591.   10. WILLIAM (DOUGLAS), EARL OF ANGUS [S.], s. and
                   h., *b*. about 1552, being 40 in 1592. He was a historian
and an antiquary, and wrote a chronicle of the House of Douglas. In
1592 he joined in a plot, known as "The Spanish Blanks," to establish
the Roman Catholic religion in Scotland, and thereby incurred forfeiture. (ᶠ) In 1608 he retired to the continent. He *m*., between 12 Apr.

granted to "Margaret Lesley, Countess of Angus," and her husband, wherein it is
stated that they had been long married. The date 1591 is erroneously given in
Douglas, vol. ii, p. 429.

(ᵃ) According to Burke's *Peerage* (1877-97) he was *suc*. by an infant s. and h.
who *d*. the same year, 1588, but he appears in fact to have had only a da.

(ᵇ) Barbara Napier was burned on 8 May 1591 for having, "with a notorious
witch," given help to "Dame Jane Lyon, Lady Angus." (*Douglas*, vol ii, p 565).

(ᶜ) According to Godscroft, he was tall, and of a spare habit of body; his visage
somewhat swarthy, but pleasant to look upon. His face was small, his countenance
grave and staid, while his limbs were well proportioned and finely shaped   V G.

(ᵈ) His claim to the Earldom as against that of the h gen was confirmed,
7 Mar. 1588/9. See note "b", page 157.

(ᵉ) See note "b", next page.

(ᶠ) In a letter of 1595, James VI speaks of him as "sometime Earl of Angus,"
and refers to his forfeiture. (*Hist. MSS Com.*, App., 9th Rep., p. 240.) V.G.

(date of cont.) and 24 June 1585, Elizabeth, 1st da. of Laurence (OLIPHANT), 7th Lᴏʀᴅ OLIPHANT [S.], by Margaret, da. of George (HAY), 7th Eᴀʀʟ ᴏꜰ Eʀʀᴏʟʟ [S.]. He *d.* 3 Mar. 1611, at Paris, in his 57th year, and was *bur.* at St. Germain des Prés, in that city. ([a]) M.I. Will dat. 1608. His widow *m.*, before 1619, James Hᴀᴍɪʟᴛᴏɴ.

XXVIII. 1611. 11. Wɪʟʟɪᴀᴍ (Dᴏᴜɢʟᴀs), Eᴀʀʟ ᴏꜰ Aɴɢᴜs [S.], s. and h. On 17 June 1633 he was *cr.* MARQUESS OF DOUGLAS, Eᴀʀʟ ᴏꜰ Aɴɢᴜs &c., [S.], having on the 13th *resigned his claim* (as Earl of Angus) " *to the privilege* and prerogative *of the first sitting and voting* in His Majestie's Parliaments, " &c. ([b])

([a]) " Qui primus eram Regni Scotorum Comes, et in bellis Dux primæ aciei, &c. " See M.I. in *Riddell*, p. 158.

([b]) Tʜᴇ Pʀᴇᴄᴇᴅᴇɴᴄʏ ᴏꜰ ᴛʜᴇ Eᴀʀʟs ᴏꜰ Aɴɢᴜs [S.]

The precedence *claimed* by the Earls of Angus was that of Premier Pᴇᴇʀs; the precedence *recognised* as their right was that of Premier Eᴀʀʟs. It was connected with the privilege of leading the van in battle, and bearing the Crown in Parl., and is therefore, perhaps, first (distinctly) to be traced in 1567 *(vide supra)* ; but as the then Earl was a boy at the time, it was, probably, at least as old as the 6th Earl. When William Douglas, the h. male, had proved his right to succeed as (9th) Earl of Angus, he obtained a charter in 1591 confirming all the ancient privileges of the family of Douglas to himself and his heirs male, *viz* :—*The first vote in council or parliament; to be the King's hereditary Lieutenant ; to have the leading of the van of the army in the day of battle, and to carry the Crown at coronations.* " After his death, and to the detriment of his s. and h., William, the 10th Earl (then 35 years old and upwards), the Duke of Lennox [S.] twice (1590 and 1592) carried the Crown, but Earl William was confirmed in the right of his ancestors to the " first place in first sitting and voting in all Parliaments &c., first place and leiding of wanguard in battailis and bearing the Crown " (*Acts of Parl.*, vol. iii, p. 588). These privileges were again recognised 15 Dec. 1599, and then stated to have been granted to the Earls of Angus and "utheris of the surname of Douglas* for their mony notable and guide offices, &c. " See *Riddell*, pp. 156-157.

* [It was under the changed order of things, after the war of Succession [S.], that Dᴏᴜɢʟᴀs (as the representative of Bruce's chief comrade in arms, Sir James Douglas, " the Good, " who commanded at Bannockburn in 1314) came to the forefront among the Earls. What the exact nature was of the prerogative asserted, in 1371, by the Earl at the coronation of Robert II (which some historians have imagined to have been a rival claim to the throne) does not clearly appear, but some sort of compromise regarding it seems to have been adjusted, a condition of which was the marriage of the Earl's eldest son, James Douglas (afterwards the 2nd Earl), with Isabel, da. of the said King. The important part sustained by the 3rd and 4th Earls Douglas (1388-1424) in the days of the Regent Albany, &c., is a matter of history, the 4th Earl having *m.* the da. of the King (Robert III), while his sister was wife to Prince David, the h. ap. to the Crown. On the accession (1437) of James II, the 5th Earl (Lieutenant General of Scotland) occupied a position entitling him to look down, from a vantage ground of superiority, on the highest nobles of the land; he had his Barons who held of him, as also his Council of retainers, analogous to the Parl. of the Country. The Earl of Crawford, alone, with his Heralds and Pursuivants, occupied a somewhat similar position, and, it is well known how formidable these two great Earls became

See "Douglas," Marquessate of [S.], *cr.* 1633 ; and see "Douglas," Dukedom of [S.], *cr.* 1703, *extinct* 1761.   From 1633 to 1703 the Earldom of Angus, and from 1703 to 1761 the Marquessate of Angus [S.] (*cr.* 1703) was used as the courtesy title of the eldest son of the Marquess of Douglas or Duke of Douglas [S.].

In 1761, the Duke of Hamilton [S.], as h. male of the abovenamed William (Douglas), Earl of Angus and (1st) Marquess of Douglas [S.], *suc.* (apparently) (*) to those titles, his right to the Earldom of Angus [S.] being under the regrant of 1547.   Since that time the Earldom of Angus has apparently (b) continued *merged* in that Dukedom.   See "Hamilton," Dukedom of [S.], *cr.* 1643, under the 7th Duke. (c)

---

when they leagued together against the Royal House.   That *Douglas* was in all respects *the premier Earl* during nearly the whole of the reigns (1406-60) of James I and James II, cannot admit of doubt, and it was only after the attainder of the 9th and last Earl, in 1455, when, as was popularly said, "The Red Douglas put down the Black," that the former (then represented by George, Earl of Angus, a stedfast adherent of the Crown during the Douglas rebellion), seems to have been *tacitly* allowed to step into all the privileges of the latter.   (*Ex inform.* G. Burnett, sometime Lyon.)]

Lastly, in the confirmation of the *Comitatus* of Angus by charter under the Great Seal to the Earl in liferent and to his s. in fee (13 Feb. 1602), there was included " primum locum in sedendo in omnibus nostris Parliamentis, conventionibus et conciliis ; primum locum et ductionem primæ aciei et gerendi coronam in omnibus nostris Parliamentis."   This charter was confirmed by Parl. in 1606 (*Acts of Parl.*, vol. iv, p. 311), and in virtue of it " the Earls of Angus obtained by the decreet of ranking in that year, the precedence of all the Earls, and sat in Parl. accordingly " See *Riddell*, p. 159.

In 1611, however, the " fiar " of 1602 became Earl, and in 1633, he, by arrange- ment, resigned (*ut supra*) these privileges, the resignation being duly registered six days later (*Acts of Parl.*, vol. v, p. 10).   Notwithstanding this, the family subse- quently endeavoured to disavow the resignation, on the ground that the Resigner was only a liferenter, the *comitatus* having been at the time (under a charter of 1631) in his s. in fee ; consequently, on the hypothesis that the original precedence was not only over Earls, but over all Peers, the Marquesses of Douglas (as Earls of Angus) persistently protested their right to " the first seatt and vote in Parl."from the Restor- ation (1660) to the eve of the Union, 16 Jan. 1707.

(a) In the article on " *The Peerage* " in the *Quarterly Review* for Oct. 1893 (p. 389) the Earldom of Angus is only spoken of as *claimed* by the Dukes of Hamilton.

(b) The Earldom of Angus [S.] has never officially been allowed to the Dukes of Hamilton [S.], and the petition of the Duke in 1762 for that Earldom, though referred to the House of Lords, was never followed up.

(c) The claim of the Earldom of Angus [S.], by petition of Archibald Douglas, formerly Stewart, only s. of Sir John Stewart, of Grandtully, Bart [S.], by " the deceased Lady Jean Douglas, only sister of Archibald, Duke of Douglas and Earl of Angus [S.], lately deceased, " was presented, with the King's reference thereof, to the House 22 Mar 1762.   It was founded on an appointment, stated to have been made 28 Oct. 1699, by the then Marquess of Douglas and Earl of Angus (by virtue of a charter 24 June 1698) that, failing heirs male of his own body, the Earldom should be inherited by " the eldest h. female of the body of his s., Lord Angus, and the heirs whatsomever of the body of the said eldest h. female of the Marquis' own body."

i.e. "ANGUS" Earldom [S.] *(Douglas)*, *cr.* 1643 with the MARQUESSATE OF DOUGLAS [S.], which see.

i.e. "ANGUS AND ABERNETHY," Marquessate [S.] *(Douglas)*, *cr.* 1703 with the DUKEDOM OF DOUGLAS [S.], which see ; *extinct* 1761.

ANNALY OF ANNALY AND RATHCLINE

BARONY.

I. 1863.

1. HENRY WHITE, of Woodlands (formerly Luttrellstown), co. Dublin, and subsequently of Rathcline, co. Longford, 4th, but only surv. s. of Luke W., bookseller, of Woodlands (ª) afsd., (who *d.* 25 Feb. 1824) by his 1st wife, Elizabeth, da. of Andrew DE LA (ᵇ) MAZIERE, was *b.* 1791. He served in the 14th Light Dragoons in the Peninsular War, was M.P. (ᶜ) for co. Dublin 1823-32, for co. Longford 1837-47, and 1857-61. Lord Lieut. of co. Longford 1841-73, and, having *suc.* to the Longford estates on the death of his next elder br., Luke W., in Aug. 1854, was, on 19 Aug. 1863, *cr.* BARON ANNALY OF ANNALY AND RATHCLINE, (ᵈ) co. Longford. (ᵉ) He *m.*, 3 Oct. 1828, Ellen, da. of William Soper DEMPSTER, by Hannah, only da. and h. of John Hamilton DEMPSTER, of Skibo Castle, Sutherland. She *d.* 12 May 1868. He *d.* 3 Sep. 1873, at Sunbury Park, Midx., aged 84.

II. 1873.

2. LUKE (WHITE), BARON ANNALY, s. and h., *b.* 26 Sep. 1829. Ed. at Eton. Capt. 13th Light Dragoons, 1847-53:

This is stated to have been confirmed by charter signed by Queen Anne, 10, and ratified by Parl. 26, Mar. 1707. See *Robertson*, p. 309. The whole matter was referred to the Lords' Committee for Privileges, but no further steps appear to have been taken, and the Earldom (under the regrant of 1547) passed to the h. *male*. By decision of the House of Lords, 27 Feb. 1769, the petitioner was found h. *gen.*, and was *cr.* a Peer. See "DOUGLAS," Barony, *cr.* 1790, *extinct* 1857.

(ª) The estate of Luttrellstown was purchased by this Luke White from the Earl of Carhampton [I.], in whose family (Luttrell) it had been since the time of Hen. VI. G.E.C.

He was M.P. (Whig) for co. Leitrim, 1812-24, and was the "celebrated Luke White, bookseller and lottery office keeper in Dublin, who is said to have realised the largest fortune ever made by trade in Ireland." See *Annual Reg.* for 1854, p. 330. In Hare's *Story of two noble Lives*, 1893, vol. i, pp. 13-17, is a curious account of his career, which mentions "his keeping a stall for books, on Essex bridge, near the Castle." V.G.

(ᵇ) *Andrew* de la Maziere, of Fleet Str., Dublin, *m.*, in 1738, Mary, da. of Mark White, of Pill Lane, grocer, and had, with other issue, a da. Elizabeth, most probably the lady in question.

(ᶜ) In Parl. he gave steady support to the Whig-Liberal party. V.G.

(ᵈ) Rathcline, an old castle of the O'Ferrals, is in Annaly.

(ᵉ) White, Lord Annaly, bears arms of Silver a cheveron engrailed between three roses gules, with a crosslet gold on the cheveron. The crosslet in this shield granted to the first Lord Annaly is its only difference from that of the ancient family of White of Leixlip, from whom no descent has otherwise been suggested. (*ex inform.* Oswald Barron.) V.G.

Lieut. Col. of the Longford Rifles. He was M.P. (Liberal), for Clare
1859-60, for Longford 1861-62, and for Kidderminster 1862-65.   Sheriff
of co. Dublin 1861, of co. Longford 1871.   A junior Lord of the Treasury
1862-66.   State Steward to (Earl Spencer) the Lord Lieut. [I.] 1868-73.
K P 9 Feb. 1885.   He *m.*, 24 Aug. 1853, Emily, da. of James STUART.
He *d* at Funchal, Madeira, 16, and was *bur.* 31 Mar. 1888, at Holdenby,
Northants, aged 58

III. 1888.   3. LUKE (WHITE), BARON ANNALY OF ANNALY AND
                     RATHCLINE [1863], 1st s. and h., *b.* 25 Feb 1857.   In the
Scots Guards 1877-96, serving in the Egyptian Campaign, 1882 (medal, clasp,
and bronze star); Capt. 1888; retired 1896.   A Lib. Unionist in politics.
He *m.*, 24 July 1884, at St. James's, Westm., Lilah Georgiana Augusta
Constance, 2nd, but only surv. da. and [1895] h. of Henry (AGAR-ELLIS),
3rd VISCOUNT CLIFDEN OF GOWRAN [I.], by Eliza Horatia Frederica, 2nd
da. of Frederick Charles William SEYMOUR.   She was *b.* 6 Aug. 1862.

[LUKE HENRY WHITE, only s. and h. ap., *b.* 7 Aug. 1885.   Lieut.
11th Hussars.]

Family Estates.—These, in 1883, consisted of about 12,500 acres in
co. Longford and about 4,000 in co. Dublin.   Total about 16,500 acres
of the yearly value of about £15,000.   *Principal Residences.*—Luttrellstown, (*) near Clonsilla, co. Dublin ; Rathcline House, co. Longford.

ANNALY OF TENELICK

BARONY [I.]   1. JOHN GORE, 2nd s. of George G., (b) 2nd Justice of
I. 1766   the Court of Common Pleas [I.], by Bridget, da. and
   to   eventually sole h of John SANKEY, of Tenelick, co.
  1784.   Longford, was *b.* 2 Mar. 1718.   Barrister King's Inns,
                 Mich. 1742 ; K.C. 1749 ; and in Mar. 1758 *suc.* his
eldest br., Arthur Gore, sometime M.P. for co. Longford ; was (himself)
M.P. for Jamestown 1747-60, and for co. Longford 1761-64, and, having
been King's Counsel, Counsel to the Commissioners of Revenue, and
Solicitor Gen. [I.] 1760-64, was, in Sep. 1764, made Chief Justice of the
King's Bench and P.C. [I.], and on 17 Jan. 1766 was *cr.* BARON AN-
NALY OF TENELICK, co. Longford [I.], taking his seat in the House
on 27 Jan.   On 20 Oct. 1767, and again in 1769, he was elected Speaker
of the House of Lords [I.], in the absence of the Lord Chancellor.   He
m., 26 Nov. 1747, Frances, 2nd da. of Richard (WINGFIELD), 1st VISCOUNT

(*) The 3rd Lord has sensibly reverted to the historic name, abandoning that
of ' Woodlands. ' V.G.

(b) He was 4th s. of Sir Arthur Gore, of Newtown Gore, co. Mayo, 1st Bart.
[I.], ancestor of Arthur G., *cr.* EARL OF ARRAN [I.] 1762.   He was a Barrister
in 1742, and was one of the "nine Gores" who sat simultaneously in the Irish Parl.
See-as to the Bank of 'Malone, Clements and Gore,' which broke in 1758, *N. & Q.*,
8th Ser., vol. viii, pp. 363 and 423.

POWERSCOURT [I.], by his 2nd wife, Dorothy Beresford, da. of Hercules ROWLEY. He *d. s.p.*, 3 Apr. 1784, at his residence in St. Stephen's Green, Dublin, and was *bur.* at Tisherig, co. Longford, aged 66, when the title became *extinct.*([a]) Will pr. 1784 [I.]. His widow, who was *b.* 2 June 1728, *d.* 31 July, and was *bur.* 16 Aug. 1794, at St. Marylebone, Midx.

II. 1789   1. Lt. Col. HENRY GORE, of Tenelick, co. Longford,
to   br. and h. of John, BARON ANNALY [I.] abovenamed, *b.*
1793.   8 Mar. 1728, M.P. for co. Longford 1758-60, 1768-89,
   and for Lanesborough 1761-68 ; Sheriff of co. Longford
1765. Examiner of the Customs, 1770. He was, on 23 Sep. 1789, ([b]) *cr.*
BARON ANNALY OF TENELICK, co. Longford [I.]. He *m.* (Lic.
Prerog. Ct. [I.] 13 July), 4 Aug. 1764, ([c]) Mary, only da. of Skeffington
Randal SMYTH, of Leigh, Queen's Co., ([d]) by Mary, ([e]) da. of the Hon.
and Rev. John MOORE, D.D. He *d. s.p.*, 5 June 1793, in Dublin, when the
title became *extinct.* Will pr. 1793. M.I. at St. Anne's, Dublin. His
widow *d.* 1 Mar. 1812, aged 75, at Mount Hervey, Queen's Co. M.I. at
St. Anne's, Dublin.

ANNAND

i.e. " ANNAND, " Viscountcy [S.] *(Murray)*, *cr.* 1622. See " AN-
NANDALE," Earldom [S.], *cr.* 1625, *extinct* 1658.

i.e. " ANNAND, " Viscountcy [S.] *(Johnston)*, *cr.* 1661 with the
EARLDOM OF ANNANDALE AND HARTFELL [S.], which see ; *dormant* 1792.

i.e. " ANNAND " Viscountcy [S.] *(Johnston)*, *cr.* 1701 with the MAR-
QUESSATE OF ANNANDALE [S.], which see, *dormant* 1792.

ANNANDALE

The Lordship of Annandale was obtained by Robert Bruce from
David I, about 1124, and thus, when his descendant Robert Bruce
became King of Scotland in 1306, merged in the Crown. It appears to
have been re-granted, in or before 1455, to Alexander (Stewart), Duke of
Albany [S.], 2nd s. of James II, by whom it, together with the Earldom of March [S.], was *forfeited* in 1483 ; both dignities being shortly
afterwards, *viz.* by Act. of Parl., 1 Oct. 1487, annexed inalienably to the
Crown. See " ALBANY, " Dukedom of [S.], *cr.* 1456.

([a]) He was one of the characters in *Baratariana.* See *N. & Q.*, 3rd Ser.,
vol. viii, p. 211, and *idem*, 8th Ser., vol. viii, p. 361.

([b]) See note *sub.* George, MARQUESS OF WATERFORD [1789].

([c]) Nevertheless he gave the date as 4 Aug. 1770, in Lords' Entries, Ulster's
Office, 22 Jan. 1790, when certifying his Pedigree, but added " as to Persons and
alliances, cant be sure as to dates. " *(ex inform.* G. D. Burtchaell.) V.G.

([d]) He was s. and h. of Edward Smyth, Bishop of Down and Connor, by the
Hon. Mary Skeffington.

([e]) ? Elizabeth, as in *Gent. Mag.*

EARLDOM [S.]   1. JOHN MURRAY, 9th and yst s. of Sir Charles
I. 1625.   Murray, of Cockpool, by Margaret, 1st da. of Hugh
    (SOMERVILLE), 5th LORD SOMERVILLE [S.], was formerly
Gent. of the Bedchamber and Master of the Horse to James VI, by whom
he was knighted, and, coming with that King to England, was made one
of the Gentlemen of the Privy Chamber there, receiving large grants of
land formerly belonging to the Abbeys of Dundrenan, Linclondane, &c.
On 28 June 1622, he was cr. LORD MURRAY OF LOCHMABEN
and VISCOUNT OF ANNAND [S], (ᵃ) and on 13 Mar. 1624/5 he was
cr. EARL OF ANNANDALE and LORD MURRAY OF TYNN-
INGHAM [S.], his long and faithful services to the King being recited in
the patent. In 1636 he suc. to the family estate of Cockpool (as h. male
of his father), on the death of his br., Sir Richard Murray, Bart. [S.].   He
m. Elizabeth, da. of Sir John SCHAW, of Broich.   He d. in London, Sep.,
and was bur. 13 Oct. 1640, at Hoddam. (ᵇ)   Fun. entry at Lyon Office.

II. 1640   2. JAMES (MURRAY), EARL OF ANNANDALE, VISCOUNT
to   OF ANNAND, and LORD MURRAY OF LOCHMABEN [S.], only
1658.   s. and h., served h. to his father 30 Mar. 1641.   On the
    death of Mungo (MURRAY), 2nd VISCOUNT STORMONT [S.],
in Mar 1642, he suc. (under the limitations in the patent of that title,
16 Aug. 1621) as VISCOUNT STORMONT [S.].   On 17 Nov. 1643
he was made Steward of Annandale.   After the battle of Kilsyth, in Aug.
1645, he joined the army of Montrose, and subsequently retired to England.
He m. (cont. dat. 26 June 1647) (ᶜ) Jean, da. of James (CARNEGIE), 2nd
EARL OF SOUTHESK [S.], by Isabel, da of Robert (KERR), 1st EARL OF
ROXBURGHE [S.].   He d. s.p., 28 Dec. 1658, in St. Clement Danes, Midx.,
when the VISCOUNTCY OF STORMONT [S.] devolved on David (MURRAY),
2nd LORD BALVAIRD [S.], (ᵈ) and the EARLDOM OF ANNANDALE, VISCOUNTCY
OF ANNAND, and the BARONY OF MURRAY OF LOCHMABEN [S.], became
extinct.   Admon. 3 Mar. 1664/5 to a creditor.   His widow m, 9 Aug
1659, at Kinnaird, David (MURRAY), 4th VISCOUNT STORMONT [S.], who
d. 24 July 1668.   She d. Mar. 1671.

III. 1661.   1. JAMES (JOHNSTON), 2nd EARL OF HARTFELL, (ᵉ) &c.
    [S.], s. and h. of James, 1st EARL OF HARTFELL [S.], by his
1st wife, Margaret, 1st da. of William (DOUGLAS), 1st EARL OF QUEENS-

---

(ᵃ) There is a charter to him dated 20 Feb. 1623/4, under the name of " *John,
Viscount of Annand,* " granting him the palace in Dumfries, the lands of Staikheuch
and Carlaverock.   See also *Maidment*, p. 3, where there is much curious information
about this family.

(ᵇ) " By no means nice as to whom he sold his influence, or from whom he took
money, he rapidly acquired one of the best estates in Scotland. "   (Note to Godman's
Court of King James.)   V G.

(ᶜ) Mansfield Charter Chest.

(ᵈ) See *sub* iv VISCOUNT STORMONT.

(ᵉ) Hartfell is the name of a high hill in Annandale.   The date of the cr. of the

BERRY [S.]. He was *b.* 1625, *suc.* his father in Mar. 1653, and was served h. to him 1 Oct. 1653. He was fined £2000 in 1654 under Cromwell's Act of Indemnity. M.P. for co. Dumfries in the Parl. [E.] 1654-56, as James, Earl of Hartfell. At the restoration he was made P.C., and having resigned his peerage honours to the King (the peerage of "Annandale," *cr.* 1625, having become *extinct* as above), he received a grant of the EARLDOM OF ANNANDALE, &c., 13 Feb. 1661 (with the precedency of the resigned Earldom of Hartfell, *viz.* 18 Mar. 1643), under the designation of "EARL OF ANNANDALE AND HARTFELL, VISCOUNT OF ANNAND, LORD JOHNSTON OF LOCHWOOD, LOCHMABEN, MOFFAT-DALE AND EVANDALE" [S.], with rem. to the heirs male of his body, rem. to the eldest heirs female of his body and the eldest heirs male of the body of such heirs female bearing the name and arms of Johnston, whom all failing to his nearest heirs whomsoever. He obtained a grant of the offices of Hereditary Constable of Lochmaben Castle and of Hereditary Steward of Annandale. He *m.* (cont. dat. 29 May 1645) Henrietta, da. of William (DOUGLAS), 1st MARQUESS OF DOUGLAS [S.], by his 2nd wife, Mary, da. of George (GORDON), 1st MARQUESS OF HUNTLY [S.]. He *d.* 17 July 1672, aged 47. His widow *d.* 1 June 1673, aged 40.

IV. 1672.

MARQUESSATE [S.]

I. 1701.

2 and 1. WILLIAM (JOHNSTON), EARL OF AN-NANDALE AND HARTFELL, &c. [S.], 2nd, but 1st surv. (*) s. and h., *b.* 17 Feb. 1663/4, was ed. at the Univ. of Glasgow. After first plotting against James II and subsequently for him, he, in 1690, made terms with William III and was sworn P.C. [S.]. Extraord. Lord of Session 1693 till his death ; Pres. of the Council [S.] 1693-95, and 15 May 1702 to 28 Feb. 1705/6 ; and of the Parl. [S.] 1695; Lord Treasurer [S.] 1696-1705 ; Lord High COMMISSIONER to the Gen. Assembly of the Church [S.] 1701, and again 1705 and 1711. On 24 June 1701 he was *cr.* MARQUESS OF ANNANDALE, EARL OF HARTFELL, VISCOUNT OF ANNAND, LORD JOHNSTON OF LOCHWOOD, LOCHMABEN, MOFFATDALE, AND EVANDALE, to him and his heirs male whomsoever. LORD PRIVY SEAL 6 May to 15 Dec. 1702 ; K.T. 7 Feb. 1703/4 ; one of the Principal Secretaries of State 9 Mar. to 29 Sep. 1705. Though opposed to the Union, he was a Rep. Peer [S.] 1708-13, and 1715 till his death. P.C.[U.K.] 19 Apr. 1711. GREAT SEAL[S.] 1714-16. P.C. again on the accession of George I, 1714, and PRIVY SEAL again 1715 till his death. He was active in support of the Government during the rebellion of 1715, at which time (and till his death) he was Lord Lieut. of Dumfries, Kircudbright and Peebles. He *m.*, 1stly, 2 Jan. 1682, at Edinburgh, Sophia, only da. and h. of John FAIRHOLM, of Craigiehall, co. Linlithgow, by Sophia, da. of Joseph JOHNSTON, of Hilton. She was *b.*

Earldom of Hartfell is 18 Mar. 1643. That of the Barony of Johnston of Lochwood [S.] (by which title the 1st Earl was raised to the Peerage) is 20 June 1633. See HARTFELL, " Earldom of [S.].

(*) His elder br., James, *b.* 17 Dec. 1660, *d.* an infant. V.G.

19 Mar. 1668, and (having been a mother at 14 and a grandmother at 31) *d.* 13, and was *bur.* 18 Dec. 1716, in Westm. Abbey. M I. He *m.*, 2ndly, 20 Nov. 1718, " without consent of the father, and perhaps mother," at the Fleet Chapel, London, Charlotte VAN LORE, only da. and h. of John VAN DEN BEMPDÉ, of Hackness Hall, co York, and of Pall Mall, Midx, by Temperance, (ᵃ) da. of John PACKER. With her he obtained a very large fortune. He *d.* 14 Jan. 1720/1, at Bath, Somerset, and was *bur.* at Johnstone, aged 66.(ᵇ) Will dat. 29 Dec. 1720, pr. Aug. 1721. His widow *m* Lieut. Col. John JOHNSTONE, who *d.* 1741, being killed at Carthagena. She *d.* 23 Nov. 1762, at Bath afsd. (ᶜ) Will pr. Dec. 1762.

MARQUESSATE [S]

II.

EARLDOM [S.]

V.

1721.

3. JAMES (JOHNSTON), MARQUESS OF ANNANDALE, &c. [S.], s and h. by 1st wife. He was *chosen* as M.P for co. Dumfries 1708, but, being the eldest s. of a Peer, was *not allowed* to take his seat. (ᵈ) He surrendered his honours, 1 Oct. 1726, and the regrant is made subject to certain conditions, one of which is mentioned in a disposition executed on the same day, whereby he declared it not leisome or lawful for any of his heirs to marry into a certain family of the name of Johnstone, whom, he adds, in that event, he excludes for ever from all right and succession " to my said honours. (ᵉ) He *d.* unm., aged 42, of consumption, at Naples, 10 Feb., and was *bur.* 25 Sep. 1730, in Westm. Abbey. (ᶠ) M.I.

MARQUESSATE [S.]

III.

EARLDOM [S.]

VI.

1730 to 1792.

4. GEORGE (JOHNSTON *afterwards* VAN DEN BEMPDÉ) MARQUESS OF ANNANDALE, (1701), EARL OF ANNANDALE AND HARTFELL(1643), EARL OF HARTFELL (1701), VISCOUNT OF ANNAND (1643 and 1701), LORD JOHNSTON OF LOCHWOOD, LOCHMABEN, MOFFATDALE

(ᵃ) They were *m.* 28 Aug. 1699, at St. James's, Duke Place, London, he 40, and she 30.

(ᵇ) " Tall, lusty and well shaped, with a very black complexion; extremely carried away by his private interests, possessing both good sense and a manly expression, but not much to be trusted." Daniel Defoe writes of him to Robert Harley, 19 Feb. 1710/1, as "of no reputation on either side because steady to none." V.G.

(ᶜ) Their s., Richard VAN DEN BEMPDÉ JOHNSTONE, of Hackness, in the North Riding of Yorkshire, inherited, in 1792, the estates of his mother, and was *cr.* a Baronet in 1795. His grandson, the 3rd Bart., was *cr.* LORD DERWENT in 1881.

(ᵈ) See *ante*, p. 2, note "a."

(ᵉ) See *Riddell*, p. 271.

(ᶠ) On his death the estate of Craigie Hall (which came from his mother) went to his sister (of the whole blood) Henrietta, wife of Charles (HOPE), 1st EARL OF HOPETOUN [S.]. She *d* 29 Nov. 1750, in her 69th year. Her grandson James, 3rd Earl of Hopetoun, became in 1792 (on the death of his grand-uncle George, 3rd Marquess of Annandale [S]) the *heir gen. of the 1st Earl of Annandale* [S.], and, as such, claimed the dignities under the regrant of 1661.

AND EVANDALE (1643 and 1701) [S.], br. of the half blood and h., being s. of the 1st Marquess by his 2nd wife. He was *b.* 29 May 1720. (ª) The loss of his only surv. br. John (who *d.* Oct. 1742, aged 21) so affected him that he became insane, and by inquest in Chancery, 5 Mar. 1748, he was declared to have been a lunatic since 12 Dec. 1744. By Act of Parl. 1744, he took the name of VAN DEN BEMPDÉ, pursuant to the will of John van den Bempdé. Under the Act for abolishing hereditary jurisdictions in 1747, he was allowed £2200 for the Stewartry of Annandale, and £800 for the Regality of Moffat. He *d.* unm., in his 72nd year, at Turnham Green, Midx., 29 Apr., and was *bur.* 7 May 1792, at Chiswick. Admon. May 1792.

After his death, his personalty, amounting to £415,000, was divided in three parts—*viz.*, one to each of his two uterine brothers, and one to the descendants (next of kin) of his sister *(ex parte paternâ)*, of the half blood, the Countess of Hopetoun [S.]. His Scotch estates went to his grand nephew (of the half blood) and heir of line, James (HOPE), 3rd EARL OF HOPETOUN [S.], grandson of his said half sister, while his English estates, which he had inherited through his mother, went to his uterine br. Richard VAN DEN BEMPDÉ JOHNSTONE, afterwards *cr.* a Baronet. His *peerage dignities* became *dormant.* (ᵇ)

(ª) Mrs. Pendarves (afterwards Mrs. Delany) writes of him in 1741, as " very tall, what is called handsome, and much commended for his dancing. " V.G.

(ᵇ) Among the many claimants to these Honours, some as heirs of entail, under the regrant of 1661, to the Earldom, &c., (with the precedency of 1643), and some as heirs male whosoever, to the Marquessate and other honours granted in 1701, may be enumerated—

1. James (HOPE), EARL OF HOPETOUN [S.], in 1794, as h. gen. and h. of entail, being grandson and h. of Henrietta, Countess of Hopetoun [S.], the only child that left issue of William, 2nd Earl and 1st Marquess of Annandale.

This claim was continued by John James HOPE JOHNSTONE, of Annandale, his grandson and h. of line (being s. and h. of his 1st da.) in 1825. *Disallowed* 11 June 1844. Revived on the ground of " res noviter." See *Maidment*, pp. 89, 107, 109 and 121. This last claimant *d.* 11 July 1876, aged 80, and was *suc.* in the Annandale estates and his claim by his grandson and h. male. Lord Campbell in his *Life of Brougham*, remarks : " When I was Attorney Gen. [1834-41], Brougham was about to create *another Earl* [besides the Earl of Devon], by making Mr. Hope Johnstone EARL OF ANNANDALE, and he had actually congratulated Mrs. Hope Johnstone as the Countess ; but, with the assistance of Sir William Follett, I prevented him completing the creation, and the claim was disallowed."

2. Sir John Lowther JOHNSTONE of Westerhall, Bart. [S.], in 1805, as h. male. This claim was continued by his s. and h., Sir George Frederick Johnstone, Bart. [S.], who petitioned 30 June 1834. Continued also after Sir George's death by his (posthumous) s. and h. Sir Frederick John William Johnstone, Bart. [S.]. See *Maidment*, p. 108, and 119 to 121.

3. John Henry GOODINGE, afterwards GOODINGE JOHNSTONE, in 1830 and 1839, as h. of entail. He was s. and h. of Sarah (wife of William Goodinge), only child that had issue of John Johnstone, s. and h. of John Johnstone, alleged to be 2nd s. of the 1st Earl of Annandale. This claim was *disallowed* 11 June 1844. See *Maidment*, p. 107, but a fresh petition was lodged in 1851.

ANNER

i.e. " CARLETON OF ANNER " co. Tipperary, Barony [I.] *(Carleton)*, *cr.* 1789, see " CARLETON OF CLARE, " Viscountcy [I.], *cr.* 1797, *extinct* 1826.

ANNESLEY OF CASTLEWELLAN

BARONY [I.]   1. WILLIAM ANNESLEY, of Castlewellan, in the parish
I. 1758.   of Kilmegan, co. Down, 6th s. (ª) of Francis A., of the
same, and of Thorganby, co. York, by his 1st wife,
Elizabeth, da. of Sir Joseph MARTIN, of London, was *b.* about 1710 ; was
a Barrister at Law (Dublin) 1738 ; M.P. for Midleton, co. Cork, 1741-
58 ; *suc.* his father (though not his h male) in the estate of Castlewellan,
7 Aug. 1750 ; was Sheriff for co. Down, 23 Nov. 1750 ; and on 20 Sep.
1758, was *cr.* BARON ANNESLEY of Castle Wellan, co. Down (ᵇ) [I.].
He took his seat in the House 29 Nov. 1759.   On 14 Nov. 1766, he was
cr. VISCOUNT GLERAWLY (ᶜ) of co. Fermanagh (ᵇ) [I.], and took
his seat accordingly 27 Jan. 1768.   He *m.* (lic. Prerog. Ct. [I.] 5 Aug.),
16 Aug. 1738, at St. Mary's, Dublin, Anne, 1st da. of Marcus (BERES-
FORD), 1st EARL OF TYRONE [I.], by Catharine, *suo jure* BARONESS LA POER
[I]. (ᵈ)   She *d.* 12 May 1770.   He *d.* at Clontarf, 12 Sep. 1770, in
his 61st year.   Will pr. 1770.

---

4. Dougal CAMPBELL, M D , as h of entail (through Mary, 1st da. of the 1st
Earl of Annandale, wife of William (Lindsay), Earl of Crawford [S.]).   This claim
also was *disallowed* 11 June 1844.

5. Sir Robert GRAHAM of Esk, Bart. (claim pending 1841), as h of entail,
through the same lady, in contradiction to the generally received pedigree which makes
him such h. to her aunt, the *sister* (not the *da*) of the 1st Earl of Annandale.

6 James JOHNSTONE of Dromore, co. Monaghan (claim made before 1841), as
h. male.   Continued by his only s. and h. Charles Johnstone.

7. Edward Douglas JOHNSTONE, of Snow Hill, co. Fermanagh. ⎫
8. Edward JOHNSIONE, of Fulford, co. Warwick, Barrister at ⎬ Presumed to be
Law.   Claim referred 28 May 1876.   ⎭ as h. male.

9 James F GYLES, a citizen of the United States in America, in 1875.

(ª) He was indeed the eldest *surv.* s. at his father's death, but his eldest br. the
Rev. Francis Annesley, LL.D , Rector of Winwick, co. Lancaster (who *d. v.p.*, 1 May
1740), left issue, being ancestor of Arthur Annesley who, in 1844, becoming
(apparently) the head of the house of Annesley, assumed the family honours of
VISCOUNT VALENTIA and LORD MOUNTNORRIS [I.].

(ᵇ) The three patents (1758, 1766, and 1789) are printed *in extenso* in the claim
to the Peerage by the 4th Earl in July 1855.   In the patent of 1758 the name is
written Castle Wellan, but in that of 1789 Castlewellan.

(ᶜ) This name is intended for GLENAWLEY (sometimes called Clanawley), a
Barony on the west side of co. Fermanagh ; the error was caused by the clerk having
inadvertently written R for N and having omitted the E in the patent.

(ᵈ) Mrs. Delany writes of him and his wife in Sep. 1744, " She is daughter to
my Lord Tyrone, such another slatternly ignorant hoyden I never saw, and the worst

23

II. 1770.   2 and 1. FRANCIS CHARLES (ANNESLEY), VISCOUNT
EARLDOM [I.]   GLERAWLY and LORD ANNESLEY of Castle Wellan [I.],
                       s. and h., b. 27 Nov. 1740. M.P. for Downpatrick
I. 1789.   1761-70. Took his seat in the House of Lords
                       1 Mar. 1771. On 17 Aug. 1789 (ª) he was cr. EARL
ANNESLEY (ᵇ) of Castlewellan, co. Down (ᶜ) [I.], with a *spec. rem.*, failing
heirs male of his body, to his br. Richard Annesley in like manner. He
took his seat on the Earls' Bench 21 Jan. 1790. He *m.*, 8 Feb. 1766,
Mary, (a fortune of £30,000) da. and h. of Robert GROVE, of Ballyhim-
mock, co. Cork, by Mary, only child of Richard RYLANDS, of Dungarvan.
She *d.* 25 Aug. 1791. He subsequently went through the marriage ceremony at Mountpanther, co. Down, with a woman who was already married,
viz. Sophia CONNOR, *wife* of one of his gate-keepers. By her (besides
a son *b. before*) he had 2 sons *b. after* this ceremony, both of whom, as
well as their mother, assumed the rank to which a legit. marriage would
have entitled them. (ᵈ) He *d. s.p. legit.*, 19 Dec. 1802, at Mountpanther
afsd., and was *bur.* at Kilmegan, afsd., aged 62. Will pr. 1803, Prerog. Ct.[I.].

EARLDOM [I.]   ⎫   2 and 3. RICHARD (ANNESLEY), EARL AN-
                      ⎪   NESLEY, *&c.* [I.], 3rd, but 2nd surv. br. and
II.   ⎪   h., inherited the Earldom according to the
                      ⎬ 1802. spec. rem. He was *b.* 14 Apr. 1745 ; Bar-
BARONY [I.]   ⎪   rister at Law, Dublin 1770 ; was M.P. (ᵉ)
                      ⎪   [I.] for Coleraine 1776-83, and for St. Canice
III.   ⎭

_____

of it is she is very good humoured, but will be familiar : her husband is very like the
Duke of Bedford, and well enough. " She writes of them again in Nov. 1752,
" They are very rich and know it, and spend their lives in increasing not enjoying
their fortune ; but he is a very honest man in all his dealings, still would be more
agreeable as well as more useful if he thought less of his possessions. His lady suits
him exactly; she does not want sense, and is comical enough is a satirical way." V.G.
    (ª) See note *sub* ii EARL CADOGAN.
    (ᵇ) See note *sub* i MARQUESS OF WATERFORD.
    (ᶜ) See note " b " on previous page.
    (ᵈ) The elder of these 2 sons was *bap.* " George de la Poer Beresford. " He
was a student in the Royal Military Coll., Sandhurst, Berks, where he *d.* unm., and
was *bur.* 18 Feb. 1814, at Sandhurst, as " George, Earl of Annesley, aged 15. " The
yr s., *called* " the Hon. Francis Charles Annesley, " *d.* an infant, 9 Mar. 1803,
at the residence of " the Countess Annesley " (*i.e.* his mother), in Sackville St., Dublin.
This *so called* Countess *d.* in Paris about 1852. Her 1st s. by the Earl (*b.* before the
marriage ceremony) *d.* at sea, aged 14. By Dorothy *McIlroy* the Earl had 4 *other*
sons, *b.* in his wife's lifetime, one of whom was living 1855. These last four are
here mentioned because they are so often confused with the three sons of Sophia
Connor, two of whom claimed to be legitimate as above mentioned.
    (ᵉ) " In his parliamentary exhibitions, Mr. Annesley is but little befriended by
his voice, as it is feeble, indistinct, confined, and inharmonious, with a childishness of
tone uncommon and offensive ; whilst his management of it is very defective in that
art which would conceal its deficiencies, and meliorate its harshness. Variety is the
most striking characteristic of his delivery, as he frequently passes, with a very sudden

1783-90, for Newtownards 1790-96, for Blessington 1797-1800, (ª) for Clogher Feb.-Mar. 1800, and for Midleton Apr.-Dec. 1800. Sheriff of co. Down, 1783. Commissioner of the Customs [I.] 1786-95, and 1802-06 ; Commissioner of the Excise [I.] 1795-1810. P C. [I] 1798. He *m.*, 25 Sep. 1771, at Swanlinbar, co. Cavan, Anne, (with £15,000 *p.a.*) only da. and h. of Robert LAMBERT, of Dunlady, co Down, by Alice, widow of John CORRY, of Newry, da. of the Rev. John VAUGHAN, Rector of Dromore, Ireland. She, who was *b.* in 1752, *d.* 30 June 1822, at Belfast He *d.* at Clontarf, 9, and was *bur.* 16 Nov. 1824, at Kilmegan afsd., aged 79. Will pr. 23 Dec. 1824.

EARLDOM [I.]		3 and 4. WILLIAM RICHARD (ANNESLEY),
III.		EARL ANNESLEY, &c., s. and h., *b.* 16 July 1772.
	1824.	M.P. (Whig) for Downpatrick, 1815-20 ;
BARONY [I.]		Sheriff of co. Down, 1822, as Viscount
		Glerawley. He *m.*, 1stly, 19 May 1803,
IV.		Isabella, 2nd da. of William (St. LAWRENCE),

2nd EARL OF HOWTH [I.], by his 1st wife, Mary, da. and coh. of Thomas (BERMINGHAM), EARL OF LOUTH [I.]. This marriage was dissolved by Act of Parl. 8 June 1821. (ᵇ) She *d.* Apr. 1827. He *m.*, 2ndly, 15 July 1828, at Kilmegan afsd., Priscilla Cecilia, 2nd da. of Hugh MOORE, of Eglantine House, in the parish of Blaris, co. Down, by Priscilla Cecilia, widow of Robert SHAW, and da of Col. Robert ARMITAGE, of Kensington. He *d.* at Oriel Lodge, Cheltenham, 25 Aug., and was *bur* 1 Sep 1838, at Kilmegan afsd., aged 66. Will dat. 29 June 1836 to 16 Aug. 1838, pr. 2 Oct. 1838. His widow, who was *bap.* 8 Sep. 1808, at Lisburn Cath., *d.* 29 Mar. 1891, aged 83, at Donard Lodge, Newcastle, co. Down, and was *bur.* at Castlewellan. Will pr. 6 May 1891.

EARLDOM [I.]		4 and 5. WILLIAM RICHARD (ANNESLEY),
IV.		EARL ANNESLEY, &c. [I.], s. and h. by 2nd
	1838.	wife, *b.* 21 Feb., in Rutland Sq., Dublin, and
BARONY [I.]		*bap.* 11 May 1830, at St. Thomas's, Dublin.
		M.P. (Conservative) for Great Grimsby,
V.		1852-57. He established his claim as a

---

transition, from the extreme of an embarrissing [*sic*] rapidity to the sleepy langour [*sic*] of monotonical preaching . and his manner has much vehemence without fire, and much impetuosity without force. " *Review of the Principal Characters of the I. H. of C.*, by " Falkland " [the Rev. John R. Scott], pub 1789. (*ex inform.* the Rev. A B Beaven) V G.

(ª) He was compelled to resign his seat in Jan. 1800, by the patron of the borough, the Marquess of Downshire, for having voted for the Union. He was one of the 3 Commissioners appointed, after the Union, to assess the sums to be paid in compensation to the patrons of the disfranchised boroughs. (*ex inform.* the Rev A. B Beaven.) V G

(ᵇ) The cause was her *crim. con* with Henry John Burn, sometime Lieut. 10th Hussars, with whom she eloped from Versailles in July 1819 Damages (laid at £20,000) were obtained for £1,500 in June 1820. She *d.* Apr. 1827, aged 44.

Peer [I.] 24 July 1855, and was elected a Rep. Peer [I.] 1867.   He *d.* unm., 10 Aug. 1874, at Cowes, in the Isle of Wight, aged 44.   Will pr. 15 Sep. 1874.

| EARLDOM [I.] V.   BARONY [I.] VI. | 1874. | 5 and 6. HUGH (ANNESLEY), EARL ANNESLEY OF CASTLEWELLAN, VISCOUNT GLERAWLY and BARON ANNESLEY OF CASTLEWELLAN [I.], br. and h., *b.* 26 Jan. 1831, in Rutland Sq., Dublin. Ed. at Eton, and at Trin. Coll., Dublin; B.A. 1851. Entered the army 1851. |

Served in the 43rd Foot and the Scots Fusilier Guards. Lieut. and Capt. 1855. Lieut. Col. 1860. Severely wounded in the Kaffir war, 1851-53, and also at the battle of Alma. Retired 1871. Was M.P. (Conservative) for Cavan, 1857-74. Claim to Peerage allowed 16 Feb. 1875. Elected a Rep. Peer [I.], 28 Apr. 1877. He *m.*, 1stly, 4 July 1877, at St. Marylebone, Midx., Mabel Wilhelmina Frances, 1st da. of Col. William Thomas MARKHAM, of Cufforth Hall (formerly Becca), co. York, by Ann Emily Sophia, da. of Sir Francis GRANT, sometime President of the Royal Academy. She, who was *b.* at Cufforth Hall, 5 Apr. 1858, *d.* 17, and was *bur.* 22 Apr. 1891, at Castlewellan. He *m.*, 2ndly, 2 July 1892, at St. Marylebone, his cousin, Priscilla Elizabeth, da. of William Armitage MOORE, of Arnmore, co. Cavan, by Mary, da. of W. H. METCALFE. He *d.* of heart failure following influenza, at Castlewellan, 15, and was *bur.* there 18 Dec. 1908, aged 77. Will pr. Aug. 1909, over £75,000. His widow living 1909. He was *suc.* by his s. and h., who is outside the scope of this work.

Family Estates.—These, in 1883, consisted of 24,350 acres in co. Down; 24,221 acres in co. Cavan, and 2489 in Queen's County. Total about 51,000 acres, valued at about £30,000 a year. *Principal Residence*, Castlewellan, co. Down.

ANNESLEY OF NEWPORT PAGNEL

i.e. "ANNESLEY OF NEWPORT PAGNEL, co. Buckingham," Barony *(Annesley)*, *cr.* 1661 with the EARLDOM OF ANGLESEY, which see; *extinct* 1761.

ANSON OR ANSON OF SOBERTON

| BARONY. I. 1747 to 1762. | 1. GEORGE ANSON, 2nd and yst s. of William ANSON, of Shugborough, co. Stafford, (who *d.* 1720) by Isabella, da. and coh. of Charles CARRIER, of Wirkworth, co. Derby, was *b.* at Colwich, co. Stafford, 23 Apr. and *bap.* there 21 May 1697; entered the navy 2 Feb. 1711/2, becoming |

a Post Captain 1724; in 1740 he commanded five ships against the Spaniards, when also he made his famous voyage round the world, (*) being appointed, on his return, 23 June, Rear Adm. of the Blue. A Lord

---

(*) He was said, in allusion to his modesty and simplicity, to have been "round the world, but never in it." V.G.

of the Admiralty, 27 Dec. 1744 to June 1751.   He was M.P. (Whig) for
Hedon, 1744-47.   F.R.S. 5 Dec. 1745   Rear Adm. of the White,
20 Apr. 1745 ; Vice Adm. of the Blue, *per saltum*, 14 July 1746 ; Commander in chief of the Channel Fleet, 31 July 1746. In May 1747 he
completely defeated a French fleet of inferior strength, off Cape Finisterre,
taking six men of war.   On 13 June 1747 he was *cr.* LORD ANSON,
BARON OF SOBERTON, co. Southampton.(ᵃ)   He was made Vice
Adm. of the Red, 15 July 1747 ; Adm. of the Blue, 12 May 1748.   In
1748 he commanded the squadron that convoyed George II to and from
Holland.   Vice Adm. of Great Britain, 1749-62 ; Elder Brother of the
Trin. House, 1749-62, and Master thereof 1752-56 ; P.C. 29 Mar. 1750.
First Lord of the Admiralty, 17 June 1751 to 20 Nov. 1756, and again
2 July 1757 till his death.   A Lord Justice of Great Britain 30 Mar.
1752, and 28 Apr. 1755.   Adm. of the White 24 Feb. 1757, and Commander in chief of the Channel Fleet a 2nd time, 15 May 1758.   Finally
he was Adm. and Commander in chief of the Fleet, 30 July 1761 till his
death, his last service being to convoy, Aug. to Sep 1761, Charlotte,
afterwards Consort of George III, to England.   He *m.*, 25 Apr. 1748 (ᵇ)
Elizabeth, 1st da. of Philip (YORKE), 1st EARL OF HARDWICKE, sometime
Lord High Chancellor, by Margaret, da. of Charles COCKS, of Worcester.
She, who was *b.* Aug. 1725, *d.* 1, and was *bur.* 26 June 1760, at Colwich.
He *d.s.p.*, suddenly, while walking in his garden, (ᶜ) at Moor Park,
Herts, 6, and was *bur.* 14 June 1762, at Colwich, aged 65, when his *peerage*
became *extinct*.   Will dat. 28 Aug. 1760, pr. 16 June 1762.

ANSON OF SHUGBOROUGH AND ORGRAVE

VISCOUNTCY.   1. THOMAS ANSON, formerly ADAMS, of Shug-
I. 1806.   borough and Orgrave, co. Stafford, s. and h. of George
             ANSON, formerly ADAMS, (ᵈ) of the same, by Mary,
da. of George Venables (VERNON), 1st LORD VERNON, was *b.* 14 Feb.
1767, and *suc.* his father 27 Oct. 1789.   Was M.P. (Whig) for Lichfield 1789-1806, and, on 17 Feb. 1806, was *cr.* (on the recommend-

---

(ᵃ) Lord Anson of Soberton bore arms of Silver three bends engrailed gules with
a crescent gules in the cantel.   The Ansons, Earls of Lichfield (formerly Adams)
bear the same, quartering Adams   William Anson, the Admiral's grandfather, failed
to prove his arms at the Heralds' Visitation of co. Stafford in 1663.

(ᵇ) Mrs Delany writes of him and his wife in Nov. 1749.   "She is a little
coxcombical, and affects to be learned, which may sometimes put him out of countenance ; but Lord A. is a most generous goodnatured amiable man, and he deserved a
wife of more dignity." V.G.

(ᶜ) At this very time a patent was being prepared to *cr.* him a Viscount, with a
spec. rem. to his sister's s , George Adams, of Orgrave. V G.

(ᵈ) He took the surname of ANSON by Royal lic. 30 Apr. 1773, being s and
h. of Sambrooke Adams, of Sambrooke, Salop, by Janette, only sister of Admiral
Lord Anson abovenamed.   He was M.P. (Whig) for Lichfield from 1770 till his
death

ation of Fox) BARON SOBERTON of Soberton, co. Southampton, and
VISCOUNT ANSON of Shugborough and Orgrave, co. Stafford. He
m., 15 Sep. 1794, at Holkham, Norfolk, Anne Margaret, 2nd da. of Thomas
William (COKE), 1st EARL OF LEICESTER OF HOLKHAM, by his 1st wife,
Jane, sister of James, 1st LORD SHERBORNE, and da. of James Lennox
DUTTON. He *d.* in St. James's Sq., 31 July, and was *bur.* 10 Aug. 1818, at
Shugborough, co. Stafford, aged 51. M.I. Will pr. Sep. 1818. His
widow, who was *b.* at Holkham, 23 Jan., and *bap.* there 23 Feb. 1779,
d. in Harley Str., 23, and was *bur.* 31 May 1843, at Shugborough. Will
dat. 5 Oct. 1839, pr. 15 July 1843

II. 1818.   2. THOMAS WILLIAM (ANSON), VISCOUNT ANSON, &c.,
                   s. and h., *b.* 20 Oct. 1795, and *bap.* at Colwich afsd.
On 15 Sep. 1831 he was *cr.* EARL OF LICHFIELD. See "LICHFIELD,"
Earldom of, *cr.* 1831.

ANTRIM

EARLDOM [I.]   1. RANDAL MAC SORLEY MAC DONNELL, of Dunluce,
                    co. Antrim, 2nd, but 1st surv. s. and h. of Sorley Buoy
I. 1620.   MAC DONNELL, Lord of the Route, co. Antrim, by Mary,
da. of Con Baccach (O'NEILL), 1st EARL OF TYRONE [I], *suc.* his father in
1589, and greatly distinguished himself in the pacification of Ulster, having
raised 500 foot and 40 horse at his own charge. He was knighted, 13 May
1602, by the Lord Deputy Mountjoy, and obtained a grant, from James I,
of the Route and the Glyns, co. Antrim, lands which his father had
conquered from the Mac Quillans On 28 May 1618 he was *cr.* VISCOUNT
DUNLUCE, co. Antrim [I.], and on 12 Dec. 1620 he was *cr.* EARL OF
ANTRIM [I.], with the annual creation fee of £20 from that co., ([a]) having
been made Lord Lieut. ([b]) of the same and P.C. the same year. On
14 July 1634 he first took his seat in the House, but, shortly afterwards,
had leave to go into the country on account of his age and weakness. He
m., 1604, Alice, da. of Hugh (O'NEILL), EARL OF TYRONE [I], by his 2nd
wife, Joanna, da. of Hugh McManus O'DONNELL. ([c]) He *d.* 10 Dec. 1636,
at Dunluce, and was *bur.* with his father at Bunnamairge (now Bonamargy).
His widow, celebrated for her beauty, was restored to her house of Ballycastle, co. Antrim, Nov. 1661, and was living 19 Aug. 1663, and then
aged 80.

II. 1636.   2 and 1. RANDAL (MAC DONNELL), EARL OF
                                   ANTRIM, &c. [I.], s. and h., *b.* 1609. He was
MARQUESSATE [I.]   knighted, 17 Mar. 1638/9, at Dublin, by the Lord

---

([a]) The preambles of the three creations (1618, 1620, and 1644/5), in which the
merits of the grantee are set forth, are given in *Lodge*, vol. 1, pp. 205, 206, and 210
([b]) There were Lieuts. of counties in Ireland down to the reign of James II,
when they were styled Governors, until the present system came in *temp.* Will IV.
(*ex inform.* G. D. Burtchaell.) V.G.
([c]) *State Papers* [I.], 1625-32, p. 66. V.G.

I. 1645   Deputy Wentworth (afterwards Earl of Strafford).
  to   Took his seat in the House 17 June 1640. He
1682.   exerted himself greatly in the Royal cause, and,
                           by Royal warrant dat. at Oxford 26 Jan. 1644/5,
was *cr.* MARQUESS OF ANTRIM (ª) [I.], with the annual fee of £40
from the customs of the port of Coleraine.   He undertook to raise an army
in Ireland and to transport it to Scotland in the King's cause, believing that
" all the clan of the Mac Donnells in the Highlands might be persuaded to
follow him. "   In Aug. 1651 he was " quartered by the rebels not far from
Kilkenny in a very obscure and unregarded condition " and apparently then
opposed to the Loyalists, but, writes Lord Clanricarde, " I apprehend little
danger from him unless he find a contrivement to appear for his Majesty,
having gained the reputation of pulling down the side he is on."   In and about
Dec. 1660, he was a prisoner in the Tower for some months on a charge of
treasonable correspondence with the Confed. Rom. Cath. Irish, 1640-45. (ᵇ)
He *m.*, 1stly, (ᶜ) Apr. 1635, Catherine, Dowager DUCHESS OF BUCKINGHAM,
da and h. of Francis (MANNERS), 6th EARL OF RUTLAND, by his 1st wife,
Frances, da. of Sir Henry KNYVETT.   She, who, in 1632, had become *suo
jure* BARONESS DE ROS, *d.* at Waterford, late in Oct. 1649. (ᵈ)   Admon.
20 Nov. 1663, as " late of the Kingdom of Ireland, " to her husband.
He *m.*, 2ndly, before 20 Mar. 1655/6, Rose, da. of Sir Henry O'NEILL, of
Edenduffe Carrick, otherwise Shane's Castle, co Antrim (who brought
these estates to her husband's family), by Martha, da. of Sir Francis
STAFFORD, Governor of Ulster.   He *d. s.p.*, 3 Feb. 1682, and was *bur.* at
Bonamargy, aged 73, when the MARQUESSATE OF ANTRIM [I.] became *extinct.*
His widow was living 4 Jan. 1689/90. (ᵉ)

EARLDOM [I.]   3. ALEXANDER (MAC DONNELL), EARL OF ANTRIM,
                        &c., [I.], only br. and h., *b.* 1615.   He commanded
III. 1683.   a regiment of Irish in 1641, was *attainted* by Cromwell,
but *restored* in 1660.   P.C. 1685.   Lord Lieut. (ᶠ) of co. Antrim.   He
sat in the Irish Parl. of James II, 7 May 1689. (ᵍ)   Adhering to
James II, for whom he commanded a Regiment of Infantry, he was again
attainted, but was again (in 1697) *restored.*   He *m*, 1stly, Elizabeth, 2nd

---

(ª) See p. 174, note " a "

(ᵇ) Clarendon describes him as a handsome man, very extravagant "of excessive
pride and vanity, and of a marvellously weak and narrow understanding. "   Of his
first wife, he remarks that " besides her great extraction and fortune, she was of a very
great wit and spirit. "   V.G.

(ᶜ) He was affianced before 1627 to Lucy, 3rd da of James (Hamilton), 1st Earl
of Abercorn, but refusing to complete the marriage, was ordered to pay £3000 to the
lady. (Stirling's Register MS.)

(ᵈ) She had been deeply engaged with the Rom. Cath. Irish rebels in 1642-43. V.G.

(ᵉ) " Mons. Schomberg's marriage to the widow Lady Antrim is great town
talk. " (Letter of Lady Chaworth, 4 Jan. 1689/90.) V.G.

(ᶠ) See p. 174, note " b. "

(ᵍ) For a list of peers present in, and absent from, this Parl, see vol. iii,
App. D. V.G.

da. of Arthur (ANNESLEY), 1st EARL OF ANGLESEY, by Elizabeth, da. and h. of Sir James ALTHAM. She *d. s.p.*, 4 Sep. 1672, and was *bur.* in St. John's Church, Dublin. He *m.*, 2ndly, Helena, 3rd da. of Sir John BURKE, of Derrymaclaughna, co. Galway, by Mary, 1st da. and coh. of Richard (BURKE), 6th EARL OF CLANRICKARD [I]. He was *bur.* at Holy-well, co. Flint, 11 June 1699, aged 84. His widow *d.* in Dublin, 7, and was *bur.* 9 Oct. 1710, at Christ Church there.

IV 1699   4. RANDAL (MAC DONNELL), EARL OF ANTRIM, &c. [I.], only s. and h. by 2nd wife, *b.* 1680. ([a]) He *m* Rachael, 1st da. of Clotworthy (SKEFFINGTON), 3rd VISCOUNT MASSE-REENE [I.], by Rachael, da. of Sir Edward HUNGERFORD, K.B. He *d.* 19 Oct. 1721, and was *bur.* at Christ Church, Dublin. His widow *m.* Robert HAWKINS-MAGILL, of Gill Hall, co. Down, and *d.* 14 Apr. 1739.

V. 1721.   5 ALEXANDER (MAC DONNELL), EARL OF ANTRIM, &c. [I], only s. and h , *b.* 22 July 1713. Being a Protestant, he took his seat in the House, 17 Oct. 1733. P.C. and Governor of co. Antrim. He *m.*, 1stly, 10 Apr. 1735, Elizabeth, ([b]) da. of Matthew PENNEFATHER, Comptroller and Accountant Gen. of Ireland, by Catharine, da of Sir Randal BERESFORD, 2nd Bart. [I.]. She *d. s.p.s.*, 18, and was *bur.* 22 Mar. 1736/7, at Christ Church, Dublin, in her 25th year He *m.*, 2ndly, 2 Jan. 1739, Anne, 1st da and coh. of Charles Patrick PLUNKETT, of Dillonstown, co. Louth, (s. of Matthew, 7th LORD LOUTH [I.]), by Elizabeth, sister of John (STRATFORD), 1st EARL OF ALDBOROUGH [I.], and da. of Edward STRATFORD, of Belan, co Kildare. She *d.* at Glenarm, 15 Jan. 1755, and was *bur.* at Bonamargy. He *m.*, 3rdly, 5 July 1755, Catharine, widow of James TAYLOR (who *d.* 1747), yst da. of Thomas MEREDYTH, of Newtown, co. Meath, by Catharine, da of (—) BALDWIN. He *d* 13 Oct. 1775, and was *bur.* at Ballycastle, co. Antrim, aged 62. His widow was *bur.* 27 Sep. 1794, in St. Patrick's, Dublin. Will pr. 1794.

VI. 1775   6 and 1. RANDAL WILLIAM (MAC DONNELL),
to   EARL OF ANTRIM AND VISCOUNT DUNLUCE, [I.],
1791   only s. and h. by 2nd wife, *b* 4 Nov. 1749. M.P.
                for co. Antrim, 1768-75; ([c]) Sheriff of co. Antrim,
EARLDOM [I]   as VISCOUNT DUNLUCE, 1771. Took his seat in the
VI. 1785.   House 13 Mar. 1776. K.B. 5 May 1779. On

([a]) A letter of Alice Hatton, describing a ball to her father, Viscount Hatton, which, though undated, can be fixed at about 7 Sep. 1696, says :—"The best of the men was Lord Antrim, Lord Anglesey and Lord Essex. But my lord Antrim has cut off his hair and got one of the new fashioned perukes, which have so much hair in them that a good one cant cost less than £60, and that monstrous bigness with his little face did not look so well. " At this date Lord Antrim was over 80, and not likely to be the best man at a ball, so she must mean his s. and successor. V.G.

([b]) A celebrated beauty. V.G.

([c]) Sir John Blaquiere writes of him then as " an idle, unsteady young man, not to be depended upon." V.G.

MARQUESSATE [I.] 5 Feb. 1783, he was *nom.* as K P. (at the institut-
II. 1789   ion of that order), but never installed, as, being
to   unwilling to resign the Order of the Bath, he
1791.   " relinquished the stall intended for him, " as a
              Knight of St Patrick, 8 Mar. following.   Having
              no male issue, he was, on 19 June 1785, *cr.*
VISCOUNT DUNLUCE and EARL OF ANTRIM [I.], with a *spec. rem.*
of those dignities, failing heirs male of his body, to his daughters in order of
seniority, and the heirs male of their bodies respectively.   P.C. [I.] 1786.
On 18 Aug. 1789,(ª) he was *cr.* MARQUESS OF ANTRIM [I.], but
without such spec. rem.   He *m.*, 3 July 1774, Letitia, widow of the Hon.
Arthur Trevor (who *d.* 19 June 1770), 1st da. of Harvey (Morres), 1st
Viscount Mountmorres [I.], by his 1st wife, Letitia, 4th da. of Brabazon
(Ponsonby), 1st Earl of Bessborough [I.].   He *d.* 29 July 1791, at
Antrim House, Merrion Sq., Dublin, and was *bur.* at Bonamargy.   On
his death the Marquessate of Antrim [I.] *and such peerage honours as
he had inherited (viz. the* Earldom of Antrim [I.] *cr. in* 1620, *and the*
Viscountcy of Dunluce [I.], *cr. in* 1618), became *extinct*, but the creations
of 1785 devolved as below.   Will dat. 14 Aug. 1790, pr. at Dublin
15 Aug. 1791.   His widow *d.* of cancer, in Grosvenor Sq., 7, and was
bur. 14 Dec. 1801, at St. James's, Westm.   Will, with nine codicils,
pr. 21 Jan. 1802.

EARLDOM [I.]   2. Anne Katharine, *suo jure* Countess of Antrim and
VII. 1791.   Viscountess Dunluce [I. 1785], 1st da. and coh , who,
                under the *spec. rem.* of 1785, inherited the abovenamed
peerages.   She was *b.* (being a twin with her sister Letitia Mary), 11 Feb.
1778.   She *m.*, 1stly, 25 Apr. 1799, (spec. lic.) in her mother's house in
Han. Sq., Sir Henry Vane-Tempest, Bart., of Wynyard, co. Durham.
He *d s.p.m.*, 1 Aug. 1813.(ᵇ)   She *m.*, 2ndly, by spec. lic., in Bruton
Str., St. James's, Westm., 24 May 1817, Edmund Phelps, who, by Royal
lic. 27 June 1817, took the name of McDonnell only, and *d.* at Rome,
30 May 1852, aged 72.   She *d. s.p m*, in Park Lane, Midx., 30 June, and
was *bur.* 7 July 1834, at St. James's, Westm., aged 56.   Will pr. Aug.
1853 and July 1854.

VIII. 1834.   3. Charlotte, *suo jure* Countess of Antrim and
                Viscountess Dunluce [I.], only surv. sister and h., who,
under the *spec. rem.* of 1785, inherited the abovenamed peerages.   She
was *b.* 12 Aug. 1779.(ᶜ)   She *m.* (as Lady Charlotte McDonnell, spinster),

(ª) See note *sub* George, Marquess of Waterford [1789].
(ᵇ) Frances Anne Emily, their only da and h , *m* , as his 2nd wife, 3 Apr. 1819,
Charles William (Vane, formerly Stewart), 1st Lord Stewart, who, in 1822,
became 3rd Marquess of Londonderry [I.]   She *d.*, his widow, 20 Jan 1865,
having inherited the large estates of her father.   Her 1st son, Earl Vane, *suc.* his
(half) br. as 5th Marquess of Londonderry [I.] in 1872, and *d.* 1884.
(ᶜ) *The Scots Peerage* says 11 Feb. 1778.   V.G.

18 July 1799, at her mother's house in Han Sq., Vice Admiral Lord Mark Robert KERR, 3rd s. of William John, 5th MARQUESS OF LOTHIAN [S.]. She *d.* at Holmwood, near Henley, 26 Oct., and was *bur.* 4 Nov. 1835, at Shiplake, Oxon. Her husband, who was *b* 12 Nov. 1776, *d.* 9 Sep. 1840

[CHARLES FORTESCUE KERR, *styled* VISCOUNT DUNLUCE, 5th (ᵃ) but 1st surv s. and h. ap , *b.* 4 Apr. and *bap.* 30 May 1810, at Binfield, Berks, *d.* unm. and *v.p.*, at Holmwood, 26 July, and was *bur* 4 Aug. 1834, at Shiplake afsd., aged 24]

IX. 1835.   4 HUGH SEYMOUR (KERR, *afterwards* McDONNELL), EARL OF ANTRIM, &c. [I.], 6th, but 1st surv. s. and h., *b.* in Portman Sq., 7 Aug., and *bap.* 4 Sep. 1813, at St. Marylebone, Midx. By royal lic , 27 June 1836, he took the name of McDONNELL only. He *m.*, at St Geo , Han. Sq., 3 May 1836, Laura Cecilia, 6th da. of Thomas (PARKER), 5th EARL OF MACCLESFIELD, being 1st da. by his 2nd wife, Eliza, da. of William Breton WOLSTENHOLME. He *d. s.p.m.*, at Glenarm Castle, in his 42nd year, 19, and was *bur.* 30 July 1855, at Bonamargy. His widow, who was *b.* 1809, *d.* at Beaufort Gardens, South Kensington, 26 Jan. 1883.

X. 1855.   5. MARK (KERR, *afterwards* McDONNELL), EARL OF ANTRIM, &c. [I.], br. and h. male, *b.* in Portman Sq., 3, and *bap.* 21 Apr. 1814, at St. Marylebone, Midx Captain R.N By royal lic., 8 Nov. 1855, he took the name of McDONNELL only. He established his claim as an Irish Peer 15 July 1858. He *m* , 27 Apr. 1849, Jane Emma Hannah, 2nd da. of Turner MACAN, of Carriff, co. Armagh, Major in the army, by Harriet, da of Ralph Henry SNEYD, also a Major in the army. He *d.* 19 Dec. 1869, at Glenarm Castle, aged 55. Will pr 24 Mar. 1870, under £25,000. His widow *d.* 21 Apr. 1892, at Fettercairne House, co. Kincardine, and was *bur.* at Southill, Beds, aged 67.

XI 1869.   6. WILLIAM RANDAL (McDONNELL), EARL OF ANTRIM and VISCOUNT DUNLUCE [I.], s. and h., *b.* 8 Jan. 1851, in in London. Ed. at Eton, and at Ch Ch. Oxford. Claim to Peerage allowed 18 June 1872. He *m* , 1 June 1875, at St James's, Westm., Louisa Jane, 3rd da. of Gen. the Hon. Charles GREY (2nd s. of Charles, 2nd EARL GREY), by Caroline Eliza, 1st. da. of Sir Thomas Harvie FARQUHAR, 2nd Bart. She was *b.* 15 Feb. 1855, at St. James's Palace. She was a lady of the Bedchamber to Queen Victoria 1890-1901, and to Queen Alexandra 1901. V. and A. 3rd class.

[RANDAL MARK KERR McDONNELL, *styled* VISCOUNT DUNLUCE, *b.* 10 Dec. 1878, at St. James's Palace, Midx. Lieut. Royal Lancashire Regt. He *m* , 2 July 1904, at Markbeech, Kent, Margaret, yst. da. of the Rt. Hon. John Gilbert TALBOT, by Meriel Sarah, 1st da. of George William (LYTTELTON), 4th BARON LYTTELTON.]

(ᵃ) His 1st br., Sidney, *d.* young. The 2nd, William, *d* 1819, aged 17. The 3rd, Mark, *d.* young. V G.

Family Estates —These, in 1883, besides about 100 acres in co Londonderry, consisted of about 34,300 acres in co. Antrim. Total about 34,400 acres, valued at about £21,000 a year. *Principal Residence.*—Glenarm Castle, co. Antrim.

AP ADAM ([a])

BARONY
BY WRIT

I. 1299
to
1311.

Cary, Somerset.

1 Sir John ap Adam, of Gorste, near Chepstow, and Beachley in Tidenham, co. Gloucester, s. and h. of Reynold ap Adam, by Joan de Knoville, his wife. ([b]) He was *b.* before 1267. He *m.*, before 1291, Elizabeth, da. and h of John de Gurnay, of Beverstone Castle, co. Gloucester, &c , by Olive, da. of Henry Lovel, of Castle He did homage, and had livery, 18 Feb. 1290/1, of the

---

([a]) For this article, and the notes thereto, the editor is indebted to G W Watson V.G.

([b]) *Inspeximus,* 25 June 1285, of a charter dated 1267, whereby the Abbot and convent of Grace Dieu gave to Joan de Knoville, sometime the wife of Reynold Abadam, the manor of Penyard Regis, co Hereford, to be held of them by Joan and her heirs and assigns This Joan had a grant, 27 Feb. 1280/1, of free warren in all her demesne lands of Penyard. (*Charter Rolls*, 13 Edw I, *m.* 19, and 9 Edw. I, *m.* 10) Penyard Regis was alienated by her grandson, Thomas ap Adam, 2 June 1329. By two fines, Easter and Trinity, 25 Edw. I, between John de Badeham, or Abadam, and Elizabeth his wife, and John de Knoville, the manors of Beverstone, Purton, and Redwick, co. Gloucester, East Harptree and Barrow Gurney, Somerset, Sharncote, Wilts, and East Hampnett, Sussex, were settled on John and Elizabeth, and the heirs of their bodies, rem. to Elizabeth's right heirs. (*Feet of Fines*, case 285, file 24, nos. 233, 236)

Dr. Ormerod, in his memoir of this Baron (*Strigulensia*, 1861, pp. 96-108) avers " that he never met with any document giving proof of his parentage in any way, and he therefore *commences with him*, without any disparagement of Herbert descent. " This descent appears first in the (alleged) commission, 12 Aug. 1460, issued by Edward IV to investigate the ancestry of William Herbert, Earl of Pembroke. Meyrick (Dwnn's *Visitations*, vol. i, pp. 196-7) shows, from the occurrence in it of the title " hys magestye, " that it must be " a forgery and not earlier than the reign of Henry VIII. " It states that Herbert fitz Herbert *m* the da of Milo fitz Walter, and was father of Peter, who inherited Betsley [Beachley] from his mother, father of Reignold, lord of Llanllowel, father of Adam, father of Sir Thomas Adam and of Jenkin Adam of Wernddu [the reputed ancestor of the Herberts]. This account, elaborated by various Welsh genealogists, now appears in the following form.—(1) Reginald fitz Peter, *d* 1286, father of (2) Peter fitz Reginald, who, by Alice, da of Bleddyn Broadspere, Lord of Llanllowel and Beachley, was father of (3) Herbert fitz Peter, father of (4) Adam ap Herbert, father of (5) Sir Thomas ap Adam (and of Jenkin ap Adam, as above), who, by Margaret, da. of Llewelyn ap Howel, was father of (6) Sir John ap Thomas ap Adam, sum to Parl. 19 Edw. I, who, by Joyce, da. of Andrew Winston, had a da and h (7) Margery, wife of John Tomlyn *alias* Huntley, of Tre Owen. (Bradney's *Monmouthshire*, 1904, vol. i, p. 199). Burke, *Extinct Peerage*, under *Herbert*, gives nearly the same account, with great impartiality, as it is utterly at variance with his statements under *Ap Adam*. In this tissue of

lands of John de Gurnay, and, 19 July 1296, of those of Olive, afsd·(ᵃ) Having thus become the possessor of vast estates, (ᵇ) he was sum., 26 Jan. (1296/7) 25 Edw I, to attend the King at Salisbury, (ᶜ) and was sum to Parl., 6 Feb. (1298/9) 27 Edw. I to 13 Dec. (1309) 3 Edw. II, by writs directed *Johanni ap Adam, ab Adam*, or *Abbadam*, whereby he may be held to have become LORD AP ADAM. He subscribed the Barons' letter to the Pope, 12 Feb. 1300/1, as *Johannes ab Adam dominus de Beveriston*. He was sum., 18 Jan. 1307/8, to attend the coronation of Edward II He *d.* in May or June 1311. (ᵈ)

None of his descendants were ever sum. to Parl in respect of this Barony. (ᵉ) His s. and h., Sir Thomas ap Adam, having proved his age, did homage and had livery of his lands, 4 July 1325. (ᶠ) Immediately afterwards, he began a series of alienations, to different persons, of his extensive property. (ᵍ) He *m.*, 1stly, Margery, who was living 13 Oct.

errors, (3) and (4) are, perhaps, wholly imaginary persons Peter fitz Reginald—whose only known wife was named Maud—was a minor in 1286 (*Close Roll*, 14 Edw. I, *m.* 1d), but he is here made the ancestor in the 3rd degree of a man who was of age in 1325 Further, the Baron himself is omitted for the John here described as " sum. 19 Edw. I " is obviously his grandson. As to Llanllowel (near Usk), a great authority, Thomas Wakeman, believed that the Ap Adams never held it, and that it was acquired, long afterwards, by the Huntleys.

(ᵃ) *Fine Rolls*, 19 Edw I, *m* 16, and 24 Edw I, *m* 7.

(ᵇ) Beverstone, Kingsweston, and Elberton, 1 fee, held of the King in chief; Over, and Purton in Lydney, ½ a fee, of the Earl of Warwick ; Redwick in Northwick, of the Bishop of Worcester , all co. Gloucester · East and West Harptree, Farrington and Barrow Gurney, Babington, Middlecote, Sandford Orcas, &c , Somerset, and Sharncote, Wilts, 22½ fees, of the Earl of Gloucester · Weare, Somerset, of John de Cogan and East Hampnett, Sussex, the marriage portion of Olive Lovel all derived from De Gurnay (*i.e.*, FitzJohn of Harptree). Salisbury, Multon, Brendehyroc, Allt-y-Bela, and Llanbadock, co Monmouth, and Talyvan, co. Glamorgan, likewise held by John ap Adam of the Earl of Gloucester, were probably inherited from his father.

(ᶜ) Concerning the validity of a writ of this date as a regular writ of summons to Parl., see Preface. V.G.

(ᵈ) 25 Apr 1311, being about to go beyond seas on pilgrimage, his attorneys were nominated for a year . 15 June 1311, the custody of his lands and those of Elizabeth his wife, was granted to Ralph de Montherner for 6000 marks (*Patent Rolls*, 4 Edw. II, *pars* 11, *m.* 17, 8 : 5 Edw. II, *pars* i, *m* 5) The writ of *diem. cl. ext.* was not issued till 6 July (*Fine Roll*, 4 Edw II, *m.* 2) There is no inquisition extant, except those following two writs of *plenius certiorari*, 3 Sep. and 1 Feb 6 Edw II, on the small property in Tidenham. (Ch. *Inq. p. m.*, Edw. II, file 28, no. 14).

(ᵉ) As to how far these early writs of summons did in fact create any peerage title, see Appendix A in the last volume. V G

(ᶠ) *Close Roll*, 18 Edw II, *m.* 1

(ᵍ) Monewden, Suffolk, to Isabella de Hastings for life, Thursday the feast of St. James [25 July] 1325 : Purton, to John de Walton for life, Sunday after St. James 1325 . Penyard Regis, *La Lee*, co. Gloucester, and East Hampnett, &c., to Sir John Inge, Friday the morrow of the Ascension [2 June] 1329 . Weare, Gorste, East Harptree, &c , to Thomas de Gurnay for life, for the settling of divers

1331. He *m.*, 2ndly, before 1341, Joan, da. of Sir John Inge, of Corton Denham, Somerset, by Alice Basset, his wife (ª) She *d. s.p.*, before 9 July 1349. He *d.* before 1342-43, leaving 3 sons, Robert, Hamund, and John. The two elder of these were living in 1342-43, (ᵇ) and *d s p.* The yst., John, living 28 May 1375, (ᶜ) was father of John ap Adam, who, together with Margaret, his wife, sold the manor of Sharncote, Wilts, to Thomas, Lord of Berkeley, in (1414-15) 2 Hen. V. (ᵈ) He *d. s.p.*, 20 Nov. 1424, leaving John Huntley, s. of his sister, Elizabeth, his h., (ᵉ) among whose representatives any hereditary Barony, that may be held to have existed, is in *abeyance.* (ᶠ)

---

disputes between them, 4 June 1329 the castle and manor of Beverstone, Over, Barrow Gurney, and Monewden, to Thomas de Berkeley and his heirs, and Kings-weston and Elberton to Maurice de Berkeley, by licences dated 11 and 12 Apr. 1330. (*Close Rolls,* 19 Edw. II, *m* 31d, 20d; 3 Edw. III, *m* 18d *Patent Roll,* 4 Edw III, *pars* 1, *m.* 32.) The clue, that Dr Ormerod desiderated, "to the rapid dissipation by the son of the wealth so suddenly obtained by the father," is probably to be found in two complaints by Thomas ap Adam that during his minority his castle of Beverstone had been entered by force and wrecked, and some 70 charters, &c., relating to his inheritance, stolen—commission thereon, appointed 12 Jan. 1325/6 : that Thomas de Gurnay and others had abducted his wife, Margery, at Beverstone, taken away his goods, and still withheld his wife—commission thereon, 13 Oct. 1331. (*Patent Rolls,* 19 Edw. II, *pars* 1, *m* 10d , 5 Edw. III, *pars* 11, *m.* 11d).

(ª) By a fine, Hilary term, 14 Edw. III, the manor of Corton Denham, Somerset, was granted to Sir John Inge for life, rem to Alice Basset for life, rem. to Thomas ap Adam and Joan his wife and their issue, rem. to John, Hildebrand, Alice, and Elizabeth, brothers and sisters of Joan, and the heirs of their bodies, in succession (*Feet of Fines,* case 199, file 23, no 33) On 9 July 1349, John [Inge], s. of Alice Basset, and br. of Joan late the wife of Thomas ap Adam, did homage for Corton and had livery thereof. (*Close Roll,* 23 Edw. III, *pars* 1, *m.* 4).

(ᵇ) In 16 Edw III, Thomas, Lord of Berkeley, confirmed to Robert, s. of Sir Thomas ap Adam, and the heirs of his body, lands in Gorste, Beachley, Tidenham, &c., rem to Hamund his br. and the heirs of his body, rem. to the right heirs of Thomas ap Adam for ever. (Harl. MSS., no 6079, f. 108 d.)

(ᶜ) By deed without date, John, s. of Sir Thomas Ap Adam, released to Katherine de Berkeley, Lady of Wotton, John de Berkeley, her s., and his heirs male, and Thomas, Lord of Berkeley, and his heirs and assigns, all his rights in the castle and manor of Beverstone, Over, Barrow Gurney, &c. On 28 May 1375, he acknow-ledged the sd deed in Chancery. (*Close Roll,* 49 Edw. III, *m.* 34d).

(ᵈ) Smyth, *Lives of the Berkeleys,* vol. 11, p. 15. It should be noticed that Smyth appears to be the only writer who knew that the father of the John ap Adam, who *d* in 1311, was named Reynold. (*Idem,* vol 1, p 54).

(ᵉ) Writ of *melius sciri* 28 June 18 Hen. VI *Inq* co Gloucester, 4 Nov. 19 Hen VI. The jurors say that John ap Adam held in Redwick within the hundred of Henbury an acre of land of the King in chief by fealty and the rent of a penny a year, and two messuages of the Bishop of Worcester by fealty "Et quod predictus Johannes obiit vicesimo die Novembris Anno regni dicti domini Regis tertio et quod quidam Johannes Hunteley est consanguineus et heres propinquior ipsius Johannis ap Adam videlicet filius Elizabethe sororis ejusdem Johannis ap Adam et quod idem Johannes Huntley est etatis quadraginta annorum et amplius." (Ch. *Inq. p. m.,* Hen VI, file 97, no 10)

(ᶠ) This John is said to have been s of Thomlyn Huntley ap Philipot (Benolt's

APPIN

DUGALD STEWART, 2nd, but only surv. s. and h. of Robert S., 8th Chief of Appin, by his 2nd wife, Anne, da. of Sir Duncan CAMPBELL, of Lochnell, was *cr.*, by the titular King, James III, 6 June 1743, BARON APPIN [S.], with rem. to heirs male. (ª)   He did not join in the Rising of 1745.   He *m.* Mary, da. of Alexander MACKENZIE.   He sold Appin in 1765, and *d. s.p.m.*, 1769.   For his successors see Ruvigny's *Jacobite Peerage.*

APSLEY

i.e. "APSLEY, Sussex," Barony (*Bathurst*), *cr.* 1771; see "BATHURST," Earldom, *cr.* 1772, under the 2nd Earl, who *suc.* to that Earldom in 1775.

APULDERCOMBE

i.e. "WORSLEY OF APULDERCOMBE in the Isle of Wight," Barony (*Anderson-Pelham*), *cr.* 1837, with the EARLDOM OF YARBOROUGH, which see.

AQUITAINE (ᵇ)

EDWARD, PRINCE OF WALES, &c., s. and h. ap. of Edward III, was

Visitation—Coll. Arm. MSS., H8).   He and Joan, his wife, demised Badamscourt in Tidenham, 10 Sep.(1448) 27 Hen. VI.   John ap Thomlyn, his s. and h., is described as "dominus de Beatisley" in a conveyance of 20 Mar. (1498/9) 14 Hen. VII.   He *m.* the da. and h. of John Roulf of Llanllowel, and had 4 daughters and coheirs. (1) Margaret, mother of William Edmond, who is described in a deed, 26 Nov. 1536, as "dominus de Betisley filius et heres Edmundi ap Gwyllym ap Hopkin et Margarete uxoris ejus unius filiarum et heredum Johannis ap Thomlyn."   (2) Margery, wife of Thomas Parker, of Monmouth, ancestress of the Parkers of Llanllowel.   (3) Jane, wife of Reynalt ap Gwillym.   (4) Elizabeth.   Thus Dr. Ormerod, partly on the authority of Thomas Wakeman.   The Welsh genealogists, who omit two generations altogether, and on whose statements no reliance can be placed, describe these coheirs as (1) Margery, h. of Llanllowel, wife of Thomas Parker, (2) Margaret, h. of Tre Owen and half Llanarth, wife of David ap Jenkin (Herbert) of Cefn-y-ddwy-glwyd (slain at Edgcott Field in 1469), (3) Anne or Matilda, h. of half Llanarth, wife of David ap Gwillym (Herbert), (4) Joan, wife of Robin Wallis, and (5) Alice, wife of Thomas William.   (Bradney, *ut supra*, vol. i, p. 44 : &c.).
    (ª) For a list of the Jacobite Peerages, see Appendix F, in this volume.
    (ᵇ) It appears from *The Glory of Regality*, by Arthur Taylor, F.S.A., 1820, p. 104, &c., that, among the Principal State officers of France, who act at the Coronation, " of the lay Peers, the Duke of Burgundy carries the Crown ; the DUKE OF AQUITAINE, OR GUIENNE, the 1st banner ; the Duke of Normandy, the second," &c. : "and here," adds Mr. Taylor, "I take occasion to notice two attendants on

by charter, (ª) 19 July 1362, *cr.* PRINCE OF AQUITAINE, and *as* PRINCE OF AQUITAINE AND WALES was sum. to Parl. 24 Feb. (1367/8) 42 Edw. III; 8 Jan. (1369/70) 44 Edw. III; and 6 Oct. (1372) 46 Edw. III; though in the last writ (having apparently resigned the principality of Aquitaine) (ᵇ) as PRINCE OF WALES (only) on 28 Dec. (1375) 49 Edw. III. He *d. v.p.*, 8 June 1376. See "CORNWALL," Dukedom of, 1337 to 1376.

JOHN, (ᶜ) DUKE OF LANCASTER, &c. ("*John of Gaunt*") 4th s. of Edward III, having shortly before resigned the style of "KING OF CASTILLE AND LEON," was, on 2 Mar. 1389/90, *cr.* in Parl. DUKE OF AQUI-TAINE "for his whole life"; and *as* "DUKE OF AQUITAINE AND LANCASTER" was sum. to Parl. 23 July and 8 Sep. (1392) 16 Ric. II, 13 Nov. (1393) 17 Ric. II, 30 Nov. (1396) 20 Ric. II, and 18 July and 5 Nov. (1397) 21 Ric. II. After this creation he styled himself "Duc de Guyene et de Lancastre," and in his M.I. at St. Paul's was styled "*Locum tenens Aquitaniæ*." He *d.* 23 Feb. 1398/9. See "LANCASTER," Dukedom of, *cr.* 1362.

HENRY, PRINCE OF WALES, DUKE OF CORNWALL AND EARL OF CHESTER, s. and h. ap. of Henry IV, was declared in Parl., 10 Nov. 1399, DUKE OF LANCASTER, and was granted the titles of PRINCE OF WALES, DUKE OF AQUITAINE, OF LANCASTER AND OF CORNWALL, AND EARL OF CHESTER. On 20 Mar. 1412/3 he ascended the throne as HENRY V, when all his honours became *merged* in the Crown.

---

our *English* coronations who have been transplanted from those of France. It is usual for two Gentlemen of the Court to walk in the procession as DUKES OF NORMANDY AND GUIENNE, habited in the ancient dress of the Ducal Peers of France . . . in representation, as is stated in a book of the age of Henry VII, '*of the King's twoo Duchesses of Gyen and Normandie.*' Of the first appearance of these characters in our corona-tions I have not found any account, but it may be conjectured that they were introduced after the conquests of Edward III, and for the purpose of perpetuating the claims of our Norman and Angevine Princes."

(ª) This patent, engraved in *facsimile* by James Basire, was published by the Record Commission.

(ᵇ) Aquitaine was erected into a *principality* in 1362, for Edward, Duke of Cornwall, 1st s. and h. ap. of Edward III, but was confiscated by the King of France, by act dated 14 May 1370. The province was reconquered by Henry V in 1418, but finally lost by his successor.

(ᶜ) It is much to be wished that the surname 'Plantagenet,' which, since the time of Charles II, has been freely given to all the descendants of Geoffrey of Anjou, had some historical basis which would justify its use, for it forms a most convenient method of referring to the Edwardian kings and their numerous descendants. The fact is, however, as has been pointed out by Sir James Ramsay and other writers of our day, that the name, although a personal emblem of the aforesaid Geoffrey, was never borne by any of his descendants before Richard Plantagenet, Duke of York (father of Edward IV), who assumed it, apparently about 1448. V.G.

ARAM

See "LEXINGTON OF ARAM, co. Nottingham," Barony (*Sutton*), *cr.* 1645 ; *extinct* 1723.

ARANE

The orthography of the Barony of AVANE AND HAMILTON [S.] (*Stewart*), *cr.* 1581 with the EARLDOM OF ARRAN [S.], has sometimes been considered as being ARANE [*i.e.* Arran] AND HAMILTON.

ARASE

i.e., "ORANSAY, DUNOON AND ARASE," Barony [S.] (*Campbell*), *cr.* 1706 with the EARLDOM OF Ilay [S.], and *extinct* therewith, 1761 ; see "ARGYLL," Dukedom [S.], *cr.* 1701, under the 3rd Duke.

ARBROATH, see ABERBROTHWICK

ARBUTHNOTT

VISCOUNTCY [S.]   1. SIR ROBERT ARBUTHNOTT, or Arbuthnott, co.
I.   1641.   Kincardine, s. and h. of Sir Robert A., of the same, by his 2nd wife, Margaret, da. of Simon (FRASER), 6th LORD LOVAT [S.], *suc.* his father 16 Mar. 1633, and, for his fidelity to Charles I, was raised by him to the peerage, being *cr.*, 16 Nov. 1641, VISCOUNT OF ARBUTHNOTT, and LORD INVERBERVIE, both in co. Kincardine [S.], to him and his heirs male.   He was a ruling elder in the Gen. Assembly of the church [S.] in that year.   P.C. 1649.   He m., 1stly, before 1639, Marjory, widow of William HALIBURTON, of Pitcur, and 4th da. of David (CARNEGIE), 1st EARL OF SOUTHESK [S.], by Margaret, da. of Sir David LINDSAY.   She *d.* 22 Dec. 1651.   He *m.*, 2ndly, 30 June 1653, his 1st cousin, Catharine, widow of Sir John SINCLAIR, of Dunbeath, and 3rd da. of Hugh (FRASER), 7th LORD LOVAT [S.], by Isabel, da. of Sir John WEMYSS.   He *d.* 10 Oct. 1655.   Fun. entry at Lyon office.   His widow, who was *b.* 1619, *m.*, 3rdly (as his 1st wife), about 1660, Andrew (FRASER), 3rd LORD FRASER [S.], who *d.* at Muchalls, 22 May 1674.   She *d.* 18 Oct. 1663.

II.   1655.   2. ROBERT (ARBUTHNOTT), VISCOUNT ARBUTHNOTT, &c. [S.], s. and h. by 1st wife.   He *m.*, 1stly, (cont. dat. 25 Mar. 1658) Elizabeth, 2nd da. of William (KEITH), 7th EARL MARISCHAL [S.], by his 1st wife, Elizabeth, 1st da. of George (SETON), 2nd EARL OF WINTON [S.].   She *d.* Feb. 1664.   He *m.*, 2ndly, (cont. 30 July 1667) Catharine, da. of Robert GORDON, of Pitlurg and Straloch.   He *d.* 16 June 1682.   His widow *m.*, in 1684, Sir David CARNEGIE, of Pittarrow, Bart. [S.], and *a.* Oct. 1692.

III. 1682.   3. ROBERT (ARBUTHNOTT), VISCOUNT ARBUTHNOTT, &c. [S.], s. and h. by 1st wife, *bap.* 8 Oct. 1661. He *m.*, 3 May 1683, at Stoke Newington, Midx., Anne, only da of George (GORDON), EARL OF SUTHERLAND [S.], by Jane, 1st da. of David (WEMYSS), 2nd EARL OF WEMYSS [S]. He *d.* Aug. 1694, in his 31st year. Fun. entry at Lyon office. His widow *d.* June 1695.

IV. 1694.   4. ROBERT (ARBUTHNOTT), VISCOUNT ARBUTHNOTT, &c. [S.], s. and h., *bap.* 24 Nov. 1686. He *d.* unm , 8, and was *bur.* 10 May 1710, at Bath Abbey.

V. 1710.   5. JOHN (ARBUTHNOTT), VISCOUNT ARBUTHNOTT, &c. [S.], br. and h. He was a Jacobite and Nonjuror. He *m.*, soon after May 1710, Jean, (ª) da. of William MORRISON, of Preston-grange, co. Haddington. He *d. s.p.*, 8 May 1756, aged 64, at Arbuthnott.

VI. 1756.   6. JOHN (ARBUTHNOTT),VISCOUNT ARBUTHNOTT, &c.(ᵇ) [S.], cousin and h. male, being 2nd, but 1st surv. s and h. of John A., of Fordun (by Margaret, da. of James FALCONER, of Phesdo, a Lord of Session), which John A. was s. of Robert, the 2nd Viscount, by his 2nd wife. He *m.*, 1stly, (cont. dat. 16 Apr. 1740) Mary, 2nd and yst. da. and coh. of Robert DOUGLAS, of Bridgeford, by Margaret GRAY. She *d. s.p.* He *m.*, 2ndly (cont. dat. 4 July 1749), in 1749, Jean, 3rd da. of Alexander ARBUTHNOTT, of Findowrie, by Margaret Ochterlony. She *d.* 18 Mar. 1786. He *d.* 20 Apr. 1791, at Arbuthnott, aged 88.

VII. 1791.   7. JOHN (ARBUTHNOTT), VISCOUNT ARBUTHNOTT, &c. [S.], 2nd, but 1st surv. s. and h. by 2nd wife, *bap.* 25 Oct. 1754. (ᶜ) He *m.*, 27 Dec. 1775, Isabella, 2nd da. of William GRAHAM, of Morphie, co. Kincardine. He *d* 27 Feb. 1800, in Queen Str., Edinburgh. His widow *d.* 4 Mar. 1818, in Edinburgh.

VIII. 1800.   8. JOHN (ARBUTHNOTT), VISCOUNT ARBUTHNOTT, &c. [S.], 1st s. and h., *b.* 16 Jan. 1778. Cornet in 7th Reg. of Dragoon Guards, and Capt. in 52nd Foot. Lord Lieut. of Kincardine 1805-47 ; Rep. Peer [S.] (Tory) 1818-20 and 1821-47 ; Rector of King's Coll Aberdeen, 1827-37. He *m.*, 25 June 1805, at Cortachy, Margaret, sister of David, EARL OF AIRLIE [S], being 1st da. of Walter OGILVY, of Clova (who, but for the attainder, would have been EARL OF AIRLIE), by his 2nd wife, Jean, da. of John OGILVY. He *d.* 10 Jan. 1860, at Berlin. His widow *d.* 12 Dec. 1870, at Arbuthnott House.

IX. 1860.   9. JOHN (ARBUTHNOTT), VISCOUNT ARBUTHNOTT, &c., [S.], 1st s. and h., *b.* 4 June 1806. Sometime a Capt in the

---

(ª) For her sisters see *sub* SUTHERLAND.
(ᵇ) " Bred a writer, [*i.e.* attorney] he had acted as factor to his predecessor for 9 years before he succeeded. " V.G.
(ᶜ) His elder br., Robert, *d.* unm and *v.p*, before 1 Aug. 1785. V.G.

Army, but retired in 1830. He *m.*, 5 June 1837, at Cortachy afsd., his 1st cousin, Jean Graham Drummond, 1st da. of his maternal uncle, David (OGILVY), the restored EARL OF AIRLIE [S.], by his 1st wife, Clementina, only da. and h. of Gavin DRUMMOND. He *d.* 26 May 1891, aged 85. Personalty £18,448. She, who was *b.* 27 Feb. 1818, *d.* 4 Mar. 1902, at Arbuthnott House, aged 84.

X. 1891.   10. JOHN (ARBUTHNOTT), VISCOUNT ARBUTHNOTT, &c., [S.], 1st s. and h. ; *b.* 20 July 1843 ; sometime Lieut. 49th Foot. He *m.*, 20 Apr. 1871, at Inchmartine House, near Inchture, co. Perth, Anna Harriett, only da. of Edmund ALLEN. She *d.* 23 Apr. 1892. He *d. s.p.*, 30 Nov. 1895, at Arbuthnott House, aged 52. Will pr. at £49,308 personalty.

XI. 1895.   11. DAVID (ARBUTHNOTT), VISCOUNT ARBUTHNOTT and BARON INVERBERIE [S. 1641], br. and h. ; *b.* 29 Jan. 1845 ; unm. in 1909. Imbecile from his boyhood. (ª)

Family Estates.—These, in 1883, consisted of about 13,500 acres in co. Kincardine, worth about £13,000 a year. *Principal Residence.*—Arbuthnott House, near Fordoun, co. Kincardine.

ARCEDEKNE (ᵇ)

BARONY   1. SIR THOMAS L'ARCEDEKNE, (ᶜ) of Ruan Lanihorne,
BY WRIT.   Cornwall, s. and h. of Otes l'A. (*d.* 1289-90), by Amice,
              his wife, was Governor of Tintagel Castle 1312, and Sheriff
I. 1321   of Cornwall, Mich. 1313-14. He was sum. to Parl.
  to   15 May (1321) 14 Edw. II to 13 Sep. (1324) 18 Edw. II,
1331.   by writs directed *Thome Lercedekne*, whereby he may
be held to have become LORD ARCEDEKNE. He *m.*, 1stly, Alice, 3rd da. of Thomas DE LA ROCHE, (ᵈ) of Roch Castle, co. Pembroke.

(ª) His next br. and h. presumptive, Hugh, sometime Lieut. 81st Foot, *b.* 10 Sep. 1847, *d.* unm. 17 July 1906, at Arbuthnott House, co. Kincardine, aged 58. V.G.

(ᵇ) The re-writing of this article has been most kindly undertaken by G.W. Watson.

The continental family of Archdeacon emigrated from Ireland to Bruges in comparatively recent times, and are descendants of the Cornish folk,—not ancestors, as M.A.Lower, in *Family Names*, suggests. V.G.

(ᶜ) The arms of Sir Thomas Arcedekne were Silver with three cheverons sable. (*ex inform.* Oswald Barron.) V.G.

(ᵈ) A pedigree of this family of Roch, in Dwnn's *Visitations*, vol. i, p. 164, from George Owen's records, states that *Alissia*, 3rd da. (but not coh.) of *Tomas le Roech*, *m. Tomas le Archdecon*, and was mother of his s., John. But in Grandisson's *Register* (ed. Hingeston-Randolph, p. 855), a document, dated 14 Nov. 1337, mentions " unam marcam pro obitu Domine Matillidis Lercedeakne matris dicti Domini Johannis Lercedekne et ejusdem Johannis cum ab hac luce migraverint. "

He *m.*, 2ndly, Maud (ᵃ)   He *d.* shortly before 21 Aug. 1331. (ᵇ)   His widow was living 11 June 1362. (ᵃ)

None of his descendants were ever sum. to Parl. in respect of this Barony. (ᶜ)   His s. and h , Sir JOHN l'Arcedekne, of Ruan Lanihorne, aged 25 and more at his father's death, had livery of his lands 15 Sep. 1331. (ᵈ)   He was sum to a Council 25 Feb. (1341/2) 16 Edw. III.   He served in the French wars 1345.   He had pardon 6 Nov. 1351, and again 26 May 1352, for having escaped from Launceston Castle, where he had been imprisoned. (ᵉ)   He *m.*, by Papal disp dated 23 Dec. 1327 (ᶠ) (being within the fourth degree of consanguinity), Cecily, da and h of Jordan Haccombe, of Haccombe, Devon, by Isabel, da. of Mauger de St. Aubin. She was living in 1365.   He was living 13 Feb. 1370/1, (ᵍ) and *d.* before 21 Dec. 1377. (ʰ)   Will pr. at Clyst 27 Jan. 1390/1 [*sic*]. (ᵉ)   His 1st s., Ralph (or Stephen), *suc.* him, but *d. s.p.*, also before 21 Dec. 1377.   He was *suc.* by his next br., Sir Warin l'Arcedekne.   He *m.* Elizabeth, da. of Sir John Talbot, of Richard's Castle, co. Hereford (by Catherine his wife), and 1st sister and coh. of John Talbot, of the same (who *d.* 3 July 1388).   He *d s p.m.*, shortly before 10 Dec 1400. (ⁱ)   His widow *d.* 3 Aug. 1407. (ʲ)   Will dat. 12 Dec. 1406, pr. at Crediton 7 Aug. 1307. (ᵏ)   He left

---

(ᵃ) Genealogists call her, without proof, da. of John de Mules.   She was one of the heirs of John Tracy, from whom she inherited half a small fee in Trevisquite.   In July 1334, being then widow of Sir Thomas l'A., she was accused of adultery with one Jullan de Tregenhay   (Grandisson's *Register*, pp 758, 1484).

(ᵇ) Writ of *diem cl. ext* , 21 Aug. 5 Edw III , Cornwall, Monday before the Nativity of the Virgin [2 Sep] 1331.   (Ch. *Inq. p. m.*, Edw. III, file 27, no. 2).

(ᶜ) As to how far these early writs of summons did in fact create any peerage title, see Appendix A in the last volume   V G

(ᵈ) *Close Roll*, 5 Edw. III, *pars* 1, *m.* 5.

(ᵉ) *Patent Rolls*, 25 Edw. III, *pars* 3, *m* 17 , 26 Edw. III, *pars* 1, *m.* 2.

(ᶠ) 10 kal. Jan. 12 John XXII.   (*Cal Papal Registers*, vol ii, p. 266).

(ᵍ) Brantyngham's *Register*, pp 14, 712   Stafford's *Register*, p 388

(ʰ) Writ of *diem cl. ext* missing   Inq , Cornwall, Monday the feast of St Thomas the Apostle, 1 [*not* 2] Ric II [21 Dec 1377].   His 1st son, here called Stephen (but Ralph in a fine of 1365), survived him, but was now dead, *s.p*   (Ch. *Inq. p m.*, Ric. II, file 5, no 30).

(ⁱ) Writ of *diem cl ext* 10 Dec 2 Hen IV   Inq , Devon (much defaced), 10 Jan. 1400/1.   (Ch *Inq p m* , Hen. IV, file 24, no 53)

(ʲ) Writ of *diem cl. ext.* 3 Sep 8 Hen IV.   Inq , each dated Wednesday the feast of St. Matthew [21 Sep.] 1407.   Cornwall.   " dicunt quod prefata Elizabetha obiit tertio die Augusti ultimo preterito   Et dicunt quod Alianora uxor Walteri Lucy Philippa uxor Hugonis Courtenay de Baunton Chivaler et Margeria uxoi Thome Arundell sunt dictorum Warini et Elizabethe propinquiores heredes et plene etatis Quia dicunt quod predicta Alianora uxor predicti Walteri Lucy est etatis xxiiij annorum et amplius et quod predicta Philippa uxor predicti Hugonis Courtenay est etatis xxj annorum et amplius et quod predicta Margeria uxor Thome Arundell est etatis xvj annorum et amplius, "   Hereford and the Marches of Wales.   " dicta Elizabetha obiit die mercurii proximo post festum sancti Petri quod dicitur advincla ultimo preteritum. "   Heirs as before.   (Ch. *Inq. p. m.*, Hen. IV, file 58, no. 39   Exch. *Inq. p m* , I, file 89, no. 7)

4 daughters and coheirs. (1) Alienor, wife of Walter Lucy. (2) Philippe, wife of Sir Hugh Courtenay. (3) Margery, wife of Thomas Arundell. (4) Elizabeth, who was betrothed, 12 Mar. 1400/1, to Otes, s. and h. of Sir John Trevarthian, (ª) but *d. s.p., v.m.* Among their representatives any hereditary Barony, that may be held to have existed, is in *abeyance.*

ARCHER

BARONY.

I. 1747.

1. Thomas Archer, of Umberslade, co. Warwick, and of Pirgo, Essex, s. and h. of Andrew A., of Umberslade, M.P. for co. Warwick 1705-10, and 1713-22, by Elizabeth, da. of Sir Samuel Dashwood, sometime Lord Mayor of London, was *b.* 21 July 1695, at Knoll, co. Warwick, *suc.* his father 31 Dec. 1741, was M.P. (Whig) for Warwick 1735-41, and for Bramber 1741-47, Recorder of Coventry, &c. On 14 July 1747, he was *cr.* LORD ARCHER, BARON OF UMBERSLADE, co. Warwick. (ᵇ) He was Custos Rotulorum of co. Flint, Mar. 1750. He *m.*, 11 Aug. 1726, at the Chapel Royal, St. James's, Midx., Catharine, yst. da. and coh. of Sir Thomas Tipping, 1st Bart. (by Anne, da. of Thomas Cheek, of Pirgo afsd.), and sister and coh. of Sir Thomas T., 2nd Bart. (ᶜ) She *d.* 20 July 1754, at Pirgo, and was *bur.* in Tanworth Church, co. Warwick. He *d.* at Pirgo, 19 Oct., and was *bur.* 3 Nov. 1768, at Tanworth afsd. Will pr. Oct. 1768.

II. 1768
to
1778.

2. Andrew (Archer), Lord Archer, Baron of Umberslade, only s. and h., *b.* 29 July, and *bap.* 31 Aug. 1736, at Pirgo. Recorder of Coventry. M.P. (Whig) for Coventry 1761-68, and chosen for Bramber 1761, but did not sit. He *m.*, 23 July 1761, at Pirgo, Sarah, 1st da. of James West, of Alscot, co. Gloucester (M.P. for St. Albans, and sometime Pres. of the Royal Soc.), by Sarah, da. and h. of Sir Thomas Steavens, of Bermondsey. He *d. s.p.m.s.,* 18, or 25, Apr. 1778, in Portman Sq., Midx., and was *bur.* at Tanworth, when the title became *extinct.* (ᵈ) Admon. 12 May 1778, as "late of Marylebone, Midx.," to Sarah, the relict. His widow, who was *b.* 11, and *bap.* 25 May 1741, at Lincoln's Inn Chapel, *d.* in Charles Str., Grosvenor Sq., 18, and was *bur.* 27 Feb. 1801, at Tanworth. (ᵉ) Will dat. 5 July 1793, pr. 16 June 1801.

(ª) *Ancient Deeds,* vol. v, no. 13222. V.G.

(ᵇ) The Lords Archer of Umberslade bore a shield of Azure with three arrows gold, the points downward, being the arms of their ancient family, long settled at Umberslade, followers of the old Earls of Warwick. (*ex inform.* Oswald Barron.) V.G.

(ᶜ) See *N. & Q.,* 5th ser., vol. xii, p. 469, &c.

(ᵈ) His only s., *b.* 27 Nov. 1771, *d.* at Umberslade, young and *v.p.* Of his three daughters and coheirs, the eldest, Sarah, who *m.,* 1stly in 1788, the 5th Earl of Plymouth, and 2ndly the 1st Earl Amherst, appears to have inherited the chief part of the estates. She *d.* 27 May 1838.

(ᵉ) As to her keeping a 'faro-table,' see *sub* Mount Edgcumbe.

ARDAGH

See " SUNDON OF ARDAGH, CO. Longford, " Barony [I.] *(Clayton)*, *cr.* 1735 ; *extinct* 1752.

ARDEE

i.e. " LORD BRABAZON, BARON OF ARDEE, (ª) co. Louth " [I], see " BRABAZON, " Barony [I.] *(Brabazon)*, *cr.* 1616.

(ª) A Claim to the Barony of Ardee [I], as *heir general*, on the supposition that a Barony [I.] of that name (other than the Barony of 1616) had been *cr.* by a *Writ of Summons*, in 1665, was made, in 1762, by Chidley Coote, of Mount Coote, co. Limerick, s. and h of Charles Coote, of the same (who *d.* 1761), who was s and h. of Sir Philips Coote, by Lady Elizabeth Brabazon, 1st da and coh. (and in her issue, sole h.) of Edward, 2nd Earl of Meath, Lord Brabazon and Baron Ardee [I.]. It appears from a case laid, in 1836, before the eminent Peerage lawyer, Sir N. Harris Nicolas, by Chidley Coote, of Mount Coote afsd. (grandson and h. gen. of the abovenamed Chidley Coote, the Petitioner), that the said petition was, on 22 Apr. 1762, referred to the Attorney Gen. and the Solicitor Gen. [I], and that the latter (alone) gave his opinion thereon, which was in favour of the Petitioner, " in consequence of which a writ was ordered to issue, but the Petitioner, C. C., dying in the meantime [24 Feb. 1764], the subject was not brought forward again. "

The facts of the case were these—William Brabazon, s. and h ap of Edward, 2nd Earl of Meath [I.], was called *v p.* to the House of Peers [I] by writ of summons, 30 Oct. 1665, as Lord Ardee, or Lord Brabazon of Ardee (the title is " Atherdee " on the *Lords' Journals* [I] of 21 Dec. 1665), and sat and voted in the House as *Junior* Baron till his father's death, when he inherited the Earldom of Meath [I.]. His father's title as given in the patent which *cr.* him a Baron [I.], 19 July 1616, was " Lord Brabazon, Baron of Ardee. "

Nicolas' opinion was (1) that the decision in the case of the Barony of Sydney in 1782 (20 years after the report in this case) was conclusive against any *new* Barony of Ardee being *cr.* by such writ of summons and sitting, unless there was " a material variation " from the name of the Barony enjoyed by the father of the Peer so summoned ; and (2) that though the fact of Lord Brabazon having sat as *Junior* Baron " is entitled to some weight, still, I fear, it would not in itself be deemed sufficient to prove a *new* creation. "

The opinion that the precedence assigned to a Barony is not, of itself, sufficient to determine the date of its creation, is strengthened by the cases of Strange, Clifford, &c. In the former case we read in *Cruise* (p. 227) that the newly summoned Baron's " *rank and precedence* is a matter *merely collateral* . . . . . and if any question arises upon the *place* given [to such Baron] by the Heralds, it is to be *decided by the Lords of Parl.*, in the House of Lords, as a matter of privilege ; whereas the *right of Peerage itself* the Lords *never* have judged, *but upon a reference by the Crown.* " G.E.C. J. H Round however considers that this is a hazardous proposition, and instances the well-known Delawarr case *temp.* Eliz , in which stress was laid on the fact that William West sat as junior Baron, under a new creation, and not in the seat of his ancestors. V.G.

With respect to this claim it must moreover, be borne in mind that " Ardee, "

By privy seal, 28 June, and writ 30 Oct. 1665, William BRABAZON, s. and h. ap. of Edward, 2nd EARL OF MEATH [I.], was *sum. v.p.*, ([a]) to the House of Lords [I.] in his father's Barony as Lord BRABAZON OF ARDEE [I.]. On 25 Mar. 1675, he *suc.* his said father as EARL OF MEATH &c. [I.].

By writ 9 Mar. 1714/5, Chaworth BRABAZON, s. and h. ap. of Chambre, 5th EARL OF MEATH [I.], was *sum. v.p.*, ([a]) to the House of Lords [I.] in his father's Barony as LORD BRABAZON OF ARDEE [I.]. On 1 Apr. 1715, he *suc.* his said father as Earl of Meath &c. [I.].

ARDELVE

i.e. "ARDELVE, co. Wicklow," Barony [I.] (*Mackenzie*), *cr.* 1766 with the VISCOUNTCY OF FORTROSE [I.], see "SEAFORTH," Earldom [I.], *cr.* 1771; all honours becoming *extinct* 1781.

ARDEN AND ARDEN OF LOHORT

BARONY [I.]   1. CATHARINE, 3rd da. of the Hon. Charles COMPTON
I. 1770.   (by Mary, da. and h. of Sir Berkeley Lucy, Bart.), and sister of Charles and Spencer, 7th and 8th EARLS OF NORTHAMPTON, was *b.* 4 June 1731, at Quinta, near Lisbon. She *m.* (as his 2nd wife), 26 Jan. 1756, ([b]) at Charlton, Kent, John (PERCEVAL), 2nd Earl of Egmont [I.]. On 23 May 1770, she was *cr.* BARONESS ARDEN of Lohort Castle, co. Cork [I.], with rem. of the Barony to the heirs male of her body. Her husband *d.* 20 Dec. 1770. She *d.* at Langley, Bucks, 11, and was *bur.* 21 June 1784, at Charlton. (For fuller account see "EGMONT," Earldom of [I.], under the 2nd Earl.)

II. 1784.   2 and 1. CHARLES GEORGE (PERCEVAL), BARON ARDEN
BARONY [U.K.]   [I.], s. and h. of his mother, *b.* at Charlton, Kent, 1, and *bap.* there 4 Oct. 1756. Ed. at Trin. Coll.
I. 1802.   Cambridge. M.A. 1777. Took his seat in the House [I.] 8 Feb. 1787. He was M.P. (Tory) for Launceston 1780-90; for Warwick, 1790-96, and for Totnes 1796-1802. Lord of the Admiralty, 1783-1801 ; F.R.S. 19 Feb. 1786 ; Registrar of the Court of Admiralty, 1790-1840; P.C. 20 Feb. 1801; Master of the Mint 1801-2 ; Commissioner of the India Board 1801-3 ; a Lord of the Bedchamber 1804-12 ; Lord Lieut. of Surrey 1830-40. On 28 July 1802, he was *cr.* BARON ARDEN of Arden, co. Warwick [U.K.]. He *m.*, 1 Mar.

---

is not an English Barony (*i.e.* one capable of being *cr.* by writ), but an Irish Barony, where the writ is merely incidental to, and not creative of, the Peerage. See Appendix A at the end of this volume.

([a]) See *ante*, p. 2 note "c" for a list of eldest sons of peers' [I.], being in all only nine, so *sum. v.p.*

([b]) This marriage and the issue therefrom, as in the Family Bible, are set forth in Crisp's *Frag. Gen.*, vol. iv, pp. 73-75.

1787, (ᵃ) at Charlton, Kent, Margaretta Elizabeth, 1st da. of Gen Sir Thomas Spencer WILSON, 6th Bart., by Jane, da of John BADGER-WELLER, of Charlton afsd. He *d.* in St. James's Place, 5, and was *bur.* 11 July 1840, at Charlton, aged 83. (ᵇ) Will dat. 3 Mar 1826 to 27 Apr. 1840, pr. 18 Sep. 1840, under £800,000 His widow, who was *b.* 4 and *bap* 24 Apr. 1768, at St. Margaret's, Westm., *d.* at York House, near Guildford, 20, and was *bur.* 28 May 1851, at Charlton afsd, aged 82. Will dat. 6 Jan. 1846, pr. 7 Nov. 1851.

BARONY, &c. [I.] III BARONY [U.K.] II.	1840.	3 and 2. GEORGE JAMES (PERCEVAL), BARON ARDEN [I], and BARON ARDEN [U K.], 3rd, but 1st surv. s. and h., (ᶜ) who, on 23 Dec. 1841, *suc.* his cousin as EARL OF EGMONT, &c. [I] and BARON LOVELL AND HOLLAND [G.B.] See "EGMONT," Earldom [I.], under the 6th Earl.

ARDENERIE

BARONY [I.] 1. Sir John BOURKE, otherwise DE BURGO, (ᵈ) "the *Mac*
I. May 1580. *William* Oughter," known as "*Johannes Magnus*," was
s. and h. of Oliver BOURKE, of Tyrawley, Ardenerie, (ᵉ)
&c., co Mayo, by(—)da. of(—)O'DONNELL On 14 June 1570, he defended that county against the encroachments of Fitton, President of Connaught. He was knighted at Athlone, Apr. 1576, and in 1577 was Sheriff of co Mayo; being, in May 1580, (ᶠ) *cr.* BARON OF ARDENERIE [I.], with rem. to the heirs male of his body. He *d* 24 Nov. 1580

II. Nov. 1580 2. WILLIAM BOURKE, only legit. s and h., (ᵍ) *b.* pro-
to bably in or before 1560, was sent in July 1579 by Sir
1591. Nicholas Malby, President of Connaught, to Sir Francis Walsingham, with whom he remained 2 or 3 years, and

(ᵃ) See previous p., note "b"
(ᵇ) His next yr. br., the Rt. Hon. Spencer Perceval (*b.* 1 Nov. 1762, in North Audley Str.), was 1st Lord of the Treasury, and was assassinated in the House of Commons, 11 May 1812. V G.
(ᶜ) His 1st br, Charles Thomas, *d.* an infant, 11 Feb. 1793, at the Admiralty. His 2nd br., John, *m.*, in 1816, Elizabeth Anne, 1st da. of Robert, 6th Earl of Cardigan, and *d. s.p.* and *v.p.* 15 Mar. 1818, at Madeira. V.G.
(ᵈ) Some account of this branch of the Bourke family is in *Lodge*, vol. IV, p. 288, *sub* MAYO.
(ᵉ) This is evidently Ardnaree, co. Sligo, on the border of Mayo; it is now a suburb of Ballina, the largest town in Mayo. The river Moy separates the places, and is the boundary of the two counties. (G.D.Burtchaell to V G, Oct. 1909.)
(ᶠ) Pat. Roll, 21 Eliz. no 1176, p. 2, *m.* 2 (44), as quoted in *Creations*, 1483-1646, in App, 47th Rep. D.K. Pub. Records. His arms as Baron Ardenerie are recorded in Ulster's Office.
(ᵍ) He had no less than 7 bastard brothers, of whom David Bourke, *b.* about

hence became known as " Walsingham's man " ; ([a]) Sheriff of co. Sligo in 1583, but did not assume the peerage (to which he was apparently, in 1580, entitled), nor did any of his descendants, who were seated in Castle Lacken, co. Mayo, down to the middle of the 18th century. He was accidentally killed in 1591, since which time the peerage has remained *dormant*.

ARDES

See " MONTGOMERY OF THE GREAT ARDES, CO. Down," Viscountcy [I.] (*Montgomery*), *cr.* 1662 ; *extinct* 1757.

ARDFERT

i.e. " CROSBIE OF ARDFERT, CO. Kerry," Viscountcy [I.] (*Crosbie*), *cr.* 1771 ; *extinct*, with the EARLDOM OF GLANDORE [I.], 1815 ; see "BRANDEN," Barony [I.], *cr.* 1758 ; *extinct* 1832, under 2nd Baron.

ARDFRY

See " WALLSCOURT OF ARDFRY, CO. Galway," Barony [I.] (*Blake*), *cr.* 1800.

ARDGLASS

EARLDOM [I.]   1. THOMAS CROMWELL, only s. and h. of Edward, 3rd LORD CROMWELL, by his 2nd wife, Frances, da. of
I. 1645.   William RUGGE, of Norfolk, was *b.* 11 June 1594, and, having *suc.* his father as BARON CROMWELL 24 Sep. 1607, was on 22 Nov. 1624, *cr.* VISCOUNT LECALE in Ulster [I.], and, continuing firmly attached to the King during the Civil War (for whom he commanded a Regiment of Horse [I.]), was *cr.*, 15 Apr. 1645 (privy seal at Oxford 7 Jan. 1644/5), EARL OF ARDGLASS [I.]. He subsequently made his peace with the Parl., paying £460 for his "delinquency." He *m.* Elizabeth, da. and h. of Robert MEVERELL ([b]), of Throwleigh and Ilam, co. Stafford,

---

1570, matric. at Oxford (Magd. Coll.) 9 Feb. 1587/8, aged 17 ; he was admitted to the Middle Temple, 30 Oct. 1594, as " s. and h. of John Bourke of Tireawly, Kt., " and was J. P. for co. Mayo 1598. Another s., Walter B. of Belleky in Tyrawley, called " Kittagh " (left-handed), *m.* a da. of (—) O'Donnell of Tyrconnel, and was father of Theobald B., who by the influence of O'Donnell was declared the " *MacWilliam* " in 1595, which style had, however, been interdicted by the Government. After defeating the English, in 1596, under Sir John Norris, he was himself shortly after defeated and attainted. He fled to Spain, and was *cr.*, by Philip II of Spain, *Marquis of Mayo*, a dignity which expired on the death of his s., Walter Bourke, *s.p.*

([a]) *State Papers* [I.].

([b]) He *d.* 5 Feb. 1627/8, and Elizabeth, his widow, *d.* 5 Aug. 1628, both being *bur.* at Blore, co. Stafford.

by Elizabeth, da. of Sir Thomas FLEMING, Lord Chief Justice of the King's
Bench. He *d.* 1653, aged 59, and was *bur.* at Tickencote, Rutland. Will
dat. 26 Mar. 1653, pr. 1661 in Prerog. Court [I.]. His widow *d.* the
same year, and was also *bur.* there.

II. 1653.　　　2. WINGFIELD (CROMWELL), EARL OF ARDGLASS, &c.,
　　　　　　　[I.], and BARON CROMWELL [E.], only s. and h., *b.* 12 Sep.
1624, at Throwleigh, co. Stafford. Ed. at Stone, co. Stafford, and afterwards at Finglas, co. Dublin Matric. Trin. Coll Dublin as Fellow Com.
20 Mar. 1637/8.　D C.L Oxford, Nov. 1642.　He was taken prisoner at
Chester in the Royal cause, Apr. 1649. He *m.* Mary, da. of Sir William
RUSSELL, Bart., of Strensham, co Worcester, by Frances, da of Sir Thomas
READE.　He *d.* 3 Oct. 1668, and was *bur.* at Ilam afsd.　His widow (who
had a jointure of £1,500 a year) *m.*, between 1670 and 1675, as his 2nd
wife, Charles COTTON (ᵃ), of Beresford Hall, Notts (the Angler and Poet),
who was *bur* at St James's, Westm , 16 Feb 1686/7.　She survived him,
though probably somewhat his senior, and was living 12 Sep 1687. (ᵇ)

III. 1668.　　　3. THOMAS (CROMWELL), EARL OF ARDGLASS, &c., [I.],
　　　　　　　and BARON CROMWELL [E.], only s. and h , *b.* 29 Nov.
1653, at Strensham, afsd.　Matric. at Oxford (Ch. Ch.) 29 Oct. 1668.　He
m. Honora, sister and in her issue coh. of Murrough, 1st VISCOUNT
BLESSINGTON [I.], being da of Michael BOYLE, ARCHBISHOP OF ARMAGH
and LORD CHANCELLOR [I], by his 2nd wife, Mary, da. of Dermot
(O'BRIEN), 5th BARON INCHIQUIN [I.].　He *d. s.p.*, 11 Apr 1682, and was
bur. at Ilam afsd (ᶜ)　His widow *m.*, before 1687, Francis CUFFE, M P
for co. Mayo, (s. of Sir James C. of Ballinrobe) who was *b.* 12 Sep. 1656,
and *d.* 26 Dec. 1694.　She *m.*, 3rdly, Capt. Thomas BURDETT, of Garahill,
co. Carlow, who subsequently (1723) was *cr.* a Bart. [I], and who *d.*
14 Apr 1727　She *d.* in Dublin, and was *bur* 14 Nov 1710, in
St Patrick's, in that city.

IV. 1682　　　4. VERE ESSEX (CROMWELL), EARL OF ARDGLASS, and
to　　　　　　VISCOUNT LECALE [I.], and BARON CROMWELL [E.], uncle
1687.　　　　and h., *b.* 2 Oct. 1625, at Throwleigh, co Stafford　Ed.
　　　　　　at Stone, co. Stafford, and afterwards at Finglas, co.
Dublin. Ent. Trin. Coll. Dublin as Fellow Com. 20 Mar. 1637/8.
He *m.*, in 1672, Catharine, da. of James HAMILTON, of Newcastle, co.

(ᵃ) He was *b.* 28 Apr. 1630, and *m.*, as his 1st wife, Isabella Hutchinson,
30 June 1656, at St Mary's, Nottingham　She was living 1664, when he entered
his pedigree at the Heralds' Visitation of that county. He *d.* in debt, admon being
granted, 12 Sep. 1687, to a creditor, his widow and five children having renounced
　(ᵇ) She was certainly *b.* before 1634, at which date her eldest br was six years
old.　See Heralds' Visitation of co. Worcester of that date
　(ᶜ) A letter of 30 Mar. 1675, describing the loss of the packet 5 days before, when
the Earl of Meath was drowned, says :—"We do not as yet hear of any saved but that
drunken Earl of Ardglass, and he was the cause of the loss of the rest, for he carried
many dozens of wine with him, and the captain and seamen drank excessively." V.G.

Down, by Margaret, da. of Francis KYNASTON, of Saule, co. Down. He *d. s.p.m.*, at his house at Booncastle, co. Down, 26 Nov., and was *bur.* 29 Dec. 1687, in the Abbey of Downpatrick, the ancient burial place of his ancestors, (Fun. Ent.) when all his *Peerage Honours* (ª) became *extinct.* Will pr. 24 Jan. 1687/8, Prerog. Court [I.]. His widow *m.* Nicholas PRICE, of Hollymount, co. Down, who *d.*, a Lieut. Gen., 29 Sep. 1734. Will pr. 1734.

See "PIERREPONT OF ARDGLASS," Barony [I.] *(Pierrepont)*, *cr.* 1703 ; *extinct* with the Barony of PIERREPONT OF HANSLAPE [E.], 1714.

See "BARRINGTON OF ARDGLASS, co. Down," Viscountcy [I.] *(Barrington)*, *cr.* 1720.

See "LECALE OF ARDGLASS, co. Down," Barony [I.] *(Fitzgerald)*, *cr.* 1800 ; *extinct* 1810.

ARDKILL

See "DE BLAQUIERE OF ARDKILL, co. Londonderry," Barony [I.] *(Blaquiere)*, *cr.* 1800.

ARDILAUN OF ASHFORD

BARONY.

I. 1880.

1. SIR ARTHUR EDWARD GUINNESS, Bart., of Ashford, co. Galway, s. and h. of Sir Benjamin Lee GUINNESS, Bart., (ᵇ) by Elizabeth, 3rd da. of Edward GUINNESS, of Dublin, was *b.* 1 Nov. 1840, at St. Anne's, Clontarf, co. Dublin, ed. at Eton, and at Trin. Coll., Dublin ; B.A. 1863 ; M.A. 1866 ; *suc.* his father 19 Mar. 1868 ; was M.P. (Conservative) for the City of Dublin 1868-69, and again 1874-80, and was *cr.*, 1 May 1880, BARON ARDILAUN OF ASHFORD, co. Galway. Hon. LL.D. Dublin, 1891. He *m.*, 16 Feb. 1871, at Bantry, co. Cork, Olivia Charlotte, 2nd da. of William Henry Hare (HEDGES WHITE), 3rd EARL OF BANTRY [I.], by Jane, da. of Charles John HERBERT, of Muckross Abbey, co. Kerry. She was *b.* 27 Aug. 1850.

(ª) A Barony of Cromwell, supposed to have been *cr.* by writ, 28 Apr. 1539, was considered to have devolved on Elizabeth, only da. of the last Earl of Ardglass [I.], and this Lady appeared as "Baroness Cromwell" at the funeral of Queen Mary, and at the coronation of Queen Anne. It appears, however, that there was no *sitting* in Parl. under the writ of 1539, which, of itself, would be fatal to such writ having *cr.* a Barony in fee. In the same writ his father is *sum.*, *also* as Lord Cromwell, though, being Vicar Gen., he is placed (as such ?) at the head of the list. However five months after the death of his father, the Earl of Essex, (who had been so *cr.* in Apr., but who was attainted, and beheaded July 1540) the said Gregory Cromwell was *cr. by patent,* 18 Dec. 1540, Baron Cromwell "to him and *the heirs male of his body.*" The Barony thus *cr.* by the *patent* of 1540, appears to have been the only Barony of Cromwell vested in the Earls of Ardglass [I.].

(ᵇ) So *cr.* in 1867, in recognition of his munificent restoration of the Cathedral of St. Patrick, Dublin, at his own sole expense. He was head of the well known firm of "Arthur Guinness and Co," Dublin, Brewers.

Family Estates.—These, in 1883, consisted of about 27,000 acres in co. Galway, about 4,000, co. Mayo, and about 500, co. Dublin. Total about 31,500 acres, worth about £6,500 a year. *Principal Residences.*—Ashford, (ᵃ) near Cong, co. Galway ; St. Anne's, Clontarf, co. Dublin.

ARDMANACH, ARDMANNACH or ARDMANNOCH (ᵇ)

i.e. "BRECHIN, NAVAR AND ARDMANACH," Barony [S.] *(Stewart)*, cr. 1481, with the EARLDOM OF ROSS [S.], which see ; *extinct*, with the DUKEDOM OF ROSS [S.], 1504.

i.e. "EDIRDALE OR ARDMANACH," Earldom [S.] *(Stewart)*, cr. 1488, with the DUKEDOM OF ROSS [S.], which see ; *extinct* 1504.

i.e. "ARDMANNOCH," Barony [S.] *(Stuart)*, cr. May 1565, with the EARLDOM OF ROSS [S.] ; see "ALBANY," Dukedom [S.], cr. *July* 1565, the grantee being the King Consort [S.]; *merged in the Crown* [S.] 24 July 1567.

i.e. "Ardmannoch," Barony [S.] *(Stuart)*, cr. 1600, with the DUKEDOM OF ALBANY [S.], which see ; *merged in the Crown*, 1625.

ARDROSSAN

i.e. "ARDROSSAN of Ardrossan, co. Ayr," Barony *(Montgomerie)*, cr. 1806; see "EGLINTON," Earldom [S.], cr. 1508, under the 12th Earl.

(ᵃ) A correspondent of *The Times* newspaper (15 Sep. 1884) writes as follows—"It was in 1852 that the late Sir Benjamin Guinness bought Ashford of Lord Oranmore as a small residential estate, being captivated by the extreme beauty of the spot, and intending merely to build a cottage ornée. In 1860 he added the adjacent Rosshill, sold to him by Lord Charlemont and Lord Leitrim, who had married the two Miss Berminghams, who were co-heiresses. Oddly enough, the next purchase in 1864 was also from co-heiresses—from the Misses Blake, nieces of the late Sir Valentine Blake. It was that of Doon, and the picturesquely situated island ruin of Castle Kirk is a part of it. I have not visited the Doon property, where there is a handsome shooting lodge, but it is said to be as rich in natural attractions as Ashford. It was about the same time, I think, that 2,000 of the most poverty-stricken of the acres which I passed through in the neighbourhood of Maan were acquired from Sir Richard O'Donnell. Lastly, in 1870, the 6,000 acres around the white shooting lodge on the Lake of Kylemore, were bought from Mr. Finlay, a newspaper proprietor in Belfast, who had himself purchased them not very long before from the D'Arcy's of Clifden, one of the oldest of the Mayo families The average price of these lands was 20 years of the former rents ; of course the rents since then have in many cases been considerably reduced. "

(ᵇ) 'Ardmannach was a generic name, including Avach and Eddirdale, held by the Douglas family previous to their forfeiture, the chief messuage of Avach being Ormond (known also as Douglas) Castle.' (Letter of G Burnett, sometime Lyon). See also note *sub* ORMOND.

ARDS see ARDES

ARDSALLAGH or ARDSALLA

i.e. "LUDLOW OF ARDSALLAGH, co. Meath," Barony [I.] *(Ludlow)*, *cr.* 1755, see "LUDLOW," Earldom [I.], *cr.* 1760, *extinct* 1842.

---

i.e. "PRESTON OF ARDSALLAGH, co. Meath," Viscountcy [I.] *(Ludlow)*, *cr.* 1760, with the EARLDOM OF LUDLOW [I.], which see ; *extinct* 1842.

---

i.e. "AMBERLEY OF AMBERLEY, CO. Gloucester, AND OF ARDSALLA, CO. Meath," Viscountcy *(Russell)*, *cr.* 1861, with the EARLDOM OF RUSSELL OF KINGSTON RUSSELL, which see.

ARGENTINE ([a])

BARONY
BY WRIT.

I. 1283.

1. REYNOLD D'ARGENTINE, ([b]) of Melbourn, co. Cambridge, and Great Wymondley, Herts, s. and h. of Giles d'A., of the same, by Margery, da. of Sir Robert Aiguillon, *suc.* his father in 1282, ([c]) before 24 Nov., being then aged 40 and more, and, 20 Dec. 1282, he had livery of his inheritance. ([d]) He was sum. to attend the King at Shrewsbury, ([e]) 28 June (1283) 11 Edw. I, and also at Salisbury, ([f]) 26 Jan. (1296/7) 25 Edw. I, by writs directed *Reginaldo de Argenteyn* and *de Argenteyme*. He *m.* Laura, da. of Hugh (DE VERE), 4th EARL OF OXFORD, by Hawise, da. of Saher (DE QUINCY), EARL OF WINCHESTER. She *d.* in 1292, and

---

([a]) The re-writing of this article has been kindly undertaken by G.W.Watson.

([b]) This family took its name from Argenton in Poitou, and not from Argenton in Berry, nor from Argentan in Normandy. The French branch of the family existed till the 16th century. Their pedigree is given by A.Du Chesne, *Maison de Chastillon*, 1621, p. 494-499, and by Beauchet-Filleau, *Dictionnaire des Familles du Poitou*, vol. i, 1891, p. 100-103. They bore for arms, Or, semé of cross crosslets Az. and 3 roundlets Gu. (Gilles le Bouvier, *dit* Berry, *Armorial* (compiled about 1455), ed. Vallet de Viriville, 1866, no. 1094). The English branch bore, Gu., 3 covered cups Arg., in allusion to the tenure of Great Wymondley, for which see under ALINGTON, p. 106, note " d. " Giles d'Argentine, who was slain at Bannockburn, bore the latter arms, the field being semé with cross crosslets Arg., as his difference.

([c]) Writ of *diem cl. ext.* 24 Nov. 11 Edw. I (*Fine Roll*, 11 Edw. I, m. 26). Inq., cos. Cambridge, Herts, and Suffolk, undated. (Ch. *Inq. p. m.*, Edw. I, file 33, no. 16).

([d]) *Fine Roll*, 11 Edw. I, m. 25.

([e]) As to this supposed Parl., see Preface : and as to how far these early writs of summons did in fact create any peerage title, see Appendix A in the last volume. V.G.

([f]) Concerning the validity of a writ of this date as a regular writ of summons to Parl., see Preface. V.G.

was *bur.* in the Church of the White Friars at Norwich.   He *d.* shortly before 3 Mar. 1307/8. (ª)

None of his descendants were ever sum. to Parl. in respect of this supposed barony.   His s. and h., John d'Argentine, aged 30 and more at his father's death, did homage and had livery of his inheritance, 4 Apr. 1308.(ᵇ) He *m.*, 1stly, Joan, da. and h. of Sir Roger Brien, of Throcking, Herts.   She *d. s.p.m.*   He *m.*, 2ndly, Agnes, da. of William Bereford, of Burton, co. Leicester.(ᶜ)   He *d.* shortly before 20 Oct. 1318, (ᵈ) leaving John d'Argentine, his s. and h., then aged 6 months, whose marriage was granted, 8 July 1325, to Robert Darcy.(ᵉ)   This John had livery of his father's lands, when still a minor, 6 Mar. 1337/8. (ᶠ)   He *m.* Margaret, da. and h. of Robert Darcy afsd., of Great Sturton, co. Lincoln, by Joan, his wife.   She *d.* 1 Sep. 1383. (ᵍ)   He *d. s.p.m. legit.* (ʰ) 18 or 26 Nov. 1382, (ⁱ) leaving his 3 daughters, or their issue, his coheirs.   (1) Joan, wife of Sir Bartholomew Naunton.   She *d. v.p.*, leaving Margaret her da. and h., wife of Robert Bokenham.   (2) Elizabeth, wife of Sir Baldwin St. George.   She *d. v.p.*, leaving Baldwin her s. and h.   (3) Maud, wife of Sir Ives FitzWarin.   Among their representatives any hereditary barony, that may be held to have existed, is in *abeyance.*

(ª) Writ of *diem cl. ext.* 3 Mar. 1 Edw. II (*Fine Roll*, 1 Edw. II, *m.* 7).   Inq. cos. Cambridge, Norfolk, and Wilts, 10, 16, and 22 Mar. 1307/8.   (Ch. *Inq. p.m.*, Edw. II, file 2, no. 14).

(ᵇ) *Fine Roll*, 1 Edw. II, *m.* 4.

(ᶜ) This Agnes *m.*, 2ndly, Sir John Narford, or Nerford, of Wissett, Suffolk, who *d. s.p.*, 5 Feb. 1328/9; and 3rdly, before 26 Feb. 1330/1, as 2nd wife, Sir John Mautravers the younger [Lord Mautravers], who *d.* 16 Feb. 1363/4.   Her will was dat. 18 Feb. 1374/5.

(ᵈ) Writ of *diem. cl. ext.* 20 Oct. 12 Edw. II.   Inq., Herts, Suffolk, Norfolk, Cambridge, and Hunts, 4, 15, 17, 27 Nov. and 9 Dec. 1318.   (Ch. *Inq. p. m.*, Edw. II, file 62, no. 43).

(ᵉ) *Patent Roll*, 19 Edw. II, *pars* 1, *m.* 36.

(ᶠ) *Close Roll*, 12 Edw. III, *pars* 1, *m.* 26.

(ᵍ) Writs of *diem. cl. ext.* 1 and 3 Sep. 7 Ric. II.   Inq., Suffolk, Thursday after the Nativity of the Virgin [10 Sep.] 1383.   " obiit die martis proximo post festum Decollationis sancti Johannis Baptiste anno supradicto. "   Inq., Herts and Essex, Monday and Tuesday before St. Martin [9 and 10 Nov.] 1383.   " obiit die martis in festo sancti Egidii Abbatis ultimo preterito. "   (Ch. *Inq. p. m.*, Ric. II, file 29, no. 4 : Exch. *Inq. p. m.*, *Enrolments*, file 1169, no. 8).

(ʰ) His illeg. s., Sir William Argentine, received the manor of Great Wymondley, and was father of John, whose da. and coh., Elizabeth, brought that manor to her husband, William Alington (who *d.* 5 July 1459), ancestor in the 8th degree of William Alington, 1st Lord Alington of Killard.

(ⁱ) Writs of *diem. cl. ext.* 14 Dec. 6 Ric. II.   Inq., co. Cambridge, Saturday after St. Gregory the Pope [14 Mar.] 1382/3.   " obiit die martis proximo ante festum sancte Katerine ultimo preterito [18 Nov.]. "   Inq., Suffolk and Norfolk, Thursday before, and Monday the vigil of, St. Matthias [19 and 23 Feb.] 1382/3.   " obiit die mercurii proximo post festum sancte Katerine virginis ultimo elapsum [26 Nov.]. "   (Ch. *Inq. p. m.*, Ric. II, file 29, no. 4 : Exch. *Inq. p. m.*, *Enrolments*, file 1169, nos. 1, 3, 5).

ARGYLL

EARLDOM [S.]   1. COLIN (CAMPBELL), LORD CAMPBELL [S.], (ª) s.
and h of Archibald CAMPBELL, of Lochow, Argyll,
I. 1457.   *styled* MASTER OF CAMPBELL, by Elizabeth, da of John
(SOMERVILE), 3rd LORD SOMERVILE, which Archibald was s. and h. ap. of
Duncan, 1st LORD CAMPBELL [S.], but *d. v.p.*, between Apr. 1431 and
Mar. 1440. He *suc.* to the dignity of a Lord of Parl. [S.] by the death of
his said grandfather, in 1453, being then a minor, and was *cr.* by James II,
in 1457, EARL OF ARGYLL [S] (ª) He was employed in various
embassies to England and France, was Master of the Household 1464, and
Chancellor [S.] 1483 to Feb. 1488, and again June 1488 till his death.
In 1460 he had a commission as Bailie of Cowal. In 1471 he had a
charter of the heritable offices of Justiciary and Sheriff within the lordship
of Lorne. In 1479 he had a charter confirming to him the offices of
Lieutenant and Commissary of Argyll, as held by his ancestors Gillespic
and Colin Cambel under a charter of 1382. In 1487 he joined the
conspiracy of the nobles against James III. He *m.*, before 9 Apr. 1465,
Elizabeth or Isabel, da. and senior coh. of John (STEWART), 2nd LORD
LORNE [S.]. On the resignation of her uncle, Walter STEWART, the h
male of the family, till then usually designated LORD LORNE, but afterwards LORD INNERMEATH [S.], he obtained a crown charter of the Lordship
of Lorne *(dominium de Lorne)*, 17 Apr 1470, to him and the heirs male
of his body, with rem. to Sir Colin Campbell of Glenorchy, to Colin
Campbell Nelesoun, to Duncan Campbell (br. of Sir Colin, of Glenorchy),
&c., each in like manner respectively. It was made a condition of this
resignation that the resigner should continue a Lord of Parl. by the style
of Lord of Innermeath " or any other honourable place that pleases him. "
From that time the Earl is usually designated (as are his successors) " Earl
of Argyll, Lord Campbell and *Lorne*. (ᵇ) After the rebellion in 1487, which
ended in the death of James III at Sauchieburn, he was deprived of the
office of Chancellor, but was reinstated by James IV in 1488, as above.
He *d* 10 May 1493. His widow *d.* 26 Oct. 1510, at Dunbarton, and was
bur. at Kilmun. (ᶜ)

II. 1493.   2. ARCHIBALD (CAMPBELL), EARL OF ARGYLL, &c. [S.],
s and h. He, like his father, was in the confidence of
James IV, to whom, in Mar. 1494/5, he was Master of the Household. (ᵈ)

(ª) Both the Barony and the Earldom (of which the former was *cr* 1445) belong
to periods at which the Great Seal is defective, and no document connected with
either is extant. The usual form and spelling is " *Ergile*, " or, when Latinized,
" *Ergadia* " It was in the time of the 1st Earl that the form of " *Campbell* " began
to supersede the old spelling of " *Cambel* "

(ᵇ) Walter Stewart, who had resigned the title of " Lorne, " became, according
to the proviso contained in the resignation thereof, Lord Innermeath [S.]

(ᶜ) Fortirgall's *Chronicle*

(ᵈ) The statement, in *Dict. Nat. Biog*, that he was designated High Chan. of

In addition to the offices inherited from his father, enumerated in his service of 1493 (Sheriff, Justiciary, Chamberlain and Coroner of Argyll and Lorne, and Lieut. within the said Sheriffdom), he had, by a charter of 1504, those of Justiciary, Sheriff, Coroner and Chamberlain of Kintyre and Knapdale, and Captain of Tarbert. In 1500 he was made Lieut. Gen. of the Isles. He *m* Elizabeth, 1st da. of John (STEWART), 1st EARL OF LENNOX [S], by Margaret, da. of Alexander (MONTGOMERY), 1st LORD MONTGOMERY [S.]. He *d.* 9 Sep. 1513, being slain at the battle of Flodden, (ª) where he and his br.-in-law, the Earl of Lennox [S.], commanded the right wing of the army, and was *bur.* at Kilmun.

III. 1513.   3. COLIN [CAMPBELL], EARL OF ARGYLL, &c. [S.], s. and h.   He was a prominent statesman both during the minority of James V, when he exerted himself to procure the tranquility of the Isles, and throughout the reign of that King ; besides holding the heritable offices of Sheriff, Justiciary, Chamberlain, and Coroner of Argyll, and the offices of Justiciary, Sheriff, Coroner, Bailie, and Chamberlain of Kintyre and Knapdale, held by his father, he was also made HIGH JUSTICIAR, or Justice Gen., OF SCOTLAND July 1514, and Lieut. of the Isles in 1516   Vice-regent and Lieut. of the Kingdom, May 1511 ; Lieut of the Borders and Warden of the Marches, July 1528.   In 1528 he was confirmed in the appointment of JUSTICIAR [S.], and had that of Master of the Household [S.] conferred on him.   In 1528 he obtained the barony of Abernethy, part of the forfeited estate of Archibald (Douglas), 5th Earl of Angus [S]   In 1529 (shortly before his death) he resigned nearly the whole of his lands, together with the offices of Sheriff of Argyll, Kintyre, and Knapdale, in favour of his s. and h. ap , Archibald Campbell, *styled* Master of Argyll.   He *m.*, before 28 Feb. 1506/7, Jean, 1st da of Alexander (GORDON), 3rd EARL OF HUNTLY [S.], by his 1st wife, Janet, da. of John (STEWART), EARL OF ATHOLL [S.].   He *d.* in 1529, before 26 Mar. (ᵇ)

IV. 1529.   4. ARCHIBALD (CAMPBELL), EARL OF ARGYLL, &c. [S.], s. and h.   On 19 Aug. and 2 Sep. 1529, he had *(v.p.)* sasine of the lands and offices conveyed to him by his father, and on 28 Oct. 1529, he was (as Archibald, Earl of Argyll) appointed JUSTICIAR OF SCOTLAND, and Master of the Household.   Master of the King's wine cellar, 28 Mar 1542.   In 1543, the lands of Muckart, co. Perth, were bestowed on him for his services in the defence of the Church against heresies.   In 1545 he was made Justiciary of Bute.   He commanded a body of Highlanders at Pinkie 10 Sep. 1547, and was at the siege of Haddington in 1548, but was soon afterwards won over (by English gold)

Scotland in 1494, apparently arises from confusing him with Archibald, Earl of Angus, who then held that office.   The discrepancies in dates and statements in this from that work must generally be regarded as deliberate.   V.G.

(ª) See list of nobles there slain *sub* LENNOX.

(ᵇ) Date of the will of James, 2nd Earl of Arran [S], who mentions his da. (wife of the 4th Earl) as Countess of Argyll.   V.G.

to side with England. Being one of the first Scottish nobles to adopt the cause of the reformed religion, he became, in 1557, one of the Lords of the Congregation. He *m.*, 1stly, before 26 Mar. 1529, ([a]) Helen, 1st da. of James (HAMILTON), 1st EARL OF ARRAN [S.], by his 2nd wife, Janet, da of Sir David BETOUN. To her, for her life, he resigned his barony of Menstrie, co Clackmannan, on 27 Aug. 1529. He *m.*, 2ndly, 21 Apr. 1541, at the Priory of Inchmahome, Margaret, da. of William (GRAHAM), 3rd EARL OF MENTEITH [S.], by Margaret, da. of John MOUBRAY, of Barnbougle. He *m.*, 3rdly, before 23 Jan. 1546, Catharine Maclean. ([b]) He *d.* between 21 Aug and 2 Dec 1558, " in tempore congregationis " at Dulnynn, (? Dunoon) and was *bur.* at Kilmun. His widow *m*, 2ndly, about 1559, Callough (or Calvagh) O'DONNELL, whose creation, as Earl of Tyrconnell [I.], was ordered by Queen Elizabeth 27 May 1561, though this was never carried out. He *d.* Dec. 1567. She *m.*, 3rdly, shortly before 6 Apr 1575, when her *m.* cont is mentioned in a disposition of lands to herself, John STEWART, of Appin, who *d.* in or shortly before 1595.

V 1558.　　5. ARCHIBALD (CAMPBELL), EARL OF ARGYLL, &c. [S.], s. and h. by 1st wife, *b.* about 1532. In 1552 he had a grant of the hereditary offices on his father's resignation. In 1558 he had a charter (from Francis and Mary) of the office of JUSTICIAR OF SCOTLAND for life, confirmed, by Queen Mary, in 1561, but in 1565 he appeared in arms against her ; he also participated in the plot for Darnley's murder, but afterwards supported the cause of the Queen, for whom he fought at Langside, 13 May 1568, being appointed her Lieut. on the day of that battle, and exhibiting incapacity and irresolution. P.C. 1571. In 1572 he came to terms of accommodation with the Regent Morton, and on 15 Jan 1572/3 was made CHANCELLOR [S.], for life. He *m.*, 1stly, (cont. dat. 1 July 1553) Jean, illegit. da. of JAMES V, by Elizabeth, da. of Sir John BETHUNE, of Creich. She was present with the Queen at the murder of Rizzio, 9 Mar. 1566. In that same year, also, she stood proxy for Queen Elizabeth, as Godmother to James VI. The Earl was censured by the Gen Assembly in Dec. 1567, for having separated from her. She, who continued a Catholic, was taken prisoner at the surrender of Edinburgh Castle, 28 May 1573. She had endeavoured to stipulate that she should not be surrendered to her husband, fearing to come to " a hard end " at Inveraray. From her he obtained a divorce " for desertion, " 23 June 1573. ([c]) In Aug. 1573 he *m.*, 2ndly, (cont. dat. 5 Aug 1573) Janet, da.

([a]) See note " b " on previous page.

([b]) *Hist. MSS. Com*, 4th Rep, Part 1, p. 477.

([c]) This is the first case in Scotland of a divorce being obtained for " non-adherence. " In 1572 the Earl had obtained a decree of 'adherence,' and on 25 Apr. 1573 she was excommunicated On 30 Apr following he obtained an Act of Parl falsely declaring the law as to non adherence entitling to a divorce to have existed since Aug. 1560, and the divorce was granted as stated in the text. The Earl's interest with the party of the Reformation, as also that of the father of his new wife, tended to their being able to carry this measure. However, perhaps owing to the above fraud, it was not fully recognized after the Earl's death, and the countess

of Alexander (CUNNINGHAM), 5th EARL OF GLENCAIRN [S.], by his 2nd wife, Janet, da. of Sir John CUNNINGHAM, of Caprington. He *d. s.p*, of the stone, 12 Sep. 1573, (ᵃ) aged about 43. Will pr. 25 May 1576, at Edinburgh. His widow *m.*, in 1583, Humphrey COLQUHOUN, of Luss, and *d. s.p*, 1584.

VI. 1573.   6. COLIN (CAMPBELL), EARL OF ARGYLL, &c. [S.], half br. and h, being s. of the 4th Earl by his 2nd wife. He was known before he succeeded to the Earldom as Sir Colin Campbell of Boquhan. In 1571, on his brother's resignation, he had the hereditary offices conferred upon him. A quarrel with the Regent Morton, arising out of a demand that he should restore certain royal jewels (of which his countess had become possessed when wife of the Regent Moray), combined with other sources of irritation, led him, in coalition with John, Earl of Atholl [S.], to obtain possession of the young King, who was made to take the sceptre in his own hands, effecting thereby Morton's retirement from the regency   Morton, however, recovering the power, though not the name of Regent, an accommodation was effected, and on 10 Aug 1579, Argyll was made CHANCELLOR [S], which office he retained till his death. He *m*, 1stly, (cont. dat. 14 Oct. 1551, when she was not yet of full contracting age) Joan, (legitimated 1551) da of Henry (STEWART), 1st LORD METH-VEN [S.], by his 3rd wife, Janet, Dowager COUNTESS OF SUTHERLAND [S.], da. of John (STEWART), 2nd EARL OF ATHOLL [S.]. She *d s p*.(ᵇ) He *m.*, 2ndly, between May 1571, and 26 Feb. 1571/2, Annabel, or Agnes, widow of James, EARL OF MORAY [S.] (the well-known REGENT, assassinated 1570), da. of William (KEITH), 4th EARL MARISCHAL [S], by Margaret, da. and coh. of Sir William KEITH. He *d.* 10 Sep. 1584, at Darnaway. Will dat. 5 Sep. 1584, pr. 23 June 1586, at Edinburgh. His widow, who was excommunicated for non-adherence to her husband, about 25 Apr. 1573, *d.* 16 July 1588, at Edinburgh, and was *bur.* at St. Giles's there, with her 1st husband. Funeral entry at Lyon office   Will pr. 9 Aug. 1591, at Edinburgh.

VII. 1584.   7. ARCHIBALD (CAMPBELL), EARL OF ARGYLL, &c. [S.], s. and h. by 2nd wife, *b.* 1575. At the age of 18, in 1594, he was sent, as the King's Lieut, against Huntly and Erroll, the Catholic Lords, by whom he was completely defeated, 3 Oct. 1594, at Glenlivat or Balrinnes. In the decreet of ranking, 5 Mar. 1606, he was placed (not according to the precedence of the *creation* of his Earldom, but) in the exalted rank of 2nd Earl [S.], owing to his office as JUSTICE

Jean continued to hold the dower lands   She was legitimated under the great seal, 18 Oct 1580, and *d.* 7 Jan. 1587/8, being *bur.* as Countess of Argyll, at Holyrood. Her will, as Dame Jane Stewart, spouse of Alexander [*sic*] Earl of Argyll, was pr. at Edinburgh, 26 Mar. 1588

    (ᵃ) The date 1575, in *Douglas*, is an error.

    (ᵇ) The bill for Lady Lorne's [*sic*] funeral in the Westm. Abbey records is dated 22 June 1576. (*Lords' Journals.*) This may refer to her. V.G.

GENERAL. (^a) In 1610 he had, on his resignation, a charter to himself in life rent, and to his s. and h. ap., Archibald, in fee, of his Earldom and hereditary offices. Having expelled the Macdonalds of Kintyre, he obtained a grant of the whole of that Lordship, including the island of Jura, in 1617. In 1618, having become a Roman Catholic after his 2nd marriage with a lady of that faith, he served, under Philip III of Spain, against Holland. (^b) On 16 Feb. 1618/9, he was formally declared a rebel and traitor at the Market Cross, Edinburgh, which sentence was reversed 22 Nov. 1621. He *m.*, 1stly, 24 July 1592, Agnes, 5th da. of William (DOUGLAS), 8th EARL

(^a) THE PRECEDENCY OF THE EARLS OF ANGUS, ARGYLL, CRAWFORD, ERROLL AND MARISCHAL

Over the other Earls [S.] of more ancient creation.

As in England, by the ranking of Henry VIII, several of the King's Officers of State were placed (*during their tenure of office*) at the top of that class of the nobility of which they happened to be members, so in Scotland (on a somewhat similar principle) certain Earls who held high office (though, in some cases, *hereditary* office) were ranked above other Earls of more ancient creation

The precedency of Angus, above all other Earls, (which apparently was originally one more by *privilege* than *office*) had been conferred by James VI, under charter of the Great Seal [S.] in 1602, and, consequently, was ratified four years later at the " Decreet of Ranking " in 1606. (For a fuller account of the precedency of Angus see *ante* p. 160 note " b. ") In this decree the 1st place was allotted to ANGUS, the next to ARGYLL, and the 3rd, 4th and 5th places, to CRAWFORD, ERROLL and MARISCHAL respectively. This was according to " the old established Precedences from Office or Privilege a matter about which much evidence may be gleaned from the Scottish Records. *Privilege* or *office*, and *not priority of creation* was the cause why Angus, Argyle [owing to his office as Justice General], Crawford, Erroll and Marischal, preceded all the other Earls. Next came the two oldest Earls [according to priority of creation, *viz.*] Sutherland and Mar, the former producing title deeds dating from 1347, the latter from 1395 and 1404. Then followed Rothes, &c. . . . . Till the middle of the sixteenth century there seems to have been no recognition of precedency in virtue of priority of creation In the fifteenth century the idea of the great Earls of Douglas or Crawford yielding the *pas* to an Earl of older date (*e g.* Ross or Sutherland) would have been unintelligible. The right of ANGUS (who came in the place of Douglas) to bear the Crown and precede all Earls (if not Dukes) was recognized in Parl. in 1592, and by charter of 1599. On public occasions, when Angus bore the Crown, ARGYLE, who also held the hereditary office of Justiciary, bore the sceptre ; and, by contemporary evidence, CRAWFORD's privilege of bearing the sword was equally acknowledged. As the Constable [*i.e.* the Earl of ERROLL] and [the Earl] MARISCHAL, were both Commissioners [in the decreet of ranking, in 1606], it would have been strange if their official precedence, often alluded to in the records, had been unrecognised. It was the clashing of the new ideas with the old that had caused the unseemly scenes in Parl , and that led to the appointment of the Commission of 1606. " See an able article on " Jurisdiction in Scottish Peerages, " by George Burnett, sometime Lyon, in the *Journal of Jurisprudence*, &c., vol 27 (No. 317), p. 241 and note thereto.

(^b) It is to this that Alexander Craig refers in his bitter lines, which are quoted in Scot's *Staggering State* :—

" Now Earl of Guile and Lord Forlorn thou goes
Quitting thy Prince to serve his foreign foes. "   V.G

of Morton [S], by Agnes, da. of George (Leslie), 4th Earl of Rothes [S.]. She, who was *b.* 1574, *d* 3 May 1607 He *m.*, 2ndly, 30 Nov 1610, at St. Botolph's, Bishopsgate, London, Anne, da. and eventually coh. of Sir William Cornwallis, of Brome, Suffolk, by his 1st wife, Lucy, da and coh. of John (Neville), Lord Latimer. She was distinguished as an authoress of some note. She *d.* at the Earl's house, in Drury Lane, Midx., 12, and was *bur.* 13 Jan. 1634/5, at St. Martin's-in-the-Fields. Fun certif. at the Coll. of Arms, London (*) He *d.*, in Oct or Nov. 1638, in London, aged about 63. Will dat. 9 Oct., pr. 29 Nov. 1638, in the Commissary Court of London.

VIII. 1638. MARQUESSATE [S.] I. 1641 to 1661.	8 and 1. Archibald (Campbell), Earl of Argyll, &c. [S.], s. and h., being only s. by 1st wife, *b.* between Aug. 1605 and Apr. 1607, probably in 1607. Matric. at St. Andrew's 15 Jan. 1622. In 1618, his father having left the kingdom, the care of the Western Highlands devolved on him, and to him, being a Protestant, his father

was directed to make over all his estates (*b*) In 1625 the office of Justice General [S.] was conferred on him and his successors, Earls of Argyll, but in 1628 it was resigned by him to the King P.C. 12 June 1628. On 14 Jan. 1634, he was (under the *style* of "*Lord Lorn*") one of the Extraordinary Lords of Session. On his accession to the Earldom he subscribed the "Covenant"; in 1639 he sent 500 Highlanders to swell the covenanting force at Aberdeen, and in 1640, in the cause of the "Covenant," he carried fire and sword through Atholl, Badenoch, and Angus. But when Charles I came to Scotland, Aug. 1641, he made his peace with him, and was *cr.*, 15 Nov. 1641, MARQUESS OF ARGYLL [S.], a pension of £1000 a year being, at the same time, settled upon him. Soon afterwards he again joined the Covenanters, but was signally defeated at Inverlochy, 2 Feb. 1644/5, and at Kilsyth, 15 Aug. 1645, by Montrose. In Oct. 1648 he conducted Cromwell to Edinburgh, where the "Covenant" was renewed. He assisted, however, in bringing Charles II to Scotland in June 1650, (*c*) and placed the Crown on his head at Scone, 1 Jan. 1650/1,

---

(*) James Campbell, her 1st s, was (*v p*), on 22 Feb. 1626, *cr* Lord of Kintyre [S.] " to him, his heirs male and successors in that Lordship. " He was afterwards, 1642, *cr.* Earl of Irvine and Lord of Lundie [S.], with rem to the heirs male of his body On his death the title of "Lord of Kintyre" [S.] was inherited, under the spec. rem., by his br, the Marquess of Argyll [S.].

(*b*) On this occasion his father is reported by Clarendon to have given the following account of him to the King. "Sir, I must know this young man better than you can do · you have brought me low that you may raise him, which I doubt you will live to repent; for he is a man of craft and subtlety and falsehood, and can love no man; and if ever he finds it in his power to do you a mischief he will be sure to do it " V.G.

(*c*) A letter to him from Charles II, dat 24 Sep. 1650, is extant, promising to make him a Duke and K.G., and Gent of the Bedchamber, "on the word of a King!" V.G.

having obtained a promise to be made a Duke and K.G.   Subsequently,
however, he was present at the proclamation of Cromwell as Lord Protector,
and signed a promise to live peaceably under that Government.   He was
M.P. for co. Aberdeen 1658-59. (ª)   On the death of his half br. James,
Earl of Irvine [S.], *s.p.*, in Sep. 1645, he inherited the title of LORD OF
KINTYRE [S.], *cr.* 22 Feb. 1626.   In July 1660 he went to London, to
wait on the newly arrived King, but this, the last of his many tergiversations,
availed him nothing, as he was ordered to the Tower, and thence taken to
Edinburgh Castle.   He was tried for high treason and sentence pronounced
against him 25 May 1661, when, having been attainted, *all his honours*
became *forfeited*.   He *d.* 27 May 1661, being executed (ᵇ) at the Cross of
Edinburgh ; his head was exposed (where Montrose's had been) on the
top of the Tolbooth till 8 June, when it was *bur.* with his body at Kilmun. (ᶜ)
He *m.*, in 1626, shortly before 6 Aug., his cousin, Margaret, 2nd da. of
William (DOUGLAS), 9th EARL OF MORTON [S.], by Anne, 1st da. of
George (KEITH), 5th EARL MARISCHAL [S.].   His widow, who was *b.*
1610, *d.* 13 Mar. 1677/8.

* * * * * * *

EARLDOM [S.]   9. ARCHIBALD CAMPBELL, *styled* LORD LORNE and
IX. 1663   MASTER OF ARGYLL in his father's lifetime, and for
to   some period after his death, s and h., *b.* 26 Feb.
1665.   1628/9, at Dalkeith.   He was appointed Col. of the
                Foot Guards and fought at Dunbar, 3 Sep. 1650, and
at Worcester, 3 Sep. 1651, on behalf of Charles II, and being then Lieut.
Gen., was excepted from Cromwell's Act of Grace 1654.   He afterwards,
however, submitted, but was compelled to find £5000 security.   At the
Restoration he was imprisoned and sentenced to death, 26 Aug. 1662, but
was released 4 June 1663, and, by patent, 16 Oct. 1663, wherein he is
styled " *Dominus de Lorne,* " was *restored* to the titles of EARL OF ARGYLL,
LORD CAMPBELL, LORNE and KINTYRE [S.]. (ᵈ)   F.R.S. 28 Oct. 1663; nom.
P.C. Apr. and sworn 9 June 1664.   On 15 Oct 1667, he received a new
charter of all his lands and offices. (ᵉ)   From 11 July 1674 to Nov. 1681,

(ª) Though a peer of Scotland, he sat in the House of Commons, as did the 2nd,
4th, and 5th VISCOUNTS FALKLAND.
(ᵇ) See *N. & Q*, 3rd Ser, vol. 11, p. 260, &c.   Lord Clarendon describes him
as " a person of extraordinary cunning, " one, who " carried himself so, that they,
who hated him most, were willing to compound with him, " and as having " no
martial qualities, nor the reputation of more courage than violent and imperious
persons, whilst they meet with no opposition, are used to have "
(ᶜ) He was a small, wiry, squinting, blue eyed, red haired man, with a high
forehead and hooked nose   V.G.
(ᵈ) See note " a " on previous page.
(ᵉ) The office of JUSTICE GEN. OF SCOTLAND was not included, as it had ceased
to be in the family.   It was not, strictly speaking, hereditary, excepting from 1625 to
1628, but it was virtually so, having been held by the 2nd down to the 8th inclusive.
In 1561, in the confirmation thereof to the 5th Earl, the moving cause is said to be

he was an Extraordinary Lord of Session. On 19 Dec. 1681, he was sentenced to death for high treason, for refusing to subscribe to the "Test Act," but escaped from Edinburgh Castle to Holland, when, having been attainted, *all his honours* became *forfeited* (ª) On 17 Apr. 1685, he was chosen General of the forces which invaded Scotland in support of Monmouth's rebellion. After a short and inglorious campaign, he was taken prisoner at a ford of the Inchinnan, was *executed* on his former sentence (at the same place as his father had been) on 30 June 1685, (ᵇ) and *bur.* in Greyfriars churchyard. M.I. He *m.*, 1stly, 13 May 1650, in the Canongate, Edinburgh, Mary, 1st da. of James (STUART), 4th EARL OF MORAY [S.], by Margaret, 1st da. of Alexander (HOME), 1st EARL OF HOME [S.]. She *d.* May 1668. He *m*, 2ndly, 28 Jan. 1670, Anne, Dowager COUNTESS OF BALCARRES [S.], 2nd da. of Colin (MACKENZIE), 1st EARL OF SEAFORTH [S.], by Margaret, 1st da. of Alexander (SETON), 1st EARL OF DUMFERMLINE [S.]. By her he had no issue. She was a prisoner in Edinburgh Castle at the time of her husband's execution in 1685, and was *bur.* at Balcarres 29 May 1707.

* * * * * * *

X 1689.
DUKEDOM [S.]
I. 1701.

10 and 1. ARCHIBALD CAMPBELL, *styled* LORD LORNE and MASTER OF ARGYLL in the lifetime, and for some period after the death of his father, s. and h. by 1st wife. On his father's afsd. invasion, in 1685, he offered to serve against him, placing himself in the hands of King James. This King, however, he soon afterwards deserted, and assisted the Prince of Orange in his expedition against him to his utmost power. In 1689 he was admitted as EARL OF ARGYLL [S.] into the convention of estates [S.], made P C. 1 May, and, on 5 June in that year, his father's *attainder* was *rescinded* From 14 Dec. 1694 until his death, he was an Extraordinary Lord of Session. He commanded a regiment, chiefly of his own clan, in Flanders, and was Col. of the (Scottish regt.) 4th troop of Horse Guards 1696-1703. A Lord of the Treasury [S.] 1696-1703 On 23 June 1701, he was *cr.* DUKE OF ARGYLL, MARQUESS OF KINTYRE and LORN *(sic)*, EARL OF CAMPBELL AND COWALL, VISCOUNT OF LOCHOW and GLENYLA, LORD OF INVERARY, MULL, MORVERN and TIRIE [S.], with rem. to his

---

that the office had been held and the duties well discharged by the grantee's father and grandfather ; and in the charter of 1625 it is stated that the predecessors of the Earl had for ages past exercised this office. On the other hand the JUSTICIARYSHIP OF ARGYLL AND OF THE ISLES (comprised in this charter) were, in the strictest sense, hereditary and continued in the family till 1747 The office of GRAND MASTER OF THE HOUSEHOLD (which still continues in the family) was also confirmed by this charter as a hereditary office. (*ex inform.* G.Burnett, sometime Lyon)

(ª) Halifax remarks on this, "I know nothing of the Scotch law, but this I know, that we should not hang a dog here, on the grounds on which my Lord Argyle has been sentenced. " V G

(ᵇ) His letter written to his s. John on the morning of his execution is simple and dignified. It is printed in *Hist. MSS Com.*, various MSS, vol. v, p. 178. V.G.

heirs male whosoever. (*) He *m*, 12 Mar. 1677/8, probably at Edinburgh, Elizabeth, 3rd da of Sir Lionel TOLLEMACHE, Bart, by Elizabeth, *suo jure* COUNTESS OF DYSART [S.]. He *d.* (ᵇ) 25 Sep. 1703, at Cherton House, near Newcastle. (ᶜ) His will, made long before his creation as a Duke, in which he styles himself " Earl of Argyll, Lord Kintyre, Campbell and Lorne, " dat 26 Sep. 1690, at Inveraray, was produced 2 Oct 1703, at Edinburgh, and pr. 1 July 1704. His widow, who was *bap* 10 July 1659, at Great Fakenham, Suffolk, and who had been separated from her husband many years before his death, *d.* 9 May 1735, at Campbelltown.

DUKEDOM [S.]
II.

EARLDOM [S.]
XI.

1703

2 and 11. JOHN (CAMPBELL), DUKE OF AR-GYLL, &c. [S.], s. and h., *b* 10 Oct. 1680, at Ham House, Petersham. (ᵈ) K.T. 4 Feb. 1703/4. An extraordinary Lord of Session 1704-08. High Commissioner of the Parl. [S] 1705. He exerted himself greatly in favour of the Protestant succession, and of the Union between England and Scotland. On 26 Nov. 1705, he was *cr.* BARON OF CHATHAM, and EARL OF GREENWICH, Kent [E.]. Col. of the 4th troop of Horse Guards 1703-15 ; Col of the 3rd Regt. of Foot (or Buffs) 1707-11 ; Col of the Royal Horse Guards 1715-17, 1733-40, and Feb. to Mar. 1742 , Col. of the 3rd Horse (now 2nd Dragoon Guards) 1726-33. Brig. Gen. 1704 ; Major Gen. 1706 ; Lieut. Gen. 1709 ; Gen. 1711 ; Field Marshal 14 Jan. 1735/6. He served in the wars under Marlborough with great distinction, 1708-10. P.C. [G.B] 3 Feb. 1708/9. El. K.G. 22 Mar. 1709/10, when he resigned the Order of the Thistle, (ᵉ) inst. 22 Dec. 1710. AMBASSADOR to Charles III of Spain Jan. 1710/1. Governor of Minorca June 1712 to Apr. 1714, and 5 Oct 1714 to July 1716 ; Governor of Edinburgh Castle 1712-14. At the Council of 30 July 1714, whereby the undisputed succession of the House of Hanover was chiefly secured, he and the Duke of Somerset boldly presented themselves without having been summoned. He was one of the Lords Justices, Regents of the Realm (1 Aug. to 18 Sep. 1714),

---

(ᵃ) The patent is made out in the plural—*i e.* " *Duces* de Argyll, &c., " the word " Lorn " being spelt therein without the final " e " It is to be remarked that " the limitation of the *Dukedom* of Argyll is so expressed that the Earldom can never subsist independently of it. " (Riddell, *Scotch Peerage Law*, 1833, p. 109, note 1.)

(ᵇ) Of the black jaundice, " in the arms of his whore. " V.G.

(ᶜ) In personal qualities, one of the most insignificant of the long line of nobles who have borne that great name. " (Macaulay) Two letters to Robert Harley, of 1 and 5 Oct 1703, describe his death, and mention his " eminent parts and endowments of mind, " as well as " his vices and scandalous course of life. " V.G

(ᵈ) A letter to Robert Harley, 5 Oct. 1703, speaks of him as " a very hopeful person, being sober, thoughtful, a good husband, and having to a more than ordinary degree the promising character of being a strict observer of his word. " V G.

(ᵉ) He was the first (ordinary) Knight of the Thistle who was honoured with the Order of the Garter. See p 16, note " d. "

appointed by the King. (ᵃ) On 13 Nov. 1715, he defeated the adherents
of the exiled House of Stuart at Sheriffmuir. Lord Lieut. of Surrey
1715-16, and of cos. Argyll and Dunbarton 1715-43. On 27 Apr. 1719,
he was *cr.* DUKE OF GREENWICH [G.B.]. Lord Steward of the
Household 1718/9-25 ; Master Gen. of the Ordnance 1725-30, and Feb.
to Mar. 1742 ; Governor of Portsmouth 1730-37. (ᵇ) He *m.*, 1stly,
(cont. dat. 30 Dec 1701) Mary, da. of John BROWN, afterwards DUNCOMBE,
of St. James's, Westm., Receiver Gen. of the Excise, by Ursula, da. of
Anthony DUNCOMBE, of Drayton, Bucks She, who had been separated
from her husband, *d s.p.*, after a long illness, 16, and was *bur.* 19 Jan.
1716/7, in Westm. Abbey, aged 35. He *m.*, 2ndly, 6 June 1717, Jane (ᶜ)
(formerly maid of honour to Queen Anne, and to Caroline, Princess of
Wales), da. of Thomas WARBURTON, of Winnington, co. Chester, by Anne,
da. and coh. of Sir Robert WILLIAMS, Bart , of Penrhyn. He *d. s p.m* , at
Sudbrooke, in the parish of Petersham, Surrey, 4, and was *bur.* 15 Oct.
1743, in Westm. Abbey, when the titles of DUKE OF GREENWICH, EARL
OF GREENWICH AND BARON OF CHATHAM became *extinct.* (ᵈ) M.I. Will

---

(ᵃ) See for a list of these, note *sub* William, DUKE OF DEVONSHIRE [1707].

(ᵇ) From 1733 he was a leading opponent of Walpole, voting steadily with the
Tories and "Patriots" until the fall of that Minister in 1742 According to his
M.I. he was "a General and Orator exceeded by none in the age he lived," which
"terminological inexactitude" is versified by Pope as
> "Argyle the State's whole thunder born to wield,
> And shake alike the Senate and the Field."

                        V G.

(ᶜ) "A goodnatured, plain, honest, ill-educated woman, to whom her husband
was always devotedly attached." "Though she was very ugly he [the Duke]
thought her perfection." (Lady Waterford.) V G.

(ᵈ) Bishop Burnet's character of him, with Dean Swift's remarks thereon in
italics, is as follows :—"Few of his years have a better understanding, nor a more
manly behaviour. He has seen most of the Courts of Europe ; is very handsome in
his person ; fair complexioned , about twenty-five years old. *Ambitious, covetous,
cunning Scot, has no principle but his own interest and greatness.* " Swift also writes of
"his unquiet spirit, never easy while there is any one above him." "This great Duke
was in his political life but a petty intriguer, a greedy courtier, and a factious
patriot " (*Suffolk Correspondence*, vol. ii, p 119) He "was graceful in his figure,
ostentatious in his behaviour, impetuous in his passions, prompt to insult, even where
he had wit to wound and eloquence to confound, and what is seldom seen, a miser as
early as a hero. . . . . He had a great thirst for books, a head admirably turned to
mechanics , was a patron of ingenious men, a promoter of discoveries, and one of the
first great encouragers of planting in England. . . . . But perhaps too much has been
said on the subject of a man who had so little great either in himself or his views . .
that posterity will probably interest themselves very slightly in the history of his
fortunes." (Horace Walpole, *George II*, vol i, pp. 275-8) An excellent Memoir
of him, by Lady Louisa Stuart, was published in 1899. She describes him as very
handsome, "warm hearted, frank, honourable, magnanimous, but rash, fiery tempered,
ambitious, haughty, impatient of contradiction . . whose shining abilities, and
loftiness of mind did not prevent his harbouring the most illiberal contempt of

dat. 3 Dec. 1741, pr. 31 Oct. 1743. His widow, by whom he had five daughters, (*) *d.* aged 84, in Bruton Str., 16, and was *bur.* 23 Apr. 1767, with her husband. Will dat 31 Dec. 1750, pr. 24 Apr. 1767.

DUKEDOM [S.]		3 and 12. ARCHIBALD (CAMPBELL), DUKE

DUKEDOM [S.] III.

EARLDOM [S.] XII.

1743. 3 and 12. ARCHIBALD (CAMPBELL), DUKE OF ARGYLL, &c. [S.], br. and h male, *b.* at Ham House, Surrey (the seat of the Countess of Dysart [S.], his maternal grandmother) June 1682. Ed. at Eton, and Glasgow Univ., and at Utrecht   Gov. of Dunbarton Castle in the reign of Anne.   A Lord of the Treasury [S.] 1705-06.   One of the Commissioners for the treaty of the Union of Scotland with England.   On 19 Oct. 1706, he was *cr.* EARL AND VISCOUNT OF ILAY, (b) LORD ORANSAY, DUNOON AND ARASE [S.].   He was a REP. PEER [S.] 1707-13, and again 1715-61. An extraordinary Lord of Session 1708 till his death ; Lord Justice Gen. [S.], 1710 for life.   P C. 13 Dec. 1711.   He was a great promoter of the succession of the House of Hanover, and was Lord Clerk Register, Aug. 1714 to July 1716.   He fought and was wounded at Sheriffmuir.   Lord Lieut. of Midlothian from 1715, and of co. Haddington from 1737, till his death   Privy Seal [S], 1721-33 ; Keeper of the Great Seal [S.], 1733-61, being a steadfast supporter of Walpole's administration.   Under the Jurisdiction Act of 1747, four years after he had *suc.* to the Dukedom, he was allowed £21,000 for the hereditary offices of Justiciary of Argyllshire and the Isles, the Sheriffship of Argyll, and the Regality of Campbell. (c) Trustee of the Brit. Museum 1753 till his death.   He collected a large library, and was the builder of the Castle of Inveraray.   He *m.* (Lic. Fac. Off., 19 Jan. 1712/3) Anne, da. of Major Walter WHITFIELD, M.P. for Romney, and Paymaster of Marines.   She *d. s.p.*, in Kensington, 1, and was *bur.* 7 Sep. 1723, as "LADY ILEY," at Kensington.   He *d.* suddenly, *s.p. legit*, in London, 15 Apr. 1761, in his 79th year. (d)   Will,

women. "   She also speaks of his taking "pleasure in wit, poetry and the *belles lettres.*"   Sir Walter Scott gives a very favourable presentment of his character in *The Heart of Midlothian.*   V.G.

(a) Caroline, his eldest da and coh., wife of the Hon. Charles Townshend, was *cr.*, 19 Aug. 1767, Baroness Greenwich, which dignity became *extinct* at her death.

(b) A very interesting letter from the Earl of Mar, dat. 29 Oct. 1706, states that the title originally selected for the Earldom and Viscountcy, was Dundee, and describes the natural indignation of the Earl of Montrose that a title borne by the most distinguished cadet of his house should pass to a Campbell.   It further details the great difficulty experienced in persuading the Duke of Argyll to agree to his brother's title being changed. (*Hist. MSS. Com.,* Mar MSS., pp. 303-4)   V.G.

(c) See *ante*, p. 204, note " e. "

(d) He appears to have been very profligate, but is described, by Lady Louisa Stuart, as of " strong clear sense, sound judgment, and thorough knowledge of mankind. . .   Cool, shrewd, penetrating, argumentative, an able man of business, and a wary if not crafty politician . . . . interested in philosophical experiments, mechanics and natural history. "   He " was slovenly in his person, mysterious, not to

leaving his English property to Mrs Ann Williams, otherwise Shireburn, who had been his mistress, dat. 14 Aug. 1760, pr. May 1761.([a])   At his death the EARLDOM AND VISCOUNTCY OF ILAY, and the other Scottish honours *cr.* therewith in 1706, became *extinct*.

DUKEDOM [S.] IV. EARLDOM [S] XIII.	} 1761.	4. and 13. JOHN (CAMPBELL), DUKE OF ARGYLL, &c, [S.], 1st cousin and h. male, being s. and h. of the Hon John CAMPBELL, (who *d.* 7 Apr. 1729) of Mamore, by Eliza-beth (who *d.* 13 Apr. 1758), 1st da. of John, (ELPHINSTONE), 8th LORD ELPHINSTONE [S],

which John Campbell was 2nd s. of Archibald, 9th Earl, by his 1st wife.   He was *b* about 1693, and was a Lieut. Col. as early as 1712 , Col. of the 39th Foot, 1737-38 ; Col. of the 21st Foot 1738-52 ; Col. of the North British Dragoons (now Scots Greys) 1752-70. Brig. Gen. 1743 ; Major Gen. 1744 ; Lieut. Gen 1747 , Gen. 1765   He distinguished himself in the wars in Flanders, and at the battle of Dettingen in 1741.   Groom of the Bedchamber 1727-60.   M P. (Whig) for co. Bute 1713-15, for Elgin burghs 1715-22 and 1725-27, and for co. Dunbarton in six parliaments, 1727-61.   Governor of Limerick 1761-70. In 1761 he *suc.* his cousin in the Dukedom as h. male of the grantee under the *spec. lim.* in the patent.   REP. PEER [S] 1761-70.   P.C. 2 Jan. 1762. K.T. 7 Aug. 1765.   He *m* , 1720, Mary ([b]) (formerly Maid of Honour to the Princess of Wales), 3rd da of John (KERR, *afterwards* BELLENDEN), 2nd LORD BELLENDEN [S.], by Mary, Dowager COUNTESS DALHOUSIE [S.], 2nd da. of Henry (MOORE), 1st EARL OF DROGHEDA [I.].   She was celebrated for her wit and beauty, and obtained the post of Keeper of the Palace of Somerset House, in the Strand.   She *d* 18, and was *bur.* 23 Dec. 1736, at St. Anne's, Soho, " with unusual honours. "   He *d.* in London, 9 Nov. 1770, in his 77th year.   Will pr. Nov. 1770.

DUKEDOM [S.] V. EARLDOM [S] XIV.	} 1770.	5 and 14. JOHN (CAMPBELL) DUKE OF ARGYLL, &c. [S.], s. and h., *bap* June 1723. Was Lieut. Col. as early as 1745 ; Aide-de-camp to the King, 1755-59 ; Col. of the 56th (afterwards 54th) Foot 1755-57 ; Col. 14th Dragoons 1757-65 , Col. of the 1st Foot (Royal Regt.) 1765-82 ; Col. of the 3rd Regt.

---

say with an air of guilt, in his deportment, slow, steady, where suppleness did not better answer his purpose, revengeful, and, if artful, at least, not ingratiating.   He loved power too well to hazard it by ostentation, and money so little, that he neither spared it to gain friends or to serve them. "   (Horace Walpole, *George II*, vol. i, p. 276).   " A man of parts, quickness, knowledge, temper, dexterity and judgment, a man of little truth, little honour, little principle, and no attachment but to his interest "   (Lord Hervey, *Memoirs*, vol. i, p. 334.)   V G.

([a]) See account of this will and of the legatees therein in *Douglas*, vol. i, p. 115.
([b]) The Poet Gay calls her " smiling Mary, soft and fair as dawn. "   Horace

of Foot Guards (now Scots Guards) 1782-1806. Commander in chief in Scotland 1767-78; Major Gen 1759; Lieut. Gen 1765; Gen. 1778, Field Marshal 30 July 1796. M.P. (Whig) for Glasgow burghs 1744-61, for Dover 1765-66. Provost of Dunbarton 1754. On 22 Dec. 1766 he was *cr.* *(v.p)* BARON SUNDRIDGE of Coomb Bank, Kent [G.B.], with rem., failing heirs male of his body, to his two brothers in like manner. After his accession to the Dukedom, he was (the 1st) President of the Highland and Agric. Soc., Scotland, 1785 till his death. Lord Lieut. co. Argyll 1794-1800. He *m.*, 3 Mar. 1759, in London, Elizabeth, (*) Dowager Duchess of Hamilton [S.], 2nd da. of John Gunning, of Castle Coote, co. Roscommon, by Bridget, da. of Theobald (Bourke), 6th Viscount Bourke of Mayo [I.] She was *b.* at Hemingford Grey, co Huntingdon, and *bap.* there 7 Dec. 1733; was Lady of the Bedchamber to Queen Charlotte, 1761-84, and on 20 May 1776 was *cr.* BARONESS HAMILTON of Hameldon, co. Leicester [G.B.], with rem. of that Barony to the heirs male of her body. She *d.* 20 Dec. 1790, in Great Argyll Str., aged 57, and was *bur.* at Kilmun. He, being then the 2nd Field officer in seniority, *d.* at Inveraray Castle, 24 May, and was *bur.* 10 June 1806, at Kilmun, aged 82. (ᵇ) Will pr. Jan. 1807.

[George John Campbell, *usually spoken of as* Earl of Campbell, 1st s. and h. ap. of his father, at that time *styled* Marquess of Lorn, *b.* 17 Feb. 1763, in London, *d.* 9 July 1764, at Roseneath, co. Dunbarton.]

DUKEDOM [S.] VI. EARLDOM [S.] XV.	6 and 15.	George William (Campbell), Duke of Argyll, &c. [S.], Lord Sundridge, &c. [G.B], 2nd, but 1st surv. s. and h., *b.* at Argyll House, London, 22 Sep., and *bap.* 20 Oct. 1768. M.P (Whig) for St. Germans 1790-96. On 3 Aug. 1799 (by

the death of his uterine br, the Duke of Hamilton [S.]), he *suc.*, in right of his mother, to the Peerage as BARON

Walpole also writes of her, "Her face and person were charming lively she was, almost to *étourderie*, and so agreeable that I never heard her mentioned afterwards by one of her contemporaries, who did not prefer her as the most perfect creature they ever knew. " V.G.

(*) "It is a match that would not disgrace Arcadia . . . . besides, exactly, like antediluvian lovers, they reconcile contending clans—the great houses of Hamilton and Campbell," writes Horace Walpole, who elsewhere calls her "the picture of majestic modesty " She was of irreproachable character, and the object of the life long admiration of George III. By her two husbands she was the mother of 4 Dukes and one courtesy Earl. Her portrait was painted by Allan Ramsay. V.G.

She was the 2nd of the 3 sisters (of whom the eldest was Countess of Coventry, and the yst. *m.* Robert Travis, 6 May 1769) who "of surpassing loveliness and captivating manners long reigned supreme in the circles of the *beau monde.*" See *Romance of the Aristocracy*, by Sir B Burke, 1855, vol. i, p 63.

(ᵇ) His marriage, in Oct. 1793, at Yeovil, Somerset, with ' Lady Mary Taylor, da. of the Earl of Bective, ' is in the *Hibernian Mag.* V.G.

HAMILTON of Hameldon [G.B.]. Lord Lieut. of co. Argyll 1800-39. Was Vice Admiral of the West Coast of Scotland 1807 Pres. of the Highland and Agric. Soc., Scotland, 1819-23. Grandmaster of Freemasons [S.], 1822-24. Keeper of the Great Seal [S.] 1827-28, and 1830-39. Lord Steward of the Household 1833-34 and 1835-39, to William IV and Victoria, and P.C. 11 Sep. 1833 G.C H. (Civil) 1833. He *m.*, 29 Nov. 1810, at Edinburgh, Caroline Elizabeth (who had been, at her own suit, divorced in 1810 from the 1st MARQUESS OF ANGLESEY), 3rd da. of George Bussey (VILLIERS), 4th EARL OF JERSEY, by Frances, da. of Philip TWISDEN, BISHOP OF RAPHOE [I.]. She *d.* 16 June 1835, and was *bur.* at Kensal Green. Admon. Nov. 1835. He *d s.p.*, at Inveraray Castle, 22 Oct., and was *bur.* 10 Nov. 1839, at Kilmun, aged 71. Will pr. Jan. 1840.

DUKEDOM [S.]
VII.   ·

EARLDOM [S]
XVI.

}1839.

7 and 16. JOHN DOUGLAS EDWARD HENRY (CAMPBELL), DUKE OF ARGYLL, &c. [S], LORD SUNDRIDGE, &c. [G.B.], br. and h., *b.* 21 Dec. 1777, and *bap.* 18 Jan. 1778, at St. James's, Westm. Sometime an officer in the army. M P. (Whig) for co Argyll ([a]) 1799-1822. F.R.S. 20 May 1819. Keeper of the Great Seal [S.] 1841-46. He *m,* 1stly, 3 Aug. 1802, Elizabeth, 1st da. of William CAMPBELL, of Fairfield, co. Ayr, by his 1st wife, Sarah CUNNINGHAM, of Cambridge, New England She *d. s.p ,* 9 Aug. 1818. He *m.,* 2ndly, 17 Apr 1820, Joan, only da. and h. of John GLASSELL, of Long Niddry, East Lothian, by Helen, da. of John BUCHAN, of Letham. She *d.* 22 Jan. 1828 He *m.,* 3rdly, 8 Jan. 1831, Anne Colquhoun, widow of Dr. George Cunningham MONTEATH, of Glasgow, and 1st da. of John CUNINGHAM, of Craigends, by Margaret, da of Sir William CUNING- HAME, Bart. [S.], of Robertland. He *d.* 25 Apr. 1847, at Inveraray, aged 69. Will pr. Oct. 1847. His widow, who was *b.* 1801, *d. s.p.,* (in the Roman Catholic faith) 25 Feb. 1874, at Rutland Gate, Midx.

DUKEDOM [S.]
VIII.

EARLDOM [S.]
XVII. 1847.

DUKEDOM [U.K.]
I. 1892.

8, 17, and 1. GEORGE DOUGLAS (CAMPBELL, otherwise GLASSELL CAMPBELL), DUKE OF ARGYLL, &c. [S.], LORD SUNDRIDGE, &c., [G B.], 2nd, but 1st surv. s. and h., by 2nd wife, *b.* 30 Apr. 1823, at Ardencaple Castle, co. Dunbarton. F.R.S. 19 June 1851; Chancellor of the Univ. of St. Andrews 1851-1900; LORD PRIVY SEAL 1852-55; P.C. 4 Jan. 1853; Rector of the Univ. of Glasgow 1854-56; Pres. of the Brit. Association 1855; POSTMASTER GEN. 1855-58; K.T. 2 May 1856; LORD PRIVY SEAL (2nd time) 1859-66; Pres. of the Royal Soc. of Edin- burgh 1860-64; LL.D Cambridge, 1862; Pres. of the Highland and Agric. Soc., Scotland, 1862-66; Elder Brother of the Trinity House 1862-

---

([a]) In his later years as a peer he was a moderate Conservative, and an adherent of Peel. V.G

1900; Lord Lieut. of Argyll from 1862, and Trustee of the Brit. Museum from 1865, till death. SECRETARY OF STATE FOR INDIA 1868-74; D.C.L. Oxford, 1870; LORD PRIVY SEAL (3rd time) 1880-81. K.G. 22 Oct. 1883, inv. 15 July 1884, retaining therewith the order of the Thistle. (ᵃ) He was *cr.*, 7 Aug. 1892, DUKE OF ARGYLL [U.K.]. In politics he was reckoned a Peelite till 1855, a Liberal 1855-86, and thereafter a Liberal Unionist. He *m.*, 1stly, at Trentham, 31 July 1844, Elizabeth Georgiana, 1st da. of George Granville (SUTHERLAND LEVESON GOWER), 2nd DUKE OF SUTHERLAND, by Harriet Elizabeth Georgiana, 3rd da. of George (HOWARD), 6th EARL OF CARLISLE. She was *b.* 30 May 1824, and was Mistress of the Robes to the Queen from Dec. 1868 to Jan. 1870. (ᵇ) She *d.*, suddenly, 25 May 1878, at Carlton House Terrace, Midx., and was *bur.* at Kilmun. He *m.*, 2ndly, 19 Aug. 1881, at Danbury Palace, Essex, Amelia Maria, widow of Col. the Hon. Archibald Henry Augustus ANSON, and 1st da. of Thomas Legh CLAUGHTON, BISHOP OF ST. ALBANS, by Julia Susanna, 1st da. of William Humble (WARD), 10th LORD WARD. She *d.* 4 Jan. 1894, at Inveraray, aged 50, and was *bur.* at Cannes with her 1st husband. Will pr. at £1357 gross, and at *nil* net. He *m.*, 3rdly, 30 July 1895, at the Chapel in the Bishop's Palace, Ripon, Ina Erskine, da. of Archibald McNEILL, of Colonsay, Argyll. She was an extra Lady of the Bedchamber to Queen Victoria. He *d.* 24 Apr. 1900, (ᶜ) at Inveraray, and was *bur.* at Kilmun, aged nearly 77. Will pr. above £92,000 personalty.

DUKEDOM [U.K.]		2, 9 and 18. JOHN DOUGLAS SUTHER-LAND (CAMPBELL), (ᵈ) DUKE OF ARGYLL
II.		[U.K. 1892], DUKE OF ARGYLL, MARQUESS
	1900.	OF KINTYRE AND LORN *(sic)* [1701]; EARL
DUKEDOM [S.]		OF ARGYLL [1457]; EARL OF CAMPBELL
IX.		AND COWALL [1701]; VISCOUNT LOCHOW

(ᵃ) He was one of the (ordinary) Knights of the Thistle (of whom his ancestor, the 3rd Duke, was another) who have obtained the Garter; but, in his case, was added the *very rare* distinction of being one (out of four) of those Knights who were permitted to retain *both* orders. See *ante*, p. 16, note "d."

(ᵇ) For a list of these ladies see note *sub* MANCHESTER.

(ᶜ) He is thus described in *Gent. Mag.*, Feb. 1857. "Remarkable for an extreme juvenility of appearance, and hair which his enemies might call red. A slim person, features intelligent and regular, a good voice and excellent delivery, great confidence and self possession of manner, and considerable industry, constitute some of his characteristics." In later life he proved himself a very able man, both in politics (as a Liberal), and in other fields, but was somewhat too arrogant and cocksure. On his retirement from Gladstone's Goverment in 1881, *Punch* insinuated the Ducal surprise, that the Ministry did not instantly collapse, by putting in his mouth Macbeth's lines, "The time has been
                That when the brains were out the man would die."
He was author of a work called *The Reign of Law*, written with the object of reconciling the claims of Science and Religion. V.G.

(ᵈ) He was gazetted (on the announcement of his marriage) 25 Oct. 1870, as "John *George Edward Henry* Douglas Sutherland," which was corrected as above

EARLDOM [S.]   }   AND GLENYLA [1701]; LORD CAMPBELL
                } 1900   [1445], LORD LORNE *(sic)* [1470],
XVIII.   }   LORD OF KINTYRE [1626]; and LORD OF
                               INVERARY, MULL, MORVERN AND TIRIE
[1701], all in the Peerage of Scotland, also LORD SUNDRIDGE [1764], and
LORD HAMILTON [1776], both in the Peerage of G.B., Hereditary
Master (*) of the Royal Household [S.], 1st s. and h. by 1st wife, *b.* 6 Aug.
1845, at Stafford House, St. James's, Westm.   Ed. at Eton, and at Trin.
Coll., Cambridge   Private Sec. to his father at the India Office 1868-71
M.P. for Argyllshire (Liberal) 1868-78, and for Manchester South (Lib.
Unionist) 1895-1900.   K.T. (extra) 21 Mar. 1871.   P.C. 17 Mar. 1875.
G.C.M.G. 14 Sep. 1878.   Gov. Gen. of Canada Oct. 1878-83. (b)   Pres.
of the Royal Geog. Soc. 1884-85; Constable of Windsor Castle 1892.
Lord Lieut. of Argyll 1900 ; G C V.O. 2 Feb. 1901.   He *m*, 21 Mar.
1871, at St. George's Chapel, Windsor Castle, H.R.H PRINCESS LOUISE
Caroline Alberta,(c) 4th da of QUEEN VICTORIA.   She was *b.* 18 Mar. 1848.

Family Estates.—These, in 1883, were about 168,000 acres in co
Argyll, and about 7,000 in co. Dunbarton.   Total about 175,000 acres,
worth about £51,000 a year. (d)   *Principal residences.*—Inveraray Castle,
Argyll ; and Roseneath, co. Dunbarton

ARKLOW

        The existence of the Barony of Arklow as an Irish Peerage, though
believed in by some, can hardly be maintained.   In the elaborate account
of the Butler family given (1754 and 1789) by John Lodge, in his Peerage
of Ireland (vol. iv., pp. 1-76), the title of "Baron of Arklow" is not
even mentioned.   William Lynch, however (who may be considered as
an authority on Feudal Institutions in Ireland), classes it (p. 92) as "an
ancient feudal Barony" descending (in accordance with his views on these
"prescriptive or feudal dignities") to the heir *male*.   He contends (p. 81)
that the first holder of this "Barony" was Theobald Walter, (e) the first

---

(by the omission of the names "George Edward Henry") in the Gazette of
25 Nov following.

(*) This office was confirmed as *hereditary* in 1676.   See *ante*, p 204, note "e. "

(b) "Of pleasant, picturesque appearance, thoroughly courteous and kindly, of
reflective habits, studious tastes and no mean intellectual endowments. " (*Society in
London*, 1885, p. 17.)   Short, stout, with yellow hair, regular features, good complexion.   V.G.

(c) She and her husband have each a descent from James I of Scotland
(1394-1437).

(d) The Duke of Argyll is one of the 28 noblemen who possess above
100,000 acres in the United Kingdom, being in point of acreage (though by no
means of rental) the 11th.   See note *sub* DUKE OF BUCCLEUCH.

(e) J.H Round, in an article on Theobald Butler, in *Dict. of Nat. Biog.*, says that
he "received from John (before 1189) the fief of Arklow, afterwards confirmed to him

"Butler" [who was possessed, possibly in 1177, but certainly in 1205, of the Lordship of Arklow], and that from him it has descended to his heirs male, thereby vesting in each successive Earl of Ormonde of the house of Butler. In support of this assertion he urges (p 219) that "it continued to be enjoyed by the heir male of the Butler family, even when, under Henry VIII, the heir male had ceased to hold the Earldom," and that it was "so enjoyed by the successive heirs male who became Earls." (*) He also mentions (p 220) its recognition, under Charles II, "in various Royal instruments," and speaks of "the multiplicity of proofs and documents still to be found respecting his Lordship's [Lord Ormonde's] right, as heir male, to the ancient feudal Barony of Arklow" (p. 91). In accordance with this view the holder of this Earldom has very frequently been considered as "BARON ARKLOW OF ARKLOW" [1]

On the other hand, the claim of the family of Butler to this title (such claim having in June 1881 been specially insisted upon in a circular, issued by Lord James W. Butler (b)), has been discussed by J. Horace Round, in an able article in *Coll Gen.*, pp 42-48. He very truly observes (1) "that there is not one scrap or tittle of direct evidence to prove that a Barony of Arklow [I.] was ever *cr.*, or even that any lineal ancestor of the present Marquess ever sat as Baron Arklow in any Parl. of Ireland;" (2) that

---

by William Marshal on becoming, *jure uxoris*, Lord of Leinster. It is in virtue of this fief that Lynch and others have attempted to claim a feudal Barony for him and his descendants."

(*) In the British Museum is a curious letter from this Walter, Earl of Ormonde [1614], the h male (then imprisoned in the Fleet by James I, who had espoused the cause of the h. gen.), to Camden, running thus—"I entreated you some fortnight past to do me the favour to make search to see if Tibbot Fitz Walter was Lord Barron of Arclo, he went over in King John's time and Henry the Second's tyme. What troble you shal receave for this busness shal be thankfully requiring [*Qy.* requited?] by your loving friend, Walter Ormond and Oss."

(b) His Lordship thus, more forcibly than grammatically, ends his letter— "I may conclude by adopting the distich of the head of the De Coucy family (freely Englished)—

'I am no Duke nor Prince, I know,
I am son of the twenty fifth Lord of Arklow,'
With Lord James Wandesford Butler's compliments."

On this statement J.H.Round sensibly remarks, "*Twenty fifth Lord of Arklow* his father indeed was, but in the sense that Ingelram de Ghysnes was hereditary *Sire de Coucy*, in the sense that John Hampden is described in his epitaph as 24*th hereditary Lord of Great Hampden.*"

Even, however, in this *limited* sense one can hardly see how the title of "Lord of Arklow" can belong to the more recent Earls, to whom that "Lordship" never belonged, inasmuch as "the Lordship of Arklow, co Wicklow," appears not only, as Round shews, to have belonged to the Boleyn family, during *their* tenure of the Earldom of Ormonde [I], but to have been *completely alienated* from the Butler family after the attainder of 1715 In 1750 it was settled by Margaret, Dowager Viscountess Allen [I.], as a marriage portion for her da. the Hon. Frances Allen, spinster, with John Proby, afterwards Lord Carysfort [I.]. See will of the said Viscountess, pr. Nov. 1758.

when, in 1791, the Ormonde honours were successfully claimed by the h. male of the family, his claim to the Barony of Butler and the Barony of Arklow was disallowed by the Law officers on the ground that he did not produce " any evidence " in support of it. Moreover (3) when the h. male of the house of Butler was, 23 Feb. 1527/8, *cr.* Earl of Ossory [I.] " to compensate him for the loss of the Earldom of Ormonde," he was " duly described " as *Sir Piers Butler*, and not as Baron Arklow ([a]) which expressly militates against Lynch's statement (as above quoted) that the Barony was continuously enjoyed by the h. male. To this may be added (4) that the solitary instance quoted by Lynch out of " the multiplicity of proofs " as to the right of the h male to the Barony of Arklow, consists of the very unimportant fact of the 2nd Duke of Ormonde having been enrolled a Bencher of King's Inn, Dublin, in 1702, under the style of *(inter alia)* " *Vicecomes de Thurles et Dingle, Baro de Arklow et Louthinia,*" a singularly careless way of recording the titles of Viscount Thurles [I.], *Baron* Dingwall [S.], Baron of Arklow [I.], and Baron *Butler of Llanthony* [E.].

It appears, therefore, that nothing whatever was heard of this Barony till the year 1588, when the words " *Baro de Arclo* " appear on the Garter plate of Thomas, xith Earl of Ormonde, who *d s p.m.* in 1614, in which year also he was called Baron of Arkloe in his funeral entry in Ulster's office. These words again appear in the fun. entry of his nephew, Walter, xiith Earl, who *d.* 1622/3, as also does the title in Latin on the Garter plate, in 1661, of James, xiiith Earl, 1st Marquess, and, subsequently, 1st Duke. As the Marquess was h. male, though *not* h. gen. (which, however, his wife was) to the xith Earl, this certainly gives some force to the argument that the Barony of Arklow was a title descending to heirs *male*. Such recognitions, however (though of more value than the inaccurate record quoted by Lynch) are as nothing in comparison with the recognition contained in the patents of 1642 and 1661, wherein James the xiiith Earl (being *cr.* Marquess and Duke respectively) is styled (among other titles) LORD BARON OF ARKLOW, as he is also in letters patent 2 Apr. 1662, restoring to him the co. of Tipperary (see *Lodge*, vol. iv, p. 51, note) ([b]) Yet even this recognition *in letters patent* of the existence of a Barony of Arklow, can only be held, on the most favourable hypothesis, to constitute a creation of that date, and cannot therefore in any case be appealed to after the extinction of the male issue of the person so recognised, which in this instance took place 17 Dec. 1758, at which date any Barony of Arklow, constituted by the " recognitions " of 1642, 1661 and 1662, must be considered as having become *extinct*.

The decision of the House in 1791 (above referred to), in which the claim of " John Butler, Esq. " to the title of Earl of Ormond and Ossory, Viscount of Thurles, Baron Butler and Baron of Arklow [I.] was allowed

([a]) This is from an article by J H Round (in *Coll. Gen.*, pp. 84-91) on " the Earldoms of Ormond [I.]; " see p. 89 thereof

([b]) J.H.Round has collected evidence, in his paper on the baronies of Mowbray and Segrave, in *Studies in Peerage and Family History*, showing the worthlessness of such recognitions in Letters Patent. V.G.

as to the Earldoms and Viscountcy ONLY, is entirely in accordance with this view, and it was probably held by the Law officers of the Crown that no such Barony was vested in the family of Butler, when, ten years later, the title was granted as a Peerage [U.K.] to a s of the reigning monarch

At the same time it must be borne in mind that the Butler family was not promoted to an Earldom till 1328, (ª) and that if there were, at that period, Baronies, in the sense of Peerage dignities, existing in Ireland, it is more than probable that some Barony (ᵇ) (whether under the name of "BUTLER," "LE BOTILLER," "ARKLOW" or "CARRICK") was vested in this leading House, and, if so, such Barony, according to *Lynch* would have been a prescriptive dignity descendible to heirs male. In this case such Barony (whatever its name) would be vested *de jure* in the Marquess of Ormonde [I.], but, in the present state of our knowledge of this intricate subject, the matter must remain only one of opinion.

i.e. "ARKLOW IN IRELAND," Barony (*H.R.H. Prince Augustus Frederick*), *cr.* 1801 with the DUKEDOM OF SUSSEX, which see , *extinct* 1843.

i e. "ARKLOW," Barony (*H.R.H. Prince Leopold*), *cr.* 1881 with the DUKEDOM OF ALBANY, which see.

ARLINGTON (ᶜ)

BARONY.	I. SIR HENRY BENNET, of Euston, Suffolk, 2nd s. of
I. 1665	Sir John B., of Dawley, Midx., by Dorothy, da. of Sir John
and	CROFTS, of Saxham, Suffolk (which Henry was a yr. br. of
1672.	Sir John Bennet, of Dawley, K.B., *cr.*, in 1682, LORD
	OSSULSTON), was *b.* about 1620. Ed. at Westm. Matric.
EARLDOM.	at Oxford (Ch. Ch.) 6 Nov. 1635, being then 15 ; was
	sometime a student there. M.A. 1642. Sec to the
I. 1672.	Duke of York 1649-58. Knighted Mar. 1656/7. Envoy
	to Madrid 1658-61. M.P. for Callington 1661-65.

Keeper of the Privy Purse 1661. P.C. 15 Oct. 1662. Sec. of State

(ª) *i e.* the date of the Earldom of *Ormonde* The question as to the Earldom of *Carrick* [I.], of which the creation charter was 1315 (the year *before* the Earldom of Kildare), is ably discussed by J.H.Round in his article on "the Earldoms of Ormond" (see previous p., note "a"), who comes to the well sustained conclusion that the Carrick charter "was simply inept "

(ᵇ) A full account of the holders of this Barony will be given under the name of " BUTLER ; " beginning with Theobald Fitz Walter, who may be considered as the 1st Baron, as on him Henry II conferred the honourable office of Chief Butler, an office which of itself would probably confer, or imply, the rank of a BARON, and which henceforth gave the name to the family. Under the name of Butler or Le Botiller (without any territorial designation) these Barons appear in every roll of Parl. to which they were summoned, and under this name in like manner the grant of the Earldom of Carrick [I.] was made, in 1315, to the 7th Baron, as also that of the Earldom of Ormonde [I.] in 1328, to his son, the 8th Baron.

(ᶜ) Usually called *Harlington*, a parish near Hounslow, Midx

1662-74. *Cr.* D.C.L. Oxford 28 Sep 1663; On 14 Mar. 1664/5, he was *cr.*
BARON ARLINGTON of Arlington, Midx., (ª) with a *spec. rem.*, failing
his issue male, *to the heirs of his body.* (ᵇ) Postmaster Gen. 1665 till his
death. In 1670 he was one of the five principal members of the Council
for foreign affairs (ᶜ) to whom alone the King revealed his policy. He
was also one of those sent to Holland to treat with Louis XIV concerning
a peace with the States. On 22 Apr 1672, he was *cr.* BARON ARLING-
TON of Arlington, Midx., VISCOUNT THETFORD, Norfolk, and
EARL OF ARLINGTON, with a similar *spec. rem.*, (ᵈ) and in default of
heirs of his body, with a further *rem.* to his br., Sir John Bennet, K B.,
abovenamed, and the heirs male of his body. El. K.G. 15, and installed
(by proxy) 22 June 1672. Lord Chamberlain of the Household from
1674, and Grand Master of Freemasons from 1679, till death. Lord Lieut.
of Suffolk 1681-84, during the minority of the Duke of Grafton. He

(ª) The arms of Bennet, Earl of Arlington, were Gules with a bezant between
three demi-lions silver, bearings which were granted by Camden to Sir Thomas
Bennet, the Lord Mayor. (*ex inform.* Oswald Barron.) V.G.

(ᵇ) Dugdale, in his MS. additions to his Baronage, states that this patent was
surrendered before the granting of that of 1672, but this is apparently a mistake, as he
is styled Baron Arlington in the 2nd patent. G.E.C For the curious reason alleged
for his not caring to be called Lord Bennet, see *Cal. State Papers Dom.*, 1664-65,
pp. 247, 257. "Sec. Bennet will not have his own name in his title to avoid any
appearance of evil in his future lady, Lady Bennet being of too famous reputation in
the world." V.G.

(ᶜ) What Macaulay calls "the whimsical coincidence" of the initial letters of
their names, *i e.* Clifford, Ashley, Buckingham, Arlington and Lauderdale, forming the
Arabic word "Cabal" has led to its being inseparably associated with them. Though
1673 is the earliest date given for the use of the word in Murray's *New Eng. Dict.*,
it occurs as early as 27 Apr. 1660, and probably much earlier, being said to be derived
from the Hebrew word "Kabbala" Of its members, says Hume (vol. vi, p. 9, edit.
1848), "Arlington was the least dangerous either by his vices or his talents. His
judgment was sound, though his capacity was but moderate, and his intentions were
good, though he wanted courage and integrity to persevere in them. Clifford and he
were secretly Catholics." Lord Clarendon gives him a somewhat contemptible
character as being "unversed in any business," one "who had not the faculties to
get himself beloved," &c.

> "Long with the royal wanderer he roved,
> And firm in all the turns of fortune proved,
> Such ancient service and desert so large
> Well claimed the royal household for his charge."
>
> (*Absalom and Achitophel*, pt. ii)

He figures as 'Eliab' in the poem, and the next lines refer to his daughter
being allied "To David's stock, and made young Othniel's bride," 'David' being
Charles II, and 'Othniel' Grafton.

"Lord Arlington speaks well and hath pretty slight superficial parts I believe,"
writes Pepys, on 24 Feb. 1666/7. V G

(ᵈ) It is difficult to account for the extensive limitation in 1665. As to that in
1672, the King had probably in view the match of the little heiress (*expectant*) with
his own son, which took place about three months later.

purchased the estate of Euston, Suffolk, from the family of Fielding, and the plot of land lying west of St. James's Park, Midx. (whereon he built Arlington House), from Hugh Audley, Registrar of the Court of Wards, the well known miser. He *m.*, soon after Mar. 1664/5, Isabella, da. of Louis DE NASSAU, BARON OF LECK AND BEVERWAET, in Holland, by Elisabeth, da. of Jean, COUNT OF HORNES, SEIGNEUR DE KESSEL. He *d. s.p.m.*, 28 July 1685, aged 67, at Arlington House, afsd., and was *bur.* at Euston. His widow *d.* 18, and was *bur.* 25 Jan. 1717/8, in her 87th year, at Euston. Will pr. Feb. 1717/8.

II. 1685.   2. ISABELLA, DUCHESS OF GRAFTON, and *suo jure* COUNT-ESS OF ARLINGTON, *&c.*, only da. and h., wife of Henry (FITZROY), 1st DUKE OF GRAFTON, K.G., to whom (when he was aged 9 and she about 4 years) she was *m.*, 1 Aug. 1672, and again 6 Nov. 1679. He *d.* 9 Oct. 1690, and was *bur.* at Euston, aged 27. She *m.*, 2ndly, 1698, (Lic. Bp. of London, 14 Oct. 1698, to marry at Whitechapel, he aged about 24, and she about 25) Sir Thomas HANMER, 3rd Bart. (*a*) He *d. s.p.*, 5 May 1746. She *d.* 7 Feb. 1722/3, in her 56th year.

III. 1723.   3. CHARLES (FITZROY), DUKE OF GRAFTON, *&c.*, who had *suc.* his father as such in 1690, and who *suc.* his mother as EARL OF ARLINGTON, *&c.*, in 1722/3, only s. and h. See "GRAFTON," Dukedom of, *cr.* 1675, (under the 2nd Duke), in which title the *Earldom and the two Baronies of Arlington* and the *Viscountcy of Thetford* became *merged.*

ARMAGH (*b*)

See "CHAWORTH OF ARMAGH," Viscountcy [I.] *(Chaworth)*, *cr.* 1627, *extinct* 1644.

See "ROKEBY OF ARMAGH," Barony [I.] *(Robinson)*, *cr.* 1777, *extinct* 1883.

i.e. "ARMAGH" Earldom [I.] (*H.R.H.* Prince *Ernest Augustus*), *cr.* 1799 with the DUKEDOM OF CUMBERLAND, which see.

ARMSTRONG OF CRAGSIDE

BARONY.	
I. 1887 to 1890.	WILLIAM GEORGE ARMSTRONG, only s. of William ARMSTRONG, Alderman, of Newcastle-upon-Tyne, by Anne, da. of William POTTER, of Walbottle Hall, Northumberland, was *b.* at the Shieldfield in Newcastle, 26 Nov., and *bap.* Dec. 1810, at All Saints there. Ed. at Bishop

---

(*a*) He was Speaker of the House of Commons 1713-15, and editor of Shakespear. V.G.

(*b*) Turlough Lynach O'Neill asked to be appointed President of Ulster, and to be *cr.* Earl of Armagh, and Baron of the Benburbe, 4 July 1579. A patent creating him Baron of Clogher, and Earl of Clanconnell, had passed the Seal 18 May 1578. He never assumed any of these titles, and in 1587 petitioned to be *cr.* Earl of Omagh for life. For fuller particulars see *sub* CLANCONNELL. V.G.

Auckland Grammar School   He was in practice as a solicitor until 1844, but subsequently became eminent as an engineer; was inventor of the hydraulic crane, and of the celebrated Armstrong guns; F.R S. 7 May 1846 ; Engineer of Rifled Ordnance to the War Department, 1858-63 ; knighted 23 Feb. 1859; C.B. (Civil) 25 Mar. 1859 ; President of the British Association, 1863, and of the Institution of Civil Engineers, 1882, and thrice President of the Institution of Mechanical Engineers ; was founder of the Elswick Works, and Chairman of that Company, *cr*. LL.D. of Cambridge, 1862 ; and D.C.L. of Oxford 21 June 1870, and of Durham, 1882 ; Grand Officer of the order of St. Maurice and Lazarus of Italy, 1876 ; Knight Commander of the Dannebrog of Denmark, of Charles III of Spain, and of Francis Joseph of Austria.   Sheriff of Northumberland, 1883 ; and on 6 July 1887, being a Liberal Unionist, was *cr*. BARON ARMSTRONG OF CRAGSIDE,(ᵃ) Northumberland.(ᵇ)   Hon. Master in Engineering, Dublin, 1892.   He *m*., 1 May 1835, Margaret, da. of William RAMSHAW, of Bishop Auckland.   She *d. s.p.*, 31 Aug. 1893, in her 86th year, at Jesmond Dene House, near Newcastle-upon-Tyne. Will pr. at £120,972.   He *d.* at Cragside, 27, and was *bur.* 31 Dec. 1900, at Rothbury, aged 90, when the peerage became *extinct*.   Will pr. above £1,399,000 gross, and above £1,232,000 net, leaving all save £7000 and an annuity of £2000 p.a., to his nephew, William Henry Armstrong Fitzpatrick WATSON-ARMSTRONG, who was *cr*, 4 Aug. 1903, BARON ARMSTRONG OF BAMBURGH AND CRAGSIDE.

Family Estates —These, in 1883, consisted of 2,265 acres in Northumberland, worth £6,606 a year   *Principal Residences :*—Cragside, near Rothbury, and Jesmond Dene, near Newcastle, both in Northumberland.

ARRACAN

See "AMHERST OF ARRACAN in the East Indies, " Earldom *(Amherst)*, *cr*. 1826.

ARRAN (in Scotland)

EARLDOM [S.]	1. THOMAS BOYD, (ᶜ) *styled* MASTER OF BOYD, s. and
1. 1467	h. ap. of Robert, 1st LORD BOYD OF KILMARNOCK [S.],
to	Governor of Scotland 1466-69, by Mariot, da. of Sir
1469.	Robert MAXWELL, of Calderwood, was, by his father's
	influence, *m*., before 26 Apr 1467, to Mary, 1st da. of

(ᵃ) The arms of Armstrong, Lord Armstrong of Cragside, were Gules a jousting spear fessewise gold, the head silver, between two right arms in armour fessewise, the elbows bent, the open hands bare.   (*ex inform.* Oswald Barron)   V G.

(ᵇ) He was one of the 8 " Jubilee " Barons *cr*. that month   For a list of these see note *sub* CHEYLESMORE

(ᶜ) John Paston writes of him as " the most corteys, gentylest, wysest, kyndest, most compenabyll, freest, largeest, most bowntesous, knyght..   Herto he is one the lyghtest, delyverst, best spokyn, fayrest archer ; devowghtest, most perfyghte and trewest to hys lady of all the knyghtys that ever I was aqweyntyd with. "   V.G

JAMES II, and sister of the reigning monarch (then a minor) JAMES III.
The island of Arran, within the Sheriffdom of Bute, was given as her
dower, and by charter, 26 Apr. 1467, he was *cr.* EARL OF ARRAN
[S.], and sat in Parl. as such 16 Oct. following.   He proceeded to Denmark in 1469 to escort Margaret of Denmark to Scotland for her espousal
to James III, but, during his absence, that King had become alienated
from him, and he had to fly his country, and was *attainted* 22 Nov. 1469,
as also were his father, and his uncle, Sir Alexander.   He was in England
at a later date, and is said to have *d.*, about 1473, at Antwerp.   M.I. (ª)
His wife, who was *b.* about 1450, *m.*, 2ndly (she being still under 21, and
her new husband about 70), in 1468, as his 2nd wife, by the King's wish,
("although her husband Thomas BOYD was neither dead nor divorced
from her") (ᵇ) James (HAMILTON), 1st LORD HAMILTON [S.], who *d.*
12 Nov. 1479, and whose s. by her was *cr.*, in 1503, EARL OF ARRAN [S.]
as below.   She *d.* about May 1488.

II. 1503.   1. JAMES (HAMILTON), LORD HAMILTON [S.], s. and h.
                 of James, LORD HAMILTON [S.], by his 2nd wife, Mary,
previously wife of Thos. BOYD, EARL OF ARRAN [S.] abovenamed, and
da. of JAMES II.   He *suc.* his father 12 Nov. 1479, being then about
four years old.   In 1502 he was sent to Denmark to aid in a naval
expedition against Sweden.   He was P.C. in 1503, when he was sent to
conclude a marriage between James IV and Margaret, da. of Henry VII;
after which, by charter, 11 Aug. 1503, he was *cr.* EARL OF ARRAN
[S.], his cousinship to the King being therein recited. (ᶜ)   In 1513, before
Flodden, he was in command of a Scottish fleet against England, but effected
nothing.   On the death of the King at Flodden, he yielded his claim to be
appointed Regent, to Albany, by whom he was, in 1517, made one of the
Lords of Regency.   He commanded the army for the King against Lennox

---

(ª) James Boyd, his only s and h , was restored to the estates of the family on
14 Oct. 1482   He appears to have been recognized as Lord Boyd in 1482, though
not as Earl of Arran, but *d.* young and unm. in 1484, leaving Margaret, his only
sister and h., who *m.*, 1stly, Alexander (Forbes), 4th Lord Forbes [S.], and 2ndly,
David (Kennedy), 1st Earl of Cassillis [S.].   She was living 1516, but *d. s.p.*

(ᵇ) Gordon, *Hist of Sutherland*, p. 76.   The *Dict of Nat Biog* gives the
account, usual in peerages, that his *widow m.* Lord Hamilton in 1474.   *Scots Peerage*
also discredits the earlier date, and considers that she *m.* about 1473/4.   V.G.

(ᶜ) The original limitation was to heirs male of the body of the grantee, but
possibly it was altered on 13 Jan. 1512/3, when the limitation of the lands and Baronies
of Hamilton, Machanshire, &c , was extended to several of his bastard sons and the
heirs male of their bodies, with rem. to others therein specially named , with a final
rem. to the nearest h. male whosoever of the grantee bearing the name and arms of
Hamilton   Four days afterwards three of these bastard sons were legitimated on the
ground that the Earl " had no heirs of his body lawfully procreated to succeed to him in
his inheritance, and in consideration of his propinquity to the King, &c. "   See also
another charter granted, 1540, to the 2nd Earl.

at Linlithgow, 4 Sep. 1526. He *m.*, 1stly, (ª) shortly before 28 Apr. 1490, when he was aged about 15, and she about 13, Elizabeth, widow of Sir Thomas Hay (s. and h. ap. of Lord Hay of Yester), da. of Alexander (Home), 2nd Lord Home, by his 2nd wife, Nichola, da. and h. of George Ker, of Samuelstown. (ᵇ) From her he obtained a divorce in the Eccles. Court, Glasgow, 16 Nov. 1504, on the ground that her 1st husband, Sir Thomas Hay, though then dead, had been alive (though supposed to be dead) at the time of her 2nd marriage. (ᶜ) He *m.*, 2ndly, between 11 and 23 Nov. 1516, Janet, widow of Sir Robert Livingston, of Easter Weemyss, da. of Sir David Beaton, of Creich, Comptroller of Scotland. She *d.* about 1522. He *d.* between 26 Mar. and 21 July 1529, at his place of Kinneil. Will dat. 26 Mar. 1529.

III. 1529.   2. James (Hamilton), Earl of Arran, &c. [S.], s. and h. by 2nd wife. He accompanied James V into France in 1536. On 15 Sep. 1540, he had a new charter of the Earldom of Arran, &c. [S.], to him and the heirs male of his body, with rem. to his br. and other persons of the name of Hamilton, in like manner, successively, whom failing, to his nearest heirs bearing the arms and name of Hamilton. On the death of the King in 1542, he was chosen Regent of Scotland, and, on 13 Mar. 1542/3, was declared Second person of that realm and heir presumptive of the Crown. As Regent he tried to trim between the two parties, but ultimately favoured the Reformers. In June 1548, when the Queen was sent to France, he was made, in that Kingdom, a Knight of the Order of St. Michael, and on 8 Feb. 1548/9 received from Henry II of France the grant of the Duchy of Châtellerault, in Poitou, by reason of which he is supposed, by some, to have acquired a hereditary French title, (ᵈ) as DUC DE CHATELLERAULT. In 1554 he re-signed the Regency to the Queen-mother. He opposed the match of the Queen with Darnley, and consequently had to leave the Kingdom 1565-69, but he returned to oppose the Regency of Moray and Lennox, though finally he submitted to the Regent Morton, 23 Feb. 1572/3. He *m.*, shortly before 23 Sep. 1532, Margaret, 1st da. of James (Douglas), Earl of Morton [S.], by Catharine, illegit. da. of James IV. He *d.* 22 Jan. 1574/5,

---

(ª) He is usually, but wrongly, said to have *m.*, 1stly, Beatrice, da. of John (Drummond), 1st Lord Drummond [S.], by Elizabeth, da. of Alexander (Lindsay), Earl of Crawford, but she was his mistress, and by her he had a da., Margaret, who *m.* Andrew (Stewart), Lord Ochiltree. V.G.

(ᵇ) She is, in Wood's *Douglas*, erroneously said to be sister (not da.) of this lord, but for proof that she was sister to Marion, Countess of Crawford [S], to George Lord Home [S], to John Home, the Abbot, &c., see *Hist. MSS. Com.*, 12th Rep., App., part viii, pp. 157 (240-242) and 161 (255). V.G.

(ᶜ) There seems to have been some doubt as to the validity of this divorce, possibly because the 1st marriage was never consummated. The decree was, however, confirmed 11 Mar. 1509/10. She *d* in 1544. V.G.

(ᵈ) The matter of the Dukedom of Châtellerault is fully discussed in Appendix B at the end of this volume

at Hamilton. (*) Will pr. 16 June 1576 at Edinburgh. His widow was living 24 May 1579.

IV. 1575 to 1581,   3. JAMES (HAMILTON), EARL OF ARRAN &c. [S.],
and 1586 to   s. and h. (b) *b.* 1537 or 1538. In May 1543 nego-
1609.   tiations were in progress for his marriage with the
Princess Elizabeth. Being taken prisoner by the murderers of Cardinal Betoun, he was deprived, by Act. of Parl. 14 Aug. 1546, of all right of succession, until he was free. In 1554 he was commander of the Scots Guards in France. In 1560 he was again suggested by the Lords of the Congregation as a husband for the afsd. Elizabeth, when Queen [E.], and, in 1561, he openly aspired to be husband of Mary, Queen of Scots. Soon afterwards, however, he was declared to be *insane*, notwithstanding which, he was imprisoned 9 Apr. 1562, and in 1579 was included in the attainder of his brothers, whereby his *titles* became *forfeited*, and so continued for six years, till the act of forfeiture was repealed, 10 Dec. 1585. During this period, however, he, in 1581, *resigned the Earldom of Arran* [S.] in favour of James Stewart (as mentioned below), which resignation was "reduced" by the Court of Session (c) in 1586 " as the act of a person incompetent in consequence of insanity," whereby he was *restored* to his honours. (d) He *d. s.p.*, Mar. 1609, aged about 71.

V. 1581   1. JAMES STEWART, of Bothwellmuir, 2nd s. of Andrew,
to   2nd LORD OCHILTREE [S.], by Agnes, da. of John CUNN-
1585.   INGHAM, of Caprington, and grandson of Andrew, 1st
Lord Ochiltree [S], by Margaret, da. (by Beatrice, his 1st wife) of James (HAMILTON), 1st EARL OF ARRAN [S.]. He served the States of Holland against the Spaniards, returned in 1579 to Scotland, and was made, by the King, a Gentleman of the Bedchamber, P.C., Capt. of the Guard, and tutor to the insane Earl of Arran [S.] above mentioned. Under pretence that he was the lawful h. of that family, and that the children of the abovenamed James (Hamilton), 1st Earl of Arran by his *second* wife (from whom sprang the succeeding Earls), were illegitimate, he obtained, 22 Apr.

(a) He is said to have been of gentle nature, but appears to have been fickle and vacillating, and without any convictions either in politics or religion. V.G.

(b) According to *Douglas*, vol. i, p. 702, the French Dukedom of Châtellerault did not descend to him, having been resumed by the Crown of France.

(c) See Hewlett's *Jurisprudence*, p. 24, where the absolute supremacy of the Court of Session in adjudicating on Scottish Peerages is recognized, and where it is stated that " There can be no doubt that, on sufficient cause, *the Court of Session had jurisdiction* to reduce a resignation, and, if a resignation were reduced, *to reduce all titles* flowing from, or grounded upon it. "

(d) He is stated, in 1592, to be " married to this Lord Glamis' aunt, " but nothing is known of any such match. He appears to have been " crackbrained and fantastic " rather than actually insane. V.G.

1581, a grant of the *comitatus* of Arran, the Baronies of Hamilton, &c., and on 28 Oct. 1581, was *cr* EARL OF ARRAN, LORD OF AVANE and HAMILTON [S.], to him and his heirs male His influence over the King having become supreme, he was appointed CHANCELLOR OF SCOTLAND, Sep. 1584, LIEUT. OF THE REALM, &c. He fled, however, after the taking of Stirling, was declared an enemy to his country, and was *attainted* in Nov. 1585. He *m.*, 6 July 1581, (*) Elizabeth, recently wife of Robert (STEWART), EARL OF LENNOX, afterwards EARL OF MARCH [S.], against whom she had obtained a decree of nullity of marriage, 19 May 1581, and formerly widow of Hugh (FRASER), LORD LOVAT [S.], being 1st da. of John (STEWART), 4th EARL OF ATHOLL [S.], by his 1st wife, Elizabeth, da. of George (GORDON), 4th EARL OF HUNTLY [S]. Her rapacity equalled that of her husband She *d.* "miserablie" in Sep 1595. He, after his disgrace, lived (as Capt. Stewart) on his own estate in Ayrshire, but returned to Court in 1592, where he was well received by the King. He *d.* 5 Dec. 1595, being assassinated by Sir James Douglas, of Parkheid, at Symontown, co. Lanark, in revenge for the death of his uncle, the 4th Earl of Morton.

VI. 1609. 4. JAMES (HAMILTON), MARQUESS OF HAMILTON, EARL OF ARRAN, and LORD HAMILTON [S.], nephew and h. of the (ivth) 3rd Earl of Arran, being s. and h. of John Hamilton, 1st Marquess of Hamilton [S.], to whose peerage he had *suc.* in 1604, which John was next br. of James, the insane Earl of Arran [S] abovenamed, and had been *cr.*, *v.f.*, 17 Apr. 1599, Marquess of Hamilton, Earl of Arran, &c. [S.] He *d* 2 Mar 1624/5, aged 36.

For fuller particulars see "HAMILTON," Marquessate and Dukedom of [S.]

(*) This is the date always given, and is doubtless correct *The Scots Peerage* gives no place, particulars, or authority, but states that the marriage was 'hurriedly arranged,' the reason therefor being shown by the birth of a child, 8 Jan. 1581/2, for which premature event the parents had to do ecclesiastical penance. A letter, dated 25 Feb. [1587] mentions the Earl's *approaching* marriage with "Athole's sister," as also that of the Earl of Angus with "Jean Lyonne," which latter event took place in July 1587. The "approaching" ceremony must have been of a confirmatory character.

Fontenay, writing to the Queen of Scots, 15 Aug 1584, describes him and his wife, and their influence over James VI as follows :—"D'argent et la grandeur sont les moyens de la gaigner, estans propres instruments pour se servir de leur ambition et avarice Et luy et elle également ont l'esprit vif pénétrant fin, convoiteux de bien et grandeurs, haultain, hardy à entreprendre et capable de beaucoup d'affaires, bref qui possèdent si avant le Roy que la plus part du people et des seigneurs estime véritablement qu'il a esté par eulx ensorcelé. "

Calderwood calls her "a meete matche for suche a spous, depending upon the response of witches, and enemie to all human societie." V G

In 1585 the Earl submitted a 'Protest' or 'Renunciation,' to Parl bearing on the legitimacy of Walter Stewart of Morphie. (*ex inform.* M.J.Shaw Stewart).

VII. 1625.   6. JAMES (HAMILTON), MARQUESS OF HAMIL-
          TON, EARL OF ARRAN, &c. [S.], s. and h. On
12 Apr. 1643, he was *cr.* DUKE OF HAMILTON, MARQUESS
OF CLYDESDALE, EARL OF ARRAN, (ª) &c. [S.], with a
spec. rem. He *d. s.p.m.*, 9 Mar. 1649. (ᵇ)

[CHARLES HAMILTON, *styled* EARL OF ARRAN, s. and h. ap. He
d. unm. *v.p.*, and was *bur.* 30 Apr. 1640, in Westm. Abbey.]

VIII. 1649.   7. WILLIAM (HAMILTON), DUKE OF HAMILTON,
          MARQUESS OF CLYDESDALE, EARL OF ARRAN,
&c. (under the above mentioned patent of 1643,) MARQUESS OF
HAMILTON (1599) and EARL OF ARRAN (1503, under the
charter of 1540), all in the Kingdom of Scotland, br. and h. male.
He *d. s.p.m.*, 12 Sep. 1651, when the Marquessate of Hamilton [S.],
cr. 1559, became *extinct;* but the EARLDOM OF ARRAN [S.], *cr.* 1643,
devolved, with the Dukedom of Hamilton and the other honours
[S.] of that date, *under the spec. rem.*, on his niece, while the *ancient*
EARLDOM OF ARRAN [S.], *cr.* 1503, and regranted 1540, has since
that time remained *dormant.* (ᶜ)

For fuller particulars see "HAMILTON, Marquessate and Dukedom of [S.]"

---

i.e. "ARRAN" Earldom [S.] *(Hamilton)*, *cr.* (ª) 1599 with the MAR-
QUESSATE OF HAMILTON [S.], which see.
     i.e. "ARRAN" Earldom [S.] *(Hamilton)*, *cr.* (ª) 1643 with the DUKE-
DOM OF HAMILTON [S.], which see.

ARRAN AND CAMBRIDGE

     i.e. "ARRAN AND CAMBRIDGE" Earldom [S.], conferred 12 Apr. 1643
with the DUKEDOM OF HAMILTON [S.] and again mentioned in the *novodamus* of that Dukedom, 10 Aug. 1698, under which it still (1909) exists.
It was not, however, included in the life grant of the Dukedom, 20 Sep.
1660, to the husband of the *suo jure* Duchess, the only Earldoms granted
therein being "ARRAN LANARK AND SELKIRK."

     (ª) It seems to have been very usual in Scotland to repeat all the minor titles in
the patent whereby an Earl or Marquess was advanced to a higher title. This, if
there were no resignation, would be a new creation. (*ex inform.* R.R.Stodart, sometime Lyon Clerk Depute.)
     (ᵇ) After his death, his 1st da., Anne, afterwards (1651) *suo jure* (under the
spec. rem. of 1643) Duchess of Hamilton &c. [S.], became the *heir of line* to the Earls
of Arran [S.], but the charter of 1540 seems to render such Earldom a *male* fief.
     (ᶜ) The h. male of the body of the 2nd Earl of Arran [S.], to whom the regrant
in 1540 had been made, was in 1651 his great grandson James (Hamilton), 2nd Earl
of Abercorn [S.], but neither he nor any of the succeeding Earls took any steps
towards establishing their claim to the ancient Earldom of Arran [S.]. See tabular
pedigree shewing such descent and representation on p. 4.

ARRAN (in Ireland)

EARLDOM [I.]

I. 1662
to
1686.

I. LORD RICHARD BUTLER, 5th s. of James, 1st DUKE OF ORMONDE, by Elizabeth, *suo jure* BARONESS DINGWALL [S.], was *b.* 15 June 1639, and was *cr.*, 13 May 1662, BARON BUTLER OF CLOUGH-GRENAN, VISCOUNT TULLOGH and EARL OF ARRAN [I.], (*) with a *spec. rem.*, failing the heirs male of his body, to his younger br , John Butler. P.C. [I.] 26 Aug. 1663. Alnager of Ireland, 2 Sep. 1666 till his death. In 1673 he distinguished himself in the sea fight with the Dutch, for which he was *cr.*, 27 Aug 1673, BARON BUTLER of Weston, co. Huntingdon [E.]. D.C.L. Oxford 6 Aug. 1677. He was Custos Rot. of co. Carlow in 1682, and on 2 May 1682, was made Deputy to his father, then Lord Lieut. of Ireland, during his absence ; and on 10 Sep. 1684, being Col of a Regiment of Guards, he was made Marshal of Array [I.], and held that office till his death. He *m.*, 1stly, before 16 Mar. 1666/7, Mary, *de jure* (ᵇ) *suo jure* (after 1660) BARONESS CLYFTON DE LAYTON BROMSWOLD, sister and h. of Esme, DUKE OF RICHMOND, and da. of James (STUART), DUKE OF RICHMOND [E.] and DUKE OF LENNOX [S.], by Mary, da of George (VILLIERS), DUKE OF BUCKINGHAM. She, who was *bap.* 10 July 1651, at St. Martin's-in-the-Fields, was h. to her only br., who *d.* a minor, and unm., 14 Aug 1660. She *d s.p.*, 4 July, and was *bur.* 19 Aug 1668, (ᶜ) at Kilkenny Cathedral, aged 16. He *m*, 2ndly, before 7 (ᵈ) June 1673, Dorothy, da. of John FERRERS, of Tamworth Castle, by Anne, da. of Sir Dudley CARLETON. He *d.* in London, *s p.m.s.*, 25, (ᵉ) and was *bur.* 27 Jan. 1685/6, in Westm. Abbey, aged 46, when (his abovenamed br., John, EARL OF GOWRAN [I], having *d.* before him *s.p.*) *all his peerage honours* became *extinct.* Will dat. 7 Jan 1677/8, "intending to embark for England," pr. 13 Jan. 1686/7. His widow *d.* 30 Nov. 1716. Will dat. 23 Mar. 1716, in which she directs to be *bur.* at Tamworth, near her father, pr. 7 Dec. 1716.

[JAMES BUTLER, *styled* LORD TULLOGH, s and h. ap., *bap.* 19 Feb. 1673/4 at Westm. Abbey, *bur.* there 10 Oct. 1676.]

(*) He had purchased the Isles of Arran, co Galway, from Erasmus Smith.

(ᵇ) According to the decision as to that dignity, 7 Feb. 1674.

(ᶜ) His mother writes, in Sep. of that year, of finding him "in great sadness. " The Duke writes, 16 Mar. 1666/7, " My son Arran's wife grows a lovely person .. I never saw so much discretion in so few years, nor so little humour or trouble in any of her sex of what age soever. " V.G.

(ᵈ) His mother writes in May 1673 of " the marriage near concluded of my son Arran to the daughter of one Ferrars, one of the best and ancientest families of England, formerly Earls of Essex. The portion is £12,000, and but one sickly young man between her and £3000 *p.a.* after his father's decease. " This young man, her only br., Sir Humphrey Ferrers, *d. s p.m.*, being drowned in the Trent, Sep. 1678 V.G.

(ᵉ) " He had a singular address in all kinds of exercises, played well at tennis and on the guitar, and was pretty successful in gallantry. " (Gramont, *Memoirs*) V.G.

30

[Thomas Butler, *styled* Lord Tullogh, 2nd, but 1st surv. s. and h. ap., *b.* before Nov. 1680, *bur.*, an infant, 7 June 1881, at Christ Church, Dublin.]

[Thomas Butler, *styled* Lord Tullogh, 3rd, but 1st surv. s. and h. ap., *bur.*, an infant, 24 Aug. 1685, at Kensington, Midx.]

II. 1693   1. Charles Butler, nephew of Richard (Butler),
to   Earl of Arran [I.] abovenamed, being 2nd and yst. surv.
1758.   s. of Thomas Butler, *styled* Earl of Ossory (the s. and
      h. ap. of James, 1st Duke of Ormonde), by Amelia, 1st
da. of Henry de Nassau, Baron of Beverwaet and Auverquerque, in
Holland, was *b.* 4 Sep. 1671. On 8 Mar. 1693, he was *cr.* (ᵃ) BARON
OF CLOUGHGRENAN, VISCOUNT OF TULLOGH and EARL
OF ARRAN [I.]. On 23 Jan. 1693/4 he was *cr.* BARON BUTLER
OF WESTON, co. Huntingdon [E.]. He was Lord of the Bedchamber
to William III, 1699-1702. Col. of the 6th Horse (now 5th Dragoon
Guards) 1697-1703 ; Col. of the 3rd Troop of Horse Guards 1703-15 ;
Brig. Gen. 24 Jan. 1702 ; Major Gen. 1 Jan. 1704 ; Lieut. Gen. 22 Apr.
1708 ; Master of the Ordnance [I.], Nov. 1712-14 ; Chancellor of the
Univ. of Oxford, 10 Sep. 1715 ; D.C.L. 14 Sep. 1715 ; and High Steward
of Westminster, 28 Feb. 1715/6, holding both these offices till his death.
By Act. of Parl. [E.] 1721, he was enabled to repurchase the family estates
(forfeited by the attainder of his br., the Duke of Ormonde, in 1715), which
were thus preserved in the family. On 2 Jan. 1721/2 he was *cr.* DUKE OF
ARRAN [E.] by the *titular* James III of England. (ᵇ) Nothwithstanding
this *titular* creation, and that (some 23 years subsequently) by the death of his
br., James, 2nd Duke of Ormonde [I.], *s.p.m.*, on 16 Nov. 1745, he became
de jure DUKE OF ORMONDE, &c. [I.], (ᶜ) he appears never to have styled
himself otherwise than Earl of Arran [I.], (ᶜ) the popular idea at that time
being that the *Irish* titles (as well as the English) of his said br. had been
forfeited by the act of attainder of the *English* Parl., 20 Aug. 1715. He
m., (Lic. Fac. Off. 26 May 1705) 3 June 1705, at Oatlands, Weybridge,
Surrey, Elizabeth, 4th da. and coh. of Thomas (Crew), 2nd Lord Crew of
Stene, by his 2nd wife, Anne, da. and coh. of Sir William Airmine, Bart.,
of Osgodby. She *d.* 21 May 1756, in her 77th year, and was *bur.* (as
Countess of Arran) at Stean, co. Northampton. M.I. Will dat. 6 June
1732, pr. with nine codicils 2 Feb. 1757. He *d. s.p.*, in his 88th year, (ᵈ)

(ᵃ) See the preamble to this creation in *Lodge*, vol. iv, p. 64, note.

(ᵇ) For a list of Jacobite Peerages, see Appendix F at the end of this volume.

(ᶜ) On 20 Apr. 1750, by the death, unm., of his niece, Lady Elizabeth Butler
(the only remaining issue of his br. the 2nd Duke), he became entitled to the Barony of
Dingwall [S.], which was at that time (like the Irish titles) considered (erroneously),
to have been forfeited by the *English* attainder in 1715. The right to this Barony
passed on his death (1758) to the heirs general, *i.e.* his sisters and their issue. See
" Dingwall, " Barony [S.], *cr.* 1609.

(ᵈ) " An inoffensive old man, the last male of the illustrious house of Ormond ;

at his lodgings next the Tilt yard, Whitehall, 17, and was *bur.* 23 Dec.
1758, at St. Margaret's, Westm., when *all the Honours* [I. and E.] which
had been conferred on him, as also the DUKEDOM AND MARQUESSATE OF
ORMONDE [I.] (which had been conferred on his grandfather, whose sole
remaining issue male he was) became *extinct;* while the right to the EARL-
DOM OF OSSORY AND ORMONDE, &c. [I.], devolved on the h. male of the
body of the grantee. See "ORMONDE," Earldom of [I.]. Will dat.
19 Jan. 1757, pr. with two codicils 17 Jan. 1759. (ª)

III. 1762   1. SIR ARTHUR GORE, Bart. [I.], of Castle Gore, co.
                Mayo, s. and h. of Sir Arthur Gore, Bart. [I.], of the
same, by Elizabeth, 1st da of Maurice ANNESLEY, of Little Rath, co. Kil-
dare, *b.* 1703 ; Matric. 5, and ent. 15 Nov. 1718 as Fellow Commoner at
Trin. Coll., Dublin, B.A. 1722 ; adm. to Mid. Temple 25 July 1724 ;
M.P. for Donegal borough 1727-58 ; Barrister King's Inns, Trin. 1730;
Sheriff of co. Wexford 1738, *suc.* his father 10 Feb. 1741/2, was made P.C.
[I.] 27 May 1748, and, on 15 Aug. 1758, was *cr.* BARON SAUNDERS
OF DEEPS, co. Wexford, and VISCOUNT SUDLEY OF CASTLE
GORE, co Mayo [I.].   He took his seat in the House 16 Oct 1759
On 12 Apr. 1762, he was *cr.* EARL OF ARRAN OF THE ARRAN
ISLANDS, co. Galway [I.], and took his seat, as such, four days later.
Custos Rot. of co Mayo, 1762 till his death.   He *m,* 16 Mar. 1730/1,
at St. Mary's, Dublin, Jane, widow of William WORTH, of Rathfarnham,
only da. and h of Richard SAUNDERS, (ᵇ) of Saunders Court, co. Wexford,
by (—) his wife.   She was *bap.* 20 Dec. 1704, and *d.* 20 Mar 1747.
He *d.* 17 Apr. 1773, aged 70.   Will pr. 1773, Prerog. Court [I.].

IV. 1773.   2. ARTHUR SAUNDERS (GORE), EARL OF ARRAN, &c.,
                [I.], s. and h., *b.* 25 July 1734   Sheriff of co. Wexford
1757, and of co Mayo, 1765, as Viscount Sudley.   M.P. for Donegal
borough 1759-60, 1768-73, and for co. Wexford 1761-68   P.C. [I.] 1771.
Custos Rot. of co. Mayo, 1773-86.   Took his seat in the House 26 Apr.
1774.   On 5 Feb. 1783, he was nom. K.P., being one of the 15 original
knights of that order. (ᶜ)   He *m.,* 1stly, (mar. lic. Prerog. Ct. [I.] 12)

---

much respected by the Jacobites, who had scarce any partizans left in whom they
might venerate even a noble name. " (Horace Walpole.)   " The Earl of Arran
is a person of middle size, (much about the same height with his br. the Duke) and is
of a sanguine complexion, and seems to be as modest as he is goodnatured. "
(T.Hearne, 1715)   V.G.
          (ª) Bishop Burnet's character of him, with Dean Swift's remarks thereon in
italics, is as follows—" of very good sense, though seldom shews it ; of a fair complexion, middle stature, towards 40 years old.   *This is right, but he is the most negligent
of his own affairs.* "
          (ᵇ) He was s. of Joseph S., by Jane, da. of Henry Whitfield
          (ᶜ) THE IRISH ORDER OF ST. PATRICK was instituted by George III on
5 Feb. 1783, consisting of 15 Knights Companions who were then mentioned ; but,

14 July 1760, (ª) Catharine, only da. of William (ANNESLEY), 1st VISCOUNT GLERAWLY [I.], by Anne, da. of Marcus (BERESFORD), 1st EARL OF TYRONE [I.]. She *d.* 23 Nov. 1770, in Dublin. He *m.*, 2ndly, in 1771, Anne, da. of the Rev. Boleyn KNIGHT, of Otley, co. York. She *d.* shortly before Oct. 1779. (ᵇ) He *m.*, 3rdly, in Feb. 1780/1, at Dublin, Elizabeth, da. of Richard UNDERWOOD, of Dublin, by Christiana, da. of Caleb GOOLD, of Dublin. He *d.* 8 Oct. 1809, aged 75, in Ireland. (ᶜ) Will. pr. 1809, Prerog. Court [I.]. His widow *d.* 5 June 1829, in Brussels. (ᵈ) Will pr. June 1829.

V. 1809.   3. ARTHUR SAUNDERS (GORE), EARL OF ARRAN, &c.
                [I.], s. and h., by 1st wife, *b.* 20 July 1761. M.P. (Tory) for Baltimore, 1783-90, and for co. Donegal 1800-06. His claim to vote at the election of Rep. Peers [I.] was admitted 30 Mar. 1821. He *m.*, 29 Dec. 1787, at St. Geo., Han. Sq., Mary, 1st and only surv. da. and h.

---

of these, the Earl of Antrim [I.] desiring to relinquish the stall *intended* for him (being unwilling to resign, as was required of him, the order of the Bath), letters patent were passed nominating the Earl of Arran to be one of the original Knights of St. Patrick in his room. These fifteen original Knights were as under, *viz* :—

1. H.R.H. PRINCE EDWARD, 4th s. of the King, *afterwards* (1799) DUKE OF KENT AND STRATHEARN [G.B.], and EARL OF DUBLIN [I.].

2. William Robert (Fitz Gerald), DUKE OF LEINSTER [I.].

3. Henry Smyth (de Burgh), EARL OF CLANRICARDE [I.], *cr.* Marquess [I.] 1789.

4. Thomas (Nugent), EARL OF WESTMEATH [I.].

5. Murrough (O'Brien), EARL OF INCHIQUIN [I.], afterwards *cr.* MARQUESS OF THOMOND [I.] 1800.

6. Charles (Moore), EARL OF DROGHEDA [I.], afterwards *cr.* MARQUESS [I.] 1791.

7. George (de la Poer Beresford), EARL OF TYRONE [I.], afterwards *cr.* MARQUESS OF WATERFORD [I.] 1789.

8. Richard (Boyle), EARL OF SHANNON [I.].

9. James (Hamilton), EARL OF CLANBRASSIL [I.].

10. Richard (Colley-Wellesley), EARL OF MORNINGTON [I.], afterwards *cr.* MARQUESS WELLESLEY [I.] 1799.

11. Arthur Saunders (Gore), EARL OF ARRAN [I.].

12. James (Stopford), EARL OF COURTOWN [I.].

13. James (Caulfeild), EARL OF CHARLEMONT [I.].

14. Thomas (Taylour), EARL OF BECTIVE [I.].

15. Henry (Loftus), EARL OF ELY [I.]. He was out of the Kingdom at the time of the installation (27 Mar. 1783), and died shortly afterwards (8 May 1783) without having been invested or installed.

(ª) Mrs. Delany's *Memoirs*, under date 18 July 1760. V.G.

(ᵇ) *Gent. Mag.* V.G.

(ᶜ) *Gent. Mag.* states that "he was a nobleman of the mildest disposition, and most elegant manners." V.G.

(ᵈ) Her 2nd da., Cecilia Letitia, widow of Sir George Buggin, by Royal lic., 2 Mar. 1834, took the name of UNDERWOOD (being her mother's maiden name), and on 10 Apr. 1840 was *cr.* Duchess of Inverness. She *d. s.p.*, 1 Aug. 1873.

of Sir John Tyrrell, of Heron, Essex, 5th and last Bart. [E. 1666], by
Mary, only da. and h. of Thomas Crispe, of Parbold Hall, co Lancaster.
She, who was sometime Governess to Princess Charlotte of Wales, and "a
leader in the fashionable world," d. 31 Aug. 1832, aged 65, at Bognor, and
was bur at Felpham, Sussex. Will pr. Oct. 1832   He d. s.p., at his seat,
Arran Lodge, near Bognor, 20, and was bur. 28 Jan. 1837, near there, at
Felpham afsd., aged 75. Will pr. Mar. 1837.

VI. 1837.   4. Philip Yorke (Gore), Earl of Arran, &c. [I.],
                     nephew and h , being s. and h. of Col. the Hon. William
John Gore, sometime Master of the Horse to the L. Lieut (by Caroline,
yst. da. and coh of Sir Thomas Pym Hales, Bart.), which William John
was next br., of the whole blood, to the last Earl, and d. 15 Jan. 1836.
He was b. 23 Nov. 1801, at Dublin Castle. In Aug. 1820 he was appointed
Attaché to the legation at Stockholm, in Feb. 1825 to the embassy at Paris,
and in June 1826 to that at Lisbon.   Secretary of legation at Buenos Ayres
1827-37, and Chargé d'affaires there from Oct. 1832 to Oct. 1834.   K.P.
6 May 1841.   He m., 1 Mar. 1838, at Freshfield, Somerset, Elizabeth
Marianne, 2nd da. of Gen. Sir William Francis Patrick Napier, K.C.B,
by Caroline Amelia, 2nd da. of Gen. the Hon. Henry Edward Fox.
He d. 25 June 1884, in his 83rd year, at 27 Chesham Str., Belgrave Sq.,
Midx. His widow d. there 27 Apr. 1899. Will pr above £45,000.

VII. 1884.   5. Arthur Saunders William Charles Fox (Gore),
                     Earl of Arran, Viscount Sudley and Baron Saunders
[I.], s. and h., b. 6 Jan. 1839, at Bath, Somerset. Ed. at Eton. Attaché
at Hanover, 1859; at Stuttgardt, 1860, at Lisbon 1861, and at Paris 1863.
Retired Dec. 1864   Sheriff of co. Donegal 1863-64, as Viscount Sudley.
Spec. Commissioner of Income tax 1865-81. Commissioner of Customs
1883-84. On 7 Nov. 1884 he was cr. BARON SUDLEY OF CASTLE
GORE, co Mayo. [U K.]   His claim to vote at the election of Rep.
Peers [I.] was admitted 4 Dec 1884.   In politics he was a Liberal. (ª)
Lord Lieut. of co. Mayo 1889 till his death. El K.P. 9 and inst 15 Mar
1898.   He m., 21 Feb. 1865, at St Geo., Han. Sq, Edith Elizabeth
Henrietta, sister and, in her issue, sole h. of Robert, 4th Earl of Roden
[I.], and da. of Robert Jocelyn, styled Viscount Jocelyn, by Frances
Elizabeth, da. of Peter Leopold Louis Francis (Cowper), 5th Earl Cowper.
She was b. 10 Feb. 1845, and d 3 Oct 1871, at Basle, aged 26   He m.,
2ndly, 29 July 1889, at the Royal Chapel, Cumberland Lodge, Windsor
Park, Winifred Ellen, widow of the Hon. John Montagu Stopford, yst.
da. of John Reilly, of St. Bridget's, co. Dublin, by Augusta, da. of Edward
(Sugden), 1st Baron St. Leonards. He d. at 16 Hertford Str., Mayfair,
14, and was bur. 19 Mar. 1901, in Windsor Cemetery, aged 62. Will pr.
May 1901, gross £44,800, net £36,700. He was suc. by his only s. and
h., who is outside the scope of this work.

(ª) In 1886, like almost every Liberal peer, excepting a few placemen, he
remained a Unionist when Gladstone broke up the party by giving way to the Irish
demand for Home Rule. V G.

Family Estates.—These, in 1883, consisted of about 30,000 acres in co. Mayo, and about 7,000 in co. Donegal. Total about 37,000 acres of the yearly value of about £10,000 ; exclusive of about 7,000 acres let on perpetual leases, and of fisheries, &c. *Principal Residence.*—Castle Gore, co. Mayo.

ARRASS

See "Macdonnell and Arrass," Barony [S.] *(Macdonnell)*, cr. 1660, *extinct* 1680.

ARTAGH

See "De Freyne of Artagh, co. Roscommon," Barony *(French)*, cr. 1839, *extinct* 1856.

ARUNDEL (ª) (co. Sussex)

EARLDOM. 1. Roger de Montgomery (who, in right of his 1st
I. 1067. wife, Mabel de Bellême, da. of William Talvas, was
    Lord of Alençon, Seez, &c, in Normandy), having during the invasion of England, remained, as Regent, in Normandy, came over thence, for the first time, with King William, in Dec. 1067, and, at the Christmas festival, was *cr.* an EARL, receiving, among other large

---

(ª) The old Sussex tradition is that—" Since William rose and Harold fell,
       There have been Earls of Arundel. "
(See *N. & Q*, 6th Ser , vol. ix, 341.) And such (unless, perhaps, for a year or so) is the case if only for " *of*" we read " *at*," leaving it as an open question whether the earlier Earls were not (more properly) Earls of a greater territory, though styled as " *of Arundel* " from their chief residence
 In treating of these Earls the Editor has followed Vincent in considering Roger de Montgomery (to whom the Conqueror gave the Castle of Arundel) to have been the 1st Earl of Arundel. Whether or no he and his sons (undoubted *possessors* of Arundel) are *numbered* among such Earls, is not, however, very material.
 A truly marvellous work entitled *The early Genealogical History of the House of Arundel,* has been written by " John Pym Yeatman, Esq , Barrister at Law, &c." Herein is contained " An account of the origin of the families of Montgomery, Albini, Fitz Alan and Howard *(sic)* from the time of the Conquest of Normandy by Rollo the Great. " Such researches are beyond the scope of *this* publication, and so far as it concerns the actual *Earls of Arundel* the Editor has not generally seen his way to adopt the conclusions arrived at. The enormous amount of documents examined, as also the labour that must have been undergone by its author, is appalling, yet must it be said of this voluminous work (as was said of that of a still more eminent author eighteen centuries earlier), that therein are " *things hard to be understood.* " An accurate and lucid history of the great family of d'Aubigny is yet to be written, and it is to be regretted that it was not undertaken by Chester Waters, as belonging to that period in which his genealogical knowledge was so great.

grants from the Conqueror, about one third of the county of Sussex, including the city of Chichester and the CASTLE OF ARUNDEL. (ª) By this last grant he *may* be considered to have become EARL OF ARUNDEL, according to the remarkable admission (ᵇ) in 1433 on the claim to that

(ª) This formed the *Honour of Arundel*, which consisted of the rapes of Arundel and Chichester, being two out of the six rapes into which Sussex is divided. It contained, besides the city of Chichester and the Castle of Arundel (as abovenamed), $84\frac{1}{2}$ knights' fees, ten hundreds (with their forests, woods and chases), three lordships (Halnaker, Petworth and Midhurst), eighteen parks and seventy-seven manors. See Tierney's *Hist. of Arundel*, p. 12. G.E.C.

It is pointed out however to the Editor by J.H.Round that, according to the latest view of archæologists, the castle may have been erected by Roger of Montgomery himself, after obtaining possession of the Honour. V.G.

(ᵇ) The claim to the Earldom as being one *by tenure* of the Castle of Arundel was made by John Arundel, who had been sum. to Parl. in 1429, the writ being directed "Johanni Arundell' de Arundell' Chivaler " In 1433 (11 Hen. VI) he petitioned [as Earl of Arundel] to be sum. to Parl. and considered as Earl of Arundel, a dignity or name united and annexed to the Castle and Lordship of Arundel, for time whereof memory of man was not to the contrary—a peculiar and distinct claim (as stated in the *First Report on the Dignity of a Peer*, p 406), " not connected with any general, but asserting a special right, and which being founded on prescription, was to be supported by evidence of constant and immemorial enjoyment of the asserted right, which right if not shown to have been so constantly enjoyed, the title by prescription failed This claim, though opposed by John (Mowbray), Duke of Norfolk, was admitted by the Crown, notwithstanding that the assertion of the constant annexation of the title to the Castle of Arundel could not have been sustained, had it been (which it was not) made the subject of an enquiry. " (*Courthope*, p. 30)

The claim then of 1433 was, as is stated above, "admitted by the Crown, or so far admitted as that the assertion in the petition is made the consideration (with others not connected with the question) for the King's acceding to it, with a saving, nevertheless, of the right of the King, of the Duke of Norfolk (who, being a coh of the Earls of Arundel, had opposed the Earl's claim) and of every other person ; which saving clause, as is remarked in the *First Report on the Dignity of a Peer*, ' was that species of saving which is deemed in law illusory, operating nothing ' " (*Courthope*, p. xx). See also Tierney's *History of Arundel* (vol. i, p. 106), where the judgment is set out, reciting " that Richard Fitz Alan was seized of the Castle, Honour and Lordship [of Arundel] in fee , that, by reason of his possession thereof, he was, without other reason or creation, EARL OF ARUNDEL, &c. "; and stating also, that "the King, contemplating the person of the present claimant, now Earl of Arundel, &c , has, with the advice and assent of the Prelates, Dukes, Earls and Barons in this present Parl. assembled, *admitted* John, now Earl of Arundel, to the place and seat anciently belonging to the Earls of Arundel in Parl. and council. "

Almost similar words are used in the Act of Parl obtained in 1627, which, in form of a petition to the King recites that the *Earldom of Arundel* had been real and *local* from the time whereof the *memory of man* was not to be contrary, and had, from the time aforesaid, been used and enjoyed by the petitioner and such of his ancestors as had possessed the Castle of Arundel, &c. Now it is to be noted that the claimant of 1433 alleged that his ancestors, the possessors of Arundel, were *Earls of Arundel*, both *before*, as well as after, *the Conquest* Fortunately, however, King Harold and his father, Earl Godwin, have not to be included, and still less a long shadowy race of

Earldom. (ª) At all events he was frequently so styled, though, occasionally, he is styled EARL OF CHICHESTER. Dugdale and many later writers consider him to have been EARL OF SUSSEX. (ᵇ) On the dismemberment of Mercia, in 1070, another Earldom was conferred on him, by the grant of nearly the whole of Shropshire (with, apparently, *Palatine* authority), together with the Castles of Shrewsbury and Montgomery, and the Lordship of the West Marches. (ᶜ) He was thenceforth generally known as EARL OF SHREWSBURY, though occasionally (according to modern views, more correctly) as EARL OF SHROPSHIRE. He is the " COMES ROGERUS " of the

---

Earls extending upwards towards (even if not including) primeval man. The words " memory of man " must, of course, be read in their strict legal significance, as indicating the reign of Richard I, so that the Act of 1627 (and, possibly, the admission of 1433 also) would not apply to any Earl of Arundel, *prior* to 1189.

The Redesdale Committee remarks on these proceedings that they " ought to be considered as an anomaly influenced by political views, and decided apparently without much discussion, and without the assistance of the Judges. " Moreover the assertion of fact by the claimant as to the Earldom having always depended on possession of the Castle in the past " seems not to have been true, and not to have been made the subject of enquiry when the question was decided. " For a similar case of a charter creating a peerage, and setting out, as facts, unfounded statements of the grantee, see the Barony of LISLE, *cr.* 1444, in the same reign.

(ª) In the Berkeley Case (1861) it was argued for the petitioner that Arundel was and is an earldom by tenure. But this contention was discussed and rejected by Lord St. Leonards, Lord Chelmsford, and Lord Redesdale in their judgments on the Berkeley claim (VIII H.L.C. 52, 101-2, 104, 137-8, 144-5). They agreed that, whatever might have been the original *status* of the dignity, it has not been held by tenure since the Act of 3 Car. I has governed its descent. (*ex inform.* J.H.Round.) V.G.

(ᵇ) In an article, in the *Archæological Journal*, on the "Earls of Sussex," by J.R. Planché (Somerset Herald, 1866-80), the writer (after stating that *without the third penny* of the pleas of the county "the greatest authorities have denied that a man *could* be an English Earl, " argues that Earl Roger, having the custody of Chichester, may (as did the Earl in the time of King Edward) have had a *third* of the annual rental of the city of CHICHESTER, and might, therefore, with good reason, be considered EARL OF CHICHESTER. Planché states, however, that, on the other hand (to quote a parallel case) William de Warenne, who, in the Domesday survey, held the borough of *Lewes* and the Rape of Pevensey, *receiving a third* of the profits thereof, is never styled Earl (either of *Lewes*, or of Sussex) but simply William de Warenne.

The fact, however, appears to be that Roger de Montgomery was AN EARL (*i.e.* Earl of some one county or more) and that (as was usual in those early times) his *Earldom* was *indifferently styled* either from his county of Sussex, or of SHROPSHIRE, or from the Castles of ARUNDEL, CHICHESTER, SHREWSBURY, or MONTGOMERY, which were, respectively, the " caput " of the Earldom. (See J.H.Round's *Geoffrey de Mandeville.*)

A parallel case, in which the Earl of a county is indifferently styled either from the capital or from his stronghold therein, is that of William, *Earl of Gloucester*, who, on 29 Sep. 1155, attests a charter to Shrewsbury Abbey as *Earl of Bristol* (Eyton's *Itin. of Henry II*, p. 12). (*ex inform.* J.H.Round.)

(ᶜ) The *(palatine)* Earldom of Chester (by gift of the county thereof), was, with similar power and privileges, granted, at the same time, to Gherbod the Fleming.

Domesday survey, where, of course, no *local* designation is attributed to him   He *d.* 27 July 1094

II. 1094.   2. HUGH (DE MONTGOMERY), EARL OF SHREWSBURY, *&c.*, and EARL OF ARUNDEL, 2nd s., (ª) but h. to his father's English possessions.   He *d. s.p.*, 1098.

III. 1098   3. ROBERT (DE BELLÊME), COUNT OF ALENÇON afsd.
to   (having, in 1082, *suc.* his mother as such) was permitted,
1102.   by William II, to succeed to the English Earldoms of his
        yr. br.   He became therefore EARL OF SHREWSBURY, *&c.*,
and EARL OF ARUNDEL.   He was exiled and *attainted* in 1102, whereby *all his English honours* and estates became *forfeited* to the Crown. (ᵇ)

IV. 1138 or 1139   1. WILLIAM D'AUBIGNY (ᶜ) *de Albiniaco*, or in the
to   Anglo-Latin of Dugdale and other writers, DE AL-
1176.   BINI, (ᵈ) surnamed 'the strong hand,' (ᵉ) Lord of the
        manor of Buckenham, Norfolk, s. and h. of William
D'A., (ᶠ) of the same, (*d.* 1139) (ᵍ) *Pincerna Regis*, (ʰ) by Maud, da. of Roger LE BIGOD, was *b.* early in the reign of Henry I.   On his marriage with the Queen Dowager (for which see below), he acquired with her, in

(ª) Sir Henry Howorth, in *The Academy* for June 1882, alleges that he was 1st. s.
(ᵇ) For fuller particulars of the foregoing see "SHREWSBURY," Earldom of, *cr.* 1071.
(ᶜ) Aubigny is in the arrond of Coutances, dept. of La Manche.   It was confiscated in 1204 by Philip Augustus, who made known by his charter that " terra comitis de Harundel " (and that of many others) was " de dominico nostro " (*Bibl. Nat*, MS. 8408, 2, 2, B, f 179 d)   He gave it to the Count of Ponthieu, and in the Register of Philip Augustus it is stated that " Comes Pontivi tenet Albigni de domino Rege per servicium duorum militum et dimidii "   Marie, Countess of Ponthieu, gave it back to Louis VIII, in July 1225.   (*Trésor des Chartes, Ponthieu*, I, no. 46).   (*ex inform.* G.W.Watson).   V.G.
(ᵈ) Of course no one ever bore such a name as de Albini ; the modern surname Daubeney indicates what the name of these Earls was.   V G
(ᵉ) This was from (or, more probably, itself suggested) the legend that, at Bourges in France, in 1137 (the year previous to his marriage) he had pulled out the tongue of a lion let loose to destroy him by Adeliz, the Queen Dowager of France, out of jealousy from his having rejected her for the sake of her namesake of England.   This tale Vincent, in his *Errors of Brooke* (Brooke having related it as fact), calls that of the " Lye-on. "
(ᶠ) He migrated from the Côtentin to England *temp.* Hen. I, as J.H.Round has pointed out.
(ᵍ) See *Chron* of Jon de Oxenedes.
(ʰ) This office of " Chief Butler " (*Pincerna*) appears, in the division of 1243, not to have followed the Manor of Buckenham in Norfolk (which was the principal estate of the *grantee*), but the Castle of Arundel, which was the " caput Baroniæ " of Earl Hugh, the *last holder*   It is now held as appendant to the Earldom of Arundel, the fees being the gold basin, ewer, and cup used by the King at the Coronation banquet.

1138 or 1139, the *Castle and Honour of Arundel*, which had been settled on her in dower,(ᵃ) whereby it may be considered that, according to the admission of 1433,(ᵇ) he became EARL OF ARUNDEL.(ᶜ)   There is conclusive evidence from various charters, that at, or about the time of, and probably soon after, his said marriage, he was recognised as EARL OF LINCOLN, and he may be assumed to have been so *cr.* in the summer of 1139.   In this year he gave shelter to the Empress Maud, at Arundel Castle, but ever after adhered to Stephen.   He can be shown to have very soon lost the Earldom of Lincoln, and in 1141 he attested a charter of Stephen as EARL OF SUSSEX, (ᵈ) (being from time to time thereafter so described, as, *e.g.* where he witnesses(ᵉ) a charter to the Abbey of Barking under that name) and may be assumed to have been so *cr.* by Stephen in 1141, after that King had regained his freedom.   Early in 1142, the Earldom of Lincoln had already passed to another, *viz.* William de Roumare.   In his own later charters he is styled, and in a charter, before 1150, of the Queen Dowager to the Abbey of Reading, she styles him EARL OF CHICHESTER.(ᶠ)   He was influential in arranging the treaty of 1153, whereby the Crown continued with King Stephen *for life*, though the inheritance thereof was secured to Henry II.   To this instrument he subscribed as "Comes Cicestrie."   Henry II, by a grant undated, but supposed to have been in 1155 (the year after his accession), *confirms* to him as " William, EARL OF ARUNDEL, the Castle of Arundel, with the whole honour of Arundel and all its appurtenances," and, by the same instrument, bestows on him the third penny of the pleas of the county of

---

(ᵃ) For evidence in a virtually contemporary MS. Chronicle (*ante* Ric. 1) that William d'Aubigny did *not* become Earl of Arundel till some time after his marriage with Queen Adeliz, and so did not take it with the Castle, see J.H.Round's *Geoffrey de Mandeville*, p. 322.

(ᵇ) See p. 231, note " b. ", but see *per contra* note by J.H.Round *sub* i Earl of Sussex.

(ᶜ) "In the elaborate discussion oɪ the title of Earl of Arundel by the Lords' committees in their Reports upon the Dignity of a Peer, it has been doubted whether even the Earldom of Arundel was ever possessed by the family of Albini, as a title of dignity.   Historians and numerous contemporary evidences have, however, constantly styled the family of Albini by the title of Earls of Arundel, and they [*i.e.* these Earls] could not with propriety be omitted in this place; nevertheless, it must be observed that the assertion made, upon the claim of John, Earl of Arundel (*temp.* Hen. VI.), that the dignity of Earl of Arundel had been constantly and invariably enjoyed by the Lords of the Castle of Arundel, cannot, under any circumstances, be maintained." (*Courthope*, p. 27).   See also observations at the beginning of the article " AUMALE " in this work.

(ᵈ) As to the different styles of his Earldom, see note *sub* i EARL OF SUSSEX.

(ᵉ) " *Testibus Matilda Regina* (shewing it was in the reign of King Stephen) *et Willelmo Comite de Sussexa* "—Confirmation charter.   Patent Roll 2 Hen. VI.   See Planché's *Earls of Sussex* referred to in note " b, " p. 232.

(ᶠ) For fuller details see Round's *Geoffrey de Mandeville*, and G.F. Warner's and H.J. Ellis's *Facsimiles of Royal Charters* &c., vol. i, 14, 27, which valuable works have been consulted and utilised in the rewriting of this article.

Sussex *unde Comes est* (ª) No doubt, however, he was more generally
known as "Earl of Arundel," and as such *(only)* he is spoken of by his
s. and h. (who styles *himself* Earl of *Sussex*) in a charter to the Priory of
Wymondham ; and as Earl of *Arundel* (only) he is described in the record
of his death in the Annals of Waverley. He was justly held in great
esteem by Henry II, and was one of the embassy to Rome in 1163/4, and to
Saxony (on the espousal of the Princess to the Duke of Saxony) in 1168
He was also in command of the Royal army in Aug. 1173, in Normandy,
against the King's rebellious sons, where he distinguished himself for his
" swiftness and velocity, " and, on 29 Sep. following he assisted at the
defeat, near Bury St. Edmunds, of the Earl of Leicester, who, with his
Flemings, had invaded Suffolk. He *m.*, in 1138 (the 3rd year of her
widowhood) Adeliz, Queen Dowager of England (widow of Henry I),
1st da. of Godefroy *à la Barbe*, Duke of Lothier (*i.e.* Lorraine Inférieure),
Count of Brabant and Louvain, by his 1st wife, Ide, da of Albert III,
Count of Namur. His wife, the Queen Dowager, retired in 1150
to a nunnery at Afflighem, in South Brabant, where she *d.*, and was *bur.*
23 Apr. 1151, aged about 48. He survived her 25 years, and *d.* 12 Oct.
1176, (ᵇ) at Waverley Abbey, Surrey, and was *bur*, with his father, at
Wymondham Priory, Norfolk.

V. 1189.   2 William (d'Aubigny), Earl of Sussex, (ᶜ) s. and
                  h., in 1176/7, was confirmed in *that* dignity, but the
Castle and Honour of *Arundel* having, in accordance with the policy of
Henry II, been retained by the Crown, on the death of the last holder, (ᵈ)

(ª) This was apparently but a *confirmation* to him of the Earldom of Sussex and
its third penny (as well as of the Honour and Castle of Arundel) which he had
enjoyed before, unless (indeed) the deed signed by him as Earl of Sussex, *temp*
Stephen (see p. 234, note " e, ") is a forgery.

Dugdale, speaking of this Earl (vol i, p 119) says :—" After the death of King
Stephen he did not only obtain [from King Henry II] the castle and honour of
Arundel to himself and his heirs, but a confirmation of the Earldom of Sussex (for
though the title of Earl was most known by Arundel and Chichester, at which places
his chief residence used to be, yet it was of the county of Sussex that he was really
Earl) by the *tertium denarium* of the Pleas of Sussex granted to him, which was the
usual way of investing such great men (in ancient times) with the possession of any
Earldom, after those ceremonies of girding with the sword and putting on the robes
performed, which have ever, till of late, been thought essential to their creation. "
See also p. 232 of this work, note " b. "

(ᵇ) For an account of this Earl and of his Earldom of Lincoln, see J.H.Round's
Geoffrey de Mandeville.

(ᶜ) For references to him as Earl of Sussex before 1189, see Benedictus, vol. ii,
p. 3, Christmas 1186, and Add. Charter 15688, before Mich 1188 *(ex inform*
H J.Ellis.) Richard I granted him the Honour after his coronation, 3 Sep. 1189,
when he is styled Earl of Sussex, and before 18 Sep. 1189, when he is styled Earl
of Arundel. V G.

(ᵈ) It certainly was not because the successor was a minor (as suggested in the
Lords' Reports on the Dignity of a Peer, vol. i, p. 410), *if* it be allowed (as in the text)

he did not obtain restoration of them till Richard I restored them to him, 27 June 1190, when (according to the admission (ᵃ) of 1433 abovenamed) he became EARL OF ARUNDEL. He was, however, styled Earl of Arundel *before* he received possession of the Castle and Honour, namely, on 18 Sep. 1189, and on 26 Nov. of the same year he witnessed King Richard's Charter as "Will. Earl of Arundel." (ᵇ) He received also at the same time, the third penny of the pleas of Sussex in the precise words of the grant made to his father. In 1191 he was made Custos of Windsor Castle, and in 1194 one of the Receivers of the money raised for the King's ransom. He *m.* Maud, widow of Roger (DE CLARE), EARL OF HERTFORD (who had *d.* 1173), da. and h. of James DE ST. HILAIRE DU HARCOUET, by Aveline, his wife. He *d.* 24 Dec. 1193, (ᶜ) and was *bur.* at Wymondham Priory.

VI. 1193.   3. WILLIAM (D'AUBIGNY), EARL OF SUSSEX, and EARL OF ARUNDEL, s. and h. He was a favourite of King John, whose concession of the Kingdom to the Pope, 15 May 1213, he witnessed, and whom he accompanied to Runnymede, 15 June 1215. (ᵈ) When, however, King John abandoned Winchester, 14 June 1216, to Louis (afterwards Louis VIII) of France, he joined that Prince, but (consistently taking the winning side) returned to his allegiance 14 July 1217, after the Royalist victory at Lincoln. Shortly afterwards he acted as JUSTICIAR, the young King, Henry III, having restored to him his forfeited possessions. He *m.* Mabel, 2nd da. of Hugh (LE MESCHIN, surnamed KEVELIOC), EARL OF CHESTER, by Bertrade, da. of Simon, COUNT OF EVREUX in Normandy. She, in her issue, was (1232) one of the four coheirs to her br. Ranulph (surnamed BLUNDEVILLE), EARL OF CHESTER. He embarked in the crusade of 1218, and was at the taking of Damietta in Nov. 1219, but *d.* at Cainell, near Rome, ("quoddam oppidulum Kainel nomine") shortly

that such successor was s. of Adeliz, for, in that case, his (said) mother would have been dead above a quarter of a century. Moreover the Earl himself had been receiving, since 1180, the third penny of the county of Sussex. See Madox, *Baronia Ang.*, p. 139. G.E.C.

At Mich. 1179, Walter de Coutances (afterwards Archbishop of Rouen) renders an account of the Honour of Arundel for the years since 1176, but from 1179 to 1189, when it was restored to the d'Aubignys, it was held, presumably for the Crown, by one of the family of Fitz Reinfred. There is evidence that Walter de Coutances was of the Fitz Reinfred family, being br., or possibly br.-in-law, of Roger Fitz R. (*Notes on Facsimile Charters*, Warner and Ellis, no. 54.) V.G.

(ᵃ) See p. 231, note "b."

(ᵇ) *Hist. MSS. Com.*, Wells MSS., vol. i, p. 309. There are not many instances of any of the d'Aubignys being styled Earl of Arundel after the death of Earl William in 1176. V.G.

(ᶜ) His death is thus entered in the annals of Waverley Abbey :—"1193 anno 5 Ric. I. obiit Willelmus Comes junior de Arundel in vigilia natalis Domini." It is curious how generally the date is wrongly given as 1196. V.G.

(ᵈ) His namesake of Belvoir became one of the sureties for the King's observance of *Magna Charta* as ' William d'Aubigny, Sheriff of Warwick and Leicester. '

PEDIGREE OF THE EARLS OF ARUNDEL, OF THE HOUSE OF AUBIGNY.

According to Courthope and the (now) received version.

According to Dugdale, the Lords' Reports, [a] *&c.*

I. William d'Aubigny, Earl of Arundel, *d.* 12 Oct. 1176. = Adeliz, the Queen Dowager, *m.* 1138, *d.* 1151, aged 48.

I. William d'Aubigny, Earl of Arundel, *d.* 12 Oct. 1176. = Adeliz the Queen Dowager.

II. William, Earl of Arundel and Sussex, *d.* 24 Dec. 1193. = Maud, widow of Roger (de Clare), Earl of Hertford, which Earl *d.* 1173.

III. William, Earl of Arundel, &c., *d.* abroad Mar. 1220/1. = Mabel, sister of Ranulph (le Meschin), Earl of Chester.

II. William, Earl of Arundel, *d.* abroad 1221. = Maud, widow of Roger, Earl of Clare.

IV, William, Earl of Arundel, &c.who, according to Dugdale, was the Earl William who *m.* Mabel, sister of the Earl of Chester, but it is certain that this lady *left issue* by her said husband. He *d. s.p.* 1224.

―

V. Hugh, Earl of Arundel, &c., *d. s.p.* 1243.

Maud, eldest da., *m.* Robert of Tatshall. Her s. & h. Robert of Tatshall, inherited the Castle and Manor of BUCKEN-HAM, Norfolk, which had been the "*caput Baroniæ*" of William d'Aubigny "*Pincerna.*"

丕

Isabel, second da. *m.* John Fitz Alan. Her s. and h. John Fitz Alan inherited the Castle and Honour of AR-UNDEL. (*See pedigree p* 253).

丕 253

Nicole, 3 da., *m.* Roger de Somery, and obtained, as her 4th share, the manor of Barrow on Soar, co. Leicester, &c.

―

Cicely *m.* Roger of Mold (*de Monte alto*) and obtained, as her 4th share, the manor of KENNING-HALL, the Castle of Rising &c. Norfolk.

―

Colette obtained lands from her uncle, the Earl of Chester, 1233, but *d.* unm., *v.f.*

―――――――――――

[a] Dugdale, *Baronage*, vol. i, p. 121, has wrongly treated William the 3rd (d'Aubigny) Earl, and his s. William the 4th Earl, as the same man, and misled the Lords' Committee on the Dignity of a Peer, who followed his version. (*ex inform.* J.H.Round.) V.G.

before 30 Mar. 1221 (ᵃ) (when the news reached England), and was *bur.* at Wymondham Priory.

VII. 1221.   4. WILLIAM (D'AUBIGNY), EARL OF SUSSEX,(ᵇ) and EARL OF ARUNDEL, s. and h.   Being just of age at his father's death he did homage for his inheritance in Apr. 1221.(ᶜ)   He *d. s.p.*, and probably unm., "adolescens" in the 4th year after his father, and a few days before 7 Aug. 1224, (ᵈ) and was *bur.* at Wymondham Priory. (ᵉ)

VIII. 1224.   5. HUGH (D'AUBIGNY), EARL OF SUSSEX, and EARL OF ARUNDEL, br. and h.   He is said to have been aged about nine years at his brother's death in 1224.   On 10 May 1235, he was of age and had seizin of all his Castles, (ᶠ) hitherto in the King's hand. (ᵍ)   His wardship was obtained by the famous Justiciar, Hubert de Burgh, Earl of Kent, 14 July 1227.   He *m.*, in 1234, Isabel, da. of William (DE WARENNE), EARL OF SURREY, by his 2nd wife, Maud, da. of William (MARSHAL), EARL OF PEMBROKE, the said Earl of Surrey having given 300 marks for the right so to dispose of him.   This same Earl also performed the office of *Pincerna* at the King's nuptials (1236) on behalf of his said son-in-law, who was still a minor and, at that time, excommunicated. (ʰ)   Notwithstanding his minority he had, in 1234, obtained, for 2500 marks, possession not only of his *paternal* estates, but also of those which he inherited by the death of his *maternal* uncle, Ranulph, Earl of Chester.   In 1242 he was one of the seven Earls who accompanied the King in his expedition to Guienne.   He *d. s.p.*, "in the flower of his

---

(ᵃ) On 30 Mar. 1221, the Sheriff of Norfolk and Suffolk was ordered to take into the King's hand the lands which were " Comitis Arundell'. " (*Fine Roll*, 5 Hen. III, *m.* 7). (*ex inform.* G.W.Watson.) V.G.

(ᵇ) " In his father's confirmation charter to Robertsbridge (Dugdale, *Monast.*, vol. ii, p. 120) he signs himself son to the 3rd Earl of Sussex, and in a Charter of King Hen. III (aᵒ 12, *m.* 6) he is called *Willelmus comes Sussex* [Qy. *Sussexie*] *quartus.* " See *Courthope*, p. 28.

(ᶜ) By writ undated, but between two others dated 12 and 21 Apr. 1221, " Willelmus de Albin' filius Comitis Arundell' " had livery of his father's lands. (*Fine Roll*, 5 Hen. III, *m.* 6). (*ex inform.* G.W.Watson.) V.G.

(ᵈ) On 7 Aug. 1224, the Sheriff of Norfolk and Suffolk was ordered to take into the King's hand the lands which were " Comitis Arundell'. " (*Fine Roll*, 8 Hen. III, *m.* 4). (*ex inform.* G.W.Watson.) V.G.

(ᵉ) See Dunstable Register.   According to Dugdale he did not die till 1234, but various entries in Close and Patent Rolls prove that this in an error.   V.G.

(ᶠ) On 8 Nov. 1233, " Hugo de Albin' frater et heres Willelmi de Albin' quondam Comitis Arundell' " fined 2500 marks for having seizin of his brother's lands (with some reservations till he reached his age), and also of those of his uncle, " R. Comitis Cestrie et Lincolnie. " (*Fine Roll*, 18 Hen. III, *m.* 11). (*ex inform.* G.W.Watson.) V.G.

(ᵍ) Patent Roll, where he is called simply " Hugo de Albiniaco. " V.G.

(ʰ) This excommunication was by Edmund (Rich, or of Abingdon), Archbishop of Canterbury (1233-45), on account of his Grace's dogs having been seized in the forest of Arundel.

youth," 7 May 1243, (ᵃ) and was *bur.* with his ancestors at Wymondham Priory. On his death the large estates of the family were divided between his four sisters (ᵇ) and coheirs, or their issue, while the EARLDOM OF SUSSEX *reverted to the Crown.* His widow (ᶜ) survived him nearly forty years, during which long period the family of Fitz Alan, though in possession of the Castle of Arundel, *never assumed the title of* EARL OF ARUNDEL. She *d.* before 23 Nov. 1282, and was *bur.* at Marham, Norfolk, in the conventual church which she had founded.

> IX. 1243.   6? JOHN FITZ ALAN, feudal LORD OF CLUN AND OSWESTRY, Salop, s. and h. of John FITZ ALAN of the same, by his 1st wife, Isabel, 2nd sister and, in her issue, coh. of Hugh, and da. of William (D'AUBIGNY), EARLS OF SUSSEX, &c., abovenamed, *suc.* his father (whom his mother had predeceased) in 1240. To him, by writ dat. 27 Nov. 1243, was awarded (in right of his deceased mother) the Castle and Honour of Arundel, whereby (according to the admission (ᵈ) of 1433 abovenamed) he must be regarded as *de jure* EARL OF ARUNDEL. He obtained possession, 26 May 1244, of his paternal estates in Salop on payment of £1000. By the title, however, of EARL of ARUNDEL he *never appears to have been known* (either in his lifetime or afterwards), although he lived 24 years after the acquisition of that Castle and Honour. In an award dat. Friday after the Circumcision 1258, he is expressly called *Dominus de Arundel* (i.e. Lord of the Honour of Arundel), and in the Fine Roll, 10 Mar. 1261/2, he is called *Baro noster*, while in his *Inq. p. m.* he is described (merely) as *Johannes filius Alani*, and the endorsement says that he held a quarter of the Earldom of Arundel. He took part in the Welsh war 1258, and, though sometimes leagued with the Barons against the Crown, was, while fighting on the Royal side, taken prisoner at the battle of Lewes, in 1264, together with the King. He *m.* Maud, da. of Theobald LE BOTILLER, [2nd BARON BUTLER [I.]], by his 2nd wife, Rohese, (ᵉ) da. of Nicholas DE

(ᵃ) On 10 May 1243, the Sheriffs of 11 counties were ordered to take into the King's hand the lands which were of "H. de Albin' Comitis Arundell'." (*Fine Roll*, 27 Hen. III, m. 4). (*ex inform.* G.W.Watson.) V.G.

(ᵇ) "Of the lands late of Hugh, Earl of Arundel, the King has assigned to Robert de Tateshall, s. of Robert de T., the eldest born of the heirs of the said Earl, the castle and manor of Buckenham [Norfolk]; to John, s. of John Fitzalan, the castle and manor of Arundel; to Roger de Sumery, who espoused Nicholaa, sister and one of the heirs of the said Earl, the manor of Barrow [on Soar, co. Leicester]; to Roger de Montaut, who espoused Cecily, 2nd sister and 4th heir of the said Earl, the castle and manor of Rising [Norfolk]." (*Pat. Roll*, 27 Nov. 1243). V.G.

(ᶜ) Her marriage was granted, 29 May 1243, to Piers, son of the Count of Geneva, and the fine if she married anyone else. (*Pat. Roll.*) V.G.

(ᵈ) See page 231, note "b."

(ᵉ) For some discussion on mediæval English names, see Appendix C at the end of volume iii.

VERDUN, of Alton, co. Stafford. (*) He *d.* 1267, before 10 Nov. Will dat. Oct. 1267. His widow *m.* Richard D'AMUNDEVILLE, and *d.* 27 Nov. 1283. He was living 1286/7.

X. 1267.   7 ? JOHN FITZ ALAN, feudal LORD OF CLUN AND
                OSWESTRY, and (according to the admission (ᵇ) of 1433 abovenamed) EARL OF ARUNDEL, only s. and h., *b.* 14 Sep. 1246. He did homage for his estates 10 Dec. 1267. He, also (as Courthope remarks), though " 22 years at his father's decease, was never known (ᶜ) as Earl of Arundel, and it is incredible that, if he had ever borne that title, as annexed to the Castle and Honour, the fact would have been omitted in the inquisition which finds him to have died seized (1272), 56 Hen. III, of that Castle and Honour *held by the 4th part of a Barony.* " He *m.* Isabel, da. of Roger DE MORTIMER, of Wigmore, by Maud, da and coh. of William DE BRIOUZE, of Brecknock. He *d.* 18 Mar. 1271/2, (ᵈ) and was *bur.* in Haughmond Abbey, Salop. His widow *m.*, before (1273) 1 Edw. I, Ralph D'ARDERNE, (living Apr. 1283) and *m.*, 3rdly, 2 Sep. 1285, at Poling, Sussex, (privately) Robert DE HASTINGS, for which marriage, having omitted to obtain the Royal lic., she was fined £1000. He was living June 1287. She was living in 1300.

XI. 1272,   8 or 1. RICHARD FITZ ALAN, feudal LORD OF CLUN
   1289,   AND OSWESTRY, and (according to the admission of
    or   1433 (ᵉ) abovenamed) EARL OF ARUNDEL, only s. and h.
   1291.   He was *b.* 3 Feb. 1266/7, and was consequently only five
                        years old at his father's death. He had seizin of his lands, 8 Dec. 1287. According to Glover (ᶠ) he was *cr.* EARL OF

(*) This Rohese's children bore her name of *Verdun* and not their father's of *Butler*. V.G.

(ᵇ) See p. 231, note " b. "

(ᶜ) These words must, Planché says, be qualified, and should run " never known *during his lifetime,* " as, in a patent of 35 Edw. I, in reference to Edmund Fitz Alan, s. of Richard, Earl of Arundel, we find the words *sub nomine Johannis filii Alani, quondam Comitis Arundelliæ, antecessoris præfati Edmundi,* which is certainly an acknowledgment, however late, that Edmund's grandfather, John Fitz Alan, *was* Earl of Arundel ;—yet in 8 Edw. I (1280) (a few years only after the death of the said John) we find his widow Isabel, to whom the custody of the Castle and Honour of Arundel was committed, spoken of, not as the widow of the Earl of Arundel, but (merely) as ' *que fuit uxor Johannis filii Alani.* "

(ᵈ) Ch. *Inq. p. m.,* Hen. III, file 42, no. 5.

(ᵉ) See p. 231, note " b. "

(ᶠ) " If Glover (a most careful and learned genealogist of the time of Elizabeth) has stated this upon good authority, which all who know his character will feel confident to be the case, it disproves Vincent's assertion that Richard Fitz Alan never had the county of Sussex. " (Planché, *Earls of Sussex.*)

Sussex ([a]) in 1289, when (being just of age) he was knighted and "received the sword of the county of Sussex" from Edward I "*ut vocatur* [*Qy ? vocetur*] *Comes ;* " but it seems more probable that this creation was as EARL OF ARUNDEL. ([b])   At all events no more is heard of the former title (Sussex) as connected with this family, but only of the title of Arundel. On 12 Feb. 1290/1 there is a grant to him as Richard de Arundel, Earl of Arundel. ([c])   In Oct. (1292) 20 Edw. I he was summoned by a writ directed to the Earl of Arundel, ([d]) and was sum. to Parl. 24 June (1295) 23 Edw. I, by a writ directed *Ricardo filio Alani Comiti Arundell'*, ranking him as *junior* to all the other Earls.   He fought in the Welsh wars 1288, in Gascony 1295-97, and in the Scottish wars 1298-1300, being present at the siege of Carlaverock in 1300.   He signed the Barons' letter to the Pope, 12 Feb. 1300/1.   He *m.*, before 1285, (when he was but 18) Alasia, ([e]) da. of Tommaso I, Marquis of Saluzzo in Piedmont [1244-1299], by Luisa, da. of Giorgio, Marquis of Ceva.   She *d.* 25 Sep 1292, and was *bur.* at Todingham Priory.   He *d.* 9 Mar. 1301/2, in his 36th year, and was *bur.* with his ancestors.

XII. 1302   9 or 2. Edmund (Fitz Alan), Earl of Arundel, s.
to   and h., *b* 1 May 1285, in the Castle of Marlborough.
1326.   His wardship was obtained by John, Earl of Surrey and
Sussex, whose granddaughter he *m*   He was knighted,

([a]) " The Earldom of Sussex must at this period have been a subject of contention between the De Warrens and Fitz Alans, for John de Warren, Earl of Surrey, was receiving, at the very time that this investiture occurred, writs directed to him as Earl of Sussex   John de Warren was perhaps the greatest noble of the time in which he lived, and his power and influence may have operated to induce Fitz-Alan to abandon his claim upon the Earldom of Sussex and to adopt that [i.e the Earldom of Arundel] by which his descendants have ever since been known. " (*Courthope*, p 29)

([b]) It is worthy of remark, in connection with the *very* doubtful right, either of his father or grandfather, to the Earldom of Arundel, that it was not till 1282, viz. sometime after their death and during this Earl's minority, that Isabel, Countess of Arundel, * widow of Hugh (d'Aubigny), died.   It would almost appear (possibly owing to the largeness of her dower) that the Earldom was not dealt with during her lifetime.   A somewhat parallel case occurs, later on, in this same family, when Richard, Earl of Arundel, who, in 1347, had suc. his maternal uncle the Earl of Surrey, did not assume the Earldom of Surrey till the death of Joan, widow of the afsd Earl, in 1361.

* Planché, in his *Earls of Sussex*, has hopelessly confused the abovenamed Isabel, the *widow*, with Isabel the *sister* and (in her issue) coh of Earl Hugh.   Had this last-named lady been alive, *she* (and not her son, grandson, and great-grandson), would (according to the decision of 1433) have been entitled to the Earldom of Arundel ; but this lady died before her husband, who himself died three years before the said Earl Hugh.

([c]) *Patent Roll,* 19 Edw. I, m. 18.   V.G.
([d]) *Placita de quo warranto,* p. 681.   V.G
([e]) Her father's sister, another Alasia, *m.* Edmund (de Lacy), Earl of Lincoln, whom see.   V.G.

32

with Edward, the King's son, and many others, 22 May 1306. On
9 Nov. (1306) 34 Edw. I, he was sum. to Parl. as EARL OF ARUNDEL, and
took part in the Scottish wars of that year. On 25 Feb. 1307/8 he officiated
as *Pincerna* (ª) at the coronation of Edward II. In 1316 he was Captain
Gen. north of the Trent. For a long time he was in opposition to the
King, and was violent against Piers Gavaston, who had beaten him in a
tournament. However, in 1321 he changed sides, and married his 1st s.
to a da. of Hugh le Despenser, being thereafter one of the few nobles who
adhered to the King. In 1323 he was Chief Justiciar of North and South
Wales. Warden of the Welsh Marches 1325. He *m.*, in 1305, while still
a minor, Alice, only da. of William DE WARENNE (only s. and h. ap. of
JOHN, EARL OF SURREY AND SUSSEX), by Joan, da. of Robert (DE VERE),
EARL OF OXFORD. Having been captured in Shropshire by the Queen's
party, he was, without trial, *beheaded* at Hereford, 17 Nov. 1326, in his
42nd year. He was subsequently attainted, when his estates and *honours*
became *forfeited*. His widow (who, in her issue was, in 1347, sole h. of
her br. John, Earl of Surrey and Sussex, and consequently of the great
family of Warenne) was living 1330, but *d.* before 23 May 1338. (ᵇ)

XIII. 1327 ? EDMUND, (ᶜ) EARL OF KENT, 6th s. of
to   Edward I, received the Castle and Honour
1330.   of Arundel, whereby (according to the ad-
               mission (ᵈ) of 1433) he may be considered to
have become EARL OF ARUNDEL. (ᵉ) He was *beheaded*
3 Sep. 1330, and, being attainted, all his honours became
forfeited, but the Castle and Honour of Arundel were retained
by his widow, on whom they had been settled.

For fuller particulars see "KENT," Earldom of, *cr.* 1321.

XIV. 1331.   10 or 3. RICHARD FITZ ALAN, called "Copped Hat,"
              s. and h. of Edmund, (xii) 9th or 2nd Earl of Arundel,

---

(ª) See p. 233, note "h." A petition, however, is recited in Taylor's *Glory
of Regality* (pp. 120-124), stating that the Earl "by his great power, though he never
had any of the manors attached to it, obtained the office." The manor of Kenning-
hall in Norfolk, which was one of these (three) manors, was subsequently in possession
of the Earls of Arundel, and, late in the 17th century, the office is said to belong to the
then Duke of Norfolk "*as* Earl of Arundel *and* Lord of the Manor of Kenninghall."

(ᵇ) *Patent Roll*, 12 Edw. III, *pars* ii, *m.* 33.

(ᶜ) As to his supposed name of 'Plantagenet' see *ante*, p. 183. V.G.

(ᵈ) See p. 231, note "b."

(ᵉ) "It may not be presumed that the grant to the Earl of Kent made him Earl
of Arundel, or that the restoration of the Castle and lands to Richard, s. and h. of
Edmond, made him Earl of Arundel either; inasmuch as there was in the Act of
Restoration a special provision applying to the title of Earl of Arundel as a name of
dignity, which would have been unnecessary had the restitution of the Castle and
Honour been considered as sufficient." (*Courthope*, p. 29). As to the latter part of
this remark, it is however more probable that such "special provision" was only added
ex abundanti cautelâ.

b about 1313.   He was in (1330-1) 4 Edw. III, fully restored in blood and honours (confirmed 1351 and again 1354), and in Dec. of that year obtained restitution of the Castle and Honour of Arundel from the widow of John, Earl of Kent.   By such restorations he doubtless became EARL OF ARUNDEL([a])   He was made Justiciar of North Wales for life 1334 ; Gov. of Carnarvon Castle, 1339 ; Sheriff of Shropshire for life 1345.   He took a distinguished part in the wars with France, was Admiral of the West 1340-41 and 1345-47, commanded the 2nd division ([b]) at the battle of Crécy, and was at the fall of Calais in 1347   He had shortly before, *viz*, on 30 June 1347, *suc.* to the vast estates of the family of WARENNE, by the death, *s.p. leg.*, of his mother's br., John, Earl of Surrey and Sussex.   By fine levied (1349-50) 23 Edw. III, he settled the Castle, town, and manor of Arundel on himself and his (then) wife Eleanor, for their joint lives, with rem to the heirs male of his body by his said wife   On the death of Joan, the widow of his said uncle, John, Earl of Surrey, in 1361, but *not before*, ([c]) he assumed the title of EARL OF SURREY, and in 1366 settled the Warenne estates on his issue.   He *m.*, 1stly, 9 Feb. 1320/1, in the King's Chapel at Havering-atte-Bower (he about 7, she about 8), Isabel, da. of Sir Hugh LE DESPENSER the younger, [LORD LE DESPENSER], by Eleanor, da. and coh of Gilbert (DE CLARE), EARL OF GLOUCESTER   He obtained, 4 Dec. 1344, a Papal mandate for the annulment of this marriage, on the ground of his minority and of his never having willingly consented to the match ([d])   He *m*, 2ndly, 5 Feb 1344/5, at Ditton, (a lady with whom

---

([a]) See note " e " on previous page
([b]) During almost the whole of his long life he was taking a leading part in warfare either by land or sea.   As heir to his mother he was a man of enormous wealth.   V.G
([c]) See third sentence of note " b, " p. 241
([d]) By his 1st wife he had a s who was said to have been 20 in 1347, and who, if this be true, must have been begotten when his father was still very young, about 15, and 2 daughters   The grounds on which the divorce was obtained were that 'prefatus Ricardus cum eadem Isabella in eodem thoro per metum et verbera positus eandem cognovit carnaliter et filium ex ea etiam procreavit ' (Grandisson's *Register*, ed Hingeston-Randolph, p 988).   The same story is told in the Papal Mandate.— ' On the petition of Richard, Earl of Arundel and Isabel, daughter of Hugh Despencer, who at the respective ages of 7 and 8, not by mutual consent, but by fear of their relations, contracted espousals, and on coming to years of puberty expressly renounced them, but were forced by blows to cohabit, so that a son was born.— Mandate by canonical procedure to annul the marriage, they having constantly lived apart, and providing for their son, so that they may be free to intermarry with others '
    It is not very easy to accept all this indecent stuff as a satisfactory explanation of a son having been born to the parties, and though in none of the documents bearing on the case is there any mention of daughters, yet there appear to have been two (see note ([b]) next p.), and if so, the '*per metum et verbera*' tale breaks down altogether, unless indeed, the boy and girls were triplets ! Obviously, what really happened, was this The powerful Earl desired to get rid of the woman to whom he had been married as a child, and who, since her father's attainder and execution, had ceased to be of any importance, that he might marry the woman with whom he was then living in

he had previously cohabited), Eleanor, widow of JOHN DE BEAUMONT, [2nd LORD BEAUMONT], da. of Henry,([a]) EARL OF LANCASTER, by Maud, da. and h. of Sir Patrick DE CHAWICES or CHAWORTH. She, who was 1st cousin to his 1st wife, and 2nd cousin once removed to the Earl, d. 11 Jan. 1372, at Arundel, and was bur. at Lewes. He d. 24 Jan. 1375/6,([b]) also at Arundel, in his 70th year, and was also bur. at Lewes. Will dat. 5 Dec. 1375.([c])

XV. 1376   11 or 4. RICHARD (FITZ ALAN), EARL OF ARUNDEL,
    to   and EARL OF SURREY, s. and h., by 2nd wife, b. in 1346.
    1397.   He was bearer of the Crown at the coronation of Richard II,
            16 July 1377, was a member of the Council, and was
made Admiral of the West and South, 1377, and subsequently, 1386, of all England. K.G. 1386. He distinguished himself in the French wars, gaining a brilliant naval victory over the allied French, Spanish, and Flemish fleets, off Margate, 24 Mar. 1387, and was made Gov. of Brest in 1388, being one of the 5 Lords Appellant in the Parl. of that year. Together with the Duke of Gloucester he took an active part against the King, who, in 1388, was entirely in that Duke's power. In 1394 he obtained pardon for all political offences, but was treacherously seized, 12 July 1397, tried at Westm., and beheaded in Cheapside, 21 Sep. 1397.([d]) He m. (cont. dat. 28 Sep., Papal disp. same month, 1359) Elizabeth, da. of William

adultery ; and the Pope very obligingly annulled the marriage and bastardised the issue : a very unfair proceeding as far as Edmund d'Arundel was concerned. The following Papal letters further illustrate the case, but need no comment.

Papal dispensation 4 Mar. 1344/5 to Richard, Earl of Arundel, to remain in marriage contracted with Eleanor, daughter of Henry, Earl of Lancaster, at Ditton in King Edward's presence, though he had carnally known Isabella, related in the 3rd and 4th degree to Eleanor.—Papal mandate 31 July 1347 on petition of Edmund d'Arundel — " Earl Richard and Isabella married and begot Edmund, but Robert, Bishop of Chichester, pronounced sentence of divorce, thus bastardising Edmund ; Richard thereupon married Joan [sic] de Bellomonte daughter of the uncle [sic] of Isabella. Papal commission was issued to cite the said Richard, Isabella, and Joan, Edmund being then 18 years old. It appeared that Joan should have been called Eleanor, and that she was not soror patruelis but neptis ex amita to Isabella. Edmund was by this time 20. "—Indult to Edmund d'Arundel, eldest son of the Earl of Arundel, and Sibyl his wife, July, 1364. (Papal Letters.) V.G.

([a]) As to his supposed name of ' Plantagenet, ' see ante, p. 183.
([b]) By his 1st wife, Isabel, he had 3 children. (1) Edmund, who m., before July 1349, Sibyl, da. of William (Montagu), Earl of Salisbury. He was knighted 1352, and was living 1377. He had a da., Alice, who m. Sir Leonard Carew (b. 1342, d. 1370), from whom descended George (Carew), Earl of Totness (1626). (2) Philippe, who m. Sir Richard Sergeaux (d. 30 Sep. 1393), whose da. Alice m., 1stly, Guy St. Aubyn, and 2ndly, about 1405, Richard (de Vere), Earl of Oxford, who d. 1417. (3) Isabel, who m. John, 4th Lord Strange of Blackmere. V.G.
([c]) He alienated the manor of Nether Bilsington, Kent, which had been held by the preceding Earls since the time of Henry I, by serjeanty. See Taylor's Glory of Regality, p. 144.
([d]) " No more shrinking or changing colour than if he were going to a banquet. " (Walsingham, vol. ii, pp. 225-6). V.G.

(BOHUN), EARL of NORTHAMPTON, by Elizabeth, da. of Bartholomew BADLESMERE. She *d.* 3 Apr. 1385, and was *bur.* at Lewes. He *m.*, 2ndly (without Royal lic., for which he was fined 500 marks), 15 Aug. 1390, Philippe, widow of John HASTINGS, (ᵃ) and da. of Edmund (MORTIMER), EARL OF MARCH, by Philippe, da. and h. of Lionel, (ᵇ) DUKE OF CLARENCE. He *d.* as afsd., 21 Sep 1397, (ᶜ) and was *bur.* in the church of the Augustin Friars, in Bread Str., London, and, having been *attainted*, all his *honours* were *forfeited*. Will dat. 4 Mar. 1382/3 at " Mon Chastel Philipp. " (ᵈ) His widow (by whom he had had no issue) was *b.* 21 Nov. 1375, at Ludlow ; she *m.*, 3rdly, after Apr. 1398, Thomas (POYNINGS), LORD ST. JOHN OF BASING, and *d.* 24 Sep. 1401, at Halnaker, Sussex, being *bur.* at Boxgrove.

XVI. 1398 ?   1. JOHN (HOLAND), DUKE OF EXETER,
to   K.G., had a grant of the Castle and Hon-
1399.   our of Arundel (ᵉ) (with all lands appert-
aining thereto in Surrey, Sussex, Essex and Herts) whereby (according to the admission (ᶠ) of 1433) he may be considered to have become " EARL OF ARUNDEL. " He was *degraded* in Parl. in 1399, and *beheaded* in 1400, whereby *all his honours* and estates became *forfeited*.

For fuller particulars see " EXETER, " Dukedom of, *cr.* 1397.

XVII. 1400.   12 or 5. THOMAS FITZ ALAN, 2nd, but only surv. s. and h. of Richard (xv) 11th or 4th Earl of Arundel, by his 1st wife, *b.* 13 Oct. 1381. He was for some time in ward to John (Holand) Duke of Exeter, by whom he was very harshly treated, but managed to escape to the Continent, and joined his uncle, Thomas, the deposed Archbishop, (ᵍ) at Utrecht, with whom he lived in great poverty. About 4 July 1399 he landed in England, with Henry, Duke of Lancaster (afterwards Henry IV), who is said to have delivered the captive King into his custody (though under 18), making him Gov. of the Tower of

---

(ᵃ) See under PEMBROKE.

(ᵇ) As to his supposed name of ' Plantagenet, ' see *ante*, p 183   V.G.

(ᶜ) A gallant, hot tempered, popular man, the persistent political opponent and bitter personal enemy of Richard II. He was one of the best sea-captains of the time. A full account of his trial is to be found in the *Chronicle* of Adam of Usk   Fabyan's *Chronicle* says that " he patiently and meekly took his death 22 Sep "   V.G.

(ᵈ) *Test Vet.*, and Nichols' *Wills*. It is a very curious and interesting document In it he styles himself " Earl of Arundel and Surrey "

(ᵉ) They were valued at £600 a year.

(ᶠ) See p. 231, note " b. "

(ᵍ) His br. Thomas, the 3rd s , was Bp of Ely in 1373, when aged 21, Chancellor 1386-88 and 1391-96, Archbp. of York in 1388, and of Canterbury 1396-1414 He was a leading statesman in that turbulent time, and is remembered for his proceedings against the Lollards. He *d* 19 Feb 1413/4. V G.

London. He was made K.B. 12 Oct 1399, and at Henry's coronation, 13 Oct, officiated as *Pincerna*. Early in 1400 he defeated the insurgent nobles, when his former guardian, John Holand, was captured and beheaded In Oct. 1400 his father's attainder was reversed, and he was *restored* in blood and in honours as EARL OF ARUNDEL AND SURREY, taking his seat, though still a minor. He also had livery of all his father's estates. K.G. 1400 He fought with moderate success against the Welsh 1401-5, and was victorious against the rebels under Archbp Scrope in 1405, and against the French in 1411. By Henry V he was made High Treasurer 21 Mar. 1412/3, and Warden of the Cinque Ports. He was at the taking of Harfleur, 1415. He *m.*, 26 Nov 1405, at Lambeth, in the presence of the Court, Beatrice, illegit. (but probably legitimated) da. of John I, KING OF PORTUGAL, (ª) by Inez PEREZ. She was one of the thirteen ladies for whom, on the feast of St. George, in 1413, robes of the Order of the Garter were provided. (ᵇ) Her right to dower being disputed, she, in 1421, was naturalised The Earl *d.* 13 Oct 1415, *s.p.*, of dysentery (contracted shortly before at the siege of Harfleur), on his birthday, aged 34, at Arundel, and was *bur* in the chapel there. (ᶜ) Will dat 10 Oct. 1415. On his death, the estates and representation of the family of Warenne (Earls of Surrey) devolved on his three sisters and coheirs (ᵈ) His widow *m.* (lic 20 Jan 1432/3) John (HOLAND), 2nd EARL OF HUNTINGDON, who was Lieut. of Aquitaine (1437) and afterwards (1442/3) DUKE OF EXETER She *d. s p.*, 23 Oct 1439, at Bordeaux, and was *bur.* at Arundel. M.I. (ᵉ)

(ª) See an exhaustive article by Sir N H. Nicolas, in *Coll Top. et Gen.*, vol. i, pp. 80-90 Her br Affonso, Duke of Braganza (ancestor of the future [1640] Kings of Portugal) was legitimated 20 Oct. 1401. See also a paper by Planché, 30 June 1860, in the *Archæological Journal*. Her arms, without any mark of bastardy, are on her seal, her tomb, &c

(ᵇ) A list of these, from 50 Edw III to 3 Hen VII, is in Beltz's *Order of the Garter*, p. ccxxi, &c It appears to have been *an actual dignity conferred*, as, in several cases, the ladies so decorated were neither the wives nor widows of Knights of the Order.

(ᶜ) He was a capable military man, but savage, revengeful, and self-seeking V G

(ᵈ) *Viz* (1) Elizabeth, Duchess of Norfolk, whose descendants (as senior heirs general) opposed the claim of the junior branch of the family of Fitz Alan (as heirs male) to the Earldom of Arundel. Her great-grandson John Mowbray (afterwards Duke of Norfolk), was in 1451 *cr.* EARL OF WARENNE AND SURREY, being ancestor to the present (1909) LORD MOWBRAY, who in her right is coh to the *ancient* Earls of Arundel, of the family of Fitz Alan, *prior* to 1415 , as also is he (by the marriage, in 1749, of his paternal ancestor, William, Lord Stourton, with Winifred Howard) to all the *succeeding* Earls of Arundel, whether of the family of Fitz Alan or of Howard, from 1415 (the above date) to 1777 (2) Joan, Baroness Abergavenny, widow, who *d.* 1434. (3) Margaret, wife of Sir Rowland Lenthal. See pedigree, *post*

(ᵉ) She is erroneously stated, in the Visit of Berks and elsewhere, to have *m.* Gilbert, 5th Lord Talbot, which lord did marry another Portuguese lady, also named Beatrice. V.G.

XVIII. 1415.   13 or 6. John d'Arundel, (who, according to the admission of 1433 ([a]) abovenamed, may be considered) Earl of Arundel by tenure of the Castle, cousin and h. male, being s and h of John d'Arundel (by Elizabeth, da of Edward ([b]) le Despenser), which last-named John (who never was sum. as a Baron) was s. and h. of John d'Arundel (sum. to Parl. ([c]) 1377-1379), who was br. of the whole blood of Richard (xv) 11th or 4th Earl of Arundel He was b 1 Aug. 1385, at Ditton manor, in Stoke Pogis, Bucks, suc his father 14 Aug 1390, was cr. K B 12 Oct 1399, became de jure Lord Mautravers by the death of his grandmother [suo jure Baroness Mautravers] on 10 Jan 1404/5, but was never sum. to Parl. as a Baron, though frequently styled Lord Mautravers. He was in the French wars in 1415, in which year he suc. to the Castle and Honour of Arundel as afsd., and (according to some authorities) is said to have been sum. to Parl. as EARL OF ARUNDEL, 3 Sep. 1416, ([d]) 4 Hen. V, though (probably owing to the opposition of the great family of Mowbray, the heirs gen of the former Earls of Arundel) never afterwards He m , before 1407, Eleanor, da. of Sir John Berkeley, of Beverstone, co Gloucester, by his 1st wife, Elizabeth, da. and h. of Sir John Betteshorne, of Betteshorne in Sopley, Hants. He d. 21 Apr. 1421, and was bur. at Arundel. His widow m., about 1423, Sir Richard Poynings, who was s and h ap. of Robert, Lord Poynings, but who d v.p., about 1430. She m, 3rdly, before 8 May 1439, Walter (Hungerford), Lord Hungerford, K G., who d. 1449. She d Aug 1455, and was bur. at Arundel. Will (in which she styles herself "Countess of Arundel and Lady Mautravers," and speaks of her 1st husband as " John, Earl of Arundel ") dat. 20 July 1455, pr. 23 Aug. following.

XIX 1421   14 or 7. John d'Arundel (who, in right either of his father's writ, or of the admission of 1433 ([a]) abovenamed, may be considered) Earl of Arundel, s. and h. He was b. 14 Feb. 1407/8, at Lytchett Mautravers, Dorset. On 19 May 1426 he was cr. K B at Leicester, by the young King, under the name of " Dominus de Maultravers. " His claim to the Earldom of Arundel not having been

---

([a]) See p 231, note " b "

([b]) See pedigree in Topographer and Genealogist, vol ii, p. 336.

([c]) The writs were directed Johanni de Arundell, and were probably issued owing to his marriage with Eleanor, suo jure Baroness Mautravers Neither his s nor grandson was so sum , nor his great-grandson (John) till 1429 (when the Baroness was dead), while his great-great-grandson (Thomas) was sum in 1452 as Thomas Arundell' de Matravers miles , and (Henry) the grandson of this last was sum in 1533 as Henricus Fitz Alan de Maltravers Chivaler

([d]) See full account of this mysterious sum. and its subsequent partial erasure (between 1658 and 1688) from the roll, in Tierney's History of Arundel, vol. i, p. 101, note. Sir C.G.Young states of this Lord that " it does not appear that the title [of Earl] was ever attributed to him during his lifetime, " and that the will of his widow was not made till " some years after her son was recognised as Earl " See Coll. Top. et Gen., vol. vi, p. 16. See also Betham's Dignities, p 180.

recognised, ([a]) he was, when of age, sum. to Parl. on 12 July and 3 Aug. (1429) 7 Hen. VI, by writs directed *Johanni Arundell' de Arundell' Chivaler*, whereby he is held to have become LORD ARUNDEL.([b])   In Dec. 1431 he was at the coronation of Henry VI at Paris.   He greatly distinguished himself in the French wars, and was made Capt. of the Castle of Rouen in Feb. 1431/2.   On 22 Apr. 1432 he was *cr.* K.G. ; and in Nov 1433 his petition to be considered EARL OF ARUNDEL, ([c]) *by tenure of the Castle of Arundel*, was allowed, but he was never afterwards sum. to Parl either as an Earl or a Baron.   He was *cr.*, in 1434, DUKE OF TOURAINE in France, by the Regent Bedford.   He *m.*, 1stly (or, more probably, was contracted when a minor to), Constance, da. of John (CORN-WALL), LORD FANHOPE, by Elizabeth, da. of John *of Gaunt*, ([d]) DUKE OF LANCASTER.   She *d s.p.* and *v.p.*, before 1429   He *m.*, 2ndly, before 1429, ([e]) Maud, widow of Sir Richard STAFFORD (who *d.* about 1427), da. of Robert LOVELL, by Elizabeth, da and coh. of Sir Guy BRYENE, who was 1st s. and h. ap of Sir Guy de Bryene [Lord Bryene].   The Earl having been severely wounded and taken prisoner at the siege of Gerberoy, in the Beauvaisis, in May 1435, was carried to Beauvais, where his leg was amputated. He *d.* there a few weeks afterwards, 12 June 1435, and was *bur.* in the Grey Friars there, though, in accordance with his will dat. 8 Apr. 1430, pr. 15 Feb. 1435/6, his body was reinterred in a noble tomb at Arundel. ([f]) His widow *d.* 19 May 1436.   Will, directing her burial to be at the Abbey of Abbotsbury, dat. 11 May 1436, pr. 25 Oct. following.

XX. 1435.   15 or 8. HUMPHREY (FITZ ALAN), EARL OF ARUNDEL, &c., only child by 2nd wife, *b.* 30 Jan. 1429, *d.* unm. 24 Apr. 1438, in his 10th year, when the DUKEDOM OF TOURAINE ([g]) became *extinct.* ([h])

XXI. 1438.   16 or 9. WILLIAM (FITZ ALAN otherwise Mautravers), EARL OF ARUNDEL, &c., uncle and h.   He was *b* 23 Nov. 1417, and, when of full age, obtained livery of his lands in Nov. 1438.

([a]) " Qui se dicit Com Arundell'. "   (*Rot. Exit.*, Mich., 8 Hen. VI.)

([b]) In Early Chanc. Proc., Bundle 9, no. 467, he is spoken of, 15 Hen. VI (1436-7), as 'sometime Lord of Arundell and Maltravers. '   V.G.

([c]) See page 231, note " b. "

([d]) As to his supposed name of ' Plantagenet, ' see *ante*, p. 183.   V.G.

([e]) On 4 Kal. May 1429, as John de Arundell' et de Mawtrewers, Knight, he and ' his *present* wife ' had a Papal indult.   V.G.

([f]) He was a dashing partisan leader, standing over 6ft. high, equally brilliant in tournaments and real war.   He was known as the English Achilles, and indeed " Impiger, iracundus, inexorabilis, acer " seems very fairly to describe him.   Polydore Vergil calls him " a man of singular valour, constancy, and gravity. "   V.G.

([g]) The title of Duke of Touraine was afterwards conferred by the French King, Charles VII, on Archibald (Douglas), 3rd Earl of Douglas [S.], in 1424, but became *extinct* on failure of his issue male, in 1440.

([h]) His maternal inheritance, the property of the Bryene family, passed to his half sister, Avice Stafford, *b.* 4 Dec. 1423, who *m.* James Butler, afterwards Earl of Wiltshire.   See an article, by B.W.Greenfield, in *N. & Q*, 5th Ser, vol. iii, p. 172

On 3 Dec. 1441 he was sum. to Parl. (ᵃ) as EARL OF ARUNDEL. (ᵇ)   He was Justice in Eyre of all forests south of the Trent 1459-61 and 1483-85. He took part with the Yorkists in their defeat at the second battle of St. Albans, 17 Feb. 1461   On 1 May 1471, he was Constable of Dover Castle, and Warden of the Cinque Ports, and again 1483 till his death. K.G. 1471.   He assisted as *Pincerna* at the coronation of Richard III, (ᶜ) as also at that of Henry VII, which King received knighthood at his hands shortly before that ceremony.   He founded the " Arundel Mass " (by gift of the manor of Aynho, co. Northampton), to be celebrated at Magd. Coll., Oxford.   He *m.*, after 17 Aug. 1438 (when his marriage was granted to his future father-in-law), Joan, 1st da. of Richard (NEVILL), EARL OF SALIS-BURY, by Alice, *suo jure* Countess of Salisbury.   She (who was sister of Richard, EARL OF WARWICK) *d.* shortly before 9 Sep. 1462, and was *bur.* at Arundel.   He *d.* late in 1487, in his 71st year, and was *bur.* there. Admon. 15 Dec. 1487, at Lambeth.

XXII. 1487.   17 or 10. THOMAS (FITZ ALAN, otherwise ARUNDELL, otherwise Mautravers), EARL OF ARUNDEL, &c., s. and h., *b.* 1450.   He (as " *Lord Fitz-Alan* ") was *cr.* K.B. at the coronation of Edward IV, 27 June 1461, and el. K.G. 26 Feb. 1473/4.   It appears from the Rolls of Parl. that in (1471) 11 Edw. IV, he sat as LORD MAUTRAVERS, though there is no *record* (ᵈ) of his having been so sum. till 15 Nov. (1482), 22 Edw. IV, when the writ was directed to him *(v.p.)* as " *Thome Arundell' de Matravers militi* " (ᵉ) in which title (LORD ARUN-DELL DE MAUTRAVERS) he sat, till in 1488 he *suc.* to the Earldom. As ' Lord Mautravers ' he was one of the peers at the coronation or

----

(ᵃ) This summons was not till eight years after the admission (1433) which confirmed the Earldom of Arundel to the Fitz Alan family.   The delay is accounted for by the absence in France of Earl John, and the minority of his successor.   It is probable, also, that this William may have been sum. some two or three years earlier, but the lists of summonses from 1438 to 1441 are unfortunately lost.

(ᵇ) PRECEDENCY OF THE EARLS OF ARUNDEL.

In 1446, Thomas (Courtenay), Earl of Devon, challenged the precedence of the Earl of Arundel.   The decision of the King, with consent of the Lords of Parl, was " that William, now Earl of Arundel, have, keep, and enjoy his seat, place and pre-eminence in the High Court of Parl., and in the King's Councils and elsewhere in the King's high presence, as Earl of Arundel, *by reason of the Castle, Honour and Lordship of Arundel*, as worshipfully as ever did any of his ancestors, Earls of Arundel, afore his time, *above* the said Earl of Devonshire and his heirs, without letting, challenge or interruption of the said Earl of Devonshire or of his heirs or of any other person " (*Rot. Parl.*, vol. v, p. 140)   " Thus ended, " adds Canon Tierney, " a controversy which, in its results, confirmed this Parliamentary decision of 1433 and established the Earldom in its original supremacy of honour above every other similar title of dignity. "   Tierney, *Hist. of Arundel*, vol. i, p. 138.

(ᶜ) Being one of the 35 nobles there present.   For a list of them, see note *sub* Humphrey, LORD DACRE DE GILLESLAND [1473].

(ᵈ) From 18 to 21 Edw. IV there are no writs, for there were no Parls.

(ᵉ) For a list of eldest sons of peers sum. to Parl. before the accession of James I, see Appendix G. in this volume. V.G.

33

Richard III. (ᵃ) In Sep. 1486 he was one of the Godfathers to Prince Arthur. Bearer of the Rod and Dove at the Coronation of Elizabeth, Queen Consort, 25 Nov. 1487. Lieut. of the Order of the Garter, 19 July 1489, and again 1517. In 1489 he was made Warden of the New Forest. He *m.*, in Oct. 1464, (ᵇ) Margaret, 2nd da. of Richard (WIDVILE), EARL RIVERS, by Jacqueline, da. of Pierre DE LUXEMBOURG, COUNT OF ST. POL and BRIENNE. She was sister of Elizabeth, QUEEN CONSORT of EDWARD IV. She *d.* before 6 Mar. 1490/1, and was *bur.* at Arundel. He *d.* 25 Oct. 1524, at Downly Park, in Singleton, Sussex, and was *bur.* at Arundel, aged 74. Will dat. 12 Aug., pr. 29 Nov. 1524.

XXIII. 1524. 18 or 11. WILLIAM (FITZ ALAN), EARL OF ARUNDEL, &c. s. and h. He was *b.* about 1476, being above 16 on 4 Aug. 1492, as found in the *Inq. p. m.* on his uncle, Richard, Earl Rivers, to whom he was coh. He was *cr.* K.B., with Prince Arthur, 29 Nov. 1489, el. K.G. 23 Apr., and inst. 25 June 1525. He bore the Rod and Dove at the coronation (1 June 1533) of Queen Anne Boleyn, and took part (1536) in her trial. He obtained, at the Reformation, a grant of the Priory of Michelham, and numerous lands formerly belonging to the Priory of Lewes. He is said to have *m.*, 1stly, Elizabeth, da. of Robert (WILLOUGHBY), LORD WILLOUGHBY DE BROKE, who is said to have *d. s.p.m.* He *m.*, 2ndly, 15 Feb. 1510/11, Anne, da. of Henry (PERCY), 4th EARL OF NORTHUMBERLAND, by Maud, da. of William (HERBERT), 1st EARL OF PEMBROKE. He *d.* 23 Jan. 1543/4, and was *bur.* at Arundel. Will dat. 23 Jan. 1543/4, pr. 5 Mar. following. His widow, who was *b.* before 27 July 1485, *d.* 1552. Will dat. 4 Mar. 1551/2, pr. 14 Dec. 1552.

XXIV. 1544. 19 or 12. HENRY (FITZ ALAN), EARL OF ARUNDEL, &c., only s. and h. by Anne, his 2nd wife, *b.* 23 Apr. 1512 (ᶜ), was named after Henry VIII, who in person was one of his sponsors. Ed. at Cambridge; page of honour to Henry VIII. He was sum. to Parl. *(v.p.),* 5 Feb. (1533/4) 25 Hen. VIII, &c., (ᵈ) in his father's Barony, as LORD MAUTRAVERS, and from 2 July 1540 to Feb. 1544, was Deputy Gov. of Calais. On 24 Apr. 1544, he was el. K.G., and was inst. 18 May following. In July of that year he was "Marshal of the Field" against the French, and distinguished himself at the taking of Boulogne. Lord Chamberlain July 1546 to Jan. 1549/50. P. C. July 1546. He was one of the Council of Twelve named by Henry VIII in 1547, and acted as HIGH CONSTABLE at the coronation of Edward VI. He was however, fined, and imprisoned in the Tower, for more than a year, 8 Nov. 1551 to 3 Dec. 1552, through the hostility of the Duke

(ᵃ) For a list of these see note *sub* Humphrey, LORD DACRE DE GILLESLAND [1473].
(ᵇ) "Item the Erle of Arundell ys son hath weddyd the Quyne ys suster." (John Wykes to Sir John Paston, 17 Feb. 1465/6.) V.G.
(ᶜ) See a printed broadside entitled "A moorning dity." (*ex inform.* Sir H.C. Maxwell Lyte.) V.G.
(ᵈ) See note "e" on previous page.

of Northumberland, on whom, however, he took ample revenge by pretending to join him in setting up Lady Jane Grey as Queen, and then betraying him to Queen Mary, and arresting him at Cambridge   He was not only among the 26 peers (ª) who signed the letters patent settling the Crown on Lady Jane Grey, (having done so, together with the Marquess of Winchester with a deliberate intention of deserting) (ᵇ) but was actually one of the 4 peers (with the Marquess of Northampton, the Earl of Huntingdon, and the Earl of Pembroke) who, together with the Duke of Northumberland, did homage to her as Queen, 9 July 1553. (ᶜ)   The Queen made him Lord Steward of the Household in Sep. 1553, and he acted as HIGH CONSTABLE at her coronation; Lord High Steward at the trial of the Duke of Suffolk, 17 Feb. 1553/4.   His offices were continued to him by Queen Elizabeth.   That Queen indeed he aspired to marry, but being rejected, he resigned all his offices in 1564.   High Steward of Oxford Univ. 1555-59, and Chancellor thereof 6 Feb. to 12 June 1559.   In 1568 he was on the Commission for the trial of the Queen of Scots, and aided in the design of his son-in-law, the Duke of Norfolk, for obtaining her in marriage.   For this he was again imprisoned, and was not finally released till after Norfolk's execution in 1572. (ᵈ)   He m., 1stly, Catharine, da. of Thomas (GREY), 2nd MARQUESS OF DORSET, by his 2nd wife, Margaret, da. of Sir Robert WOTTON, which Catharine was aunt of the unfortunate Queen, Jane Grey, abovenamed.   She d. 1 May 1532.   He m., 2ndly, 19 Dec. 1545 (Lic. Fac. Off. 6 Sep. 1545), Mary, widow of Robert

---

(ª) For a list of these see note *sub* Edward, EARL OF DERBY [1521].

(ᵇ) Froude's *Queen Mary*, p. 73.

(ᶜ) He was " of the middle size, well proportioned in limb, 'stronge in bone, furnished with cleane and firme flesh, voide of fogines and fatnes.'   His countenance was regular and expressive, his voice powerful and pleasing , but the rapidity of his utterance often made his meaning 'somewhat harde to the unskilfull ' " (*Dict. of Nat. Biog.*)   He was leader of the old nobility and catholics, was constantly conspiring, and apparently always ready to play the part of Judas, at short notice.   See a masterly character of him in Froude's *Elizabeth*, vol. i, pp. 43-4.   " A piercing apprehension, a strong memory, a large and capacious judgment, a dexterous prudence, a discerning wisdom was the least of his happiness. " (Lloyd, 1665)   V G.

(ᵈ) He was probably the earliest patron of Thomas Vautrollier (or Vautroullier), the learned printer, who dedicates his first printed work to him in 1570.   See *N. & Q.*, 2nd Ser., vol. iv, p. 84.   He was the purchaser (for £41. 6s. 6d.) of what was afterwards known as ARUNDEL HOUSE, in the Strand, which, having been originally the old town house of the Bishops of Bath, had passed, *temp.* Edward VI, " without recompence, " into the hands of the King's uncle, Thomas, Lord Seymour of Sudeley, after whose death and attainder in 1549, it was sold as above.   Here were stored the statues and other rarities collected by the Earl's great grandson, Thomas (Howard), Earl of Arundel, and here Hollar drew his well known view of London.   Here also the meetings of the Royal Society were held, after the fire of London.   The house was taken down in 1678, when Arundel street, Surrey street, Norfolk street, and Howard street were erected on its site, which still (1910) belongs to the Earl's descendant, Henry (Fitz Alan Howard), Duke of Norfolk, Earl of Arundel, Surrey, and Norfolk, &c.

(RADCLYFFE), EARL OF SUSSEX, da. of Sir John ARUNDELL, of Lanherne, Cornwall, by his 2nd wife, Katharine, da. of Sir Thomas GRENVILLE, of Stow, Devon. By her he had no issue. She *d.* at Arundel House, Strand, 20, and was *bur* 28 Oct. 1557, at St. Clement Danes, but afterwards removed to Arundel. (ª)   The Earl *d.* at the same place, *s.p.m.s.*, 24 Feb. 1579/80, (ᵇ) and was *bur.* at Arundel, aged 67. (ᶜ)   M I. (ᵈ)   Will dat. 30 Dec. 1579, pr. 27 Feb. 1579/80.

[HENRY FITZ ALAN, *styled* LORD MAUTRAVERS, only s. and h. ap. by 1st wife, *b.* in 1538   Knighted as a K B, being 5th in order of the 40 knights so *cr.* at the coronation of Edward VI, (ᵉ) 20 Feb. 1546/7. Matric. Cambridge (Queens' Coll.) May 1549.   He *m.* (Lic. 12 Apr. 1555) Ann, widow of Sir Hugh RICH, 3rd da. and coh. of Sir John WENTWORTH, of Gosfield, Essex.   Being sent Ambassador to the King of Bohemia, he caught a fever, and *d. s.p.* and *v.p.*, 30 June 1556, at Brussels, and was *bur.* in the Cathedral there, aged 18.   His widow *m*, between 1573 and 1580, William DEANE. She was *bur.* 10 Jan. 1580/1, at Gosfield afsd., as "Ann, Lady Maltravers, uxor William Deane Esq." In her will dat. 26 Mar. 1573, she styles herself 'late wife of the Rt. Hon. Henry Earl of Arundel' and bequeaths her residue to "my servant" William Deane, who pr. the said will 15 Feb. 1580/1.   He, who, in 1571, bought Dynes Hall, Great Maplestead, Essex, *m*, 2ndly, Anne, widow of George BLYTHE, clerk to the Council of York, and da. of Thomas EGERTON, and had issue, and *d.* 4 Oct. 1585. (ᶠ)]

XXV. 1580   20 *or* 13. PHILIP (HOWARD), EARL OF ARUNDEL, for-
to   merly *styled* EARL OF SURREY, (ᵍ) grandson & h., being s.
1589   and h. of Thomas, (xth) 4th DUKE OF NORFOLK, EARL OF
         SURREY, &c. (who was *attainted* 16 Jan. and beheaded

(ª) Here her coffin was found in the 19th century with her death date thereon, as in the text   She was "A noted scholar, she translated the wise sayings and antient actions of the Emperor Severus." Many of her MSS. are in the Royal Library.

(ᵇ) Arthur Gounter of Racton in his confession (Hatfield MS. 797) evidently speaks of him as the White Horse (the Fitzalan badge).   In an injudicious conversation Gounter had said (the spelling being modernized) "I trust the White Horse will be in quiet; . . . . it is well known his blood as yet was never attaint, nor was he ever a man of war, wherefore it is like that we shall sit still; but if he should stomach it, he were able to make a great power." (*ex inform.* Oswald Barron.) V.G.

(ᶜ) The Earls of Arundel of the house of Aubigny bore arms as early as the twelfth century, the seal of Earl William showing the rampant lion about 1180. The earls of the Fitzalan line bore the golden lion on a field of gules   (*ex inform* Oswald Barron)   V G.

(ᵈ) By his death the male line of Fitz Alan, Earls of Arundel, owners of the Castle of Arundel for upwards of 300 years, became *extinct*. See tabular pedigree illustrating their descent on next page

(ᵉ) See note as to these *sub* Henry, EARL OF DERBY [1572].

(ᶠ) See Essex *Arch. Soc. Publications*, N. S., vol. III.

(ᵍ) PRE-EMINENCE OF THE EARLDOM OF ARUNDEL OVER THE EARLDOM OF SURREY.
   In the settlement made by Henry (Fitz Alan), Earl of Arundel, of the Earldom

PEDIGREE OF THE EARLS OF ARUNDEL OF THE HOUSE OF FITZ ALAN.

John Fitz Alan, feudal=Isabel, 2nd sister and, in her issue, coh. of Hugh (d'Aubiguy),
Lord of Clun, &c. | Earl of Arundel, &c. (See pedigree, p. 237).

I. John Fitz Alan, who *suc.* to the Castle, &c., of Arundel in 1243 and=
was (according to the admission of 1433) Earl of Arundel, *d.* 1267.

II. John Fitz Alan, Earl of Arundel, as above, s. and h. *d.* 1272.=

III. Richard, Earl of Arundel, sum. to Parl *as such*, s. and h. *d.* 1302.=Alasia di Saluzzo.

IV. Edmund, Earl of Arundel, =Alice de Warenne, who, in her issue, was heir
s. and h., *attainted* and *d.* 1326. | to the Earls of Surrey and Sussex.

V. Richard Fitz Alan, *restored* as Earl of Arundel in 1331=Eleanor.
s. and h. *styled* himself Earl of Surrey in 1361, *d.* 1376.

VI. Richard, Earl of Arundel, &c., s.= John, Lord Arundel, sum. to=Eleanor, *suo jure* Baroness
and h. Beheaded and *attainted* 1397. Parl. as such 1377-79, *d.* 1379. | Mautravers, *d.* 1405.

VII. Thomas | Elizabeth,(*) 1st | Joan,(*) 2nd sister | Margaret,(*) 3rd | John Fitz Alan, other-=
Fitz Alan, *re-* | sister and coh., | and coh., widow of | sister and coh., | wise d'Arundel, *d.*
stored in 1400 | relict of Thomas | William (Beau- | wife of Sir Row- | 1391.
as Earl of | (Mowbray), | champ), Lord | land Lenthall,
Arundel and | Duke of Nor- | Abergavenny, and | and aged 33 in | VIII. John, Lord Mau-=
Surrey, *d. s.p.* | folk, and aged | aged 40 in 1415. | 1415. | travers (1405) and Earl
1415. | upwards of 40 | | | of Arundel (1415) *d.*
| in 1415. | | | 1421.

Sir Robert Howard,=Margaret, whose issue | Thomas John Isabel=James, Lord Berkeley
d. 1436. | became coheirs

John, *cr.* Duke of Norfolk | IX. John, Earl of Arundel=| XI. William, Earl of Arundel,=
d. 1485. | &c., s. and h., *d.* 1435. | &c. uncle and h., *d.* 1488.

Thomas, Duke of Norfolk
cr. Earl of Surrey 1483, *d.* | X. Humphrey, Earl of Ar- | XII. Thomas, Earl of=
1524. | undel, &c., only s. and h., | Arundel, &c. s. and h., *d.*
| *d. s.p.* 1438. | 1524.
Thomas, D. of Norfolk, *d.* 1554.

Sir Henry Howard, K.G., *styled* Earl | XIII. William, Earl of Arundel, &c., *d.* 1544.=Anne Percy.
of Surrey, beheaded *v.p.*, 1547.

XIV. Henry, Earl of Arundel, &c., the last heir *male* of the=Catharine
house of Fitz Alan, Earls of Arundel, *d. s.p.m.s.* 1580. | Grey.

Thomas (Howard),=Mary, in her issue | Henry Fitz Alan, only s. and | Joan, *m.* John, Lord
Duke of Norfolk, | sole h. to her father, | h. ap., *styled* Lord Mautravers, | Lumley, and *d. v.p.*
&c., beheaded 1572 | *d. v.p.* 1557. | *d. v.p.* and *s.p.* 1556. | and *s.p.* 1576.

Philip (Howard), Earl of Arundel, who, in 1580, *suc.* his maternal grandfather in the
Castle and Honour of Arundel. He *d.* 1595, being great grandfather of Thomas
(Howard), Earl of Arundel, restored, in 1660, to the Dukedom of Norfolk. See tabular
pedigree, under "NORFOLK," Dukedom of.

(*) *In the descendants of these three Ladies vests the representation of the earlier Earls of Arundel.
In* 1895 *the coheirs of the eldest (the Duchess of Norfolk) were, as to one moiety, the* suo jure *Baroness
Berkeley, and, as to the other (the Howard) moiety,* (1) *Lord Mowbray, Segrave and Stourton, and* (2)
Lord Petre. See p. 246, *note* "d."

2 June 1572) and only child, by (his *first* wife) Mary, 2nd da. (by 1st wife) and only child that had issue, of Henry (FITZ ALAN), EARL OF ARUNDEL (°) abovenamed. He was *b.* 28 June 1557, at Arundel House, Strand, and *bap.* 2 July following at the Chapel Royal, Whitehall, the King, Philip, after whom he was named, being in person one of his Godfathers. On 25 Aug. following, his mother *d.* in her 17th year. He was ed at the Univ. of Cambridge. M.A. Nov. 1576. On 24 Feb. 1579/80 he *suc.* his maternal grandfather and, on the *same day,* Lord Lumley, on whom (jointly with Joan his wife, who had *d. s.p.* some four years previously, being the elder of the two daughters of the late Earl of Arundel) the Arundel estates had in 1570 been settled, conveyed his life interest in the Castle and Honour of Arundel to him, whereby (according to the admission (ᵇ) of 1433) he became EARL OF ARUNDEL. On 28 May 1580, he took the arms of Fitz Alan only. He was sum. to Parl. as "*Earl of Arundel*" 16 Jan. (1580/1) 23 Eliz., and took his seat as such 11 Apr. following. By Act. of Parl 23 Eliz., he was, on 15 Mar. 1580/1, restored in blood. In Sep 1584 he became (as his wife had previously become) a Roman Catholic, and, having endeavoured to escape from England without licence, was taken prisoner 25 Apr. 1585, and lodged in the Tower of London,

---

of Arundel, on Philip Howard, *styled* Earl of Surrey, (being s. and h. ap of Thomas, Duke of Norfolk), the said Earl of Arundel, "after reciting that forasmuch as the said Earldom was the most ancient Earldom of this Realm, and that, in a certain event, the same was to descend to the Earl of Surrey or to the heirs of his body, covenanted with the said Duke of Norfolk, that after such time as the same honour or dignity of Duke of Norfolk shall descend to the said Earl of Surrey, or to the heirs of his body, then *the son and heir apparent* of the said Earl of Surrey and the heirs of his body, in all writings and in all common appellations and callings *shall be* written, named, and *called* the EARL OF ARUNDEL AND SURREY   Although this covenant is since annulled by the resettlement of the estates (Act of Parl., 3 Car. I), the Duke of Norfolk, on his accession in 1842, styled his eldest son EARL OF ARUNDEL AND SURREY, and to evince a further regard for the House of Fitz Alan, was desirous that the name of Fitz Alan should be borne by his issue. "—MS. note by T.W.King, York Herald (1848-72), in his copy of *Nicolas.*

(ᵇ) An interesting little work (London, 1857), was edited by the late (1856-1860) Duke of Norfolk, from the original MS. in his possession entitled "The life and death of the Renowned Confessor, Philip Howard, Earl of Arundel, &c. " and "The life of the Rᵗ Hon. Lady, the Lady Anne, Countesse of Arundell and Surrey, Foundresse of the English College of the Society of Jesus in Gant. " The author was probably a Jesuit priest. It appears herein that the Earl in his youth was somewhat wild, and had behaved so undutifully to his grandfather (the Earl of Arundel) and his aunt, the Lady Lumley, that "they both were so aversed from him that they alienated unto others a great part of their estates which otherwise would have come from them to him ; " also by his profuse expenditure "in tiltings and tourneys, " in entertaining ambassadors, as also the Queen herself, once at Keninghall, Norfolk, and again at his house in Norwich, he became to be so deeply indebted that he was forced to make "sale of a good quantity both of his own and his Lady's lands. " After his conversion, however, his manner of life was very different, and indeed truly exemplary.

(ᵇ) See p. 231, note "b. "

where he was detained till his death, and fined £10,000. He was *attainted* 14 Apr. 1589 on a charge of high treason, when *all his honours* became *forfeited*. He *m.*, in 1571, at "the age of 12 years complete," and again, "about 2 years after that, when he was at years of full consent, that is after 14 complete," Anne, one of the children of his stepmother, Elizabeth, Duchess of Norfolk, being 1st of the three sisters (ª) and coheirs of George, Lord Dacre of Gillesland, and da. of Thomas (Dacre), Lord Dacre of Gillesland, by Elizabeth (the abovenamed Duchess) da. of Sir Francis Leyburn. He *d.*, as afsd., 19 Nov. 1595, aged 38, after nearly eleven years of imprisonment, (ᵇ) (being by some supposed to have been poisoned) and was *bur.* in the chapel of the Tower of London, but removed thence, in 1624, to West Horsley, Surrey, the seat of the widow, and finally to Arundel. His widow, who was *b.* 21 Mar. 1557, at Carlisle, and who brought her husband the estate of Greystock, *d.* 19 Apr. 1630, at Shifnal Manor, Salop, in her 74th year, and was *bur.* at Arundel. Will pr. 4 July 1630.

XXVI. 1604.   21 or 14. Thomas Howard, only s. and h., *b.* 7 July 1585, at Finchingfield, Essex. Ed. at Westm. School, and at Trin. Coll. Cambridge. By Act of Parl. 18 Apr. (1604) 2 Jac. I, he was *restored in blood*, and to the titles of Earl of Arundel and Earl of Surrey, and to such honours as his father had enjoyed, and such Baronies *as had been possessed by* his grandfather, *the attainted Duke of Norfolk*. Many of the estates, however, were in the hands of other members of the family. Joint Lord Lieut. of Sussex 26 Aug. 1608 ; Lord Lieut. of Norfolk 18 Apr. 1615 ; and joint Lord Lieut. of Northumberland, Westmorland, and Cumberland 20 May 1633. El. K.G. 24 Apr. and inst. 13 May 1611. On 14 Feb. 1613, he carried the sword of state at the marriage of Elizabeth, da. of James I, soon after which he went to Italy, and began acquiring the celebrated collection known as "the Arundel Marbles," &c. (ᶜ) On 25 Dec. 1615, he publicly professed the Protestant

---

(ª) The two other sisters and coheirs *m.* his two brothers of the half blood. One of these *d. s p.*, and the other brought the estate of Naworth to her husband, Lord William Howard, by whom she was ancestress to the Earls of Carlisle.

(ᵇ) During his long imprisonment, which he spent in devotional and ascetic exercises, he was treated with great hardship, and, even when dying, Elizabeth cruelly refused him permission to see his wife and children unless he would abandon the Roman Communion His funeral cost his frugal sovereign £2 Lloyd (1665) calls him "as good an Englishman in his heart, as he was a Catholick in his conscience." V.G.

(ᶜ) At Evelyn's request, the Earl's grandson, Henry Howard "of Norfolk" (afterwards Duke of Norfolk) gave (1) to the University of Oxford "those celebrated and famous inscriptions, Greek and Latine . . . . whatever I found had inscriptions on them that were *not* statues ; " and (2) to the Royal Society the Earl's library and such MSS. as were not reserved for the College of Arms ; of this a catalogue was printed in 1681, entitled *Bibliotheca Norfolciana*. The Duke also gave (3) to the College of Arms (of which, as Earl Marshal, he was head) all MSS. relating to Genealogy and kindred subjects, including what are known as *The Shrewsbury MSS*.

religion, and, becoming high in Court favour, was made P.C. 16 July 1616 ; on 25 Sep. of that year he was one of the six commissioners of the office of Earl Marshal, and on 29 Aug. 1621, was made for life ([a]) EARL MARSHAL solely. On 1 Aug. 1622 his power to act as such, independently of the High Constable, was declared by patent. He assisted at the coronation 2 Feb. 1625/6, but, next year, was imprisoned and heavily fined, owing to the clandestine marriage of his 1st s. and h. ap. with Lady Elizabeth STUART. In 1627 (3 Car. I) he obtained an Act. of Parl. " For the annexing of the Castle, honour, manor and lordship of Arundel, &c., with the titles and dignities of the BARONIES OF FITZ ALAN, CLUN AND OSWALDESTRE AND MALTRAVERS,([b]) and with divers other lands, &c., being now parcels of the possessions of [him the said] Thomas, Earl of Arundel and Surrey, Earl Marshal of England, to the same title, name and dignity of EARL OF ARUNDEL, " ([c]) settling the same on *him* and the heirs *male* of his body, with rem. to the *heirs of his body*, with rem. to his *uncle* Lord William Howard([d]) *and his issue* (male and general) in like way, with rem. to the *said Earl and his heirs* for ever. To this is added a clause of precedency granting " all places, *pre-eminences*, arms, ensigns and dignities, to the said Earldom, Castle, Honour and Baronies belonging. " ([e])   In Dec. 1632 he was sent as Ambassador from the King to his sister, the widowed Queen of Bohemia, and again in 1636 to Holland, on the

as well as *The Arundel MSS.*,—of which a catalogue was printed in 1829 (8vo, pp. 136), edited by C.G.Young, afterwards Garter King of Arms.   As to the statues, most of them were sold in 1720 (for £6,335), but many, especially those in any way mutilated, had been removed as early as 1678, by Cuper (the Earl's gardener) to his public pleasure gardens at Bankside, Southwark. See Cunningham's *London*, under " Tart Hall, " and " Cuper's Gardens. "

([a]) See creations 1483-1646, App., 47th Rep. D. K. Public Records.   The office only became hereditary in 1672

([b]) In his petition the Earl calls them " the titles names and dignities of *Lora Fitz Alan, Lord of Clun and of Oswaldestre* and *Lord Maltravers.* "

([c]) " The Dukes of Norfolk are Earls of Arundel not by possession of Arundel Castle only, but under the special entail of the dignity cr. by Act. of Parl., in 1627." (*Quart. Rev.*, Oct. 1893, p. 414.) V G

([d]) He was the younger (but the survivor) of the two brothers of the half blood (neither of whom had for their mother the heiress of the Fitz Alan family) of the last Earl, so that (probably owing to this fortunate survivorship) the Earls of Suffolk, who descend from the *elder* of these two brothers, and, consequently, are next in rem to the *paternal* honour of the family, viz· the Dukedom of Norfolk, &c , are *postponed* (in the Act of Parl. of 1627), as to the Earldom of Arundel &c., to the Earls of Carlisle and all other issue, male *or female*, of this Lord William Howard, their ancestor's *younger* brother. Both these Earls, (i e Suffolk and Carlisle) though not descended from the heiress of the last Earl of Arundel of the family of Fitz Alan, have a descent from Richard (Fitz Alan), Earl of Arundel and Surrey (who d. 1397) through his 1st da. Elizabeth, wife of Thomas (Mowbray), Duke of Norfolk, and grandmother of their ancestor Sir John Howard, cr. Duke of Norfolk. Such descent, however, carries with it no *representation* either of the Fitz Alan or of the Mowbray family.

([e]) See p. 231, note " b. "

subject of the Palatinate.   Said to have been Grand Master of Freemasons
1633-35.   Chief Justice in Eyre North of Trent 25 Feb. 1634 till his
death.   In Dec. 1638 he had command of the train bands against the
Scottish Covenanters. (ª)   Lord Lieut. of Cumberland 31 Aug. 1639.
Lord Steward of the Household Apr. 1640 to Aug. 1641.   In Mar. 1641
he presided as LORD HIGH STEWARD at the trial of Strafford.   In Feb.
1642 he embarked with the Princess Mary to conduct her to her husband,
the Prince of Orange, and never returned to England.   In answer to a
petition (which he had presented in 1641), signed by sixteen Peers,
praying to be *restored to the Dukedom* of his grandfather, the King, by patent,
dated at Oxford 6 June 1644, *cr.* him EARL OF NORFOLK, with rem ,
failing the heirs male of his body, to those of his uncle Thomas, late Earl
of Suffolk, rem to his uncle, Lord William Howard, with like remainder.
He *m.*, in Sep. 1606, Alathea, 3rd da. and coh., but eventually sole h , of
Gilbert (TALBOT), 7th EARL OF SHREWSBURY, by Mary, da. of Sir William
CAVENDISH.   He *d.* 4 Oct. 1646, at Padua, (M I. there) aged 61, and was
bur. at Arundel.   Admon. 13 Nov. 1646.   One will is dat. 28 Mar. 1617,
another, dat. 3 Sep. 1641, pr. at York 23 July 1647. (ᵇ)   His widow, who
on 7 Dec. 1651 (on the death of her surv. sister *s.p.*) inherited the BARONIES
OF FURNIVAL (1295), STRANGE OF BLACKMERE (1308), and TALBOT (1331),
d. 24 May/3 June 1654, at Amsterdam, and was *bur.* at Rotherham, co.
York. (ᶜ)   Admon. 1659, in Court of Delegates, to William (Howard),
Viscount Stafford, yr. s of deceased.   Further admon. 8 Jan. 1714/5 to
Henry (Stafford-Howard), Earl of Stafford, grandson and next of kin

---

(ª) Having, according to Clarendon " nothing martial about him but his presence
and his looks. " V.G.

(ᵇ) See notes concerning him in *N. & Q.*, 3rd Ser., vol. ii, p. 403.   The unflat-
tering character given of him by Clarendon suggests over-weening pride and
incompetence—*e.g.*, that he went to court but seldom " because *there*, only, was a
greater man than himself "—that " He was willing to be thought a scholar " because
of his purchase of statues and collection of medals, but " as to all parts of learning he
was most illiterate "—that his dress was " very different from that of the time, such
as men had only beheld in the pictures of the most considerable men, all which drew
the eyes of most and the reverence of many towards him "—that he was " not much
concerned for religion, " nor " inclined to this or that party, " but " had little other
affection for the nation than as *he* had a share in it, in which, like the great Leviathan,
he might sport *himself*, from which he withdrew as soon as he discerned the repose
thereof was likely to be disturbed and died in Italy under the same doubtful character
of religion in which he lived. "   A 17th century poem says of his life in that
country :—
" Remaining in that calm delightful air
Till death removed him thence, the Lord knows where. "
Evelyn, however, speaks of him very differently as " *the magnificent* Earl of
Arundel, my noble friend while he lived. "

(ᶜ) For her was built, by Nicholas Stone, in 1638, " TART HALL, " near
Buckingham House, but just *outside* St James's Park   This descended to her 2nd s.,
Lord Stafford, whose name is still preserved in Stafford Row —See Cunningham's
London.   It was through her that the Howard family inherited the Manor of Worksop,
Notts, held by Grand Serjeantry.   See Taylor's *Glory of Regality*, p. 138.

34

[SIR JAMES HOWARD, *styled* LORD MALTRAVERS, s. and h. ap., *bap.* 17 July 1607, at the Chapel Royal, Whitehall, the King, James I, being his Godfather. On 4 Nov. 1616 he was *cr.* K B. at the creation of the Prince of Wales. He *d.* (of the small pox), aged 17, and unm., July 1624, at Ghent in Flanders, and was *bur.* at Arundel]

XXVII. 1646.   22 or 15. HENRY FREDERICK (HOWARD), EARL OF ARUNDEL, &c., 2nd, but 1st surv. s and h., *b.* 15 Aug. 1608. He, together with his eldest br., was *cr.* K.B. 4 Nov. 1616. M.P. for Arundel 1628-29, for Callan [I.] 1634, for Arundel again, 1640. P.C. [I.] 10 Aug. 1634. On 21 Mar. 1639/40 he was sum. to Parl (in his father's Barony) as LORD MOWBRAY,(*) and placed at the upper end of the Barons' Bench on 16 Apr. following. He was a zealous Royalist, was present at the battle of Edgehill, and was with the Court at Oxford, by which University, on 1 Nov. 1642, he was made M.A. In 1648 he was fined by Parl. £6,000, but allowed to compound for his estates. He appears to have contested his father's will, and to have behaved very undutifully to his mother, who had brought an annual revenue of more than £30,000 to the family, and to whom he allowed but a paltry sum. She, however, outlived him. He *m.*, 7 Mar. 1625/6, (a marriage for which his father suffered fine and imprisonment) Elizabeth, da. of Esme (STUART), 3rd DUKE OF LENNOX [S.], by Katharine, only da. and h. of Gervase (CLIFTON), LORD CLIFTON DE LAYTON BROMSWOLD He *d.* 17 Apr. 1652, at Arundel House, Strand, in his 44th year, and was *bur.* at Arundel. His widow *d.* 23 Jan. 1673/4. Will (in which she directs to be *bur.* by her husband) dat. 3 Nov. 1673, *pr.* 30 Mar. 1674.

XXVIII. 1652.   23 or 16. THOMAS (HOWARD), EARL OF ARUNDEL, EARL OF SURREY, EARL OF NORFOLK, &c., s. and h., *b.* 9 Mar. 1627/8, at Arundel House, Strand. Ed. at Utrecht. While with his grandfather in 1645, at Padua, he had a fever, from which his mental faculties never recovered. On 29 Dec. 1660 he was *restored* (together with the heirs male of the body of the 1st Duke of Norfolk) to the DUKEDOM OF NORFOLK. He *d.* unm. 13 Dec. 1677, at Padua, and was *bur.* at Arundel. See fuller account under "NORFOLK," Dukedom of.

(*) The *entirety* of the Barony of MOWBRAY (and not a moiety only, as till recently has been generally supposed) was vested in his father, the abeyance of it (as well as that of the Barony of SEGRAVE) having (doubtless) been terminated by Richard III in favour of the Howard family (who, with the Berkeley family, were *coheirs* to a *moiety* of it), inasmuch as it is certain that that King addressed the Duke of Norfolk (John Howard) as "*Lord Mowbray and Segrave.*" The House of Lords, (when the Barony of Mowbray was assigned, on 27 July 1877, to Lord Stourton (the senior coh. of the Barony thus [by Richard III] terminated), though they did not *expressly* state that the abeyance had been terminated by Richard III, came to the resolution that at some period subsequent to 1481 but before the time of Elizabeth, it was terminated in favour of the Howard family, a resolution which (coupled with the recognition of the Barony above quoted and the fact that no other such recognition took place in the 16th century) amounts (practically) to the same thing.

The Earldom of Arundel and the other honours entailed therewith by the Act. of Parl. of 1627, have been, since 1660, *merged* in the Dukedom of Norfolk ; the Duke of Norfolk in 1660 and each of his successors being *heir male of the body* of Thomas (Howard), xxvith (21st or 14th), Earl of Arundel, on which class of heirs the *first* limitation is made. If, however, such heirs male were to become *extinct*, the Earldom of Arundel, &c, would pass (under the *next* rem. in the entail of 1627) to the heirs *general* of the body of the said Thomas (which are numerous), and would consequently become separated from the Dukedom of Norfolk, and could only become re-united therewith on the failure of such heirs general, when the subsequent limitation would take effect.

ARUNDEL

BARONY
BY WRIT.

I 1377.

1. JOHN D'ARUNDEL,(*) yr. s. of Richard (FITZ ALAN) xivth (10th or 3rd) EARL OF ARUNDEL, by his 2nd wife, Eleanor, da. of Henry,(*b*) EARL OF LANCASTER, *m.*, 17 Feb. 1358/9, Eleanor, 2nd and yst. da. of Sir John MAU-TRAVERS, by Gwenthlian, his wife, which Eleanor was found granddaughter and coh. (she eventually was sole h.) of Sir John Mautravers [Lord Mautravers] on 16 Feb. 1364/5, at which date she was aged 19. In consequence, probably, of such marriage, he was sum. to Parl., from 4 Aug. (1377) 1 Ric II to 20 Oct. (1379) 3 Ric. II by writs directed " *Johanni de Arundell*', " whereby he may be (*c*) held to have become LORD ARUNDEL. (*d*)   He was MARSHAL OF ENGLAND in that same year, 1377, and also 9 Apr. 1378   Being in command of a naval expedition in aid of the Duke of Brittany, he defeated the French fleet off the coast of Cornwall, but was later, 15 or 16 Dec. 1379,(*e*) wrecked and drowned in

(*) The family of Fitz Alan, otherwise Arundel, affords an instance of the name of the dignity being adopted as the surname.

Sir John Arundel, knight, son and heir of Sir John Arundel, by Eleanor Mautravers, seals in 1388 with a shield of Fitzalan quartering Mautravers. (*ex inform.* Oswald Barron.)   V G.

(*b*) As to his supposed name of ' Plantagenet, ' see p. 183.

(*c*) This Barony of Arundel would probaby be held to be the same Barony as that of Mautravers, and the summons of 1377 to be one *jure uxoris*, and consequently not one creating any new dignity   The s. and h of the Baron (so sum. in 1377), *d.* before his mother, Baroness Mautravers, and (consequently ?) was never sum.; the grandson and h of the Baroness became Earl of Arundel within six years after he came of age, and is said to have been sum. as an *Earl* the following year.   Notwithstanding this, however, his s. and h. was sum. in 1429 (*not* as an Earl, but) as a Baron (and that too by the title of Lord Arundel, not Lord Mautravers), until his claim to the Earldom of Arundel was allowed (four years later) in 1433. If the Barony of Arundel be held to be a *separate* one from that of Mautravers, it is now (1910) in abeyance between the Lords Mowbray and Petre, the coheirs general of the Baron sum. in 1377. If, however, it be the *same* Barony as that of Mautravers, it passes (as such) under the Act of Parl. of 1627 to the Duke of Norfolk.

(*d*) There is proof in the Rolls of Parl. of his sitting.

(*e*) " Johannes darundell chivaler. " Writs of *diem cl. ext.* 26 Jan. 3 Ric. II.

the Irish sea.(ᵃ) He was *bur.* in Lewes Priory. Will dat. 26 Nov. 1379. His widow (*de jure suo jure* BARONESS MAUTRAVERS, according to modern doctrine), *m.* by disp. from the Archbp. of Canterbury, dated 9 Sep. 1384 (being within the third degree of consanguinity) (ᵇ), as 2nd wife, Reynold (COBHAM), 2nd LORD COBHAM (of Sterborough), who *d.* 6 July 1403. She *d.* 10 Jan. 1404/5.(ᵇ) Will dat. at Lytchett Matravers, 26 Sep. 1404, desiring to be *bur.* at Lewes Priory with " mon tres honorable seigneur John Arundell, " pr. 16 Jan. 1404/5 at Maidstone.

II. 1379.   2. JOHN D'ARUNDEL, s. and h., *b.* 30 Nov. 1364. He   was *never sum. to Parl.* He was with the army in Scotland in 1383, and with the English Fleet in 1388. He *m.*, before 1387, Elizabeth, da. of Edward (DESPENSER), LORD LE DESPENSER, by Elizabeth, da. and h. of Bartholomew (BURGHERSH), LORD BURGHERSH. He *d.* 14 Aug. 1390,(ᶜ) and was *bur.* in Missenden Abbey. On 15 July 1406 he is referred to as John Darundell Chivaler, and his s. as John Darundell Esquire.(ᵈ) His widow *m.* William (LA ZOUCHE), LORD ZOUCHE OF HARYNGWORTH, who *d.* 13 May 1396. She *d.* 10 or 11 Apr. 1408.(ᵉ) Will, desiring to be *bur.* in Tewkesbury Abbey, dat. 4 Apr. 1408.

Inq., Surrey, Kent, Sussex, Northumberland, 9 Feb. to 27 Mar 1379/80. He *d.* 16 Dec. last   Inq , Somerset, Dorset, Gloucester, Wilts, 20 Feb. to 1 Mar. 1379/80   He *d.* 15 Dec. last   John d'Arundell chivaler is his s and next heir " et fuit etatis xv annorum in festo sancti Andree apostoli ultimo preterito. " (Ch. *Inq. p. m.,* Ric. II, file 8, no. 1). (*ex inform.* G W Watson.) V G.

(ᵃ) He appears to have been one of the fops of the period, for he had on board 52 suits of clothes " pro proprio corpore, novos apparatus vel aureos vel aureo textos. " V G.

(ᵇ) " Alianora que fuit uxor Reginaldi de Cobham Chivaler. " Writ of *diem. cl. ext.* 21 Jan. 6 Hen. IV. Inq., Wilts, Kent, 20 Feb., 11 Mar. 1404/5. " Alianora obiit die sabbati proximo post festum Epiphanie domini [*aliter* x die Januarii] ultimo preteritum. "   " Alianora que fuit uxor Johannis Darundell senioris Chivaler. " Writs, 16 Feb. 6 Hen. IV. Inq., Wilts, Somerset, Gloucester, 12, 17, 26 Mar. 1404/5. " Alianora obiit x die Januarii ultimo preterito. " (Ch. *Inq. p. m.,* Hen. IV, file 49, no. 31). (*ex inform.* G.W.Watson.) V.G.

(ᶜ) " Johannes de Arundell chivaler. " Writ of *diem. cl ext.* 6 Oct. 14 Ric. II. Inq., Surrey, 2 Nov. 1390. " dicunt quod predictus Johannes filius Johannis obiit die dominica in vigilia assumptionis beate Marie ultimo preterito et quod Johannes filius ejus est heres ejus propinquior et fuit etatis quinque annorum in vigilia sancti Petri quod dicitur advincla ultima preterita. " (Ch *Inq. p. m.,* Ric. II, file 62, no. 1). (*ex inform.* G.W.Watson) V.G.

(ᵈ) *Pat. Roll*

(ᵉ) " Elizabetha que fuit uxor Johannis de Arundell chivaler. " Writ of *diem cl. ext.* 8 May 9 Hen. IV   Inq., co Gloucester, 19 June 1408. " Elizabetha obiit die mercurii proximo post festum dominice in ramis Palmarum ultimo preterito [11 Apr]. "   " Elizabetha que fuit uxor Willelmi la Zouche militis. " Writ 16 Apr. 9 Hen IV. Inq., Beds, Northants, London, Wilts, 25 Apr. to 19 May 1408. " Elizabetha diem suum clausit extremum die martis proximo ante [*rectius* post, *i.e.* 10 Apr.] dominicam in Ramis Palmarum ultimo preteritam. " (Ch. *Inq. p. m.,* Hen. IV, file 66, no. 20, file 69, no. 45) (*ex inform.* G.W.Watson.) V.G.

III. 1390.   3. JOHN D'ARUNDEL, s. and h., *b.* 1 Aug.
1385.(*)   In Jan 1405 he *suc.* his grand-
mother in the Barony of MAUTRAVERS, but was never sum. to
Parl. as a Baron.   In 1415 he *suc.* to the Castle and (according
to the admission of 1433) to the Earldom of Arundel.   He
d. 21 Apr. 1421.

IV. 1421.   4. JOHN D'ARUNDEL, s. and h. was sum.
to Parl. on 12 July and 3 Aug. (1429)
7 Hen. VI by writs directed " *Johanni Arundell' de Arundell'*
Chivaler," whereby he is held to have become LORD ARUN-
DEL.   He *d.* 12 June 1435.

For fuller particulars see "ARUNDELL" Earldom of, under the xviiith and xixth Earls.

ARUNDELL OF TRERICE

BARONY.   1. RICHARD ARUNDELL, of Trerice, Cornwall, s and
I. 1664.   h. of John A., (ᵇ) of the same (M.P. for Cornwall 1601,
and 1621-22, who *d.* 5 Dec. 1654), by Mary, da. of
George CARY, of Clovelly, Devon, was M.P. for Lostwithiel 1640-44, and
a Col. in the King's army   Gov. of Pendennis 1662 till his death.   Having

---

(*) Writ *de etate probanda*, 8 Aug 7 Hen. IV.   Inq at Colnbrook, 12 Aug
1406.   " predictus Johannes filius et heres predicti Johannis de Arundell Chivaler
junioris apud manerium de Ditton in parochia sancti Egidii de Stokepogeys natus
fuit in die sancti Petri quod dicitur advincla anno regni Ricardi nuper Regis
Anglie secundi post Conquestum nono et in ecclesia parochiali beate Marie virginis
de Dachet predicto manerio de Ditton adjacente in comitatu Bukinghamie eodem
die baptizatus fuit " (Ch. Inq. p. m., Hen. IV, file 49, no. 31). (*ex inform*
G.W.Watson.) V.G.

(ᵇ) This John was known as " Jack for the King, " and the following epitaph
is said to be, or to have been, in Llanidolawre churchyard.

          " Under this thing
          Lies ' John for the King '
          Who in truth and verement
          Did hate the Parliament,
          But as for the Blud Ryall
          He was trew as a Sundyall. "
                              V G.

He (as also his four sons, of whom two lost their lives in the Royal service) was
most zealous in the cause of Charles I.   His gallant defence of Pendennis Castle, of
which he was Governor, is well known   It was, however, surrendered on 31 Aug.
1646.—" Lord Clarendon's account thereof is as follows—" This Castle was defended
by the Governor thereof, John Arundel of Trerice in Cornwall, an old Gentleman,
of near four-score years of age, and of one of the best estates and interest in
that County, who, with the assistance of his son, Richard Arundel (who was then a
Col. in the Army, a stout and diligent officer, and was by the King, after his return,
made a Baron, LORD ARUNDEL OF TRERICE, in memory of his father's service and
his own eminent behaviour throughout the war) maintained and defended the same to
the last extremity. "

fought for the King at the battle of Edgehill, and been despoiled of nearly all his estates by the Parl , he was, in reward for his own and his father's loyalty, *cr.*, 23 Mar. 1663/4, BARON ARUNDELL OF TRERICE, (*) Cornwall. A Tory in politics. He *m.*, before 1648, at St. James's, Westm., Gertrude, widow of (his friend and companion in arms) Sir Nicholas SLANNING, of Bickley, Governor of Pendennis Castle (who *d.* of his wounds at the taking of Bristol, 1643, aged 25), and da. of Sir James BAGGE, of Saltram, Devon, by Grace, da. of John FORTESCUE, of Buckland Filleigh, Devon. He was *bur.* 10 Oct. 1687, at St. James's, Westm. Admon. 26 June 1688, and again 23 Aug. 1692. His widow, who was aged 6 in 1620, was *bur.* there 28 Nov. 1691.

II. 1688.　　　2 JOHN (ARUNDELL), BARON ARUNDELL OF TRERICE, only surv. s. and h., *bap.* 1 Sep. 1649 (ᵇ) at Richmond, Surrey, and named in his grandfather's will, dat. 14 June 1654. M.P. (Tory) for Truro 1666-79, and 1685-87. He *m.*, 1stly, lic. 10 May 1675, Margaret, only da. of Sir John ACLAND, of Columb John, Devon (by Margaret, da. of Dennis ROLLE, of Stevenstone in that co.), sister and h. of Sir Arthur A., who *d.* a minor in 1672. She *d.* 26 Mar. and was *bur.* 1 Apr. 1691, at Newlyn. M.I. He *m*, 2ndly, 14 Feb. 1692/3, at All Hallows, Staining, London, (Lic. Vic. Gen., she about 25) Barbara, widow of Sir Richard MAULEVERER, da. of Sir Thomas SLINGSBY, 2nd Bart. [S], by Dorothy, da and coh. of George CRADOCK. He *d.* shortly before 21, and was *bur.* 23 June 1698, at St James's, Westm, aged 48. Will dat 1 Dec 1695, pr. 27 June 1698. His widow *m.*, 3rdly, 21 Sep. 1708, at St. James's, Westm., as his 2nd wife, Thomas (HERBERT), 3rd EARL OF PEMBROKE, who *d.* 22 Jan. 1732/3. She *d.* 1, and was *bur.* 9 Aug. 1721, in Salisbury Cath. Admon. 8 May 1733, and again 30 Apr. 1759.

III. 1698.　　　3. JOHN (ARUNDELL), BARON ARUNDELL OF TRERICE, s. and h. by 1st wife, *b.* 25 Feb. and *bap.* 12 Mar. 1677/8 at St Martin's-in-the-Fields. He *m.* Jane, 6th da. of William BEAW, BISHOP OF LLANDAFF (1679-1706), by Frances, da of Alexander BOWSIE, of Southampton. She was aged 9 years in 1683. He *d.* in London, 24 Sep , and was *bur.* 30 Oct. 1706, aged 22, (ᶜ) at Newlyn. Will dat. 13 July, pr. 3 Dec. 1706. His widow *d.* 20, and was *bur.* 23 June 1744,

(ᵃ) This family, a cadet branch of the house of Lanherne, bore arms of Sable with three cheverons silver, these being the arms of Trerice of Trerice, heir of Lansladron who first bore this shield. In later times the Lords Arundell of Trerice reverted to the use of the ancient arms of Arundell, which are Sable with six swallows silver　(*ex inform.* Oswald Barron)　V G.

(ᵇ) " John, s of Richard Arundell Esq & yᵉ Lady Slannell *(sic)* his wife. " The burial, 16 July 1648, of an elder br. of this John is also reg. at Richmond as " John Arundell, s of the Lady Slannell "

(ᶜ) " He starved himself, being in love with a lady, who left him, and was married when she promised never to marry. " See " Le Neve's memoranda " in *Top. and Gen* , vol. iii, p 263.

at Thornbury, co. Gloucester, aged 70. M.I. Will dat 28 Jan 1739, proved 14 July 1744.

IV. 1706   4 JOHN (ARUNDELL), BARON ARUNDELL OF TRERICE,
to   only surv s. and h., *b.* 21 Nov. 1701. Ed. at Balliol
1768.   Coll. Oxford. In politics he was a Tory He *m.*, 2 June
                1722, at Hounslow, (*) (Lic. Lond., 1 June 1722, to
m. at St James's, Westm , he 20, and she 25 [*sic, sed rectius* 41]) Elizabeth,
"almost old enough to be his mother," (*) sister of Thomas, EARL OF
STRAFFORD, da. of Sir William WENTWORTH, of Ashby, co. Lincoln, by
Isabella, da. of Sir Allen APSLEY. She *d.* 21 Mar. 1750, aged 69, and was
bur. at Sturminster Marshall, Dorset. M.I. He *d. s.p.*, aged 66, and was
bur. 13 Aug. 1768, with his wife, when the *title* became *extinct.*

    Family estates.—These, after the death of the last Peer, went, according
to the entail in his mar settl , to William Wentworth, the nephew of his
wife, whence, by re-settlement, they passed to Sir Thomas Dyke Acland,
Bart.

ARUNDELL OF WARDOUR

BARONY.   1. THOMAS ARUNDELL, (b) of Wardour Castle, Wilts,
I. 1605.   s. and h. of Sir Matthew A., of the same, by Margaret,
            da. of Sir Henry WILLOUGHBY, of Wollaton, Notts., was
b. about 1560. He was imprisoned in the summer of 1580 for his zeal
in the cause of his communion. He subscribed £100 towards repelling
the Spanish Armada in 1588. He was known as ' the Valiant,' and served
in 1588 with the Imperialists, against the Turks, and, having taken a
standard from the enemy at Gran, in Hungary, was *cr.* by the Emperor
Rudolph II, on 14 Dec. 1595 (by patent dat. at Prague), a COUNT OF
THE HOLY ROMAN EMPIRE. (c) Any precedence, however, as such, in
England was never acknowledged by Queen Elizabeth, though the title
was recognised by her successor. In Dec. 1598, being then a knight, and
aged 36, he *suc.* his father, and on 4 May 1605, (d) was *cr.* BARON
ARUNDELL OF WARDOUR, (e) Wilts. He *m* , 1stly (lic. Lond. (f)
dat. 18, and settl. dated 19 June 1585) Mary, da. of Henry (WRIOTHES-

---

    (*) Hearne's *Collections.* V.G.
    (b) The family of Arundell is one of the five (*viz.* Arundell, Fermor, Hunloke,
Petre, and Phelips) contained in the *Roman Catholic Families of England, based on the
Lawson, MSS.*, a magnificent work edited by J J Howard.
    (c) This patent is duly recorded in the College of Arms, London
    (d) For a list of the seven peers *cr.* on this day, see note *sub* Thomas, EARL OF
EXETER [1605].
    (e) The Lords Arundell of Wardour, cadets of the house of Lanherne, bear the
whole coat of that house, which is Sable with six swallows silver—the *hirondelles*
playing upon the name of Arundell   (*ex inform* Oswald Barron) V.G
    (f) " 18 June 1585. Sir *Matthew* [*sic*] Arundle Kt. to *m.* Mary Wrisley [*sic*]
da. of Henry, late Earl of Southampton, at the chapel in St. Andrew's, Holborn "

LEY), 2nd EARL OF SOUTHAMPTON, by Mary, da. of Anthony (BROWNE), 1st
VISCOUNT MONTAGUE. She was *bur.* 27 June 1607, at Tisbury, Wilts.
He *m.*, 2ndly, 1 July 1608, at St. Andrew's, Holborn, Anne, da. of Miles
PHILIPSON, of Crook, Westmorland, by Barbara, sister and coh. of Francis
SANDYS, of Conishead, co. Lancaster. She *d.* at Lennox House, Drury
Lane, 28 June, and was *bur* 4 July 1637, at Tisbury. M.I. Admon. as
of St. Giles'-in-the-Fields, Midx., 1 Feb. 1639/40, granted to her da.
Catharine Eure, widow. He *d.* 7 Nov. 1639, ([a]) aged about 79, at
Wardour Castle, and was *bur.* at Tisbury. M.I. Will dat. 5 Nov., pr.
3 Dec 1639 *Inq. p m.* 17 Car. I.

II. 1639.   2. THOMAS (ARUNDELL), BARON ARUNDELL OF WARD-
             OUR, s. and h. by 1st wife, *b* about 1586. He was a
devoted Royalist, and raised a Regiment of Horse for the King. He *m.*
(settl. after marriage, 11 May 1607) Blanche, 6th da. of Edward (SOMER-
SET), 4th EARL OF WORCESTER, by Elizabeth, da of Francis (HASTINGS),
2nd EARL OF HUNTINGDON. She gallantly defended Wardour Castle
against the Parliamentary forces under Sir Edward Hungerford, but was
finally forced to surrender on honourable terms, which, however, were not
observed, and the castle was sacked, and the lady removed as a prisoner to
Dorchester. He *d.* at Oxford, 19 May, of wounds received at the battle
of Stratton, 16 May 1643, aged about 57, and was *bur.* at Tisbury. M.I.
Will dat. 7 Jan. 1641/2 to 14 May 1643, pr. 27 Nov. 1648. His widow
d. 28 Oct 1649, at Winchester, in her 66th year, and was also *bur.* at
Tisbury. M.I. Will dat. 28 Sep., pr. 2 Nov. 1649.

III. 1643.   3. HENRY (ARUNDELL), BARON ARUNDELL OF WARDOUR,
             s. and h, *bap.* 23 Feb. 1607/8, at St. Andrew's, Holborn.
Master of the Horse to Queen Henrietta Maria. He also was very
active for the King, and in Mar. 1644 re-took Wardour Castle from the
rebels, and destroyed it to prevent its being used by them as a fortress.
Having been second to his br. in law, Col. Henry Compton, when he was
killed by Lord Chandos in a duel, 13 May 1652, they were found guilty
of manslaughter, 17 May 1653, and sentenced to be burned in the hand. ([b])
From Oct. 1678 to Feb. 1683/4, he was, with other "popish" Peers,
imprisoned in the Tower, on the accusation of Titus Oates. ([c])   P.C.

([a]) His portrait by Vandyke is (1910) at Wardour   V.G.
([b]) "Lord Chandos and my Lord Arundel of Wardour were this day upon their
trial in the Upper Bench upon the indictment for killing Mr. Compton which had
been found at Kingston but manslaughter. They pleaded their peerage that so
according to the statute they might not be put to read, but the house of peers being
taken away, that plea would not be allowed, so they read but the burning in the
hand was respited till Monday." (Letter of T Harley, 21 May 1653. *Hist. MSS.
Com.*, 14th Rep., App., Pt. 2, p. 201.) "The Lord Arundell of Wardour, and the
Lord Shandoys were indicted at sessions and found guilty of manslaughter, and had
sentence to be burned in the hand (a strange doom for noblemen)." (*Newsletter*,
21 May 1653)   V.G.
([c]) The other Lords impeached with him were the Earl of Powis, and Lords

17 July 1686 till Feb. 1688/9 ; Lord Privy Seal 11 Mar 1686/7-88.
He was one of the five Lords to whom James II committed the administration of his affairs in 1688 , and on the expulsion of that King he
retired to Breamore, Hants. (ª) He *m.* Cicely, widow of Sir John Fermor,
of Somerton, Oxon, da. of the Hon. Sir Henry Compton, K.B., of
Brambletye, Sussex, by Cicely, da. of Robert (Sackville), Earl of Dorset.
She *d.* 24 Mar. 1675/6, and was *bur.* 1 Apr. 1676, at Tisbury, aged 66.
M.I.   He *d.* at his residence, Breamore, afsd, 28 Dec. 1694, aged 88, and
was *bur.* with his wife. (ᵇ)   Will, no date, pr. 12 Aug. 1695.

IV. 1694.   4. Thomas (Arundell), Baron Arundell of Ward-
                   our, s. and h., *b.* 1633. (ᶜ)   He *m.* Margaret, widow of
Robert Lucy, of Charlecote, co Warwick, and da of Thomas Spencer, or
Ufton in that co.   She *d.* 23 Dec. 1704.   Will dat. 12 June 1693.   He
d. 10 Feb. 1711/2, at Breamore, afsd., and was *bur* at Tisbury, aged
about 79.   Will dat. Jan. 1704/5.

V. 1712.   5. Henry (Arundell), Baron Arundell of Ward-
                  our, s. and h.   He *m.*, between 5 and 9 Aug. 1691
(settl. before marriage, 5 Aug.) Elizabeth, sister of Lt. Gen. Thomas
Panton (*d.* 20 July 1753), and da. of Col. Thomas Panton, of St.
Martin's-in-the-Fields, Midx , a large proprietor in that parish (being the
"celebrated Gamester" (ᵈ) who *d.* 24 July 1685), by Dorothy, da. of
John Stacy, of London, and Elinor, da. of Thomas Blake, of Easton,
Hants.   She *d.* 9, and was *bur.* 11 May 1700, at St. James's, Westm. (ᵉ)
He *d.* at Wardour Castle, 20 Apr , and was *bur.* 2 May 1726, at Tisbury.
Admon. 13 June 1726 to his s. Henry.

VI. 1726.   6. Henry (Arundell), Baron Arundell of Ward-
                   our, s. and h , *b* 4 Oct. 1694   He *m* , 1stly, (cont. dat.
28 Sep. 1716) Elizabeth Eleanor, da. and h. of Raymond Everard, of
Fethard, co. Tipperary, and of Liège, a Baron of the Holy Roman Empire.
She, who was *bap.* 1 Jan. 1696/7, at Reckheim, in Belgium, *d.* at Wardour

---

Belasyse, Petre, and Stafford, while Lords Aston and Castlemaine, Lady Powis,
Lady Abergavenny and others were imprisoned on baseless charges of a similar
kind.   For another preposterous accusation against him see note *sub* William, Baron
Powis [1667].   V.G.

(ª) Here he kept a pack of hounds which were the progenitors of the famous
Quorn pack (as to which see note *sub* John, Baron Manners of Foston [1864]).
He is said to have been a great gambler.   V.G

(ᵇ) Wardour Str., Soho, built about 1686, was called after him, as, also, was
Arundel Str. (Panton Sq.), which first appears, under that name, in 1673 in the rate
books of St. Martin's-in-the-Fields.

(ᶜ) He went in the suite of the Earl of Castlemaine on the Embassy to Pope
Innocent XI, in 1686.

(ᵈ) See Cunningham's *London* (1850), under "Panton Street. "

(ᵉ) It is stated in Jackson Howard's *Catholic Families* that she was *bur.* at
Tisbury, so probably the burial at St. James's was merely temporary.

Castle, 22 May 1728, in her 31st year, and was *bur.* at Tisbury. M.I.
He *m.*, 2ndly, (cont. dat. 18 Jan. 1728/9) Anne, da. of William (HERBERT),
2nd MARQUESS OF POWIS, by Mary, da. and coh. of Sir Thomas PRESTON,
Bart. He *d.* at Richmond, Surrey, 30 June, and was *bur.* 17 July 1746,
at Tisbury, aged 51. Will, dat. 13 to 30 Oct. 1739, pr. 8 July 1746
His widow *d. s.p.*, at Salisbury, 2, and was *bur.* 5 Oct 1757, at Tisbury.
Will dat. 17 May to 27 Aug., pr. 2 Nov. 1757.

VII 1746.   7. HENRY (ARUNDELL), BARON ARUNDELL OF WARD-
                     OUR, s. and h , by 1st wife, *b* 4 Oct. 1717, or 4 Mar.
1717/8. He *m.*, 27 Jan. 1738/9, (settl. 26 Jan.) Mary, (with £70,000)
yr. da. and coh. [eventually sole h.] of Richard BELLINGS-ARUNDELL,([ª]) of
Lanherne, Cornwall, by Anne, da. of Joseph GAGE, of Sherborne, Oxon.
He *d.*, in his 38th year, at Wardour Castle, 12, and was *bur.* 22 Sep. 1756,
at Tisbury. M.I. Will dat 10 May 1739, and 27 Feb. 1754, pr. 26 Jan.
1757, by Mary, the widow and universal legatee. She, who was *b.* 1716,
d. 21 Feb , and was *bur.* 5 Apr. 1769, at Tisbury. Will dat. 6 June
1767, pr. 29 Mar. 1769.

VIII. 1756   8. HENRY (ARUNDELL), BARON ARUNDELL OF WARD-
                     OUR, only s. and h., *b.* 31 Mar., and *bap.* 11 Apr. 1740.
Ed. at St. Omer, under the name of Bellings, 16 Aug. 1753 to 1 May
1758. In 1769 he *suc.* to his mother's Cornish property at Lanherne.
He rebuilt the Castle at Wardour, beginning the work in 1771. He *m.*,
31 May 1763, at St Geo., Han Sq, Mary Christina, only da. and h. of
Benedict CONQUEST, of Irnham Hall, co Lincoln, by Mary Ursula, da. of
Thomas MARKHAM, of Ollerton, Notts. He *d. s.p.m.*, at Wardour Castle,
4, and was *bur* 20 Dec. 1808, in Wardour Chapel, aged 68. Will pr.
July 1809 His widow *d* 20 June 1813, aged 70, at Irnham, and was
bur. there. Will dat. 5 Nov. 1812, pr. Sep. 1813.

IX. 1808   9. JAMES EVERARD (ARUNDELL), BARON ARUNDELL OF
                     WARDOUR, cousin and h. male, being 1st surv. s. and h.
of the Hon. James Everard A. (by Ann, da. and h. of John WYNDHAM,
of Ashcombe, Wilts), who was 3rd s. of Henry, 6th Lord He was *b.*
4 Mar. 1763, and *bap.* the same day at Salisbury. He *suc.* his father
20 Mar. 1803. He *m.*, 1stly, 3 Feb 1785, Mary Christina, 1st da. and
coh. of (his paternal uncle) Henry (ARUNDELL), 8th LORD ARUNDELL OF
WARDOUR, by Mary Christina abovenamed. She, who was *b.* 10 Aug.
1764, at Wardour Castle, *d.* 14 Feb. 1805, at Irnham, and was *bur.* there.
M.I. He *m.*, 2ndly, 18 Sep. 1806, at St. Geo., Han. Sq., Mary, 3rd da.
of Robert Burnet JONES, of Ades, Sussex, said to have been sometime
Attorney-Gen. of Barbados, by Elizabeth Susannah, da. of Samuel EST-
WICKE, of Barbados. He *d.*, aged 54, at Bath 14, and was *bur.* 22 July

---

([ª]) He was s. of Sir Richard Bellings, by Frances, da and coh of Sir John Arundell, of Lanherne, Cornwall. By this marriage the two branches of the Arundell
family, separated for above two centuries, were united.

1817, at Tisbury. Will pr. Feb. 1818. His widow *d.* 19, and was *bur*
25 Nov. 1853, at Tisbury. Will pr. Dec. 1853.

X. 1817.   10. JAMES EVERARD (ARUNDELL), BARON ARUNDELL OF
                WARDOUR, s. and h. by 1st wife, *b.* 3 Nov. 1785, in
Clifford Str, Midx He was a Tory in politics. (ª) He *m.*, 26 Feb.
1811, at Buckingham House, Pall Mall, (spec. lic) and again next day at
the house of the Dowager Lady Arundell of Wardour in Baker Str.,
Marylebone, Mary Anne, only da. of George (NUGENT-TEMPLE-GRENVILLE),
1st MARQUESS OF BUCKINGHAM, by Mary Elizabeth, 1st da. and coh. of
Robert (NUGENT), 1st EARL NUGENT [I]. He *d. s.p.*, 21 June 1834, at
Rome, and was *bur.* in the Gesù, aged 48. M.I. Will pr. Jan. 1835. His
widow, who was *b.* 8 July 1787, at Stowe, *d.* 1 June 1845, aged 57, at
Loughborough, co. Leicester, and was *bur.* in Ratcliffe Collegiate Church.
M.I. Will pr. July 1845.

XI. 1834.   11. HENRY BENEDICT (ARUNDELL), BARON ARUNDELL
                OF WARDOUR, br. (of the whole blood) and h., *b.* 12 Nov.
1804, at Irnham Hall. (ᵇ) He *m*, 1stly, 8 Aug. 1826, at the R.C. Chapel,
Bath, and at Bathwick Church, Lucy, only child of Hugh Philip SMYTHE,
of Acton Burnell, Salop, by Lucy, 2nd da. of Edward SULYARDE, of
Haughley Park, Suffolk. She *d. s.p.*, 22 Feb. 1827, and was *bur.* in
Wardour Chapel. He *m.*, 2ndly, 22 Sep. 1829, at Tichborne Park,
Hants, Frances Catharine, 2nd da. of Sir Henry Joseph TICHBORNE, 8th
Bart., by Anne, 4th da. of Sir Thomas BURKE, Bart., of Marble Hill. She,
who was *b.* 18 Mar. 1809, at Alresford, *d.* 19 Apr. 1836, at Wardour
Castle, and was *bur.* in the Chapel there. He *m*, 3rdly, 19 June 1838, at
the R.C. Chapel, Chelsea, Theresa, 5th da of William (STOURTON), 17th
LORD STOURTON, by Catharine, da. of Thomas WELD, of Lulworth, Dorset.
He *d.* 19 Oct. 1862, at Wardour Castle, in his 58th year. His widow *d.*
26 Oct. 1878, aged 66, at North Court House, Abingdon, Berks, and was
bur. in Wardour Chapel.

XII. 1862.   12. JOHN FRANCIS (ARUNDELL), BARON ARUNDELL OF
                WARDOUR, s. and h. by 2nd wife, *b.* 28 Dec. 1831, at
Wardour Castle, and *bap.* there the same day. Ed. at Stonyhurst Coll.
In politics he was a Conservative. He *m.*, 13 Oct 1862, at the R C.
Chapel, Hexham, Anne Lucy, da. of John ERRINGTON, of High Warden,
Northumberland, by his 1st wife, Anne Mary, 3rd da. of Vincent Henry
EYRE, of Highfield, co. Derby. She was *b* 22 Oct. 1842. He *d.* 26, and
was *bur.* 31 Oct. 1906, in Wardour Chapelry, aged 74. Will pr. Mar.
1907, gross £189,789, net £54,854. He was *suc.* by his br., who is
outside the scope of this work.

Family Estates.—These, in 1883, besides 182 acres in Cornwall worth

---

(ª) He was the only Roman Cath. peer who, in 1832, voted against the
Reform Bill

(ᵇ) He seldom voted, and when he did, it was with the Liberals

£120 a year (said to have been in the family since 12 Edw. I), consisted of over 6,000 acres in Wilts, worth over £9,000 a year. Total, 6,219 acres, of the yearly value of £9,174. *Principal Residence.*—Wardour Castle, near Tisbury.

ASCELES see ATHOLL

ASCOTT

i e. "Ascott, co. Hertford," Viscountcy *(Dormer)*, *cr.* 1628 with the Earldom of Carnarvon, which see ; *extinct* 1709.

ASHBOURNE

BARONY.

I. 1885.

1. Edward Gibson, 2nd s of William Gibson (*d.* 20 Feb. 1872), of Gaulstown, co. Meath, and Merrion Sq., Dublin, by his 1st wife, Louisa (*d.* 4 Dec. 1853), da. of Joseph Grant, of Dublin, Barrister-at-Law, was *b.* 4 Sep. 1837, and bap. at St. Thomas's, Dublin. He was ed. at Trin. Coll. Dublin ; B A. and 1st gold medallist, 1858; M A. 1861; and, finally, Hon. LL D. 1881. Barrister [I.] 1860 ; Q.C. [I] 1872 ; Attorney Gen [I.] 1877-80. He was M.P. (Conservative) for Dublin Univ. 1875-85. (*) · P.C. [I.] 15 Feb. 1877 and Bencher of the King's Inns, Dublin, the same year P.C. [G.B.] 24 June 1885. In June 1885 he was made Lord Chancellor [I.], and on 4 July following was *cr.* BARON ASHBOURNE (*b*) of Ashbourne, co. Meath (*c*) He resigned office in Feb. 1886, was re-appointed Aug. following, but again resigned in 1892, again re-appointed in 1895 and again held that office, 1895-1905. (*d*) He *m.*, 4 Apr. 1868, at St. Stephen's, Dublin, Frances Maria Adelaide, 2nd da. of Henry Jonathan Cope Colles, Barrister-at-Law She was *b.* 24 Dec. 1849, and *bap* 14 Feb 1850, at St. Peter's, Dublin.

[William Gibson, 1st s. and h ap., *b.* 16 Dec. 1868. M A of Oxford and Dublin. He *m.*, 7 Jan 1896, Marianne, da. of M. de Monbrison, of Paris]

Family Estates.—These in 1883 were under 2,000 acres.

(*) "Mr. Gibson is famous for his white head, his fluent, fearless utterance, his Irish brogue, his spirit and energy, and his copious imagination." (*Society in London,* 1885, p. 224.) V G.

(*b*) Lord Ashbourne's arms are Ermine three keys barwise azure with three trefoils vert in the chief. The keys in this modern grant are borrowed from the arms of the Scottish house of Gibson of Durie *(ex inform.* Oswald Barron) V G.

(*c*) This was one of a dozen Baronies *cr.* in June and July 1885, for a list of which see *sub* Hobhouse.

(*d*) He was spoken of by Lord Randolph Churchill as " the family lawyer of the Tory party. " V.G.

ASHBROOK

VISCOUNTCY [I.]   1. HENRY (FLOWER), BARON CASTLE-DURROW [I.],
was only surv s. and h of William, 1st BARON
I. 1751.   CASTLE-DURROW [I.], by Edith, da. of the Hon Toby
CAULFEILD, of Clone, co. Kilkenny. In Aug. 1710, he was cornet of a troop
of Hoise, and, soon after, a captain.   On 29 Apr. 1746, he *suc.* his father
as LORD CASTLE-DURROW [I.], and took his seat in the House 28 Oct. 1747.
On 30 Sep. 1751, he was *cr.* VISCOUNT ASHBROOK [I.], and took
his seat, as such, on 8 Oct. following. He *m.*, 9 Mar. 1740/1, at St. Paul's,
London, Elizabeth, sister of Col. Nevill TATTON, da. of William TATTON,
of Hillingdon, Midx, Lieut. Gen. in the army. He *d.* at St. Stephen's
Green, Dublin, 27 June 1752, and was *bur.* at Finglas, near Dublin.   Will,
in which, failing his own issue, he devised the reversion of all his estates
to his wife absolutely, dat. 25 June, pr. 31 July 1752, in Dublin, and June
1753, in London   His widow *d.* 10, and was *bur.* 13 Feb. 1759, (with
her father) at Hillingdon. Will dat 27 Nov. 1758, pr. Feb 1759

II. 1752.   2. WILLIAM (FLOWER), VISCOUNT ASHBROOK, &c. [I.],
only s. and h., *b.* 25 June 1744, at Castle-Durrow, co.
Kilkenny. Matric. Oxford (Ch. Ch.) 29 Nov. 1762   He *m*, 9 Mar.
1766, Elizabeth, (ª) da. of Thomas RIDGE, of co. Oxford   He *d.* 30 Aug.
1780, (ᵇ) at Shillingford, Berks, and was *bur.* there, aged 36. M.I.
Will pr. Oct. 1780. His widow, who was *b.* 18 July 1746, *m.*, 20 Jun.
1790, the Rev. John JONES, D.D, and *d.* 22 Feb 1808, at Shipston
upon Stour, co. Worcester, and was *bur.* at Shillingford afsd. Will pr.
May 1808.

III. 1780.   3. WILLIAM (FLOWER), VISCOUNT ASHBROOK, &c. [I.],
s. and h, *b.* 16 Nov. 1767. Ed. at Eton Matric.
Oxford (Trin. Coll), 13 July 1785. He *d.* unm., 6 Jan. 1802, at Wadley
House, Berks, aged 34. Will pr. Feb 1802.

IV. 1802.   4. HENRY JEFFERY (FLOWER), VISCOUNT ASHBROOK, &c
[I.], only br. and h., *b.* 16 Nov. 1776. Sometime Capt.
58th Foot. Claim to Peerage allowed 25 Aug. 1831. Lord of the Bedchamber 1832-37. He *m.*, 1stly, by spec. lic. 26 May 1802, at St. Geo.,
Han. Sq., Deborah Susanna, (fortune £30,000) only da. and h. of the Rev.
William Maximilian FREIND, Rector of Chinnor, co. Oxford, by Deborah, da.
and h. of Thomas WALKER, of New Woodstock in that co. She *d.* 24 Mar.
1810, aged 30, and was *bur.* at Hurley, Berks. M.I Admon. July 1812.
He *m.*, 2ndly, 22 June 1812, by spec. lic., at St Geo., Han. Sq, Emily

(ª) According to George Montagu, writing in 1766 to Horace Walpole, she was
"a waterman's daughter, near Oxford." V.G.

(ᵇ) There is an abusive account of him, purporting to be an epitaph, which
refers to his insignificance, boorishness, stupidity, &c, in *The Abbey of Kilkhampton*, by
Sir Herbert Croft, 1780, *part* ii

Theophila, sister of Charles Theophilus, LORD METCALFE, 1st da. of Sir Thomas Theophilus METCALFE, 1st Bart., by Susannah Selina Sophia, da. of John DEBONNAIRE. He *d.* 4 May 1847, at his seat, Beaumont Lodge, Old Windsor, aged 70. Will pr. June 1847. His widow, who was *b* 16 June 1790, in Portland Place, Marylebone, *d.* 9 Apr. 1885, aged 94, at 26 Queen's Gate Terrace. Will pr. 9 May 1885, above £73,000.

V. 1847.   5 HENRY (WALKER, *afterwards* FLOWER), VISCOUNT ASHBROOK, &c. [I], 2nd but 1st surv. ([a]) s. and h by 1st wife, *b.* 17 June and *bap* 5 July 1806, reg at Old Windsor, Berks By royal lic. 23 Nov. 1827, he took the name of Walker only ; and by a subsequent one, 15 July 1847, resumed the name of Flower only. Sheriff co. Kilkenny 1834. Claim to Peerage allowed 15 July 1847. He *m.*, 7 June 1828, at St. Geo., Han. Sq , Frances, 9th da. of the Rev. Sir John ROBINSON, 1st Bart , of Rokeby Hall, co. Louth, by Mary Anne, da. of James SPENCER, of Rathangan. He *d* 3 Aug. 1871, aged 65. His widow *d.* 15 June 1886, aged 83, at Knockcatrina, near Durrow.

VI. 1871.   6. HENRY JEFFERY (FLOWER), VISCOUNT ASHBROOK, &c., [I.], sometime (1829-47) HENRY JEFFERY WALKER, s and h., *b.* 26 Mar. 1829. Ensign 52nd Foot, 1848. Retired 1853 Dep. Lieut. of Queen's County. Sheriff 1856. Claim to Peerage allowed 3 May 1872. He *m* , 4 Sep. 1860, at Leamington, co Warwick, Emily, 1st da. of John Frederick ABINGDON, of Esher, Surrey. She was divorced, decree *nisi* 28 Feb. 1877.([b]) He *d. s.p.s.*, 14 Dec. 1882, at Castle-Durrow, aged 53.

VII. 1882.   7. WILLIAM SPENCER (FLOWER), VISCOUNT ASHBROOK (1751) and BARON CASTLE-DURROW (1733) [I.], sometime (1830-47) WILLIAM SPENCER WALKER, br. and h., *b.* 23 Mar. 1830. Ed. at Eton, and at Trin. Coll , Dublin. B.A. 1851. Sometime an officer in the 52nd Foot. He *m.*, 25 June 1861, at Capernwray, Augusta Madeline Henrietta, 1st da. of George MARTON, of Capernwray Hall, co Lancaster, by Lucy Sarah, da. of the Rt. Hon. Sir Robert DALLAS, Lord Chief Justice of the Common Pleas She *d.* 5 Jan. 1906, suddenly, of heart failure after bronchitis, at Castle-Durrow. Will pr. above £5000 gross and net, exclusive of settled funds. He *d.* 26 Nov. 1906, at Castle-Durrow, aged 76. He was *suc.* by his br., who is outside the scope of this work

Family Estates —These, in 1883, consisted of about 9,300 acres in co. Kilkenny, 7,700 in King's County, 4,600 in Queen's County, 860 in co. Limerick, and 500 in Dublin. Total 23,050 acres of the yearly value of £13,911. *Principal Residence.*—Castle-Durrow, co. Kilkenny.

([a]) An elder br. *d.* an infant.
([b]) The cause was her *crim con.* with Capt. Hugh Sydney Baillie

ASHBURNHAM (ᵃ)

BARONY.   1. John Ashburnham, of Ashburnham, Sussex, s. and
h. of William A. (who *d. v.p.*, 1665), (ᵇ) by Elizabeth,
I. 1689.   da. of John (Poulett), 1st Lord Poulett, was *b.* 15 Jan.
1655/6, at Chiswick, Midx. M.P. (Tory) for Hastings 1679-81, 1685-87,
1689. On 20 May 1689, he was *cr.* BARON ASHBURNHAM (ᶜ) of
Ashburnham, Sussex. From 19 Oct. 1702 till his death, he was Custos
Rotulorum of co. Brecon. He *m.*, 22 July 1677, at Westm. Abbey,
Bridget, da. and h. of Walter Vaughan, (ᵈ) of Porthammel House, co
Brecon. He *d.*, (ᵉ) at his house in Southampton Str., Bloomsbury, 21 Jan.,
and was *bur.* 1 Feb. 1709/10, at Ashburnham, aged 44. Will pr. Feb.
1710. His widow *d.* 12, and was *bur.* 19 May 1719, in her 59th year, at
Ashburnham. Will dat. 12 Sep. 1717, pr. 22 May 1719

II. 1710.   2. William (Ashburnham), Baron Ashburnham, s.
and h., *b.* 21 and *bap* 22 May 1679, at St. Martin's-in-
the-Fields ; reg at Ashburnham. M.P. (Tory) for Hastings, 1702-10.
He *m.*, 16 Oct. 1705, at Carby, co. Lincoln, Catharine, da. and eventually
sole h. of Thomas Taylor, of Clapham, Beds, by Ursula, his wife. (ᶠ)

(ᵃ) This is one of the twelve families given in Drummond's *Noble British
Families* See p 118, note "b."

"The common account [writes a correspondent] of the descent of this family
given by Fuller and others is mythical. The true descent is probably from Criol, to
which name belongs the oldest quartering. Hence also the name Bertram."

(ᵇ) This William was s. and h. ap. of John A, of Ashburnham, Groom of the
Bedchamber to Charles I, and well known for his close relations with that King, who
d. 15 June 1671. It seems remarkable that this John Ashburnham, who had done
so much for the House of Stuart, should not have been raised to the Peerage immediately after the Restoration of that House, while his grandson (whose chief claim to
distinction appears to have been that he *was* such grandson) should have been *cr.* a
Baron by the very King who had driven the House of Stuart into banishment.
Clarendon explains the neglect of John the elder by the general opinion (not shared
by him) that John A had been outwitted, if not corrupted, by Cromwell at the
time of Charles I leaving Hampton Court.

(ᶜ) The Ashburnhams of Ashburnham bear Gules a fesse between six molets
silver. In old times the molets were pierced, and thirteenth century seals show that
Ashburnham bore for a time a fretty coat derived from a match with Mautravers.
(*ex inform.* Oswald Barron) V.G.

(ᵈ) Walter was s. and h. of Sir Charles Vaughan, by Frances, da. of Sir Robert
Knollys. A pedigree of him is given in Jones's *Brecknockshire*, vol. 11, p. 341, but the
name of his wife (about whom there seems some mystery) is not stated therein.

(ᵉ) According to Macky he was (1704) "a thin brown man."

(ᶠ) Among the sixteen "delinquents" of co. Bedford, whose estates were
"decimated" in 1655, the amount (£90) levied on "Richard Taylor of Clopham
Esq." was only exceeded by two others, *viz.* Conquest of Houghton Conquest (£120)
and Leigh of Leighton Buzzard (£135) See *Thurloe State Papers*, vol. iv, p 513.
The property of Clapham (more anciently *Clopham*) passed (by sale, or entail) to the

He *d. s.p.*, 16 June 1710, aged 31, at his seat in Sussex, and his widow *d.* 11 July following, aged 23 years, 10 months and 14 days   Both *d.* of small pox, and were *bur.* at Ashburnham.   His will pr. July 1710.   The admon. of his widow granted, 26 July 1710, to her mother Ursula Taylor, widow.

III. 1710.	3 and 1. JOHN (ASHBURNHAM), BARON ASHBURNHAM, br. and h., *bap.* 13 Mar. 1687, at St. Margaret's, Westm.
EARLDOM.	M.P. (Tory) for Hastings Feb. to June 1710. Col. of
I. 1730.	the 1st troop of Horse Guards 1713-15. From Dec. 1728 to June 1731 he was Lord of the Bedchamber to the

Prince of Wales   On 14 May 1730, he was *cr.* VISCOUNT ST. ASAPH of the Principality of Wales, and EARL OF ASHBURNHAM.   Capt. of the Yeomen of the Guard 23 Nov. 1731 till death. (ª)   He *m.*, 1stly, 21 Oct 1710, Mary, da. of James (BUTLER), 2nd DUKE OF ORMONDE, by his 2nd wife, Mary, da. of Henry (SOMERSET), 1st DUKE OF BEAUFORT. She *d. s p.*, 2 Jan. 1712/3, in childbed, (ᵇ) in her 23rd year, and was *bur.* at Ashburnham.   He *m.*, 2ndly, 24 July 1714, at the Chapel Royal, Whitehall, Henrietta Maria, Dowager COUNTESS OF ANGLESEY, 1st da. and coh. of William Richard George (STANLEY), 9th EARL OF DERBY, by Elizabeth, da of Thomas BUTLER, *styled* EARL OF OSSORY.   She *d. s.p.m.*, 26 June 1718, in her 31st year, and was *bur.* at Ashburnham.   Admon 26 July 1718 to her husband   He *m.*, 3rdly, 14 Mar. 1723/4 (spec. lic.), at St James's, Westm., Jemima, 2nd da and coh. of Henry (DE GREY), 1st DUKE OF KENT, by his 1st wife, Jemima, da. and coh. of Thomas (CREWE), 2nd LORD CREWE of Stene.   She *d.* 7 July 1731, in her 33rd year, and was *bur.* at Ashburnham.   He *d.* 10 Mar. 1736/7, at his house in St. James's Sq., Westm., in his 49th year, and was *bur.* at Ashburnham. Will pr. Mar. 1737.

EARLDOM.	⎫	2 and 4. JOHN (ASHBURNHAM), EARL OF
	⎪	ASHBURNHAM, *&c.* only s and h. by 3rd wife,
II	⎪	*b.* 30 Oct. 1724. A Lord of the Bedchamber
	⎬ 1737.	1748-62. LL D. of Cambridge 3 July 1749;
BARONY.	⎪	L. Lieut. of Sussex 1754-7. Keeper of Hyde
IV.	⎪	Park and of St. James's Park, 1753-62. P.C.
	⎭	12 July 1765, Master of the Great Wardrobe

---

family of Ashburnham, by whom it is still held, the Manor House having long been used as a farm.   The ped of Taylor is recorded in the Visit. of Beds, 1634.

(ª) In 1730 he sold to the Crown the long lease of " Ashburnham House " in Little Dean's Yard, Westminster, which had been built for his ancestor by Inigo Jones, and which, as to internal structure, the graceful staircase, *&c.*, is reckoned one of the finest of his works.   Part of the house was shortly afterwards (23 Oct. 1731) destroyed by fire, with nearly a fourth part of the celebrated Cottonian MSS then deposited therein.

(ᵇ) Swift writes at this time, —" She was my greatest favourite, and I am in excessive concern for her death, I hardly knew a more valuable person on all accounts. "   V.G.

1765-75. First Lord of the Bedchamber and Groom of the Stole, 1775-82. He *m.*, 28 June 1756, at St. Geo., Han. Sq. (spec. lic.), Elizabeth, (a fortune of £200,000) da. and coh. of John CROWLEY, of Barking, Suffolk, Alderman of London (who was only s. and h. of Sir Ambrose CROWLEY, Alderman of London), by Theodosia, (ª) da. of the Rev. Joseph GASCOYNE, D.D., Rector of Enfield, Midx. She *d.* at Bath, 5, and was "carried away" (Abbey Reg.) 15 Feb. 1781, aged 53. He *d* 8 Apr. 1812, aged 87. (ᵇ) Will pr. June 1812. Both were *bur.* at Ashburnham. (ᶜ)

[GEORGE ASHBURNHAM, *styled* VISCOUNT ST. ASAPH, s. and h. ap., *b.* 2, and *d.* 13 Feb. 1758, and was *bur.* at Ashburnham.]

EARLDOM.
III.

BARONY.
V.

1812.

3 and 5. GEORGE (ASHBURNHAM), EARL OF ASHBURNHAM, &c., 2nd, but 1st surv. s. and h., *b.* 25 Dec. 1760, and *bap* 29 Jan 1761, at St. Geo., Han. Sq., the King, the Duke of Newcastle, and the Princess Dowager of Wales, being sponsors. Ed. at Trin. Coll. Cambridge. M.A. 1780. Lord of the Bedchamber to the Prince of Wales, 1784-95. Trustee of the Brit. Museum 1810 till death. He was sum. by writ, 23 Mar. 1803, *v.p.*, in his father's Barony, as LORD ASHBURNHAM. F.S.A., G.C H., 1827; el. K.G. 10, and inst. 22 June 1829. In politics he was a Tory. He *m*, 1stly, 28 Aug. 1784, (spec. lic.) at her father's house in Arlington Str., St. Geo, Han. Sq., Sophia, 3rd da. of Thomas (THYNNE), 1st MARQUESS OF BATH, by Elizabeth Cavendish, da. of William (BENTINCK), 1st DUKE OF PORTLAND. She was *b.* 19 Dec 1763, and *d* 9 Apr. 1791, in childbed, as VISCOUNTESS ST. ASAPH. He *m*, 2ndly, 25 July 1795, at Orwell Park, near Ipswich, Charlotte, (ᵈ) 1st da. of Algernon (PERCY), 1st EARL OF BEVERLEY, by Isabella Susanna, 2nd da.

(ª) Through this lady the estate of Barking in Suffolk came to the family of Ashburnham, her mother, Anne, being da. and h. of Sir Francis THEOBALD, of Barking. This Theodosia Crowley survived all her children, and *d.* 17 May 1782, aged 89, when Barking devolved on her grandson, George Ashburnham, afterwards the 5th Earl.

(ᵇ) "A most decent, reserved and servile courtier. He did not want sense, but it all centred in self interest" (Horace Walpole). George Selwyn writes of him in 1782.—"I have the greatest opinion of his judgment in the conductive part of life. I really believe, if any man ever went through life with consummate discretion, it has been himself, and he has preserved his reputation at the same time." He was originally a Whig, and protested against the disqualification of Wilkes, but became a Tory late in life. V.G.

(ᶜ) For them apparently (the arms of Ashburnham, with those of Crowley in pretence, being on the screen in front) was built Ashburnham House, in Dover street, Midx., one of the few old patrician mansions still (1885) remaining in the Metropolis, but which has, alas, now (1910) been gone some few years.

(ᵈ) The Earl's 4th da. by his 2nd wife, Jane Henrietta, was mother of Algernon Charles Swinburne, *b.* 5 Apr. 1837, *d.* 10 Apr 1909, the last of the great Victorian poets. V G

36

of Peter BURRELL, of Beckenham, Kent. He *d.* 27 Oct. 1830, (ᵃ) at
Ashburnham, aged 69. Will pr. Dec. 1830. His widow, who was *b.*
3 June 1776, *d.* 26 Nov. 1862, in Eaton Sq., Midx., in her 87th year.

[GEORGE ASHBURNHAM, *styled* VISCOUNT ST. ASAPH from Apr. 1812,
s. and h. ap. by 1st wife, *b.* 9 Oct. 1785. Ed at Trin Coll. Cambridge ;
M.A. 1805. M.P. (Tory) for New Romney 1807-12, for Weobley,
1812 till his death. He *d.* unm., *v.p.*, in Dover Str., 7, and was *bur.*
15 June 1813, at Ashburnham, aged 27.]

EARLDOM.		4 and 6. BERTRAM (ASHBURNHAM), EARL OF
IV.		ASHBURNHAM, &c., 4th s., being 2nd, but 1st
		surv. s. and h. by 2nd wife, *b.* 23 Nov. 1797.
	1830.	Ed. at St. John's Coll., Cambridge. A Con-
BARONY.		servative in politics. He *m*, 8 Jan. 1840,
VI.		Katherine Charlotte, sister to George, 10th

EARL OF HADDINGTON [S.], 4th da. of George
BAILLIE, of Jerviswood, by Mary, da. of Sir James PRINGLE, Bart. [S.].
He *d.* 22 June 1878, at Ashburnham, and was *bur.* there, aged 80. (ᵇ) His
widow, who was *b.* 10 May 1819, *d* 6 Feb. 1894.

(ᵃ) By him was edited a well-known book entitled " *A Narrative by John
Ashburnham of his Attendance on King Charles the First, &c. To which is prefixed a
Vindication of his Character and Conduct, from the Misrepresentations of Lord Clarendon,
by his lineal Descendant and present Representative.* " 2 vols., 1830.

(ᵇ) He was the Collector of an extensive library of early and rare books, both
English and Foreign, and of a vast assemblage of MSS.   It comprised four divisions—
viz (i) the LIBRI collection, purchased in 1848, containing numerous ancient codices,
illuminated MSS., works of mediæval literature, literary and scientific correspondence,
&c   (ii) The BARROIS collection, rich in old French poetry and romances.   (iii) The
STOWE collection, purchased, at the sale of the Duke of Buckingham's effects, in 1849,
containing many early charters, monastic registers, state papers, and antiquarian
gatherings concerning England [including the MSS. of the well-known Thomas
Astle, Keeper of the Records], as well as many valuable Irish MSS.   (iv) A portion
known as the " appendix," comprising Lord Ashburnham's miscellaneous collections.
These four portions, containing nearly 4000 MSS , were, in 1883, offered to Government for £160,000.   The French Government, however, claiming between 160 and
170 of the MSS. in the Libri and Barrois collections as having been stolen (which
MSS. were valued at £24,000), the trustees of the British Museum recommended
(17 Mar. 1883) the purchase of the remainder at £136,000, but the Treasury
declined the proposal   (*ex inform.* H.Gough).

Finally, however, in July 1883, the Government purchased the Stowe collection
(which in 1849 was sold for £8000) for £45,000, presenting the English portion to
the British Museum, and the Irish (on loan) to the Royal Irish Academy, Dublin ;
while in May 1884, the Italian Government bought for £23,000, for the Laurenzian
library at Florence, the larger portion of the Libri collection (the whole of which,
some 1923 MSS. had, in 1846, been sold for £8000), as also the Dante MSS. (some
dozen or so) from the " Appendix , " while the Barrois collection, some 704 MSS.
(which had been offered in 1848 to the British Museum for £6000), and the
" Appendix " (except as above stated), were returned to Lord Ashburnham

EARLDOM.   5 and 7. BERTRAM (ASHBURNHAM), EARL OF
V.   ASHBURNHAM (1730), VISCOUNT ST. ASAPH
              (1730) AND BARON ASHBURNHAM (1689), s. and
        1878.   h., *b.* 28 Oct. 1840, (ª) at Ashburnham Place,
BARONY.   Sussex   Ed. at Westm. school.   D L for
VII.   co Brecon.   He became a Roman Catholic in
             1872. (ᵇ)   In politics he was a Conservative
until 1888, when he became a Liberal.   He *m.*, 25 Feb. 1888, at the Reg.
Office, St Geo., Han. Sq., (marriage not announced in *The Times* until
Mar. 1893) Emily, da of " Richard CHAPLIN, Gent.," then deceased, the
residence of both parties being 30 Montpelier Sq., Brompton.   She *d.* of
pleurisy, 12, and was *bur.* 16 Feb. 1900, at Ashburnham.   Will pr.
over £5,900.

[BERTRAM RICHARD ASHBURNHAM, *styled* VISCOUNT ST. ASAPH, s. and
h. ap, *b.* (a few days after his parents' marriage) 2, and *d.* 4 Mar. 1888.]

Family Estates.—These, in 1883, consisted of about, 14,000 acres in
Sussex, 3,400 in Suffolk, 5,700 in Carmarthen, and 1,400 in co Brecon.
Total about 24,500 acres, worth about £24,000 a year.   *Principal Resi-
dences.*—Ashburnham Place, near Battle, Sussex ; and Barking Hall, near
Ipswich, Suffolk.

ASHBURTON

BARONY.   1. JOHN DUNNING, 2nd, but only surv. s. and h. of
I. 1782.   John D., of Ashburton, Devon (who *d.* there 1 Dec.
          1780, aged 80), by Agnes, da. of Henry JUDSHAM, of
Oldport, in Modbury, in that co., was *b.* 18 Oct. near, and *bap.* 29 Oct.
1731, at Ashburton, and ed. at the Grammar school there.   He was a
Barrister, adm. to the Middle Temple, 8 May 1752, and one of the
most popular Pleaders of his time.   Recorder of Bristol 1766 till death ;
Solicitor-Gen. 1768-1770 ; M.P. (Whig) for Calne 1768-82. (ᶜ)   P.C.

A very full account of the contents of the whole of the Ashburnham MSS. will
be found in *Hist. MSS. Com.*, 8th Rep., App., part 3.   The remainder of the
Ashburnham library was sold in 1897.

(ª) John, his next br, and (1909) h. presumptive, *b.* 6 Mar. 1845, sometime
2nd Sec. Diplomatic Service, *m*, 21 May 1907, at St. Cuthbert's, Philbeach Gdns,
Maud Mary, 2nd da. of Charles Royal-Dawson, of South East Wynaad, Madras
Presidency. V.G.

(ᵇ) For a list of Peers and Peeresses who have joined this faith since 1850, see
App. G in vol. III. V.G.

(ᶜ) It was he who moved the celebrated resolution in the H. of Commons that
" the power of the Crown has increased, is increasing, and ought to be diminished. "
He and one Lucy Charlton appear in 1774 as " the powerful Pleader and Miss C ,
in the notorious tête à tête portraits in the *Town and Country Mag.*, as to which see
ante, p. 94.   He was remarkably ugly.   Lord Thurlow is said, in Rogers' *Table Talk*,
to have caused a note to him at once to reach its destination by telling a waiter at

27 Mar. 1782. Through the influence of Lord Shelburne, he was *cr*, on 8 Apr. 1782, BARON ASHBURTON (ᵃ) of Ashburton, Devon. At the same time he was made Chancellor of the Duchy of Lancaster, receiving some £4000 *p. a.*, though always loud against pensions and sinecures. He *m.*, 31 Mar. 1780, at St. Leonard's, near Exeter, Devon, Elizabeth, da. of John BARING, of Larkbeare, near Exeter, merchant, by Elizabeth, da. of John VOWLER, of Bellair, Devon. He *d.* 18 Aug. 1783, of paralysis, at Exmouth, aged 52, "just as he had attained the fond object of his ambition," (ᵇ) and was *bur.* at Ashburton. Will pr. Sep. 1783. His widow, who was *b.* 21 July 1744, at Larkbeare, *d.* 23 Feb 1809, in Cadogan Place. Will pr. Mar. 1809.

II. 1783 to 1823. 2. RICHARD BARRÉ (DUNNING), BARON ASHBURTON, 2nd, but only surv. s. and h., *b.* 20 Sep. 1782. In politics he was a Whig. He *m.*, 17 Sep 1805, at Lainshaw, Anne Selby, 3rd da. of William CUNNINGHAM, of Lainshaw, by Margaret Nicholson, da of the Hon George CRANSTOUN. He *d. s p.*, 15 Feb 1823, at Friar's Hall, co. Roxburgh, when the *title* became *extinct.* (ᶜ) Will pr. May 1823. His widow, who is said to have possessed a fortune of £200,000, (ᵈ) resided at Edinburgh. She *m.*, 30 June 1826, at Glenlee, N B., the CHIEF OF CLANRANALD. (ᵉ) She *d.* 8 July 1835, in Gt. Stanhope Str, and was *bur.* at Kensal Green. Will pr. July 1835, leaving her property and late husband's estates to her maternal cousin, Lord Cranstoun. The Chief, *i.e.* Ranald George Macdonald, *titular* 6th Baron Clanranald under the Jacobite creation of 1716, (ᶠ) *d.* 11 Mar. 1873, in Clarendon Rd., Midx., and was *bur.* in Brompton Cemetery.

III. 1835. 1 ALEXANDER BARING, 2nd s. of Sir Francis B, 1st Bart. [1793], by Harriet, da. of William HERRING, of

---

Dunning's club " to deliver it to the ugliest man at the card table—to him who most resembles the knave of spades. " See also, as to his appearance, Wraxall's *Memoirs*, 1884, vol ii, p. 257, and *ibid*. p. 259 as to the remarkable way in which his peerage was obtained ; see also *ibid.* p 39 A splendid portrait, by Reynolds, of him and his sister is (1910) *penes* Sir Edgar Vincent, K.C M.G. V.G.

(ᵃ) The Lords Ashburton of the Dunning family bore arms of Bendy gold and vert of eight pieces sinisterwise with a lion sable over all. These arms, save for the ' sinisterwise ' colouring of the bendy field, are those allowed in the sixteenth century to a family of Donning at Rye and Chichester in Sussex, with whom the Devonshire family claims no kinship (*ex inform.* Oswald Barron.) V.G.

(ᵇ) Brydges' *Biographical Peerage*. See a refutation of what in Campbell's life of Lord Chancellor Charles Yorke is (erroneously) called " one of the best specimens of *Dunning's eloquence* " in *N. & Q.*, 2nd ser., vol v, p. 12.

(ᶜ) He was author of a valuable work entitled *Genealogical Memoirs of the Royal House of France*, with copious tabular pedigrees. London. 1825, large 4to., pp. 200.

(ᵈ) See *N & Q*, 2nd ser., vol vi, p 151

(ᵉ) He is the hero of a recent novel by Maurice Hewlett, *The Stooping Lady.* V.G

(ᶠ) For a list of Jacobite Peerages, see Appendix F in this volume.

Croydon, Surrey (which Sir Francis was br. of Elizabeth, wife of John (Dunning), 1st Lord Ashburton abovenamed), was *b.* 27 Oct. 1774, and was for 18 years head of the firm of Baring Brothers, Merchants(*) in London. M.P. for Taunton, 1806-26; for Callington, 1826-31; (ᵇ) for Thetford, 1831-32; and for North Essex, 1832-35. Trustee of the Brit Museum from 1829, and of the Nat. Gallery from 1835, till his death Master of the Mint and President of the Board of Trade 1834-35; P.C 15 Dec. 1834; D.C.L. On 10 Apr. 1835, he was *cr.* BARON ASHBURTON(ᶜ) of Ashburton, Devon. AMBASSADOR (Special Mission) to the U.S.A, 1842 (ᵈ) He *m.*, 23 Aug. 1798, in N. America, Anne Louisa, 1st da. of William BINGHAM, of Philadelphia, a Senator of the U.S.A. He *d.* 12 May 1848, at Longleat, Wilts, aged 73, and his widow *d* 5 Dec following, at Bay House, near Gosport.

IV. 1848. 2. WILLIAM BINGHAM (BARING), BARON ASHBURTON, s. and h., *b.* June 1799 Ed. at Oriel Coll. Oxford; B.A. 1821, 2nd class classics. M.P. for Thetford, 1826-30; for Callington, 1830-31; for Winchester, 1832-37; (ᵉ) for North Staffordshire, 1837-41; and for Thetford, 1841-48. Secretary to the Board of Control, 1841-45; Paymaster Gen of the Forces 1845-46. P.C. 30 June 1845; Trustee of Nat. Gallery 1850 till death; Pres. Roy. Asiat. Soc. 1852-55; of the Roy. Agric. Soc. 1853, and of the Roy. Geog. Soc. 1860-62. F.R.S. 29 Apr 1854. Commander of the Legion of Honour He *m*, 1stly, 12 Apr 1823, at her mother's house in Dover Str., St. Geo, Han. Sq., Harriet Mary, 1st da of George John (MONTAGU), 6th EARL OF SANDWICH, by Louisa, da. of Armar (LOWRY-CORRY), 1st EARL OF BELMORE[I.]. She, who was *b* 14 May 1805, *d. s p.s.*, 4 May 1857, at Paris He *m*, 2ndly, 17 Nov. 1858, at Bath House, Piccadilly, Louisa Caroline, 3rd and yst. da of the Rt. Hon. James Alexander Stewart MACKENZIE, by Mary Elizabeth Frederica, 1st da. and coh. of Francis Humberston (MACKENZIE), LORD SEAFORTH He *d. s.p m.*, 23 Mar. 1864, at the Grange, Hants. Will pr. 1 June 1864, under £180,000. His widow, who was *b* 5 May 1827, and who inherited the Mackenzie estate of nearly 30,000 acres in co Ross, *d.* 2 Feb. 1903, at Kent House, Knightsbridge, aged 76. Will pr. over £285,000 gross, and over £109,000 net.

(*) Of this great mercantile house, the Duc de Richelieu wittily said, "There are six great powers in Europe, *viz.* England, France, Russia, Austria, Prussia, and Baring Brothers." See also as to this house, and as to the number of peerages acquired by the Baring family, notes *sub* REVELSTOKE V G.

(ᵇ) From 1806 to 1831 he sat as a Whig, but thereafter acted with the Tories. V.G.

(ᶜ) The Barings, Lords Ashburton, bear arms of Azure a fesse gold with a bear's head in its proper colours, cut off at the neck, in the chief, having a golden muzzle and ring (*ex inform* Oswald Barron.) V G

(ᵈ) He then concluded the 'Ashburton Treaty' delimiting the frontiers of British North America and the U.S.A. V.G.

(ᵉ) From 1826 to 1831 he sat as a Whig, but thereafter as a Conservative. V.G.

V. 1864. 3. FRANCIS (BARING), BARON ASHBURTON, br. and h. male, b. 20 May 1800. M.P. (ª) for Thetford, 1830-31, 1832-41, and 1848-57. He m, Jan. 1833, Hortense Eugenie Claire, da. of Hugues Bernard MARET, DUKE OF BASSANO in France, (the celebrated Minister of Napoleon), by Marie Madeleine, da. of Martin, Count LEJFAS CHARPENTIER. He d. 6 Sep. 1868, leaving personalty to the amount of £250,000 His widow d. 15 Dec. 1882, aged 70, at her residence in the Champs Elysées, Paris. Will dat. 30 Oct 1878, pr. (as an English subject) Apr. 1883 in London.

VI. 1868. 4. ALEXANDER HUGH (BARING), BARON ASHBURTON, only surv. s. and h., b. 4 May 1835 Ed. at Harrow, and at Ch Ch. Oxford. B.A 1857. M.P. (Conservative) for Thetford, 1857-67. He m., 5 Jan. 1864, Leonora Caroline, 2nd da. of Edward St. Vincent (DIGBY), 9th LORD DIGBY [I.], by Theresa Anna Maria, da. of Henry Stephen (FOX-STRANGWAYS), 3rd EARL OF ILCHESTER. He d. 18 July 1889, aged 54, at Bath House, Piccadilly. His widow, who was b. 8 Nov. 1844, d. 18 Jan. 1904, at 17 Hertford Str., Mayfair.

VII. 1889. 5. FRANCIS DENZIL EDWARD (BARING), BARON ASH-BURTON [1835], 1st s and h. ; b. 20 July 1866. A Conservative in politics. He m., 25 July 1889 (seven days after his father's death), at St. Geo., Han. Sq., Mabel Edith, 1st da. of Francis Wheler (HOOD), 4th VISCOUNT HOOD OF WHITLEY, by Edith, da. of Arthur W. WARD. She, who was b 26 May 1866, d. 18 Jan. 1904. He m., 2ndly, 19 Feb. 1906, at the Mairie, Paris, and afterwards in the Rue d'Aguesseau there, Frances, da. of J. C. DONNELLY, of New York, an American actress, known as " Frances Belmont. " (ᵇ)

Family Estates —These, in 1883, consisted of about 15,500 acres in Hants, 10,000 in Wilts, 6,500 in co. Hereford, 4,000 in Essex and 1,000 in Somerset. Total about 37,000 worth about £47,000 a year. Besides this, in 1883, Louisa, the Dowager Baroness, had about 2,500 acres in Devon, about 2,000 in Cornwall and about 200 in Hants, as also about 28,500 in co. Ross, which last named estate, though " of the nominal value of £1,885, practically produces no income. " Total (for this lady) about 33,000 acres worth about £6,000 a year. (ᶜ) *Principal Residence.*— The Grange, near Alresford, Hants.

(ª) He sat as a Whig 1830-31, but thereafter joined the Tories, changing his politics precisely as his two predecessors in title had done. V.G.

(ᵇ) For a list of peers who have m. Singers, Dancers, or Actresses, see note *sub* Charles, EARL OF PETERBOROUGH [1697]. V G

(ᶜ) The whole of the estates near Taunton were offered at auction in May 1894, the portion sold amounting to £70,000. Fitzhead Court was withdrawn. V.G.

ASHCOMBE OF DORKING AND OF BODIAM CASTLE

BARONY.

I. 1892.

1. GEORGE CUBITT, 1st s and h. of Thomas CUBITT, of Denbies, the eminent builder (ª) (who *d.* 20 Dec. 1855, in his 68th year), by Mary Anne, da. of Samuel WARNER, was *b.* 4 June 1828, at Clapham Common ; ed. at Trin. Coll. Cambridge ; B.A., 1851 ; M.A, 1854 ; was M.P. (Conservative) for West Surrey 1860-85, and for Mid Surrey, 1885-92 ; Second Church-Estates Commissr., 1874-79; P.C. 24 Mar. 1880; Member of the Council of Selwyn College, 1887. On 22 Aug. 1892, he was *cr.* (ᵇ) BARON ASHCOMBE OF DORKING, Surrey, AND OF BODIAM CASTLE, (ᶜ) Sussex. He *m.*, 14 June 1853, at Dorking, Laura, yst. da. of the Rev. James JOYCE, Vicar of Dorking, by Sarah, da. of (—) Brakspear, of Henley on Thames. She, who was *b* 13 Aug. 1826, *d.* 7 July 1904, at 17 Prince's Gate, Midx, and was *bur.* at Ranmore, Surrey.

[HENRY CUBITT, 3rd, (ᵈ) but 1st surv. s. and h. ap., *b.* at 17 Prince's Gate afsd., 14 Mar , and *bap* 1 May 1867, at All Saints, Ennismore Gardens, Midx ; ed. at Eton, and at Trin. Coll. Cambridge ; B.A. 1889 ; M.A. 1891. M.P. (Conservative) South East Surrey 1892-1906 ; Lord Lieut. and Custos Rotulorum, Surrey, 1905. He *m*, 21 Aug. 1890, at Ockley, Surrey, Maud Marianne, yr. of the 2 daughters of Archibald Motteux CALVERT, Col. R A , of Ockley Court, Surrey, by Constance, da. of Henry PETERS, of Betchworth Park. She was *b.* in 1865, at Charlton, near Woolwich.]

Family Estates —These, in 1883, consisted of 3,989 acres in Surrey ; 2,200 in Devon, and 600 in Sussex. *Total.*—6,789 acres ; worth £8,509 a year. *Principal Residence.*—Denbies, near Dorking, Surrey. *Note.* In 1909 the Surrey property, consisting of 4,200 acres, had become the property of his Lordship's h. ap.

(ª) The buildings on the Westminster and Lowndes estates, (including Belgrave Sq., Lowndes Sq , Chesham Place, and the vast district known as South Belgravia, between Eaton Sq. and the Thames) as also those erected at an earlier date in Tavistock Sq , Gordon Sq. and Woburn Place, on the estates of the Duke of Bedford and Lord Southampton, form the chief part of his undertakings. His yr. br., William Cubitt, for two years (1860-62) L. Mayor of London (*d.* 1863), was sometime in the same business.

(ᵇ) This was one of 8 Baronies conferred at the recommendation of Lord Salisbury on leaving office, for a list of which see note *sub* LLANGATTOCK.

(ᶜ) Lord Ashcombe's arms, a modern grant, are Checky gold and gules with a pile silver and a lion's head razed sable on the pile. The Cubitts are a yeoman family of East Norfolk, of whom the branch settled at Catfield showed, on their eighteenth century monuments, a shield of a bent bow with an arrow. (*ex inform.* Oswald Barron) V.G.

(ᵈ) Of his two elder brothers, (1) Geoffrey George, *b.* 31 May 1854, *d.* 6 June 1855, (2) Thomas Edmund Wiltred, *b.* 5 Aug. 1859 at Denbies, *d.* 17 May 1865.

ASHFIELD

See "Thurlow of Ashfield, co. Suffolk," Barony (*Thurlow*), *cr.* 1778; *extinct* 1806, the Barony of Thurlow of Thurlow (*cr.* 1792) remaining.

ASHFORD

i.e. "Ashford of Ashford, Kent," Barony *(Keppel)*, *cr.* 1697 with the Earldom of Albemarle, which see.

See "Ardilaun of Ashford, co. Galway," Barony *(Guinness)*, *cr.* 1880.

ASHLEY

i.e. "Ashley of Wimborne St. Giles, Dorset," Barony (*Cooper*), *cr.* 1661; see "Shaftesbury," Earldom, *cr.* 1672.

ASHTON

BARONY.   1. James Williamson, of Ashton, co. Lancaster, 2nd s.
I. 1895.   of James Williamson, of Parkfield in Scotforth, co.
Lancaster, sometime Mayor of Lancaster (*d.* 3 Jan. 1879), by Eleanor, da. of Leonard Miller, of Lancaster, was *b.* 31 Dec., 1842; ed. at the Lancaster Grammar School; became a successful manufacturer of linoleum([a]) at Ashton, afsd.; High Sheriff for co. Lancaster, 1885; M.P. (Liberal) for the Lancaster div. of N. Lancashire, 1886-95, and was *cr.* 25 July 1895,([b]) BARON ASHTON([c]) of Ashton, co. Lancaster. He was not, however, introduced into the House of Lords till (nearly two years later) 25 Mar. 1897. He *m.*, 1stly, 23 Sep. 1869, Margaret, 1st da.

([a]) *The Morning Post*, 1 July 1895, under "Resignation Honours," states that this grantee " is described as a manufacturer."

([b]) This was one of the four Baronies conferred on the retirement of the Earl of Rosebery from the Premiership. There would seem at first sight little to justify two out of these four creations, *viz.* this and 'Wandsworth,' but as the bad days of jobbery are long gone by, and it is impossible that a Minister desirous of mending the House of Lords should recommend anyone for a peerage except on the ground of merit and public service, it is clear that the grantees must have privately advanced solid reasons for their promotion, though these have not been, and are not likely to be, revealed to the outside world. See also note *sub* Wandsworth. V.G.

([c]) The arms of Lord Ashton, a modern grant, are Party cheveronwise gold and silver with a cheveron nebuly between two trefoils and a demi-eagle of sable. These arms are a version of those of the old Nottinghamshire family of Williamson of Wakeringham and Burton. No kinship with this family is alleged by Lord Ashton. (*ex inform.* Oswald Barron.) V.G.

of Joseph GATEY, of Keswick, Cumberland. She *d. s.p.m.*, 10 Apr. 1877.
He *m.*, 2ndly, 23 Nov. 1880, Jessy Henrietta, 2nd and yst. da. of James
STEWART, of Clapham, in the West Riding of co. York. She *d. s.p.*, of
apoplexy, at Ryelands, 5, and was *bur.* there 10 Oct. 1904. He *m*, 3rdly,
30 July 1909, at Trinity Church, Sloane Str , Florence Maude, widow of
Col J. Lawson WHALLEY, of Richmond House, Lancaster, da. of the Rev.
Robert DANIEL, Vicar of Osbaldwick, co. York.

Family Estates.—These, in 1883, were under 2,000 acres. *Principal
Residence.*—Ryelands, near Lancaster.

ASHTOWN

BARONY [I.]   1. FREDERIC TRENCH, of Woodlawn (formerly called
1. 1800.   Moate), in Kilconnel, co. Galway, s. and h. of Frederic
                  T., of Moate, afsd., by Mary, 1st da. and coh. of Francis
SADLEIR, of Sopwell Hall, co. Tipperary, *b.* 17 Sep. 1755, *suc.* his father
27 Nov. 1797, was M.P. for Maryborough 1785-90, and for Portarlington,
1798-1800, [I.] and 1800 [U.K] (ª) when, having been bribed thereby to
support the Union with Ireland, to which he had formerly been opposed,
he was, on 27 Dec. 1800, *cr.* BARON ASHTOWN (ᵇ) of Moate, co.
Galway (ᶜ) [I.], such creation being with a *spec. rem.* (very unusual in the
case of a *Commoner* when raised to Peerage rank) (ᵈ) to the heirs male of the
body of his father (who were numerous), failing those of his own body,
who did not exist. He *m.*, 25 May 1785, Elizabeth, only da. and h. of
Robert ROBINSON, M.D., by Elizabeth, da. of Thomas LYSTER, of Lyster-
field, co. Roscommon, and niece of Christopher Robinson, a Judge of the
King's Bench [I.]. He *d. s.p.*, aged 84, at Bath, 1, and was *bur.* 13 May
1840, at Kilconnel afsd. Will pr. May 1840. His widow *d.* June 1844,
at Dublin, aged 77. Will pr. July 1844.

II 1840.   2. FREDERIC MASON (TRENCH), BARON ASHTOWN [1],
                  nephew and h., according to the *spec. lim.* in the patent,

---

(ª) He was elected by lot for this place in the 1st Parl. [U.K.], but his creation as
an Irish peer of course prevented his taking his seat, though he would have been
eligible for an English or Scottish constituency. (*ex inform.* G.D. Burtchaell.) V.G.

(ᵇ) Trench, Lord Ashtown, bears for arms Silver, a lion passant gules between
three fleurs-de-lys, with a chief azure charged with a golden sun. (*ex inform.* Oswald
Barron.) V.G.

(ᶜ) The patent is given *in extenso* in the claim of his successor, to establish his
right to the Peerage, July 1855. Sir Jonah Barrington in his *Rise and Fall of the
Irish Nation* is particularly severe on the Grantee—saying that "His change of sides
and the majority of *one* to which it contributed [against Mr. Ponsonby's motion]
were probably the remote causes of persevering in an Union. Mr. Trench's venality
excited indignation in every friend of Ireland." Later on a speech of his is quoted
in which he says "he had, *since the night before*, been fully convinced of the advantages
of an Union, and would certainly support it " For a list of the creations and promotions in the Irish Peerage at the time of the Union [I.], see vol. ii, Appendix E.

(ᵈ) For a list of *spec. rem.* granted to commoners, see vol. iii, Appendix F.

37

being 2nd, but 1st surv, s. and h. of Francis TRENCH, of Sopwell Hall, afsd. (by Mary, (*) 2nd da. and coh. of Henry MASON, of Shrewsbury), which Francis was next br. to the 1st Lord Ashtown [I.], but d. before him, Nov. 1829, aged 72. He was b. 25 Dec. 1804 ; was Sheriff of co. Galway 1840. Claim to Peerage allowed 12 July 1855. He m, 1stly, 29 Aug. 1831, Harriet Georgiana, yst. da. of Thomas COSBY, of Stradbally Hall, Queen's County, by Charlotte Elizabeth, da. of the Rt. Hon. Thomas KELLY, 2nd Justice of the Common Pleas [I.]. She d. 25 Feb. 1845, at Woodlawn, aged 34, and was bur. there. He m., 2ndly, 10 Feb. 1852, at Aberford, co. York, Elizabeth, 2nd da. and coh. of Richard Oliver GASCOIGNE, of Castle Oliver, co. Limerick, and of Parlington, co. York, by Mary, da. of Sir Charles TURNER, of Kirkleatham, Bart.   He d. at Clonod-foy, co. Limerick, in his 76th year, 12, and was bur. 17 Sep. 1880, at Woodlawn. Will dat. 10 July 1879, pr. 29 Nov. 1880. His widow d. at the Hôtel National, Montreux, Switzerland, 23, and was bur. 25 Feb. 1893, at Territet, Switzerland. Will dat. 2 Nov. 1890 to 24 Sep. 1892, pr. 25 May 1893.

III. 1880.   3. FREDERIC OLIVER (TRENCH), BARON ASHTOWN [I.], grandson and h., being s. and h. of the Hon. Frederic Sidney Charles TRENCH (by Anne, 1st da. of William Thomas (LE POER TRENCH), 3rd EARL OF CLANCARTY [I.]), which Frederic was s. and h. ap. of the last Lord by his 1st wife, but d. v.p., 2 Mar. 1879, in his 40th year. He was b. at the Villa, Galway, 2 Feb, and bap. 5 Apr. 1868, at Kilconnell. Ed. at Eton. Matric. Oxford (Magd. Coll.) 22 Oct. 1887. Rep. Peer [I.], (Conservative) Nov. 1908. He m., 11 Jan. 1894, at Stradbally afsd., his 2nd cousin, Violet Grace, yst. da. of Col Robert Ashworth Godolphin COSBY, by his 1st wife, Alice Sophia Elizabeth, only da. of Sir George Edward POCOCK, Bart.

[FREDERICK SYDNEY TRENCH, 1st s. and h. ap., b. 9 Dec. 1894, at Woodlawn, and bap. there 20 Jan. 1895.]

Family Estates —These, in 1883, consisted of about 6,400 acres in co. York, worth about £7,700 a year, and of about 37,200 acres in Ireland (chiefly in the counties of Limerick, Galway, Tipperary, and Waterford), worth about £27,000 a year. Total about 43,600 acres, worth about £34,700 a year. But query if the Yorkshire estates were not those of the family of Gascoigne, belonging to the Dowager Baroness ? *Principal Residence.*—Woodlawn, co Galway.

ASKE

See " DUNDAS OF ASKE, co. York, " Barony *(Dundas), cr.* 1794.

(*) Francis Trench and Mary Mason were m 11 June 1802, at St. Chad's, Shrewsbury.

ASPALL

i.e. "KITCHENER OF KHARTOUM AND OF ASPALL," Suffolk, Barony (*Kitchener*), *cr.* 1898, see "KITCHENER" Viscountcy, *cr* 1902.

i.e. "KITCHENER OF KHARTOUM THE VAAL AND OF ASPALL," Suffolk, Viscountcy (*Kitchener*), *cr.* 1902, which see.

ASTLEY or ESTLEIGH

BARONY.   1. ANDREW OF ASTLEY, ([a]) of Astley and Bentley, co.
I 1295.   Warwick, s and h. of Sir Thomas of A., of the same, ([b])
by his 1st wife, Joan, da. of Ernald DU BOIS, of co Leicester, *suc.* his father (who was slain at Evesham) 4 Aug. 1265, and was by the composition called the *dictum de Kenilworth*, on payment of a fine, put into possession of his father's estates, which had been confiscated. He was in the Scottish wars and at the Battle of Falkirk. He *m* Sibyl. He was sum. to attend the King at Shrewsbury 28 June (1283) 11 Edw I ([c]) by writ directed *Andree de Estleye.* From 24 June (1295) 23 Edw. I, to 3 Nov. (1306) 34 Edw. I, he was sum. to Parl. by writs directed *Andree de Estlegh'*, whereby he may be held to have become LORD ASTLEY. ([d]) He *d.* however shortly before 18 Jan. (1300/1) 29 Edw. I, ([e]) so that the later summons must have been in error.

II. 1301.   2. NICHOLAS OF ASTLEY, s. and h., aged 24 at his
father's death. He was sum. to Parl. 4 July (1302) 30 Edw. I, 11 June (1309) 2 Edw. II, and 26 Oct. (1309) 2 Edw. II. He was taken prisoner, not as some say, slain, at Bannockburn in 1314. He *d. s.p.*, 1325.

III. 1325.   3. THOMAS OF ASTLEY, nephew and h., being s. and h.
of Sir Giles of A. (*d.* before 1316), br. of the last Lord, by Alice, (living 1344-5), ([f]) 2nd da. and coh. of Sir Thomas WOLVEY. He had seizin 27 Mar. 1326, having proved his age. He was sum. to Parl. from 25 Feb. (1342/3) 17 Edw. III, to 10 Mar. (1349/50) 23 Edw. III. He founded a chantry in the parish church of Astley. He *m.*, before

---

([a]) Astley of Astley in Warwickshire bore arms of Azure with a cinqfoil ermine. (*ex inform.* Oswald Barron.) V.G.

([b]) This Thomas was s. and h. of Walter A, who was s and h. of Thomas A. (who by his wife, Maud, sister and h. of Roger Camville of Creek [1210] had much increased the family estates), s. and h. of Philip A., lord of Astley, co. Warwick, in 1165.

([c]) As to this and other supposed Parls. see Preface.

([d]) As to how far these early writs of summons did in fact create any Peerage title, see last vol., Appendix A   V.G.

([e]) *Inq. p. m.*, 29 Edw. I, no. 155.

([f]) An undated deed gives the names of 5 younger children of Thomas (*Ancient Deeds*, vol. v, A. 12138.) V.G.

1336/7, when she was living,(ª) Elizabeth, da. of Guy (DE BEAUCHAMP), 2nd EARL OF WARWICK, by Alice, da. of Ralph DE TONI. He was living 3 May 1366. (ᵇ)

IV. 1370?　　　4. WILLIAM (OF ASTLEY), LORD ASTLEY, s. and h., *b.* before 1344-5. (ᶜ)　He was never sum. to Parl., though included in several commissions by Henry IV and Henry VI. He *m.* Joan, da. of John WILLOUGHBY, [LORD WILLOUGHBY OF ERESBY]. He *d. s.p.m.*

After his death, the Barony of Astley, if an hereditary Peerage (there being no proof of any sitting) would have devolved on his only da. and h., Joan, and the heirs of her body. She *m.*, 1stly, Thomas RALEIGH, of Farnborough, co. Warwick, by whom she had no surv. male issue. She *m.*, 2ndly (as his 2nd wife), Reynold (GREY), 3rd LORD GREY OF RUTHIN, who *d.* 1440, leaving, by his said wife, Edward Grey (s. and h. to his mother), who was sum. to Parl. in 1446 as LORD FERRERS OF GROBY. The Barony of Astley (if then existing) would thenceforth have followed the course of that of Ferrers of Groby, and have been *forfeited* therewith on the attainder of Henry (GREY), DUKE OF SUFFOLK, &c., in 1554.—See "FERRERS OF GROBY," Barony of.

ASTLEY OF READING

BARONY.　　1. JACOB ASTLEY, 2nd s. of Isaac A., of Hill Morton, I. 1644.　co. Warwick, and of Melton Constable, co. York, by Mary, da. of Edward WALDEGRAVE, of Borley, Essex, was knighted 17 July 1624 ; Gov. of Plymouth 1638, was Col. of the 3rd Reg. of Foot in the King's campaign against the Scots (1640), Serjeant Major Gen. of the King's army on the outbreak of the Civil War (1642). On 4 Nov. 1644, he was *cr.* BARON ASTLEY OF READING,(ᵈ) Berks. He was wounded at the battle of Edgehill ; Governor of Reading ; Commander of the King's Infantry at Naseby (1645), where he "performed his part with great gallantry." (ᵉ)　He was taken prisoner at Stow-on-the-Wold, in 1646.(ᶠ) He was soon afterwards released on being admitted

(ª) Thomas Astley and *Margaret* his wife were living 15 July 1334. (*Pat. Rolls.*) V.G.

(ᵇ) *Ancient Deeds,* vol. iv, A. 10248.

(ᶜ) See note "f" on previous page.

(ᵈ) The Lords Astley of Reading bore the arms of Astley or Astley with a golden border engrailed. (*ex inform.* Oswald Barron.) V.G.

(ᵉ) *Whitelocke.*

(ᶠ) Here he is said to have uttered the well-known speech "You have done your work now, and may go to play unless you fall out among yourselves." Lord Clarendon says of him "Sir Jacob Astley was an honest, brave, plain man and as fit for the office he exercised of Major Gen. of the Foot as Christendom yielded, and was so generally esteemed ; very discerning and prompt in giving orders as the occasions required, and most cheerful and present in any action. In council he used few but pertinent words ; and was not at all pleased with the long speeches usually made there and which rather confounded than informed his understanding ; so that

to composition. He *m.* Agnes (a German lady), da. of Henry IMPLE. He *d.* Feb. 1651/2, in the old Palace of Maidstone, and was *bur.* at Maidstone.

II. 1652.   2. ISAAC (ASTLEY), BARON ASTLEY OF READING, s and h._ Knighted at Oxford 23 Feb. 1642/3. He *m*, 27 Dec 1650, at St Giles's, Cripplegate, as 'Sir Isaac Astley,' Anne, 4th da of Sir Francis STYDOLFE, of Mickleham, Surrey, by Mary, da of Sir James ALTHAM, of Oxhey, Herts, one of the Barons of the Exchequer. He *d.* 1662, and was *bur.* at Maidstone. His widow *d.* at Maidstone afsd. Admon. 21 Nov. 1674 to her s. Jacob, "Lord Astley, *Baron of Reading.*"

III. 1662   3. JACOB (ASTLEY), BARON ASTLEY OF READING, s. and
to   h., *b.* before 1654. Adm. Fellow Com. of St. John's
1688.   Coll. Cambridge, 28 Jan 1668/9. He *m* Frances, da.
and coh. of his maternal uncle, Sir Richard STYDOLFE, of Norbury, Surrey, Bart., by Elizabeth, da of Sir George STONEHOUSE, of Radley, Berks. He *d. s.p.s.*, 1688, at St. Margaret's, Westm., and was *bur.* at Maidstone, when the *title* became *extinct* Admon. 8 May, 1689. His widow *d.* 11, and was *bur.* 22 July 1692, at Maidstone.

ASTON OF FORFAR

BARONY [S].   1. SIR WALTER ASTON, Bart, of Tixall, co. Stafford,
I. 1627.   1st surv. s. and h. of Sir Edward A., of the same (whose
                estates exceeded the annual value of £10,000), by his 2nd
wife, Anne, da. of Sir Thomas LUCY, of Charlecote, co Warwick, was *bap.* 9 July 1584, at Charlecote, *suc.* his father 1 Feb 1596/7, was *cr* K B (25 July 1603) at the coronation of James I, and was *cr.* a Bart., 22 May 1611, on the institution of that order. He was a Statesman of distinction and served on several missions, where his princely magnificence greatly injured his private fortune Ambassador to Spain 1620-25, and again 1635-38 While in that country he became a Rom Cath On 28 Nov. 1627, he was *cr.* (ª) LORD ASTON OF FORFAR [S.], with rem. to him and his heirs male for ever bearing the name and arms of Aston. (ᵇ) He *m.*, about 1607, Gertrude, only da. of Sir Thomas SADLEIR, (ᶜ) of Standon,

---

he rather collected the ends of the debates, and what he was himself to do, than enlarged them by his own discourses, though he forbore not to deliver his own mind "

(ª) "Creavimus, facimus et constituimus præfatum Dominum Walterum Aston *Dominum Aston de Forfar* infra vicecomitatum nostrum de Forfar in dicto regno nostro, ac dedimus, &c., eidem suisque heredibus masculis in perpetuum, cognomen et insignia de Aston gerentibus, titulum, honorem, ordinem et dignitatem *Dominorum Baronum* parliamenti dicti Regni, &c. Tenen. et Haben. dict. titulum, &c., dicti *Domini Baronis de Forfar* cum suffragio in parliamento, &c." (*ex inform* R. R. Stodart, sometime Lyon Clerk Depute.) See, as to the rare use of the word 'Baron' in Scottish creations, note *sub* Elizabeth, BARONESS CRAMOND [1628].

(ᵇ) This was as a reward for his services in negotiating for the marriage of Charles Prince of Wales with the Infanta of Spain. V.G.

(ᶜ) He was s. of the well-known diplomat and statesman Sir Ralph Sadleir. V G

Herts, by his 2nd wife, Gertrude, da. of Robert Markham, of Cotham, Notts. She, who was confirmed by the Bp. of Chalcedon, 1 Apr. 1627, and had a pension of £50 p a from the King in 1628, was living 3 June 1635, and, in her issue, was h. to her br. Ralph Sadleir, of Standon, who d s.p. 12 Feb. 1660. He d 13 Aug. 1639, and was bur. at St. Mary's, Stafford. (ª) Will dat. 3 June 1635, pr. 31 Oct. 1639

II. 1639   2. WALTER (Aston), LORD ASTON OF FORFAR [S], 1st surv s. and h., b. 1609. He was a gallant adherent of Charles I, and was at the siege of Lichfield, 1646, and at the surrender of Oxford, after which he had to compound for his estates and live in retirement. In 1660 he inherited the estate of Standon, Herts., from his maternal uncle, Ralph Sadleir, abovenamed. He m., in 1629, Mary, 2nd da. of Richard (Weston), 1st EARL OF PORTLAND, by his 1st wife, Elizabeth, da of William Pincheon, of Writtle, Essex. He d. 23 Apr. 1678, aged 69, at Tixall, and was bur. at St. Mary's, Stafford, above 1000 people accompanying his corpse. (ᵇ) His widow, who was bap. 2 Jan. 1602/3, at Roxwell, Essex, was living Aug. 1678. (ᶜ)

III. 1678.   3. WALTER (Aston), LORD ASTON OF FORFAR [S.], s. and h., b. 1633 at Tixall. Along with other ' Popish Lords ' (ᵈ) he was strictly imprisoned in the Tower in 1679, being charged with misprision of treason, May 1680, for his supposed share in the plot fabricated by Titus Oates. He was not released until June 1685. He was Lord Lieut. co. Stafford 1687-89, and remained loyal to James II on the landing of William of Orange. At the election of Scottish Rep. Peers, 8 Oct. 1713, a protest was made by him that the patent granted to his grandfather in 1627 should be read, and his name enrolled according to the date thereof. (ᵉ) He m., 1stly, about 1657, Eleanor, widow of Robert Knightley, of Offchurch, co. Warwick, da. of Sir Walter Blount, of Sodington, 1st Bart., by Elizabeth, da. of George Wylde, of Droitwich. She d. 3 Dec. 1674. He m., 2ndly, apparently after 1680, Catherine, da.

(ª) He was patron of the poet Drayton. V.G.

(ᵇ) " The munificent Lord Aston " removed from Tixall to Standon. His table was daily served with 20 dishes at a course, 3 courses the year about, and 4 servants waited behind his own chair—his gentleman, his house Steward, his chief park-keeper, and his footman. For his services at Lichfield the King wrote him a special letter, 6 June 1646, in which he said, " The greatest of my misfortunes is, that I cannot reward such gallant and loyal subjects as you are, as I ought or would " (ex inform. Major Francis Skeet) V.G.

(ᶜ) " She grew melancholy and lost her wits, keeping almost perpetual silence, and refusing nourishment. " (Letter of Sir Edward Southcote, her daughter's husband.) V.G.

(ᵈ) See, for a list of these, ante, p. 264, note " c. "

(ᵉ) His predecessors, having been Roman Catholics, were precluded from sitting in the Scottish Parl. It is probably owing to this fact that the title is not on the Union Roll (1707), nor in the return made by the Lords of Session to the House of Lords in 1740.

of Sir Thomas GAGE, of Firle, 2nd Bart., by Mary, da. of John CHAMBER-LAIN, of Shirburn, Oxon. He *d.* 24 Nov. 1714, in his 82nd year, and was *bur.* at Standon. M.I. Will dat. 2 Nov., pr. 10 Dec. 1714 His widow *d.* 2 Apr. 1720, and was also *bur.* at Standon.

IV. 1714   4. WALTER (ASTON), LORD ASTON OF FORFAR [S.],
           3rd (*) but 1st surv , s. and h by 1st wife, *b.* 1660 He *m.*, about 1 Oct. 1698, Mary, sister of Thomas and Edward, 8th and 9th DUKES OF NORFOLK, only da. of Lord Thomas HOWARD, of Worksop, Notts., by Mary Elizabeth, da. and h. of Sir John SAVILE, of Copley, Bart. She *d.* 23 May 1723, in childbed of her 11th child, and was *bur.* at Standon. M.I. He *d.* at Tixall, 4, and was *bur.* 8 Apr. 1748, at Standon, aged 88. M I. Will dat. 4 July 1746, pr. 15 Aug. 1748.

V. 1748.   5. JAMES (ASTON), LORD ASTON OF FORFAR [S.],
           5th (b) but 1st surv., s. and h , *b.* 23 May 1723. He lived in retirement at Standon Lordship, owing to the severity of the penal laws. He *m.*, 30 June 1742, at Twickenham, Midx , Barbara, sister of George, 14th EARL OF SHREWSBURY, 1st da. of George TALBOT, by Mary, da. of Thomas (FITZ WILLIAM), 4th VISCOUNT FITZ WILLIAM [I.]. He *d. s p.m.*, 24 Aug. 1751, of the small pox, at Tixall, aged 28, and with him expired the issue male of the first Peer, when the *Baronetcy* became *extinct.* Will dat. 11 Aug., pr. 5 Dec. 1751. His widow *d.* 9 Nov. 1759, at Paris. (c) Admon. 26 July 1760, and again 3 July 1766.

Note.—On the death of the 5th lord, the peerage, in accordance with the terms of the patent, devolved upon the h. male *general* of the grantee ; this appears to have been William Aston of Beaulieu, whose descent is given below. It should be noted, however, that H.W.F.Harwood, in his excellent article on 'Aston' in *The Scots Peerage*, is unable to *prove* the extinction of the lines of Herbert A. or of John A., brothers of the 2nd Lord, or of Thomas A., his uncle, and that the heir of anyone of these three, if such existed, would have taken precedence of the afsd. William A.

(*) Of his elder brothers, (1) Edward Walter, *b.* 1658, *d.* at Clermont Coll., Paris, unm. and *v.p.*, 1678. (2) Francis *d. s.p* and *v p*, 1694, and was *bur*. at Standon. V.G

(b) Of his 4 elder brothers, (1) Walter, *b.* 16 Feb. 1711, *d. v.p.*, 19 June 1717, and was *bur.* at Standon. (2) Edward Richard, *b.* 17 Jan. 1713, *d.* young (3) Thomas William Anthony, *d* between 16 June and 25 Oct. 1739. (4) Charles Joseph, *b.* 19 Mar. 1719, *d.* 12 and was *bur.* 15 Apr. 1730, at Standon. V.G.

(c) Of their two daughters and coheirs (1) Mary, *b.* and *bap.* at Standon 14 Aug. 1743, *m.*, 21 Sep. 1766, at Worksop Manor, Notts, her cousin, Sir Walter Blount, of Sodington, 6th Bart., and had issue. She *d.* 30 Jan. 1805, aged 62, being burnt to death at Basford, Staffs., the house of her s George. (2) Barbara, who inherited the estate of Tixall, *b* 4 and *bap* 8 Sep. 1744, at Standon, *m.*, 2 Feb. 1762, at St James's, Westm., the Hon Henry Thomas Clifford, and was mother of Sir Thomas Hugh Clifford (afterwards Clifford-Constable), of Tixall, *cr.* a Baronet in 1815 Standon House was sold in 1767.

VI.? 1751.   6? WILLIAM ASTON, of Beaulieu, co. Louth, and
                Rathbone Place, London, distant cousin, and in all
probability h. male, was only s. and h. of Tichborne A., of Beaulieu afsd.
(M.P. for Ardee 1741, Sheriff of co. Louth 1742, d. 4 Mar. 1747/8), by
Jane (m. 1746) only da. of William Rowan, K. C., which Tichborne was
2nd, but 1st surv., s. of William Aston, of Beaulieu (Sheriff co. Louth
1715, M.P. for Dunleer 1721-27, and for co. Louth 1727-44, d. 23 Aug.
1744), by Salisbury, da. and h. of Henry (Tichborne), Lord Ferrard of
Beaulieu [I.], which last named William A. was 1st s. and h. of Thomas
Aston (b. 1662), by Margaret, da. of Col. Robert Sandys, of Roscommon,
which Thomas was 3rd s. of Sir William A., (b. 1615, d. 1671/2) 2nd
Justice of the King's Bench [I.], being 1st s. by his 3rd wife, Ursula, da.
of Thomas Stockton, Justice of the King's Bench [I.], which Sir William
was 1st s. and h. of John A. (d. 1640), of Tean, co. Stafford, by Margery,
da. of James Walton, of Fole, in that co., which John was 4th and yst. s.
of Robert A. (d. 1623), of Park Hall, co. Stafford, by Joyce, 2nd da. of
William Dalison, a Judge of the King's Bench, which Robert (d. 1623)
was next br. of Sir Edward A., father of Walter, the 1st Lord.   He was
b. 8 Apr. 1747, and bap. the same day in St. Anne's, Dublin.   He
never claimed the title, and d. unm., Feb. 1769   Will dat. 5, pr.
10 Feb. 1769. ([a])

Note.—On or shortly after the death of the 5th Lord, the peerage
was assumed as below.   Of these claimants it is obvious that the first two
were not entitled to it, as their descent was from the 4th s. of Sir Walter
A. (grandfather of the 1st Lord), while the above named William A. (their
distant relative in Ireland, of whose existence they were probably unaware),
descended from the 2nd s.   As regards the 3rd claimant to this title,
however, *viz.* Walter A., the watchmaker, the succession must have opened
to him on the death of William A. in 1769, (assuming that the issue male
of Robert A. of Park Hall then became extinct) subject only to the remote
possibility of the uncle or one of the 2 brothers of the 2nd lord having
then a surviving h. male.

PHILIP ASTON, styling himself LORD ASTON OF FORFAR [S.], cousin,
and wrongly supposing himself to be *h.* male, being s. and h. of Walter A.
(by Penelope, da. of John WHITFIELD, of Lincoln), who was s. and h. of
Edward A., 4th s. (and, in his issue, h. male) of Edward A., of Milwich,
co. Stafford, who was s. and h. of William A., of the same, the 4th s. of
Sir Walter Aston, of Tixall, co. Stafford, which Sir Walter Aston (who
d. 1589) was ancestor of the first Lord, being father of Sir Edward A.,
of Tixall (who d. 1597), leaving Walter his s. and h., who was *cr.* LORD

([a]) Valuable assistance in rewriting the account of this peerage, has been received
from H.W.F.Harwood, from G.D.Burtchaell, and from Major Francis Skeet.   V.G.

Aston of Forfar [S.] in 1627, as above mentioned. He was *b.* 3 Aug. 1709, in the parish of St. Giles's-in-the-Fields, Midx., and *suc.* his father 6 Jan. 1721/2. He is said to have been a Rom. Cath. priest. He *d.* unm., 29 Apr. 1755, and was *bur.* at St. Geo. the Martyr, Bloomsbury.

Walter Aston, styling himself, in error, Lord Aston of Forfar [S.], only br. and h., *b.* 24 Feb. 1712, in the parish of St. Giles's, abovenamed. He *m.* Anne, da. of [? Wright]. He *d.* 25 Mar. 1763, and was *bur.* at St. Geo. the Martyr afsd. (ª) Admon. 11 Apr. 1763 to his widow. She *d.* 11 Aug. 1764. Admon. of her goods granted 1 Oct. 1764, to Frances Wright, her mother.

VII ? 1769.   7. Walter Aston, styling himself Lord Aston of Forfar [S.], cousin and h., being s. and h. of Edward A. (by Anne, da. of Thomas Bayley, of Stafford), who was uncle of Philip, the supposed 6th Lord. He was *b.* 10 Oct. 1732, and was sometime in trade as a watchmaker. His vote at the election of Scottish Rep. Peers was objected to in 1768, on the grounds of the Peerage of Aston not being on the Union roll. In 1769, however, George III granted him a pension of £300 *p.a.* on the Scottish establishment under the name of "Walter, *Lord Aston, Baron of Forfar.*" (ᵇ) He *m.*, 28 May 1766, at Hampstead, Midx., Anne, da. of Peter Hutchinson, of Gales, co. York. He *d.* (ᶜ) 29 July 1805, in Bolton Row, Piccadilly, in his 73rd year, and was *bur.* in Grosvenor Chapel, St. Geo., Han. Sq. Will pr. Feb. 1806. A 'Lady Aston,' conceivably his widow, was *bur.* at Bath Abbey, 2 Apr. 1808. The will of Anne, Dowager Lady Aston, was pr. Feb. 1821.

VIII ? 1805   8. The Rev. Walter Hutchinson Aston, styling
to   himself Lord Aston of Forfar [S.], 1st and only surv.
1845.   s. and h., *b.* 15 Sep. 1769, and *bap.* at St. Geo., Han.
                    Sq. Matric. at Oxford (Ch. Ch.), 12 June 1789, as
"the son of a Baron." B.A. 1793. M.A. 1796. After officiating at Caversham, Berks., and at Tamworth, co. Warwick, he became Vicar of Tardebigg, co. Worcester, 1821. J.P. for co. Worcester. In Feb. 1819 he presented a petition to the Crown, claiming the Barony of Aston of Forfar [S.]. He *m.*, 14 June 1802, at St. Mary's, Nottingham, Elizabeth, da. of the Rev. Nathan Haines, D.D., by Susan, sister of Sir John Chudleigh, 6th Bart., and da. of George Chudleigh, of Chalm-

---

(ª) *The Gent. Mag.* for Apr. 1763 states, "Died lately Rt. Hon. Lord Aston, formerly cook to Sir [Charles] Mordaunt, Bart. He is succeeded by Mr. Walter Aston, a watchmaker." V.G.

(ᵇ) On 5 Dec. 1778 he had a patent of arms at the Lyon office, on delivering up thereto a patent (not recorded) granted by Brodie, Lyon, to Philip, Lord Aston. (*ex inform.* R.R.Stodart, Lyon Clerk Depute.)

(ᶜ) "His Lordship, who had been engaged in trade in the early part of his life... was an inoffensive man of rather a convivial turn." (*Gent. Mag.*) V.G.

38

ington, Dorset. She *d.* 24 Aug. 1833, aged 67, at Tardebigg. Admon. July 1834. He *d.* there *s.p.*, aged 75, 21 Jan. 1845.([a])   Will pr. Apr. 1845. Both *bur.* at Tardebigg.

[*Note.*—It is most likely that an h. male exists of the first peer, who would be entitled to this peerage. Failing nearer heirs (though nearer there are bound to be) he could be found among the family of Aston of Whorcross, co. Stafford, a numerous race, descended from Richard, next br. to Sir John A., the first of Tixall, who *d.* 1523. See *Hewlett,* p. 28.]

ASTON-CLINTON

See "LAKE of Delhi and Laswary, and ASTON-CLINTON, Bucks," Barony *(Lake),* cr. 1804 ; Viscountcy *(Lake),* cr. 1807 ; both *extinct* 1848.

ASTON HALL

See "AMESBURY of Kintbury-Amesbury and Barton Court, Berks., and ASTON HALL, co. Flint," Barony *(Dundas),* cr. 1832, *extinct* 1832.

ATHBOY([b])

See "DARNLEY OF ATHBOY, co. Meath," Viscountcy [I.] *(Bligh),* cr. 1722 ; Earldom [I.] *(Bligh),* cr. 1725.

ATHENRY, anciently ATHNERY

[*Observations.*—The origin of this Peerage is obscure, but its position is undoubted, and has been acknowledged in almost every Parl. during its existence. Its possessor in 1489 was ranked third of the eleven Irish Barons who (with two Earls) obeyed the summons by Henry VII to Greenwich in that year, ([c]) the fourth of such Barons being Kingsale, while the fifth was Gormanston].

ROBERT BERMINGHAM or BREMINGHAM, not improbably a yr. s. of Piers, LORD OF BIRMINGHAM, co. Warwick, ([d]) appears to have been the

([a]) See anecdotes of this supposed Peer and his ancestors in *N. & Q.*, 3rd ser., vol. viii, p. 120, &c.

([b]) See also Appendix A in this volume.

([c]) For the ranking of Irish peers on various occasions, see Appendix A, *circa finem,* in this volume.

([d]) The name of the Founder is uncertain, by some it is said to be Piers or Peter, and by others William, although neither of these names appears in any Irish document of this date. The family were called Mac Feorais (or Phioris), which is the Erse equivalent for Fitz Piers, after Piers B., *temp.* Henry III, so no inference can

first, or at any rate a very early member, of this family to settle in Ireland.([a]) Under the name of Robert de Bermyngeham he was witness to important Irish charters, 1175-79. The statements that he accompanied Henry II in his invasion of Ireland in 1172, and that he obtained the *status* of a Peer as LORD ATHENRY [I.], rest on no discoverable satisfactory evidence. He *d.* before 1218.

PIERS BERMINGHAM, s. and h., received in 1234 twenty marks a year from Henry III. In 28 Hen. III (1243-44) he and nine other of the Anglo-Irish Feudal nobility (together with 22 of the native chiefs) were specially thanked by the King for their zeal in his service. He is by some regarded as having obtained or inherited the *status* of a Peer, as LORD ATHENRY [I.]. He *d.* 1254. ([b])

MEILER MAC PHIORIS, ([b]) or BERMINGHAM, of Athenry, co. Galway, s. and h., is said to have taken an important part in the Conquest of Connaught, and to have been known as 'Mor' (*i.e.* the Great), being styled (by Ware) *Dynast* (or Petty Prince) *of Athenry*. On 10 June 1244 he was granted a market at Athenry. He founded the monastery for Dominicans at Athenry. He is by some regarded as having obtained or inherited the *status* of a Peer as LORD ATHENRY [I.]. He *m.* Basile, ([c]) sister and h. of Ralph of WORCESTER, and da. of William of W., who brought him a large territory in co. Tipperary, which he exchanged for other lands. He *d.* 1263, near Cashel, and was *bur.* in the Priory at Athenry, aged 50. ([d]) His widow was living 1275.

---

be drawn therefrom, as to the name of the first of the Berminghams to settle in Connaught. G.E.C. writing in 1887, denounced the early part of the pedigree as most untrustworthy, and unfortunately the charge still holds good down to the middle of the 16th century. Documentary evidence is scarce, and the stories of Lodge, Betham, and O'Ferrall are vague, contradictory, and in places demonstrably inaccurate. G.D.Burtchaell, Athlone Pursuivant, has spent much time in collating the different accounts and endeavouring to improve this article, which, maugre his kind efforts, still leaves much to be desired. V.G.

([a]) "An ancient monument, valued at £200, on which was represented in brass the landing of the first ancestor of the family of Birmingham in Ireland," is said to have been entrusted to the charge of the Portreeve of Athenry and by him sold in foreign parts during the Civil Wars, for which a bill in Chancery was filed against him in 1667.

([b]) The Bermingham family were lords of Dunmore; and according to *The Annals of Lough Ké*, (ed. by William Hennessy M.R.I.A., 1871) Piers Pramister, lord of Conmaicne of Dunmore, *d.* in 1254. This doubtless is the abovenamed Piers Bermingham, who was ancestor of all the various septs of the family of Bermingham who settled in Ireland, and who, from him, usually styled themselves *Mac Phioris*, or Mac Feorais, *i.e.* sons of Piers, or Peter. His 2nd s., James, was Lord of Thetmoy, and grandfather of John (Bermingham), the celebrated Earl of Louth [I.], so *cr.* 1319. See pedigree, p. 298, and Appendix A. in this volume.

([c]) For some discussion on mediaeval English names see vol. iii, Appendix C. V.G.

([d]) William, consecrated Archbishop of Tuam in 1289, is said to have been his yst. son.

I. 1280 ?   1 PIERS (MAC PHIORIS, ([a]) or BERMINGHAM), LORD
                   ATHENRY [I.], s. and h.   He was fined 100s. for non-
attendance in Parl. (1284), 12 Edw I, and was placed as 7th Baron ([b]) in
the Parl. of 1295. On 23 Feb. 1321/2 he was sum. to the Scottish
expedition. He may be regarded as the first of his family to obtain
recognition as LORD ([c]) ATHENRY [I.], although any date given for
the origin of early prescriptive Irish titles such as this must be of the
nature of guess work. On 2 Dec. 1302, he presented a petition to the
Parl. at Kilkenny, mentioning the death of his s Meiler, and the minority
of that son's 2 daughters. ([d]) He distinguished himself against the native
Irish. He *m* , 1stly, (—). He *m.*, 2ndly, Maud, da. of Richard of Rokeby, who gave her the lands of Kencloy in Roscommon. ([e]) He *d.* 2 Apr.
1307, and was *bur.* at Athenry Priory.

II. 1307.   2. RICHARD (MAC PHIORIS, ([a]) or BERMINGHAM),
                   called "of the Battles," LORD ATHENRY [I.], 2nd, but
1st surv., s. and h. male. ([f])   Sheriff of Connaught 1299, 1310 and 1316.
He assisted in the victories gained over Edward Bruce and the tribe of
O'Connor in 1316, ([g]) and is said to have been a Lord of the Great
Council [I.] 1317. He *m.* Finola. He *d.* before 1322, and was *bur.* at
Athenry Priory. His widow had dower 1322. ([h])

III. 1321.   3. THOMAS (MAC PHIORIS, ([a]) or BERMINGHAM), LORD
                   ATHENRY [I.], s. and h. He was a minor in 1334. On
30 Jan 1346 he was made King's Chief Sergeant of co Connaught. On
4 Aug. 1356 he received a writ from the King (directed to him as " his
beloved *Thomas de Birmingham, Lord of Athenry*") to restrain him from
making war with the Clanricardes. He *m.* Edina, da. of (—) Mc Egan. ([i])
He *d.* 1373, and was *bur.* at Athenry Priory. His widow *d.* 1384.

([a]) See note " b " on previous page.
([b]) It is probable, however, that any such placing at this early date is immaterial.
The Baron placed next to him was his first cousin, another Piers Bermingham, Baron
of Thetmoy, in Offaley. See Appendix A. at the end of this volume.
([c]) As to certain Irish peers being described as *Dominus* and others as *Baro*, see
Appendix A in this volume   V.G
([d]) Justiciary Rolls, Ireland.
([e]) Plea Roll
([f]) As to the succession of the heir *male* in the case of ancient Baronies of Ireland,
see note *sub* Randall, LORD DUNSANY [1781].
    Meiler, his elder br., being the 1st s. and h. ap of the last Lord, having *m.* Joan
(in the presence of the English court), *d. s.p.m., v.p.,* before 2 Dec. 1302, leaving two
daughters his coheirs, the heirs gen. of the earlier Barons   See pedigree, p. 298.
([g]) The battle of Athenry, 10 Aug 1316, was the turning point in the subjug-
ation of Ireland by the English, which was completed by the battle of Dundalk,
14 Oct. 1318, won by John (of Bermingham), Earl of Louth [I]   V.G.
([h]) Plea Roll.
([i]) This lady has hitherto figured with the surname of " Snymecaga " !! Though
having a secure feeling that this was nonsense, the Editor could do nothing to " make

IV. 1374. 4. WALTER (BERMINGHAM), LORD ATHENRY [I.], 3rd
but 1st surv., s. and h. (ᵃ) He was called " Mor " or
" the Great. " After having been fined 100 s. (ᵇ) for absenting himself
from the Parl. held at Dublin 1377, he was again sum 11 Sep. 1380, and
29 Apr. 1381. Sheriff of Connaught 1388 and again 1400. He d. in
1428, at a great age, and was bur. at Athenry Priory.

V. 1428. 5. THOMAS FITZ WALTER (BERMINGHAM), LORD ATH-
ENRY [I.], s. and h. He was enfeoffed by his cousin,
Sir Walter Bermingham, 3 Hen. IV (1402), in the manors of Knockgraffin
and Kiltenenan, (ᶜ) co. Tipperary, and was sum. to Parl. in the reign of
Hen. VI. He is said to have d " in senectute bona " 1473 ? [Qy. aged
90 years and upwards ?]

VI. 1473 ? 6. THOMAS (BERMINGHAM), LORD ATHENRY [I.], (ᵈ)
s. and h. He was called " Oge " or junior. His succession to the Peerage was disputed by Richard MacFeorais called " of the
wine " or " old Richard, " (ᵉ) apparently his uncle, being 2nd s. of Walter
the 4th Lord, which Richard was presumably the chieftain elected by the
native Irish. He was one of the 15 Irish Barons who obeyed the sum. of
Hen. VII in 1489 to Greenwich, being ranked as " L. Bremingham de
Athenrie, " next below " L. Roche de Fermoye " and " L. Barre de Buttevant, " which last was next below the Earl of Ormond. (ᶠ) He m. Annabel
DE BURGH or BOURKE. He d. 1489 ?

---

known the interpretation, " but a Daniel was found in C.M.Tenison, who explained
that ny is Erse for daughter, and MacCagan an old form of McEgan. The McEgans
were a Galway sept. V.G.

(ᵃ) According to W.F. Carter, editor of The Midland Antiquary, in his continuation of Dugdale's Warwickshire (so far as that work relates to Birmingham), this
Walter's exact relationship to his predecessor is unknown, and he further remarks
that " thenceforward up to the middle of the 16th cent. the ped. of the family and
the descent of the Barony are quite uncertain. " V.G.

(ᵇ) This was the fine of a Peer of Parl., being greater than that of a Commoner.
It continued in force till 70 years later, when, by Act 28 Hen. VI, the fines of Peers
and Commoners were made equal

(ᶜ) These manors, after 1500, were vested in the family of Butler, Lords Caher
[I.], through the match of Piers Butler with the h. gen. of this line of the family of
Bermingham, viz. Elizabeth, da. and h. of John, 1st s. and h. ap. of Thomas, 6th
Lord Athenry, which John d v p. in 1488, s.p.m. See pedigree p. 298.

(ᵈ) The Lords Athenry and the Lords Kerry [I.] appear to have held no correspondence with the King's Government from temp Richard II to temp. Henry VII,
and had become Irish Chieftains and assumed Irish names.

(ᵉ) It was his descendant who succeeded to the peerage on the death of John the
11th Lord about 1547. If it be true as stated in the Annals of the Four Masters that
Richard " of the wine " established his claim to the title, then he and his successors as
set out under the 9th Lord should take the place of the 6th, 7th, and 8th Lords
of the text. V G.

(ᶠ) See Appendix A. to this volume, and note sub DESMOND.

VII. 1489 ?   7. MEILER (BERMINGHAM), LORD ATHENRY [I.], 2nd,
        but 1st surv., s. and h. male. (ª) He *m.* Honor, da. of
Richard "Oge," or *junior*, BOURKE, of Clanricarde. He *d.* 1529.

VIII. 1529.   8. JOHN (BERMINGHAM), LORD ATHENRY [I.], s. and
        h. He attended the Parl. of 1541, in which Hen. VIII
was declared *King* of Ireland. He *d. s.p.m.*, (ᵇ) being slain in the disturb-
ances of the country, [1547 ?] before 1550 According to Betham,
however, he *d. v.p.* before 1529.

IX. 1547 ?   9. RICHARD (BERMINGHAM), LORD ATHENRY [I.], 3rd
        cousin once removed and h. male, (ᶜ) being s and h. of
Edmund B., the s. and h. of Richard, the s. and h. of Edmund, the s. and
h. of Richard, 2nd s. of Walter, the 4th Lord. (ᵈ) He sat in the Parl. of
1559-60. In 1568, having surrendered all his "manors, castells, lord-
shippes, &c.," he received a regrant thereof to him and the heirs male of
his body by letters patent enrolled in the Exchequer [I] In 1572 he
attended the Lord Deputy Sidney in his progress through Galway, who
writes of him that he was "as poore a Baron as lyveth and yet agreed on
to be the *auntientest Baron* in this lande" He *m*, before 1540, Catharine,
da. of Teige O'KELLY, of Gallagh, Chief of his name, by Sabine, da of
Thomas MacRichard Oge BURKE, of Derrymaclaghtny. He *d.* 1580.

X. 1580.   10. EDMOND (BERMINGHAM), LORD ATHENRY [I.], s
        and h., *b* 1540. He sat in the Parl. at Dublin, 26 Apr.
1585, by the style of "*The Lord Bermyngham of Athynrie.*" He *m.*, about
1560, Cecily, da. of Teige O'KELLY, of Mullaghmore She *d.* 1593.
According to *Lodge*, (ᵉ) he *m.*, in 1560, a da. of Sir Dermod O'SHAUGH-
NASSIE, of Gortinshigorie, co. Galway. He *d.* 1614. A bill in Chancery
was filed in 1629 by "Dame *Una*, Baronesse of Athenry, the widow and
relict of Edmond, late Lord Baron of Athenry," claiming dower.

XI. 1614   11. RICHARD (BERMINGHAM), LORD ATHENRY [I.], s.
        and h., *b.* 1570. He sat in the Parl. 1613, 1615, and (as

(ª) Up to this time the history and succession of these Lords, as far back as Meiler,
who in the 13th century founded the Monastery of Athenry, is taken from a copy of
the "Registry of Athenry" in the British Museum (Sloane MSS , no. 4784) This,
however, ends in 1526, neither must it be implicitly relied upon, for the *Annals of
the four Masters* (*sub.* 1473) shew that the succession to the Peerage of Thomas the
6th lord in the text was disputed. There is also a good deal of uncertainty as to the
succession between 1473 and the reign of Elizabeth. The authorities for the 34 years
from 1526 to 1560 are mostly the statements given in "the case of Edward Birmingham of Dalgan, co Galway, claiming to be Lord Birmingham, Baron of Athenry and
Premier Baron of Ireland."

(ᵇ) Anne, his only da. and h., is said to have *m.* William Legge, and to have
been mother of Edward Legge, *b* 1543, ancestor of the Earls of Dartmouth.

(ᶜ) See *ante* p. 292, note f.

(ᵈ) See pedigree p. 298.

(ᵉ) Vol III, p. 42.

Premier (ª) Baron) in 1634. He *m.*, 1stly (—), da. of William LALLY, Archbishop of Tuam. He *m.*, 2ndly, Gille, widow of Dermot O'SHAUGH-NESSY, da. of Ulick Bourke McHUBERT, of Dysert Kelly, co. Galway. She *d.* 20 Nov. 1635, and was *bur.* in the Abbey of Athenry. Fun. Cert. He *d.* 1645, at Turlovaughane, and was *bur.* at Athenry.

XII. 1645 ?   12. EDMOND BERMINGHAM, *de jure hereditario* LORD ATHENRY [I.], grandson and h., being s. and h. of Edward B. (by Mary, da. of Feagh BOURKE, of Dunamon, co. Galway), who was s. and h. ap., by his 1st wife, of the last Lord, and *d. v.p.* before 1641. He was a Dominican Friar, and, accordingly, by deed dat. 3 May 1641, stating that he was grandchild and next h. to "Richard, Lord Birmingham, Lord Baron of Athenry," conveys "as much as in him lieth, all his birthright and title and possibility of descent to the honour and estate of LORD BIRMINGHAM, BARON OF ATHENRY, (ᵇ) to his dearest br. Francis Birmingham, &c., that after the death of his said grandfather, the name, title, honour and estate of Lord Birmingham, Baron of Athenry, be and remain to his said br. Francis and his *heirs male.*" (ᶜ) He *d. s.p.* The date of his death is unknown.

XII. 1645 ?   12. FRANCIS (BERMINGHAM), LORD ATHENRY [I.], grandson, and *de facto* h. of Richard, Lord Athenry abovenamed, being next br. to Edmond, *de jure*, Lord, abovenamed. By virtue of the resignation of his elder br., he appears to have *suc.* to the Peerage in 1645, immediately on the death of his grandfather, and to have been in possession thereof during the Civil Wars. The exercise of Martial Law in Connaught was granted to him in 1649. He maintained the King's cause in Ireland to the last, and was excepted from the pardon of 12 Aug. 1652. He, as "Francis Lord Baron of Athenree," and "Mary Bermingham, widow," his mother, appear, under date 4 Sep. 1655, among the transplanted Irish in Connaught. On 9 May 1661 (when, not improbably, his elder br. was dead) he took his seat in the House of Lords [I.]. In 1667 he filed a bill in Chancery against the Portreeve of Athenry, referred to above. (ᵈ) He *m.* Bridget, da. of Sir Lucas DILLON, of Lough Glyn, co. Roscommon, by Jane, da. of Garret MOORE, of Ball, co. Mayo. He *d.* 12 Apr. 1677, and was *bur.* at Athenry. His widow *d.* 2 Jan. 1687, and was *bur.* at Turlovaughane.

(ª) Journals of the Irish House of Lords 1634, which begin in that year.

(ᵇ) A somewhat similar case occurs in the Viscountcy of Buttevant [I.], where Richard, *de jure* Viscount, 1581-1622 (being deaf and dumb, though of sound understanding), was passed over in favour of his yr. br. David Barry—the *de facto* Viscount 1581-1617, as also in that of Slane, 1629. See that title.

(ᶜ) The original deed (price 60s.) was for sale in Dec. 1883, by J. Coleman, Bookseller, Tottenham, Midx. It is stated that he is therein styled "*Sir* Edmond Birmingham, of the Blessed Order of St. Dominick, &c."

(ᵈ) See *ante*, p. 291, note "a."

XIII. 1677.   13. EDWARD (BERMINGHAM), LORD ATHENRY [I.], s. and h. Lord Lieut. of co. Mayo. He served as Capt. in the army of James II in Ireland, 1689, (Earl of Clanricarde's Reg. of Infantry) (ᵃ) and was *outlawed* 11 May 1691, but the attainder was reversed 25 Nov. 1698, and *full pardon* granted by patent 5 June 1700. He *m.*, 1stly, Mary, widow of Sir John BURKE, of Derrymaclaghtny, co. Galway, 1st da. of Richard (DE BURGH), 6th EARL OF CLANRICARDE [I.], by Elizabeth, da. of Walter (BUTLER), EARL OF ORMONDE [I]. By her he had no surv. issue. She *d* of small pox, at Merchant's Key, Dublin, 13, and was *bur.* 14 Aug. 1685, at Christ Church, Dublin Fun. ent. He *m.*, 2ndly, Bridget, 1st da. of Col. John BROWNE, of Westport, co. Mayo, by his 2nd wife, Maud, da. of Theobald (BOURKE), 3rd VISCOUNT MAYO [I.]. She *d.* 13 Jan. 1702, and was *bur.* at Athenry. He *d.* 3, and was *bur.* 9 May 1709, at Athenry. Fun. Entry [I.] signed Athunry by his successor.

XIV. 1709.   14. FRANCIS (BERMINGHAM), LORD ATHENRY [I.], only surv. s. and h. by 2nd wife, *b.* 1692. Conformed to the Established Church [I.] 19 June 1709. Took his seat in the House of Lords [I.] 25 Nov. 1713. He *m.*, 1stly, 22 Sep. 1716, Mary, 1st da and, in her issue, coh. of Thomas (NUGENT), 4th EARL OF WESTMEATH [I.], by Margaret, da of John (BELLEW), 1st LORD BELLEW [I.]. She was *b.* 1694, and *d.* at Galway, July 1725. He *m.*, 2ndly, 17 Aug. 1745, Ellis, widow of Theobald (BOURKE), VISCOUNT MAYO [I.], da. of James AGAR, of Gowran, co. Kilkenny, by his 2nd wife, Mary, da. of Sir Henry WEMYSS. He *d.* in Dublin, 4 Mar. 1749/50. His widow, who on 1 Aug. 1758, was *cr.* COUNTESS OF BRANDON [I.], *d. s.p.*, 11 Mar. 1789, in Merrion Sq., Dublin. See "BRANDON," Countess of [I.], *cr.* 1758 ; *extinct* 1789.

XV. 1750   15. THOMAS (BERMINGHAM), LORD ATHENRY [I.], 1st, to   and only surv. (ᵇ) s. and h. by 1st wife, *b.* 16 Nov. 1799.   1717. M.P. for co. Galway 1745-49/50. Took his seat in the House of Lords [I] 19 Mar. 1749/50. On 23 Apr. 1759 he was *cr.* EARL OF LOUTH, co. Louth [I.], and took his seat as such 23 Nov. following. P.C. [I.], but was turned out of the Council by Lord Townshend. He *m.*, 1stly, Nov. 1745, Jane, 1st da. of Sir John BINGHAM, 5th Bart. [S.], by Anne, da. of Agmondesham VESEY. She *d. s.p.s.*, 11 Sep. 1746, at Castlebar, co. Mayo. He *m.*, 2ndly, 10 Jan. 1750, Margaret, yst. da. and eventually coh. of Peter DALY, of Quansbury, co. Galway, by Elizabeth, da. of Richard BLAKE, of Ardfry. She *d.* in or before 1793. Admon. 18 May 1793. He *d. s.p.m.s.*, 11 Jan 1799, at his house at Bermingham, co. Galway, when the EARLDOM OF LOUTH [I.] became *extinct*, and the BARONY OF ATHENRY [I] *dormant* (ᶜ) The latter title was, however, assumed as under.

(ᵃ) For a list of the Irish peers present in, and absent from, the Parl. of 1689, see vol iii, Appendix D.

(ᵇ) He had 2 yr. brothers living 4 May 1736, then aged about 15 and 11 (*Hist. MSS. Com.*, 15th Rep., App., Pt. 1, p. 156).

(ᶜ) On his death any Barony *in fee* that might have been vested in him would

XVI ? 1799.   16. ? JOHN BIRMINGHAM, of Dalgan, co. Galway, assumed the title of LORD ATHENRY [I.], as h. male of the grantee, being 1st surv. s. and h. of John B., of Dalgan (who *d.* Nov. 1771, aged 85), by Maud, da. of John BIRMINGHAM, of Ross Hill or Killbeg, which John B. of Dalgan was s. and h. of Francis B. (who *d.* 1728), s. and h. of Myles B. (who *d.* 1707), s. and h. of Redmond B. (who *d.* 1695), s. and h. of Meiler B. (called Meiler Buy), all of Dalgan afsd., this Meiler being said to be 2nd s. of Edmond, 10th Lord Athenry. He was J.P. for co. Galway. On the death of the EARL OF

---

have fallen into abeyance between (1) Elizabeth, his 1st da., who *m.*, 1stly, Thomas Baily Heath Sewell; 2ndly, 19 June 1779, Francis Duffield (who was living May 1793); 3rdly, Joseph Russell; and who *d.* 1838. (2) The four daughters and coheirs of Mary, *styled* Viscountess St. Lawrence, his 2nd da. (who *d. v.p.* 24 July 1793), *viz.*—Harriet (the petitioner of 1827), Isabella, Mary, and Matilda ; (3) Louisa Catherine Mary, his 3rd and yst. da., *b.* 20 July 1764, *m.*, 1stly, Joseph Henry (Blake), 1st Lord Wallscourt [I.], 2ndly, 21 Apr. 1804, James Daly, and *d.* 28 May 1827.

The petition of "Thomas Bermingham Daly Henry SEWELL, Esq.," *b.* 13 Feb. 1774, only s. of Lady Elizabeth DUFFIELD, by her former husband " Thomas Baily Heath Sewell, Esq.," deceased, " to put an end to the abeyance of the said Barony of Athenry in behalf of his said mother, 1st of the three daughters and coheirs of Thomas, late Earl of Louth and Baron of Athenry [I.], deceased, " was reported upon, 3 Nov. 1800, * by the Law officers [I.] of the Crown, *viz.*, John Toler (Attorney Gen.), John Stewart (Solicitor Gen.), and St. George Daly (Prime Serjeant), who pronounced as their opinion " that the Barony of Athenry, appearing to be the most ancient on the list of Barons and being of so great antiquity and *consequently* [sic] a Barony in fee, is now, as stated in the petition, in abeyance between (1) the said Lady Elizabeth, the mother of the Petitioner, (2) the said daughters of Lady St. LAWRENCE and (3) the said Lady WALLSCOURT. " These learned gentlemen also state " that it belongs now to His Majesty alone to determine whether the said Barony shall vest in any of the said coheiresses, or whether he " shall vouchsafe to bestow his consideration and favour " [*to the exclusion of all of them,* and in favour of one who was *not* a coheir] " on the Petitioner, as the son of the eldest daughter, *&c.*" Many years afterwards, another petition, alleging (as a fact) the Barony of Athenry to be *a Barony in fee* and consequently in abeyance between the heirs gen. of the late Earl of Louth [I.], was presented, in 1827, by Lady Harriet ST. GEORGE, da. of William (St. Lawrence), Earl of Howth [I.], by his 1st wife, Mary (*styled* Viscountess St. Lawrence), who was 2nd da. and, in her issue, coh. of the abovenamed Earl of Louth. A report was made thereon by the Attorney Gen. (Scarlett), but in this petition, also, there was the same *fatal* defect as in the one of 1800, *viz.* that " no attempt was made on the part of the Petitioner to prove herself to be an heir gen. of the *first* Baron. " The case was referred to the House together with that of Edward Birmingham, who claimed as h. male. Lady Harriet *d.* 2 Feb. 1830.

* On the same date they reported the BARONY OF DELVIN [I.] " *to be an antient Barony in fee,* " and now in abeyance between (1) " John NUGENT, Lieut. Gov. of Tortola " and (2) the coheirs of Lady Mary Nugent, *i.e.* the three (abovenamed) daughters of the late Earl of Louth [I.] (who was s. and h. of the said Lady Mary, by Francis, Lord Athenry abovenamed), or their representatives.

PEDIGREE

(which, though probable, is unsupported by conclusive evidence) shewing the succession of the Lords Athenry [I.] and the relationship of those claiming that Peerage.

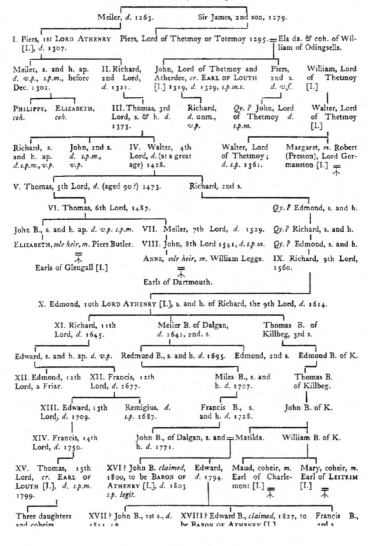

Robert of Bermingham or Birmingham.

Piers of Bermingham *d.* 1254.

Meiler, *d.* 1263.   Sir James, 2nd son, 1279.

I. Piers, 1st LORD ATHENRY Piers, Lord of Thetmoy or Totemoy 1295. = Ela da. & coh. of Wil-
[I.], *d.* 1307.   liam of Odingsells.

Meiler, s. and h. ap. II. Richard, John, Lord of Thetmoy and Piers, William, Lord
d. v.p., s.p.m., before 2nd Lord, Atherdee, *cr.* EARL OF LOUTH 2nd s. of Thetmoy
Dec. 1302.   *d.* 1321. [I.] 1319, *d.* 1329, *s.p.m.s.* *d. v.f.* [I.]

PHILIPPE, ELIZABETH, III. Thomas, 3rd Richard, *Qy. ?* John, Lord Walter, Lord
coh. *coh.* Lord, s. & h. *d.* *d.* unm., of Thetmoy *d.* of Thetmoy
    1373. *v.p.* *s.p.m.* [I.]

Richard, s. John, 2nd s. IV. Walter, 4th Walter, Lord Margaret, *m.* Robert
and h. ap. *d. s.p.m.*, Lord, *d.* (at a great of Thetmoy ; (Preston), Lord Gor-
d. s.p.m., v.p. *v.p.* age) 1428. *d. s.p.* 1361. manston [I.] =

V. Thomas, 5th Lord, *d.* (aged 90 ?) 1473.   Richard, 2nd s.

VI. Thomas, 6th Lord, 1487.   *Qy. ?* Edmond, s. and h.

John B., s. and h. ap. *d. v.p. s.p.m.* VII. Meiler, 7th Lord, *d.* 1529. *Qy. ?* Richard, s. and h.

ELIZABETH, *sole heir, m.* Piers Butler. VIII. John, 8th Lord 1541, *d. s.p.m.* *Qy. ?* Edmond, s. and h.

Earls of Glengall [I.]   ANNE, *sole heir, m.* William Legge. IX. Richard, 9th Lord, 1560.

Earls of Dartmouth.

X. Edmond, 10th LORD ATHENRY [I.], s. and h. of Richard, the 9th Lord, *d.* 1614.

XI. Richard, 11th Meiler B. of Dalgan, Thomas B. of
Lord, *d.* 1645. *d.* 1641, 2nd. s. Killbeg, 3rd s.

Edward, s. and h. ap. *d. v.p.* Redmond B., s. and h. *d.* 1695. Edmond, 2nd s. Edmond B. of K.

XII. Edmond, 12th XII. Francis, 12th Miles B., s. and Thomas B.
Lord, a Friar. Lord, *d.* 1677. h. *d.* 1707. of Killbeg.

XIII. Edward, 13th Remigius, *d.* Francis B., s. John B. of K.
Lord, *d.* 1709. *s.p.* 1687. and h. *d.* 1728.

XIV. Francis, 14th John B., of Dalgan, s. and = Matilda. William B. of K.
Lord, *d.* 1750. h. *d.* 1771.

XV. Thomas, 15th XVI? John B. *claimed,* Edward, Maud, coheir, *m.* Mary, coheir, *m.*
Lord, *cr.* EARL OF 1800, to be BARON OF *d.* 1794. Earl of Charle- Earl of LEITRIM
LOUTH [I.], *d. s.p.m.* ATHENRY [I.], *d.* 1803   mont [I.] [I.]
1799. *s.p. legit.*

Three daughters XVII? John B., 1st s., *d.* XVIII? Edward B., *claimed,* 1827, to Francis B.,
and coheirs 1811, *s.p.* be BARON OF ATHENRY [I.] 3rd s.

LOUTH [I.], he petitioned (as " John Birmingham, Esq., ") to be sum.
" by the style and title of BARON OF ATHENRY " [I.], as h. male
(of the body) of Piers, who sat as such in (1243-44) 28 Hen. III. This
was referred to the Law officers [I.] Mar. 1800. He *m.*, 1stly, Jennet,
da. of John PUECH, of St. Christopher's. She *d.* 1768. He *m.*, 2ndly,
Dorothea MATHEWS, of Demarara. He *d. s.p. legit.* 1803. (ª)

XVII. ? 1803.   20. ? JOHN BIRMINGHAM, of Dalgan afsd., nephew
                and h., being s. and h. of Edward B. (by Anne, da. of
James WADDELL), yst. br. of the above, who *d.* 1794. He appears,
however, never to have assumed or claimed the title. He *d. s.p.*, being
slain at the siege of Badajos 1811. (ª)

XVIII. ? 1811.   18. ? EDWARD BIRMINGHAM, of Dalgan, afsd., br. and
                h. In 1827 he petitioned that, *as heir male*, he should
be declared "to be entitled to the honours and dignities of LORD BIRMING-
HAM, BARON OF ATHENRY and Premier Baron of Ireland as a prescriptive
dignity which had been enjoyed by his ancestors from time immemorial." (ᵇ) The Attorney Gen. (Denman) reported to the King thereon
that in his opinion " the petitioner has proved himself to be the h. male
of Richard, LORD ATHENRY, who sat in Parl. in the reign of Queen
Eliz." The petition was referred to the House, and the minutes of
evidence before the Committee of Privileges were ordered to be printed
10 Mar. 1836. (ᶜ) See tabular pedigree at p. 298.

ATHERDEE or ARDEE see ARDEE

ATHLONE

See "WILMOT OF ATHLONE," Viscountcy [I.] *(Wilmot)*, cr. 1621,
extinct with the Earldom of Rochester, 1681.

(ª) See Pedigree p. 298.
(ᵇ) On like grounds, 4 Oct. 1721, the Irish House of Lords resolved in favour
of Gerald de Courcy, who, being h. male, had claimed the Barony of Kingsale [I.]
as a *Barony by Prescription* for " that his ancestors have been, *time out of mind*, Peers
of this Realm and sitting members of this House." The h. gen. (female) was passed
over in this resolution of 1721, as was also the case, 38 years later, on the death of
this same Lord Kingsale, *s.p.m.*, 1759, when John de Courcy, the then h. male, was
declared h. to the Peerage, and took his seat, in 1762, accordingly.
(ᶜ) At the funeral, in 1884, of John Birmingham of Millbrook, a grandson
of John, the claimant of 1799 (who *d. s.p. legit* in 1803), there was present
another John Birmingham, said to be 2nd cousin of the deceased. (*ex inform.*
W.F.Carter).

EARLDOM [I.]   1. GODARD (ª) VAN REEDE (ᵇ) s. and h. of Godard
I. 1692.   Adriaan van R., 1st BARON VAN REEDE (ᶜ) [in Denmark,
    so *cr.* 25 May 1671] Lord of Amerongen, Middachten,
Lievendaal, Ginkel, &c., in the United Provinces, several times Ambassador
to England and Denmark (who *d.* 1691), by his wife Brilliana (or Margaret),
da of George TURNOR, by his wife Salomé VAN MEETKERCKEN.   He was *b.*
4 June 1644 (O.S.) at Amerongen Castle, in Utrecht, his family belonging
to the old feudal nobility of that province.   He was made Lieut. Gen. of
Cavalry in the United Provinces 20 Oct. 1683, and was appointed, by
William III, Lieut. Gen. and Commander in Chief of the army in Ireland.
Having distinguished himself by the capture of Athlone, 20 June 1691, and
at the battle of Aughrim on 10 July following, he was naturalised as ' Baron
de Ginkel' by Act of Parl 24 Feb. 1691/2, and was *cr.* (ᵈ) 4 Mar. 1691/2,
BARON OF AGHRIM, co. Galway, and EARL OF ATHLONE, (ᵉ)
co. Roscommon [I].   On 13 Oct. 1693 the King granted him the forfeited
estates (26,481 acres) (ᶠ) of William Dongan, the attainted Earl of Limerick
[I], but this grant was reversed by Parl. on 15 Dec. 1699.   Commander
in Chief of the allied armies in Flanders, and, in 1702, was Veldt-Marshal
of the armies of the States Gen.   He *m.*, (cont. 31 July), 26 Aug. 1666, at
Ellekom, in Gelderland, Urselina Philopota, da of Reinier VAN RAESVELD,
Lord of Middachten, by Margaretha VAN LEEFDAEL, his wife.   He *d.*
11 Feb. 1702/3, of apoplexy, at Utrecht, and was *bur.* at Amerongen.
His widow *d.* 30 Sep. 1721, at Middachten Castle, and was also *bur.* at
Amerongen.   Their mutual testament dat. 11 Apr. 1701.

II. 1703.   2. FREDERIK CHRISTIAAN (VAN REEDE), EARL OF ATH-
    LONE, &c, [I.], s. and h., *b.* 20 Oct. 1668, at Utrecht.
He was a member of the Nobles in that province.   Naturalised in England
1696.   Lieut. Gen. of the Dutch Forces, and Governor of Sluys.   In 1710

(ª) The Editor desires to acknowledge the valuable help which he has received
in the re-writing of this article from G D Burtchaell, Athlone Pursuivant, and from
the Marquis de Ruvigny, the latter having examined the Dutch, and the former the
Irish sources of information, including the original certificate of " the nobles and
knights representing the second estate of the country of Utrecht " dated 3 Jan. 1780,
which is filed with an English translation in Ulster's office, and which has been followed as to the spelling of most of the proper names in this article.   V.G.

(ᵇ) It would appear that this is the correct family name, although ' Ginkel '
was the one by which they were known in England ; this latter, however, was only
one of several Dutch Lordships which they held.   V.G.

(ᶜ) His cousin german, Jan van Reede, Heer van Renswoude, is said to have
been *cr* a Baron [E], by Charles I, by letters patent dated 24 Mar. 1644.   His
line is extinct.   (*ex inform.* the Marquis de Ruvigny.)   V.G.

(ᵈ) See the preamble to the patent in *Lodge*, vol. ii, p 155.

(ᵉ) The Dutch Earls of Athlone bore arms of Silver, two dances sable.   (*ex
inform* Oswald Barron.)   V G

(ᶠ) This grant to the man who had won Ireland for him, was less than a quarter
of that to the lad Keppel, who had done no public service.   For a list of the largest
of these grants, and some remarks thereon, see p 92, note " a. "   V.G.

he was taken prisoner after the siege of St. Venant. He *m.*, (cont same day) 2 Mar. 1715, at Zuylestein Castle, Henrietta (ª), yst. da. of William Henry (DE NASSAU-ZUYLESTEIN), 1st EARL OF ROCHFORD, by Jane, da and h. of Sir Henry WROTH. He *d.* 15 Aug. 1719, (ᵇ) at Sluys.

III. 1719.   3. GODARD ADRIAAN (VAN REEDE), EARL OF ATHLONE, &c., [I.], s. and h , *b.* 25 Jan. 1715/6, at Utrecht. He *d.* unm. 8 Oct. 1736, of the small pox, at Marburg, in Hesse (where he was a student at the University), and was *bur.* at Amerongen, aged 20 years and 8 months.

IV. 1736.   4 FREDERIK WILLEM (VAN REEDE), EARL OF ATHLONE, &c., [I.], only br. and h., *b.* 1 Apr. 1717, at Utrecht, and *bap.* at the Walloon Church there, 3 days later. Ed. at the University of Marburg. " Though only 30 years of age, he had a seat in several Colleges of the generality, in behalf of the province of Utrecht. " (ᶜ)   He *m.* (cont. 13 Apr.), 2 May 1742, at Voorschoten, Louisa Isabella Herme-lina, da. and coh. of Arent, BARON VAN WASSENAAR [H.R.E.], Lord of Duvenvoirde, Voorschoten, &c., in the United Provinces, Ambassador from the States Gen. to the Court of St. James, by Anna Margaretha, da. of Hans Willem (BENTINCK), 1st EARL OF PORTLAND. He *d.* 1 Dec. 1747, at Arnhem. His widow, who was *b.* at the Hague, and *bap.* there 19 Feb. 1718/9, *d.* 23 Apr. 1756, at Amerongen. Will dat. 12 Nov. 1754.

V. 1747.   5. FREDERIK CHRISTIAAN REINHART (VAN REEDE), EARL OF ATHLONE, &c., [I.], s. and h., *b.* 31 Jan. 1743, at the Hague. He was a member of the Nobles in the province of Utrecht, was Ranger of the said province, and was Chief Magistrate for that city in 1790. He was *cr.*, 25 Sep. 1790, Count of the Holy Roman Empire, as COUNT VAN REEDE. In 1795, the French having occupied Holland, he accompanied the Stadtholder to England, and took his seat in the House of Lords [I.] 10 Mar. 1795, (ᵈ) his signed pedigree being ' delivered in ' to the Lords by Ulster King of Arms at the same time. (ᵉ) On 1 Aug. 1800 he obtained an annuity from that House as a poor Peer. He *m.*, 29 Dec. 1765, at the Hague, his cousin, Anna Elisabeth Christina, da. of Jan

---

(ª) Her eldest sister, Maria, *m.* Godard van Reede, lord of Harweld, 2nd s of the 1st Earl of Athlone [I]. V G.

(ᵇ) The Dutch accounts and *Dict. Nat. Biog* say 1719, and *Burke* 1729, but 1720 is the date given in the ped. signed by the 5th Earl in 1795. V G.

(ᶜ) *Lodge*, vol ii, p. 157, where, however, this statement is applied to *Godert*, Earl ot A., a supposed yr. br. of the 3rd Earl, who does not appear in fact to have had any existence V G.

(ᵈ) The decision of the House enabling him so to do seems questionable, as it appears that he was an *alien*. The Crown, however, would not have been bound by such decision.

(ᵉ) " According to the Resolutions of the House of Peers of 12 June 1778. " This interesting document, from *Lords Entries*, vol. iii, pp. 453-54, of which a copy has been most kindly furnished, to the Editor, by G.D.Burtchaell, Athlone Pursui-vant, corrects several serious errors into which Lodge has fallen, as, *e g* , in note (ᶜ) above.

Maximilian, Baron van Tuyll van Serooskerken, Lord of Westbroek and Vleuten in the United Provinces, by his 1st wife, Ursula Christina Reimera, da. of Frederik Christiaan (van Reede), 2nd Earl of Athlone [I.]. He *d.* 13 Dec. 1808, at Teddington, Midx., and was *bur.* there. Will pr. Jan. 1810. His widow, who was *b.* 9 Sep. 1745, at Zuylen Castle, *d.* 16 Jan. 1819, at the Hague, aged 73.

VI. 1808.   6. Frederik Willem (van Reede), Earl of Athlone, &c., [I.], s. and h., *b.* 22 Oct. 1766, at Utrecht. He is said to have been a Capt. in the British Army in 1795. He *m.*, 1stly, in Mar. 1789, at Utrecht, Cornelia Adriaana, da. of Willem Munter, Councillor and Echevin of Amsterdam, by Wendela Eleanora ten Hove, Lady of Doorn, den Bosch, and Sleeburg. She, who was *b.* 30 Jan. 1770, at Amsterdam, was divorced(ᵃ) 5 July 1794. He *m.*, 2ndly, 11 Nov. 1800, (spec lic) at Windlestone, co. Durham, Maria, 2nd da. of Sir John Eden, 4th Bart., of West Auckland, by his 2nd wife, Dorothea, da. and h. of Peter Johnson. He *d. s.p.*, insane, at Croom's Hill, Greenwich, of water on the brain, 5, and was *bur.* 13 Dec. 1810, at Greenwich. Admon. Mar. 1811. His widow *m.*, 30 Oct. 1821, at St. James's, Westm. (as his 2nd wife), Vice Admiral Sir William Johnstone Hope, G.C.B., who *d.* 2 May 1831, aged 64. She *d. s.p.*, 5 Mar 1851, aged 81, in South Str., Grosvenor Sq. Will pr. Mar. 1851.

VII. 1810.   7. Reynoud Diederik Jacob (van Reede), Earl of Athlone, &c, [I], br. and h, being 3rd (ᵇ) s. of the 5th Earl, *b.* 24 July 1773, at Utrecht. Major in the Army 28 Jan. 1808; Lieut. Gen 4 June 1814. He *m.*, 19 Mar. 1818, at the British Embassy, Paris, Henrietta Dorothea Maria, sister, and in her issue, h. of William Williams Hope, of Rushton Hall, co. Northampton, and da. of John Williams Hope, of Amsterdam (formerly John Williams), by Ann, da. of John Goddard, of Rotterdam, and of Woodford Hall, Essex. He *d.* 31 Oct. 1823, of apoplexy, at the Hague. Will pr. Feb. 1824. His widow *m.*, 4 May 1825, in Gt. Cumberland Str., William, 1st. s. of Sir James Gambier, by whom also she had issue. She *d.* 3 Sep. 1830, in London. Admon. Nov 1830.

VIII. 1823.   8. George Godard Henry(ᶜ) (van Reede), Earl of Athlone, &c., [I.] only s. and h., *b.* 21 Nov. 1820, at the Hague. He *d.* unm., 2 Mar. 1843, aged 22, at Bath. Will pr. Mar. 1843.

IX. 1843.   9. Willem Gustaaf Frederik (ᵈ) (van Reede), Earl of Athlone and Baron of Aghrim [I.], 10th Baron

---

(ᵃ) The cause being her *crim. con.* with a German officer, Col. von Bosc. She *d.* 24 Oct 1828, at Dresden   V.G

(ᵇ) The 2nd s , Karel Willem Louis, *b.* 27 Mar. 1772, *d.* unm. and *v p*, 21 Dec. 1793. V.G.

(ᶜ) The Dutch accounts give his name as Henry not Hendrik. V.G.

(ᵈ) He is called 'William' only, in the ped. signed by his father. V.G.

van Reede [Denmark, 1671], 5th Count van Reede [H R.E. 1790], Lord of Amerongen, Middachten, Lievendaal, Ginkel, &c. [United Provinces], uncle and h male, being 5th(ª) and yst. s. of the 5th Earl, b 21 July 1780, at Utrecht. He m., 7 Sep. 1814, at Amsterdam, Wendela Eleanora, da. of Sir James Boreel, 8th Bart. [1645], of the Hague, Jonkherr [Neth. 28 Aug. 1814], Member of the Equestrian Order and States of Holland, by Margaretha Johanna, da. of Willem Munter, Echevin of Amsterdam. He d. s.p., 21 May 1844, at the Hague, when his peerage titles, and all his foreign honours, became *extinct.* His widow, who was b. 11 July 1792, at Amsterdam, d. 30 Jan. 1868, at Avegoor Castle, in the village of Ellekom afsd.

---

i.e. "Athlone" Earldom *(H.R.H. Prince Albert Victor Christian Edward),* cr. 1890, with the Dukedom of Clarence and Avondale, which see ; *extinct* 1892.

ATHLUMNEY OF SOMERVILLE AND DOLLARDSTOWN

BARONY [I.]
I. 1863.

1. William Meredyth Somerville, of Somerville, co. Meath, s. and h. of Sir Marcus S., of the same, 4th Bart. [I. 1748], by his 1st wife, Mary Anne, only da and h. of Sir Richard Gorges-Meredyth, Bart. [I. 1787], b 1802. Matric. Oxford (Ch. Ch.) 18 Feb. 1822, aged 19. He was M.P. (Liberal) for Drogheda 1837-52, for Canterbury 1854-65, Under Secretary Home Department 1846-47, Chief Secretary for Ireland 1847-52, and P.C. 22 July 1847. He was raised to the Peerage of Ireland (ᵇ) 14 Dec. 1863, being cr. BARON ATHLUMNEY OF SOMERVILLE AND DOLLARDSTOWN, co. Meath [I.], and, within three years, was cr., 3 May 1866, BARON MEREDYTH of Dollardstown, co. Meath [U.K.]. He was a respectable Parliamentary official. He m., 1stly, 22 Dec. 1832, (spec. lic.) in Hamilton Place, St. Geo., Han. Sq., Maria Harriet, yst. da. of Henry (Conyngham), 1st Marquess Conyngham [I], by Elizabeth, da. of Joseph Denison. She d. s.p m.s., 3 Dec. 1843. He m., 2ndly, at the British Embassy, Paris, 16 Oct. 1860, Maria Georgiana Elizabeth, only da. of Herbert George Jones, Serjeant at Law, by Maria Alicia, 2nd da. of Sir George William Leeds, 1st Bart. [1812]. He d. at Waterloo Crescent, Dover, Kent, 7, and was bur. 13 Dec. 1873, at Kentstown, co. Meath. Will pr. 20 Jan 1874. His widow, who was b. 24 June 1831, d., aged 67, at Frant, Sussex, 6, and was bur. 11 Jan. 1899, at Kentstown. Will dat. 21 Apr. 1897, pr. 16 Feb. 1899. (ᶜ)

(ª) The 4th s, Jan Reinhart Gerard, b. 12 Dec 1774, d. s.p.m., 18 Mar. 1818.
(ᵇ) The three extinctions used for this purpose, according to the Act of Union [I.], were Caher (Earl of Glengall), Riversdale, and Dungannon
(ᶜ) William Henry Marcus S., only s. by 1st wife, d. v p., an infant, 11 Sep 1837.

II 1873.   2 JAMES HERBERT GUSTAVUS MEREDYTH (SOMERVILLE), BARON ATHLUMNEY [I], BARON MEREDYTH [U.K.], and a Baronet [I.], only surv. s. and h. by 2nd wife, *b.* at Somerville House, 23 Mar., and *bap.* at Kentstown 25 Apr 1865. Ed. at Harrow school. Lieut. 5th batt Royal Canadians, 1882. Lieut. Coldstream Guards 1886 ; served in the Dongola Expedition 1896, mentioned in Despatches ; served in S. Africa 1900, medal and 4 clasps (ª) In politics he is a Conservative

Family Estates —These, in 1883, consisted of about 10,200 acres in co. Meath, and about 300 in co. Dublin. Total about 10,500 acres worth about £11,400 a year.—*Principal Residence* :—Somerville House, near Navan, co. Meath.

ATHNERY, see ATHENRY

ATHOLL(ᵇ) or ATHOLE *sometimes anciently called* ASCELES(ᶜ)

[This Earldom, with GOWRY (now together forming the north and east part of Perthshire), was one of the *Seven original Mormaerships* of Scotland (ᵈ) the Rulers of which were styled *Mormaers* in the 10th century, and early in the 12th were known as Earls.]

EARLDOM [S]   1 MADACH, s (ᵈ) of Melmare (br. of Malcolm III, KING OF SCOTLAND, 1057-98) was witness to the charter I. 1115 ?   of Scone dat 1115 as 'Madach Comes,' *i.e.* Madach EARL OF ATHOLL or ATHOLE (ᵉ) [S.]. He *m.*, about 1133, (probably as a 2nd wife) Margaret, (ᶠ) da. of Haco, JARL OF ORKNEY, which island was then part of the Kingdom of Norway, and *d.* between 1142 and 1152. His widow *m.* Erland Ugni, JARL OF ORKNEY, who was killed 1156.

II. 1150 ?   2. MALCOLM, EARL OF ATHOLL [S.], s. of Malcolm, who was probably s. of Madach by a prior marriage. He made a donation to the Priory of St. Andrews at some date before 1174, and to Dunfermline between 1183 and 1186. He *m.*, as his 2nd wife, Hextild, da. of Waltheof, or Uchtred, and widow of Richard COMYN. He *d.* between 1186 and Aug 1198

(ª) For a list of peers, and heirs ap. of peers, serving in this war, see vol. III, Appendix B. V G.

(ᵇ) See remarks under ANGUS, p. 141.

(ᶜ) See *N. & Q*, 7th Ser, vol VIII, pp. 271-2, as to this appellation.

(ᵈ) He is, however, sometimes called s. of Donald Bane. (*N. & Q*, 7th Ser, vol. VIII, p 271.

(ᵉ) Skene's *Celtic Scotland*, vol III, p 54

(ᶠ) Her son suc. to Orkney, but not to Atholl.

III. 1190 ?   3. HENRY, EARL OF ATHOLL [S], s. and h., confirmed his father's grants. He *m.* Margaret, and *d.* shortly before Jan. 1210/1, *s.p.m s.*

IV. 1210 ?   4. ISABEL, *suo jure* COUNTESS OF ATHOLL [S.], 1st da. and h. She *m.*, before Jan 1210/1, Thomas OF GALLO-WAY (br. to the well-known Alan, Lord of Galloway), who in her right is then called EARL OF ATHOLL [S.]. (*) They jointly (as Earl and Countess) made a grant to the Abbey of Dunfermline He *d.* 1231. She seems to have *m.*, 2ndly, Alan DE LUNDIN, "Ostiarius Regis," who is designated EARL OF ATHOLL in 1233 and 1235, but as his signature appears afterwards without that designation, he probably held the Earldom in wardship (only) during the minority of his step-son.

V. 1231 ?   5. PATRICK (OF GALLOWAY), EARL OF ATHOLL [S.], only s. and h. Having been successful at a tournament against Walter Bisset, he was burnt to death by him at Haddington, 1242. He *d.* unm. (b)

VI. 1242.   6. FERNELITH, *suo jure* COUNTESS OF ATHOLL [S.], aunt and h , being the yr. of the two daughters and coheirs of Earl Henry abovenamed. She *m.*, before 1242, David HASTINGS, who, in her right, became EARL OF ATHOLL [S.], and, as such, was one of the guar-antors of a treaty of peace with Henry III, in 1244. She surv. him.

VII. 1250?   7. ADA, *suo jure* COUNTESS OF ATHOLL [S.], da. and h. She *m.* John OF STRATHBOGIE, s. and h. of David, who was 3rd s. of Duncan, EARL OF FIFE [S.]. By this match her husband became, in her right, EARL OF ATHOLL [S.], and, as such, he, with his Countess, in 1254, confirmed a donation made by the father of the latter to the monastery of Coupar.

VIII. 1260?   8. DAVID (OF STRATHBOGIE), EARL OF ATHOLL [S.], s. and h., *suc.* before Christmas 1264. He *m.*, 1stly, Helen. He *m.*, 2ndly, before 1265, Isabel (*b.* after 1245), da. of Richard OF CHILHAM, or OF DOVER, by Maud, *suo jure* COUNTESS OF ANGUS, da. and h. of Malcolm, EARL OF ANGUS. (c) He *d.* in the seventh Crusade, 6 Aug. 1270, at Carthage. His widow *m.*, without lic., shortly after 7 Nov. 1270, (when her marriage was granted to Philip d'Aubigny) Alexander DE BALLIOL

(a) A charter of Roger de Quency, Earl of Winchester and Constable of Scot-land, and Helen, his wife, confirms lands on the Tweed granted by " Thomas fil. Rolandi comes Atholl " to St. Andrew's Priory, Northampton. Royal MS. 11 B. IX f. 103 b. (*ex inform.* H.J.Ellis) V.G

(b) In *Patent Roll*, 30 Jan. 1251/2, there is a pardon to " Alan, s. of Thomas, Earl of Athell, " for killing some men in Ireland.

(c) This Richard of Dover was s. and h. of Richard Fitzroy (living 1232), by Rose, (*d.* before 1232), da and h of Robert of Dover, which last Richard was bastard s. of King John. (G.J.Turner, in *The Genealogist*, N. S., vol. xxii, pp. 109-10).

of Cavers [LORD BALLIOL], who survived her, and was living 1307. She *d.* Feb. 1292, and is said to have been *bur.* in Canterbury Cathedral. (ᵃ)

IX. 1270.   9. JOHN (OF STRATHBOGIE), EARL OF ATHOLL [S], s. and h. by 2nd wife. He was one of the Nobles who, 5 Feb. 1283/4, acknowledged Margaret, Maid of Norway, as their Sovereign. In 1292 he swore fealty to Edward I, but fought on the side of the Scots in their defeat at Dunbar, 28 Apr 1296, and was taken prisoner to London, the order for his release from the Tower being dated 31 July 1297. Having *m.* Margaret, (ᵇ) da. of Donald, EARL OF MAR, by Helen, da. of Llewellyn, PRINCE OF NORTH WALES, and sister to the 1st wife of King Robert Bruce, he became a staunch adherent of Bruce, at whose coronation he assisted, 27 Mar. 1306. In the English invasion of Scotland that followed, the Earl was taken prisoner to London, *executed* 7 Nov. 1306 (his body burnt and his head fixed on London Bridge), and his *title forfeited.*

X. 1306.   1. RALPH (DE MONTHERMER), EARL OF GLOUCESTER, on whom his father-in-law, Edward I, conferred, 12 Oct. 1306, the whole of Annandale, with the title of EARL OF ATHOLL [S.]. He, however, for 5,000 marks, resigned such title in favour of the s. of the late Earl, 24 June 1307, as below.   See "GLOUCESTER," Earldom of, *cr.* 1299.

XI. 1307.   10. DAVID OF STRATHBOGIE, of Chilham, Kent, s. and h. of John, 9th Earl, was restored by Edward II as EARL OF ATHOLL [S.], between 21 Aug. 1307, and 20 May 1308. On 23 Dec. 1300, he was a prisoner in England. On 16 Nov. 1316 he had pardon as "David Earl of Ascelles." (ᶜ) Before Feb. 1311/2 he had been constituted High Constable [S.] by King Robert Bruce, but, rebelling against him in 1314, his lands, office *and title* were *forfeited* by that monarch. In consideration, however, of his services to England, he was sum. (ᵈ) to the English Parl. from 14 Mar. (1321/2) 15 Edw. II to 3 Dec. (1326) 20 Edw. II, by writs directed "*David de Strabolgi comiti Athol*," whereby he may be held to have acquired an English Barony in fee (LORD STRATHBOGIE), though not an English Earldom. (ᵉ)   He was chief

(ᵃ) An article, by W.H. St. John Hope, in *Arch. Cantiana*, vol. xxvii, p. 209, (1905) shows that the tomb supposed to be that of this Countess, who *d.* 1292, is really that of Dame Elizabeth Tryvet, who *d.* 1483 ! V.G.

(ᵇ) In *Patent Roll*, under date 11 Mar. 1285/6, there is a "Royal assent to the marriage of John de Asceles with one of the daughters of William de Sules" [Soulis] This entry presumably refers to Earl John, but no evidence has been found of such marriage having actually taken place. V.G.

(ᶜ) *Patent Roll.*

(ᵈ) In *Courthope*, p. 451, it is stated that such summons was "in virtue of his English Barony of Chilham, co. Kent, *says Dugdale,*" but *Query*

(ᵉ) He, his son and grandson continued to be so sum. till 1369. "They must,

Warden of Northumberland, 1322, and commander of the English troops in Gascony, 1325. He *m.* Joan, sister and coh. of John Comyn, of Badenoch (who fell at Bannockburn 24 June 1314), da. of John Comyn, of Badenoch (stabbed by Bruce 10 Feb 1305/6), by Joan, da of William de Valence, Earl of Pembroke. She *d.* between 8 June and 24 July 1326. (ᵃ) He *d.* 28 Dec. 1326

XII. 1326.   11. David (of Strathbogie), Earl of Atholl [S.](ᵇ) and Lord Strathbogie [E.], s. and h. He was *b.* 1 Feb. 1308/9, at Newcastle-on-Tyne, and *bap.* at St. Nicholas's Church there. He had livery of some of his lands, though under age, 28 July 1327, (ᶜ) and had complete livery 6 May 1330, "though he had not proved his age before the King as is customary." (ᵈ) He was sum. to Parl. [E.] 25 Jan. (1329/30) 4 Edw. III, to 24 July (1334) 8 Edw. III, the writs being directed "*David de Strabolgi comiti Athol*." In 1332 he accompanied Balliol into Scotland, and was at the victory over the Scots, 12 Aug., at Dupplin, after which he was restored by Balliol to his title [S.] and estates. He, however, rebelled in 1334, but was pardoned at the treaty of peace, 18 Aug. 1335. He *m.* Catharine, da. of Henry (de Beaumont), Earl of Buchan [S.], by Alice, 1st da. and h. of line of John (Comyn), 4th Earl

however, be considered as having been sum as *Barons*, though by the appellation of a Scotch Earldom Edward de Baliol, King of Scotland, was sum in 1348 as an English Baron, though the writ was addressed *Magnifico Principi Regi Siotiæ* ; Henry, Lord Bourchier, was also sum. by his Norman title of *Earl of Ewe* (1435), 13 Hen. VI." (*Courthope*, p.34). See also *ante*, p. 147 of this work, note "e" to the case of "Angus." V.G

(ᵃ) Three inquisitions state her age. (1) " Adomarus Comyn." Writ of *diem cl. ext* 25 Oct. 10 Edw II. Inq, Northumberland, 15 Nov. 1316. " Johanna uxor David Comitis Adtholie et Elizabetha soror predicte Johanne sorores Johannis Comyn patris predicti Adomari Comyn sunt amite et propinquiores heredes predicti Adomari. Et predicta Johanna est etatis viginti et quatuor annorum. Et Elizabetha est etatis sexdecim annorum." (2) "Johannes Comyn de Badenoch." Writ —May 19 Edw II Inq, same co, 8 June 1326. " Johanna Comitissa Athollie est de etate xxx annorum x die Mail ultimo preterito. (3) *Idem.* Writ 9 July 20 Edw. II. Inq., same co., 24 July 1326. " dicta Johanna quondam Comitissa Athollie die obitus dicti Johannis Comyn fratris sui videlicet die lune in festo Nativitatis Sancti Johannis Baptiste anno r. r. E. nunc viij [*sic*] fuit de etate xviij annorum et supervixit post mortem dicti Johannis fratris sui per xj annos et amplius." (Ch.*Inq p.m.*,Edw.II, file 53, no. 10, file 97, no. 86). Bain, *Cal. Doc. Scot.*, vol. iii, preface, p. lxvii, argues from nos. 2 and 3 that Joan was thus under 12 at the birth of her son [1 Feb. 1308/9], "a fact scarcely credible." It will be seen that the earlier inquisition makes her some 4 years older. The truth is that inquisitions cannot be treated as arithmetically exact, least of all when they disagree, or lead to an absurdity. (*ex inform.* G.W.Watson). V.G

(ᵇ) As in the somewhat similar case of Angus, the real fact appears to have been that the Earldom was a *Scottish* Dignity and was *forfeited*, according to the view of the Scottish King ; but was *extant* according to the view of the King of England.

(ᶜ) *Close Roll.*

(ᵈ) *Patent Roll.*

OF BUCHAN [S.]. He was *slain* at the conflict of Kilblane, 30 Nov. 1335, in his 27th year. Writ of *diem cl. ext* 8 Dec. 1335. His widow defended Lochindorb Castle, when besieged, from Nov. 1335 to June 1336, and *d.* 11 Nov. 1368, ([a]) having held Brabourne, Kent, and lands in Herts, in dower from 28 Mar. 1337. ([b])

XIV. * 1335
to
1369.

12 DAVID (OF STRATHBOGIE), EARL OF ATHOLL [S. ? or ([c]) E. ?], also LORD STRATHBOGIE [E.], only s. and h. He was three years old in 1335. He had seizin 8 May 1355. In 1355 he, who was then of age, accompanied Edward, Prince of Wales, into France. He was sum. to Parl. 20 Jan. (1365/6) 39 Edw. III, to 6 Apr. (1369) 43 Edw. III, the writ being directed to him (as it had been to his father and grandfather) as " *David Strabolgi comiti Athol'*." He *m.*, between 24 Sep. 1342 and 1361, Elizabeth [not Catharine], da. of Henry (FERRERS), 2nd LORD FERRERS OF GROBY, by Isabel, da. and coh. of Theobald (VERDON), 2nd LORD VERDON. He *d. s.p.m.*, 10 Oct. 1369 ([d]) aged 48, when any *English* BARONY OF STRATHBOGIE (and any right to an Earldom of Atholl as far as created by the *English* writ of summons in 1321) fell into *abeyance*, ([e]) while the *Scottish* EARLDOM

([a]) " Katerina nuper Comitissa Athollie. " Writs of *diem cl. ext.* 26 and 30 Nov. 42 Edw. III Inq., Northumberland, 25 Jan. 1368/9 " Et dicunt dicta Katerina obiit in festo sancti Martini in yeme ultimo preterito Et dicunt quod David de Strabolgy Comes Athollie filius dicte Katerine est filius et heres predicti David nuper Comitis Et est etatis xxxij annorum et amplius " Inq., Kent, defaced. (Ch *Inq. p. m.*, Edw. III, file 241, no. 4). (*ex inform.* G.W.Watson).

([b]) *Close Roll*

(*) These numbers XIII and XIV are transposed so as to enable the Earls of the Strathbogie family to be kept together. V.G.

([c]) See note " b " on previous page.

([d]) " David de Strabolgy Comes Athollie " Writs of *diem cl ext.* 15 Oct. 43 Edw. III. Inq., Norfolk and Kent, 22 Oct., 8 Nov 1369. " Et dicunt quod predictus comes obiit x die Octobris ultimo preterito. Et quod Elizabetha et Philippa filie predicti comitis sunt filie et heredes ejusdem comitis propinquiores et quod Elizabetha fuit etatis vij annorum primo die Martii ultimo preterito et quod Philippa soror ejus fuit etatis vj annorum xxj die Martii ultimo preterito. " Inq. co. Lincoln, 6 Dec 1369. " Et [dicunt] quod idem Comes obiit die mercurii proximo ante festum sancti Edwardi Confessoris [10 Oct.] anno supradicto Et quod Elizabetha filia predicti Comitis etatis septem annorum videlicet die martis proximo post festum Conversionis sancti Pauli [30 Jan] anno supradicto et Philippa soror predicte Elizabethe etatis sex annorum videlicet die mercurii proximo post festum Annunciationis beate Marie Virginis [28 Mar.] anno supradicto sunt propinquiores heredes predicti comitis. " Inq., Northumberland, 18, 20 Jan. 1369/70. (Ch. *Inq. p m*, Edw III, file 241, no. 4). Dugdale gives the date of the Earl's death, incorrectly, as 10 Oct. 49 Edw. III, doubtless owing to the fact that the inquisitions on the Earl, his wife, and his mother, were all mixed up together in Dugdale's time: they are so still. (*ex inform.* G.W Watson). V.G.

([e]) He left 2 daughters his coheirs. (1) Elizabeth. Having proved her age, she had livery, 2 July 1376, of her lands in Kent, Wilts, and Norfolk. (*Close Roll*, 50 Edw. III, *pars* i, m. 2). She *m.*, istly, in 1376 or 1377, Sir Thomas Percy (2nd s.

OF ATHOLL (excepting only as far as acknowledged by the *English writs* of summons) had been more than sixty years *forfeited.* His widow had a writ of livery 12, and an order for assignment of dower 14 Feb. 1369/70. She *m.,* 2ndly, John MALEWAYN. She *d.* 22 or 23 Oct. 1375,(ᵃ) at Ashford, Kent, and was *bur.* there. M.I.

[The Earldom of Atholl [S.] having (as above said) been forfeited,

---

of Henry, 1st Earl of Northumberland), who *d.* in Spain about 1388. She *m.,* 2ndly, before Mich. 1391, Sir John le Scrope (5th s. of Henry, 1st Lord Scrope of Masham), whose will, dat. 18 Dec 1405, was pr 23 Dec following. By him she had 2 daughters, his coheirs. She *m* , 3rdly, Robert de Thorley, and was living in 1416. Her s. and h., Sir Henry Percy, " of Atholl, " *d.* 25 Oct. 1432, leaving 2 daughters his coheirs. (i) Elizabeth, who *m* , 1stly, Thomas Burgh, and 2ndly, Sir William Lucy, who was slain at the battle of Northampton in 1460, *s.p.* She *d.* 28 Sep (Inq , Northumberland) or 16 Oct. (Inq, co York) 1455 (writs of *diem cl. ext* dated 29 Sep [*sic*] 34 Hen. VI), leaving Thomas Burgh her s and h , aged 24 and more [see BURGH] (ii) Margery, who *m* , 1stly, Henry, 6th Lord Grey of Codnor, by whom she had an only child, Henry, 7th Lord, who *d. s p.* [see GREY OF CODNOR]. She *m* , 2ndly, Sir Richard Veer [yr. s. of John, 12th Earl of Oxford]. She *d.* 28 Sep. 1464. (2) Philippe. Having proved her age (*viz.,* aged 15 on 21 Mar 1376/7), she had livery, 6 May 1377, of her lands in Lincoln, Norfolk, and Northumberland. (*Close Roll,* 51 Edw. III, *m.* 2). She *m* , before 20 Mar. 1376/7, Sir Ralph Percy (next br. of Thomas afsd), but this marriage must have been annulled. He *d. s p* , 15 Sep. 1397, " in partibus transmarinis. " She *m.,* 2ndly (apparently under the name of *Philippe Michell,* by banns publ. in the churches of West Grinstead and Coombs), as 1st wife, John Halsham, of Coombs, Sussex She *d* Tuesday [2 Nov.] the feast of All Saints [1 Nov.] 1395, according to two inquisitions (1 Nov.—Brass at West Grinstead), leaving John Halsham her s and h , aged 10 and more, 11, or 11 and more. He *d. s.p.,* before 8 Feb. 1404/5. His father *d.* 16 Apr. 1415, leaving Hugh " filius et heres ipsorum Johannis Halsham et Philippe de corporibus ipsorum Johannis Halsham et Philippe legitime procreatus, " aged 24 and more. Hugh's legitimacy had been disputed, but the inquiry by the Bp. of Chichester, 6 June 1405, in pursuance of the King's writ of 8 Feb. 1404/5, found that he was legit. s. " Johannis Halsham et Philippe Atheles. " (Exch., K.R., *Eccles* , 7/18) This Sir Hugh *d. s.p* , 28 Feb. 1441/2 (Brass, *ibid.*), when Joan, da. of his br., Richard, was found to be his h. and aged 20 and more, and then wife of John Lewkenor, who was slain at the battle of Tewkesbury in 1471 She *d. s.p* , 12 May 1495, leaving Sir Henry Roos, grandson of John Halsham afsd., her next h. The dates of death, &c., given above, are all taken from the inquisitions. (*ex inform.* G.W.Watson). V.G.

(ᵃ) " Elizabetha que fuit uxor Johannis Malewayn nuper Comitissa Atholie " Writs of *diem. cl. ext.* 28 Oct. and 8 Nov. 49 Edw. III. Inq., co. Lincoln, 12 Dec. 1375 " Et dicunt quod dicta Elizabetha obiit apud Asshford in comitatu Kantie xxiij° die Octobris. Et dicunt quod Elizabetha et Philippa filie David de Strabolgi nuper Comitis Atholie quondam viri prefate Elizabethe que fuit uxor Johannis Malwayn sunt filie et propinquiores heredes predicte Elizabethe. Et dicunt quod predicta Elizabetha est etatis xiiij annorum et amplius. Et Philippa est etatis xij annorum et amplius. " Inq., Kent, Norfolk, 17 Nov , 7 Dec 1375 Similar findings. Inq., Cumberland, Westmorland, York, 1, 18 Feb., 12 Mar. 1375/6. (Ch *Inq. p. m.,* Edw. III, file 241, no. 4). On her brass at Ashford (Weever, *Fun. Mon.,* p. 275) the Countess is stated to have *d.* 22 Oct. (*ex inform.* G.W.Watson) V.G.

soon after 1314, in *Scotland* by the Strathbogie family (though acknowledged more than 60 years later, in *England*) was re-granted by the Scottish Kings as under.]

XIII. * 1320 ?   1. SIR JOHN CAMPBELL, of Moulin, 2nd s. of Sir Niel
to   C., of Lochow (to whom and to his wife the forfeited
1333.   estates of the Earl of Atholl [S.] had been granted), being
          (by his mother Mary, sister of Robert Bruce) cousin to
David II, was by him *cr.* EARL OF ATHOLL [S.].   He *m.* Joan,
widow of Malise, EARL OF STRATHERN [S.], da. of Sir John MENTEITH.
He *d. s.p.*, aged about 20, being slain at the Scots defeat on Halidon hill,
19 July 1333, when the *title* became *extinct*.   His widow *m.* (dispensation
dat 11 July 1339) Sir Maurice MORAY, of Drumsargard, who had the
Earldom of Strathern conferred on him in 1343/4, and who *d.* 17 Oct. 1346.
She *m.*, 4thly, before Nov. 1347, William (SUTHERLAND), 4th EARL OF
SUTHERLAND, who *d.* 1370.   She was living 1367.

XV. 1341.   1. SIR WILLIAM DOUGLAS, of Liddesdale, known as
            "the Flower of Chivalry," s. and h. of Sir James DOUG-
LAS, of Lothian (ancestor of the EARLS OF MORTON [S.]), was *cr.* EARL OF
ATHOLL [S.], 18 July 1341, and almost immediately afterwards *resigned
that Earldom*, at Aberdeen, in favour of Robert Stewart, the High STEWARD
[S.].   He obtained lands from the Grahames, and is usually said to have
m. Margaret, sister and coh. of John GRAHAM, of Dalkeith and Abercorn.
He *m.* Elizabeth. (*)   Having entailed (under the style of "Dominus
Vallis de Lydel"), on 3 Nov. 1351, his lands of Liddesdale on the sons
of his br., John Douglas, he *d. s.p.m.*, in Aug. 1353, being assassinated by
his kinsman, William (Douglas), 1st Earl of Douglas [S.].   His widow
Elizabeth *m.* Hugh DACRE. (*)

XVI. 1342   1. ROBERT STEWART, HIGH STEWARD OF SCOTLAND, s.
to   and h. of Walter S., also High Steward, by Marjory (who
1371.   *d.* 1316), 1st da. of ROBERT I, King of Scotland, was *b.*
2 Mar. 1316, *suc.* his father 9 Apr. 1327, and was in
command at Halidon hill, 19 July 1333, in consequence of which his
estates were forfeited and conferred, by Balliol, on David (of Strathbogie),
Earl of Atholl.   From 1338 to 1341 he was REGENT OF SCOTLAND, and,
on 16 Feb. 1341/2, was *cr.* EARL OF ATHOLL [S.] on the resignation
of William Douglas, Earl of Atholl [S.], as mentioned above.   From 1346
to 1357, during the imprisonment of David II in England, he was again
REGENT [S.].   In 1358 he was *cr.* EARL OF STRATHERN [S.].   On
22 Feb. 1370/1 he *suc.* his uncle, David II, as KING OF SCOTLAND,
under the name of ROBERT II, when *his Dignities* became (apparently)

(*) See note " * " p. 308.
(*) *New Fœdera*, vol. iii, pt. i, p. 304.   V.G.

merged in the Crown [S.]. He *m.*, 1stly, by Papal dispensation dat. 22 Nov. 1347 (in which he is styled " Robertus, *Dominus de Stratgrif* "), Elizabeth, (ª) da. of Sir Adam Mure, of Rowallan, co. Ayr, (ᵇ) their issue (born before marriage) being legitimated by the dispensation, and their right of succession to the Crown being further confirmed by act, dat. 1373. He *m.*, 2ndly, by Papal dispensation dat. 2 May 1355, Eupheme, widow of John, Earl of Moray [S.], da. of Hugh, 6th Earl of Ross [S.], by his last wife, Margaret Graham. She *d.* in 1387. He *d.* at Dundonald Castle, 19 Apr. 1390.

XVII 1398   1. David (Stewart), Duke of Rothesay, &c. [S.],
to   s. and h. ap. of Robert III, having been *cr.* Earl of
1402.   Carrick [S.], on, or shortly after his father's accession to
             the throne, 19 Apr. 1390, was *cr.* Duke of Rothesay [S.],
28 Apr. 1398, and was, by charter dat. 6 Sep. 1398, *cr.* EARL OF ATHOLL [S.]. He *d. s.p.*, 26 Mar. 1402, when his *Peerage honours* became *extinct* or reverted to the Crown. See fuller account under " Rothesay, " Dukedom of [S.], *cr.* 1398.

XVIII. 1403   1. Robert (Stewart), Duke of Albany, &c. [S.],
to   3rd, but 2nd surv. s. of Robert II, having been *cr.*
1406.   Earl of Fife [S.] in 1371 and Duke of Albany [S.]
             28 Apr. 1398, was, by charter dat. 2 Sep. 1403, *cr.* EARL OF ATHOLL [S.], *during the life of King Robert III*, with remainder, should he die in the lifetime of the said King, to the grantee's 2nd s., John Stewart. By the death of the King, 4 Apr. 1406, in the lifetime of the grantee, the *dignity* became *extinct* at that date. See fuller account under " Albany, " Dukedom of [S.], *cr.* 1398.

XIX 1404   1. Walter Stewart, 6th and yst. s. of Robert II,
to   King of Scotland, being his 2nd s. by his 2nd wife,
1437.   Eupheme, abovenamed, was *cr.*, about 1402, and before
             July 1402, Earl of Caithness [S.] on the resignation of his niece, Eupheme, Countess Palatine of Strathern and Countess of Caithness [S.], who was da. and h. of his elder br. David, the possessor of those dignities. He was afterwards, shortly before 8 June 1404 (ᶜ) *cr.* EARL OF ATHOLL [S.]. He was Great Justiciar [S.], and on 22 July 1427

(ª) A marriage between Hugh Giffard of the diocese of St Andrew's, and *Elizabeth Mure*, of the diocese of Glasgow, contracted when he was 9, and she 11, was dissolved by the Pope, xiii Kal. Junii 1345. Presumably this is the Elizabeth of the text.

(ᵇ) Sir Adam's 1st wife was Joan, widow of Hugh Houston, [Hutsconperi] da. of (—) Cunningham ; his 2nd wife was Janet Mure, heiress of Polkelly; it is not known which was mother of Elizabeth. V.G.

(ᶜ) He is so called in a document of 8 June 1404, printed in Rymer's *Fœdera*.

was *cr* EARL PALATINE OF STRATHERN [S.] for life   He *m*, before 19 Oct. 1378, Margaret, da and h. of Sir David BARCLAY, Laird of Brechin, co. Forfar, by Janet, (ª) da of Sir Edward KEITH, of Synton.   By her he acquired the Lordship of Brechin.   She *d*. before 1 Aug 1404, when he had dispensation to *m*. Elizabeth, da. of Sir William GRAHAME, of Kincardine, (possibly 1st LORD GRAHAM [S]) but there is no evidence that the marriage took place, and on 3 Feb. 1407/8, this Elizabeth *m*. the Earl's half br., Sir John STEWART, of Dundonald, illegit. s of Robert III. Though greatly trusted by his nephew, James I, he long cherished a design to supplant him on the throne, to which, as representative of the 2nd marriage of his father, he conceived himself to have a better right than the doubtfully legitimate issue of his father's 1st wife.   Accordingly he and his grandson and h. ap. (as mentioned below), were among the chief contrivers of the murder of James I, 20 Feb. 1436/7.   They were both put to death, the Earl being *executed* at Edinburgh 26 Mar. 1437, when his *titles* and extensive estates became *forfeited*.

[DAVID (ᵇ) STEWART, probably *styled* MASTER OF ATHOLL, 1st s. and h. ap.   In May 1424 he was one of the hostages for the ransom of James I, and *d* in England, *v.p.*, after Feb. 1433/4.]

[SIR ROBERT STEWART, undoubtedly (ᶜ) *styled* MASTER OF ATHOLL, s. and h. of the above David, on 29 Jan 1428/9 had dispensation to marry Margaret OGILVY.   He joined in the conspiracy of his grandfather, and was *executed* a few days before him, in Mar. 1437.]

XX. 1457?   1. SIR JOHN STEWART (who, in right of his wife, was
and   of Balveny, co. Fife), s. and h. of Sir James Stewart "the
1482.   Black Knight of Lorn," by Joan, QUEEN DOWAGER OF
   SCOTLAND, was *b*. about 1440 and was *cr*. EARL OF
ATHOLL [S.] in, or shortly before, 1457.   He had a new charter of this Earldom 18 Mar. 1481/2, to him and the heirs male of his body, with rem. to the Crown. (ᵈ)   He is there described as "frater carnalis" of

---

(ª) Janet *m*., 2ndly, Sir Thomas Erskine, by whom she had a s and h, Robert, who, through her, *suc*. to the Earldom of Mar [S.], of which he was deprived in 1457.

(ᵇ) This David is misprinted as *James* in the Preface to vol. iv of the *Exch. Rolls* [S.], p. clxi.   (*ex inform* G.Burnett, sometime Lyon)

(ᶜ) See *ante*, p 2 note "a" as to this being an early use of the designation 'Master.'

(ᵈ) "Some perplexity has arisen from the fact that while Sir John Stewart is designated Earl of Athole as far back as 1457 (*Rotuli Scotiæ*, vol. ii, p. 383) he has nevertheless, on 18th Mar. 1481/2, a charter from James III conveying to him, as if for the first time, the Earldom of Athole, and designating him Sir John Stewart of Balveny (*Reg. Mag. Sig.*, x, 7)   The explanation seems to be that the Queen's dower having been secured on the Earldom of Athole, the alienation of it by the Crown, during her lifetime, was a questionable proceeding, and, for the security of Earl John's rights, it became important to have a confirmation of it after the death of Mary of Gueldres" (Preface to vol. vi (p. lxxxv) of *The Exchequer Rolls of Scotland*, edited by G.Burnett, sometime Lyon King of Arms.)

the late King James II. He took an active part in suppressing the rebellion of John, Earl of Ross [S.], the last "Lord of the Isles."(ᵃ) He was AMBASSADOR TO ENGLAND 1484, and commanded in the army of King James III against the rebel Lords. He *m.*, 1stly, in 1459/60, Margaret, Dowager COUNTESS OF DOUGLAS [S.] (widow of William, 8th Earl, who *d.* Feb. 1451/2, and the divorced wife of his br. James, 9th Earl), only da. of Archibald, 5th EARL OF DOUGLAS, [S.] by Eupheme GRAHAM, da. of Eupheme, *suo jure* COUNTESS OF STRATHERN [S.]. She, who was called "*the fair maid of Galloway*," was h. to her br. William, 6th EARL OF DOUGLAS [S.], who *d s.p.*, 24 Nov. 1440. On this marriage the King bestowed on them the Lordship of Balveny (ᵇ) (one of the forfeited possessions of the family of Douglas) and other large estates. She was living 21 Jan. 1472/3, but *d.* in or before 1475. He *m.*, 2ndly, before 19 Apr 1475, Eleanor, da. of William (SINCLAIR), EARL OF ORKNEY AND CAITHNESS [S.], by his 2nd wife, Marjory, da. of Alexander SUTHERLAND, of Dunbeath. By her he had eleven children. He *d.* 15 Sep. 1512, at the Laighwood, and was *bur.* in Dunkeld Cathedral. His widow *d.* 21 Mar 1518, and was *bur.* with him.

XXI. 1512.   2. JOHN (STEWART), EARL OF ATHOLL [S.], s. and h. by 2nd wife. He *m.* Janet, 3rd da. of Archibald (CAMPBELL), 2nd EARL OF ARGYLL [S.], by Elizabeth, 1st da. of John (STEWART), 1st EARL OF LENNOX [S.]. He is usually said to have been slain 9 Sep. 1513, at the battle of Flodden, but he did not die till 1521. His widow *d.* about 2 Feb. 1545/6.

XXII. 1521.   3. JOHN (STEWART), EARL OF ATHOLL [S.], only s. and h., *b.* 6 Oct. 1507; enfeoffed 3 May 1522. He was celebrated for his magnificent hospitality. In 1529 he entertained James V, the Pope's nuncio, &c. He *m.*, 1stly, before Oct. 1533, Grizel, da. of Sir John RATTRAY, of that ilk, which lady was living 1537. He *m.*, 2ndly, less than 6 months before his death, Jean, yst. da. of John (FORBES), 6th LORD FORBES [S.], by his 3rd wife, Elizabeth BARLOW, widow of Alexander, 1st LORD ELPHINSTONE [S]. He *d* 1542, about Nov., aged 35. His widow *m.*, after 17 Nov. 1545, Alexander HAY, of Dalgety, and 3rdly, before 17 Jan. 1549/50, as his 1st wife, William LESLIE, of Balquhain. She had a charter (wherein she is called "*Jonet Forbes, Countess of Atholl*"), dat. 9 Jan. 1546/7, of part of Balquhain.

(ᵃ) On this occasion it is reported that his nephew, King James III, said to him—"Furth fortune and fill the fetters," the motto assumed by the succeeding Earls of Atholl.

(ᵇ) Though the Castle of Balveny came to the Earl by his 1st wife, he did not leave it to *her* issue (two daughters) by him (she had none by her former husbands), but to his own s and h by his *second* wife. It was sold in 1610 (soon after the death of the 5th Earl in 1595, *s.p m*) to John (Abernethy), 8th Lord Saltoun [S.], whose issue became *extinct* in 1669 In 1687 Alexander Duff, of Braco, agent to Arthur Forbes, got possession of it, and succeeded, after many law suits (all of which were settled in 1743), in retaining it.

XXIII. 1542.   4. JOHN (STEWART), EARL OF ATHOLL [S.], s. and h.
by 1st wife. He was a zealous Roman Catholic. P.C.
[S.] 1561. In 1576 he opposed the Regent Morton, but on 29 Mar.
1578 was made CHANCELLOR [S.], and so remained till his death. Being
reconciled to the Regent, he was feasted by him in Apr. 1579, at Stirling,
but *d.* a few days afterwards, not without suspicion of poison. He *m.*, 1stly,
before 26 May 1547, Elizabeth, 1st da of George (GORDON), 4th EARL OF
HUNTLY [S.], by Elizabeth, 1st da. of Robert KEITH, *styled* LORD KEITH.
She *d. s p.m*, before 1557. He *m.*, 2ndly, (cont. dat. 1 Apr. 1557) Margaret, widow of Robert GRAHAM, *styled* LORD GRAHAM, and later of Thomas
ERSKINE (*styled* MASTER OF ERSKINE), da. of Malcolm (FLEMING), 3rd LORD
FLEMING [S.], by Joan STEWART, illegit. da. of James IV. She was thought
to possess powers of incantation. The Earl *d.* as above related, at " Kin-
corne " [? Kincardine], the house of the Earl of Montrose, 24 Apr., and was
bur. 4 July 1579, in St. Giles's Church, Edinburgh. M.I. Will pr.
26 Dec. 1580, at Edinburgh. His widow was living 15 Aug. 1584.

XXIV. 1579   5. JOHN (STEWART), EARL OF ATHOLL [S.], only s. and
to   h. by 2nd wife, *b.* 22 May 1563, at Dunkeld, served h.
1595.   to his father 5 May 1579. P.C. [S.] 1590. He *m.*,
24 Jan. 1579/80, at Perth, Mary, 1st da. of William
(RUTHVEN), 1st EARL OF GOWRIE [S], by Dorothea, 2nd da. of Henry
(STEWART), LORD METHVEN [S.]. He *d. s.p.m.*, and in embarrassed
circumstances, 25 Aug. 1595, at Perth, aged 32, when the *Earldom* (according
to the charter of 1480/1) *reverted to the Crown.* His widow *m* John
(STEWART), *cr.* EARL OF ATHOLL [S.] in 1596, as below.

XXV. 1596.   1. JOHN (STEWART), LORD INNERMEATH [S.], s. and h.
of James S. (*) 5th LORD I., by Helen, da. of James
(OGILVY), 3rd LORD OGILVY OF AIRLIE [S.], was *b.* about 1566, *suc.* his
father in or before May 1579, and was *cr.*, 6 Mar. 1595/6, EARL OF
ATHOLL [S.], with rem. to the heirs male of his body. He *m.*, 1stly,
(cont. dat. 6 Oct. 1580) Margaret (dowry 9500 marks), 2nd da. of David
(LINDSAY), 9th EARL OF CRAWFORD [S.], by his 2nd wife, Catharine, da. of
Sir John CAMPBELL, of Lorn. She was living 16 June 1589. He *m*,
2ndly, (cont. dat. 31 Mar. 1596) Mary, DOWAGER COUNTESS OF ATHOLL
[S] abovenamed, but by her had no issue. He *d.* at Kincardine, in
Strathern, 1603, between Aug. and Oct., aged about 37. His widow *m.*,
before 30 Aug. 1613, James STEWART, son of James, MASTER OF BUCHAN

XXVI. 1603   2. JOHN (STEWART), EARL OF ATHOLL and LORD
to   INNERMEATH [S.], only s. and h., by 1st wife, served h. to
1625.   his father 29 July 1609. He *m.* (cont. dat. 12 Sep. 1603)

(*) This James Stewart was great-grandson of Thomas, 2nd Lord Innermeath
(killed at Flodden 1513), who was great-grandson of Sir John S. of the same, " Lord
of Lorn," who (by his s. Sir James S. "the Black Knight of Lorn") was grandfather
of John Stewart, *cr.* EARL OF ATHOLL [S] in 1457 as above stated.

Mary, 2nd da. and coh. of John (STEWART), xxivth (5th) EARL OF ATHOLL [S.], by his own step-mother (2nd wife of his father), Mary, 2nd da. of William (RUTHVEN), 1st EARL OF GOWRIE [S.] abovenamed. He *d s.p.*, 1625, when the Earldom of 1596 conferred on his father, as also, apparently, the Barony of Inermeath, became *extinct*. His widow *m.* Capt. Peter ROLLOCK.

XXVII. 1629. 1 or 6. JOHN MURRAY, only s. and h. of William MURRAY, sometime (1609-26) EARL OF TULLIBARDINE [S.], by his 2nd wife, Dorothea, 1st da. and coh. of John (STEWART), xxivth (5th) EARL OF ATHOLL [S], *suc.* his father in or shortly after 1626, but his said father had previously resigned (1 Apr. 1626) the Barony of Murray and the Earldom of Tullibardine [S.], as also, apparently, the Barony of Innermeath [S.], in favour of Sir Patrick Murray, having obtained the Royal promise that the *Earldom of Atholl* [S.] *should be revived* in the person and descendants of his wife, who was the h. of line   Accordingly, on 6 Aug. 1628, the said John Murray was served "nearest and lawful eldest h." to John (STEWART) [xx] EARL OF ATHOLL [S.], " br. uterine of King James." By patent 17 Feb. 1628/9, the service was confirmed, and the title of EARL OF ATHOLL [S.] acknowledged, (*) the grant containing a *novodamus* of the title and dignity without prejudice to the Earl's right as h. gen.   In the Civil wars the Earl raised 1800 men to support the King, but was taken prisoner by Argyll in 1640. He *m.*, 6 June 1630, (tocher 40,000 marks) Jean, yst. da. of Sir Duncan CAMPBELL, of Glenorchy, by his 2nd wife, Elizabeth, da. of Henry (SINCLAIR), 3rd LORD SINCLAIR [S.]. He *d.* June 1642.

XXVIII. 1642.

MARQUESSATE [S.]

1. 1676.

2 or 7, and 1. JOHN (MURRAY), EARL OF ATHOLL [S.], s. and h., *b.* 2 May 1631. He joined the King's Standard with 2000 men in 1653, and was excepted from Cromwell's act of indemnity in 1654. At the Restoration, in 1660, he was made P.C., Hereditary Sheriff of Fife, &c. JUSTICE GEN. [S.] 1663 to 1676. In Jan. 1670 he *suc.* his cousin James (Murray), EARL OF TULLIBARDINE and LORD MURRAY OF GASK [S.] in those titles. Capt. Gen. of the Royal Company of Archers 1670 till death. Col. of the 4th troop of Horse Guards 1671-78. KEEPER OF THE PRIVY SEAL [S.] 1672-89. An extraordinary Lord of Session 14 Jan. 1673 till

---

(*) There can be little doubt but that this was an entirely new creation, and such appears to have been Lord Hailes' view, though it is stated in *Riddell* (p. 178) that it was confirmed 17 Feb. 1629 "*with the original precedence*"   Charles I in his patent of 1629 (misinformed as to the facts) expressed himself bound in honour and conscience to ratify the dignity to the h. of line; but the Earl of Tullibardine, doubting the legal efficacy of such ratification, obtained a new patent of the honour of Atholl. The Earldom of 1457 appears, however, under the charter of *Novodamus* in 1481, to have have lapsed in 1595 by failure of the heirs therein named.

1689   On 17 Feb. 1676 (ª) he was *cr*. (to him and the heirs male of his body)
MARQUESS OF ATHOLE (ᵇ) EARL OF TULLIBARDIN, VIS-
COUNT OF BALQUHIDDER, LORD MURRAY, BALVANY AND
GASK [S.].   He was instrumental in opposing Argyll's invasion in 1685.
K.T. 29 May 1687, being one of the original Knights on the revival of
that order (ᶜ) by James II   In the Revolution, shortly afterwards, he
played a trimming and shuffling part. (ᵈ)   He *m*., 5 May 1659, Amelia
Sophia, da. and, in her issue, sole h. of James (STANLEY), 7th EARL OF
DERBY and 1st LORD STRANGE, by Charlotte, da of Claude DE LA
TRÉMOILLE, DUKE OF THOUARS, in Poitou. She *d*. 22 Feb. 1702/3, and
was *bur* at Dunkeld, co. Perth.   He *d*. 6, and was *bur* 17 May 1703, also
at Dunkeld, afsd., aged 72.   Fun. entry at Lyon office.

MARQUESSATE [S.]		
II.		2, 3, or 8, and 1 JOHN (MURRAY), MARQUESS OF ATHOLL, &c. [S.], s. and h., *b*. 24 Feb. 1659/60, at Knows-
EARLDOM [S.]	1703 (May.)	ley, co. Lancaster, the seat of his maternal uncle, Charles (Stanley), 8th
XXIX.		Earl of Derby Being blind of one eye, he was known as "Ian Cam."
DUKEDOM [S.]		He, having been a zealous supporter of William III, as one of the Principal
I. 1703 (June).		Secretaries of State [S.], &c., was in

his father's lifetime *cr*, by patent dat. 27 July 1696 (at the Castle of Atre,
a league S E of Ath, in Hainault), EARL OF TULLIBARDIN, (ᵇ)

(ª) See notes *sub* 1 DUKE OF HAMILTON and 1 DUKE OF QUEENSBERRY.

(ᵇ) The spelling of the Atholl titles is given in accordance with the (rather
variable) orthography of the Register of the Great Seal.

(ᶜ) The Scottish Order of the THE THISTLE (or St Andrew) was revived (or
rather instituted) by King James II on 29 May 1687, eight Knights being nominated
on 6 June following.   These eight original Knights were as under .—

    1. James (Drummond), 4th EARL OF PERTH.

    2. George (Gordon), 1st DUKE OF GORDON

    3 John (Murray), 1st MARQUESS OF ATHOLL, *d*. before Dec. 1703

    4. James (Hamilton), *styled* EARL OF ARRAN, afterwards (1698) DUKE OF
HAMILTON.

    5. Kenneth (Mackenzie), 4th EARL OF SEAFORTH, *d*. before 1703.

    6 John (Drummond), 1st EARL OF MELFORT.

    7. George (Douglas), 1st EARL OF DUNBARTON, *d* before 1703.

    8. Alexander (Stewart), 5th EARL OF MORAY, *d*. before 1703.

No additions were made to the order till 31 Dec 1703 (2 Anne), at which
time, out of the above eight Knights, only two, *viz*. the Duke of Gordon and the
Duke of Hamilton, were recognised as such.   *Perth* and *Melfort*, the only others who
were then living, were *passed over*, having (as had Seaforth and Dunbarton) adhered
to their founder, and gone with him in exile to St. Germain.

(ᵈ) If Lord Macaulay's superlatives are to be accepted, he was " the falsest, the
most fickle, the most pusillanimous of mankind "   Had he been more actively
disloyal to James, no doubt this unfavourable opinion would have been modified. V.G.

VISCOUNT GLENALMOND, and LORD MURRAY [S.] *for life*.
He was HIGH COMMISSIONER to the Parl. [S.] 1696-98.   Chanc. of St.
Andrew's Univ 1697-1724.   Having been P.C. [S] to William III, he
was re-appointed on the accession of Anne, and was made LORD PRIVY
SEAL [S.] in Apr 1703, a month before he *suc.* to his father's honours
On 30 June 1703 (a month after succeeding to the Marquessate, &c.), he
was *cr.* DUKE OF ATHOLE, MARQUESS OF TILLIBARDIN,
EARL OF STRATHTAY AND STRATHARDLE, VISCOUNT OF
BALWHIDDER, GLENALMOND AND GLENLYON, AND LORD
MURRAY, BALVENIE, AND GASK, ([a]) all in the co. of Perth [S],
with a spec. rem, failing the heirs male of his own body to those of his
father.   K.T. 7 Feb. 1703/4.   In 1705 he resigned his office of Privy
Seal, and warmly opposed the Union of Scotland with England   Having
joined the Tory party, he was elected a REP. PEER [S.] in 1710 and (again)
1713 ; Lord High Commissioner to the Gen. Assembly of the Church of
Scotland 1712 to 1714; an extraordinary Lord of Session 7 Nov. 1712 till
death.   P.C. [G.B.] 17 Apr. 1712 till Sep 1714.   PRIVY SEAL [S] (for 2nd
time) 1713 to 1714, Lord Lieut of co. Perth 1715 till death   His then
eldest son and h. ap. being attainted for high treason in that year, he
procured an act of Parl. (1 Geo. I) for vesting his honours and estates,
after his death, in his next surv. son, James Murray.   He *m.*, 1stly,
24 May 1683, (cont. dat. 24 Apr. 1683) Katharine, 2nd da. of William
(DOUGLAS, afterwards HAMILTON), DUKE OF HAMILTON [S.], by Anne, *suo
jure*, DUCHESS OF HAMILTON [S.].   She, who was *bap.* at Hamilton, 24 Oct.
1662, *d.* and was *bur.* there 17 Jan. 1707.   Fun entry at Lyon office.   He
m., 2ndly, (cont. dat. 26 June 1710) in 1710, Mary, 2nd da. of William
(Ross), LORD ROSS [S], by Agnes, da. and h. of Sir John WILKIE.   He *d.*
at Huntingtower, co. Perth, in his 65th year, 14, and was *bur.* 26 Nov.
1724, ([b]) at Dunkeld   Fun. entry at Lyon office.   On his death the titles
conferred on him in 1696, being *for life*, became *extinct*.   His widow,
who was *b.* 18 July 1687, *d.* 17 Jan. 1767, at Huntingtower, having
survived him 42 years, and was *bur.* with him.

[JOHN MURRAY, *styled* MARQUESS OF TULLIBARDINE, 1st s. and h. ap.
by 1st wife, *b.* 6 May 1684, at Kinneil, was, on 22 Jan. 1706, a student
at the Univ. of Leyden.   He was Col. of a regiment in the service of the
States of Holland.   He served at Oudenarde, 30 June/11 July 1708, and
at Malplaquet, 31 Aug./11 Sep. 1709, where he was killed, *v.p.*, aged 24,
and was *bur.* at Brussels.]

[WILLIAM MURRAY, *styled* MARQUESS OF TULLIBARDINE, 2nd, but 1st
surv., s. and h ap. by 1st wife, *b.* 14 Apr. 1689, at Edinburgh, matric. at
St. Andrew's 25 Jan. 1706, ent. the Navy 1707.   He was one of the first

---

([a]) See note "b" on previous page.
([b]) "Le Comte d'Errol me dit, que ce Duc est fort entier dans ses sentiments,
et d'une grande probité ; que sa parole est inviolable, et qu'on peut compter là dessus;
qu'il est hautain et emporté." (*Col Hawke's Memoirs*, vol. ii, p. 357.   Roxburghe
Club)   V.G.

to join the Rising in Aug. 1715 for the restoration of the House of Stuart, and was consequently *attainted*, 17 Feb. 1715/6, of high treason, but he escaped to Britanny. On 1 Feb. 1716/7, he was *cr.*, by the titular King James III, Duke of Rannoch, Marquess of Blair, Earl of Glen Tilt, Viscount Glenshie, and Lord Strathbran [S.], with rem. to heirs male. Since his death the Jacobite titles have remained united with the Dukedom of Atholl. Returning to Scotland with the Spanish force, he was defeated at the battle of Glenshiel, 18 June 1719. He again escaped, though £2000 was offered for his capture, and in Oct. 1734 "had been long a prisoner for debt" at Paris (ᵃ) After 26 years he accompanied the Chevalier St. George to Scotland, on whose behalf he unfurled the Royal Standard at Glenfinnan, 19 Aug. 1745,(ᵇ) but after the battle of Culloden he surrendered himself, 27 Apr. 1746, and was committed to the Tower of London (on 21 June), being then very ill. There he *d.* unm., 9 July 1746, in his 58th year, of a stoppage of urine, and was *bur.* in the Chapel of the Tower.]

DUKEDOM [S.] II.

MARQUESSATE [S.] III.

EARLDOM [S.] XXX.

1724. 2, 3, 4 or 9. JAMES (MURRAY), DUKE OF ATHOLL, &c. [S.], 3rd, but 2nd surv., s by 1st wife, who, according to the Act of Parl. of 1715, *suc.* to his father's honours and estate. He was *b.* 28 Sep. 1690, at Edinburgh. In 1712 he was Captain and Lieut. Col. of a Grenadier company in the 1st Reg. of Foot Guards, and afterwards Lieut. Col. of the 1st or Royal Scots Reg. of Foot. M.P. (Whig) for co. Perth, 1715-24. In 1733 he obtained an Act of Parl. that the attainder of his br. should extend only to that br. and his issue, and not to any other the heirs male of his father. LORD PRIVY SEAL June 1733 to 6 Apr. 1763. Elected a REP. PEER [S.] 1733 and (again) 1734. P.C. 31 Jan. 1733/4 K.T. 11 Feb 1733/4. In 1736, in accordance with the same Act of Parl. of 1715 (notwithstanding that his elder br. was still alive), he *suc.* his cousin James (STANLEY), 10th EARL OF DERBY, both in the Sovereignty of the Isle of Man as well as in the Peerage of England as LORD STRANGE, a Barony *cr.* by writ 7 Mar. 1627/8. As Lord Strange he was sum. to Parl. 14 Mar. 1736/7, sitting both as an English Baron and as a Scotch Rep. Peer for 4 years, till the gen. election of 1741. On 9 July 1746, by the death of his elder br. *s.p.*, he became the *de facto* as well as *parliamentary* h. male of his father. He accompanied the Duke of Cumberland to Scotland in 1746. KEEPER OF THE GREAT

(ᵃ) See *N & Q.*, 4th Ser., vol. x, p. 161
(ᵇ) "Tottering with age and infirmities, and supported by an attendant on each side, [he] was, as highest in rank, appointed to unfurl the banner , it was of red silk with a white space in the centre, on which, some weeks afterwards, the celebrated motto "*Tandem Triumphans*" was inscribed. . . . Tullibardine, after a little pause, read aloud the manifesto of the old Chevalier, and the commission of Regency granted to Prince Charles. " See Earl Stanhope's eloquent account of *The Forty Five*

Seal, 6 Apr. 1763 till his death. (ᵃ) He *m.*, 1stly, 28 Apr. 1726, Jane, widow of James Lannoy, of Hammersmith, merchant, sister of Sir John Frederick, Bart., (so *cr.* 1723) yst da. of Thomas Frederick, by Leonora, da. and h. of Charles Maresco, of London. She *d.* in London, 13, and was *bur.* 20 June 1748, at St. Olave's, Old Jewry, aged 55. Will pr. June 1748. He *m.*, 2ndly, at Edinburgh, 7 May 1749, Jean, (ᵇ) da. of John Drummond, of Megginch, co. Perth, but by her had no issue. He *d. s.p.m.s.*, 8 Jan. 1764, at Dunkeld, in his 74th year. Fun entry at Lyon office. His widow *m.*, 2 Sep. 1767, in St. Geo., Han. Sq., Gen. Lord Adam Gordon, 4th s. of Alexander, 2nd Duke of Gordon [S.], which Lord Adam *d.* 13 Aug. 1801, suddenly, at his seat, 'The Burn,' co. Kincardine. She *d.* 22 Feb. 1795, at Holyroodhouse. Both are *bur.* at Inveresk.

[John Murray, *styled* Marquess of Tullibardine, 1st s. and h. ap. by 1st wife, *b.* at Dunkeld, and *bap.* there 13 Sep. 1728, *d.* there, an infant and *v.p.*, 23 Apr. 1729.]

[James Murray, *styled* Marquess of Tullibardine, 2nd, but 1st surv. S. and h. ap., *b.* and *bap.* 28 Mar. 1735, at Dunkeld, *d.* there, an infant and *v.p.* 12 Feb. 1735/6.]

DUKEDOM [S.] III. MARQUESSATE [S.] IV. EARLDOM [S.] XXXI.	3, 4, 5 or 10. John (Murray), Duke of Atholl, &c. [S.], nephew and h. male, being s. and h. of Lord George Murray (by Amelia, only surv. da. and h. of James Murray, of Glencarse and Strowan), who was next surv. br. of the 2nd Duke, and 5th s. of the 1st Duke, by his 1st wife. He was *b.* 6 May 1729, and was Capt. in the 54th (Highland)

1764.

Reg. of Foot. M.P. (Tory) for co Perth 1761-64. In consequence of the attainder of his father (ᶜ) (who was Lieut. Gen. of the forces of "Charles Edward" in 1745) his right of succession to the Dukedom of Atholl, &c. [S.], being a matter of doubtful validity, he presented a petition to the Crown, claiming the same on the death of his uncle, and it was resolved, 7 Feb. 1764, by the House of Lords (to which the petition had been referred) " that the Petitioner hath a right to the titles, honours and

---

(ᵃ) The statement in *Dict. Nat. Biog* that he was at the same date made Lord Justice Gen. is altogether erroneous. V.G.

(ᵇ) " A very pretty girl " writes her br.-in-law, Lord George Murray, 28 May 1749. V.G.

(ᶜ) As to the effect of an attainder, " In the Athol case (1764) it was held that if the attainted person died in the lifetime of the person in possession of the dignity, the attainted person's son could take ; and in the Airlie case (1812) it was held that if the attainted person survived the person in possession of the dignity the title was forfeited. " See *Hewlett*, p 12, and *Robertson*, p. 315-318.

dignities of *Duke of Atholl, Marquis of Tullibardine, Earl of Strathtay and Strathardle, Viscount Balquhidar, Glenalmond and Glenlyon, Lord Murray, Balvenie and Gask* claimed by his said petition " (ᵃ) On 21 Aug. 1766 and again in 1768 he was chosen a REP. PEER [S] K.T. 23 Dec. 1767. Grand Master of Freemasons [S.] 1773 till his death. He *m.*, 23 Oct. 1753, at Dunkeld, Charlotte, only surv. da. and h. of his uncle, James (MURRAY), 2nd DUKE OF ATHOLL [S.], by Jean, his 1st wife, da. of Thomas FREDERICK, abovenamed. On her father's death, 8 Jan. 1764, she became *suo jure* BARONESS STRANGE, and inherited the Sovereignty of the Isle of Man, which had been granted by Henry IV to her ancestor Sir John Stanley, and held by that family till 1736, when it devolved in right of her father's grandmother (see under the 1st Marquess as also under the 2nd Duke of Atholl) on her said father. This Sovereignty of the Isle of Man she and her husband sold to the Government in 1765 for £70,000 and an annuity of £2,000 for their joint lives, reserving, however, their landed interest. The Duke *d.* at Dunkeld (having drowned himself in the Tay, in a fit of delirium), (ᵇ) 5 Nov. 1774, in his 46th year Will pr. Mar. 1779 His widow (ᶜ) *d.* at Barochney House, near Glasgow, 13 Oct. 1805. (ᵈ) in her 75th year. Will pr. Aug. 1806. Both *bur.* at Dunkeld.

DUKEDOM [S.] IV. MARQUESSATE [S.] V. EARLDOM [S] XXXII	4, 5, 6 or 11. JOHN (MURRAY), DUKE OF ATHOLL, &c [S.], s. and h., *b.* 30 June 1755, and *bap.* at Dunkeld. In 1777 he raised a Regiment for the public service, named the 77th Reg. of Foot or Atholl Highlanders. Grand Master of Freemasons [S] 1778-80 In 1780, being a Tory, he was elected a REP. PEER [S] F.R.S 9 Nov 1780 On 18 Aug 1786 he

was raised to the Peerage of Great Britain, being *cr.* BARON MURRAY

(ᵃ) It is curious that neither the Marquessate of Atholl, the Earldom of Atholl, nor the Earldom of Tullibardine are mentioned among these honours

(ᵇ) For an account of his death see *Hist. MSS Com.*, 11th Rep., App, pt. 5, where the writer of the letter, Sir James A. Oughton, speaks warmly of his virtues and benevolence. V G

(ᶜ) On the death of the Duke of Ancaster, in 1779, the Duchess of Atholl (being, through the families of Stanley and de Vere, senior coh., though by the *half* blood, of Henry, 18*th Earl of Oxford, High Chamberlain*), was a claimant for the office of High Chamberlain of England, as also was Hugh, Lord Percy, *styled* Earl Percy (who was the senior coh of John, *the 14th Earl*, and of *all the preceding Earls*), but the decision in May 1781 was that their rights " were barred by the statute of limitations. " See vol. ii, Appendix D.

(ᵈ) In *The Abbey of Kilkhampton*, p. 103, edition 1788, Sir Herbert Croft, probably sacrificing truth and meaning to alliteration, describes her as " mad miserable and merciless. " V.G.

of Stanley, co. Gloucester, and EARL STRANGE. On 4 Feb. 1793 he was made Capt. Gen. and Gov. in Chief of the Isle of Man. Lord Lieut. of co. Perth 1794 till death ; P.C. 28 June 1797 ; Col. of the Perthshire Militia 1798   K.T. 4 Apr. 1800. REP. PEER [S] 1780-86. On 13 Oct. 1805 he *suc.* his mother in the BARONY OF STRANGE. In 1781 he presented a petition praying for a bill to amend the provisions of the Act of 1765, as having been unjust to his family in the inadequate allowance granted for the sale of the Isle of Man. This bill, though it passed the Commons, was lost in the House of Lords. In 1790 he renewed the same, but it was postponed. In 1805 however, on a third petition, it was carried, after great opposition, and one fourth of the customs of the island was settled on him and on the heirs general of James (Stanley), 7th Earl of Derby. (ª) This fourth, however, he appears to have resigned subsequently for £409,000. Pres. of the Highland and Agric. Soc. [S.] 1807-11. He *m.*, 1stly, at her father's house in Grosvenor Place, St. Geo., Han. Sq., 26 Dec. 1774, Jane, 1st da. of Charles (CATHCART), 9th LORD CATHCART [S.], by Jean, da. of Lord Archibald HAMILTON. She, who was *b.* in London 20 May 1754, *d.* in Hanover Sq , 5, and was *bur.* 30 Dec. 1790, at Dunkeld Cathedral, in her 37th year. He *m.*, 2ndly, 11 Mar. 1794, at St. Marylebone, (spec. lic.) Margery, widow of John MACKENZIE (*styled* LORD MACLEOD), 1st da. of James (FORBES), 16th LORD FORBES [S.], by Catharine, da. of Sir Robert INNES, Bart. [S]. He *d.* 29 Sep. 1830, at St. Adamnan's Cottage, Dunkeld, aged 75, and was *bur.* there. Will pr. July 1831. His widow *d. s.p.s.,* 3 Oct. 1842.

DUKEDOM [S.] V. MARQUESSATE [S.] VI. EARLDOM [S.] XXXIII.	1830.

5, 6, 7 or 12. JOHN (MURRAY), DUKE OF ATHOLL, &c. [S.], also EARL STRANGE, LORD STRANGE and BARON MURRAY, s. and h , *b.* 26 June at Dunkeld, and *bap.* there 17 July 1778. Ed. at Eton. Ensign 61st Regt. 1797. He was of unsound mind in 1798, and is said to have been a Whig in politics. (ᵇ) He *d.* unm., in Greville Place, St. John's Wood, Midx., 14, and was *bur.* 26 Sep. 1846, at Dunkeld, aged 68.

(ª) The three daughters and coheirs of Ferdinando (Stanley), 5th Earl of Derby (who *d. s p m.* in 1594), were the heirs gen. of *(the grantee)* Sir John Stanley, to whom the Sovereignty of the Isle of Man had been granted in 1404. They are said [*but query*] to have sold their rights to their uncle William, the 6th Earl (1594-1642), whose s. and h. was James, 7th Earl, abovementioned, to whose heirs gen. (*not* of the heirs gen. of the Royal grantee) the above compensation was made See, as to the service by which this island was held, Taylor's *Glory of Regality*, p. 143.

(ᵇ) Moss's *Parl. Guide,* 1841. He, however, never voted on any matter of importance, and probably never took his seat, and why he should be so labelled, the Editor does not know. V.G.

42

DUKEDOM [S.]
VI.

MARQUESSATE [S]
VII

EARLDOM [S.]
XXXIV.

} 1846.

6, 7, 8 or 13. GEORGE AUGUSTUS FREDERICK JOHN (MURRAY), DUKE OF ATHOLL, &c. [S.], also EARL STRANGE, LORD STRANGE, BARON MURRAY AND BARON GLENLYON, nephew and h., being s. and h. of James (MURRAY), LORD GLENLYON, (so *cr.* 9 July 1821), by Emily Frances, da. and, in her issue, sole h. of Hugh (PERCY), 2nd DUKE OF NORTHUMBERLAND, which

James, Lord Glenlyon, was 2nd s. (by the 1st wife) of the 4th Duke of Atholl [S.]. He was *b.* 20 Sep. 1814, in Gt. Cumberland Place, Marylebone. Sometime (1834) an officer in 2nd Dragoon Guards, retiring 1840. Grand Master of Freemasons [S.] 1843 till his death. Hereditary Sheriff of co. Perth. On 12 Oct. 1837 he *suc.* his father as LORD GLENLYON. A Lord in Waiting Jan. to July 1846. K.T. 28 Oct. 1853. Pres. of the Highland and Agric. Soc. [S.] 1858-62. In politics he was a Conservative. He *m.*, 29 Oct. 1839, at Blair Drummond, Anne, only da. of Henry HOME-DRUMMOND, of Blair Drummond, co. Perth, by Christian, 1st da. of Charles MORAY, of Abercairny in that co. He *d.*, of cancer in the neck, at Blair Castle, 16, and was *bur.* 25 Jan. 1864, in the (ruinous) Church of Blair, aged 49. His widow, who was *b.* 17 June 1814, in Edinburgh, and who from Feb. to Dec. 1852 was Mistress of the Robes, (ª) was a Lady of the Bedchamber May 1854 to 1897, being acting Mistress of the Robes 1892. V.A. (3rd Class.) She *d.* at Dunkeld 18, and was *bur.* 22 May 1897, at Blair Atholl.

DUKEDOM [S.]
VII.

MARQUESSATE [S.]
VIII.

EARLDOM [S.]
XXXV.

} 1864.

9 or 14. JOHN JAMES HUGH HENRY (MURRAY, afterwards STEWART-MURRAY), DUKE OF ATHOLL (1703), MARQUESS (ᵇ) OF ATHOLL (1676), MARQUESS OF TULLIBARDINE (1703), EARL (ᵇ) OF ATHOLL (1457, or 1629), EARL (ᵇ) OF TULLIBARDINE (1606 and 1676), EARL OF STRATHTAY AND STRATHARDLE (1703), VISCOUNT OF BALQUHIDDER (1676), VISCOUNT OF

BALWHIDDER, GLENALMOND AND GLENLYON (1703), LORD MURRAY OF TULLIBARDINE (1604), LORD MURRAY, BALVENIE AND GASK (1676 and 1703), all in the Peerage of Scotland; also EARL STRANGE (1786), LORD STRANGE (*by writ* 1628), LORD PERCY (*by writ* 1722), BARON MURRAY OF STANLEY (1786), and BARON GLENLYON (1821), in the Peerage of England, Great Britain, or the United Kingdom, and Hereditary Sheriff of co. Perth,

---

(ª) For a list of these ladies, see note *sub* William, DUKE OF MANCHESTER [1855]. She was chief mourner at the funeral of H.R H the Duchess of Gloucester, 15 May 1857.

(ᵇ) As to the Marquessate and Earldom of Atholl and the Earldom of Tullibardine see *ante*, p. 320, note "a."

only s and h., *b* 6 Aug. and *bap.* 12 Nov. 1840, at Blair Castle. Lieut. Scots Fusilier Guards, 1859 ; Capt, 1864 to 1866. On 12 Feb. 1865 he *suc.* his maternal uncle Algernon (Percy), 4th Duke of Northumberland, *&c.* in the Barony *cr.* by writ of summons 23 Nov. 1722, (*) as LORD PERCY. On 1 Dec. 1865, he registered at the Lyon office, Edinburgh, his assumption of the name of *Stewart* before that of *Murray.* K.T. 14 May 1868. Lord Lieut. of co. Perth, 1878 Pres. of the Highland and Agric. Soc. [S.] 1887-88. In politics he is a Conservative. (ᵇ) He *m*, 29 Oct. 1863, at Moncreiffe House, Louisa, 1st da. of Sir Thomas Moncreiffe, of Moncreiffe, 7th Bart. [S.], by Louisa, 1st da. of Thomas Robert (Hay), 10th Earl of Kinnoull [S.]. She *d.*, in Italy, on a journey from Salso Maggiore to Axenfels, 8, and was *bur.* 17 July 1902, at Blair.

[John Stewart-Murray, *styled* Marquess of Tullibardine, 1st s. and h. ap., *b.* 30 Aug. 1869, at Blair Castle, *d.* the next day].

[John George Stewart-Murray, *styled* Marquess of Tullibardine, 2nd, but 1st surv. s. and h. ap., *b.* 15 Dec. 1871, at Blair Castle, co. Perth. 2nd Lieut. Royal Horse Guards 1892 ; Lieut. 1893 ; Capt. 1899 ; brevet Major 1900 ; Lieut Col. 1903 Served in the Sudan 1893 ; at the battle of Atbara ; at the battle of Khartoum ; mentioned in despatches. (D.S.O. 15 Nov. 1898 ; British and Khedive's medal with 2 clasps). Served in the S. African War, 1899-1902, three times mentioned in despatches. (ᶜ) M.V.O. 14 Oct. 1902 ; Grand Master of Freemasons [S.] 1909 ; M P. (Conservative) for West Perthshire 1910. He *m*, 20 July 1899, at St. Margaret's, Westm., Katherine Marjory, 4th da. of Sir James Henry Ramsay, of Bamff, 10th Bart. [1666], being 1st da. by his 2nd wife, Charlotte Fanning, da. and h. of William Stewart, of Ardvorlich.]

Family Estates.—These, in 1883, consisted of about 202,000 acres in co. Perth, valued at about £42,000 a year. *Principal Residence.*—The Castle, Blair Atholl, co. Perth (ᵈ)

(ᵃ) He thus became the representative of *both* of the claimants of the High Chamberlainship mentioned *ante*, in note " c, " p. 320. As such he was one of the claimants to the Lord Great Chamberlainship on the accession of King Edward VII. As to that high office see vol. ii, Appendix D. V.G.

(ᵇ) " The Duke of Atholl, of our British nobility, may claim to have the greatest number of titles. Besides his Dukedom, he holds two Marquisates, five Earldoms, three Viscountcies, eight Baronies, and is also a Knight of the Thistle. *Twenty* distinct titles in all. He is, moreover, coheir of five other baronies " Of course the above list takes no account of the shadowy Jacobite Dukedom of Rannoch and other peerage titles conferred on his collateral ancestor in 1717, of which he is the heir. In the *Edinburgh Gazette*, 26 Sep. 1893, appeared a notice to the effect that the Duke would in future revert to the original spelling and use the title of Atholl. The latter form seems first to have been started by the 6th Duke about 1854. V.G.

(ᶜ) For a list of peers, and heirs ap. of peers, serving in this war, see vol. iii, Appendix B. V.G.

(ᵈ) The Duke of Atholl is among the 28 noblemen who, in 1883, possessed above

ATHOLL

i.e. "DUNMORE in the forest of ATHOLL, co. Perth," Barony *(Murray)*, *cr.* 1831 ; see DUNMORE Earldom [I.], *cr.* 1686, under the 5th Earl.

ATON ([a])

SIR GILBERT ATON, ([b]) of West Ayton, etc., co. York, ([c]) s. and h. of William A. of the same, by Isabel, ([d]) da. of Sir Simon DE VEER, of Goxhill, co. Lincoln, and Sproatley in Holderness. He was knighted, with the Prince of Wales, 22 May 1306, ([e]) and had a grant of free warren in his demesne lands in Barlby, the Holmes, Welham, and Knapton, 7 Aug. 1308. ([f]) He established his claim to the lands of William de Vescy of Kildare [Lord de Vescy] in 1316 and 1317, ([g]) did homage 7 Nov. 1317, and had livery of Langton and Wintringham, co. York, 22 Jan 1317/8, and of Malton, 26 Nov. 1318. ([h]) In (1323-24)

100,000 acres in the United Kingdom, and he stood sixth in point of acreage, though by no means in rental. See a list of these in a note *sub* BUCCLEUCH.

([a]) The re-writing of this article has been kindly undertaken by G.W.Watson.

([b]) The arms of Aton, as quartered by their descendants, were, Barry of six Or and Azure, on a canton Gules a cross flory Argent. Gilbert assumed the arms of Vescy, Or a cross Sable. (*Boroughbridge Roll*, no. 131). His s., William, added, for some time, 5 bull's heads Argent to the cross, thereby occasioning a dispute with Sir Robert de Boveton (Boulton or Bolton), which was arranged by indenture dated 5 Apr. 1375. (Bodleian Charters, *Yorkshire*, no. 335).

([c]) He was a sub-tenant of the Earl of Lancaster in West Ayton (wapentake of Pickering Lythe): of the Bishop of Durham in Barlby and Menthorpe (liberty of Howden) : of the fief of Vescy in Knapton, and that of Moubray in Welham (wapentake of Buckrose).

([d]) She was h. of her mother, Ada, 4th sister and in her issue coh. of Roger Bertram of Mitford ; but not of her father, Simon, who, by his 1st marriage, had Sir Simon de Veer, his s. and h. The younger Simon gave the manor of Bottesford, co. Lincoln, to his uncle, Roger de Veer, prior of the knights Hospitallers, 3 Sep. 1270. (*Charter Roll*, 55 Hen. III, *m.* 3).

([e]) It was he who was knighted at this date, and not, as has hitherto been stated, his uncle, who was dead in 1303. (*Knights' fees in Yorkshire* 31 *Edw. I*, Surtees Soc., p. 242).

([f]) *Charter Roll*, 2 Edw. II, *m.* 14.

([g]) On the death of William de Vescy of Kildare, a bastard, without h. of his body (slain at Bannockburn 24 June 1314), it was found by inquisitions, cos. York and Lincoln, 2 June, 5 Aug., and 15 Nov. 1315, that Gilbert d'Aton, aged 26 and more, was h. of William de Vescy the elder [reputed father of the afsd. William], being s. and h. of William, br. and h. of Gilbert, s. and h. of William, s. and h. of Margery [wife of Gilbert d'Aton who *d.* 1235], da. and h. of Warin de Vescy [of Knapton], br. of Eustace, grandfather of the sd. William the elder. (Ch. *Inq. p. m.*, Edw. II, file 40, no. 1).

([h]) *Close Rolls*, 11 Edw. II, *m.* 13 ; 12 Edw. II, *m.* 22.

17 Edw. II, he confirmed, for 700 marks, to Henry de Percy, the grant which Anthony, Bishop of Durham, had made him of the castle of Alnwick. (ᵃ) He was sum. to three Councils, 30 Dec. (1324) and 20 Feb. (1324/5) 18 Edw. II, and 25 Feb. (1341/2) 16 Edw. III, by writs directed *Gilberto de Aton'*. Will dat. 10 Apr. 1350. (ᵇ)

BARONY   1. Sir William Aton, of Malton, Ayton, &c., s. and
BY WRIT   h., *b.* about 1299. (ᶜ) He was sum. to a Council, 10 Oct.
I. 1371.   (1359) 33 Edw. III, and to Parl. 8 Jan. (1370/1)
                44 Edw. III, by writs directed *Willelmo de Aton'*, by which
latter summons he may be held to have become LORD ATON. (ᵈ) He was Sheriff of co. York 27 Nov. 1368-70 and 12 Dec. 1372-73. On 22 Feb. 1376/7 he obtained an exemption for life from being put on assizes, juries, etc., and from being made a justice of the peace, mayor, sheriff, etc. (ᵉ) He *m.*, before Jan. 1326/7, (ᶠ) Isabel, da. of Sir Henry Percy [2nd Lord Percy], by Idoine, (ᵍ) da. of Sir Robert Clifford [1st Lord Clifford]. She *d.* before 25 May 1368. He *d.s.p.m.s.*(ʰ) before Mar. 1388/9.(ⁱ)

(ᵃ) The story, related by Dugdale and others, that the Bishop appropriated Alnwick, when holding it in trust for the bastard William de Vescy, is disproved by the deeds to lead the uses of the fines, dated Saturday before All Saints 23 Edw. I [29 Oct. 1295], whereby William de Vescy gave, in the event of his dying *s.p. legit.*, Malton, Langton, Wintringham, and Brompton, co. York, and Caythorpe, co. Lincoln, to William de Vescy of Kildare, and Alnwick and Tughall, Northumberland, to the Bishop and his heirs for ever. These deeds are printed in *Collins*, ed. 1779, vol. ii, p. 489.

(ᵇ) *Test. Ebor.*, vol. i, no. 47. He mentions in it "William mon fitz." There appears to be no inquisition extant. But it is evident from a deed dated Saturday in the 1st week of Lent 1349 [20 Feb. 1349/50] (*Monasticon*, vol. iii, p. 504) that he had before that date enfeoffed his s. William of some, if not all, of his property.

(ᶜ) He deposed in 1386 that he was " de age de iiijˣˣ et vij anz armez de lxvj ans " (*Scrope and Grosvenor Controversy*, vol. i, p. 142), whence Nicolas (*ibid.*, vol. ii, p. 347) concludes that the dates prove that he must have been brother of Gilbert, and not *son*. The dates do not prove this, nor is it true. On the feast of St. Bartholomew 1384, and the morrow thereof, he executed two charters at Malton and Aton in Pickering Lythe, respectively, styling himself Sir William d'Aton knt. s. and h. of Sir Gilbert d'Aton knt. (Bodleian Charters, *Yorkshire*, nos. 200, 199). The erroneous statement by Nicolas has been copied in Tate's *Alnwick*, and elsewhere.

(ᵈ) As to how far these early writs of summons did in fact *cr.* any peerage title, see Appendix A in the last volume. V.G.

(ᵉ) This exemption, with exemplification and confirmations thereof, dated 20 July and 12 Nov. 1377, and 28 Oct. 1379, are on the *Patent Rolls*, 51 Edw. III, *m.* 35; 1 Ric. II, *pars* i, *m.* 19, *pars* ii, *m.* 32 ; 3 Ric. II, *pars* i, *m.* 17.

(ᶠ) *Feet of Fines*, case 272, file 102, nos. 10, 11.

(ᵍ) For some discussion on mediaeval English names see vol. iii, Appendix C. V.G.

(ʰ) His son, William, *d.s.p., v.p.* The seal to a charter of Margaret, " nuper uxor Willelmi Aton militis filii Willelmi de Aton militis, " dated aᵒ 7 Ric. II, gives her arms, barry of 6, over all a bend. (Harl. MSS., no. 245, f. 123 d).

(ⁱ) On Michaelmas day 9 Ric. II, he gave his manor of Barlby to Sir Ralph

He left 3 daughters and coheirs. (1) Anastasia, wife of Sir Edward St. John. He *d.* 7 Mar. 1388/9. (ᵃ) (2) Katherine, 2nd wife of Sir Ralph Eure, of Witton Castle, co. Durham. He *d.* 10 Mar. 1421/2. (ᵇ) (3) Elizabeth, formerly wife of Sir William Playce, but then wife of Sir John Conyers, of Sockburn, co. Durham, who *d.* shortly before 6 Mar. 1395/6. (ᶜ) She *d.* shortly before 8 May 1402. (ᶜ) They made partition of their inheritance, 22 July 1389, and among their representatives any hereditary Barony, that may be held to have existed, is in *abeyance.* (ᵈ)

ATTINGHAM

See " BERWICK OF ATTINGHAM, co. Salop, " Barony *(Hill), cr.* 1784.

AUBENY see D'AUBENY

AUBIGNY (ᵉ)

Aubigny-sur-Nerre was a French seigneurie situated in Berry. From the 15th to the 17th century, however, the style of " Lord Aubigny " was frequently used both in England and Scotland by its

---

Eure, Sir John Conyers, and Sir William Playce (s. of Elizabeth Aton), for their lives, &c. (Harl. MSS., no. 245, *ibid.*). He *d.* before his son-in-law, Sir Edward St. John (*Close Roll*, 12 Ric. II, *m.* 11).

(ᵃ) "Edwardus de Sancto Johanne miles. " Writ, missing. Inq., co. York, 1 Apr. 1389. "Item dicunt predicti Juratores quod dictus Edwardus obiit septimo die Martii jam ultimo preterito. Et quod Margareta filia dicti Edwardi quam Thomas de Brounflete duxit in uxorem est heres dicti Edwardi propinquior et quod est de etate septemdecim annorum et amplius. " (Ch. *Inq. p. m.,* Ric. II, file 57, no. 51).

(ᵇ) "Radulfus de Eure Chivaler. " Writ of *diem cl. ext.* 16 Apr. 10 Hen. V. Inq., co. Northumberland, 17 June 1422. "Et dicunt quod predictus Radulfus obiit die martis proximo ante festum sancti Gregorii martyris [*sic*] ultimo preterito. Et quod Willelmus de Eure miles filius predicti Radulfi est heres ejus propinquior et est etatis xxvj annorum et amplius. " (Ch. *Inq. p. m.,* Hen. V, file 64, no. 39). Inq., Durham, 7 Sep. 1422. "Radulfus obiit x die Martii." Heir as before. (*Cursitor's Records,* no. ii, f. 214).

(ᶜ) Durham Inquisitions of these dates. (*Cursitor's Records,* no. ii, ff. 124, 140d).

(ᵈ) (1) Anastasia left an only da. and h., Margaret, who *m.* Sir Thomas Bromflete. Their s. and h., Henry, was sum. to Parl. 24 Jan. 1448/9, by writ directed *Henrico Bromflete militi baroni de Vesy.* See " VESCY, " Barony, 1449. (2) The representation of Katherine devolved on the 2 daughters and coheirs of Sir William Eure (slain at Marston Moor in 1644), *viz.,* (i) Margaret, wife of Thomas Danby, of Farnley, co. York, and (ii) Mary, wife of William Palmes, of Lindley, co. York. (3) Elizabeth left a s. and h., Sir William Playce (living 30 Mar. 1396), who was father of Robert Place, who, by his wife, Katherine, da. and h. of Halnath de Halnaby, was ancestor of the family of Place of Halnaby, co. York.

(ᵉ) The re-writing of this article has been kindly undertaken by G.W.Watson.

different possessors. Accordingly, an account of the various persons (all being members of the House of Stewart) who held it is subjoined.

1. Sir John Stewart, of Darnley, co. Renfrew, s. and h. of Sir Alexander Stewart, of the same (who *d.* before 5 May 1404), by his 1st wife, whose name is unknown. (ª) He was knighted before May 1387. He entered the service of France in Oct. 1419, and was soon afterwards appointed Constable of the Army of Scotland. Having distinguished himself at the battle of Baugé in Anjou, 22 Mar. 1420/1, he received from the Dauphin Charles, 23 Apr. 1421, the Seigneurie of Concressault in Berry, (ᵇ) and from the same (after he had become King), 26 Mar. 1422/3, the Seigneurie of Aubigny, also in Berry, (ᶜ) and in Jan. 1426/7 the Comté of Evreux in Normandy. (ᵈ) To reward his further services, 4 Feb. 1427/8, Charles VII granted him the privilege of bearing the arms of France in the 1st and 4th quarters of his shield. (ᵉ) He *m.* (disp. 23 Sep. 1406) Elizabeth, 2nd or 3rd da. and coh. of Duncan, Earl of Lennox [S.], by Ellen, da. of Gillespic Campbell, of Lochawe. He *d.* 12 Feb. 1428/9, (ᶠ) being slain at the battle "of Herrings" at Rouvray-Saint-Denis, and was *bur.* in the Cathedral of Orléans. His widow was *bur.* with him in Nov. 1429.

2. Sir John Stuart, 2nd s., inherited the Seigneuries of Concressault and Aubigny, for which he did homage to Louis XI, 2 Sep. 1461. He was Chamberlain of the King of France, a knight of the Order of St. Michael, and Capt. of the 100 Scottish Men-at-Arms. He *m.*, in 1446, Beatrix, da. of Béraud d'Apchier, Seigneur d'Apchier in Languedoc, by Anne, da. and h. of Géraud de la Gorce, Seigneur de la Gorce. He *d.* in 1482.

(ª) *Scots Peerage*, vol. v, p. 345.
(ᵇ) P. Dupuy, *Traitez touchant les Droits du Roy*, 1655, p. 785.
(ᶜ) *Anselme*, vol. v, pp. 921-2: Andrew Stuart, *History of the Stewarts*, pp. 393-5. The grant is to him "et a ses hoirs masles descendans de son corps et de ses hoirs masles en droite ligne."
(ᵈ) Le Brasseur, *Histoire d'Evreux*, 1722, pp. 119-20: *Anselme*, vol. iii, pp. 98-9: A.Stuart, pp. 141-3. The grant is to him and the heirs male of his body. On 15 Mar. 1426/7, he promised, for himself and his heirs, to resign the *comté* at any time for 50,000 *écus d'or*. Whether he did so or not is unknown, but after his death the title disappears till Evreux was made a *duché* in Oct. 1569.
(ᵉ) Thaumas de la Thaumassiere, *Histoire de Berry*, 1689, p. 697.
(ᶠ) It may be that, as La Thaumassiere states, he was suc. in the seigneurie of Aubigny by his eldest s., Alan, but there are no *aveux* nor homages before 1461 in evidence, to decide the question. This Alan was in Scotland, Nov. 1429 and Feb. 1433, and does not appear in France till 1435, when he is described as "Connestable de larmee dEcosse." In a protection against creditors, 4 Aug. 1437, from the French King, he is not described as Seigneur d'Aubigny. (A.Stuart, pp. 162-5: Fraser, *The Lennox*, vol. ii, p. 65).

3. BÉRAUD or BERNARD, STUART, SEIGNEUR D'AUBIGNY, Chamberlain of the King of France, knight of the Order of St. Michael, only s. and h., b. about 1447. He did homage for the Seigneurie of Aubigny to Charles VIII, 22 Nov. 1483. He commanded the French contingent at the battle of Bosworth, 22 Aug. 1485, and was appointed Capt. of the Scottish Archers of the Guard, Dec. 1493. He accompanied Charles VIII and Louis XII in their Italian campaigns, held the office of Grand Constable of Sicily and Jerusalem (i.e. of Naples), and was made Gov. of Calabria in 1495, with the title of Marquis of Squilazzo. Having defeated the Spaniards at Terranuova, 25 Dec. 1502, and again at Girace, he was cr., by Louis XII, Duke of Terranuova and Marquis of Girace. He m., 1stly, Guillemette DE BOUCARD. He m., 2ndly, Anne, only da. and h. of Guy DE MAUMONT, SEIGNEUR DE SAINT QUENTIN in La Marche, by Jeanne, suo jure COUNTESS OF BEAUMONT-LE-ROGER, illegit. da. of Jean II, DUKE OF ALENCON. He d. s.p.m.(ᵃ) in 1508, on or shortly after 8 June, (ᵇ) at Corstorphine, when on an embassy to Scotland. Will, directing that he should be bur. in the Church of the Black Friars, Edinburgh, dat. 8 June 1508. (ᶜ) His widow m., in 1510, Aubert DES AGES.

4. ROBERT STUART, SEIGNEUR D'AUBIGNY, Capt. of the Scottish Archers of the Guard and of the 100 Scottish Men-at-Arms, cousin of the above, being 4th s. (but 2nd surv. s. in 1508) of John, 1st Earl of Lennox [S.], who was s. and h. of Sir Alan S. of Darnley, s. and h. of Sir John S. of Darnley above-named. He did homage for the Seigneurie of Aubigny to Louis XII, 21 Aug. 1508, and was cr. a Marshal of France in 1515. He m., 1stly, his 2nd cousin, Anne, da. and coh. of Béraud STUART, SEIGNEUR D'AUBIGNY, by his 2nd wife, Anne DE MAUMONT, both above-named. She d. before 1527. He m., 2ndly, Jacqueline, da. and coh. of François DE LA QUEUILLE, SEIGNEUR DE LA QUEUILLE in Auvergne, by his 1st wife, Marguerite, da. of Jean DE CASTELNAU, SEIGNEUR DE CASTELNAU DE BRÉTENOUX ET DE SAINT SENTIN DE CAUMONT in Quercy. He received a grant, 15 June 1527, to him

---

(ᵃ) He left 2 daughters : (by his 1st wife) Guyonne, who m. Philippe Braque, Seigneur du Luat (Ile de France), and left posterity ; and (by his 2nd wife) Anne, who m. her cousin, Robert Stuart, as below. The name Braque is given wrongly as "de Brague" in The Stuarts of Aubigny, by Lady E.Cust, and elsewhere.

(ᵇ) In the Scots Peerage, vol. v, p. 347, he is said to have d. 15 June. The authority cited is Treasurer's Accounts [S.], vol. iv, p. 42. But the entry there runs "Item the xv day of Junij to the Kingis offerand at my Lord of Owbigneis saule mes, xiiij s.," and shows, on the contrary, that he d. some time before that date.

(ᶜ) This will, of "Baraldus Stewart," and an inventory, are printed by A.Stuart, p. 207, and (with some differences) by Fraser, vol. ii, p. 186. The inventory gives the value of his goods as 2004 l., and "Summa omnium bonorum debitis extractis" as 1800 l. [or 1850 l.]—incorrectly rendered in The Stuarts of Aubigny, p. 44, as "that he owed 1850 l. to different creditors."

and his 2nd wife, of the Comté of Beaumont-le-Roger, his 1st wife's inheritance. He *d. s.p.* in 1543. His wife surv. him.

5. JOHN STUART, SEIGNEUR D'AUBIGNY, grand-nephew of the above, being 3rd s. of John, 3rd Earl of Lennox [S.], s. and h. of Matthew, the 2nd Earl, who was s. and h. of John, the 1st Earl, above-named. He was *b.* about 1519, and was naturalised as a French subject by Francis I in Jan. 1536/7. He did homage for the Seigneurie of Aubigny to Charles IX, 14 July 1560. He was Capt. of the Scottish Archers of the Guard, 1536-60. He *m.,* about 1542, Anne (the half-sister of the 2nd wife of his grand-uncle above-named), da. and coh. of François DE LA QUEUILLE, SEIGNEUR DE LA QUEUILLE, by his 2nd wife, Anne, da. of Jacques D'ESPINAY, SEIGNEUR D'USSÉ ET DE SAINT MICHEL-SUR-LOIRE. (ᵃ) He *d.* 31 May 1567. His widow's will was dat. 4 Dec. 1579.

6. ESMÉ STUART, SEIGNEUR D'AUBIGNY, only s. and h. He was *b.* about 1543, and was brought up in France, but went to Scotland in Sep. 1579. On 5 Mar. 1579/80, he was *cr.* EARL OF LENNOX, &c. [S.], and, 5 Aug. 1581, DUKE OF LENNOX, &c. [S.]. He *d.* 26 May 1583. See "LENNOX," Dukedom of, under the 1st Duke.

7. ESMÉ STUART, SEIGNEUR D'AUBIGNY, 2nd s. He was *b.* about 1579, and was brought up in France. He did homage for the Seigneurie of Aubigny to Henry IV, 8 Apr. 1600. On 7 June 1619 (ᵇ) he was *cr.* EARL OF MARCH, &c. [E.]. On 16 Feb. 1623/4 he *suc.* his elder br. as

---

(ᵃ) J. le Laboureur, *Les Tombeaux des Personnes Illustres,* 1642, p. 170. According to J.B. Bouillet, *Nobiliaire d'Auvergne,* 1846-53, vol. v, p. 212, she was da. of Henry de Rohan [*sic*], Seigneur d'Espinay. But Anne, da. of Henry d'Espinay, Seigneur d'Espinay in Brittany (nephew of Jacques above-named), *m.* (cont. 22 Sep. 1511), Jacques de Beauvau, Seigneur de Tigny in Anjou, who *d.* in 1553. (Du Paz, *Plusieurs Maisons Illustres de Bretagne,* 1619, pp. 262-317, pedigree of Espinay : S. et L. de Ste. Marthe, *Histoire de la Maison de Beauvau,* 1626, p. 80). Bouillet's absurd mistake of attributing the surname of Rohan to the great family of Espinay has been freely copied by English writers. Anne de la Queuille *d.* 5 Sep. 1540 ; her heart was *bur.* in the Church of the Celestins at Paris. The arms on the tablet there were her husband's, Sable, a cross engrailed Or *(la Queuille),* quartering, Gules, a lion rampant Or (probably *Fleurac)* : and her own, Argent, a lion rampant per fesse Gules and Vert, armed langued and crowned Or *(Espinay),* quartering, Gules, 9 mascles Or, a label of 4 points Argent *(Montauban) ;* over all, Argent, a snake coiled in pale Azure, crowned Or, and swallowing an infant Gules *(Visconti of Parma).* These arms are incorrectly described in *The Stuarts of Aubigny,* p. 88, *Montauban* being attributed to "*Rohan de Montauban* " [*sic*], and *Espinay* being wrongly blazoned and attributed to *Armagnac* [Argent, a lion rampant Gules, quartering, Gules, a lion rampant guardant Or *(Rodez)*], which latter arms, though sometimes quartered by *Montauban* [not *Rohan*], do not appear on the tomb.

(ᵇ) This is the date always given, but there is no enrolment of the creation. (D.K. *Reports,* no. 47, Appendix, p. 105). He appears, however, as Lord Aubigny, 10 June 1619. *(Cal. of State Papers, Domestic,* 1619-23, p. 52).

Duke of Lennox, &c. [S.].   He *d.* 30 July 1624.   See "Lennox,"
Dukedom of, under the 3rd Duke.

8. Henry Stuart, Seigneur d'Aubigny, 2nd s., *b.* Jan. 1615/6,
and *bap.* at the Chapel Royal, Whitehall, 2 Apr. 1616, Queen Anne
being his godmother.   His father resigned the Seigneurie of Aubigny
in his favour in 1619, and he was sent with his two next brothers to
Aubigny, where they were brought up as Roman Catholics and naturalised as French subjects. (ᵃ)   He was ed. at Bourges and at Paris.   He
d. in 1632, at Venice, and was *bur.* there in the Church of SS. Giovanni
e Paolo.

9. George Stuart, Seigneur d'Aubigny, next br., *b.* 17 July
1618, at Bath House, Holborn.   Ed. at Paris.   He did homage for the
Seigneurie of Aubigny to Louis XIII, 5 Aug. 1636.   He *m.*, secretly,
in 1638, Katherine, (ᵇ) da. of Theophilus (Howard), 2nd Earl of
Suffolk, by Elizabeth, 2nd da. and coh. of George (Home), Earl of
Dunbar [S.].   He *d.* 23 Oct. 1642, being slain, *ex parte Regis,* at the
battle of Edgehill, and was *bur.* in Christ Church Cathedral, Oxford. (ᶜ)
Admon., as "of the city of Westm.," 8 June 1647 to the widow,
"Katherine Lady Aubigny," and again, on behalf of his children alone,
6 June 1650 and 24 Sep. 1660.   His widow *m.*, in or shortly before
1649, Sir James Levingston, who was *cr.* Earl of Newburgh, &c. [S.],
31 Dec. 1660.   She *d.* in exile, in 1650, at the Hague.   He was *bur.*
6 Dec. 1670.

10. Ludovic Stuart, Seigneur d'Aubigny, (ᵈ) next br., *b.* 14 Oct.

(ᵃ) "They wer naturalized in France that therby they might be capable to
inherite the lordship of Aubignay and the rest of [their father's] lands in that kingdome,
which otherwise they culd not doe, being borne in England and therefore alients in
France." (Sir Robert Gordon, *Earldom of Sutherland,* p. 127).

(ᵇ) "Lady Katherine Howard... unknown to her father, the Earl of Suffolk, she
is or will be married to the Lord d'Aubigny." (Garrard to Wentworth, 10 May
1638—*Strafford Letters,* vol. ii, p. 165).

(ᶜ) He is included in *The Loyalists' Bloody Roll,* for which see vol. ii, Appendix A.
He was "a gentleman of great hopes, of a gentle and winning disposition, and of a
very clear courage."   Evelyn, in his *Diary,* 11 Jan. 1661/2, says that he was "a
person of good sense, but wholly abandoned to ease and effeminacy." V.G.

(ᵈ) He was able to succeed to the Seigneurie, to the prejudice of his nephew
(and successor), Charles, as he was a naturalised French subject.   Charles, in a
petition to the House of Lords (which was reported on, 6 Apr. 1647), stated that
"his uncle Lodowick now liveth in France, and most wrongfully detaineth the estate
of your petitioner there," and the Lords, 23 July 1647, excluded Ludovic from his
share of the property of his brothers, John and Bernard, "in regard that the said Lord
Lodowicke receiveth a great part of the Lord Aubignie's estate, which he converteth
to his own use." (*Lords' Journals,* vol. ix, pp. 210, 351).   Charles I, 24 Oct. 1646,
wrote hoping that Lord Aubigny's children would not be put by from succeeding
their father by "the omission of some formalities." (*Letters,* Camden Soc., p. 73).

1619, at March House, Drury Lane. He was ed. at Port-Royal des Champs and took Orders, being appointed Abbé of Haute Fontaine and a canon of Nôtre Dame at Paris. He did homage for the Seigneurie of Aubigny to Louis XIV, 5 Aug. or 20 Nov. 1656. ([a]) He was Chief Almoner to the Queen Dowager of England. He *d.* 11 [not 3] Nov. 1665, a few days after he was nom. a Cardinal, at Paris, and was *bur.* there in the Church of the Chartreux. M.I. Admon. 3 Apr. 1666, to Charles, Duke of Richmond and Lennox, the nephew by the br. This was revoked, and will pr. May 1666.

11. CHARLES STUART, SEIGNEUR D'AUBIGNY, nephew of the above, being only s. and h. of George, Seigneur d'Aubigny above-named. He was *b.* 7 Mar. 1638/9, in London. On 10 Dec. 1645 he was *cr.* EARL OF LICHFIELD, &c., ([b]) and, 10 Aug. 1660, *suc.* his cousin as DUKE OF RICHMOND, &c. [E.], and DUKE OF LENNOX, &c. [S.]. After much negotiation he was recognised as Seigneur d'Aubigny by decree dat. 31 Dec. 1668, and did homage, by proxy, for that Seigneurie, to Louis XIV, 11 May 1670. ([c]) He *d. s.p.* 12 Dec. 1672. See "RICHMOND," Dukedom of, *cr.* 1641, under the 3rd Duke.

[On the death, 12 Dec. 1672, of the Duke of Richmond, above-named, Charles II and his br. James were the only remaining descendants in the male line of Sir John Stewart, the grantee of Aubigny in 1422/3. Charles II claimed the seigneurie, but Louis XIV declined to admit that a King of England could hold land in France. As a compromise, he made

---

([a]) In the instrument of homage (according to A.Stuart, p. 277, who dates it 20 Nov. 1656) he is stated to have suc. to Aubigny by the decease of his brothers, Henry, George, John, and Bernard. The two latter were junior to him, being *b.* in 1621, and 1622 or 3, respectively. The date of the homage, according to the subsequent *aveu* (which was signed by Ludovic, 26 Sep./6 Oct. 1661), was 5 Aug. 1656. (Addit. MSS., no. 21949, f. 8). There is a charter, dated 16 Sep. 1634, of "George Stuart Seigneur d'Aubigny *etc.* tant en nostre nom que comme ayant attraict le bail de Ludovic, Jean, et Bernard Stuart nos freres coheritiers de feu messire Henry Stuart nostre frere vivant chivallier seigneur dudict Aubigny *etc.*" Signed, "Ge. dAubigny. Ludovic Stuart." (Addit. Charter, no. 13335).

([b]) He was styled "Lord Stuart, Lord Aubigny" in the letters of admon. to his father and to his uncles, John and Bernard, all bearing date 6 June 1650, his title of Earl of Lichfield, etc., not being recognised either then or in the letters of admon. of 1647 ; Parl. having declared, on 11 Nov. 1643, that all patents and grants passed *since* 22 *May* 1642 were *void*. A subsequent Act of Parl., 4 Feb. 1651, enacted that all the honours granted by Charles I *since* 4 *Jan.* 1641/2 were *void*. These enactments are the cause of great confusion in the nomenclature of several of the Royalists during the Commonwealth period, many Peerages, Baronetcies, and Knighthoods, having been conferred by the King subsequent to these two dates. G.E.C.

([c]) A.Stuart, p. 280. Not 11 Mar., the date given in *The Stuarts of Aubigny*, and elsewhere. This homage was registered at the *Chambre des Comptes* at Paris by the Duke's agent 17 May 1670. (See this agent's letters (originals) in Addit. MSS., no. 21949, ff. 146-148).

a grant of " le fonds et proprieté de ladite terre d'Aubigny " to Louise
Renée de Penancoët de Keroualle, Duchess of Portsmouth, with remainder to any natural s. of Charles whom the latter might appoint, in tail
male. In this grant he affected to believe that the male line of the
original grantee was extinct. (ª) In Jan. 1683/4, Aubigny was erected
into a *duché-pairie,* in favour of the Duchess and her son, Charles. (ᵇ)
She did homage to Louis XIV for Aubigny in 1692, and was *suc.* therein
on her death, 14 Nov. 1734, by her grandson, Charles, Duke of Richmond. Aubigny was confiscated at the French Revolution].

(ª) Louis *etc.* La terre d'Aubigny sur Nierre dans nostre province de Berry
ayant esté donnée dés l'année 1422 par le roy Charles VII l'un de nos predecesseurs
à Jean Stuart comme une marque des grands et considerables services qu'il avoit rendus
dans la guerre au roy et à sa couronne et cette donation ayant esté accompagnée de
la condition que ladite terre d'Aubigny passeroit de masle en masle à tous les descendans dudit Jean Stuart avec reversion à nostre couronne lorsque la branche masculine
qui seroit venuë de luy seroit eteinte ce cas porté par lesdites lettres de donation est
arrivé l'année derniere par la mort de nostre cousin le duc de Richemond dernier de
la ligne masculine dudit Jean Stuart. Mais parce que cette terre ayant esté durant
tant d'années dans une maison qui avoit l'honneur d'appartenir de si prés à nostre tres
cher et tres amé frere le roy de la Grande Bretagne ledit roy nous auroit fait temoig-
ner qu'il seroit bien aise qu'à cette consideration nous voulussions bien la faire passer
à une personne qu'il affectionneroit et rentrer apres elle dans une maison qui fut
encore unie par le sang à la sienne. Qu'à ce sujet il nous auroit fait requerir que nous
voulussions bien accorder nos lettres de donation de ladite terre d'Aubigny sur Nierre
à la dame Louise Renée de Keroualle duchesse de Portsmouth pour passer apres sa
mort à tel des enfans naturels de nostre frere le roy de la Grande Bretagne qu'il
voudra nommer sous les mesmes clauses et conditions que la mesme terre fut pre-
mierement donnée par Charles VII en 1422 au susdit Jean Stuart et que ladite terre
estant passée à tel fils naturel dudit roy de la Grande Bretagne qu'il aura voulu
nommer elle demeure audit fils naturel et à ses descendans de masle en masle avec
droit de reversion à nostre couronne au deffaut d'enfans masles et par l'extinction de
la ligne masculine qui seroit sortie de luy. [A grant on these terms follows]. Donné
à Saint Germain en Laye au mois de decembre l'an de grace mil six cens soixante
treize et de nostre regne le trente uniesme. Signé Louis. (*Anselme,* vol. v, p. 922).

(ᵇ) Louis *etc.* Nous avons ladite ville terre chastellenie et chasteau d'Aubigny
fiefs et terres en dependans joint uni et annexé joignons unissons et annexons entant
que de besoin par ces presentes signées de nostre main pour n'estre à l'avenir qu'un
corps et territoire et le tout ensemble creé erigé et etabli et de nostre propre mouve-
ment certaine science pleine puissance et autorité royale creons erigeons et etablissons
en titre nom dignité prerogatives et preeminences de duché Pairie de France pour en
jouïr et user par ladite dame Louise Renée de Penancoet de Keroualle duchesse de
Portsmouth pendant sa vie et apres son decés par ledit sieur duc de Richemont et les
enfans et descendans masles dudit sieur duc de Richemont en nom titre et dignité de
ducs d'Aubigny et Pairs de France en tous actes lieux et endroits et tout ainsi que les
autres ducs et Pairs jouïssent et usent des droits de Pairie tant en justice seance et
jurisdiction qualitez droits honneurs autoritez prerogatives et preeminences appartenans
à dignité de duc et Pair de France et dont les ducs et Pairs de nostre royaume ont cy
devant accoustumé de jouïr et user jouïssent et usent de present lequel duché ladite

i.e., " Darnley, Aubigny and Dalkeith, " Barony [S] *(Stuart),* cr
1580 with the Earldom of Lennox [S.] ; see " Lennox, " Dukedom [S.],
cr. 1581 ; *extinct* (with the Dukedom of Richmond) 1672.

---

i e., "Aubigny, Dalkeith, Torboltoun and Aberdour," Barony [S]
(Stuart), cr. 1581, with the Dukedom of Lennox [S], which see ; *extinct*
(with the Dukedom of Richmond) 1672.

AUCHINDOUN

i.e., " Badenoch, Lochaber, Strathavon, Balmore, Auchindoun,
Garthie and Kincardine, Barony [S.] *(Gordon),* cr 1684 with the
Dukedom of Gordon [S.], which see ; *extinct* 1836.

AUCHINLECK

See " Macartney of Parkhurst, Surrey, and of Auchinleck, in
the Stewartry of Kircudbright, " Barony *(Macartney),* cr 1796 ; *extinct*
with the Earldom of Macartney [I] 1806.

AUCHMOUTIE

i.e., " Auchmoutie and Caskieberry, " Barony [S] *(Leslie),* cr. 1680
with the Dukedom of Rothes [S.], which see ; *extinct* 1681.

AUCHTERHOUSE

i.e , " Auchterhouse, " Barony [S.] *(Stewart),* cr. 1469 with the
Earldom of Buchan [S], which see.

AUCKLAND

BARONY [I.] I. 1789. BARONY [G B.] I. 1793.	1. William Eden, 3rd s. of Sir Robert Eden, 3rd Bart of West Auckland, by Mary, yst. da of William Davison, of Beamish, co Durham, *b.* 1744, was ed. at Eton, and at Ch. Ch. Oxford ; B.A., 1765 ; M.A., 1768 ; Barrister (Mid. Temple) 1769 Auditor, and a Director, of Greenwich Hospital 1771 till death.

Under Sec. of State for the North 1772-78. M.P for
Woodstock, 1774-84 ; for Heytesbury, 1784-93; and for Dungannon [I.],

---

dame duchesse de Portsmouth et ledit sieur duc de Richemont et ses enfans masles
tiendront à foy et hommage de nous et de nostre couronne.... . Donné à Versailles
au mois de janvier l'an de grace mil six cent quatrevingt quatre et de nostre regne le
quarante uniesme. Signé Louis *(Anselme,* vol. v, p. 924)

1781-83. A Lord of Trade 1776-82. He accompanied the Earl of Carlisle, as a Commissioner, to North America in 1778, and, as Chief Secretary, to Ireland 1780-82. P.C. [I.] 23 Dec. 1780, and [G B.] 7 Apr. 1783. Joint Vice Treas. [I.] 1783-84. Envoy to France, on a special mission relating to commerce, 1785-87 ; F.R.S. 23 Mar. 1786. AMBASSADOR to Spain, 1787-89, and to the United Provinces, or Netherlands, 1789-93. On 18 Nov. 1789, he was *cr.* BARON AUCKLAND [I], (ª) and (within four years) on 22 May 1793, he was *cr.* BARON AUCKLAND of West Auckland, co Durham. [G B.] (ᵇ) Chanc. of Marischall Coll. Aberdeen, 1796-1814. Joint Postmaster Gen , 1798-1804 ; Pres. of Board of Trade 1806-7. He *m.*, 26 Sep. 1776, Eleanor, sister of Gilbert, 1st EARL OF MINTO, and yst. da. of the Rt. Hon. Sir Gilbert ELLIOT, 3rd Bart [S.], by Agnes, da. and h. of Hugh DALRYMPLE MURRAY KYNYNMOUND, of Melgund, co Forfar. He *d.* 28 May 1814, (ᶜ) suddenly, of spasms, at Eden Farm, Beckenham, Kent, aged 70. Will dat. 14 Mar. 1814, pr.

(ª) See note *sub* Richard, BARON PENRHYN [1783]

(ᵇ) The arms of Lord Auckland are Gules, a cheveron between three golden sheaves banded vert, with three scallops sable on the cheveron. (*ex inform* Oswald Barron.)   V G

(ᶜ) " He had been called to the Bar, but being a bad orator had made no figure there. . . . He possessed a most insinuating gentle manner, which cover'd a deeply intriguing and ambitious spirit." (William Knox, 1 June 1779, in *Hist. MSS. Com* , Various MSS , vol. vi, pp. 265-6).

" In person he rose above the ordinary height, his figure was elegant and wanted not grace. His countenance was thin and pale, his features regular and full of intelligence, his manners calm, polite and conciliating. There equally existed in Eden's physiognomy, even in his manner and deportment, something which did not convey the impression of plain dealing, or inspire confidence " *(Wraxall's Memoirs).* He was a shifty politician, originally a Tory, but supported the Coalition Govt., 1783-85, then deserted the Whigs and joined Pitt, who made him a member of the Council for affairs of trade, and (with a salary of £6000 *p.a.*) Envoy for concluding a commercial treaty with France. When he apologised to Lord North, saying that it was not a political change, but only a temporary affair of negotiation of trade, the reply was that his Lordship " always considered the whole transaction as a mere affair of trade " ! He was attacked by the authors of the *Rolliad* for his conduct at this time, one couplet running ·

" Will you give a place ? my dearest Billy Pitt, o !
  If I can't have a whole one, o give a little bit, o ! "

and another quatrain being—

" To all you young men who are famous for changing,
  From party to party continually ranging,
  I tell you the place of all places to breed in
  For maggots of corruption's the heart of Billy Eden."

" From his proficiency in the science of corruption, he was known in England by the name of the ' man-monger ' " (Lord Charlemont's *Memoirs*)   He held office in the Ministry of All the Talents (1806-7) and thereafter till his death acted with the Whigs, so that he was successively Tory, Whig, Tory again, Whig again ! In private life he was an agreeable companion and amiable man. His 2nd br was Governor of Maryland, and the 8th and yst. was *cr.* Baron Henley [I.].   V.G.

21 July following. His widow, who was *b.* 1758, *d* 18 May 1818, at Eden Farm, in her 60th year. Will pr. June 1818.

BARONY [G.B. & I.]	2 and 1. GEORGE (EDEN), BARON AUCKLAND [G.B.], and BARON AUCKLAND [I], 2nd, (ª) but 1st surv., s.
II. 1814.	and h , *b.* 25 Aug. 1784, at Beckenham, Kent. Ed. at Eton, and at Ch. Ch. Oxford , B.A., 1806 ; M A.,
EARLDOM	1808. Barrister (Linc. Inn) 1809. Deputy Teller of the Exchequer 1809-12. M.P. (Whig) for Wood-
I. 1839 to 1849.	stock, 1810-12, and 1813-14. Auditor of Greenwich Hospital 1814-29, and Commissioner thereof 1829-34. President of the Board of Trade and Master of the Mint (with a seat in the cabinet) Nov. 1830-34. P.C.

22 Nov. 1830. Auditor of the Exchequer, Jan. to Oct. 1834. First Lord of the Admiralty, June to Nov. 1834, Apr. to Sep. 1835, and 1846-49. G.C.B , (Civil) 29 Aug. 1835. GOVERNOR GEN. OF INDIA, 1835-41, during the disastrous Afghan war. (ᵇ)   On 21 Dec. 1839 he was *cr.* BARON EDEN of Norwood, Surrey, and EARL OF AUCKLAND. Pres. of the Roy. Asiatic Soc 1843 till his death. He *d.* unm., of a paralytic stroke, 1 Jan. 1849, (ᶜ) at the Grange, Hants (the seat of Lord Ashburton), aged 64, when THE BARONY OF EDEN OF NORWOOD and the EARLDOM OF AUCKLAND became *extinct.* Will pr. Feb. 1849.

BARONY [G.B. & I.].	3. ROBERT JOHN (EDEN), BARON AUCKLAND
III. 1849.	[G.B.], and BARON AUCKLAND [I.], as also BISHOP OF SODOR AND MAN, being yst. and only surv. br.

and h. (ᵈ) He was *b.* 10 July 1799; ed. at Magd. Coll., Cambridge. M.A. 1819, D.D. 1847. Vicar of Eyam, co. Derby, 1823 ; Rector of Herting-fordbury, Herts, 1825 ; Chaplain to William IV, 1831-37, to Victoria 1837-49, and Vicar of Battersea, Surrey, 1834. BISHOP OF SODOR AND

(ª) His elder br., William Frederick Elliot Eden, M P. for Woodstock, and Teller of the Exchequer, drowned himself in the Thames, 19 Jan. 1810. V.G.

(ᵇ) His impolicy in entering on this campaign was only equalled by his pusillanimity after our disasters had been incurred. V.G

(ᶜ) " He was a man without shining qualities or showy accomplishments, austere and almost forbidding in his manner, silent and reserved in society, unpretending in public and in private life, and in the H. of Lords taking a rare and modest part in debate. Nevertheless he was universally popular. . . . . His understanding was excellent, his temper placid, his taste and tact exquisite , his disposition, notwithstanding his apparent gravity, cheerful, and under his cold exterior there was a heart overflowing with human kindness, and with the deepest feelings of affection, charity and benevolence . . . He closed a useful, honourable and prosperous life, with his faculties unimpaired, leaving behind him a memory universally honoured and regretted." (Greville's *Memoirs,* 2 Jan. 1849). V.G.

(ᵈ) A grandson of his informs me that he was offered and refused to be placed in remainder to the Earldom at the time of its creation. Such "Tales of a Grandson " should as a rule be received with caution, but as this is the case of a bishop, it is reasonable to suppose that " such outward things dwelt not in his desires. " V.G.

Man, 1847-54, Bishop of Bath and Wells, 1854 to 1869, when he resigned that see. His signature during that period was "Auckland, Bath and Wells." In politics he was a Liberal He *m*, 15 Sep. 1825, Mary, 1st da. of Francis Edward Hurt, of Alderwasley, co. Derby, by Elizabeth, da. of Richard Arkwright, of Willesley, in that co. He *d*. 25 Apr. 1870, at the Bishop's Palace, Wells, Somerset, aged 70. His widow *d*. 25 Nov. 1872, at Wells, in her 67th year.

IV. 1870.   4. William George (Eden), Baron Auckland [G B.] and Baron Auckland [I.], 1st s. and h., *b*. 19 Jan. 1829 Ed. at Rugby school. Was attached to the legation at Stockholm, Nov. 1847 ; paid attaché at Washington, Feb 1852 , at Brussels, June 1852 ; at Stuttgart, Aug. 1853. Resident chargé d'affaires at Carlsruhe 1859 to Aug. 1861. His claim to the Peerage [I.] was allowed 21 June 1870. In politics he was a Liberal. (ª) He *m*., 1stly, 8 Oct. 1857, Lucy Walbanke, yst. da of John Walbanke Childers, of Cantley, co. York, by Anne, sister of Charles, 1st Viscount Halifax, and da. of Sir Francis Lindley Wood, of Barnsley, 2nd Bart. She *d*. 18 May 1870, at Carr House, Doncaster, aged 34. He *m*., 2ndly, 6 July 1872, at St. Margaret's, Westm , Mabel Emily, 2nd da of George James (Finch-Hatton), 10th Earl of Winchilsea, by Constance Henrietta, da of Henry (Paget), 2nd Marquess of Anglesey. She *d*. *s p*., 6 Nov. following, at Carr House, Doncaster. He *m* , 3rdly, 20 July 1875, at Merrington, his cousin, Edith, yst da of Sir William Eden, 9th Bart., by Elfrida Susannah Harriet, 3rd and yst. da of William Iremonger, of Wherwell, Hants. He *d*. 17 Feb. 1890, at Edenthorpe, co. York, aged 61 Personalty £114,212. His widow *m*., 10 June 1897, at St. James's, Dover, Philip Symons, of the Grange, in Seal, Kent.

V. 1890   5. William Morton (Eden), Baron Auckland [1793], also Baron Auckland [I. 1789], 1st s and h., by 1st wife, *b*. 27 Mar. 1859, at Frankfort-on-the-Maine ; sometime, 1880-91, an officer in the army, retiring as Captain. In politics he is a Conservative. He *m* , 2 Apr. 1891, at Gate Burton, co Lincoln, Sybil Constance, 1st da. of George Morland Hutton, C.B., of Gate Burton, afsd., by Eustace Emma Millicent, only child of Eustace Arkwright.

[William Alfred Morton Eden, 1st s. and h ap., *b*. 15 June 1892.]

Family Estates.—The Edenthorpe property near Doncaster, between 3000 and 4000 acres, was sold in 1897 for £75,000

AUDLEY or ALDITHLEY (of Heleigh) (ᵇ)

[The following short notice of the earlier members of this family, who may have been feudal Barons, is subjoined.]

(ª) He remained an Unionist at the break up of the Liberal party on the Home Rule question in 1886. V.G.

(ᵇ) The description given in *Courthope* and in other Peerages of this family is

1. Henry of Aldithley, ([a]) 2nd ([b]) s. of Adam ([c]) of A., (who *d.* between 1203 and 1211) by Emma, da. of Ralf fitz Orm; was *b.* about 1175; with his father, he was witness to a charter of Harvey Bagot in 1194. He bought large estates from Eleanor Malbank in 1214; in 1227 he acquired the manors of Edgmund and Newport, and in 1230 that of Ford, all in Salop, and all held by him direct from the Crown, though not by military or knight service. ([d]) He was Under Sheriff of Salop and co. Stafford 1217-20, and Sheriff 1227-32; was in command of the Welsh Marches 1223-46. He built the castle of Heleigh, co. Stafford; and Red Castle, Salop. In 1223 he founded Hulton Abbey. He was appointed Custodian of Chester and Beeston Castle, 22 June 1237, on the extinction of the then earldom of Chester. He *m.*, in 1217, Bertred, da. of Ralf Mainwaring, Seneschal of Chester. He *d.* in 1246, shortly before Nov. His widow was living in 1249.

2. James of Aldithley, 1st or 2nd ([e]) s. and h., *b.* about 1220. Keeper of the castle of Newcastle-under-Lyme, 30 Oct. 1250. He joined in a letter of the Barons to the Pope in 1258. Witnessed, as one of the King's sworn Council, the confirmation by Henry III of the Provisions of Oxford, 1258; Lord Marcher; Sheriff of Salop, and co. Staff.,

---

very erroneous. This article has been re-written with the kind help of Josiah Wedgwood M.P. For further information on the Audleys see his valuable account in *Hist. Coll. Staff.* vol. ix, N.S., pp. 245-68. See also *Order of the Garter*, by G.F.Beltz, Lancaster Herald, 1841, p. 81; Nichols' *Herald and Genealogist*, 1870, vol. v, p. 63; J.H.Round's *Peerage and Pedigree*; and *Genealogist*, O.S., vol. vi, pp. 16-19, in connection with the Lords Martin. V.G.

([a]) Henry of Aldithley seals in 1233 with a shield of Fretty, with a quarter charged with a cross formy. His son and heir, James, and his heirs after him, bore Gules fretted with gold, the quarter and the cross disappearing. The fret is derived from the arms of the Verdons, over-lords of the earlier Audleys. Hugh Audley, of Stratton Audley, differenced the arms of his father with a blue label. Hugh Audley, Earl of Gloucester, would seem to have borne a silver border as his difference. The Tuchets, Lords Audley, quartered the arms of Audley with Ermine, a cheveron gules. Thicknesse, the last heir of the old Audley barony, bore, for Thicknesse, Silver, a cheveron sable, fretted gold, with a scythe-blade gules in the chief. (*ex inform.* Oswald Barron.) V.G.

([b]) His elder br. Adam, who was sometime constable to Hugh (de Lacy), Earl of Ulster [I.], *d. s.p.* in or shortly before 1212, having surv. his father. V.G.

([c]) This Adam appears to have been s. of Liulf, s. of Liulf, who had a grant of the manors of Aldithley (or Audley), Talke, &c. co. Staff. *temp.* Stephen, from Nicholas de Verdun. See *Charter Roll* of 1227, which disproves the allegation that this grant was made by Henry I to Adam, the supposed father of the last named Liulf. See J.H.Round's *Peerage and Pedigree*, where the matter is discussed. V.G.

([d]) There does not seem to be any evidence as to when, if ever, he became a Baron by tenure, and his ancestors of the 3 previous generations did not even hold any lands *in capite*, and were not Barons by tenure, though sometimes so described. V.G.

([e]) His br. (very possibly his elder br.) Ralf *d. v.p.* and *s.p.*, before 1240. V.G.

44

1261-62 and 1270-71 ; Justiciar of Ireland 1270-72. He took an active part on the King's side against the Barons, being in arms for the King on the Welsh Marches in 1264, and engaging in the Evesham campaign in 1265. He *m.* (*), in 1244, Ela, da. of William Longespée, often spoken of as Earl of Salisbury (who *d.* 1250), by Idoine, (*) da. and h. of Richard de Camville. She brought him the manors of Stratton, afterwards called Stratton Audley, and Wretchwick, Oxon, in frank marriage. He *d.* about 11 June (1272) 56 Hen. III, in Ireland, (*) by 'breaking his neck.' Writ for his *Inq. p. m.* 16 July 1272. His widow *d.* apparently shortly before 22 Nov. 1299. (*) *Inq. p. m.* (1325-26) 19 Edw. II.

3. James of Aldithley, s. and h., *b.* 1250. He *m.* Maud, but *d. s.p.*, in 1273. His widow had *Inq.* for dower 16 Jan. 1273/4. She *m.*, in 1274, John Deivill [Lord Deivill], and *d.* in 1276, a few days after her br.-in-law, Henry (next below), and before 22 Apr. 1276.

4. Henry of Aldithley, br. and h., *b.* 1251. He *m.* Lucy, but *d. s.p.*, in 1276. Writ for *Inq. p. m.* 22 Apr. (1276), 4 Edw. I. His widow *m.*, before 1281, Sir William Rithre [Lord Rithre]. She was living in 1303.

5. William of Aldithley, br. and h., *b.* 18 Oct. 1253. He *d. s.p.*, being slain in 1282, 11 Edw. I, in the Welsh expedition. Writ for *Inq. p. m.* 25 Dec. 1282.

6. Nicholas of Aldithley or Audley, br. and h., *b.* before 1258. On 26 Jan. (1296/7) 25 Edw. I, he was sum. to attend the King at Salisbury, but such summons cannot be considered as a regular writ of summons to Parl. (*) He *m.* Catherine, (*) da. of John Giffard, [1st Lord Giffard of Brimpsfield], by his 1st wife, Maud, widow of William Longespée, (sometimes regarded as Earl of Salisbury), da. and h. of Walter de Clifford. He *d.* 28 Aug. 1299. *Inq. p. m.*

(*) The grounds for the supposition that he *m.* a lady of unknown name, before Ela, which lady was mother of his 4 elder sons, a supposition which G.E.C., following Beltz, entertained, are that it would have been illegal for Ela to have enfeoffed his 5th s. Hugh in her manor of Stratton, which she did immediately after her husband's death, unless Hugh had been *her* eldest s. However it is clear that she did act in the way which Beltz regarded as illegal, and the apocryphal anonymous 1st wife may be disregarded, for the date of James' marriage to Ela is now known, and various Audley *Inqs.* show that none of his sons were *b.* before 1249. V.G.

(*) For some discussion on mediæval English names, see vol. iii, Appendix C. V.G.

(*) His yst. s., Hugh A., was sum. to Parl. 1321; see *sub* Audley (of Stratton Audley).

(*) *Patent Rolls.*

(*) See Preface, *circa finem.*

(*) See her pedigree from the Plea Rolls in *Coll. Top. et Gen.*, vol. i, p. 129.

27 Edw. I. His widow, who was *b.* 1272, had dower 23 Oct. 1299 ; she was living in 1322, as a nun at Ledbury.

7. Thomas of Aldithley or Audley, s. and h., *b.* 1288, was aged over 10 at his father's death. He *m.* Eve, da. and h. of John of Clavering [2nd Lord Clavering], by Hawise, da. of Robert de Tibetot. He *d. s.p.*, while still a minor, between 8 July and 14 Dec. 1307. Writ for *Inq. p. m.* 16 Jan. 1307/8. His widow *m.*, 2ndly, before 2 Dec. 1308, Sir Thomas de Ufford, who was slain at Bannockburn 24 June 1314. After his death she lived with, but did not marry, (possibly owing to some difficulty in obtaining a dispensation ; or to avoid the fine which she would have had to pay on marriage) Sir James Audley, (a) (who *d.* 1333/4) 1st cousin of her 1st husband. She *m.*, finally, Robert of Benhale, [Lord Benhale].

BARONY　　　1. Nicholas Audley or Aldithley, of Heleigh, co.
BY WRIT　　Stafford, br. and h., *b.* 11 Nov. 1289. He had seizin of
I. 1313.　　his brother's lands, having proved his age 27 Mar. 1313/4.
He was *sum.* to Parl. by writs directed *Nicholao de Audele*, 8 Jan. (1312/3) 6 Edw. II to 25 Aug. (1318) 12 Edw. II (b) whereby he may be held to have become LORD AUDLEY. He *m.*, in 1312, without lic., Joan, widow of Henry, Earl of Lincoln, the only child that had issue of William Martin [Lord Martin], by Eleanor, widow of John de Mohun, of Dunster, da. of Sir Reynold Fitz Piers. He *d.* in 1316, shortly before 9 Dec., aged 27. *Inq. p. m.* 1317, 10 Edw. II. His widow *d.* between Feb. 1319/20 and 1 Aug. 1322.

II. 1316.　　　2. James (Audley or Aldithley), Lord Audley, s.
and h., *b.* 8 Jan. 1312/3, at Knesale, co. Notts, and bap. there ; aged 3 at his father's death, and 14 in 1326, at the death of his maternal uncle, William Martin, to whose vast estates in cos. Pembroke and Devon he was coh., and eventually (by the death, in 1343, of his mother's sister, Eleanor, widow of Philip, Lord Columbers) sole heir, and would then apparently have been entitled to any Peerage which his afsd. uncle may be held to have possessed. He had seisin, though not of age, 25 May 1329. Though still a minor, 21 Mar. 1333/4, he was *sum.* to Parl. as early as 25 Jan. 1329/30 to 8 Aug. 1386. An order for his arrest issued on 28 July 1348 because he had not attended the King and Council when summoned. He had exemption for life from attending Parl. 20 Apr. 1353. He *m.*, 1stly, before 13 June 1330, Joan, da. of Roger (Mortimer), 1st Earl of March, by Joan, da. of Piers de Joinville, which Earl had been his guardian. She *d.* between 1337 and 1351. He *m.*, 2ndly, before Dec. 1351, Isabel, said to have been da. of Roger (le Strange) 5th Baron

---

(a) See *post*, p. 348, note " a. "
(b) As to how far these early writs of sum. did in fact *cr.* any peerage title see last vol., Appendix A. V.G.

STRANGE OF KNOKYN ([a]) She was living in 1366 He *d.* 1 Apr. 1386, at Heleigh, and was *bur.* at Hulton Abbey, aged 73. Will, in which he styles himself " Lord of Rouge Chastel [*i.e.* Red Castle, Salop] and of Heleigh, " dat. (1385) 9 Ric. II.

III. 1386
to
1391.

3. NICHOLAS (AUDLEY or ALDITHLEY), LORD AUDLEY [and, as some may consider, LORD MARTIN], s. and h. by 1st wife, *b.* about 1328. He was knighted before 1352, and in 1352 was in arms, with his next br. Roger, against their father, when they sacked Castle Heleigh. He was in the wars with France *(v.p.)*, 1359 and 1372, and was afterwards Chief Justice of South Wales, 1 Feb. 1381/2. He was sum. to Parl. 17 Dec. 1387 to 12 Dec. 1390. He *m.* (settl. (1329/30-1330/1) 5 Edw. III, both being then under 12) ([b]) Elizabeth, da. of Henry (BEAUMONT), LORD BEAUMONT, by Alice, *suo jure* COUNTESS OF BUCHAN [S.]. He *d. s.p.*, 22 July 1391, (Writ for *Inq. p. m.* 30 July 1391) when the BARONY OF AUDLEY, together, apparently, with the BARONY OF MARTIN, fell (in accordance with modern doctrine) into *abeyance* between his sisters or their descendants. ([c]) Will dat. the year of his death. His widow *d.* 27 Oct. 1400 *Inq. p. m.* 1400-1. Her will, in which she directs to be *bur.* in Hulton Abbey, with my very honourable husband Lord D'Audeley, dat. 30 Sep. and pr. 2 Nov. of the same year

IV. 1405.

4. JOHN TUCHET, great nephew and coh., being s. and h. of John T., who was s. and h. of Sir John Tuchet of Markeaton, co. Derby, (slain at Rochelle, 1371), by Joan, sister of the whole blood of Nicholas, 3rd Lord Audley. He was *b.* 23 Apr. 1371, and was 20 years old at the death of his said great uncle, in 1391, to whom he was found one of his next heirs He was in the Welsh wars against Glendower, and was sum. to Parl. as a Baron [LORD AUDLEY] 21 Dec. 1405 to 26 Aug. 1408, ([d]) whereby the *abeyance* of the Barony of Audley was probably *terminated* in his favour ; the writ was, however, directed

---

([a]) The present Editor can find no evidence for the statement that James Audley *m.* 2ndly " Isabell, da. and coh. of William Malbank, usually called Baron of Wich Malbank, " indeed the Malbank Barony had ended in coheirs more than 100 years before. V G.

([b]) He must have been the merest baby, for his father was not *b.* till 1312/3

([c]) These were (1) John Tuchet, his great nephew, by Joan his sister of the whole blood, as mentioned in the text (2) Margery, his other sister of the whole blood, then aged 40, and the wife, in or before 1353, of Sir Roger Hillary, but who *d. s.p.* in 1410/1, and (3) " Fulk, s of Fulk Fitz-Warin, s. of [another] Margery, half sister of the said Nicholas. " Thomas, Rowland, and James Audley, brothers of the whole blood of the last named Margery, all *d. s p.* in their half-brother's life time. In *Close Roll,* 31 Edw. III, *m.* 17d, mention is made of Katharine, da. of Sir James Audley of Rouge Chastel and Heleye, wife of Thomas Spigurnel. She therefore must have been another sister or half sister of Nicholas, Lord Audley, but must have *d v.f* and *s.p.* V.G.

([d]) There is proof in the rolls of Parl. of his sitting.

(merely) *Johanni Tuchet* (LORD TUCHET ?). He *m.* Isabel, who was living June 1405. He *d.* 19 Dec. 1408, aged about 38

V. 1408.   5. James (Tuchet), Lord Audley, s. and h., aged ten
                years in 1408 He was sum. to Parl. 26 Feb. 1420/1 to
26 May 1455, (ᵃ) the writs being directed *Jacobo de Audley*. Chief
Justice of South Wales 17 Nov. 1423. Chamberlain of S. Wales 11 Feb.
1438/9, and again 24 Oct. 1441. He distinguished himself in the wars
with France, having the chief command of some forces in 1430. On
26 Oct. 1447, he had exemption for life, as James Tuchete, Lord of Audley, from attendance in Parl (ᵇ) Having raised 10,000 men on behalf of
Henry VI, he was defeated and slain by the Yorkists at the battle of Blore
Heath, Salop. (ᶜ) He *m.*, 1stly, Margaret, da. of William (Roos), Lord
Roos, by Margaret, da. of John (Arundel), Lord Arundel (Papal Disp
6 Kal. Mar. 1415, to him to remain in marriage contracted but not consummated). She was living 15 Kal. Sep. 1423. He *m*, 2ndly, (Papal
Disp. to remain in marriage contracted but not consummated, though
related in the 3rd degree, dat 16 Kal. Mar. 1429/30) Eleanor, illegit. da.
of Thomas (Holand), Earl of Kent, by Constance, da. of Edmund, (ᵈ)
Duke of York, but, according to Mills' *Catalogue of Honour* (1610), she
was da. of Edmund Holand, by Elizabeth, widow of Edward (le Despenser), Lord Despenser, da. and h. of Bartholomew (Burghersh), Lord
Burghersh. (ᵉ) He *d.* (as afsd.) 23 Sep. 1459, aged about 61. (ᶠ)

VI 1459.   6. John (Tuchet), Lord Audley, s. and h. by 1st
                wife, who, in consideration of his father's services, had a
spec. livery of his lands (1459-60), 38 Hen. VI, without proof of age. He
was taken prisoner at Calais next year, where he joined the party of

---

(ᵃ) See note " d " on previous page.
(ᵇ) *Cal. Patent Rolls*, 1446-1452, p. 113. He must have been under 50 when
he obtained this exemption, and it suggests that attendance in the House of Lords was
then still regarded, at it previously had been, not as a privilege, but as a burdensome
obligation. V.G.
(ᶜ) He was slain by Sir Roger Kynaston, of Hordley, who took his arms, Ermine
a cheveron gules, ever after borne by that branch of the Kynastons. V.G.
(ᵈ) As to his supposed surname of ' Plantagenet, ' see *ante*, p. 183, note " c. "
(ᵉ) See *N. & Q.*, 4th Ser., vol iii, p 608 But see, also, Sandford's *Genealogical History*, 1707, p. 379, wherein it is stated that Constance of York " was the
paramour of Edmond Holand, Earl of Kent, by whom she had been so long courted
that at last she brought him a da. named Eleanor, *m.* to James Touchet, Lord
Audley, of which family the Audleys of Norfolk were descended. Which Eleanor
would fain have made herself legitimate, but the right heirs preferred their bill in
Parl thereby proving her to be a bastard, as you may see in Polton's printed statutes,
anno 9 Hen. VI, *cap.* xi. "
(ᶠ) His sons by his 2nd wife took the name of Audley. These were (1) Sir
Humphrey A , slain at Tewkesbury 1471, said to be ancestor of the Audley family
of Norfolk ; and (2) Edmund Audley, Bishop of Rochester 1480, of Hereford 1493,
and of Salisbury 1502, who *d.* 23 Aug. 1524.

Edward IV, with whom he was in great esteem. He was sum. to Parl.
26 May 1461 to 9 Dec. 1483, (ª) the writs being directed to *Johanni
de Audley*. Master of the King's Dogs, 5 July 1471. P.C 1471,
obtaining a grant of £100 a year, and being joint Commander of the army.
He was sent into Britanny, 1475, and was one of the 35 peers (ᵇ) at the
Coronation of Ric. III, who made him LORD TREASURER, 1484. He *m.*,
before 1456, Anne, widow of John ROGERS, of Bryanston, Dorset, (who
d. Aug. 1450) da and coh. (ᶜ) of Sir Thomas ECHINGHAM, probably
by his 2nd wife, Margaret, da. of John KNYVETT (senior). He *d.* 26 Sep.
1490 *Inq. p. m.* 26 Oct. 1490. His widow *d.* 7 May 1498, and was *bur.*
in Bermondsey monastery. Will dat. 11 Nov. 1497, pr. 24 June 1498 by
Henry Rogers, s. and executor.

VII. 1490   7. JAMES (TUCHET), LORD AUDLEY, s and h., K.B.,
to   having been so *cr.* at the creation of the Prince of Wales,
1497.   18 Apr. 1475, aged 27 at his father's death. He was
        sum. to Parl 12 Aug. 1492 to 16 Jan. 1496/7. (ª) He,
however, joined in the Cornish insurrection, was taken prisoner, 24, and
beheaded 28 June 1497, on Tower Hill, being *bur.* in the Blackfriars ; when
his *peerage* became *forfeited.* He *m.*, 1stly, in or before 1483, Margaret,
da. of Sir Richard DAYRELL, of Lillingstone Dayrell, Bucks, by Margaret,
widow of Humphrey STAFFORD, *styled* EARL OF STAFFORD, da. and coh. of
Edmund (BEAUFORT), DUKE OF SOMERSET. He *m* , 2ndly, at or before
Mich. 1488, Joan, da of Fulk (BOURCHIER), LORD FITZ-WARINE, by
Elizabeth, da. of Sir John DYNHAM. His widow *d.* 3 Mar. 1532. (ᵈ)

VIII. 1512.   8. JOHN TUCHET, s. and h. by 1st wife, Margaret,
        aged 6 years and no more, 6 Aug 1489, when he was h.
to his maternal grandfather   He was *restored* in blood and honours, 1512
(as LORD AUDLEY), and attended the King next year in the French
war.   He was sum. to Parl. 23 Nov. 1514 to 21 Oct 1556 (ᵉ)   He *m.*
Mary, da. of John GRIFFIN, of Braybroke, Northants, by Emmote, da. of
Richard WHEATHILL, of Calais (ᶠ)   He *d.* before 20 Jan. 1557/8.

(ª) There is proof in the rolls of Parl. of his sitting.

(ᵇ) See note *sub* Humphrey, LORD DACRE OF GILLESLAND [1473], for a list of these.

(ᶜ) *Misc. Gen. et Her* , 1st Ser., vol. 1, p 258.

(ᵈ) Her s. and h., John, aged about 7 at his father's death in 1497, who has
been confused with his elder br. of the half blood, John, who was *b.* 1483, had livery
of her lands (1533-34) 25 Hen. VIII.   V.G.

(ᵉ) The name of *John* Tuchet, Lord Audley, is improperly continued in
Dugdale's *Lists of Summons* until 23 Jan (1558/9), 1 Eliz.

(ᶠ) According to the Visit of Dorset, 1565, he *m* Katherine, da. of John
Dackombe, of Stapleton, Dorset, by Eleanor, da. of Gregory Morgan, of Chitterne,
Wilts.   According to the Visit. of co. Warwick, 1619, Elizabeth, da. of Sir John
Danvers, of Dauntsey, Wilts, by Anne, sister and h. of Sir Edward Stradling, *m.*,
1stly, (—) Borrowes [*i.e* John Abarrow, who, with her, was living 20 Nov. 1539,
the date of her mother's will] and 2ndly, 'Dominus Audley '   No such match,
however, appears in the Audley pedigree, though in 7 Hen. VIII there is an *Inq. p m.*
on *Katherine* Audley.   V.G.

IX. 1557 ?   9. GEORGE (TUCHET), LORD AUDLEY, s. and h., sum.
                      to Parl. and took his seat the same day, 20 Jan. 1557/8 ([a])
He *m.*, 1stly, Elizabeth, da of Sir Brian TUKE, Treasurer of the Chamber to
Henry VIII, by Grizel, da. of Nicholas BOUGHTON, of Woolwich ([b])   He
m., 2ndly, 23 Jan. 1559/60, at his Oratory in Chester, (Lic Bp. of
London, 22 Jan. 1559/60) Joan PLATT, of St. Andrew's, Eastcheap, London,
widow.   He was *bur.* 3 July 1560, at St. Margaret's, Westm.   Admon.
9 Sep. 1560 to Joan, the relict.

X. 1560.   10. HENRY (TUCHET), LORD AUDLEY, s. and h. by 1st
                    wife.   He was never sum. to Parl   He *m* Elizabeth,
da. of Sir William SNEYD, of Bradwell, co. Stafford, by his 1st wife, Anne,
da and h. of Thomas BARROWE, of Flookersbrooke, co. Chester.   He *d.*
30 Dec. 1563, and was *bur.* 5 Jan. 1563/4, at Betley.   His widow *d.* at
Thelwall, co Chester, Dec 1609, and was *bur.* 4 Jan. 1609/10, at Grappen-
hall, in that co.

XI. 1563.   11. GEORGE (TUCHET), LORD AUDLEY, s. and
                    h., sum. to Parl. 30 Sep 1566 to 5 Apr. 1614.
On 6 Sep. 1616 he was *cr.* BARON AUDLEY OF ORIER, co.
Armagh, and EARL OF CASTLEHAVEN, co. Cork [I.]   He
d. 1617.

XII. 1617   12. MERVIN (TUCHET), EARL OF CASTLEHAVEN,
      to   *&c.* [I] ; also LORD AUDLEY [E.], s. and h.   He
      1631.   was attainted of felony and *beheaded*, 14 May
                     1631, when his English Peerage (being descendible
to *heirs gen.*) became *forfeited*, and the Irish titles (though *in tail*)
appear (in error) to have been likewise so considered ([c])

[I 1633]   13 JAMES (TUCHET), EARL OF CASTLEHAVEN [I.],
XIII. 1678.   *&c.*, s. and h., BARON AUDLEY OF HELY [E.], to
                     him and his heirs for ever, by letters patent 3 June
1633, with the 'place and precedency of George, his grandfather,
formerly Baron Audley of Hely.' ([d])   After this restoration he
was allowed in the House of Lords the precedency of the *ancient
Barony of Audley*, but such allowance appears to have been made in
error, as the Crown *(alone)* has not the power of restoring a forfeited Peerage, and " it is clear that in former instances it had been
considered that the authority of the Legislature was necessary to
restore a dignity lost by attainder."   This authority was accordingly

(right margin, rotated:) "CASTLEHAVEN," Earldom of [I.], *cr.* 1617; *extinct* 1777. For fuller particulars see

---

([a]) There is proof in the rolls of Parl. of his sitting
([b]) Query if she be not the ' *Isabel* Audley ' *bur.* 28 June 1554, at St. Margaret's, Westm.   V G.
([c]) See *Courthope*, p. lxviii, in the *Observations on Dignities*, where, however, it is
erroneously stated that his s and h. was again *cr* Earl of Castlehaven [I].   See note
sub George, EARL OF CASTLEHAVEN [1616].
([d]) See App. to 47th Rep., Dep. Keeper of Records.

afterwards obtained, and it was enacted by Act of Parl. (29 and 30 Car. II) 1678, that " the said James Lord Audley, Baron Audley of Hely, Earl of Castlehaven, and the heirs of his body begotten, and immediately after them, Mervin Tuchet, 3rd son of the said Mervin Lord Audley, and the heirs of his body begotten, and after them, then the daughters of the said Mervin Lord Audley and their heirs, shall and may from henceforth have, hold, and enjoy, and shall be and are hereby restored unto the honour, dignity, state, authority, and title of Baron Audley of Hely, with all and every the privileges, rights, precedencies, and pre-eminences thereunto belonging, as fully, amply, and honourably to all intents and purposes as the said Mervin Lord Audley at any time or George, Lord Audley, father of Mervin, at any time during his life, did or might hold and enjoy the same, any matter, cause, or thing whatsoever to the contrary notwithstanding, and as fully, amply, and honourably as if George Tuchet, ([a]) 2nd son of the said Mervin Lord Audley, now beyond the seas, were naturally dead without issue. " ([b])　He *d. s.p.* 11 Oct. 1684.

XIV. 1684.　　　14. MERVIN (TUCHET), EARL OF CASTLEHAVEN, &c. [I], and LORD AUDLEY [E.], br. and h.　He *d.* 2 Nov. 1686.

XV. 1686.　　　15. JAMES (TUCHET), EARL OF CASTLEHAVEN, &c. [I.], and LORD AUDLEY [E.], s. and h.　He *d.* 12 Aug. 1700.

XVI. 1700.　　　16. JAMES (TUCHET), EARL OF CASTLEHAVEN, &c. [I.], and LORD AUDLEY [E.], s. and h.　He *d.* 12 Oct. 1740.

XVII. 1740.　　　17. JAMES (TOUCHET), EARL OF CASTLEHAVEN, &c. [I.], and LORD AUDLEY [E.], s. and h.　He *d.* unm. 8 May 1769.

XVIII. 1769.　　　18. JOHN TALBOT (TUCHET), EARL OF CASTLE-HAVEN, &c. [I.], and LORD AUDLEY [E.], br. and h. He *d. s.p.*, 22 Apr. 1777, when his Irish Peerage dignities (as well as any that might have been created *de novo* by the patent of 3 June 1634) became *extinct*, the English Barony by writ (1312) devolving as below.

XIX. 1777.　　　19. GEORGE THICKNESSE (afterwards THICKNESSE-TOU-CHET), LORD AUDLEY, nephew and h., being 1st surv. s. of Philip THICKNESSE, of Farthinghoe, Northants, Capt. in the army, and Lieut.

For fuller particulars see " CASTLEHAVEN," Earldom of [I.], cr. 1617, *extinct* 1777.

([a]) This exception was doubtless because George was a Benedictine Monk.
([b]) See *Courthope*, p. 36, and *4th Report on the dignity of a Peer*, pp. 318, 331-334. The reversal of the attainder applies only to the issue of Mervin, the 12th Lord, failing which the Barony would again become *forfeited*.

Gov. of Languard Fort, Suffolk, ([a]) by the 2nd of his 3 wives, Elizabeth, ([b])
only sister of the last two Barons abovenamed, and da of James (TUCHET),
5th EARL OF CASTLEHAVEN, &c [I], LORD AUDLEY. He was *b.* 4 Feb.
1758. Ensign 2nd Reg. of Foot. By Royal lic., 3 Apr. 1784, he took
the name of *Touchet* after that of *Thicknesse* In politics he was a Whig.
He *m.*, 1stly, 21 May 1781, at her father's house in Hanover Sq , Elizabeth, 2nd da and coh of Sir John Hussey DELAVAL, Bart., afterwards
LORD DELAVAL [I. and G.B.], by his 1st wife, Susannah, da of R ROBINSON
She *d.* 11 July 1785, at Sandridge Lodge, near Melksham, and was *bur*
there. He *m.*, 2ndly, 2 May 1792, Augusta Henrietta Catherina, widow
of Col. MOORHOUSE, ([c]) 2nd and yst. da. and coh of the Rev André
BOISDAUNE, by Elizabeth, 2nd da. of Edward STRODE, of Southhill, Somerset
He *d.* 24 Aug. 1818, at Sandridge Lodge afsd., and was *bur* at Melksham,
aged 60. Admon. Apr. 1819. His widow *d.* Apr. 1844, aged 82, at
Sidmouth. Will pr. May 1844.

XX. 1818.   20. GEORGE JOHN (THICKNESSE-TOUCHET), LORD AUD-
          LEY, s. and h. by 1st wife, *b* 23 Jan 1783   Ed. at Eton
In politics he was a Whig. He *m* , 18 Apr. 1816, at Brussels, Anne Jane,
1st da. of Vice Admiral Sir Ross DONELLY, K.C B   He *d* 14, and was
bur. 23 Jan. 1837, at Melksham, aged nearly 54. His widow *d* 18 Aug
1855, at Dover

XXI. 1837   21. GEORGE EDWARD (THICKNESSE-TOUCHET), LORD
    to   AUDLEY, s. and h., ([d]) *b.* 26 Jan. 1817. In politics he
   1872.   was a Liberal. He *m.*, 1stly, 16 Apr. 1857, at St Mark's,

---

([a]) This eccentric character *m.*, 3rdly, 27 Sep. 1762, Anne, da. of Thomas
Ford, Clerk of the Arraigns, by whom also he had issue, and *d.* 23 Nov. 1792, and
was *bur* at Boulogne. See his M.I. in *N. & Q.*, 9th Ser , vol. ii, p 341. In his
will, pr. 24 Jan. 1793, he desires his right hand to be cut off and sent to his s , Lord
Audley, to "remind him of his duty to God, after having so long abandoned the duty
he owed to a father, who once affectionately loved him" He appears, however, to
have been a vile rascal, and to have swindled his s , to annoy whom he put up this
notice on a board at Bath —"Boots and shoes mended, carpets beat &c , by P
Thicknesse, father of Lord Audley " See *Historic Houses in Bath*   V G
([b]) She *m.* 10 May 1749, and *d* (30 years before her husband) 28 Mar. 1762.
([c]) "Have you heard Lady Audley's first husband Mr Moorhouse is risen from
the dead, and returned to claim his wife, or at least his money ? and as Lord A.
married her for that, probably he will beg leave to part with both at once. Instead
of being killed in the E. Indies he was taken prisoner, and has been exchanged,
or made his escape lately. At least this is the story. I do not vouch for the truth
of a single syllable of it. (M J Holroyd, letter of 11 Dec. 1795) No confirmation
of this "Enoch Arden " tale has been discovered. V.G.
([d]) Of his 3 brothers, (1) John, *b* 8 Nov. 1819, sometime an officer in the
army, *m* , 6 Sep 1842, Elizabeth, 3rd da of John Henry Blennerhasset, of co. Kerry,
and *d.* 21 July 1861, of delirium tremens, in the Infirmary, Cork, leaving a s and h ,
George John, *b.* 27 Apr. 1847, who *d* , under age and unm., 11 Nov. 1866.
(2) William Ross, *b.* 23 Nov 1821, *d.* presumably unm., and long before 1900.
(3) James, *b.* 1825, *d.* an infant. V.G.

Darling Point, Sydney, Emily, 2nd da. of Sir Thomas Livingstone Mitchell, D.C.L. (the eminent Geographer), by (—) da of Gen. Richard
Blunt, Col of the 66th Foot. She *d* 1 Apr. 1860, aged 31 He *m.*,
2ndly, 15 Feb. 1868, at All Saints, Paddington, Midx., Margaret Anne,
widow of James Willing Smith, of Gloucester Sq., Paddington, and sister
of the Rev. Thomas Dawson Hudson, of Frogmore Hall, Herts He *d.*
s.p.m., 18 Apr. 1872, at Homburg, in his 55th year, and was *bur* at Frankfort-on-the-Maine, leaving, by his 1st wife, two daughters (ª) and coheirs,
between whom the Barony fell *in abeyance.* His widow *d.* 22 Aug. 1888,
at 15 Gloucester Sq. Will pr. 29 Sep 1888, above £154,000.

AUDLEY OF HELY

i.e., "Audley of Hely," Barony *(Tuchet)*, *cr.* 1633. See "Audley,"
Barony, *cr.* 1313 under the 13th holder ; *extinct*, with the Earldom of
Castlehaven [I.], 1777.

AUDLEY or ALDITHLEY

BARONY
BY WRIT.

I. 1317.

1. Hugh Audley or Aldithley *(junior)*, 2nd s. of
Hugh A , who, *afterwards (viz.* in 1321), was also sum.
to Parl., by Isolt, (ᵇ) da. of Edmund de Mortimer, of
Wigmore, was *b. c.* 1289. He was sum *v.p* , to Parl.
20 Nov.(1317) 11 Edw. II to 15 May (1321) 14 Edw II, by writs directed
Hugoni Daudele juniori. He was with his father in the insurrection of
1321/2, (ᶜ) but was pardoned. He was also sum to Parl. 3 Dec 1326 to
24 Aug. 1336, by writs directed *Hugoni de Audele* (only), his father having
died in 1325, or early in 1326. In 1336 he was in the King's service
in Scotland, and on 16 Mar. 1336/7 he was *cr.* EARL OF GLOU-
CESTER, his wife having, in 1313, become coh to her br. Gilbert, Earl
of Gloucester and Hertford In 1341 he was Ambassador to France
He *m.*, 28 Apr. 1317, at Windsor, Margaret, (ᵈ) widow of Piers (Gavaston), Earl of Cornwall, 2nd da. of Gilbert (de Clare), Earl of
Gloucester and Hertford, by Joan, da. of King Edward I. She, who
was found to be aged 22 in her brother's *Inq. p. m.* of 12 Oct. (1314)
8 Edw II, *d.* Apr. 1342, before Easter. *Inq. p. m.* 1342-3. He himself
d. s.p.m., 10 Nov. 1347, and was *bur.* in the priory of Tunbridge, when,
"although the dignity [of the Earldom of Gloucester] was to him and his
heirs, the title appears to have been considered as *extinct.*" (ᵉ)

(ª) *Viz* , Mary, *b.* 13 Aug. 1858, and Emily, *b.* 29 Nov. 1859, both (1910)
unmarried

(ᵇ) For some discussion on mediæval English names see vol. iii, Appendix C. V.G.

(ᶜ) For an account of the battle of Boroughbridge, 16 Mar. 1321/2, see
vol. ii, Appendix C V G.

(ᵈ) In 1316 she is called " Comitissa Gloucestrie et Hertfordie " *(Feudal
Aids).* V G

(ᵉ) See *Courthope*, p 241

II. 1347.   2. MARGARET, *de jure*, apparently *suo jure* BARON-
ESS AUDLEY, da. and h., *m*, probably in 1335/6,
Ralph STAFFORD, afterwards LORD STAFFORD and EARL OF STAFFORD.
She *d.* between 1347/8 and 1350/1. He *d.* 31 Aug. 1372.

III. 1350.   3. SIR RALPH STAFFORD, *de jure* LORD AUDLEY,
s. and h. of his mother He *d s p*, *v p.*, about
1358.

IV. 1358 ?   4. HUGH (STAFFORD), *de jure* LORD AUDLEY,
br. and h On 31 Aug. 1372, being then aged
28 years, he *suc.* his father as EARL OF STAFFORD, &c, with which
titles the BARONY OF AUDLEY is presumed to have been *merged*, till, on
the attainder in 1483 of Henry (Stafford), 2nd Duke of Buckingham (and 7th Earl Stafford), it was *forfeited*, and though his son, in
1486, was restored to all his father's honours, they were *again
forfeited*, in 1521, on the attainder of that Nobleman

For fuller account see " STAFFORD," Earldom, cr. 1351, forfeited 1521.

AUDLEY (of Stratton Audley)

BARONY
BY WRIT.

I. 1321
to
1325
or
1326

1 HUGH AUDLEY, of Stratton Audley, Oxon, yst. s.
of James Audley or Aldithley, of Heleigh, co Stafford, (ª)
by Ela, da. of William LONGESPÉE; was *b c.* 1267, and obtained from his mother, soon after her husband's death, a
reversionary grant, (1272-73) 1 Edw. I, of Stratton Audley, afsd, which had been her inheritance. (ᵇ) He was in
the French wars, 1294, &c; a prisoner in France 2 Apr
1299; in the Scottish wars, 1299-1302, and again 1313;
he was in Gascony in 1304/5; Justice of North Wales 1306; and was
Governor of Montgomery Castle, 1309. He was sum. to Parl. 15 May
(1321) 14 Edw. II, the writ being directed *Hugoni de Audele seniori*, to
distinguish him from his 2nd s., Hugh Audley, *Junior*, who had been so
sum in 1317.(ᶜ) In 1321/2 he joined the insurrection of the Earl of
Lancaster, but surrendered before the battle of Boroughbridge, 16 Mar
1321/2, (ᵈ) and was confined in Wallingford Castle. He *m*, before 7 Jan
1293, and probably in 1288, Isolt, widow of Sir Walter DE BALUN, of Much
Marcle, co. Hereford (who was living and *m.* to her in 1286/7), da of Sir
Edmund DE MORTIMER, (ᵉ) of Wigmore, co. Hereford, by Margaret, da
of Sir William DE FIENNES She brought him the manors of Eastington,

---

(ª) See *ante*, p. 337.
(ᵇ) See *ante*, p. 338, note " a. "
(ᶜ) See previous page.
(ᵈ) For an account of the battle of Boroughbridge, 16 Mar 1321/2, see
vol. ii, Appendix C V G
(ᵉ) Her father, Edmund de Mortimer of Wigmore, by charter, undated, gave
to her and Walter de Balun, her husband, the manor of Arley, co Stafford, for life
(Addit. MSS., no 5485, f 160). On 12 Apr. 1326, she (again) had livery of this
manor. (*Close Roll*, 19 Edw. II, *m* 8). (*ex inform* G.W. Watson). V.G.

co. Gloucester, and of Thornbury, co. Hereford. He *d.* between Nov. 1325, and Mar. 1325/6, probably while still a prisoner. No trace can be found of the pardon which he is sometimes said to have received, and any peerage which he may be held to have possessed, may be treated as having been *forfeited* by attainder. (ª) His widow was living 1336.

AUDLEY OR ALDITHLEY

JAMES AUDLEY, or ALDITHLEY, is asserted by Dugdale (ᵇ) to have been "of this family also" and to have "had summons to Parl., after the eldest branch went off with daughters and heirs, from 8 Hen. V (1420-21) until 33 Hen. VI (1454-55) inclusive." There can, however, be no doubt that this is the same person as "James (TUCHET), vth LORD AUDLEY," above named, who was sum. from 8 Hen. V to 33 Hen. VI by writs directed "*Jacobo de Audley.*"

AUDLEY OF WALDEN

BARONY.

I. 1538
to
1544.

1. THOMAS AUDLEY, s. of Geoffrey A., of Earls Colne, Essex, was *b.* there 1488, is presumed to have been ed. at Magd. Coll., Cambridge, and was admitted in 1516 a Burgess of Colchester, where he became Town Clerk. Barrister (Inner Temple) and Autumn Reader, 1526; M.P. for Essex, 1529-32; Speaker of the House of Commons, Nov. 1529, when the first attack was made on the Papal power (ᶜ); Attorney for the Duchy of Lancaster, 1530; King's Sergeant, 14 Nov. 1531; Chancellor of the Court of Augmentations; LORD KEEPER, 30 May 1532, when he

---

(ª) Sir James Audley, of Stratton Audley, his s. and h., naturally never took any steps to obtain a sum. to Parl., being quite unaware that future ages would ascribe to a writ of summons the virtue of conferring an hereditary peerage. He was styled "of Gloucestershire," and served in Gascony in 1324, and in Scotland in 1327. He *d. s.p. legit.*, shortly before 1 Mar. 1333/4. By his mistress Eve, formerly wife of his cousin, Thomas Audley (see *ante*, page 339) he was father of two illegit. sons, viz., Sir Peter Audley, who *d. s.p.* 1359, and the celebrated Sir James Audley, K.G. 1344, Governor of Aquitaine and Seneschal of Poitou; one of the Founders of that most noble Order. (See Beltz's *Memorials of the Garter*, p. 83, and *Coll. Top. et Gen.*, vol. vii, p. 51, and p. 52 note "z.") The latter was the hero of the battle of Poitiers (1356). He *d. s.p.* 1369, at his estate of Fontenay le Comte in Poitou, and was *bur.* at Poitiers, when the issue of Sir James, the elder (his father), appears to have become *extinct*, as the family estates in Oxon and co. Gloucester passed to the family of Stafford in right of descent from Hugh Audley, the younger (Earl of Gloucester), br. of the elder, and uncle of the younger, Sir James. See "AUDLEY," Barony, 1317. V.G.

(ᵇ) Vol. i, p. 751.

(ᶜ) The statement in *Dict. Nat. Biog.* that Audley succeeded Sir Thomas More in 1529 as Chancellor of the Duchy of Lancaster, is altogether erroneous. William Fitzwilliam was More's successor in that office, which Audley never held. V.G.

was knighted; LORD CHANCELLOR, 24 Jan. 1532/3, till just before his death 11 years later (*) Being a zealous promotor of the King's various schemes (whether just or otherwise) he obtained a large share of Abbey lands, particularly in 1531 those of the Holy Trinity, or Christchurch, Aldgate (subsequently called " Duke's Place "), and of the rich monastery of Walden, in Essex, in (1538-39) 30 Hen VIII. On 29 Nov. 1538, he was *cr* BARON AUDLEY OF WALDEN, Essex. (*)   El. K G. 23 Apr. and inst. 19 May 1540. He resigned the Great Seal (nine days before his death) 21 Apr 1544. He *m.*, 1stly, (? Margaret), da. of Sir Thomas BARNARDISTON,(*) of Ketton, Suffolk, by Elizabeth, da. of John (or Roger) NEWPORT, of Pelham, Herts. She *d s p*, 23 Jan 1537/8. He *m.*, 2ndly, 22 Apr. 1538, Elizabeth, da of Thomas (GREY), 2nd MARQUESS OF DORSET, by his 2nd wife, Margaret, da. of Sir Robert WOTTON. (ᵈ)   He *d. s.p.m.*, 30 Apr. 1544, aged 56, at his resid-

---

(*) These years were "a period more disgraceful in the annals of England than any of a similar extent   Within it were comprehended the King's divorce from one Queen, after a union of 22 years, under pretence of a scruple of conscience ; the repudiation of another after a few day's intercourse, on the mere ground of personal antipathy , the execution of *two* others, one of them sacrificed to obtain a new partner , and innumerable judicial and remorseless murders, those of Sir Thomas More and Bishop Fisher leading the dreadful array. "   " Audley has acquired the character of undoubtedly equalling, if he did not *exceed*, all his contemporaries in servility. "   " His interpretations of the law on the various criminal trials at which he presided are a disgrace not only to him, but to every member of the bench associated with him, while both branches of the legislature are equally chargeable with the ignominy of passing the acts he introduced, perilling every man's life by the new treasons they invented, and every man's conscience by the contradictory oaths they imposed. "   (*Judges of England*, by E Foss, F. S. A.)   He "has always been considered as the founder of Magdalene Coll Cambridge, which he endowed with large estates, and ordained that his heirs, the possessors of the late monastery of Walden, should be Visitors of the College *in perpetuum* and enjoy the exclusive right of nominating the master, which appointment is still vested in the owner of Audley End. "   (*History of Audley End*, by Richard, Lord Braybrooke, London, 1836, p 332.)   In this work is an engraving of the Lord Audley from a picture by Holbein at that mansion.   G.E.C.   Lloyd remarks of him, " The King might very well trust him with his conscience when he trusted the King with his "   V G

(ᵇ) Audley, the Lord Chancellor, shows upon his tomb at Saffron Walden, arms of Quarterly gold and azure—the parting line indented—a bend azure between two eagles gold, with a fret between two martlets gold upon the bend   This coat, probably granted at the time of his elevation to the peerage, is a peculiarly bad example of Tudor heraldry.   (*ex inform.* Oswald Barron)   V.G

(ᶜ) The Barnardiston pedigree is worked out in the *Suffolk Arch. Inst. Proceedings*, vol. vi.

(ᵈ) There is extant a metal plate, like a small Garter-plate, with the arms, enamelled, of *The noble & valyant Knyght Syre Thomas Audley Lorde Chansylleys of Yenglond*. It was lately, and probably is now [1885], in the possession of Mr. Joseph Clarke, F. S A., Architect   At the top is the date " *Anno Criste (sic)* 1538." The arms are not those usually attributed to Lord Audley (and used by Magdalene College, Cambridge), but are, Or, on a fess, azure, between 3 hares courant, sable, as many martlets, argent.   Impaled with this coat are the arms of Grey—8 quarters.

ence, Christchurch (*i.e* Cree Church), London, when the Barony became *extinct.*([a])　He was *bur* in a chapel he had erected at Saffron Walden.　M I. Will dat. 19 Apr. 1544, pr 18 Feb. 1544/5.　His widow *m.* George NORTON.

AUDLEY OF ORIER

i.e "AUDLEY OF ORIER, co. Armagh," Barony [I.] *(Tuchet)*, *cr.* 1616 with the Earldom of CASTLEHAVEN [I], which see ; *extinct* 1777.

AUGHRIM see AGHRIM

AUMALE([b])

Observations.—The town of Aumale, ([c]) on the Brêle, in Normandy, was formerly the chief place of a small *comté*, to which it gave its name.　The *comté* probably became such owing to the fact that the first Count thereof, Stephen, was already of comital rank, being son of the disinherited Count of Champagne : or because his mother, the first Countess, was of the ducal house of Normandy.　Being already Counts, the acquirement of an English Earldom did not alter the status of the family, and consequently the title of Earl of Yorkshire, bestowed on one of them by Stephen, was soon discontinued. " It may be presumed that the Norman Counts who accompanied the Conqueror to England would not deem their dignity augmented by the acquisition of a title taken from the Saxon Ealdormen or Earls " (*Courthope*, p. 19).

　　After the capture of Aumale by Philip Augustus in 1204, the " Counts of Aumale," of the family of Forz, still retained that title, though their connection with Aumale had wholly ceased.　The English Kings, in

---

The plate seems to have been made on the marriage.　Its height is rather more than 6in. and its width rather less than 5.　The armory of this family of Audley is a curious subject　The arms of Harper, Lord Mayor of London 1561, and founder of Bedford School, must be in some way connected with the *later* coat of Audley, but it is not easy to see how. (*ex inform.* H Gough, who has a tracing of the plate referred to.)　The later and well-known coat is on the Garter plate, 1540, and was probably conferred, or confirmed, in 1538, on the creation of the Peerage

　([a]) He had two daughters and coheirs by his 2nd wife, *viz* (1) Mary, who *d* unm (2) Margaret, who *m*, 1stly, Lord Henry Dudley, who *d s p.* 1557　She *m.*, 2ndly, as his 2nd wife, Thomas (Howard), 4th Duke of Norfolk, by whom she had a s (who was h to his mother), *viz.,* Thomas Howard, sum. in 1597 as Lord Howard *de Walden*, and *cr.* in 1600 Earl of Suffolk —See HOWARD DE WALDEN, Barony, *cr.* 1597.　He appears to have had two brothers, both also named Thomas, who inherited the manors of Berechurch and Gosbecks, near Colchester

　([b]) The re-writing of this article has been kindly undertaken by G.W.Watson

　([c]) Aumale *(Alba Marla, Albemarla,* or *Aumalcum)* was usually written in French, till about the end of the 13th century, Aubemarle or Albemalle· in the 14th and 15th centuries, Aubemalle, Aubmalle, Aubmale, Aumalle, or Aumale　and in the 16th and 17th centuries, Aumalle or Aumale.　In England, the title of Edward (afterwards Duke of York) was always spelt Aumarle, both in English and in Norman-French, by contemporary writers　The quaint form " Aumâle " is to be found only in English works of recent date.

fact, did not recognise the forfeiture made by the French King, though it was absolute. The case appears to be exactly parallel with those of the Umfrevilles and Strathbogies, who, after they had totally lost their Scottish Earldoms of Angus and Atholl respectively, were still accorded these titles by the Kings of England.

---

1. ADELAIDE([a]) or ADELIZ, sister of William the Conqueror,([b]) being illeg. da. of Robert, Duke of the Normans, by Herleve or Harlotte, da. of Fulbert or Robert, a *pelliparius* of Falaise, is mentioned in Domesday as *Comitissa de Albamarla*, and as holding some manors in Essex and Suffolk. In 1082, William, King of the English, and Maud, his wife, gave to the Abbey of La Trinité at Caen the bourg of Le Homme (*de Hulmo*) in the Côtentin, " sed et Comitissa A. de Albamarla concedente eo videlicet pacto ut ipsa teneret in vita sua. "([c]) Adelaide *m.*, 1stly, Enguerrand II, COUNT OF PONTHIEU, who *d. s.p.m.*, being slain in 1053.([d])

([a]) For some discussion on mediæval English names, see vol. iii, Appendix C. V.G.

([b]) The pedigree of the earlier possessors of Aumale has been investigated by T.Stapleton in *Archaeologia*, vol. xxvi, pp. 349-360. There he supposed he had proved that Orderic was wrong in stating that the wife of Count Eudes of Champagne was da. of Duke Robert, and, that she was really the Duke's grand-daughter. Later on, he discovered his own error. His amended conclusions are in *Coll. Top. et Gen.*, vol. vi, p. 265, and, at greater length, in *Rot. Scacc. Norm.*, vol. ii, pp. xxix-xxxi. He had, however, in the meantime misled Poulson (*Holderness*, vol. i, p. 24 sqq.).

([c]) *Gallia Christ.*, vol. xi, *instr.*, c. 68-72. Stapleton always misdates this charter.

([d]) A charter of the Church of St. Martin, at Auchy (now Aumale), narrates its foundation " a viro quodam videlicet Guerinfrido qui condidit castellum quod Albamarla nuncupatur in externis partibus Normannie super flumen quod Augus dicitur, " this charter being drawn up " jussu Enguerrani consulis qui filius fuit Berte supradicti Guerinfridi filie et Adelidis comitisse uxoris sue sororis scilicet Willelmi Regis Anglorum, " and mentioning " Addelidis comitissa supradicti Engueranni et supradicte Adelidis filia que post obitum illorum in imperio successit, " and also " Judita comitissa domine supradicte filia. " (*Archaeologia, ibid.*, pp. 358-60). As to Judith, in the *Vita et passio venerabilis viri Gualdevi comitis Huntendonie et Norhantonie* (an MS. of the 13th century in the Douai library), printed by F. Michel, *Chron. Anglo-Normandes*, vol. ii, it is stated, p. 112, that King William gave to Waltheof " in uxorem neptem suam Ivettam, filiam comitis Lamberti de Lens, sororem nobilis viri Stephani comitis de Albemarlia. " The following pedigree illustrates this descent.

Guerinfrey. He built the castle of Aumale. ═

Berthe, da. and h.═Hugh II, Count of Ponthieu. *d.* 20 Nov. 1052.

Enguerrand, Count═Adelaide, sister of═Lambert de Bou-═Eudes, Count of
of Ponthieu and Sire	William the Con-	logne, Count of Lens.	Champagne; deprived
d'Aumale. Slain	queror. She is styled	Slain in battle at	of Champagne by his
at the siege of Arques	Countess of Aumale.	Lille in 1054.	uncle Thibaut before
in 1053.	*d.* before 1090.		1071.

Adelaide. Living	Judith. *m.* Waltheof,	Stephen, Count
1096.	Earl of Huntingdon.	of Aumale.

She *m.*, 2ndly, Lambert, ([a]) COUNT OF LENS in Artois, who *d. s.p.m.*, being slain in 1054. She *m.*, 3rdly, Eudes, ([b]) the disinherited COUNT OF CHAMPAGNE, who had taken refuge in Normandy. ([c])   She *d.* before 1090. ([d])   Her husband obtained Holderness after the date of Domesday. ([e])   Having conspired against William II in 1094, he was imprisoned in 1096. He occurs as *Comes Odo* in the Lindsey Survey (1115-18).

2. STEPHEN, COUNT OF AUMALE, Lord of Holderness, s. and h. of the said Adelaide, by her 3rd husband. He was *b.* before 1070. In 1090 he took part with William II, and fortified his castle of Aumale against Duke Robert.   By reason of his descent from the ducal house of Normandy he was chosen by Robert de Mowbray and his confederates as the person on whom to bestow the Crown, had they succeeded in their attempt to dethrone William II in 1094. He went on Crusade in 1096 with Duke Robert, before which, 14 July 1096, as *Comes de Alba-marla*, he gave the Church of St. Martin at Auchy to the Abbey of St. Lucien at Beauvais. ([f])   He took the part of Henry I against Duke Robert in 1104, but in 1118 supported Baldwin *à la Hache*, Count of Flanders, and the French King, in their invasion of Normandy on behalf of William *Cliton*, son of Duke Robert. He persisted in his rebellion, but was reduced to submission in 1119. He often occurs, but only once as *Comes de Albamara*, in the Lindsey Survey.   He *m.* Hawise, da. of Ralph DE MORTEMER, of Wigmore, co. Hereford, Seigneur de

---

([a]) He was yr. s. of Eustace I, Count of Boulogne, by Mahaut, da. of Lambert I, Count of Louvain.

([b]) He was s. and h. of Stephen II, Count of Champagne, by Adele, whose parentage is unknown.

([c]) A charter to the Church of St. Martin at Auchy, was written by command of *Adelidis* the most noble *Comitissa*, sister to wit of William, King of the English, "confirmante viro suo videlicet Odone comite una cum filio suo Stephano." (Stapleton, *Rot. Scacc. Norm.*, vol. ii, p. xxxi).

([d]) It is here assumed that it was the sister of the Conqueror, and not her da. of the same name, who is mentioned in Domesday. Stapleton says of the former that "she did not long survive her br., King William," but there is nothing definite known beyond that she was living in 1082 and dead in 1090. There seems to be no charter in which the younger Adelaide is called Countess. The charter of her half-brother, Stephen, dated 14 July 1096, is "consensu simul et corroboratione sororis mee Adelidis," showing she had some rights on Aumale. It is not very clear what they were, though she is said in the charter quoted above to have succeeded "in imperio." Nothing further seems to be known about her, but Count Stephen had eventually the whole inheritance.

([e]) Count Eudes and his s., Stephen, gave the manor and church of Hornsea (in Holderness) to the Abbey of St. Mary at York. (*Monasticon*, vol. iii, p. 548).

([f]) *Gallia Christ.*, vol. xi, *instr.*, c. 19-20. In a charter, dated 1115, Stephen makes mention of "Willelmi regis Anglie avunculi mei." (*Neustria Pia*, pp. 731-2 : *Monasticon*, vol. vi, p. 1103).

Saint Victor-en-Caux, by Milicent, his wife. ([a]) He *d.* before 1130.

3. WILLIAM, *le Gros*, COUNT OF AUMALE, Lord of Holderness, s. and h. He witnessed two charters of King Stephen in 1136 as *Willelmus de Albamarla*, not being placed among the *comites*. He distinguished himself at the battle of the Standard in 1138, and was made Earl of Yorkshire as his reward. ([b]) He was with King Stephen in his defeat at Lincoln, 2 Feb. 1140/1. He founded the Abbey of Meaux in 1150. ([c]) He *m.* Cicely, Lady of Skipton, da. and coh. of William FITZ DUNCAN, by Alice, Lady of Skipton, da. and coh. of William LE MESCHIN, Lord of Copeland. ([d]) He *d. s.p.m.*, 20 Aug. 1179, ([e]) and was *bur.* in the Abbey of Thornton, co. Lincoln, which he had founded in 1139.

4. HAWISE, 1st (or, more probably, only) da. and h., *suc.* her father in the *Comté* of Aumale and the Lordship of Holderness. She *m.*, 1stly, 14 Jan. 1179/80, at Pleshy, Essex, ([f]) William (DE MANDEVILLE), EARL OF ESSEX, ([g]) who thereby became COUNT OF AUMALE. He *d. s.p.*, 14 Nov. 1189. ([f]) She *m.*, 2ndly, after 3 July 1190, William DE FORZ, ([h])

([a]) *Monasticon*, vol. vi, p. 1098 : Round, *Cal. of Documents*, no. 1264.

([b]) *Comitem in Eboraci sciria*, according to John, Prior of Hexham (p. 295). This can only mean Yorkshire excluding Richmondshire. As Round points out, he was not recognised as Count of Aumale till after this date (*Geoffrey de Mandeville*, p. 264). He occasionally attested charters as *comes Ebor'* (see, *e.g.*, Round's *Cal. of Documents*, no. 804), but the title was soon dropped for that of *comes Albemarle*. A very similar case is that of the Count of Meulan, who was *cr.* Earl of Worcester by Stephen. He, on his seal, has SIGILLVM GVALERANNI COMITIS MELLENTI, and on the counterseal, SIGILLVM GVALERANNI COMITIS WIGORNIE. (Douët d'Arcq, *Collection de Sceaux*, vol. i, no. 715). Here again the English title was soon dropped.

([c]) He had rashly made a vow to go on crusade, an adventure which his bulk rendered so perilous, that he founded this Abbey instead, to absolve himself.

([d]) William le Meschin, Lord of Copeland, yr. s. of Rannulf, Vicomte of the Bessin, *m.* Cicely de Rumilly, Lady of Skipton, and had 2 daughters and coheirs. (1) Alice, Lady of Skipton, who *m.* 1stly, William fitz Duncan, s. of Duncan, Earl of Moray (s. of Duncan, King of Scots), by Octreda, da. and h. of Alan, Lord of Allerdale. They had one s., William, " the Boy of Egremont, " who *d.* in the King's ward after 1155, leaving his 3 sisters his coheirs : (i) Cicely, as in the text : (ii) Amabel, Lady of Copeland (called, in the Pipe Rolls and elsewhere, *Comitissa de Couplanda*), who *m.* Reynold de Lucy : (iii) Alice de Rumilly, Lady of Allerdale, who *m.*, 1stly, Gilbert Pipard, and 2ndly, Robert de Courtenay, and *d. s.p.* (2) Avice, Lady of Harewood, who *m.*, 1stly, William Paynell, of Drax, co. York, and 2ndly, Robert de Courcy, of Stoke, Somerset. Alice, Lady of Skipton, *m.*, 2ndly, Alexander fitz Gerold.

([e]) " 1180, xiij kal. Septembris, " according to the Chron. of Thornton (*Monasticon*, vol. vi, p. 326). Benedictus, vol. i, p. 243, gives the year, correctly, as 1179. *Cf. Pipe Rolls*, 25, 26 Hen. II.

([f]) *R. de Diceto*, vol. ii, pp. 3, 73.

([g]) See ESSEX, Earldom of, under the 3rd Earl.

([h]) Stapleton (*Lib. de Antiquis Legibus*, pref., p. xxxiv) states that " the surname de Fortibus was derived from Fors, a commune of the canton of Prahecq, arrond.

who thereby became COUNT OF AUMALE. He accompanied Richard I in his Crusade, and *d.* in 1195. She *m.*, 3rdly, Baldwin DE BÉTHUNE, SEIGNEUR DE CHOQUES in Artois, 3rd s. of Robert DE BÉTHUNE, *le Roux*, SEIGNEUR DE BÉTHUNE and AVOUÉ D'ARRAS, by Adelaide, da. of Hugh III, COUNT OF ST. POL. He thereby became COUNT OF AUMALE.(ᵃ) His castle of Aumale was captured by the King of France in 1196.(ᵇ) He *d.* 13 or 14 Oct. 1212 [not 1211 nor 1213],(ᶜ) and was *bur.* in the Abbey of Meaux. His widow gave, 3 Nov. 1212, 5000 marks, to possess her

of Niort, dept. of Deux Sèvres, in Poitou, as is evident [*sic*] from the following charter, copied in the Register of Philip Augustus, at the Bibl. du Roi, no. 8408 [the original is at the *Trésor des Chartes*, J 473, no. 5]. Ego A. comitissa Augi notum... quod ego terram de Forz quam hahebam... dimisi in manu karissimi domini mei Ludovici Regis Francie illustris ad cujus manum devenerat ex eschaeta Guillelmi quondam domini de Forz et comitis Aubemarle... MCC tricesimo tertio mense februarii. [The correct text has here been substituted for Stapleton's]." It is difficult to see how this charter indicates any locality whatever for Fors. Hoveden, vol. iii, p. 36, calls the Count, *Willelmus de Forz de Ulerum* (Oléron). Beauchet-Filleau, *Dict. des Familles du Poitou*, mentions a seal of a "de Fors," bearing a cross patonce with 2 roundels in chief, arms cognate to those of the Counts of Aumale.

(ᵃ) "1195. Eodem anno obiit Willelmus de Forz comes Albemarlie, cui successit in comitatu illo Baldewinus de Betun dono Ricardi regis Anglie, et duxit uxorem comitissam Albemarlie." (*Hoveden*, vol. iii, p. 306).

(ᵇ) The *comté* of Aumale remained to Richard I by the treaty of Jan. 1195/6. (*Trésor des Chartes*, J 628, no. 2). Six months afterwards, Philip Augustus "cepit per vim castellum de Albemarlia et subvertit illud, et rex Anglie dedit ei tria millia marcarum argenti pro redemptione militum et servientum suorum qui capti fuerunt in Albemarlia." (*Hoveden*, vol. iv, p. 5). In May 1200, King John promised (in the event of his dying *s.p.*) "feodum comitis Albemarle citra mare Anglie," etc., to Louis, s. of the King of France, in marriage "cum filia regis Castelle nepte nostra." (*Trésor des Chartes*, J 628, no. 4). After the conquest of Normandy, Philip gave "comitatum Albemalle cum feodis et dominiis" to Renaud de Dammartin, Count of Boulogne, in Dec. 1204: Renaud gave the *comté* in marriage with his only child, Mahaut, to Philip *Hurepel*, s. of the King of France, in May 1210. (*Idem*, J 238, nos. 4, 8). The later Counts of Aumale were descended, but not in the male line, from Simon de Dammartin, br. of Renaud. After 1204 the connection of the Lords of Holderness with Aumale was merely nominal.

(ᶜ) The writ to the escheator was issued about Oct. 1212. (*Close Roll*, 14 John, *m.* 4). He *d.* "iij idus Octobris," according to the Obituary of Béthune, or "prid. idus Octobris," and his wife "v idus Martii," according to that of the Abbey of Choques. (Du Chesne, *Maison de Bethune*, 1639, *preuves*, p. 66.) The seal attached to a charter of William de Forz *Comes Albemarl'* bore [Gu.] a cross patonce Vair, and that to a charter of Baldwin de Béthune *Comes Albemarl'* a shield charged with a chief bendy [Bendy, Or and Azure, was the ancient arms of Béthune] (Harl. MSS., no. 245, ff. 117 d, 118). Baldwin's seal to a charter of 1199 bore the same arms, and his wife's seal bore a shield with a border compony of 16 pieces, or, as it may otherwise be described, Gyronny of 16 and an escutcheon. (Du Chesne, *ibid.*, *preuves*, p. 61: see also Addit. Charter, no. 20559, for the latter seal). He had a s. (who may have been by a former wife), "Baldevinus filius Comitis de Albe-

inheritance, and that she might not be compelled to marry again. ([a]) She *d.* 11 Mar. 1213/4.

5. WILLIAM (DE FORZ), titular COUNT OF AUMALE, Lord of Holderness, s. and h. of the said Hawise, by her 2nd husband. He had livery of his mother's lands about Sep. 1214. ([a]) He was one of the 25 Conservators of MAGNA CARTA. He *m.*, in or soon after 1214, Aveline, 2nd da., and in her issue coh., of Richard DE MONTFICHET, of Stansted, Essex, by Milicent, his wife. She *d.* about Nov. 1239, ([b]) and was *bur.* in Thornton Abbey. ([c]) He *d.* 29 Mar. 1241, in the Mediterranean. ([d])

6. WILLIAM (DE FORZ), titular COUNT OF AUMALE, Lord of Holderness, s. and h. He did homage and had livery of his father's lands, 18 Sep. 1241. ([e]) He *m.*, 1stly, before Apr. 1236, Christian, 2nd da. and coh. of Alan, LORD OF GALLOWAY, by his 2nd wife (to whom she was elder da. and coh.), Margaret, 1st da., and in her issue coh., of David (OF SCOTLAND), EARL OF HUNTINGDON. She *d. s.p.*, shortly before 29 July 1246.([f]) He *m.*, 2ndly, in 1248/9,([g]) Isabel, elder da. of Baldwin (DE REVIERS), EARL OF DEVON, by Amice, da. of Gilbert (DE CLARE), EARL OF GLOUCESTER AND HERTFORD. He *d.* 23 May 1260, ([h]) at Amiens, and was *bur.* in Thornton Abbey. ([e]) His widow, who was *b.* in July 1237, ([g]) had livery of her dower, 9 Aug. 1260, ([i]) and of the lands of her br., Baldwin, Earl of Devon, 17 Aug. 1263, ([j]), after which she styled herself Countess of Aumale and Devon, and Lady of the Isle. ([j])

---

marla," who witnessed a charter in 1204 (*Idem, preuves*, p. 64), and *d. v.p.* ; and a da., Alice, who *m.* William (Marshal), junior, Earl of Pembroke, and *d. s.p.*

([a]) *Charter Rolls,* 14 John, *m.* 3, and 16 John, *m.* 7.

([b]) *M. Paris,* vol. iii, p. 624. He calls her "mulier admirabilis pulchritudinis."

([c]) *Chron. de Melsa*, vol. ii, p. 106.

([d]) "In mari Mediterraneo peregrinans, cum nullo modo posset comedere et octo diebus jejunando martirium protelasset, die veneris proxima ante Pascha." (*M. Paris,* vol. iv, p. 174).

([e]) *Fine Roll,* 25 Hen. III, *m.* 3, and *Patent Roll,* *m.* 4.

([f]) *Fine Roll,* 30 Hen. III, *m.* 5. There she is erroneously called *Dorvorgoyl,* which was her sister's name.

([g]) "1237. Amicia filia Gileberti quondam comitis Gloucestrie peperit filiam Baldewino de Ripariis, nomine Isabel, circa Translationem beati Thome martyris [7 July]." "1248 [1248/9]. Filia comitis Devonie nupsit comiti de Aubemarla." (*Annales de Theokesberia*, pp. 104, 137).

([h]) The writ to the escheator to take his lands into the King's hand was dated 12 June. (*Fine Roll,* 44 Hen. III, *m.* 7).

([i]) *Close Roll,* 44 Hen. III, *m.* 7. *Fine Roll,* 47 Hen. III, *m.* 3.

([j]) The King granted her marriage, or the fine, if such she should make, for her said marriage, or the forfeiture due if it happened that she *m.* without licence, to his s., Edmund, 20 Nov. 1268 (*Patent Roll,* 53 Hen. III, *m.* 27). On the same roll, *m.* 7, are two *inspeximus* charters, dated 24 July, of deeds of 21 July 1269, between the Queen, Edmund, and Amice, Countess of Devon (also styled Countess of the Isle), relating to the settlements on the marriage of Aveline.

She *d. s.p.s.*, 10 Nov. 1293, at Stockwell, Surrey, and was *bur.* in Breamore Priory, Hants. (ª)

7. THOMAS DE FORZ, s. and h. by 2nd wife, *b.* 9 Sep. 1253. (ᵇ) He *d. s.p.*, before 6 Apr. 1269, and was *bur.* in the Church of the Black Friars at Stamford, co. Lincoln.

8. AVELINE DE FORZ, occasionally, but not often, styled COUNTESS OF AUMALE, sister and h. (ᶜ)   She was *b.* 20 Jan. 1258/9, at Burstwick, co. York. (ᵈ)   She *m.* (cont. 6 Apr.(ᵉ)) 8 or 9 Apr. 1269, at Westm. Abbey, as 1st wife, Edmund, afterwards EARL OF LANCASTER, 2nd s. of Henry III. She *d. s.p.*, 10 Nov. 1274 (ᶠ), and was *bur.* in Westm. Abbey. (ᵍ)

(ª) By deed, dated Monday before St. Martin [9 Nov.] 1293, she gave the King the Isle of Wight, etc., for 6000 marks.   The quittance for the subsequent payment of this sum is guilelessly dated Wednesday before St. Martin [4 Nov.], showing that these deeds (*Liber Rubeus*, pp. 1020-2) were forged some years afterwards.

(ᵇ) He was aged 7 on the morrow of the Nativity of the Virgin, 1260, according to the *Inq. p. m.* on his father, to whom he was found h. (Ch. *Inq. p. m.*, Hen. III, file 24, no. 6).   According to a petition by Thomas de Multon and Anthony de Lucy (*Coram Rege*, Easter, 9 Edw. II, *m.* 112) for the manors of Cockermouth, Skipton, etc., the Count had 5 children, John, Thomas, William, Avice, and Aveline. John must have *d.* before 11 Aug. 1260, when Thomas and William, "filii et heredes Willelmi de Fortibus comitis Albemarle," were in their mother's keeping (*Close Roll*, 44 Hen. III, *m.* 8d).   William *d.* at Oxford, and was *bur.* there in the Church of the Black Friars ; whether he survived Thomas or not is unknown.

(ᶜ) Her sister Avice *d.* before 6 Apr. 1269.   She was *bur.* (it would seem) in the Abbey of Meaux (*Chron. de Melsa*, vol. i, p. 92, vol. ii, p. 106).   In *Coll. Top. et Gen.*, vol. vi, p. 264, *Courthope*, etc., she is said to have *m.* Ingram de Percy [of Levington, co. York, who *d.s.p.*, being poisoned, in 1262].   It is true that the "maritagium filie primogenite et unius heredum Willelmi de Fortibus que fuit uxor Ingrami de Percy" was given to the Queen, 10 Oct. 1262 (*Patent Roll*, 46 Hen. III, *pars* 2, *m.* 2).   But, as the marriage of the daughters of William *Le Fort* was given to this Ingram and two others, 2 Aug. 1259 (*Fine Roll*, 43 Hen. III, *m.* 4), it is clear that Ingram *m.* the 1st da. and coh., not of the Count, but of William *Le Fort* de Vivonne, of Chewton, Somerset, *viz.*, Joan, afterwards wife of Reynold fitz Piers.

(ᵈ) She was aged 14 on the feast of SS. Fabian and Sebastian last past, according to her proof of age, undated, but taken between 20 Jan. and 2 Feb. 1272/3.   This *Inq.* states that the Count, her father, had been dead 12 years at Whitsunday last, *i.e.*, he *d.* on Whitsunday [23 May] 1260. (Ch. *Inq. p. m.*, Edw. I, file 4, no. 4).

(ᵉ) *Charter Roll*, 53 Hen. III, *m.* 10.   W. Rishanger (*Chron.*, p. 63) and the *Annales de Osencia*, p. 221, give the date of her marriage as "sexto idus Aprilis," the *Annales de Wintonia*, p. 107, as "v idus Aprilis," and the *Chron. Maiorum et Vicecomitum London.*, p. 109, as "nono die Aprilis tunc temporis Hokeday."

(ᶠ) "In vigilia sancti Martini proximo preterita," according to the writ of *diem cl. ext.*, dated 7 Nov. (*Fine Roll*, 2 Edw. I, *m.* 2).

(ᵍ) On the death of Aveline, one John d'Eston [Eshton, co. York] claimed to be her heir, as descended from Avice, da., as he averred, of William *le Gros*.   This was denied by Philip de Wyvelesby (who claimed to descend from Simon, yr. br. of William), the heirs of Peter de Brus, and those of Amabel, wife of Reynold

> Thomas of Woodstock, Duke of Gloucester (so *cr*. 6 Aug. 1385), 6th s. of Edward III, was, on 3 Sep. 1385, sum. to Parl. by writ (enrolled as) directed "Carissimo Avunculo Regis Thome Duci Albemarlie."(ª) He *d.* 8 or 9 Sep. 1397, being murdered at Calais. On 24 Sep. following he was declared in Parl. to have been guilty of treason, whereby all his honours were *forfeited*. See "Gloucester," Dukedom of, *cr*. 1385.

DUKEDOM.   1. Edward, Earl of Rutland (so *cr*., by charter,
I. 1397   25 Feb. 1389/90), s. and h. ap. of Edmund, Duke of
to   York, 5th s. of Edward III, was, on 29 Sep. 1397, *cr*., in
1399.   Parl., DUKE OF AUMALE.(ᵇ) He, the Duke of
           Surrey, and the Duke of Exeter, were adjudged by the
Lords in Parl., with the King's assent, 3 Nov. 1399, to "lese and forgo

---

de Lucy (see p. 353, note "d"). A jury found in John's favour (*Misc. Inq.*, file 35, no. 28). Sir C.G.Young, in *Coll. Top. et Gen.*, vol. vi, p. 261, suspects "that the claim of Aston was a mere fiction, to give the King a colourable pretence for retaining the honour in his own hands, as by admitting the fictitious claim and then purchasing it from him, he shut out all real claim that might have been justly made by Wivelby, who afterwards proved his descent from Stephen, Earl of Albemarle, only one generation further back than the pretended descent of Aston." The truth is that neither the English nor the French Kings at this period were over scrupulous as to the means they employed to get the great fiefs into their own hands. John d'Eston surrendered his right to the *comté* of Aumale and to all the lands in England and Normandy which had belonged to Aveline, John, Thomas, and William, de Forz, to William *le Gros* sometime Count of Aumale, and to Hawise his da. (Deed enrolled on *Close Roll*, 6 Edw. I, *m*. 2d), and on 7 Nov. 1278 he received in return 4 [or 4½] knights' fees in Thornton by Pickering [Thornton Dale] and elsewhere, valued at 100*l*. a year, to hold by the service of 1 knight (*Charter Roll*, 6 Edw. I, *m*. 3).

The heirs to the lands, in Essex, Bucks, and Surrey, which Aveline had inherited from the family of Montfichet, were :—(1) the 4 daughters of Hugh de Bolebec (s. of another Hugh who had *m*. her grandmother's elder sister Margery), *viz*., Philippe, wife of Roger de Lancaster, Margery, wife of Nicholas Corbet, Alice, wife of Walter de Huntercombe, and Maud, wife of Hugh de Laval. (2) Ralph de Playz, s. of Richard, s. of Hugh (which Hugh had *m*. her grandmother's yr. sister, Philippe). (Ch. *Inq. p.m.*, Edw. I, file 10, no. 8).

(ª) *Close Roll*, 9 Ric. II, *m*. 45d, where the word is certainly *Albemarlie*: but it is an error for *Gloucestrie*, as Thomas of Woodstock could never have possessed the former title. Four weeks before, as "Buk' et Essex' comes," he had been *cr*. Duke of Gloucester (*Charter Roll*, *m*. 15, *no*. 27), yet this undoubted title is omitted in the writ : he was invested with the Dukedom of Gloucester, and that Dukedom only, in full Parl. (*Parl. Roll*, *m*. 5, *no*. 15): in the orders, Nov. 1385, that divers rents granted him "pro statu suo ducali decencius sustinendo" should be paid him, "quem in ducem ereximus eidem ducatus Glouc' titulum assignantes et nomen" (*Close Roll*, *m*. 35), no dukedom of Aumale is mentioned, nor is this title ever again attributed to him. His full style (1394) is on his seal :—"Sigillu thome filii regis ducis glouc coitis essex buk constabular anglie." (Brit. Mus., lxxxix, no. 37). He did not obtain Holderness till 7 June 1394.

(ᵇ) *Parl. Roll*, 21 Ric. II, *m*. 11, *no*. 35 : *Charter Roll*, 21-23 Ric. II, *m*. 14, *no*. 23.

fro hem and her heirs thes names that thei have nowe os dukes and the worship and the dignite therof. " ([a]) On 1 Aug. 1402 he suc. his father as Duke of York, and in May 1414 was, in Parl., restored "a lestat noun fame et honour auxi entierment et pleinement come lavoit devaunt le juggement envers luy renduz " in 1399. ([b]) He *d. s.p.*, being slain at the battle of Agincourt, 25 Oct. 1415. See "York," Dukedom of, under the 2nd Duke.

EARLDOM.

I. 1412
to
1421.

1. Thomas of Lancaster, 2nd s. of Henry IV, was, on 9 July 1412, *cr.* EARL OF AUMALE and Duke of Clarence. ([c]) He *d. s.p.*, being slain at the battle of Baugé, 22 Mar. 1420/1, when all his honours became *extinct.* See "Clarence," Dukedom of, *cr.* 1412.

---

1. Richard (Beauchamp), xiiith Earl of Warwick, received a grant, 19 May 1419, of the Comté of Aumale to him and the heirs male of his body. ([d]) He *d.* 30 Apr. 1439. ([e]) See "Warwick," Earldom of, under the xiiith Earl.

2. Henry (Beauchamp), Earl of Warwick and Count of Aumale, ([f]) only s. and h., *b.* 22 Mar. 1424/5. On 5 Apr. 1445, he was *cr.* Duke of Warwick. He *d. s.p.m.,* 11 June 1446, ([g]) when the title of Count of Aumale became *extinct.* See "Warwick," Dukedom of, *cr.* 1445.

([a]) *Parl. Roll (Placita Corone),* 1 Hen. IV, *m.* 2, *no.* 10. The judgment was pronounced "die lune proxima post festum Omnium Sanctorum " (*Chron. Mon. S. Albani,* vol. iv, p. 314), or "Monday the morowe after alle Sowlyn day " (*Chron. of London,* edit. Kingsford, p. 58), *i.e.,* 3 Nov.

([b]) *Parl. Roll,* 2 Hen. V, *pars* 1, *m.* 7, *no.* 9. But "purveu toutfoitz que icestes presentz declaracion et restitucion ne tournent ne se extendent en prejudice de Roi ne en prejudice et disheritans des autres seignurs nautres persones en nulle manere, " and therefore excluding the restoration of the title of Aumale, which had already been bestowed elsewhere.

([c]) "… ipsum filium nostrum primo in Comitem Albe Marlie et exinde in Ducem Clarencie ereximus. " (*Charter Roll,* 13 and 14 Hen. IV, *m.* 3, *no.* 3).

([d]) The full text of the letters patent—which have hitherto escaped research—is given in Appendix J to this volume.

([e]) His style in a charter, 27 Mar. 1 Hen. VI, is "Ricardus de Bello Campo Comes Warrewichie et Albemarlie dominus de Insula " (*Inspeximus* on *Patent Roll,* 25 Hen. VI, *pars* 1, *m.* 15), and in another, 13 Mar. 1426, "Richard de beauchamp Conte de vvarrevvyk et daubmalle Seignur le despensier et de lisle " (*Addit. Charters,* no. 330). See also his seal, 6 Apr. 8 Hen. VI (*Idem,* no. 20432).

([f]) His style, in two charters, 1 and last of Feb. 23 Hen. VI, is "Henricus de bello Campo primus Comes regni Anglie Comes Warrewic' et Albemarlie ac dominus le Despencer dominus de Bergevenny Glomorgan et Morgannok. " (*Inspeximus* on *Patent Roll,* 27 Hen. VI, *pars* 2, *m.* 23).

([g]) Writs of *diem cl. ext.* 16 June and 12 July 24 Hen. VI. "obiit die sabbati xj° die Junii anno xxiiij[t]. " (Ch. *Inq. p. m.,* Hen. VI, file 123, no. 43).

AUNGIER OF LONGFORD

i.e. "AUNGIER OF LONGFORD, co. Longford, " Barony [l.] *(Aungier)*, *cr.* 1621, *extinct* 1704, with the Earldom of Longford [I.], which see.

AVA

i.e. "AVA in the province of Burma, " Earldom, see "DUFFERIN AND AVA" Marquessate *(Hamilton-Temple-Blackwood)*, *cr.* 1888.

AVALON

See "HOOD OF AVALON, Somerset, " Barony *(Hood)*, *cr* 1892.

See "MORDAUNT OF AVALON, Somerset, " Viscountcy *(Mordaunt)*, *cr* 1659, *extinct*, with the Earldoms of PETERBOROUGH and MONMOUTH, 1814

AVANDALE, AVENDALE, or AVONDALE

EARLDOM [S.]   1. JAMES DOUGLAS, of Balveny, 2nd s of Archibald,
              3rd EARL OF DOUGLAS [S], by Joan, widow of Thomas
I. 1437   Moray, of Bothwell, was, in 1437, *cr.* EARL OF
to   AVANDALE, having a charter, 22 Dec 1439 (con-
1455.   firmed 20 Sep 1440) as "EARL OF AVENDALE and
LORD OF BALVENY" [S.]. In 1440 he *suc.* as "EARL OF DOUGLAS" [S.], in which Earldom this title was *merged* till both became *forfeited* in 1455. See "DOUGLAS, " Earldom of [S.], *cr.* 1356/7

See also "STEWART OF AVONDALE AND STEWART OF OCHILTREE."

AVANE

i.e. "AVANE AND HAMILTON" [S.], Avane being doubtless a clerical error for Arane or ARRAN [S.], which see.

AVEBURY

BARONY   1. JOHN LUBBOCK, 1st s. and h. of Sir John L , 3rd
          Bart., [1806], Banker *(d.* 21 June 1865), by Harriet
I. 1900.   *(d.* 12 Feb. 1873), da. of Lieut. Col. George HOTHAM,
of York, was *b.* 30 Apr. 1834, at 22 Eaton Place, and *bap* at St. Peter's, Eaton Sq. Ed. at Eton. Senior Partner in the Bank 'Robarts Lubbock & Co.' M.P. (Liberal) for Maidstone 1870-80, and for the Univ. of London 1880-1900. D.C.L., F.R.S. 1856, and LL.D. Commander of the Legion of Honour, Member of the Order Pour le Mérite. Vice Chanc. of London Univ. 1872-80. Pres of the Brit. Assoc. 1881. Pres of the London Chamber of Commerce 1888-93. Member of the L.C.C. (City) 1889-92, Vice Chairman 1889-90, Chairman 1890-92,

Alderman 1892-98. P C. 8 Feb. 1890. Pres. of the London Institution
1894-1906. Pres. of the Statistical Soc. 1900-1902. Sec. for Foreign
Correspondence, R Academy, 1903. Pres. of Soc. of Antiquaries 1904.
Rector of St. Andrew's Univ. 1907. Trustee of the Brit Museum since
1878. On 22 Jan. 1900 (*a*) he was *cr*. BARON AVEBURY of Avebury,
Wilts. (*b*) He *m*., 1stly, 10 Apr. 1856, at Rostherne, co. Chester, Ellen
Frances, only da. of the Rev. Peter HORDERN, of Chorlton cum Hardy, co
Lancaster. She *d*. 20 Oct. 1879, at High Elms, Kent, and was *bur* at
Down. He *m*., 2ndly, 17 May 1884, at St Peter's, Eaton Sq, Alice
Augusta Laurentia Lane, da. of Gen. Augustus Henry Lane FOX-PITT
RIVERS, of Rushmore, Wilts, by Alice Margaret, da. of Edward John
(STANLEY), BARON STANLEY OF ALDERLEY. She was *b*. in London.

[JOHN BIRKBECK LUBBOCK, s. and h ap. by 1st wife ; *b*. 4 Oct. 1858
Ed. at Eton.]

Family Estates.—These are situated in Kent. Principal Residence :—
High Elms, Farnborough, in that co.

AVELAND

BARONY   1. GILBERT JOHN HEATHCOTE, s. and h. of Sir Gilbert
I. 1856.   H., 4th Bart., of Normanton Park, Rutland, by his 1st
wife, Katharine Sophia, da. of John MANNERS, of Grant-
ham Grange, co. Lincoln, by Louisa, *suo jure* COUNTESS OF DYSART [S.],
was *b*. 16 Jan. 1795, at Normanton Park afsd. Ed. at Westm. School, and
at Trin. Coll. Cambridge. M.P. (Whig)(*c*) for Boston 1820-30, and
1831-32; for South Lincolnshire, 1832-41; and for Rutland, 1841-56; *suc*.
his father 26 Mar 1851 as 5th Bart Lord Lieut of co Lincoln 1862-67.
On 26 Feb. 1856, he was *cr*. BARON AVELAND OF AVELAND, co
Lincoln. He *m*., 8 Oct 1827, at Drummond Castle, Muthill, co. Perth,
Clementina Elizabeth BURRELL-DRUMMOND, afterwards (1871) *suo jure*
BARONESS WILLOUGHBY DE ERESBY (see that title) He *d*. at 12 Belgrave
Sq., 6, and was *bur*. 13 Sep. 1867, at Normanton, aged 72. Will dat. 10 Aug.
1863 to 15 Aug 1866, pr. 5 Oct. 1867, at £400,000. His widow, who
was *b*. in Piccadilly, 2, and *bap*. 15 Sep. 1809, at St. Geo, Han. Sq., being
the elder of the two sisters of Alberic, Lord Willoughby of [*sic*] Eresby, *suc*
on her said brother's death, 26 Aug 1870, to the coheirship of that Barony,
of which the abeyance was terminated in her favour 13 Nov. 1871. By
royal lic., 4 May 1872, she took for herself and her issue the surname of
HEATHCOTE-DRUMMOND-WILLOUGHBY. She *d*. 13 Nov. 1888, aged 79,
at Grimsthorpe Castle, co. Lincoln, and was *bur*. with her husband. Will
dat 6 Aug. 1884, pr. 1 Apr. 1889.

(*a*) Since 1886 a Liberal Unionist. He is a staunch Free Trader, with large and
varied scientific and literary attainments, which were found also in his father. V.G.
(*b*) Lord Avebury's arms are Silver a stork ermine, standing on a mount vert,
and a chief gules with three silver stars. (*ex inform*. Oswald Barron) V.G
(*c*) He was never more than a very moderate Liberal. V G.

II. 1867.   2. GILBERT HENRY (HEATHCOTE-DRUMMOND-WIL-
          LOUGHBY, formerly HEATHCOTE), BARON AVELAND, and a
Baronet, only s. and h., *b.* 1 Oct. 1830.   By the death of his mother,
13 Nov. 1888, he became LORD WILLOUGHBY DE ERESBY, and joint Hered.
GREAT CHAMBERLAIN, (ª) and was *cr.*, 22 Aug. 1892, EARL OF ANCASTER.
See fuller particulars under that title.

AVEN

i.e. "AVEN AND INNERDALE" Baron [S] *(Hamilton)*, *cr.* 1643, with
the Dukedom of Hamilton [S.], which see.

AVENDALE, see STEWART OF AVONDALE

AVON see AVEN

AVONDALE

i.e., "CLARENCE AND AVONDALE," Dukedom ; see "ATHLONE."
See also " CLARENCE AND AVONDALE. "

See also " STEWART OF AVONDALE. "

AVONMORE (ᵇ)

BARONY [I.]   1. BARRY YELVERTON, s and h. of Francis Y., of
          Blackwater and Kanturk, co. Cork, (*d.* 27 Mar.
I. 1795.   1746) by Elizabeth, da. of Jonas BARRY, of Kilbrin,
VISCOUNTCY [I.]   co. Cork, *b.* 28 May 1736. Scholar Trin. Coll.
          Dublin 1755. B A. 1757; LLB. 1761; LLD. 1774.
I. 1800.   Admitted to the Middle Temple 10 Oct. 1759.
Barrister at Law (Dublin) 1764; K.C. and Bencher, 1772; M.P. for Donegal
borough 1774-76; and for Carrickfergus 1776-83, and as such "a zealous
partizan for the claims of Ireland." (ᶜ)   Attorney Gen. [I.] 1782-83 ;

(ª) For remarks on this hereditary office, see vol ıı, Appendix D
(ᵇ) It was not from Avonmore (*i e.* the Great River) in co. Wicklow that he
took his title, but probably from some river of the same name ın co. Cork.   V.G
(ᶜ) See *Rise and Fall of the Irish Nation*, by Sir Jonah Barrington, cap. vii, where
a long and interesting account of his Lordship's career is given.   The author's views,
as against the Irish Union, are well known.   At the end of the sketch he adds—
" This distinguished man, at the critical period of Ireland's emancipation, burst forth
as a meteor ın the Irish Senate, " but " after having with zeal and sincerity laboured
to attaın independence for his country ın 1782, he became one of its Sale-Masters ın
1800 " and, through the influence of the Duke of Portland, " and the absolute
necessity of a family provision, on the question of the Union, the radiance of his
public character was obscured for ever. "   " His rising sun was brilliant, his meridian

47

P.C. [I.] 13 July 1782 ; Lord Chief Baron of the Exchequer [I.] 1783-1805. On 15 June 1795 he was *cr* LORD YELVERTON, BARON AVONMORE, co. Cork [I.] On 29 Dec. 1800([a]) he was *cr*. VISCOUNT AVONMORE of Derry Island, co. Tipperary [I.]. He *m*. (Lic Prerog Ct [I.] 14 July 1761), July 1761, Mary, da and coh. of William NUGENT, (5th s. of James N., of Clonlost, co. Westmeath) by Ursula, da. of Richard AGLIONBY, of Carlisle. She, who was *b*. 28 Mar. 1733, *d*. 1802. He *d*. 19 Aug. 1805, at Forthfield, near Rathfarnham, co. Dublin, aged 69. Will pr. 1806, Prerog. Ct. [I.].

II. 1805.   2. WILLIAM CHARLES (YELVERTON), VISCOUNT AVON-
                    MORE, &c. [I.], s. and h., *b*. 5 Apr. 1762. Principal
Registrar of the High Court of Chancery [I.]. He *m*., 1 Sep. 1787, by spec. lic., in St. James's Place, in the parish of St. James's, Westm (his bride being then a minor), Mary, 1st da of John READE, of East Cams, Hants. He *d* 28 Nov. 1814, at Clythe, co. Monmouth, aged 52 Will pr. July 1815. His widow *d*. 30 May 1834.

III. 1814.   3. BARRY JOHN (YELVERTON), VISCOUNT AVONMORE,
                    &c. [I.], s. and h., *b* 21 Feb. 1790. He *m*., 1stly, 1811, Jane, 2nd da of Thomas BOOTHE, of Dublin and Whitehaven. She *d*. Oct. 1821. He *m*, 2ndly, 1 Aug. 1822, Cecilia, 1st da. of Charles O'KEEFE, of Hollybrooke Park, co. Tipperary, one of the Registrars of the Court of Chancery [I]. He *d*. 24 Oct 1870, at Dublin, in his 81st year. His widow *d*. 1 Feb. 1876, at Tritonville, co. Dublin, aged 71.

IV. 1870.   4. WILLIAM CHARLES (YELVERTON), VISCOUNT AVON-
                    MORE, &c. [I.], 3rd([b]) but 1st surv. s. and h., being 1st s. by 2nd wife, *b*. 27 Sep. 1824. Major, R A. Served in the Crimea.

---

cloudy, his setting obscure, " yet " few men possessed so much talent, so much heart, or so much weakness " G.E.C. " Mr Yelverton is said to have been born of obscure and poor parentage, being the son of a weaver in Newmarket in the county of Cork... [a story without foundation]. The leading feature of his eloquence is energetic force. His voice is full and deep, his pronunciation slow and solemn ; his arrangement masterly , his knowledge great and diversified ; his manner animated and impressive. He is allowed to be a good and a learned judge , but he has one fault... he is extremely irritable. " (*Sketches of Irish political Character* 1799) " One of the most accomplished and merciful men on the Irish Bench. After his death Curran finely said of him, that he could on his death bed have had no more selfish wish than that justice should be administered to him, in the world to come, in the same spirit with which he distributed it in this. " (Lecky, *Hist. of England in the Eighteenth Cent.*, vol. vii, p. 53) " He was a great lawyer, an admirable speaker, a statesman of sound and moderate judgment, a man of eminent accomplishments, and of a singularly sweet, simple, and even childlike nature, but . his character had been broken down by extravagance and debt. " (*Idem*, vol. viii, p. 467.) V.G.

([a]) For particulars of the creations and promotions in the Irish peerage at the time of the Union, and remarks thereon, see Appendix H in volume iii. V.G.

([b]) Of his two elder brothers of the half blood (1) Barry Charles Y., *b*. 21 Nov. 1814, in Dublin, Lieut 79th Foot, 1833, *d* unm and *v.p.*, 11 Jan 1853, aged 38,

Medal and clasp for Inkermann and Sebastopol   Knight of the Turkish
order of Medjidie, 5th class, but was "*suspended from all military duties*"
Mar 1861.(ᵃ)   He *m.*, 26 June 1858, at Trinity (Episcopal) Chapel,
Edinburgh, Emily Marianne, widow of Edward FORBES, F R S., F G S.,
&c., and yst da of Major Gen. Sir Charles ASHWORTH, K.C.B. He *d.*
1 Apr. 1883, at Biarritz, aged 58. His widow *d.* there 28 Nov. 1909.
Will pr. 7 June 1910, at £ 4,633.

V. 1883.   5. BARRY NUGENT (YELVERTON), VISCOUNT AVONMORE,
                &c [I.], s and h., *b* 11 Feb 1859. Ed. at the Royal
Military Coll. Sandhurst ; 2nd Lieut. 37th Foot, Jan. 1878 ; Lieut., Feb.
1879 ; Instructor of Musketry, Jan. 1882 ; Capt., Nov. 1884. He *d.*
unm., 13 Feb. 1885, aged 26, of enteric fever (when on service) at Kerb-
ekan, in the Soudan war.

VI. 1885   6. ALGERNON WILLIAM (YELVERTON), VISCOUNT AVON-
                MORE [1800], and LORD YELVERTON, BARON AVONMORE
[1795], all in the Peerage of Ireland, yst. but only surv. br. and h., *b.*
19 Nov. 1866. He *m.*, 17 Dec. 1890, at St. Anne's, Dungannon, co.
Tyrone, Mabel Sarah, 2nd da. of George EVANS, of Gortmerron, in that

---

at Hangle Park, co Mayo   (2) George Frederick William Y , *b* 7 Mar 1818,
sometime in the 64th reg , *m* , 12 Feb. 1857, Louisa Lenox, da of Guy Lenox
Prendergast, but *d. v.p.* and *s.p.*, 26 Feb. 1860, aged 41, at Ennismore House,
Kingstown. V.G.

(ᵃ) This was owing to the scandal occasioned by the trial, which lasted ten days
(21 Feb to 4 Mar. 1861) in the Court of Common Pleas [I.], of " *Thelwall
v Yelverton,* " wherein the actual cause of action was for £259 supplied by the
plaintiff for the use of the wife of the defendant, but the real question at issue was
whether or no the lady in question *was* legally such wife. Her maiden name was
Maria Theresa LONGWORTH, of Smedley, co. Lancaster, she being the yst. da. of a silk
merchant in Manchester, deceased. She was *b* at Chetwood, in that co ,ed. at a convent
in France, and brought up as a Roman Catholic   Having joined the French Sisters
of Charity to attend the sick at the Hospital of Galata, during the Russian war, she
there received an offer of marriage from Major Yelverton (early in 1857), and
shortly afterwards he " performed the ceremony " by reading the marriage service of
the Church of England at Edinburgh   On 15 Aug 1857 the marriage was cele-
rated by a Roman Catholic Priest at Rostrevor in the north of Ireland, after which
they travelled on the Continent together as husband and wife. Though by act
of Parl. (19 Geo. II, cap. 13) it is enacted " that a marriage between a Roman
Catholic and a Protestant, if celebrated by a Roman Catholic priest, shall be deemed
null and void, " the jury found not only that the Scotch marriage was valid, but that
the one in Ireland was good also, finding that Major Yelverton *was* a Roman
Catholic   This decision was received by the populace with the greatest applause.—
See an interesting account of the celebrated trial in the *Annual Register* for 1861
See also *N. & Q.*, 5th Ser., vol. ii, p. 466, and 9th Ser., vol. vi, p. 229.   On appeal,
however, this decision was not sustained, and, on 28 July 1864, and finally, 30 July
1867, the illegality of these marriages was decided by the House of Lords, whereby
the validity of this scoundrel's marriage in 1858 (as in the text) became established
Miss Longworth *d.* Sep. 1881, at Pietermaritzburg.

co., and formerly of Canada, by Jane, da. of Major FITZGERALD, of Kingston, Canada. (ᵃ)

Principal Residences in 1884.—Belle Isle, near Roscrea, co. Tipperary, and Hazle Rock, co. Mayo.

AXILHOLM

i.e. "LORD MOWBRAY OF AXILHOLM." See "MOWBRAY," Barony *(Mowbray)*, 1283, under the 4th Lord, 1362-66.

AYEMOUTH see EYEMOUTH

AYLESBOROUGH

See "COVENTRY OF AYLESBOROUGH, co. Worcester," Barony *(Coventry)*, cr. 1628, *extinct* 1719, the Earldom of Coventry (*cr.* 1697 with a spec. rem.) remaining.

AYLESBURY, see AILESBURY

AYLESFORD

EARLDOM
I. 1714.

1. HENEAGE FINCH, (ᵇ) 2nd s. of Heneage (FINCH), 1st EARL OF NOTTINGHAM, by Elizabeth, da. of William HARVEY, matric. at Oxford (Ch Ch) 18 Nov. 1664, being then aged 15; became a Barrister of the Inner Temple (being popularly known as "silvertongued Finch"); K.C. 1677, and was made Solicitor Gen. 13 Jan. 1678/9, (ᶜ) from which office he was removed by James II, 21 Apr. 1686. In Trinity term 1688 he was one of the counsel for the seven Bishops against the Crown. M.P. (Tory) for Oxford Univ. 1679, 1689-98, 1701-3; and for Guildford 1685-87. Was chosen by the Univ. to receive Queen Anne, in Aug. 1702, on her coming to Oxford.

(ᵃ) William Henry Morgan Yelverton, *b.* 7 Feb. 1840, then h presumptive, and only male descendant, besides the 6th Viscount, of the grantee, only s. of the Hon William Henry Y., *d.* unm., 3 Mar 1909, at Biarritz. V.G.

(ᵇ) For a note on the Arms of the Finches, Lords Aylesford, see under Winchilsea.

(ᶜ) In the trial, for high treason, of Lord Russell in 1683, he (according to Bishop Burnet) "summed up the evidence against him, but shewed more of a vicious eloquence, in turning matters against the prisoner, than law" On which Dean Swift remarks "Finch was afterwards Earl of Aylesford—an arrant r—l" It is certainly remarkable that during the reign of William III (to whose cause he was favourable) he obtained neither promotion, nor office of *any* kind. G.E.C. "His abilities were very great, he was judicious, eloquent, and industrious, and a statesman endued with strong veracity, and inflexible integrity." Note to *Absalom and Achitophel*, pt. ii. According to Macky (1704) he was "a tall thin black man" V G

On 15 Mar. 1702/3, "in consideration of his great merits and abilities," he was *cr.* ([a]) BARON OF GERNSEY *(sic)*. ([b]) P.C. 20 Mar. 1702/3 till May 1708, and 13 Dec. 1711. He was again sworn P.C. 14 Oct. 1714, and appointed Chancellor of the Duchy of Lancaster, which office he resigned 29 Feb. 1715/6 On 19 Oct. 1714, he was *cr.* EARL OF AYLESFORD, Kent ([c]) He *m*, 16 May 1678, at St. Giles's-in-the-Fields, Elizabeth, da. and coh. of Sir John BANKS, of London, Bart (so *cr.* Aug. 1661), by Elizabeth, da of Sir John DETHICK, Knt., sometime Lord Mayor of London. By her (on the death of her father), in Oct 1699, he acquired the estate of Aylesford, Kent. He *d.* at Albury, Surrey, 22 July, and was *bur.* 8 Aug. 1719, at Aylesford. Will pr. Oct. 1719. His widow *d.* 1 Sep. 1743. Will pr. Oct. 1743.

II 1719.   ,   2. HENEAGE (FINCH), EARL OF AYLESFORD, &c, s. and h, *b.* at Albury, Surrey Matric. at Oxford (Ch. Ch.) 27 June 1700, aged 17. M.P. (Tory) for Maidstone 1704-05; and for Surrey 1710-19. Master of the Jewel office, 1711-16. He *m.*, 9 Dec. 1712, at Great Packington, Mary, da. and h. of Sir Clement FISHER, of Packington, co. Warwick, 3rd Bart., by Ann, da. of Humphrey JENNENS, of Erdington, in that co With her he acquired the estate of Packington. She *d.* 28 May 1740, at Bath. Admon. 20 Feb. 1740/1 to her husband. He *d.* 29 June 1757. Will pr. July 1757.

III. 1757.   3. HENEAGE (FINCH), EARL OF AYLESFORD, &c., only s. and h, *b.* and *bap.* 6 Nov. 1715. ([d]) Matric. at Oxford (Univ Coll) 31 July 1732. Created M.A. 13 Dec. 1735, and D C.L. 14 Apr. 1761. M.P. ([e]) for co. Leicester 1739-41; for Maidstone 1741-47, and 1754-57. He *m*, 6 Oct. 1750, at St. Geo., Han. Sq., Charlotte, (a fortune of £50,000) yst. da. of Charles (SEYMOUR), 6th DUKE OF SOMERSET, by his 2nd wife, Charlotte, da. of Daniel (FINCH), EARL OF WINCHILSEA AND NOTTINGHAM. He *d* 9 May 1777, in Grosvenor Sq, and was *bur.* at Packington, aged 61. Will pr. May 1777. His widow, who was *b.* 21 Sep. 1730, *d* 15 Feb. 1805, at Aylesford, and was *bur.* at Packington. Will pr. May 1805.

([a]) This was one of the 4 peerages by some supposed to have been conferred for the purpose of creating a majority in the House of Lords. See note *sub* IV BARON CONWAY. V G.

([b]) In *Courthope* the title of creation is erroneously given as "*Lord* Guernsey, *co. Southampton*," so also, similarly, the title of Earl of Jersey, *cr.* 1697, is there said (erroneously) to have been "*co. Southampton*," the mistake possibly arising from these islands forming (ecclesiastically) part of the diocese of Winchester

([c]) This was one of the 14 peerages *cr* on the coronation, 20 Oct. 1714, of George I. For a list of Coronation peerages, see Appendix F in vol. II.

([d]) The entries in the family Bible of the births, &c., of the 6 children (1713-22) of the 2nd Earl, and those of the 11 children (1751-69) of the 3rd Earl, are given in *Misc. Gen. et Her*, 2nd Ser, vol. VIII, p. 109. V.G

([e]) In the Commons he voted with the Tories and anti-Walpoleans, but in the Lords he was a Grenville Whig, protesting against the Repeal of the Stamp Act, and opposing the Court on the Midx. election question. V.G.

IV. 1777. 4. HENEAGE (FINCH), EARL OF AYLESFORD, &c., s and h., *b.* at Sion House, 4, and *bap.* 15 July 1751 at Isleworth, Midx. (ª) Matric. at Oxford (Ch Ch.) 13 Nov. 1767 Created M A. 16 June 1770, and D.C.L. 7 July 1773. F R.S. 25 Feb 1773. M.P. (Tory) for Castle Rising 1772-74; and for Maidstone 1774-77 ; Lord of the Bedchamber 1777-83 P.C. 31 Dec. 1783. F.S.A. Capt of the Yeomen of the Guard 1783-1804 Trustee of the Brit. Museum 1787 till death. Lord Steward of the Household 1804-12 He *m* , by spec lic., 18 Nov. 1781, Louisa, 1st da. of Thomas (THYNNE), 1st MARQUESS OF BATH, by Elizabeth, 1st da of William (CAVENDISH-BENTINCK), 2nd DUKE OF PORTLAND. He *d.* 21 Oct. 1812, aged 61, of gout in the stomach, at Packington. (ᵇ) Will pr. Feb 1813. His widow, who was *b.* 25 Mar. 1760, *d.* 28 Dec. 1832. Will pr. Jan. 1833.

[CHARLES FINCH, *styled* LORD GERNSEY, s. and h. ap., *d* young, 18 July 1784, at Packington].

V. 1812. 5. HENEAGE (FINCH), EARL OF AYLESFORD, &c., 2nd but 1st surv. s. and h., *b* 24 Apr , and *bap.* 25 May 1786, at St. James's, Westm Matric. at Oxford (Ch. Ch) 19 Apr. 1804; B.A. 1807 ; M.P. (Tory) for Weobley 1807-12. An officer in the Light Dragoons 1811-12. F S A He *m* , 23 Apr. 1821, at St. Geo., Han. Sq., Augusta Sophia, da of George (GREVILLE), 2nd EARL OF WARWICK, by his 2nd wife, Henrietta, 1st da. and coh. of Richard VERNON, of Hilton, co. Stafford She *d.* 2 Mar. 1845, at Packington afsd. Admon. Aug. 1845. He *d.* there 3 Jan. 1859, aged 72.

VI. 1859. 6 HENEAGE (FINCH), EARL OF AYLESFORD, &c , s. and h., *b.* 24 Dec. 1824, at Packington M.P. (Conservative) for South Warwickshire 1849-57. He *m.*, 7 May 1846, at St. Geo., Han. Sq , Jane Wightwick, only da and h. of John Wightwick KNIGHTLEY, of Offchurch Bury, co. Warwick. He *d.* 10 Jan. 1871, at 48 Grosvenor Str , Midx., and was *bur.* at Packington, aged 46 Will pr 21 Mar. 1871 under £120,000, but resworn as under £100,000. His widow is now (1910) living at Offchurch Bury afsd.

VII. 1871. 7. HENEAGE (ᶜ) (FINCH), EARL OF AYLESFORD, &c., s and h., *b.* 21 Feb. 1849, in Upper Brook Str., Midx. Ed. at Eton. Officer of the Greek Order of the Saviour. In 1874 he entertained the Prince of Wales at Packington. (ᵈ) In politics he was a Conservative He *m.*, 8 Jan 1871, at St. Geo , Han. Sq., Edith, 3rd da. of Lieut. Col.

(ª) See note " d " on previous page

(ᵇ) Among the principal amusements of the " Men of Fashion " in 1782, his is given as " Pistol Shooting " For a list of these see Appendix H in this volume.

(ᶜ) His Lordship was the 7th Earl in *uninterrupted* succession who had borne the Christian name of " Heneage. "

(ᵈ) He was well known in the sporting world, in which, however, his career was singularly unsuccessful.

Thomas Peers Williams, of Temple House, Berks, and of Craig-y-don, Anglesey, by Emily, da. of Anthony Bacon, of Elcott, Berks   From her he was separated by deed dat. 22 May 1877.   He *d. s p.m.* ([a]) 13 Jan 1885, at Big Springs, co. Howard, in Texas, aged 34, and was *bur.* in the church of Packington   Will dat. 2 Sep. 1882.   His widow *d.* at 51 Welbeck Str., 23, and was *bur.* 28 June 1897, at Bisham, Berks.   Admon £8,742 gross, £1,127 net.

VIII. 1885.   Charles Wightwick (Finch), Earl of Aylesford [1714], and Baron Gernsey [1703], br. and h. male, *b.* 7 June 1851, in Curzon Str., Mayfair.   He established his claim to the Peerage ([b]) and had a writ of summons 31 July 1855.   In politics he is a Conservative.   He *m*, 1stly, 4 Feb. 1873, Georgiana Agnes, 1st da. of William (Bagot), 3rd Lord Bagot, by Lucia Caroline Elizabeth, da. of

---

([a]) It appeared that the Countess gave birth to a son, on 4 Nov. 1881, at No 8 Avenue Friedland, Paris, who was registered (the parents being not named) as "Guy Bertrand," and who appears, sometimes, to have been *styled* "Lord Guernsey." His reputed father was George Charles Spencer-Churchill, then *styled* Marquess of Blandford, afterwards (1883), 8th Duke of Marlborough.   Nearly two years afterwards this child was, 29 June 1883, *bap.*, under the same names, at St. Mary-le-Strand, Midx., but as son of Heneage, Earl of Aylesford, and Edith, which paternity was however subsequently disallowed by the House of Lords.

([b]) The old legal doctrine of "*Pater est quem nuptiæ demonstrant*" has been overruled by the House of Lords in the following instances —(1) In 1692/3 and (again) in 1813, in the case of the Earldom of Banbury, in which the legitimacy of Nicholas Knollys, *b.* 3 Jan. 1630/1, was disallowed by their Lordships, notwithstanding it had been allowed by the King's Bench in 1694.   (2) In 1824, in the case of the Barony of Gardner, as against the claim of Henry Fenton Gardner (better known as Henry Fenton Jadis), *b.* 8 Dec. 1802 in wedlock, but at a date which precluded the possibility of his legitimacy.   (3) On 16 May 1848, in the case of the Barony of Say and Sele, in which the right of Charles Twisleton (whose putative father "John Stein, Esq.," gave evidence as to such his paternity) was passed over, though the said Charles was *b.* 30 Mar 1797, *before* the dissolution [1798] of his mother's marriage with the Hon. Thomas James Twisleton, whose son (by a *subsequent* wife) Frederick Benjamin Twisleton (*b.* 4 July 1799) was declared to have established his claim to the Peerage   (4) In July 1885, in the case of the Earldom of Aylesford, as against the legitimacy of a child *b.* 4 Nov. 1881 in wedlock, of parties who were residing respectively in Chapel Place (Oxford Str.) and in Portugal Str. (South Audley Str.) Midx., in the months of Jan., Feb., Mar. and Apr. previous to the birth.   (5) On 3 July 1905, in the case of the Earldom of Poulett, as against the legitimacy of a child *b* 15 Dec. 1849, in wedlock, the mother having *m.* Earl Poulett 23 June 1849, and the Earl denying paternity on he ground of non-access. The same overruling has also been effected by Act of Parl, of which the following instances apply to Peerage successions, *viz.*.—(1) Act 9 and 10 Will. III, c. 11, "for dissolving the marriage between Charles [Gerard] Earl of Macclesfield and Anne his wife, and to illegitimate to children of the said Anne", and (2) Act 6 and 7 Vic., "to declare that certain persons therein named are not the children of George Ferrars [Townshend], Marquis Townshend." The case of the supposed s of the xviii Earl of Leicester, *b.* 29 Sep. 1738, 21 years after the Earl's marriage, never seems to have come before the Lords

George James (AGAR ELLIS), LORD DOVER   She, who was *b.* 22 May
1852, *d. s.p.* 12 Apr. 1874.   He m , 2ndly, 16 Feb. 1879, Ella Victoria,
widow of Charles LINTON, of Hemmingford Abbots, Hunts, yst. da. of
John Ross, of Benena, co. Cork.

[HENEAGE GREVILLE FINCH, *styled* LORD GUERNSEY, s. and h. ap., by
2nd wife, *b.* 2 June 1883.   Ed. at Eton.   Served in the S African
war at St. Helena in 1901. (ᵃ)   Lieut. 1st Batt. Irish Guards, Sep. 1904.
A.D.C. to the Gov. of Gibraltar 1905.   He *m.*, 11 June 1907, at St. Michael's, Chester Sq , Gladys Cecil Georgina, 2nd da. of William Henry
(FELLOWES), 2nd BARON DE RAMSEY, by Rosamund Jane Frances, 2nd da.
of John Winston (SPENCER-CHURCHILL), DUKE OF MARLBOROUGH.   She
was *b.* 4 Jan. 1885.]

Family Estates.—These, in 1883, consisted of about 12,500 acres in
co. Warwick, about 4,300 in co. Leicester, and 2,856 in Kent   Total about
20,000, valued at about £33,000 a year.   *Note.*—The Kentish estates, 2,864
(sic) acres, were put up for sale in Sep. 1884, under a "disentailing act"
of 1882.   Some were not at once sold, but the amount realized was
£80,000, of which £26,200 was paid for the Boxley Abbey estate (905 acres)
by the Earl of Romney, the rental being about £1000 a year.   *Principal
Residence :*—Packington Hall, co. Warwick.

AYLMER [of Balrath]

BARONY [I.]   1. MATTHEW AYLMER, 2nd s. of Sir Christopher A.,
I. 1718.   of Balrath, co. Meath, 1st Bart. [I.], by Margaret, 3rd da.
               of Matthew (PLUNKETT), 5th LORD LOUTH [I.], having
been page to the Duke of Buckingham, ent. the Navy 1678, obtained the
command of a ship, and became Rear Adm. of the Red 1692/3 ; Vice Adm.
1694; Admiral 1708; Commander in Chief of the Fleet 1708-11, and 1714
till death.   Commissioner of the Navy 1694-1702.   M.P. (Whig) for Portsmouth 1695, till unseated on petition Jan. 1696; for Dover 1697-1713, and
1715 till death.   Governor of Greenwich Hospital 6 Nov. 1714 till death.
A Lord of the Admiralty 1717-18.   On 1 May 1718 he was *cr* LORD
AYLMER, BARON OF BALRATH, co. Meath [I.]. (ᵇ)   On 18 Mar.
1717/8 he was appointed to the honorary office of Rear Adm. of Great
Britain.   Ranger of Greenwich Park and Keeper of Greenwich Palace.
He *m.* Sarah, da. of Edward ELLIS, of London.   She *d.* Nov. 1710.   He *d.*
at Greenwich Palace, 18, and was *bur.* 23 Aug 1720, at Greenwich.   Will
dat 2 June, pr 7 Sep. 1720. (ᶜ)

(ᵃ) For a list of peers, and heirs ap. of peers, serving in this war, see vol. iii,
Appendix B.
(ᵇ) The preamble to this creation is printed in Lodge's *Peerage of Ireland,* 1789,
vol. vii, p. 65.   The patent, which is in Latin, is given *in extenso* in the claim to the
Peerage in July 1860.   The titles are " *Dominus Aylmer, Baro de Balrath.* "
(ᶜ) The following is Bishop Burnet's character of him when upwards of 50,

II. 1720   2. Henry (Aylmer), Lord Aylmer &c. [I], only s
                    and h. Equerry to George I. M P. (Whig) for Rye
1722-27 Comptroller of the Mint, July 1727 till his death. He *m* (settlement 27 June 1716) Elizabeth, da of William Priestman, of Westcliffe,
near Dover, Kent, and St. Paul's, Covent Garden, Midx., by Mary, his
wife. She *d.* at Greenwich, 12, and was *bur.* there 20 Jan. 1749/50, aged 60
He *d.* 26 June, and was *bur.* 4 July 1754, at Greenwich. Will dat. 17 Sep.
1751, pr. 15 July 1754.

III 1754.   3. Henry (Aylmer), Lord Aylmer, &c. [I.], 2nd, (ᵃ)
                    but 1st surv. s. and h., *bap.* 21 May 1718, at St. Paul's,
Covent Garden. Capt. R.N. He *m.* Anne, da. of William Pierce, of
Virginia, in North America. She *d.* at the Hotwells, Bristol, 21, and was
bur. 28 Sep. 1756, at Greenwich. He *d.* at Ickleford, Herts, 7, and was
bur. 16 Oct. 1766, at Greenwich, aged 48. Will (no date) pr. 6 Dec. 1766.

IV 1766.   4 Henry (Aylmer), Lord Aylmer, &c. [I.], 2nd,
                    but only surv. s. and h , *b.* about 1750, a minor at his
father's death. (ᵇ) On 11 May 1766, on the death of his cousin, Sir Matthew Aylmer, of Balrath, co. Meath, 6th Bart. [I.], he *suc.* to that Baronetcy,
cr. in 1662. He took his seat in the House of Lords [I.], 16 Feb. 1778,
and on his petition that he was "totally unable to support the dignity of the
Peerage," was recommended by that House, 25 July 1782, "as an object
of His Majesty's bounty." He *m*, 23 Feb. 1774, at Didbrook, co
Gloucester, Catharine, divorced wife of Philip Cade, of the Exchequer
Office, (ᶜ) sister of Charles, Earl Whitworth, 2nd da. of Sir Charles
Whitworth, of Leybourne, Kent, by Martha, 1st da. of Richard Shelley.
He *d.* 22 Oct. 1785, aged 43.(ᵈ)   M.I Killarney Church. Admon. Feb
1805. His widow *m.*, 3rdly, 22 Sep. 1787, at Loughurn, co. Armagh,
Howell Price, and 4thly (—) Bowles. She *d.* 9 Jan 1805, at Middle
Hill, near Box, Somerset.

V. 1785.   5. Matthew (Aylmer, *afterwards* Whitworth-Ayl-
                    mer), Lord Aylmer, &c [I], s and h., *b.* 24 May 1775
On 1 Aug 1800 he obtained an annuity of £600 for life. Ent. the Army
1787, where he saw much service. He was in a French prison for 6 months

---

with Dean Swift's remarks thereon *in italics.* " He has a very good head , indefatigable and designing , is very zealous for the liberties of the People , makes a good
figure in the Parl. as well as the Fleet ; is handsome in his person. " *A virulent
man, born in Ireland.*

(ᵃ) His 1st br., Matthew A , *d. v p* , 2 Sep. 1748. V.G.

(ᵇ) His elder br., Henry, *bap.* 18 Apr 1742, at St Paul's, Covent Garden,
d. an infant. See Lords' Entries in Ulster's Office, vol. 1, p. 267. (*ex inform.*
G.D.Burtchaell). V.G.

(ᶜ) She *m* him 17 Feb. 1761, and the Libel for her *crim. con.* with Lord
Aylmer was exhibited, 5 Dec 1772, at Doctors Commons.

(ᵈ) The beautiful verses of Walter Savage Landor on his da. Rose Whitworth
Aylmer, beginning " Ah ! what avails the sceptred race, " are well known. V.G.

in 1798, and was present at most of the battles in the Peninsular war. Major Gen. 1813; Lieut Gen 1825; Col. of the 56th Foot 1827-32; Col. of the 18th Foot 1832-50; Gen. 23 Nov. 1841. Adjutant Gen. in Ireland 1814-23. Governor Gen. of Canada 1830-35. A D.C. to the King 1810-13. K.C.B. 2 Jan. 1815. G.C.B. 10 Sep. 1836. He *m.*, 4 Aug. 1801, Louisa Anne, 2nd da. of Sir John CALL, 1st Bart., by Philadelphia, da of William BATTY, M.D. He *d* suddenly, of aneurism of the heart, *s p.*, at 15 Eaton Sq., 23 Feb., and was *bur.* 2 Mar. 1850, in the cemetery at Norwood, Surrey, aged 74. His widow, who was *b.* in 1778, *d.* at Newton, Devon, 13 Aug. 1862, aged 84.

VI 1850.   6. FREDERICK WHITWORTH WILLIAM (AYLMER), LORD
          AYLMER, &c. [I.], only surv. br. and h., *b.* 12 Oct. 1777. Entered the Navy 1790. Was at the battle of the Nile (7 Aug. 1798), and was commander of "the Severn" (27 Aug. 1816) at the bombardment of Algiers. Naval A D.C. to the King 1830-37. Rear Adm. 1837; Vice Adm. 1848; Adm. 1854. Knight of the order of St. Ferdinand of Naples. Obtained the Turkish gold medal in 1801 in the Egyptian Campaign. C.B 19 Sep. 1816; K C.B 5 July 1855. He *d.* unm., at 20 Dawson Place, Paddington, 5, and was *bur.* 12 Mar. 1858, at Kensal Green cemetery, aged 80. Will, in which he left £5,500 to his successor, dat. 29 Feb. 1856, with two codicils, pr. 4 Aug. 1858.

VII. 1858.   7. UDOLPHUS (AYLMER), LORD AYLMER, BARON OF
          BALRATH, and a Baronet [I.], cousin and h. male, being 2nd, but 1st surv. s. and h. of John Athelmar AYLMER, of Melbourne, in East Canada, Capt. R. N. (*d.* 21 Jan. 1849), by Elizabeth, (ª) da of Henry COATES, of Burton upon Trent, which John Athelmar was only s. and h. of Adm. John A. (*d.* 1841, aged 82) s. and h. of John A, Preb. of Bristol (*d.* 1793, aged 70), who was 2nd s. of the 2nd Lord. He was *b.* 10 June, and *bap.* 2 July 1814, at St. Werburgh's, Derby His claim to the Peerage was allowed 10 July 1860. He *m*, 28 June 1841, Mary Eliza, 3rd da. of Edward JOURNEAUX, formerly of Dublin, but afterwards of Melbourne, East Canada. She *d.* 14 Sep. 1881. He *d.* 30 Nov. 1901, at Melbourne afsd., aged 87, and was *suc.* by his s. and h., who is outside the scope of this work.

AYMOUTH see AYEMOUTH

AYR see AIR

(ª) She was *m* 12 July 1812, at St. Werburgh's, Derby.

B

BACON

No Peerage dignity ever existed of this name, yet the celebrated Sir Francis Bacon (*Lord* Keeper 1616-17, *Lord* Chancellor 1617-18, who was, in 1618, *cr.* BARON VERULAM, and, in 1621, VISCOUNT ST. ALBANS), is very generally, though erroneously, spoken of as LORD BACON. (a)   See "ST. ALBANS," Viscountcy, *cr.* 1621, *extinct* 1626.

BADENOCH

i.e. "LORD OF BADENOCH" [S.], Alexander (STEWART), EARL OF BUCHAN [S.], &c., (4th son of Robert II [S.]), is so styled.   See "BUCHAN," Earldom of [S.], *cr.* 1374.

i.e. "BADENOCH or GORDON OF BADENOCH" Barony [S.] *(Gordon), cr.* apparently 1599, with the MARQUESSATE OF HUNTLY [S.] (which see), but not allowed therewith in 1838.

i.e. "BADENOCH, LOCHABER, STRATHNAVON," &c., Barony [S.] *(Gordon), cr.* 1684 with the DUKEDOM OF GORDON [S.] (which see), *extinct* 1836.

BADLESMERE

BARONY
BY WRIT.

1. BARTHOLOMEW OF BADLESMERE, of Badlesmere and Chilham Castle, Kent, s. and h. of Guncelin or Gun-

---

(a) He is styled "*Lord Bacon*" in works published as early as 1658, 1661, 1671, &c.   See *N. & Q.,* 6th Ser., vol. x, p. 502.   But see also *N. & Q.,* 3rd Ser., vol. ii, p. 200, where it is stated "that persons holding the inferior offices [*i.e.* inferior to the office of Chancellor] of Chief Judges in the Courts of Common Law were then called *Lords,* though not Peers, as *Lord* Coke, *Lord* Hailes and *Lord* Holt."   "Lord Hailes," however, is not a case in point; Sir David Dalrymple, Bart. [S.], being a Senator of the College of Justice, and having assumed that style in accordance with Scottish custom.   The titles of all these, whom the Scotch call "Paper Lords," will be found in Brunton and Haig's *Historical Account of the Senators of the College of Justice.*   (*ex inform.* H.Gough.)

I. 1309   selm B , of Badlesmere afsd., (ᵃ) Justice of Chester, by
to   Joan, da. of Ralph FITZ BERNARD, of Kingsdown, Kent
1322.   (aunt and, in her issue, h. to Thomas [LORD] FITZ
BERNARD), attended the war in Gascony (1294) 22
Edw. I ; *suc.* his father in 1301, being then aged 26 ; was in the Scottish
wars 1303 and 1304 ; Governor of Bristol Castle 1307 ; had a grant of the
Castle and Manor of Chilham, Kent, 1309, and from 26 Oct. (1309)
3 Edw. II, to 15 May (1321) 14 Edw. II, was sum. (ᵇ) to Parl by writs
directed *Bartholomeo de Badlesmere,* whereby he may be held to have become
LORD BADLESMERE. (ᶜ)   He obtained a grant of the Castle of
Leeds in Kent, and in (1314-15) 8 Edw. II, was made Governor of Skipton
Castle, and of all the castles in Yorkshire and Westmorland whereof
Robert de Clifford had *d.* seized.   He was also Steward of the King's
Household.   Notwithstanding the many favours he had received, he joined
the Earl of Lancaster in his rebellion, and was defeated with him at
Boroughbridge, 16 Mar 1322, captured at Stow Park, *attainted,* and hung
as a traitor at Canterbury, 14 Apr 1322.   He is described in the contem-
porary Boroughbridge Roll as a Banneret. (ᵈ)   He *m.,* before 30 June 1308,
Margaret, widow of Gilbert DE UMFREVILLE(ᵉ) (who *d.* before 23 May 1303,
s. and h. ap. of Gilbert vii EARL OF ANGUS), aunt and coh. of Thomas DE
CLARE, Steward of the Forest of Essex, da. of Thomas DE C (yr. s. of Richard,
EARL OF GLOUCESTER AND HERTFORD), by Julian, (not Amy), da. of Sir
Maurice FITZ MAURICE, Lord Justice of Ireland.   He *d.* as afsd, 1322. (ᶠ)
His widow, notorious for having refused the Queen admission to the Royal
Castle of Leeds in the summer of 1321, was besieged therein by Edward II,
and being captured with the Castle on 11 Nov. following, was imprisoned
in the Tower of London, but was released 3 Nov. 1322, and after staying
some time at the Minorites without Aldgate, at the King's charge (2s. a day),
had leave to go to her friends, 1 July 1324.   She, who was aged 40 in Mar.
1326/7, had dower on lands at Castlecombe, Wilts, &c., and *d.* late in 1333.

II. 1328   2. GILES OF BADLESMERE, s. and h., *b.* 18 Oct. 1314, at
to   Hambleton, Rutland, and *bap.* at St. Andrew's Church
1338.   there, was 14 years old in Nov. 1328, when he obtained
the *reversal of his father's attainder,* and though a minor,
had livery of his father's lands (1333) 7 Edw. III.   He was sum. to Parl.

(ᵃ) The Lords Badlesmere bore arms of Silver a fesse and two gimels gules.
(*ex inform.* Oswald Barron)   V.G.

(ᵇ) There is proof in the rolls of Parl. of his sitting.

(ᶜ) As to how far these early writs of summons did in fact create any peerage
title, see Appendix A in the last volume.   V G.

(ᵈ) For an account of the battle of Boroughbridge and list of the nobles who
fought on either side, see vol ii, Appendix C.   V.G

(ᵉ) She figures as " Margaret Dumfravill, Lady of Badlesmere " 19 June 1325,
and on the seal of a grant to Master Richard de Clare, 23 June 1328 ; also as
" Margaret de Umframville late the wife of Bartholomew de Badlesmere, " in *Patent
Roll,* 13 Dec. 1329.   V.G.

(ᶠ) *Inq. p. m.,* Colerne, 8 Feb. 3 Edw. III   V G.

by writs directed *Egidio de Badlismere*, 22 Jan. (1335/6) 9 Edw. III to
20 Dec. (1337) 11 Edw III.   He *m.*, after Feb. 1327/8, Elizabeth, ([*]) da.
of William (MONTAGU), 1st EARL OF SALISBURY, by Catherine, da. of
William [LORD] GRANSON. ([b])   He *d. s.p*, between 7 Apr. and 22 June
1338, aged 24, since which time any Barony, that may be supposed to have
existed, has been in *abeyance* ([c])   His widow *m.*, before May 1341, Hugh
[LORD] LE DESPENSER, who *d. s p.* 8 Feb. 1348/9.   She *m.*, 3rdly, before
10 July 1350, Guy [LORD] BRYAN, who *d.* 17 Aug. 1390.   She *d.* 31 May
1359, at Ashley, Hants, and was *bur.* in Tewkesbury Abbey. ([d])

Note —The Barony of Badlesmere was assumed by John (de Vere),
7th Earl of Oxford in right of his wife, who (though she was not the eldest
of the sisters and coheirs of the last Lord) had *suc.* to the *Lordship
of Badlesmere*, Kent.   The succeeding Earls likewise assumed the style of
Lords Badlesmere, and that, too, even after the death of John, the 14th
Earl, in 1526, *s.p.m.*, on whose *sisters* and coheirs the representation of any
Barony in fee which might have been vested in the issue of the 7th Earl
would (according to the now received law in Peerage descent) have devolved   This their assumption was on the principle (then generally believed)
that when a *Barony once* became *united with an Earldom* it continued *attendant thereon.*   At length on the death *s.p.* of Henry, the 18th Earl, in
1625, when this Barony together with other honours was claimed by
Robert de Vere, his cousin and h. male, the House, on 5 Apr. 1626
(without enquiring into the origin or nature of these dignities, or even into
the fact of their actual existence in the person of the said John, the 14th
Earl), resolved *that the Baronies of Bolebec, Sandford and Badlesmere were in
abeyance between the heirs gen. of the said John, Earl of Oxford.*   But in the

([a]) "*Mary* [sic] who was wife of Giles de Badlesmere" brings an action in
Mich. 1340. (Year Books, 14 and 15 Edw III, Rolls Series, p 200.) V.G.

([b]) For some discussion on mediæval English names see vol. iii, Appendix C. V G.

([c]) On his death his four sisters were found his coheirs, and in their issue rests
the representation of the Barony.   They were (1) Margery, then aged 32, and wife
of William de Ros, by whom she was ancestress of the Lords de Ros, &c. (2) Maud,
then aged 28, and Countess of Oxford.   She *d* (1366) 40 Edw. III, being ancestress
of John, the 14th Earl of Oxford, on whose death *s.p.* in 1526, his three sisters
became coheirs. (3) Elizabeth, then aged 25, and Countess of Northampton, who
by her 1st husband, Edmund de Mortimer, had a s. and h, Roger, Earl of March,
through whom her share in the Barony became vested in the Crown in the person
of Edward IV. (4) Margaret, then 23 years old, and wife of John, [2nd Lord]
Tiptoft or Tibetot, whose s and h., Robert, *d. s.p.m* 1372, leaving three daughters
and coheirs.   The coheirs of the Barony of Badlesmere (1855) are given in *Courthope*,
p. 38, and somewhat more fully (1822) in *Coll. Top. et Gen*, vol. viii, p 181.

([d]) "1359, apud Assteley in comitatu Hamptonie, ultimo die mensis Maii"
(*Chron. of Tewkesbury*, in *Monasticon*, vol ii, p. 62), *i.e.*, Ashley, Hants, a manor of
the Despensers.   It has been stated that there is an *Inq. p. m.* on her of date 15
Edw. III, but there is, of course, no such *Inq.*   On the tomb of Guy de Brian at
Tewkesbury, the arms of Montagu are impaled with his own · but the lady is buried
hard by, under a magnificent tomb on the North side of the High Altar, with her
2nd husband, Hugh le Despenser. (*ex inform* G. W. Watson.) V.G.

Lords' Reports (3rd) it is added that the Committee apprehend that if enquiry had been made " it would have appeared that the Barony of Badlesmere had been in abeyance between four coheirs, one of whom *m*. John, then Earl of Oxford; and unless the Crown had done some act, calling the dignity out of abeyance in favour of some Earl of Oxford, of which the committee have not found any trace, that dignity was never vested in any Earl of Oxford, and must have remained in abeyance between the four coheirs of Giles de Badlesmere and not between the coheirs of John, Earl of Oxford. " Notwithstanding this decision, Aubrey (de Vere), Earl of Oxford, in the Court of Claims for the Coronation of Charles II, in 1661, styled himself " Seigneur Bolebeck Stanford [*i e.* Sandford] Badlesmere et Scales "; while, by writ of Privy Seal, 8 June 1588, Queen Elizabeth granted Earls Colne Priory to " Edwardo de Veere Comiti Oxon Vicecomiti Bulbeck Domino de Badlesmere et de Scales " See note *sub* BEDFORD Barony and note *sub* BOLEBEC.

BAGOT OF BAGOT'S BROMLEY

BARONY.   1. WILLIAM BAGOT, of Bagot's Bromley and Blithfield,
I. 1780.   co. Stafford, 2nd, but 1st surv. s. and h. of Sir Walter
                Wagstaffe BAGOT, 5th Bart. [1627] of the same, by Barbara,
1st da. of William (LEGGE), 1st EARL OF DARTMOUTH, was *b.* 28 Feb. 1728. Matric. at Oxford (Magd. Coll.) 28 Oct 1746; M A 1749; Hon D.C.L. 1754; was M.P (Tory) for co Stafford, 1754-80; (a) *suc.* his father as 6th Bart, 20 Jan 1768; and was *cr.*, 17 Oct 1780, BARON BAGOT OF BAGOT'S BROMLEY, co. Stafford. (b) He *m*, 20 Aug. 1760, Elizabeth Louisa, sister of Frederick, 2nd VISCOUNT BOLINGBROKE, and 1st da. of John (ST. JOHN), 2nd VISCOUNT ST. JOHN, by his 1st wife, Anne, da and h of Sir Robert FURNESE, Bart. He *d.* 22 Oct. 1798, aged 70. Will pr Nov. 1798 and again Apr. 1847. His widow *d.* 4 Feb. 1820, at Blithfield afsd, aged 76. Will pr. Mar. 1820.

II. 1798.   2. WILLIAM (BAGOT), BARON BAGOT OF BAGOT'S BROM-
                LEY, 3rd, (c) but 1st surv. s and h, *b.* 11 Sep. 1773, in
Bruton Str Ed. at Westm. Matric. at Oxford (Ch. Ch.) 10 Nov. 1791; Hon. D.C.L. 1834 F.S A. He was a Tory in politics. He *m*, 1stly, 30 May 1799, in Mayfair Chapel, Curzon Str., St. Geo., Han. Sq. (spec. lic.), Emily, 4th da. of Charles (FITZ ROY), 1st LORD SOUTHAMPTON, by

---

(a) He supported Fox's India Bill, but opposed him on the Regency Question in 1788   V.G.

(b) The Lords Bagot bear arms of Ermine two cheverons azure. (*ex inform.* Oswald Barron) V.G.

(c) His 1st br , Edward, *b.* 1763, and his 2nd br., Walter, *b.* 1766, and a sister Barbara, *b* 1768, all *d.* within a few days of one another, of putrid sore throat, and were *bur.* at Blithfield, June 1773. Charles, the 4th br., a distinguished diplomatist, and intimate friend of the statesman Canning, was Gov Gen of Canada, from 1841 till his death, and *d* 19 May 1843. Richard, the 5th br , was successively Bishop of Oxford, and of Bath and Wells, and *d* 15 May 1854. V.G.

Anne, da. and coh. of Vice Admiral Sir Peter WARREN, K.B. She, who was *b.* 26 Dec. 1770, *d. s.p.m.*, 8 June 1800, of consumption, at Christ Church, Hants. He *m.*, 2ndly, at St. James's, Westm., 17 Feb. 1807, Louisa, 1st da. of his cousin, George (LEGGE), 3rd EARL OF DARTMOUTH, by Frances, da. of Heneage (FINCH), 3rd EARL OF AYLESFORD. She, who was *b.* 8 Mar. 1787, *d.* 13 Aug. 1816, of typhus fever, at Pool Park, near Ruthyn. He *d.* 12 Feb. 1856, at Blithfield, aged 82.

III. 1856.   3. WILLIAM (BAGOT), BARON BAGOT OF BAGOT'S BROM-
          LEY, s. and h. by 2nd wife, *b.* 27 Mar. 1811, at Blithfield House, co. Stafford. Ed. at Charterhouse school, and at Eton, and at Magd. Coll. Cambridge. M.P. (Conservative) for Denbighshire, 1835-52 ; Gent. of the Bedchamber to the Prince Consort 1858-59. One of the Lords in Waiting, July 1866 to Dec. 1868, and Feb. 1874 to May 1880. He *m.*, 13 Aug. 1851, Lucia Caroline Elizabeth, sister of Henry, 3rd VISCOUNT CLIFDEN [I.], and 1st da. of George James Welbore (AGAR-ELLIS), 1st LORD DOVER, by Georgiana, da. of George (HOWARD), 6th EARL OF CARLISLE. He *d.* 19 Jan. 1887, in Princes Gardens, aged 75. His widow, who was *b.* 9 Jan. 1827, *d.* 22 Jan. 1895, at Nervi, from failure of the heart.

IV. 1887.   4. WILLIAM (BAGOT) BARON BAGOT OF BAGOT'S BROM-
          LEY [1780], and a Baronet [1627], 1st s. and h., *b.* 19 Jan. 1857, at Blithfield Hall ; sometime an officer in the army ; A.D.C. to the Gov. Gen. of Canada, 1876-83 ; Gent. Usher of the Privy Chamber, 1885-87 ; a Lord in Waiting, 1896-1901 (Conservative). He *m.*, 25 July 1903, at Brompton Oratory, Lilian, da. of Henry MAY, of Maryland, U.S.A.

Family Estates.—These, in 1883, consisted of nearly 11,000 acres in co. Stafford worth above £14,000 a year, about 18,000 in co. Denbigh and about 1,600 in co. Merioneth. Total 30,543 acres worth about £22,212 a year. *Principal Residences.*—Blithfield House, near Rugeley, co. Stafford, and Pool Park, near Ruthyn, co. Denbigh.

BAGOT'S BROMLEY

See "BAGOT OF BAGOTS BROMLEY, co. Stafford, " Barony *(Bagot)*, *cr.* 1780.

BAILIEBOROUGH

See "LISGAR OF LISGAR AND BAILIEBOROUGH, co. Cavan, " Barony *(Young)*, *cr.* 1870 ; *extinct* 1876.

BALCARRES

BARONY [S.].   1. DAVID LINDSAY, of Balcarres, co. Fife, 2nd, but
I. 1633.   only surv. s. of the Hon. John LINDSAY, of the same (one of the Lords of Session being denominated as *Lord Men-*

muir, (ª) sometime PRIVY SEAL and Secretary of State [S]), by his 1st wife, Marion, widow of David BORTHWICK, of Lochhill, advocate, and da. of Alexander GUTHRIE, Town Clerk of Edinburgh, by Janet HENRYSON, which John Lindsay was 2nd s. of David, 9th Earl of Crawford [S]. He was *bap.* 17 Mar. 1587, at Edinburgh. He *suc.* his 1st br., John L., in the estate of Balcarres in Jan 1600/1, being then aged 14 years, and was served h. to him 19 May 1601. Was Knighted 1612. When Charles I visited Scotland, he was (shortly after the coronation at Holyrood) *cr.*, 27 June 1633, LORD LINDSAY OF BALCARRES [S.], to him and his heirs male bearing the name and arms of Lindsay. The original " signature " was for his being *cr.* " *Lord Lindsay of Balneill and Viscount of Balcarres* " [S]. (ᵇ) He *m.*, 16 Feb. 1611/2, at Dunfermline, his 1st cousin once removed, Sophia, 5th da. of Alexander (SETON), 1st EARL OF DUNFERM-LINE [S.], sometime Chancellor [S.], by his 1st wife, Lilias, da. of Patrick (DRUMMOND), 3rd LORD DRUMMOND [S.], by Elizabeth, da. of David (LINDSAY), 9th EARL OF CRAWFORD [S.] abovenamed. In the disputes which led to the Civil war, he steadfastly adhered to his King. He *d.* Mar. 1640/1, and was *bur.* in the Chapel of Balcarres, aged 54. (ᶜ) His will, dat. 1 June 1640, appoints his wife, who surv. him, his sole executrix. (ᵇ)

II 1641.   2 and 1. ALEXANDER (LINDSAY), LORD LINDSAY OF
EARLDOM [S].   BALCARRES [S.], s. and h. He was *b.* at Balcarres, 6 July, and *bap* 4 Aug. 1618. Ed. at school at Had-
I. 1651.   dington, and at the University of St. Andrews Unlike his father, he took the part of the Covenanters against the King, but, notwithstanding, was made P.C. [S.] 16 Nov. 1641. He was at the battle of Marston Moor, 2 July 1644, and commanded a troop of horse at the battle of Alford, 2 July 1645, where, however, he was defeated by the Royalists under Montrose, after a hard fight. On 29 Dec. 1645, he was one of the Commissioners [S.] to the King at Newcastle, whom he urged (though to no purpose) to adopt measures so as to avoid his being surrendered to the English. After this he appears to have stood high in favour with the King, who appointed him Governor of Edinburgh Castle. On the arrival of Charles II in Scotland, he persuaded many of his relations and friends to espouse the Royal cause. On 9 Jan. 1650/1, by patent dat. at Perth, he was *cr.* LORD LINDSAY AND BALNEIL, and EARL OF BALCARRES [S.], (ᵈ) " sibi, ejusque heredibus masculis

(ª) In 1586 Lord Menmuir " purchased the lands of *Balcarres*, Balniell, Pit-corthie and others in Fifeshire and obtained a Royal Charter uniting them into a free Barony in his favour [10 June 1592], an estate which, with the lands of Balmakin and Innerdoral in Angus, formed the original patrimony of the Balcarres family. "

(ᵇ) See *Lives of the Lindsays* (a work of great research) by Alexander W. C. Lindsay, *styled* Lord Lindsay, afterwards (1869-80) Earl of Crawford [S.], 3 vols. 8vo, 1849, and (a better edn.) 1858.

(ᶜ) He devoted himself to science and literature, particularly to chemistry and to the search of the (then widely sought) " Philosopher's stone. "

(ᵈ) For a list of Peerages *cr* by Charles II while in exile, see note *sub* i BARON LANGDALE OF HOLME

talliæ et provisionis in ejus infeofamentis expressis, seu exprimendis. "
He was Hereditary Governor of the Castle of Edinburgh (an office afterwards surrendered by his widow), and High Commissioner to the Gen.
Assembly of the Kirk, 16 July 1651. He was in command of the troops
north of the Forth, and by mortgage and by sale of his plate raised £8,000
for the Royal cause. After the King's defeat at Worcester in Sep. 1651,
he capitulated to Cromwell. He again took arms for Charles II in 1653,
and his estate being sequestrated, joined his King on the Continent in that
year. He was considered the head of the Presbyterians or Scottish Consti-
tutionalists, and was the King's Secretary of State for Scotland. He m., in
Apr. 1640 (cont. 22 and 23 Apr.), his 1st cousin Anne, 1st of the two
daughters and coheirs of Colin (MACKENZIE), 1st EARL OF SEAFORTH, by
(his mother's sister) Margaret, da. of Alexander (SETON), 1st EARL OF
DUNFERMLINE [S.] afsd. He d. in exile, at Breda, 30 Aug. 1659, and was
bur. 12 June 1660, aged 41, at Balcarres. His widow, who was an intimate
friend of Richard Baxter, the well-known divine, m. (as his 2nd wife),
28 Jan. 1670, Archibald (CAMPBELL), 9th EARL OF ARGYLL [S.], who was
beheaded 30 June 1685. She d. 2, and was bur. 29 May 1707, at Balcarres.
Fun. entry in Lyon office.

| EARLDOM [S.]
II.
BARONY [S.]
III. | 1659. | 2 and 3. CHARLES (LINDSAY), EARL OF BALCARRES, &c., s. and h., bap. 7 Feb. 1651, at Dundee. He d., "a large stone being found at his heart," (ᵃ) at Balcarres, 15, and was there bur. 21 Oct. 1662, aged 11. |

| EARLDOM [S.]
III.
BARONY [S.]
IV. | 1662. | 3 and 4. COLIN (LINDSAY), EARL OF BALCARRES, &c. [S.], br. and h., bap. 23 Aug. 1652, at Kilconquhar. At the age of 16 he was presented to the King, Charles II, who gave him a troop of horse and a life pension of £1000 a year. He sat in Parl. when still a minor 19 Oct. |

1669. He was with the Duke of York "in the well fought battle
of Solebay, 28 May 1672, and enjoyed a great share of his Highness' confidence. " (ᵃ) P.C. 3 June 1680. Sheriff of co. Fife, 1682.
Commissioner of the Treasury, 3 Sep. 1686, being one of the Council of
Six in whom the Scottish administration was lodged. His spirited proposition to apply the £90,000 then in the Scottish exchequer to the levying
of troops to support James II against the invasion of the Prince of Orange,
was overruled by Melfort. He and Lord Dundee [S.] were the last who
were in attendance on King James, before his final expulsion from London.
They then proceeded to Scotland to call a Parl. at Stirling, but the Earl
was taken prisoner, and kept in the Tolbooth at Edinburgh for some

---

(ᵃ) See note " b " on previous page.

months. He again joined, in 1690, in Sir James Montgomery's scheme for restoring the exiled King, whom (on its discovery) he joined at St. Germain. After an exile of ten years, he returned to Scotland in 1700, and was received at court by Queen Anne. He voted in favour of the Scottish Union. He obtained likewise a pension of £500 a year for ten years in lieu of the one of £1000 lost at the Revolution P.C. (again) Apr. 1705. His attachment to the House of Stuart led him to join the Rising of 1715, but having surrendered himself, he was included in the indemnity. (*) He *m.*, (*b*) 1stly, about 1670, when very young, Mauritia de Nassau, da. of Louis, Baron of Lecke and Beverwaet, in Holland (illegit s. of Maurice, Prince of Orange), by Elisabeth, da. of Jean, Count of Hornes, Seigneur de Kessel. She *d s.p.*, within the year, in childbed, and was *bur* at St. Margaret's, Westm., 14 Aug. 1671, as " Moriso Margreta de Naso Countice of Bellcarris. " He *m.*, (*b*) 2ndly, Jean, da. of David (Carnegie), 2nd Earl of Northesk [S.], by Jean, da of Patrick (Maule), 1st Earl of Panmure. She *d. s.p.m.s.*, about 1680. He *m.*, 3rdly, Jean, da. of William (Kerr, formerly Drummond), 2nd Earl of Roxburghe [S.], by Jean, da. of Harry Kerr, 'Master of Roxburghe,' *styled* Lord Kerr. He *m.*, 4thly, before 4 July 1689, Margaret, da of James (Campbell), 2nd Earl of Loudoun [S], by Margaret, da. of Hugh (Montgomerie), 7th Earl of Eglintoun [S.] He *d* in 1722, at Balcarres, in his 73rd year, and was *bur.* in the chapel there. (*c*) His widow *d.* May 1747.

[Colin Lindsay, " Master of Balcarres," generally *styled* Lord Cummerland, (*d*) s and h ap. by 3rd wife. Capt. of Dragoons and A D.C. to the Duke of Marlborough. He *d* unm and *v.p.*, Nov. 1708.]

EARLDOM [S.] IV.

BARONY [S.] V.

1722.

4 and 5 Alexander (Lindsay), Earl of Balcarres, &c. [S.], 1st surv s and h., by 4th wife. He served in the wars in Flanders in 1707, and was wounded at the siege of St. Venant, but owing to his father's share in the Rising of 1715, it was not till 1732 that he obtained a company in the Foot Guards. He was a Rep Peer [S] 1734 till his death. (*e*) He *m.*, in 1718 (cont. 31 July 1718), Elizabeth, da. of David Scott, of Scotstarvet, co Fife. He *d s.p*, 25 July 1736 Admon. as of Balcarres, co. Fife, 3 Aug 1737. His widow *d.* at Edinburgh, 14 Sep. 1778.

(*a*) He was a man of letters, with a taste for art as well as books. He was author of *An account of the affairs in Scotland relating to the Revolution*, 1688, and as such has a place among Walpole's *Noble Authors*.

(*b*) See romantic stories about both these weddings in the *Lives of the Lindsays*.

(*c*) His grand-daughter characterises him as " one of the handsomest and most accomplished men of his time, a man of letters, but fond of pleasure, and pleasure's favourite. " V.G.

(*d*) This title was taken from Cummerland, part of the estate of Balcarres. See *Douglas*, p 175.

(*e*) He was a friend of the celebrated Duncan Forbes, President of the Court of Session.

EARLDOM [S.]		
V.		
BARONY [S]	1736.	
VI.		

5 and 6. JAMES (LINDSAY), EARL OF BALCARRES, &c [S.], br. and h, being yst. s. of the 3rd Earl, b. 14 Nov. 1691. Lieut. R N. He joined his father in the Rising of 1715, and was Capt of a troop which acted with great gallantry at the battle of Sheriffmuir. He was, however, pardoned and made Lieut. in the 2nd or Royal North British Reg. of Dragoons (Scots Greys), under his uncle Sir James Campbell ; commanded a squadron at the battle of Dettingen in 1743, but retired after the battle of Fontenoy, 1745, in which his said uncle was slain. He devoted the rest of his life to literature, and to the improvement of his estate. When in his 60th year he m., 24 Oct. 1749, at Edinburgh, Anne, da. of Sir Robert DALRYMPLE, of Castleton, by his 2nd wife, Anne, da. of Sir William CUNNINGHAM, of Caprington. He d. 20 Feb. 1768, in his 77th year, at Balcarres, and was bur there. (a) His widow, who was b 25 Dec. 1727, d. 20 Nov. 1820, at Balcarres. (b) Will pr. June 1825.

EARLDOM [S.]		
VI.		
BARONY [S.]	1768.	
VII.		

6 and 7 ALEXANDER (LINDSAY), EARL OF BALCARRES &c. [S], s. and h, b 18 Jan. 1752. On the death of his cousin, George (LINDSAY), 20th EARL OF CRAWFORD [S.], who d s.p, 30 Jan. 1808, he should de jure have suc. to that Earldom, which was confirmed to his son after reference to the House of Lords in 1848 (23 years after his death on 27 Mar. 1825). See "CRAWFORD," Earldom of [S.]

BALFOUR OF BURLEIGH

BARONY [S] I. 1607.

1 MICHAEL BALFOUR, of Burleigh Castle, in Orwell, co. Kinross, s. and h of Sir James B, of Pittendreich, co. Fife, President of the Court of Session [S.], who d. 1583, by Margaret, da. and h of Michael BALFOUR, of Burleigh afsd., obtained charters (v.p.) of lands in co Fife and co Banff in 1569 and 1577. He

(a) His da. Anne describes him as "an accomplished gentleman, a reasoning philosopher, a judicious farmer, and a warm partisan." Of her mother she writes — "She was fair, blooming, and lively; her beauty and embonpoint charmed my dear, tall, lean, majestic father ... She had worth, honour, activity, good sense, good spirits, economy, justice, friendship, generosity—everything but softness." V G

(b) Of their eleven children, the eldest, Anne, b 8 Dec 1750, m., 31 Oct 1793, Andrew Barnard, Secretary to the Colony of the Cape of Good Hope, who d. there 27 Oct. 1807, s p. This was the celebrated Lady Anne Barnard, the authoress (1772) of "Auld Robin Gray," &c. She d 6 May 1825, in her 75th year. Her youngest sister, Elizabeth, Countess of Hardwicke (b. 11 Oct 1763, d 26 May 1858), outlived the birth of her grandfather, Earl Colin (abovenamed) by no less a period than 207 years

was knighted before 1592 ; sat in convention 1599, and had charter of the Barony of Burleigh 29 Nov. 1606, in which year he is stated to have been AMBASSADOR both to the Grand Duke of Tuscany and to the Duke of Lorraine On 16 July 1607, he was *cr.* LORD BALFOUR OF BUR-LEIGH, co. Kinross [S], without mention of heirs in the patent of creation. (ᵃ) P.C. He appears to have been one of the *Scots* peers sum. to the *Irish* House of Lords by writ 11 Mar 1613/4. (ᵇ) On 7 Sep. 1614, he obtained a charter of the Barony of Kilwinning " with the title of LORD OF KILWINNING, " to him and his heirs and assigns whatever. (ᶜ) He *m.* Margaret, (ᵈ) da. of (—) LUNDIN of that ilk. He *d.* 15 Mar. 1619. Will confirmed 10 July 1620, at St. Andrews. His widow *d.* at Kilmany, co. Fife. Will confirmed 26 Apr. 1626, at St. Andrews.

II. 1619   2. MARGARET, *suo jure* BARONESS BALFOUR OF BUR-
                 LEIGH [S.], da. and sole h. She *m.* (settl. Sep. 1606) Robert ARNOT, of Fernic, co Fife, who assumed the name of BALFOUR. By virtue of a letter from the King, he sat as a peer (LORD BALFOUR OF BURLEIGH) in the Parl. [S], 25 Jan. 1621, and on 11 June 1640 was chosen President of the Session. P.C. He was defeated by Montrose at Aberdeen, 12 Sep 1644, and again at Kilsyth, 15 Aug. 1645. He opposed the " Engagement " to march into England for the rescue of the King. In 1649 he was one of the Colonels for co. Fife, and one of the Commissioners of the Treasury and Exchequer. The Baroness *d.* June 1639, at Edinburgh, and was *bur.* at Orwell. He *d.* at Burleigh, 10, and was *bur.* 12 Aug 1663, " in his parish church. "

III. 1639   3. JOHN (BALFOUR), LORD BALFOUR OF BURLEIGH [S.],
   or   only s. and h. He *m ,* early in 1649, in London, Isabel,
  1663   da. of Sir William BALFOUR, of Pitcullo, Lieut. of the
                 Tower of London. Settl. (post nuptial) 24 Nov. 1666. This marriage his father endeavoured to get set aside. He was living 10 Dec. 1696, but *d.* before Feb. 1696/7.

IV. 1696   4. ROBERT (BALFOUR), LORD BALFOUR OF BURLEIGH [S.],
   or   s. and h., sat in the Parl. of 1698. He *m* Margaret, 1st
  1697   da. of George (MELVILLE), 1st EARL OF MELVILLE [S.],
                 by Catharine, da. of Alexander LESLIE, Master of Leven, *styled* LORD BALGONIE. He *d.* July 1713. She was *b.* 28 Oct. 1658.

(ᵃ) See note *sub* John, EARL OF CARRICK (in Orkney) [1628]

(ᵇ) See *ante*, p. 2 note ' c. "

(ᶜ) The abbey lands of Kilwinning, erected into a Lordship, were granted, 5 Jan. 1603/4, to Hugh (Montgomerie) Earl of Eglintoun, who settled them in 1611 on his cousin and successor in title, from whom they were taken. They were, however, re-conveyed to him by Lord Balfour of Burleigh for 8000 marks. V.G.

(ᵈ) Mariot Adamson, sometimes attributed to him as a first wife, was the wife of another Michael Balfour, of Montquhany. V G.

V. 1713
to
1715.

5. ROBERT (BALFOUR), LORD BALFOUR OF BURLEIGH [S.], only s. and h. He was tried, 4 Aug. 1709, for the murder of Henry Stenhouse, a Schoolmaster of Inverkeithing (who had *m.* a girl to whom he, being then the Master of Burleigh, was attached), and was sentenced (29 Nov.) to be beheaded on 6 Jan. 1709/10, but escaped by changing clothes with his sister. He engaged in the Rising of 1715 on behalf of the exiled Royal family, and (not having surrendered himself by 30 June 1716) was, under the designation of "Robert, Lord Burleigh," *attainted* from 13 Nov. 1715 (*), whereby his estate of £697 a year and his *Peerage* became *forfeited.* He *d.* unm., and was *bur.* at Grey Friars, Edinburgh, 20 Mar. 1757.

1757. MARGARET BALFOUR, spinster, 1st sister and h. of line, who, but for the attainder, would *suo jure* have been LADY BALFOUR OF BURLEIGH [S.]. She *d.* unm., 12 Mar. 1769, at Edinburgh, and was *bur.* in the Canongate there.

1769. ROBERT BRUCE, of Kennet, co. Clackmannan, nephew and h., being s. and h. of Brig. Gen. Alexander BRUCE, of the same, by Mary (sister of Margaret abovenamed), 2nd and yst da. of Robert (BALFOUR), 4th LORD BALFOUR OF BURLEIGH [S.]. He was *b.* 29 Dec. 1718, *suc.* his father 8 Aug. 1747, and his mother (who *d.* before her elder sister abovenamed) 7 Nov. 1758. He was one of the Lords of Session [S.], by the denomination of "Lord Kennet," from 1764, and a Lord of Justiciary, from 1769 till his death. On the death of his maternal aunt in 1769 (as above) he, but for the attainder, would have become LORD BALFOUR OF BURLEIGH [S.]. He *m.*, 21 May 1754, Helen, sister of the gallant Sir Ralph ABERCROMBY, K.B., and da. of George ABERCROMBY, of Tullibody, by Mary, da. of Ralph DUNDAS. He *d.* 8 Apr. 1785, aged 66. His widow *d.* 1786.

1785. ALEXANDER BRUCE, of Kennet afsd., s. and h., *b.* 17 July 1755. Sometime a merchant in China. He *m.*, 13 Feb. 1793, Hugh [*sic*], yst. da. of Hugh BLACKBURN, of Glasgow. He *d.* 12 July 1808, at Kennet, aged nearly 53. His widow, who was *b.* 13 Aug. 1768, at Killearn, near Glasgow, *d.* Dec. 1851, at Edinburgh.

1808. ROBERT BRUCE, of Kennet afsd., s. and h., *b.* 8 Dec. 1795. Ed. at Eton, and at Oxford. Ent. the Army Dec. 1813 ; Capt. in the Grenadier Guards 1820 ; served in the Peninsular war, and was at the battle of Waterloo, retiring 1824. M.P. (Tory) for co. Clackmannan, 1820-24. But for the attainder he would have been LORD BALFOUR OF BURLEIGH [S.], to which Barony he laid

---

(*) See Appendix E in this volume, for a list of the Scottish peers attainted at that date.

claim. (ᵃ)   He *m.*, 1stly, 12 Apr. 1825, Anne, 1st da. of William Murray, of Touchadam and Polmaise, by a da. of (—) Spiers, of Culcreugh,
near Fintry.   She *d. s.p.*, 19 May 1846, at Kennet.   He *m.*, 2ndly, 22
Apr. 1848, at Clackmannan, Jane Dalrymple Hamilton, da. of Sir James
Fergusson, of Kilkerran, 4th Bart. [S.], by his 2nd wife, Henrietta, da.
of Adam (Duncan), 1st Viscount Duncan of Camperdown.   He *d.*
13 Aug. 1864, aged 68.   His widow was living 1910.

VI. 1869.   6. Alexander Hugh Bruce, s. and h. by 2nd wife.
                He, but for the attainder, would have been entitled to the
Peerage in 1864.   His claim to the Barony having been allowed by the
House of Lords, 23 July 1868, he, when the *attainder* was *reversed*, by Act
of Parl., 19 Mar. 1869, became LORD BALFOUR OF BURLEIGH
[S.]. (ᵇ)   He was *b.* 13 Jan. 1849, at Kennet, and *bap.* at Clackmannan.
Ed. at Eton ; Matric. at Oxford (Oriel Coll.) 19 Oct. 1867 ; B.A. and 2nd
class, 1871.   Rep. Peer [S.], 1876 (Conservative Free Trader).   Education
Commissioner [S.], 1882-90; a Lord in Waiting 1887-88; Sec. to the Board
of Trade 1888-92 ; P.C. 28 June 1892 ; Sec. for Scotland 1895-1903 ;
Lord Rector of Edinburgh Univ. 1896-99 ; Pres. of the Highland and
Agric. Soc. 1899-1900 ; Chanc. of St. Andrew's Univ. since 1900 ; K.T.
18 Mar. 1901 ; Gov. of the Bank of Scotland 1904; Warden of the Stannaries
since 1908. (ᶜ)   He *m.*, 21 Nov. 1876, at St. Mary Abbot's, Kensington,
Katherine Eliza, yst. da. of George John (Gordon), 5th Earl of Aberdeen
[S.], by Mary, 2nd da. of George Baillie, of Jerviswood.   She was *b.*
16 Oct. 1852, at the Ranger's House, Blackheath.

[Robert Bruce, *styled* Master of Burleigh, s. and h. ap., *b.* 25 Sep.
1880, at Edinburgh.]

Family Estates.—These, in 1883, consisted of about 2,700 acres in
the counties of Clackmannan, Perth, and Stirling, worth about £3,400
a year.   The estate of Blairgowrie, co. Perth, was sold in 1891 for £20,100
to Lieut. Col. Hare.   *Principal Residence.*—Kennet House, near Alloa, co.
Clackmannan.

(ᵃ) The rival claim of Walter Francis Balfour, of Fernie, h. *male* of the body
of John, Lord Balfour, the 3rd holder of that title (through his 2nd s. Col. John B.
who had been found guilty of high treason at Carlisle in 1716) was referred, May
1861, to the committee of the House of Lords.

(ᵇ) " No claim for this peerage was ever made by my family till 1861.   No
attainder at all was reversed, I believe, until after the accession of George IV, anyhow
not till the late years of George III, and then only to direct heirs.   Reversing the
attainder in favour of collaterals was a later process.   Though my family knew their
right they could not prove it till the accidental discovery of the patent in an oak chest
here [Kennet, Alloa] in 1858." (Lord Balfour to V.G., Mar 1897.)

(ᶜ) He is one of the numerous peers who are or have been directors of public
companies.   For a list of these (in 1896) see vol. v, Appendix C.   V.G.

BALFOUR [of Glenawley]

BARONY [I.]   1. Sir James Balfour of Glenawley [*rectius* Clanawley],
I. 1619.   co. Fermanagh, yr. br. of Michael, 1st Lord Balfour of
Burleigh [S.], 2nd s. of Sir James B., of Pittendreich, co.
Fife, by Margaret, da. and h. of Michael Balfour, of Burleigh, co. Kinross,
received by charter from his parents, 28 Mar. 1587, lands at Costertoun,
co. Edinburgh, and (having risen high in favour with James I, and obtained
several grants of lands in Ireland), was, on 8 Nov. 1619, *cr.* LORD
BALFOUR, BARON OF GLENAWLEY, co. Fermanagh [I.].   He *m.*,
1stly, Grisold, da. and h. of Patrick Balfour, of Pitcullo, co. Fife, by whom
he had three sons and three daughters. (ᵃ)   He *m.*, 2ndly, Elizabeth,
formerly wife of Sir John Leslie, of Balquhain (whom she had divorced
for adultery, 9 Mar. 1597/8), da. of George (Hay), 6th Earl of Erroll
[S.], and only child by his 2nd wife, Helen, da. of Walter Bruce, of
Pitcullen, co. Perth.   He *m.*, 3rdly, before 1627, Anne, da. of Edward
(Blayney) 1st Lord Blayney [I.], by Anne, da. of Adam Loftus, Archbishop of Dublin and Chancellor [I.].   She was living Aug. 1628.   He *d.*
in London, 18, and was *bur.* 24 Oct. 1634, at St. Anne's, Blackfriars.
Fun. cert. in Ulster's office, 29 July 1635. (ᵇ)   Will. dat. 16 Oct. 1634,
pr. 5 Mar. 1634/5 at Dublin.   Admon. 15 May 1635, pending a suit
between Alexander and James Balfour, the sons of deceased.   Will pr.
(again) 2 June 1636.

II. 1634.   2. James (Balfour), Lord Balfour, Baron of Glenawley [I.], s. and h., by 1st wife.   He *m.*, before 1623,
Ann, widow of William Warren, da. of Sir Francis Gouldsmith, of
Crayford, Kent, by Catherine, da. of Edward Oundley, of Catesby, co.
Northampton.   He *d. s.p.*, 26 Feb. 1635/6.   Will as " James Balfour, of
St. Mary le Savoy, Strand, Esq., s. and h. of Sir James, late Baron of Glenawley," dat. 15 Feb. 1635/6, making his wife executrix, pr. 9 Mar. 1635/6,
by Ann, the relict.   *Inq. p.m.* taken at Newtown, co. Fermanagh, 23 May
1639, in which he is styled " Baro de Clonawley. "

III. 1636   3. Alexander (Balfour) Lord Balfour, Baron of
to   Glenawley [I.], only br. and h., was *m.* and of full age
?   when he *suc.* to the title, (ᶜ) but nothing more is known
about him.   He is presumed to have *d. s.p.*, shortly after
1636.   At his death the title became *extinct*.

(ᵃ) Of these Anne, the 2nd da., *m.*, 1stly, Sir John Wemyss ; 2ndly, before
1639, Archibald Hamilton of Ballygally co. Tyrone, who *d. s.p.*, 10 May 1659,
being br. of Hugh Hamilton, *cr.* Baron Hamilton *of Glenawley* [I.], 2 Mar. 1660.
(ᵇ) Printed in Foster's *Collectanea Genealogica*.
(ᶜ) The fact that he did so succeed has never hitherto been recognised in any
peerage.   It is proved by the following *Inq. p. m.* of the 1st Lord, dat. 23 May 1639
(the same day as another *Inq. p. m.* mentioned in text), of which a copy has been
kindly furnished me by G.D.Burtchaell.   It finds that James Balfour [*i.e.* the 2nd

BALGONIE

i.e. "BALGONIE" Barony [S.] (*Leslie*), *cr.* 1641, with the Earldom of ROTHES [S], which see.

BALGOWAN

See "LYNEDOCH OF BALGOWAN," Barony (*Graham*) *cr.* 1818 ; *extinct* 1843.

BALINHARD OF FARNELL

i.e. "BALINHARD OF FARNELL, co. Forfar" Barony (*Carnegie*), *cr.* 1869 See "SOUTHESK," Earldom [S.], *cr.* 1633, under the 6th Earl

BALINROBE

See "TYRAWLEY OF BALINROBE," Barony (*Cuffe*) [I.], *cr.* 1797 ; *extinct* 1821.

BALIOL see BALLIOL

BALLINASLOE

i.e. "DUNLO OF DUNLO and BALLINASLOE," Viscountcy [I.] *(Trench)*, *cr.* 1800 ; see 'CLANCARTY' Earldom [I.], *cr.* 1803.

BALLINBREICH OR BAMBREICH(*)

i.e. "LESLIE AND BALLINBREICH," Barony [S.] *(Leslie)*, granted in 1663 with the *novodamus* of the Earldom of ROTHES [S.], which see.

i e. "BALLINBREICH," Marquessate [S.] *(Leslie)*, *cr.* 1680, with the Dukedom of ROTHES [S.], which see ; *extinct* 1681.

Lord], by deed dated 3 Feb. 1635, demised certain lands to Francis Gouldsmith, of Gray's Inn, and William Hamilton Esq , to the use of said J B for life, and after his death to the use of Anne then wife of said James for life, and after her decease to the use of Archibald Hamilton of Ballygally and Anna Balfour *alias* Waymes [*i.e.* Wemyss, see note "a" p. 383] now wife of said Archibald and the heirs of their bodies. The said James *d.* in the month of Feb. 1635. Alexander B. his br and next h. was of full age at the time of his death afsd , and married   V.G.

(*) "Bambreich" is the form in the patent according to the report on the Rothes muniments in the *Hist. MSS. Com.*   V.G.

BALLINGARD see BELLINGUARD

BALLIOL, (^{a}) or BALIOL

> JOHN BALLIOL (^{b}) 3rd, but 1st surv. s. of John B. (sometime Regent of Scotland), by Devorgild, 2nd da. and coh. of Alan, Lord of Galloway, was *b*. about 1240, being aged 40, 29 Nov. 1280, and was sum. to attend the King at Shrewsbury, 28 June (1283) 11 Edw. I, by writ directed (^{c}) *Johanni de Balliolo*. He possessed the Barony of Bywell, Northumberland, and Barnard's Castle, co. Durham. (^{d}) In right of his descent, through his mother Devorgild, from David I, he was crowned KING of SCOTLAND at Scone, 30 Nov. 1292, having been awarded the Crown by Edward I. In 1295 he lost his English Barony of Bywell, which was given to John of Britanny, Earl of Richmond, nephew of Edward I. He abdicated 10 July 1296. After being detained for some three years as a prisoner in England, he went to France. He *m*., before Feb. 1280/1, Isabel, da. of John (WARENNE) EARL OF SURREY. He *d*. between 4 Mar. 1313/4 and 4 Jan. 1314/5, (^{e}) in France.

BARONY BY WRIT (^{f}) I. 1349 to 1363 or 1365.	1. EDWARD BALLIOL, s. and h., was a prisoner in the Tower at his father's death. He did not succeed to the Barony of Bywell which had been forfeited, but, by the English interest, was crowned KING OF SCOTLAND 24 Sep. 1332, and having fled from that Kingdom in the Dec. following, was sixteen years afterwards sum. to the English

(^{a}) The locality from which this family derived its name was generally presumed to be in Normandy, until it was shown by J.H.Round from a charter of Bernard de Balliol (*Calendar of Documents in France*, p. 513) that the family was of Picard origin, and sprang from Bailleul in the modern department of the Somme. V.G.

Though many genealogists, English and French, have supposed he took his name from Bailleul in Normandy, and have even pointed out his tomb at Bailleul-sur-Eaune, near Rouen, the place in question was, on the contrary, Bailleul-en-Vimeu (canton of Hallencourt, Somme), Vimeu being a district in Picardy (*cf.* *Genealogist*, N.S., vol. viii, p. 217). In 3 charters, of dates from 1304 to 4 Mar. 1313/4, he styles himself " Jehans rois dEscoce et sires de Bailleul en Vimeu " (R. de Belleval, *Jean de Bailleul, Roi d'Ecosse*, 1866, appendix, nos. 4, 5, 7). In betrothing his s., Edward, 23 Oct. 1295, to a da. of Charles, Count of Valois [the marriage did not take place], he gave her dower in his seigneuries of Bailleul, Hornoy, and Hélicourt, all in Vimeu. (*ex inform.* G.W.Watson.) V.G.

(^{b}) By the death of his two elder brothers (of whom Hugh *d. s.p.* before 10 Apr. 1271, and Alexander before 13 Nov. 1278) he became head of the great house of Balliol. His parents were, in 1263, founders of Balliol College, Oxford.

(^{c}) As to this supposed Parl., see Preface.

(^{d}) His arms were Gules a voided scutcheon silver. (*ex inform.* Oswald Barron). V.G.

(^{e}) He *d*. shortly before 4 Jan. 1314/5 (*New Foedera*, vol. ii, pt. i, p. 260). V.G.

(^{f}) " It seems clear that the writ of 22 Edw. III must be regarded as having *cr.* a Barony and that the title of this Barony is BALLIOL. " (*ex inform.* H. Gough.)

Parl., 1 Jan. and again 10 Mar. (1348/9) 22 Edw. III, by writs beginning "Rex Magnifico Principi et fideli suo Edwardo de Balliolo Regi Scotie consanguineo suo charissimo salutem." He *d. s.p.* (ª) between May 1363 and Sep. 1365, (ᵇ) when any *Peerage* dignity that may be supposed (ᶜ) to have been *cr* by these writs became *extinct.* (ᵈ)

BALLIOL, or BALIOL (of Cavers)

BARONY
BY WRIT.

I. 1300.

1. SIR ALEXANDER BALLIOL (ᵉ) of Cavers, co. Roxburgh, s of Sir Henry B., of the same, by Lora, (*m.* before 1233) one of the three daughters and coheirs of William DE VALOIGNES, (ᶠ) Chamberlain of Scotland, was a younger br. of Guy Balliol (standard bearer to de Montfort at the battle of Evesham

---

(ª) It is erroneously stated by Summonte, *Hist. di Napoli,* and those following him, that he *m.* Margherita, da. of Filippo, Prince of Taranto. She *m,* in 1348, Francesco del Balzo, Duke of Andria. See *Genealogist,* N S, vol. xii, pp. 247-8, and the authorities there cited. (*ex inform* G W Watson.) V.G.

(ᵇ) He was living, 27 May 1363, at Wheatley near Doncaster, where he had resided for many years on a pension from Edward III. On 6 Sep. 1365, Raoul de Coucy, knt, Seigneur de la Ferté-Gaucher, brought two suits in the Parl of Paris "ratione terre de Balloho etc ... ut consanguineus et heres proximior defuncti Edouardi domini de Balloho" (Du Chesne, *Maison de Guines et de Coucy, preuves,* pp 440-1). A document in the Scottish Calendar, vol. iv, no 168, of date 20 May 1370, cannot therefore be interpreted as the editor in his preface suggests, *viz.* that Edward Balliol was then alive (*ex inform.* G.W Watson.) V.G.

(ᶜ) As to how far these early writs of summons did, in fact, *cr* any peerage title, see Appendix A in the last volume

(ᵈ) His 4 sisters were (1) Margaret, who *d.* unm. (11) Ada, wife of William de Lindsay. (111) Cicely, wife of John de Burgh. (1v) Mary, wife of John Comyn of Badenoch. Some genealogists add (but in error) a fifth sister, Anne, wife of Brian Fitz Alan of Bedale ; see under " FITZ ALAN (of Bedale). " Christian, sole da. and h. of Ada (the 1st da. who left issue), *m* Enguerrand de Guines, Sire de Coucy, whose great-grandson, Enguerrand, Sire de Coucy (Earl of Bedford), left 3 das. and coheirs the 1st of whom, Marie, *m.* Henri de Bar Their grand-daughter and h, Jeanne de Bar, *m.* Louis de Luxembourg, Count of St Pol and Brienne, whose s and h., Pierre, left 2 daughters and coheirs, the elder of whom, Marie, *m.* François de Bourbon, Count of Vendôme, great-grandfather of Henry IV of France. Thus the heir of line to David I is in the House of Bourbon. (*ex inform.* G W.Watson). V.G.

(ᵉ) An able paper by J.A.C.Vincent in " *The Genealogist* " N.S, vol. vi, p. 1, fully proves the parentage of this Alexander, and that the commonly received notion that he was a younger br. of John Balliol, King of Scotland, is erroneous. See also Surtees' *Durham,* vol iv, p. 58, note " f, " where (as also in Hodgson's *Northumberland,* part 2, vol. ii, p. 42) an elaborate pedigree of Balliol will be found.

(ᶠ) A pedigree shewing the extinction of the Barony of Valoignes is contributed by James Greenstreet to *N. & Q,* 6th Ser, vol v, p. 142. See p. 290 of the same vol., for an amplification thereof by J A.C.Vincent, as also pp. 61 and 389 of the same See also J H Round's " Comyn and Valoignes " (*The Ancestor,* no. xi, p. 133)

and there slain, in 1265), was in possession of his paternal estate before
6 Apr. 1272, and was sometime (between 1287 and 1294) Chamberlain of
Scotland. He fought in Flanders in 1297, at Falkirk in 1298, and at
Carlaverock in 1300. Having *m.*, about 1270, after 7 Nov. 1270, Isabel,
widow of David (OF STRATHBOGIE), EARL OF ATHOLL [S.], sister and coh. of
Richard CHILHAM, or DOVER, da. of Richard Fitz Roy (a natural s. of King
John), by Roese, da. and h. of Fulbert of DOVER, all of Chilham, Kent,
he acquired that Lordship in her right, and was sum. to attend the King
at Shrewsbury 28 June (1283) 11 Edw. I, (ª) by writ addressed *Alexandro
de Balliolo de Chileham*, and to Parl. by writs addressed *Alexandro de Balliolo*,
from 26 Sep. (1300) 28 Edw. I, to 22 Feb. (1306/7) 35 Edw. I. (ᵇ) His
wife *d.* 1292, (before 1 May) and was *bur.* in Canterbury Cathedral. (ᶜ)
He was living 19 Apr. 1310, but *d.* before June 1311. (ᵈ) He was *suc.*
in the lordship of Cavers by his s., Sir Thomas BALLIOL, who was living
7 Feb. 1312/3, but ' soon disappears from record. " (ᵉ)

BALLYANE

BARONY FOR
LIFE [I.]

I. 1554
to
1555.

1. CAHIR (*i.e.* CHARLES) MC ART CAVANAGH, "Chief
of his Sept" (whose ancestors at the time of the English
invasion of Ireland were Kings of Leinster), was by
patent, 8 Feb. (1553/4), (ᶠ) 1 Mary, *cr.* BARON OF
BALLYANE, co. Wexford [I.], " with seat and place
in all Parliaments and Councils like all other Barons of
Ireland " [but merely] *for life*. For the better support of this dignity he
had a grant of the office of Captain over his kindred and others, *&c.*, also

---

(ª) As to this supposed Parl., see Preface, *circa finem.*
(ᵇ) See note " c " on previous page.
(ᶜ) The history of his descendants is obscure. Thomas Balliol (probably his
grandson), resigned the Lordship of Cavers in Mar. 1368 to William, Earl of Douglas
[S.]. This Thomas is frequently spoken of (1360, *&c.*) as " brother to the Earl
of Mar " [S.], and, to account for this relationship, some make him to be s. and h.
of another Alexander Balliol (s. and h. of the Alexander mentioned in the text), by
Isabel, widow of Donald, Earl of Mar (mother of Thomas Earl of Mar afsd.), da. of Sir
John Stewart, of Bonkil. Others make this Thomas Balliol a *son* (instead of a
grandson) of the Alexander mentioned in the text, his mother (as in the previous conjecture) being the said Isabel Countess of Mar, whom they state to have been a
2nd wife of his father. Isabel, sister of the said Thomas Balliol, appears to have been
his h., and was given by David II in marriage to Ranald More. " So ended, "
says Crawford in his *Officers of State* [S.], " the family of the Baliols after they had
continued in great lustre in this realm for upwards of 200 years. "
(ᵈ) His s. Alexander was a prisoner at Berkhampsted, 12 Oct. 1301. On
28 Mar. 1310 he was released from the Tower, his father having become surety for
his loyalty [*Close Rolls*]. Alexander B. was living 1316 [*Feudal Aids*]. Alexander
B. was living 1346 [*Feudal Aids*]. V.G.
(ᵉ) *Genealogist*, N.S., vol. iv, pp. 141-3, in an article by Joseph Bain, F.S.A. Scot.
(ᶠ) " Cahir McArte Kavanagh to be a Baron. " Instructions from Queen
Mary to the Lord Deputy St. Leger, Oct. 1553. V.G.

that he should have twenty-four soldiers (called "Kernes") for himself and twelve more for [his s. and h. ap.] Morghe (*i.e.* Maurice) Cavanagh, "qui proxime post eum in gradum *Baronis de Cowelelyene* (ª) futurus sit." He *m.* Alice, said to have been da. of Gerald (Fitz Gerald), Earl of Kildare [I.]. She was living 2 Feb. 1549/50. He *d.* about a year after his creation, before the end of the year 1555, when his *life Peerage* became *extinct.*

II. 1555
    to
    15....

1. Dermot McCahir Cavanagh, yr. s. of the above, but not of Alice Fitzgerald, "being accepted and esteemed as *Baron of Cowelelyene*," (ª) was made by patent, 17 May 1555, "*Secondary or Tanist*" in the said Captaincy, from the death of Maurice (his br.) abovenamed, and was assigned the twelve kernes which the said Maurice had enjoyed during the life of his said father. By this patent he was *cr.* BARON OF BALLYANE [I.], *for life* as his father had been. He appears to have *d. s.p.* On his death his *life Peerage* (if indeed it ever existed) became *extinct.* (ᵇ)

BALLYCRENODE

i.e. "Norbury of Ballycrenode, co. Tipperary," Barony [I.] (*Toler*), *cr.* 1800, see "Norbury" Earldom [I.], *cr.* 1827.

BALLYHIGUE

See Peerages *cr.* by James II after 1688 in Appendix F in this volume.

BALLYLAWN

i.e. "Stewart of Stewarts Court and Ballylawn, co. Donegal," Barony (*Stewart*, afterwards *Vane*), *cr.* 1814, see "Londonderry" Marquessate [I.], *cr.* 1816, under the 3rd Marquess.

BALLYLIEDY

See "Dufferin and Claneboye of Ballyliedy," co. Down, Barony [I.] (*Blackwood* born *Stevenson*), *cr.* 1800.

(ª) *i.e.* the Barony of Cowelelyene, co. Wexford, being the principal estate of the family. His 1st s., Maurice, appears to have *suc.* thereto and to have *d.* shortly afterwards.

(ᵇ) From Bryan, his yr. br., the family of Cavanagh of Borris, co. Carlow, is lineally descended.

BALLYMORE

See "WESTCOTE OF BALLYMORE," co. Longford, Barony [I.] (*Littelton*), *cr.* 1776.

BALLYMOTE

i.e. "BALLYMOTE," Barony [I.] (*Taaffe*), *cr.* 1628, with the Viscountcy of TAAFFE [I.], which see.

BALLYSHANNON

See "FOLIOT OF BALLYSHANNON," co. Donegal, Barony [I.] (*Foliot*), *cr.* 1619, *extinct* 1630.

BALLYTRAMMON

i.e. "MONCK OF BALLYTRAMMON," co. Wexford, Barony [I] (*Monck*), *cr.* 1797. See MONCK OF BALLYTRAMMON, Viscountcy [I.], *cr.* 1801.

i.e. "MONCK OF BALLYTRAMMON, co. Wexford, Barony" [U.K.] (*Monck*) *cr.* 1866. See "MONCK OF BALLYTRAMMON," Viscountcy [I.], *cr.* 1801, under the 4th Viscount.

BALLYWALTER

See "DUNLEATH OF BALLYWALTER, co. Down," Barony (*Mulholland*), *cr.* 1892.

BALMERINOCH

BARONY [S.]   1. SIR JAMES ELPHINSTONE, of Barntoun, 3rd s. of
I. 1606.   Robert, 3rd LORD ELPHINSTONE [S.], by Margaret, da.
                of Sir John DRUMMOND, was *b.* 19 Aug. 1557. He
was appointed a Lord of Session, under the designation of "Lord
Innernochtie," 4 Mar. 1586/7; one of the eight Commissioners of the
Treasury in 1595/6, known as "Octavians;" Secretary of State (*) in 1598,
P.C. [E.] 4 May 1603, and on 1 Mar. 1605 President of the Court of
Session. He acquired many grants of lands, of which those belonging to
the Cistercian Abbey of Balmerinoch, co Fife, (*b*) were erected into a
Barony in favour of him, his heirs male, and heirs of tailzie and provision,

---

(*) "Secretary Elphinstone was as wise a man as was in England or Scotland."
(Ant. Welldon, *James I*, p. 328.) V.G.

(*b*) See note *sub* "HOLYROODHOUSE," as to lands of religious houses granted with a peerage [S.] to laics.

by charter 20 Feb. 1603/4, and on 11 July 1606 he obtained a charter including the honour of a Lord of Parl., whereby he was *cr.* LORD BALMERINOCH [S.], and took his place in Parl. accordingly.   He was however found guilty of the fabrication of a letter (in 1599) purporting to be from James VI to Pope Clement VIII, and was on 10 Mar. 1608/9 sentenced to death and *attainted.* (ª)   He *m*, 1stly, 21 Mar. 1588, Sarah, da. of Sir John MENTETH, of Carse.   She was living 14 Dec. 1592.   He *m.*, 2ndly, before 23 Dec 1597, Marjory, da. of Hugh MAXWELL, of Tealing (ᵇ)   She was living 12 Aug. 1601.   He *d*, 21 June 1612, at Balmerinoch, " of a weakness in the stomach," while under attainder (ᶜ)

II. 1613.   2. JOHN (ELPHINSTONE), LORD BALMERINOCH [S.], s.
            and h. by 1st wife, was *restored* in blood, and to the peer-age, by Royal letters 4 Aug. 1613.   He was a leading Covenanter, taking a most active part against the King, being one of those who implored the assistance of Louis XIII of France against him   His trial and conviction (by a majority of one) 3 Dec. 1634 to 20 Mar. 1634/5, for joining in a petition to the Crown against grievances, greatly exasperated the feelings of the Scots towards the Monarchy.   He was President of the Parl [S] 1641, Extraord. Lord of Session 1641-49, and was one of those who were against rescuing the King from his imprisonment in 1648.   He sat in the Parl. 4 Jan. 1648/9, where those who were concerned in the " Engagement " were proscribed.   He *m.*, shortly after 30 Aug. 1613, Ann, sister of Robert, EARL OF SOMERSET, da. of Sir Thomas KER, of Fernihirst, co. Jedburgh, by his 2nd wife, Janet, da of William SCOTT, of Buccleuch.   He *d.* suddenly, 28 Feb 1648/9, of apoplexy, at Edinburgh, and was *bur* in the Logan cemetery at Restalrig. (ª)   His widow *d.* at Leith, 15 Feb. 1649/50, and was *bur* with him.

III. 1649.   3. JOHN (ELPHINSTONE), LORD BALMERINOCH [S.], s.
            and h., *b.* 18 Feb. 1623, at Edinburgh.   By reason of the heavy debts of his father and of several law suits, he was forced to sell nearly all his estate.   In 1662 he was fined by Parl. £6000 (Scots) for his compliance with Cromwell's Government.   By the death of his uncle James (Elphinstone), Lord Coupar [S.], in 1669, he *suc.* (under the *spec. rem.* of that Peerage, 20 Dec. 1607) to the title of LORD COUPAR [S.] and to the estate of Coupar in Angus.   He *m*, 30 Oct 1649, in the chapel of Holyrood House, Edinburgh, Margaret, 2nd and yst da. of John (CAMP-BELL), 1st EARL OF LOUDOUN [S.], by Margaret, *suo jure* BARONESS LOUDOUN [S].   She *d* Dec. 1665   He *d* 10 June 1704, in his 82nd year.   Both were *bur.* at Restalrig.   Fun. entry for both at Lyon office.

(ª) *State Trials*, vol. ii, p. 721.
(ᵇ) James Elphinstone, the only s by this marriage, was *cr.* in 1607, Lord Coupar [S.].   See that title.
(ᶜ) According to the gossip collected by *Scotstarvet*, p. 61, " He got an amatorious potion of cantharides from a maid in his house. "   V G
(ª) The Barony of Restalrig had been obtained by the first Lord on the resignation of the notorious Robert Logan, 16 May 1605.

IV. 1704.   JOHN (ELPHINSTONE), LORD BALMERINOCH and LORD
COUPAR [S], s. and h, *b.* 26 Dec 1652, at Edinburgh,
" a man of excellent parts, being perhaps one of the best lawyers in the
Kingdom. " P C. [S.] 16 Aug. 1687. A steadfast opposer of the Union,
but elected a REP. PEER [S.] (Tory) 1710 and 1713. Governor of the
Mint, and Sheriff of co. Edinburgh, 1710. A Commissioner of the Office
of Lord Chamberlain, 1711. On the accession of George I he was, however, removed (for no apparent reason except his politics) from all his
places. He *m*, 1stly, 16 Feb 1672, at Cramond, Christian, da. of Hugh
(MONTGOMERIE), 7th EARL OF EGLINTOUN [S.], by his 2nd wife, Mary,
da. of John (LESLIE), 6th EARL OF ROTHES. He *m.*, 2ndly, 7 June 1687,
at Edinburgh, Ann, da. of Arthur Ross, Archbishop of St. Andrew's. She
d at her lodging in the Mint, and was *bur.* 8 Nov. 1712, at Restalrig
Fun entry in Lyon office. He *d* at his house in Leith, 13, and was *bur.*
17 May 1736, at Restalrig, in his 84th year.

[HUGH ELPHINSTONE, *styled* MASTER OF BALMERINOCH, 2nd s. and h.
ap. after 1704 ; an officer in the army under the Duke of Marlborough,
d. unm., *v.p.*, being killed during the 3 months' siege of Lille, in 1708].

V. 1736.   5. JAMES (ELPHINSTONE), LORD BALMERINOCH and
LORD COUPAR [S], 3rd and yst , but 1st surv, s and h.
by 1st wife, *b.* 24 Nov. 1675, at Edinburgh. Barrister, 1703. One of
the Lords of Session, 5 June 1714, assuming the designation of " Lord
Coupar. " He *m.* (cont. 28 Apr. and 17 May 1718) Elizabeth, 2nd da.
of David (CARNEGIE), 4th EARL OF NORTHESK, by Margaret, *suo jure* COUNT-
ESS OF WEMYSS [S.]. He *d. s p.* 5 Jan. 1746, at Leith, in his 71st year
His widow, who was *b.* and *bap.* 2 Jan. 1699, in Edinburgh, *d.* 21 Sep.
1767, aged 68, and was *bur* at Restalrig.

VI. 1746.   6. ARTHUR (ELPHINSTONE), LORD BALMERINOCH and
LORD COUPAR [S.], br. (of the half blood) and h , being
1st s. of the 4th Lord, by his 2nd wife. He was *b.* 1688. In the time of
Queen Anne he commanded a company of Foot, but joined in the Rising
of 1715, escaping afterwards to France, where he continued nearly 20 years
in the French service. In 1744 he was one of the first to join the party of
the Young Chevalier in Scotland, and was made Col. of the 2nd troop of
Horse Guards. He was at the taking of Carlisle, and in the march to
Derby, but was taken prisoner at the battle of Culloden (16 Apr. 1746),
having *suc.* to the Peerage some 3 months before. He was confined in the
Tower of London, tried for high treason 29 July (together with the Earls
of Kilmarnock and of Cromarty [S], both of whom pleaded "guilty"),
pleaded "not guilty," but was unanimously found guilty by the Peers, (ª)

(ª) He remained firm in his allegiance to the Stuarts, in contrast to his fellow
sufferer, Lord Kilmarnock, who, in sight of death, acknowledged his "only rightful
sovereign King George" See *State Trials*, vol. xviii, p. 441. Horace Walpole
writes of his trial :—" He is the most natural brave old fellow I ever saw ; of the

attainted ([ª]) and sentenced to death on 1 Aug 1746. On 18 Aug. 1746 he and the said Earl of Kilmarnock were beheaded on Tower Hill, and *bur.* in the chapel of St. Peter ad Vincula there. He *m.* Margaret, da. of Capt. CHALMERS. He *d. s.p.* 18 Aug. 1746 (as afsd) in his 58th year, whereby the *issue male of the 1st Lord Balmerinoch* failed, and the Peerage of Balmerinoch [S], which had a few days previously been *attainted*, became *extinct;* while that of Coupar [S] would possibly, subject to the attainder, have passed to the h. male collateral of the 1st Lord Balmerinoch. ([ᵇ]) His widow *d.* 24 Aug. 1765, in her 56th year, in poverty, at Restalrig.

BALMORE

i.e "BADENOCH, LOCHABER, STRATHAVON, BALMORE &c.," Barony [S] (*Gordon*), *cr* 1684, with the Dukedom of GORDON [S.], which see; *extinct* 1836.

BALQUHIDDER, or BALWHIDDER

i.e. "BALQUHIDDER," Viscountcy [S.], (*Murray*), *cr.* 1676, with the Marquessate of ATHOLL [S], which see.

i.e. "BALWHIDDER," Viscountcy [S.], (*Murray*), *cr.* 1703, with the Dukedom of ATHOLL [S.], which see.

BALRATH

i.e. "BALRATH," Barony [I.] (*Aylmer*), *cr.* 1718 with the Barony of AYLMER [I.], which see.

BALNEIL

i.e. "LINDSAY AND BALNEIL," Barony [S] (*Lindsay*), *cr.* 1651, with the Earldom of BALCARRES [S.], which see.

---

highest intrepidity, even to indifference   At the bar he behaved like a soldier and a man · in the intervals of form, with carelessness and humour.   He pressed extremely to have his wife, the pretty Peggy, with him in the Tower."   Another zealous Hanoverian contemporary is constrained to even warmer praise —" Thus fell Lord Balmerino, a man of the most incredible courage, the most commendable sincerity, and the most engaging simplicity, who was an honour to the worst cause, and would have been an ornament to the best "   His dying speech on the scaffold ran .— " I am afraid there are some here who may think my behaviour bold : it arises from a just confidence in God, and from a clear conscience."   It seems pitiful to have shed the blood of this truly noble loyalist, especially after the absolute failure of the Rising; but neither generosity nor mercy were to be looked for from the " unco wee bit Garman thing " then on the throne.   V G.

([ª]) For a list of the Scots Peerages forfeited after this and the previous Rising, see Appendix E in this volume.

([ᵇ]) See note *sub* John, LORD COUPAR [1669]

BALTIMORE (ᵃ)

BARONY [I]　1 GEORGE CALVERT, of Danbywiske, co. York, s. and
h. of Leonard C., by Alice, da. of John CROSSLAND, of
I. 1625.　Crossland in that co., *b.* at Kipling, in the chapelry of
Bolton, co. York, in 1578 or 1579 ; matric. at Oxford (Trin. Coll.) as a
Gent. Commoner, 12 July 1594, then aged 14　B A Feb. 1597 , Under
Secretary of State ; Clerk of the Privy Council, 1605 ; was on a special
diplomatic mission to France 1611, and to the Elector Palatine, 1615 ;
Knighted 29 Sep. 1617 ; Secretary of State, Feb. 1618/9-25 , P.C. 16 Feb.
1618/9 ; a Lord of the Treasury Jan. to Dec. 1620.　He received a life
pension of £1000 a year, and obtained a grant of the province of Avalon,
in Newfoundland, with most extensive privileges, which province, after
expending £25,000 thereon, he had to abandon owing to the severity of
the winter climate ; was M.P. for Bossiney 1609-11 ; co York 1620-22 ;
and for Oxford Univ 1624-25.　He resigned his preferments Feb 1624/5,
having become a Roman Catholic, but inasmuch as he had received large
grants of land in Ireland, was, on 16 Feb. 1624/5, *cr.* BARON BALTI-
MORE of Baltimore (ᵇ) [I.]　He obtained from Charles I a grant of
Maryland (ᶜ) (on broader terms than he had held that of Avalon), (ᵈ) which
grant was made out to his s. and h , under the great seal, 20 June 1632,
a few weeks after his death.　He *m.*, 1stly, 22 Nov 1604, at St. Peter's,
Cornhill, Anne, da. of George MYNNE, of Hertingfordbury, Herts., by
Elizabeth, da. of Sir Thomas WROTH.　She *d* 8 Aug. 1622, and was *bur.*
at Hertingfordbury. M.I. He *m* , 2ndly, in or before 1627, Joan, who
went with him to Avalon, but *d.* before him.　He *d.* 15 Apr. 1632, and
was *bur.* at St. Dunstan's-in-the-West, London.　Will dat 14, pr. 21 Apr.
1632.　*Inq. p.m.* 13 Sep 1633, at York

II. 1632.　2. CECIL (ᵉ) (CALVERT), BARON BALTIMORE [I], s. and
h., *bap.* 2 Mar. 1605/6, at Bexley, Kent.　He was heavily
mulcted by the Parliamentary party, though he is not known to have
actually fought for the King.　He *m.* (settlement 20 Mar. 1627/8) Anne,
da. of Thomas (ARUNDELL), 1st LORD ARUNDELL OF WARDOUR, by his 2nd
wife, Anne, 3rd da of Miles PHILIPSON, of Crook, Westmorland.　She *d.* in

(ᵃ) A good deal of information in this article has been obtained from Thos.
Hearne's diaries, and more from Charles Weathers Bump, John Hopkins Univ,
Baltimore, U.S.A.　V.G.

(ᵇ) "*No County* is named in the enrolment of the Baltimore patent " (*ex
inform* the late Sir B Burke, Ulster.)　There was not (and is not) any place of that
name in co. Longford, which is the county generally assigned to this creation, but the
chartered town of Baltimore co Cork, (the only place of that name in Ireland) was
then of considerable note.

(ᶜ) So named in honour of the Queen, Henrietta Maria.

(ᵈ) It was really a Palatinate, and modelled closely on that of Durham.
V.G.

(ᵉ) After the Earl of Salisbury, who was his Godfather.　V.G.

51

her 34th year, 23 July 1649, and was *bur.* at Tisbury, Wilts. (ª)   M.I.
He was *bur.* 7 Dec. 1675, at St. Giles'-in-the-Fields, Midx   Will, dat.
22 and 28 Nov. 1675, pr. 3 Feb. 1675/6.

III. 1675.   3. CHARLES (CALVERT), BARON BALTIMORE [I.], 2nd,
                    but 1st surv. (ᵇ) s and h., *b.* 27 Aug. 1637.   He was
Governor of Maryland for his father, 1661-75, and for himself 1676, and
again 1679-84; he was deprived of the Province at the Revolution of 1689
He was not present in James II's Parl. in that year. (ᶜ)   He was outlawed
by the Wexford Grand Jury in 1691, but this was reversed by the King
25 Jan. 1691/2.   He was named as in the fabricated plot of Titus Oates,
and in the Lancashire plot of 1694, but was not arrested.   Brig. Gen. 1696,
Major Gen. 1704.   He inherited the estate of Woodcote Park in Epsom,
and Horton, under the will (pr 3 Aug. 1692) of Elizabeth Evelyn, widow,
a relative of his grandmother, Anne Mynne   He *m.*, 1stly, about 1660,
(—) sister of Sir John DARNALL, da. of Ralph D., of Loughton (or Loughton's Hope), co. Hereford.   She *d.* in childbed, in Maryland.   He *m.*,
2ndly, about 1667, Jane, widow of Henry IRWELL, M D., da. of Nicholas
Lows, of Denby, co Derby.   She *d.* on or before 19, and was *bur.* 24 Jan.
1700/1, at St. Giles'-in-the-Fields.   He *m.*,3rdly, Mary BANKES, widow of
(—), THORPE, of Thorpe, near Welwick, co. York, who was *bur.* (from St.
Andrew's Holborn) at St. Giles' afsd., 17 Mar. 1710/1.   He *m.*, 4thly,
Margaret, da of Thomas CHARLETON, of Hexham, Northumberland.   He
d. 21, and was *bur.* 26 Feb. 1714/5, at St. Pancras, Midx., aged 77.   Will
dat. 29 July 1714, pr. 20 May 1715 by his widow.   She *m.*, 9 Nov. 1718,
at Symond's Chapel, Laurence ELIOT, of Yapton Place, Sussex   She *d.*
20, and was *bur.* 26 July 1731, at St. Pancras afsd.   Will dat 15, pr.
27 July 1731.

IV. 1715.   4. BENEDICT LEONARD (CALVERT), BARON BALTIMORE
February.   [I.], 2nd, but 1st (ᵈ) surv. s. and h. by 2nd wife, *b.*
                    21 Mar. 1679.   He conformed to the established church
in 1713, and thereupon had the province of Maryland restored to him.
M.P. (Tory) for Harwich 1714-15   He *m*, 2 Jan. 1698/9 (he 21, and
she 20), Charlotte, da. of Edward Henry (LEE), 1st EARL OF LICHFIELD,
by Lady Charlotte FITZROY, illegit. da. of Charles II.   He sold Woodstock
Park (his wife's marriage jointure), to the Crown for a gift to the Duke
of Marlborough, in 1705.   He *d* 16 Apr., and was *bur.* 2 May 1715, at
Epsom, Surrey.   Will dat. 15 Aug. 1713, pr. 2 May 1716.   His widow,
from whom he was separated in 1705, *m.*, before 10 Dec. 1719, Christopher
CROWE, sometime Consul at Leghorn, who *d.* 9 Nov. 1749, aged 68.   She,
who was *b.* 13 Mar. 1678, in St James's Park, *d* at Mr Crowe's seat at

---

(ª) She is said to have been a most beautiful and accomplished woman.   V.G.
(ᵇ) His elder br., George C., *b.* 15 Sep 1634, *d. v p.*, June 1636   V.G
(ᶜ) For a list of peers present in, and absent from this Parl., see volume iii,
Appendix D.   V.G.
(ᵈ) His elder *br.*, Cecil C., *b* 1667 or 1668, *d. v.p.*, 1681.   V.G.

Woodford, Essex, of rheumatism, 22, and was *bur.* there 29 Jan. 1720/1, aged 42. M I. Admon , as of Woodford Hall, Essex, 4 Mar. 1720/1.

V. 1715.

April.

5. CHARLES (CALVERT), BARON BALTIMORE [I.], s. and h., *b.* 29 Sep 1699. Gent. of the Bedchamber to the Prince of Wales 1731-47, and Cofferer of the Household to that Prince 1747-51 , F.R S 9 Dec. 1731 ; Governor of Maryland (in person) 1732-33 ; M.P. (Tory) for St. Germans, 1734-41, and for Surrey 1741 till his death. A Lord of the Admiralty 1742-44 ; Elder Brother of the Trinity House 1744-51; Surveyor Gen. of the Duchy of Cornwall 1747-51. He *m* , 20 July 1730, Mary, da. of Sir Theodore JANSSEN, of Wimbledon, Surrey, 1st Bart., by Williamsa, da. of Sir Robert HENLEY, of the Grange, Hants. He *d.* 24 Apr. 1751, and was *bur.* at Erith, Kent aged 51. (ª) Will dat 17 Nov 1750, pr. 30 Apr. 1751. His widow *d.* 25 Mar 1770, at Chaillot, near Paris.

VI. 1751
to
1771.

6. FREDERICK (CALVERT), BARON BALTIMORE [I.], only s. and h., *b.* 6 Feb 1731/2. Ed at Eton F R.S. 26 Feb. 1767. He *m.*, 9 Mar. 1753, Diana, da. of Scrope (EGERTON), 1st DUKE OF BRIDGEWATER, by his 2nd wife, Rachael, da. of Wriothesley (RUSSELL), 2nd DUKE OF BEDFORD She, who was *b.* 3 Mar. 1731/2, *d.* 13 Aug 1758 Admon. 21 Nov. 1758 After a career of profligacy and extravagance, he was tried for a rape at Kingston assizes 26 Mar 1768, and having with difficulty escaped conviction (ᵇ) left England. He *d s p.*, 4 Sep. 1771, at Naples, and was *bur* at Epsom, aged 39, when the Peerage became *extinct.* Will pr. Jan. 1772

Family Estates.—Most of these were sold by the last Lord to John Trotter, an upholsterer of Soho, Midx.

BALTINGLASS (ᶜ)

VISCOUNTCY [I.]

I. 1541.

1. SIR THOMAS EUSTACE, of Harristown, s. of Richard E., by Anne, da. of Robert EUSTACE, of Ballyloughrane, nephew and h. male of Rowland (EUSTACE or FITZ EUSTACE), LORD PORTLESTER [I.], *b* about 1480, suc. his said uncle in the family estates 14 Dec. 1496, was *cr.* BARON KILCUL-

(ª) King George II said of him—"There is my Lord Baltimore, who thinks he understands everything, and understands nothing : who wants to be well with both Courts and is well with neither, and who, *entre nous*, is a little mad " (Lord Hervey, *Memoirs*, vol. II.) Mrs. Delaney, with whose affections he had trifled, and with whom he had been on the point of marriage, who is therefore a tainted witness as to his wife, writes of him as "very handsome, genteel and unaffected, " and of her, at a ball, as looking "like a frightened owl, her locks strutted out, and most furiously greased or rather gummed and powdered " There are many more references to him in her memoirs V.G.

(ᵇ) See *Gent. Mag.*, 1768, p. 180.

(ᶜ) For the ranking of Irish peers see Appendix A in this volume. V.G.

LEN, co. Kildare [I.], in Sep. 1535, ([a]) and subsequently, 29 June 1541, was *cr.* VISCOUNT BALTINGLASS, co. Wicklow [I.]. He is said to have possessed one half of the co. of Wicklow. He *m.* Margaret, da. of Peter Talbot, of Malahide, co. Dublin, by Catharine, illegit. da. of Gerald (Fitz Gerald), Earl of Kildare [I.]. He *d.* 31 July 1549.

II. 1549.   2. Rowland (Eustace), Viscount Baltinglass, &c.
                [I.], s. and h. Aged 35 in 1540. On 26 Oct. 1549 he had livery of the family estates. On 11 June 1567, he was ordered to be sent a prisoner to London. He *m.* Joan, da. of James (Butler), Lord Dunboyne [I.], by Joan, da. of Piers (Butler), 8th Earl of Ormonde [I.]. He *d.* 31 Mar. 1578. His widow was living Sep. 1585.

III. 1578   3. James (Eustace), Viscount Baltinglass and Baron
   to   Kilcullen [I.], s. and h. In 1576 he joined with other
   1581.   "Lords of the Pale" in a complaint as to taxes being levied without sanction of Parl., and subsequently joined the Earl of Desmond in a conspiracy to place the Queen of Scots on the English and Irish throne, which failing, he fled from his country in 1581. For this he was *outlawed*, and his title forfeited, he being described as "James Eustace *late* Viscount Baltinglass" in the Act of Parl. for the attainder of the family honours, and forfeiture of the entailed estates, passed May 1585, some six months before his death. All his brothers took part in the same rebellion and were likewise attainted. He *m.* Mary, da. and coh. of Henry Travers, of Monkstown Castle, co. Dublin, by Genet, da. of Jenico (Preston), Viscount Gormanston [I.]. He *d. s.p.*, 25 Nov. 1585, in Spain. His widow *m.* (as his 1st wife) Gerald Aylmer (who was *cr.* a Bart. [I.] in 1621), and *d.* 28 Nov., and was *bur.* 17 Dec. 1610, at Monkton. Fun. Ent.

The title was assumed as under.

IV. 1585   Edmund Eustace, next br. and h., having joined his
   to   br. in rebellion, fled to Scotland in 1583, and thence to
   1594.   Spain; and was attainted with him May 1585. On the death of the 3rd Viscount, in Nov. 1585, he assumed the title of VISCOUNT BALTINGLASS [I.], being sometimes said to have been so *cr.* by the Pope! ([b]) in 1586. He served in the Armada in 1588, and *d.* Sep. 1594, in Portugal, apparently unm. ([c])

([a]) Ware's *Annals*, p. 93. On 10 Oct. 1535, John Alen, Master of the Rolls [I.], acknowledges receipt from Secretary Thomas Cromwell of patents of creation for Thomas Eustace and Sir Richard Power to be Barons of Parliament. (*State Papers*, Ireland, 1509-1573, p. 15.) Lord Power was so *cr.* 13 Sep. V.G.

([b]) For another supposed Papal creation in the peerage, see the case of John de Mohun, pretended to have been *cr.* Earl of Somerset in King John's time. V.G.

([c]) A letter, dat. Jan. 1594/5, printed in *State Papers*, [I.], states that "my lord of Baltinglass is now in Madrid;" and a pilot of a fleet, which left Lisbon in Oct.

After his death nothing very definite is known as to any assumption of the title. He had 4 yr. brothers of whom one or possibly two surv. him. They all took part in the rebellion of 1581, and were attainted, and all apparently *d.* unm. They were (1) Thomas, 3rd s. of the 2nd Viscount, executed 1582. (2) William, ([b]) 4th s., slain in rebellion, 21 Apr. 1581.([b]) (3) Walter, taken prisoner 1583, and, as some say, then executed, ([c]) although in a list of those slain by the Earl of Kildare's troops 1 Mar. 1599/1600, appears the name of "Walter Eustace, pretended to be Viscount Baltinglass."([d]) (4) Richard, 6th and yst. s., was living in Paris 1580, and was a Priest in Rome in Jan. 1595/6.

IV. 1627.   1. THOMAS ROPER, ([e]) Knighted at Christchurch, Dublin, 16 Sep. 1603, a member of the Privy Council [I.], and a distinguished commander in that Kingdom during the reigns of Elizabeth and James I, obtained, 10 Nov. 1626, a grant of the monastery and Lordship of Baltinglass, and was, on 27 June 1627, *cr.* BARON OF

1596, reports—"In an Irish ship called *The Sonday*, cast away, were lost 14 Irish of name, capital rebels. Among the Irish lost is Edmund Eustace, called the Lord Baltinglass." The above two entries show either that the report of Edmund's death in 1594, as in the text, was incorrect, or that they refer to another Edmund, possibly his s., who assumed the title after his death. V.G.

([a]) The petition, in 1839, of the Rev. Charles Eustace (*d.* 5 Jan. 1856, at a great age) claiming to be the h. male of the body of this William, who, he alleged, was living in London and styling himself "Viscount Baltinglass" in 1610, (a statement which, though possibly true of some William Eustace, was not true of this William, who, moreover, was not as alleged in the petition, *next surv.* br. of the 3rd Viscount) seeking for the acknowledgement of his right to the title, was favourably reported upon by the law officers of Ireland and England, subject to the reversal of the attainder. See an account of these proceedings as also of the then state of the family in Burke's *Extinct Peerage*, 1883, p. 191.

([b]) "The head of William Eustace, another of Baltinglass's brethren taken this morning." (L. Bryskett to Walsingham, *Cal. State Papers* [I.]). V.G.

([c]) G.D.Burtchaell writes to G.E.C. in May 1907,—"There can be no doubt, I think, that Walter, 4th s. of the 2nd Viscount was executed in 1583. He was apprehended in that year, and the Government would never have let him escape. Had he done so, there would surely have been some reference to it. Walter Eustace, slain 1599/1600, is evidently the Viscount referred to by the Lord Deputy, 19 Aug. 1596, as "set up" by the O'Neills, and does not appear to have been a son of any of the attainted brethren. He was probably a grandson of the 1st Viscount, who had, besides his successor, Richard E., of Little Bouley, Alexander E., of Colbinstown, and Robert E., of Tulloghgowrey." V.G.

([d]) *Hist. MSS. Com.*, App., 9th Rep., p. 292. V.G.

([e]) It is difficult to suppose that he belonged to the Derbyshire family of Roper of Heanor, whose arms (*Sa.*, an eagle, *or*) differ so entirely from his own, which were "*Erm.*, 2 chevronels, paly of six *or* and *gu.*" Yet in the Heraldic Visitation of Derbyshire, in 1634, at the College of Arms (C. 33, pt. 1, p. 27), some ground is given for such (the generally received) conjecture.

BANTRY, co. Cork, and VISCOUNT BALTINGLASS, co. Wicklow [I.].
He *m.* Ann, da of Sir Henry HARINGTON, sometime of Baltinglass, by his
2nd wife, Ruth, 1st da. and coh. of James PILKINGTON, Bishop of Durham,
which Henry was br. of John, 1st LORD HARINGTON of Exton.   He *d.* at
Roper's Rest, 18, and was *bur.* 20 Feb. 1637/8, at St. John's, Dublin.
Will pr. 1637/8.   His widow *d.* 7, and was *bur.* 9 Jan. 1639/40, at
St. John's afsd   Will pr. 1639/40, Prerog Court [I.].

V. 1637.   2. THOMAS (ROPER), VISCOUNT BALTINGLASS, &c. [I.],
            s. and h.   In 1660, he was petitioning for the command
of a company of Foot, which he had held before the Commonwealth   He
m, in 1637, Anne, da. of Sir Peter TEMPLE, of Stowe, Bucks, 2nd Bart.,
being the only child, that survived infancy, of his 1st wife, Anne, (ª) da. and
coh. of Sir Arthur THROCKMORTON, of Paulerspury, Northants.   After
great losses by the Irish Rebellion "and much more by the English,"
as also by extensive law suits, he *d. s.p.*, about 1670.   Admon. to the
principal creditor, 15 Jan 1677/8, and again 30 Mar. 1685.   His widow,
who was *bap* 20 Jan. 1619, at Stowe, Bucks, *d.* in the Fleet prison,
London, 13, and was *bur.* 16 Aug. 1696, at St. Katherine's, Aldgate. (ᵇ)
Admon., 3 July 1702, to William Temple, Esq, "cousin once removed
and next of kin."

VI. 1670?   3. CARY (ROPER), VISCOUNT BALTINGLASS and BARON
    to   OF BANTRY [I.], only surv. br and h., being 5th s. of the
  1672.   1st Viscount.   He was an Ensign of Foot   He *d.* unm.,
            and was *bur.* about 1 Sep. 1672, (ᶜ) at Castle Lyons, co.
Cork, when his Peerage honours became *extinct.*

(ª) Lands of the value of £700 a year, on either side, were at her marriage settled
upon the issue thereof, by indenture, 22 June (1614), 12 James I.   This was the
subject of a long lawsuit, and of a Bill being preferred in Parl., being "The Case
and Narrative of the Sufferings of the Lord and Lady Baltinglasse, &c," wherein it
is stated that Sir Peter Temple, on his death bed in 1653, advised his eldest son (by
another marriage) thus. "Dick, your sister is poor and sickly, if you do but enter
upon her estate, the profits will maintain the suit; you may soon weary her out, or
if she dyes before the end of it, you are next heir."   Lord B   also states that he is
"in great extremity of want," having lost £10,000 by the Irish Rebellion "and 16 years
suit in Chancery," and that too "after at least £25,000 received out of the Lady
Baltinglasse her estate, betwixt Sir Peter Temple and his son Sir Richard."

(ᵇ) She, "a heap of flesh and brandy," is said, in the memoirs of Thomas, Earl
of Ailesbury, to have *m*, 2ndly, when in prison, the infamous Titus Oates.   He,
however, had lic. from the Vic. Gen., 10 Aug 1693, as a *bachelor*, to *m.* Rebecca
Weld. V.G

(ᶜ) The King, 1 Oct. 1672, granted his estate to the Earl of Arlington, but this
grant proved, apparently, to be "a mere compliment, for neither he nor his brother,
that was lord before him, had £100 a year clear these 20 years past."   (Robt. Leigh
to the Earl of Arlington, *State Papers* [I.]).   V.G.

i.e. " BALTINGLASS," Viscountcy [I.] *(Talbot)*, *cr.* 1685, with the Earldom of TYRCONNELL [I], which see ; *forfeited* 1691.

---

i.e " BALTINGLASS, co. Wicklow," Barony [I.] *(Stratford)*, *cr* 1763, see " ALDBOROUGH " Earldom [I.], *cr.* 1777 ; *extinct* 1875.

BALVAIRD

BARONY [S.] 1. ANDREW MURRAY, of Balvaird, 2nd, but 1st surv.,
I. 1641. s. and h. of David M., of Balgony and Kippo, by
Agnes, da of (——) MONCREIFFE, of Moncreiffe, was knighted 1633, had a charter of the lands of Pitlochie, 1636, was a Member of the Gen. Assembly at Glasgow in 1638, in which his conduct was so favourably represented to the King by the High Commissioner (Marquess of Hamilton), that he was *cr*, 17 Nov. 1641, LORD BALVAIRD [S], with rem. to his " heirs male." On the death, Mar. 1642, of his cousin Mungo (MURRAY), 2nd VISCOUNT OF STORMONT [S.], he *suc.* as heir of entail to the *lands* of that Lordship. (ª) He *m* Elizabeth, da. of David (CARNEGIE), 1st EARL OF SOUTHESK [S.], by Margaret, da. of Sir David LINDSAY, of Edzell. He *d.* 24 Sep. 1644.

II. 1644. 2. DAVID (MURRAY), LORD BALVAIRD [S], s. and h.
On 28 Dec. 1658, by the death of James (MURRAY), EARL OF ANNANDALE [S.], he *suc.* him in the title of VISCOUNT STORMONT and LORD SCONE [S] under the spec. limitations regulating the succession to those titles See " STORMONT," Viscountcy.

BALVANY or BALVENIE

i e. " MURRAY, BALVANY and GASK," Barony [S.] *(Murray)*, *cr.* 1676, with the Marquessate of ATHOLL [S.], which see.

---

i.e. " MURRAY, BALVENIE and GASK," Barony [S.] *(Murray)*, *cr.* 1703, with the Dukedom of ATHOLL [S], which see.

BALWEARIE

i.e. " RAITH, MONYMAIL and BALWEARIE," Barony [S.] *(Melville)*, *cr.* 1690, with the Earldom of MELVILLE, which see.

(ª) See Pedigree *sub* STORMONT.

BALWHIDDER see BALQUHIDDER

BAMBREICH see BALLINBREICH

BANBURY

EARLDOM.   1. WILLIAM KNOLLYS, of Rotherfield Greys, &c , Oxon,
              and of Cholcey, Caversham, &c., Berks, 2nd s. but h.
1. 1626   *male* of Sir Francis Knollys, (ᵃ) K G., by Mary, sister of
Henry, LORD HUNSDON, da. of William CARY (by Mary, sister of Anne
BOLEYN, Queen of Henry VIII), was *b* about 1547. Ed. at Magd. Coll.,
Oxford ; M.A. 27 Sep 1592. M.P. for Tregony 1572-83, for Oxon,
1584-86, 1592-93, 1597-98, and 1601 ; knighted 7 Oct. 1586, in Holland,
by Robert, Earl of Leicester. P.C. 30 Aug 1596 ; Lord Lieut. of Berks
from that year till his death ; Comptroller of the Household 1596-1600 ;
suc. his father in the family estates abovenamed, 19 July 1596. He was
delegate to the States of Holland, 1599 ; Treasurer of the Household
1600-16 ; and was *cr*, by James I, 13 May 1603, BARON KNOLLYS
OF GREYS, co. Oxford ; Master of the Wards, 1614-18 ; elected K.G.
24 Apr. and inst. 22 May 1615. On 7 Nov. 1616 he was *cr.* VISCOUNT
WALLINGFORD, Berks ; High Steward of Oxford 1620 , and finally,
on 18 Aug 1626, he was *cr.* EARL OF BANBURY, co. Oxford, with a
clause "that he shall have precedency as if he had been created the first
Earle after his Majestys accesse to the Crowne. " (ᵇ)   This precedency
was disputed in Parl., but the King, sending " a gracious message " to the
House of Lords, in which he " desires this may pass for once in this
particular, considering how old a man this Lord is, and *childless*, (ᶜ) &c., "
the Lords resolved, on 9 Apr. 1628, that though " the Act of Parl.,
31 Hen. VIII, is most strong and plain for the settling of the Precedency
of the Peers, according to their ancienty and times of creation, " yet that
they are contented that " the said Earl [of Banbury] may hold the same
place, as he now stands entered, for his *life only* and that place of precedency
not to go to his heirs ; " accordingly on the 15th, he took his seat and was
" placed next to the Earl of Berks " (ᵈ)   The Earl seems to have been
latterly in embarrassed circumstances, and to have alienated much of the

(ᵃ) This Francis Knollys was 5th in descent from Thomas K., Mayor of London
1399 to 1400, and 1410 to 1411. V G.

(ᵇ) For a discussion on the precedency of Peers in Parl. by Royal Warrant, see
Appendix C in this volume.

(ᶜ) He was childless at the date of the patent of precedency (18 Aug 1626),
though the Countess had given birth to a son some 10 or 11 months before the date
of this Royal message . a fact probably unknown to the Court   It is probable that
the King, to support his Royal prerogative, made a point of Lord Banbury's precedence, which, at his age of 82, and as being only over six Earls, could not have been
of much importance to his Lordship.

(ᵈ) He thus took precedence of the Earls of Cleveland, Mulgrave, Danby,
Totnes, Monmouth, and Marlborough. V.G.

family property. (ª)   He *m*, 1stly, Dorothy, widow of BARON CHANDOS
(who *d.* 11 Sep. 1573), and da. of Edmund (BRAYE), 1st LORD BRAYE,
by Jane, da. and h of Sir Richard HALLIWELL.   She *d.* 31 Oct. 1605,
at Minty, and was *bur.* at Rotherfield Greys.   The Earl *m*, 2ndly,
(settlement dated 23 Dec., in the same year, 1605), being then aged
about 58, Elizabeth, a girl of 19, da. of Thomas (HOWARD), EARL OF
SUFFOLK, by his 2nd wife, Katharine, 1st. da. and coh. of Sir Henry
KNYVETT, of Charlton, Suffolk.   Besides a da who died young, sometime
before 1610 (ᵇ) (and possibly other issue), the Countess was mother of two
sons (*b.* 1627 and 1630/1) whose paternity has been frequently called in
in question.   The Earl *d* 25 May 1632, at the house of Dr. Grant, his
physician, in Paternoster Row, (ᶜ) London, aged about 85, and was *bur* at
Rotherfield Greys   Will (no mention being therein made of any children)
leaving all, but a few legacies, to his wife, dat 19 May 1630, and pr. by
her 2 July 1632   Fun. certif. at Coll of Arms, stating that he *d. s.p* (ᵈ)
Inq. p. m. taken at Burford, Oxon, 11 Apr. 1633 (about 11 months after
his death), finding that he *d* at Caversham (ᵉ) and *without issue*, his next
heirs being the (female) issue of Henry Knollys, his 1st br.   By a subsequent *Inq.* at Abingdon, 1 Apr. 1641 (by direction of the Court of Wards,
on behalf of the infant Earl), it was found that the late Earl *d.* in London,
leaving "Edward, now Earl of Banbury, his s and next h," who was then
aged 5 years, 1 month and 15 days   His widow, who was *bap* 11 Aug.
1586, at Saffron Walden, *m.*, (within 5 weeks of her husband's death)
before 2 July 1632, Edward (VAUX), 4th LORD VAUX OF HARROWDEN,
who *d. s p.* (or, at all events, *s.p legit*), 8 Apr. 1661, aged 74, and was
bur. at Dorking, Surrey.   The Countess, "a professed Papist" (who
appears to have been an object of constant suspicion to the Parl), *d.* 17
Apr 1658, in her 72nd year, and was also *bur.* there.   M.I. (ᶠ)

(ª) On 1 Mar 1630/1, he sold the manor of Rotherfield Greys to Sir Robert
Knollys, who (with his eldest s. William K) sold it again, in May 1642, to Sir John
Evelyn and Arthur Evelyn

(ᵇ) The fact of issue born *previous* to 1627 is here mentioned, as it confutes the
argument based on the *absence* of any such between 1606 and 1627.   See Milles'
Catalogue of Honour (1610), p 546, as to this da ; and see Brooke's *Catalogue
of Nobility* (1619), where it is stated that the Earl " had issue," which issue, according
to Vincent, who *corrected* Brooke (with a vengeance) in 1622, " died young. "

(ᶜ) Deposition of his servant Robert Lloyd, *present at his death*.   This agrees
with the finding in the second *Inq. p. m*, wherein it is stated that the Earl *d.* in
London, leaving Edward his s and h.

(ᵈ) It is stated in *Dugdale* (vol II, p 413), that this certificate was signed by his
widow.   Such, however, is not the fact.

(ᵉ) The place of his death was undoubtedly wrong, and both it and the statement
as to want of issue are contradicted by the finding in the subsequent inquisition.
Neither did his nieces, who were found heirs herein, inherit any of the Earl's lands
which were heritable, whereas the s and h. named in the subsequent inquisition *did*
so inherit.

(ᶠ) Her age on the M.I. is erroneously given as in her 75th year.

II. 1632.   2. EDWARD (KNOLLYS), EARL OF BANBURY, &c., s.
               and h., *b.* 10 Apr. 1627, at Rotherfield Greys, where
the Earl (his father) was then residing.   Under the description of "Earl
of Banbury" he was party to a chancery suit, 9 Feb. 1640/1, as "an
infant, by William, Earl of Salisbury, his prochein amy and guardian." (ª)
He *d.* unm., and under age, in or before June 1645, being slain in a
quarrel on the road between Calais and Gravelines, and was *bur.* in the
church of the Friars Minims, at Calais.

III. 1646.   3. NICHOLAS (KNOLLYS, "*heretofore* VAUX"), EARL
               OF BANBURY, &c., only br. and h., *b.* 3 Jan. 1630/1, at
(Lord Vaux's House) Harrowden, Northants.   As heir to his br.
he inherited a small property (called the Bowling Place) at Henley-
upon-Thames (being part of the heritable lands of his late father which
had passed under the *Inq. p. m.* of 1641), and immediately assumed the
peerage, as appears by a deed dat. 19 Oct. 1646, whereby his step
father, Lord Vaux, settles the manors of Harrowden, &c., Northants,
on his (Lord Vaux's) wife, the Dowager Countess of Banbury, for her
life, with rem. to Nicholas, her son, the said Earl.   He sat repeatedly

---

(ª) Depositions as to his birth were then made.   The best account of the claim
to the Earldom of Banbury is *A treatise on the Law of Adulterine Bastardy, with a
report of the Banbury case, &c.,* by Sir N. Harris Nicolas, 1836, p. 588, from which
work most of the facts mentioned in the text are taken.   The learned writer is not
merely content with ably demonstrating the legitimacy *in law* of the 2nd and
3rd Earls, but brings forth many arguments to prove that they were *in fact* children
of the 1st Earl.   There certainly seems no proof to the contrary.   The fact of the
childless Lord Vaux settling his estates on his young step son, who consequently took
his name, though suspicious, is not without precedent; at p. 369 of Nicolas' treatise
a similar instance (Agsborough, *alias* Townshend) is mentioned.   It seems also
certain, that the Earl must have been aware of the birth of the elder of the two sons,
as according to the evidence of "Francis Delavall, Esq.," (1641) he "did come into
the chamber where the Countess was, a little before her delivery, and desired to have
persons sent for to give her ease, and shortly after the birth desired witness' wife to
take care of *his boy.*"   The birth of the second boy, being at Lord Vaux's house, is
in more suspicious circumstances, but, even then, there is the testimony of Anne
Delavall (1661), that the lying in was publicly known in the house, "that he [Lord
Banbury] knew shee lay in" and that "he [Nicholas] was owned by the E.
of Banbury as his son."   The general impression however doubtless was (as is noticed
by Peter Le Neve, Norroy, in an elaborate ped. of Knollys, about 1693, now in the
Harl. MSS. 5808) that the two sons were begotten by Lord Vaux.   Their *matern-
ity* is quite clear, and the singular and probably unique hypothesis of Beltz (Lancaster
Herald, 1822-41) that they were the sons of Lord Vaux, but by another woman [or
women] than the Countess, appears to be opposed to all evidence and probability.
Anyhow, whatever may have been their *actual,* their *legal* paternity (not having
been upset by Act of Parl.) appears indisputable and has been acknowledged by the
law of the land, though unacknowledged by the House of Lords.   See also
post, p. 404, note "*a.*"

in the House of Lords from June to Nov. 1660, in the "Convention Parl." and was twice appointed a member of a Committee, though on 13 July of that year it was moved "that there being a person who, as is conceived, hath no title to be a Peer, *viz.* the Earl of Banbury, it is ordered that this business shall be heard at the bar" on the 23rd. No proceedings, however, appear to have taken place. On 21 Nov. 1660 he obtained leave of absence, a permission frequently granted to other Lords, and one which was certainly a tacit admission of his *right to be present.* On 29 Dec. following, the Convention Parl. was prorogued. Although the Earl had thus sat in Parl. and exercised all the functions of a Peer for six months, yet, when the next Parl. was sum. in May 1661, no writ was issued to him. On this he presented a petition to the King, which was referred to the Committee for Privileges, who reported thereon on 1 July 1661, "that Nicholas, Earl of Banbury, is a legitimate person." The Lords, however, not adopting this report, it was referred to the Committee, as also was the matter of "the *Right of Precedence,* between the said Earl of Banbury and several Peers of this Realm." On this the Report, 19 July 1661, was, that the Earl was "in the eye of the lawe, sonne of the late William Earle of Banbury," and that "the house of Peeres should therefore advise the King to send him a writ to come to Parl.;" but that, as to the question of his precedency, they were of opinion that he "ought to have place in the House of Peeres according to the date of his patent." The House resolved to take this report into consideration, but never, apparently, did so, and on 9 Dec. following a bill was read for the first time entitled "An act for declaring Nicholas, called Earl of Banbury, to be illegitimate," inasmuch as "the illegitimation of children born in wedlock can *noeway* be declared but by Act. of Parl." This attempt to obtain an *ex post facto* law to divest a man of rights (publicly acknowledged and long enjoyed) was abandoned after the first reading of the Bill, and the Earl was left in possession of his former *status,* viz. *legal legitimacy,* for, as was said in the "Purbeck" case in 1678, "By bringing in a bill to bar him, his *right to the title* is confessed, for he cannot be barred of anything which he hath not right to." On 26 Oct. 1669 it was again referred to the Committee for Privileges to examine why the Earl's name was omitted from "the list by which the Lords were called," "he having formerly sat *as a Peer* in this House." The report thereon, 25 Nov. 1669, recited all the proceedings against the Earl, as also the statement of Garter King of Arms, that in the two Parliaments of 1640 no mention (ⁿ) is made of an Earl of Banbury, and left "the business to the consideration of the House." On the 23 Feb. 1670, the Earl presented a petition (not to the King

---

(ⁿ) This is accounted for by his having been then a minor, "it not being usual to insert the names of Peers who were under age in such lists. The Earls of Oxford and Winchelsea, Lords Delawarr, Chandos, Petre and Teynham were also minors and their names are likewise omitted."—See Nicolas' *Treatise, &c.,* p. 395.

but) to the House of Lords, stating "that he had the honour to be a Peer of this Realm," and praying his writ accordingly. No proceedings thereon took place, and within four years thereof the Earl died. He *m.*, 1stly, Isabella, da. of Montjoy (BLOUNT), 1st EARL OF NEWPORT, by Anne, yst. da. and coh. of John (BOTELER), LORD BOTELER. She *d. s.p.m.*, and was *bur.* 2 Mar. 1654/5, at St. Martin's-in-the-fields. He *m.*, 2ndly, 4 Oct. 1655, at Stapleford, co. Leicester, Anne, da. of William (SHERARD), LORD SHERARD [I.], by Abigail, da. and coh. of Cecil CAVE. He *d.* 14 Mar. 1673/4, at Boughton, Northants, and was *bur.* there, aged 43. Admon. 28 Jan. 1674/5 to his widow, again 21 June 1681, and again 4 July 1683. His widow *d.* at Harrowden Magna, 6, and was *bur.* 10 Mar. 1679/80, at Boughton. Admon. 21 June 1681 and 4 July 1683.

IV. 1674.   4. CHARLES (KNOLLYS), EARL OF BANBURY, &c., s. and h. by 2nd wife, *bap.* 3 June 1662, at Boughton afsd., as "*Viscount Wallingford*, s. and h. ap. of the Rt. Hon. Nicholas, *Earl of Banbury.*" About a year after attaining his majority, he, on 10 June 1685, petitioned the House for his writ of summons, which was reported on by the Lords' Committee, and a day fixed for hearing counsel thereon, but no further proceedings were taken. The Earl, however, having killed in a duel his br.-in-law, Capt. Philip Lawson, was indicted 7 Dec. 1692 as "*Charles Knollys, Esq.*," on which, on the 13th, he presented his petition to the House, praying, as a Peer, to be tried by his Peers. This being a legal question, it was moved that the Judges be heard as "to the points of law in this case," which equitable motion, however, was rejected by a majority of 38 Peers to 29 ; after which it was carried, 17 Jan. 1692/3, that the *Petitioner had no right to the Earldom of Banbury*, and his petition was dismissed accordingly. Against this resolution no less than 20 Peers "protested," the majority being (probably) only eight.([a]) The indictment had been removed, from Midx., by *certiorari*, in Hilary term 1692/3, to the King's Bench, where the prisoner pleaded a misnomer, which plea (after about a year's delay, caused by the Attorney Gen. insisting that the resolution of the House was a proof of the non-existence of the Peerage, and by "demurrers" and "counter demurrers" on either side) was confirmed in Trin. term 1694 by the unanimous judgment of Lord Chief Justice Holt and the three other Judges of the King's Bench, who adjudged "the replication [of the Attorney Gen. against the peerage] bad, and the Resolution of the Lords invalid." ([b]) Four years afterwards the Earl again petitioned for his writ, which on 18 Jan. 1698 was again referred to the Lords, who

([a]) See Nicolas' *Treatise, &c.*, p. 411, note 1. See also *ante*, under "Aylesford," p. 367, note "b," for later instances in which the House of Lords have overruled the *legal* doctrine of "*Pater est quem nuptiæ demonstrant.*"

([b]) See *State Trials*, vol. xii, p. 1167.

referred the King to their former resolution, taking the opportunity, however (somewhat to the detriment of the dignity of their house), to endeavour to browbeat the Judges for their official judgment.   On 19 Mar. 1712 the Earl again petitioned the Crown, who referred it to the Privy Council, but the death of the Queen stopped further proceedings ; again, on the accession of George II, he presented a like petition to that King, but Sir Philip Yorke, the Attorney Gen. (to whom it had been referred), pointed out in his report thereon, Jan. 1727/8, the inadvisability in this case, of referring the matter to the *House of Lords* (as was the usual course) considering the disagreement as to the law governing this claim between that House and the King's Bench.   Accordingly no such reference was made and nothing more was done in the matter till the lapse of some 80 years.   The Earl *m.*, 1stly, 16 May 1689, at the Nag's Head Coffee-house, James Str., Covent Garden, (Dr. William Cleaver, the notorious Fleet Parson officiating) Elizabeth,(ᵃ) da. of Michael LISTER, of Burwell, co Lincoln, by Ann, da. of Abraham BURRELL, of Medloe, Hunts.   She, who was *bap.* 7 June 1663, at South Carlton, co. Lincoln, was *bur.* 31 Dec. 1699, at Egham, Surrey, as Countess of Banbury.   He *m.*, 2ndly, 30 Apr. 1702, at St. Bride's, London, Mary, da. of Thomas WOODS, of St. Andrew's, Holborn, merchant,(ᵇ) by Mary HARWOOD, his wife.   He *d.* at Dunkirk, 26, and was *bur.* 28 Aug. 1740, aged 78.   His widow *d.* 12 May 1762, at Bath, and was *bur.* at St. James's there.   Admon. 28 July 1762.

[CHARLES KNOLLYS, *styled* VISCOUNT WALLINGFORD, s. and h. ap. by 1st wife, *b.* 15 Oct., and *bap.* 12 Nov. 1694, at St. James's, Westm. He *d.* an infant, and was *bur.* there 23 Apr. 1695.]

[WILLIAM KNOLLYS, *styled* VISCOUNT WALLINGFORD, 2nd, but 1st surv. s. and h. ap. by 1st wife (twin with Charles).   Major in the Horse Guards.   M.P. (Whig) for Banbury 1733-40.   He *m.* his 1st cousin,

---

(ᵃ) A certain Elizabeth Price, said to have been a lady at the Court of St. Germain, claimed to be his 1st wife, alleging that she was *m.* to him at Verona, 7 Apr. 1692.   See *The true Countess of Banbury's Case* * *relating to her marriage, rightly stated in a letter to the Lord Banbury*, London, printed 1696, small folio, pp. 34.   In this "Case" the lady states that Lord B. took her a house in Pall Mall in May 1689, and then travelled with her abroad from Nov. 1689 till Easter 1692, when the marriage took place as above stated.   A certificate thereof from the Archbishop of Verona to Dr. Oxenden, Dean of the Arches, is given.   G.E.C.   The Court of Delegates, after three and a half years trial, pronounced, 13 Jan. 1696/7, against the marriage with 'Mrs. Price' and in favour of that with 'Mrs. Lister,' who 'was a gentlewoman of good reputation, and had children by his Lordship,' whereas the other had none such, and 'had been a Player and mistress to several persons.'   (See Luttrell's *Diary*, 14 Jan. 1696/7.)   V.G.

(*) A copy is in the private collection of the College of Arms, London, marked "C.G.Y.," No. 203.

(ᵇ) For a pedigree of this family of Woods see *Her. and Gen.*, vol. viii, p. 191.

Mary Katherine, da. of John Law, the celebrated financier, by Katherine, 3rd da. of Nicholas (Knollys), titular 3rd Earl of Banbury. He *d. s.p.* and *v.p.*, June 1740, suddenly, of cramp, aged 45, and was *bur.* in the chapel in South Audley Str., St. Geo., Han. Sq. Will dat. 6, pr. 14 June 1740. His widow, who survived her husband over 50 years, *d.* 14 Oct. 1790, in Park Str., Grosvenor Sq., aged 79, and was *bur.* with him. (ᵃ) Will dat. 23 Dec. 1784, pr. 27 Oct. 1790].

V. 1740.   5. Charles (Knollys), Earl of Banbury, &c., 3rd, but 1st surv. s. and h. by 2nd wife, *b.* 26 Mar. and *bap.* 14 Apr. 1703, at St. James's, Westm. Matric. at Oxford (Ch. Ch.), 9 May 1722, as "s. of the Earl of Banbury;" B.A. 1725; M.A. 1728; Vicar of Burford, Oxon., 1750-71. He *m.* Martha, da. of (—) Hughes, of Southampton. He *d.* at Burford, 13, and was *bur.* there 19 Mar. 1771, aged nearly 68. Admon. 6 Apr. 1771 to his widow. Further admon. 4 Oct. 1771. His widow only surv. him for 6 months, and was *bur.* with him 17 Sep. 1771. Will pr. Nov. 1771.

VI. 1771.   6. William (Knollys), Earl of Banbury, &c., s. and h., *b.* 21 Oct. 1726, and *bap.* 21 July 1727, at St. Michael's, Southampton. Lieut. Col. in the army. He *d.* unm., 29 Aug., and was *bur.* 5 Sep. 1776, at Burford afsd., aged 49. Will pr. Sep. 1776.

VII. 1776.   7. Thomas Woods (Knollys), Earl of Banbury, &c., br. and h., *b.* 6 Dec. 1727, in Hawkmore Str., and *bap.* 15 Jan. 1727/8, at Cowley, Oxon. He was an officer in the 3rd. Reg. of Foot. He *m.*, 30 Mar. 1761, at St. Thomas's, Winchester, Mary, da. of William Porter, of Winchester, Attorney at Law. He *d.* at his house in Winchester, 18, and was *bur.* 27 Mar. 1793, in the Cathedral there, aged 65. Will *pr.* May 1793. His widow *d.* 22 Mar. 1798.

VIII. 1793.   8. William (Knollys), Earl of Banbury, &c., s. and h., *bap.* 2 Mar. 1763, at St. Thomas's, Winchester. Ensign 3rd Reg. Foot Guards, 1778; Lieut. 1788; Lieut. Col. 1793; Col. (brevet) 1795; Major Gen. 1802; Lt. Gen. 1808; General 1819; Lieut. Gov. of St. John's (Newfoundland) 1818-27; Governor of Limerick 1826 till his death. In 1806, by the style of "*William, Earl of Banbury*," he petitioned the Crown for his writ, which was referred to the Attorney Gen. (Sir Vicary Gibbs), whose report thereon, 17 Jan. 1808, was that, in his opinion, the resolution of the House of Lords in 1692/3 was "not a conclusive judgment" against the Peerage; that no steps had been taken to upset the judgment of the King's Bench, which if erroneous "might have been removed by a writ of

---

(ᵃ) Mrs. Delany writes of her, in 1740, as 'civil and goodnatured.'   V.G.

error to the House of Lords and there reversed," but that, though
the birth during marriage is proved, "the legitimacy of Nicholas is left
in a considerable degree of doubt." The petition was referred to the
House. After five years' discussion, the Committee for Privileges, on a
division, of 21 to 13, reported "that the Petitioner *hath not made out
his claim* to the title, honour, and dignity of Earl of Banbury."
Whereupon, on 15 Mar. 1813, the House resolved (a) (a much more
comprehensive resolution) "that the Petitioner *is not entitled* to the
title, &c., of Earl of Banbury." A "forcible and eloquent" protest (b)
drawn up by Lord Erskine, and signed by himself and ten other Peers,
was entered on the Lords' Journal. After this decision the Petitioner
discontinued the usage of the title. He *m.*, 23 June 1795, (Lic.
22 June, at Winchester, he 21, she 18, both of St. Thomas's, in that
city) Charlotte Martha, da. of Ebenezer BLACKWELL, of Lombard Str.,
London, Banker, by Mary, his wife. She *d.* 5 Feb. 1818, in Paris. Gen.
Knollys (as he was subsequently called) *d.* 20 Mar. 1834, of influenza,
at Paris, aged 71.

IX. 1834.　　　　9. WILLIAM THOMAS KNOLLYS, s. and h., who, till
　　　　　　　　1813 (but not afterwards), was *styled* VISCOUNT WAL-
LINGFORD, and who in his will styles himself "by hereditary descent and
by the law of the land EARL OF BANBURY, VISCOUNT WALLINGFORD and
BARON KNOLLYS OF GREYS, co. Oxon." (c) He was *b.* 1 Aug. 1797,
ed. at Harrow and at Sandhurst College. (d) In Dec. 1813 he joined
the Scots Fusilier Guards serving in the Peninsular War. Major Gen.
1854 ; Lieut. Gen. 1860 ; Gen. 1866 ; Col. 62nd Regiment, 1858, and
(four days before his death) gazetted Col. of the Scots Guards, 19 June

---

(a) "How far this Resolution is a conclusive judgment, and whether it does or does
not bar the heir of the Petitioner from prosecuting his claim are grave constitutional
questions." See Nicolas' *Treatise*, &c., p. 530. See also *ante*, p. 404, note "a."

(b) "Upon this protest Lord Erskine observed, in a letter to Gen. Knollys, the
late [1836] Claimant, dated 21 July 1813—*The protest gives them every fact and all
their arguments, but, giving them both,* leaves them without a single voice in Westm.
Hall, from one end to the other." See Nicolas' *Treatise*, &c., p. 530, note 2. The
"Protest" itself is printed pp. 531 to 551 of that work. It was signed by three
Royal Dukes, Kent, Sussex, and Gloucester.

(c) Letter signed "William Wallingford Knollys, Lieut. Col. H. P., claiming
to be Earl of Banbury, &c.," in *The Times* newspaper, 25 Aug. 1883. In this the
writer makes "a public protest against the decision [of 1692/3] by no means final"
and recites a passage in a letter of his father to the Morning Post, dat. 7 Mar. 1863,
as follows—"But the law of the land cannot be *changed, or constituted,* by such a vote
of *one* branch of the Legislature, and the voice of Westm. Hall, from Lord Coke and
Chief Justice Holt, to the present day, has repudiated, with some rare exceptions,
being governed by the law as thus laid down."

(d) The order book of Sandhurst College in 1813 contains the following note:—
"Gentleman Cadet Viscount Wallingford will henceforth be designated as Gentleman Cadet Knollys."

1883. Governor of Guernsey, 1854-55; in command of the camp at Aldershot (then first formed) 1855; Vice President of the Council of Military Education, 1861 to 1862; Treasurer and Comptroller of the Household of the Prince of Wales, 1862-77; K.C.B., 1867; P.C. 19 Mar. 1872; Gentleman Usher of the Black Rod to the House of Lords, 1877 till his death; Groom of the Stole to the Prince of Wales from 1877, and Receiver Gen. of the Duchy of Cornwall from 1878 till his death; Hon. D.C.L. (Oxford); Hon. LL.D. (Cambridge). He *m.*, 29 Sep. 1830, at St. Geo., Han. Sq., Elizabeth, illegit. da. of Sir John St. Aubyn, 5th Bart., of Clowance, and sister of Sir Edward St. Aubyn, *cr.* a Bart. 1866. She *d.* 28 Jan. 1878. He *d.* 23 June 1883, at his official residence in the House of Lords, aged 85. Will pr. 30 Aug. 1883, above £32,000, by his yst. s., Francis K., C.B., afterwards, 21 July 1902, *cr.* BARON KNOLLYS, who inherited the family estates of Blount's Court, Oxon, to the exclusion of his elder br. as below.

X. 1883.   10. WILLIAM WALLINGFORD KNOLLYS [Qy. EARL OF BANBURY, VISCOUNT WALLINGFORD AND BARON KNOLLYS OF GREYS?], who did not assume the title, though after his father's death he published a letter laying claim to the Earldom, (*) s. and h., *b.* 13 Nov. 1833, in London. Ed. at Sandhurst. Served in the Scots Guards during the Crimean Campaign; exchanged into the 93rd Highlanders June 1858. Lieut. Col. 1878, retiring Dec. 1883. He *m.*, 1860, Sophia Elizabeth Tuckfield, 1st. da. of Thomas GOLDSWORTHY, by Sophia, da. of (—) TUCKFIELD. She was *b.* 6 Dec. 1840. He *d.* 13 Aug. 1904, (*b*) suddenly, of heart failure, at Perham House, Perham Road, West Kensington, aged 70. His widow was living in 1910. He was *suc.* by his s., who is outside the scope of this work.

BANDON

i.e. "BOYLE OF BANDON, co. Cork," Viscountcy [I.] *(Boyle)*, *cr.* 1756, with the Earldom of SHANNON [I] which see.

BARONY [I.]
I. 1793.

VISCOUNTCY [I.]
I. 1795.

EARLDOM [I.]
I. 1800.

1. FRANCIS BERNARD, of Castle Bernard, near Bandon, co. Cork, s. and h. of James B., of the same, (M.P. for co. Cork, in three Parls.) by Esther, widow of Robert Gookin, da. of Percy SMITH, and sister and coh. of William S., of Headborough, was *b.* 26 Nov. 1755. Was M.P. [I.] for Ennis 1778-83, for Bandon Bridge, 1783-90; *suc.* his father 7 July 1790; and was, on 26 Nov. 1793, *cr.* BARON BANDON of Bandonbridge, co. Cork [I]; on 4 Oct. 1795

VISCOUNT BANDON of Bandonbridge, co. Cork [I.]; and on 29 Aug. 1800, VISCOUNT BERNARD and EARL OF BANDON [I.] ([a]) REP. PEER [I.] (Tory) 1801-30, being one of the original 28 elected at the time of the Union. He *m.*, 12 Feb. 1784 (mar. lic. 11 Feb. at Dublin), Catharine Henrietta, da. of Richard (BOYLE), 2nd EARL OF SHANNON, by Catharine, da. of the Rt. Hon. John PONSONBY. She, who was *b.* 12 Jan. 1768, *d.* 8 July 1815, at Castle Bernard, and was *bur.* at Ballymodan, co. Cork. He *d.* 26 Nov. 1830, suddenly, at Castle Bernard, on his 75th birthday. ([b])

II 1830.   2. JAMES (BERNARD), EARL OF BANDON, &c. [I.], s.
          and h., *b.* 14 June 1785. M.P. (Tory) for Youghal 1806-07, 1818-20; for co. Cork 1807-18; for Bandon 1820-26, and Aug. to Nov. 1830   Hon. D C L. (Oxford) 1832 ; REP. PEER [I.] 1835. ([c])   LL.D (Cambridge) ; Lord Lieut. of co. Cork 1842 till his death ; F R.S. 5 June 1845 ; Recorder of Bandon, &c.   He *m.*, 13 Mar. 1809, at the Cathedral, Cashel, Mary Susan Albinia, 1st. da. of the Hon. Charles BRODRICK, Archbishop of Cashel, by Mary, da. of Richard WOODWARD, Bishop of Cloyne.   He *d* at Castle Bernard, 31 Oct , and was *bur* 5 Nov. 1856, at Bandon, aged 71.   M.I   Will pr. Feb. 1857.   His widow, who was *b.* 9 Oct. 1787, *d.* 23, and was *bur.* 29 Apr. 1870, at Bandon.   M.I.

III. 1856.   3. FRANCIS (BERNARD), EARL OF BANDON, &c. [I.], s.
          and h., *b.* 3 Jan. 1810, in Grosvenor Str., Midx.   Ed. at Oriel Coll. Oxford ; B A 1830 ; M.A. 1834 , M.P. (Conservative) for Bandon, Jan. to July 1831, and 1842-56 ; REP. PEER [I] 1858 , D.C.L., Lord Lieut of co. Cork 1874 till his death   He *m.*, 16 Aug. 1832, at Brighton, Catherine Mary, 1st da. of Thomas WHITMORE, of Apley, Salop, by Catherine, da. and h. of Thomas THOMASON, of York.   She *d* 15 Dec. 1873, at Castle Bernard   He *d.* there, 17 Feb. 1877, aged 67

IV. 1877.   4. JAMES FRANCIS (BERNARD), EARL OF BANDON, VIS-
          COUNT BANDON, VISCOUNT BERNARD and BARON BANDON [I.], only s. and h., *b.* 12 Sep. 1850; ed. at Eton.   Sheriff of Co. Cork 1875, as Viscount Bernard ; State Steward to the Lord Lieut. [I.] 1876-77; Lord Lieut. of co. Cork, since 1877; REP. PEER [I.] (Conservative) 1881. K.P. 29 Aug. 1900.   He *m.*, 22 June 1876, at St. Michael's, Chester Sq., Midx., Georgiana Dorothea Harriet, only child of George Patrick Percy (EVANS-FREKE), 7th LORD CARBERY [I.], by Harriet Maria Catherine, da. of Lieut. Gen. Edmund William SHULDHAM, of Dunmanway, co Cork. She was *b.* 3 Nov. 1853.

---

it for many years, acting as war correspondent, editor, and military critic. " (Obit. notice *Morning Post*)   V.G.

     ([a]) See volume iii, Appendix H, for a list of the 47 peerages [I] *cr.* in the last 12 months before the Union   V.G.

     ([b]) In 1799 his Irish estates were stated to be worth £18,000 *p.a.* See vol. iv, Appendix C, for a list of the largest resident Irish landlords at that date.   V.G.

     ([c]) He voted for the repeal of the Corn Laws in 1846.   V.G.

Family Estates.—These, in 1883, consisted of about 40,940 acres, co. Cork, of the annual value of about £19,215. *Principal Residence* —Castle Bernard, near Bandon, co. Cork.

BANDONBRIDGE

i.e. "BANDONBRIDGE, co. Cork" Barony [I.] *(Boyle)*, *cr.* 1628, with the Viscountcy BOYLE OF KYNALMEAKY [I.], which see.

---

i.e. "BANDON OF BANDONBRIDGE, co. Cork" Barony [I.], *cr.* 1793 ; Viscountcy [I.] *(Boyle)*, *cr.* 1795 , see 'BANDON' Earldom [I.].

BANFF

BARONY [S.]   1. GEORGE OGILVY, of Banff and Dunlugus, co Banff,
                   s. and h. of Sir Walter O., of the same, by Helen,
I. 1642.   da of Walter URQUHART, of Cromarty, was *cr* a BARON-
ET [S], 30 July 1627, and having distinguished himself against the Covenanters, 19 June 1639, at the bridge of Dee, was *cr* by the King, by patent dat at Nottingham, 31 Aug 1642, LORD OF BANFF [S.], "to him and his heirs male for ever bearing the name and arms of Ogilvy." (a) In revenge for the part he had taken against them, his fine house and gardens at Banff were wrecked by the Covenanting army. The King gave him 10,000 marks towards repairing his losses In 1654 he was fined £1000 by Cromwell. He *m.*, 1stly, before 9 Mar. 1610/1, Margaret, da. of Sir Alexander IRVINE, of Drum She *d s.p.m.* He *m* , 2ndly, Janet, da. of William SUTHERLAND, of Duffus. On 30 July 1629 she complained to the Privy Council of his cruelty to her and her children. He *d.* 11 Aug. 1663.

II. 1663.   2. GEORGE OGILVY, LORD BANFF [S.], s. and h by 2nd
                   wife   M P. for co Nairn 1644. Like his father, an
active loyalist, and fought for Charles II at Worcester. He *m.* Agnes, da. of Alexander (FALCONER), 1st LORD FALCONER OF HALKERTOUN [S.], by Ann, only child of John (LINDSAY), 9th LORD LINDSAY OF THE BYRES [S.]. He *d* Mar 1668   His widow *d.* Mar. 1708. Fun entry at Lyon office. (b).

III. 1668.   3. GEORGE (OGILVY), LORD BANFF [S.], s. and h., *bap.*
                   9 Sep. 1649. He renounced the Roman Catholic faith,
and taking his seat in Parl., 3 Oct. 1706, was a zealous supporter of the

---

(a) The preamble to the patent is in *Douglas*, p. 192.
(b) At that date she is there entered as '*Grizel* Falconer, Lady Banff,' yet her name was probably, as in Wood's *Douglas*, *Agnes*, and her death as '*Agnes* Falconer, Lady Banff' on 4 Jan. 1711 [*sic*] *æt.* 85, at Forglen, is recorded in the Diary of John Row, Principal of King's Coll. V.G.

Union (ᵃ) He *m.* (cont 22 Sep. 1669), Jean, 3rd and yst da. of William (KEITH), 7th EARL MARISCHAL [S.], by his 1st wife, Elizabeth, da. of George (SETON), 2nd EARL OF WINTOUN [S.].   On 5 Feb. 1685 she made complaint of her husband refusing to cohabit with her   She was living 1687.   He *d.* Nov. 1713, aged 64, perishing in the fire which destroyed his house at Inchdruer, co. Banff (ᵇ)

IV. 1713.   4. GEORGE (OGILVY), LORD BANFF [S.], s. and h., *bap.* 4 Aug. 1670, at Banff.   He *m.*, 11 Jan. 1712, Helen, da. of Sir John LAUDER, 2nd Bart. [S.], of Fountainhall, a Lord of Session, by Janet, da. of Sir Andrew RAMSAY, Bart. [S.]   He *d* 1717/8, before 12 Jan., aged 47.   His widow *m.*, 27 June 1721, Alexander GORDON, of Glengerrack.   She *m*, 3rdly, James HAY, Merchant in Banff, and *d.* 22 Oct. 1742

V. 1718.   5. JOHN GEORGE (OGILVY), LORD BANFF [S.], 3rd, but 1st surv (ᶜ) s. and h., *b.* 18 Feb. 1717.   He *m.*, 18 Aug. 1735, in the Fleet Prison, Mary, da. of Capt. James OGILVY. He *d. s.p.*, being drowned while bathing at the Black rocks, near Cullen, 29 July, and was *bur* 1 Aug. 1738, at Banff, aged 21.   His widow *m.* the Rev. Thomas KEMP, D D , Rector of St Michael's, Crooked lane, London, who *d.* 21 July 1769, aged 69.   She *d.* 31 Jan. 1784, aged 69.   Both *bur.* at Cheam, Surrey.   M.I.   Her will, dat. 1 Oct. 1773 to 28 Jan. 1784, pr. 11 Feb. 1784.

VI. 1738.   6. ALEXANDER (OGILVY), LORD BANFF [S.], br. and h., *bap.* 12 July 1718, at Banff, being a posthumous child.   Ent. the Navy 16 Feb. 1732/3. (ᵈ)   Capt R N., 1741 ; Commander, 1742-43, of the 'Hastings' man of war, when he captured a Spanish Privateer.   In recognition of his gallantry, he received the freedom of the City of Glasgow, in 1743.   He *d.* unm , at Lisbon, Nov. 1746, and was *bur.* 10 May 1747, at St. Martin's-in-the-Fields, in his 29th year.   Admon 5 July 1750 and 12 June 1751 on behalf of his uterine brothers, " Hon. Charles Hay, James Hay and William Hay, Esquires, " minors.

VII. 1746.   7. ALEXANDER (OGILVY), LORD BANFF [S.], cousin and h. male, being s. and h. of Alexander O., the younger, of Forglen, co. Banff, by Jane, da. of Benjamin FREND, of Ballyrehy, King's Co., which Alexander O. was s. and eventually h. ap. (dying *v.p.*) of the

---

(ᵃ) " Never was a vote more cheaply purchased, as it appears from the account of the Earl of Glasgow, exhibited upon oath, that Lord Banff's share of the £20,000 distributed on this occasion was only £11 2s 0d " (*Douglas*, p. 193)

(ᵇ) The date given in Row's Diary, quoted above, is 30 Jan. 1713, and he is there called " an man of an very eivell life. " (*Scottish Notes and Queries*)   V.G.

(ᶜ) The 1st s., George, *bap.* 20 Feb. 1714, and the 2nd s , George, *bap.* 28 Nov 1715, both *d.* infants   V G

(ᵈ) The particulars of his outfit, and the sums disbursed therefor, are given in *The Genealogist*, vol. xxv, pt. 4, pp. 264-5.   V.G.

Hon. Sir Alexander Ogilvy, Bart. [S.], of Forglen afsd (so *cr* 1701), who was 2nd s. of George, 2nd Lord Banff [S]   He *suc.* his said grandfather in his estate and Baronetcy in 1727, some 19 years before he *suc.* his cousin in the peerage. He *m.*, 2 Apr. 1749, at Edinburgh, Jean, (ª) da. of William NISBET, of Dirleton, co. Haddington. He *d.* 1 Sep. 1771, at Forglen. Will dat. 2 Aug. 1766, pr. 19 Mar. 1773. His widow *d* 29 Aug. 1790, at Forglen.

[ALEXANDER OGILVY, *styled* MASTER of BANFF, s. and h. ap.   He *d.* young and unm., *v.p.*, 1763]

VIII. 1771   8. WILLIAM (OGILVY), LORD BANFF, 2nd, but 1st surv.
to   s. and h. He served, under the Duke of York, as an
1803.   officer in the Enniskillen (6th) Reg. of Dragoons; Cornet,
               1773 ; Lieut , 1778 ; Capt., 1780 , retired 1794. He *d.*
unm., 4 June 1803, at Forglen, when the issue male of the 1st Lord became *extinct*, and the *Peerage* (if not *extinct*) became *dormant.* (ᵇ)

The Peerage was claimed by petition in June 1812, and again in June 1819, (ᶜ) by Sir William Ogilvy of Boyne (*d* at Edinburgh, 8 June 1825) as the descendant and h male of George O. of Boyne, elder br. of Sir Walter O of Dunlugus, the great grandfather of the first Lord Banff [S.] See *Lords' Journals*, vol. 48, p 920 ; vol. 52, p 790. In Burke's *Extinct Peerage* for 1866 it was stated to be then "claimed" by Alexander Ogilvie, M.D., Dep. Inspector Gen Royal Artillery, as "male descendant and representative of George Ogilvy, 2nd Baron Boyne, and as heir male of George, 1st Baron Ogilvy of Banff. "   This claimant, who was *b* 9 May 1789, left an only child, Alexander Walter Armstrong Ogilvie, Capt. R A. (*b* 20 Jan 1834, *m.* 5 June 1860, *d.* 21 June 1865), who left an only child Alexander Ogilvie.

BANGOR

i.e. "BANGOR, co Down " Earldom [I.] *(Schomberg)*, *cr.* 1691, with

---

(ª) She was sister of the wife of the 8th Earl of Leven, and of the 1st wife of the so-called 5th Lord Ruthven of Freeland   V G

(ᵇ) The estates, which were all in co. Banff, went to Jane, his eldest sister, wife of Sir George Abercromby, 4th Bart [S] of Birkenbog, co Banff, and afterwards of Forglen House, which thereafter became the principal residence of the Abercromby family.

(ᶜ) The claim is very absurd   William Ogilvy was, 19 Feb 1812, served h male of his cousin, Sir Patrick O , of Boyne, Bart., and h gen of his great-great-grandfather, Alexander O , of Boyne   Sir Patrick, however, was not a Baronet, and why serve to him, as he left at least two sons who long surv. him ?   Alexander O. of Boyne, who *d* an old man in 1606, could not be so few generations removed from the claimant   Then in the Banff line extinctions would need to be proved up to about 1500   (*ex inform.* R R Stodart)

Robert Riddle Stodart, *b.* 16 Nov 1827, Lyon Clerk 1863, to whose unfailing kindness the former editor was indebted for able revision of the earlier notices in the Scottish Peerage, *d* before the 1st vol. was completed, 19 Apr. 1886. An appreciative notice of him is in *The Genealogist*, N.S , vol iii, pp. 129-135

the Dukedom of LEINSTER [I.]. See "SCHOMBERG" Dukedom, *cr.* 1689, under the 3rd Duke , all titles becoming *extinct* 1719.

BARONY [I.]

I. 1770.

VISCOUNTCY [I.]

I. 1781.

1. BERNARD WARD, of Bangor, co. Down, only surv. s. and h. of Michael W., (*d.* 1758) one of the Justices of the Court of King's Bench [I.] (1727-58), by Anne Catharina, da. and coh. of James HAMILTON, of Bangor afsd. (by Sophia da. of John (MORDAUNT), 2nd EARL OF PETERBOROUGH), was *b* Aug. and *bap.* 6 Sep. 1719 ; M.P. for co. Down 1745-70. On 30 May 1770, he was *cr.* BARON BANGOR of Castle Ward, co. Down, and took his seat 11 Mar. 1771. On 11 Jan. 1781 (ª) he was *cr.* VISCOUNT BANGOR of Castle Ward, co. Down [I]. He *m*, Dec. 1747, Ann, widow of Robert HAWKINS-MAGILL, of Gill Hall, co Down, (*d* 1745) da. of John (BLIGH), 1st EARL OF DARNLEY, by Theodosia, da. and h. of Edward (HYDE), 3rd EARL OF CLARENDON. He *d.* 20 May 1781, at Castle Ward, afsd., aged 61. Will pr. 1781. His widow *d.* at Bath, Somerset, 7, and was "carried away" 20 Feb 1789. Will pr. 1793, Prerog. Court [I.]

II. 1781.   2 NICHOLAS (WARD), VISCOUNT BANGOR, &c. [I.], s. and h , *bap.* 5 Dec. 1750. Matric. at Oxford (Ch. Ch.) 18 Apr. 1769 ; M P for Bangor 1771-76 (ᵇ) He was a lunatic before 11 Apr. 1785, when the Committees of his person and estates obtained a bill in the House of Lords to make leases, &c. He *d.* unm , 11 Sep. 1827, at Castle Ward, aged 76.

III. 1827.   3. EDWARD SOUTHWELL (WARD), VISCOUNT BANGOR, &c [I], nephew and h., being 3rd but 1st surv. s and h. of the Hon. Edward WARD, M.P. for co. Down, by Arabella, da. of William (CROSBIE), 1st EARL OF GLANDORE [I.], which Edward was 2nd surv s of the 1st Viscount, and *d.* Nov. 1812. He was *b.* Mar. 1790. He *m.*, 14 Feb. 1826, Harriet Margaret, 2nd da. of Henry (MAXWELL), 6th LORD FARNHAM [I], by Anne, da of Henry Thomas (BUTLER), 2nd EARL OF CARRICK [I]. He *d.* 1 Aug 1837, aged 47. Will pr. May 1840. His widow *m*, 4 Oct. 1841, in Dublin, Andrew NUGENT, of Portaferry, Major 36th Reg. She *d* 4 July 1880, at Castle Ward, aged 76

IV. 1837.   4. EDWARD (WARD), VISCOUNT BANGOR, &c [I.], s. and h., *b.* 23 Feb. 1827, in London. REP. PEER [I.] (Conservative) 1855. He *d.* unm., 14 Sep 1881, at Brighton, aged 54.

V. 1881.   5. HENRY WILLIAM CROSBIE (WARD), VISCOUNT BANGOR and BARON BANGOR [I.], br. and h., *b.* 26 July 1828,

---

(ª) King's Letters, 15 Dec 1780.
(ᵇ) When Sir John Blaquiere writes of him—" more than half an idiot, requires watching. "   V G

in London. Ed. at Rugby School, and at Sandhurst Coll. Officer in 43rd Reg.; served in Kaffir war 1851-53, and retired as Capt. 1854. REP. PEER [I.] (Conservative) since Nov. 1885. He *m.*, 1stly, 6 Dec. 1854, Mary, yst. da. of the Rev. Henry KING, of Ballylin, King's Co., by Harriet, da. of John LLOYD, of Gloster, King's Co. She *d.* 31 Aug. 1869, being killed by an accident at Parsonstown. He *m.*, 2ndly, 8 Apr. 1874, Elizabeth, only surv. da. and h. of Hugh ECCLES, of Cronroe, co. Wicklow, by Harriet Anne, 3rd da. of Sir Richard Bligh ST. GEORGE, 2nd Bart. [I.]. She was *b.* 9 Dec. 1828.

[MAXWELL RICHARD CROSBIE WARD, 3rd, but only surv. s. ([a]) and h. ap., *b.* 4 May 1868; Capt. R.A. He *m.*, 5 Jan. 1905, at Monaghan, Agnes Elizabeth, 3rd da. of Dacre HAMILTON, of Cornacassa, co. Monaghan, by Helen, da. of Walter NUGENT, Baron of the Austrian Empire.]

Family Estates.—These, in 1883 (besides three acres in Berks valued at £87 a year), consisted of 9,861 acres in co. Down, of the yearly value of £13,156. *Principal Residence* :—Castle Ward, co. Down.

BANHEATH

See "KEITH OF BANHEATH, co. Dunbarton, " Barony *(Elphinstone)*, *cr.* 1803, *extinct* 1867.

BANNOW

i.e. BANNOW co. Wexford, " Barony [I.] *(Cheevers)*, *cr.* by James II after his deposition from the *English* throne, with the Viscountcy of MOUNT LEINSTER [I.], which see ; *extinct* 1693.

BANTRY

i.e. "BANTRY, co. Cork" Barony [I.] *(Roper)*, *cr.* [27 June] 1627, with the Viscountcy of BALTINGLASS [I.], which see ; *extinct* 1693.

BANTRY

FRANCES, widow of Sir George HAMILTON, elder da. and coh. of Richard JENNINGS, of Sandridge, Herts, became in 1679 wife of Richard TALBOT, afterwards EARL OF TYRCONNELL ; she was intended in 1677 to

([a]) Of his 2 elder brothers (1) Henry Somerset Andrew, *b.* 30 Aug. 1857, *d. v.p.*, 10 July 1860. (2) Edward William Henry, *b.* Jan. 1863, sometime Lieut. Rifle Brigade, *d.* unm. and *v.p.*, 10 July 1887. V.G.

have been *cr.* COUNTESS OF BANTRY(ᵃ) or COUNTESS OF BEREHAVEN [I.],(ᵇ) but no patent ever passed the seals. For fuller particulars see *sub* TYRCONNELL, Earldom, *cr.* 1685.

---

i.e. " SAUNDERSON OF BANTRY, co. Cork " Barony [I.] *(Saunderson), cr.* [11 July] 1627, with the Viscountcy of CASTLETON [I.], which see ; *extinct* with the Earldom of CASTLETON, 1723.

BARONY [I.]

I. 1797.

VISCOUNTCY [I.]

I. 1800.

EARLDOM [I.]

I. 1816.

1. RICHARD WHITE, (ᶜ) of Bantry, co. Cork, s. and h. of Simon W., of the same, by Frances Jane, da. of Richard HEDGES, of Macroom, in that co., *b.* 6 Aug. 1767, *suc.* his grandfather Richard White, of Bantry afsd., and for his exertions in repelling the French invasion (1797) at Bantry Bay, was *cr.*, 24 Mar. 1797, (ᵈ) BARON BANTRY, of Bantry, co. Cork, and, subsequently, 29 Dec. 1800, (ᵉ) VISCOUNT BANTRY of Bantry, co. Cork, and finally, 22 Jan. 1816, VISCOUNT BEREHAVEN and EARL OF BANTRY, co. Cork [I.]. He *m.*, (spec. lic.) 3 Nov. 1799, at Cork, Margaret Anne, (fortune £30,000) 1st da. of William (HARE), 1st EARL OF LISTOWEL [I.], by his 1st wife, Mary, da. of Henry WRIXON. She was *b.* 1779, and *d.* 19 Jan. 1835. He *d.* 2 May 1851, at Glengariff Lodge, co. Cork, aged 83. (ᶠ)

(ᵃ) In an MS. entitled " Irish Nobility " *(circa* 1690-1710 ? by Peter le Neve ?) *penes* Sir Arthur Vicars, she appears as " Countess of Bantry." *(ex inform.* G.D. Burtchaell). " 18 June 1677. Reference to the Lord Treasurer of the petition of the Countess of Bantry for a pension which she was informed after marriage to Sir G.Hamilton his Majesty would grant her, if she outlived him." *(State Papers Dom.,* Entry Book 46, p. 187.) V.G.

(ᵇ) 9 July 1677. Warrant to the Earl of Peterborough, Deputy E. M. after reciting the creation of Dame Frances Hamilton, the relict of Sir G.Hamilton to be Countess of Berehaven in Ireland, ordaining that Elizabeth, Mary Frances, and Henrietta Hamilton, the daughters of the said Sir George Hamilton should enjoy the the privilege and precedence of the daughters of a Countess of Ireland. *(State Papers Dom.,* Entry Book 40A, f. 209. *(ex inform.* the Marquis de Ruvigny.) V.G.

(ᶜ) See *Misc. Gen. et Her.,* N.S., vol. i, p. 60, for an interesting account of this family.

(ᵈ) King's Letters, 11 Mar. 1797.

(ᵉ) For an account of the Irish peerages *cr.* at the time of the Union, see vol. iii, Appendix H. V.G.

(ᶠ) In 1799 his Irish estates were said to be worth £9000 *p.a.* For a list of the largest resident Irish landlords at that date see vol. iii, Appendix G. " He possesses large property which he inherits through his grandfather, who made an immense fortune in the profession of the law. He is a warm supporter of all the measures of government, and an advocate for the union. " *(Sketches of Irish political character,* 1799.) V.G.

II. 1851.   2. Richard (White), Earl of Bantry, &c. [I.], s.
and h , *b.* 16 Nov. 1800, at St. Finbarr, Cork.   Sheriff of
co. Cork, 1835, as Viscount Berehaven.   Rep. Peer [I.] (Conservative) (ᵃ)
1854.   He *m*, 11 Oct. 1836, at St. Geo , Han Sq , Mary, 3rd and yst
da and coh. of William (O'Brien), 2nd Marquess of Thomond [I], by
Elizabeth, da. and h. of Thomas Trotter.   She *d.* 19 July 1853, at
Bantry House.   He *d. s.p.*, 16 July 1868, at Exmouth House, Hants,
aged 67.   Will pr. Nov. 1868, under £90,000.

III. 1868.   3. William Henry Hare (Hedges-White), Earl of
Bantry, &c. [I.], br. and h., *b.* 10 Nov. 1801, in Dublin.
Ed. at Downing Coll., Cambridge ; M.A 1823.   By royal lic., 7 Sep.
1840, he took the additional name of Hedges. (ᵇ)   Sheriff of co. Cork, 1848
Rep Peer [I.] (Conservative) 1869.   He *m.*, 16 Apr. 1845, at St. Geo ,
Han. Sq., Jane, 1st da. of Charles John Herbert, of Muckross Abbey, co.
Kerry, by Louisa Middleton, his wife.   He *d* 15 Jan 1884, at Bantry
House, co. Cork, in his 83rd year.   Will pr. above £107,000 personalty
[E. and I.].   His widow *d.* 7 July 1898, at Torquay, and was *bur.* at
Bantry.   Will pr. above £3000 personalty.

IV. 1884   4. William Henry Hare (Hedges-White), Earl of
to   Bantry, Viscount Bantry, Viscount Berehaven and
1891.   Baron Bantry [I.], only s. and h , *b.* 2 July 1854.   He
m , 18 Feb. 1886, at Rome, Rosamund Catharine, da. of
the Hon. Edmund George Petre, by Mary Anne Jane, da. of Loraine
M. Kerr.   He *d. s p.*, 30 Nov. 1891, aged 37, at Mount Merrion, co.
Dublin, when all his honours became *extinct*   Will pr. at £18,639 net.
His widow, who was *b.* 25 Aug. 1857, *m.*, 7 Dec. 1897, at Christ Church,
Down Str , Arthur William, 2nd Baron Trevor of Brynkinalt, and was
living 1910.

Family Estates.—These, in 1883, consisted of 69,500 acres in co.
Cork, of the annual value of £14,561.   *Principal Residences* :—Macroom
Castle and Bantry House, both co. Cork.

BANYARD, see BAYNARD

BARD OF DROMBOY

i.e. "Bard of Dromboy, co. Meath " Barony [I.] *(Bard)*, cr. 1645,
with the Viscountcy of Bellomont [I], which see ; *extinct* 1660

(ᵃ) This word appears to have been coined by Croker for the use of a political
party in a *Quarterly Review* article, in 1831.   V.G.
(ᵇ) Out of gratitude to, and respect for the memory of, his maternal uncle,
Robert Hedges Eyre, of Macroom Castle, co. Clare, who had devised him certain
estates. (*ex inform* G.D. Burtchaell)   V.G.

BARDOLF OR BARDOLF
OF WIRMEGAY OR WORMEGAY ([a])

WILLIAM BARDOLF, s. of William B., ([b]) (who *d.* 1275) of Wormegay, Norfolk, and Shelford, Notts, &c., was sum. to attend the King at
Shrewsbury 28 June (1283) 11 Edw. I, ([c]) by writ directed *Willelmo
Bardolf'.* He *m.* Julian, da. and h. of Hugh DE GOURNAY, of Mapledur-
ham, Oxon. He *d.* 1 Dec. 1289. His widow *d.* in 1295.

BARONY   1. HUGH BARDOLF, ([d]) of Wormegay, and Shelford, afsd.,
BY WRIT.   s. and h., *b.* about 29 Sep. 1259. He had seizin of his
            mother's lands 29 Nov. 1295. He took an active part in
I. 1299.   the French and Scottish wars, and was among the retainers
of Henry (de Lacy), Earl of Lincoln, at Carlaverock. He was knighted.
In addition to the irregular sum. of 8 June 1294, which would not serve
to *cr.* a Barony, ([e]) he was sum. to Parl. from 6 Feb. (1298/9) 27 Edw. I,
to 2 June (1302) 30 Edw. I, by writs directed *Hugoni Bardolf'*, whereby
he may be held to have become LORD BARDOLF. ([f]) He *m.*, before
1282, Isabel, da. and (15 Feb. 1285/6) sole h. of Sir Robert AGUILLON,
of Addington, ([g]) Surrey, Watton at Stone, Herts., &c., by his 1st wife,
Joan, one of the seven daughters (and coheirs of the 1st wife) of William
(DE FERRERS), EARL OF DERBY. He *d.* Sep. 1304. His widow, who was

([a]) See Stapleton's preface to *Liber de Antiquis Legibus*, Camden Soc., 1846.

([b]) This William was s. and h. of Doun B., by Beatrice, da. and h. of William
de Warenne, of Wormegay afsd., which Doun or Dodo B. was s. and h. of Thomas
B., by Rose, da. of Ralph Hauselyn. V.G.

([c]) As to this supposed Parl. see Preface.

([d]) The Bardolfs of Wormegay bore arms of Azure three cinquefoils gold.
The stall-plate of Sir William Phelipp, knight of the Garter, shows his shield of
Quarterly gules and silver with an eagle gold in the quarter. (*ex inform.* Oswald
Barron.) V.G.

([e]) There is proof in the Rolls of Parl. of his sitting, before the record of Writs
of Summons began : if the Lords had to adjudicate on the question and were to
follow the precedent set in 1841 as to the Barony of Hastings, the date of such
sitting and not that of the first writ, 1298/9, would determine the precedency of this
Barony. As to the summons of 1294, see Preface. V.G.

([f]) As to how far these early writs of summons did in fact create any peerage
title, see Appendix A in the last volume. V.G.

([g]) He held a manor, afterwards called Bardolf's manor, in the parish of
Addington, by Grand Serjeantry, by the service of making a mess called " *gerout* " for
the King's table. The manor had been held at the time of Domesday by Tezelin,
the King's Cook, which accounts for the origin of a *culinary* service. This service
was performed for George III by Mr. Spencer, Lord of the manor of Addington (both
manors being then united), but in 1807 the property was sold to the See of Canterbury. See Taylor's *Glory of Regality*, 1820, p. 147, and Stapleton's *Liber de Antiquis
Legibus*, p. lxxxviii, note *.

b. 25 Mar. 1257/8, had livery of Ruskington, co. Lincoln, 15 Oct 1304, and was of Addington afsd, in 1316.   She *d.* shortly before 28 May 1323.

II. 1304.   2 THOMAS (BARDOLF), LORD BARDOLF, s. and h., *b.*
                    4 Oct. 1282, at Watton at Stone, Herts.   Knighted
22 May 1306   He was sum. to Parl. from 26 Aug. (1307) 1 Edw. II,
to 23 Oct. (1330) 4 Edw. III.   He *m.* Agnes, perhaps da. of William
DE GRANDSON, SEIGNEUR DE GRANDSON, on the Lake of Neuchâtel in
Switzerland, by Blanche, da. of LOUIS DE SAVOIE, BARON DE VAUD. (ᵃ)   He
d. 15 Dec. 1328, and was *bur.* at Shelford Priory, Notts, aged 46.   Writ
for *Inq. p. m.* 30 Dec. 1328.   His widow, who had a protection, Aug.
1337, as being "by birth of the parts of Almain," *d.* 11 Dec. 1357, at
Ruskington, co. Lincoln. (ᵇ)

III. 1328.   3. JOHN (BARDOLF), LORD BARDOLF, s. and h., *b.* 13 Jan.
                    1311/2.   He had seizin of his lands 26 Mar. 1335   He
served in Scotland, Germany, and Brittany, and in (1345) 19 Edw. III,
was a Knight Banneret.   He was sum to Parl 22 Jan. (1335/6) 9 Edw. III,
to 1 June (1363), 37 Edw. III, the last two writs being directed *Johanni
Bardolf' de Wirmegey.* (ᶜ)   He *m* , 1326, Elizabeth, only da. and h. of Roger

---

(ᵃ) Stapleton, in his so-called "Preface" to the *Liber de Antiquis Legibus*, after remarking that the continuator of Blomfield's *Norfolk* states that the wife of Thomas Lord Bardolf was Agnes, da of the Lord Grandisson, proceeds to prove that "Agnes, da. of William de Grandisson a Baron of Parl.," *m.* someone else [as indeed she did]. In an appendix he adds "hence [no sufficient reason is advanced] it may be assumed, as an unquestionable fact, that Agnes, wife of Thomas Lord Bardolf, was the seventh da. of Thomas Beauchamp, Earl of Warwick. .According to the pedigree of this family, compiled by John Rous, this earl had a da , Agnes, who is described to have been the wife of—Cokesey, and afterwards of—Bardolf   Hence we may infer that Agnes was the wife, first of Thomas Lord Bardolf, whose eldest son John was *b.* 13 Jan. 1312 ; and that after his decease on the 15th day of Feb [*sic*] 2 Edw. III 1328 she re-married Sir Walter de Cokesey, of Cokesey, com. Worc. " (p. ccxxxv). As Thomas Beauchamp, Earl of Warwick, was not *m* till 1337, his seventh da was not likely to have a son *b* in 1312, and the above "unquestionable fact " is a gross mistake.   Agnes was perhaps, as above stated, da. of William, Seigneur de Grandson, which would explain her having been *b.* in the parts of Almain, as mentioned in the the text. (*ex inform.* G W.Watson)   V G

(ᵇ) "Agnes que fuit uxor Thome Bardolf "   Writs of *diem cl. ext* 22 Dec. 31 Edw. III   Inq , co. Lincoln, Tuesday after the Epiphany [9 Jan.] 1357/8. "obiit apud Riskyngton die lune proximo post festum Conceptionis beate Marie virginis [11 Dec.] anno etc. tricesimo primo. "   Inq., Essex, Thursday after Ash Wednesday [15 Feb].   "obiit die lune proximo ante festum sancte Lucie ultimo preteritum [11 Dec.]."   Inq , co Notts, 12 Jan   "obiit die lune proximo post festum sancti Nicholai ultimo preterito [11 Dec]. "   Inq., co. Leicester, Saturday before St. Hilary [6 Jan.].   "obiit die martis proximo post festum sancti Nicholai [12 Dec.] anno etc. tricesimo primo. "   Inq., cos. Derby and Northants, 18, 20 Jan.   " obiit xij die Decembris ultimo preterito. "   Inq , Sussex, 9. Jan.   "obiit xxij [*sic*] die Decembris proximo preterito "   (Ch *Inq p m.*, Edw. III, file 137, no. 48).   (*ex inform.* G W Watson).   V G

(ᶜ) There is proof in the Rolls of Parl. of his sitting.

[LORD] D'AMORIE, by Elizabeth, 3rd and yst da. of Gilbert (DE CLARE), EARL OF GLOUCESTER AND HERTFORD, and Joan, da. of King Edward I. She, who was *b.* shortly before 23 May 1318, brought him large estates in Dorset, and was living 1360 (ª) He *d.* in July or Aug. 1363, at Assisi, in Italy, aged 51 (ᵇ)

IV. 1363   4 WILLIAM (BARDOLF), LORD BARDOLF, s and h., *b* 21 Oct. 1349. He served in the wars in France and Ireland   He was sum. to Parl. 28 Dec (1375) 49 Edw. III, to 3 Sep. (1385) 9 Ric. II, by writs directed *Willelmo Bardolf'*, with, from 16 July 1381, the suffix *de Wirmegeye*. (ᶜ)   He *m.* Agnes, da. of Michael [LORD] POYNINGS (to whom he had been in ward), by Joan, formerly wife of Sir John DE MOLEYNS, (ᵈ) da. of Sir Richard ROKESLEY. He *d.* 29 Jan. 1385/6, aged 36. Will, in which he directs to be *bur* at the Friar Carmelites at Lynn, in Norfolk, dat 12 Sep. (1385) 9 Ric II. His widow *m.*, (probably shortly) after 10 Apr 1386, when she had lic. to *m* whom she would, Sir Thomas MORTIMER, who *d.* before 9 Jan 1402/3, and *d.* 12 June 1403 Will, in which she desires to be *bur.* at Trinity Priory, Aldgate, London, dat. 9 Jan. 1402/3, pr. 13 June 1403.

V 1386   5. THOMAS (BARDOLF), LORD BARDOLF, s. and h., *b.*
to   22 Dec 1369, (ᵉ) at Birling, Sussex. He was sum. to
1406.   Parl. from 12 Sep. (1390) 14 Ric. II, to 25 Aug (1404)
         5 Hen. IV, (ᶜ) by writs directed *Thome Bardolf' de Wor-*

(ª) See seals of him and his wife, *Top and Gen.*, vol 1, p 222, and *Her. and Gen.*, vol. iv, p 414.

(ᵇ) "Johannes Bardolf de Wormegeye." Writs of *diem cl. ext.* 13 Oct. 37 Edw. III. Inq., Herts, Norfolk, Suffolk, 6 Nov., 12, 14, 18 Dec. 1363. "Et dicunt quod idem Johannes obiit tertio die Augusti ultimo preterito. Et quod Willelmus filius ejus est heres ejusdem Johannis propinquior et etatis xiiij annorum et xj septima-narum." Inq , co. Lincoln, Thursday before SS Simon and Jude [26 Oct.] 1363. "Item dicunt quod predictus Johannes Bardolf obiit apud civitatem de Assise ultra mare die sabbati proximo ante festum sancti Petri Advincla proximo preteritum [29 July] secundum rumores qui venerunt de partibus illis. Et dicunt quod Willel-mus Bardolf filius ejusdem Johannis est heres propinquior ejusdem Johannis et est etatis xiiij annorum et amplius." Inq., Notts, Derby, 12, 20 Jan 1363/4. "Et dicunt quod idem Johannes Bardolf obiit die lune proximo post festum sancti Petri Advincla ultimo preterito [7 Aug.] Et quod Willelmus filius ejus est propinquior heres ejusdem Johannis et etatis xviij annorum." Writs of *melius sciri* 10 Sep. 45 Edw. III. By inq., cos. Derby, Surrey, Sussex, Bucks, Dorset, 15 to 26 Sep. 1371, it was found that the h. was aged 21 and more, 22, 22 and more, or 22 and 3 weeks And co. Gloucester, 24 Sep., that "Johannes [*sic*] Bardolf chivaler filius predicti Johannis Bardolf est heres ejus propinquior et fuit etatis viginti unius anni [*sic*] xxjᵒ die Octobris ultimo preterito," the date of death being given in all 6 inq as 5 Aug. 37 Edw. III. (Ch. *Inq. p. m.*, Edw. III, file 180, no 7). (*ex inform.* G.W. Watson, who has corrected Stapleton's numerous mistakes in dates &c.) V.G.

(ᶜ) See note "c" on previous page.

(ᵈ) Pedigree of Poynings, in *Sussex Archæol Coll.*, vol. xv, p. 15.

(ᵉ) In the inquisitions taken immediately after his father's death, Feb and Mar

megey He *m.*, before 8 July 1382, Anice or Amice, da of Ralph (Cromwell), Lord Cromwell of Tattershall, by Maud, da. of John de Bernake,
heiress of Tattershall, co. Lincoln. In 1405 he joined the Earl of Northumberland in his rebellion, and with him fled to Scotland, and was declared
by Parl to be a traitor, 4 Dec. 1406, (ª) when the *peerage* became *forfeited.*
Returning, however, he was defeated at Bramham Moor, co. York, 19 Feb.
1407/8, (ᵇ) and *d. s.p m* , of his wounds, a few hours subsequently, aged 38,
his remains being afterwards quartered, and his head placed on one of the
gates of Lincoln.(ᶜ) His widow *d.* 1 July 1421.

VI. 1437 ? to 1441.	1. Sir William Phelip, of Dennington, co Suffolk, Erpingham, co. Norfolk, &c., s. and h of Sir William P., of Dennington, by Julian, da and in her issue h of Sir

Robert Erpingham, of Erpingham, was *b.* 1383. He
m., before 1407, Joan, (ᵈ) 2nd and yst. of the two daughters and coheirs
of Thomas (Bardolf), Lord Bardolf, and Anice, his wife abovenamed.
He served at Agincourt, 25 Oct 1415, and again in Normandy, and,
during his absence there, was, in 1418 or early in 1419, elected K.G
In 1421-22 he was Capt of Harfleur, and subsequently Treasurer of the
Household to Henry V. He was P C. and Chamberlain to Henry VI, and
on 13 Nov. 1437 is thought by some to have been *cr.* a Baron, as after

---

1385/6, it is stated that he was 16 on Friday after St Thomas the Apostle last
[22 Dec] (Sussex) 16 on 30 Dec. last (Surrey) : 17 and more (Lincoln, Notts,
Derby) 18 on 25 Dec last (Leicester). Pursuant to a further writ, 25 Oct. 13 Ric. II,
it was found (Essex) that he was 20 on 4 Jan last, *i. e.* 1389/90. (*ex inform.* G.W.
Watson) V G

(ª) His estates were then declared to be forfeited as from 6 May 1405 In *Patent
Roll*, 11 Aug 1405, the wife of Thomas, late Lord of Bardolf appears in print as
Amice, and, in *Patent Roll* 26 Apr. 1407, the name is printed *Avice* , possibly the
correct form is Amice. For some discussion on mediæval english names see vol iii,
Appendix C V G

(ᵇ) " Thomas Bardolf chivaler " Writs of *diem. cl. ext* , 30 May 9 Hen. IV
Inq., Herts, Sussex, Oxon, Leicester, Notts, 17 Sep. to 3 Nov. 1408. " Thomas
Bardolf chivaler obiit die dominica proxima post festum sancti Valentini ultimo preterito
[19 Feb.]." (Ch *Inq. p.m.*, Hen. IV, file 67, no 31). The date of the battle was
xi kal Martii (T. *Walsingham*, vol. ii, p 278, Otterbourne, p 263). Ramsay, *Lancaster and York*, vol. i, p. 113, misconstruing Otterbourne, places the battle on the
Monday (*ex inform.* G W Watson). V.G.

(ᶜ) The order to give up his head and quarters to his widow Anice for burial, is
dated 13 Apr 1408 V.G.

(ᵈ) By letters patent 19 July 1408, the reversion of the manors of Wormegay,
Bradwell, Birling, and others in Norfolk, Suffolk and Sussex (which had been granted
to divers people for life), with the remaining portions of the forfeited lands, were
confirmed to Sir William Clifford, Knt., and Anne his wife, and to William Phelipp
and Joan his wife, for their lives and the life of the longest liver, with rem. to the
heirs of their bodies and reversion in default thereof to the King. Of these two
daughters and coheirs of the attainted Lord, Anne, the elder, who was *b.* 24 June
1389, and *bap* at Tattershall, *m.*, 2ndly, (as 2nd wife) Reynold (Cobham), Lord
Cobham, and *d. s p.* 6 Nov. 1453.

this date he is sometimes described as William Phelip, LORD BARDOLF.([a]) His name, however, does not appear on the list of Peers([b]) sum to Parl. 26 Sep 1439 He *d. s p.m.*, 6 June 1441, ([c]) when any *Peerage*, if *cr.* by patent, would have become *extinct* He was *bur*, under a sumptuous monument, at Dennington. Will, dat. 1 Dec. 1438 to 30 May 1441, describing himself as *Dominus Bardolff*, pr. 28 June 1441 at Lambeth His widow, who was *b.* and *bap.* 11 Nov. 1390, at Tattershall Castle, co. Lincoln, *d.* 12 Mar. 1446/7, and was *bur.* with her husband ([d]) Will dat. 11 Mar. to 7 Sep. 1446, pr. 3 Apr. 1447 at Norwich

BARFLEUR ([e])

i e. "BARFLEUR," Viscountcy *(Russell)*, *cr.* 1697, with the Earldom of OXFORD, which see ; *extinct* 1727.

BARGANY OR BARGENY

BARONY [S]   1. SIR JOHN HAMILTON, of Bargeny, co. Ayr, s. and h.
I. 1641.   of Sir John H., of the same (who *d.* about 1638), by Jean, da. of Alexander CAMPBELL, Bishop of Brechin, (which Sir John was an illegitimate but legitimated s. of John, 1st MARQUESS

([a]) See *ante*, p. 417, note "a", yet in the *Patent Rolls*, 4 Mar. 1437/8, and 14 Apr. 1440, he is called simply "Wil Phelip knight." V.G.

([b]) It is not clear why Stapleton should describe this list as "apparently imperfect" for practically the same number of lay peers were sum to this and the two preceding Parls.

([c]) "Willelmus Phelip miles." Writs of *diem cl. ext.* 16 June 19 Hen VI Inq., Norfolk, Suffolk, Lincoln, Sussex, Oxon, Derby, Notts, Leicester, Cambridge, Herts, 30 Oct. to 4 Nov. 1441. The jurors (all ten cos) say "quod predictus Willelmus Phelip obiit sexto die Junii ultimo preterito Et dicunt quod Henricus filius Johannis Vicecomitis Beaumont et Elizabethe nuper uxoris ejus filie predicti Willelmi Phelip et Johanne est consanguineus et heres ejusdem Willelmi Phelip propinquior et etatis septem annorum et amplius." (Ch. *Inq p m*, Hen. VI, file 103, no. 30). (*ex inform.* G W Watson). V.G.

([d]) The representation of any Barony in fee which might have been acquired *(de novo)* by her husband, but not that of the old Barony of Bardolf, vested on her death in the s and h of her only da. and h. Elizabeth, wife of John (Beaumont), 1st Viscount Beaumont, which Elizabeth *d.* before 30 Oct. 1441. This s. and h. was William Beaumont, afterwards (1460) 2nd Viscount Beaumont, who, as early as 1448, and when but a boy, is styled, *v.p.*, in the *Charter Roll*, 8 Nov 1448, *dominus de Bardolf*, and who *d. s p.* 1507, being called '*Viscount Beaumont and Lorde Bardolfe*' on his tomb in Wivenhoe church, Essex, and elsewhere. It was not, however, till the death, 6 Nov. 1453, of Anne, Lady Cobham, the elder sister of his mother, that he represented the *entirety* of this Barony. The representatives, in 1910, are (1) the 2 daughters and coheirs of the 10th Lord Beaumont and (2) the Earl of Abingdon, between whom any Barony of Bardolf, that may be held to have been *cr.* in 1299, is (subject to the attainder) in abeyance

([e]) For a list of names of peerages taken from places abroad, see vol. iii, Appendix E.

OF HAMILTON [S.]). On 16 Nov. 1641, (ª) he was *cr.* LORD BARGENY [S.]. (ᵇ) He was served h. to his father 23 Apr. 1642. He accompanied the Duke of Hamilton [S.], in 1648, on his unfortunate expedition into England, and being captured after his defeat, was imprisoned for a year. He then joined Charles II in the Netherlands, and when the King invaded England in 1651, Lord B. was sent to Scotland by him, to raise a force there. He was again taken prisoner at Elliott, in Perthshire, 28 Aug 1651, and imprisoned in the Tower for about a year, and was excepted from Cromwell's Act of Grace. He *m.*, in 1632, Jean, 2nd da. of William (DOUGLAS), 1st MARQUESS OF DOUGLAS [S.], by his 1st wife, Margaret, da. of Claud (HAMILTON), LORD PAISLEY [S.]. He *d.* Apr. 1658. His widow *d* 1669.

II. 1658.   2. JOHN (HAMILTON), LORD BARGENY [S.], s. and h., served h. to his father 17 Oct. 1662. In Nov. 1679 he was imprisoned on an indictment for high treason, *viz*, for a conspiracy against Episcopacy, against the life of the Duke of Lauderdale [S.], &c., but was never brought to trial, and was released June 1680, on finding security in 50,000 marks. (ᶜ) In 1689 he raised a regiment of 600 foot to promote the Revolution He *m.*, 1stly, in 1662, Margaret, 2nd da. of William (CUNNINGHAM), 9th EARL OF GLENCAIRN [S.], by his 1st wife, Anne, da of James (OGILVY), 1st EARL OF FINDLATER [S.]. He *m.*, 2ndly, in 1676, Alice, widow of Henry (HAMILTON), EARL OF CLANBRASSILL [I.], da. of Henry (MOORE), 1st EARL OF DROGHEDA [I.], by Alice, da. of William (SPENCER), 2nd BARON SPENCER OF WORMLEIGHTON. She *d. s p*, 25 Dec. 1677, at Roscommon House, Dublin, He *d.* 15 May 1693, and was *bur.* at Ballantrae, co. Ayr. Will pr. Prerog. Court [I.] 1696.

[JOHN HAMILTON, *styled* MASTER OF BARGENY, 1st s. and h. ap. by 1st wife. He *m.*, 19 June 1688, Jean, da. of Sir Robert SINCLAIR, Bart [S.], of Longformacus. He *d. v p.* and *s p m*, and was *bur.* 27 Mar. 1690, at St Giles's Church, Edinburgh. His widow *d.* 12, and was *bur.* 16 Dec. 1700, in New Church (St. Giles's Edinburgh). Fun. entry of both at Lyon office.] (ᵈ)

III. 1693.   3. WILLIAM (HAMILTON), LORD BARGENY [S.], 2nd, but 1st surv. s. and h. male. He took the oaths and his seat in Parl. 9 May 1695. He was a strenuous opposer of the Union.

(ª) The date in the text is from the original diploma, *penes* the Hon. Hew Hamilton 1904 Nisbet, *Heraldry*, vol 1, p 394, gives 14 Nov 1641, and an MS. collection of patents in the Advocate's Library [S], gives 22 Oct. 1639, which year is adopted in *Dict. Nat. Biog.*

(ᵇ) " Expressions in the Bargeny entail have led to a surmise that there may have been a rem to heirs female, failing the male line of the Patentee. " (*ex inform* G.Burnett, sometime Lyon.)

(ᶜ) *State Trials*, vol xi, p 65.

(ᵈ) The issue of Joanna, their only child, *b.* 1690, who *m.*, 23 Feb. 1707, Sir Robert Dalrymple, inherited the Bargeny estates by decision of the House of Lords See *Douglas*, pp. 197-199, where a full account of such succession is given.

He *m.*, 1stly, Mary, sister of William, 1st Viscount Primrose [S.], and 1st da. of Sir William Primrose, Bart [S], by Mary, da. of Patrick Scott, of Thirlestane. She, who was *b.* 20 June 1677, *d. s.p m.* He *m*, 2ndly (cont dat. 6 Aug 1708), Margaret, 1st. da. of Robert Dundas, of Arniston, a Lord of Session. He *d.* about 1712 (*) His widow *d.* 30 Mar. 1717. Fun. entry at Lyon office.

IV. 1712 to 1736.   4. James (Hamilton), Lord Bargeny [S.], only s. and h. by 2nd wife, *b.* 29 Nov. 1710. He completed his education by foreign travel, but *d.* unm., at Edinburgh, 28 Mar., and was *bur.* 5 Apr. 1736, in the Church of Holyrood House, aged 25. On his death the issue male of the grantee, and in all probability the Peerage itself, became *extinct.* (ᵇ)

BARHAM

BARONY.   1. Charles Middleton, 2nd s. of Robert M., (ᶜ) Col-
I. 1805.   lector of the Customs at Bo'ness, co. Linlithgow, by
Helen, da. of Charles Dundas, of Arniston, co. Midlothian, *b.* at Leith 14 Oct. 1726 ; Lieut. R.N. 1745, Post Capt. 22 May 1758 ; distinguished himself, in 1761, when in command of the *Emerald* frigate, in the West Indies ; Comptroller of the Navy 1778-90 ; Elder Brother of the Trinity House 1781-1813. He, being of Barham Court, and Teston, Kent, was *cr.* a Baronet on 23 Oct. 1781 (with a *spec. rem* , (ᵈ) failing his issue male, to his s.-in-law, Gerard Noel Edwardes) ; M.P. (Tory) for Rochester 1784-90 ; Rear Adm. 1787 ; Vice Adm. 1793 ; a Lord of the Admiralty 1794-95 ; Adm. of the Blue 1795 ; First commissioner for revising the civil affairs of the navy ; and 1st Lord of the Admiralty (ᵉ) 30 Apr. 1805-06 P.C. 1 May 1805. On 1 May 1805, he

---

(ª) " With kind Bargeny faithful to his word, whom Heaven made good and social, tho' a Lord. " (Epitaph, by Hamilton of Bangour). V.G.

(ᵇ) The Lords of Session [S.] in their return, 1740, report that as they cannot discover from the records the limitation of the dignity "they cannot take upon them to say whether it is *extinct* or not." (See *Robertson*, p 213) The Peerage must have been a male fief, as the succession of the 3rd Lord, the h *male* was allowed, instead of that of the h *gen.* And even supposing the patent to have been to heirs male *whomsoever*, these, the grantee being illegitimate, would have ended with the heirs male *of his body.*

(ᶜ) This Robert was grandson of Alexander M., next yr. br. of John, 1st Earl Middleton [S.] 1660. V.G.

(ᵈ) A rare instance at that date of a rem. to one whose relationship was not in the *male* line See, however, the Barony of Basset of Stratton, in 1797, as also the Dukedom of Marlborough, for a yet more extended rem. in 1706. See also vol. iii, Appendix F.

(ᵉ) This appointment led to a quarrel between Pitt and Sidmouth, the latter desiring to appoint the Earl of Buckinghamshire, and to the two last leaving the Ministry. V.G.

was *cr*. BARON BARHAM of Barham Court and Teston, Kent, with a *spec. rem.* of that dignity, in default of issue male, to his only da. and the heirs male of her body.   Adm of the Red, 9 Nov. 1805   He *m*., 21 Dec. 1761, at St. Martin's-in-the-Fields, Margaret, (ᵃ) da. of James GAMBIER, Barrister at Law and Warden of the Fleet Prison, by Mary, da. of (—) MEAD.   She *d* 10 Oct. 1792, at Teston.   He *d. s.p m*., 17 June 1813, aged 87, at Barham Court. (ᵇ)   Will, in which he left £10,000 to each of his 14 grandchildren, pr Aug. 1813, and again Jan. 1848.

II. 1813.   2. DIANA, *suo jure*, BARONESS BARHAM, only child and h., *b*. 18 Sep. 1762, *suc*. to the Peerage under the *spec. rem*. in the patent thereof.   She *m*., (as 1st wife) 21 Dec. 1780, at St. Geo., Han. Sq , Gerard Noel EDWARDES, afterwards Sir Gerard Noel NOEL, Bart., of Exton Park, Rutland.   She *d*. 12 Apr. 1823, at her seat, Fairy Hill, near Swansea, aged 60, and was *bur* at Teston, afsd   Admon. May 1823.   Her husband, who was *b*. 17 July 1759, at Tickencote, Rutland, and who, by royal lic., 5 May 1798, took the name of NOEL in compliance with the will of Henry (Noel), 6th Earl of Gainsborough, *suc*. in 1813 to the Baronetcy conferred (1781) on his wife's father, under the *spec. rem*. in the patent thereof, and *d* 25 Feb 1838, aged 78, at Exton Park, and was *bur*. at Exton afsd.   Will pr. Apr. 1838.

III. 1823.   3. CHARLES NOEL (NOEL), BARON BARHAM, s. and h., *b*. 2 Oct. 1781.   On 16 Aug. 1841 he was *cr*   BARON NOEL, VISCOUNT CAMPDEN AND EARL OF GAINSBOROUGH.   See " GAINSBOROUGH," Earldom of ; *cr*. 1841.

BARHAM COURT

See " BARHAM OF BARHAM COURT AND TESTON, Kent " Barony *(Middleton* afterwards *Noel), cr*. 1805.

BARMEATH

See "BELLEW OF BARMEATH, co. Louth," Barony [I.] *(Bellew), cr*. 1848.

(ᵃ) An accomplished woman, and the friend of Samuel Johnson and Hannah More   She was one of the first actively to oppose the slave trade   V.G.

(ᵇ) He was an early member of the Evangelical party, whose chances for distinction *at sea* were small, although, " As a naval administrator and reformer he has had few equals in the whole history of the Navy ; as a naval thinker, the inspirer of thought in others and the confidential sharer of the best thoughts of his best contemporaries, he stands not less indisputably in the front rank ; and that on the one occasion which called his strategic faculties into play he displayed a sureness of insight and a rapidity of decision which were not unworthy of NELSON himself. " *(The Times*, 3 May 1910.)   The explanation of his receiving a peerage with a *spec. rem* (an honour always very sparingly conferred except during Lord Salisbury's administration, and which his public services hardly justified) is perhaps to be sought in the fact that through his mother he was a near relative of Henry (Dundas), Lord Melville.   V.G.

BARNARD

BARONY.

I. 1698.

1. CHRISTOPHER VANE, 7th and yst s. of the well-known Sir Henry VANE, of Raby Castle, co. Durham, (executed for high treason 14 June 1662) by Frances, da. of Sir Christopher WRAY, Bart , was *b.* 21 May 1653, and *suc.* his elder and only surv. br., Thomas Vane, 1673, in the family estates. M.P. (Whig) for co. Durham 1675-79.([a]) P.C. 6 July 1688 till Feb. 1688/9. Finally, "probably as a reward for his father's sufferings in the cause of liberty,"([b]) he was *cr.*, 25 July 1698, ([c]) BARON BARNARD OF BARNARD'S CASTLE in the Bishopric of Durham. ([d]) He *m* (lic. Vic Gen., 9 May 1676, he about 22, she about 19), Elizabeth, 1st sister and coh. of John, DUKE OF NEWCASTLE, da. of Gilbert (HOLLES), EARL OF CLARE, by Grace, da. of William PIERREPONT, of Thoresby, Notts. He *d.* 28 Oct 1723, at Fairlawn in the parish of Shipborne, Kent, and was *bur.* in the church there, ([e]) aged 70. Will, dat. 27 Sep. 1715 to 26 May 1716, pr. 11 Nov. 1723 His widow *d.* 9 Nov. 1725. Will dat. 3 Sep., pr. 10 Nov. 1725.

II. 1723.

2. GILBERT (VANE), BARON BARNARD, 2nd, but 1st surv. s. and h , *bap.* 17 Apr. 1678, in London In politics he was an opponent of Walpole. He *m.*, Jan. 1704/5, Mary, da. and coh. of Morgan RANDYLL, of Chilworth, Surrey, sometime M.P. for Guildford, by Anne, da. of Sir Thomas GOLD, Alderman of London. She, who was *b.* 30 Jan. 1682, *d.* 4 Aug 1728, in her 47th year,([f]) and was *bur* at Bushey. M.I. ([g]) He *d.* 27 Apr. 1753, aged 75. Admon. 11 May 1753.

([a]) When a peer he supported the Tories. V G.

([b]) See Sir Egerton Brydges' note in *Collins*, vol. iv, p. 522.

([c]) Not 1699, as in *Dict. Nat. Biog.* V.G.

([d]) "It is a curious fact that the attainder of his father has never been reversed, notwithstanding the evidence which the elevation of his son to the Peerage and the still higher honours [*sic*] conferred upon his descendants afford of the estimation in which they have been held by their Sovereign By an attainder the right to *armorial ensigns*, as well as to other honours, is destroyed, and upon the creation [*sic*] of Christopher Vane to the Peerage, the then Garter King of Arms, finding himself in a dilemma as to what arms he should assign to the Peer, applied to the Crown for instructions, when a licence was granted authorising him to allow to Christopher, Lord Barnard, and his descendants the arms and quarterings of his father, notwithstanding his attainder , the legality of this exercise of the Royal Prerogative is not free from doubt, for it is held that nothing but an express legislative enactment can relieve an individual from any of the penalties of an attainder The Crown may, however, assign to a subject whatever armorial ensigns it pleases *de novo*, and, in this construction of the licence, it was, of course, valid. " (*Courthope*, p. 41.)

([e]) For copious extracts from his fun. sermon, by the Rev. Thomas Curteis, at Wrotham, see *Collins*, vol. iv, p. 522.

([f]) She is spoken of as " scandalous " in the will of her step-father, Lord Barnard.

([g]) Her 1st da., Anne, well known from Samuel Johnson's line—
"Yet Vane can tell what ills from beauty spring,"

III. 1753.

VISCOUNTCY

I. 1754.

3. HENRY (VANE), BARON BARNARD, s. and h. On 3 Apr. 1754 he was *cr.* VISCOUNT BARNARD of Barnard's Castle, and EARL OF DARLINGTON, co. Durham. He *d.* 6 Mar. 1758.

VISCOUNTCY

II. 1758.

BARONY

IV.

4. HENRY (VANE), EARL OF DARLINGTON, VISCOUNT BARNARD and BARON BARNARD, s. and h. He *d* 8 Sep. 1792.

For fuller account see " DARLINGTON," Earldom of, cr. 1754

VISCOUNTCY

III. 1792.

BARONY

V.

5. WILLIAM HENRY (VANE), EARL OF DARLINGTON, &c, VISCOUNT BARNARD AND BARON BARNARD, s. and h. On 5 Oct. 1827 he was *cr* MARQUESS OF CLEVELAND; and on 29 Jan. 1833 BARON RABY and DUKE OF CLEVELAND He *d.* 29 Jan. 1842.

Dukedom of, cr. 1833

VISCOUNTCY

IV. 1842.

BARONY

VI.

6. HENRY (VANE), DUKE OF CLEVELAND, &c., VISCOUNT BARNARD AND BARON BARNARD, s. and h. He *d. s.p* , 18 Jan 1864.

VISCOUNTCY

V. 1864.

BARONY

VII.

7. WILLIAM JOHN FREDERICK (VANE, formerly POWLETT), DUKE OF CLEVELAND, &c., VISCOUNT BARNARD AND BARON BARNARD, br. and h. He *d s p.* 6 Sep. 1864

For fuller account see "CLEVELAND," Dukedom of, cr. 1833

VISCOUNTCY

VI. 1864

BARONY

VIII.

8. HARRY GEORGE (VANE, afterwards POWLETT), DUKE OF CLEVELAND, MARQUESS OF CLEVELAND, EARL OF DARLINGTON, VISCOUNT BARNARD, BARON BARNARD and BARON RABY, br. and h , *b.* 19 Apr. 1803. He *d. s.p.*, 21 Aug 1891, aged 88, when all his honours, save the BARONY OF BARNARD, became *extinct.*

IX. 1891.

9. HENRY DE VERE (VANE), BARON BARNARD OF BARNARD'S CASTLE [1698], cousin and h. male, being 1st s. and h. of Sir Henry Morgan VANE, Sec to the Charity Commission 1853 till his death, by Louisa, yr. da. and coh. of the Rev. Richard FARRER, of Ashley, Northants, which Sir Henry (who *d.* 22 Apr 1886, aged 77) was s. and h. of John Henry VANE (*d* 10 June 1849, aged 61), who was 2nd son of Morgan VANE, of Bilby Hall, Notts, Comptroller of the Stamp office

was the mother, by Frederick, Prince of Wales, of a s , Fitz-Frederick, *b* 4 June 1732. She *d* unm., 11 Mar. 1735/6, at Bath , the child *d.* before her. V.G.

(*d* 11 Nov. 1789, aged 51), s. of the Hon. Morgan VANE, of Bilby Hall afsd. (*d.* 14 Nov. 1779, aged 73), who was yr. br. of the 1st EARL OF DARLINGTON, both being sons of the 2nd BARON BARNARD. He was *b.* 10 May 1854; ed at Eton, and at Brasenose Coll., Oxford; B A, 1876; Barrister (Inner Temple) 1879 His right to the Peerage was allowed (*) by the Committee for Privileges, 30 May 1892. He *m.*, 28 June 1881, at St. Thomas's, Portman Sq, Catherine Sarah, 3rd surv. da. of William Alleyne (CECIL), 3rd MARQUESS OF EXETER, by Georgiana, da. of Thomas (PAKENHAM), EARL OF LONGFORD [I.]. She was *b* 8 Apr. 1861.

Family Estates —The 'Raby estates,' devised to him by the Duke of Cleveland, were in the counties of Durham, Northampton, Salop, Stafford and Middlesex. In 1883, that Duke held 55,837 acres in co. Durham; 25,604 in Salop; and 3,482 in co. Northampton. *Total,* 84,923 acres, worth £67,014, besides an unknown quantity in co Stafford, worth £3,970 a year. *Principal Seat.*—Raby Castle, near Darlington, co. Durham.

[HENRY CECIL VANE, 1st s. and h., *b.* 1882. A.D.C. to Lord Ampthill, Governor Gen. of Madras.]

BARNARD'S CASTLE

See "BARNARD OF BARNARD'S CASTLE, in the Bishopric of Durham," Barony *(Vane), cr.* 1698.

---

i e., "BARNARD OF BARNARD'S CASTLE, co Durham," Viscountcy *(Vane), cr.* 1754, with the Earldom of DARLINGTON, which see; *extinct* (with the Dukedom of CLEVELAND), 1891.

BARNEWALL OF TRIMLESTON see TRIMLESTON

BARNEWALL OF KINGSLAND

VISCOUNTCY [I.]. 1. NICHOLAS BARNEWALL, s. and h. of Sir Patrick
I. 1646.   B, of Turvey, Gracedieu, and Fieldston, co Dublin,
       by Mary, da. of Sir Nicholas BAGNALL, Knight
Marechal [I.], *b.* 1592, was 30 years old at the time of his father's death, 11 Jan. 1621/2. He was ed. at Douay, Dec. 1600. M.P. for co. Dublin

---

(*) The claim was resisted by Capt. Francis Forester, of Croom, co Limerick, great nephew of the late Duke, to some of whose estates he would have suc. if the right to the Peerage had been disallowed The grounds were the illegitimacy of claimant's father, who was *b* 29 Nov. 1808, at Brigg, co Lincoln, but it was proved (by the evidence of Miss Nicholson, maternal aunt of the said child) that the parents 'who had previously misconducted themselves,' were married at Louth, the 13th of June previous to such birth.

1634-35, and 1639-46. Having, though a Rom. Cath., adhered to the
English interest, for his own loyalty and that of his then eldest surv. s., Col.
Patrick B., Col. of a troop of Horse in the English service (who is specially
named in the patent, but who *d. v.p* , and *s.p*), he was *cr.* 29 June 1646 (the
privy seal dat. 12 Sep 1645 at Ragland), BARON OF TURVEY and VIS-
COUNT BARNEWALL OF KINGSLAND [in the parish of Donabate]
co Dublin [I]. (ª) In June 1654 he was in prison, being charged with
complicity in a plot against the Lord Protector, by whom his property had
been sequestrated, it being afterwards restored to him in 1660. He *m* , in
1617, before 7 July, Bridget, widow of Roderick (O'DONNELL), 1st EARL
OF TYRCONNELL [I.], 1st da and coh. of Henry (FITZ GERALD), EARL OF
KILDARE [I], by Frances, 2nd da. of Charles (HOWARD), EARL OF NOTT-
INGHAM. She was living in 1661. He *d.* at Turvey, 20 Aug , and was
bur 3 Sep. 1663, in the church of Luske, aged 91. Will, without date,
pr. 11 Sep. 1663, Prerog. Court [I.].

II. 1663.   2. HENRY (BARNEWALL), VISCOUNT BARNEWALL OF
            KINGSLAND, &c [I], 3rd, but 1st surv. s. and h. On
17 May 1671, he had a release of the quit rents which had been imposed
by the acts of settlement, and in 1685 had a grant of lands under the Act
of Grace. He *m* , istly, in 1661, Mary, 1st da. of John (NETTERVILLE),
2nd VISCOUNT NETTERVILLE [I.], by Elizabeth, 1st da of Richard (WESTON),
EARL OF PORTLAND, Lord High Treasurer [E.]. She *d. s.p m.*, 28 Oct.
1663, and was *bur.* at Luske afsd. He *m* , 2ndly, 11 Dec (marr. settl.
29 Nov.) 1664, Mary, 1st da. of Richard (NUGENT), 1st EARL OF WEST-
MEATH [I.], by Jane, da. of Christopher (PLUNKETT), LORD KILLEEN [I]
She, who was *b.* 21 Feb. 1648, *d.* 25 June 1680, and was *bur.* at Luske. He
d. 1, and was *bur.* 3 June 1688. Will, without date, pr. Prerog. Court [I]
1691, and at Dublin, by order of the Court, 14 Oct. 1693.

III. 1688.   3 NICHOLAS (BARNEWALL), VISCOUNT BARNEWALL OF
            KINGSLAND, &c. [I.], s. and h. by his 2nd wife. He was
b. 15 Apr 1668. He sat in King James's Parl [I.] in May 1689. (ᵇ)
He *m* , 15 May 1688, Mary, 3rd and yst. da. and coh. of Sir George
HAMILTON (Comte Hamilton and Maréchal du Camp in France), by
Frances, subsequently DUCHESS OF TYRCONNELL [I.], (ᶜ) da. and coh. of
Richard JENNINGS, of Sandridge, Herts. With her he received a portion
of £3000, and soon afterwards *suc* to estates worth £3,500 a year He
served in Lord Limerick's Dragoons, 1688, on behalf of James II, and
was consequently *outlawed*, but being comprehended in the treaty of
Limerick this outlawry was reversed. (ᵈ) He delivered his writ of summons, 28 Oct. 1692, to the House, but refusing to subscribe according to

---

(ª) Copy of the preamble of the patent is in *Lodge*, vol v, p 49
(ᵇ) For a list of the Irish peers present in, and absent from, that Parl., see
vol. iii, Appendix D.
(ᶜ) See note *sub* TYRCONNEL, and *ante*, p. 415, notes " a " and " b. "
(ᵈ) See *Lords' Journals* [I], vol. i, p 675

the act made in England, had to withdraw. He *d.* 14, and was *bur.* 16 June 1725, "in his monument" ([a]) at Luske, aged 57. Will pr. 1727. His widow, who was *b.* in France, *d.* 15 Feb 1735/6, at Turvey, and was *bur.* with him. Will, dat. 17 Jan. to 11 Feb. 1731/2, pr. 10 Apr. 1740, Prerog. Court [I]

IV. 1725.   4. HENRY BENEDICT (BARNEWALL), VISCOUNT BARNE-
                   WALL OF KINGSLAND, &c. [I], s. and h., *b* 1 Feb. 1708.
On 31 Mar. 1740 he delivered his writ of summons, and took the oath of fidelity, but, being a Roman Catholic, was disqualified from taking his seat. Grand Master of Freemasons [I] 1733-35. He *m.*, 22 May 1735, at Arbour Hill, Honora, 1st da. and coh. of Peter DALY, of Quansbury, co. Galway, by Elizabeth, da. of Richard BLAKE, of Ardfry in that co. He *d. s.p.*, 11 Mar. 1774, at Quansbury, aged 66. Will pr. 1800, Prerog. Court [I.]. His widow *d.* 1784.

V. 1774   5. GEORGE (BARNEWALL), VISCOUNT BARNEWALL OF
   to   KINGSLAND, &c. [I.], nephew and h , being only child and
   1800.   h. of the Hon. George B., by Barbara, 2nd da. of Thomas
                 (BELASYSE), 1st EARL FAUCONBERG, which George was
next br. to the 4th Lord and *d.* June 1771 aged 60. He was *b* 12 July 1758, in London, and being of the established religion, took his seat in the House of Lords [I.] 18 Jan. 1787. He *d.* unm , 5 Apr. 1800, at Pontoise in France, and was *bur.* there, when the title remained *dormant* for 14 years ([b]) Will dat 23 Mar. 1800, pr 2 Feb 1801.

VI 1800   6 MATTHEW (BARNEWALL), VISCOUNT BARNEWALL OF
   or   KINGSLAND and BARON OF TURVEY [I], 3rd cousin and h
   1814   male, being yst. but only surv. s. and h. of Matthew B.,
   to   of Stoney Batter, in Dublin, by Anne, da. of Thomas
   1834.   McCAN, his 2nd wife, which Matthew (who *d.* 1773)
                 was s. and h. of Nicholas B , of Woodpark, co Meath
(*d.* 1735), who was s. and h. of the Hon Francis B., of Woodpark afsd. and of Beggstown, co. Meath, who was 4th, but 2nd surv. s. of the 1st Viscount, and who *d* 1697 He was *b.* in Dublin, and is said to have been in a very humble position ([c]) His claim to the Peerage was allowed ([d]) in 1814, and he subsequently received a small pension. He *m* , 1stly, in

---

([a]) *Lords' Entries.* V.G
([b]) The vast estates passed to his cousin and h at law, Nicholas (Barnewall), 14th Lord Trimlestown [I], s and h of his aunt Frances (*d.* 19 Mar. 1735, aged 35), by the Hon. Richard Barnewall, 3rd s. of John, 11th Lord Trimlestown [I.]   On the death of their grandson Thomas, 16th Lord Trimlestown, on 4 Aug. 1879, that peerage also became *dormant.*
([c]) See an amusing account of him in Sir B Burke's *Vicissitudes,* 3rd series, 1863, pp. 16-21
([d]) His claim was opposed by Thomas Barnewall, who stated that he was h. male of the body of Christopher B., alleged to have been the 2nd s of Henry, the 2nd Viscount. This Christopher, however, who was *b* 22 Feb 1680, appears to have *d* young—no mention of him being made in the family settlement of 21 July 1698.

early life, a woman who *d.* leaving a son John, who was living 1815, but *d.* unm *v.p.* He *m.*, 2ndly, in 1819, Mary Anne, 1st da. of John BRAD-SHAW, of Cork, by Elizabeth, 2nd da. of Sir Robert WARREN, 1st Bart. [I.]. She *d s.p*, and was *bur.* from St Bride's, Fleet Str., 16 Oct. 1819, at Lambeth, aged 37. He *m*, 3rdly, 2 Jan. 1820, at St. Mary's, Lambeth, Julia, da. of John WILLIS, of Walcot Place, Lambeth, Surrey. He *d. s.p m.s.*, 15 Nov. 1834, at Walcot Place, and was *bur.* at Lambeth, when the Peerage became *extinct.* (a) His widow, who was *b* 28 Feb. 1804, was from 1875, a Pensioner of the "Universal Beneficent Society," Soho Sq., Midx. She *d.* 10 Jan. 1890, aged 86, and was *bur.* at East Finchley.

BARNS

i.e. "RAMSEY OF BARNS, co. Haddington," [S] *(Ramsay)*, *cr.* 1606, with the Viscountcy of HADDINGTON [S.], see "HOLDERNESSE," Earldom, *cr* 1621, all such honours becoming *extinct*, 1626.

BARONSTOWN

See "SUNDERLIN OF BARONSTOWN, co. Westmeath," Barony [I.] *(Malone)*, *cr.* 1797 with a spec. rem., *extinct* (with another Barony of Sunderlin [I], *cr.* 1785) 1816.

BARRE DE BUTEVANT see BARRY

BARREFORE, *i.e.* BURFORD

See "CARRINGTON OF BURFORD in Connaught," Viscountcy [I] *(Smyth)*, *cr.* 1643 ; *extinct* 1706.

BARRELS

i.e. "BARRELS, co Catherlough" Viscountcy [I.] *(Knight)*, *cr* 1763, with the Earldom of CATHERLOUGH [I.], which see ; *extinct* 1772.

(a) In 1835 a petition claiming this title was presented by Thomas Barnewall, Capt in the Longford militia, s and h of Christopher B., who was s. and h of George B., both of Wimbledon, co. Dublin, which George was s. and h of Col. James B., alleged to have been the 6th and yst. s. of the 1st Viscount. This James was in fact son *in law* of the 1st Viscount, being the 2nd husband of his da Mabel, Countess of Fingall. No further proceedings were taken in this matter. In the two deeds of settlement of the estates on the heirs male of the Barnewall family, dat 31 Dec 1661 and 21 July 1698, *no* mention is made of such a 6th s. (James), or of his issue, who (had they existed) would doubtless have been placed in remainder before the very distant branches of the Barnewall family mentioned therein. The extinction of the title was acted upon in the creation, 4 May 1836, of the Barony of Oranmore [I], according to the Act of Union [I.]

BARRETT OF NEWBURGH

BARONY [I]   1 EDWARD BARRETT, s and h. of Charles B (who *d.*
I. 1627   *v.p.*, 8 Aug. 1584), by Christian, da of Sir Walter MILD-
  to   MAY, was *b.* 21 June 1581, and *bap.* at Aveley ; *suc.* his
1645.   grandfather Edward Barrett, of Belhouse, or Belhus, in the
             parish of Aveley, Essex, 31 Jan. 1585/6 ; Matric Oxford
(Queen's Coll), aged 16, 17 Mar 1597/8 ; Adm. Lincoln's Inn, 1602 ; he
had livery of his lands 27 Nov. 1602 ; went with the Earl of Nottingham,
in 1605, to conclude peace with Spain ; knighted by James I, 17 Apr. 1608;
M.P. for Whitchurch 1614, and for Newport (Cornwall) 1621-22. He had
lic. to empark Belhus 23 Dec. 1618 , AMBASSADOR to France, 1625 ; was *cr.*
(to him and the heirs male of his body), 17 Oct. 1627, LORD BARRETT
OF NEWBURGH, co. Fife [S.]; P.C. 10 July 1628, and Chancellor of
the Exchequer 15 Aug 1628-29. (ª) On 2 Oct 1628, being already a Peer
[S], he was *cr.* " a baronet of Nova Scotia, and received a grant of, presumably, 16,000 acres in that region, whereof he obtained seizin in the following January. " (ᵇ) Chancellor of the Duchy of Lancaster, 1629-44 ; a Lord
of the Treasury, 1641-43. He was a staunch supporter of the Stuarts.
He *m.*, 1stly, between 22 Apr. and 3 May 1608, Jane, sister of Henry,
1st VISCOUNT FALKLAND [S], 5th da. of Sir Edward CARY, of Aldenham,
Herts, by Catharine, da of Sir Henry KNYVETT, of Buckenham, Norfolk.
She *d. s.p.m.*, and was *bur.* 2 Jan 1632/3, at Aveley, aged 38. He *m.*,
2ndly, in Aug. 1635, (ᶜ) Catharine, (with whom he had £10,000) widow of
Hugh PERRY (*d.* Jan. 1634/5), Alderman of Queenhithe Ward, London, da.
of Hugh FENN, of Wotton under Edge, co. Gloucester. He *d. s.p.s* , and
was *bur.* 2 Jan. 1644/5, at Aveley, aged 63, when the *Peerage* became *extinct.*
Will dat. 17 Mar. 1633/4, pr. 7 Feb. 1645/6, " by the Lady Barrett, widow
and executrix." (ᵈ) She *m.*, 29 Sep. 1653, at St. Giles's-in-the-Fields, William
MORGAN, of Cawthrop, Oxon, her steward, and was living as his wife
19 Oct. 1664. (ᵉ) She appears to have *m.*, 4thly, a Frenchman named
BUSSY. (ᶠ) She *d.* 22 July 1674 (ᵍ)

BARRETT'S COUNTY

i e. "BARON OF BARRETT'S COUNTY and VISCOUNT KINGSALE," both
co. Cork [I.]. See " SARSFIELD OF KILMALLOCK," VISCOUNTCY [I.] *(Sarsfield)*, which title was substituted for "Kingsale, " by royal authority.

(ª) See extracts from his Diary in *The Families of Lennard and Barrett*, privately
printed, 1908, p 380. V G
  (ᵇ) *Complete Baronetage*, by G E.C
  (ᶜ) *The Cal. of State Papers*, 1635, speaks of her as worth £10,000, and as one
who " useth to be a little mad sometimes. " V.G.
  (ᵈ) See copy of this will and a good account of Aveley in *More about Stifford*,
by the Rev. W. Palin, 1872, pp. 81-90.
  (ᵉ) *Hatton Correspondence*, Camden Soc., vol. i, p 40. V G
  (ᶠ) *Idem*, vol. ii, p. 140   V.G.
  (ᵍ) *The Families of Lennard and Barrett*, p. 402. V.G.

BARRINGTON OF ARDGLASS,
AND BARRINGTON OF NEWCASTLE

VISCOUNTCY [I.]

BARONY [I.]

I 1720.

1. JOHN BARRINGTON, of Becket, in the parish of Shrivenham, Berks., formerly John SHUTE, being 3rd and yst s. of Benjamin SHUTE,(ª) by Elizabeth, da of the Rev. Joseph CARYL, was *b.* in 1678, at Theobald's, Herts; ed at Utrecht. He became a Barrister of the Inner Temple, London ; was Commissioner of the Customs, 1708 to 1711; inherited in 1710 the estate of Becket, and considerable property in Berkshire, by devise of John Wildman, of Becket afsd., and soon afterwards inherited the estate of Tofts, in Little Baddow, Essex, by settlement of Francis Barrington, Merchant, whose wife, Elizabeth, (by whom he had no issue), was Shute's cousin german, being da. of his uncle, Samuel Shute. (ᵇ) By Act of Parl. 1716, he took the name of BARRINGTON. He was M.P. (Whig) for Berwick upon Tweed, 1715 until expelled the House of Commons, 15 Feb. 1722/3, for having promoted "an infamous fraudulent project, " the lottery of Harbourg. (ᶜ) On 5 July 1717 he had the reversion of the office of Master of the Rolls [I.], which, however, he surrendered 10 Dec. 1731. On 1 July 1720 was *cr.* BARON BARRINGTON OF NEWCASTLE, co. Limerick, and VISCOUNT BARRINGTON OF ARDGLASS, co. Down [I.] (ᵈ) He *m*, 23 June 1713, at St. Benet's, Paul's Wharf, (settl. dat. 26 June 1713) Anne, da. and coh. of Sir William DAINES, sometime Mayor of, and M.P. for, Bristol. He *d.* at Becket, 14, and was *bur.* 27 Dec 1734, at Shrivenham, in his 56th year.(ᵉ) Will dat. 2 Mar. 1726, pr. 13 June 1738. His widow *d.* 8 Feb. 1763. Admon. 10 Mar. 1763.

(ª) This Benjamin was "yst. s. of Francis Shute of Upton, co. Leicester, Esq., who was descended from Robert Shute of Hockington, co. Cambridge, one of the twelve Judges in the reign of Queen Elizabeth. " See M.I. to the 1st Viscount Barrington in *Lodge,* vol v, p 203.

(ᵇ) He was no relation to either of his benefactors, of whom (1) J. Wildman adopted him *more Romano* as " most worthy, " though, it seems, after " one fortnight's acquaintance. " (Le Neve's *Mem*) (2) F.Barrington adopted him as being a cousin of his *wife,* devising to him the estate of the ancient family of Barrington, though he had no descent whatever therefrom.

(ᶜ) Notwithstanding this disgrace he was (according to *Lodge*) a person of *great judgment* and learning, being the author " of divers pamphlets in favour of such as dissent from the established church. "

(ᵈ) See *Lodge,* vol v, p 202, where the preamble of the patent of Peerage is given.

(ᵉ) He is described by Swift, in 1708, as " the shrewdest head in England " Horace Walpole writes of him to the Rev. Mr. Cole, 18 Sep. 1778, " I believe was a very dirty fellow, for besides being expelled the H. of C. on the affair of the lottery, he was reckoned to have twice sold the dissenters to the Court. " V.G.

II. 1734.   2. WILLIAM WILDMAN (BARRINGTON-SHUTE), (ª) VIS-
COUNT BARRINGTON OF ARDGLASS, &c. [I.], s. and h., b.
15 Jan. 1717, and ed. at Geneva. M.P. (ᵇ) for Berwick, 1740-54 ; for
Plymouth, 1754 to 1778. Took his seat in the House of Lords [I.],
8 Oct. 1745. A Lord of the Admiralty, 1746-54 ; Master of the Great
Wardrobe, 1754-55 ; P.C 11 Mar. 1755, and Secretary at War, 1755-61;
Chancellor of the Exchequer, (ᶜ) Mar. 1761 to June 1762 ; Treasurer of
the Navy, 1762-65; Secretary at War, (2nd time), July 1765 to Dec. 1778;
Joint Postmaster Gen., Jan. to Apr. 1782, when he retired from public
life. He m., 16 Sep. 1740, at Harleston, Northants, Mary, (" with
£5000 p a ") widow of the Hon. Samuel GRIMSTON, da. and h. of Henry
LOVELL, of Northampton, Merchant, by Mary, da. and coh. of Thomas
COLE, of London. She d. 24 Sep. 1764, at Becket House, Berks, and was
bur. at Shrivenham. Will, dat. 2 Nov. 1761 to 19 May 1764, pr. 3 Nov.
1764. He d. s.p.s., 1 Feb. 1793, in Cavendish Sq., and was bur. at
Shrivenham, aged 76. (ᵈ) M.I. Will dat. 21 Apr. 1787 to 9 Dec. 1792, pr.
8 Feb. 1793.

III. 1793.   3. WILLIAM (BARRINGTON), VISCOUNT BARRINGTON
OF ARDGLASS, &c. [I.], nephew and h., being s. and h. of
Major Gen. the Hon. John BARRINGTON, Deputy Governor of Berwick, by
Elizabeth, da. of Florentius VASSAL, of Jamaica, which John was 3rd s. of

(ª) These names are so given in Lodge, vol. v, p. 206, whose article (1784) was
based on the " information of Lord Viscount Barrington. "

(ᵇ) He entered Parl. as an opponent of Walpole, and was for a long time classed
as a Whig, but acted with the Tories after Lord North became Premier. He was
one of "The King's friends." His steady hold on office in spite of changes of
administration is commented on in some satirical lines, for which see Appendix H in
this volume. Horace Walpole, in the same letter as that in which he refers to his
father (see note " e " previous p.), speaks of his " forty years of servility which even in
this age makes him a proverb ; " and in his George II (vol. ii, p. 142) he says that he
" had a lisp and a tedious precision that prejudiced me against him, yet he did not
want a sort of vivacity." Lecky calls him "one of the most servile politicians of the
time " He figures, in 1771, (" The Hostile Scribe and the Stable-yard Messalina ")
among the notorious tête-à-tête portraits, in the Town and Country Mag, vol. iii, p. 9,
the lady to whom allusion is made being Lady Harrington. See Appendix B, in the
last volume. V.G.

(ᶜ) The 1st Lord Holland writes of this appointment,—" 1st Lord B., a frivolous
little minded man is not honester or abler than his predecessor [Henry Bilson Legge],
he will do well in this now (that there is another head to the Treasury, and another
head of the House of Commons) insignificant [sic !] employment. In his last year
he pleased nobody. He has no regard to truth, but perhaps by what are not so material faults, being trifling, tedious, and circumstantial, he was very disagreeable to King,
General, and Minister." V G

(ᵈ) Both he and 3 of his brothers were of sufficient note in their day to find a
place in the Dict. Nat Biog. Daines B., 4th s of the 1st Viscount, is still remembered as an antiquary, lawyer, and naturalist. Samuel, the 5th s., was a distinguished
Admiral, and Shute, the 6th and yet s., was Bishop of Llandaff 1769, Bishop of
Salisbury 1782, and Bishop of Durham 1791 till his death, s p , 25 Mar. 1826. V G

the 1st Viscount, and *d.* 2 Apr 1764. He *m.* Anne, da. of James MURR-ELL, of Thetford Abbey, Norfolk. He *d s.p*, 13 July 1801, at his house near Bath, aged 40. Will dat. 20 Jan 1801, pr. 4 July following. His widow *m.*, 1 Feb. 1812, at Uley, co. Gloucester, Edward THORNYCROFT, of Thornycroft Hall, Cheshire, and *d.* there May 1816. Will pr. June 1816.

IV. 1801   4. RICHARD JAMES (BARRINGTON), VISCOUNT BARRING-TON OF ARDGLASS &c. [I.], br. and h. He *m*, in 1783, Susan, da. of William BUDDEN, of Philadelphia, U.S.A. He *d. s.p*, Jan. 1814, at Valenciennes. His widow *d.* 1830.

V. 1814.   5. GEORGE (BARRINGTON), VISCOUNT BARRINGTON OF ARDGLASS, &c [I], br. and h., *b.* 16 July 1761, in London. King's scholar, Westm., 1774. Matric. at Oxford (Ch. Ch), 17 June 1778. B A. 1782. M.A. 1785. In Holy Orders. Rector of Sedgefield, co. Durham. Prebendary of Durham 1796 till his death. He *m.*, 12 Feb. 1788, Elizabeth, 2nd da. of Robert ADAIR, of Stratford Place, Marylebone, Midx., by Caroline, 2nd da. of William Anne (KEPPEL), 2nd EARL OF ALBEMARLE. He *d.* 4 Mar. 1829, at Rome. Will pr. Sep. 1829. His widow *d* 2 Mar. 1841, at Shrivenham, aged 72. Will pr. June 1841.

VI. 1829.   6. WILLIAM KEPPEL (BARRINGTON), VISCOUNT BAR-RINGTON OF ARDGLASS, &c. [I.], s. and h, *b.* 1 Oct 1793, in London. Ed. at Westm. school. Matric at Oxford (Ch. Ch.), 28 May 1811. B A. 1813. M.P. (Conservative) for Berkshire, 1837-57. Chair-man Great Western Railway 1856-57. He *m.*, 21 Apr. 1823, (spec. lic.) in Portland Place, Marylebone, Jane Elizabeth, 4th da. of Thomas Henry (LIDDELL), 1st LORD RAVENSWORTH, by Isabella Horatia, da. of Lord George SEYMOUR. He *d* 9 Feb. 1867, at Becket House, aged 73. His widow, who was *b.* 29 Sep. 1804, and who was Lady of the Bedchamber to Adelaide, the Queen Dowager, *d.* 22 Mar. 1883, at 20 Cavendish Sq. Both were *bur.* at Shrivenham.

VII. 1867   7. GEORGE WILLIAM (BARRINGTON), VISCOUNT BAR-RINGTON OF ARDGLASS, &c, [I.], s and h, *b.* 14 Feb 1824, in Lower Brook Str., Midx. Matric. at Oxford (Ch Ch.) 20 Oct 1841. M.P (Conservative) for Eye, 1866-80. Vice-Chamberlain of the House-hold, 1874-80. P.C. 2 Mar. 1874; Capt. Yeomen of the Guard, 1885-86; Capt Gent at Arms, Aug to Nov 1886. Sometime Private Sec. to the (14th) Earl of Derby, when Prime Minister. On 17 Apr. 1880, he was *cr.* BARON SHUTE of Beckett, co. Berks, [U.K.] *with a spec. rem.*, failing issue male, to his br., the Hon. Percy Barrington and the heirs male of his body. He *m*, 19 Feb 1846, at St. Geo., Han. Sq., Isabel Elizabeth (then a minor), da and h. of John MORRITT (*) of the family of Morritt of Rokeby Park, co. York, by Mary, da. of Peter BAILLIE,

---

(*) He is called "my late nephew" in the will, dat. 13 June 1842, of John Bacon Sawrey Morritt, of Rokeby Park, who *d. s.p.*, 12 July 1843.

of Dochfour. He *d. s p*, 6 Nov. 1886, after a few hours' illness, when on a visit at Grimsthorpe Castle, co. Lincoln, and was *bur.* at Shrivenham, aged 62. Will pr. 10 Feb. 1887, over £43,000. His widow *d.* at 39 Devonshire Place, 1, and was *bur.* 4 Feb 1898, at Shrivenham, aged 71. Will pr at £21,269 personalty.

VIII 1886   8. PERCY (BARRINGTON), VISCOUNT BARRINGTON OF ARDGLASS AND BARON BARRINGTON OF NEWCASTLE[I 1720], also BARON SHUTE OF BECKETT [U.K. 1880], next br. and h., *b* 22 Apr. 1825, in Lower Brook Str. Ed at Eton ; sometime (1841-45) an officer in the Rifle Brigade and Scots Fusilier Guards ; Sheriff of Bucks, 1864. He inherited the Barony [U.K] under the spec rem in the creation of that dignity, and was a Conservative in politics. He *m.*, 3 July 1845, at St. Geo, Han. Sq., Louisa, da. and h. of Tully HIGGINS She *d.* 17 May 1884, aged 59, at Westbury Manor, Bucks. He *d.* there, 29 Apr., and was *bur* 3 May 1901, at Brackley, with his wife, aged 76. Will pr. above £62,000 gross, and above £17,000 net personalty. He was *suc.* by his s and h., who is outside the scope of this work.

Family Estates.—These, in 1883, consisted of 3,477 acres in Berks, 1,635 in the West Riding of Yorkshire, and 1,275 in Northumberland. Total 6,387 acres, of the annual value of £17,387. *Principal Residence .*— Becket House, Shrivenham, Berks.

BARROGILL

i.e. " BARROGILL OF BARROGILL CASTLE, co. Caithness " Barony *(Sinclair)*, *cr.* 1886 ; *extinct* 1889 ; see " CAITHNESS, " Earldom [S], under the 14th Earl.

BARROWFIELD

i e " NEWLANDS OF NEWLANDS AND BARROWFIELD AND OF MAUDSLIE CASTLE " Barony *(Hozier)*, *cr* 1898, which see.

BARRY

See " ROMILLY OF BARRY, co. Glamorgan, " Barony *(Romilly)*, *cr.* 1866.

BARRY, BARRYMORE or BUTTEVANT (*)

Observations.—This is one of the Irish Peerages by prescription, *i.e.*

(*) The Editor is indebted to G.D.Burtchaell, Athlone Pursuivant, for entirely re-writing the earlier portion of this article, for a very able revision of the whole, and for the chart pedigree (p 451) showing the very distant relationship of James Fitz Richard Barry, afterwards Viscount Buttevant, who (20 Mar. 1557/8) succeeded to the

Peerages which were recognised in 1489 by Henry VII ([a]) but of the date or mode of whose creation nothing certain is known. Its existence as the premier Barony [I.] was acknowledged in 1489, 1490, 1541, 1560, and 1585. ([b])

PHILIP DE BARRY, ([c]) 2nd s. ([d]) of WILLIAM DE BARRY, by Angareth, ([e]) da. of STEPHEN, Constable of Cardigan Castle (by Nesta, da. of RHYS AP GRIFFITH, Prince of South Wales), received from his maternal uncle, Robert Fitz Stephen, about 1180, ([f]) a grant of the cantred of Olethan and of two others (Muscry-Donnegan and Killyde) in co. Cork. He *m.* (—), da. of Richard FITZ TANCRED. The statements that he or his immediate successors obtained the *status* of a Peer, as LORD BARRY [I.], are unsupported by evidence. He *d.* about 1200.

WILLIAM DE BARRY, of Olethan, &c. afsd., s. and h., to whom King John, on 21 Feb. 1206, confirmed the three cantreds abovenamed.

DAVID DE BARRY, of Olethan, &c., to whom was granted, 24 Sep.

---

estates of (his 6th cousin once removed) James, 3rd Viscount. He writes, " The succession of the feudal Lords of the cantred of Olethan, afterwards known as the Barony of Barrymore, has been traced, and the various pedigrees English and Irish of the different branches of the Barry family have been critically examined and collated with public and private records and the Irish annals, by the late Rev. E. Barry, P.P., M.R.I.A., Vice Pres. R.S.A. Ireland, in a series of papers entitled " Barrymore, " published in the *Journal of the Cork Historical and Archæological Soc.*, 2nd Ser., vols. v, vi, vii, viii (1899-1902). The succession which, as attempted by Lodge, is in hopeless confusion, was unravelled to a certain extent by Sir William Betham, Ulster (Betham's MSS., Ulster's Office), and somewhat more fully by Denis O'Callaghan Fisher (Fisher's MSS., Ulster's Office), but their efforts fall very far short of the extensive work and research of the said Rev. E. Barry, upon which the following account is founded. " G.D.Burtchaell adds that though following him generally, he has not " in all cases accepted his identification of the various parties," and states that the Rev. E. Barry " makes no suggestion as to the origin of the peerage." V.G.

([a]) In " The Order of placing the Lords of Ireland in the Procession at the Court of Greenwich. " See Appendix A in this volume.

([b]) See Appendix A in this volume.

([c]) Camden in his *Britannia* states that " the name is derived from the island of Barry, co. Glamorgan, and from their great riches and large estates the family have been called Barry-more, or Barry the Great." J.H.Round, however, points out that Philip's father, William, was of Manorbier Castle on the coast, west of Tenby, and adds that Philip joined his uncle in Ireland at the end of February, 1183, and that his father-in-law, Richard Fitz Tancard, of Tankarston in Brawey, was Constable of Haverfordwest.

([d]) The yst s., Gerald, was the celebrated *Giraldus Cambrensis*, author of the *Itinerarium Cambriae, Topographia Hibernica,* &c. The 1st s., Robert, who was slain at Lismore about 1185, was " for his worthiness " called Barry-More.

([e]) For some discussion on mediæval English names see vol. iii, Appendix C. V.G.

([f]) Henry II bestowed the county of Cork on Robert Fitz-Stephen (and another) in May 1177.

1234, a weekly market and a yearly fair at his manor of Botavant [*i.e.*
Buttevant, co. Cork].([a]) In 1235 he enlarged the friary of Ballybeg.
It was probably he who was styled Barrach *Mor* [*i.e.* the great Barry]
by the Irish, and who was slain at the battle of Callan, in Desmond, in
1261. ([b])

I. 1261 ?   1. DAVID DE BARRY, of Olethan, &c., s. and h., called
             David *Oge* [junior] and *Anbuille* [*i.e.* of the blows]. He
was Lord Justiciar of Ireland 1267. According to a grotesquely untrue
statement in *Lodge* he " was styled the 1st Viscount of Buttevant."([c]) He
may perhaps be regarded as the first of his family to obtain the *status* of a
Peer as LORD BARRY, BARRYMORE, or BUTTEVANT [I.], although
any date given for the origin of early prescriptive Irish titles such as this
must be in the nature of guess work. He *d.* in 1278.

II. 1278.   2. JOHN (BARRY), LORD BARRY, BARRYMORE or BUT-
             TEVANT [I.], s. and h. On 1 July 1283 a distraint was
served on him by the Lord Justiciar [I.] to compel him to receive knighthood. In 1284 he surrendered Olethan, and in 1285 Muscry-Donnegan,
to his brother David, as below. ([d])

III. 1285.   3. DAVID FITZ DAVID (BARRY), LORD BARRY, BARRY-
             MORE or BUTTEVANT [I.], br. and h., of Olethan in 1284,

---

([a]) The name of Buttevant is said to have been derived from the war
cry "Boutez en avant," used in a victory over the MacCarthies near that place,
about 1267, gained by David de Barry, and ever after adopted as a *motto* by his
descendants. Although as an Irish chieftain he was much more likely to be acquainted
with Norman French than with English, it is not easy to accept this derivation. V. G.

([b]) The Rev. E. Barry suggests that this David may have been succeeded at an
earlier date than 1261 by a brother, John, who was slain at Callan in 1261. But
the introduction of a John Barry into one of the Carew Pedigrees (where he is made
grandfather of the 1st so-called Viscount Buttevant) appears to be a mistake. V. G.

([c]) In the dateless pedigrees of these Lords drawn up in the latter half of the
16th Century (Carew MSS., Lambeth Library), the Viscountcy of Buttevant is
ascribed to them as early as the 13th century, *i.e.* at least 150 years before the style
of "Viscount" as a Peerage dignity was known in England ! Of course, none of
these Lords is ever styled "Viscount" in any existing contemporary document.
There is, indeed, a deed enrolled 26 Nov. (1614) 12 Jac. I, on the Patent Roll [I.],
on the petition of one John Barry Esq., but this must be received with the gravest
suspicion as to its genuineness. It purports to be a grant by "Jacobus Dñus Vic. de
Buttevant" dated Monday before the Epiphany (4 Jan. 1405/6) 7 Hen. IV. At that
date, however, the Lord of Buttevant was *John* Barry, who never in any official
document of his own time was styled *Dominus*, but who may then (as he undoubtedly
was in 1401 and 1413-15) have been "Vicecomes" [*i.e.* Sheriff, not Viscount] of
county Cork. See Appendix A in this volume. V.G.

([d]) He is not mentioned in the pedigrees, having presumably *d. s.p.*, and so being
out of the line of descent.

and of Muscry-Donnegan in 1285, on the surrender of his brother as afsd. He is said to have *m*. Maud de Boulltron,(ª) of Wales.   He *d*. about 1290.

IV. 1290 ?   4. JOHN (BARRY), LORD BARRY, BARRYMORE or BUT-
          TEVANT [I.], s. and h.   He had lic. (1301) 29 Edw. I to alienate land to the value of £20 a year in Muscry, Olethan and Obawne [*i.e*. Ibawne], and appears accordingly to have alienated Ibawne to his younger brother(ᵇ) William.(ᶜ)   He was sum. to the Parl [I] at Kilkenny, 8 Jan (1309/10) 3 Edw. II, and was present in the Parl. [I.] at Dublin, Easter (1324/5) 17 Edw. II.   He seems to have *d. s.p* , about 1330. (ᵈ)

V. 1330 ?   5. DAVID (BARRY), LORD BARRY, BARRYMORE or BUT-
          TEVANT [I.], next br. and h.   He was sum. to Parl. [I.] in 1339, and was Sheriff of co Cork 1344   He *d* 12 May 1347.

VI. 1347.   6. DAVID (BARRY), LORD BARRY, BARRYMORE or
          BUTTEVANT [I.], s and h , a minor at the time of his father's death.   He was sum. to Parl. [I.] 22 Nov. (1374) 48 Edw. III, to 25 Apr. (1382) 5 Ric II, being on this last occasion fined 100s. for absence, for which he pleaded a pardon.   He *d*. 6 Sep. 1392.

VII. 1392.   7. JOHN (BARRY), LORD BARRY, BARRYMORE or BUT-
          TEVANT [I.], called *kittagh* [*i e* left handed], s. and h. Sheriff of Cork 1401, and 1403-15.   He *m*. Ellice, da. of Gerald Fitz Maurice (FITZ GERALD), EARL OF DESMOND [I.].   He *d*. about 1420.

VIII. 1420 ?   8. WILLIAM (BARRY), (ᵉ) LORD BARRY, BARRYMORE
          or BUTTEVANT [I], s. and h (ᶠ)   He was Sheriff of co Cork 1433, 1451, and 1461; a Commissioner for the peace of that co. 1434.

(ª) So also in *Lodge*, though it is there added " but we find that the wife of David de Barry, living 1298, was named Joan ; that she afterwards *m*. Eustace le Poer, and assigned to her son John de Barry, for all her dower in Olethan, &c., the moiety of the cantred of Muskery, except 2 parts of the marriage of Philip, son and heir to Philip de Barry." This seems as if this Joan (not mentioned in the text, following the Carew MSS) was the mother of John, the 1st s. and successor of this David and of his 2 younger brothers.

(ᵇ) Escheator's *Inq*.

(ᶜ) James Fitz Richard Barry, who on the death of James, Viscount Buttevant [I.], 20 Mar. 1557/8, succeeded to his estates and honours, was 6th in descent from this William Barry.   See pedigree, *post*, pp. 452, 453.

(ᵈ) He also is not mentioned in the pedigrees.

(ᵉ) These three Lords are *all* omitted (as such) in the claim of J. R Barry to the Viscountcy of Buttevant in 1825.   The Lords Barry, as well as the Lords Athenry, Lords Kingsale and Lords Kerry became, during most of that period, mere Irish Chieftains, many of them assuming Irish names, and being entirely hostile to the English Government.

(ᶠ) He had three younger brothers, Richard, David, and James, from all of whom there were male descendants living in 1600, and consequently nearer heirs male to the Viscount who *d* in 1557/8 than James Barry, who succeeded him.

He apparently it was who, as "William Lord Barry, Esquire" signed a public testimonial dat. 9 Jan. (1442/3) 21 Hen VI. ([a]) He had a grant from Edward IV, 8 Nov. 1461, of 20 marks a year for life out of the customs of Cork, under the style of *Dominus de Barry.* He *m.* Ellen, da. of Lord Roche [I]. He *d.* about 1480.

IX. 1480?   9. John (Barry), ([b]) Lord Barry, Barrymore, or Buttevant [I.], called *baccagh,* [*i.e.* the lame], s. and h. He *m.,* 1stly, (—), by whom he had an only s. He *m,* 2ndly, Sheely, da. of MacCartie Reach, by whom he had seven sons. He was slain on Christmas day 1486, by Donogh *oge* MacCartie, lord of Ealla, against whom he had gone on a predatory expedition. ([c])

X. 1486.   10. Thomas (Barry), ([b]) Lord Barry, Barrymore, or Buttevant [I.], s. and h. by 1st wife. On 27 June 1488, he took the oath of allegiance to the King's Commissioner in Ireland. He *d. s.p.* soon after.

XI. 1488?   11. William (Barry), Lord Barry, Barrymore, or Buttevant [I.], br. and h, being 1st s. and h of John *baccagh,* by his 2nd wife. He was one of the fifteen Irish Peers sum. to Greenwich by Henry VII in 1489, being ranked as Premier Baron, "Lord Barre de Buttevant," next immediately after the Earls. ([d]) He also sat in the Parl. [I.] in 1491. He *m* Sheely, da. of Cormac Mac-Teig MacCartie, of Muskerry. He *d.* 1500, being slain by his br. David, Archdeacon of Cork.

XII. 1500.   12. John (Barry), Lord Barry, Barrrymore, or Buttevant [I.], s. and h In 1520 he took the oath of allegiance as Lord Barry before the King's Commissioners. He *d s.p.,* *circa* 1530, being slain at Ballynecranagh, by Thomas, Earl of Desmond.

XIII. 1530?   13. John Fitz John (Barry), Lord Barry, Barrymore, or Buttevant, [I.], called *reogh* [*i.e.* the striped], uncle and h, being 2nd s. of John *baccagh,* by his 2nd wife. He *m.* Ellen, da. of Fitz Gibbon, the White Knight. He *d circa* 1534.

XIV. 1534?
VISCOUNTCY [I.]   14 and 1 John Fitz John (Barry), Lord Barry, Barrymore, or Buttevant, [I.], called *Bowleragh,* ([e]) s. and h., *b.* 1517 or 1518. ([f]) He sat in the Parl.

([a]) See *Carew Papers,* vol. vi, p. 461. (*ex inform.* J. H Round, to whom G E C was indebted for much information and for many suggestions and emendations in this article)
([b]) See note "e" on previous page
([c]) *Annals of the Four Masters.*
([d]) See Appendix A in this volume.
([e]) The translation of this word is doubtful, but it probably means "fostered by the Bowlers," *i.e* the Bowler family of Kerry (*ex inform* M.J.McEnery.) V.G
([f]) Steven ap Parry writes to Cromwell, 6 Oct. 1535, "moreover there

I. 1541. [I.] in June 1541 (ª) as Premier Viscount as "Dñs Barry, Vic. Barry," being the first of his family who sat under this designation. There appears never to have been any creation of this Viscountcy, which seems to have been simply assumed. (ᵇ) In 1542 he, with other Irish magnates, entered into an indenture of allegiance &c., with the Lord Deputy [I] as "the Lord Barre, *alias* the Great Barry" (ᶜ) He *m.*, 1stly, Ellen, da. of LORD ROCHE, and 2ndly, (—), da. of Gerald Fitz John FITZGERALD, of the Decies, co. Waterford. He *d. s p*, between May and Nov. 1553. (ᵈ)

VISCOUNTCY [I.] II. BARONY [I.] XV.	1553.	2 and 15. EDMOND (BARRY), VISCOUNT BARRY, BARRYMORE, or BUTTEVANT &., [I.], br. and h., being 2nd s. of John *reogh*. He styles himself "Edmond Lord Barrymor" in a memorandum dated 28 Nov. 1553 (ᵉ) He is said to have entailed his lands, in default of issue male of himself

and his brother, on James Barry fitz Richard, who eventually became Viscount Buttevant. He *m.*, 1stly, Joan, da. of James (FITZ GERALD), EARL OF DESMOND. She left him, and *d.* 1600. He *m.*, 2ndly, while his 1st wife was living, Sheely, da. of Donal MacCartie REAGH. He *d. s p.*, about 1556.

VISCOUNTCY [I.] III. BARONY [I.] XVI.	1556?	3 and 16. JAMES FITZ JOHN (BARRY), VISCOUNT BARRY, BARRYMORE, or BUTTEVANT, &c. [I.], br. and h., being 3rd s. of John *reogh*. He executed a deed, 9 Feb. 1556/7, whereby he settled his estates of Buttevant, Olethan, &c., on himself and the heirs male of his body, with rem. to

James Fitz Richard BARRY *roe* [i e red], Lord of Ibawne, and his heirs male, with similar rem. to Richard fitz David Barry, and to David Fitz

came in to my lord James [Butler] one called Lord Barrowe, who can speak very good English and is not more than 17 or 18 years old He is a great inheritor." (*Cal. State Papers* [I.]). (*ex inform.* G.D.Burtchaell.) V.G.

(ª) "In the Parl, 1541, wherein Henry VIII was declared King of Ireland, there were present, the Earls of Ormond and Desmond, the Lord Barry, McGilla Phadrig, Chieftain of Ossory, the sons of O'Bryan, MacCarthy More, with many Irish Lords." (MS. in Trin. Coll., Dublin).

(ᵇ) See Appendix A in this vol., and for a similar case see *sub* FERMOY. V.G.

(ᶜ) The Mayor of Cork, writing to the Lord Deputy in 1548, styles him "Lord Barrymore." (*ex inform* G D.Burtchaell.) V.G

(ᵈ) Sir Thomas Cusack writes to the Duke of Northumberland, 8 May 1553, "... the lords and captains of those countries as the Earl of Desmond, the *Viscount* Barrie, the *Lord* Roche, the Lord Fitz Morris and divers other... beeth now in the commission with the justices of the Peace to hear and determine causes " (*Cal. Carew MSS.*) This may refer to his successor. (*ex inform.* G D.Burtchaell.) V.G.

(ᵉ) Roche Papers , Smith's *Hist. of Cork.* (*ex inform.* G.D. Burtchaell) V.G.

David Barry *roe*, &c. He *m.*, 1stly, Ellis, da. of Maurice Fitz Gerald, of the Shean, co. Waterford. She *d. s.p.* He *m.*, 2ndly, Ellen, da. of Teig Mac-Cormac oge MacCartie, of Muskerry. He *d. s.p.m.*, ([a]) 20 Mar. 1557/8. ([b]) His widow *m.* (as his 2nd wife) John (Power), 3rd Lord le Power [I.], who *d.* 8 Nov. 1592

VISCOUNTCY [I]		1. James Fitz Richard (Barry roe),
IV.		Viscount Barry, Barrymore, or Butte-
	1558.	vant, &c. [I.], cousin, but not h. male,
BARONY [I]		being 1st s. of Richard Barry of the Rath,
		which Richard was 1st s. (but illegit.
XVII.		according to a decision of the spiritual

court) of James Barry *roe*, which James was s. of Richard, s. of James, s. of Laurence 1st Barry *roe*, s. of William fitz David Barry called *moyle* [*i.e.* bald], of Ibawne, which William was a yr s. of David Barry the 3rd Lord. ([c]) In consequence of the illegitimacy of his father, Ibawne and the chieftainship of Barry *roe* passed to the sons of his grandfather's 2nd marriage. To secure the lordship of Ibawne and make himself Barry *roe* he is said to have murdered his cousins Redmond and John   Their brothers Richard and David fled to the Earl of Desmond, and were apparently living at the date of the entail of 1557; but he is said to have procured them also to be made away with. On 28 Apr. 1558 he had a pardon as James Barry of Barrescourt Viscount Barrymore otherwise James called Barrymore and Barryroe. He was sum. to the Parl [I.] which met 12 Jan. 1559/60, where he sat next after the Earls as *Jacobus le Barry Dns. de Buttevant*. By indenture dated 18 Mar. 1560/1, he, as " james Barrie Lord Barrie mor and Barrie roe," obtained from Edmond Barry of Rathgobbane, the rightful heir to the Peerage ([d]) a surrender of the estates to him and his heirs for ever. On 27 Apr. of that year he had livery of these lands as "James Barry, Viscount Barrymore, kinsman and h. of James late Lord," the Crown thus apparently finally acquiescing in his succession to *the title* as well as to the

---

([a]) By her he had an only da., Catherine, who *m* Richard, Lord le Power, who began a suit against David, Lord Barry, for the whole lordship in right of his wife. "The Queen, to avoid contention, persuaded that the Lord Barry's son should marry the Lord Power's da. " (*Cal. Carew MSS.*, vol. v, p 391.) (*ex inform.* G.D. Burtchaell.) V.G.

([b]) On his death the title of Lord Barry, Barrymore, or Buttevant, should have passed to his h male, *viz.* Edmond *more* Barry of Rathgobbane, co. Cork, eldest surv. s of Gerrot, 2nd s. of Richard Barry, 2nd s. of John *kittagh*, but under the entail made by him the estates passed to James Fitz Richard Barry Roe, the 4th Viscount as in the text. (*ex inform* G.D Burtchaell.) V.G.

([c]) In the pedigrees in the Carew MSS., William *moyle* is represented as a brother of John *kittagh*, but the Rev. E. Barry has demonstrated that he must have been grand-uncle, not brother, to the latter. (*ex inform.* G D.Burtchaell.) V.G.

([d]) Edmond Barry of Rathgobbane was *suc.* by his s., Robert Barry, living 1573, whose s., William, was living, blind and landless, in 1617. David, 3rd s., and James, 4th s., of John *kittagh*, had numerous descendants. (*ex inform.* G.D.Burtchaell.) V.G.

estates.   Having been knighted, 30 Mar. 1566/7, at Limerick by the Lord
Deputy, as James fitz Richard Barry, Viscount Buttevant, on 5 Apr. 1567
he had a Commission to execute martial law as " Sir James Barry knt, Lord
Barrye more, Viscount Bowtyvant, " while 12 Mar. 1567/8, he received a
Crown lease of lands, co. Cork, as " *Viscount Barrymore.*" (ª)   He *m.* Ellen,
da. of Cormac MacCarthy REAGH.   He *d.* 10 Apr. 1581.   *Inq. p.m.* at
Youghal 31 Mar. (1624) 22 Jac. I, in which he is called " James Fitz
Richard, Lord Barry, Viscount Buttevant. "

VISCOUNTCY [I.] V. BARONY [I.] XVIII. 1581.	2. RICHARD BARRY, who apparently was *de jure* VISCOUNT BARRY, BARRYMORE, or BUTTEVANT, &c. [I.], s. and h., but being deaf and dumb (though of sound understanding) was passed over in the succession. (ᵇ) He *d. s.p.*, 24 Apr. 1622, at Liscarroll.

VISCOUNTCY [I.]

V.

$\left.\begin{array}{l}\\ \\ \\ \\ \\ \end{array}\right\}$ 1581.

BARONY [I.]

XVIII.

3. DAVID BARRY, *de facto* VISCOUNT
BARRY, BARRYMORE, or BUTTEVANT, &c.
[I.], who, being 2nd s. of James, the 4th
Viscount, entered into possession of the
estate and assumed the title.   He was of
Barry Court, co. Cork.   He was sum. to
Parl. [I.], and appears in the list of Peers
present, 26 Apr. 1585, as the " Viscount of Barry, *alias* Buttevant ; " and,
in the Parl. of 1613, was placed as "Viscount Barry *of* Buttevant," next to
the Earls. (ᶜ)   He joined Desmond's rebellion, and is said (in a letter of
Queen Elizabeth, dat. 8 Aug. 1593) to have done so as "Viscount Barry,"
but abandoned the rebel cause in or before 1599, and as " Viscount Buttevant" (which designation (ᵈ) henceforth became the usual one) was pardoned
15 Nov. 1602, and is frequently so styled in inquisitions, &c.   In 1601 he
had a warrant " to levy all the risings out of the country," and in 1602
commanded 1,600 men.   On 20 May 1615 he was one of the Council for
the province of Munster.   He *m.*, 1stly, Ellen, da. of David (ROCHE),
VISCOUNT ROCHE OF FERMOY [I.], by Ellen, da. of James (BUTLER), LORD
DUNBOYNE [I.].   She was living as his wife, Oct. 1593, and apparently in
1599.   He *m.*, 2ndly, Julia, 2nd da. of Cormac MACCARTHY, of Muskerry.
He *d.* (in the lifetime of his elder br., the *de jure* Viscount) 10 Apr. 1617,
at Barry's Court.   His widow *m.* Sir Roger O'SHAUGHESSY.

(ª) *Patent Rolls.*

(ᵇ) A similar case occurred in the succession to the Barony of Slane [I.] in 1629,
and in that of the Barony of Athenry [I.] in 1645.

(ᶜ) *Cal. Carew MSS.*

(ᵈ) He is styled in a warrant of 31 Jan. 1609/10 (Docquet Roll) " the Lord
Barry, Viscount Buttevant, " and in royal letters dat. 22 Oct. (1618) 16 Jac. I,
confirmed 13 May (1625) 1 Car. I, " David, Lord Butevant, lately deceased. "   In
both of these letters also, his grandson and h. is styled " David, Lord Barry, Lord
Viscount Buttevant. "   (*ex inform.* J. H. Round.)

[DAVID BARRY, s. and h. ap. by 1st wife. He *m.* Elizabeth, 3rd da. of Richard, 4th LORD LE POWER [I], by Catherine, da. and coh of James Fitz John, 3rd VISCOUNT BARRY abovenamed. ([a]). He *d. v.p.*, in 1604 or 1604/5].

VISCOUNTCY [I.] VI. BARONY [I.] XIX. 1617. EARLDOM [I.] I. 1628.	4. DAVID (BARRY), VISCOUNT BARRY, BARRYMORE, or BUTTEVANT, &c. [I.], grandson and h., being posthumous s. and h. of David Barry and Elizabeth abovenamed. At the death of his grandfather he was twelve years and one month old ; and was there-fore *b.* on or about 10 Mar. 1604/5 ([b]) He had livery of his lands, 13 May 1625. For his fidelity to the English interest in Ireland he was *cr.* ([c]) 28 Feb. 1627/8, EARL OF BARRYMORE, co. Cork [I.], and took his seat as such 14 July 1634. From

1639 to 1642 he took an active part as a Royalist, and was mortally wounded at the battle of Liscarrol He *m.*, 21 July 1621, Alice, 1st da. of Richard (BOYLE), 1st EARL OF CORK [I.], by Catherine, da. of Sir Geoffrey FENTON. He *d.* 29 Sep 1642, aged 38, and was *bur* in the Boyle vault at Youghal. His widow, who was *b.* 20 Mar. 1607, at Youghal, *m.* John BARRY, of Liscarrol She *d.* 23, and was *bur.* 25 Mar. 1666, as "Mrs Barry," at St. Patrick's, Dublin. Fun. entry.

EARLDOM [I] II. VISCOUNTCY [I] VII. BARONY [I.] XX.	} 1642.	5. RICHARD (BARRY), EARL OF BARRY-MORE, &c. [I.], s. and h., *bap.* 4 Nov. 1630, at St Werburgh's, Dublin. On 5 Feb. 1660/1 he was appointed Col of Foot. On 11 May 1661, and again (after the Revolution) on 7 Oct. 1692, he took his seat in the House. He sat in James II's Parl. [I.] in May 1689 ([d]) He is said to have *m* , 1stly, Susan, ([e]) da. of Sir William KILLEGREW. He *m.*, 2ndly, Nov 1656, (banns publ. at

([a]) See *ante*, p. 441, note " a. "

([b]) By the *Inq. p. m.* 31 Mar. (1624) 22 Jac. I, he was found heir to the family estates by reason of the deaths of David Fitz David, David Fitz James Fitz Richard, Richard Fitz James Fitz Richard, James Fitz Richard " Dominus Barry, Vicecomes Buttevant" and James Fitz John " Dominus Barry, Vicecomes Buttevant," *i.e* his father [who *d. v.p.*], his grandfather, his great uncle (the *de jure* Lord), his great grandfather, and (lastly) the cousin and predecessor of his said great grandfather. He had livery of his estates as "Lord Barry, Viscount Buttevant," 12 Dec 1626.

([c]) The preamble to the patent is given in *Lodge*, vol. 1, p. 296. In it he is styled " *Dominus Barry, Vicecomes Buttevant, &c.,* " as also in his M.I. For a list of the creations and promotions in the Irish peerage (1628) see vol. iii, Appendix H.

([d]) For a list of peers present in, and absent from, this Parl , see volume iii, Appendix D.

([e]) *Qy* if this was not Susan, da. of Sir W K. (Vice Chamberlain to the Queen Consort, Catharine), by Mary, da. of John Hill. She was *bap.* 1 Apr. 1629, at St Margaret's, Lothbury, London, and was living 1633.

St. Margaret's, Westm.) Martha, da. of Henry LAWRENCE, of London (President of Cromwell's Council), by Amy, da. of Sir Edward PEYTON, Bart. She *d.* 1664, and was *bur.* at Thele, otherwise St. Margaret's, Herts. [a] He *m.*, 3rdly, Feb. 1666, Dorothy, da. and h. of John FERRAR, of Dromore, co. Down. He *d.* Nov. 1694. His widow *m.* (as his 3rd wife) Sir Matthew DEANE, 1st Bart. [I. 1710], of Dromore, who *d.* 10 Jan. 1710/1, aged 84.

EARLDOM [I.] III.
VISCOUNTCY [I.] VIII.
BARONY [I.] XXI. } 1694.

6. LAURENCE (BARRY), EARL OF BARRYMORE, &c. [I.], s. and h. by 2nd wife. He was *attainted* in 1689 by the Parl. of James II, but *restored* soon after. He took his seat in the House of Lords, 27 Aug. 1695, and 2 Dec. 1697 signed the association in defence of William III. He *m.*, in 1682, Katharine, da. of Richard (BARRY), 2nd BARON BARRY OF SANTRY [I.], by Elizabeth, da. of Henry JENERY. He *d. s.p.*, 17 Apr. 1699. Admon. 11 Nov. 1699, at Dublin. His widow, who was *bap.* 9 May 1663, at St. Michan's, Dublin, *m.*, 2ndly, in 1699, Francis GASH, one of the Revenue Collectors [I.]. She *m.*, 3rdly, 8 Dec. 1729, Sir Henry PIERS, Bart. [I. 1661], of Tristernagh, who *d.* 14 Mar. 1733/4. She *d.* 8, and was *bur.* 10 June 1737, at St. Mary's, Dublin. Will dat. 3 June 1737, pr. 1744.

EARLDOM [I.] IV.
VISCOUNTCY [I.] IX.
BARONY [I.] XXII. } 1699.

7. JAMES (BARRY), EARL OF BARRYMORE, &c. [I.], br. (of the half blood) and h., being s. of the 2nd Earl by his 3rd wife, *b.* 1667. Lieut. Col. in the army of William of Orange, 31 Dec. 1688; Col. of the 13th Foot 1702-15. He commanded a regt. under Lord Galway in Spain, and was taken prisoner in the English defeat, at Almanza, 25 Apr. 1707. Brig. Gen. 1707; Major Gen. 1709; Lieut. Gen. 1710/11. On 14 Feb. 1703/4 he took his seat in the House of Lords. M.P. (Tory) for Stockbridge 1710-13, 1714-15; and for Wigan 1715-27, and 1734-47. P.C. [I.] 29 Jan. 1713/4. He was arrested on suspicion of treason in 1715, but nothing was proved against him. He was *cr.* D.C.L. (Oxford) 1735/6. He *m.*, 1stly, Elizabeth, da. of Charles (BOYLE), LORD CLIFFORD, by his 1st wife, Jane, da. of William (SEYMOUR), DUKE OF SOMERSET. She, who was sister to Charles (BOYLE), 3rd EARL OF CORK [I.], was *bap.* 13 Feb. 1662, and had a fortune of £10,000. She *d. s.p.m.s.* Admon. 10 Oct. 1703 granted to

---

[a] A Bill for her naturalisation was rejected Oct. 1622, being unnecessary, as she was *b.* of English parents. V.G.

her husband. He *m.*, 2ndly, in June 1706 (unknown to her father), (ª) Elizabeth, da. and h. of Richard (SAVAGE), 4th EARL RIVERS, by Penelope, da. and h of Roger DOWNES. She *d.* (in childbed) *s p.m s*, 19 Mar. 1713/4. He *m.*, 3rdly, 12 July 1716, at St. Anne's, Soho, Anne, da. of Arthur (CHICHESTER), 3rd EARL OF DONEGAL [I.], by his 2nd wife, Catharine, da. of Arthur (FORBES), EARL OF GRANARD [I.]. He *d.* 5 Jan. 1747/8, in his 80th year, and was *bur.* at Castle Lyons, co. Cork. M.I. (ᵇ) Will dat. 20 Aug. 1744 to 23 Jan. 1746/7, pr. 2 July 1753. His widow *d.* 6 Dec. 1753, and was also *bur.* at Castle Lyons. Will pr. 1754, Prerog. Ct. [I.].

[A s. and h. *styled* LORD BUTTEVANT, *d* an infant, 30 May 1707.]

EARLDOM [I] V. VISCOUNTCY [I.] X. BARONY [I.] XXIII.	1748.	8. JAMES (BARRY), EARL OF BARRYMORE, *&c.* [I.], 1st surv. s. and h. by 3rd wife, *b.* 25 Apr. 1717, in London Matric. at Oxford (Brasenose Coll.), 12 Jan. 1732/3; *cr.* M.A 1735/6 He *m*, 8 June 1738, Margaret, (" with £30,000 ") sister and coh. of Edward, 3rd VISCOUNT MOUNT-CASHELL [I.], being yst da. of Paul (DAVYS), 1st VISCOUNT MOUNTCASHELL [I], by Catharine, da. of Callaghan (M'CARTY), EARL OF CLANCARTY [I.].

He *d.* 19 Dec 1751, in Dublin. Will dat. 16 Dec. 1751, pr. 1752, Prerog. Ct [I.]. His widow *d.* 2 Dec. 1788, at an advanced age, in Dublin. Will pr Mar. 1791.

EARLDOM [I.] VI. VISCOUNTCY [I.] XI. BARONY [I] XXIV.	1751.	9. RICHARD (BARRY), EARL OF BARRYMORE, *&c.* [I.], only s. and h , *b.* Oct. 1745 Ed at Westm. school, and at Eton. He is said to have been at Oxford, but does not appear to have matriculated Capt. in 9th Reg of Dragoons Oct. 1767. He *m.*, 16 Apr. 1767, at St. Martin's-in-the-Fields, Emily, 3rd da. of William (STANHOPE), 2nd EARL OF HARRINGTON, by Caroline, da of Charles (FITZROY), 2nd DUKE OF GRAFTON.

He *d.* 1 Aug. 1773, at Dromana, of fever, aged 27, and was *bur.* at Castle Lyons. Admon. 13 Sep. 1773 to his widow, and again, 28 May 1781, to his mother on behalf of his children. His widow, who was *b.* 24 May 1749, *d.* 5 Sep. 1780, in France. Will pr. Apr. 1781.

(ª) *Hist MSS. Com.*, Marquess of Bath's MSS., vol. 1, p. 87. V.G.
(ᵇ) On his monument he is styled " Comes de Barrymore, Vicecomes de Barry et Buttevant, Baro de Ibawne et Olethan "

EARLDOM [I.]
VII.

VISCOUNTCY [I.]
XII.

BARONY [I.]

XXV.

} 1773.

10. RICHARD (BARRY), EARL OF BARRY-MORE, &c. [I.], s. and h., b. 14 Aug. 1769, and bap. at St. Marylebone. M.P. (Whig) for Heytesbury 1791-93. Though of considerable talents, his career was wild and perhaps only equalled in profligacy by the Duke of Buckingham. (ª) It was terminated in his 24th year by the explosion of his musket, near Folkestone, while escorting (as Capt. in the Berks Militia) some French prisoners to Dover. He m., about 7 (ᵇ) June 1792, Charlotte, da. of (—) GOULDING, (a sedan chairman) by Phillis, (sister of Lætitia, the wife of Sir John Lade, Bart.) da. of (—) SMITH. (ᶜ) He d. s.p., 6, and was bur. 17 Mar. 1793, at Wargrave, Berks. Admon. 26 Mar. 1794, under £5000. His widow, who was a minor aged 18 in Mar. 1794, m., 22 Sep. 1794, Robert WILLIAMS, Capt. 3rd Regt. Foot Guards.

EARLDOM [I.]
VIII.

VISCOUNTCY [I.]
XIII.

BARONY [I.]

XXVI.

} 1793 to 1823.

11. HENRY (BARRY), EARL OF BARRY-MORE, VISCOUNT BUTTEVANT AND LORD BARRY [I.], br. and h., b. 21 Oct. 1770, at Marylebone. Matric. at Oxford (Ex. Coll.) 21 Apr. 1788. He m., 24 Jan. 1795, at Cork, by spec. lic., Anne, 1st da. of Jeremiah COGHLAN, of Ardo, co. Waterford. He d. s.p. legit., 18 Dec. 1823, of apoplexy, aged 53, at the house of the Duc

---

(ª) See his character in Sir Egerton Brydges' *Biographical Peerage* (1817), vol. iv, p. 37. Also a vast amount of information as to the character, position, &c., of various members of this family is given in " *N. & Q.*," 5th Ser., vol. xi, p. 276, *et ante*. In 1790 he and a lady figure as " The theatrical peer of Berks and Antonietta " in the scandalous tête-à-tête portraits in the *Town and Country Mag.*, vol. xxii, p. 59. (See Appendix B in the last volume of this work). He and his family received, from their friend the Prince Regent, the following nicknames—he himself, "Hellgate;" his br. and successor Henry, who had a club foot, " Cripplegate ; " his yst br. Augustus, " Newgate ; " and his sister, owing to the flow and vigour of her language, " Billingsgate." A caricature by Gillray, entitled *Les trois Magots*, shows the three men as " A Hellgate blackguard, " " A Cripplegate Monster, " and " A Newgate Scrub. " *The last Earls of Barrymore*, by John Robert Robinson, 1894, contains much gossip of the period. Sir Herbert Croft, in the *Abbey of Kilkhampton*, p. 101, ed. 1788, mentions his fondness for racing, " his courage, his fickleness, his merriment, " and calls him " a comely youth, son of a comely mother. " In 1797 the annual rental from his estates was said to be £7500. For a list of the largest resident Irish landlords at that date see vol. iv, Appendix C. V.G. He sold the Barrymore estates, including Castle Lyons and Buttevant, to John Anderson, of Fermoy, reserving £4,000 a year for himself and £1,000 for his widow, for life. Castle Lyons was burnt down about 1775.

(ᵇ) On 6 June 1792, he started from London with Miss Goulding for Gretna Green, but neither the place nor exact date of the marriage is certainly known. V.G.

(ᶜ) " Joseph Darby, Esq., " presumably her mother's br.-in-law, appears as her

de Castries, husband of his wife's sister. (ª) Admon Dec. 1829. His widow *d.* 6 May 1832, in Paris. Will pr. July 1832. On the Earl's death in 1823, the Earldom (ᵇ) certainly, and the Viscountcy (ᶜ) (if it ever existed) and Barony probably, became *extinct.*

BARRY OF SANTRY (ᵈ)

BARONY [I.]
1. 1661.

1. Sɪʀ Jᴀᴍᴇs Bᴀʀʀʏ, of Santry, co. Dublin, s. and h. of Richard B., Alderman and sometime (1610) Mayor of Dublin, by Anne, da. and h , or coh., of James Cusᴀᴄᴋ, was *b* 1603, ed. at Trin Coll Dublin B.A 27 Apr. 1621 ; M A. June 1624 ; incorporated, Oxford, 10 July 1627, and Cambridge, same year. Admitted Linc Inn., 11 July 1621 ; barrister 1628, and King's Inns, 15 Apr. 1630. He was made Prime Serjeant [I.] 6 Oct. 1629, second Baron of the Exchequer [I] 5 Aug. 1634; M P. for Lismore 1634; was Knighted [I.] Aug. 1640 ; was Chairman of the Royalist Convention which met at Dublin, 7 July 1659, in defiance of the then Government, and, in reward of his services, was, at the Restoration, made P.C. [I.] and Chief Justice of the King's Bench [I.] in Nov. 1660, and was *cr* , 18 Feb. 1660/1, BARON BARRY OF SANTRY, co. Dublin [I], taking his seat 8 May 1661. He *m* , Catharine, 1st da. of Sir William Pᴀʀsoɴs, Bart. [I.],

uncle in the proceedings as to her husband's administration, which her mother, and guardian, Phillis Chapman, formerly Goulding, wife of William Chapman, renounced The notorious "Lady Barrymore" (mentioned in *N. & Q.* as above), who *d.* of drink, in poverty, 30 Oct. 1832, in Charles Court, Drury Lane, was (probably) mistress (not wife) of this (the 7th) Earl.

(ª) At his death his sister, Lady Caroline, assumed the title of Baroness de Barry.

(ᵇ) The extinction of the Earldom of Barrymore was acted upon as one of the three used, is accordance with the Act of Union [I.], for the creation of the Viscountcy of Guillamore. Had the Viscountcy of Buttevant (or any other peerage [I] which was *held at the time of the Union* by the then Earl) continued, the Earldom would not have been *such* an extinction as could have been used for a new creation. This point was decided (as regarding the Earldom of Mountrath and the Barony of Castle Coote [I] which, at the time of the Union, were united) at the creation of the Barony of Fermoy [I] in 1856.

(ᶜ) The Viscountcy of Buttevant was assumed by James Redmond Barry, of Donoughmore, co Cork, as h. male of the body of James, 4th Viscount His claim to vote at the election of an Irish Rep. Peer was before the House of Lords in 1825. He was only s. and h. of James B. (*d. v.p.* 1800), the only s. who had issue of James B., of Mount Barry, co Cork (*d.* 1802), said to be s and h. of William Fitz James B., of Ballymacraheen, co. Cork (*d.* about 1760), s. and h. of James B. of the same, said to be only s and h. of William B. of Lislee, co. Cork (living 1656), s and h. of James B., who was s and h of William B., both of the same, which William (who *d* before 1594) was said to be the same as William Barry, 3rd s. of James, 4th Viscount, who *d.* 1581.

(ᵈ) A full account of this branch of the family of Barry, with an engraving of the tomb of Richard, the 2nd Lord, is in the *History of Santry and Clogran parishes, co. Dublin,* by B. W. Adams, D.D., 1883

Lord Deputy [I.], by Elizabeth, da. of John Lany, Alderman of Dublin. He *d* 9, and was *bur.* 14 Feb. 1672/3, at St Mary's Chapel, Christ Church, Dublin

II. 1673.   2 Richard (Barry), Baron Barry of Santry [I.], s. and h. Matric. Oxford (Jesus Coll.) 5 Dec. 1651 ; admitted to Linc. Inn, 17 Aug 1660 ; barrister, 1666. He did not sit in James II's Irish Parl., May 1689, (ª) by which he was provisionally attainted, but took his seat in Oct. 1692. He *m.* (lic. Vic. Gen. 11 Sep 1660, he aged 23 and she aged 15) Elizabeth, da. of Henry Jenery, of the Court of King's Bench [I.]. She *d.* 6, and was *bur.* 17 Feb. 1682, at Santry. He *d.* Oct 1694, and was *bur.* at Santry. Will dat. 25 Oct., pr. 10 Nov. 1694, in Dublin.

III. 1694.   3. Henry (Barry), Baron Barry of Santry [I], 4th, but 1st surv. s. and h., *b.* 1680. Ed. at Eton 1698. Gov. of Londonderry and Culmore fort. P.C. [I.] 30 Nov. 1714. (ᵇ) He *m*, 9 Feb. 1702, Bridget, da. of Sir Thomas Domvile, Bart. [I. 1686], of Templeogue, co. Dublin, by his 1st wife, Elizabeth, da. of Sir Lancelot Lake, of Canons, in Whitchurch, Midx. He *d.* at Santry, 27, and was *bur.* there 29 Jan. 1734/5. Will pr. 1736, Prerog. Court [I.]. His widow *d.* 21 Aug., and was *bur.* 8 Sep. 1750, at Santry.

IV. 1734   4. Henry (Barry), Baron Barry of Santry [I.], only
to   s. and h., *b.* 3 Sep. 1710, at St. Mary's, Dublin. He was
1739   tried for the murder of Laughlin Murphy, a footman
(whom in a fit of passion he had stabbed 9 Aug. 1738, but who did not die till 25 Sep following), and being found guilty was *attainted* and condemned to death, 27 Apr. 1739, whereby his Peerage as well as his estates were *forfeited*, but as regards the former only for the period of his own life. (ᶜ) On 17 June following he obtained pardon under

(ª) For a list of peers present in, and absent from this Parl., see volume III, Appendix D

(ᵇ) His signature (together with those of the 2nd Duke of Bolton, the 1st Baron Midleton, and other notables) appears on a document, dated 17 Aug 1719, seriously recommending the castration of all unregistered priests and friars, with a view to making the common Irish protestants. V.G.

(ᶜ) J.H. Round points out that by the attainder for felony the Barony was forfeited *for life*, though preserved for the heirs by the statute *De Donis*, as now interpreted (see Palmer's *Peerage Law in England*, 1909, p. 199) The peculiarity of this case is that he survived his attainder. V.G.

At the time Lord Santry's peerage was supposed to have been forfeited *absolutely*, and the same view was entertained in the case of Mervin (Tuchet), Earl of Castlehaven [I.] (see under that title), though, in both cases, the peerages being *in tail* would not have been forfeited by the heirs according to the now received opinion, and to the precedent afforded by the Stourton case (1557) and confirmed (1760) in that of Ferrers. In the former case Charles, Lord Stourton, was attainted for felony and hanged for murder, as also, in the latter case, was Earl Ferrers, but in neither was there any forfeiture by the heirs, and consequently no act of restoration. See *Courthope* in " Observations on Dignities, " p. lxviii.

the Great Seal, as to his life, and, in 1741, a regrant of his estates. He *m.*, 1stly, 8 May 1737, at Finglass, Anne, da. of William Thornton, of Finglass. She *d.* Mar 1742, at Nottingham. He *m*, 2ndly, 7 Nov 1750, at Flawford, Notts, Elizabeth Shore, spinster, of the parish of St. Nicholas, Nottingham (Ruddington Register). He *d. s.p*, 18, and was *bur.* 22 Mar. 1750/1, at St. Nicholas', Nottingham, (ª) when, in all probability, the *Peerage* became *extinct* (ᵇ) Will dat. 19 Mar 1749, pr. 14 Jan. 1750/1, Prerog Court [I.]. His widow *d.* 28 Dec. 1816, at Nottingham, aged 80.

BARRYMORE, see BARRY

BARTON COURT

See "Amesbury of Kintbury, Amesbury and Barton Court, Berks," Barony *(Dundas)*, *cr.* and *extinct* both in 1832.

BASING (ᶜ)

See "St John," Barony *(St. John)*, 1299; but sum from 1322 to 1325 as "St. John de Basing;" *in abeyance* 1347.

See "Pawlet de Basing," Barony *(St. John)*, *cr.* 1717, *extinct* 1754.

BASING OF BASING BYFLETE AND OF HODDINGTON

BARONY.   1. George Sclater-Booth (formerly Sclater), 1st s
I. 1887.   and h. of William Lutley Sclater, (ᵈ) of Hoddington House, Hants (*d* 15 Dec. 1885, aged 96), by Anna Maria, da. of William Bowyer, of the King's Remembrancer's office, was

---

(ª) The entry in the parish register is "The Hon. Henry Barry, Esq , formerly Lord Santry of the Kingdom of Ireland."

(ᵇ) By his will he devised his estates to his maternal uncle (of the half blood), Sir Compton Domvile, Bart. [I.].

(ᶜ) It is generally considered that the Barony of St. John, *cr.* in 1539, and held by the family of Paulet, was "St. John of Basing." Such, however, is not the case ; see that title.

(ᵈ) This William was 1st s. of the Rev. Bartholomew Lutley Sclater, Rector of Whitlington, Northumberland (*d* 1804), and grandson of Richard Sclater, Alderman of London, by his 2nd wife, Penelope, da. of Philip Lutley, of Bromcroft Castle, Salop The Alderman's 1st wife was Magdalen, da. and eventually h. of John Limbrey, of Tangier Park, and Hoddington House with Basing Byfleet, Hants, estates which were inherited by her children, both of whom, however, *d.* (1809-1814) unm , when the last named property passed to their nephew of the half blood, the said William Lutley Sclater.

b 19 May 1826, in London ; ed at Winchester (gold medal for Latin verse 1844), and at Balliol Coll Oxford ; B A and 2nd class classics, 1847 ; M A. 1850 , Barrister (Inner Temple) 1851 ; took the name of Sclater Booth in lieu of that of Sclater 30 Nov. 1857 (in compliance with the will of Anna Maria Booth) ; was M.P. for North Hants, 1857-85, and for the Basingstoke div of Hants, 1885-87 ; Parl. Sec. to the Poor Law Board, 1867-68 ; Financial Sec. to the Treasury, Feb. to Dec 1868 ; P C. 2 Mar. 1874 , Pres. of the Local Govt. Board, 1874-80 ; a Gov. of Winchester School , F.R.S. 20 Jan. 1876, Official Verderer of the New Forest, 1877. On 7 July 1887, he was *cr.* BARON BASING OF BASING BYFLETE AND OF HODDINGTON, both in co Southampton (ᵃ) He *m.*, 8 Dec. 1857, at Crondall, Hants, Lydia Caroline, only da. of Major George Birch, H.E.I.C S., of Clare Park in that co , by Lydia Diana, da of Samuel Francis Dashwood, of Stanford, Notts. She *d.* 5 July 1881, and was *bur.* at Upton Grey, Hants He *d* at Hoddington House afsd., 22 Oct. 1894, aged 68, and was *bur.* at Upton Grey. (ᵇ) Will pr. at £49,147 gross and £24,732 net personalty.

II. 1894   2. George Limbrey (Sclater-Booth), Baron Basing OF Basing Byflete and of Hoddington [1887], 1st s. and h. ; *b.* 1 Jan. 1860, in New Str., Spring Gardens, Whitehall ; ed. at Eton, and at Balliol Coll., Oxford ; B.A. 1862 ; sometime Capt. 1st Dragoons. He *m*, 12 Dec. 1889, at Maiden Earley, Berks, Mary, 2nd da. of John Hargreaves, of Maiden Earley afsd., and of Whalley Abbey, co. Lancaster, by Mary Jane, da. of Alexander Cobham Cobham, of Shinfield, Bucks.

[John Limbrey Robert Sclater-Booth, s and h , *b.* 1890.]

Family Estates.—These in 1833, were under 2,000 acres. *Principal Residence.*—Hoddington House, near Odiham, Hants.

(ᵃ) He was one of the 8 " Jubilee " Barons *cr.* that month.   For a list of these see note *sub* " Cheylesmore. "

(ᵇ) Lord Randolph Churchill speaks of him in, apparently unduly, disparaging fashion as " Mediocrity distinguished by a double-barrelled name. " He is elsewhere called " A painstaking useful man, but not of the sort to fill the House at the dinner hour. " (*Men and Manners in Parl.*, 1874.) V.G.

PEDIGREE
OF BARRY

face p 450

Philip
Olethan

William DE BARRY, *s. & *
of the grant of Olethan

David DE BARRY, *s. & h.*, was granted a
at his manor of Botavant 25 Sep. 1234.

I. David DE BARRY, 1st Lord
Justiciar of Ireland 1267;

II. John, *s. & h.*, 2nd Lord, surrendered Olethan
1284, and Muscry Donnegan 1285.

IV. John, *s. & h.*, 4th Lord. He appears to have alienated Obawn [Ibawne]
to his br. William *(moyle)*, ancestor of James Fitz Richard Barry, who
suc. as 4th Viscount. He *d. c.* 1330 ?

V. David, *br. & h.*, 5th
d. 12 May 1347.

VI. David, *s. & h.*, 6th Lord, a minor in 1347, *d.* 6 Sep. 1392.⊤.........

VII. John (*kittagh*), *s. & h.*, 7th Lord, *d. c.* 1420 ?=Ellice, da. of Gerald, Earl of Desmond.

VIII. William, *s. & h.* 8th Lord, *d. c.* 1480 ?=Ellen, da. of Lord Roche.

Richard   Davi

All had male desce
after 16

(1) (.........)⸗IX. John (*baccagh*) *s. & h.*, 9th Lord,⸗(2) Sheely, da. of Mac-
slain on Christmas Day 1486.   Cartie Reagh.

X. Thomas, *s. & h.* 10th Lord,
d.s.p. 1488.

XI. William, *br. & h.*,⸗Sheely, da. of Cormac MacTeig
11th Lord, slain | MacCartie, of Muskerry.
1500.

XIII. John (*rea*
13th Lor

XII. John,
s. & h.,
12th Lord,
slain, *c.*
1530.

XIV. John (*Bowieragh*), *s. & h.* 1st Viscount, *b.* 1517 or 1518, *d.s.p.*
1553. He *m.* (1) Ellen, da. of Lord
Roche ; (2) ...... da. of Gerald
Fitz Gerald of the Decies.

XV. Edmond, *br. & h.*, 2nd Viscount,
d.s.p., c. 1556. He *m.* (1) Joan,
da. of James, Earl of Desmond.
(2) Sheely, da. of Donal Mac-
Cartie Reagh.

(1) Ellis, da. of=XVI.
Maurice Fitz
Gerald of the
Shean. She *d.s.p.*

Richard, 1

BARRY

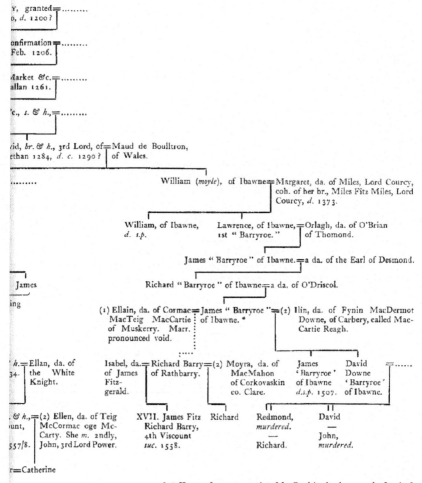

y, granted= ....
o, d. 1200?

onfirmation= ....
Feb. 1206.

Market &c.= ....
allan 1261.

'c., s. & h.,= ....

id, br. & h., 3rd Lord, of=Maud de Boulltron,
ethan 1284, d. c. 1290? of Wales.

....

William (moyle), of Ibawne=Margaret, da. of Miles, Lord Courcy,
coh. of her br., Miles Fitz Miles, Lord
Courcy, d. 1373.

William, of Ibawne,   Lawrence, of Ibawne,=Orlagh, da. of O'Brian
d. s.p.   1st "Barryroe."   of Thomond.

James   James "Barryroe" of Ibawne.=a da. of the Earl of Desmond.
ing

Richard "Barryroe" of Ibawne.=a da. of O'Driscol.

(1) Ellain, da. of Cormac=James "Barryroe"=(2) Ilin, da. of Fynin MacDermot
MacTeig MacCartie : of Ibawne. *   Downe, of Carbery, called Mac-
of Muskerry. Marr. :   Cartie Reagh.
pronounced void.   :

h.=Ellan, da. of   Isabel, da.=Richard Barry=(2) Moyra, da. of   James   David   = ...
34. the White   of James   of Rathbarry.   MacMahon   'Barryroe'   Downe
     Knight.   Fitz-   of Corkovaskin of Ibawne   'Barryroe'
                    gerald.   co. Clare.   d.s.p. 1507. of Ibawne.

. & h.,=(2) Ellen, da. of Teig   XVII. James Fitz   Richard   Redmond,   David
unt,   McCormac oge Mc-   Richard Barry,   murdered.   ——
        Carty. She m. 2ndly,   4th Viscount   ——   John,
557/8. John, 3rd Lord Power.   suc. 1558.   Richard.   murdered.

r=Catherine

* " He was first contracted to MacCartie's da. but m. the Lord of
Muskre's da. and had issue Richard; but repenting his error took
MacCartie's da. to wife and repudiated the other, reputing his
son Richard a bastard, being so censured by the spiritual Court."
(Carew MSS.)

APPENDICES

APPENDIX A [*]

SOME OBSERVATIONS ON EARLY
IRISH BARONIES

It was the Editor's original intention to give here a list of the Irish peerage before the 16th century, but he has deemed it advisable to postpone it to vol xi. This Appendix is therefore confined to some observations on the early Irish Baronies, (which may, and probably will, require to be supplemented when the work has proceeded further) and to transcripts of the Rankings of the Peers at various dates.

Fabulously early dates are often assigned to the early Irish Baronies. This apparently arises from the date of origin of the feudal barony being regarded as if it were that of the peerage.

All peerages in Ireland, except three Baronies, *cr.* by James II in 1689 [b] and those of which the origin is unknown, but which have become such by prescription, were created by charter or patent, the unreasonable theory of hereditary dignities being created by writ of summons to Parliament (as now held in England) being unknown there either before or after 1689. [c] Charters or patents of creation of Irish peerages before 1500 are, however, rare, there being, apparently, but eleven such documents known. Of these eleven, seven are Earldoms,

Ulster	Carrick	Kildare
Louth	Ormond	Desmond
	Waterford	

---

[*] The references to this Appendix in the following notes should be concelled as the matter referred to is dealt with in vol. xi, Appendix A

Notes "a" p. 24 , "b" p. 290 , "b" p 291 , "b" p 292 ; "c" p 292.

[b] These were Fitton of Gosworth, Nugent of Riverston, and Bourke of Bophin, all *cr.* when James II had been expelled from England but was still enjoying his Royal rights in Ireland.

[c] The decision of 19 Dec. 1767 whereby the Irish "Barony of La Poer" was allowed to the Dowager Countess of Tyrone [I.] "in fee by descent from her grandfather Richard, who sat and voted in Parliament as Baron La Poer till 28 Car. II" was clearly anomalous. See Preface to 1st edition, as reprinted in this volume, *ante*, p. xxviii, note "a."

One is a Viscountcy,

Gormanston 1478.

The other three are Baronies, (*)

Trimleston 1462   Portlester 1462   Ratowth 1468.

RANKING OF IRISH PEERS

The first Ranking of the Irish Peers was in 1489, in "the order of placing the Lords of Ireland in the procession of the Court of Greenwich where the King himself was." (See table of Rankings, *post*) Two Earls and eleven Barons were present, but of only two of these Barons, Trimleston and Gormanston, is the date of creation known, thus the order of placing is very important as showing the ranking of the other nine among themselves at that time. To these nine should be added the Barony of Fitzmaurice of Kerry (the owner of which was summoned in 1489 but did not attend); these ten may be called Baronies by Prescription acknowledged as Peerage Baronies in 1489. The holder of the Barony of Portlester was not summoned to Greenwich; the Barony of Ratowth became extinct about 1480.

While the ranking at Greenwich shows the precedency which the Barons there present were assigned at that date, it probably has little bearing on the actual antiquity of their Baronies. Reference to the rankings of later dates also suggests that precedence then depended solely on the importance possessed or assumed by the holders of the peerage dignities at the time of the ranking, having no basis in antiquity, and being uninfluenced by the precedence held on a former occasion.

DATE OF CREATION OF EARLY BARONIES

As has been pointed out in the body of this work, the ascription of dates of creation to the early baronies is in the nature of guess work. Although the principle obtaining in England may be deemed unhistoric and even absurd, it is convenient, because it provides a definite starting point, which in the case of Ireland is lacking in most of the early peerages; for, as we have seen, the patents of creation of only three Baronies and one Viscountcy are known to date before 1500, although as many as twelve Barons were summoned by Henry VII to Greenwich as early as 1489

In assigning the date at which the status of a peer may be held to have been acquired, the Editor has been guided mainly by historical evidence as to the public position and influence of the individual concerned. But it must be borne in mind that in the absence of proof as to the actual creation of a peerage dignity, the dating in this manner of an early Irish Barony is tentative only.

(*) Rathwire (1475) is included in *Lynch* (p. 189) among the peerage creations on the ground, apparently, of a grant of certain manors to "Thomas Daniell Knight, Lord and Baron of Rathwire." These seems no reason, however, to consider him as other than a feudal baron

The first Irish Viscountcy is that of Gormanston, created by patent 1478. In England there had been three earlier creations of a Viscount, *viz.*, Beaumont (1440), Bourghchier (1446), Lisle (1451), the fourth English Viscountcy, that of Berkeley (1481), being *cr.* only three years later than that of Gormanston.

A reference to the lists of Rankings will show that Gormanston, although created a Viscount in 1478, only ranked fifth among the Barons in 1489, being then described as "Lord Preston of Gormanston." In 1541 he was ranked second; in 1560, fifth; in 1585, third.

The anomalous position of Gormanston has prompted G D. Burtchaell to compare the extant Patents of creation of the earliest Viscountcies. The patent creating Viscount Bourghchier is not in existence. With regard to the others named above, the patent creating Gormanston proves to be almost identical with that creating Berkeley But while Beaumont and Lisle were specifically given precedency over "all barons," these words do not occur in the Gormanston Patent, which gives him "the Status of a Viscount of our land aforesaid [Ireland]"—the only status at that time being that of a sheriff. The Irish peers, therefore, seem to have considered that he was not given (or, at any rate, would not recognise him as having) precedence over barons, consequently his name was not put above them in the oldest lists extant. As to Berkeley, on the other hand, that being the fourth Viscountcy created in England, the status of Viscount in that country had already been definitely settled. As to the Viscountcies of Barry (or Buttevant) and Roche of Fermoy, it has been pointed out in the text under Barry that the Lords Barry were never styled Viscounts in any documents prior to 1541, and no evidence as to the *creation* of a Viscountcy at any time is forthcoming.

The Lords Roche of Fermoy appear to have been first styled Viscounts in the list of Ranking in 1584, and in their case also there is no known evidence of the *creation* of a Viscountcy. Indeed both of these seem to be cases of the audacious and successful assumption of a higher title, which could hardly have occurred anywhere but in Ireland. G.D. Burtchaell, who has investigated this question thoroughly, writes; "I am convinced that the titles of *Viscount* Buttevant and *Viscount* Fermoy were unknown before the reign of Henry VIII, and that such titles were never created; and that Lord Barry and Lord Roche managed to get themselves acknowledged as *Viscounts* with precedence before Gormanston, who was the first and only Viscount until Barry and Roche insisted on being treated as such."

RANKING OF

THE IRISH PEERS

face p. 460

RANKING OF T[

GREENWICH 1489 (ᵃ)

"Book of Howth," Carew MSS.

Earl of Kildare
Earl of Ormond
Lord Barre de Buttevant
Lord Roche de Fermoy
Lord Bermingham de Athenry
Lord Coursey de Kinsale
Lord Preston de Gormanston
Lord Nugent de Delvin
Lord Fleming de Slane
Lord Plunket de Killeen
Lord Saint Lawrence de Howth
Lord Barnewall de Trimleston
Lord Plunket de Dunsany

DUBLIN 1490

Lord Primates (Ussher) MSS., Copy in
Ulster's Office.

Dns. de Buttevant
Dns. de Fermoy
Dns. de Athenry
Dns. de Kinsale
nunc (interlined) Vic. de Gormanston
Baro de Delvin
Baro de Slane
Dns. de Killeen
Dns. de Howth
Dns. de Trimleston
Dns. de Dunsany

DUBLI[

State Papers, Lync[
p. [

Earl of Ormond an[
Earl of Desmond
Dns. Barry, Vic. E[
Vic. de Gormansto[
Vic. de Clontarf
Vic. de Baltinglas
Dns. de Kerry
Dns. Roche
Dns. Bermingham [
Baro de Slane
Baro de Delvin
Dns. de Killeen
Dns. de Dunsany
Dns. de Howth
Dns. de Trimlesto[
Dns. de Power
Baro de Dunboyne
Baro de Upper Oss[
Baro de Lowth
Baro de Carbery

(ᵃ) The Earl of Desmond and Lord Kerry
were also summoned, but did not attend.

41	Dublin Jan. 1560	Dublin April 15
dal Dignities,	Parliament Roll, Lynch's *Feudal Dignities,* P. 343.	Parliament Roll, Lynch's *Feudal* P. 347.
ory	Earl of Ormond and Ossory, Treasurer	Earl of Kildare
	Earl of Kildare	Earl of Ormond and Ossory
	Earl of Desmond	Earl of Tyrone
	Earl of Thomond	Earl of Clanrickard
	Earl of Clanrickard	Earl of Thomond
	Dns. de Buttevant	Earl of Clancare
	Dns. de Fermoy	Vic. Buttevant
	Dns. de Athenry	Vic. Fermoy
henry	Dns. de Kinsale	Vic. Gormanston
	Vicecomes de Gormanston	Vic. Montgarrett
	Vicecomes de Baltinglas	Lord Athenry
	Vicecomes de Montgarret	Lord Coursey
	Baro de Delvin	Lord Slane
	Baro de Slane	Lord Delvin
	Dns. de Killeen	Lord Killeen
	Dns. de Howth	Lord Howth
	Dns. de Trimlestown	Lord Dunsany
	Baro de Lacknsnawy, de Kerry	Lord Trimleston
	Dns. de Dunsany	Lord Dunboyne
	Dns. de Dunboyne	Lord Upper Ossory
	Dns. de Louth	Lord Lowth
	Dns. de Curraghmore	Lord Curraghmore
	Dns. de Upper Ossory	Lord Dungannan
		Lord Inchiquin
		Lord Burke of Conell
		Lord Cahir

APPENDIX B

THE DUKEDOM OF CHÂTELLERAULT

James Hamilton, who succeeded to the Marquessate of Abercorn in 1818 was styled DUKE OF CHÂTELLERAULT in France, inasmuch as " he was served h. male of the body of the 1st Duke of Châtellerault by the Sheriff of Chancery in Scotland, 13 Jan. 1862, and, as such h. male of the 1st Duke, asserts his hereditary right to the original title of Duke of Châtellerault of 1549. By the edict of Louis XIV, May 1711, the descent of French Dukedoms was declared " to be to heirs *descendus de mâles en mâles.* " (*)

" It has been doubted of late whether the title of *Duc de Châtellerault* ever existed as a *peerage dignity*, and it has even been argued by the late R. R. Stodart (in his paper on the Dukedom of Châtellerault in *Her. & Gen.*, vol. IV, pp. 97-107), that no creation of a Duchy took place, and that the object of the grant made by Henry II (5 Feb. 1548/9) to James, Earl of Arran, and his heirs was merely to secure a yearly revenue of 12,000 livres to the grantee. This opinion was fortified by the fact that the letters patent of Châtellerault differ from those by which, three years later, the Constable de Montmorency was created Duke ; Mr. Stodart concluded therefore that the title of Duke was never regularly conferred at all, and was only a title of courtesy given to Arran as Lord of the Duchy. But, (though in a later part of his paper he seems to be aware of it) Mr. Stodart has overlooked the fact that in France, *Dukes* were not necessarily *Peers.* It is quite clear that, in the sense of being a *duché-pairie*, the duchy created by Henry II for Arran was not " a peerage dignity ; " but that did not at all affect the fact that the Duchy was nevertheless an *hereditary* dignity. The difference in the letters patent, on which Mr. Stodart lays stress, is fully accounted for by the fact that Montmorency *was* created (while Arran was *not*) ' *Duc et pair* ; ' and it must be added that no further argument can be based upon the difference in the letters-patent, if it be remembered that Montmorency was the first French subject created ' Duc

---

(*) See *Burke's Peerage*, 1868-87.

et pair ' by letters patent ; (ᵃ) of this fact Mr. Stodart seems to be unaware.

It must be noted that by the treaty signed at Châtillon, 27 Jan. 1547, Henry II expressly engaged ' a conférer au Comte d'Arran *le titre de duc, avec duché en ce royaume de France de douze mille livres de rente, pour lui, ses hoirs et ayants cause, à perpétuité.*' The after proceeding shows clearly that this engagement was carried out to the letter by Henry. On 5 Feb. 1548 the act of cession of the duchy of Châtellerault received the sign manual. In the same month letters patent of investiture were delivered by the King at St Germain-en-Laye. In the month of July letters *de grand naturalité* were granted to the ' Comte d'Arran, duc de Châtellerault, pour lui et ses héritiers ;' and moreover the King divested himself and his successors of the ' droict d'aubeyne ' with regard to the duchy, in favour of the Duke, his heirs and successors. In 1550, the Bishop of Ross, as procurator for Arran, did homage for the Duchy, and the needful proceedings in fulfilment of the provisions of the treaty were thus completed. There is really no doubt whatever that a hereditary duchy was fully and legally created, and that it was not merely a rental of 12,000 *livres* which was secured to Arran and his heirs. The King thoroughly carried out the stipulation of the treaty, and we may be sure that no other arrangement would have satisfied the Earl. No doubt could have arisen on the subject had it been remembered of how very few persons the ' pairs de France ' consisted at this time, and that the two dignities of the *duché* and *pairie* were, and continued to be, distinct. Arran as a foreigner would care nothing for the special privileges of the *pairie* ; the Duchy of Châtellerault, with its hereditary title and its guaranteed revenue of 12,000 *livres*, would be all that he would value. The seizure of the Duchy in 1559, after Henry's death, by the ' parlement de Poitiers, ' did not destroy Arran's rights ; and in 1560, in the treaty between England, France, and Scotland, it was particularly stipulated that the Scottish *seigneurs, particulièrement le duc de Châtellerault rentreraient en possession et jouissance de toutes les terres, possessions, héritages, estats, et offices dont ils jouissaient en France avant le sixième Mars 1558, non obstant toutes saisies, dont par ce traité, Sa Majesté consentit par ses Ambassadeurs une pleine et entière mainlevée.* As a matter of fact the full restitution of the Duchy was hindered by various causes ; though money payments were made in partial satisfaction of the claim ; but the hereditary rights granted to Arran and his heirs in the Duchy, and therefore to the title of Duke of Châtellerault, were never legally annulled. It must be added that no argument can be drawn from the fact that the Earl of Arran was not always styled in documents ' Duc de Châtellerault ' by the French King, in the face of many others in which his full title was accorded to him. " (ᵇ)

The *tenure* of the Duchy ceased, as far as the Hamilton family are

---

(ᵃ) Artus de Gouffier had been created in 1519 *Duc et pair* de Rouanne, but died before investiture.

(ᵇ) G.E.C was indebted to the Rev. John Woodward, F.S.A., for these remarks on the Dukedom.

concerned, eleven years after its creation, though the pension thereby secured of 12,000 *livres* was continued to the heir of the grantee (which h was *h. male* as well as *h gen*) till the death of the 1st Duke of Hamilton [S], *s.p.m.*, in 1649, when (for two years) it was paid to his br., the 2nd Duke, who was *h. male* (but *not h. gen.*) of the grantee. Since his death in 1651 the French government appears to have recognised the claim of the *h. of line*, Anne, *suo jure*, Duchess of Hamilton [S.], by repeated grants (but apparently not by actual payment) of the said pension, and in 1714 arrangements were made for payment to the said Duchess Anne of 500,000 *livres* as an equivalent for her claims. The then Earl of Abercorn [S], however, protested, as *h. male*, against such recognition, and it was agreed that one-fourth of the sum so recovered should be paid over to him. The money, however, appears never to have been actually received

Although there appears to have been some recognition of the title of Duc de Châtellerault to the Hamilton family *previous* to 1649, *after* that date, when the h. male ceased to be the h. gen, there is none whatever. The rights of the *h. male*, however, were asserted by a protest of the then Earl of Abercorn [S], 14 July 1652, against the rights of the Duchess Anne, as *h. of line* to her father, which general protest hardly seems to apply to this special point. There is also a protest of the 6th Earl, 9 Sep. 1712, stating that, as the ambassadors at Utrecht were to obtain from the French King justice as to the restitution of the Duchy of Châtellerault, he himself reclaimed the said Duchy with all its privileges, and on the coffin plate of the 8th Earl, who *d.* 1789, he is styled " Duc de Châtellerault " On the other hand, the Dukes of Hamilton [S.], from 1651 to 1799, during which time they were the *heirs* of line to the grantee, never assumed or claimed such title. Since 1799, the family of Stanley, Earls of Derby (as descendants and representatives of the 6th Duke) have been such heirs ; but they also, never assumed nor claimed such title The family of La Trémoille, the *possessors* of the Duchy, however, long since adopted it, and made use of it in 1748, when the then Duc de la Trémoille styled himself *Duc de Châtellerault* in his protest as to his right to the Kingdom of Naples.

After the restoration of the French monarchy the 10th Duke of Hamilton advanced his claim to the Dukedom of Châtellerault, which was, however, opposed by the Abercorn line, the heirs male. In 1819, he assumed the title, and his wife was received at the French Court as a Duchess (which indeed she was), but probably only as a *foreign* lady of that rank. Charles X of France took advantage of the disputed succession to drop all recognition of the title. The 11th Duke of Hamilton [S] (s. of the 10th Duke) having *m.* a cousin of Napoleon III, renewed his claim. His rank and that of his wife was in 1855 settled in the French Court as being next to that of the Imperial family. Nothing, however, was said of the title of Duc de Châtellerault till (shortly after his death in July, 1863) the following paragraph relating to his s., the 12th Duke, appeared on 25 Aug. 1864, in the " Bulletin des Lois, " *viz.*, that the " Duc d'Hamilton a été maintenu et confirmé, par décret du 20 Avril 1864, dans le titre héréditaire de *Duc de Châtellerault*, crée par le Roi de

France, Henri II, en 1548, en faveur de Jacques Hamilton, Comte d'Arran." Such "confirmation," however, appears only to apply to a creation of 20 April 1864, for with respect to the creation of 1548/9, the opinion of W. B. D. Turnbull, in his "Factum touching the restitution of the Duchy of Chatelherault" (Edinburgh, 1843), is doubtless correct, viz., "that his Grace of Hamilton being neither heir male nor heir female [h. of line] has as much right to it as he has to the throne of China."

The decree of the Emperor was so far favourable to the Abercorn line (the heirs male), in that it acknowledged the creation of an hereditary French Dukedom which his predecessors had ignored; and, this being acknowledged, it would appear to follow that its descent would be (as set out in the decree of Louis XIV) to the h. male of the body of the grantee. Inasmuch, however, as the decree assigned the said title to the Duke of Hamilton [S.], the Marquess of Abercorn appealed against it in 1864-5. The "Conseil d'Etat aux Contentieux," nevertheless, decided against him, and found him "liable in expenses," which decision was "approved of" 11 Aug. 1866 by the Emperor. It is stated (see *The Times*, 22 Sep. 1866), that the appeal was not "rejected by the 'Council' on a question of right, but solely on the incompetence of the [said] 'Council' to reconsider or reverse the decree of the Emperor, who, in 1864, re-created that title in favour of his relative, without any consideration being given to the claims of the Marquis of Abercorn to the original title." See the able article on "The Dukedom of Châtellerault," by R. R. Stodart, already referred to, from which most of the above remarks are taken; see also *Requeste et Pièces pour Milord Comte d'Aran, touchant la restitution de Duché de Chastellerault et des autres choses comprises dans le don fait par le Roy Henry II, &c.*, 1685, 4to., pp. 26; also see *Mémoire Justificatif de droit qui appartient à M. Le Duc d'Hamilton de porter le titre de Duc de Châtellerault*, Paris, 8vo., pp. 64, where the argument of "A. Teulet, Archiviste aux Archives d'Empire," against the right of the h. of line in 1799, but in favour of the right of such h. in 1652 (which two points are necessary for his case), is rather amusing; see also (a much more able work) *Consultation pour James Hamilton, Marquis d'Abercorn, &c., contre le Duc d'Hamilton*, Paris, privately printed, 1865, 8vo., pp. 95, signed "E. Reverchon, Avocat à la Cour Impériale, &c."

APPENDIX C

PRECEDENCY OF PEERS IN PARLIAMENT
BY ROYAL PREROGATIVE

The prerogative of the Crown as to the precedence of Peers of the same grade *inter se*, has been frequently exercised, as in the case of SOMERSET (1397) by Richard II; of DORSET (1441), of EXETER, of WARWICK, of BUCKINGHAM, of DE LISLE, of RICHMOND, and of PEMBROKE, by Henry VI; of DACRE OF GILLESLAND by Edward IV, and of PEMBROKE (Marchioness) by Henry VIII. This precedency, however, as regards *place in Parliament* was disputed in the case of the patent of the Earldom of Banbury, in 1626, as being contrary to the Statute of Precedency of 31 Henry VIII, which regulates the order of certain great offices and which enacts "that all Dukes not afore mentioned, Marquesses, Earls, Viscounts and Barons not having any of the offices afsd., shall sit and be placed after their anciently as it hath been accustomed." As to the meaning of the above phrase, Sir Harris Nicolas remarks (in his "Observations on precedency in patents of Peerage") that "the purport of the clause appears to be that the former practise respecting the Precedency of Peers, excepting in the instances of those who held certain high offices, should remain as before the passing of the act." Anyhow, very shortly after that act (1) Edward Courtenay, a descendant, through the *female* line, of the old Earls of Devon, (*temp.* Stephen), was *cr.* (1553) EARL OF DEVON "to him and his heirs *male*" with a clause of precedency, *viz.* that he and his successors "were to enjoy *in Parliament*, as well as in all other places whatsoever, such place and *precedence* as any of the ancestors of the said Earl, heretofore Earls of Devon, had ever had or enjoyed." (2) In 1557, Thomas, Lord Percy (who had been so *cr.* in *tail male* the previous day, being s. and h. of the attainted Sir Thomas Percy, next br. and, in his issue, h. to Henry, Earl of Northumberland) was *cr* EARL OF NORTHUMBERLAND also in *tail male* with a spec. rem. of each peerage in favour of his yr. br. (such creation in no way amounting to a restitution), and with an especial clause granting the *ancient place* of the Earldom as it had been held by his ancestors, under which clause he sat in Parliament (as the second Earl of the realm) between the Earl of Arundel and the Earl of Westmorland (*Lords' Journals*, vol. 1, 533). (3) William

Parr, the attainted MARQUESS OF NORTHAMPTON, being restored in blood but not in honours was, on 13 Jan. 1559, again *cr.* by such title with the *precedency* of the former creation (1547), to which no objection was ever made by the Lords   (4) In 1603, the King having awarded the BARONY OF ABERGAVENNY to Edward Nevill (who was neither heir nor a coheir of any former Baron), the House assigned to him its old *precedency*, though, in this case without, apparently, a royal warrant to that effect; while, on the other hand, (5) without consulting Parliament, and simply *by royal warrant*, 31 March 1613, the EARL OF ABERCORN, a *Scottish* Earl, was authorised "to hold the place and PRECEDENCY OF AN EARL" in the *Parliament* of *Ireland*. (6) In 1618 the King granted to Charles (Howard), EARL OF NOTTINGHAM, a descendant (but not the representative nor even a coheir) of John (Mowbray,) Earl of Nottingham in 1377, the same "place and precedency as well *in Parliament* as in the Star chamber, &c.," as was possessed by his said ancestor, and "above all Earls of a later creation," in which precedency (of 1377) he sat for the remainder of his life.   Such then were the precedents which Charles I followed when (7) in 1626 the precedency of the previous year was granted to the EARLDOM OF BANBURY, a precedency which was, *after protest, acquiesced in* by the House of Lords *for the Earl's life*, and not for his heirs.   No such acquiescence, however, was given to (8) the precedency of the BARONY OF MONTJOY conferred, 5 June 1627, on Montjoy (Blount), Baron Montjoy in Ireland.   In this creation the clause of precedency was over all (they were but two) Barons *cr.* after the 20th day of May last past.   On complaints being preferred by these two Barons, (*viz.* by Lord Fauconberg, who had been *cr.* 25 May, and by Lord Lovelace, who was *cr.* 30 May in the same year), the point was referred to the Lords' Committee for Privileges, who reported 29 April 1628 that the Committee had considered thereof, and are of opinion, " That according to the statute 31 Henry VIII, and according to a former judgment of this House, in the like case of precedency (granted to the Earl of Banbury), that the said Baron Fauconberg and the said Baron Lovelace are to have place and precedence according to the ancienties and dates of their several patents before the said Baron Montjoy, whose patent of creation bears date afterward, notwithstanding the said clause in his patent to the contrary." See *Lords' Journals*, vol. iii, p. 174.   The natural result of this report was that Lord Montjoy was, on 3 Aug. following, raised to the rank of an Earl, as Earl of Newport.   Before, however, the date of the report of the Lords' Committee, the King (9) on 7 Apr. 1628 granted a patent to Henry (Percy), Earl of Northumberland and BARON PERCY (under the limitation of the creations of 1557 above mentioned, in which a spec. precedence had been granted to the *Earldom* but not to the *Barony*), "that he and his heirs male " should enjoy " the same seat, place and degree of Baron Percy as well *in Parliament* as elsewhere," as any the said Earl's ancestor.   Under this patent the Earl's son and h. ap., who had already been sum. in his father's Barony, sat in the old precedence (in lieu of that of 1557), and his claim to precede Lord Abergavenny came before the Lords' Committee in 1628-9. It is to be remembered that this Earl, though inheriting the Barony of

Percy under the spec. rem. of the creation of 1557 was *not* the heir gen.
nor even a coheir of the ancient Lords Percy. (10) On 12 Sep. 1640, Sir
William Howard and Mary his wife, sister and h. of Henry, Lord Stafford,
were *cr.* respectively BARON STAFFORD and BARONESS STAFFORD, with a
warrant of precedency "to possess such place and precedency of Baron of
Stafford as well *in Parliament, &c*, as Henry, late br. of the said Mary, in
his lifetime Baron of Stafford, ever held or enjoyed." Sir William took
his seat in the old Barony of Stafford, *cr.* 1298, which seems to have been
then under forfeiture. The question of his right to do so having been
referred to the Committee for Privileges, the King, to prevent controversy
(as in the similar case of Montjoy in 1627), raised him to a higher rank,
11 Nov. 1640, as Viscount Stafford. In Garter's list of Peeresses at the coronation of James II, this early precedence (1298) was allowed to his widow,
suo jure Baroness Stafford (her husband's Viscountcy and Barony being
under attainder), such list having been duly approved of by the King in
Council. When, however, in 1829, the attainder of her husband was
reversed and their h. gen. inherited his and her Barony, the place assigned
to it was according to the patent of creation (1640), the Lord Chancellor
Eldon stating that, having the case of Banbury in view, the clause of precedency was void.

The last case of a warrant of precedency of higher date than the
creation of the Peerage is one that does not involve any rank *in Parliament*,
being that of Alice Dudley, *cr.* 23 May 1644, DUCHESS DUDLEY for her life.
Her husband had been *cr* a Duke by Ferdinand II of Tuscany, by patent
dat. 9 March 1620 at Vienna, and her precedence was to date from the
time of such creation. The words in the grant are "out of our Prerogative
Royal which we will not have drawn into dispute."

So late, however, as February 1645/6 (as has been pointed out to the
Editor by J. H. Round), the Crown *endeavoured* to follow the Abergavenny
precedent by diverting the descent of the Barony of Windsor (a barony in
fee), *with its ancient precedence*, in favour of the heirs *male* of the body of a
coheir, though the endeavour was abandoned. (See *Studies in Peerage and
Family History*, pp. 360-361). The same informant mentions the similar
attempt previously made by the Crown in the Patent granted to Sir
Conyers Darcy in 1641 which made him Baron Darcy, with the *precedence*
of Henry IV's reign, and with a limitation of the Barony to the heirs *male*
of his body. The House, however, appears to have ignored this grant.

APPENDIX D

PRECEDENCY ANOMALOUSLY ALLOWED

The precedency due to certain Baronies of ancient creation has been allowed in the following cases to the person sum. therein, though such person has not been the h. gen. or even a coheir of the Barony, and would not, according to the now accepted notion, have been entitled to such precedence   There is some ground for supposing that to certain ancient Baronies (say those before *temp.* Henry VI.) certain seats in the House of Lords were formerly assigned, and that to such seats the persons sum. in the name of such Baronies (whether entitled thereto by descent or otherwise), were deemed to be entitled.

(1) In 1421 James Berkeley, h. male (but *not* h. gen.) of Thomas, LORD BERKELEY (sum. by writ 1295) was himself sum. by writ as a Baron, and he (probably) was, and his heirs (certainly) were, allowed the *precedency* of the old Barony, in which his grandson Thomas sat (1529-33), though, as the latter was not in possession of the Castle or estate of Berkeley, the precedence could not (in his case, at all events) be due to a Barony by tenure.

(2) In 1533/4 Henry Pole was sum. by writ as LORD MONTAGU, and sat in the *precedency* of the Barony of that name (under a sum. by writ 1299), though his *mother*, through whom his claim was derived, was *then living.*

(3) In 1558 Henry (Stafford), LORD STAFFORD, (who having been declared BARON STAFFORD, with rem. to the heirs *male* of his body by Act of Parliament 1547 had taken his seat as junior Baron in 1548) claimed and was allowed the *precedency* of the BARONY OF STAFFORD (under a sum. by writ 1298), which, so far from being vested in him, was then actually under *forfeiture*

(4) In 1571 (on 4 April) Thomas Paget was sum. by writ in a Barony of that name, cr. by writ 1549, and was ranked accordingly. If the date of death of Elizabeth, da. and h. of the last Baron (*viz.* 29 June 1571) be correct, he would not have been so entitled till two months later, *viz.*, after her death, *s.p.*

(5) In 1597, Thomas (West) LORD DE LA WARR, whose father had sat as junior Baron under a creation of 1570, was allowed the *precedency* of the

ancient Barony of De la Warr (*cr.* by writ), of which he was not, apparently, h. gen.

(6) In 1604 Edward Nevill, a descendant, but neither h. nor coheir of William (Beauchamp), LORD BERGAVENNY (who was sum by writ 1392), was himself sum. by writ as LORD BERGAVENNY and allowed the precedency of the older lords, that is to say, a much higher precedency than that of 1392, the earliest to which he would have been entitled had the Barony been treated as a Barony by writ *E g., temp.* Henry VIII Bergavenny was ranked above Zouche (1308), Willoughby (1313), de la Warr, Dacre, Ferrers, &c. (See J. H Round's *Peerage and Pedigree*).

In the cases subsequent to this date the writs were issued by inadvertence, *viz.* :—

(7) On 7 Feb. 1627/8 Henry Clifford, s. and h. ap. of the EARL OF CUMBERLAND, being sum. by writ as LORD CLIFFORD (under the erroneous impression that that ancient Barony was vested in his father), sat in the *precedency* of the BARONY OF CLIFFORD, under a sum by writ 1299. In 1691 the claim of the h. gen to the old Barony of 1299 was allowed, and in 1737 the claim of the h. gen. to the Barony of 1627/8 was also allowed, but *not* (of course) *the ancient precedency* of 1299, this latter Barony being ranked as one *cr.* by the writ of 1627/8, *de novo*, notwithstanding the high precedency which had formerly (though erroneously) been assigned to it.

(8) On 7 Mar. 1627/8, (a few weeks later) James Stanley, s. and h. ap. of the EARL OF DERBY, was sum. by writ as LORD STRANGE (under a like erroneous impression), and sat in the *precedency* of the BARONY OF STRANGE, *cr.* by writ 1299 In 1736/7 the claim of the h. gen to the Barony *cr.* by the writ of summons of 1627/8 was allowed, but *not the precedency* of the old Barony of 1299, which last was then, as now, in abeyance, the Lord Strange (in 1754) taking his place, as a Baron of 1627/8, next immediately below Lord Maynard.

(9) In 1722 Algernon Seymour (*styled* Earl of Hertford), s. and h. ap. of the DUKE OF SOMERSET was sum. by writ as Lord Percy (under a like erroneous impression that that ancient Barony had become vested in him on the decease of his mother), and sat in the *precedency* of the BARONY OF PERCY, *cr.* by writ 1299. This precedency was also allowed to his grandson and h. in 1777, and again to his great-grandson in 1817. There can, however, be no question that the old Barony of 1299, though under attainder, is in abeyance between the descendants of the daughters and coheirs of the 5th Earl of Northumberland, who *d* 1572, and that the precedency, allowed in 1722 and subsequently, was probably (like the issue of the writ) in ignorance of the real facts of the case.

Note.—To the BARONY OF PERCY, *cr.* in *tail male* 1557, the ancient precedency (*i.e.*, that of 1299) "in Parliament as elsewhere" was granted by Charles I, by patent 2 Apr. 1628. In virtue of this grant, Algernon Percy (s. and h. ap. of the EARL OF NORTHUMBERLAND), who sat in his father's Barony, 1626 to 1632, as BARON PERCY, was after (though not before) 1628 rightly placed in the *precedency* of 1299. This barony, however, and *the precedency* of 1299 (so granted thereto in 1628), became *extinct* in 1670

The following errors have also occurred in writs of summons, but in no way affect the question of *precedency* :—

In 1717 Charles Pawlet (*styled* Marquess of Winchester), s. and h. ap. of the Duke of Bolton, was sum. as a Baron, by writ directed " Carolo Pawlet de Basing, &c., " and sat as Lord Pawlet of Basing. This was under the erroneous impression that this Barony was vested in his father, whereas the name of his father's Barony was St John of Basing It was held to be a writ of fresh creation, and he was placed as the lowest Baron and thereby obtained a Barony in fee On his death, however, *s.p* , in 1754, this Barony become *extinct.*

In 1833 Francis Russell (*styled* Marquess of Tavistock), s. and h. ap. of the Duke of Bedford, was sum. as a Baron, by writ erroneously directed to " Francis Russell of Streatham, co. Surrey, chevalier. " The Barony, which was vested in his father, was that of Howland [not Russell] of Streatham, co. Surrey, *cr.* 1695. In this case, however, it having been declared from the chair that his Lordship's summons was "in his father's Barony, " in that Barony (*i.e.,* " Howland, " *cr.* 1695) the Marquess was placed, and consequently no new Barony in fee was created.

Judging from these cases (more especially from those of Strange and Clifford), it would appear that, in spite of a wrongful placing in the House, a writ of summons to a person *not* being an heir or coheir to the Barony in which he is sum. creates a Barony *de novo* and one of no higher date than the writ.

APPENDIX E

1715

By the Rising of 1715 no less than 19 Scottish Peerages, together with the Earldom of DERWENTWATER, the Barony of WIDDRINGTON, and the Dukedom of ORMOND in England (which last, however, was held with the Barony of Dingwall [S.], and so is included among the 19 Scotish Peerages abovenamed) were *forfeited* by attainder. This, however, in ten cases (those marked *) was reversed by acts of Parl. in 1824, 1826, and subsequently, while in one case, that of Sinclair, it came to an end. This list [S.] is (alphabetically arranged) as under :—

* * AIRLIE *(Ogilvie)*, Earldom ; after death [1717] of the then [1715] Earl. *Restored* 26 May 1826.
* * BALFOUR OF BURLEIGH *(Balfour)*, Barony   *Restored* 19 March 1869.
* * CARNWATH *(Dalzell)*, Earldom.   *Restored (nominatim)* 26 May 1826
* * DINGWALL *(Butler)*, Barony, held, in 1715, with the Dukedom of Ormond [E.] *Restored* 31 July 1871.
* * DUFFUS *(Sutherland)*, Barony.   *Restored (nominatim)* 26 May 1826; *dormant* or *extinct* 30 Jan. 1827
* * KENMURE *(Gordon)*, Viscountcy.   *Restored (nominatim)* 17 June 1824 , *dormant* or *extinct* 1 Sept. 1847.
* KILSYTH *(Livingston)*, Viscountcy.   The Grantee's heirs male of the body, *extinct* 12 Jan. 1733
* KINGSTON *(Seton)*, Viscountcy ; *extinct* about 1726.
* LINLITHGOW and CALENDAR *(Livingston)*, Earldom.   The Grantee's heirs male of the body, *extinct* 25 April 1723.
* * MAR *(Erskine)*, Earldom.   *Restored (nominatim)* 17 June 1824, and, again, 6 Aug. 1885.
* MARISCHAL *(Keith)*, Earldom.   The Grantee's heirs male of the body existed down to 1833, and possibly later.

* NAIRNE *(Nairne)*, Barony. *Restored (nominatim)* 17 June 1824.

NITHSDALE *(Maxwell)*, Earldom. *The attainder reversed* 9 June 1848, as far as relates to the issue of the forfeited Earl, whereby the Barony of HERRIES OF TERREGLES, held therewith in 1715, was *restored* to the heir general.

PANMURE *(Maule)*, Earldom. The Grantee's heirs male of the body, *extinct* 4 Jan. 1782.

* PERTH *(Drummond)*, Earldom ; after death [1716] of the then [1715] Earl. *Restored* 28 June 1853.

SEAFORTH *(Mackenzie)*, Earldom. The Grantee's heirs male of the body, *extinct* 11 Jan. 1815.

SINCLAIR *(Sinclair)*, Barony. The effect of the attainder came to an end 30 Nov. 1762, and the Peerage was allowed accordingly.

* SOUTHESK *(Carnegie)*, Earldom. *Restored* 2 July 1855.

WINTOUN *(Seton)*, Earldom. The Earl *d. s p.* 19 Dec. 1749.

The holders of five of these peerages—Carnwath, Kenmure, Nairne, Nithsdale and Wintoun, together with the English Lords, Derwentwater and Widdrington, were condemned to death. Derwentwater and Kenmure were beheaded 24 Feb 1715/6, Nithsdale having effected his escape the previous day. Carnwath, Nairne, and Widdrington were respited till preserved by the act of indemnity, while Wintoun, on 4 Aug. 1716, also effected his escape. "A large breadth of land was forfeited by special statutes passed for attainting the Lords Mar, Tullibardine [s. and h. ap. of the Duke of Atholl], Linlithgow, Drummond [s. and h. ap. of the Earl of Perth], Marischal, Southesk, Seaforth, and Panmure." "The epoch of a change of dynasty is not an appropriate time for a sanguinary retaliation," and "there was a palliation on this occasion which did not attend the subsequent rebellion of 1745." The celebrated Duncan Forbes, Lord Advocate [S], truly "predicted that excessive penalties and forfeitures following the first outbreak against the Hanover succession would infallibly lay the foundation of another." See J. H. Burton's *Scotland*, under 1716-18.

1745

By the Rising of 1745, seven Scottish Peerages were *forfeited* by attainder. This act, however, in three cases (those marked *) was reversed by acts of Parl. in 1824, 1826 and 1854 The list is as under :—

BALMERINOCH and COUPAR *(Elphinstone)*, Barony. The grantee's heirs male of the body, *extinct* 18 Aug. 1746.

CROMARTY *(Mackenzie)*, Earldom. The grantee's heirs male of the body, *extinct* 4 Nov. 1796.

FORBES OF PITSLIGO *(Forbes)*, Barony. The grantee's heirs male of the body, *extinct* 30 Aug. 1781.

KILMARNOCK *(Boyd)*, Earldom. The heir male of the body of the attainted Earl is the Earl of Erroll [S].

* LOVAT *(Fraser)*, Barony [*forfeited* 19 March 1746/7] *Restored* 10 *July* 1854.

[Pitsligo, see Forbes of Pitsligo].

* STRATHALLAN *(Drummond)*, Viscountcy. *Restored* 17 June 1824.
* WEMYSS *(Wemyss)*, Earldom, *forfeited* after the death [1756] of the then (1745) Earl. *Restored* 26 May 1826.

In the act of 19 Geo. II., there were also included ;

Alexander (Erskine) EARL OF KELLIE, who having surrendered before 12 July 1746 (before the attainder took effect), was pardoned.

" James DRUMMOND, Esq.," 1st s. and h. ap. of William, VISCOUNT OF STRATHALLAN.

" Simon FRASER, Esq., " 1st s. and h. ap. of Simon, LORD LOVAT.

" James DRUMMOND, taking upon himself the title of DUKE OF PERTH " [*i e.* James then *styled* Lord Drummond, *attainted* by act 1 Geo I , s. and h ap. of the Earl of Perth, to whose dignities he was accordingly barred from succeeding].

" James GRAHAM, late of Duntroon, taking upon himself the title of VISCOUNT OF DUNDEE " [*i.e.*, the collateral heir male of that Viscountcy, *cr.* 1688 ; *forfeited* 1690]

" John NAIRN taking upon himself the title or style of LORD NAIRN" [*i.e.*, John, s. and h of William, Lord Nairne, who was *attainted* by act, 1 Geo. I.].

" David OGILVIE taking upon himself the title of LORD OGILVIE " [*i e* , David, s. and h. ap. of John, who, but for the attainder of his brother, by act, 1 Geo. I , would have been from 1731 to 1761, Earl of Airlie. He himself, but for such attainder, would have been, in 1761, EARL OF AIRLIE]

The list also contains the following persons connected with the Scottish nobility, *viz* , LORD GEORGE MURRAY (br. to the Duke of Atholl), LORD LEWIS GORDON (br. to the Duke of Gordon), "John Drummond taking upon himself the style or title of LORD JOHN DRUMMOND, br. to James, taking on himself the title of Duke of Perth, " five of the clan of Macdonald, four of that of Cameron, &c.

The holders of four of these seven Peerages were condemned to death, of whom Balmerinoch and Kilmarnock were (accordingly) beheaded on 18 August 1746, Lovat on 9 April 1747, while Cromarty was subsequently pardoned. " A list of Persons attainted after the '45, " is in *The Scottish Antiquary*, (Ed. by A. W. G. Hallen, F.S A) for Sep. 1890, vol. v, pp. 49—53

RESTORATIONS

The following is a return, pursuant to an order of the House of Lords, dat 15 June 1885, of " All Acts of Parl. passed during the last 200 years by which a *Peerage* has been *restored to the person entitled to hold the same :*"—

1. 1742/3 March 21. Dignity and title of EARL OF DONCASTER and of BARON SCOTT OF TINDAL restored to Francis (SCOTT), Duke of Buccleuch [S.].

2 1824 June 17. Ditto of EARL OF MAR [S] to " John Francis ERSKINE of Mar. "

3. „   „   „   „   „ VISCOUNT KENMURE [S.] to " John GORDON, Esq., of Kenmure. "

4. „   „   „   „   „ VISCOUNT STRATHALLAN [S.] to " James DRUMMOND, Esq "

5. „   „   „   „   „ LORD NAIRN [S.] to "William NAIRNE, Esq. "

6. 1826 May 26.   „   „ BARON DUFFUS [S.] to " James SUTHERLAND, Esq. "

7. „   „   „   „   „ EARL OF CARNWATH [S.] to " Major-Gen. Robert Alexander DALZELL. "

To which may now be added

8. 1885 August 6. "An act for restitution of the ancient dignity and title of EARL OF MAR " [S.] to John Francis Erskine GOODEVE-ERSKINE.

With the exception of the first one in this list, all these restorations were of peerages forfeited in connexion with the Risings of 1715 and 1745.

It should be observed that the restoration of 1742/3 applied only to the Duke of Buccleuch [S.] and the heirs male of his body, whereas all the other restorations are to the persons entitled to succeed the restored person in the specified dignities   This partial restoration, whereby the inferior dignities held by the attainted Duke of Monmouth were restored, excluding the Dukedom, is probably accounted for by the Earldom of Monmouth, *cr.* in 1689, being still in existence in the family of Mordaunt. Had it been extinct, no doubt the interest that prevailed for the restoration of the Earldom belonging to this cowardly and self-seeking traitor would have prevailed as to the restoration of his Dukedom, which, had it been restored, would now (1910) rank as the 3rd English Dukedom.   A somewhat similar partial restoration of honours was that in 1858 of those of the Earl of Nithsdale [S], attainted in 1715, whose attainder as far as concerned the Barony of Herries of Terregles [S] was reversed, whereby the heir general became entitled to the Barony, whilst the Earldom, which was to heirs male, was still left under attainder.

As to the 7 Peerages restored from 1685 to 1885 in the above table, those only are included which were so restored *nominatim*, but many were restored indirectly, as

The EARLDOM of WEMYSS [S. 1633] and the Barony of Wemyss of Elcho [S. 1628] were so restored by an Act dated 26 May 1826 "to restore Francis, Baron Wemyss and others from the effects of the attainder of David Wemyss, commonly called Lord Elcho. "

The EARLDOM OF AIRLIE [S. 1639], the Barony of Ogilvy of Airlie [S. 1491], and the Barony of Ogilvy of Alith and Lintrathen [S 1639], were restored by an Act of like date " to restore David Ogilvy Esq., and others from the effects of the attainder of James, eldest son of David, Earl of Airlie, and of David Ogilvy taking upon himself the title of Lord Ogilvy."

The EARLDOM OF PERTH [S] was restored in 1853 ; the EARLDOM OF SOUTHESK [S] in 1855; the BARONY OF LOVAT [S.] in 1857; the BARONY OF HERRIES [S.] in 1858 ; the BARONY OF BALFOUR [S.] in 1869 ; the BARONY OF DINGWALL [S.] in 1871.

APPENDIX F

JACOBITE PEERAGES

James II was declared, by the English Parliament (6 Feb 1688/9), to have abdicated the throne on 11 Dec. 1688.

In *Scotland* no similar declaration was made till 4 Apr. 1689, but only one Scottish peerage, and that only for life, was *cr* by James II between 11 Dec. 1688 and that date. He however *cr*. 6 Irish Peers, when in Ireland, during a time when the government was carried on *solely* in his name (which was the case till the landing of Gen. Schomberg in Ulster in Aug. 1689), and when he was at all events the *de facto* King of *Ireland*.

The acts of a King in possession have, as a rule, been recognised by his successor . *e.g.*, the Peerages *cr* by Henry VI were acknowledged by Edward IV ; those *cr* by Richard III were acknowledged by Henry VII; though in both these cases (unlike the case of 1689) the preceding monarch was considered as an usurper by his successor

There remains indeed the *constitutional question*, whether Ireland, being " a dependent, subordinate kingdom," and " inseparably united " to the Crown of England (see Blackstone, i, 99-104, and Coke, *Inst*, iv, 349, *&c*), an " Abdication " in England would not override all kingly rights in Ireland, and the soundest legal opinion would, in all probability, be that it does so. By an Irish Statute, 33 Henry VIII, it is enacted that the King of England is *ipso facto* King of Ireland. The statutes relating to the Crown were not re-enacted in Ireland after the Revolution.

Such Irish Peerages, however, as were *cr* by James II in 1689—at a time when he was in full possession of all his Regal Rights as King of Ireland, all of which creations, moreover, were duly enrolled on the Patent Rolls of that Kingdom, from which they have never been erased—stand in a very different category from other Peerages *cr* by that King after his (so called) " abdication " of the throne of England on 11 Dec. 1688. By a singular coincidence, however, nearly all these Irish Peerages, at no long time after their creation, became either *extinct* or *merged*. ' In 1839, in the case of " Nugent of Riverston " (the only one then existing *per se*), the dignity was claimed but no decision was pronounced thereupon ; and in 1871 this peerage also (assuming its existence) *merged* into the Earldom of Westmeath [I].

IRISH PEERAGES

CREATED BY JAMES II IN 1689

(while he was *de facto* King of Ireland) are as follows,—being (besides the minor incidental creations) one Dukedom, three Viscountcies, and three Baronies :—

1689. Mar. 30, Warrant, 25 Mar. Richard (Talbot), Earl of Tyrconnell [I], *cr.* MARQUESS AND DUKE OF TYRCONNELL [I.]. *Attainted,* 1691. He *d. s p.m* , 14 Aug. 1691.

1689. Apr. 2, Warrant same day. John Bourke, *cr.* BARON BOURKE OF BOPHIN, co Galway [I.]. In 1705 any Peerage so *cr.* became *merged* in the Earldom of Clanricarde [I.]

1689. Apr. 3, Warrant same day Thomas Nugent, *cr.* BARON NUGENT OF RIVERSTON, co Westmeath [I]. In 1871 any Peerage so *cr.* became *merged* in the Earldom of Westmeath [I.].

1689. Apr. 20, Warrant same day. Sir Valentine Browne, Bart. [I.], *cr.* BARON CASTLEROSSE AND VISCOUNT KENMARE [I] *Attainted* 1690. On 14 Feb. 1798, his great-grandson and h. male (the attainder never having been reversed) was *cr.* a Peer by the same titles, and subsequently (2 Jan. 1801) was *cr.* EARL OF KENMARE [I.].

1689. May 1, Warrant same day. Sir Alexander Fitton, Lord Chancellor [I.], *cr.* BARON FITTON OF GOSWORTH, co. Limerick [I.].   He *d s p.m.* about Nov. 1699.

1689. May 23, Warrant May. Lieut. Gen. Justin McCarty, *cr.* BARON CASTLEINCH AND VISCOUNT MOUNTCASHELL, both in co. Tipperary [I.]. He *d. s p.* July 1694.

1689 Aug. 23. Edward Cheevers, *cr* BARON BANNOW, co. Wexford, AND VISCOUNT MOUNT-LEINSTER, co. Carlow [I.].   He *d. s.p.* 1693.

PEERAGES CREATED

BY JAMES II AFTER 11 DEC. 1688

Other than the seven Irish Peerages mentioned above.

As far as these can be ascertained they are, in chronological order, as under :—

1688/9. Jan. 3/13. Donna Victoria Montecuculi Davia, *c†.* COUNTESS OF ALMOND [S.] for life.

1688/9. Jan. 21 Richard (Graham), Viscount Preston [S.], *cr.* BARON OF LIDDAL, Cumberland, and VISCOUNT PRESTON in Amounderness, co Lancaster, with a spec. rem. On 9 Nov. 1689, he claimed his privilege

as an English peer, in right hereof, but the creation was disallowed.(ᵃ)
Attainted 1690. His issue male *extinct* 1739.

1689 (before 1 June). William (Herbert), Marquess of Powis, *cr.* MARQUESS OF MONTGOMERY and DUKE OF POWIS. *Attainted* 1690. K.G. by James II 1692 His issue male *extinct* 1748

1689. July 9, Warrant same day. Henry (Jermyn), Lord Dover, *cr.* LORD JERMYN OF RAYSTOWNE, [*i.e.* Royston], BARON OF IPSWICH, VISCOUNT CHEVELEY, Suffolk, and EARL OF DOVER. He *d. s p.,* 1708.

1689. Aug. 7. John (Drummond), Earl of Melfort [S.], *cr.* BARON OF CLEWORTH [*i.e* CLEWER], BERKS, with like *spec rem* as that with which that Scottish Earldom had been conferred. (ᵇ) See " Melfort," Dukedom of, *cr.* 1692, by James II, as below.

1689 or 1690? [——]. Dominick Roche, Alderman of Limerick, *cr.* BARON TARBERT and VISCOUNT CAHIRAVAHILLA [I.]. (ᶜ)

1690/1. Jan. [—]. Patrick Sarsfield (the celebrated Irish General), *cr.* BARON ROSBERRY, VISCOUNT OF TULLY, and EARL OF LUCAN, co. Dublin [I], by a patent brought over from St. Germain to Ireland by the Lord Deputy Tyrconnell [I.]. His only son *d. s.p.*

1692 ? [——] Piers (Butler), Viscount Galmoye [I.], *cr.* EARL OF NEWCASTLE [I]. *Attainted* 1697. His issue male *extinct* 1740.

1692. Apr 17, Warrant same day. John (Drummond), Earl of Melfort [S.], *cr.* DUKE OF MELFORT, as also " MARQUIS OF FORTH, EARL OF ISLA AND BURNTIZLAND, VISCOUNT OF RIKERTON, LORD CASTLEMAINS AND GALSTON " [S], (ᵈ) with the like *spec. rem.* as his former honours. *Attainted* 1695. [His heir was *restored* 28 June 1853]

1692. May. 3. Sir Edward Hales, of Woodchurch, Kent, Bart. ; *cr.* EARL OF TENTERDEN, VISCOUNT TUNSTALL AND BARON HALES OF EMLEY, Kent, 3 May 1692, with a *spec. rem* His issue male *extinct* 1829.

1691 ? Sir Edward Herbert, sometime (1685-87) Lord Chief Justice of the Court of King's Bench, was appointed by James II, when in exile, his Lord Chancellor, and *cr.* EARL OF PORTLAND. He *d. s p.* Nov. 1698.

1691 ? [——]. Kenneth (Mackenzie), Earl of Seaforth [S.], *cr.* Earl, Viscount, or Baron, FORTROSE and MARQUESS OF SEAFORTH [S.]. *Attainted* 1716. His issue male *extinct* 1815.

1696, Warrant, 13 Jan. 1695/6. Henry Fitz James, *cr.* BARON OF ROMNEY, EARL OF ROCHFORD, and DUKE OF ALBEMARLE [E.]. He *d. s.p.* 1702.

(ᵃ) It has been pointed out to the Editor by J H. Round that, as William and Mary were not offered the Crown and proclaimed Sovereigns till 13 Feb 1688/9, this (and the preceding) creation took place during an interregnum, a point which was raised at the time. V.G.

(ᵇ) See *Riddell,* pp 963-965

(ᶜ) See Ferrar's *History of Limerick*

(ᵈ) See *Riddell,* pp. 963-965. On 28 June 1853, the h. male of his body, George Drummond, Duc de Melfort in France, was *restored* in blood, and consequently became entitled to the Earldoms of Perth and Melfort [S] , inasmuch as his ancestor, the 1st Earl of Melfort (*cr.* Duke by James II in 1689 as above) was 2nd s. of the 3rd Earl of Perth, and next br to the 4th Earl (*cr.* Duke of Perth by the *titular* James III) whose issue male had failed in 1760.

1698. Apr. 12. Virgilio Davia, Senator of Bologna, *cr.* BARON DAVIA, VISCOUNT MONEYDIE and EARL OF ALMOND [S]

[——] . . . Purcell, said to have been *cr.* BARON LOUGHMORE [I.] but query ? Nicholas Purcell, Lord of the Barony of Lougmow, co. Tipperary, was Col of a Regiment of Horse in James II's army [I.] 1689. Many of that name "followed the fortunes of James the Second to the Continent." (*)

[——] . . . De Cantillon, said to have been *cr.* BARON BALLYHIGUE [I.], but query if not a French creation ? (b)

[——] Humphrey Borlase of Treludro, Cornwall, is said to have been *cr.* by James II after his dethronement LORD BORLASE OF BORLASE, and BARON OF MITCHELL, Cornwall. He *d. s.p.s.* 1709

[——] Walter Pye is said to have been *cr.* BARON KILPEE [E.].

The abovenamed creations of James II (after 11 Dec. 1688), if arranged according to the highest dignity conferred (omitting the incidental titles), amount to 4 Dukedoms, *viz.*—Tyrconnell [I.], Powis [E], Melfort [S.], and Albemarle [E]; one Marquessate, *viz.*—Seaforth [S.]; 7 Earldoms, *viz*—Almond [S.] for life, Dover [E.], Newcastle [I.], Lucan [I.], Tenterden [E.], Portland [E], and Almond [S.]; 5 Viscountcies, *viz:*—Kenmare [I.], Mountcashell [I.], Mount Leinster [I], Preston [S.], and Cahiravahilla [I]; and 5, or possibly 9 Baronies, *viz:*—Fitton [I.], Bourke of Bophin [I], Nugent of Riverston [I.], Liddal [E.], Cleworth [E.], and (Qy.) Loughmore [I.], Ballyhigue [I.], Borlase [E.], and Kilpee [E.]. In all 21 or 25 creations, of which 6 (Tyrconnell, Powis, Jermyn, Galmoy, Melfort, and Seaforth) were already Peers of the Kingdom in which they were thus granted a dignity of a higher grade.

PEERAGES CREATED

BY JAMES FRANCIS EDWARD STUART *titular* "JAMES III" 1701-66

Note.—The list is arranged according to the rank of the Peerage conferred. It is to be observed that there are some *Scottish* creations among them *after* 1707, inasmuch as the Union with Scotland was not recognised by the exiled House of Stuart

DUKES

1701. James (Drummond), Earl of Perth [S.], *cr.* 22 Oct. 1716 BARON

(*) See *King James' Irish Army List,* 1689, by J. D'Alton, 1st Edit, pp 239-245.
(b) The arms of "Cantillon de Ballyhigue" are blazoned in H. Gourdon de Genouillac, *Recueil d'Armoires des Maisons Nobles de France,* Paris, 1860, 8vo. "The Chevalier Antoine Sylvain de Cantillon, Baron de Ballyheige *in France*" is mentioned in Sir B. Burke's *Gen Armory,* 1878. J H. Round suggests that the grantee may have been Sir Richard Cantillon, of the court of James III. V.G.

CONCRAIG, VISCOUNT CARGILL, EARL OF STOBHALL, MARQUESS OF DRUMMOND and DUKE OF PERTH [S.]. His s and h. ap. was *attainted, v.p.*, in 1715. Issue male of the grantee *extinct* 1760.

1715 John (Erskine), Earl of Mar, [S.], *cr.* LORD OF ALLOA, FERRITON, and FORREST, VISCOUNT GARIOCH, EARL OF KILDRUMMIE, MARQUESS ERSKINE, and DUKE OF MAR. [S.]. *Attainted* 1716 His issue male *extinct* 1766, but the limitation was to his heirs in tail general.

1717. William Murray, *styled* Marquess of Tullibardine (being s. and h ap. of John, Duke of Atholl [S]), *cr.* 1 Feb 1716/7 LORD STRATH-BRAN, VISCOUNT GLENSHIE, EARL OF GLEN TILT, MARQUESS OF BLAIR, and DUKE OF RANNOCH [S.]. He had been previously (1715) *attainted*, but at the Court of St. Germain was (of course) recognised, on his father's death (14 Nov. 1724), as Duke of Atholl [S.] He *d s p.*, 9 July 1746, in the Tower of London.

1717. Don Jose de Bozas, Conde del Castelbianco, *cr.* 4 Feb. 1716/7, DUKE OF CASTELBIANCO, DUKE OF ST. ALBANS, MARQUESS OF BORLAND, EARL OF FORDAN, VISCOUNT OF THE BASS, and LORD DIVRON [S.]

1721. George (Granville), Lord Lansdowne (so *cr.* by Queen Anne), who, on 6 Oct. 1721, as George Granville, Esq., had been *cr.* LORD OF LANSDOWN, Devon, VISCOUNT of —, co. —, and EARL OF BATH, Somerset [E.], with *rem*, to heirs male, was *cr.* 3 Nov. following BARON LANSDOWN OF BIDEFORD, Devon, VISCOUNT BEVEL, EARL OF BATH, MARQUIS MONK AND FITZHEMON, and DUKE OF ALBEMARLE [E], with a *spec. rem.* He *d. s.p.m.*, 8 Jan. 1734/5.

1722. Charles (Butler), Earl of Arran [I.], *cr.* a Duke.* *Qy* DUKE OF ARRAN [I.]? On 16 Nov. 1745 he became, *de jure*, DUKE OF ORMONDE [I], but never assumed that title. He *d s p*, 1758

1722. Thomas (Wentworth), Earl of Strafford (so *cr.* by Queen Anne), *cr.* DUKE OF STRAFFORD [E] 5 Jan. 1721/2. His issue male *extinct* 1791.

1716. Philip (Wharton), Duke of Wharton (so *cr.* by George I.), was, 22 Dec 1716 *cr.* by the *titular* James III, DUKE OF NORTHUMBER-LAND, MARQUESS OF WOBURN, co. Bedford, EARL OF MALMESBURY, Wilts, and VISCOUNT WINCHENDEN, Bucks [E]. *Attainted* in 1728. He *d. s p.*, 1731.

1718 Col. the Hon. John Hay, of Cromlix (3rd s. of Thomas, 6th Earl of Kinnoul [S]) having joined in 1715 in proclaiming " James Francis " as " King " at Inverness, and having been *attainted* in 1716 accordingly, was *cr.* 5 Oct. 1718 EARL OF INVERNESS, VISCOUNT INNERPEFFRAY, and LORD CROMLIX AND ERNE [S.] ; on 3 Apr. 1727 he was *cr.* BARON HAY [E], and finally, 4 Apr. 1727, DUKE OF INVERNESS [S.].

1740. Simon (Fraser), Lord Lovat [S], *cr.* 14 Mar 1739/40 DUKE OF FRASER, MARQUESS OF BEAUFORT, EARL OF STRATHERRICK AND ABER-TARF, VISCOUNT OF THE AIRD AND STRATHGLASS, and LORD LOVAT OF BEAULIEU [S.]. *Attainted* in 1747. His issue male *extinct* 1815.

1725 ? Henry Benedict Maria Clement Stuart, 2nd and yst. s of the *titular*

---

* The name of the title unknown

James III, attaining the age of twenty-one years on 21 Mar. 1746, was (probably at his birth) *cr.* (by his father) DUKE OF YORK. When he was made a Cardinal, he was popularly known as "Cardinal *York.*" He *d.*, unm , 13 July 1807, in his 83rd year, being the last legitimate descendant of James II.

MARQUESSES

1715. James Paynter, of ' Trelisk ' [Trelissick], Cornwall, was *cr.* 20 June 1715, at the Court of St Germain, MARQUIS [*sic*] OF TRELISSICK, with rem to the heirs male of his body.

1720 ? James Francis Fitz James, *styled* Earl of Tinmouth (being s and h. ap. of James, *(attainted)* Duke of Berwick), is stated to have been *cr.* MARQUESS OF JAMAICA, but no proof has been found of such creation. He was also *cr* a Spanish Duke, as DUKE OF LIRIA. In 1734 he *suc* his father, and *d.* 1738. His issue male still (1910) exists.

EARLS

1701. Charles (Middelton), 2nd Earl of Middelton [S], one of the Principal Secretaries of State to the late King James II (*attainted* 1695), *cr.* EARL OF MONMOUTH. His son *d. s.p.m.s.*

1705. Giovanni Baptista Gualterio, br. of Cardinal Gualterio, *cr.,* shortly before 12 Nov 1705, EARL OF DUNDEE [S.]. He *d.* 1740 leaving a s. and h.

1715. Henry (St. John), Viscount Bolingbroke (so *cr.* by Queen Anne), *cr.* 26 July 1715 EARL OF BOLINGBROKE [E.] *Attainted* 1714. He *d s p*, 1751

1716. William (Villiers), Earl of Jersey (whose father had been so *cr.* by William III), *cr.,* in Apr. 1716, (by the description of " William Villiers, s of Sir Edward Villiers and Barbara, his wife ") EARL OF JERSEY, VISCOUNT OF DARTFORD and BARON OF HOO [E]. He *d* 1721, being ancestor of the succeeding Earls of Jersey

1716. Barbara, widow of Edward, 1st Earl of Jersey (so *cr.* by William III) was on the same date as her son William next above mentioned, granted the title and precedency of a Countess, as COUNTESS OF JERSEY [E.].

1721. The Hon. James Murray (2nd s. of David, 5th Viscount Stormont [S.], and elder br. of William, *cr.,* in 1776, Earl of Mansfield), who had been one of Queen Anne's Commissioners for settling the trade with France, was *cr*, 2 Feb. 1720/1, EARL OF DUNBAR, VISCOUNT DRUMCAIRN, and LORD OF HADYKES [S.] He *d. s.p.*, at Avignon, Aug. 1770, aged 30.

1721 The Hon. John Nairne, *cr.* 24 June 1721, EARL OF NAIRNE and VISCOUNT STANLEY. He was s. and h. ap. of William, Lord Nairne [S.], *suc.* his father 1725 as Lord Nairne [S.], and was *attainted* 1746. He *d* 1770, being ancestor of the succeeding Lords, the attainder having been *reversed* in 1824.

1721. General The Hon. Arthur Dillon, who had previously, 1 Feb. 1716/7 been *cr.* a Baron * and a Viscount * [I.] with rem. to the heirs male of his body, was *cr.*, 24 June 1721, a Baron *, a Viscount * and an Earl * [S.] with rem to his heirs male. He was 3rd s. of Theobald, 7th Viscount Dillon [I]. He commanded an Irish regiment before he was twenty. In 1705 was Marechal de Camp and Governor of Toulouse , subsequently, a Lieut. Gen. He *d* 5 Feb. 1732/3, leaving five sons, of whom Charles and Henry were successively Viscounts Dillon [I.], the latter being ancestor of the succeeding Viscounts.

1722. William (North), Lord North and Lord Grey of Rolleston, 5 Jan 1721/22 *cr.* EARL NORTH [E.] He *d. s.p.*, 1734.

1722. Lucius Henry (Cary), Viscount Falkland [S], *cr* 13 Dec. 1722, EARL OF FALKLAND [E.]. He was the 6th Viscount, having *suc* to the Peerage in 1694. He *d.* at Paris 31 Dec 1730, being ancestor of the succeeding Viscounts.

1722. Mrs. Ann Henrietta Oglethorpe, *cr.* 6 Oct. 1722 a Countess * [I.]. She was 1st da. of Sir Theophilus O , and sister of Theophilus, *cr.* a Baron in 1717, as under. She *d.* unm. in or after 1714.

1726. Lieut. Gen. George Browne, of the Imperial service, *cr.* 12 Apr. 1726, an Earl [? Browne].

1745. Antoine Vincent Walsh, who conveyed "Prince Charles Edward" to Scotland, *cr.* 22 Oct. 1745, EARL WALSH. The issue male of his body became *extinct* 20 Oct. 1884

1746 Sir Thomas Arthur Lally, titular 2nd Bart. was *cr.*, 16 Jan. 1745/6, EARL OF MOENMOYNE, VISCOUNT OF BALLYMOLE, and BARON OF TOLLENDALLY [I.]. The issue male of his body became *extinct* 11 Mar. 1830.

1746. Col. Daniel O'Brien, who had previously, 17 Mar 1725/6, been *cr.* BARON CASTLE LYONS [I.], *cr* 11 Oct. 1746, EARL OF LISMORE and VISCOUNT TALLOW [I.] The issue male of his body became *extinct* before 1789.

1759. The Hon. Alexander Murray, 4th s. of Alexander, 4th Lord Elibank [S.], *cr.* 12 Aug. 1759, EARL OF WESTMINSTER [E.]. He had taken an active part in the election of 1750 against the ministerial candidate. He was generally known as COUNT MURRAY. He *d.* unm., in 1777.

1760. John Græme, who had been *cr* a Bart. by James III on 6 Sep. 1726, was *cr.*, 20 Jan. 1760, LORD NEWTON, VISCOUNT FALKIRK and EARL OF ALFORD [S.].

---

* The name of the title unknown.

APPENDIX F 487

VISCOUNTS

1722. Sir Henry Goring, Bart., *cr.* 2 Jan. 1721/2, VISCOUNT GORING and
BARON BULLINGHEL [E.]. ([a])
„ Col. Donald McMahon, *cr.* a Viscount. *
1723 Sir Redmond Everard, Bart. [I.], *cr.* 20 June 1723, VISCOUNT
EVERARD. He *d. s.p.* in or about 1744.
1731. Owen O'Bourke of Carha [I.], *cr.* 31 July 1731, VISCOUNT OF
BREFFNEY IN CONNAUGHT [I.].

BARONS

1701. John Caryll, Secretary of Requests to the Queen mother, *cr.*,
between 8 and 28 Mar., BARON CARYLL, of Durford, in Harting,
Sussex. He *d. s.p.*, 4 Sep. 1711.
1708. Col. Nathaniel Hooke, *cr.*, 19 Feb. 1708, BARON HOOKE [I].
1716. Francis Cottington, *cr.* Apr. 1716, BARON COTTINGTON of Fonthill
Gifford, Wilts [E.].
„ Ranald McDonald, of Clanranald, *cr.* 28 Sep. 1716, BARON CLAN-
RANALD [S].
„ Penelope Mackenzie (widow of Clanranald, slain at Sheriffmuir), *cr.*
BARONESS CLANRANALD [S] 28 Sep. 1716
„ Alister McDonald, of Glengarry, *cr.* BARON MACDONALD [S.]
28 Sep. 1716
„ Sir Hector McLean, *cr.* BARON MCLEAN [S.] 17 Dec. 1716.
„ Norman McLeod, of McLeod, *cr* BARON MACLEOD [S] 8 Dec. 1716
„ Sir Donald McDonald, of Sleat, *cr.* BARON SLEAT [S.] 23 Dec 1716
1717. Lauchlan McIntosh, of McIntosh, *cr.* BARON MACKINTOSH [S.]
21 Jan. 1716/7.
„ John Cameron, of Lochiel, *cr* LORD LOCHIEL [S.] 27 Jan. 1716/7
„ Theophilus Oglethorpe, *cr.* BARON OGLETHORPE OF OGLETHORPE
[E.] 20 Dec. 1717. He was M P for Haslemere 1708-13, but soon
afterwards retired to Messina, in Sicily. He *d. s.p.*, in France, before
1720.
1721. James Grant, of Grant, *cr.* BARON GRANT [S.] 24 June 1721.
„ Sir Peter Redmond, *cr.* BARON REDMOND [I.] 15 Dec. 1721. He
had been *cr.* a Bart. also by the *titular* James III, in 1717.
1723. Charles Fraser, of Inverallochy, was *cr*, 20 July 1723, LORD FRASER
OF MUCHALLS [S.].
1724. Robert Sempill, is said to have been *cr* BARON SEMPILL. ([b])

([a]) For his successors see *The Complete Baronetage*, by G. E. C.
* The name of the title unknown.
([b]) It appears however that there was no Jacobite creation of, but only a recognition of Robert's claim, as h. male, to the Barony of Sempill; see under that title. V G

1727. Sir Toby Bourke, *cr* BARON BOURKE [I.] 3 Feb. 1726/7.
  ,,   Richard Butler, " Esq., " *cr.* BARON BUTLER [I] 1 Apr. 1727.
1728. Brigadier [—] Crone, Governor of Lerida, *cr.* BARON CRONE [I.] 16 Feb. 1727/8.
1743. Dugald Stewart, of Appin, *cr* BARON APPIN [S.] 6 June 1743
1760. Laurence Oliphant, of Gask, *cr.* 14 July 1760, a Baron. *

After the death of the *titular* James III (1 Jan 1766) his s and h., " Prince Charles Edward " (*titular* Charles III), assumed for himself the title of EARL OF ALBANY *(Comte d'Albanie)*, and by deed 30 Mar 1783 *cr.* his illegit. da. Charlotte, DUCHESS OF ALBANY It is not known that he conferred any other titles, neither are any supposed to have been conferred by his br. and h , " Cardinal York " (*titular* Henry IX), on whose death, 13 July 1807, the legitimate issue of James II became *extinct*

Note.—In " *N.* and *Q.,* " 3rd Ser., vol. ix, p. 71, there is a notice signed " B. B. Woodward " (the well-known Librarian at Windsor Castle) concerning the whereabouts of the records of many Jacobite titles of honour, and a list of Peerages, Baronetages, K G.'s, and K.T.'s, so *cr.,* is given. See also Oliphant's *Jacobite Lairds of Gask*, "The Stuart Papers, " *Hist. MSS. Com.*, and Ruvigny's *Jacobite Peerage*

---

    * The name of the title unknown

APPENDIX G

ELDEST SONS OF PEERS
SUMMONED TO PARLIAMENT *V P.* IN ONE OF
THEIR FATHERS' PEERAGES

In "Writs of Summons to the eldest son of a Peer in his father's Barony" (*Courthope*, p. xxxix) the effect of such writ is fully discussed in an able and lucid manner. It is there mentioned that "the only instance of a son sum in his father's Earldom" is that of the Earl of Warwick (1552-53), 6 and 7 Edw. VI. It is also stated that in 1628 the s. of a Viscount (*i.e.* Edward Conway, s. and h. ap. of Edward, Baron Conway and Viscount Conway) was sum *v p.* in his father's Barony, and that in 1680 the s. of a Baron (*i.e* Conyers Darcy, s. and h. of Conyers, Baron Darcy and Baron Conyers) was sum. *v p.* in one of his father's Baronies. There is, however, a later such instance, when, in May 1723, Charles Townshend s. and h. ap of Charles Viscount Townshend was sum *v.p* in his father's Barony. In no other cases has the s. of anyone below the rank of an Earl been so sum.

Among the nine instances of eldest sons of Irish Peers sum. to the House of Lords [I.] in one of their father's titles (see *ante*, p 2, note "c") it is to be noted that the s. of the Duke of Ormonde was sum. in 1662 as Earl of Ossory ; the s. of the Earl of Clancarty, also in 1662, as Viscount Muskerry ; the s. of the Earl of Cork, in 1662/3, as Viscount Dungarvan, while the s. of a Viscount (Viscount Strabane), was sum. in 1735/6, as Baron Mountcastle

As to the right of the eldest son of an Earl to be sum. to Parl., compare the writ (1336) 10 Edw III to Hugh (Courtenay), Earl of Devon, "quod ipse &c vel filium suum primogenitum ibidem mittat." See Dugdale's *Summons*, p. 187.

For convenience of reference the list here given is printed in tabular form on the next page.

Those summoned down to the end of the 19th century are as under. (ª) *Note.* In every case only the date of the *first* summons is given, and in every case, except where it is otherwise specified, it may be assumed the men once summoned in their fathers' baronies continued to be regularly so sum. until they *suc.* to higher titles on their fathers' death.

[HENRY PERCY, "Hotspur," s. and h. ap. of Henry, Earl of Northumberland, sat in the Parl. of 6 Oct (1399) 1 Hen. IV, and is by some considered to have been sum. in his father's Barony as Lord Percy. (ᵇ)]

1. THOMAS FITZ ALAN, otherwise ARUNDELL, otherwise MAUTRAVERS, s. and h. ap. of William, Earl of Arundel, sum. as LORD ARUNDEL DE MAUTRAVERS, Nov 1482. (ᶜ)

2. HENRY POLE, s. and h. ap. of Margaret, *suo jure* Countess of Salisbury, sum. as LORD MONTAGU, Nov. 1529, (ᵈ) attainted 1538.

3. GEORGE BOLEYN, „ „ Thomas, Earl of Wiltshire and Ormond, „ „ LORD ROCHFORD, Feb. 1532/3, (ᵉ) attainted 1536.

4. HENRY FITZ ALAN, „ „ William, Earl of Arundel, „ „ LORD MALTRAVERS, Jan 1533/4.

5. FRANCIS TALBOT, „ „ George, Earl of Shrewsbury, „ „ LORD TALBOT, Jan 1533/4

6. JOHN DUDLEY, „ „ John, Duke of Northumberland, „ „ EARL OF WARWICK, Mar. 1552/3, attainted Aug. 1553.

7. GEORGE TALBOT, „ „ Francis, Earl of Shrewsbury, „ „ LORD TALBOT, Mar. 1552/3.

8. FRANCIS RUSSELL, „ „ John, Earl of Bedford, „ „ LORD RUSSELL, „ „

9. THOMAS RAICLYFFE, „ „ Henry, Earl of Sussex, „ „ LORD FITZWALTER, Aug. 1553

10. JOHN PAULET, „ „ William, Marquess of Winchester, „ „ LORD ST JOHN, Oct. 1554

11. HENRY STANLEY, „ „ Edward, Earl of Derby, „ „ LORD STRANGE, Jan. 1558/9.

(ª) A similar list down to 32 Car. II is given at p 579 of Dugdale's *Summons*: the Editor is indebted to the Rev. A B Beaven for pointing out various errors into which Dugdale has fallen, and for carrying on the list as far as the end of last century. V G.

(ᵇ) In the Editor's opinion, however, the idea that a summons to Parl. could confer a peerage title had not then entered the mind of man. V.G.

(ᶜ) He sat in the Parl. of (1471) 11 Edw. IV, but there is no record of his having been then sum V G

(ᵈ) He was sum in a Barony then vested in his *mother*, so the summons though omitted by Dugdale is clearly of the same class as the others given in this list. V.G.

(ᵉ) J H. Round in his *Peerage and Family History*, p 335 note (2), points out that "strictly this was a new creation, as his father was only coheir of the Barony of Rochford." V.G.

12. HENRY HASTINGS,	s. and h. ap. of Francis, Earl of Huntingdon,	sum. as LORD HASTINGS,	,,	,,
13. WILLIAM PAULET,	,, John, Marquess of Winchester,	,, LORD ST. JOHN, May 1572.		
14. JOHN RUSSELL,	,, Francis, Earl of Bedford,	,, LORD RUSSELL, Jan 1580/1 (*) *d v p.* 1584.		
15. FERDINANDO STANLEY,	,, Henry, Earl of Derby,	,, LORD STRANGE, Feb. 1588/9.		
16. GILBERT TALBOT,	,, George, Earl of Shrewsbury,	,, LORD TALBOT, ,, ,,		
17. HENRY SOMERSET,	,, Edward, Earl of Worcester,	,, LORD HERBERT, Mar. 1603/4 (*)		
18. WILLIAM HOWARD,	,, Charles, Earl of Nottingham,	,, LORD HOWARD OF EFFINGHAM, Mar. 1603/4, (*) *d v p* 1615		
19. THOMAS CLINTON,	,, Henry, Earl of Lincoln,	,, LORD CLINTON DE SAY, Feb. 1609/10		
20. THEOPHILUS HOWARD,	,, Thomas, Earl of Suffolk,	,, LORD HOWARD DE WALDEN, Feb. 1609/10.		
21. JOHN PAULET,	,, William, Marquess of Winchester,	,, LORD ST. JOHN, Feb. 1623/4		
22. HENRY LEY,	,, James, Earl of Marlborough,	,, LORD LEY, Mar 1625/6.		
23. ALGERNON PERCY,	,, Henry, Earl of Northumberland,	,, LORD PERCY, Mar. 1626.		
24. SPENCER COMPTON,	,, William, Earl of Northampton,	,, LORD COMPTON, Apr. 1626 (*)		

(*) The summons to John Russell is omitted by Dugdale, and Courthope is answerable for spreading the entirely erroneous statement that no notice of him appears on the Journals of the House On this matter the Rev. A. B. Beaven writes :—

"'Dominus Russell,' for the Journals in such cases never give the Christian name, appears for the first time on the list of peers in the Journals on the second day of the session (Jan 18) and is retained thereon throughout the remainder of the Parliament which sat for the last time on March 18 following."

In place of John Russell Dugdale gives "*William Paulet'* Lord St. *John* eldest son to *William* Marquess of *Winchester*, 23, 28 Eliz," but a careful investigation of the Lords' Journals by the Rev. A. B. Beaven seems to show that this is an error, and that no St. John title other than that of Oliver, Lord St. John of Bletsoe, who sat in his own right, was represented in Parl at this time. V.G.

(*) After Henry Somerset, sum as Lord Herbert, Dugdale gives "*Charles* Lord *Herbert* of *Shurland*, eldest son to *Philip*, Earl of *Montgomery* 18, 19, 21 Jac. I." He also omits Henry from his lists of these Parliaments, though inserting him in his lists for 3, 5, 7, 8, 12 Jac I, and again in 1 Car. I It is obvious that Dugdale has wrongly put "Charles" for "Henry," for in 21 Jac. I Charles was an infant of only about 4 years. V.G.

(*) After William Howard, sum, as Lord Howard of Effingham, Dugdale gives "*William Parker* Lord *Monteagle* eldest son to *Edward* Lord *Morley* 1, 3, 4, 7, 8, 12 Jac II" This is clearly an error, for though his father was then alive, the Barony of Monteagle was never vested in him; and his mother, from whom he *inherited* the Barony in the ordinary course, must have *d.* before 12 July 1599, when her son, who had then *suc* as Lord Monteagle but had not yet been sum. as such, was knighted as "Lord Monteagle," by the Earl of Essex V G

(*) After Spencer Compton, sum, as Lord Compton, Dugdale gives "*Ulick* Lord *Burgh* eldest son to *Richard* Earl of St. Albans,

25	Edward Montagu,	s. and h. ap. of Henry, Earl of Manchester,	sum as Lord Kimbolton, May 1626.
26.	Henry Clifford,	" Francis, Earl of Cumberland,	" " Lord Clifford, Feb. 1627/8 (ᵃ)
27.	James Stanley,	" William, Earl of Derby,	" " Lord Strange, " " (ᵃ)
28	Basil Feilding,	" William, Earl of Denbigh,	" " Lord Newnham Paddox, Feb 1627/8.
29	Edward Conway,	" Edward, Viscount Conway,	" " Lord Conway, Apr. 1628.
30.	Henry Frederick Howard,	" Thomas, Earl of Arundel,	" " Lord Mowbray, Apr. 1640.
31.	Montagu Bertie,	" Robert, Earl of Lindsey,	" " Lord Willoughby d'Eresby, Oct 1640.
32.	Ferdinando Hastings,	" Henry, Earl of Huntingdon,	" " Lord Hastings,
33.	Thomas Wentworth,	" Thomas, Earl of Cleveland,	" " Lord Wentworth, Oct. 1640, d.v.p. 1664/5.
34.	John Carey,	" Henry, Earl of Dover,	" " Lord Hunsdon, Nov. 1640
35.	Charles Howard,	" Thomas, Earl of Berkshire,	" " Lord Howard of Charlton, Nov. 1640.
36.	Henry Pierrepont,	" Robert, Earl of Kingston,	" " Lord Pierrepont, Jan. 1640/1.
37.	Robert Rich,	" Robert, Earl of Warwick,	" " Lord Rich, " "
38.	Oliver St. John,	" Oliver, Earl of Bolingbroke,	" " Lord St John of Bletso, May 1641. d.v.p. 1642
39.	George Digby,	" John, Earl of Bristol,	" " Lord Digby, June 1641
40.	Henry Howard,	" Henry, Duke of Norfolk,	" " Lord Mowbray, Mar. 1678/9.
41.	Conyers Darcy,	" Conyers, Baron Darcy and Conyers, (ᵇ)	" " Lord Conyers, Mar. 1679/80.
42.	Charles Berkeley,	" George, Earl of Berkeley,	" " Lord Berkeley, July 1689
43.	Robert Sydney,	" Philip, Earl of Leicester,	" " Lord Sydney of Penshurst, July 1689.
44.	Charles Granville,	" John, Earl of Bath,	" " Lord Granville, " "
45.	Charles Boyle,	" Richard, Earl of Burlington,	" " Lord Clifford of Lanfsborough, July 1689,(ᶜ) d. v.p. 1694.

3, 4 Car. I," but beyond Dugdale's authority there is no evidence for this statement. It is, as the Rev. A. B Beaven writes, when criticising Dugdale's list, not easy to prove a negative, but two things are certain, (1) that this Ulick, if he ever was sum. to, never attended the above Parliaments, nor is his name on the lists of peers in the Journals, during their continuance, (2) in 3 Car. I his father had not yet been cr Earl of St. Albans. V.G.

(ᵃ) This was really a new Barony, but he was allowed the precedency of 1299, on the erroneous assumption that the ancient Barony was vested in his father. V.G.

(ᵇ) cr, Earl of Holdernesse, Dec. 1682. V.G.
(ᶜ) The s. and h. of this Charles Boyle claimed and received a summons in this Barony in Nov. 1694. V.G.

46.	PEREGRINE OSBORNE,	s. and h. ap. of	Thomas, Marquess of Carmarthen,(a)	sum. as	LORD OSBORNE, Mar 1689/90.
47.	ROBERT BERTIE,	"	Robert, Earl of Lindsey,	"	LORD WILLOUGHBY D'ERESBY, Apr. 1690.
48.	JAMES BERKELEY,	"	Charles, Earl of Berkeley,	"	LORD BERKELEY, Mar. 1704/5.
49.	JAMES COMPTON,	"	George, Earl of Northampton,	"	LORD COMPTON, Dec 1711.
50.	CHARLES BRUCE,	"	Thomas, Earl of Aylesbury,	"	LORD BRUCE OF WHORLTON, Dec. 1711.
51.	PEREGRINE HYDE OSBORNE,	"	Peregrine, Duke of Leeds,	"	LORD OSBORNE, Jan. 1712/3.
52.	PEREGRINE BERTIE,	"	Robert, Marquess of Lindsey,(b)	"	LORD WILLOUGHBY D'ERESBY, Mar. 1714/5.
53.	RICHARD LUMLEY,	"	Richard, Earl of Scarbrough,	"	LORD LUMLEY, Mar. 1714/5
54.	ANTHONY GREY,	"	Henry, Duke of Kent,	"	LORD LUCAS OF CRUDWELL, Nov. 1718, d.v.p. 1723
55.	CHARLES TOWNSHEND,	"	Charles, Viscount Townshend,	"	LORD TOWNSHEND OF LYNN REGIS, May 1723.(c)
56.	JOHN HERVEY,	"	John, Earl of Bristol,	"	LORD HERVEY, June 1733,d v.p. 1743.
57.	JOHN POULETT,	"	John, Earl Poulett,	"	LORD HINTON, Jan 1733/4.
58.	HENRY HYDE,	"	Henry, Earl of Clarendon and Rochester,	"	LORD HYDE OF HINDON, Jan 1750/1, d.v.p. 1753.
59.	WILLIAM CAVENDISH,	"	William, Duke of Devonshire,	"	LORD CAVENDISH, June 1751.
60.	FRANCIS GODOLPHIN OSBORNE,	"	Thomas, Duke of Leeds,	"	LORD OSBORNE, May 1776.
61.	ROBERT HOBART,	"	George, Earl of Buckinghamshire,	"	LORD HOBART, Nov. 1798.
62.	GEORGE GRANVILLE LEVESON-GOWER,	"	Granville, Marquess of Stafford,	"	LORD GOWER, Feb. 1799.
63.	GEORGE LEGGE,	"	William, Earl of Dartmouth,	"	LORD DARTMOUTH, June 1801.(d)
64.	THOMAS PELHAM,	"	Thomas, Earl of Chichester,	"	LORD PELHAM, June 1801.
65.	ROBERT BANKS JENKINSON,	"	Charles, Earl of Liverpool,	"	LORD HAWKESBURY, Nov. 1803
66.	GEORGE ASHBURNHAM,	"	John, Earl of Ashburnham,	"	LORD ASHBURNHAM, Oct. 1804.
67.	GEORGE SPENCER,	"	George, Duke of Marlborough,	"	LORD SPENCER, Mar. 1806.

(a) cr. Duke of Leeds, May 1694. V.G.
(b) cr. Duke of Ancaster, July 1715. V G
(c) In the *Journals* of the House he is erroneously styled "Lord Lynn." V.G.
(d) He never sat in this Barony, as he suc. to the Earldom in the following month. V.G.

68. ALEXANDER HAMILTON,	s. and h. ap. of Archibald, Duke of Hamilton and Brandon,	sum. as	LORD DUTTON, Nov. 1806
69. CHARLES WILLIAM HENRY MONTAGU-SCOTT,	Henry, Duke of Buccleuch,	„	LORD TYNDALE, Apr. 1807.
70. GEORGE GORDON,	Alexander, Duke of Gordon,	„	LORD GORDON OF HUNTLY, Apr. 1807.
71. HUGH PERCY,	Hugh, Duke of Northumberland,	„	LORD PERCY, Mar. 1812.
72. GEORGE HORATIO CHOL-MONDELEY,	George James, Marquess of Cholmon-deley,	„	LORD NEWBURGH, Jan. 1822.
73. GEORGE GRANVILLE LE-VESON-GOWER,	George Granville, Marquess of Stafford,(a),	„	LORD GOWER, Nov. 1826.
74. FRANCIS RUSSELL,	John, Duke of Bedford,	„	LORD HOWLAND, Jan 1833.
75. HENRY PAGET,	Henry William, Marquess of Anglesey,	„	LORD PAGET, Jan. 1833.
76. GEORGE HARRY GREY,	George Harry, Earl of Stamford and Warrington,	„	LORD GREY OF GROBY, Jan 1833, d.v.p 1835.
77. GEORGE CHARLES PRATT,	John Jeffreys, Marquess Camden,	„	LORD CAMDEN, Jan 1835.
78. FRANCIS GODOLPHIN D'AR-CY OSBORNE,	George William Frederick, Duke of Leeds,	„	LORD OSBORNE, July 1838.
79. GEORGE WILLIAM FREDE-RICK BRUDENELL-BRUCE,	Charles, Marquess of Ailesbury,	„	LORD BRUCE OF TOTTENHAM, July 1838.
80. HUGH FORTESCUE,	Hugh, Earl Fortescue,	„	LORD FORTESCUE, Mar 1839.
81. HENRY CHARLES HOWARD,	Bernard Edward, Duke of Norfolk,	„	LORD MALTRAVERS, Aug 1841.
82. WILLIAM LOWTHER,	William, Earl of Lonsdale,	„	LORD LOWTHER, Sep. 1841.
83. EDWARD GEOFFRY SMITH-STANLEY,	Edward, Earl of Derby,	„	LORD STANLEY OF BICKERSTAFFE, Nov. 1844.
84. GEORGE STEVENS BYNG,	John, Earl of Strafford,	„	LORD STRAFFORD, Apr 1853
85. HENRY PETTY FITZMAU-RICE,	Henry, Marquess of Lansdowne,	„	LORD WYCOMBE, July 1856.
86. CHARLES BENNET,	Charles Augustus, Earl of Tankerville,	„	LORD OSSULSTON, May 1859
87. HUGH FORTESCUE,	Hugh, Earl Fortescue,	„	LORD FORTESCUE, Dec. 1859
88. EDWARD ADOLPHUS FER-DINAND SEYMOUR,	Edward Adolphus, Duke of Somerset,	„	LORD SEYMOUR, July 1863, d.v.p. 1869.

(a) cr. Duke of Sutherland, Jan. 1833   V.G.

89. WILLIAM GORDON CORN-
    WALLIS ELIOT,   s. and h. ap. of Edward Granville, Earl St. Germans, sum. as LORD ELIOT, Sep. 1870.

90. GEORGE HENRY CHARLES
    BYNG,   ,,   George Stevens, Earl of Strafford,   ,,   ,, LORD STRAFFORD, Feb 1874.

91. WILLIAM COATTS KEPPEL ,,   ,,   George Thomas, Earl of Albemarle,   ,,   ,, LORD ASHFORD, Sep. 1876.

92. WILLIAM ARCHER AM-
    HERST,   ,,   William Pitt, Earl Amherst,   ,,   ,, LORD AMHERST, Apr. 1880.

93 HENRY GEORGE PERCY, ,,   ,,   Algernon George, Duke of Northum-
    berland,   ,,   ,, LORD LOVAINE, July 1887.

94. HENRY JOHN BRINSLEY
    MANNERS,   ,,   John James Robert, Duke or Rutland, ,,   ,, LORD MANNERS OF HADDON, June 1896.

APPENDIX H

AMUSEMENTS OF MEN OF FASHION IN 1782

In the *Morning Herald* of 6 Aug. 1782, is " one of those little bits of information which Historians like, and know how to make use of."—See *N. and Q.*, 7th Ser., vol. i, p. 45, where it is reprinted. This relates to the best known characters of that period (1782), and is entitled " Amusements that ye following *Men of Fashion* principally delight in." Alphabetically arranged, these fashionable gentlemen are as under:—

Abingdon, Earl of	Flute playing.
Aylesford, Earl of	Pistol shooting.
Berkeley, Earl of	Hare hunting.
*Bessborough, Earl of [I.]	Virtu [vertu].
Buckinghamshire, Earl of	An old coat.
Camden, Lord (*cr.* in 1786 Earl Camden) .	Agriculture.
Cornwallis, Earl	Military glory.
Cumberland, Duke of	Fresh water.
Dartmouth, Earl of	The tabernacle.
Devonshire, Duke of	Retirement.
Dorset, Duke of	Cricket.
Draper, Sir William (K.B., 1765; Lieut Gen.; *d.* 8 Jan. 1787)	Tennis.
Effingham, Earl of . . A dirty scirt [*i.e.* shirt or skirt].	
Egmont, Earl of [I.].	Fox hunting.
Egremont, Earl of	Street riding.
Fox, Mr. (The Right Hon. Charles James, *d.* 15 Sep. 1806, aged 57)	Popular tumult.
Grosvenor, Lord (*cr.* in 1784 Earl Grosvenor)	The turf.
Hamilton, " Lord " (Qy. Duke of [S.]) . .	Skaiting.
Hillsborough, Earl of (*cr.* in 1789 Marquess of Downshire [I.])	A nap.
Howe, Viscount (*cr.* in 1788 Earl Howe) . .	Naval practice.

* Had this list appeared in 1882 (in lieu of 1782) " cricket " would have taken the place of " virtu."

Keppel, Viscount	A warm cot.
Lade, Sir John, Bart. (posthumous s. and h. of Sir John Lade, *cr.* a Bart. in 1758), *b.* 1759, *d. s.p.* 10 Feb. 1838	Gig driving.
Malden, Lord (*suc.* in 1799 as Earl of Essex)	Violoncello
Montfort, Lord	Menageries.
Norfolk, Duke of	Toping.
North, Lord (afterwards, 1790, Earl of Guilford)	A festive board.
Orford, Earl of	Coursing.
Pembroke, Earl of	The menage.
†Rigby, Mr. (Richard Rigby, Sec. to the Duke of Bedford, when Lord Lieut. [I]; Master of the Rolls [I.], 1761; P.C.; *d.* 8 Apr. 1788 at Bath .	Conviviality.
Sandwich, Earl of	Ancient music.
Townshend, Viscount (*cr.* in 1787 Marquess Townshend)	Caricature.
Westcote, Lord [I.] (*cr.* in 1794 Baron Lyttelton)	A parenthesis.
Weymouth, Viscount (*cr.* in 1789 Marquess of Bath)	Burgundy.
Wynn, Sir Watkin Williams, Bart. (of Wynnstay, co. Denbigh, *suc.* his father Sep. 1749, *d* July 1789)	Acting.

AN ANONYMOUS SATIRE ON THE NOBILITY
EARLY IN 1773

Specifying their faults and foibles, being an early instance of what in the twentieth century would be called a topical song.   V.G.

> "You I love my dearest life,
> More than Georgey loves his wife;
> More than ministers to rule,
> More than North to play the fool,
> More than Camden to grimace,
> More than Barrington his place,
> More than Clive his black jagueer,
> More than Bute the Royal ear;
> More than patriots their price,
> More than Fox loves cards and dice,
> More than cits the Court to spite,
> More than Townshend not to fight,

---

† Rigby, who was *b.* in 1722, held the lucrative office of Paymaster of the Forces from 1768 to 1781. His "blushing merit" [from wine] is alluded to by Junius. He is often mentioned in Wraxall's *Memoirs*, and Horace Walpole speaks of his Essex seat, Mistley Hall, as "the charmingest place by nature, and the most trumpery by art that ever I saw."

More than Colebrook heaps of pelf,(a)
More than Elliot loves himself,(b)
More than Alderman his gut,
More than Hillsborough to strut,
More than cullies love a jilt,
More than Grosvenor horns well gilt;
More than Dartmouth loves field preachers,
More than Huntingdon her teachers,
More than Carlisle those who cheat him,
More than Long Tom those who treat him,(c)
More than Pomfret a lead mine
More than Weymouth play and wine,
More than fools at wits to nibble,
More than Walpole loves to scribble,
More than Lyttleton to write,
More than blackleg March to bite,
More than country squires their dogs,
More than Mawbey loves his hogs,(d)
More than demireps a spark,
More than Martin a sure mark;(e)
More than Grafton loves his pimps,
More than Devil loves his imps,
More than Tories love the Stuarts,
More than Whigs love all true hearts,
Thus my fair, I love you more
Than ever man loved fair before."

(a) Sir George Colebrooke, Bt., M.P. for Arundel, chairman of the East India Company, head of the bank, Colebrooke, Lessingham & Binns He was supposed to be very wealthy, but his bank stopped payment 31 Mar. 1773, very shortly after these lines were circulated

(b) Sir Gilbert Elliot, father of the 1st Lord Minto.

(c) Sir Thomas Robinson of Rokeby, on whom Lord Chesterfield wrote the epigram

> "Unlike my subject now shall be my song,
>   It shall be witty and it shan't be long."

(d) He is the Sir Joseph of *the Rolliad*, M.P. for Southwark, then a strong Wilkesite. He was the butt of both sides, being a frequent and rather grotesque speaker, he affected the pursuits of a country gentleman and took prizes for fat hogs.

(e) Samuel Martin, secretary to the Treasury at the time of the prosecution of the *North Briton*, he challenged, fought, and wounded Wilkes in a duel, and was alleged by the latter's friends to have practised steadily at a target before sending the challenge.

APPENDIX I

POLITICS OF PEERS

The Rev. A. B. Beaven writes as follows in explanation of the principles by which he has been guided in assigning the party designations which the Editor has adopted, on his authority, in describing the politics of individual peers.

"So far as I know no one has ever attempted to determine in a comprehensive list, embracing the whole period from the reign of Charles II to the writer's own times, the political bias of individual members of the two Houses of Parliament. For the three-quarters of a century since the passing of the Reform Act we have the successive issues of Dod's *Parliamentary Companion*, which publication records throughout the politics of the members of the House of Commons, and (explicitly from 1857 onward, as well as inferentially in its earlier issues), though with frequent omissions, those of the peers. But we have no similar authority for the pre-Reform era. The Biographical Indexes to the House of Lords and the House of Commons respectively by Joshua Wilson, published in 1806 and 1808, are of some service for the parliaments with which they deal, but the attempts of Stooks Smith (*Parliaments of England*, 3 vols, 1844-50) and Crosby (*Parliamentary Record*, 1841) to identify the political opinions of many of the members of the House of Commons in the 18th century with those of the Whig or the Tory party are more praiseworthy in intention than successful in execution· their numerous demonstrable inaccuracies render them practically worthless as authorities on this point, except to those who possess the requisite 'expert' knowledge for correcting them.

"The Protests of the Lords and the Division Lists in both houses, with the records of contemporary newspapers, periodicals and correspondence, afford the only trustworthy evidence on which the party allegiance of the less prominent political personages before 1832 can be determined with any degree of accuracy, and this material, which exists to a fairly adequate degree up to the fall of Walpole, is of comparatively scanty extent for the latter half of George II's reign, and not only during that period, but also through the greater part of the reign of his successor, political connexions were so variable and transient that the knowledge we possess as to the apparently inconsistent votes of individuals, on various questions and at various stages of their public careers, increases the difficulty of classification.

"Throughout the 230 years which have elapsed since party nomenclature became a permanent feature of our parliamentary system, there has been a more or less continuous supply of those sturdily 'independent' members—men of the type of the first Lord Lilford, William Wilberforce, John Arthur Roebuck, and Harold Cox—who were the despair alike of contemporary Whips and of future historians. By whatever party name, if any, they may have elected to be called at any given date, the label of a single epithet would be delusive without some annotation   We are on surer ground when we have to deal with those whose political opinions, whether in the normal course of some evolutionary process or through the operation of more expeditious inducements, underwent complete transformation—those for whom party malignity or the attractiveness of monosyllabic emphasis has provided the ineuphonious but expressive designation 'rats,' and for not a few of whom, especially in these later days, a change of political connexion has been found to be the precursor of a coronet or of the Ulster hand.

"Politicians like Godolphin and Peterborough and Haversham in the Lords, or 'Jack' Howe in the Commons, who boxed the party compass in the days of William III and Anne, were early practitioners of that fine art of political tergiversation, which in the master hands of Charles Fox and the first Lord Auckland and Peel and Graham and Gladstone was reduced almost to an exact science, and is still illustrated by no unskilled exponent in the ranks of the leading statesmen of the year 1910.

"From 1679 to the death of George I the distinction of Whig and Tory was sufficiently marked to ensure a fairly accurate discrimination, except in the case of those members of either House who rarely took part in important debates or divisions.

"For the later years of Walpole's government (1730-42) I have used the simple term 'Whig' to denote the Prime Minister's adherents, distinguishing those of his opponents who were not Tories pure and simple by the epithet 'Anti-Walpolean.'

"From the fall of Walpole till the rise of the new Tory party under the younger Pitt, the Tories became less and less an organised political connexion, and in fact had almost ceased to exist under that name when George III ascended the throne: politicians like Egremont, Halifax, Barrington, Nugent, even Lord North himself, who were ranged on the side of the Court in its struggle with the old Whig families, regarding themselves as being no less genuine Whigs than the Bentincks and Cavendishes and Lennoxes and Wentworths, who affected to monopolise, by a kind of divine right of permanent tenure, the trusteeship of the Revolution settlement.

"The difficulty of precise classification is complicated by the action of the Grenville and Bedford Whigs. Both these sections protested against the Repeal of the Stamp Act, and supported the measures taken against the American Colonists, while the former section, although the original proceedings against Wilkes had been initiated by their leader in 1763, joined the Chatham and the Rockingham Whigs (the Bedford group, irreverently termed by their opponents 'the Bloomsbury gang,' standing aloof), in vehement opposition to the action of the Grafton ministry with regard to the Middlesex election of 1769 and the agitation to which it gave occasion.

"In dealing with the period from 1780 to 1783 I have had regard to facts rather than to names, and have classified the adherents of Lord North's administration generally as Tories and its opponents as Whigs, though probably most of the former would have disclaimed the party name which I have assigned to them.

"Many of North's colleagues and adherents, as Loughborough, Carlisle, Eden, Stormont, Sandwich, &c., followed their leader into the disastrous Coalition of 1783, and continued afterwards to act, some for a time only and some permanently, with the Whig opposition to Pitt's ministry, whilst leading Whigs, as Camden, Gower, Carmarthen, Thomas Townshend, Wilkes, &c., gave their support to Pitt, most of them ultimately becoming indistinguishable from Tories, though they did not adopt the name.

"From the Regency Bill of 1789 to the close of the 18th century the main body of Pitt's supporters may for historical purposes be classed as Tories, though Pitt himself and Grenville, his leader in the House of Lords, would hardly have accepted the designation: these were reinforced in 1794 by the Portland-Burke section of the Whigs, some of whom were with Portland himself finally incorporated in the Tory party, whilst others, as Windham, Spencer, Minto, &c., reverted to their old Whig connexion after the Peace of Amiens. For some years after Pitt's resignation the Grenville and Addington sections were disturbing elements as political combinations, till they were merged (the latter in 1812, and the former in 1822), in the main body of the Tory party. The Canningite group and (at a later date) the Peelites have also to be considered; with few exceptions, after the deaths of their respective leaders, they gravitated towards and were finally swallowed up by the Liberals. The Liberal Unionists of 1886 are of too recent date to cause any difficulty in identification, although in one or two cases such authorities as *Dod* and *Who's Who* regard the same individual as 'Conservative' and 'Liberal Unionist' respectively in the same year, and some Liberal peers who avowed their opposition to Home Rule in 1886 are classed with their old party in *Dod* till 1892 or 1893.

"As I have said, it is not in my judgment possible to indicate with precision, by the simple use of the terms 'Whig' and 'Tory,' the avowed principles and the course of action (often tortuous and evasive) of politicians in the half century that followed the fall of Walpole, or even in the time of the French Revolution and the Napoleonic Wars. I am conscious that where I have used those terms without modification my *fundamentum divisionis* may not commend itself to every student of the subject, but I think the explanation I have given will render my classification intelligible.

"I ought to add that for any errors whether of fact or judgment,

64

in the statements made in this work as to the politics of individual peers, I accept the sole responsibility. What I have written above will show that they are not due to inadequate appreciation of the difficulties inherent in the task I have undertaken. On the other hand, whatever degree of accuracy has been attained is due in no small measure to the perspicacity of the Editor, whose vigilant eye detected many items in my original contribution which required reconsideration, or notes explanatory of doubtful points which they suggested to him."

APPENDIX J[a]

GRANT OF THE COMTÉ OF
AUMALE TO RICHARD, EARL OF WARWICK

In the *Chambre des Comptes* at Parıs there was formerly a volume entitled:—"Cest le Lıvre et Registre des Chartes et Lettres patentes du Roy nostre souverain Seigneur des dons par luy faıts de plusieurs fiefs terres rentes et seigneuries commenceantes a Pasques 1420(b) lunziesme jour davril apres Pasques."

Thıs Register ıs not now ın the *Archives Natıonales*, and has doubtless perıshed But ın the unarranged mass of *Preuves* collected by Gılles André de la Roque ın hıs *Histoire de la Maıson de Harcourt*, ten documents are reproduced (pp. 1439-73) therefrom. Of these some have been also entered on the *Norman Rolls*, some not. Among the latter ıs the followıng·—

Henrıcus Deı gracia Rex Francie et Anglie et Dominus Hibernıe omnıbus ad quos presentes littere pervenerınt salutem Scıatıs quod ınter cetera quıbus nostra sollıcıtudo resıdet et versatur votıs nostrıs occurrıt precipuum universa loca dominacionı nostre subdita et subjecta et eorum incolas ın pace et tranquıllıtate firmare eaque nobilıbus et potentıbus fulcire et ornare et eorum amplıs consiliis et favorıbus contra hostiles ınvasıones et incursus protecta et munıta sub pacis et quıetis dulcedine securıus perseverent et certe potıssime ducatum nostrum Normannie quem sanıtate operante multıformı gracıa Salvatoris sumus undıque conquestı hınc est quod nos ad preclarıssımum consanguıneum nostrum Rıcardum Comıtem Warrewıc' mentıs nostre acıem ıntime dırıgentes actusque suos vırtuosos ecıam preclara et laudabılıa merıta quıbuscum vırtutıs donıs nobilıter ınsıgnıtur nutu ponderantes de gracıa nostra speciali dedimus et concessimus eidem

---

(a) Contrıbuted by G. W. Watson.

(b) So descrıbed, but several of the documents mentıoned above are of earlıer date. There ıs no doubt about the date of the one here gıven, for Henry V was certaınly at Vernon on 19 May 1419 La Roque has made a few blunders ın hıs transcript and extensıons —*omnıa* for *onera*, *facere ımpı imum* for *facıant ımperpetuum*, etc.; *stuffura* he gave up as hopeless.

consanguineo nostro totum Comitatum daumarle una cum terra de Pleville in quantum se extendunt tam in feodis nobilibus quam in membris cum pertinenciis et dependenciis suis quibuscumque infra ducatum nostrum predictum habendum et tenendum totum Comitatum et terram predicta cum omnibus pertinenciis et dependenciis suis predictis prefato consanguineo nostro et heredibus suis masculis de corpore suo exeuntibus de nobis et heredibus nostris imperpetuum adeo plene integre quiete et honorifice sicut Johannes nuper Comes de Harcourt eundem Comitatum daumarle et terram habuit tenuit et possedit per homagium nobis et heredibus nostris predictis faciendo et reddendo nobis et eisdem heredibus nostris unam cerotecam de plata pro dextra manu et unum vantbras pro dextro brachio ac unum gladium primo die Augusti per manus suas proprias nisi obstante impedimento sive causa racionabili et tunc vice et nomine suis per quendam militem tam ortu quam gestu nobilem et potentem singulis annis imperpe-tuum Proviso semper quod idem consanguineus noster et heredes sui predicti decem homines ad arma et viginti sagittarios ad equitandum nobiscum seu heredibus nostris aut locumtenente nostro durante presenti guerra ad custus suos proprios invenire teneantur finitaque guerra hujus-modi onera et servicia in hac parte debita et consueta faciant imperpetuum Et quod competens et sufficiens stuffura hominum ad arma et sagittariorum in castris et villis firmatis Comiti predicto pertinentibus ad ea contra hostiles invasiones et incursus tempore eminenti munienda et defendenda semper habeatur In cujus rei testimonium has litteras nostras fieri fecimus patentes Teste meipso apud Castrum nostrum de Vernon super Sayne xix die Maii anno regni nostri septimo

Ita signatum per ipsum Regem

Sturgeon

Note.—When Aumale was besieged and taken by Henry V in 1419, Jean d'Harcourt VIII (only legitimate son of Jean VII, Count of Harcourt), was Count of Aumale and Mortain. He was slain at the battle of Verneuil, 17 Aug. 1424, aged 28, being then "Lieutenant et Capitaine General pour Monseigneur le Roy es pais de Normandie danjou et du Maine." He *d. s.p. legit.* Aumale was captured by the French under the Sire de Longueval in 1429, but was shortly afterwards recaptured by the Earl of Suffolk. Jean d'Harcourt VII *d. s.p.m. legit.*, 18 Mar. 1452/3, aged 82 His elder da. (the only legitimate child who left issue), Marie, *m.* Antoine de Lorraine, Count of Vaudemont. The *comté* of Aumale was erected *en duché Pairie* in July 1547 in favour of their great-great-grandson, François, styled Monsieur d'Aumale, eldest son of Claude de Lorraine, Duke of Guise.

END OF VOLUME ONE

CPSIA information can be obtained
at www.ICGtesting.com
Printed in the USA
BVOW06*1540181017
497893BV00046B/600/P